THE OFFICIAL PRICE GUIDE TO

Elvis Presley

Records and Memorabilia

SECOND EDITION

Jerry Osborne

MOVIE MEMORABILIA EDITOR: STEVE TEMPLETON

HOUSE OF COLLECTIBLES
THE BALLANTINE PUBLISHING GROUP • NEW YORK

Important Notice. All of the information, including valuations, in this book has been compiled from the most reliable sources, and every effort has been made to eliminate errors and questionable data. Nevertheless, the possibility of error, in a work of such immense scope, always exists. The publisher will not be held responsible for losses which may occur in the purchase, sale, or other transaction of items because of information contained herein. Readers who feel they have discovered errors are invited to *write* and inform us, so they may be corrected in subsequent editions. Those seeking further information on the topics covered in this book are advised to refer to the complete line of *Official Price Guides* published by the House of Collectibles.

Copyright ©1998 by Jerry Osborne

HC This is a registered trademark of Random House, Inc.

All rights reserved under International and Pan-American Copyright Conventions.

Published by: House of Collectibles
                 The Ballantine Publishing Group
                 201 East 50th Street
                 New York, New York 10022

Distributed by The Ballantine Publishing Group, a division of Random House, Inc., New York, and simultaneously in Canada by Random House of Canada Limited, Toronto.

Cover design by Dreu Pennington-McNeil
Cover photos by George Kerrigan

Manufactured in the United States of America

ISSN: 1075-2145

ISBN: 0-676-60141-3

Second Edition: August 1998

10 9 8 7 6 5 4 3 2 1

CONTENTS

ACKNOWLEDGMENTS

The single most important element in updating and revising a price and reference guide is reader input. From dealers and collectors scattered throughout the country we receive suggestions, additions and corrections. Every single piece of data we receive is carefully reviewed, with all appropriate and usable information utilized in the next edition of this guide.

As enthusiastically as we encourage your contribution, let us equally encourage that when you write, you will either type or print your name clearly on both the envelope and contents. It's as frustrating for us to receive a mailing of useful information, and not be able to credit the sender, as it probably is for the sender to not see his or her name in the Acknowledgments section.

In compiling this edition, information supplied by the people whose names appear below was of great importance. To these good folks, our deepest gratitude is extended. The amount of data and investment of time, of course, varied, but without each and every one of them this book would have been something less than it is.

A special thank you is extended to Judith Ebner, for editorial assistance; to John R. Diesso, who loaned us most of the collectibles seen on the front cover; to Steve Templeton, for sharing his movie memorabilia expertise; and to Betty Harper, whose art adorns the "About the Author" page.

Here then, alphabetically listed, are the contributors to this edition:

Bob Alaniz
Carol Alaniz
Patsy Andersen
Nicholas Anez
Loren Ayresman
Steve Banas
Howard F. Banney
John Barancyk
Kenneth Baumgartner
Aaron Benneian
Jean Blankenship
Luuk Bonthond
Chris G. Bowman
Frank Bowman
Susan Bowman
Ernie L. Boyes
Anthony Britch
Denise Brown
Gary Brown
Pat Brown
William Brown
Jimmy Carpenter
Knox Christie
Lorena Christie
William Clavery
Morris Coffey Jr.
Steve Colbert
Carlo Colla
Perry Cox
Sharon Creed
Judy Davis
Chuck Dawson
Devon Dawson
Vance A. De Lozier
John R. Diesso
David Dombroski
Susan Duncan

Dorothy I. Dunn
Judith M. Ihnken Ebner
Frank Evans
Mike Everett
F. James Flanagan
Robert Furrer
Arnie Ganem
Jean-Marc Gargiulo
Jim Gibbons
Ray Gora
Jean Haffner
Eddie Hammer
Dale Hampton
Jim Hannaford
Betty Harper
Nick Head
Gary Hein
Karen Heizing
Larry Holloway
Robert L. Hostler
Pauline Hubbard
Sheila James
Terry Mike Jeffrey
Pamela E. Jenkins
Chuck Jett
Bill Kelly
John Kelly
Slade Kitchens
Tony Kolodziej
Tracy Kolodziej
Rocky Kruegel
Doug Legrand
Paul Lichter
René Lucas
Jeanne MacMillen
Robert Mauriello
Roger Meyer

Donald E. Mielke
Andrrey Mrozowski
Charlie Neu
Gerry Parrish
John Perretta
Seth Poppel
Don Pressman
Darrell Privett
Chuck Proske
Chester Prudhomme
Dennis Quintavalle
Danny Reijne
David J. Rennicke
Pam Ridell
George Rittenhouse Sr.
Tim Robinson
Bob Ruggieri
Ernie Ruggieri
Mike Safran
Larry Sanford
Stuart Shergold
Jeff Stark
Maria Stark
Skip Sullivan
Linwood Sutton
Paul Sweeney
Mark Takayesu
Steve Templeton
Eliza R. Testerman
Walter Unglaub
Frankie Vee
Bill R. Waddell
Daniel Scott Wade
Ed Wall
Annamarie Weichey
Danny A. White
Lee Williamson

THE OFFICIAL® PRICE GUIDE TO

Elvis Presley

Records and Memorabilia

INTRODUCTION

For those who may have missed the previous edition of this guide, we introduced there the two most consequential modifications in Elvis price guide history: separate pricing for all the pieces that make up a "package," and precise individual identification of pressings.

By way of review:

There may be 30 or so different pressings made of an album during a period with only three different label designs in use.

Our introduction of separate identification of the minor as well as the major variations enables one to accurately match a disc and its appropriate, or original, cover – along with any germane insert, inner sleeve, bonus, or sticker.

Lacking this information, one could not easily distinguish whether a cover for a black label dog on top *Blue Hawaii* is really one from 1961, or one that came with a 1973 orange label reissue.

Despite the extensive research involved in preparing the information for this edition, and the many additions and corrections made since the first edition (1992), there are still some releases that have yet to be validated. Each of these mavericks is marked "Verification Pending." Any input as to what makes these covers different from previous ones would be appreciated and will be incorporated in future editions.

One of the most revealing aspects of cover appraising occurs when the exact same jacket is used on later issues. Whether RCA reprinted from earlier cover slick artwork, or simply continued using covers from an earlier printing, the effect still creates a lower price on the original printing than usual. To indicate this anomaly, something along the lines of: "Price reflects RCA's continued use of this same cover, with no discernible differences" will appear.

This should make it possible to know whether a cover for a late '60s issue is identical to ones used in the early '60s, or if an early '60s disc is in fact in a late '60s cover.

As with every new Presley guide we do, label and cover descriptions have once again been expanded. To merely identify a cover as having the catalog number at the upper right, or lower left, as in earlier guides, doesn't begin to adequately describe and differentiate cover variations.

As to the separate pricing for each part, the feedback we have received is that, while it takes some getting used to, it is truly the only sensible approach – especially when it comes to Elvis Presley collectibles.

Only then can the difference between packages where the bulk of the value is in the cover, such as the Chicken of the Sea *Aloha from Hawaii Via Satellite* or International Hotel box sets, be sorted out from those where the greater value is in the disc, such as *Elvis* (LPM-1382) with the alternate take of *Old Shep*.

Separate pricing appears in all three sections of the guide, although only in the EP and LP chapters are grand totals given for complete packages. Adding up all of the parts of a package for you will eliminate your having to total the appropriate numbers.

Do not, however, automatically use the total package price if any of the significant parts are missing.

For singles, where the individual parts are pretty much limited to a disc and a picture sleeve, the totals are quite easy to figure.

Whenever possible, we provide recording serial numbers. Having these serial – or identification – numbers in hand, it is not necessary to play the record to know if it is the 35 rpm single of *He Touched Me*, or *It's Now Or Never* without the piano track, or *Elvis: A Legendary Performer, Vol. 2* without the false starts and outtakes. Each of these oddities has a take number unique unto itself.

RCA's production procedure becomes clearer all the time and makes it easier for us to understand how many of their manufacturing errors came to be, as well as why so many corrections are found on their stampings.

Also in this edition is a supplement to our record manufacturing chapter. By William Brown, this essay digs even deeper into RCA's pressing plants, label makers, and identification coding.

How the Prices Are Determined

Since the previous edition we have regularly received suggested additions and changes from fans worldwide

This is important because, as with most collectibles, record prices can vary drastically from one region to another. Having reviewers and annotators everywhere affords us a realistic average of current asking prices.

Other sources for price updates include: set sale and auction lists in record trading publications, personal want lists, record convention trading, and, as always, many hours in consultation with collectors and retailers.

One frequently asked question regarding pricing is: "How do you handle outrageously high winning bids?"

Briefly, while some dealers send us only the winning bids, others also submit an average of bids received. A few even send along all of the bid amounts they get.

When we only learn of the winning bid, we'll do one of two things:

1. If the item is extremely rare and another sale is unlikely any time soon, our pricing will probably position the winning bid in the middle of price range. This allows for price movement in either direction.

2. If the item is not so scarce, and other sales are likely, we'll put the winning bid at the high end of the range. This usually provides a realistic price range, since the winning bid is by no means the medium offering – merely the top dollar bid. The average sale price is going to be something less.

Condition Gap Is Expanding

It will surprise no one to learn that the gulch between GOOD and MINT is gradually becoming a canyon. The drift toward widening the grading gap that began about 10 years ago shows no signs of slowing. To keep pace with this phenomena, changes have been made in the guide to reflect the ever-increasing premiums being paid for mint condition items.

A value spread that a decade ago rated GOOD at about 20% of MINT is now at around 10%. Look for the gap to widen further in years ahead. Most industry observers do not foresee a narrowing trend during this millennium.

Grading and the Price Range

The pricing column in this edition represents the price range for near-mint condition copies of the records listed. Though the range is for near-mint, it also allows for the countless variables that affect record pricing, of which condition is only one.

If the price range indicates, for example, $300 to $400, that doesn't anymore mean $400 than it does $300. Sometimes those wanting to sell look only at the higher end of the price range, while prospective buyers focus on the low end. The reason for using a range is because prices have been found at both ends and probably in the middle. Please don't overlook this point regardless of whether you are buying or selling.

One standardized system of record grading, used and endorsed by Osborne Enterprises as well as buyers and sellers worldwide is as follows:

MINT: A *mint* item must be absolutely perfect. Nothing less can be honestly described as mint. Even brand new purchases can easily be flawed in some manner and not qualify as mint. To allow for tiny blemishes, the highest grade used in our record guide series is *near-mint.* An absolutely pristine mint, or still sealed, item may carry a slight premium above the near-mint range shown in this guide.

VERY GOOD: Records in *very good* condition should have a minimum of visual or audible imperfections, which should not detract much from your enjoyment of owning them. This grade is halfway between good and near-mint.

GOOD: Practically speaking, the grade of *good* means that the item is good enough to fill a gap in your collection until a better copy becomes available. Good condition merchandise will show definite signs of wear and tear, probably evidencing that no protective care was given the item. Even so, records in good condition should play all the way through without skipping.

Most older records are going to be in something less than near-mint, or "excellent" condition. It is very important to use the near-mint price range in this guide only as a starting point in record appraising. Be honest about actual condition. Apply the same standards to the records you trade or sell as you would want one from whom you were buying to observe. Visual grading may be unreliable. Accurate grading may require playing the record (play-grading).

Use the following formula to determine values on lesser condition copies:

For **VERY GOOD** condition, figure about 40% to 60% of the near-mint price range given in this guide.

With many of the older pieces that cannot be found in near-mint, VG or VG+ may be the highest grade available. This significantly narrows the gap between VG and the near-mint range.

For **GOOD** condition, figure about 10% to 20% of the near-mint price range given in this guide.

The 10 Point Grading System

Another recommended grading system is based on the often-used 10 point scale. Many feel that grading with the 10 point system allows for a more precise description of records that are in less than mint condition. Instead of vague terms, such as VG++ (is this the same as M- -?), assigning a specific number provides a more accurate classification of condition.

Most of the records you are likely to buy or sell will no doubt be graded somewhere between 5 and 10.

After using this system ourselves for a few years, we are inclined to agree that it is more precise. Customers who have purchased records from us have, without exception, been pleased with this way of grading.

The table below shows how the 10 point system equates with the more established terms:

10: MINT
9: NEAR-MINT
8: Better than VG but below NM
7: VERY GOOD
6: Better than G but below VG
5: GOOD
4: Better than POOR but below G
3: POOR
2: Really trashed
1: It hurts to think about it

Remember, though, that all of the price guides in the world – no matter how authoritative – will not change the certainty that true value is nothing more than what one person is willing to accept and another is willing to pay. In the end, true value is always a product of scarcity and demand.

In general, just because something is old does not necessarily mean that it is valuable, although with Elvis collectibles everything is valuable to some extent. Even recent Elvis releases can have high value, as in often the case with promotional issues.

Promotional Issues

In this guide, a "promotional issue" is normally a record with a special label or sleeve, usually marked "Not for Sale," "Dee Jay Copy," etc.

Another variation of a promotional issue is the "designate promo," a term we coined in the '70s to describe copies that are identical to commercial releases, except that they have been earmarked for promotional purposes. Such releases may be rubber stamped, mechanically perforated, stickered, written on by hand, have cut corners, or altered in some other way to accommodate use for promotional purposes.

Imports

This guide, by design, lists only U.S. vinyl releases; however, there are some exceptions. A few albums were widely distributed in the United States and sold via widespread U.S. advertising, even though manufactured outside this country. Since many U.S. collectors bought these, they are included.

Bootlegs and Counterfeits

Bootleg and counterfeit records are not priced in this or any of our guides. Nevertheless, many folks over the years have asked us to at least document bootleg releases, if only for identification purposes.

This we do for vinyl records, and it should eliminate the confusion that sometimes exists. Especially with those new to the field, it can be difficult to know the difference between original, legitimate issues, and boots that are so professionally manufactured as to appear lawful.

As with all the other listings in the guide, a checklist box is also provided for each bootleg recording, for those of you keeping an inventory.

It's a good idea to inspect each label and/or number carefully, as some bootlegs have titles identical to or very similar to legitimate issues.

By definition, a "bootleg" recording is one illegally manufactured, usually containing material that has not previously appeared on a legitimate release. If the material is easily and legally available, there would be no appeal to buy the boot.

There are also a number of bootleg picture sleeves, most of which were made by ambitious collectors for Elvis singles that did not originally come with sleeves.

Beginning in 1970 with the European release of *Please Release Me*, the flow of bootleg Elvis recordings, both albums and CDs, has been endless.

Although most of the recent Elvis boots are exclusively on compact disc, the market for otherwise unreleased Elvis tracks seems as brisk as ever.

In the late '70s, many significant Elvis boots were made in the United States; however, in the last 10 years most have originated in European countries where lax copyright laws make their manufacture more allowable.

A "counterfeit" record is one manufactured as close as possible in appearance to the source disc from which it was taken. Not all counterfeits are created to fool an unsuspecting buyer, but some were. Many are marked in a way so as to distinguish them from the originals.

The primary value of counterfeits is to fill the gap in a collection until the real thing comes along.

Amazingly, many bootlegs – singles as well as albums – have sold for prices once thought possible only for rare originals.

Since most of the valuable Elvis Presley records have been counterfeited, it is always a good idea to consult with an expert when there is doubt. The trained eye can usually spot a fake.

Throughout the guide, you'll find helpful tips regarding counterfeit identification.

Another breed of goods are "unauthorized" releases. These are legitimate releases that, for whatever reasons, are unauthorized by one entity or another. These are not necessarily bootlegs or counterfeits, and unauthorized certainly does not mean illegal.

What to Expect When Selling Your Records to a Dealer

There can be a substantial difference between the prices reported in the guide and what one should expect a dealer to pay when buying records for resale.

Unless a dealer is buying for a personal collection and without plans to resell, he or she is simply not in a position to pay full price.

Dealers work on a percentage basis, largely determined by the total dollar investment, quality and quantity of material offered, as well as their general financial condition and inventory at the time.

Another important consideration is the length of time it will take the dealer to recoup *at least* the amount of the original investment.

The quicker the demand for the stock, and the better the condition, the quicker the return and therefore the greater the percentage that can be paid.

Most dealers will pay from 25% to 50% of guide prices. And that's assuming they are planning to resell at guide prices. If they traditionally sell below guide, that difference may be reflected in what they will pay.

If you have records to sell, it would be wise to check with several shops. In doing so, you'll begin to get a good idea of the value of your collection to a dealer.

Consult the Buyer-Seller Directory at the back of this guide for the names of dealers who not only might be interested in buying but from whom many collectible records are available for purchase.

Wax Fax and E-mail

Two frequently used methods of forwarding data to us is by fax and by e-mail. For your convenience, we have a dedicated fax line: (360) 385-6572. Use this service to easily and instantly transmit additions, corrections, price updates, and suggestions. Be sure to include (legibly) your name, address, and phone number so we can acknowledge your contribution and, if necessary, contact you.

Our e-mail address is **jo@jerryosborne.com.** Again, remember to provide your full name separately since Internet letters normally relay only the sender's e-mail address.

If you help, we want to credit you properly. Just make sure we have — and can read — the information with which to do it.

Send all additions, corrections, and suggestions to:

Jerry Osborne
Box 255
Port Townsend, WA 98368
Fax: (360) 385-6572
e-mail: jo@jerryosborne.com
web site: www.jerryosborne.com.

And when you are online, remember you can stay informed on all of our publications – past, current and future – by regularly visiting our fun and informative site (URL above). Bookmark this page!

More Tips to Using This Book

➢ In most cases, the side listed first in the singles chapter is the one indicated as the top side by its recording serial number (the side with the lower serial number). There are a few exceptions, ones where the acknowledged A-side is the lower number. For these, the established A-side is listed first.

➢ Following the singles chapter is a complete listing of flip sides, from which any B-side can be quickly cross referenced to the side listed first in the guide.

➢ As part of our in-depth label analysis, the wording on the label of the artist (and other) credits is provided. Even something as simple as whether or not Elvis is singing with the Jordanaires can vary from pressing to pressing. And sometimes when he is, they remain unaccredited.

➢ Credits shown in the guide are copied directly from the labels, meaning text in capital letters on the label is in caps in the guide.

➢ With any listing in the guide, when you see recording serial, or identification numbers you can be sure of all of the accompanying information. Documenting the numbers is proof positive that the information here was taken directly from the record and/or cover.

➢ When there is no price difference between one variation and another, all of them may be found under the same listing. For the convenience of collectors who seek every possible variation, a separate checklist box also appears to each individual stamping.

➢ We have tried to limit our description of covers to those characteristics most likely to signal a change from one release to the next. While a comment or two about the covers may be found, we are certainly not trying to condense to text a thorough depiction of each cover. Such things as one cover being inked slightly more or less than another, not uncommon on reissues, is often skipped in our sketch. Rather than get into a situation where you need both copies in order to compare, we've opted for more definitive ways to identify reissues.

➤ It may never be possible to track down every reissue cover for every Elvis LP release. When you see "Verification Pending" following a cover listing, it means we have not compared that particular cover to ones preceding it. In some cases, there may be no difference whatsoever between covers, which theoretically would lower the value of the earlier cover, or covers, at least slightly.

➤ When we have not yet had the opportunity to compare covers, we operate on the assumption that there is *something* different – no matter how slight – between the covers. As readers and those on our research team make these comparisons, each future edition of the guide will have fewer lines reading "Verification Pending."

➤ When RCA began issuing albums on flexible vinyl, circa 1971, many of the earlier Elvis LPs were reissued using this process. In each case where we are certain a flexible vinyl press exists, it is listed. When we fail to show such an issue, it means we have yet to verify one and would welcome additional data from readers.

➤ Various artists compilations, radio programs, and other oddities are listed alphabetically along with the 100% Elvis recordings, in both the EP and LP chapters. Each is clearly identified under the title as a "Various artists collection."

➤ Extended play various artists samplers without titles are found in alphanumeric sequence by their release number. For example, "SPA-7-61" is found at the beginning of the "S" section.

➤ Untitled long play samplers are all listed under RCA UNTITLED SAMPLERS, at the beginning of the "R" section.

➤ In the contents section, following each various artists listing, the Elvis Presley tracks are shown in boldface type.

➤ For the sake of consistency we have identified as an "insert" a number of items that, while not necessarily *inserted* inside the cover, still came with the album.

➤ Often with record labels and covers (ahem, as with publishing) typographical errors occur in the titles or text. When we catch a mistitled song, we will show the correct title followed by the incorrect one. Example: *Baby Let's Play House* (shown as "I Wanna Play House with You").

➤ Some trivial inconsistencies may be found with regard to the compilation of information from labels and covers. This is because each review and contributor, as well as the editor, submits data in a slightly distinct format.

➤ All discs in this edition are presumed to be vinyl. Any that are polystyrene pressings are indicated as such.

➤ All album covers in this edition are presumed to be cardboard stock, with separately produced and printed slicks applied. Covers with printing done directly on them are indicated as such.

➤ The articles "A," "An," "And" and "The" have been dropped from the alphabetized titles, even though they may appear on the records as part of the name. Try to find *An American Trilogy* under "AN," and you will encounter a cross-reference which sends you to *AMERICAN TRILOGY* (which, in this case, is not far away).

➤ The value of a "Total Package" may or may not be mathematically equal to the sum of its parts. At times it makes more sense to round off odd amounts, such as using $2,000 when the exact package total is $2,005.

➢ Regarding mono and stereo, following each applicable listing one of the following notations will be found:

(M): MONAURAL.

(S): STEREO. Labeled stereo, but may in truth be either true stereo, electronically reprocessed stereo (i.e. fake stereo), or a combination of both. Not yet played for verification.

(SE): Completely electronically reprocessed stereo.

(ST): Completely true stereo.

(SP): Part electronically reprocessed stereo and part true stereo.

(Q): Quadraphonic.

Concluding Thoughts

The purpose of this guide is to report as accurately as possible the most recent prices asked and paid for Elvis collectibles. There are two key words here that deserve emphasis: **Guide** and **Report**.

We cannot stress enough that this book is only a guide. There always have been and always will be instances of records selling well above and below the prices shown within these pages. These extremes are recognized in the final averaging process; but it's still important to understand that just because we've reported a 30-year-old record as having a $25 to $50 near-mint value, doesn't mean that a collector of that material should be hesitant to pay $75 for it. How badly he or she wants it and how often it's possible to purchase it *at any price* should be the prime factors considered, not the fact that we last reported it at a lower price.

We may report a record for, say, $500 to $1,000, which may have been an accurate appraisal at press time. However, before the new edition hits the streets, the price might be $1,000 to $2,000. One or two transactions and six months later it jumps to $2,000 to $4,000. By the time we're close to a new edition, this same disc may be considered a bargain at $5,000.

At that point, people may look at the book and wonder how we could show $500 to $1,000 for a $5,000 record. "That price is a joke," you'll hear. And, at that point, it is.

Check the copyright page (usually page ii) to learn this edition's publication date – then make appropriate inflationary allowances.

Our objective is to report and reflect record marketplace activity; not to *establish* prices. For that reason, and if given the choice, we'd prefer to be a bit behind the times rather than ahead.

Finally, the wise fan will also keep abreast of current trends and news through the pages of the fanzines and publications devoted to collecting Elvis memorabilia.

DISC RECORDS:
METALLIZING & PLATING

To fully understand the assorted code numbers, and to interpret each ingredient of the recording serial numbers adds an exciting dimension to the enjoyment of collecting Elvis records.

Before 1992, when we first published this chapter, in *Presleyana III*, most Elvis collectors had their own theories about what some of those funny little numbers and letters found on records really mean. Then there were other markings that we wouldn't even bother to try and figure out. They didn't mean anything anyway. Right?

Wrong!

Thanks to our discovery at the RCA Indianapolis plant of a late '70s, in-house pamphlet titled "Disc Records: Metallizing and Plating," these little mysteries are solved.

Rather than rewrite or editorialize, we will reproduce faithfully the text of this pamphlet. However, when we feel a clarification to be helpful, it will appear in brackets, so you'll know that portion is not from the pamphlet:

Marking Metal Parts

This notice specifies the procedure, location, and coding for marking of metal parts and marking factory identification on stampers.

I. Recording Serial Number.

The recording serial number stamped or engraved between the lead out grooves [commonly referred to as the "vinyl trail-off," or "dead wax"] shall be used as a reference from which all subsequent factory markings shall be located. The position of the recording serial number and transfer number shall be at 12 o'clock [referring to the top center position on the face of a clock].

II. Duplication History

The marking of the duplication history shall be located between the lead out grooves, as close to the 3 o'clock position as possible.

a) Identifying Master (#1, #2, etc.). Stamp with a letter (A, B, C, etc.). These letters are assigned in alphabetical sequence to each master made from a lacquer recording or a mold. The sequence is repeated for each different mold or lacquer transfer from which the parts are duplicated.

[In the disc production system, a "master," or "mother," is one of the parts (made from a lacquer) of the process, and should not be confused with a master tape, as made in a recording studio.]

b) Identifying Molds (#1, #2, etc.). Stamp with numbers (1, 2, 3, etc.). These letters are assigned in numerical sequence for each mold made from the same master. The sequence of numbers is repeated for each different master from which the parts are duplicated.

[Example: "A1" indicates the first mold made from the first master. "A3" would be the third mold made from the first master. "C2" identifies the second mold made from the third master.]

Note: The letters and numbers identifying masters and molds are to be assigned to both rejected and acceptable parts. This is necessary in order that the number of duplications will be indicated by the particular letter or number of any metal part.

Plant Identification of Stampers

The following code letters system shall be used by the plant in identifying stampers:

Plant	Code Letter
Indianapolis	I
Hollywood	H
Rockaway	R

The code shall be used as follows:

a) The plant producing the stamper shall stamp its code letter between the lead out grooves, in the 6 o'clock position [as close as possible to being directly across from the recording serial number]. For parts used in the production of cheap, low-quality records having no quality warranty, the plant shall stamp its letter twice in the area mentioned (using 1/16" reverse reading stamps).

b) In order to identify records made from exported stampers, Indianapolis will add a horizontal bar across the plant code (i.e. "I") to form this configuration on all exported metal parts.

General Recording and Matrix Procedure

a) Commercial Composite Master Tape Lacquer Coding: The first four characters of the serial number will be coded with respect to year recorded, label designation, size and speed, and groove description per the chart that follows below [which covers all of Elvis' recordings for the label. Information for pre-1963 releases has been added based on independent research].

b) The first four characters will be followed by a four-digit numerical sequence starting with 0001. The first four characters will be separated from the numerical sequence by a hyphen (example: WPKM-5766).

c) The take number for a specific recording shall be designated by a number following the serial number and separated from the serial number by a hyphen, as follows: WPKM-5766-1 for take one, WPKM-5766-2 for take two.

[Remember, this "take" has nothing to do with the different takes made in the recording studio. In metallizing and plating, a new take number is assigned when they go back to the master tape and make a new lacquer, mold, and stamper. This return to the master tape procedure is necessary since there is a limit to the life of a stamper, and the greater the sales of a record the greater the number of new stampers needed.]

The take number is almost always followed immediately by the letter "S," such as WPKM-5766-1S. No one we've spoken with at RCA knows why the letter "S" was chosen, as opposed to say "T" for take. They say it does not stand for stamper, although that also seems to make some sense.

At any rate, with a "1S" in the vinyl (never on the label although the rest of the serial number is) you can be certain you have a copy made from the first set of parts – a record that can truly be called a first pressing.

Even though many in fandom use the term "matrix number" to mean the entire serial number, the manufacturer refers only to the take number when using the "matrix number." [In the preceding example only the "1S" is the matrix number.]

d) The serial number shall be stamped or marked on all original tapes by the Recording Section.

e) The selection-master tape serial number code, as such, will not be used for rerecorded or composite-master tapes, lacquers, production transfers, matrix parts, or record labels.

f) The year used must coincide with the year recorded and not when the serial numbers were used.

Pre-1963 Coding

Only the years after 1962, beginning with *One Broken Heart for Sale* (45) and *It Happened at the World's Fair* (LP), are covered by the RCA coding that follows. To better understand pre-1963 codes, beginning in 1955 and ending with *Return to Sender* (45) and *Girls! Girls! Girls!* (LP), review this list:

When the second character is "2" it indicates a commercial, popular music release. (Appears on all formats through 1962.)

When the second character is "7" on singles, it indicates a promo only recording.

When the second character is "8" it indicates a promo only recording.

When the second character is "Q" it indicates a promo only Compact 33 Single.

When the third character is "N" (on EPs) it indicates there is more than one artist on the record – mostly various artists samplers.

When the third character is "N" (on LPs) it indicates there is more than one artist on the record – mostly various artists samplers. (Effective from 1956 through 1962.)

When the third character is "P" (on 45s) it indicates a film song supplied to RCA. (Effective from *Hard Headed Woman* through *Return to Sender*.) We have yet to determine the meaning of "P" as the third character on EPs, as it occurs with both RCA studio and film song releases.

When the third character is "P" (on LPs) it indicates a 12-inch 33 rpm. (Effective from *Elvis Presley* through *Girls! Girls! Girls!*)

When the third character is "W" (on 45s) it indicates an RCA studio recording (not film songs turned over to RCA).

When the third character is "W" (on EPs) it indicates only one artist on the record.

When the fourth character is "A" it indicates a "Living Stereo" 45.

When the fourth character is "B" (on singles) it indicates a 78 rpm single. (After 78s were dropped from the catalog, "B" then meant a mono EP.)

When the fourth character is "H" it indicates a mono EP.

When the fourth character is "I" it indicates a mono Compact 33 Single.

When the fourth character is "O" it indicates a stereo Compact 33 Single.

When the fourth character is "P" (on LPs) it indicates monaural. (Effective from *Elvis Presley* through *Girls! Girls! Girls!*)

When the fourth character is "Y" (on LPs) it indicates "Living Stereo" or "Electronically Reprocessed Stereo." (Effective *G.I. Blues* through *Girls! Girls! Girls!*)

When the fourth character is "W" it indicates a mono 45 rpm single. (From *One Broken Heart for Sale* through *Fool*, a mono 45 rpm is indicated by using a "K" as the third character. Note RCA considered *TV Guide Presents Elvis* a single ("G8MW.")

Before the advent of the stereo disc (1958), grooves were classified either as "Fine" (LP & 45 rpm) or "Standard" (78 rpm). The "H," "L," "P" and "W" codes in the fourth position, for example, were indicated as "Fine" before being changed to "Mono."

Commercial Composite Master
Tape Lacquer Coding

Year Code	Label Designation	Size and Speed	Description
F (1955)	A – Grunt	A/B/C – Master Tape 3¾-ips	A – EP Stereo
G (1956)	B – TMI	K – 7-inch 45 rpm	B – EP Mono
H (1957)	C – Camden	L – 7-inch 33 1/3 rpm	M – Mono
J (1958)	D – Neon	P – 10-inch 33 1/3 rpm	S – Stereo
K (1959)	E – Educational	R – 12-inch 33 1/3 rpm	T – Quadraphonic
L (1960)	F – Wooden Nickel		
M (1961)	G – Groove		
N (1962)	H – (1963-'64) Hugo & Luigi		
P (1963)	H – (1972-'73) Chelsea		
R (1964)	J – Children		
S (1965)	K – Daybreak		
T (1966)	L – Wheel		
U (1967)	M – George Jones Musicor Masters		
W (1968)	N – Promotional & Premium		
X (1969)	P – Popular		
Z (1970)	R – Red Seal		
	S – International		
A (1971)	T – (1970-'71) Gregar		
B (1972)	T – (1972-'73) Metromedia		
C (1973)	V – Victrola		
D (1974)	W – Country & Western		
E (1975)	X – Chart		
F (1976)	Y – Kirshner		
G (1977)	Z – Colgems		
H (1978)			
J (1979)			
K (1980)			
L (1981)			
M (1982)			
N (1983)			
O (1984)			
P (1985)			
R (1986)			
S (1987)			

From Lacquers to Masters — The Five Steps

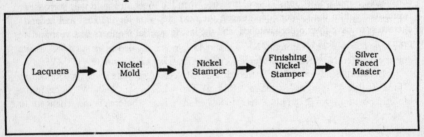

LABELS & NUMBERS
A CLOSER LOOK

By William Brown

Digging deeper into RCA Victor serial numbers, record label printing, and pressings has revealed even more information than previously published in the Osborne Elvis guides. Here are the results of said digging:

Serial Numbers

What follows is a composite list made of serial number codes used by RCA between 1942 (when the system was first concocted) and the early 1990s, along with correspondence from Claudia Depkin of the BMG Archives who, in turn, sent copies of a proposed manuscript, by the late Victorologist, Ted Fagan, titled "The Victor Alphabet," which explains the origins of many codes.

I must add, however, that the only information on serial number codes BMG has is for pre-1958 codes; unlike the information already printed in *Presleyana* for post-1963 codes, BMG only has specific information on codes from 1951 to 1957.

As for the "S" on a take in the end of an identification number (i.e. WPKM-5766-1S), it does indeed mean "stamper," as previously reported in *Presleyana*.

To quote the dear departed Mr. Fagan, "When preceded by a "1" through "10" ("1S," "2S" etc.), it indicates Stamper parts numbers assigned by Mr. Pulley for Parts Shipped." This code dates back to the 1940s.

A "30S" at the end of an identification number of post-1969 Elvis singles indicates the first master lacquer from the New York studio; the first takes (1S, 2S, etc.) were mastered at other studios, including – in Elvis' case – the Nashville studio.

As to why the serial number of the special promo copy of *Blue Christmas/Blue Christmas*, from November 1957, is HO7W-0808 while *Old Shep* (CR-15, early 1957) is H7OW-3721, there is a reason for the transposed "07."

Between 1955 and 1969, on pressings from RCA Custom, if the sequential numbers passed the 9999 threshold before the year ended, the order of the second and third characters in a prefix would then be switched. (It seems that by RCA's standards, the Elvis recordings between 1955 and 1962 which were regular studio sides and not soundtrack music, fell under the canon of Country & Western, hence the "W" as the third character of such recordings, while his soundtrack works with the "P" code were considered Popular selections.) Once, in 1966, when the 9999 threshold was surpassed twice over within the Custom department, the next step was for the first and second characters to have their order switched, and the last few serial numbers that year had a prefix of, say, 4TKM for mono 45s.

The "KM" in the third and fourth characters of post-1963 mono 45s and "KS" on stereo 45s were put in place of other codes assigned to masters when originally recorded:

A1 - Recorded in New York.
A2 - Recorded in Chicago
A3 - Recorded in Hollywood
A4 - Recorded in Nashville
A5 - Recorded in outside studios in U.S.A.
A6 - Recorded outside U.S.A.

For example, *Burning Love*, when recorded in Hollywood on March 28, 1972, was assigned a master serial number of BPA3-1257. When issued on single 74-0769, the number is shown as BPKS-1257 on the commercial (stereo) copies, and BPKM-1257 on the mono promo copies.

Record Label Printing

I have some new information regarding the origins and printing location of the examples of labels, pictured and described in the following chapter, "The Primary RCA Record Labels."

Labels shown as S#1, S#12L, S#14, S#16, S#22, EP#1, EP#2, EP#8, EP#9, EP#10, EP#11 and LP#6 all emanated from the Rockaway, New Jersey, factory and were printed by a Newark printer named Co-Service.

It is Co-Service – not RCA – who is responsible for adding the horizontal silver line across 45 labels through mid-1957. Co-Service printed labels for RCA's Rockaway plant through early 1959, after which the RCA printed its own, with some label copy artwork from Indianapolis and others from the plant itself.

As for Co-Service, by the mid-'60s they moved to Mountainside, N.J. Renamed Shell Press, they printed labels on what amounted to an exclusive basis for that town's Bestway Products pressing plant through the early 1980s. (The *Roustabout Theatre Lobby Spot* label was printed by this same company.)

A few early (pre-1959) RCA stereo LPs pressed in Rockaway had labels similar in design to LP#6, except that the top said "Stereo-Orthophonic" instead of "New Orthophonic;" and "LIVING STEREO" instead of LONG 33 1/3 PLAY." This does not apply to Elvis, of course, since by the time he cut his first stereo sides (1960), Co-Service was no longer printing labels for RCA in Rockaway.)

I believe we now know the identity of the printing company that supplied the Hollywood plant with labels S#2, S#3, S#6, S#8, S#9, S#12, S#19, S#20, S#24, S#25, S#27, GS#2, GS#3, GS#5, GS#7, GS#8, EP#3, EP#15, LP#1, LP#4, LP#7, LP#9, LP#10, LP#13 and LP#16.

Based on: 1) Ads in Billboard's International Buyer's Guide, in which some of the typefaces used on RCA's West Coast labels are present, and, 2) Sept. 16, 1967 issue of Billboard, wherein they put in a message of congratulations to Capitol Records (home of The Beatles) in regard to their 25th anniversary – the printer is the Los Angeles-based Bert-Co Press.

In addition to doing label copy for RCA's Hollywood factory, Bert-Co did likewise for the Los Angeles pressing plant of Capitol Records and the West Coast plants (Hollywood and Santa Maria) of Columbia Records through the early-to-mid-'60s.

Bert-Co also put "His Master's Voice" atop the dog and the "78 RPM (or R.P.M.)" line on 78s. They also added "'New (or Stereo) Orthophonic High Fidelity" on all LPs and 45s between 1962 (at which point Rockaway and Indianapolis ceased to do so) and 1965.

And the actual name of the printing company that printed the RCA Radio Victrola spot record label was MacMurray Press, located for years in New York's Greenwich Village, now on Canal Street in lower Manhattan.

Labels S#4, S#11, EP#4, EP#7, LP#2, LP#3, LP#5, LP#8, LP#11 and LP#14 all originated at the RCA Indianapolis plant (although, after 1959, the Rockaway plant also used such label copy artwork). The typefaces in these label examples were made by Monotype, one of several hot-metal typesetting companies – the others being Linotype, Intertype and Ludlow.

Labels S#13, LP#12 and LP#15 also came from Indianapolis, but these are Linotype typefaces.

On labels S#5, S#7, S#10, S#15, S#21, GS#1, GS#4, EP#5, EP#6 and EP#12, the typefaces shown came courtesy of Varitype (whose typefaces were used by Columbia's Santa Maria plant from circa 1966 to 1977 – their best known use being on West Coast labels like Warner/Reprise and ABC/ Dunhill). These were from – you guessed it – Indianapolis.

Labels S#17, S#18, S#23, S#26, GS#6(?), GS#10, GS#11, GS#12, EP#13, EP#14 and EP#16 were also set on Varitype machines, but these came out of Rockaway. One important detail on labels from each of the two plants, to distinguish one from the other, are opening and closing quotes. Rockaway label artwork has thin quote marks that are very close together, whereas Indianapolis quotes are rather bold and further apart.

In early 1972, approximately, Rockaway spaced each quote apart, a la Indianapolis, but the marks remained thin. It should also be noted that in the first year of RCA's orange label, Hollywood label copy typesetting copied Rockaway's style, instead of Indianapolis. Varitype fonts, called Megaron and that company's equivalent of Helvetica, were used on orange labels and other colors from 1968 to 1975.

Some slight changes came after '75, but Hollywood's label copy was nonetheless closer to the Rockaway style than to that of Indianapolis.

With singles from 1969 on, one can distinguish a Rockaway pressing from a Hollywood one – aside from engraved vs. stamped identification numbers in the plastic, and that Hollywood did not have mold numbers (i.e. "A1 E") – by Hollywood's use of slightly glossy paper stock, whereas the other two factories used cast-coated, or extra shiny stock.

Another important fact about 1968-'76 labels regards the change in paper color in late 1974, which only affected Indianapolis. Hollywood still used orange labels and continued to do so until that plant's closure in early 1976. Rockaway shut down in early 1973, soon after pressing some of the first copies of the *Elvis Aloha From Hawaii Via Satellite* album.

That *Bringing It Back/Pieces Of My Life* (PB-10401) became the last orange Elvis single is because the Hollywood factory closed before the release of *For The Heart/Hurt* (PB-10601). First pressings *of For The Heart/Hurt* are on the tan label; the black, dog near top pressings came later. Indianapolis, by the way, ceased to press records in late 1987.

Labels for both the *Old Shep* promo (CR-15) and the *RCA Radio Victrola Spot* record (GM9E-0401) were made by a printer named McMurray, whose typefaces came from Ludlow.

Shelley Who?

As for those polystyrene records, from circa 1977-'81, that have "Shelley" engraved in the trail-off area, that refers to Shelley Products, a pressing plant in Huntington Station, New York. Shelley worked for RCA on a subcontracting basis in the absence of an East Coast factory of its own (remember, Rockaway closed in 1973). Shelley also pressed some LPs for RCA which are distinguished by a 3 7/8" diameter label as opposed to the standard 4" labels used by all the other companies.

RCA itself first pressed polystyrene 45s around 1979, when its Indianapolis factory moved from 501 North La Salle Street to 6550 East 30th Street.

Exploring Rigid Orange Indents

Here is some new information about 1968-'70 orange label rigid vinyl LPs. There are at least two easily distinguishable types of such pressings, the most recognizable difference being the diameter of the circular indent around the label.

From October 1968 through mid-'69, the circular indent is 1 1/4" from the edge of the playing hole (diameter of circle is 2 3/4"). These pressings are very rigid, with virtually no flexibility whatsoever.

Discs made from mid-'69 through mid-'70 have a circular indent that is only 3/8" from the edge of the hole (1" diameter). Though still categorized as "rigid" by collectors, these pressings are noticably more flexible than those with the large indent circle (yet not quite as flexible as the ones we call "flexible," and nowhere nearly as flexible as Dynaflex).

It is the smaller circular indent that is used on post-1970 Dynaflex pressings.

For awhile, we entertained the assumption that a rigid orange label of any pre-mid-'69 disc, with the larger indent circle, would an earlier release – by perhaps a year or two – than a rigid orange of the same album with the smaller circle. However, after checking dozens of orange rigids, it seems that no precise pattern exists. Several albums turned up that shattered what appeared to be a worthy theory.

Circular 2 ¾ " indent, used from October 1968 through mid-'69

ELVIS INNER SLEEVES

During the first few years after Elvis signed with RCA Victor, generic paper inner sleeves were used to hold the discs in his albums. By 1959, however, the company had discovered the value of using the inner sleeves to carry promotional announcements and pictures of releases by their hottest artist, Elvis, as well as other acts on their roster.

Described and priced directly below are five various artists inner sleeves that picture an Elvis album. There may be other sleeves like these, and if so we'd like to learn of them.

❑ **RCA Victor No Number** .... '57   10-15
Full color. Pictures *Elvis Presley* and *Elvis* as two of the LPs in the "Best-Selling Long Play Pop Albums" category.

❑ **RCA Victor No Number** .... '57   10-15
Full color. Pictures *Elvis Presley* and *Elvis* as two of the LPs in the "Best-Selling Long Play Pop Albums" category.

❑ **RCA Victor No Number** .... '58   8-12
Black, white and red. Pictures *Loving You* as one of five LPs in the "Popular" category.

❑ **RCA Victor No Number** .... '58   5-8
Black, white and red. Pictures no records, but lists 35 "Current Best-Selling RCA Victor Albums," including *Loving You* as one of five LPs in the "Popular" category.

❑ **RCA Victor No Number** .... '58   5-8
Black, white, and multi-color. Pictures no records, but lists 43 RCA "New Albums," including *Elvis' Golden Records* (column 3).

❑ **RCA Victor No Number** .... '59   8-12
Black, white and red. Pictures *A Date with Elvis* (Side 1, row 1, column 3).

❑ **RCA Victor 21-112 Pt. 22B** .... '59   8-12
Black, white and red. Pictures *A Date with Elvis* (Side 1, row 1, column 3).

❑ **RCA Victor 21-112-1 Pt. 22C** .... '60   8-12
Black, white and red. Pictures *Elvis' Gold Records, Volume 2* (Side 1, row 2, column 4).

❑ **RCA Victor 21-112-1 Pt. 22D** .... '60   8-12
Black, white and red. Pictures *Elvis' Is Back* (Side 1, row 1, column 1).

In late 1960, the first of what would eventually be 28 all-Elvis inner sleeves, came with the *G.I. Blues* LP. This sleeve prominently featured *Elvis Is Back* with additional photos and promotional plugs for eight of Elvis' first nine long playing albums (*Elvis' Christmas Album* is not mentioned). The back side pictures 16 Elvis extended plays.

Besides *G.I. Blues*, RCA also used the "Elvis Is Back" sleeve with random albums by other Victor artists. It is also possible that this sleeve came with some of the Elvis albums issued between *G.I. Blues* and *It Happened at the World's Fair*, although this is only speculation.

When *Elvis' Golden Records, Vol. 3* appeared in late '63, we discovered a new breed of Elvis inner sleeve, one picturing 16 previous Elvis LPs on the front and 21 EPs on the back.

LISTEN
to these recent RCA Victor releases

Now available in NEW ORTHOPHONIC and LIVING STEREO versions...already acclaimed for their musical excellence and technical perfection.

Neither of these first two all-Elvis inner sleeves were numbered; however, beginning with the next one – issued in 1964 – identification numbers appeared on every Elvis inner sleeve.

Over the years, paper inner sleeves were used to promote virtually all of the formats besides vinyl records where Elvis' music could be heard: Stereo 8 (tape cartridge), Twin Pack Stereo 8, cassette tapes, reel to reel tapes, and the very short lived Q8 tape cartridges (quadraphonic 8-track tapes). Separate inner sleeves are even devoted to Elvis' Camden LPs and tapes.

Values have been assigned to all custom Elvis inner sleeves, both as individual pieces as well as part of the total package. Also noted are albums issued with either a plain white sleeve, or a generic sleeve which makes no mention of Elvis. For these sleeves, we attach no monetary value.

Though the research required to determine which sleeves came with which albums was fairly conclusive, there's a chance that any LP may have come with any of several sleeves from the same time period. Use our information only as a guide, then allow for the improbable.

Listed and priced in this chapter, using the same basic format as the records in the guide, are all of the Elvis inner sleeves. Each album documented has its inner sleeve accounted for in some manner.

The sleeves appear in chronological order here. They are not listed numerically! The distinction is important since RCA did not number their Elvis sleeves in the order of release.

Among the 28 inner sleeves are four that we have yet to verify and, therefore, cannot accurately describe. Despite not having these sleeves available, we have taken a crack at explaining them based on what we know about RCA's sleeve patterns. They are:

RCA Victor 21-112-1 PT 56B
RCA Victor 21-112-1 PT 56C
RCA Victor 21-112-1 PT 57C
RCA Victor 21-112-1 PT 55C

These four mystery sleeves are accompanied below by the comment: "Verification Pending." Any assistance or input regarding these maverick sleeves would be greatly appreciated – especially a clear photocopy of both sides.

For your convenience, a checkbox is provided with each sleeve listed.

❑ **RCA Victor No Number** .... **10/60**　　**10-20**
Brown, black and white. Front: RCA Elvis LP catalog, most recent of which is *Elvis Is Back!* (Side 1, row 1). Back: RCA Elvis EPs and an explanation of stereophonic sound.

❑ **RCA Victor No Number** .... **9/63**　　**8-10**
Turquoise, black and white. Front: RCA Elvis LP catalog, most recent of which is *It Happened at the World's Fair* (Side 1, row 4, column 5). Back: RCA Elvis EPs and 45s catalog.

❑ **RCA Victor 21-112-1 40A** .... **10/64**　　**4-8**
Red, black and white. Front: RCA Elvis LP catalog, most recent of which is *Kissin' Cousins* (Side 1, row 1, column 6). Back: RCA Elvis EPs and 45s catalog.

❑ **RCA Victor 21-112-1 40B** .... **4/65**　　**4-6**
Red, black and white. Front: RCA Elvis LP catalog, most recent of which is *Roustabout* (Side 1, row 1, column 5). Back: RCA Elvis EPs and 45s catalog.

HERE IS ELVIS'
GREAT LP CATALOG
ON RCA VICTOR RECORDS

All available through your RCA Victor Dealer

All available through your RCA Victor Dealer

HERE IS ELVIS' GREAT
LP CATALOG
ON RCA VICTOR RECORDS

❑ **RCA Victor 21-112-1 40C**...**3/67**   **4-6**
Blue, black and white. Front: RCA Elvis LP catalog, most recent of which is *Spinout* (Side 1, row 2, column 7). Back: RCA Elvis Stereo 8 catalog.

❑ **RCA Victor 21-112-1 40D**...**6/68**   **4-6**
Red, black and white. Front: RCA Elvis LP catalog, most recent of which is *Elvis' Gold Records, Vol. 4* (Side 1, row 4, column 5). Back: RCA Elvis LP and Twin Pack Stereo 8 catalog.

❑ **RCA Victor 21-112-1 pt 54**...**8/70**   **3-5**
Black-and-white. Pictures RCA Elvis LP catalog front and back, most recent of which is *Worldwide Gold Award Hits, Vol. 1* (Side 2, row 4, column 4).

❑ **RCA Victor 21-112-1 pt 55**...**8/70**   **3-5**
Black-and-white. Pictures RCA Elvis Stereo 8 tape catalog front and back, most recent of which is *Worldwide 50 Gold Award Hits, Vol. 1* (Side 2, row 3, column 5).

❑ **RCA Victor 21-112-1 pt 56**...**8/70**   **3-5**
Black-and-white. Pictures RCA Elvis cassette tape catalog front and back, most recent of which is *Worldwide 50 Gold Award Hits, Vol. 1* (Side 2, row 3, column 4).

❑ **RCA Victor 21-112-1 pt 57**...**8/70**   **3-5**
Black-and-white. Front: Pictures Camden Elvis catalog, most recent of which is *Elvis' Christmas Album.* (Side 1, row 2, column 1). Back: RCA Elvis 3¾-ips reel tapes.

❑ **RCA Victor 21-112-1 PT 54A**...**8/71**   **3-5**
Black-and-white. Pictures RCA Elvis LP catalog front and back, most recent of which is *Love Letters from Elvis* (Side 2, row 4, column 5.)

❑ **RCA Victor 21-112-1 PT 55A**...**8/71**   **3-5**
Black-and-white. Pictures RCA Elvis Stereo 8 tape catalog front and back, most recent of which is a four-tape issue of *Worldwide 50 Gold Award Hits, Vol. 1* (Side 2, row 3, column 6).

❑ **RCA Victor 21-112-1 PT 56A**...**8/71**   **3-5**
Black-and-white. Pictures RCA Elvis cassette tape catalog front and back, most recent of which is four-tape issue of *Worldwide 50 Gold Award Hits* (Side 2, row 3, column 5).

❑ **RCA Victor 21-112-1 PT 57A**...**8/71**   **3-5**
Black-and-white. Front: Pictures Camden Elvis catalog, most recent of which is *C'mon Everybody* (side 1, row 2, column 3). Back: RCA Elvis 3 ¾-ips reel tapes.

❑ **RCA Victor 21-112-1 PT 56B**...**9/72**   **4-8**
Verification pending. Assumption: Black-and-white. Pictures RCA Elvis cassette tape catalog front and back, most recent of which is *Elvis As Recorded at Madison Square Garden* (Probably: Side 2, row 3, column 5).

❑ **RCA Victor 21-112-1 PT 56C**...**11/72**   **4-8**
Verification pending. Assumption: Black-and-white. Pictures RCA Elvis cassette tape catalog front and back, most recent of which might be *Elvis As Recorded at Madison Square Garden* (Probably: Side 2, row 3, column 5).

❑ **RCA Victor 21-112-1 PT 57B** 11/72 **2-4**
Black-and-white. Front: Pictures Camden Elvis catalog, most recent of which is
Elvis Sings Hits from His Movies, Volume 1 (Side 1, row 3, column 3). Back:
RCA Elvis 3¾-ips reel tapes.

❑ **RCA Victor 21-112-1 PT 54B** 7/73 **2-4**
Black-and-white. Pictures RCA Elvis LP catalog front and back, most recent of
which is *Elvis As Recorded at Madison Square Garden* (Side 2, row 4, column
2).

❑ **RCA Victor 21-112-1 PT 57C** 1973 **4-8**
Verification pending. Assumption: Black-and-white. Front: Pictures Elvis
Camden Tapes and Q8 Tape Cartridges, most recent of which is ? (Side ?, row
?, column ?). Back: ?

❑ **RCA Victor 21-112-1 PT 54C** 11/73 **2-4**
Black-and-white. Pictures RCA Elvis LP catalog front and back, most recent of
which is *Elvis As Recorded at Madison Square Garden* (Side 2, row 4, column
2).

❑ **RCA Victor 21-112-1 PT 57D** 11/73 **4-8**
Black-and-white. Front: Pictures Elvis Camden Tapes and Q8 Tape Cartridges,
most recent of which is *Aloha from Hawaii via Satellite* (Side 1, row 2, column 5).
Back: Camden Elvis LP catalog.

❑ **RCA Victor 21-112-1 PT 55B** 4/74 **2-4**
Black-and-white. Pictures RCA Elvis Stereo 8 tape catalog front and back, most
recent of which is *Elvis As Recorded at Madison Square Garden.* (Side 2, row 4,
column 3).

❑ **RCA Victor 21-112-1 PT 55C** 6/74 **4-8**
Verification pending. Assumption: Black-and-white. Pictures RCA Elvis Stereo
8 tape catalog front and back, most recent of which might be *Elvis Sings Burning
Love and Hits from His Movies* (Side ?, row ?, column ?).

❑ **RCA Victor 21-112-1 PT 55D** 6/74 **2-4**
Black-and-white. Pictures RCA Elvis Stereo 8 tape catalog front and back, most
recent of which is *Separate Ways* (Side 1, row 4, column 6).

❑ **RCA Victor 21-112-1 PT56D** 6/74 **2-4**
Black-and-white. Pictures RCA Elvis cassette tape catalog front and back, most
recent of which is *Elvis, Aloha from Hawaii via Satellite.* (Side 2, row 3, column
5).

❑ **RCA Victor 21-112-1 PT 54D** 6/75 **2-4**
Black-and-white. Pictures RCA Elvis LP catalog front and back, most recent of
which is *Elvis As Recorded at Madison Square Garden* (Side 2, row 4, column
2).

❑ **RCA Victor 21-112-1 PT 54D** 6/75 **2-4**
Black-and-white. Pictures RCA Elvis LP catalog front and back, most recent of
which is *Raised on Rock/For Ol' Times Sake* (Side 2, row 1, column 5). We have
no explanation as to why two different sleeves with this number exist.

❑ **RCA Victor 21-112-1 PT 54E** 4/77 **2-4**
Black-and-white. Pictures RCA Elvis LP catalog front and back, most recent of
which is *From Elvis Presley Boulevard, Memphis, Tennessee* (Side 2, row 4,
column 5).

❑ **RCA Victor 21-112-1 PT 54F**..7/77   **2-4**

Black-and-white. Pictures RCA Elvis LPs front and back, most recent of which is
Moody Blue (Side 2, row 5, column 1).

THE PRIMARY RCA RECORD LABELS (1955-1968)

Between the time Elvis signed with RCA Victor (November 1955) and late 1968, when the company switched to their orange label, the primary RCA labels are black.

For this 13-year period, virtually all of the black RCA Victor labels have the familiar bull terrier logo – RCA's dog "Nipper" listening to "His Master's Voice."

Until late 1964 or early 1965, the Nipper/gramophone logo is centered horizontally on the label, and centered vertically between the "RCA Victor" logo and the spindle hole. This label design, known as "black label, dog on top," is found on all formats: 33, 45 and 78 rpm singles, EPs, and LPs.

By the spring of 1965, all RCA Victor Elvis releases came on a reworked black label, on which Nipper and gramophone are centered horizontally on the left side. This label design is referred to as "black label, dog on side."

Sounds simple enough, only two different labels to deal with, right? Wrong! Within just these two basic label designs – dog on top and dog on side – there are nearly 50 different RCA Victor labels on records made by Elvis Presley.

Sometimes the differences between two dog on top labels are obvious at a glance; however, often only by close inspection can the variances be spotted.

Each of the primary RCA Victor black labels is pictured and described in this chapter, with subtle as well as not so subtle variations noted.

Among the listings are several promotional labels, selected from those issued during the time period covered (1955-1968). Issues on these promos came on both white and yellow RCA Victor labels. There are also a few black label special products and promo only labels, but these are included primarily to see if readers turn up other Elvis-related releases with similar labels. No attempt is made here to picture or describe every black label promo or special products label.

RCA STANDARD CATALOG SINGLES LABELS

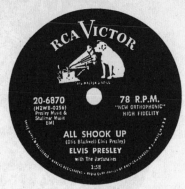

S#1
RCA VICTOR
RCA "Nipper" dog logo
"NEW ORTHOPHONIC"   **Selection number**
HIGH FIDELITY   **Identification number**
    Publisher
Song title
Artist credits
Time

Typestyle is mostly extra bold. Playing speed is not shown on label. Differs from S#3, which does not have "His Master's Voice" under the dog. Also, speed is not shown on this label and it is on S#3.

S#3
RCA VICTOR
RCA "Nipper" dog logo
"HIS MASTERS VOICE"
Selection number   **78 R.P.M.**
Identification number   **"NEW ORTHOPHONIC"**
Publisher   **HIGH FIDELITY**
Song title
Artist credits
Time

Typestyle is mostly extra bold. Nearly identical to S#8 except has the time at bottom, whereas S#8 has it at left. Also see S#1.

S#2
RCA VICTOR
RCA "Nipper" dog logo
"HIS MASTERS VOICE"
Selection number   **78 R.P.M.**
Identification number   **"NEW ORTHOPHONIC"**
    HIGH FIDELITY
Song title
Artist credits

Typestyle is mostly condensed regular bold and normal, but speed is in extra bold. Typestyle is the most noticeable difference between this 78 rpm label and S#1 and S#3, both of which have extra bold titles.

S#4
RCA VICTOR
RCA "Nipper" dog logo
Selection number   **"NEW ORTHOPHONIC"**
Publisher   **HIGH FIDELITY**
Identification number
Song title
Artist credits
Time

Typestyle is mostly condensed regular bold. Does not show speed. Some discs, using this label, do not have "New Orthophonic High Fidelity," and that area is left blank. Similar to S#5, but has time at bottom, whereas S#5 has it at right. Also, selection number is in regular bold type here but is in condensed regular bold on S#5.

S#5
RCA VICTOR
RCA "Nipper" dog logo
Selection number   "NEW ORTHOPHONIC"
Publisher   HIGH FIDELITY
Identification number   Time
Song title
Artist credits

Typestyle is mostly condensed regular bold. Does not show speed. Nearly identical to S#10 except for type on the selection number, which is condensed regular bold here and regular bold on S#10. Also see S#4.

S#7
RCA VICTOR
RCA "Nipper" dog logo
Selection number   "NEW ORTHOPHONIC"
Publisher   HIGH FIDELITY
Identification number
Time
Song title
Artist credits

Typestyle is mostly condensed regular bold. Does not show speed. Nearly identical to S#11 except selection number is condensed regular bold here and regular bold on S#11. Also, position of middle text is a bit lower on S#11 than it is here.

S#6
RCA VICTOR
RCA "Nipper" dog logo
"HIS MASTERS VOICE"
Selection number   78 RPM
Publisher   "NEW ORTHOPHONIC"
Identification number   HIGH FIDELITY
Song title
Artist credits
Time

Typestyle is mostly condensed regular bold. Does show speed. Similar to S#9 except has time at bottom, whereas S#9 has it at left. Also, this label has the identification number at left and S#9 has it at the bottom.

S#8
RCA VICTOR
RCA "Nipper" dog logo
"HIS MASTERS VOICE"
Selection number   78 R.P.M.
Identification number "NEW ORTHOPHONIC"
Publisher   HIGH FIDELITY
Time
Song title
Artist credits

Typestyle is mostly extra bold. Identical to label S#19 (45 rpm), except for the speed—shown here as 78 R.P.M. of course. Also, S#19 does not have "His Master's Voice." Also see S#1 and S#3.

S#9
RCA VICTOR
RCA "Nipper" dog logo
"HIS MASTERS VOICE"
Selection number   **78 RPM**
Publisher   **"NEW ORTHOPHONIC"**
Time   **HIGH FIDELITY**
Song title
Artist credits
Identification number
Typestyle is mostly condensed regular bold, Does show speed. Also see S#6.

S#11
RCA VICTOR
RCA "Nipper" dog logo
Selection number   **"NEW ORTHOPHONIC"**
Publisher   **HIGH FIDELITY**
Time
Song title
Artist credits
Identification number
Typestyle is mostly condensed regular bold, though selection number is in regular bold. Does not show speed. Also see S#7.

S#10
RCA VICTOR
RCA "Nipper" dog logo
Selection number   **"NEW ORTHOPHONIC"**
Publisher   **HIGH FIDELITY**
Identification number   **Time**
Song title
Artist credits
Typestyle is mostly condensed regular bold. Does not show speed. Also see S#5.

S#12
RCA VICTOR
RCA "Nipper" dog logo
Selection number   **45 R.P.M.**
Identification number **"NEW ORTHOPHONIC"**
                             HIGH FIDELITY
Song title
Artist credits
Time
Typestyle is regular bold and extra bold. Identical to S#12L, except does not have the horizontal silver line across label. Also similar to S#19 except has time at bottom instead of at left.

S#12L
RCA VICTOR
RCA "Nipper" dog logo

Selection number	45 R.P.M.
Identification number	"NEW ORTHOPHONIC"
	HIGH FIDELITY

Song title
Artist credits
Time

Typestyle is mostly regular bold and extra bold. The most noticeable difference between this label and both S#12 and S#13 is the horizontal silver line across label. Otherwise, this and S#12 are identical. Unlike here, typestyle on S#13 is mostly normal—not bold.

Label S#14 also has the silver line; however, unlike S#12L, it has the time at the left and the identification number at the bottom.

S#14
RCA VICTOR
RCA "Nipper" dog logo

Selection number	45 R.P.M.
Publisher	"NEW ORTHOPHONIC"
Time	HIGH FIDELITY

Song title
Artist credits
Identification number

Typestyle is mostly extra bold. See S#12L.

S#13
RCA VICTOR
RCA "Nipper" dog logo

Selection number	45 RPM
Publisher (If shown)	
Identification number	"NEW ORTHOPHONIC"
	HIGH FIDELITY

Song title
Artist credits
Time (If shown)

Typestyle is mostly normal, but is bold on selection number and "45 RPM 'New Orthophonic' High Fidelity." Does not have the horizontal silver line. Label S#15 also has no silver line; however, it has selection number in a normal typestyle, whereas here it is in either bold or extra bold. This label may or may not show time, but if so it is at bottom. Also see S#15.

S#15
RCA VICTOR
RCA "Nipper" dog logo

Selection number	45 RPM
Publisher	"NEW ORTHOPHONIC"
Identification number	HIGH FIDELITY
	Time

Song title
Artist credits

Typestyle is mostly normal and condensed normal. Does not have the horizontal silver line. Unlike S#17, which has the time at left, here it is at right. Also see S#13.

31

S#16
RCA VICTOR

Selection number	45 R.P.M.
Identification number	"NEW ORTHOPHONIC"
Publisher	HIGH FIDELITY
Song title	
Artist credits	
Time	

Typestyle is regular bold and extra bold. Nearly identical to S#12L except this label has no dog.

S#18
RCA VICTOR
RCA "Nipper" dog logo

Selection number	45
Publisher	RPM
Identification number	
Time	
Song title	
Artist credits	

Typestyle is mostly normal and condensed normal, except speed which is extra bold. Does not have "New Orthophonic High Fidelity." Also see S#17.

S#17
RCA VICTOR
RCA "Nipper" dog logo

Selection number	45 RPM
Publisher	"NEW ORTHOPHONIC"
Identification number	HIGH FIDELITY
Time	
Song title	
Artist credits	

Typestyle is mostly normal and condensed normal. Similar to S#18 except has "New Orthophonic High Fidelity." S#18 which does not. Also see S#15.

S#19
RCA VICTOR
RCA "Nipper" dog logo

Selection number	45 R.P.M.
Identification number	"NEW ORTHOPHONIC"
Publisher	HIGH FIDELITY
Time	
Song title	
Artist credits	

Typestyle is regular bold and extra bold. Identical to S#12, except has the time at the left instead of at the bottom. Also see S#8.

S#20
Song title

Selection number
RCA "Nipper" dog logo
Publisher
Identification number   45 RPM
                                                              RCA
                                                           VICTOR
                                                             Time
Artist

A combination of typestyles are used, but has
condensed regular bold on title and artist. This is the
main difference between this and S#21, which does not
have condensed type on title and artist.

S#22
RCA Victor
RECORD PREVUE

RCA Victor Camden logo   RCA Corp. logo
Publisher   NOT FOR SALE
                                              Selection number
Identification number "NEW ORTHOPHONIC"
                                              HIGH FIDELITY
Song title
Artist credits
Time

Distinctive Elvis single. There are no other Elvis U.S.
RCA Record Prevue singles.

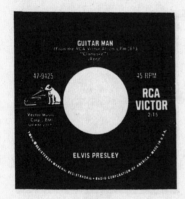

S#21
Song title

Selection number
RCA "Nipper" dog logo
Publisher
Identification number   45 RPM
                                                              RCA
                                                           VICTOR
                                                             Time
Artist

Typestyle is mostly normal and regular bold. Also see
S#20.

S#23
RCA Victor
Artist credit

Selection number   45
Publisher   RPM
Identification number   NOT FOR SALE
Time
Song title

Typestyle is mostly normal and condensed normal, but
is condensed regular bold on title and artist, and extra
bold on speed. The main difference between this and
S#26, is that S#26 does not have condensed type on
title and artist.

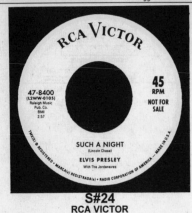

S#24
RCA VICTOR
                                                45
Selection number   **RPM**
Identification number   **NOT FOR**
Publisher   **SALE**
Time
            Song title
          Artist credits

Typestyle is mostly regular bold and extra bold. Distinctive promo single, as there are no others with a label like this. It combines elements of labels S#19 and S#25.

S#26
RCA Victor
Artist credit
Selection number   45
Publisher   **RPM**
Identification number   **NOT FOR SALE**
Time
            Song title

Typestyle is mostly normal and condensed normal, but, unlike S#25, is regular bold—not condensed—on title and artist.

S#25
RCA Victor
Artist credit
                                                45
Selection number   **RPM**
Identification number   **NOT FOR**
Publisher   **SALE**
Time
            Song title

A combination of typestyles are used, but has condensed regular bold on title and artist. Nearly identical to S#27, except NOT FOR SALE is on two lines here and on one line on S#27.

S#27
RCA Victor
Artist credit
                                                45
Selection number   **RPM**
Identification number   **NOT FOR**
Publisher   **SALE**
Time
            Song title

A combination of typestyles are used, but has condensed regular bold on title and artist. Nearly identical to S#25, except NOT FOR SALE is on one line here and on two lines on S#25.

RCA GOLD STANDARD SINGLES LABELS

GS#1
RCA VICTOR
RCA "Nipper" dog logo
Selection number   **45**
Identification number   **RPM**
Recording date
     Song title
     Artist credits
This is the predominant Gold Standard label for the dog on top issues. GS#2 and GS#3 are two exceptions.

GS#3
RCA VICTOR
RCA "Nipper" dog logo
Selection number   **45 R.P.M.**
Identification number   **"NEW ORTHOPHONIC"**
Publisher   **HIGH FIDELITY**
Time
     Song title
     Artist credits
Nearly identical to standard catalog singles label S#19. We know of no other Gold Standard single using this label.

GS#2
RCA VICTOR
RCA "Nipper" dog logo
Selection number   **45**
Identification number   **RPM**
Recording date
     Song title
     Artist credits
Distinctive label. Has extra large extra bold lettering on "45 RPM" and condensed regular bold type on selection number. We only know of three Elvis RCA singles, Gold Standard or otherwise, using this label.

GS#4
     Song title
Selection number   **45 RPM**
RCA "Nipper" dog logo   **RCA**
Identification number   **VICTOR**
     Recording date
     Artist credits
Very similar to GS#6, except here recording date is on right side.

GS#5
Song title

Selection number	45 RPM
RCA "Nipper" dog logo	RCA
Publisher	VICTOR
Identification number	Time

Artist credits

Differs from other Gold Standard labels by its use of a condensed typestyle on artist credits and title.

GS#7
RCA VICTOR
Artist credit

Selection number	45
Identification number	RPM
Publisher	NOT FOR
Time	SALE

Song title

Speed, artist, title, identification number, and "NOT FOR SALE" are in condensed bold or condensed extra bold. Everything else is in a normal typestyle.

GS#6
Song title

Selection number	45 RPM
RCA "Nipper" dog logo	RCA
Identification number	VICTOR
Recording date	

Artist credits

Very similar to GS#4, except here the recording date is on left side.

GS#8
RCA VICTOR

Selection number	45
Identification number	RPM
Recording date	NOT FOR
	SALE

Song title
Artist credit

Except for label name top is blank. This is the only Gold Standard promo using this label, which is very similar to standard catalog singles label S#24.

GS#9
RCA VICTOR
Artist credit

Selection number   **45**
Identification number   **RPM**
                                    NOT FOR SALE
Recording date
                    Song title

Speed is condensed extra bold. Everything else is in normal, condensed normal, or regular bold type.

GS#11
RCA VICTOR
Artist credits

Selection number   **45**
Publisher   **RPM**
Identification number   **NOT FOR SALE**
Time
Recording date
                    Song title

Speed, artist and title are extra bold or condensed extra bold. Everything else, including "NOT FOR SALE," is in normal, condensed normal, or regular bold type. Has recording date on left, which on GS#10 is on right.

GS#10
RCA VICTOR
Artist credit

Selection number   **45**
Publisher   **RPM**
Identification number   **NOT FOR SALE**
Time   Recording date
                    Song title

Speed, artist, title, and "NOT FOR SALE" are extra bold or condensed extra bold. Everything else is in normal, condensed normal, or regular bold type. Has recording date on right, which on GS#11 is on left. Very similar to standard catalog singles label S#26.

GS#12
RCA VICTOR
Artist credits

                                                    45
Selection number   **RPM**
Publisher   **NOT FOR SALE**
Identification number
Time
                    Song title

Except for speed, which is condensed extra bold, everything else is in normal, condensed normal, or regular bold type. Artist and title are in condensed regular bold. We know of no other Gold Standard promo singles using this label.

RCA VICTOR EP LABELS

EP#1
RCA VICTOR
RCA "Nipper" dog logo
Selection number   Side number
Identification number   "NEW ORTHOPHONIC"
                              HIGH FIDELITY
Song titles
Artist credits

Has the horizontal silver line. Though location of label information is identical to EP#8, a dash is used on EP#8 between the side and number ("Side — 1"). Here, there is no dash. Unlike EP#2, does not show speed. Side number is in a different position than on EP#2.

EP#3
RCA VICTOR
RCA "Nipper" dog logo
Selection number   45 EP
Side number   "NEW ORTHOPHONIC"
Identification number   HIGH FIDELITY
Song titles
Artist credits

Though location of label information is identical to EP#5 and EP#6, the side number is in a sans serif typeface here ("I"). On EP#5 and EP#6 those numbers are in a serif typeface ("1"). Also see EP#4.

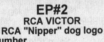

EP#2
RCA VICTOR
RCA "Nipper" dog logo
Selection number   45 EP
Identification number "NEW ORTHOPHONIC"
                              HIGH FIDELITY
                              Side number
Song titles
Artist credits

Has the horizontal silver line. Unlike EP#1, has "45 EP." Also has side number under "NEW ORTHOPHONIC HIGH FIDELITY." Label EP#1 has the side number above these lines.

EP#4
RCA VICTOR
RCA "Nipper" dog logo
Selection number   45 EP
Side number   "NEW ORTHOPHONIC"
Identification number   HIGH FIDELITY
Song titles
Artist credits

Though location of label information is identical to EP#3, the side number is in a serif typeface here ("1"). On EP#3, the numbers are in a sans serif typeface ("I"). Also "NEW ORTHOPHONIC HIGH FIDELITY" is in a condensed regular bold typestyle here. On EP#3 and EP#6, the regular bold is not condensed.

EP#5
RCA VICTOR
RCA "Nipper" dog logo

Selection number   45 EP
Side number   "NEW ORTHOPHONIC"
Identification number   HIGH FIDELITY
Song titles
Artist credits

Though location of label information is identical to EP#3, the side number is in a serif typeface here ("1"). On EP#3, the numbers are in a sans serif typeface ("I"). Also, this label differs from EP#4 in that "NEW ORTHOPHONIC HIGH FIDELITY" is in a regular bold typestyle here. On EP#4, it is in condensed regular bold.

EP#7
RCA VICTOR
RCA "Nipper" dog logo

Selection number   45
Side number   EP
Identification number
Song titles
Artist credits

Though location of label information is identical to EP#6, the selection number is in a regular bold typestyle here, and is condensed medium on EP#6. Also, the type size on song titles and artist credits is noticeably smaller here than on EP#6.

EP#6
RCA VICTOR
RCA "Nipper" dog logo

Selection number   45
Side number   EP
Identification number
Song titles
Artist credits

Though location of label information is identical to EP#7, the selection number is in a condensed medium typestyle here, and is regular bold on EP#7.

EP#8
RCA VICTOR
RCA "Nipper" dog logo

Selection number   Side number
Identification number "NEW ORTHOPHONIC"
HIGH FIDELITY
Song titles
Artist credits

Though location of label information is identical to EP#1, a dash is used here between the side and number (i.e. Side — 1). On EP#1 there is no dash. We know of no copies of this label with a horizontal silver line. Thus far, we have found this label only on the 1958 releases, *King Creole* and *King Creole, Vol. 2*.

EP#9
RCA VICTOR
RCA "Nipper" dog logo
Selection number   "NEW ORTHOPHONIC"
Side number   HIGH FIDELITY
Identification number
               Song titles
               Artist credits

Though location of label information is identical to
EP#10, a condensed regular bold typestyle is used
here—especially noticeable on selection number and
artist credit. Thus far, we have found this label only on
the 1957 release, *Elvis Sings Christmas Songs.*

EP#11
RCA VICTOR
Selection number   Side number
Identification number "NEW ORTHOPHONIC"
                              HIGH FIDELITY
               Song titles
               Artist credits

RCA's dogless EP label. Found only on Elvis EPs in
1956.

EP#10
RCA VICTOR
RCA "Nipper" dog logo
Selection number   "NEW ORTHOPHONIC"
Side number   HIGH FIDELITY
Identification number
               Song titles
               Artist credits

Though location of label information is identical to
EP#10, a regular bold (not condensed) typestyle is used
here—especially noticeable on selection number and
artist credit. Thus far we have found this label only on
the 1957 release, *Jailhouse Rock.*

EP#12
Song titles
Selection number   45 EP
RCA "Nipper" dog logo   RCA
                              VICTOR
Identification number   Side number
               Artist credits

The most noticeable difference between this and EP#14
is the type size used on the titles. Though not indicated
as such on the label this is a Gold Standard EP. A slight
variation of this label exists, one identical but without the
side numbers.

EP#13
EP title

Selection number	45 EP
RCA "Nipper" dog logo	RCA
	VICTOR
Identification number	Side number
Song titles	
Artist credits	

Though location of label information is similar to EP#12, the song titles are at the top on EP#12 and at the bottom here. Also, side number is in a san serif typeface ("I"). On EP#12, the numbers are in a serif typeface ("1").

EP#15
Song titles

Selection number	45 EP
RCA "Nipper" dog logo	RCA
	VICTOR
Side number	"NEW ORTHOPHONIC"
Identification number	HIGH FIDELITY
Artist credits	

Found only on the 1965 release, *Tickle Me*. There is no other Elvis-related release known with this label.

EP#14
Song titles

Selection number	45 EP
RCA "Nipper" dog logo	RCA
	VICTOR
Identification number	Side number
Artist credits	

See EP#12. A slight variation of this label exists, one identical but without the side numbers.

EP#16
EP title
Artist credit

Selection number	45 EP
RCA "Nipper" dog logo	RCA
	VICTOR
Identification number	Side number
Song titles	

Found only on the 1967 release, *Easy Come, Easy Go*. There is no other Elvis-related release known with this label.

RCA VICTOR LONG PLAY LABELS

LP#1

Differs slightly from LP#2 in that title and artist credit is in a bold typestyle. On LP#2 these are in a normal typestyle.

Differs from LP#3 and LP#4, neither of which have "New Orthophonic High Fidelity" on right.

May or may not have "Camden, N.J." at bottom of label.

LP#3

Differs from LP#4 which has only the side number ("1"). This label has "Side 1," etc.

Differs from LP#5 slightly in that artist credit is larger here than on LP#5.

See LP#1 for additional notes about this label.

LP#2

Like LP#1, may or may not have "Camden, N.J." at bottom of label. See LP#1 for additional notes about this label.

LP#4

See LP#1 and LP#3 for additional notes about this label.

LP#5

See LP#3 for additional notes about this label.

LP#8

See LP#7 for additional notes about this label.

LP#6

No differences noted. We know of no noteworthy variations of this specific label.

LP#9

No differences noted. We know of no noteworthy variations of this specific label.

LP#7

Differs from LP#8, which does not have "Stereo Orthophonic High Fidelity" under side number. This label does.

LP#10

Differs from LP#11 which does not have "New Orthophonic High Fidelity" on right. This label does.

LP#11.

See LP#10 for additional notes about this label.

LP#14

Differs from LP#13, which has "Stereo Orthophonic High Fidelity" under side number. This label does not.

LP#12

No differences noted. We know of no noteworthy variations of this specific label.

LP#15

No differences noted. We know of no noteworthy variations of this specific label.

LP#13

See LP#14 for additional notes about this label.

LP#16

No differences noted. We know of no noteworthy variations of this specific label.

SINGLES

AIN'T THAT LOVING YOU BABY / Ask Me

❑ RCA Victor 47-8440 .... 9/64   6-10
Black label, dog on top.
J2WW-3255-3S/RPKM-1005-3S. Label S#18. Credits "ELVIS
PRESLEY" on Ain't That Loving You Baby and "ELVIS
PRESLEY with the Jordanaires" on Ask Me.

❑ RCA Victor 47-8440 .... 9/64   20-30
Picture sleeve. Reads: "Coming Soon!
Roustabout LP Album."

❑ RCA Victor 47-8440 .... 10/64   30-40
Picture sleeve. Reads: "Ask For *Roustabout*
LP Album."

❑ RCA Victor 47-8440 .... 9/64   40-50
White label. Promotional issue only.
J2WW-3255-4S/RPKM-1005-4S. Label S#25. Credits "ELVIS
PRESLEY with the Jordanaires."

❑ RCA Victor 447-0649 ...... 11/65   6-10
Gold Standard. Black label, dog on side.
J2WW-3255-3S/RPKM-1005-3S. Label GS#6. Has playing
times and publisher. Credits "ELVIS PRESLEY" on *Ain't That
Loving You Baby* and "ELVIS PRESLEY with the Jordanaires"
on *Ask Me.*

❑ RCA Victor 447-0649 .... '70   10-12
Gold Standard. Red label.

❑ RCA Victor 447-0649 .... '77   3-5
Gold Standard. Black label, dog near top.

ALL SHOOK UP / (Let Me Be Your) Teddy Bear

❑ RCA Victor PB-13888 ...... 12/84   3-4
Gold vinyl. Originally included as one of the
singles in the boxed set *Elvis' Greatest Hits –
Golden Singles, Vol. 1.*

❑ RCA Victor PB-13888 ...... 12/84   3-4
Picture sleeve.

ALL SHOOK UP / That's When Your Heartaches Begin

❑ RCA Victor 20-6870 .... 3/57   75-125
Black label 78 rpm.
H2WB-0256-5S/H2WB-0260-5S. Label S#3. Credits "ELVIS
PRESLEY with The Jordanaires."

❑ RCA Victor 20-6870 .... '70s   250-500
White label 78 rpm. Reads: "Record Prevue,
Disc Jockey Sample." Unlike others in this
series, this one does not have the rectangular
"Not for Sale" box printed on label. We're not
yet certain as to the history, purpose and
legitimacy of this series.
H2WW-0256/H2WW-0260. Credits "Elvis Presley with The
Jordanaires." Identification numbers are engraved, but may
be scratched over.

❑ RCA Victor 47-6870 .... 3/57   20-30
Black label, dog on top, without horizontal
silver line.
H2WW-0256-1S/H2WW-0260-3S. Label S#15. Credits "Elvis
Presley with The Jordanaires."

❑ RCA Victor 47-6870 .... 3/57   30-40
Black label, dog on top, with horizontal silver
line.
H2WW-0256-5S/H2WW-0260-4S. Label S#12L. Credits
"ELVIS PRESLEY WITH THE JORDANAIRES."

❑ RCA Victor 47-6870 .... 3/57   50-100
Picture sleeve.

❑ RCA Victor 447-0618 .... 3/59   10-20
Gold Standard. Black label, dog on top.
J2PW-6015-2S/J2PW-6016-2S. Label GS#1 Credits "ELVIS
PRESLEY with The Jordanaires."

❑ RCA Victor 447-0618 .... 6/64   250-300
Gold Standard picture sleeve.

❑ RCA Victor 447-0618 .... 6/64   75-125
Gold Standard. White label. Promotional issue
only.
J2PW-6015-3S/J2PW-6016-3S. Label GS#9. Credits "ELVIS
PRESLEY with The Jordanaires."

❑ RCA Victor 447-0618 .... '65   6-10
Gold Standard. Black label, dog on side.
J2PW-6015-2S/J2PW-6016-2S. Label GS#4. Credits "ELVIS
PRESLEY with The Jordanaires."

❑ RCA Victor 447-0618 .... '68   50-75
Gold Standard. Orange label.
J2PW-6015-2S/J2PW-6016-2S. Credits "ELVIS PRESLEY with
The Jordanaires."

❑ RCA Victor 447-0618 .... '70   10-12
Gold Standard. Red label.
J2PW-6015-5S/J2PW-6016-2S. Credits "ELVIS PRESLEY with
The Jordanaires."

❑ RCA Victor 447-0618 .... '77   3-5
Gold Standard. Black label, dog near top.

❑ RCA Victor PB-11106 ...... 10/77   3-4
Originally included as one of the singles in the
boxed sets *15 Golden Records – 30 Golden
Hits* and *20 Golden Hits in Full Color Sleeves.*

❑ RCA Victor PB-11106 ...... 10/77   3-4
Picture sleeve.

ALMOST IN LOVE / A Little Less Conversation

❑ RCA Victor 47-9610 .... 9/68   10-15
Black label, dog on side.
WPKM-5766-9S/WPKM-5767-8S. Label S#27. Credits "ELVIS
PRESLEY with The Jordanaires."

❑ RCA Victor 47-9610 .... 9/68   30-40
Picture sleeve.

❑ RCA Victor 47-9610 .... 9/68   35-45
Yellow label. Promotional issue only.
WPKM-5766-4S/WPKM-5767-4S. Label S#26. Film mention,
under title on both sides, is on two lines. Credits "ELVIS
PRESLEY with The Jordanaires."
WPKM-5766-7S/WPKM-5767-9S. Label S#27. Film mention,
under title on both sides, is on one line. Credits "ELVIS
PRESLEY with The Jordanaires."

❑ RCA Victor 447-0667 .... 12/70   25-30
Gold Standard. Red label.
WPKM-5766-4S/WPKM-5767-5S. Credits "ELVIS PRESLEY"
(no mention of Jordanaires).

❑ RCA Victor 447-0667 .... '77   3-5
Gold Standard. Black label, dog near top.

ALWAYS ON MY MIND / Always on My Mind

❑ RCA Victor JK-14090
(PB-14090) 6/85   15-20
Promotional issue. Purple vinyl. Gold Elvis
50th Anniversary label.
PB-14090A-1/PB-14090A-2. Both sides are stereo. Credits "ELVIS PRESLEY."
Identification numbers are engraved.

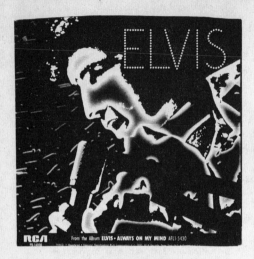

ALWAYS ON MY MIND / My Boy

❑ RCA Victor PB-14090........6/85   10-15
Purple vinyl. Gold Elvis 50th Anniversary
label.
PB-14090A-2/PB-14090B-2. Label states: "NOT FOR SALE."
Both sides are stereo. Credits "ELVIS PRESLEY."
Identification numbers are engraved.

❑ RCA Victor PB-14090.......6/85   5-10
Picture sleeve.

AMAZING WORLD OF SHORT WAVE LISTENING (SIDE 1) / Amazing World of Short Wave Listening (Side 2)

❑ Amazing World of Short Wave
Listening 4434-1...................'62   25-75
N9MW-4434-1/N9MW-4435-1.
Front: Gold with black print. Narrated by Alex
Dreier, "Radio/TV's Man on the Go." Back:
Text and picture of Dreier. Reportedly
includes an excerpt of an Elvis tune.

AMERICAN TRILOGY / The First Time Ever I Saw Your Face

❑ RCA Victor 74-0672 ....4/72   10-20
Orange label.
BPKS-1147-4S/APKS-1255-3S. Both sides are stereo.
Credits "ELVIS PRESLEY" on *An American Trilogy* and "ELVIS
PRESLEY, Vocal accomp. by The Nashville Edition and The
Imperials Quartet" on *The First Time Ever I Saw Your Face.*

❑ RCA Victor 74-0672 ....4/72   50-75
Picture sleeve. Sleeve reads: "From Elvis'
Standing Room Only Album," which was
never released. Instead, *Elvis As Recorded at
Madison Square Garden* came out.

❑ RCA Victor 74-0672 ....4/72   20-25
Yellow label. Promotional issue only.
BPKM-1147-1S/APKM-1255-1S. Both sides are mono.
Credits "ELVIS PRESLEY" on *An American Trilogy* and "ELVIS
PRESLEY, Vocal accomp. by The Nashville Edition and The
Imperials Quartet" on *The First Time Ever I Saw Your Face.*

AMERICAN TRILOGY / Until It's Time for You to Go

❑ RCA Victor 447-0685 ....5/73   10-12
Gold Standard. Red label.
BPKS-1147-6S/APKS-1255-5S. Both sides are stereo.
Credits "ELVIS PRESLEY" on *An American Trilogy* and "ELVIS
PRESLEY, Vocal accompaniment by The Imperials Quartet"
on *Until It's Time for You to Go.*

❑ RCA Victor 447-0685 ....'77   3-5
Gold Standard. Black label, dog near top.

AN AMERICAN TRILOGY: see *AMERICAN TRILOGY*

ARE YOU LONESOME TONIGHT / Can't Help Falling in Love

❑ RCA Victor PB-13895......12/84   3-4
Gold vinyl. Originally included as one of the
singles in the boxed set *Elvis' Greatest Hits –
Golden Singles, Vol. 2.*

❑ RCA Victor PB-13895......12/84   3-4
Picture sleeve.

ARE YOU LONESOME TONIGHT / I Gotta Know

❑ RCA Victor 47-7810.........11/60   8-10
Black label, dog on top.
L2WW-0106-7S/L2WW-0104-7S. Label S#19. Credits "ELVIS
PRESLEY with The Jordanaires."

❑ RCA Victor 47-7810.........11/60   20-30
Picture sleeve.

❑ RCA Victor 61-7810.........11/60   600-800
Living Stereo.
L2WA-3838-1S/L2WA-3837-1S. Credits "ELVIS PRESLEY
with The Jordanaires."

❑ RCA Victor 447-0629.........2/62   10-20
Gold Standard. Black label, dog on top.

❑ RCA Victor 447-0629...........'65   6-10
Gold Standard. Black label, dog on side.
L2WW-0106-1S/L2WW-0104-1S. Label GS#6, Credits
"ELVIS PRESLEY with The Jordanaires."

❑ RCA Victor 447-0629...........'68   50-75
Gold Standard. Orange label.
L2WW-0106-4S/L2WW-0104-2S. Credits "ELVIS PRESLEY
with The Jordanaires."

❑ RCA Victor 447-0629...........'70   10-12
Gold Standard. Red label.
L2WW-0106-12S/L2WW-0104-9S. Credits "ELVIS PRESLEY
with The Jordanaires."

❑ RCA Victor 447-0629...........'77   3-5
Gold Standard. Black label, dog near top.

❑ RCA Victor PB-11104......10/77   3-4
Originally included as one of the singles in the
boxed sets *15 Golden Records – 30 Golden
Hits* and *20 Golden Hits in Full Color Sleeves.*

❑ RCA Victor PB-11104......10/77   3-4
Picture sleeve. Title may also be shown as
Are You Lonesome Tonight.

ARE YOU SINCERE / Solitaire

❑ RCA Victor PB-11533........5/79   3-5
Black label, dog near top.
PB-11533-A-4S/PB-11533-B-3S. Both sides are stereo.
Credits "ELVIS PRESLEY, Unreleased version Produced by
Joan Deary" on *Are You Sincere* and "ELVIS PRESLEY,
Reissue Produced by Joan Deary / Original version produced
by Felton Jarvis" on *Solitaire.* Identification numbers are
engraved. Polystyrene pressing.

❑ RCA Victor PB-11533........5/79   8-10
Picture sleeve.

❑ RCA Victor JB-11533
(PB-11533) 5/79   10-12
Light yellow label. Promotional issue only.
PB-11533-A-3S/PB-11533-B-4S. Both sides are stereo.
Credits "ELVIS PRESLEY, Unreleased version Produced by
Joan Deary" on *Are You Sincere* and "ELVIS PRESLEY,
Reissue Produced by Joan Deary / Original version produced
by Felton Jarvis" on *Solitaire.* Identification numbers are
engraved. Polystyrene pressing.
For the Gold Standard release of *Are You
Sincere* see *UNCHAINED MELODY / Are You
Sincere*

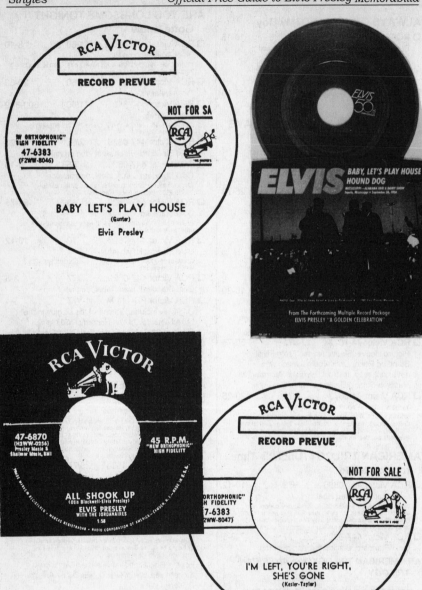

BABY, LET'S PLAY HOUSE / Hound Dog

❑ RCA Victor PB-13875........8/84   15-25
Gold vinyl. Gold Elvis 50th Anniversary label.
PB-13875-A-1S/PB-13875-B-2S. Both sides have "January 8th, 1935" stamped in trail off, but identification numbers are engraved. Neither side indicates mono or stereo. Credits "ELVIS PRESLEY." Also states: "Conceived & Produced by Joan Deary."
PB-13875-A-2S/PB-13875-B-1S. Both sides have "January 8th, 1935" stamped in trail off, but identification numbers are engraved.

❑ RCA Victor PB-13875........8/84   15-25
Picture sleeve.

❑ RCA Victor JB-13875
(PB-13875).......................8/84   350-400
Promotional issue. Gold vinyl. Gold Elvis 50th Anniversary label on *Baby Let's Play House* and white label on *Hound Dog*.

❑ RCA Victor PB-13875........8/84   20-40
Promotional issue. Gold vinyl. Gold Elvis 50th Anniversary label.
PB-13875-A-2S/PB-13875-B-1S. Both sides have "January 8th, 1935" stamped in trail off, but identification numbers are engraved. Label states: "NOT FOR SALE." Both sides shown as stereo. Credits "ELVIS PRESLEY." Also states: "Conceived & Produced by Joan Deary."
PB-13875-A-2S/PB-13875-B-1S. Both sides have "January 8th, 1935" stamped in trail off, but identification numbers are engraved. Label on *Hound Dog* is mostly blank, except for some print, which is backwards. Credits "ELVIS PRESLEY," but print is backwards. Print on *Baby, Let's Play House* is normal.
PB-13875-A-2S/PB-13875-B-2S. Both sides have "January 8th, 1935" stamped in trail off, but identification numbers are engraved. Label states: "NOT FOR SALE." Both sides shown as stereo. Credits "ELVIS PRESLEY." Also states: "Conceived & Produced by Joan Deary."

❑ RCA Victor JB-13875
(PB-13875).......................8/84   75-100
Promotional issue. Gold vinyl. Gold Elvis 50th Anniversary label on both sides.
PB-13875-A-1S/PB-13875-B-1S. Both sides have "January 8th, 1935" stamped in trail off, but Identification numbers are engraved. Label states: "NOT FOR SALE." Neither side indicates mono or stereo. Credits "ELVIS PRESLEY." Also states: "Conceived & Produced by Joan Deary."

RCA's Joan Deary appeared in Tupelo, Mississippi, August 16, 1986, when copies of this were distributed, and some have her autograph. For those, add 10% to 15% to price range. Actually, all copies are promotional issues, though only JB-13857 is marked "Not for Sale." Regardless of what is printed on label, both sides are monaural.

BABY LET'S PLAY HOUSE / I'm Left, You're Right, She's Gone

❑ Sun 217 ....4/55   800-1200
78 rpm.
U-143-2 △3445/U-142 △3289. Spacing between words is missing on second side (i.e. "I'mLeft, You'reRight, She'sGone"). Credits "ELVIS PRESLEY" (on line one) and "SCOTTY & BILL" (line two). Identification numbers are engraved.
Counterfeit Identification: Any colored plastic Sun 78 is an unauthorized (circa 1978) issue.

❑ Sun 217 ....4/55   700-1100
U-143X-45-2-72/U-142-45-72. Credits "ELVIS PRESLEY" (on line one) and "SCOTTY & BILL" (line two). Release number is at bottom of label. Push marks are present. Spacing between words is missing on second side (i.e. "I'mLeft, You'reRight, She'sGone"). Identification numbers are engraved.
Counterfeit Identification: Fakes of Sun 45s are numerous; however, some are easily identified. Any with "Issued 1973" engraved in the vinyl are fakes, and any on colored vinyl are boots. On some fakes, the brown sunrays, circling top half of label, fail to go all the way to the edge of the hole, though we are not prepared to state unequivocally that there are no originals printed this way. When compared to the label of an original, some fakes have noticeably darker brown print on noticeably lighter yellow stock. Any discs with "RE" or "Reissue" engraved in the vinyl are fakes. Any Sun singles with three push marks (three circular indentations, that if connected by a line would form a triangle) are original pressings.
Only bootleg picture sleeves exist for this release.

❑ RCA Victor 20-6383........12/55   100-150
Black label, 78 rpm.
F2WB-8046-3S/F2WB-8047-1S. Label S#2. Credits "ELVIS PRESLEY." Identification numbers are engraved, but may be scratched over.

❑ RCA Victor 20-6383...........'70s   250-500
White label 78 rpm. Reads: "Record Prevue, Disc Jockey Sample." Has rectangular "Not for Sale" box printed on label. We're not yet certain as to the history, purpose and legitimacy of this series.
F2WB-8046/F2WB-8047. Credits "ELVIS PRESLEY."

❑ RCA Victor 47-6383........12/55   40-50
Black label, dog on top, without horizontal silver line.
Only bootleg picture sleeves exist for this release.

❑ RCA Victor 47-6383........12/55   50-60
Black label, dog on top, with horizontal silver line.
F2WW-8046-4S/F2WW-8047-3S. Label S#12L. Credits "ELVIS PRESLEY."
Only bootleg picture sleeves exist for this release.

❑ RCA Victor 47-6383........12/55   200-300
White "Record Prevue" label. Promotional, Canadian issue only.

❑ RCA Victor 447-0604........3/59   10-20
Gold Standard. Black label, dog on top.
J2PW-5689-2S/J2PW-5690-3S. Label GS#1. Credits "ELVIS PRESLEY."

❑ RCA Victor 447-0604...........'65   6-12
Gold Standard. Black label, dog on side.
J2PW-5689-2S/J2PW-5690-3S. Label GS#6. Credits "ELVIS PRESLEY."

❑ RCA Victor 447-0604...........'70   10-12
Gold Standard. Red label.

❑ RCA Victor 447-0604...........'77   3-5
Gold Standard. Black label, dog near top.

❑ Collectables 4502 ....'86   3-4
Black vinyl.
DPE1-1002-A-1/DPE1-1002-B-1. Credits "ELVIS PRESLEY." Polystyrene pressing.

❏ Collectables 4502 .... 7/92   5-6
Gold vinyl.
DPE1-1002-A-1/DPE1-1002-B-1. Credits "ELVIS PRESLEY."
Polystyrene pressing.
May be shown as *Baby, Let's Play House*
(with comma) on some labels.

BABY LET'S PLAY HOUSE / Let Yourself Go

❏ Marquis M-101: Bootleg. Listed for
identification only.

BEATLEMANIA / ELVISMANIA

❏ Professional JCL-7777: Bootleg. Listed for
identification only.

BEGINNINGS – ELVIS STYLE, PART I / Beginnings Part II

Memphis Flash 92444 .... '78   10-20
First issue of Bob Neale's 1954 interview with
Elvis (and others).

BIG BOSS MAN / Paralyzed

❏ Collectables 4521 .... '86   3-4
Black vinyl.
DPE1-1021-A-1/DPE1-1021-B-1. Credits "ELVIS PRESLEY."
Identification numbers are engraved. Polystyrene pressing.

❏ Collectables 4521 .... 7/92   5-6
Gold vinyl.
DPE1-1021-A-1/DPE1-1021-B-1. Credits "ELVIS PRESLEY."
Identification numbers are engraved. Polystyrene pressing.

BIG BOSS MAN / You Don't Know Me

❏ RCA Victor 47-9341 .... 9/67   6-10
Black label, dog on side.
UPKM-2771-5S/UPKM-2766-5S. Label S#20. Credits "ELVIS
PRESLEY" on *Big Boss Man* and "ELVIS PRESLEY with the
Jordanaires" on *You Don't Know Me*.

❏ RCA Victor 47-9341 .... 9/67   20-30
Picture sleeve.

❏ RCA Victor 47-9341 .... 9/67   35-40
White label. Promotional issue only.
UPKM-2771-4S/UPKM-2766-4S. Label S#27. Credits "ELVIS
PRESLEY" on *Big Boss Man* and "ELVIS PRESLEY with the
Jordanaires" on *You Don't Know Me*. This seems to be the
first time a label S#27 pressing (with narrow bold label
print) has a lower take number than one on label S#26
(standard bold print).
UPKM-2771-7S/UPKM-2766-7S. Label S#26. Credits "ELVIS
PRESLEY" on *Big Boss Man* and "ELVIS PRESLEY with the
Jordanaires" on *You Don't Know Me*.

❏ RCA Victor 447-0662 .... '70   10-12
Gold Standard. Red label.
UPKM-2771-8S/UPKM-2766-8S. Label S#26. Credits "ELVIS
PRESLEY" on *Big Boss Man* and "ELVIS PRESLEY with The
Jordanaires" on *You Don't Know Me*.

❏ RCA Victor 447-0662 .... '77   3-5
Gold Standard. Black label, dog near top.

BIG HUNK O' LOVE / My Wish Came True

❏ RCA Victor 47-7600 .... 7/59   10-15
Black label, dog on top.
J2WW-3254-5S/H2PW-5524-6S. Label S#19. Credits "ELVIS
PRESLEY with The Jordanaires."

❏ RCA Victor 47-7600 .... 7/59   30-40
Picture sleeve.

❏ RCA Victor 447-0626 .... 2/62   10-20
Gold Standard. Black label, dog on top.
J2WW-3254-9S/H2PW-5524-10S. Label GS#1. Credits
"ELVIS PRESLEY with The Jordanaires."

❏ RCA Victor 447-0626 .... '65   6-10
Gold Standard. Black label, dog on side.
J2WW-3254-9S/H2PW-5524-10S. Label GS#6. Has playing
times. Credits "ELVIS PRESLEY with The Jordanaires." The
line "with The Jordanaires" is off center to the left on *A Big
Hunk O' Love* and off center to the right on *My Wish Came
True*.

❏ RCA Victor 447-0626 .... '68   50-75
Gold Standard. Orange label.
J2WW-3254-10S/H2PW-5524-9S. Credits "ELVIS PRESLEY
with The Jordanaires."

❏ RCA Victor 447-0626 .... '70   10-12
Gold Standard. Red label.
J2WW-3254-11S/H2PW-5524-9S. Credits "ELVIS PRESLEY
with The Jordanaires."

❏ RCA Victor 447-0626 .... '77   3-5
Gold Standard. Black label, dog near top.

❏ Collectables 4508 .... '86   3-4
Black vinyl.
DPE1-1008-A-1/DPE1-1008-B-1. Credits "ELVIS PRESLEY
with The Jordanaires." Polystyrene pressing.

❏ Collectables 4508 .... 7/92   5-6
Gold vinyl.
DPE1-1008-A-1/DPE1-1008-B-1. Credits "ELVIS PRESLEY
with The Jordanaires." Polystyrene pressing.

BLUE CHRISTMAS / Blue Christmas

❏ RCA Victor H07W-
0808 .... 11/57   2000-3000
White label. Listed by identification number
since no selection number is used. This disc
is usually referred to as "0808." Promotional
issue only.
HO7W-0808-1/HO7W-0808-1. Identification numbers are
engraved. Credits "ELVIS PRESLEY."

BLUE CHRISTMAS / Santa Claus Is Back in Town

❏ RCA Victor 447-0647 .... 11/65   6-10
Gold Standard. Black label, dog on side.
H2PW-5525-3S/H2PW-5532-2S. Label GS#6. Has playing
times and publisher. Does not show recording dates. Credits
"ELVIS PRESLEY."

❏ RCA Victor 447-0647 .... 11/65   30-35
Picture sleeve. Reads: "Gold Standard
Series" in upper left corner.

❏ RCA Victor 447-0647 .... 11/65   35-40
Gold Standard. White label. Promotional issue
only.
H2PW-5525-1S/H2PW-5532-1S. Label GS#3. Credits "ELVIS
PRESLEY."
H2PW-5525-7S/H2PW-5532-3S. Label GS#10. Credits
"ELVIS PRESLEY."

❏ RCA Victor 447-0647 .... '68   50-75
Gold Standard. Orange label.
H2PW-5525-8S/H2PW-5532-7S. Credits "ELVIS PRESLEY."
H2PW-5525-9S/H2PW-5532-7S. Credits "ELVIS PRESLEY."

❏ RCA Victor 447-0647 .... '70   10-12
Gold Standard. Red label.
H2PW-5525-3S/H2PW-5532-2S. Credits "ELVIS PRESLEY."

❏ RCA Victor 447-0647 .... 11/77   3-5
Gold Standard. Black label, dog near top.
H2PW-5525-3S/H2PW-5532-12. Credits "ELVIS PRESLEY."

❏ RCA Victor 447-0647 .... 11/77   8-10
Picture sleeve. Does not mention Gold
Standard Series.

BLUE CHRISTMAS / Santa Claus Is Back in Town (Cassette)

❏ RCA 0647-4-RS 11/87   3-5
Cassette single, one song on each side.

❏ RCA 0647-4-RS 11/87   3-5
Tape cover/holder.

BLUE CHRISTMAS / Wooden Heart

❏ RCA Victor 447-0720 ...... 11/64   10-20
Gold Standard. Black label, dog on top.
H2PW-5525-4S/L2PW-3681-6S. Label GS#3. Credits "ELVIS PRESLEY."

❏ RCA Victor 447-0720 ...... 11/64   45-55
Gold Standard picture sleeve.

❏ RCA Victor 447-0720 ...... 11/64   35-40
Gold Standard. White label. Promotional issue only.
H2PW-5525-4S/L2PW-3681-6S. Label GS#7. Credits "ELVIS PRESLEY."

Despite a higher Gold Standard selection number, this single came out one year before 447-0647.

BLUE HAWAII / Blank

❏ Paramount Pictures
SP-1800 .... 10/61   500-750
Promotional issue for play in theatre lobbies. Has excerpts of several film songs. Side two is a blank pressing. Label does not identify Elvis as the singer.

BLUE HAWAII / Hawaiian Wedding Song

❏ Shaker 1835 (record or picture sleeve): Bootleg. Listed for identification only.

BLUE MOON / Just Because

❏ RCA Victor 20-6640 .... 9/56   75-100
Black label, 78 rpm.
F2WB-8117-3S/F2WB-8118-3S. Label S#3. Credits "ELVIS PRESLEY."

❏ RCA Victor 47-6640 .... 9/56   40-50
Black label, dog on top, without silver horizontal line.
Only bootleg picture sleeves exist for this release.

❏ RCA Victor 47-6640 .... 9/56   50-60
Black label, dog on top, with silver horizontal line.
F2WW-8117-5S/F2WW-8118-5S. Label S#12L. Credits "ELVIS PRESLEY."
Only bootleg picture sleeves exist for this release.

❏ RCA Victor 447-0613 .... 3/59   15-20
Gold Standard. Black label, dog on top.
J2PW-6005-2S/J2PW-6006-1S. Label GS#1. Credits "ELVIS PRESLEY."

❏ RCA Victor 447-0613 .... '65   6-12
Gold Standard. Black label, dog on side.
J2PW-6005-2S/J2PW-6006-4S. Label GS#6. Credits "ELVIS PRESLEY."

❏ RCA Victor 447-0613 .... '68   50-75
Gold Standard. Orange label.

❏ RCA Victor 447-0613 .... '70   10-12
Gold Standard. Red label.
J2PW-6005-2S/J2PW-6006-6S. Credits "ELVIS PRESLEY."

❏ RCA Victor 447-0613 .... '77   3-5
Gold Standard. Black label, dog near top.

BLUE SUEDE SHOES / Blue Suede Shoes

❏ RCA Victor JK-13929 (PB-13929) 12/84   15-25
Promotional issue. Blue vinyl. Gold Elvis 50th Anniversary label.
PB-13929-A-5/PB-13929-A-5. Label states: "NOT FOR SALE." Both sides shown as mono. Credits "ELVIS PRESLEY." Identification numbers are engraved.

BLUE SUEDE SHOES [Elvis Presley] / El Paso [Marty Robbins]

❏ For Your Classic Juke Box
G-509 .... '80s   50-75
78 rpm. Made for juke box use.

BLUE SUEDE SHOES / Promised Land

❏ RCA Victor PB-13929 ...... 12/84   10-15
Blue vinyl. Gold Elvis 50th Anniversary label.
PB-13929-A-5/PB-13929-B-5. *Blue Suede Shoes* shown as stereo, *Promised Land* shown as mono. Credits "ELVIS PRESLEY." Identification numbers are engraved.

❏ RCA Victor PB-13929 ...... 12/84   8-12
Blue vinyl. Gold Elvis 50th Anniversary label.
PB-13929-A-5/PB-13929-B-5. *Blue Suede Shoes* shown as mono, *Promised Land* shown as stereo. Credits "ELVIS PRESLEY." Identification numbers are engraved.

❏ RCA Victor PB-13929 ...... 12/84   10-15
Picture sleeve.

BLUE SUEDE SHOES / Tutti Frutti

❏ RCA Victor 20-6636 .... 9/56   75-100
Black label, 78 rpm.
G2WB-1230-1S/G2WB-1255-1S. Label S#4. Credits "ELVIS PRESLEY."

❏ RCA Victor 47-6636 .... 9/56   60-90
Black label, dog on top, without horizontal silver line.
Only bootleg picture sleeves exist for this release.

❏ RCA Victor 47-6636 .... 9/56   90-100
Black label, dog on top, with horizontal silver line.
G2WW-1230-3S/G2WW-1255-3S. Label S#12L. Credits "ELVIS PRESLEY."
Only bootleg picture sleeves exist for this release.

❏ RCA Victor 447-0609 .... 3/59   15-20
Gold Standard. Black label, dog on top.

❏ RCA Victor 447-0609 .... '65   6-10
Gold Standard. Black label, dog on side.
J2PW-5697-3S/J2PW-5698-2S. Label GS#4. Credits "ELVIS PRESLEY."

❏ RCA Victor 447-0609 .... '70   10-12
Gold Standard. Red label.
J2PW-5697-4S/J2PW-5698-2S. Credits "ELVIS PRESLEY."

❏ RCA Victor 447-0609 .... '68   50-75
Gold Standard. Orange label.
J2PW-5697-3S/J2PW-5698-2S. Credits "ELVIS PRESLEY."

❏ RCA Victor 447-0609 .... '77 3-5
Gold Standard. Black label, dog near top.
J2PW-5697 PB-11107A-7/J2PW-5698 PB-11107B-6S. Credits "ELVIS PRESLEY."

❏ RCA Victor PB-11107......10/77 3-4
Originally included as one of the singles in the boxed sets *15 Golden Records – 30 Golden Hits* and *20 Golden Hits in Full Color Sleeves.*

❏ RCA Victor PB-11107......10/77 3-4
Picture sleeve.

❏ RCA Victor PB-13885......12/84 3-4
Gold vinyl. Originally included as one of the singles in the boxed set *Elvis' Greatest Hits – Golden Singles, Vol. 1.*

❏ RCA Victor PB-13885......12/84 3-4
Picture sleeve.

BOSSA NOVA BABY / Such a Night

❏ Collectables 4513................ '86 3-4
Black vinyl.
DPE1-1013-A-1/DPE1-1013-B-1. *Such a Night* has the false starts and studio chatter first heard on *Elvis: A Legendary Performer, Volume 2.* Credits "ELVIS PRESLEY with The Jordanaires." Polystyrene pressing.

❏ Collectables 4513.............. 7/92 5-6
Gold vinyl.
DPE1-1013-A-1/DPE1-1013-B-1. *Such a Night* has the false starts and studio chatter first heard on *Elvis: A Legendary Performer, Volume 2.* Credits "ELVIS PRESLEY with The Jordanaires." Polystyrene pressing.

BOSSA NOVA BABY / Witchcraft

❏ RCA Victor 47-8243 .... 10/63 6-10
Black label, dog on top.
PPKM-4431-4S/PPKM-0295-3S. Label S#18. Credits "ELVIS PRESLEY With THE JORDANAIRES."
PPKM-4431-5S/PPKM-0295-5S. Label S#19. Credits "ELVIS PRESLEY With The Jordanaires."

❏ RCA Victor 47-8243 .... 10/63 20-30
Picture sleeve. Reads: "Coming Soon! *Fun in Acapulco* LP Album" across bottom.

❏ RCA Victor 47-8243 .... 1/64 200-300
Picture sleeve. Has makes no mention of the *Fun in Acapulco* LP.

❏ RCA Victor 447-0642 .... 8/64 20-25
Gold Standard. Black label, dog on top.

❏ RCA Victor 447-0642 .... '65 6-10
Gold Standard. Black label, dog on side.
PPKM-4431-4S/PPKM-0295-3S. Label GS#6. Has playing times and publisher. Credits "ELVIS PRESLEY with The Jordanaires."

❏ RCA Victor 447-0642 .... '68 50-75
Gold Standard. Orange label.

❏ RCA Victor 447-0642 .... '70 10-12
Gold Standard. Red label.
PPKM-4431-3S/PPKM-0295-4S. Credits "ELVIS PRESLEY with The Jordanaires."

❏ RCA Victor 447-0642 .... '77 3-5
Gold Standard. Black label, dog near top.

BRIDGE OVER TROUBLED WATER / Lawdy Miss Clawdy

❏ R.S. Productions R-91858: Bootleg. Listed for identification only.

BRINGING IT BACK / Pieces of My Life

❏ RCA Victor PB-10401......10/75 200-300
Orange label.
This is the last Elvis RCA single issued on the orange label.

❏ RCA Victor PB-10401......10/75 8-10
Tan label.
PB-10401-A-30S/PB-10401-B-3S. Both sides are stereo. Credits "ELVIS PRESLEY, Vocal Accompaniment: Voice/The Holladays" on *Bringing It Back* and "ELVIS PRESLEY, Vocal Accompaniment: Voice" on *Pieces of My Life.*

❏ RCA Victor PB-10401......10/75 10-15
Picture sleeve.

❏ RCA Victor JA-10401
(PB-10401) 10/75 20-25
Light yellow label. Promotional issue only.
PA-10401-C-10S/PA-10401-D-2S. Both sides are mono. *Bringing It Back* side has identification numbers engraved, but *Pieces of My Life* has them stamped. Credits "ELVIS PRESLEY, Vocal Accompaniment:Voice/The Holladays" on *Bringing It Back* and "ELVIS PRESLEY, Vocal Accompaniment: Voice" on *Pieces of My Life.*

BURNING LOVE / Can't Help Falling in Love

❏ Prime PRN 78-19 .... '72 75-100
78 rpm. Made for juke box use.

BURNING LOVE / It's a Matter of Time

❏ RCA Victor 74-0769..........8/72 250-300
Gray label.
BPKS-1257-1S/BPKS-1260-5S. Both sides are stereo. Credits "ELVIS PRESLEY, Vocal accomp.: J.D. Sumner & The Stamps."

❏ RCA Victor 74-0769..........8/72 4-6
Orange label.
BPKS-1257-4S/BPKS-1260-4S. Both sides are stereo. Credits "ELVIS PRESLEY, Vocal accomp.: J.D. Sumner & The Stamps."

❏ RCA Victor 74-0769..........8/72 10-15
Picture sleeve.

❏ RCA Victor 74-0769..........8/72 15-20
Yellow label. Promotional issue only.
BPKM-1257-4S/BPKM-1260-4S. Both sides are mono. Credits "ELVIS PRESLEY, Vocal accomp.: J.D. Sumner & The Stamps."

BURNING LOVE / Steamroller Blues

❏ RCA Victor GB-10156 ....3/75 10-12
Gold Standard. Red label.

❏ RCA Victor GB-10156 ....'77 3-5
Gold Standard. Black label, dog near top.

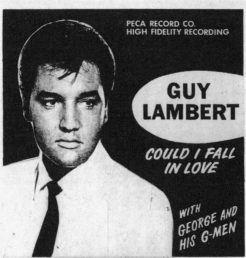

CAN'T HELP FALLING IN LOVE / Rock-a-Hula Baby

❑ RCA Victor 47-7968.........12/61   8-10
Black label, dog on top.
M2PW-2988-4S/M2PW-2989-6S. Label S#19. Indicates *Rock-A-Hula Baby* is a "TWIST SPECIAL." Credits "ELVIS PRESLEY with The Jordanaires."

❑ RCA Victor 47-7968.........12/61   20-30
Picture sleeve.

❑ RCA Victor 37-7968.........12/61   5000-8000
Compact 33 single.
M2PI-5480-2S/M2PI-5479-2S. Has LP-size (¼-inch) hole. Credits "ELVIS PRESLEY with The Jordanaires."

❑ RCA Victor 37-7968.........12/61   5000-8000
Picture sleeve for Compact 33 single.

❑ RCA Victor 447-0635 ...... 11/62   8-12
Gold Standard. Black label, dog on top.

❑ RCA Victor 447-0635 ....'65   6-10
Gold Standard. Black label, dog on side.
M2PW-2988-5S/M2PW-2989-3S. Label GS#6. Has playing times and publisher. Does not show recording dates. Credits "ELVIS PRESLEY with The Jordanaires."

❑ RCA Victor 447-0635 ....'68   50-75
Gold Standard. Orange label.
M2PW-2988-5S/M2PW-2989-3S. Credits "ELVIS PRESLEY with The Jordanaires."

❑ RCA Victor 447-0635 ....'70   10-12
Gold Standard. Red label.
M2PW-2988-7S/M2PW-2989-7S. Credits "ELVIS PRESLEY with The Jordanaires."

❑ RCA Victor 447-0635 ....'77   3-5
Gold Standard. Black label, dog near top.

❑ RCA Victor PB-11102......10/77   3-4
Originally included as one of the singles in the boxed sets *15 Golden Records – 30 Golden Hits* and *20 Golden Hits in Full Color Sleeves.*

❑ RCA Victor PB-11102......10/77   3-4
Picture sleeve.

CHRONOLOGY OF AMERICAN MUSIC (A Countdown of All the Number One Songs 1955 to Now) / A Short Version

❑ More Music Productions
MM-02-202-72.................12/72   25-50
Gold Label with black print. Promotional single issued only to subscribing radio stations which may have been included in a programmer's packet to promote the five-hour, 21-disc radio show of the same title (listed in LONG PLAY ALBUM chapter). Includes excerpts of several No. 1 Elvis songs.
CF-847-1/CF-847-2. Identification numbers are engraved.

❑ MM-02-202-72.................12/72   50-75
Titles sleeve. Black and white gatefold sleeve with description of contents on upper inside of sleeve. Back of sleeve is blank.

CLEAN UP YOUR OWN BACK YARD / The Fair Is Moving On

❑ RCA Victor 47-9747 ....6/69   3-5
Orange label.
XPKM-3976-6S/XPKM-1276-5S. Credits "ELVIS PRESLEY."

❑ RCA Victor 47-9747..........6/69   15-20
Picture sleeve.

❑ RCA Victor 47-9747..........6/69   25-30
Yellow label. Promotional issue only.
XPKM-3976-6S/XPKM-1276-6S. Credits "ELVIS PRESLEY."

❑ RCA Victor 447-0672.......12/70   10-12
Gold Standard. Red label.
XPKM-3976-3S/XPKM-1276-3S. Credits "ELVIS PRESLEY."

❑ RCA Victor 447-0672...........'77   3-5
Gold Standard. Black label, dog near top.

COULD I FALL IN LOVE / Blank

❑ PECA.....................7/66   4000-8000
Picture sleeve. Pictures Elvis but makes no mention of him by name. Credits "Guy Lambert with George and His G-Men." Guy Lambert is Elvis' character in the film *Double Trouble.* This full color sleeve was made as a prop for the film. No Peca records were made.

COUNTRY SIDE – ELVIS / The Country Music's Radio Magazine

❑ Creative Radio...................5/82   50-100
Demo disc, issued to radio stations only.

CRYING IN THE CHAPEL / I Believe in the Man in the Sky

❑ RCA Victor 447-0643.........4/65   6-10
Gold Standard. Black label, dog on side.
L2WW-0385-4S/L2WW-0375-4S. Label GS#5. Credits "ELVIS PRESLEY with the Jordanaires."

❑ RCA Victor 447-0643.........4/65   20-30
Gold Standard picture sleeve.

❑ RCA Victor 447-0643.........4/65   25-30
Gold Standard. White label. Promotional issue only.
L2WW-0385-1S/L2WW-0375-3S. Label GS#12. We know of no other Elvis pressings with this label, promo or otherwise. On both sides, the line "with the Jordanaires" is slightly crooked. Credits "ELVIS PRESLEY with the Jordanaires."
L2WW-0385-4S/L2WW-0375-4S. Label GS#7. Credits "ELVIS PRESLEY with the Jordanaires."

❑ RCA Victor 447-0643...........'70   10-12
Gold Standard. Red label.
L2WW-0385-6S/L2WW-0375-6S. Credits "ELVIS PRESLEY with The Jordanaires."

❑ RCA Victor 447-0643...........'77   3-5
Gold Standard. Black label, dog near top.

❑ RCA Victor PB-11113......10/77   3-4
Originally included as one of the singles in the boxed set *15 Golden Records – 30 Golden Hits.*

❑ RCA Victor PB-11113......10/77   3-4
Picture sleeve.

(YOU'RE THE) DEVIL IN DISGUISE / Please Don't Drag That String Around

❑ RCA Victor 47-8188 .... 6/63   500-700
Black label, dog on top. This pressing incorrectly shows the flip side title as *Please Don't Drag That String ALONG.*
PPKM-0292-7S/PPKM-0291-16S. Label S#12L. Credits "ELVIS PRESLEY With The Jordanaires."

❑ RCA Victor 47-8188 .... 6/63   6-10
Black label, dog on top. Shows flip side title correctly.
PPKM-0292-6S/PPKM-0291-15S. Label S#19. Credits "ELVIS PRESLEY With The Jordanaires."
PPKM-0292-7S/PPKM-0291-15S. Label S#19. Credits "ELVIS PRESLEY With The Jordanaires."

❑ RCA Victor 47-8188 .... 6/63   20-30
Picture sleeve.

❑ RCA Victor 447-0641 .... 8/64   20-25
Gold Standard. Black label, dog on top.

❑ RCA Victor 447-0641 .... '65   6-10
Gold Standard. Black label, dog on side.
PPKM-0292-5S/PPKM-0291-13S. Label GS#4. Has playing times and publisher. Credits "ELVIS PRESLEY with The Jordanaires."

❑ RCA Victor 447-0641 .... '70   10-12
Gold Standard. Red label.
PPKM-0292-5S/PPKM-0291-17S. Credits "ELVIS PRESLEY with The Jordanaires."

❑ RCA Victor 447-0641 .... '77   3-5
Gold Standard. Black label, dog near top.
PPKM-0292/PPKM-0291. Credits "ELVIS PRESLEY with The Jordanaires." Identification numbers are engraved. Also has "Shelley" engraved on both sides.

DO THE CLAM / You'll Be Gone

❑ RCA Victor 47-8500 .... 2/65   6-10
Black label, dog on top.
SPKM-2009-7S/N2WW-0691-7S. Label S#19. Credits "ELVIS PRESLEY with the Jordanaires; Jubilee Four & Carole Lombard Trio" on *Do the Clam* and "ELVIS PRESLEY with the Jordanaires" on *You'll Be Gone.*

❑ RCA Victor 47-8500 .... 2/65   20-30
Picture sleeve.

❑ RCA Victor 47-8500 .... 2/65   40-45
White label. Promotional issue only.
SPKM-2009-4S/N2WW-0691-4S. Label S#23. Credits "ELVIS PRESLEY with the Jordanaires; Jubilee Four & Carole Lombard Trio" on *Do the Clam* and "ELVIS PRESLEY with the Jordanaires" on *You'll Be Gone.*

❑ RCA Victor 447-0648 ...... 11/65   6-10
Gold Standard. Black label, dog on side.

❑ RCA Victor 447-0648 .... '70   10-12
Gold Standard. Red label.
SPKM-2009-6S/N2WW-0691-9S. Credits "ELVIS PRESLEY with the Jordanaires; Jubilee Four & Carole Lombard Trio" on *Do the Clam* and "ELVIS PRESLEY with the Jordanaires" on *You'll Be Gone.*

❑ RCA Victor 447-0648 .... '77   3-5
Gold Standard. Black label, dog near top.

DON'T / I Beg of You

❑ RCA Victor 20-7150 .... 1/58   75-150
Black label, 78 rpm.
H2PB-5529-2S/H2WB-0259-5S. Label S#5. Credits "ELVIS PRESLEY With The Jordanaires."

❑ RCA Victor 47-7150 .... 1/58   10-15
Black label, dog on top.
H2PW-5529-5S/H2WW-0259-5S. Label S#15. Credits "ELVIS PRESLEY With The Jordanaires."

H2PW-5529-8S/H2WW-0259-9S. Label S#12L. Has expanded spacing between each letter of the title (i.e. "D O N ' T "). Credits "ELVIS PRESLEY with The Jordanaires." Identification numbers are stamped.
H2PW-5529-10S/H2WW-0259-11S. Label S#12L. Has normal letter spacing on "DON'T." Credits "ELVIS PRESLEY with The Jordanaires."

❑ RCA Victor 47-7150 .... 1/58   50-60
Picture sleeve.

❑ RCA Victor 47-7150 .... 1/58   200-300
White "Record Prevue" label. Promotional, Canadian issue only.

❑ RCA Victor 447-0621 .... '61   10-15
Gold Standard. Black label, dog on top.
H2PW-5529-1S/H2WW-0259-15S. Label GS#1. Credits "ELVIS PRESLEY with The Jordanaires."

❑ RCA Victor 447-0621 .... '65   6-10
Gold Standard. Black label, dog on side.
H2PW-5529-3S/H2WW-0259-16S. Label GS#6. Credits "ELVIS PRESLEY with The Jordanaires."

❑ RCA Victor 447-0621 .... '68   50-75
Gold Standard. Orange label.

❑ RCA Victor 447-0621 .... '70   10-12
Gold Standard. Red label.
H2PW-5529-4S/H2WW-0259-17S. Credits "ELVIS PRESLEY with The Jordanaires."

❑ RCA Victor 447-0621 .... '77   3-5
Gold Standard. Black label, dog near top.

DON'T / Wear My Ring Around Your Neck

❑ RCA Victor SP-45-76 .... 1/60   800-1000
Black label, dog on top. Promotional issue only.
H2PW-5529-1S/J2WW-0181-1S. Label S#13. Label has "NOT FOR SALE." Credits "ELVIS PRESLEY with The Jordanaires."

❑ RCA Victor SP-45-76 .... 1/60   1200-2000
Picture sleeve.

DON'T BE CRUEL / Ain't that Lovin' You Baby

❑ RCA Victor 07863-
62402-7 .... '92   3-5
Black vinyl, silver label.
07863-62402-7-A-2/07863-624042-B-2. Identification numbers are engraved. Polygram International. Credits "ELVIS PRESLEY."

❑ RCA Victor 07863-
62402-7 .... '92   1-2
Plain white picture sleeve. Has aqua sticker with white letters reading: "Elvis The King of Rock 'N' Roll EP-7."

❑ RCA Victor 62402-7 .... '92   5-8
Juke box title strips. Five color strips with picture of Elvis. Released in conjunction with the CD box set *Elvis – The King of Rock 'N' Roll – The Complete 50's Masters.*

DON'T BE CRUEL / Don't Be Cruel

❑ Qualiton 101 (record or picture sleeve): Bootleg. Listed for identification only.

DON'T BE CRUEL / Hound Dog

❑ RCA Victor 20-6604 .... 7/56   75-100
Black label, 78 rpm.
G2WB-5936-1S/G2WB-5935-1S. Label S#6. Credits "ELVIS PRESLEY."
G2WB-5936-7S/G2WB-5935-8S. Label S#6. Credits "ELVIS PRESLEY."

❑ RCA Victor 20-6604 .... '70s   250-500
White label 78 rpm. Reads: "Record Prevue, Disc Jockey Sample." Has rectangular "Not for Sale" box printed on label. We're not yet certain as to the history, purpose and legitimacy of this series.
G2WB-5936/G2WB-5935. Credits "ELVIS PRESLEY." Identification numbers are engraved, but may be scratched over.

❑ RCA Victor 47-6604 .... 7/56   20-30
Black label, dog on top, without horizontal silver line.
G2WW-5936-1S/G2WW-5935-2S. Label S#13. Credits "ELVIS PRESLEY."
G2WW-5936-2S/G2WW-5935-3S. Label S#13. Credits "ELVIS PRESLEY."

❑ RCA Victor 47-6604 .... 7/56   30-40
Black label, dog on top, with horizontal silver line.
G2WW-5936-14S/G2WW-5935-11S. Label S#12L. Credits "ELVIS PRESLEY."

❑ RCA Victor 47-6604 .... 7/56   65-75
Picture sleeve. Front of sleeve has *Hound Dog!* on top of *Don't Be Cruel*. This black and white sleeve was the first one issued with an Elvis photograph, and has a different one on each side.
Counterfeit Identification: On fake sleeves, reproduction of the black and white Elvis photos are slightly out of focus – looking very much like a copy. On originals, the photos are sharp and precise.

❑ RCA Victor 47-6604 .... 7/56   75-85
Picture sleeve. Front of sleeve has *Don't Be Cruel* on top of *Hound Dog!*

❑ RCA Victor 47-6604 .... 7/56   200-300
White "Record Prevue" label. Promotional, Canadian issue only.

❑ RCA Victor 447-0608 .... 3/59   10-20
Gold Standard. Black label, dog on top.
J2PW-5696-4S/J2PW-5695-3S. Label GS#1. Credits "ELVIS PRESLEY."
J2PW-5696-?S/J2PW-5695-?S. Label GS#2. Credits "ELVIS PRESLEY."

❑ RCA Victor 447-0608 .... 6/64   250-300
Gold Standard picture sleeve.

❑ RCA Victor 447-0608 .... 6/64   75-125
Gold Standard. White label. Promotional issue only.
J2PW-5696-4S/J2PW-5695-3S. Label GS#9. Credits "ELVIS PRESLEY."

❑ RCA Victor 447-0608 .... '65   6-10
Gold Standard. Black label, dog on side.
J2PW-5696-6S/J2PW-5695-7S. Label GS#4. Credits "ELVIS PRESLEY."

❑ RCA Victor 447-0608 .... '68   50-75
Gold Standard. Orange label.
J2PW-5696-6S/J2PW-5695-7S. Credits "ELVIS PRESLEY."

❑ RCA Victor 447-0608 .... '70   10-12
Gold Standard. Red label.
J2PW-5696-7S/J2PW-5695-8S. Credits "ELVIS PRESLEY."

❑ RCA Victor 447-0608 .... '77   3-5
Gold Standard. Black label, dog near top.

❑ RCA Victor PB-11099 ...... 10/77   3-4
Originally included as one of the singles in the boxed sets *15 Golden Records – 30 Golden Hits* and *20 Golden Hits in Full Color Sleeves*.

❑ RCA Victor PB-11099 ...... 10/77   3-4
Picture sleeve.

❑ RCA Victor PB-13886 ...... 12/84   3-4
Gold vinyl. Originally included as one of the singles in the boxed set *Elvis' Greatest Hits – Golden Singles, Vol. 1*.

❑ RCA Victor PB-13886 ...... 12/84   3-4
Picture sleeve.

DON'T CRY DADDY / Rubberneckin'

❑ RCA Victor 47-9768 .... 11/69   4-6
Orange label.
XPKM-1149-1S/XPKM-1156-2S. Credits "ELVIS PRESLEY."

❑ RCA Victor 47-9768 .... 11/69   10-20
Picture sleeve.

❑ RCA Victor 47-9768 .... 11/69   20-30
Yellow label. Promotional issue only.
XPKM-1149-5S/XPKM-1156-6S. On *Rubberneckin'*, has incorrect identification number ("XP11-2377") in trail off, with the "2377" crossed out (with X's). Correct number ("1156") follows other number. Credits "ELVIS PRESLEY."

❑ RCA Victor 447-0674 .... 12/70   10-12
Gold Standard. Red label.

❑ RCA Victor 447-0674 .... '77   3-5
Gold Standard. Black label, dog near top.
XPKM-1149-5S/XPKM-1156-31S. Credits "ELVIS PRESLEY."

EASY COME, EASY GO THEATRE LOBBY SPOT (COMING SOON)

❑ Paramount Pictures .... '67   800-1000
Promotional issue to theaters for lobby play in advance of the film *Easy Come, Easy Go*. Label does not identify Elvis as the singer.

(SUCH AN) EASY QUESTION / It Feels So Right

❑ RCA Victor 47-8585 .... 5/65   6-10
Black label, dog on side.
N2WW-0687-3S/L2WW-0086-5S. Label S#21. Shows title on two lines, with first line in uppers and second in all caps: "(Such An) EASY QUESTION." Label is flat black. Credits "ELVIS PRESLEY with The Jordanaires."
N2WW-0687-4S/L2WW-0086-5S. Label S#21. Shows title on one line in all caps: "(SUCH AN) EASY QUESTION." Label is glossy black. Credits "ELVIS PRESLEY with The Jordanaires."

❑ RCA Victor 47-8585 .... 5/65   20-25
Picture sleeve. Reads: "Coming Soon! Special Tickle Me EP."

❑ RCA Victor 47-8585 .... 6/65   30-35
Picture sleeve. Reads: "Ask For Special Tickle Me EP."

❑ RCA Victor 47-8585 .... 6/65   40-45
White label. Promotional issue only.
N2WW-0687-7S/L2WW-0086-7S. Label S#27. Credits "ELVIS PRESLEY with the Jordanaires."

❑ RCA Victor 447-0653 .... 11/66   6-10
Gold Standard. Black label, dog on side.

❑ RCA Victor 447-0653 .... '70   10-12
Gold Standard. Red label.

❑ RCA Victor 447-0653 .... '77   3-5
Gold Standard. Black label, dog near top.

ELVIS' GREATEST HITS – GOLDEN SINGLES, VOL. 1 (12 Golden Hits in Picture Sleeves)

❑ RCA Victor PB-13897 ...... 12/84   20-25
COMPLETE SET: Package of six gold vinyl
singles in color sleeves, individually
numbered PB-13885 through PB-13890. Price
is for all records, sleeves and cardboard box.

❑ RCA Victor PB-13897 ...... 12/84   3-5
BOX: Price for just the box. Gold stock with
black and white photo of Elvis on front.

ELVIS' GREATEST HITS – GOLDEN SINGLES, VOL. 2 (12 Golden Hits in Picture Sleeves)

❑ RCA Victor PB-13898 ...... 12/84   20-25
COMPLETE SET: Package of five gold vinyl
singles in color sleeves, individually
numbered PB-13891 through PB-13896. Price
is for all records, sleeves and cardboard box.

❑ RCA Victor PB-13897 ...... 12/84   3-5
BOX: Price for just the box. Gold stock with
black and white photo of Elvis on front.

ELVIS HOUR / Gary Owens Supertracks

❑ Creative Radio.................... 1/86   20-30
Demo disc for radio stations, with samples of
syndicated programs.
L-23610 M-0374-EH-D1/L-21003-X M-0227-ST-D-2.
Identification numbers are engraved.

ELVIS LIVE (Side One) / Elvis Live (Side Two)

❑ Eva-Tone
1037710A&BX.................... 4/78   25-30
Plastic 33 soundsheet containing Elvis' 1961
Memphis press conference. No label used –
print is on the plastic. This soundsheet
originally came bound in the magazine
Collector's Issue. This price is for the
magazine with soundsheet still intact.

❑ Eva-Tone
1037710A&BX.................... 4/78   10-15
Price for soundsheet only.

ELVIS MEDLEY / Always on My Mind

❑ RCA Victor PB-13351 ...... 11/82   3-5
Black label, dog near top.
PB-13351-A-3/PB-13351-A-3. Both sides are stereo.
Inscribed in trail off on *The Elvis Medley* is "MR-108020,"
and "MR-108020-X" on *Always on My Mind.* Both sides have
"Denny Woodland" engraved in trail off. Credits "ELVIS
PRESLEY, Produced and Arranged by David Briggs" on *The
Elvis Medley* and "ELVIS PRESLEY" on *Always on My Mind.*
Identification numbers are engraved.

❑ RCA Victor PB-13351 ...... 11/82   10-15
Picture sleeve.

❑ Collectables 4564................ '87   3-4
Black vinyl.

DPE1-1046-A-1/DPE1-1046-B-1. Credits "ELVIS PRESLEY."
Identification numbers are engraved. Polystyrene pressing.

❑ Collectables 4564 .... 7/92   5-6
Gold vinyl.
DPE1-1046-A-1/DPE1-1046-B-1. Credits "ELVIS PRESLEY."
Identification numbers are engraved. Polystyrene pressing.

ELVIS MEDLEY (LONG VERSION) (3:54) / The Elvis Medley (Short Version) (3:36)

Medley: *Jailhouse Rock; (Let Me Be Your)
Teddy Bear; Hound Dog; Don't Be Cruel (To a
Heart That's True); Burning Love; Suspicious
Minds.*

❑ RCA Victor JB-13351
(PB-13351) 11/82   100-150
Gold vinyl. Gold label. Promotional issue only.
PB-13351-A-11/PB-13351-D-3. Both sides are stereo.
Inscribed in trail off on both sides is "Denny Woodland." On
the "Short Version" side, the matrix "PA-13351-B" has an
error, so the "B" is crossed out and next to it is a "D."
Credits "ELVIS PRESLEY, Produced and Arranged by David
Briggs." Identification numbers are engraved.

❑ RCA Victor JB-13351
(PB-13351) 11/82   10-15
Light yellow label. Promotional issue only.
PB-13351-A-3/PB-13351-D-1. Both sides are stereo.
Inscribed in trail off on both sides is "MR-108020" and
"Denny Woodland." Credits "ELVIS PRESLEY, Produced and
Arranged by David Briggs." Identification numbers are
engraved.

ELVIS PRESLEY MEDLEY / Elvis Presley Press Conference

❑ Ace NSP-71: Bootleg. Listed for identification
only.

ELVIS PRESLEY SHOW / Blank

❑ Royal 4/56   200-300
78 rpm, single-sided disc. Made for radio
station use to promote Elvis' early '56 concert
appearances. Includes an excerpt of
Heartbreak Hotel.

ELVIS PRESLEY "SPEAKS – IN PERSON!" / Directions for Playing This Disc

❑ Rainbo Records............... 11/56   300-400
Cardboard, 6¾" 78 rpm, single-sided. Has
Elvis speaking to his fans. Originally attached
to the cover of the *Elvis Answers Back!*
magazine. This price is for magazine and disc
still intact. Both disc and magazine came in
two variations. Besides the difference in titles
between this disc and *ELVIS PRESLEY "THE
TRUTH ABOUT ME,"* the labels are different
shades of blue. Magazines exist with both red
and green lettering.

❑ Rainbo Records............... 11/56   100-150
Price for cardboard disc only.
No identification number used.

ELVIS PRESLEY STORY / Blank

❑ Eva-Tone 726771XS 7/77   8-15
Black vinyl. 33 rpm, 5½", stereo soundsheet.
Single-sided. No label used – print is on the
plastic. Promotional Candlelite Music test
sampler, with excerpts of 11 Elvis tracks from
The Elvis Presley Story boxed set. 10,000
copies made.
EV-726771XS.

ELVIS PRESLEY "THE TRUTH ABOUT ME" / Directions for Playing This Disc

❑ Rainbo Records...............11/56   300-400
Cardboard, 6¾" 78 rpm, single-sided. Has
Elvis speaking to his fans. Originally attached
to the cover of the *Elvis Answers Back!*
magazine. This price is for magazine and disc
still intact. Both disc and magazine came in
two variations. Besides the difference in titles
between this disc and *ELVIS PRESLEY
"SPEAKS – IN PERSON!,"* the labels are
different shades of blue. Magazines exist with
both red and green lettering.

❑ Rainbo Records...............11/56   100-150
Price for cardboard disc only.
No identification number used.

ELVIS PRESLEY "THE TRUTH ABOUT ME"

❑ Rainbo Records.................3/97   40
Reissue package. Includes: 1) Single-sided,
gold foil vinyl soundsheet of *The TRUTH
About Me* disc. 2) Reprint of the (green) 1956
Elvis Answers Back! magazine. 3) 10" gold
vinyl disc. 4) compact disc. Both CD and LP
contain about 20 minutes of Elvis speaking,
whereas 1956 version has only about two
minutes. Both also have Elvis' picture on
them. Everything is packaged in a 12", plastic
gatefold case. Widely available at press time
for $39.95.

❑ Rainbo Records.................3/97   5-10
Price for soundsheet only.

❑ Rainbo Records.................3/97   10-15
Price for 10" LP only. Copies used for
publicity purposes are stamped: "Not for Sale
Promotional Copy."

ELVIS REMEMBERED: see Extended Plays

ELVIS SHOW /

❑ Rainbo 6/56   150-250
78 rpm, may be single-sided. Issued to radio
stations to promote a June 3, 1956 Elvis
concert appearance. Label also plugs May
Company's record department.

ELVIS SPEAKS! "THE TRUTH ABOUT ME" / Blank

❑ Lynchburg Audio
LYN1-042 ....12/56   125-150
Black vinyl. 45 rpm, single-sided. Blue label.
Promotional issue only. Label reads: "An
intimate message for readers of "TEEN
PARADE" your ALL COLOR music - mag."
LYN1-042. Label indicates: "Copyright 1956 (USA &
Canada)." Identification numbers are engraved.

❑ Eva-Tone EV-38713T...............   30-40
Black vinyl. 45 rpm. No label used – print is on
the plastic. Promotional issue only. Label
reads: "An intimate message for readers of
"TEEN PARADE" your ALL COLOR music
mag."
EV-38713T. No copyright date indicated – release date not
yet known. Identification numbers are engraved.

ELVIS 10TH ANNIVERSARY / The Elvis Hour

❑ Creative Radio...................5/87   15-20
Demo disc for radio stations, with samples of
syndicated programs.
L-26705/M-0374-EH-D1. Identification numbers are
engraved.

ELVIS – THE 50TH BIRTHDAY RADIO SPECIAL / The Day the Music Died

❑ Creative Radio.................11/84   20-30
Demo disc for radio stations, with a sample of
syndicated programs.
L-19416/L19416X. Has "1-8-85, Elvis 50th Birthday"
engraved in the trail-off. Also, print size of titles is smaller
than on second pressings. Identification numbers are
engraved.

❑ Creative Radio...................1/87   10-20
Demo disc for radio stations, with a sample of
syndicated programs.
L-29580X/L29580. Instead of "1-8-85, Elvis 50th Birthday,"
has only "Elvis" engraved in the trail-off. Print size of titles
is larger than on first pressings. Identification numbers are
engraved.

15 GOLDEN RECORDS / 30 GOLDEN HITS

❑ RCA Victor PP-11301......10/77   65-75
COMPLETE SET: Package of 15 singles in
color sleeves, individually numbered PB-
11099 through PB-11113. Price is for all
records, sleeves and cardboard box, but does
not include browser carton.

❑ RCA Victor PP-11301......10/77   15-20
BOX: Price for just the box. Black stock with
mustard color lettering.

❑ RCA Victor PP-11301......10/77   35-40
BROWSER CARTON: Specially printed
browser. Made for retailers to display six 15-
record packages. Mustard color box with
black lettering.

50,000,000 ELVIS FANS WEREN'T WRONG / Blank

❏ Eva-Tone 831942.............7/83　　5-10
Red vinyl. 33 rpm soundsheet. No label used
– print is on the plastic. Offered as a bonus to
buyers of the book *Presleyana, 2nd Edition*.
EV-831942-T. Reads: "Produced And Edited by Jerry
Osborne." Identification numbers are engraved.

FOLLOW THAT DREAM / When My Blue Moon Turns to Gold Again

❏ Collectables 4515................'86　　3-4
Black vinyl.
DPE1-1015-A-1/DPE1-1015-B-1. Credits "ELVIS PRESLEY."
Identification numbers are stamped on *Follow That Dream*
and engraved on *When My Blue Moon Turns to Gold Again*.
Polystyrene pressing.

❏ Collectables 4515..............7/92　　5-6
Gold vinyl.
DPE1-1015-A-1/DPE1-1015-B-1. Credits "ELVIS PRESLEY."
Identification numbers are stamped on *Follow That Dream*
and engraved on *When My Blue Moon Turns to Gold Again*.
Polystyrene pressing.

FOLLOW THAT DREAM (Take 2) / You Gave Me a Molehill

❏ Royal Caribbean Cruise Lines
RCCL-12690 ....1/90　　10-15
Promotional, souvenir issue given to Elvis
fans taking the January 1990 "Follow That
Dream" cruise.
RCCL-12690A U-26439-M-A/RCC-12690B U-24639M-B. Both
sides are mono. Has a previously unissued alternative take
of *Follow That Dream*. Elvis not credited as singer, though
label reads: "In Commemoration of Elvis' 55th Birthday."
Identification numbers are engraved.

FOOL / Steamroller Blues

❏ RCA Victor 74-0910 ....4/73　　4-6
Orange label.
BPKS-1258-4S/CPKS-4728-4S. Both sides are stereo.
Credits "ELVIS PRESLEY, Strings arranged by Glen (sic) D.
Hardin, Vocal accomp. by J.D. Sumner and The Stamps" on
Fool and "ELVIS PRESLEY, Vocal accomp. by J.D. Sumner
and The Stamps, Kathy Westmoreland and The Sweet
Inspirations" on *Steamroller Blues*.

❏ RCA Victor 74-0910 ....4/73　　10-15
Picture sleeve.

❏ RCA Victor 74-0910 ....4/73　　10-15
Light yellow label. Promotional issue only.
BPKM-1258-3S/CPKM-4728-3S. Both sides are mono.
Credits "ELVIS PRESLEY, Strings arranged by Glen (sic) D.
Hardin, Vocal accomp. by J.D. Sumner and The Stamps" on
Fool and "ELVIS PRESLEY, Vocal accomp. by J.D. Sumner
and The Stamps, Kathy Westmoreland and The Sweet
Inspirations" on *Steamroller Blues*. Identification numbers
are engraved. *Fool* has yet to appear on a Gold Standard
single. *Steamroller Blues* is the flip side of *Burning Love* on
Gold Standard.

FOOLS FALL IN LOVE / Blue Suede Shoes

❏ Collectables 4522................'86　　3-4
Black vinyl.
DPE1-1022-A-1/DPE1-1022-B-1. Credits "ELVIS PRESLEY
with The Jordanaires" on *Fools Fall in Love* and "ELVIS
PRESLEY" on *Blue Suede Shoes*. Identification numbers are
engraved. Polystyrene pressing.

❏ Collectables 4522..............7/92　　5-6
Gold vinyl.

DPE1-1022-A-1/DPE1-1022-B-1. Credits "ELVIS PRESLEY
with The Jordanaires" on *Fools Fall in Love* and "ELVIS
PRESLEY" on *Blue Suede Shoes*. Identification numbers are
engraved. Polystyrene pressing.

FOR THE HEART / Hurt

❏ RCA Victor PB-10601........3/76　　4-6
Tan label.
PB-10601-A-2/PB-10601-B-2. Both sides are stereo. Credits
"ELVIS PRESLEY." Identification numbers are engraved.

❏ RCA Victor PB-10601........3/76　　10-12
Picture sleeve.

❏ RCA Victor JB-10601
(PB-10601) ....3/76　　20-25
Light yellow label. Promotional issue only.
PB-10601-A-2/PB-10601-B-2. Both sides are stereo. Credits
"ELVIS PRESLEY." Identification numbers are engraved.

❏ RCA Victor PB-10601........4/76　　90-100
Black label, dog near top. This pressing
became the first Elvis single issued with the
recent RCA black label – with the dog just to
the right of the top.
PB-10601-A-1/PB-10601-B-1. Both sides are stereo. Credits
"ELVIS PRESLEY."
For the Gold Standard release of *For the
Heart*, see *MOODY BLUE / For the Heart*.

FRANKIE AND JOHNNY / Love Letters

❏ Collectables 4516................'86　　3-4
Black vinyl.
DPE1-1016-A-1/DPE1-1016-B-1. Credits "ELVIS PRESLEY
with The Jordanaires." Polystyrene pressing.

❏ Collectables 4516..............7/92　　5-6
Gold vinyl.
DPE1-1016-A-1/DPE1-1016-B-1. Credits "ELVIS PRESLEY
with The Jordanaires." Polystyrene pressing.

FRANKIE AND JOHNNY / Please Don't Stop Loving Me

❏ RCA Victor 47-8780...........3/66　　6-10
Black label, dog on side.
SPKM-7378-5S/SPKM-7384-5S. Label S#21. Credits "ELVIS
PRESLEY."

❏ RCA Victor 47-8780...........3/66　　20-30
Picture sleeve.

❏ RCA Victor 47-8780...........3/66　　40-45
White label. Promotional issue only.
SPKM-7378-7S/SPKM-7384-6S. Label S#27. Credits "ELVIS
PRESLEY."

❏ RCA Victor 447-0656.........2/68　　6-10
Gold Standard. Black label, dog on side.

❏ RCA Victor 447-0656...........'68　　50-75
Gold Standard. Orange label.
SPKM-7378-5S/SPKM-7384-5S. Credits "ELVIS PRESLEY."

❏ RCA Victor 447-0656...........'70　　10-12
Gold Standard. Red label.
SPKM-7378-8S/SPKM-7384-8S. Credits "ELVIS PRESLEY."

❏ RCA Victor 447-0656...........'77　　3-5
Gold Standard. Black label, dog near top.

GENTLE ON MY MIND / Faded Love

❏ Siesta S-45-101: Bootleg. Listed for
identification only.

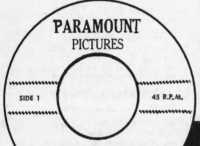

GIRLS! GIRLS! GIRLS! ADVANCE (COMING SOON) THEATRE LOBBY SPOT / Girls! Girls! Girls! (Now Playing) Theatre Lobby Spot

❑ Paramount Pictures
SP-2017 .... 10/62   800-1000
Promotional issue to theaters for lobby play in advance of and during the run of the *Girls! Girls! Girls!* film.
SP-2017/SP-2018. Label does not identify Elvis as the singer.

GOOD LUCK CHARM / Anything That's Part of You

❑ RCA Victor 47-7992 .... 3/62   8-10
Black label, dog on top.
M2WW-1003-3S/M2WW-1004-1S. Label S#18. Thus far, this is the earliest first take ("1S") to appear on this style (without "New Orthophonic High Fidelity") label. Credits "ELVIS PRESLEY with The Jordanaires."

❑ RCA Victor 47-7992 .... 3/62   20-30
Picture sleeve. Has titles in blue and pink letters.

❑ RCA Victor 47-7992 .... 3/62   20-30
Picture sleeve. Has titles in rust and lavender letters.

❑ RCA Victor 37-7992 .... 3/62   8000-12000
Compact 33 single.
N2WI-1307-1S/N2WI-1308-1S. Has LP-size (¼-inch) hole. Credits "ELVIS PRESLEY with The Jordanaires." Identification numbers are engraved.

❑ RCA Victor 37-7992 .... 3/62   8000-12000
Picture sleeve for Compact 33 single.

❑ RCA Victor 447-0636 ...... 11/62   8-12
Gold Standard. Black label, dog on top.

❑ RCA Victor 447-0636 .... '65   6-10
Gold Standard. Black label, dog on side.
M2WW-1003-4S/M2WW-1004-4S. On some copies, *Anything That's Part of You* label text is off center, well below its intended position. Label itself is properly applied, as dog and RCA Victor logo are centered. Label GS#6. Has playing times and publisher. Credits "ELVIS PRESLEY with The Jordanaires."

❑ RCA Victor 447-0636 .... '68   50-75
Gold Standard. Orange label.

❑ RCA Victor 447-0636 .... '70   10-12
Gold Standard. Red label.
M2WW-1003-4S/M2WW-1004-4S. Credits "ELVIS PRESLEY with The Jordanaires."

❑ RCA Victor 447-0636 .... '77   3-5
Gold Standard. Black label, dog near top.

GOOD ROCKIN' TONIGHT / I Don't Care If the Sun Don't Shine

❑ Sun 210 .... 9/54   1000-1500
78 rpm.
U-131-72 Δ1121/U-130-2-72 Δ1120. Credits "ELVIS PRESLEY" (on line one), "SCOTTY and BILL." Identification numbers are engraved.
Counterfeit Identification: Any colored plastic Sun 78 is an unauthorized (circa 1978) issue.

❑ Sun 210 .... 9/54   900-1400
U-131-45-72/U-130-45-72. Credits "ELVIS PRESLEY." Release number is at bottom of label. Push marks are present. Identification numbers are engraved.

Counterfeit Identification: Fakes of Sun 45s are numerous; however, some are easily identified. Any with "Issued 1973" engraved in the vinyl are fakes, and any on colored vinyl are boots. On some fakes, the brown sunrays, circling top half of label, fail to go all the way to the edge of the hole, though we are not prepared to state unequivocally that there are no originals printed this way. When compared to the label of an original, some fakes have noticeably darker brown print on noticeably lighter yellow stock. Any discs with "RE" or "Reissue" engraved in the vinyl are fakes. Any Sun singles with three push marks (three circular indentations, that if connected by a line would form a triangle) are original pressings.
Only bootleg picture sleeves exist for this release.

❑ RCA Victor 20-6381 .... 12/55   100-150
Black label, 78 rpm.
F2WB-8043-1S/F2WB-8042-3S. Label S#4. Credits "Elvis Presley." (Rarely does Elvis' name appear in uppers and lowers on an RCA label.)

❑ RCA Victor 47-6381 .... 12/55   40-50
Black label, dog on top, without horizontal silver line.
Only bootleg picture sleeves exist for this release.

❑ RCA Victor 47-6381 .... 12/55   50-60
Black label, dog on top, with horizontal silver line.
F2WW-8043-8S/F2WW-8042-8S. Label S#12L. Credits "ELVIS PRESLEY."
Only bootleg picture sleeves exist for this release.

❑ RCA Victor 447-0602 .... 3/59   15-20
Gold Standard. Black label, dog on top.
J2PW-5686-7S/J2PW-5685-7S. Label GS#2. Credits "ELVIS PRESLEY."

❑ RCA Victor 447-0602 .... 6/64   250-300
Gold Standard picture sleeve.

❑ RCA Victor 447-0602 .... 6/64   75-125
Gold Standard. White label. Promotional issue only.
J2PW-5686-6S/J2PW-5685-6S. Label GS#9. Credits "ELVIS PRESLEY."

❑ RCA Victor 447-0602 .... '65   6-12
Gold Standard. Black label, dog on side.
J2PW-5686-8S/J2PW-5685-5S. Label GS#4. Credits "ELVIS PRESLEY."

❑ RCA Victor 447-0602 .... '70   10-12
Gold Standard. Red label.
J2PW-5686-8S/J2PW-5685-5S. Credits "ELVIS PRESLEY."

❑ RCA Victor 447-0602 .... '77   3-5
Gold Standard. Black label, dog near top.

❑ Collectables 4500 .... '86   3-4
Black vinyl.
DPE1-1000-A-1/DPE1-1000-B-1. Credits "ELVIS PRESLEY."

❑ Collectables 4500 .... 7/92   5-6
Gold vinyl.
DPE1-1000-A-1/DPE1-1000-B-1. Credits "ELVIS PRESLEY."

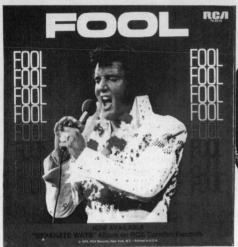

GRACELAND TOUR / Blank

❑ Record Digest/Eva-Tone
25794X 2/79   5-10
Red vinyl. 33 rpm, 6" soundsheet. No label
used – print is on the plastic. All-Elvis novelty
break-in, offered as a bonus to buyers of the
'79 Osborne book, *Our Best to You*.
EV-25794XT. Credits read: "With Jerry Osborne as Dan
Rathernot." Identification numbers are engraved.

GREEN, GREEN GRASS OF HOME /
Home Is Where the Heart Is
(Cassette)

❑ RCA/BMG
RDJ-62026-4 .... 8/91   5-10
Cassette single, one song on each side.

❑ RCA/BMG
RDJ-62026-4 .... 8/91   5-10
Tape cover/holder. Pictures Elvis' birthplace in
Tupelo, Miss. Promotional issue only.
Available only in Tupelo, in conjunction with
Elvis' birthplace festivities.

GUITAR MAN / Faded Love

❑ RCA Victor PB-12158 .... 1/81   3-5
Black label, dog near top.
PB-12158-A-2S/PA-12158-C-1S. Both sides are stereo. At
this time, stamped numbers were the exception rather than
the rule. Also inscribed in trail off is "Randy's Roost." Credits
"ELVIS PRESLEY, Produced by Felton Jarvis." Polystyrene
pressing.

❑ RCA Victor PB-12158 .... 1/81   6-10
Picture sleeve.

GUITAR MAN (Stereo) / Guitar Man
(Mono)

❑ RCA Victor JH-12158
(PB-12158) 1/81   150-200
Red vinyl. Mustard label. Promotional issue
only.
PB-12158-A-1S/PA-12158-C-1S. One side is stereo, the
other mono. Also inscribed in trail off is "Randy's Roost."
This was the first standard issue Elvis promo made on
colored vinyl. Credits "ELVIS PRESLEY, Produced by Felton
Jarvis." Identification numbers are engraved.

❑ RCA Victor JH-12158
(PB-12158) 1/81   10-15
Light yellow label. Promotional issue only.
PB-12158-A-7S/PA-12158-C-2S. One side is stereo, the
other mono. Also inscribed in trail off is "Randy's Roost."
Credits "ELVIS PRESLEY, Produced by Felton Jarvis."
Identification numbers are engraved. Both tracks on PB-
12158, taken from the *Guitar Man* LP, have completely
reworked backings and instrumentations than previously
issued.

GUITAR MAN / High Heel Sneakers

❑ RCA Victor 47-9425 .... 1/68   6-10
Black label, dog on side.
UPKM-2765-4S/UPKM-2770-5S. Label S#21. Credits "ELVIS
PRESLEY." Label is identical to label S#21 pressing below,
except there is no blank space between the time ("2:15")
and the word "Victor" on the line above.
UPKM-2765-5S/UPKM-2770-5S. Label S#21. Credits "ELVIS
PRESLEY." Label is identical to pressing above, except there
is about a sixteenth-inch blank space between the time
("2:15") and the word "Victor" on the line above.

❑ RCA Victor 47-9425 .... 1/68   20-25
Picture sleeve. Reads: "Coming Soon, Elvis'
Gold Records, Volume 4."

❑ RCA Victor 47-9425 .... 2/68   25-30
Picture sleeve. Reads: "Ask for Elvis' Gold
Records, Volume 4."

❑ RCA Victor 47-9425 .... 1/68   20-30
Yellow label. Promotional issue only.
UPKM-2765-9S/UPKM-2770-7S. Label S#27. Credits "ELVIS
PRESLEY.

❑ RCA Victor 447-0663 .... '70   10-12
Gold Standard. Red label.
UPKM-2765-4S/UPKM-2770-5S. Credits "ELVIS PRESLEY.

❑ RCA Victor 447-0663 .... '77   3-5
Gold Standard. Black label, dog near top.
Some copies of this release show *High Heel
Sneakers* as *Hi-Heel Sneakers*.

HARD HEADED WOMAN / Don't Ask
Me Why

❑ RCA Victor 20-7280 .... 6/58   200-300
Black label, 78 rpm.
J2-PB-3603-1S/J2-PB-3610-1S. Label S#7. Credits "ELVIS
PRESLEY with The Jordanaires."
J2-PB-3603-3S/J2-PB-3610-3S. Label S#8. Credits "ELVIS
PRESLEY with The Jordanaires."

❑ RCA Victor 47-7280 .... 6/58   10-15
Black label, dog on top.
J2PW-3603-5S/J2PW-3610-5S. Label S#19. Credits "ELVIS
PRESLEY with The Jordanaires."

❑ RCA Victor 47-7280 .... 6/58   45-50
Picture sleeve.

❑ RCA Victor 447-0623 .... '61   10-20
Gold Standard. Black label, dog on top.
J2PW-3603-10S/J2PW-3610-10S. Label GS#1. Has playing
times. Credits "ELVIS PRESLEY with The Jordanaires."

❑ RCA Victor 447-0623 .... '65   6-10
Gold Standard. Black label, dog on side.
J2PW-3603-11S/J2PW-3610-10S. Credits "ELVIS PRESLEY
with The Jordanaires."

❑ RCA Victor 447-0623 .... '68   50-75
Gold Standard. Orange label.

❑ RCA Victor 447-0623 .... '70   10-12
Gold Standard. Red label.
J2PW-3603-12S/J2PW-3610-11S. Credits "ELVIS PRESLEY
with The Jordanaires."

❑ RCA Victor 447-0623 .... '77   3-5
Gold Standard. Black label, dog near top.

HARBOR LIGHTS / Tiger Man

❑ Sun 520 (record or picture sleeve): Bootleg.
Listed for identification only.

HE TOUCHED ME / Bosom of
Abraham

❑ RCA Victor 74-0651 .... 3/72   125-150
Orange label. A production error caused this
issue to be pressed at approximately 35 rpm
on the *He Touched Me* side only.
APKS-1277-4S/APKS-1295-4S. Though label shows the
identification number as "APKS-1277," stamped in the trail
off is "AWKS-1277." Both sides are stereo. Credits "ELVIS
PRESLEY, Vocal accomp. by The Imperials Quartet."

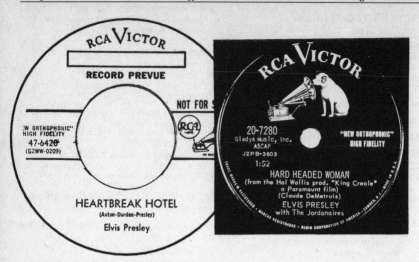

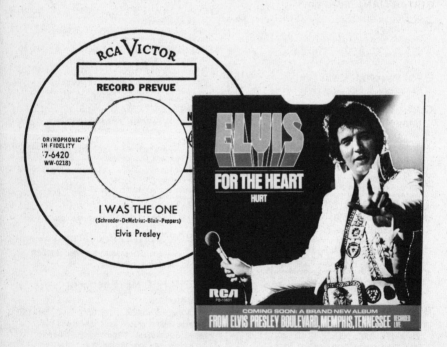

❑ RCA Victor 74-0651 ....3/72   4-6
Orange label. Both sides play at 45 rpm.
APKS-1277-3S/APKS-1295-4S. Credits "ELVIS PRESLEY, Vocal accomp. by The Imperials Quartet."
APKS-1277-5S/APKS-1295-6S. Credits "ELVIS PRESLEY, Vocal accomp. by The Imperials Quartet."

❑ RCA Victor 74-0651 ....3/72   100-150
Picture sleeve.

❑ RCA Victor 74-0651 ....3/72   125-150
Yellow label. Promotional issue only.
APKM-1277-4S/APKM-1295-4S. Though label shows the identification number as "APKM-1277," stamped in the trail off is "AWKM-1277." Both sides are mono. Credits "ELVIS PRESLEY, Vocal accomp. by The Imperials Quartet."

HEARTBREAK HOTEL [Elvis Presley] / Heartbreak Hotel [David Keith]

❑ Popular Library/Fawcett
Books ....'88   300-400
Picture sleeve. Promotional issue made to promote the book, *Heartbreak Hotel*, by Anne Rivers Siddons. However, accompanying disc is black label, dog near top, Gold Standard (447-0605) – not '88 reissue (8760-7-R).

❑ RCA Victor 8760-7-R...........'88   3-5
Red label. Printing on both sides of label.
8760-7-RA/8760-7R-1. Elvis side shown as Side A; Keith side shown as Side 1. Credits "ELVIS PRESLEY" on Side A, and "David Keith & Charlie Schlatter with Zulu Time" on Side 1. Identification numbers are engraved.

❑ RCA Victor 8760-7-R...........'88   4-8
Red label. Printing on Elvis side only. Though only the RCA logo is on the Keith side label, his music track is there.
8760-7-RA/8760-7R-1. Elvis side shown as Side A; Keith side shown as Side 1. Credits "ELVIS PRESLEY." Identification numbers are engraved.

❑ RCA Victor 8760-7-R...........'88   4-8
Red label. Printing on David Keith side only. Though only the RCA logo is on the Presley side label, his music track is there.
8760-7RA/8760-7R-1. Keith side shown as Side 1. Credits "David Keith & Charlie Schlatter with Zulu Time" on Side 1. Identification numbers are engraved.

❑ RCA Victor 8760-7-R...........'88   4-8
Picture sleeve. Blue; pictures Elvis and four others in a pink Cadillac.

❑ RCA Victor 8760-7-R...........'88   10-15
Picture sleeve. Blue – pictures Elvis and four others in a pink Cadillac. Has "NOT FOR SALE – DEMONSTRATION" on back. Promotional issue only.

❑ RCA Victor 8760-7-R...........'88   20-25
Picture sleeve. Red – pictures an unidentified man (RCA employee, Butch Waugh) in a white jumpsuit. Promotional issue only.

❑ RCA Victor 8760-7-RA1 ......'88   20-25
White label. Promotional issue only.
8760-7-RA/8760-7R-1. Elvis side shown as Side A; Keith side shown as Side 1. Credits "ELVIS PRESLEY," and "David Keith & Charlie Schlatter with Zulu Time" on Side 1. Identification numbers are engraved.
Both tracks are "From the Original Motion Picture Soundtrack, *Heartbreak Hotel*."

HEARTBREAK HOTEL [Elvis Presley] / Heartbreak Hotel [David Keith] (Cassette)

❑ RCA Victor 8760-4-RS ....'88   4-6
Cassette tape, one song on each side.

❑ RCA Victor 8760-4-RS ....'88   4-6
Tape cover/holder.

HEARTBREAK HOTEL / Hound Dog

❑ RCA Victor 07863
62449-7 ....'92   3-5
Black label, silver label.
07863-62449-A-2/07863-62449-B-2. Identification numbers are engraved. Polygram International. Credits "ELVIS PRESLEY."

❑ RCA Victor 07863-
62449-7 ....'92   1-2
Plain white picture sleeve. Has aqua sticker with white letters reading: "Elvis The King of Rock 'N' Roll EP-7."

❑ RCA Victor 62449-7.............'92   5-8
Juke box title strips. Five color strips with picture of Elvis. Released in conjunction with the CD box set *Elvis – The King of Rock 'N' Roll – The Complete 50's Masters*.

HEARTBREAK HOTEL / I Was the One

❑ RCA Victor 20-6420...........1/56   75-100
Black label, 78 rpm.
G2WB-0209-2S/G2WB-0218-2S. Label S#9. Credits "ELVIS PRESLEY."

❑ RCA Victor 20-6420...........'70s   250-500
White label 78 rpm. Reads: "Record Prevue, Disc Jockey Sample." Has rectangular "Not for Sale" box printed on label. We're not yet certain as to the history, purpose and legitimacy of this series.
G2WB-0209/G2WB-0218. Credits "ELVIS PRESLEY." Identification numbers are engraved, but may be scratched over.

❑ RCA Victor 47-6420...........1/56   20-30
Black label, dog on top, without horizontal silver line.
G2WW-0209-5S/G2WW-0218-5S. Label S#13. Credits "ELVIS PRESLEY."
Only bootleg picture sleeves exist for this release.

❑ RCA Victor 47-6420...........1/56   30-40
Black label, dog on top, with horizontal silver line.
G2WW-0209-4S/G2WW-0218-3S. Label S#12L. Credits "ELVIS PRESLEY."
Only bootleg picture sleeves exist for this release.

❑ RCA Victor 47-6420...........1/56   40-50
Turquoise label, dog on top.
G2WW-0209-?S/G2WW-0218-?S. Credits "ELVIS PRESLEY."
Only bootleg picture sleeves exist for this release.

❑ RCA Victor 47-6420...........1/56   200-300
White "Record Prevue" label. Promotional, Canadian issue only.

❏ RCA Victor 447-0605 ....3/59   10-20
Gold Standard. Black label, dog on top.
J2PW-5691-2S/J2PW-5692-1S. Label GS#1. Credits "ELVIS
PRESLEY."
J2PW-5691-?S/J2PW-5692-?S. Label GS#2. Credits "ELVIS
PRESLEY."

❏ RCA Victor 447-0605 ....6/64   250-300
Gold Standard picture sleeve.

❏ RCA Victor 447-0605 ....6/64   75-125
Gold Standard. White label. Promotional issue
only.
J2PW-5691-2S/J2PW-5692-3S. Label GS#9. Credits "ELVIS
PRESLEY."

❏ RCA Victor 447-0605 ....'65   6-10
Gold Standard. Black label, dog on side.
J2PW-5691-4S/J2PW-5692-2S. Label GS#6. Credits "ELVIS
PRESLEY."

❏ RCA Victor 447-0605 ....'68   50-75
Gold Standard. Orange label.
J2PW-5691-4S/J2PW-5692-2S. Credits "ELVIS PRESLEY."

❏ RCA Victor 447-0605 ....'70   10-12
Gold Standard. Red label.
J2PW-5691-7S/J2PW-5692-2S. Credits "ELVIS PRESLEY."

❏ RCA Victor 447-0605 ....'77   3-5
Gold Standard. Black label, dog near top.

❏ RCA Victor PB-11105......10/77   3-4
Originally included as one of the singles in the
boxed sets *15 Golden Records – 30 Golden
Hits* and *20 Golden Hits in Full Color Sleeves*.

❏ RCA Victor PB-11105......10/77   3-4
Picture sleeve.

❏ For Your Classic Juke Box
G-118 ....'80s   50-75
78 rpm. Made for juke box use.
For a 1983 reissue of I Was the One, see
WEAR MY RING AROUND YOUR NECK / I
Was the One

HEARTBREAK HOTEL / Jailhouse Rock

❏ RCA Victor PB-13892......12/84   3-4
Gold vinyl. Originally included as one of the
singles in the boxed set *Elvis' Greatest Hits –
Golden Singles, Vol. 2*.

❏ RCA Victor PB-13892......12/84   3-4
Picture sleeve.

HEARTBREAK HOTEL / Shake, Rattle and Roll

❏ Sun 227: Bootleg. Listed for identification
only.

(MARIE'S THE NAME) HIS LATEST FLAME / Little Sister

❏ RCA Victor 47-7908 ....8/61   8-10
Black label, dog on top.
M2WW-0860-2S/M2WW-0861-1S. Label S#19. This release
marks the first time a label S#19 (bold print label) appears
on a "1S" or "2S" take. Credits "ELVIS PRESLEY."

❏ RCA Victor 47-7908 ....8/61   25-30
Picture sleeve. Reads: "HIS LATEST
FLAME," whereas disc shows "Marie's The
Name HIS LATEST FLAME."

❏ RCA Victor 37-7908 ....8/61   4000-6000
Compact 33 single

M2WI-2965-1S/M2WI-2964-1S. Has LP-size (¼-inch) hole.
Credits "ELVIS PRESLEY."

❏ RCA Victor 37-7908...........8/61   4000-6000
Picture sleeve for Compact 33 single. Has
"New-Orthophonic" under RCA logo at upper
right.

❏ RCA Victor 37-7908...........8/61   4000-6000
Picture sleeve for Compact 33 single. Has
"Stereo-Orthophonic" under logo at upper
right.

❏ RCA Victor 447-0634.......11/62   8-12
Gold Standard. Black label, dog on top.

❏ RCA Victor 447-0634...........'65   6-10
Gold Standard. Black label, dog on side.
M2WW-0860-4S/M2WW-0861-4S. Label GS#4. Has playing
times and publisher. Credits "ELVIS PRESLEY."

❏ RCA Victor 447-0634...........'68   50-75
Gold Standard. Orange label.
M2WW-0860-4S/M2WW-0861-4S. Credits "ELVIS PRESLEY."

❏ RCA Victor 447-0634...........'70   10-12
Gold Standard. Red label.
M2WW-0860-7S/M2WW-0861-4S. Credits "ELVIS PRESLEY."

❏ RCA Victor 447-0634...........'77   3-5
Gold Standard. Black label, dog near top.

❏ RCA Victor PB-13894......12/84   3-4
Gold vinyl. Originally included as one of the
singles in the boxed set *Elvis' Greatest Hits –
Golden Singles, Vol. 2*.

❏ RCA Victor PB-13894......12/84   3-4
Picture sleeve.

HOW GREAT THOU ART / His Hand in Mine

❏ RCA Victor 74-0130...........4/69   20-25
Orange label.
TPKS-0909-1S/L2WA-0374-1S. Both sides are marked
STEREO. Credits "ELVIS PRESLEY with the Jordanaires and
The Imperials Quartet" on *How Great Thou Art* and "ELVIS
PRESLEY with the Jordanaires" on *His Hand in Mine*.

❏ RCA Victor 74-0130...........4/69   150-200
Picture sleeve.

❏ RCA Victor 74-0130...........4/69   75-125
Yellow label. Promotional issue only.
TPKS-0909-3S/L2WA-0374-3S. Both sides are in stereo
though only *How Great Thou Art* is identified as stereo.
Credits "ELVIS PRESLEY With The Jordanaires and The
Imperials Quartet" on *How Great Thou Art* and "ELVIS
PRESLEY With The Jordanaires" on *His Hand in Mine*.

❏ RCA Victor 447-0670.......12/70   12-15
Gold Standard. Red label.
TPKS-0909-3S/L2WA-0374-3S. Both sides are stereo.
Credits "ELVIS PRESLEY with the Jordanaires and The
Imperials Quartet" on *How Great Thou Art* and "ELVIS
PRESLEY with the Jordanaires" on *His Hand in Mine*.

❏ RCA Victor 447-0670...........'77   3-5
Gold Standard. Black label, dog near top.

❏ Collectables 4520 ....'86   3-4
Black vinyl.
DPE1-1020-A-1/DPE1-1020-B-1. Credits "ELVIS PRESLEY
with The Jordanaires and The Imperials Quartet" on *How
Great Thou Art* and "ELVIS PRESLEY with The Jordanaires"
on *His Hand in Mine*. Identification numbers are stamped on
How Great Thou Art and engraved on *His Hand in Mine*.
Polystyrene pressing.

❏ Collectables 4520 ....7/92   5-6
Gold vinyl.
DPE1-1020-A-1/DPE1-1020-B-1. Credits "ELVIS PRESLEY
with The Jordanaires and The Imperials Quartet" on *How
Great Thou Art* and "ELVIS PRESLEY with The Jordanaires"
on *His Hand in Mine*. Identification numbers are stamped on
How Great Thou Art and engraved on *His Hand in Mine*.
Polystyrene pressing.

HOW GREAT THOU ART / So High

❑ RCA Victor SP-45-162 ...... 4/67   150-175
White label. Promotional issue only.
UNKM-3825-1S/UNKM-3826-1S. Credits "ELVIS PRESLEY."

❑ RCA Victor SP-45-162 ...... 4/67   150-200
Picture sleeve, black and white.

Counterfeit Identification: On fake covers, the reproduction of the black and white Elvis photo is slightly out of focus – it is grainy and looks like a copy. On originals, the photo is sharp and precise.

I FEEL SO BAD / Wild in the Country

❑ RCA Victor 47-7880 .... 5/61   8-10
Black label, dog on top.
M2WW-0571-2S/L2PW-5383-2S. Label S#17. Credits "ELVIS PRESLEY" on *I Feel So Bad* and "ELVIS PRESLEY with The Jordanaires" on *Wild in the Country*. This is the first Elvis single with different credits on each side.

❑ RCA Victor 47-7880 .... 5/61   20-30
Picture sleeve.

❑ RCA Victor 37-7880 .... 5/61   1000-1500
Compact 33 single.
M2PI-2569-4S/M2PI-2570-4S. Has LP-size (¼-inch) hole. Credits "ELVIS PRESLEY" on *I Feel So Bad* and "ELVIS PRESLEY with The Jordanaires" on *Wild in the Country*. Identification numbers are engraved.

❑ RCA Victor 37-7880 .... 5/61   1500-2000
Picture sleeve for Compact 33 single.

❑ RCA Victor 447-0631 .... 2/62   8-12
Gold Standard. Black label, dog on top.
M2WW-0571-2S/L2PW-5383-3S. Matrix stamped as "2S" on *Lonely Man*, but the "2" is stamped over with a "3." Credits "ELVIS PRESLEY."

❑ RCA Victor 447-0631 .... '65   6-10
Gold Standard. Black label, dog on side.
M2WW-0571-11S/L2PW-5383-3S. Label S#1. Has playing times and publisher. Credits "ELVIS PRESLEY."

❑ RCA Victor 447-0631 .... '68   50-75
Gold Standard. Orange label.
M2WW-0571-11S/L2PW-5383-3S. Label GS#1. Has playing times and publisher. Credits "ELVIS PRESLEY."

❑ RCA Victor 447-0631 .... '70   10-12
Gold Standard. Red label.
M2WW-0571-11S/L2PW-5383-3S. Label GS#6. Has playing times and publisher. Credits "ELVIS PRESLEY."

❑ RCA Victor 447-0631 .... '77   3-5
Gold Standard. Black label, dog near top.

❑ Collectables 4510 .... '86   3-4
Black vinyl.
DPE1-1010-B-1/DPE1-1010-A-1. Credits "ELVIS PRESLEY with The Jordanaires." Polystyrene pressing.

❑ Collectables 4510 .... 7/92   5-6
Gold vinyl.
DPE1-1010-B-1/DPE1-1010-A-1. Credits "ELVIS PRESLEY with The Jordanaires." Polystyrene pressing. The Collectables discs show *Wild in the Country* as the A-side.

I GOT A FEELIN' IN MY BODY / There's a Honky Tonk Angel (Who Will Take Me Back In)

❑ RCA Victor PB-11679........ 8/79   12-15
Black label, dog near top.

PB-11679-A-1S/PB-11679-B-1S. Both sides are stereo. Credits "ELVIS PRESLEY, Reissue Produced by Joan Deary, Original Version produced by Felton Jarvis, Vocal Accompaniment by VOICE/J.D. Sumner & The Stamps" on *I Got a Feelin' in My Body* and "ELVIS PRESLEY, Reissue Produced by Joan Deary, Original Version produced by Felton Jarvis, Vocal Accompaniment by VOICE, Strings Arranged by Mike Leech" on *There's a Honky Tonk Angel (Who Will Take Me Back In)*. Since both tracks on this single were deliberately pressed without the vocal and string accompaniment, those credits are printed in error. Identification numbers are engraved.

❑ RCA Victor PB-11679........ 8/79   3-5
Black label, dog near top.
PB-11679-A-3S/PB-11679-B-3S. Both sides are stereo and have hand engraved identification numbers in the trail off. Credits corrected to read: "ELVIS PRESLEY, Reissue Produced by Joan Deary, Original Version produced by Felton Jarvis." Polystyrene pressing.

❑ RCA Victor PB-11679........ 8/79   8-10
Picture sleeve.

❑ RCA Victor JB-11679
(PB-11679) 8/79   10-12
Light yellow label. Promotional issue only.
PB-11679-A-4S/PB-11679-B-4S. Both sides are stereo. Credits "ELVIS PRESLEY, Reissue Produced by Joan Deary, Original Version produced by Felton Jarvis, Vocal Accompaniment by VOICE/J.D. Sumner & The Stamps" on *I Got a Feelin' in My Body* and "ELVIS PRESLEY, Reissue Produced by Joan Deary, Original Version produced by Felton Jarvis, Vocal Accompaniment by VOICE, Strings Arranged by Mike Leech" on *There's a Honky Tonk Angel (Who Will Take Me Back In)*. Identification numbers are engraved. Polystyrene pressing.

I GOT A WOMAN / I'm Counting on You

❑ RCA Victor 20-6637........... 9/56   75-100
Black label, 78 rpm.
G2WB-208-2S/G2WB-211-2S. Label S#1. Credits "ELVIS PRESLEY."

❑ RCA Victor 47-6637........... 9/56   40-50
Black label, dog on top, without horizontal silver line.
G2WW-208-4S/G2WW-211-4S. Label S#12. (Hollywood pressing.) Credits "ELVIS PRESLEY."
Only bootleg picture sleeves exist for this release.

❑ RCA Victor 47-6637........... 9/56   50-60
Black label, dog on top, with horizontal silver line.
G2WW-208-5S/G2WW-211-6S. Label S#12L. (Indianapolis pressing.) Credits "ELVIS PRESLEY."
Only bootleg picture sleeves exist for this release.

❑ RCA Victor 447-0610......... 3/59   15-20
Gold Standard. Black label, dog on top.

❑ Collectables 4503 .... '86   3-4
Black vinyl.
DPE1-1003-A-1/DPE1-1003-B-1. Credits "ELVIS PRESLEY." Polystyrene pressing.

❑ Collectables 4503 .... 7/92   5-6
Gold vinyl.
DPE1-1003-A-1/DPE1-1003-B-1. Credits "ELVIS PRESLEY." Polystyrene pressing.

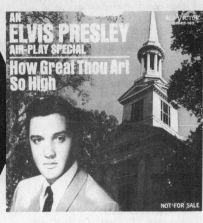

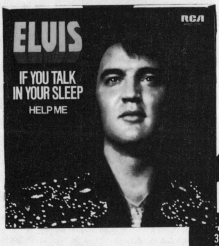

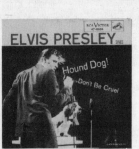

I NEED YOUR LOVE TONIGHT /(Now and Then There's) A Fool Such As I

❏ RCA Victor 47-7506 .... 3/59   10-15
Black label, dog on top.
J2WW-3253-2S/J2WW-3256-2S. Label S#19. Credits "ELVIS PRESLEY with The Jordanaires."

❏ RCA Victor 47-7506 .... 3/59   300-500
Picture sleeve. Has promotion of *Elvis Sails* EP on back of sleeve. Sleeve shows title as "A Fool Such as I," whereas record label gives full title: "(Now and Then There's) A Fool Such As I."

❏ RCA Victor 47-7506 .... 4/59   35-45
Picture sleeve. Has listing of Elvis EPs and Gold Standard singles. Sleeve shows title as "A Fool Such as I," whereas record label gives full title: "(Now and Then There's) A Fool Such As I."

❏ RCA Victor 447-0625 .... '61   10-15
Gold Standard. Black label, dog on top.

❏ RCA Victor 447-0625 .... '65   6-10
Gold Standard. Black label, dog on side.
J2WW-3253-9S/J2WW-3256-9S. Label GS#6. Has playing times. Credits "ELVIS PRESLEY with The Jordanaires."

❏ RCA Victor 447-0625 .... '68   50-75
Gold Standard. Orange label.
J2WW-3253-9S/J2WW-3256-9S. Credits "ELVIS PRESLEY with The Jordanaires."

❏ RCA Victor 447-0625 .... '70   10-12
Gold Standard. Red label.
J2WW-3253-10S/J2WW-3256-9S. Credits "ELVIS PRESLEY with The Jordanaires."

❏ RCA Victor 447-0625 .... '77   3-5
Gold Standard. Black label, dog near top.

I REALLY DON'T WANT TO KNOW / There Goes My Everything

❏ RCA Victor 47-9960 .... 12/70   4-6
Orange label.
ZPKM-1616-8S-A3B/ZPKM-1624-7S-A1F. Credits "ELVIS PRESLEY, Vocal Accompaniment: The Imperials Quartet." Identification numbers are engraved.

❏ RCA Victor 47-9960 .... 12/70   10-20
Picture sleeve. Reads: "Coming Soon – New Album."

❏ RCA Victor 47-9960 .... 1/71   20-25
Picture sleeve. Reads: "Now Available – New Album."

❏ RCA Victor 47-9960 .... 12/70   20-25
Yellow label. Promotional issue only.
ZPKM-1616-1S/ZPKM-1624-2S. Credits "ELVIS PRESLEY, Vocal Accompaniment: The Imperials Quartet."

❏ RCA Victor 447-0679 .... 2/72   10-12
Gold Standard. Red label.
ZPKM-1616-30S/ZPKM-1624-30S. Credits "ELVIS PRESLEY, Vocal Accompaniment: The Imperials Quartet."

❏ RCA Victor 447-0679 .... '77   3-5
Gold Standard. Black label, dog near top.

I WANT YOU, I NEED YOU, I LOVE YOU / Hound Dog

❏ Sun 224: Bootleg. Listed for identification only.

I WANT YOU, I NEED YOU, I LOVE YOU / Love Me

❏ RCA Victor PB-13887 ...... 12/84   3-4
Gold vinyl. Originally included as one of the singles in the boxed set *Elvis' Greatest Hits – Golden Singles, Vol. 1.*

❏ RCA Victor PB-13887 ...... 12/84   3-4
Picture sleeve.

I WANT YOU, I NEED YOU, I LOVE YOU / My Baby Left Me

❏ RCA Victor 20-6540 .... 5/56   75-100
Black label, 78 rpm.
G2WB-0271-3S/G2WB-1231-1S. Label S#4. Credits "ELVIS PRESLEY."

❏ RCA Victor 20-6540 .... '70s   250-500
White label 78 rpm. Reads: "Record Prevue, Disc Jockey Sample." Has rectangular "Not for Sale" box printed on label. We're not yet certain as to the history, purpose and legitimacy of this series.
G2WB-0271/G2WB-1231. Credits "ELVIS PRESLEY." Identification numbers are engraved, but may be scratched over.

❏ RCA Victor 47-6540 .... 5/56   20-30
Black label, dog on top, without horizontal silver line.
G2WW-0271-4S/G2WW-1231-1S. Label S#13. Songwriter Maurice Mysels is mistakenly shown as "Maurice Myself." Credits "ELVIS PRESLEY."

❏ RCA Victor 47-6540 .... 5/56   30-40
Black label, dog on top, with horizontal silver line.
G2WW-0271-6S/G2WW-1231-6S. Label S#12L. Credits "ELVIS PRESLEY."
Picture sleeves for this single are bootlegs. The RCA "This Is His Life," cartoon sleeve, previously and mistakenly, thought to have been issued with this single, is now found under *MYSTERY TRAIN.*

❏ RCA Victor 47-6540 .... 5/56   200-300
White "Record Prevue" label. Promotional, Canadian issue only.

❏ RCA Victor 447-0607 .... 3/59   15-20
Gold Standard. Black label, dog on top.
J2PW-5693-2S/J2PW-5694-1S. Label GS#1. Credits "ELVIS PRESLEY."

❏ RCA Victor 447-0607 .... '65   6-10
Gold Standard. Black label, dog on side.
J2PW-5693-3S/J2PW-5694-2S. Label GS#6. Credits "ELVIS PRESLEY."

❏ RCA Victor 447-0607 .... '68   50-75
Gold Standard. Orange label.
J2PW-5693-3S/J2PW-5694-2S. Credits "ELVIS PRESLEY."

❏ RCA Victor 447-0607 .... '70   10-12
Gold Standard. Red label.
J2PW-5693-3S/J2PW-5694-2S. Credits "ELVIS PRESLEY."

❏ RCA Victor 447-0607 .... '77   3-5
Gold Standard. Black label, dog near top.

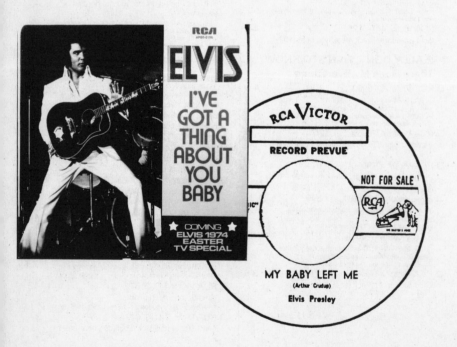

I WAS THE ONE / Wear My Ring Around Your Neck

❑ RCA Victor PB-13500........4/83   3-5
Black label, dog near top.
PB-13500-A-9/PB-13500-B-6. Both sides shown as stereo. Inscribed on *I Was the One* is "MRΔ109179," and on *Wear My Ring Around Your Neck* is "MRΔ109179X." Has "Denny Woodland" in trail off on both sides. Credits "ELVIS PRESLEY, Reissue Produced by Tony Brown and David Briggs." Identification numbers are engraved.

❑ RCA Victor PB-13500........4/83   5-10
Picture sleeve.

❑ RCA Victor JB-13500........4/83   100-200
Gold vinyl. Yellow label, red print. Promotional issue only.
PB-13500-A-1/PB-13500-B-1. Both sides shown as stereo. Has "Denny Woodland" in trail off on both sides. Credits "ELVIS PRESLEY, Reissue Produced by Tony Brown and David Briggs." Identification numbers are engraved.

❑ RCA Victor JB-13500........4/83   10-15
Light yellow with black print. Promotional issue only.
PB-13500-A-9/PB-13500-B-6. Both sides shown as stereo. Inscribed on *I Was the One* is "MRΔ109179," and on *Wear My Ring Around Your Neck* is "MRΔ109179X." Has "Denny Woodland" in trail off on both sides. Has a dingbat (❋) printed on the label, to indicate that *I Was the One* is the plug side. Credits "ELVIS PRESLEY, Reissue Produced by Tony Brown and David Briggs." Identification numbers are engraved.

These tracks, both from the *I Was the One* LP, have some additional instrumentation added to the original masters. Neither track was originally recorded in stereo; however, the added instrumentation creates an overall stereo effect.

I'LL BE BACK / Blank

❑ RCA Victor 4-834-115 ....9/66   5000-8000
White label. Single-sided. Reads: "For Special Academy Consideration Only." Made for submission to the Academy of Motion Picture Arts and Sciences.
TPKM-5313-1S. Credits "ELVIS PRESLEY with the Jordanaires."

I'LL NEVER LET YOU GO (LITTLE DARLIN') / I'm Gonna Sit Right Down and Cry (Over You)

❑ RCA Victor 20-6638 ....9/56   75-100
Black label, 78 rpm.
F2WB-8116-2S/G2WB-1254-2S. Label S#1. Credits "ELVIS PRESLEY."

❑ RCA Victor 47-6638 ....9/56   40-50
Black label, dog on top, without horizontal silver line.
F2WW-8116-4S/G2WW-1254-4S. Label S#12. (Hollywood pressing.) Credits "ELVIS PRESLEY."
Only bootleg picture sleeves exist for this release.

❑ RCA Victor 47-6638 ....9/56   50-60
Black label, dog on top, with horizontal silver line.
F2WW-8116-5S/G2WW-1254-5S. Label S#12L. (Indianapolis pressing.) Credits "ELVIS PRESLEY."
Only bootleg picture sleeves exist for this release.

❑ RCA Victor 47-6638...........9/56   200-300
White "Record Prevue" label. Promotional, Canadian issue only.

❑ RCA Victor 447-0611.........3/59   15-20
Gold Standard. Black label, dog on top.

❑ Collectables 4504 ....'86   3-4
Black vinyl.
DPE1-1004-B-1/DPE1-1004-A-1. Credits "ELVIS PRESLEY." Polystyrene pressing.

❑ Collectables 4504 ....7/92   5-6
Gold vinyl.
DPE1-1004-B-1/DPE1-1004-A-1. Credits "ELVIS PRESLEY." Polystyrene pressing.

I'M LEAVIN' / Heart of Rome

❑ RCA Victor 47-9998...........7/71   4-6
Orange label.
APKM-1285-1S/ZPKM-1614-2S. Credits "ELVIS PRESLEY, Vocal accompaniment: Imperials Quartet" on *I'm Leavin'* and "ELVIS PRESLEY" on *Heart of Rome*.

❑ RCA Victor 47-9998...........7/71   25-30
Picture sleeve.

❑ RCA Victor 47-9998...........7/71   20-25
Yellow label. Promotional issue only.
APKM-1285-4S/ZPKM-1614-4S. Credits "ELVIS PRESLEY, Vocal accompaniment: Imperials Quartet" on *I'm Leavin'* and "ELVIS PRESLEY" on *Heart of Rome*.

❑ RCA Victor 447-0683.........5/72   10-12
Gold Standard. Red label.
APKM-1285-4S/ZPKM-1614-4S. Both sides shown as mono. Credits "ELVIS PRESLEY, Vocal accomp.: Imperials Quartet" on *I'm Leavin'* and "ELVIS PRESLEY" on *Heart of Rome*.

❑ RCA Victor 447-0683...........'77   3-5
Gold Standard. Black label, dog near top.

I'M YOURS / (It's a) Long Lonely Highway

❑ RCA Victor 47-8657...........8/65   6-10
Black label, dog on side.
M2WW-0859-3S/PPKM-0303-2S. Label S#21. Credits "ELVIS PRESLEY" on *I'm Yours* and "ELVIS PRESLEY with The Jordanaires" on *(It's A) Long Lonely Highway*.

❑ RCA Victor 47-8657...........8/65   20-30
Picture sleeve.

❑ RCA Victor 47-8657...........8/65   40-45
White label. Promotional issue only.
M2WW-0859-3S/PPKM-0303-3S. Label S#26. Credits "ELVIS PRESLEY" on *I'm Yours* and "ELVIS PRESLEY with The Jordanaires" on *(It's A) Long Lonely Highway*.

❑ RCA Victor 447-0654...........11/66   6-10
Gold Standard. Black label, dog on side.

❑ RCA Victor 447-0654...........'70   10-12
Gold Standard. Red label.

❑ RCA Victor 447-0654...........'77   3-5
Gold Standard. Black label, dog near top.

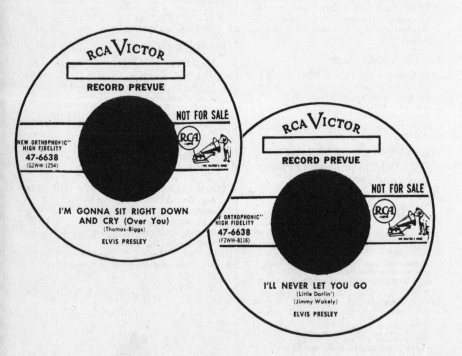

I'VE LOST YOU / The Next Step Is Love

❑ RCA Victor 47-9873 ....7/70   4-6
Orange label.
ZPKM-1594-5S/ZPKM-1619-4S. On *I've Lost You* side, the number in the trail off is "1595," but with the last "5" crossed out. Above the "5" is a "4." Credits "ELVIS PRESLEY Horns & Strings arranged by Bergen White."

❑ RCA Victor 47-9873 ....7/70   10-15
Titles sleeve – no picture.

❑ RCA Victor 47-9873 ....7/70   20-25
Yellow label. Promotional issue only.
ZPKM-1594-4S/ZPKM-1619-5S. On *I've Lost You* side, the identification number in the trail off has the "4" in "1594" crossed out. Above the "4" is a "5," which is also crossed out. Below those numbers is another "4." Credits "ELVIS PRESLEY Horns & Strings arranged by Bergen White."

❑ RCA Victor 447-0677 ....8/71   10-12
Gold Standard. Red label.
ZPKM-1594-5S/ZPKM-1619-4S. On *I've Lost You* side, the identification number in the trail off was "1595." The "5" is crossed out and a "4" put next to is. This is a different correction than found on the promo copy. Credits "ELVIS PRESLEY Horns & Strings arranged by Bergen White."

❑ RCA Victor 447-0677 ....'77   3-5
Gold Standard. Black label, dog near top.

IF EVERY DAY WAS LIKE CHRISTMAS / How Would You Like to Be

❑ RCA Victor 47-8950 ....11/66   6-10
Black label, dog on side.
TPKM-0984-1S/PPKM-2722-1S. Label S#21. *If Every Day Was Like Christmas*, credits "ELVIS PRESLEY" on one line and "with The Jordanaires and" on the second line and "The Imperials Quartet" on the third line. Credits "ELVIS PRESLEY with The Mello Men" on *How Would You Like to Be*.

❑ RCA Victor 47-8950 ....11/66   25-35
Picture sleeve.

❑ RCA Victor 47-8950 ....11/66   40-45
White label. Promotional issue only.
TPKM-0984-4S/PPKM-2722-4S. Label S#26. *If Every Day Was Like Christmas*, credits "ELVIS PRESLEY" on one line and "with The Jordanaires and The Imperials Quartet" on a second line. Credits "ELVIS PRESLEY with The Mello Men" on *How Would You Like to Be*.
TPKM-0984-8S/PPKM-2722-8S. Label S#27. *If Every Day Was Like Christmas*, credits "ELVIS PRESLEY" on one line, "with The Jordanaires and" on the second line, and "The Imperials Quartet" on the third line. Credits "ELVIS PRESLEY with The Mello Men" on *How Would You Like to Be*.

❑ RCA Victor 447-0681 ....5/72   10-12
Gold Standard. Red label.

❑ RCA Victor 447-0681 ....'77   3-5
Gold Standard. Black label, dog near top.

IF I CAN DREAM / Edge of Reality

❑ RCA Victor 47-9670 ....11/68   4-6
Orange label.
WPKM-8029-9S/WPKM-5769-17S. Credits "ELVIS PRESLEY."

❑ RCA Victor 47-9670 ....11/68   15-20
Picture sleeve. Reads: "As Featured On His NBC-TV Special."

❑ RCA Victor 47-9670 ....1/69   15-20
Picture sleeve. No mention of TV special.

❑ RCA Victor 47-9670 ....11/68   25-35
Yellow label. Promotional issue only.
WPKM-8029-9S/WPKM-5769-18S. Credits "ELVIS PRESLEY." Corresponding with the change to the orange commercial label, RCA's yellow promo labels now were nearly identical to commercial issues, except that the name "Victor" on the right side is replaced with the words "NOT FOR SALE."

❑ RCA Victor 447-0668 ....12/70   10-12
Gold Standard. Red label.

❑ RCA Victor 447-0668 ....'77   3-5
Gold Standard. Black label, dog near top.

IF YOU TALK IN YOUR SLEEP / Help Me

❑ RCA Victor APBO-0280.....5/74   10-15
Orange label. Has title, "If You Talk in Your Sleep," on one line.
APBO-0280-A-1/APBO-0280-B-1. Both sides are stereo. Credits "ELVIS PRESLEY" on *If You Talk in Your Sleep* and "ELVIS PRESLEY, Vocal accompaniment: Voice/J.D. Sumner & The Stamps, Strings arranged by Mike Leech" on *Help Me*. Identification numbers are engraved.

❑ RCA Victor APBO-0280.....5/74   4-6
Orange label. Has title, "If You Talk in Your Sleep," on two lines.
APBO-0280-A/APBO-0280-B. Both sides are stereo. Credits "ELVIS PRESLEY" on *If You Talk in Your Sleep* and "ELVIS PRESLEY, Vocal accompaniment: Voice/J.D. Sumner & The Stamps, Strings arranged by Mike Leech" on *Help Me*.

❑ RCA Victor APBO-0280.....5/74   20-25
Picture sleeve.

❑ RCA Victor DJAO-0280
(APBO-0280).....................5/74   15-20
Light yellow label. Promotional issue only.
APBO-0280-C-1/APBO-0280-D-1. Both sides are mono. Credits "ELVIS PRESLEY" on *If You Talk in Your Sleep* and "ELVIS PRESLEY, Vocal accompaniment: Voice/J.D. Sumner & The Stamps, Strings arranged by Mike Leech" on *Help Me*.

For the Gold Standard release of *If You Talk in Your Sleep* see *RAISED ON ROCK / If You Talk in Your Sleep*.

IMPOSSIBLE DREAM (THE QUEST) / An American Trilogy

❑ RCA Victor JH-13302 ....8/82   75-100
Gold label. Souvenir, given to visitors to Elvis' birthplace in Tupelo.
JH-13302-B-1S/JH-13302-B-1S. Both sides are stereo. Label states: "NOT FOR SALE," and "Commemoration, Tupelo, Mississippi, August 16, 1982." Credits "ELVIS PRESLEY, Produced by Joan Deary." Identification numbers are engraved.

❑ RCA Victor JH-13302 ....8/82   75-100
Titles sleeve – no picture. Black and white.

IN THE GHETTO / Any Day Now

❑ RCA Victor 47-9741...........4/69   4-6
Orange label.
XPKM-1154-6S/XPKM-1274-5S. Credits "ELVIS PRESLEY."

❑ RCA Victor 47-9741...........4/69   15-20
Picture sleeve. Reads: "Coming Soon *From Elvis in Memphis* LP Album."

❑ RCA Victor 47-9741...........5/69   20-25
Picture sleeve. Reads: "Ask For *From Elvis in Memphis* LP Album."

❑ RCA Victor 47-9741...........4/69   20-30
Yellow label. Promotional issue only.
XPKM-1154-4S/XPKM-1274-4S. Credits "ELVIS PRESLEY." Identification numbers are engraved.

❑ RCA Victor 447-0671.......12/70   10-12
Gold Standard. Red label.
XPKM-1154-3S/XPKM-1274-7S. Numbers are engraved in trail off on *In the Ghetto* (the earliest Gold Standard single we've found with engraved numbers), and stamped on *Any Day Now*. Credits "ELVIS PRESLEY."

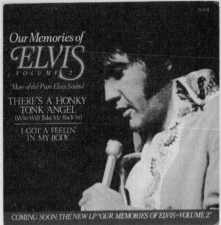

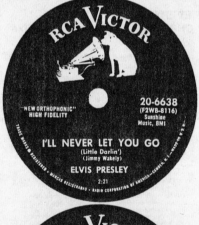

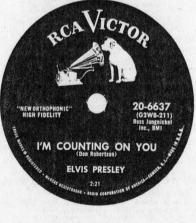

❑ RCA Victor 447-0671 .... '77　　3-5
Gold Standard. Black label, dog near top.

❑ RCA Victor PB-11100 ...... 10/77　　3-4
Originally included as one of the singles in the boxed sets *15 Golden Records – 30 Golden Hits* and *20 Golden Hits in Full Color Sleeves*.

❑ RCA Victor PB-11100 ...... 10/77　　3-4
Picture sleeve.

IN THE GHETTO / If I Can Dream

❑ RCA Victor PB-13890 ...... 12/84　　3-4
Gold vinyl; originally included as one of the singles in the boxed set *Elvis' Greatest Hits – Golden Singles, Vol. 1*.

❑ RCA Victor PB-13890 ...... 12/84　　3-4
Picture sleeve.

INDESCRIBABLY BLUE / Fools Fall in Love

❑ RCA Victor 47-9056 .... 1/67　　6-10
Black label, dog on side.
TPKM-0982-2S/TPKM-0925-2S. Label S#21. *Indescribably Blue*, credits "ELVIS PRESLEY" on one line, "with The Jordanaires" on the second line, and "and The Imperials Quartet" on the third line. Credits "ELVIS PRESLEY with The Jordanaires" on *Fools Fall in Love*.
TPKM-0982-7S/TPKM-0925-8S. Label S#20. *Indescribably Blue*, credits "ELVIS PRESLEY" on one line, "with The Jordanaires and The" on the second line, and "Imperials Quartet" on the third line. Credits "ELVIS PRESLEY with The Jordanaires" on *Fools Fall in Love*.

❑ RCA Victor 47-9056 .... 1/67　　20-30
Picture sleeve.

❑ RCA Victor 47-9056 .... 1/67　　35-40
White label. Promotional issue only.
TPKM-0982-2S/TPKM-0925-2S. Label S#26. Credits "ELVIS PRESLEY with The Jordanaires and The Imperials Quartet" on *Indescribably Blue* and "ELVIS PRESLEY with The Jordanaires" on *Fools Fall in Love*.
TPKM-0982-7S/TPKM-0925-7S. Label S#27. Credits "ELVIS PRESLEY with The Jordanaires and The Imperials Quartet" on *Indescribably Blue* and "ELVIS PRESLEY with The Jordanaires" on *Fools Fall in Love*.

❑ RCA Victor 447-0659 .... '68　　50-75
Gold Standard. Orange label.

❑ RCA Victor 447-0659 .... '70　　10-12
Gold Standard. Red label.

❑ RCA Victor 447-0659 .... '77　　3-5
Gold Standard. Black label, dog near top.

IT'S NOW OR NEVER / A Mess of Blues

❑ RCA Victor 47-7777 .... 7/60　　750-1000
Black label, dog on top.
Does not have the piano track on *It's Now Or Never*.
L2WW-0100-3S/L2WW-0085-9S. Label S#19. Credits "ELVIS PRESLEY with The Jordanaires."
L2WW-0100-4S/L2WW-0085-7S. Label S#19. Credits "ELVIS PRESLEY with The Jordanaires."

❑ RCA Victor 47-7777 .... 7/60　　8-12
Black label, dog on top.
L2WW-0100-25S/L2WW-0085-5S. Label S#19. Credits "ELVIS PRESLEY with The Jordanaires."

❑ RCA Victor 47-7777 .... 7/60　　20-30
Picture sleeve.

❑ RCA Victor 61-7777 .... 7/60　　500-700
Living Stereo.
L2WA-3514-1S/L2WA-3515-1S. Credits "ELVIS PRESLEY with The Jordanaires."

❑ RCA Victor 447-0628 .... 2/62　　8-12
Gold Standard. Black label, dog on top.

❑ RCA Victor 447-0628 .... '65　　6-10
Gold Standard. Black label, dog on side.
L2WW-0100-10S/L2WW-0085-1S. Label GS#6. Credits "ELVIS PRESLEY with The Jordanaires."

❑ RCA Victor 447-0628 .... '68　　50-75
Gold Standard. Orange label.
L2WW-0100-18S/L2WW-0085-11S. Credits "ELVIS PRESLEY with The Jordanaires."

❑ RCA Victor 447-0628 .... '70　　10-12
Gold Standard. Red label.
L2WW-0100-19S/L2WW-0085-11S. Credits "ELVIS PRESLEY with The Jordanaires."

❑ RCA Victor 447-0628 .... '77　　3-5
Gold Standard. Black label, dog near top.

❑ RCA Victor PB-11110 ...... 10/77　　3-4
Originally included as one of the singles in the boxed set *15 Golden Records – 30 Golden Hits*.

❑ RCA Victor PB-11110 ...... 10/77　　3-4
Picture sleeve.

IT'S NOW OR NEVER / I Walk the Line (Jaye P. Morgan)

❑ U.S.A.F. Pgm. No. 125/6 ... 2/61　　300-400
Public service, five-minute radio show, part of the U.S. Air Force's "Music in the Air" series. Plays a slightly edited version of *It's Now or Never*.
E-6491 OSS-MA-126/E-6492 OSS-MA-125. Mistakenly shows Elvis' publishing company, Gladys Music Inc., as "Glady's Music Inc." Credits "ELVIS PRESLEY." Identification numbers are engraved. Polystyrene pressing. May have been the first Elvis 45 on polystyrene.

❑ U.S.A.F. Pgm. No. 125-128 .... 2/61　　100-125
Cardboard mailer. Printed information on this mailer indicates "Programs 125, 126, 127, 128" are included.

IT'S NOW OR NEVER / Surrender

❑ RCA Victor PB-13889 ...... 12/84　　3-4
Gold vinyl. Originally included as one of the singles in the boxed set *Elvis' Greatest Hits – Golden Singles, Vol. 1*.

❑ RCA Victor PB-13889 ...... 12/84　　3-4
Picture sleeve.

IT'S ONLY LOVE / The Sound of Your Cry

❑ RCA Victor 48-1017 .... 9/71　　4-6
Orange label.
APKM-1287-6S/ZPKM-1596-6S. Credits "ELVIS PRESLEY, Vocal accompaniment by The Imperials Quartet" on *It's Only Love* and "ELVIS PRESLEY" on *The Sound of Your Cry*.

❑ RCA Victor 48-1017 .... 9/71　　20-25
Picture sleeve.

❑ RCA Victor 48-1017 .... 9/71　　25-30
Yellow label. Promotional issue only.
APKM-1287-6S/ZPKM-1596-6S. Credits "ELVIS PRESLEY, Vocal accompaniment by The Imperials Quartet" on *It's Only Love* and "ELVIS PRESLEY" on *The Sound of Your Cry*.

❑ RCA Victor 447-0684 ....5/72   10-12
Gold Standard. Red label.
APKM-1287-6S/ZPKM-1596-6S. Both sides shown as mono.
Credits "ELVIS PRESLEY, Vocal accomp. by The Imperials
Quartet" on *It's Only Love* and "ELVIS PRESLEY" on *The
Sound of Your Cry.*

❑ RCA Victor 447-0684 ....'77   3-5
Gold Standard. Black label, dog near top.

JAILHOUSE ROCK / Baby I Don't Care

❑ Laurel 41 624 ....5/57   75-100
Picture cover. Pictures Elvis but credits Vince
Everett. This black-and-white, cardboard, EP-
like cover may have been made as a prop for
the film *Jailhouse Rock*, in which Elvis'
character was named Vince Everett. While
some researchers question the authenticity –
and therefore the production date – of this
item, prices in this range are nevertheless
paid for it. No Laurel records of this title exist.

JAILHOUSE ROCK / Treat Me Nice

❑ RCA Victor 20-7035 ....9/57   75-125
Black label, 78 rpm.
H2WB-6779-1S/H2WB-6778-1S. Label S#5. Credits "ELVIS
PRESLEY."

❑ RCA Victor 20-7035 ....'70s   250-500
White label 78 rpm. Reads: "Record Prevue,
Disc Jockey Sample." Has rectangular "Not
for Sale" box printed on label. We're not yet
certain as to the history, purpose and
legitimacy of this series.
H2WB-6779/H2WB-6778. Credits "ELVIS PRESLEY."
Identification numbers are engraved, but may be scratched
over.

❑ RCA Victor 47-7035 ....9/57   20-30
Black label, dog on top, without horizontal
silver line.
H2WW-6779-5S/H2WW-6778-8S. Label S#12. Credits
"ELVIS PRESLEY."

❑ RCA Victor 47-7035 ....9/57   30-40
Black label, dog on top, with horizontal silver
line.
Black vinyl. This is the final RCA Elvis single
with the horizontal silver line label.
H2WW-6779-1S/H2WW-6778-2S. Label S#15. Credits
"ELVIS PRESLEY."

❑ RCA Victor 47-7035 ....9/57   2500-3500
Gold label, dog on top. Gold vinyl. Specific
purpose not yet known. May be promotional
though not marked as such. Similar to other
gold label, gold vinyl singles, by assorted
RCA artists popular at the time.
H2WW-6779-1S/H2WW-6778-2S. Label S#15. Credits
"ELVIS PRESLEY."

❑ RCA Victor 47-7035 ....9/57   50-100
Picture sleeve.

❑ RCA Victor 47-7035 ....10/57   1000-1500
MGM special press preview theatre
ticket/sleeve. Sent wrapped around the
standard *Jailhouse Rock* picture sleeve, with
a 45 rpm inside. Promotional issue only,
distributed only to media film reviewers. Price
is for ticket with stub still attached.

Counterfeit Identification: Ticket/Sleeve is in
absolutely perfect condition. This flawless
reproduction can only be identified by its
immaculate condition. Originals should show
some aging signs.

❑ RCA Victor 47-7035.........10/57   500-750
Same as above, except stub has been
detached from ticket.

❑ RCA Victor 447-0619...........'61   10-20
Gold Standard. Black label, dog on top.

❑ RCA Victor 447-0619...........'65   6-10
Gold Standard. Black label, dog on side.
H2WW-6779-6S/H2WW-6778-6S. Label GS#6. Credits
"ELVIS PRESLEY."

❑ RCA Victor 447-0619...........'68   50-75
Gold Standard. Orange label.

❑ RCA Victor 447-0619...........'70   10-12
Gold Standard. Red label.
H2WW-6779-18S/H2WW-6778-13S. Credits "ELVIS
PRESLEY."

❑ RCA Victor 447-0619...........'77   3-5
Gold Standard. Black label, dog near top.

❑ RCA Victor PB-11101......10/77   3-4
Originally included as one of the singles in the
boxed set *15 Golden Records – 30 Golden
Hits.*

❑ RCA Victor PB-11101......10/77   3-4
Picture sleeve.

JAILHOUSE ROCK / Young and Beautiful

❑ Soundtrack 102: Bootleg. Listed for
identification only.

JOSHUA FIT THE BATTLE / Known Only to Him

❑ RCA Victor 447-0651.........3/66   20-25
Gold Standard. Black label, dog on side.
L2WW-0380-1S/L2WW-0384-2S. Label GS#6. Has playing
times and publisher. Credits "ELVIS PRESLEY with The
Jordanaires."

❑ RCA Victor 447-0651.........3/66   200-250
Gold Standard picture sleeve.

❑ RCA Victor 447-0651.........3/66   75-125
Gold Standard. White label. Promotional issue
only.
L2WW-0380-1S/L2WW-0384-2S. Label GS#11. Credits
"ELVIS PRESLEY with The Jordanaires."

❑ RCA Victor 447-0651...........'70   12-15
Gold Standard. Red label.

❑ RCA Victor 447-0651...........'77   3-5
Gold Standard. Black label, dog near top.

❑ RCA Victor 447-0651.........4/66   900-1200
"Special Easter Programming Kit." Includes
picture sleeve mailer and promo copies of
both 1966 Easter singles: *Joshua Fit the
Battle* and *Milky White Way* in their picture
sleeves. Also has a 1966 Easter card from
Elvis.

❑ RCA Victor 447-0651.........4/66   800-1000
"Special Easter Programming Kit." Price is for
sleeve-mailer by itself. Has a black-and-white
Elvis photo on front.

JOY OF CHRISTMAS / Joy of Christmas Promos

❑ Creative Radio (SP) 9/86   20-30
Programmed for adult contemporary formats. Issued to radio stations only.

❑ Creative Radio (SP) 9/86   20-30
Programmed for country music formats. Issued to radio stations only.

JUDY / There's Always Me

❑ RCA Victor 47-9287 .... 8/67   6-10
Black label, dog on side.
M2WW-0577-8S/M2WW-0574-8S. Label S#21. Credits "ELVIS PRESLEY" on Judy and "ELVIS PRESLEY with The Jordanaires" on There's Always Me.

❑ RCA Victor 47-9287 .... 8/67   20-30
Picture sleeve.

❑ RCA Victor 47-9287 .... 8/67   35-40
White label. Promotional issue only.
M2WW-0577-6S/M2WW-0574-4S. Label S#27. Credits "ELVIS PRESLEY" on Judy and "ELVIS PRESLEY with The Jordanaires" on There's Always Me.

❑ RCA Victor 447-0661 .... '70   12-15
Gold Standard. Red label.

❑ RCA Victor 447-0661 .... '77   3-5
Gold Standard. Black label, dog near top.

KENTUCKY RAIN / My Little Friend

❑ RCA Victor 47-9791 .... 2/70   4-6
Orange label.
XPKM-1271-5S/XPKM-1153-6S. Credits "ELVIS PRESLEY."

❑ RCA Victor 47-9791 .... 2/70   10-20
Picture sleeve.

❑ RCA Victor 47-9791 .... 2/70   20-30
Yellow label. Promotional issue only.
XPKM-1271-5S/XPKM-1153-6S. Credits "ELVIS PRESLEY."

❑ RCA Victor 447-0675 .... 8/71   10-12
Gold Standard. Red label.
XPKM-1271-3S/XPKM-1153-4S. Credits "ELVIS PRESLEY."

❑ RCA Victor 447-0675 .... '77   3-5
Gold Standard. Black label, dog near top.

KING IS DEAD LONG LIVE THE KING (Elvis Presley Is Still the King!) / Blank

❑ Eva-Tone 52578X 5/78   25-75
Yellow vinyl soundsheet sampler, made for Universal Sounds Unlimited to promote a proposed Elvis radio special. No label used – print is on the plastic.

KING OF THE WHOLE WIDE WORLD / Home Is Where the Heart Is

❑ RCA Victor SP-45-118 ...... 8/62   200-250
Black label, dog on top. Promotional issue only.
N2PW-3131-2S/N2PW-3134-2S. Credits "ELVIS PRESLEY, The Jordanaires." (Not "with" the Jordanaires.)

❑ RCA Victor SP-45-118 ...... 8/62   200-250
Titles sleeve – no picture. Black and white.
Counterfeit Identification: Fakes look perfect: however, the ink on them is red. Originals have black ink.

❑ RCA Victor 62-35,
Aug. 21, 1962 .... 8/62   3-5
"Deejay Notes from RCA Victor," a one-page publicity sheet with a promotional pitch for *King of the Whole Wide World* and *Home Is Where the Heart Is*. Also plugs new RCA releases by Jimmy Elledge and Sam Fletcher. Value is minimal since we know of now way to distinguish an original from photocopies.

KISS ME QUICK / Suspicion

❑ RCA Victor 447-0639......... 4/64   8-12
Gold Standard. Black label, dog on top.
M2WW-0657-3S/N2WW-0694-3S. Label GS#1. Credits "ELVIS PRESLEY with The Jordanaires."

❑ RCA Victor 447-0639......... 4/64   50-75
Gold Standard picture sleeve.

❑ RCA Victor 447-0639......... 4/64   40-50
Gold Standard. White label. Promotional issue only.
M2WW-0657-4S/N2WW-0694-4S. Label GS#8. Credits "ELVIS PRESLEY with The Jordanaires."

❑ RCA Victor 447-0639.......... '68   50-75
Gold Standard. Orange label.
M2WW-0857-3S/N2WW-0694-5S. Credits "ELVIS PRESLEY with The Jordanaires."

❑ RCA Victor 447-0639.......... '70   10-12
Gold Standard. Red label.
M2WW-0857-3S/N2WW-0694-6S. Credits "ELVIS PRESLEY with The Jordanaires."

❑ RCA Victor 447-0639.......... '77   3-5
Gold Standard. Black label, dog near top.

KISSIN' COUSINS / It Hurts Me

❑ RCA Victor 47-8307........... 1/64   6-10
Black label, dog on top.
RPKM-0219-6S/RPKM-1006-6S. Label S#19. Credits "ELVIS PRESLEY with The Jordanaires."

❑ RCA Victor 47-8307........... 1/64   20-30
Picture sleeve.

❑ RCA Victor 447-0644......... 5/65   6-10
Gold Standard. Black label, dog on side.
RPKM-0219-5S/RPKM-1006-8S. Label GS#6. Has playing times and publisher. Credits "ELVIS PRESLEY with The Jordanaires."

❑ RCA Victor 447-0644.......... '68   50-75
Gold Standard. Orange label.

❑ RCA Victor 447-0644.......... '70   10-12
Gold Standard. Red label.
RPKM-0219-5S/RPKM-1006-9S. Credits "ELVIS PRESLEY with The Jordanaires."

❑ RCA Victor 447-0644.......... '77   3-5
Gold Standard. Black label, dog near top.

KU-U-I-PO / Nostalgia Party

❑ Shaker: Bootleg. Listed for identification only.

LADY LOVES ME / C'Mon Everybody

❑ Soundtrack 101: Bootleg. Listed for identification only.

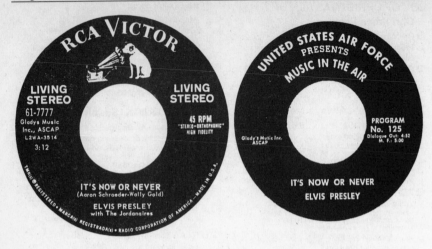

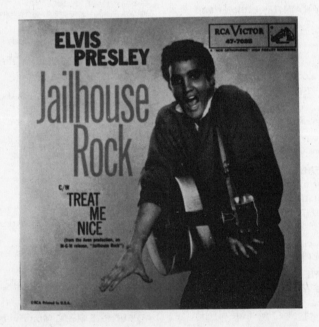

LAWDY, MISS CLAWDY / Shake, Rattle and Roll

❑ RCA Victor 20-6642 ....9/56   75-100
Black label, 78 rpm.
G2WB-1293-2S/G2WB-1294-2S. Label S#1. Credits "ELVIS PRESLEY."

❑ RCA Victor 47-6642 ....9/56   40-50
Black label, dog on top, without horizontal silver line.
Only bootleg picture sleeves exist for this release.

❑ RCA Victor 47-6642 ....9/56   200-225
Black label, no dog on label, with horizontal silver line.
Only bootleg picture sleeves exist for this release.

❑ RCA Victor 47-6642 ....9/56   50-60
Black label, dog on top, with horizontal silver line.
G2WW-1293-3S/G2WW-1294-3S. Label S#12L. Credits "ELVIS PRESLEY."
Only bootleg picture sleeves exist for this release.

❑ RCA Victor 447-0615 ....3/59   15-20
Gold Standard. Black label, dog on top.
J2PW-6010-4S/J2PW-6009-3S. Label GS#1. Credits "ELVIS PRESLEY."

❑ RCA Victor 447-0615 ....'65   6-12
Gold Standard. Black label, dog on side.
J2PW-6010-4S/J2PW-6009-4S. Label GS#4. Credits "ELVIS PRESLEY."

❑ RCA Victor 447-0615 ....'68   50-75
Gold Standard. Orange label.

❑ RCA Victor 447-0615 ....'70   10-12
Gold Standard. Red label.
J2PW-6010-4S/J2PW-6009-4S. Credits "ELVIS PRESLEY."

❑ RCA Victor 447-0615 ....'77   3-5
Gold Standard. Black label, dog near top.

LET ME BE THERE (Stereo) / Let Me Be There (Mono)

❑ RCA Victor JH-10951 ....6/74   150-200
Light yellow label. Promotional issue only. Distributed by Al Gallico Publishing to radio stations only.
JH-10951A-1/JH-10951C-1. Credits "ELVIS PRESLEY, Vocal accomp. by VOICE/J.D. Sumner & The Stamps/The Sweet Inspirations/Kathy Westmoreland."

LET'S HAVE A PARTY / Got a Lot O' Livin to Do

❑ Soundtrack 103: Bootleg. Listed for identification only.

LIFE / I Don't Know How to Love Him (Helen Reddy)

❑ What's It All About TRAV PGM #278/277 ....'77   45-55
Public-service religious program, also has interviews with Hugh Jarrett of the Jordanaires and with Helen Reddy.

LIFE / Only Believe

❑ RCA Victor 47-9985...........5/71   4-6
Orange label.
ZPKM-1613-5S/ZPKM-1626-5S. Credits "ELVIS PRESLEY" on *Life* and "ELVIS PRESLEY," Vocal accompaniment by The Imperials Quartet" on *Only Believe.*

❑ RCA Victor 47-9985...........5/71   20-30
Picture sleeve.

❑ RCA Victor 47-9985...........5/71   25-30
Yellow label. Promotional issue only.
ZPKM-1613-4S/ZPKM-1626-3S. Credits "ELVIS PRESLEY" on *Life* and "ELVIS PRESLEY," Vocal accompaniment by The Imperials Quartet" on *Only Believe.*

❑ RCA Victor 447-0682.........5/72   10-12
Gold Standard. Red label.
ZPKM-1613-6S/ZPKM-1626-5S. Both sides shown as mono. Credits "ELVIS PRESLEY" on *Life* and "ELVIS PRESLEY, Vocal accomp. by The Imperials Quartet" on *Only Believe.*

❑ RCA Victor 447-0682...........'77   3-5
Gold Standard. Black label, dog near top.

LITTLE SISTER / Paralyzed

❑ RCA Victor PB-13547........6/83   3-5
Black label, dog near top.
PB-13547-A-4/PB-13547-B-4. Both sides shown as stereo. Inscribed on *Little Sister* is "MR△109070," and on *Paralyzed* is "MRΔ109070X." Has "Denny Woodland" in trail off on both sides. Credits "ELVIS PRESLEY, Reissue Produced by Tony Brown and David Briggs." Identification numbers are engraved.

❑ RCA Victor PB-13547........6/83   20-25
Picture sleeve.

❑ RCA Victor JB-13547 ....6/83   10-15
Light yellow label. Promotional issue only.

❑ RCA Victor JB-13547 ....6/83   200-250
Blue vinyl. Blue label.
PB-13547-A-1/PB-13547-B-1. Both sides shown as stereo. Has "Denny Woodland" in trail off on both sides. Credits "ELVIS PRESLEY, Reissue Produced by Tony Brown and David Briggs." Identification numbers are engraved.

These tracks, both from the *I Was the One* LP, have some additional instrumentation added to the original masters. Neither track was originally recorded in stereo; however, the added instrumentation creates an overall stereo effect.

LITTLE SISTER / Rip It Up

❑ RCA Victor EP-0517..........6/83   125-150
Promotional only, 12" single. Black label with pink print and dog near top. Issued in a plain white cover.
EP-0517-A/EP-0517-B. Identification numbers are engraved. Both sides shown as stereo. Has "Denny Woodland" engraved on both sides. Credits only "ELVIS."

LONG LEGGED GIRL (WITH THE SHORT DRESS ON) / That's Someone You Never Forget

❑ RCA Victor 47-9115...........5/67   8-12
Black label, dog on side.
UPKM-3937-3S/M2WW-0858-3S. Label S#21. Credits "ELVIS PRESLEY with The Jordanaires."
UPKM-3937-6S/M2WW-0858-6S. Has "That's Someone You Never Forget" on two lines. Label S#21. Credits "ELVIS PRESLEY with The Jordanaires."
UPKM-3937-7S/M2WW-0858-7S. Has "That's Someone You Never Forget" on one line. Label S#21. Credits "ELVIS PRESLEY with The Jordanaires."
UPKM-3937-7S/M2WW-0858-8S. Label S#20. Credits "ELVIS PRESLEY with the Jordanaires."

"I WAS THE ONE"
ELVIS

NOT FOR SALE
PROMOTIONAL USE ONLY

SIDE A
EP-0517-A
33 1/3 RPM
STEREO

1. LITTLE SISTER 2:29

(From The LP-AHL1-4678)

TMK(s) ℗ RCA CORP. Made In U.S.A.
© 1983 RCA Records

DJ Preview Special

ELVIS

sings

KING OF THE WHOLE WIDE WORLD (2:07) BMI
HOME IS WHERE THE HEART IS (1:50) ASCAP

TWO (2) ORIGINAL SOUND TRACK SELECTIONS

FROM HIS NEW MOVIE

"KID GALAHAD"

Mirisch Bros. Production — United Artists Release

THESE SOUND TRACK RECORDINGS
PLUS 4 OTHERS AVAILABLE ONLY IN ELVIS'
NEW 45 E.P. - KID GALAHAD (EPA-4371)

SP45-118

RCA VICTOR

SP-45-118
Elvis Presley
Music Inc., BMI
N2PW-3131
2:07

45
RPM

NOT FOR
SALE

KING OF THE WHOLE WIDE WORLD
(from the Mirisch Co. Presentation "Kid Galahad"
A UA Release) (from the RCA Victor album
EPA-4371 "Kid Galahad")
(Ruth Batchlor-Bob Roberts)
ELVIS PRESLEY
The Jordanaires

Deejay notes FROM **RCA VICTOR**

✱ ✱
#62-35, Aug. 21, 1962

ELVIS!

Here's that man again! Mr. Elvis Presley brings you two songs (culled just for
you!) from his upcoming Original Soundtrack EP of his new movie, "Kid Galahad."
First, there's a striking rocker with the style of belting that made Elvis
famous - THE KING OF THE WHOLE WIDE WORLD. You'll dig Elvis' flashy, swinging
delivery with the vocal backdrop by those fabulous Jordanaires. Singers may
come and go, but there's just no one who creates the dynamic excitement of
Elvis Presley. THE KING OF THE WHOLE WORLD is backed by a lovely, simple ballad,
HOME IS WHERE THE HEART IS. And our Elvis is "home" on your turntables. Enjoy!
KING OF THE WHOLE WIDE WORLD, Elvis Presley Music, Inc., BMI, 2:07/
HOME IS WHERE THE HEART IS, Gladys Music, Inc., ASCAP, 1:50

JIMMY ELLEDGE

Popular young Nashville chanter Jimmy Elledge has one of his best sides to
date in the Roger Miller original, A GOLDEN TEAR. Jimmy's wailing delivery of
the blueser is charged with vocal electricity. Elledge has a unique quality
to his voice that has a tendency to fascinate the listener. His styling of
A GOLDEN TEAR is no exception. I'LL GET BY (Don't Worry) is another strong
blues side. This thing builds to a wild climax with Elledge and those Nashville
musicians finishing together. Chet Atkins produced.
A GOLDEN TEAR, Tree Pub. Co., Inc., BMI, 2:03/I'LL GET BY (Don't Worry),
Tree Pub., BMI, 2:02

SAM FLETCHER

Here's a guy who's one of your favorites. It looks like Sam Fletcher has a
winner in the rhythmic ballad, ME AND THE ONE THAT I LOVE. Sam gives the number
a moving interpretation with his exceptionally fine phrasing and inherent feeling
for "beat." The orchestral background, by co-producer Hugo (of Hugo & Luigi)
Peretti, has an uncommon touch with its emphasis on strings - but swingin'
strings! THE ANSWER TO EVERYTHING is an uptempo backer with an infectious tune.
Conclusion: this fellow named Sam is about to make it big!
ME AND THE ONE THAT I LOVE, Chalet Music Corp., ASCAP, 2:30/
THE ANSWER TO EVERYTHING, Dolfi Music, Inc., ASCAP, 2:37

❑ RCA Victor 47-9115 ....5/67   20-30
Picture sleeve. Reads: "Coming Soon –
Double Trouble LP Album."

❑ RCA Victor 47-9115 ....6/67   30-40
Picture sleeve. Reads: "Ask For – *Double
Trouble* LP Album."

❑ RCA Victor 47-9115 ....5/67   35-45
White label. Promotional issue only.
UPKM-3937-6S/M2WW-0858-6S. Label S#26. Has "That's
Someone" on first line and "You Never Forget" on second.
Credits "ELVIS PRESLEY with the Jordanaires."
UPKM-3937-8S/M2WW-0858-8S. Label S#27. Has "That's
Someone You Never Forget" all on one line. Credits "ELVIS
PRESLEY with the Jordanaires."

❑ RCA Victor 447-0660 ....'70   25-50
Gold Standard. Red label.

LOVE LETTERS / Come What May

❑ RCA Victor 47-8870 ....6/66   6-10
Black label, dog on side.
TPKM-0914-7S/TPKM-0924-8S. Credits "ELVIS
PRESLEY" on *Love Letters* and "ELVIS PRESLEY With The
Jordanaires" on *Come What May*. Identification numbers are
stamped, except for "8S," which is engraved.

❑ RCA Victor 47-8870 ....6/66   20-30
Picture sleeve. Reads: "Coming Soon –
Paradise Hawaiian Style."

❑ RCA Victor 47-8870 ....7/66   50-75
Picture sleeve. Reads: "Ask For – *Paradise
Hawaiian Style*."

❑ RCA Victor 47-8870 ....6/66   40-45
White label. Promotional issue only.
TPKM-0914-2S/TPKM-0924-3S. Label S#26. Credits "ELVIS
PRESLEY" on *Love Letters* and "ELVIS PRESLEY With The
Jordanaires" on *Come What May*. Identification numbers are
stamped.

❑ RCA Victor 447-0657 ....2/68   6-10
Gold Standard. Black label, dog on side.
TPKM-0914-4S/TPKM-0924-4S. Label GS#6. Has playing
times and publisher. Does not show recording dates. Credits
"ELVIS PRESLEY" on *Love Letters* and "ELVIS PRESLEY with
the Jordanaires" on *Come What May*.

❑ RCA Victor 447-0657 ....'70   10-12
Gold Standard. Red label.
TPKM-0914-11S/TPKM-0924-11S. Credits "ELVIS PRESLEY"
on *Love Letters* and "ELVIS PRESLEY with the Jordanaires"
on *Come What May*.

❑ RCA Victor 447-0657 ....'77   3-5
Gold Standard. Black label, dog near top.

LOVE ME / Flaming Star

❑ Collectables 4514 ....'86   3-4
Black vinyl.
DPE1-1014-A-1/DPE1-1014-B-1. Credits "ELVIS PRESLEY"
on *Love Me* and "ELVIS PRESLEY with The Jordanaires" on
Flaming Star.

❑ Collectables 4514 ....7/92   5-6
Gold vinyl.
DPE1-1014-A-1/DPE1-1014-B-1. Credits "ELVIS PRESLEY"
on *Love Me* and "ELVIS PRESLEY with The Jordanaires" on
Flaming Star.

LOVE ME TENDER / Anyway You
Want Me (That's How I Will Be)

❑ RCA Victor 20-6643 ....10/56   50-100
Black label, 78 rpm. Time is shown for
Anyway You Want Me (That's How I Will Be)
but not for *Love Me Tender*.
G2WB-4767-7S/G2WB-5937-3S. Label S#3. Refers to the
"20th Century-Fox film, "Love Me Tender," without mention
of "CinemaScope." Credits "ELVIS PRESLEY."

G2WB-4767-9S/G2WB-5937-9S. Label S#1. Refers to the
"20th Century-Fox CinemaScope film, "Love Me Tender."
Credits "ELVIS PRESLEY."
G2WB-4767-11S/G2WB-5937-9S. Label S#1. Refers to the
"20th Century-Fox CinemaScope film, "Love Me Tender."
Credits "ELVIS PRESLEY."

❑ RCA Victor 20-6643 ....'70s   250-500
White label 78 rpm. Reads: "Record Prevue,
Disc Jockey Sample." Has rectangular "Not
for Sale" box printed on label. We're not yet
certain as to the history, purpose and
legitimacy of this series.
G2WW-4767/G2WW-5937. Credits "ELVIS PRESLEY."
Identification numbers are engraved, but may be scratched
over.

❑ RCA Victor 47-6643 ....10/56   20-30
Black label, dog on top, without horizontal
silver line.

❑ RCA Victor 47-6643 ....10/56   30-40
Black label, dog on top, with horizontal silver
line. Time is shown for *Anyway You Want Me
(That's How I Will Be)* but not for *Love Me
Tender*.
G2WW-4767-10S/G2WW-5937-11S. Label S#12L. Credits
"ELVIS PRESLEY."
G2WW-4767-15S/G2WW-5937-12S. Label S#12L. Credits
"ELVIS PRESLEY."
G2WW-4767-24S/G2WW-5937-28S. Label S#12L. Credits
"ELVIS PRESLEY."

❑ RCA Victor 47-6643 ....10/56   100-150
Picture sleeve. Black and white.

❑ RCA Victor 47-6643 ....10/56   75-100
Picture sleeve. Black and green.

❑ RCA Victor 47-6643 ....10/56   50-75
Picture sleeve. Black and dark pink.

❑ RCA Victor 47-6643 ....10/56   40-60
Picture sleeve. Black and light pink.
All sleeves show the B-side title as Any Way
(two words) You Want Me (That's How I Will
Be).

Counterfeit Identification: On fake sleeves,
the reproduction of the Elvis photo is slightly
out of focus – it looks like a *copy*. On
originals, the photo is sharp and precise.

❑ RCA Victor 447-0616 ....3/59   10-20
Gold Standard. Black label, dog on top.
J2PW-6012-1S/J2PW-6011-2S. Label GS#1. Credits "ELVIS
PRESLEY."

❑ RCA Victor 447-0616 ....'65   6-10
Gold Standard. Black label, dog on side.
J2PW-6012-2S/J2PW-6011-2S. Label GS#6. Credits "ELVIS
PRESLEY."

❑ RCA Victor 447-0616 ....'68   50-75
Gold Standard. Orange label.
J2PW-6012-2S/J2PW-6011-1S. Credits "ELVIS PRESLEY."

❑ RCA Victor 447-0616 ....'70   10-12
Gold Standard. Red label.
J2PW-6012-5S/J2PW-6011-5S. Credits "ELVIS PRESLEY."

❑ RCA Victor 447-0616 ....'77   3-5
Gold Standard. Black label, dog near top.

❑ RCA Victor PB-11108 ......10/77   3-4
Originally included as one of the singles in the
boxed sets *15 Golden Records – 30 Golden
Hits* and *20 Golden Hits in Full Color Sleeves*.

❑ RCA Victor PB-11108 ......10/77   3-4
Picture sleeve.

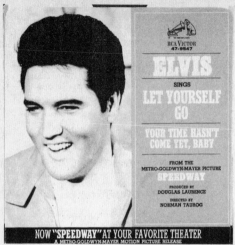

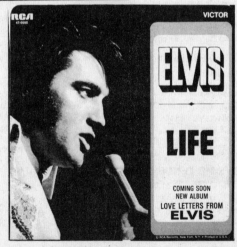

LOVE ME TENDER / Blue Christmas

❏ RCA Victor 07863-
62403-7 .... '92   3-5
Black vinyl, silver label.
07863-62403-A/07863-62403-B. Identification numbers are
engraved. Polygram International. Credits "ELVIS PRESLEY."

❏ RCA Victor 07863-
62403-7 .... '92   1-2
Plain white picture sleeve. Has aqua sticker
with white letters reading: "Elvis The King of
Rock 'N' Roll EP-7."

❏ RCA Victor 62403-7 .... '92   5-8
Juke box title strips. Five color strips with
picture of Elvis. Released in conjunction with
the CD box set *Elvis – The King of Rock 'N'
Roll – The Complete 50's Masters.*

LOVE ME TENDER / The Lady Loves Me

❏ Sun 601: Bootleg. Listed for identification
only.

LOVE ME TENDER / Hurt

❏ Kosac 1277: Bootleg. Listed for identification
only.

LOVE ME TENDER / Love Me Tender

❏ Duet 101 (record or picture sleeve): Bootleg.
Listed for identification only.

LOVE ME TENDER / Loving You

❏ RCA Victor PB-13893 ...... 12/84   3-4
Gold vinyl. Originally included as one of the
singles in the boxed set *Elvis' Greatest Hits –
Golden Singles, Vol. 2.*

❏ RCA Victor PB-13893 ...... 12/84   3-4
Picture sleeve.

LOVIN' ARMS / You Asked Me To

❏ RCA Victor PB-12205 .... 4/81   3-5
Black label, dog near top.
PB-12205-A-2S/PB-12205-B-2S. Both sides are stereo. Also
engraved is "Randy's Roost" on *Lovin' Arms* and "RR" on *You
Asked Me To.* Credits "ELVIS PRESLEY, Produced by Felton
Jarvis." Polystyrene pressing.

❏ RCA Victor JB-12205
(PB-12205) 4/81   250-300
Green vinyl. Yellow label. Promotional issue
only.
PB-12205-A-1S/PB-12205-B-1S. Both sides are stereo. Also
inscribed in trail off is "Randy's Roost." Credits "ELVIS
PRESLEY, Produced by Felton Jarvis." Identification numbers
are engraved.

❏ RCA Victor JB-12205
(PB-12205) 4/81   10-15
Light yellow label. Promotional issue only.
PB-12205-A-4S/PB-12205-B-4S. Both sides are stereo. Has
a dingbat (✱) indicating *Lovin' Arms* is the plug side. Also in
the trail off is "RR" (for Randy's Roost) and "R-7007."
Credits "ELVIS PRESLEY, Produced by Felton Jarvis."
Identification numbers are engraved. Polystyrene pressing.

Counterfeit Identification: This was the first
standard catalog Elvis release since 1956 not
issued with a picture sleeve of some type. Any
sleeve for this single is a bootleg.

MARIE'S THE NAME: see *HIS LATEST FLAME*

MEAN WOMAN BLUES / Loving You

❏ Soundtrack 104: Bootleg. Listed for
identification only.

MEMORIES / Charro

❏ RCA Victor 47-9731 .... 3/69   4-6
Orange label.
WPKM-8044-7S/WPKS-8091-7S. *Memories* is mono; *Charro*
is stereo though not marked as such on label. This was the
first stereo Elvis single since *Surrender*, in 1961. The last
letter ("S") of the identification prefix on the *Charro* side,
WPKS, indicates stereo. The prefix ends with "M," for
monaural, on the *Memories* side ("WPKM"). Credits "ELVIS
PRESLEY."

❏ RCA Victor 47-9731 .... 3/69   20-25
Picture sleeve.

❏ RCA Victor 47-9731 .... 3/69   20-30
Yellow label. Promotional issue only.
WPKM-8044-8S/WPKS-8091-7S. *Memories* is mono; *Charro*
is stereo, as explained above. Credits "ELVIS PRESLEY."

❏ RCA Victor 447-0669 .... 12/70   10-12
Gold Standard. Red label.
WPKM-8044-5S/WPKS-8091-5S. *Memories* is mono; *Charro*
is stereo. This is the earliest stereo Gold Standard single.
Credits "ELVIS PRESLEY.

❏ RCA Victor 447-0669 .... '77   3-5
Gold Standard. Black label, dog near top.

MEMORIES OF ELVIS / The Elvis Hour

❏ Creative Radio 7/87   40-50
Black vinyl. Demo disc for radio stations, with
samples of syndicated programs.
L-26191 MEM-ED/L-23610 M-0374-EH-D1. Identification
numbers are engraved.

❏ Creative Radio 7/90   25-35
Red vinyl. Demo disc for radio stations, with
samples of syndicated programs.
L-37298 MOE-D/L-37380 EH-D1. Identification numbers are
engraved.

MERRY CHRISTMAS BABY / O Come, All Ye Faithful

❏ RCA Victor 74-0572 .... 12/71   15-20
Orange label.
APKS-1849-6S/APKS-1270-6S. Both sides are stereo.
Credits "ELVIS PRESLEY" on *Merry Christmas Baby* and
"ELVIS PRESLEY, Vocal accompaniment: The Imperials
Quartet" on
O Come, All Ye Faithful."

❏ RCA Victor 74-0572 .... 12/71   40-50
Picture sleeve.

❏ RCA Victor 74-0572 .... 12/71   25-30
Yellow label. Promotional issue only.
APKM-1849-1S/APKM-1270-1S. Both sides are mono.
Credits "ELVIS PRESLEY" on *Merry Christmas Baby* and
"ELVIS PRESLEY, Vocal accompaniment: The Imperials
Quartet" on
O Come, All Ye Faithful.

MERRY CHRISTMAS BABY / Santa Claus Is Back in Town

❏ RCA Victor PB-14237......12/85   10-15
Black vinyl. Gold "Elvis 50th Anniversary" label.
PB-14237A-1/PB-14237B-1. Merry Christmas Baby is stereo, Santa Claus Is Back in Town, mono. Credits "ELVIS PRESLEY." Identification numbers are engraved. Polystyrene pressing.

❏ RCA Victor PB-14237......12/85   15-20
Green vinyl. Gold "Elvis 50th Anniversary" label. Promotional issue only.
PB-14237A-5/PB-14237B-5. Merry Christmas Baby is stereo, Santa Claus Is Back in Town, mono. Credits "ELVIS PRESLEY." Identification numbers are engraved.

❏ RCA Victor PB-14237......12/85   3-5
Black vinyl. Black label, dog near top.
PB-14237A-?/PB-14237B-?. Merry Christmas Baby is stereo, Santa Claus Is Back in Town, mono. Credits "ELVIS PRESLEY." Identification numbers are engraved.

❏ RCA Victor PB-14237......12/85   10-15
Picture sleeve.

MILKCOW BLUES BOOGIE / You're a Heartbreaker

❏ Sun 215............................1/55   1500-2000
78 rpm.
U-140-72/U-141-2-72. Credits "ELVIS PRESLEY" (on line one), and "SCOTTY and BILL" (line two). Identification numbers are engraved.
Counterfeit Identification: Any colored plastic Sun 78 is an unauthorized (circa 1978) issue.

❏ Sun 215............................1/55   1400-1900
U-140-45-72/U-141-45-72. Credits "ELVIS PRESLEY" (on line one), and "SCOTTY and BILL" (line two). Release number is at bottom of label. Push marks are present. Identification numbers are engraved.
Counterfeit Identification: Fakes of Sun 45s are numerous; however, some are easily identified. Any with "Issued 1973" engraved in the vinyl are fakes, and any on colored vinyl are boots. On some fakes, the brown sunrays, circling top half of label, fail to go all the way to the edge of the hole, though we are not prepared to state unequivocally that there are no originals printed this way. When compared to the label of an original, some fakes have noticeably darker brown print on noticeably lighter yellow stock. Any discs with "RE" or "Reissue" engraved in the vinyl are fakes. Any Sun singles with three push marks (three circular indentations, that if connected by a line would form a triangle) are original pressings.
Only bootleg picture sleeves exist for this release.

❏ RCA Victor 20-6382 ....12/55   100-150
Black label, 78 rpm.
F2WB-8044-2S/F2WB-8045-2S. Label S#9. Credits "ELVIS PRESLEY."

❏ RCA Victor 20-6382 ....'70s   250-500
White label 78 rpm. Reads: "Record Prevue, Disc Jockey Sample." Has rectangular "Not for Sale" box printed on label. We're not yet certain as to the history, purpose and legitimacy of this series.

F2WW-8044/F2WW-8045. Credits "ELVIS PRESLEY." Identification numbers are engraved, but may be scratched over.

❏ RCA Victor 47-6382.........12/55   40-50
Black label, dog on top, without horizontal silver line.
F2WW-8044-10S/F2WW-8045-1S. Label S#13. Credits "ELVIS PRESLEY."
Only bootleg picture sleeves exist for this release.

❏ RCA Victor 47-6382.........12/55   50-60
Black label, dog on top, with horizontal silver line.
Only bootleg picture sleeves exist for this release.

❏ RCA Victor 47-6382.........12/55   200-300
White "Record Prevue" label. Promotional, Canadian issue only.

❏ RCA Victor 447-0603.........3/59   15-20
Gold Standard. Black label, dog on top.
J2PW-5687-3S/J2PW-5688-2S. Label GS#1. Credits "ELVIS PRESLEY."

❏ RCA Victor 447-0603...........'65   6-12
Gold Standard. Black label, dog on side.
J2PW-5687-3S/J2PW-5688-2S. Label GS#4. Credits "ELVIS PRESLEY."

❏ RCA Victor 447-0603...........'68   50-75
Gold Standard. Orange label.
J2PW-5687-2S/J2PW-5688-3S. Credits "ELVIS PRESLEY."

❏ RCA Victor 447-0603...........'70   10-12
Gold Standard. Red label.
J2PW-5687-2S/J2PW-5688-5S. Credits "ELVIS PRESLEY."

❏ RCA Victor 447-0603...........'77   3-5
Gold Standard. Black label, dog near top.

❏ Collectables 4501 ....'86   3-4
Black vinyl.
DPE1-1001-A-1/DPE1-1001-B-1. Credits "ELVIS PRESLEY." Polystyrene pressing.

❏ Collectables 4501 ....7/92   5-6
Gold vinyl.
DPE1-1001-A-1/DPE1-1001-B-1. Credits "ELVIS PRESLEY." Polystyrene pressing.

MILKY WHITE WAY / Swing Down Sweet Chariot

❏ RCA Victor 447-0652.........3/66   15-25
Gold Standard. Black label, dog on side.
L2WW-0373-5S/L2WW-0381-4S. Label GS#6. Has playing times and publisher. Credits "ELVIS PRESLEY with The Jordanaires."
L2WW-0373-7S/L2WW-0381-7S. Label GS#5. Has playing times and publisher. Credits "ELVIS PRESLEY with The Jordanaires."

❏ RCA Victor 447-0652.........3/66   200-250
Gold Standard picture sleeve.

❏ RCA Victor 447-0652.........3/66   75-125
White label. Promotional issue only.
L2WW-0373-1S/L2WW-0381-1S. Label GS#11. Credits "ELVIS PRESLEY with The Jordanaires.

❏ RCA Victor 447-0652...........'70   12-15
Gold Standard. Red label.
See *JOSHUA FIT THE BATTLE / Known Only to Him* for listing of the "Special Easter Programming Kit."

MONEY HONEY / Blue Moon

❑ Sun 522: Bootleg. Listed for identification only.

MONEY HONEY / I Got a Woman

❑ RCA Victor 47-6689 .... 10/56   200-300
White "Record Prevue" label. Promotional, Canadian issue only.

MONEY HONEY / One-Sided Love Affair

❑ RCA Victor 20-6641 .... 9/56   75-100
Black label. 78 rpm.
G2WB-210-3S/G2WB-1232-3S. Label S#3. Credits "ELVIS PRESLEY."

❑ RCA Victor 47-6641 .... 9/56   40-50
Black label, dog on top, without horizontal silver line.
Only bootleg picture sleeves exist for this release.

❑ RCA Victor 47-6641 .... 9/56   50-60
Black label, dog on top, with horizontal silver line.
G2WW-210-5S/G2WW-1232-5S. Label S#12L. Credits "ELVIS PRESLEY."
Only bootleg picture sleeves exist for this release.

❑ RCA Victor 47-6689 .... 10/56   200-300
White "Record Prevue" label. Promotional, Canadian issue only.

❑ RCA Victor 447-0614 .... 3/59   15-20
Gold Standard. Black label, dog on top.

❑ RCA Victor 447-0614 .... '65   6-12
Gold Standard. Black label, dog on side.
J2PW-6007-1S/J2PW-6008-5S. Label GS#6. Credits "ELVIS PRESLEY."

❑ RCA Victor 447-0614 .... '68   50-75
Gold Standard. Orange label.
J2PW-6007-1S/J2PW-6008-5S. Credits "ELVIS PRESLEY."

❑ RCA Victor 447-0614 .... '70   10-12
Gold Standard. Red label.
J2PW-6007-1S/J2PW-6008-5S. Credits "ELVIS PRESLEY."

❑ RCA Victor 447-0614 .... '77   3-5
Gold Standard. Black label, dog near top.

❑ Collectables 4506 .... '86   3-4
Black vinyl.
DPE1-1006-A-1/DPE1-1006-B-1. Credits "ELVIS PRESLEY." Polystyrene pressing.

❑ Collectables 4506 .... 7/92   5-6
Gold vinyl.
DPE1-1006-A-1/DPE1-1006-B-1. Credits "ELVIS PRESLEY." Polystyrene pressing.

MOODY BLUE / For The Heart

❑ RCA Victor GB-11326 .... 8/78   3-4
Gold Standard. Black label, dog near top.
GB-11326A/GB-11326B. Both sides are stereo. Identification numbers are engraved. Both sides also have the original Identification numbers ("PB-10857A/PB-10601A") stamped in the trail off, but crossed out. Credits "ELVIS PRESLEY, Executive Producer: Elvis Presley, Associate Producer: Felton Jarvis, Vocal accompaniment by J.D. Sumner & Stamps Qt., Kathy Westmoreland, Myrna Smith, Strings and Horns arranged by Bergen White" on *Moody Blue* and credits "ELVIS PRESLEY" on *For the Heart*.

MOODY BLUE / She Thinks I Still Care

❑ RCA Victor PB-10857 ...... 12/76   3-5
Black label, dog near top.
PB-10857-A-1/PB-10857-B-2. Both sides are stereo. Has a "2" at the end of the identification number, which is crossed out and a "1" stamped next to it. Credits "ELVIS PRESLEY, Vocal accomp. by J.D. Sumner & Stamps Qt., Kathy Westmoreland, Myrna Smith, Strings and Horns arr. by Bergen White, Exec. Prod.: Elvis Presley, Associate Prod.: Felton Jarvis." Polystyrene pressing.
PB-10857-A-2/PB-10857-B-2. Same as above.

❑ RCA Victor PB-10857 ...... 12/76   10-20
Picture sleeve.

❑ RCA Victor PB-10857 ...... 12/76   5-8
Black label, dog near top. Promotional issue only.
PB-10857-A-1/PB-10857-B-2. Has white "NOT FOR SALE" sticker on *She Thinks I Still Care* label. Both sides are stereo. Has a "2" at the end of the identification number, which is crossed out and a "1" stamped next to it. Credits "ELVIS PRESLEY, Vocal accomp. by J.D. Sumner & Stamps Qt., Kathy Westmoreland, Myrna Smith, Strings and Horns arr. by Bergen White, Exec. Prod.: Elvis Presley, Associate Prod.: Felton Jarvis."

❑ RCA Victor JB-10857 (PB-10857) 12/76   15-20
Light yellow label. Promotional issue only.
PB-10857-A-2/PB-10857-B-2. Both sides are stereo. This is the first Elvis RCA promo single to have a dingbat (✳) printed on the label, used here to indicate that *Moody Blue* is the plug side. Credits "ELVIS PRESLEY, Vocal accomp. by J.D. Sumner & Stamps Qt., Kathy Westmoreland, Myrna Smith, Strings and Horns arr. by Bergen White, Exec. Prod.: Elvis Presley, Associate Prod.: Felton Jarvis." Polystyrene pressing.

❑ RCA Victor JB-10857 .... 5/77   2000-3000
Black label, dog near top. Colored vinyl experimental production singles done in red, white, gold, blue, and green. Price is for any of the five colors.

MY BABY'S GONE / Baby Let's Play House

❑ Sun 45T: Bootleg. Listed for identification only.

MY BABY'S GONE / Blue Suede Shoes

❑ Sun 521: Bootleg. Listed for identification only.

MY BABY'S GONE / My Baby's Gone

❑ Please Release Me (No Number Used): Bootleg. Listed for identification only.

MY BABY'S GONE / That's All Right

❑ Hillbilly Cat HC-101: Bootleg. Listed for identification only.

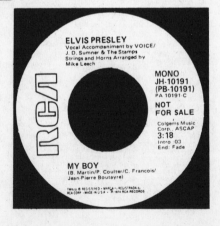

MY BOY / Loving (sic) Arms

❑ RCA Victor 2458EX............. '74   650-750
Gray label. Manufactured in the U.S. for
distribution overseas.
2458-A/2458-B. Both sides are stereo.

❑ RCA Victor 2458EX............. '74   150-200
Insert – a green, black and white insert sheet,
printed on one side. Not a sleeve. Reads:
"Elvis Presley" and "My Boy."

MY BOY (Stereo) / My Boy (Mono)

❑ RCA Victor JH-10191
(PB-10191).......................1/75   25-30
Light yellow label. Promotional issue only.
PB-10191-A-2/PA-10191-C2. One side is stereo, one side is
mono. Credits "ELVIS PRESLEY, Vocal Accompaniment by
VOICE/J.D. Sumner & The Stamps, Strings and Horns
Arranged by Mike Leech."

MY BOY / Thinking About You

❑ RCA Victor PB-10191........1/75   20-25
Tan label.
PB-10191-A-1/PA-10191-B-1. One side is stereo, one side is
mono. Credits "ELVIS PRESLEY, Vocal Accompaniment by
VOICE/J.D. Sumner & The Stamps, Strings and Horns
Arranged by Mike Leech."

❑ RCA Victor PB-10191........1/75   15-20
Orange label.
PB-10191-A-2/PA-10191-B-2. Both sides are stereo. Credits
"ELVIS PRESLEY, Vocal Accompaniment by VOICE/J.D.
Sumner & The Stamps, Strings and Horns Arranged by Mike
Leech."

❑ RCA Victor PB-10191........1/75   40-50
Picture sleeve.

❑ RCA Victor GB-10489 ....2/76   10-12
Gold Standard. Red label.
PB-10191-A-1 GB-10489A-1/PA-10191B-1 GB-10489B-1.
Both sides are stereo and have original identification
numbers ("PB") stamped, along with GB series numbers
hand engraved in trail off. Credits "ELVIS PRESLEY, Vocal
Accompaniment by VOICE/J.D. Sumner & The
Stamps/Strings and Horns Arranged by Mike Leech."

❑ RCA Victor GB-10489 .... '77   3-5
Gold Standard. Black label, dog near top.

MY WAY / America

❑ RCA Victor PB-11165......11/77   3-5
Black label, dog near top.
PB-11165-A-11S/PA-11165-B-10S. *My Way* is stereo,
America is mono. Credits "ELVIS PRESLEY, Vocal
Accompaniment by J.D. Sumner & Stamps, The Sweet
Inspirations and Kathy Westmoreland, Exec. Prod.: Elvis
Presley, Associate Prod.: Felton Jarvis" on *My Way* and only
"ELVIS PRESLEY" on *America*. Identification numbers are
engraved. Polystyrene pressing.

❑ RCA Victor PB-11165......11/77   10-15
Picture sleeve.

❑ RCA Victor JH-11165
(PB-11165).......................11/77   15-20
Light yellow label. Promotional issue only.
PB-11165-A-10S/PA-11165-B-10S. *My Way* is stereo,
America is mono. Has a dingbat (✳) printed on the label, to
indicate *My Way* is the plug side. Credits "ELVIS PRESLEY,
Vocal Accompaniment by J.D. Sumner & Stamps, The Sweet
Inspirations and Kathy Westmoreland, Exec. Prod.: Elvis
Presley, Associate Prod.: Felton Jarvis" on *My Way* and only
"ELVIS PRESLEY" on *America*. Identification numbers are
engraved. Polystyrene pressing.

MY WAY / America the Beautiful

❑ RCA Victor PB-11165......11/77   20-25
Black label, dog near top.
PB-11165-A-12S/PA-11165-B-12S. *My Way* is stereo,
America the Beautiful is mono (also indicated by the "PA"
instead of "PB"). Both sides have stamped identification
numbers in trail off. Credits "ELVIS PRESLEY, Vocal
Accompaniment by J.D. Sumner & Stamps, The Sweet
Inspirations and Kathy Westmoreland, Exec. Prod.: Elvis
Presley, Associate Prod.: Felton Jarvis" on *My Way* and
"ELVIS PRESLEY, Vocal Accompaniment by Kathy
Westmoreland, J.D. Sumner and The Stamps, The Sweet
Inspirations, Sherrill Nielsen" on *America the Beautiful*.

❑ RCA Victor PB-11165......11/77   20-25
Black label, dog near top.
PB-11165-A-13S/PA-11165-B-13S. *My Way* is stereo,
America the Beautiful is mono. Credits "ELVIS PRESLEY,
Vocal Accompaniment by J.D. Sumner & Stamps, The Sweet
Inspirations and Kathy Westmoreland, Exec. Prod.: Elvis
Presley, Associate Prod.: Felton Jarvis" on *My Way* and only
"ELVIS PRESLEY" on *America the Beautiful*.

❑ RCA Victor PB-11165......11/77   30-40
Picture sleeve.

❑ RCA Victor PB-11165......11/77   20-25
Black label, dog near top.
For Gold Standard release of *My Way* see
WAY DOWN / My Way.

MYSTERY TRAIN / I Forgot to Remember to Forget

❑ Sun 223 ....9/55   800-1000
78 rpm.
U-156 Δ5377/U-157 Δ5379. Credits "ELVIS PRESLEY" (on
line one), and "SCOTTY and BILL" (line two). Identification
numbers are engraved.
Counterfeit Identification: Any colored
plastic Sun 78 is an unauthorized (circa 1978)
issue.

❑ Sun 223 ....9/55   700-900
45 rpm.
45-U-156X-20/45-U-157X-20. Has "M.S.I. Co." embossed in
vinyl.
45-U-156X-20/45-U-157X-20. Credits "ELVIS PRESLEY" (on
line one), and "SCOTTY and BILL" (line two). Release
number is at bottom of label. No push marks. Identification
numbers are engraved.
Counterfeit Identification: Fakes of Sun 45s
are numerous; however, some are easily
identified. Any with "Issued 1973" engraved in
the vinyl are fakes, and any on colored vinyl
are boots. On some fakes, the brown sunrays,
circling top half of label, fail to go all the way
to the edge of the hole, though we are not
prepared to state unequivocally that there are
no originals printed this way. When compared
to the label of an original, some fakes have
noticeably darker brown print on noticeably
lighter yellow stock. Any discs with "RE" or
"Reissue" engraved in the vinyl are fakes. Any
Sun singles with three push marks (three
circular indentations, that if connected by a
line would form a triangle) are original
pressings.
Only bootleg picture sleeves exist for this
release.

❑ RCA Victor 20-6357.........11/55   100-150
Black label, 78 rpm.
F2WB-8001-2S/F2WB-8000-2S. Label S#2. Credits "ELVIS
PRESLEY with SCOTTY and BILL."

❏ RCA Victor 20-6357 .... '70s   250-500
White label 78 rpm. Reads: "Record Prevue,
Disc Jockey Sample." Has rectangular "Not
for Sale" box printed on label. We're not yet
certain as to the history, purpose and
legitimacy of this series.
F2WW-8001/F2WW-8000. Identification numbers are
engraved, but may be scratched over.

❏ RCA Victor 47-6357 .... 11/55   40-50
Black label, dog on top, without horizontal
silver line.
F2WW-8001-1S/F2WW-8000-1S. Label S#13. Credits "Elvis
Presley with Scotty and Bill."
Only bootleg picture sleeves exist for this
release.

❏ RCA Victor 47-6357 .... 11/55   50-60
Black label, dog on top, with horizontal silver
line.
F2WW-8001-3S/F2WW-8000-3S. Label S#12L. Credits
"ELVIS PRESLEY With SCOTTY and BILL."
Only bootleg picture sleeves exist for this
release.

❏ RCA Victor 47-6357 .... 11/55   300-400
White "Record Prevue" label. Promotional
issue only.
F2WW-8001-4S/F2WW-8000-4S. Label S#22. Credits
"ELVIS PRESLEY."
This single is both the first standard catalog
RCA Elvis release and the first Gold Standard
Elvis single. There are several Canadian
"Dealer Prevue" singles other than *Mystery
Train*; however, this is the only USA-issued
white label Dealer's Prevue Elvis 45 rpm.

❏ RCA Victor 47-6357 .... 11/55   1000-2000
Picture sleeve. One of a series of promotional
"This Is His Life" issues, made for many RCA
artists. Though not numbered, this is the first
picture sleeve of any type issued with an Elvis
record. Unfortunately, the "life story" is
somewhat fabricated.

❏ RCA Victor........................ 12/55   50-100
Dee Jay Digest Vol 2, No. 50, dated Dec. 2,
1955. Four-page RCA record newsletter, sent
to radio stations with "Record Prevue" promo
of *Mystery Train / I Forgot to Remember to
Forget* (47-6357). As with above cartoon
sleeve, some Elvis "facts" in the *Digest* bio
are untrue.

❏ RCA Victor 447-0600 .... 3/59   15-20
Gold Standard. Black label, dog on top.

❏ RCA Victor 447-0600 .... '65   6-12
Gold Standard. Black label, dog on side.
J2PW-5682-4S/J2PW-5681-3S. Label GS#6. Credits "ELVIS
PRESLEY."

❏ RCA Victor 447-0600 .... '68   50-75
Gold Standard. Orange label.
J2PW-5682-4S/J2PW-5681-3S. Credits "ELVIS PRESLEY."

❏ RCA Victor 447-0600 .... '70   10-12
Gold Standard. Red label.
J2PW-5682-4S/J2PW-5681-4S. Credits "ELVIS PRESLEY."

❏ RCA Victor 447-0600 .... '77   3-5
Gold Standard. Black label, dog near top.

NEARER MY GOD TO THEE / You Gave Me a Molehill

❏ Creative Radio Shows 7/89   8-10
Given as a bonus single with the promotional
three-LP set, *Between Takes with Elvis*. Only
500 made. Has LP-size (¼-inch) hole.
Promotional issue only. See *BETWEEN
TAKES WITH ELVIS* for more information.
L-33141X/L-33141. Identification numbers are engraved.

1955 TEXARKANA INTERVIEW / The Truth About Me

❏ Spoken Word 100 .... '78   8-12
Has picture of Elvis on label.

1967 ELVIS MEDLEY (AS ORIGINALLY BROADCAST JANUARY 8, 1967 ON KYOS, MERCED, CALIFORNIA) / The #1 Hits Medley (1956-69) (From the First Elvis to the Last Beatles' #1 Hits)

❏ Osborne Enterprises 6/88   10-15
First pressing, 400 made. Promotional,
souvenir issue only.
L-31914/L-31914X. Both sides are mono. Identification
numbers are engraved.

❏ Osborne Enterprises 6/88   1-2
Black and white printed insert explaining the
origin of the medley on one side and a listing
of the No. 1 songs (1956-1970) on the
reverse.

1967 ELVIS MEDLEY (AS ORIGINALLY BROADCAST JANUARY 8, 1967 ON KYOS, MERCED, CALIFORNIA) / The #1 Hits Medley (1956-70) (From the First Elvis to the Last Beatles' #1 Hit)

❏ Osborne Enterprises 7/88   15-25
Second pressing, 100 made. Corrects B-side
title to show "1956-70" and "Hit" instead of
"1956-69" and "Hits." Promotional, souvenir
issue only. Logo and print is larger than on
first pressing. Inserts were not included with
second pressings.
L-31914/L-31914X. Both sides are mono. Identification
numbers are engraved.

OLD SHEP / Blank

❏ RCA Victor CR-15 .... 12/56   700-800
White label, single-sided disc. Promotional
issue only.
H7OW-3721-1/45 SPIRAL-1-B. Identification numbers are
stamped on *Old Shep*, but are engraved on the blank side.
Credits: "ELVIS PRESLEY."

Counterfeit Identification: Fakes are easily
identified since the identification numbers are
engraved. Originals have the numbers
stamped in the vinyl.

OLD SHEP / You'll Never Walk Alone

❏ Collectables 4518 .... '86   3-4
Black vinyl.
DPE1-1018-A-1/DPE1-1018-B-1. Credits "ELVIS PRESLEY" on *Old Shep* and "ELVIS PRESLEY with The Jordanaires" on *You'll Never Walk Alone*. Identification numbers are engraved. Polystyrene pressing.

❏ Collectables 4518 .... 7/92   5-6
Gold vinyl.
DPE1-1018-A-1/DPE1-1018-B-1. Credits "ELVIS PRESLEY" on *Old Shep* and "ELVIS PRESLEY with The Jordanaires" on *You'll Never Walk Alone*. Identification numbers are engraved. Polystyrene pressing.

ONE BROKEN HEART FOR SALE / They Remind Me Too Much of You

❏ RCA Victor 47-8134 .... 2/63   8-10
Black label, dog on top.
PPKM-2724-1S/PPKM-2725-1S. Label S#18. Identification numbers are engraved making this the earliest commercial RCA Elvis single we've found with identification numbers engraved. Credits "ELVIS PRESLEY with The Mello Men."

❏ RCA Victor 47-8134 .... 2/63   25-35
Picture sleeve.

❏ RCA Victor 447-0640 .... 8/64   20-25
Gold Standard. Black label, dog on top.

❏ RCA Victor 447-0640 .... '65   6-10
Gold Standard. Black label, dog on side.
PPKM-2724-4S/PPKM-2725-4S. Label GS#6. Has playing times and publisher. Does not show recording dates. Credits "ELVIS PRESLEY with The Mello Men."

❏ RCA Victor 447-0640 .... '68   50-75
Gold Standard. Orange label.
PPKM-2724-4S/PPKM-2725-4S. Credits "ELVIS PRESLEY with The Mello Men."

❏ RCA Victor 447-0640 .... '70   10-12
Gold Standard. Red label.
PPKM-2724-4S/PPKM-2725-4S. Credits "ELVIS PRESLEY with The Mello Men."

❏ RCA Victor 447-0640 .... '77   3-5
Gold Standard. Black label, dog near top.

ONE BROKEN HEART FOR SALE / (You're the) Devil in Disguise

❏ Collectables 4512 .... '86   3-4
Black vinyl.
DPE1-1012-A-1/DPE1-1012-B-1. Credits "ELVIS PRESLEY with the Mello Men" on *One Broken Heart for Sale* and "ELVIS PRESLEY with The Jordanaires" on *Devil in Disguise*. Identification numbers are engraved. Polystyrene pressing.

❏ Collectables 4512 .... 7/92   5-6
Gold vinyl.
DPE1-1012-A-1/DPE1-1012-B-1. Credits "ELVIS PRESLEY with the Mello Men" on *One Broken Heart for Sale* and "ELVIS PRESLEY with The Jordanaires" on *Devil in Disguise*. Identification numbers are engraved. Polystyrene pressing.

ONE NIGHT / I Got Stung

❏ RCA Victor 20-7410 .... 10/58   500-750
Black label, 78 rpm.
H2WB-0415-1S/J2WB-3257-1S. Label S#10. Credits "ELVIS PRESLEY" on *One Night* and "ELVIS PRESLEY with The Jordanaires" on *I Got Stung*. This is the final RCA Elvis 78 rpm issued in the United States.

❏ RCA Victor 47-7410 .... 10/58   10-15
Black label, dog on top.
H2WW-0415-6S/J2WW-3257-6S. Label S#19. Credits "ELVIS PRESLEY" on *One Night* and "ELVIS PRESLEY With The Jordanaires" on *I Got Stung*.
H2WW-0415-9S/J2WW-3257-8S. Label S#19. Credits "ELVIS PRESLEY" on *One Night* and "ELVIS PRESLEY with The Jordanaires" on *I Got Stung*. Print is smaller on the "Jordanaires" line than on H2WW-0415-6S/J2WW-3257-6S.

❏ RCA Victor 47-7410 .... 10/58   40-50
Picture sleeve.

❏ RCA Victor 447-0624 .... '61   10-15
Gold Standard. Black label, dog on top.

❏ RCA Victor 447-0624 .... '65   6-10
Gold Standard. Black label, dog on side.
H2WW-0415-3S/J2WW-3257-11S. Label GS#6. Credits "ELVIS PRESLEY with The Jordanaires."

❏ RCA Victor 447-0624 .... '68   50-75
Gold Standard. Orange label.
H2WW-0415-3S/J2WW-3257-10S. Credits "ELVIS PRESLEY with The Jordanaires."

❏ RCA Victor 447-0624 .... '70   10-12
Gold Standard. Red label.
H2WW-0415-3S/J2WW-3257-12S. Credits "ELVIS PRESLEY with The Jordanaires."

❏ RCA Victor 447-0624 .... '77   3-5
Gold Standard. Black label, dog near top.

❏ RCA Victor PB11112 .... 10/77   3-4
Originally included as one of the singles in the boxed set *15 Golden Records – 30 Golden Hits*.

❏ RCA Victor PB-11112 ...... 10/77   3-4
Picture sleeve.

POOR BOY / An American Trilogy

❏ Collectables 4519 .... '86   3-4
Black vinyl.
DPE1-1019-A-1/DPE1-1019-B-1. Credits "ELVIS PRESLEY." Identification numbers are engraved. Polystyrene pressing.

❏ Collectables 4519 .... 7/92   5-6
Gold vinyl.
DPE1-1019-A-1/DPE1-1019-B-1. Credits "ELVIS PRESLEY." Identification numbers are engraved. Polystyrene pressing.

PRESS INTERVIEWS ELVIS / That's All Right, Mama

❏ Spinout 81677: Bootleg. Listed for identification only.

PROMISED LAND / It's Midnight

❏ RCA Victor PB-10074 ...... 10/74   10-15
Orange label.
PB-10074-B-2/PB-10074-A-2. Both sides are stereo. Credits "ELVIS PRESLEY" on *Promised Land* and "ELVIS PRESLEY, Vocal accompaniment: J.D. Sumner & The Stamps, Strings arranged by Mike Leech" on *It's Midnight*. Identification numbers are engraved.

❏ RCA Victor PB-10074 ...... 10/74   10-20
Gray label.

❏ RCA Victor PB-10074 ...... 10/74   15-25
Tan label.

❏ RCA Victor PB-10074 ...... 10/74   10-15
Picture sleeve.

❏ RCA Victor JA-10074 (PB-10074) 10/74   20-25
Light yellow label. Promotional issue only.
PA-10074-D-2/PA-10074-C-3. Both sides are mono. Credits "ELVIS PRESLEY" on *Promised Land* and "ELVIS PRESLEY, Vocal accompaniment: J.D. Sumner & The Stamps, Strings arranged by Mike Leech" on *It's Midnight*. Identification numbers are engraved.

❏ RCA Victor GB-10488 ....2/76   10-12
Gold Standard. Red label.
GB-10488B/GB-10488A. Both sides are stereo. Both have original identification numbers stamped (PA-10074A/PA-10074B) in trail off, but crossed out. Credits "ELVIS PRESLEY" on *Promised Land* and "ELVIS PRESLEY, Vocal Accompaniment: VOICE/J.D. Sumner & The Stamps" on *It's Midnight*. (These credits differ from original commercial and promo issues, which do not credit "VOICE." This pressing, however, makes no mention of "strings arranged by Mike Leech.") Identification numbers are engraved.

❏ RCA Victor GB-10488 ....'77   3-5
Gold Standard. Black label, dog near top.

PUPPET ON A STRING / Wooden Heart

❏ RCA Victor 447-0650 ......10/65   6-10
Gold Standard. Black label, dog on side.
SPKM-2010-3S/L2PW-3681-5S. Label GS#6. Has playing times and publisher. Credits "ELVIS PRESLEY with The Jordanaires" on *Puppet on a String* and "ELVIS PRESLEY" on *Wooden Heart*.

❏ RCA Victor 447-0650 ......10/65   40-50
Gold Standard picture sleeve.

❏ RCA Victor 447-0650 ......10/65   30-35
Gold Standard. White label. Promotional issue only.
SPKM-2010-4S/L2PW-3681-9S. Label GS#7. Credits "ELVIS PRESLEY with the Jordanaires" on *Puppet on a String* and "ELVIS PRESLEY" on *Wooden Heart*.

❏ RCA Victor 447-0650 ....'70   10-12
Gold Standard. Red label.
SPKM-2010-7S/L2PW-3681-10S. Credits "ELVIS PRESLEY with The Jordanaires" on *Puppet on a String* and "ELVIS PRESLEY" on *Wooden Heart*.

❏ RCA Victor 447-0650 ....'77   3-5
Gold Standard. Black label, dog near top.

RAGS TO RICHES / Where Did They Go, Lord

❏ RCA Victor 47-9980 ....2/71   4-6
Orange label.
ZPKM-1800-3S/ZPKM-1798-3S. Credits "ELVIS PRESLEY, Vocal accompaniment: The Imperials Quartet" on *Rags to Riches* and "ELVIS PRESLEY, Vocal accompaniment: The Imperials Quartet & The Jordanaires" on *Where Did They Go, Lord*.

❏ RCA Victor 47-9980 ....2/71   35-40
Picture sleeve.

❏ RCA Victor 47-9980 ....2/71   25-30
Yellow label. Promotional issue only.
ZPKM-1800-4S/ZPKM-1798-4S. Credits "ELVIS PRESLEY, Vocal accompaniment: The Imperials Quartet" on *Rags to Riches* and "ELVIS PRESLEY, Vocal accompaniment: The Imperials Quartet & The Jordanaires" on *Where Did They Go, Lord*.

❏ RCA Victor 447-0680 ....2/72   10-12
Gold Standard. Red label.

❏ RCA Victor 447-0680 .,........'77   3-5
Gold Standard. Black label, dog near top.

RAISED ON ROCK / For Ol' Times Sake

❏ RCA Victor APBO-0088 ....9/73   5-8
Orange label.
APAO-0088A-4S/APAO-0088B-4S. Both sides are stereo. Credits "ELVIS PRESLEY."

❏ RCA Victor APBO-0088 ....9/73   25-30
Picture sleeve.

❏ RCA Victor APBO-0088 ....9/73   8-10
Orange label. Promotional issue only.
APAO-0088A-4S/APAO-0088B-4S. Has white "NOT FOR SALE" sticker on *For Ol' Times Sake* label. Both sides are stereo. Credits "ELVIS PRESLEY." Identification numbers are engraved.

❏ RCA Victor DJAO-0088
(APBO-0088).....................9/73   20-25
Light yellow label. Promotional issue only.
APAO-0088C1/APAO-0088D1. Both sides are mono. Credits "ELVIS PRESLEY." Identification numbers are engraved.

RAISED ON ROCK / If You Talk in Your Sleep

❏ RCA Victor GB-10157 ....3/75   10-12
Gold Standard. Red label.
GB-10157-A-1S/GB-10157-B-1. Both sides are stereo. Credits "ELVIS PRESLEY" on *Raised on Rock* and "ELVIS PRESLEY, Strings & Horns arranged by Mike Leech" on *If You Talk in Your Sleep*.

❏ RCA Victor GB-10157 ....'77   3-5
Gold Standard. Black label, dog near top.

RETURN TO SENDER / (Now and Then There's) A Fool Such As I

❏ For Your Classic Juke Box
G-119 ....'80s   50-75
78 rpm. Made for juke box use.

RETURN TO SENDER / Where Do You Come From

❏ RCA Victor 47-8100.........10/62   8-10
Black label, dog on top.
N2PW-3279-7S/N2PW-3274-7S. Label S#19. Credits "ELVIS PRESLEY with the Jordanaires."

❏ RCA Victor 47-8100.........10/62   20-30
Picture sleeve.

❏ RCA Victor 447-0638.........6/63   8-12
Gold Standard. Black label, dog on top.

❏ RCA Victor 447-0638...........'65   6-10
Gold Standard. Black label, dog on side.
N2PW-3279-4S/N2PW-3274-4S. Label GS#6. Has playing times and publisher. Does not show recording dates. Credits "ELVIS PRESLEY with The Jordanaires."

❏ RCA Victor 447-0638...........'68   50-75
Gold Standard. Orange label.

❏ RCA Victor 447-0638...........'70   10-12
Gold Standard. Red label.
N2PW-3279-9S/N2PW-3274-4S. Credits "ELVIS PRESLEY with The Jordanaires."

❏ RCA Victor 447-0638.....,......'77   3-5
Gold Standard. Black label, dog near top.

❏ RCA Victor PB-11111......10/77   3-4
Originally included as one of the singles in the boxed sets *15 Golden Records – 30 Golden Hits* and *20 Golden Hits in Full Color Sleeves*.

❏ RCA Victor PB-11111......10/77   3-4
Picture sleeve.

ROUSTABOUT / One Track Heart

❏ RCA Victor SP-45-139.....11/64   225-275
White label. Promotional issue only.
RNKM-7088-1S/RNKM-7089-1S.

ROUSTABOUT THEATRE LOBBY SPOT (COMING SOON) / Roustabout Theatre Lobby Spot (Now Playing)

❑ Paramount Pictures
SP-2413 .... 10/64   2000-3000
Promotional issue to theaters for lobby play in
advance of and during the run of the
Roustabout film. This take is different than the
one on the *Roustabout* LP and the RCA
promo 45. Blue label.
SP-2413/SP-2414. Label does not identify Elvis as the singer.

SEPARATE WAYS / Always on My Mind

❑ RCA Victor 74-0815 .... 11/72   4-6
Orange label.
BPKS-1149-2S/BPKS-1259-2S. Both sides are stereo.
Credits "ELVIS PRESLEY, Strings arr. by Glen (sic) D.
Hardin, Vocal Background: J.D. Sumner & The Stamps" on
Separate Ways and "ELVIS PRESLEY, Strings & Horns arr. by
Glen (sic) D. Hardin, Vocal Background: J.D. Sumner & The
Stamps" on *Always on My Mind*.

❑ RCA Victor 74-0815 .... 11/72   10-15
Picture sleeve.

❑ RCA Victor 74-0815 .... 11/72   20-25
Yellow label. Promotional issue only.
BPKM-1149-2S/BPKM-1259-2S. Both sides are mono.
Credits "ELVIS PRESLEY, Strings arr. by Glen (sic) D.
Hardin, Vocal Background: J.D. Sumner & The Stamps" on
Separate Ways and "ELVIS PRESLEY, Strings & Horns arr. by
Glen (sic) D. Hardin, Vocal Background: J.D. Sumner & The
Stamps" on *Always on My Mind*.

❑ RCA Victor GB-10486 .... 2/76   10-12
Gold Standard. Red label.
BPKM-1149-2S GB-10486-A/BPKM-1259-2S GB-10486-B.
Both sides are stereo and have original identification
numbers ("BPKM") stamped, along with GB series numbers
hand engraved in trail off. Credits "ELVIS PRESLEY, Strings
arr. by Glen (sic) D. Hardin, Vocal Background: J.D. Sumner
& The Stamps" on *Separate Ways* and "ELVIS PRESLEY,
Strings & Horns Arranged by Glen (sic) D. Hardin/Vocal
Background: J.D. Sumner & The Stamps" on *Always on My
Mind*.

❑ RCA Victor GB-10486 .... '77   3-5
Gold Standard. Black label, dog near top.

SHAKE, RATTLE AND ROLL / I Got a Woman

❑ White Knight WK-SP-1-28 (record or picture
sleeve): Bootleg. Listed for identification
only.

SHE'S NOT YOU / Jailhouse Rock

❑ Collectables 4511 .... '86   3-4
Black vinyl.
DPE1-1011-A-1/DPE1-1011-B-1. Credits "ELVIS PRESLEY
with The Jordanaires." Polystyrene pressing.

❑ Collectables 4511 .... 7/92   5-6
Gold vinyl.
DPE1-1011-A-1/DPE1-1011-B-1. Credits "ELVIS PRESLEY
with The Jordanaires." Polystyrene pressing.

SHE'S NOT YOU / Just Tell Her Jim Said Hello

❑ RCA Victor 47-8041 .... 7/62   8-10
Black label, dog on top.

N2WW-0695-6S/N2WW-0693-6S. Label S#19. Credits
"ELVIS PRESLEY with The Jordanaires."

❑ RCA Victor 47-8041 .... 7/62   20-30
Picture sleeve.

❑ RCA Victor 447-0637 .... 6/63   8-12
Gold Standard. Black label, dog on top.

❑ RCA Victor 447-0637 .... '65   6-10
Gold Standard. Black label, dog on side.
N2WW-0695-8S/N2WW-0693-8S. Label GS#6. Has playing
times, publisher and production credit. Does not show
recording dates. Credits "ELVIS PRESLEY with The
Jordanaires."

❑ RCA Victor 447-0637 .... '68   50-75
Gold Standard. Orange label.

❑ RCA Victor 447-0637 .... '70   10-12
Gold Standard. Red label.
N2WW-0695-11S/N2WW-0693-10S. Credits "ELVIS PRESLEY
with The Jordanaires."

❑ RCA Victor 447-0637 .... '77   3-5
Gold Standard. Black label, dog near top.

SILVER BELLS (UNRELEASED VERSION) / Silver Bells (Released Version)

RCA/BMG 62411-7 .... 11/93   15-20
Silver and gray label, dog on top. Made for
juke box operators. Side 1 is an alternative
take of *Silver Bells* that up until 1993 was
unavailable. Side 2 has the standard release.

RCA/BMG 62411-7 .... 11/93   3-5
RCA red die-cut sleeve.

RCA/BMG 62411-7 .... 11/93   3-5
Title strip for juke box use.

SPECIAL EASTER PROGRAMMING KIT: see *JOSHUA FIT THE BATTLE / Known Only to Him*

SPINOUT / All That I Am

❑ RCA Victor 47-8941 .... 9/66   6-10
Black label, dog on side.
TPKM-5311-1S/TPKM-5307-2S. Label S#21. Credits "ELVIS
PRESLEY with the Jordanaires."

❑ RCA Victor 47-8941 .... 9/66   20-30
Picture sleeve. Reads: "Watch For Elvis'
Spinout LP."

❑ RCA Victor 47-8941 .... 10/66   30-40
Picture sleeve. Reads: "Ask For Elvis' *Spinout*
LP."

❑ RCA Victor 47-8941 .... 9/66   40-45
White label. Promotional issue only.
TPKM-5311-1S/TPKM-5307-1S. Label S#26. Credits "ELVIS
PRESLEY with Jordanaires." (Not with "The" Jordanaires.)

❑ RCA Victor 47-8941 .... 9/66   25-30
TPKM-5311-7S/TPKM-5307-9S. Label S#27. Credits "ELVIS
PRESLEY With The Jordanaires."

❑ RCA Victor 447-0658 .... 2/68   6-10
Gold Standard. Black label, dog on side.
TPKM-5311-4S/TPKM-5307-1S. Label GS#6. Has playing
times and publisher. Does not show recording dates. Credits
"ELVIS PRESLEY with the Jordanaires."

❑ RCA Victor 447-0658 .... '70   10-12
Gold Standard. Red label.
TPKM-5311-10S/TPKM-5307-10S. Credits "ELVIS PRESLEY
with the Jordanaires."

❑ RCA Victor 447-0658 .... '77   3-5
Gold Standard. Black label, dog near top.

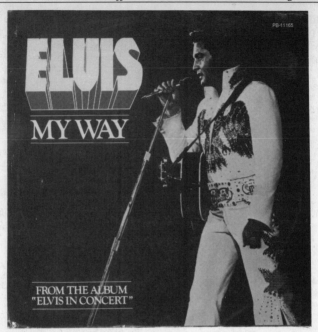

STUCK ON YOU / Fame and Fortune

❑ RCA Victor 47-7740 ....4/60　　8-10
Black label, dog on top.
L2WW-0083-12S/L2WW-0084-14S. Label S#17. Credits
"ELVIS PRESLEY With The Jordanaires."

❑ RCA Victor 47-7740 ....4/60　　30-35
Picture sleeve. Has die-cut sleeve which, with
disc inside, displays the record label.

❑ RCA Victor 61-7740 ....4/60　　400-500
Living Stereo.
L2WA-1838-1S/L2WA-1839-1S. Credits "ELVIS PRESLEY
with The Jordanaires."

❑ RCA Victor 447-0627 ....2/62　　8-12
Gold Standard. Black label, dog on top.

❑ RCA Victor 447-0627 ....'65　　6-10
Gold Standard. Black label, dog on side.
L2WW-0083-23S/L2WW-0084-24S. Label GS#6. Has playing
times. Credits "ELVIS PRESLEY with The Jordanaires."

❑ RCA Victor 447-0627 ....'68　　50-75
Gold Standard. Orange label.

❑ RCA Victor 447-0627 ....'70　　10-12
Gold Standard. Red label.
L2WW-0083-23S/L2WW-0084-24S. Credits "ELVIS PRESLEY
with The Jordanaires."

❑ RCA Victor 447-0627 ....'77　　3-5
Gold Standard. Black label, dog near top.

❑ Collectables 4509 ....'86　　3-4
Black vinyl.
DPE1-1009-A-1/DPE1-1009-B-1. Credits "ELVIS PRESLEY
with The Jordanaires." Polystyrene pressing.

❑ Collectables 4509 ....7/92　　5-6
Gold vinyl.
DPE1-1009-A-1/DPE1-1009-B-1. Credits "ELVIS PRESLEY
with The Jordanaires." Polystyrene pressing.

SUCH A NIGHT / Never Ending

❑ RCA Victor 47-8400 ....7/64　　6-10
Black label, dog on top.
L2WW-0105-2S/PPKM-0293-2S. Label S#18. Credits "ELVIS
PRESLEY with The Jordanaires." Has "#15" engraved after
the identification number in the trail off on *Such a Night*.

❑ RCA Victor 47-8400 ....7/64　　20-30
Picture sleeve.

❑ RCA Victor 47-8400 ....7/64　　5000-7500
White label. Promotional issue only.
L2WW-0105-5S/PPKM-0293-5S. Label S#24. Credits "ELVIS
PRESLEY With The Jordanaires."

❑ RCA Victor 447-0645 ....5/65　　25-35
Gold Standard. Black label, dog on top.

❑ RCA Victor 447-0645 ....5/65　　6-10
Gold Standard. Black label, dog on side.
L2WW-0105-4S/PPKM-0293-3S. Label GS#6. Has playing
times and publisher. Has an unexplained "R" above
recording date on *Such a Night* side. Credits "ELVIS
PRESLEY with The Jordanaires."

❑ RCA Victor 447-0645 ....'68　　50-75
Gold Standard. Orange label.
L2WW-0105-4S/PPKM-0293-3S. Credits "ELVIS PRESLEY
with The Jordanaires."

❑ RCA Victor 447-0645 ....'70　　10-12
Gold Standard. Red label.

❑ RCA Victor 447-0645 ....'77　　3-5
Gold Standard. Black label, dog near top.

SURRENDER / Lonely Man

❑ RCA Victor 47-7850 ....2/61　　8-10
Black label, dog on top.

L2WW-0377-1S/L2PW-5381-3S. Label S#17. Credits "ELVIS
PRESLEY with The Jordanaires."

❑ RCA Victor 47-7850 ....2/61　　20-30
Picture sleeve. hole.

❑ RCA Victor 61-7850 ....2/61　　750-1000
Living Stereo.
M2PA-1881-1S/M2PA-1882-1S. Credits "ELVIS PRESLEY with
The Jordanaires."

❑ RCA Victor 37-7850 ....2/61　　500-700
Compact 33 single.
M2PI-1859-11S/M2PI-1860-8S. Surrender has identification
numbers engraved, on *Lonely Man* they are stamped. Has
LP-size (¼-inch) hole. Credits "ELVIS PRESLEY with The
Jordanaires." Unlike the other five Compact 33s, which have
"RCA VICTOR" in mustard color print, this one has orange
letters.

❑ RCA Victor 37-7850 ....2/61　　800-1000
Picture sleeve for Compact 33 single.

❑ RCA Victor 68-7850 ....2/61　　1000-1500
Living Stereo Compact 33 single.
M2PO-1883-1S/M2PO-1884-1S. Surrender has identification
numbers engraved, but on *Lonely Man* they are stamped.
Has LP-size (¼-inch) hole. Credits "ELVIS PRESLEY with The
Jordanaires."

❑ RCA Victor 447-0630 ....2/62　　10-20
Gold Standard. Black label, dog on top.

❑ RCA Victor 447-0630 ....'65　　6-10
Gold Standard. Black label, dog on side.
L2WW-0377-3S/L2PW-5381-1S. Label GS#6. Has playing
times and publisher. Credits "ELVIS PRESLEY with The
Jordanaires."

❑ RCA Victor 447-0630 ....'68　　50-75
Gold Standard. Orange label.

❑ RCA Victor 447-0630 ....'70　　10-12
Gold Standard. Red label.
L2WW-0377-12S/L2PW-5381-2S. Credits "ELVIS PRESLEY
with The Jordanaires."

❑ RCA Victor 447-0630 ....'77　　3-5
Gold Standard. Black label, dog near top.

SURRENDER / Out of a Clear Blue Sky (Lawrence Welk)

❑ U.S.A.F. Pgm. Nr. 159/
160 ....3/61　　300-400
Public service, five-minute radio show, part of
the U.S. Air Force's "Music in the Air" series.
GZS-80183-1A/GZS-80184-1A. Credits "ELVIS PRESLEY."
Polystyrene pressing.

❑ U.S.A.F. Pgm. Nr. 159/
160 ....3/61　　100-125
Cardboard mailer. Printed information on this
mailer indicates "Programs 157, 158, 159,
160" are included.

SUSPICIOUS MINDS / Burning Love

❑ RCA Victor PB-13896 ......12/84　　3-4
Gold vinyl. Originally included as one of the
singles in the boxed set *Elvis' Greatest Hits –
Golden Singles, Vol. 2.*

❑ RCA Victor PB-13896 ......12/84　　3-4
Picture sleeve.

SUSPICIOUS MINDS / Funny How Time Slips Away

Rooster 45-5001 (record or picture sleeve):
Bootleg. Listed for identification only.

SUSPICIOUS MINDS / You'll Think of Me

❏ RCA Victor 47-9764 .... 9/69   4-6
Orange label.
XPKM-1227-5S/XPKM-1146-5S. Credits "ELVIS PRESLEY."

❏ RCA Victor 47-9764 .... 9/69   10-15
Picture sleeve.

❏ RCA Victor 47-9764 .... 9/69   20-30
Yellow label. Promotional issue only.
XPKM-1227-4S/XPKM-1146-3S. This is the first Elvis promo single to have the intro time printed on the label. Intro time is the number of seconds before the singer begins, allowing dee jays to "talk up" to the vocal. Credits "ELVIS PRESLEY." Identification numbers are engraved.

❏ RCA Victor 447-0673 ...... 12/70   10-12
Gold Standard. Red label.
XPKM-1227-3S/XPKM-1146-3S. Credits "ELVIS PRESLEY." Identification numbers are engraved.

❏ RCA Victor 447-0673 .... '77   3-5
Gold Standard. Black label, dog near top.

❏ RCA Victor PB-11103 ...... 10/77   3-4
Originally included as one of the singles in the boxed set *15 Golden Records – 30 Golden Hits*.

❏ RCA Victor PB-11103 ...... 10/77   3-4
Picture sleeve.

❏ RCA Victor GB-13275 .... 1/83   3-4
Gold Standard. Black label, dog near top.
GB-13275-A PB-11103A XPKM-1227-31/GB-13275-B-32. Both sides are stereo. On *You'll Think of Me*, numbers "PB-11103A XPKM-1227-31" are stamped in the trail off, but are crossed out. Credits "ELVIS PRESLEY."
This is both the first polystyrene Gold Standard single, and the first Gold Standard single reissued using a different Gold Standard number. Polystyrene pressing.

TAKE GOOD CARE OF HER / I've Got a Thing About You Baby

❏ RCA Victor APBO-0196 .... 1/74   4-6
Orange label.
APBO-0196A-4/APBO-0196B-4. Both sides are stereo. Credits "ELVIS PRESLEY, Strings arranged by Glen Spreen, Vocal accompaniment J.D. Sumner & The Stamps." Identification numbers are engraved.

❏ RCA Victor APBO-0196 .... 1/74   10-15
Picture sleeve.

❏ RCA Victor DJBO-0196
(APBO-0196) 1/74   20-25
Light yellow label. Promotional issue only.
APBO-0196A-2/APBO-0196B-2. Both sides are stereo. Credits "ELVIS PRESLEY, Strings arranged by Glen Spreen, Vocal accompaniment J.D. Sumner & The Stamps."

❏ RCA Victor GB-10485 .... 2/76   10-12
Gold Standard. Red label.
APBO-0196A-1 GB-10485A/APBO-0196B-2 GB-10485B. Both sides are stereo and have original identification numbers ("APBO-0196") stamped, along with GB series numbers engraved. Credits "ELVIS PRESLEY, Strings Arranged by Glen Spreen, Vocal Accompaniment: J.D. Sumner & The Stamps."

❏ RCA Victor GB-10485 .... '77   3-5
Gold Standard. Black label, dog near top.

(LET ME BE YOUR) TEDDY BEAR / Loving You

❏ RCA Victor 20-7000 .... 6/57   75-100
Black label, 78 rpm.

❏ RCA Victor 20-7000 .... '70s   250-500
White label 78 rpm. Reads: "Record Prevue, Disc Jockey Sample." Has rectangular "Not for Sale" box printed on label. We're not yet certain as to the history, purpose and legitimacy of this series.
H2WW-2193/H2WW-0418. Credits "ELVIS PRESLEY WITH THE JORDANAIRES." Identification numbers are engraved, but may be scratched over.

❏ RCA Victor 47-7000 .... 6/57   20-30
Black label, dog on top, without horizontal silver line.
H2WW-2193-3S/H2WW-0418-3S. Label S#15. Has no parentheses around "Let Me Be Your." Credits "Elvis Presley with The Jordanaires."

❏ RCA Victor 47-7000 .... 6/57   30-40
Black label, dog on top, with horizontal silver line.
H2WW-2193-5S/H2WW-0418-6S. Label S#12L. Has parentheses around "Let Me Be Your." Credits "ELVIS PRESLEY WITH THE JORDANAIRES."

❏ RCA Victor 47-7000 .... 6/57   25-35
Black label, dog on top, does not have parentheses around "Let Me Be Your."

❏ RCA Victor 47-7000 .... 6/57   50-100
Picture sleeve. This, the first full color sleeve, has a different Elvis photo on each side.

❏ RCA Victor 47-7000 .... 6/57   200-300
White "Record Prevue" label. Promotional, Canadian issue only.

❏ RCA Victor 447-0620 .... '61   10-20
Gold Standard. Black label, dog on top.
H2WW-2193-10S/H2WW-0418-11S. Label GS#1. Credits "ELVIS PRESLEY with The Jordanaires."

❏ RCA Victor 447-0620 .... '65   6-10
Gold Standard. Black label, dog on side.

❏ RCA Victor 447-0620 .... '68   50-75
Gold Standard. Orange label.
H2WW-2193-10S/H2WW-0418-13S. Credits "ELVIS PRESLEY with The Jordanaires."

❏ RCA Victor 447-0620 .... '70   10-12
Gold Standard. Red label.
H2WW-2193-11S/H2WW-0418-14S. Credits "ELVIS PRESLEY with The Jordanaires."

❏ RCA Victor 447-0620 .... '77   3-5
Gold Standard. Black label, dog near top.

❏ RCA Victor PB-11109 ...... 10/77   3-4
Originally included as one of the singles in the boxed sets *15 Golden Records – 30 Golden Hits* and *20 Golden Hits* in Full Color Sleeves.

❏ RCA Victor PB-11109 ...... 10/77   3-4
Picture sleeve.

(LET ME BE YOUR) TEDDY BEAR / Puppet on a String

❏ RCA Victor PB-11320 .... 8/78   3-5
Black label, dog near top.
PA-11320-A-1S/PB-11320-B-1S. *(Let Me Be Your) Teddy Bear* is mono, *Puppet on a String* is stereo. Credits "ELVIS PRESLEY, Vocal accompaniment by The Jordanaires."

❏ RCA Victor PB-11320 .... 8/78   8-10
Picture sleeve.

❑ RCA Victor JH-11320
PB-11320) 8/78   10-15
Light yellow label. Promotional issue only.
PA-11320-A-3S/PB-11320-B-3S. *(Let Me Be Your) Teddy Bear* is mono, *Puppet on a String* is stereo. Credits "ELVIS PRESLEY, Vocal accompaniment by The Jordanaires." Identification numbers are engraved. Polystyrene pressing.

TELL ME PRETTY BABY / Tell Me Pretty Baby

Elvis Classic EC-5478

Credits "Elvis" and has his likeness on a picture sleeve. Nevertheless, this recording is not by Elvis Presley. He had no involvement whatsoever. It is, in fact, a total fraud.

TELL ME WHY / Blue River

❑ RCA Victor 47-8740 .... 12/65   6-10
Black label, dog on side.
H2WW-0254-3S/SPKM-7357-3S. Label S#21. Credits "ELVIS PRESLEY With The Jordanaires" on *Tell Me Why* and Credits "ELVIS PRESLEY" on *Blue River*.

❑ RCA Victor 47-8740 .... 12/65   20-30
Picture sleeve.

❑ RCA Victor 47-8740 .... 12/65   40-45
White label. Promotional issue only.
H2WW-0254-5S/SPKM-7357-5S. Label S#27. Credits "ELVIS PRESLEY with the Jordanaires" on *Tell Me Why* and Credits "ELVIS PRESLEY" on *Blue River*.

❑ RCA Victor 447-0655 .... 2/68   6-10
Gold Standard. Black label, dog on side.
H2WW-0254-4S/SPKM-7357-2S. Label GS#6. Has playing times and publisher. Credits "ELVIS PRESLEY with the Jordanaires" on *Tell Me Why* and Credits "ELVIS PRESLEY" on *Blue River*.

❑ RCA Victor 447-0655 .... '70   10-12
Gold Standard. Red label.

❑ RCA Victor 447-0655 .... '77   3-5
Gold Standard. Black label, dog near top.

THAT'S ALL RIGHT / Blue Moon of Kentucky

❑ Sun 209 .... 7/54   1200-1600
78 rpm.
U-128-2-72/U-129-2-72. Credits "ELVIS PRESLEY" (on line one), and "SCOTTY and BILL" (line two). Identification numbers are engraved.
Counterfeit Identification: Any colored plastic Sun 78 is an unauthorized (circa 1978) issue.

❑ Sun 209 .... 7/54   1100-1500
U-128-45-72/U-129-45-72. Credits "ELVIS PRESLEY" (on line one), and "SCOTTY and BILL" (line two). Release number is at bottom of label. Push marks are present. Identification numbers are engraved.
Counterfeit Identification: Fakes of Sun 45s are numerous; however, some are easily identified. Any with "Issued 1973" engraved in the vinyl are fakes, and any on colored vinyl are boots. On some fakes, the brown sunrays, circling top half of label, fail to go all the way to the edge of the hole, though we are not prepared to state unequivocally that there are no originals printed this way. When compared to the label of an original, some fakes have noticeably darker brown print on noticeably lighter yellow stock. Any discs with "RE" or "Reissue" engraved in the vinyl are fakes. Any Sun singles with three push marks (three

circular indentations, that if connected by a line would form a triangle) are original pressings.
Only bootleg picture sleeves exist for this release.

❑ RCA Victor 20-6380 .... 12/55   100-150
Black label, 78 rpm.
F2WB-8040-4S/F2WB-8041-3S. Label S#11. Credits "Elvis Presley." (Rarely on an RCA label does Elvis' name appear in upper and lower case letters.)

❑ RCA Victor 47-6380 .... 12/55   40-50
Black label, dog on top, without horizontal silver line.
Only bootleg picture sleeves exist for this release.

❑ RCA Victor 47-6380 .... 12/55   50-60
Black label, dog on top, with horizontal silver line.
F2WW-8040-4S/F2WW-8041-6S. Label S#14. Credits "ELVIS PRESLEY."
Only bootleg picture sleeves exist for this release.

❑ RCA Victor 447-0601 .... 3/59   15-20
Gold Standard. Black label, dog on top.
J2PW-5683-3S/J2PW-5684-3S. Label GS#1. Credits "ELVIS PRESLEY."

❑ RCA Victor 447-0601 .... 6/64   250-300
Gold Standard picture sleeve.

❑ RCA Victor 447-0601 .... 6/64   75-125
Gold Standard. White label. Promotional issue only.
J2PW-5683-4S/J2PW-5684-4S. Label GS#9. Credits "ELVIS PRESLEY."

❑ RCA Victor 447-0601 .... '65   6-12
Gold Standard. Black label, dog on side.
J2PW-5683-3S/J2PW-5684-6S. Label GS#6. Credits "ELVIS PRESLEY."

❑ RCA Victor 447-0601 .... '70   10-12
Gold Standard. Red label.
J2PW-5683-7S/J2PW-5684-7S. Credits "ELVIS PRESLEY" on *That's All Right*, but mistakenly credits "ELVIS PRESLEY" on *Blue Moon of Kentucky*. We do not yet know if all red label copies have this error, or only certain ones – such as "7S."

❑ RCA Victor 447-0601 .... '77   3-5
Gold Standard. Black label, dog near top.

❑ RCA Victor PB-13891 ...... 12/84   3-4
Gold vinyl. Originally included as one of the singles in the boxed set *Elvis' Greatest Hits – Golden Singles, Vol. 2.*

❑ RCA Victor PB-13891 ...... 12/84   3-4
Picture sleeve.

THAT'S ALL RIGHT / Blue Moon of Kentucky

❑ Chicken 101: Bootleg. Listed for identification only.
❑ Qualiton 100 (record or picture sleeve): Bootleg. Listed for identification only.

THERE GOES MY EVERYTHING / You'll Never Walk Alone

❑ RCA Victor PB-13058 .... 2/82   3-5
Black label, dog near top.
PB-13058-A-1S/PB-13058-B-1S. Both sides are stereo. Credits "ELVIS PRESLEY, Vocal accompaniment: The Imperials Quartet" on *There Goes My Everything* and "ELVIS PRESLEY with The Jordanaires" on *You'll Never Walk Alone*. Identification numbers are engraved.

❑ RCA Victor PB-13058........2/82   10-15
Picture sleeve.

❑ RCA Victor JB-13058
(PB-13058)........................2/82   10-15
Light yellow label. Promotional issue only.
PB-13058-A-8S/PB-13058-B-8S. Both sides are stereo.
Inscribed in trail off on *There Goes My Everything* is "MR-
Δ107597," and on *You'll Never Walk Alone* is "MR-
Δ107597X." Credits "ELVIS PRESLEY, Vocal accompaniment:
The Imperials Quartet" on *There Goes My Everything* and
"ELVIS PRESLEY with The Jordanaires" on *You'll Never Walk
Alone*. Identification numbers are engraved.

THOMPSON VOCAL ELIMINATOR (TVE) / Thompson Analog Delay

❑ Eva-Tone 12-27785........12/78   15-20
Promotional 8" soundsheet used as a publicity
item for LT Sound's Thompson Vocal
Eliminator, contains a portion of *You Don't
Have to Say You Love Me*. No label used –
print is on the plastic.

THOMPSON VOCAL ELIMINATOR / More of the Thompson Vocal Eliminator

❑ Eva-Tone........................12/78   15-20
Soundsheet used as a promotional item for LT
Sound's Thompson Vocal Eliminator, probably
contains the same Elvis track as the previous
Thompson soundsheet, a portion of *You Don't
Have to Say You Love Me*. No label used –
print is on the plastic.

TOO MUCH [Elvis Presley] / Cattle Call [Eddy Arnold]

❑ For Your Classic Juke Box
G-520 ....'80s   50-75
78 rpm. Made for juke box use.

TOO MUCH / Playing for Keeps

❑ RCA Victor 20-6800 ....1/57   75-100
Black label, 78 rpm.
G2WB-4928-5S/G2WB-4920-5S. Label S#3. Credits "ELVIS
PRESLEY with The Jordanaires." This is the first RCA Elvis
label to credit the Jordanaires.

❑ RCA Victor 20-6800 ....'70s   250-500
White label 78 rpm. Reads: "Record Prevue,
Disc Jockey Sample." Has rectangular "Not
for Sale" box printed on label. We're not yet
certain as to the history, purpose and
legitimacy of this series.
G2WW-4928/G2WW-4920. Credits "ELVIS PRESLEY with The
Jordanaires." Identification numbers are engraved, but may
be scratched over.

❑ RCA Victor 47-6800 ....1/57   20-30
Black label, dog on top, without horizontal
silver line.
G2WW-4928-2S/G2WW-4920-2S. Label S#13. Credits
"ELVIS PRESLEY with The Jordanaires." This is the first RCA
Elvis label to credit the Jordanaires.

❑ RCA Victor 47-6800 ....1/57   200-225
Black label, no dog on label, with horizontal
silver line.
G2WW-4928-16S/G2WW-4920-16S. Label S#16. Credits
"ELVIS PRESLEY with The Jordanaires."

❑ RCA Victor 47-6800..........1/57   30-40
Black label, dog on top, with horizontal silver
line.
G2WW-4928-11S/G2WW-4920-11S. Label S#12L. Credits
"ELVIS PRESLEY with The Jordanaires."

❑ RCA Victor 47-6800..........1/57   50-100
Picture sleeve.

❑ RCA Victor 47-6800..........1/57   200-300
White "Record Prevue" label. Promotional,
Canadian issue only.

RCA Victor 447-0617.............3/59   10-20
Gold Standard. Black label, dog on top.

❑ RCA Victor 447-0617...........'65   6-10
Gold Standard. Black label, dog on side.
J2PW-6013-4S/J2PW-6014-1S. Label GS#6. Credits "ELVIS
PRESLEY with The Jordanaires."

❑ RCA Victor 447-0617...........'68   50-75
Gold Standard. Orange label.

❑ RCA Victor 447-0617...........'70   10-12
Gold Standard. Red label.
J2PW-6013-4S/J2PW-6014-3S. Credits "ELVIS PRESLEY with
The Jordanaires."

❑ RCA Victor 447-0617...........'77   3-5
Gold Standard. Black label, dog near top.

❑ Collectables 4507 ....'86   3-4
Black vinyl.
DPE1-1007-A-1/DPE1-1007-B-1. Credits "ELVIS PRESLEY
with The Jordanaires." Polystyrene pressing.

❑ Collectables 4507 ....7/92   5-6
Gold vinyl.
DPE1-1007-A-1/DPE1-1007-B-1. Credits "ELVIS PRESLEY
with The Jordanaires." Polystyrene pressing.

TREAT ME NICE / Nellie Was a Lady

❑ Laurel 41 623.....................5/57   5000-10000
Picture sleeve. Pictures Elvis but credits
"Vince Everett." This black-and-white sleeve
was made as a prop for the film *Jailhouse
Rock*, in which Elvis' character is named
Vince Everett. The printed sheet had no
reverse side and was applied to a randomly
selected EP. In one case, the EP used was
Charlie Mariano (Imperial 125). Other sleeves
were probably attached to various EPs, or
even plain pieces of cardboard. There are no
Laurel records of this title.

TRIBUTE TO ELVIS PRESLEY (PART 1) / A Tribute to Elvis Presley (Part 2)

❑ Tribute 501 ....'56   50-100
In addition to a few words from Elvis, also has
the voices of: Edward R. Murrow, Steve Allen,
Ed Sullivan, Danny Kaye, Jimmy Durante,
Gabriel Heater, Sid Caesar, Liberace,
Mantovani, Jack Benny, Gene Vincent, Gloria
DeHaven, Nat King Cole, Nelson Eddy, and
Jane Russell.

T-R-O-U-B-L-E / Mr. Songman

❏ RCA Victor PB-10278........4/75   8-10
Tan label.
PB-10278-A-20S/PB-10278-B-1. Both sides are stereo. *T-r-o-u-b-l-e* side has identification numbers engraved, but *Mr. Songman* side has them stamped. This is the first known occurrence of this technique. Credits "ELVIS PRESLEY" on *T-r-o-u-b-l-e* and "ELVIS PRESLEY, Strings arranged by Mike Leech" on *Mr. Songman.*

❏ RCA Victor PB-10278........4/75   200-300
Gray label.
PB-10278-A-21S/PB-10278-B-1. Both sides are stereo. Credits "ELVIS PRESLEY" on *T-r-o-u-b-l-e* and "ELVIS PRESLEY, Strings arranged by Mike Leech" on *Mr. Songman.*

❏ RCA Victor PB-10278........4/75   20-25
Orange label.
This is the second to last Elvis RCA single issued on the orange label.
PB-10278-A-22S/PB-10278-B-3. Both sides are stereo. Credits "ELVIS PRESLEY" on *T-r-o-u-b-l-e* and "ELVIS PRESLEY, Strings arranged by Mike Leech" on *Mr. Songman.* Identification numbers are engraved.
PB-10278-A-25S/PB-10278-B-3.

❏ RCA Victor PB-10278........4/75   10-15
Picture sleeve.

❏ RCA Victor PB-10278........4/75   25-30
Orange label. Promotional issue only.
PB-10278-A-22S/PB-10278-B-3. Both sides are stereo. Has white "NOT FOR SALE" sticker on *Mr. Songman* label. Credits "ELVIS PRESLEY" on *T-r-o-u-b-l-e* and "ELVIS PRESLEY, Strings arranged by Mike Leech" on *Mr. Songman.* Identification numbers are engraved.

❏ RCA Victor GS-10487 ....2/76   10-12
Gold Standard. Red label.

❏ RCA Victor GB-10487 .... '77   3-5
Gold Standard. Black label, dog near top.

T-R-O-U-B-L-E (Stereo) / T-r-o-u-b-l-e (Mono)

❏ RCA Victor JH-10278
(PB-10278) 4/75   30-35
Light yellow label. Promotional issue only.
PB-10278-A-228/PA-10278-C-228. One side is stereo, one side is mono. Credits "ELVIS PRESLEY." Identification numbers are engraved.

TRYIN' TO GET TO YOU / I Love You Because

❏ RCA Victor 20-6639 .... 9/56   75-100
Black label, 78 rpm.
F2WB-8039-1S/G2WB-1086-1S. Label S#4. Credits "ELVIS PRESLEY."

❏ RCA Victor 47-6639 .... 9/56   40-50
Black label, dog on top, without horizontal silver line.
Only bootleg picture sleeves exist for this release.

❏ RCA Victor 47-6639 .... 9/56   50-60
Black label, dog on top, with horizontal silver line.
Only bootleg picture sleeves exist for this release.
F2WW-8039-3S/G2WW-1086-3S. Label S#12L. Credits "ELVIS PRESLEY."

❏ RCA Victor 47-6639 .... 9/56   200-300
White "Record Prevue" label. Promotional, Canadian issue only.

❏ RCA Victor 447-0612 ....3/59   15-20
Gold Standard. Black label, dog on top.

J2PW-6003-1S/J2PW-6004-1S. Label GS#1. Credits "ELVIS PRESLEY."

❏ Collectables 4505 .... '86   3-4
Black vinyl.
DPE1-1005-A-1/DPE1-1005-B-1. Credits "ELVIS PRESLEY." Polystyrene pressing.

❏ Collectables 4505 ....7/92   5-6
Gold vinyl.
DPE1-1005-A-1/DPE1-1005-B-1. Credits "ELVIS PRESLEY." Polystyrene pressing.

TWEEDLE DEE / Happy, Happy Birthday Baby

❏ Sun 525: Bootleg. Listed for identification only.

TWEEDLE DEE / Lawdy, Miss Clawdy

❏ Sun 526: Bootleg. Listed for identification only.

TWEEDLE DEE / Louisiana Hayride Interview

❏ Sun 600: Bootleg. Listed for identification only.

TUTTI FRUTTI / I'll Never Let You Go

❏ Sun 523: Bootleg. Listed for identification only.

20 GOLDEN HITS IN FULL COLOR SLEEVES

❏ RCA Victor PP-11340 ......12/77   65-75
COMPLETE SET: Package of 10 singles in color sleeves, individually numbered PB-11099 through PB-11111. Price is for all records, sleeves and cardboard box.

❏ RCA Victor PP-11340 ......12/77   10-15
BOX: Price for just the box, which is red stock with white lettering.

U.S. MALE / Stay Away

❏ RCA Victor 47-9465...........3/68   6-10
Black label, dog on side.
WPKM-1807-7S/WPKM-1002-7S. Label S#20. Credits "ELVIS PRESLEY with The Jordanaires."

❏ RCA Victor 47-9465...........3/68   15-20
Picture sleeve.

❏ RCA Victor 47-9465...........3/68   25-35
Yellow label. Promotional issue only.
WPKM-1807-6S/WPKM-1002-7S. Label S#27. Credits "ELVIS PRESLEY with the Jordanaires."

❏ RCA Victor 447-0664...........'70   10-12
Gold Standard. Red label.
WPKM-1807-4S/WPKM-1002-4S. Credits "ELVIS PRESLEY with The Jordanaires."

❏ RCA Victor 447-0664...........'70   3-5
Gold Standard. Black label, dog near top.
WPKM-1807-8S/WPKM-1002-9. Credits "ELVIS PRESLEY with The Jordanaires."

U.S. MALE / Until It's Time for You to Go

❑ Collectables 4517 .... '86   3-4
Black vinyl.
DPE1-1017-A-1/DPE1-1017-B-1. Credits "ELVIS PRESLEY with The Jordanaires" on *U.S. Male* and "ELVIS PRESLEY, Vocal accompaniment by The Imperials Qt." on *Until It's Time for You to Go*. Identification numbers are stamped on *U.S. Male* and engraved on *Until It's Time for You to Go*. Polystyrene pressing.

❑ Collectables 4517 .... 7/92   5-6
Gold vinyl.
DPE1-1017-A-1/DPE1-1017-B-1. Credits "ELVIS PRESLEY with The Jordanaires" on *U.S. Male* and "ELVIS PRESLEY, Vocal accompaniment by The Imperials Qt." on *Until It's Time for You to Go*. Identification numbers are stamped on *U.S. Male* and engraved on *Until It's Time for You to Go*. Polystyrene pressing.

UNCHAINED MELODY / Are You Sincere

❑ RCA Victor GB-11988 .... 5/80   3-4
Gold Standard. Black label, dog near top.
GB-11988A/GB-11988B. Both sides are stereo. Has PB-11212A on *Unchained Melody* and PB-11533A on *Are You Sincere* (their original identification numbers) stamped in trail off, but both are crossed out. Credits "ELVIS PRESLEY, Produced by Joan Deary, Executive Producer: Elvis Presley, Associate Producer: Felton Jarvis" on *Unchained Melody* and "ELVIS PRESLEY, Produced by Joan Deary" on *Are You Sincere*.

UNCHAINED MELODY / Softly, As I Leave You

❑ RCA Victor PB-11212 .... 3/78   10-15
Black label, dog near top.
Mistakenly has "Vocal Accompaniment by Sherrill Nielsen" on *Unchained Melody*. Identification numbers (not yet known) are engraved. Polystyrene pressing.

❑ RCA Victor PB-11212 .... 3/78   5-10
Black label, dog near top.
PB-11212-A-3S/PA-11212-B-4S. Identification numbers are engraved. Mistakenly has "Vocal Accompaniment by Sherrill Nielsen" on *Unchained Melody*. Identification numbers are engraved. Polystyrene pressing.
PB-11212-A-4S/PA-11212-B-4S. *Unchained Melody* is stereo, *Softly, As I Leave You* is mono. Credits "ELVIS PRESLEY, Executive Producer: Elvis Presley, Associate Producer: Felton Jarvis" (Omits "Vocal Accompaniment by Sherrill Nielsen," as is shown in error on promo pressing) on *Unchained Melody* and "ELVIS PRESLEY, Vocal Accompaniment by Sherrill Nielsen" on *Softly, As I Leave You*. Identification numbers are engraved. Polystyrene pressing.

❑ RCA Victor PB-11212 .... 3/78   10-15
Picture sleeve.

❑ RCA Victor JH-11212 (PB-11212) 3/78   10-15
Light yellow label. Promotional issue only.
PB-11212-A-4S/PA-11212-B-4S. *Unchained Melody* is stereo, *Softly, As I Leave You* is mono. Credits "ELVIS PRESLEY, Executive Producer: Felton Jarvis, Vocal Accompaniment by Sherrill Nielsen" (printed on this side by mistake) on *Unchained Melody* and "ELVIS PRESLEY, Vocal Accompaniment by Sherrill Nielsen" on *Softly, As I Leave You*. Identification numbers are engraved. Polystyrene pressing.

For Gold Standard release of Unchained Melody see UNCHAINED MELODY / Are You Sincere.

UNTIL IT'S TIME FOR YOU TO GO / We Can Make the Morning

❑ RCA Victor 74-0619 .... 1/72   4-6
Orange label.

APKS-1289-2S/APKS-1286-1S. Both sides are stereo. Credits "ELVIS PRESLEY, Vocal accompaniment by The Imperials Qt."

❑ RCA Victor 74-0619 .... 1/72   20-25
Picture sleeve.

❑ RCA Victor 74-0619 .... 1/72   25-30
Yellow label. Promotional issue only.
APKM-1289-7S/APKM-1286-1S. Both sides are mono. Credits "ELVIS PRESLEY, Vocal accompaniment by The Imperials Qt."

For Gold Standard release of *Until It's Time for You to Go* see *AMERICAN TRILOGY / Until It's Time for You to Go*.

VIVA LAS VEGAS / What'd I Say

❑ RCA Victor 47-8360 .... 4/64   6-10
Black label, dog on top.
RPKM-0234-2S/RPKM-0235-2S. Label S#18. Credits "ELVIS PRESLEY with the Jordanaires" on *Viva Las Vegas* and "ELVIS PRESLEY with the Jubilee Four and Carole Lombard Quartet" on *What'd I Say*. Although the same take numbers ("2S") are stamped on this pressing, as on the white label promotional copy, this disc has a "3" engraved in the trail off after the "2S" on both sides.

❑ RCA Victor 47-8360 .... 4/64   30-40
Picture sleeve. Reads: "Coming Soon" regarding the *Viva Las Vegas* EP.

❑ RCA Victor 47-8360 .... 4/64   75-100
Picture sleeve. Reads: "Ask For" the *Viva Las Vegas* EP.

❑ RCA Victor 47-8360 .... 4/64   45-50
White label. Promotional issue only.
RPKM-0234-2S/RPKM-0235-2S. Label S#23. Credits "ELVIS PRESLEY with the Jordanaires" on *Viva Las Vegas* and "ELVIS PRESLEY with the Jubilee Four & Carole Lombard Quartet" on *What'd I Say*.

❑ RCA Victor 447-0646 .... 5/65   25-35
Gold Standard. Black label, dog on top.

❑ RCA Victor 447-0646 .... 5/65   6-10
Gold Standard. Black label, dog on side.
RPKM-0234-5S/RPKM-0235-4S. Has playing times and publisher. Does not show recording dates. Credits "ELVIS PRESLEY with the Jordanaires" on *Viva Las Vegas* and "ELVIS PRESLEY with the Jubilee Four and Carole Lombard Quartet" on *What'd I Say*.

❑ RCA Victor 447-0646 .... '68   50-75
Gold Standard. Orange label.
RPKM-0234-4S/RPKM-0235-4S. Credits "ELVIS PRESLEY with the Jordanaires" on *Viva Las Vegas* and "ELVIS PRESLEY with the Jubilee Four and Carole Lombard Quartet" on *What'd I Say*.

❑ RCA Victor 447-0646 .... '70   10-12
Gold Standard. Red label.
RPKM-0234-4S/RPKM-0235-5S. Credits "ELVIS PRESLEY with the Jordanaires" on *Viva Las Vegas* and "ELVIS PRESLEY with the Jubilee Four and Carole Lombard Quartet" on *What'd I Say*.

❑ RCA Victor 447-0646 .... '77   3-5
Gold Standard. Black label, dog near top.

WAY DOWN / My Way

❑ RCA Victor GB-11504 .... 5/79   3-4
Black label, dog near top.
GB-11504A/GB-11504B. Both sides are stereo. Identification numbers are engraved. Both sides also have original identification numbers (PB-10998-A-1S/PB-10998-B-1S) stamped in trail off, but crossed out. Credits "ELVIS PRESLEY, Exec. Prod.: Elvis Presley, Associate Producer: Felton Jarvis, Vocal accomp. by J.D. Sumner & Stamps Qt./Kathy Westmoreland, Sherrill Nielsen and Myrna Smith" on *Way Down* and "ELVIS PRESLEY, Exec. Prod.: Elvis Presley, Associate Producer: Felton Jarvis, Vocal accomp. by J.D. Sumner & Stamps, The Sweet Inspirations and Kathy Westmoreland" on *My Way*.

WAY DOWN / Pledging My Love

❏ RCA Victor PB-10998........7/77   3-5
Black label, dog near top.
PB-10998-A-1S/PB-10998-B-1S. Both sides are stereo.
Credits "ELVIS PRESLEY, Vocal accomp. by J.D. Sumner &
Stamps Qt., Kathy Westmoreland, Sherrill Nielsen and
Myrna Smith, Exec. Prod.: Elvis Presley, Associate Prod.:
Felton Jarvis." Polystyrene pressing.

❏ RCA Victor PB-10998........7/77   10-15
Picture sleeve.

❏ RCA Victor JB-10998 ....7/77   150-175
White label. Promotional issue only.
PB-10998-A-1S/PB-10998-B-1S. Both sides are stereo.
Credits "ELVIS PRESLEY."

❏ RCA Victor JB-10998
(PB-10998)........................7/77   15-20
Light yellow label. Promotional issue only.
PB-10998-A-1S/PB-10998-B-1S. Both sides are stereo.
Credits "ELVIS PRESLEY, Vocal accomp. by J.D. Sumner &
Stamps Qt., Kathy Westmoreland, Sherrill Nielsen and
Myrna Smith, Exec. Prod.: Elvis Presley, Associate Prod.:
Felton Jarvis." Polystyrene pressing.

WEAR MY RING AROUND YOUR NECK / Doncha' Think It's Time

❏ RCA Victor 20-7240 ....4/58   200-300
Black label, 78 rpm.
J2WB-0181-2S/J2WW-0179-2S. Label S#1. Credits "ELVIS
PRESLEY With THE JORDANAIRES."

❏ RCA Victor 47-7240 ....4/58   10-15
Black label, dog on top.
J2WW-0181-6S/J2WW-0179-6S. Label S#19. Credits "ELVIS
PRESLEY With THE JORDANAIRES."

❏ RCA Victor 47-7240 ....4/58   50-60
Picture sleeve.

❏ RCA Victor 47-7240 ....4/58   200-300
White "Record Prevue" label. Promotional,
Canadian issue only.

❏ RCA Victor 447-0622 ....'61   10-15
Gold Standard. Black label, dog on top.
J2WW-0181-12S/J2WW-0179-11S. Label GS#1. Credits
"ELVIS PRESLEY with The Jordanaires."

❏ RCA Victor 447-0622 ....'65   6-10
Gold Standard. Black label, dog on side.
J2WW-0181-13S/J2WW-0179-13S. Label GS#6. Credits
"ELVIS PRESLEY with The Jordanaires."

❏ RCA Victor 447-0622 ....'68   50-75
Gold Standard. Orange label.
J2WW-0181-13S/J2WW-0179-14S. Credits "ELVIS PRESLEY
with The Jordanaires."

❏ RCA Victor 447-0622 ....'70   10-12
Gold Standard. Red label.
J2WW-0181-14S/J2WW-0179-14S. Credits "ELVIS PRESLEY
with The Jordanaires."

❏ RCA Victor 447-0622 ....'77   3-5
Gold Standard. Black label, dog near top.
Wear My Ring Around Your Neck is also on a
special promotional 45. See *DON'T / Wear My
Ring Around Your Neck* for that listing. Also
see *I WAS THE ONE / Wear My Ring Around
Your Neck.*

WHAT'S IT ALL ABOUT?

❏ MA-3025 (Pgm 633/634) .....'82   50-75
Outlines Elvis' life story, with his music and
interviews. Hosted by Bill Huey, for the
Presbyterian Church. Provided as religious
programming for radio stations.
MA-1840-555/MA-1840-556. Identification numbers are
engraved.

WONDER OF YOU / Mama Liked the Roses

❏ RCA Victor 47-9835...........5/70   4-6
Orange label.
ZPKM-1300-1S/XPKM-1152-2S. Credits "ELVIS PRESLEY
Arranged by Glenn D. Hardin" on *The Wonder of You* and
"ELVIS PRESLEY" on *Mama Liked the Roses.* Identification
numbers are engraved.

❏ RCA Victor 47-9835...........5/70   10-20
Picture sleeve.

❏ RCA Victor 47-9835...........5/70   25-30
Yellow label. Promotional issue only.
ZPKM-1300-4S/XPKM-1152-6S. Credits "ELVIS PRESLEY
Arranged by Glenn D. Hardin" on *The Wonder of You* and
"ELVIS PRESLEY" on *Mama Liked the Roses.* This is the first
Elvis promo label to alert dee jays as to how the song ends
– whether by fading out or "cold" (abrupt).

❏ RCA Victor 447-0676........8/71   10-12
Gold Standard. Red label.
ZPKM-1300-4S/XPKM-1152-30S. Credits "ELVIS PRESLEY,
Arranged by Glenn D. Hardin" on *The Wonder of You* and
"ELVIS PRESLEY" on *Mama Liked the Roses.*

❏ RCA Victor 447-0676...........'77   3-5
Gold Standard. Black label, dog near top.

YOU DON'T HAVE TO SAY YOU LOVE ME / Patch It Up

❏ RCA Victor 47-9916........10/70   4-6
Orange label.
ZPKM-1608-9S/ZPKM-1628-9S. Credits "ELVIS PRESLEY
Horns and Strings arranged by Bergen White" on *You Don't
Have to Say You Love Me* and "ELVIS PRESLEY, Horns
arranged by David Briggs" on *Patch It Up.*

❏ RCA Victor 47-9916........10/70   10-20
Picture sleeve.

❏ RCA Victor 47-9916........10/70   20-25
Yellow label. Promotional issue only.
ZPKM-1608-5S/ZPKM-1628-5S. Credits "ELVIS PRESLEY
Horns and Strings Arranged by Bergen White" on *You Don't
Have to Say You Love Me* and "ELVIS PRESLEY,
Arranged by David Briggs" on *Patch It Up.*

❏ RCA Victor 447-0678........2/72   10-12
Gold Standard. Red label.
ZPKM-1608-4S/ZPKM-1628-6S. Credits "ELVIS PRESLEY,
Horns and Strings arranged by Bergen White" on *You Don't
Have to Say You Love Me* and "ELVIS PRESLEY, Horns
arranged by David Briggs" on *Patch It Up.*

❏ RCA Victor 447-0678...........'77   3-5
Gold Standard. Black label, dog near top.

YOU'LL NEVER WALK ALONE / We Call On Him

❑ RCA Victor 47-9600 .... 4/68   6-10
Black label, dog on side.
UPKM-2772-7S/UPKM-2773-8S. Label S#20. Credits "ELVIS PRESLEY with the Jordanaires."

❑ RCA Victor 47-9600 .... 4/68   75-125
Picture sleeve.

❑ RCA Victor 47-9600 .... 4/68   25-35
Yellow label. Promotional issue only.
UPKM-2772-8S/UPKM-2773-8S. Label S#27. Credits "ELVIS PRESLEY with the Jordanaires."

❑ RCA Victor 447-0665 ...... 12/70   12-15
Gold Standard. Red label.
UPKM-2772-5S/UPKM-2773-4S. Credits "ELVIS PRESLEY with the Jordanaires."

❑ RCA Victor 447-0665 .... '77   3-5
Black label, dog near top.

YOUNG AND BEAUTIFUL / Don't Leave Me Now

❑ Laurel 41 625 .... 5/57   75-100
Picture cover. Pictures Elvis but credits Vince Everett. This black-and-white, cardboard, EP-like cover may have been made as a prop for the film *Jailhouse Rock*, in which Elvis' character was named Vince Everett. While some researchers question the authenticity – and therefore the production date – of this item, prices in this range are nevertheless paid for it. No Laurel records of this title exist.

YOUR TIME HASN'T COME YET, BABY / Let Yourself Go

❑ RCA Victor 47-9547 .... 6/68   15-20
Black label, dog on side.
WPKM-1023-9S/WPKM-1029-9S. Label S#20. Credits "ELVIS PRESLEY with The Jordanaires."

❑ RCA Victor 47-9547 .... 6/68   30-40
Picture sleeve. Reads: "Coming Soon – *Speedway* LP."

❑ RCA Victor 47-9547 .... 7/68   40-50
Picture sleeve. Reads: "Ask For – *Speedway* LP."

❑ RCA Victor 47-9547 .... 6/68   50-60
Yellow label. Promotional issue only.
WPKM-1023-6S/WPKM-1029-4S. Label S#26. Credits "ELVIS PRESLEY With The Jordanaires."

❑ RCA Victor 447-0666 ...... 12/70   20-25
Gold Standard. Red label.
WPKM-1023-4S/WPKM-1029-5S. Credits "ELVIS PRESLEY with the Jordanaires."

❑ RCA Victor 447-0666 .... '77   3-5
Gold Standard. Black label, dog near top.

With these two labels – as with all of the Canadian "Record Prevue" singles pictured in this edition – the photocopies supplied to us were made with the discs still in their paper sleeves. Therefore some text on the sides, and the "Made in Canada," etc. line at the bottom does not show.

ALPHABETICAL LISTINGS OF ELVIS FLIP SIDES

When you can think of only one side of an Elvis disc, and when that one tune happens to be listed as a flip side in our pricing section, this handy listing will give you the "A" side. Then simply look up that title.

TO LOCATE:	LOOK FOR:
A Fool Such As I	**I Need Your Love Tonight**
All That I Am	Spinout
Always on My Mind	**Separate Ways**
Always on My Mind	**The Elvis Medley**
America (The Beautiful)	My Way
American Trilogy	Impossible Dream
American Trilogy	Poor Boy
Any Day Now	In the Ghetto
Anyway You Want Me	Love Me Tender
Anything That's Part of You	Good Luck Charm
Ask Me	**Ain't That Loving You Baby**
Blue Moon of Kentucky	That's All Right
Blue River	Tell Me Why
Blue Suede Shoes	Fools Fall in Love
Bosom of Abraham	He Touched Me
Charro	Memories
Come What May	Love Letters
Devil in Disguise	One Broken Heart for Sale
Doncha' Think It's Time	**Wear My Ring Around Your Neck**
Don't Ask Me Why	**Hard Headed Woman**
Edge of Reality	If I Can Dream
Elvis Hour	**Elvis 10th Anniversary**
Elvis Hour	Memories of Elvis
Faded Love	Guitar Man
Fair Is Moving On	**Clean Up Your Own Backyard**
Fame and Fortune	Stuck on You
First Time Ever I Saw Your Face	**American Trilogy**
Flaming Star	Love Me
Fool Such As I	**I Need Your Love Tonight**
Fools Fall in Love	Indescribably Blue
For Ol' Times Sake	Raised on Rock
For the Heart	Moody Blue
Heart of Rome	I'm Leavin'
Help Me	If You Talk in Your Sleep
High Heel Sneakers	Guitar Man
His Hand in Mine	How Great Thou Art
Home Is Where the Heart Is	**King of the Whole Wide World**
Hound Dog	Baby, Let's Play House
Hound Dog	Don't Be Cruel
Hound Dog (live)	Baby, Let's Play House
How Would You Like to Be	**If Everyday Was Like Christmas**
Hurt	For the Heart
I Beg of You	Don't
I Believe in the Man in the Sky	Crying in the Chapel

I Don't Care If the Sun Don't Shine	**Good Rockin' Tonight**
I Forgot to Remember to Forget	**Mystery Train**
I Got a Woman (Canadian)	**Money Honey**
I Got Stung	One Night
I Gotta Know	Are You Lonesome Tonight
I Love You Because	Tryin' to Get to You
If You Talk in Your Sleep	Raised on Rock
I'm Counting on You	I Got a Woman
I'm Gonna Sit Right Down and Cry (Over You)	**I'll Never Let You Go (Little Darlin')**
I'm Left, You're Right, She's Gone	**Baby Let's Play House**
I've Got a Thing About You Baby	**Take Good Care of Her**
It Feels So Right	Easy Question
It Hurts Me	Kissin' Cousins
It's a Matter of Time	Burning Love
It's Midnight	Promised Land
Jailhouse Rock	She's Not You
Just Because	Blue Moon
Just Tell Her Jim Said Hello	She's Not You
Known Only to Him	Joshua Fit the Battle
Let Yourself Go	**Your Time Hasn't Come Yet Baby**
Little Less Conversation	Almost in Love
Little Sister	His Latest Flame
Lonely Man	Surrender
Long Lonely Highway	I'm Yours
Love Letters	Frankie and Johnny
Love Me	**I Want You, I Need You, I Love You**
Loving Arms	My Boy
Loving You	Teddy Bear
Mama Liked the Roses	The Wonder of You
Mess of Blues	It's Now Or Never
Mr. Songman	T-R-O-U-B-L-E
My Baby Left Me	**I Want You, I Need You, I Love You**
My Boy	Always on My Mind
My Little Friend	Kentucky Rain
My Wish Came True	Big Hunk O' Love
Next Step Is Love	I've Lost You
Never Ending	Such a Night
Now and Then There's A Fool Such As I	**I Need Your Love Tonight**
Number 1 Hits Medley	1967 Elvis Medley
O Come, All Ye Faithful	Merry Christmas Baby
One Sided Love Affair	Money Honey
One Track Heart	Roustabout
Only Believe	Life
Paralyzed	Big Boss Man
Paralyzed	Little Sister
Patch It Up	**You Don't Have to Say You Love Me**
Pieces of My Life	Bringing It Back
Playing for Keeps	Too Much
Please Don't Drag That String Along	**Devil in Disguise**
Please Don't Drag That String Around	**Devil in Disguise**
Please Don't Stop Loving Me	**Frankie and Johnny**
Pledging My Love	Way Down
Promised Land	Blue Suede Shoes

Puppet on a String.......................................Teddy Bear
Rip It Up...Little Sister
Rock-A-Hula Baby ....Can't Help Falling in Love
Rubberneckin'.....................................Don't Cry Daddy
Santa Claus Is Back in Town................Blue Christmas
Santa Claus Is Back in Town.....Merry Christmas Baby
Shake, Rattle and Roll.................Lawdy Miss Clawdy
She Thinks I Still Care ....Moody Blue
So High...How Great Thou Art
Softly, As I Leave You ....Unchained Melody
Solitaire.....................................Are You Sincere
Sound of Your Cry ....It's Only Love
Stay Away...U.S. Male
Steamroller Blues ....Fool
Such a Night ....Bossa Nova Baby
Suspicion .... Kiss Me Quick
Swing Down Sweet Chariot ....Milky White Way
That's Someone You Never Forget ... Long Legged Girl
That's When Your Heartaches Begin ....All Shook Up
There Goes My Everything.........I Really Don't Want to
   Know
There's a Honky Tonk Angel (Who'll Take Me
   Back In) .... I Got a Feelin' in My Body
There's Always Me ....Judy
They Remind Me Too Much of You.. One Broken Heart
   for Sale
Thinking About You .... My Boy
Treat Me Nice.......................................Jailhouse Rock
Tutti Frutti ....Blue Suede Shoes
Until It's Time for You to Go...............American Trilogy
Until It's Time for You to Go............................U.S. Male
We Call on Him......................You'll Never Walk Alone
We Can Make the Morning.... Until It's Time for You to
   Go
Wear My Ring Around Your Neck...........I Was the One
What'd I Say ....Viva Las Vegas
When My Blue Moon Turns to Gold Again ....Follow
   That Dream
Where Did They Go Lord......................Rags to Riches
Where Do You Come From ....Return to Sender
Wild in the Country ....I Feel So Bad
Witchcraft..Bossa Nova Baby
Wooden Heart ....Blue Christmas
Wooden Heart ....Puppet on a String
You Asked Me To .... Lovin' Arms
You Don't Know Me .... Big Boss Man
You Gave Me a Molehill ....Follow That
   Dream (Take 2)
You Gave Me a Molehill ....Nearer My God to Thee
You'll Be Gone..Do the Clam
You'll Never Walk Alone .... Old Shep
You'll Never Walk Alone .....There Goes My Everything
You'll Think of Me .... Suspicious Minds
You're a Heartbreaker ....Milkcow Blues Boogie
You're the Devil in Disguise.........One Broken Heart for
   Sale

EXTENDED PLAYS

ALOHA FROM HAWAII VIA SATELLITE

❑ RCA DTF0-2006................5/74   60-70
DISC 1: Issued for play on stereo juke boxes.
DTFO-2006A/DTFO-2006B. Has LP-size (¼-inch) hole. This is the only stereo RCA Elvis EP, and the only one showing just "RCA" (not "RCA Victor") on the label and cover.

❑ RCA DTF0-2006................5/74   90-100
COVER 1: Front: RCA logo and number at lower right. Same basic cover and Elvis photo as on the LP of the same title. Back is blank.

❑ RCA DTF0-2006................5/74   20-30
INSERT 1: Sheet of 10 juke box title strips. Reads: "RCA Stereo Album VPSX-6089," which is the number for the LP of *Elvis Aloha from Hawaii via Satellite*.

RCA DTF0-2006 ....5/74   170-200
TOTAL PACKAGE 1: Disc, cover, insert.

Side 1
Something
You Gave Me a Mountain
I Can't Stop Loving You

Side 2
My Way
What Now My Love
I'm So Lonesome I Could Cry

ANYWAY YOU WANT ME

❑ RCA Victor EPA-965 ....10/56   20-30
DISC 1: Black label, dog on top, without horizontal silver line.
G2WH-7105-1S/G2WH-7106-1S. Label EP#4.
G2WH-7105-3S/G2WH-7106-3S. Label EP#3.

❑ RCA Victor EPA-965 ....10/56   80-100
COVER 1: Front: Titles at top in white print on black stock. RCA Victor logo and number at upper right. Black and white Elvis photo. Back: Text only. Front and back of cover show title as "*Any Way You Want Me*," but disc (correctly) shows "*Anyway You Want Me (That's How I Will Be)*."

**RCA Victor
EPA-965 ....10/56   100-130**
TOTAL PACKAGE 1: Disc, cover.

❑ RCA Victor EPA-965 ....10/56   30-40
DISC 2: Black label, dog on top, with horizontal silver line.

❑ RCA Victor EPA-965 ....10/56   80-100
COVER 2: Same as cover 1.

RCA Victor EPA-965 ....10/56   110-140
TOTAL PACKAGE 2: Disc, cover.

❑ RCA Victor EPA-965 ....10/56   170-200
DISC 3: Black label, no dog on label, with horizontal silver line.

G2WH-7105-4S/G2WH-7106-4S. Label EP#11.

❑ RCA Victor EPA-965 ....10/56   80-100
COVER 3: Same as cover 1.

RCA Victor EPA-965 ....10/56   250-300
TOTAL PACKAGE 3: Disc, cover.

❑ RCA Victor EPA-965 ....'65   20-30
DISC 4: Black label, dog on side.
G2WH-7105-7S/G2WH-7106-7S. Label EP#13.

❑ RCA Victor EPA-965 ....'65   40-50
COVER 4: Verification pending.

RCA Victor EPA-965 ....'65   60-80
TOTAL PACKAGE 4: Disc, cover.

❑ RCA Victor EPA-965 ....'68   50-65
DISC 5: Orange label.
G2WH-7105-7S/G2WH-7106-7S.

❑ RCA Victor EPA-965 ....'68   50-65
COVER 5: No song titles or catalog number. RCA logo at upper right.

RCA Victor EPA-965 ....'68   100-130
TOTAL PACKAGE 5: Disc, cover.

Side 1
Anyway You Want Me (That's How I Will Be)
I'm Left, You're Right, She's Gone

Side 2
I Don't Care If the Sun Don't Shine
Mystery Train

BABY LET'S PLAY HOUSE

❑ Sun EP-102: Bootleg. Listed for identification only.

BEGINNING OF ELVIS

❑ Show-Land SL-1001............'79   30-40
DISC 1: Verification pending.

❑ Show-Land SL-1001............'79   30-40
COVER 1: White, paper sleeve. Reads: "Elvis His First Live Recorded Performance of Early 50's." Front: Black and white photocopy of the "First Picture Known of Elvis from a Live Stage Performance." Back: Text only.

Show-Land SL-1001.........'79   60-80
TOTAL PACKAGE 1: Disc, cover.

BEGINNING

❑ Sun LPM-500: Bootleg. Listed for identification only.

RCA STEREO ALBUM
SOMETHING ● YOU GAVE ME A MOUNTAIN
I CAN'T STOP LOVING YOU
SATELLITE - ELVIS PRESLEY
MY WAY ● WHAT NOW MY LOVE
I'M SO LONESOME I COULD CRY

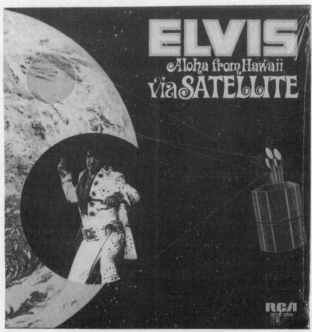

CHRISTMAS WITH ELVIS

❑ RCA Victor EPA-4340 ..... 11/58   75-100
DISC 1: Black label, dog on top.
K2PH-2461-1S/K2PH-2462-1S. Label EP#5.

❑ RCA Victor EPA-4340 ..... 11/58   125-150
COVER 1: Front: Titles at left in blue print.
RCA Victor logo and number at upper right.
Color Elvis photo. Same basic cover as on
Elvis' Christmas Album (LPM/LSP-1951). Has
copyright notice and "Printed in U.S.A." at
lower right. Back: Pictures *Elvis Sings
Christmas Songs* and *Peace in the Valley*
EPs.

RCA Victor EPA-4340 .. 11/58   200-250
TOTAL PACKAGE 1: Disc, cover.

❑ RCA Victor EPA-4340 .... '65   50-75
DISC 2: Black label, dog on side.
K2PH-2461-4S/K2PH-2462-4S. Label EP#14.

❑ RCA Victor EPA-4340 .... '65   50-75
COVER 2: Same as cover 1, except does not
have copyright notice and "Printed in U.S.A."
at lower right on front.

RCA Victor EPA-4340 ...... '65   100-150
TOTAL PACKAGE 2: Disc, cover.

❑ RCA Victor EPA-4340 .... '68   75-100
DISC 3: Orange label.
K2PH-2461-5S/K2PH-2462-6S.

❑ RCA Victor EPA-4340 .... '68   75-100
COVER 3: Same as cover 2 except has white
border around the edges. Construction of
cardboard and slick are different from the first
two covers.

RCA Victor EPA-4340 ...... '68   150-200
Side 1
White Christmas
Here Comes Santa Claus
Side 2
Oh Little Town of Bethlehem
Silent Night

DJ-7 (Elvis Presley / Jean Chapel)

❑ RCA Victor DJ-7 (47-6643/
47-6681) 10/56   150-200
DISC 1: White label. Promotional issue only.
G2NH-7341-1S/G2NH-7342-1S
COVER 1: None made.

RCA Victor DJ-7 (47-6643/
47-6681) 10/56   150-200
TOTAL PACKAGE 1: Disc.

Side 1 (Elvis Presley)
Love Me Tender
Anyway You Want Me (That's How I Will Be)
Side 2 (Jean Chapel)
Welcome to the Club
I Won't Be Rockin' Tonight

DJ-56 (Elvis Presley / Dinah Shore)

❑ RCA Victor DJ-56 (47-6800/
47-6792) 12/56   150-200
DISC 1: White label. Promotional issue only.

G2NH-9644-1S/G2NH-9645-1S
COVER 1: None made.

RCA Victor DJ-56 (47-6800/
47-6792) 12/56   150-200
TOTAL PACKAGE 1: Disc.

Side 1 (Elvis Presley)
Too Much
Playing for Keeps
Side 2 (Dinah Shore)
Chantez-Chantez
Honkytonk Heart

DEALERS' PREVUE
Various artists collection

❑ RCA Victor SDS-7-2 .... 6/57   800-1000
DISC 1: White label. Promotional issue only.
H2NH-4361-1S/H2NH-4362-1.
Has eight tracks – two each by four different
artists, including *Loving You* and *(Let Me Be
Your) Teddy Bear* by Elvis.

❑ RCA Victor SDS-7-2 .... 10/57   1500-2000
MAILER 1: Paper envelope used to mail
SDS-7-2. Front: Black and white Elvis photo.
Reads: "Elvis Presley at His Greatest." The
only selection number shown on the mailer is
47/20-7000 (for 45 and 78 rpm singles of *(Let
Me Be Your) Teddy Bear / Loving You.*

RCA Victor SDS-7-2 .... 6/57   2300-3000
TOTAL PACKAGE 1: Disc, mailer.

Side 1
Loving You (Elvis Presley)
(Let Me Be Your) Teddy Bear (Elvis Presley)
Now Stop (Martha Carson)
Just Whistle Or Call (Martha Carson)
Side 2
The Wife (Lou Monte)
Musica Bella (Lou Monte)
Mailman, Bring Me No More Blues (Herb Jeffries)
So Shy (Herb Jeffries)

DEALERS' PREVUE
Various artists collection

❑ RCA Victor SDS-57-39 .... 10/57   800-1000
DISC 1: White label. Promotional issue only.
H2NH-6567-1S/H2NH-6568.

❑ RCA Victor SDS-57-39 .... 10/57   1500-2000
MAILER 1: Paper envelope used to mail
SDS-57-39.

RCA Victor
SDS-57-39 .... 10/57   2300-3000
TOTAL PACKAGE 1: Disc, mailer.

Side 1
The Old Rugged Cross (Stuart Hamblen)
Old Time Religion (Stuart Hamblen)
Jailhouse Rock (Elvis Presley)
Treat Me Nice (Elvis Presley)
Till the Last Leaf Shall Fall (Statesmen Quartet)
Every Hour and Every Day (Statesmen Quartet)

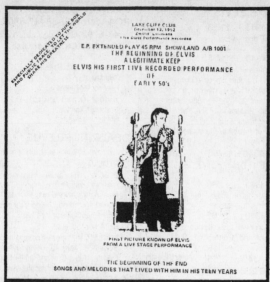

Side 2
A Slip of the Lip (Kathy Barr)
Welcome Mat (Kathy Barr)
Just Born (Perry Como)
Ivy Rose (Perry Como)
Sayonara (Eddie Fisher)
That's the Way It Goes (Eddie Fisher)

EASY COME, EASY GO

❏ RCA Victor EPA-4387 .... 2/67   25-30
DISC 1: Black label, dog on side.
UPKB-3811-4S/UPKB-3812-4S. Label EP#16.

❏ RCA Victor EPA-4387 .... 2/67   35-50
COVER 1: Front: Titles at right in black print
on yellow stock. RCA Victor logo at upper
right, number at upper left. Color Elvis (circa
1965) photo. Reads: "Ask for Elvis' 1967
Complete Full Color Catalog" at bottom. Back:
Black and white Elvis photo. Reads: "Ask for
Elvis' 1967 Complete Full Color Catalog" at
bottom.

RCA Victor EPA-4387 .... 2/67   60-80
TOTAL PACKAGE 1: Disc, cover.

❏ RCA Victor EPA-4387 .... 2/67   110-120
DISC 2: White label. Promotional issue only.
UPKB-3811-1S/UPKB-3812-2S. Condensed bold lettering.
Paramount Pictures credits at top.

❏ RCA Victor EPA-4387 .... 2/67   40-50
COVER 2: Front: Titles at right in black print
on yellow stock. RCA Victor logo at upper
right, number at upper left. Color Elvis (circa
1965) photo. Reads: "Ask for Elvis' 1967
Complete Full Color Catalog" at bottom. Back:
Black and white Elvis photo. Reads: "Ask for
Elvis' 1967 Complete Full Color Catalog" at
bottom.

RCA Victor EPA-4387 .... 2/67   150-170
TOTAL PACKAGE 2: Disc, cover.

❏ RCA Victor EPA-4387 .... 2/67   110-120
DISC 3: White label. Promotional issue only.
UPKB-3811-7S/UPKB-3812-7S. Normal bold lettering.
Paramount Pictures credits at bottom.

❏ RCA Victor EPA-4387 .... 2/67   40-50
COVER 3: Same as cover 2.

RCA Victor EPA-4387 .... 2/67   150-170
TOTAL PACKAGE 3: Disc, cover.

Side 1
Easy Come, Easy Go
The Love Machine
Yoga Is As Yoga Does
Side 2
You Gotta Shop
Sing You Children
I'll Take Love
This is the only standard catalog RCA Elvis
EP not reissued on the orange label.

ELVIS (VOLUME 1)

❏ RCA Victor EPA-992 .... 11/56   20-30
DISC 1: Black label, dog on top, without
horizontal silver line. Songwriting credits for
Paralyzed read: "Otis Blackwell – Elvis
Presley."

G2WH-7209-1S/G2WH-7210-1S. Label EP#4.

❏ RCA Victor EPA-992 .... 11/56   55-70
COVER 1: Front: Titles at top in white print on
black stock. RCA Victor logo and number at
upper right. Color Elvis photo. Back: Text only
– excerpted from the liner notes on LPM-
1382. Portion beginning "Of special note"
refers to the Jordanaires.

RCA Victor EPA-992 .... 11/56   75-100
TOTAL PACKAGE 1: Disc, cover.

❏ RCA Victor EPA-992 .... 11/56   30-40
DISC 2: Black label, dog on top, with
horizontal silver line. Songwriting credits for
Paralyzed show only "Otis Blackwell."
G2WH-7209-2S/G2WH-7210-2S. Label EP#1, with a little
extra space added between side number and "New
Orthophonic." Copies crediting only Otis Blackwell also exist
with label EP#3.

❏ RCA Victor EPA-992 .... 11/56   55-70
COVER 2: Same as cover 1.

RCA Victor EPA-992 .... 11/56   85-110
TOTAL PACKAGE 2: Disc, cover.

❏ RCA Victor EPA-992 .... 11/56   170-200
DISC 3: Black label, no dog on label, with
horizontal silver line.

❏ RCA Victor EPA-992 .... 11/56   55-70
COVER 3: Same as cover 1.

RCA Victor EPA-992 .... 11/56   225-270
TOTAL PACKAGE 3: Disc, cover.

❏ RCA Victor EPA-992 .... '65   20-30
DISC 4: Black label, dog on side.

❏ RCA Victor EPA-992 .... '65   65-70
COVER 4: Verification pending.

RCA Victor EPA-992 .... '65   85-100
TOTAL PACKAGE 4: Disc, cover.

❏ RCA Victor EPA-992 .... '68   50-65
DISC 5: Orange label.
G2WH-7209-5S/G2WH-7210-6S.

❏ RCA Victor EPA-992 .... '68   50-65
COVER 5: Front: RCA Victor logo at upper
right. *A "NEW ORTHOPHONIC" HIGH
FIDELITY RECORDING* below logo. Color
Elvis photo. EPA-992 and EPA-993 at lower
right in white border. *RCA printed in U.S.A* at
lower right of photo. Back: Text only –
excerpted from the liner notes on LPM-1382.
Portion beginning "Of special note" refers to
the Jordanaires."

RCA Victor EPA-992 .... '68   100-130
TOTAL PACKAGE 5: Disc, cover.

Side 1
Rip It Up
Love Me
Side 2
When My Blue Moon Turns to Gold Again
Paralyzed

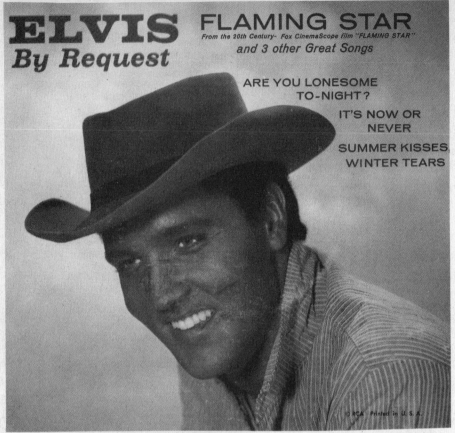

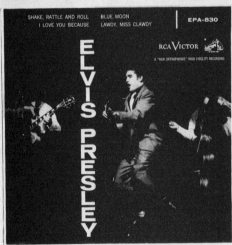

ELVIS (VOLUME 2)

❑ RCA Victor EPA-993 .... 11/56   20-30
  DISC 1: Black label, dog on top, without
  horizontal silver line.
  G2WH-7211-3S/G2WH-7212-3S. Label EP#3.

❑ RCA Victor EPA-993 .... 11/56   55-70
  COVER 1: Front: Titles at top in white print on
  black stock. RCA Victor logo and number at
  upper right. Color Elvis photo (same as on
  EPA-992). Back: Text only – excerpted from
  the liner notes on LPM-1382. Portion
  beginning "Of special interest" refers to Elvis
  playing piano on *Old Shep*.

RCA Victor EPA-993 .... 11/56   75-100
  TOTAL PACKAGE 1: Disc, cover.

❑ RCA Victor EPA-993 .... 11/56   30-40
  DISC 2: Black label, dog on top, with
  horizontal silver line.

❑ RCA Victor EPA-993 .... 11/56   55-70
  COVER 2: Same as cover 1.

RCA Victor EPA-993 .... 11/56   85-110
  TOTAL PACKAGE 2: Disc, cover.

❑ RCA Victor EPA-993 .... 11/56   170-200
  DISC 3: Black label, no dog on label, with
  horizontal silver line.
  G2WH-7211-2S-A1/G2WH-7212-2S. Label EP#1.

❑ RCA Victor EPA-993 .... 11/56   55-70
  COVER 3: Same as cover 1.

RCA Victor EPA-993 .... 11/56   225-270
  TOTAL PACKAGE 3: Disc, cover.

❑ RCA Victor EPA-993 .... '65   20-30
  DISC 4: Black label, dog on side.
  G2WH-7211-8S/G2WH-7212-8S. Label EP#14.

❑ RCA Victor EPA-993 .... '65   40-50
  COVER 4: Same as cover 1, except no titles
  are shown on front.

RCA Victor EPA-993 .... '65   60-80
  TOTAL PACKAGE 4: Disc, cover.

❑ RCA Victor EPA-993 .... '68   50-65
  DISC 5: Orange label.
  G2WH-7211-8S/G2WH-7212-8S.

❑ RCA Victor EPA-993 .... '68   50-65
  COVER 5: Verification pending.

RCA Victor EPA-993 .... '68   100-130
  TOTAL PACKAGE 5: Disc, cover.

  Side 1
  So Glad You're Mine
  Old Shep
  Side 2
  Reddy Teddy
  Anyplace Is Paradise

ELVIS (VOLUME 3): see *STRICTLY ELVIS*

ELVIS / JAYE P. MORGAN (2 EPs)

Two-EP, promotional sampler, though the
discs were standard commercial pressings.
This package was made to encourage retail
stores to establish themselves in the
music/record business. The idea of the
Elvis/Jaye P. Morgan coupling was both to
emphasize that the Elvis EP (EPA-992) sold
1,000 times better than the Jaye P. Morgan
EP (EPA-689) and that record and
phonograph sales were on the rise.

❑ RCA Victor EPA-992 .... 12/56   40-50
  DISC 1A: Black label, dog on top, without
  horizontal silver line. Songwriting credits for
  Paralyzed read: "Otis Blackwell – Elvis
  Presley."
  G2WH-7209-5S/G2WH-7210-1S. Label EP#4. This is
  definitely the original pressing included with this EP and is
  not just a random copy of EPA-992 used to fill the set.

❑ RCA Victor EPA-689 .... 12/56   10-20
  DISC 1B: Black label, dog on top
  F2PH-8325-1S/F2PH-8236-1S. Label EP#3.

❑ RCA Victor EPA-992/
  EPA-689 .... 12/56 8000-12000
  COVER 1: Double pocket jacket. Front: Titles
  are not printed anywhere. RCA Victor logo at
  upper right, numbers (for both EPs) at lower
  right. Color Elvis photo. Back: Color slick from
  Jaye P. Morgan EP. Both inside panels have
  the promotional pitch; however, at least two
  variations exist. One is imprinted for "Mr. L.F.
  Koranda, Associated Merchandising Corp,
  1440 Broadway, New York, New York." and
  another for "Mr. Walter H. Awe, Mutual Buying
  Syndicate, 11 West 42st Street, New York 36,
  New York." Other than the representative's
  imprint, all text is identical.

**RCA Victor EPA-992/
  689............................ 12/56 8000-12000**
  TOTAL PACKAGE 1: Discs, cover.

  Side 1
  Rip It Up
  Love Me
  Side 2
  When My Blue Moon Turns to Gold Again
  Paralyzed

ELVIS BY REQUEST (FLAMING STAR AND 3 OTHER GREAT SONGS)

❑ RCA Victor LPC-128.......... 1/61   40-50
  DISC 1: Compact 33 Double.
  M2PQ-1972-1S/M2PQ-1973-1S. Has LP-size (¼-inch) hole.

❑ RCA Victor LPC-128.......... 1/61   40-50
  COVER 1: Front: Titles at right in red print on
  blue stock. RCA Victor logo and number at
  upper right. Color Elvis photo. Back: Text
  only.

RCA Victor LPC-128....... 1/61   80-100
  TOTAL PACKAGE 1: Disc, cover.

Side 1
Flaming Star
Summer Kisses, Winter Tears

Side 2
Are You Lonesome Tonight
It's Now or Never
This is the only Elvis Compact 33 Double
made by RCA in the U.S.A.

ELVIS INTERVIEWS
❑ Arch 001 .... '70s   10-15

ELVIS – MY LIFE
❑ Memphis Flash 92444 .... '78   50-75
Two 7" picture discs in gatefold, die-cut cover.
Spoken word content from interviews, etc.
"Collector Series" number on front cover.
Reportedly 3,000 made.

ELVIS PRESLEY
❑ RCA Victor EPA-747 .... 3/56   20-30
DISC 1: Black label, dog on top, without
horizontal silver line. The disc originally
shipped in the temporary paper sleeve (cover
1) was on a label without the horizontal line.
G2WH-1854-7S/G2WH-1855-7S. Label EP#4.
❑ RCA Victor EPA-747 .... 3/56   1000-1800
COVER 1: Temporary paper envelope/sleeve.
Used until standard EP covers were available.
Paper stock is white, with dark blue print.
❑ RCA Victor EPA-747 .... 3/56   3-5
INSERT 1: Typed note of explanation to
retailers regarding the use of temporary
sleeves. Value is minimal since we know of no
way to distinguish an original from
photocopies.

RCA Victor EPA-747 ...... 3/56   1000-1800
    **TOTAL PACKAGE 1: Disc, paper cover,
    insert.**

Counterfeit Identification: One fake exists
with black print, instead of blue. Another found
is printed on gray paper instead of white and
is therefore easy to identify. On this sleeve
the printed area is much smaller than on
originals.
❑ RCA Victor EPA-747 .... 3/56   20-30
DISC 2A: Black label, dog on top, without
horizontal silver line.
❑ RCA Victor EPA-747 .... 3/56   80-95
COVER 2: This disc may be found in any of
the covers shown as 2A through 2E,
individually described below.

RCA Victor EPA-747 ...... 3/56   100-125
    TOTAL PACKAGE 2A: Disc, cover.

❑ RCA Victor EPA-747 .... 3/56   30-40
DISC 2B: Black label, dog on top, with
horizontal silver line.
❑ RCA Victor EPA-747 .... 3/56   80-95
COVER 2: This disc may be found in any of
the covers shown as 2A through 2E,
individually described below.

RCA Victor EPA-747 ...... 3/56   110-135
    TOTAL PACKAGE 2B: Disc, cover.

❑ RCA Victor EPA-747 .... 3/56   170-200
DISC 2C: Black label, no dog on label, with
horizontal silver line.
❑ RCA Victor EPA-747 .... 3/56   80-95
COVER 2: This disc may be found in any of
the covers shown as 2A through 2E,
individually described below.

RCA Victor EPA-747 ...... 3/56   250-300
    TOTAL PACKAGE 2C: Disc, cover.

❑ RCA Victor EPA-747 .... 3/56   80-95
COVER 2A: Front: Titles at top in black print
on white stock. RCA Victor logo and number
at upper right. "ELVIS" is in dark pink letters.
Black and white Elvis photo. Same basic
cover as on LPM-1254. Back: Color pictures
of (clockwise): *I Love You (Eddie Fisher)*;
*Como's Golden Records; Dinah Shore Sings
the Blues; Mark Twain; That Bad Eartha.*
❑ RCA Victor EPA-747 .... 3/56   80-95
COVER 2B: Same as cover 2A, except back
pictures (clockwise): *Collaboration; Inside
Sauter-Finegan; East Coast, West Coast
Scene; Jazz for People Who Hate Jazz; Louis
Armstrong Sings the Blues.*
❑ RCA Victor EPA-747 .... 3/56   80-95
COVER 2C: Same as cover 2A, except back
pictures (clockwise): *Soft and Sweet; Sax in
Silk; Music for Two People Alone; Passion in
Pink; Music By Starlight.*
❑ RCA Victor EPA-747 .... 3/56   80-95
COVER 2D: Same as cover 2A, except back
has a black and white Elvis photo, and the
same text as used on the back of EPA-830,
Elvis Presley. No other RCA releases are
pictured.
❑ RCA Victor EPA-747 .... 3/56   80-95
COVER 2E: Same as cover 2A, except back
has only the text, as found on the back of
EPA-830, *Elvis Presley.* Discs 2A through 2C
may be found in any of the covers shown as
2A through 2E.
❑ RCA Victor EPA-747 :.......... '65   20-30
DISC 4: Black label, dog on side.
❑ RCA Victor EPA-747 .... '65   40-50
COVER 4: Verification pending.

RCA Victor EPA-747 .... '65   60-80
    TOTAL PACKAGE 4: Disc, cover.

❑ RCA Victor EPA-747 .... '68   50-65
DISC 5: Orange label.
G2WH-1854-7S/G2WH-1855-7S.
❑ RCA Victor EPA-747 .... '68   50-65
COVER 5: Front: Same as cover 1, except no
titles are shown. Back: Text only. Area where
other RCA releases are pictured on cover 1 is
left blank.

RCA Victor EPA-747 .... '68   100-130
    TOTAL PACKAGE 5: Disc, cover.

Side 1
Blue Suede Shoes
Tutti Frutti
Side 2
I Got a Woman
Just Because

ELVIS PRESLEY (2 EPs)

❑ RCA Victor EPB-1254 .... 4/56   20-30
  DISCS 1A: Black label, dog on top, without horizontal silver line.
  Disc 1 (Side 1) G2WH-1850-5S/(Side 4) G2WH-1853-5S. Label is EP#5 style, with an extra line of identification numbers added on left side.
  Disc 2 (Side 2) G2WH-1851-5S/(Side 3) G2WH-1852-5S. Label is EP#5 style, with an extra line of identification numbers added on left side.
  Disc 1 (Side 1) G2WH-1850-6S/(Side 4) G2WH-1853-6S. Label is EP#5 style, with an extra line of identification numbers added on left side.
  Disc 2 (Side 2) G2WH-1851-6S/(Side 3) G2WH-1852-6S. Label is EP#5 style, with an extra line of identification numbers added on left side.

❑ RCA Victor EPB-1254 .... 4/56   250-350
  COVER 1: For variations see COVERS 1A through 1C, individually described below.

RCA Victor EPB-1254 .... 4/56   300-400
  TOTAL PACKAGE 1A: Discs, cover.

❑ RCA Victor EPB-1254 .... 4/56   30-40
  DISCS 1B: Black label, dog on top, with horizontal silver line.
  Disc 1 (Side 1) G2WH-1850-7S/(Side 4) G2WH-1853-7S. Label is EP#2 style, with an extra line of identification numbers and side number above "New Orthophonic" instead of below.
  Disc 2 (Side 2) G2WH-1851-7S/(Side 3) G2WH-1852-7S. Label is EP#2 style, with an extra line of identification numbers and side number above "New Orthophonic" instead of below.
  Disc 1 (Side 1) G2WH-1850-8S/(Side 4) G2WH-1853-8S. Label is EP#2 style, with an extra line of identification numbers and side number above "New Orthophonic" instead of below.
  Disc 2 (Side 2) G2WH-1851-8S/(Side 3) G2WH-1852-8S. Label is EP#2 style, with an extra line of identification numbers and side number above "New Orthophonic" instead of below.

❑ RCA Victor EPB-1254 .... 4/56   250-350
  COVER 1: For variations see COVERS 1A through 1C, individually described below.

RCA Victor EPB-1254 .... 4/56   325-425
  TOTAL PACKAGE 1B: Discs, cover.

❑ RCA Victor EPB-1254 .... 4/56   170-200
  DISCS 1C: Black label, no dog on label, with horizontal silver line.

❑ RCA Victor EPB-1254 .... 4/56   250-350
  COVER 1: For variations see COVERS 1A through 1C, individually described below.

RCA Victor EPB-1254 .... 4/56   425-550
  TOTAL PACKAGE 1B: Discs, cover.

❑ RCA Victor EPB-1254 .... 4/56   250-350
  COVER 1A: Titles at top in black print on white stock. RCA Victor logo and number at upper right. Same basic cover as on LPM-1254. Back: Color pictures of (clockwise): *Beautiful Garden of Prayer; Gone with the Wind; Mambo By the King; Fox Trots; Music for Relaxation*. Has paragraph regarding: "For best reproduction, RCA Victor records should be played with the R.I.A.A. or 'New Orthophonic' curve adjustment, etc." Inside front panel: Titles and black and white Elvis photo. Inside back panel: Text only.

❑ RCA Victor EPB-1254 .... 4/56   250-350
  COVER 1B: Same as cover 1A, except pictures (clockwise): *Waltzes; Sunday Band Concert; Inside Sauter-Finegan; Glenn Miller; Music for Dining*. Has paragraph regarding: "For best reproduction, RCA Victor records should be played with the R.I.A.A. or 'New Orthophonic' curve adjustment, etc."

❑ RCA Victor EPB-1254 .... 4/56   250-350
  COVER 1C: Same as cover 1A, except back cover pictures (clockwise): *With Love from a Chorus; Victory at Sea; The Student Prince (Mario Lanza); Rhapsody in Blue; The Family All Together (Boston Pops)*. Has paragraph regarding: "For best reproduction, RCA Victor records should be played with the R.I.A.A. or 'New Orthophonic' curve adjustment, etc." Discs 1A and 1B may be found in any of the covers shown as 1A through 1C.

❑ RCA Victor EPB-1254 .... 4/56   20-30
  DISCS 2: Same as discs 1A.

❑ RCA Victor EPB-1254 .... 4/56   30-40
  DISCS 3: Same as discs 1B.

❑ RCA Victor EPB-1254 .... '56   200-300
  COVER 2: Front: Titles at top in black print on white stock. RCA Victor logo and number at upper right. Same basic cover as on LPM-1254. Back: Black and white Elvis photo. Does not picture other RCA releases and does not have paragraph about "For best reproduction, RCA Victor records should be played with the R.I.A.A. or 'New Orthophonic' curve adjustment, etc." This cover mistakenly reverses the contents of sides 2 and 3, as follows:

Side 1
Blue Suede Shoes
I'm Counting on You
Side 2
Tutti Frutti
Tryin' to Get to You
Side 3
I Got a Woman
One Sided Love Affair
Side 4
I'm Gonna Sit Right Down and Cry (Over You)
I'll Never Let You Go

Though the titles are wrong on the back cover, they are listed correctly on the inside front panel. We have yet to learn of a copy of this EP with the titles either listed wrong on the labels, or pressed wrong. This cover came with either set of Discs 2 or 3.

RCA Victor EPB-1254 ...... '56   325-450
TOTAL PACKAGE 2: Discs, cover.

Counterfeit Identification: Fake discs have engraved identification numbers. Originals have those numbers stamped in the vinyl. Any copy on a white label is a fake. Counterfeit covers exist, but the reproduction of the black and white Elvis photo is noticeably grainy. On originals, the photo is sharp and clear.

Side 1
Blue Suede Shoes
I'm Counting on You

Side 2
I Got a Woman
One Sided Love Affair

Side 3
Tutti Frutti
Tryin' to Get to You

Side 4
I'm Gonna Sit Right Down and Cry (Over You)
I'll Never Let You Go (Little Darlin')

ELVIS PRESLEY (2 EPs)

❑ RCA Victor SPD-22 .... 10/56   500-750
DISCS 1: Black label, dog on top, with horizontal silver line. Double EP, given as a bonus to buyers of a $32.95 Victrola.
Disc 1 (Side 1) G2WH-1850-8S/(Side 4) G2WH-1852-9S. Label is EP#2 style, with an extra line of identification numbers and side number above "New Orthophonic" instead of below.
Disc 2 (Side 2) G2WH-1851-9S/(Side 3) G2WH-1853-8S. Label is EP#2 style, with an extra line of identification numbers and side number above "New Orthophonic" instead of below.

❑ RCA Victor SPD-22 .... 10/56   1500-1750
COVER 1: Double pocket jacket. Titles at top in black print on white stock. RCA Victor logo and number at upper right. "ELVIS" is in dark pink letters. Back: Text only – same basic notes as on the back of EPA-992, minus the "Of special note" portion. Inside panels are blank.

RCA Victor SPD-22 ...... 10/56   2000-2500
TOTAL PACKAGE 1: Discs, cover.

❑ RCA Victor SPD-22 .... 10/56   500-750
DISCS 2: Same as discs 1.
❑ RCA Victor SPD-22 .... 10/56   1500-1750
COVER 2: Same as cover 1, except "ELVIS" is in light pink letters.

RCA Victor SPD-22 ...... 10/56   2000-2500
TOTAL PACKAGE 2: Discs, cover.

Side 1
Blue Suede Shoes
I'm Counting on You

Side 2
I Got a Woman
One Sided Love Affair

Side 3
I'm Gonna Sit Right Down and Cry (Over You)
I'll Never Let You Go

Side 4
Tutti Frutti
Tryin' to Get to You

ELVIS PRESLEY (3 EPs)

❑ RCA Victor SPD-23 .... 10/56   1200-1600
DISCS 1: Black label, dog on top. Triple EP, given as a bonus to buyers of a $47.95 Victrola.
Disc 1 (Side 1) G2WH-1850-8S/(Side 6) G2WH-6137-2S. Label is EP#2 style, with an extra line of identification numbers and side number above "New Orthophonic" instead of below.
Disc 2 (Side 3) G2WH-1853-8S/(Side 4) G2WH-1852-8S. Label is EP#2 style, with an extra line of identification numbers and side number above "New Orthophonic" instead of below.
Disc 3 (Side 2) G2WH-1851-9S/(Side 5) G2WH-6136-2S. Label is EP#2 style, with an extra line of identification numbers and side number above "New Orthophonic" instead of below.

❑ RCA Victor SPD-23 .... 10/56   2200-2800
COVER 1: Triple pocket jacket. Titles at top in black print on white stock. RCA Victor logo and number at upper right. "ELVIS" is in light pink letters. Back: Text only – same basic notes as on the back of EPA-992, minus the "Of special note" portion. Inside panels are blank.

❑ RCA Victor SPD-23 .... 10/56   75-100
INSERT 1: Six-page brochure titled "How to Use and Enjoy Your RCA Victor Elvis Presley Autograph, Automatic 45 Victrola Portable Phonograph." Supplied to buyers of the $47.95 Victrola.

RCA Victor SPD-23 ...... 10/56   3500-4500
TOTAL PACKAGE 1: Discs, cover, insert.

Side 1
Blue Suede Shoes
I'm Counting on You

Side 2
I Got a Woman
One Sided Love Affair

Side 3
I'm Gonna Sit Right Down and Cry (Over You)
I'll Never Let You Go

Side 4
Tutti Frutti
Tryin' to Get to You

Side 5
Don't Be Cruel
I Want You, I Need You, I Love You

Side 6
Hound Dog
My Baby Left Me

ELVIS PRESLEY

❑ RCA Victor EPA-830 ....9/56   20-30
DISC 1: Black label, dog on top, without horizontal silver line.

❑ RCA Victor EPA-830 ....9/56   80-95
COVER 1: Front: Titles at top in white print on black stock. RCA Victor logo and number at upper right. Back: Black and white Elvis photo, same as on the back of EPB-1254, cover 2A.

RCA Victor EPA-830 ......9/56   100-125
TOTAL PACKAGE 1: Disc, cover.

❑ RCA Victor EPA-830 ....9/56   30-40
DISC 2: Black label, dog on top, with horizontal silver line.
G2WH-3462-2S/G2WH-3463-2S. Label EP#2L.

❑ RCA Victor EPA-830 ....9/56   80-95
COVER 2: Same as cover 1.

RCA Victor EPA-830 ......9/56   110-135
TOTAL PACKAGE 2: Disc, cover.

❑ RCA Victor EPA-830 ....9/56   170-200
DISC 3: Black label, no dog on label, with horizontal silver line.
G2WH-3462-2S/G2WH-3463-2S. Label EP#11.

❑ RCA Victor EPA-830 ....9/56   80-95
COVER 3: Same as cover 1.

RCA Victor EPA-830 ......9/56   250-300
TOTAL PACKAGE 3: Disc, cover.

❑ RCA Victor EPA-830 ....'65   20-30
DISC 4: Black label, dog on side.

❑ RCA Victor EPA-830 ....'65   60-70
COVER 4: Verification pending.

RCA Victor EPA-830 ....'65   80-100
TOTAL PACKAGE 4: Disc, cover.

❑ RCA Victor EPA-830 ....'68   50-65
DISC 5: Orange label.
G2WH-3462-8S/G2WH-3463-13S

❑ RCA Victor EPA-830 ....'68   50-65
COVER 5: Verification pending.

RCA Victor EPA-830 ....'68   100-130
TOTAL PACKAGE 5: Disc, cover.

Side 1
Shake, Rattle and Roll
I Love You Because
Side 2
Blue Moon
Lawdy, Miss Clawdy

ELVIS PRESLEY

❑ Rockin' 45-001: Bootleg. Listed for identification only.

ELVIS PRESLEY LIVE ON THE LOUISIANA HAYRIDE

❑ Rockin' 45-006: Bootleg. Listed for identification only.

ELVIS PRESLEY STORY: see Singles

ELVIS REMEMBERED / (Frank Sinatra – Nat King Cole)

❑ Creative Radio Shows ....'79   40-50
DISC 1: Sales demonstration disc for a three-hour Elvis radio program. Side two is a demo for shows about Frank Sinatra and Nat King Cole. Promotional issue only.
816/DL-40. Has LP-size (¼-inch) hole.
COVER 1: None made.

Creative Radio Shows .....'79   40-50
TOTAL PACKAGE 1: Disc.

ELVIS SAILS

❑ RCA Victor EPA-4325 .....10/58   25-55
DISC 1: Black label, dog on top.
L2PH-7305-1S/L2PH-7306-1S. Label is #5, with time added to left and publishing house shown on right side.

❑ RCA Victor EPA-4325 .....10/58   75-95
COVER 1: Front: RCA Victor logo and number at upper right. Black and white Elvis photo. Back: Cover is "Elvis' 1959 Calendar." Has five color Elvis photos. Cover has a hole punched at top-center, suitable for hanging.

RCA Victor EPA-4325 ..10/58   100-150
TOTAL PACKAGE 1: Disc, cover.

❑ RCA Victor EPA-4325 .....10/58   25-30
DISC 2: Same as disc 1.

❑ RCA Victor EPA-4325 .....10/58   75-95
COVER 2: Same as cover 1, except printing is done directly on the cover stock, not on a slick.
Counterfeit Identification: Fake discs have identification numbers engraved. Originals have those number stamped in the vinyl. Fake covers do not have the hole at top center, for hanging the calendar.

RCA Victor EPA-4325 ..10/58   100-125
TOTAL PACKAGE 2: Disc, cover.

❑ RCA Victor EPA-5157 ....4/65   25-35
DISC 3: Black label, dog on top.
L2PH-7305-6S/L2PH-7306-6S. Unlike 1958 pressings, which have "45 EP" on label, this has "45 RPM" on both sides – identical to many of the dog on top Gold Standard singles.

❑ RCA Victor EPA-5157 ....4/65   50-65
COVER 3: Front: RCA Victor logo, Gold Standard Series logo, and number at upper right. Has "Re-released by popular request for your collection" at upper left. Black and white Elvis photo. Back: Pictures four other Elvis RCA EPs, and lists another 20. Reads: "Now Available 'Crying in the Chapel' on 45 rpm Single" at bottom.

RCA Victor EPA-5157 ....4/65   75-100
TOTAL PACKAGE 3: Disc, cover.

ELVIS SINGS CHRISTMAS SONGS
Santa Bring My Baby Back (To Me) · Blue Christmas
Santa Claus Is Back in Town · I'll Be Home for Christmas

❏ RCA Victor EPA-5157 .... '68   75-100
DISC 4: Orange label.
L2PH-7305-8S/L2PH-7306-8S.

❏ RCA Victor EPA-5157 .... '68   75-100
COVER 4: Verification pending.

RCA Victor EPA-5157 ...... '68   150-200
TOTAL PACKAGE 4: Disc, cover.

On all Gold Standard EPs, the term "Gold Standard" appears only on covers – not on labels.

Side 1
Press Interview with Elvis Presley

Side 2
Elvis Presley's Newsreel Interview
Pat Hernon Interviews Elvis in the Library of the U.S.S. Randall at Sailing

ELVIS SINGS CHRISTMAS SONGS

❏ RCA Victor EPA-4108 ..... 11/57   25-30
DISC 1: Black label, dog on top.
H2PH-6528-10S/H2PH-6529-6S. Label EP#5.
H2PH-6528-17S/H2PH-6529-15S. Label EP#9.

❏ RCA Victor EPA-4108 ..... 11/57   50-70
COVER 1: Front: Titles at top in black print on white stock. RCA Victor logo and number at upper left. Below titles. Has "45 EP Economy Package," the earliest Elvis EP so designated. Color Elvis photo (same basic cover as LOC-1035). Back: Two black and white Elvis photos.

RCA Victor EPA-4108 .. 11/57   75-100
TOTAL PACKAGE 1: Disc, cover.

❏ RCA Victor EPA-4108 .... '65   20-30
DISC 2: Black label, dog on side.
H2PH-6528-21S/H2PH-6529-18S.

❏ RCA Victor EPA-4108 .... '65   40-50
COVER 2: Verification pending.

RCA Victor EPA-4108 ...... '65   60-80
TOTAL PACKAGE 2: Disc, cover.

❏ RCA Victor EPA-4108 .... '68   75-100
DISC 3: Orange label.
H2PH-6528-18S/H2PH-6529-21S.

❏ RCA Victor EPA-4108 .... '68   75-100
COVER 3: Verification pending.

RCA Victor EPA-4108 ...... '68   150-200
TOTAL PACKAGE 3: Disc, cover.

Side 1
Santa Bring My Baby Back (To Me)
Blue Christmas

Side 2
Santa Claus Is Back in Town
I'll Be Home for Christmas

ELVIS: SIX HOUR SPECIAL / Jamboree USA / Listen!

❏ Eva-Tone
10287733BX 11/77   15-20
Black vinyl. 33 rpm, 6 ¾", square soundsheet. From the Chicago Radio Syndicate to promote their six-hour Elvis broadcast. No label used – print is on the plastic. *Jamboree USA* (actually the first track) is another radio feature. The flip side, *Listen!*, is also a promotional message.
EV-A-10287733BXT/EV-A-10287733AXT. Identification numbers are engraved.

FLAMING STAR: see *ELVIS BY REQUEST*

FOLLOW THAT DREAM

❏ RCA Victor EPA-4368 .... 5/62   30-35
DISC 1: Black label, dog on top. Song titles are not accompanied by playing times.

❏ RCA Victor EPA-4368 .... 5/62   30-40
COVER 1: Front: No titles shown. RCA Victor logo and number at upper right. Color Elvis photo. Back: Four black and white Elvis photos. Reads: "Coming Soon, Elvis' New LP, POT LUCK. Watch for It!" at bottom. Playing times are incorrectly listed for three of the four tracks: *Follow That Dream,* shown as 1:35, should be 1:38; *Angel,* shown as 2:35, should be 2:40; and *I'm Not the Marrying Kind,* shown as 1:49, should be 2:00.

RCA Victor EPA-4368 .... 5/62   60-75
TOTAL PACKAGE 1: Disc, cover.

❏ RCA Victor EPA-4368 .... 5/62   50-75
DISC 2: Black label, dog on top. Each song title is followed by its correct playing time. Though there is no mention on the label of this being the "Coin Operator / DJ Prevue" disc, the addition of the playing times (for dee jay use) support that theory.
N2PH-1603-5S/N2PH-1604-6S. Label EP#3.

❏ RCA Victor EPA-4368 .... 5/62   150-225
COVER 2: Paper sleeve. Reads: "Coin Operator / DJ Prevue" at top. White stock with red print. Back is blank.
Counterfeit Identification: Fakes can be identified by their black print. Print on originals is red.

RCA Victor EPA-4368 .... 5/62   200-300
TOTAL PACKAGE 2: Disc, cover.

❏ RCA Victor EPA-4368 .... '65   20-30
DISC 3: Black label, dog on side.
❏ RCA Victor EPA-4368 .... '65   40-50
COVER 3: Same as cover 1, except playing times are correct.

RCA Victor EPA-4368 ...... '65   60-80
TOTAL PACKAGE 3: Disc, cover.

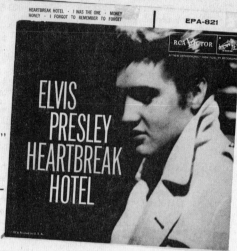

COIN OPERATOR   DJ PREVUE
EPA 4368

ELVIS
SINGS

FOUR GREAT SONGS

Side 1 Follow That Dream (1:38 ASCAP)
        Angel (2:40 ASCAP)
Side 2 What A Wonderful Life (2:28 ASCAP)
        I'm Not The Marrying Kind (2:00 ASCAP)

FROM HIS NEW MOVIE

"FOLLOW THAT DREAM"

AVAILABLE NOW ONLY ON 45 EP

HEARTBREAK HOTEL · I WAS THE ONE · MONEY
HONEY · I FORGOT TO REMEMBER TO FORGET

EPA-821

RCA VICTOR

ELVIS
PRESLEY
HEARTBREAK
HOTEL

Eddy Arnold · Chet Atkins
Jim Edward, Maxine and Bonnie Brown
Homer and Jethro · Johnnie and Jack · Pee Wee King
Elvis Presley · Jim Reeves · Hank Snow
Sons of the Pioneers · Porter Wagoner · Del Wood

GREAT COUNTRY/WESTERN HITS

RCA VICTOR

SPD-26
SIDE 6
599-9141
(H2WH-1996)

45 EP
"NEW ORTHOPHONIC"
HIGH FIDELITY

1—BLUE MOON OF KENTUCKY (Bill Monroe)
2—LOVE ME TENDER (from the 20th Century-Fo
CinemaScope production "Love Me Tender")
(Elvis Presley-Vera Matson)

Elvis Presley

❏ RCA Victor EPA-4368 .... '68   50-65
DISC 4: Orange label.
N2PH-1603-7S/N2PH-1604-8S.

❏ RCA Victor EPA-4368 .... '68   50-65
COVER 4: Same as cover 1, except playing
times are correct, and a tiny "2" is at lower left
on back.

RCA Victor EPA-4368 ...... '68   100-130
TOTAL PACKAGE 4: Disc, cover.

Side 1
Follow That Dream
Angel
Side 2
What a Wonderful Life
I'm Not the Marrying Kind

GOOD ROCKIN' TONIGHT

❏ Sun EP-101: Bootleg. Listed for identification
only.

GREAT COUNTRY / WESTERN HITS (10 EPs)

Various artists collection

❏ RCA Victor SPD-26/
599-9141 .... 11/56   350-750
DISCS 1: Black labels, dog on top. Boxed set
of 10 black label extended plays. Includes 10
printed paper separator inserts. Has one Elvis
EP, numbered 599-9141, representing sides 6
and 15 of 20. Elvis disc priced separately
below (disc 2).

❏ RCA Victor SPD-26 .... 11/56   800-1200
BOX 1: Textured brown, gold print on spine.
Front: Color photo of ranch scene. Back is
blank.

❏ RCA Victor 11/56   15-25
INSERTS 1: Includes an introductory Contrary
to Custom (Form 3K693) insert, plus two to
four copies of each of the following separator
inserts: "All-Time Pop Best Sellers," which
lists EPA-747, *Elvis Presley* (45 EP-POP-
Insert 1); "All-Time Red Seal Best Sellers" (45
EP-RS 1); and "New Orthophonic High
Fidelity Albums" (45 EP-RS-Insert 2), for a
total of 10 inserts.

RCA Victor SPD-26 ...... 11/56   1200-2000
TOTAL PACKAGE 1: Discs, box, inserts.

❏ RCA Victor SPD-26/
599-9141 .... 11/56   300-400
DISC 2: Black label, dog on top. Price for just
the Elvis EP from the SPD-26 boxed set.
H2WH-1996-1S/H2WH-1997-1S. Label is #5, but with an
extra line of identification numbers added on left side.

**RCA Victor SPD-26/
599-9141 .... 11/56   300-400**
TOTAL PACKAGE 2: Disc.

Side 6
Blue Moon of Kentucky
Love Me Tender
Side 15
Mystery Train

Milkcow Blues Boogie (shown as "Milkcow Boogie
Blues")

HEARTBREAK HOTEL

❏ RCA Victor EPA-821 .... 4/56   20-30
DISC 1: Black label, dog on top, without
horizontal silver line.
G2PH-2942-1S/G2PH-2943-10S. Label EP#4.

❏ RCA Victor EPA-821 .... 4/56   80-95
COVER 1: Front: Titles at top in black print on
white stock. RCA Victor logo and number at
upper right. Duotone Elvis photo. Back: Black
and white Elvis photo.

RCA Victor EPA-821 ...... 4/56   100-125
TOTAL PACKAGE 1: Disc, cover.

❏ RCA Victor EPA-821 .... 4/56   30-40
DISC 2: Black label, dog on top, with
horizontal silver line.
G2PH-2942-5S/G2PH-2943-5S. Label EP#1.

❏ RCA Victor EPA-821 .... 4/56   80-95
COVER 2: Same as cover 1.

RCA Victor EPA-821 ...... 4/56   110-135
TOTAL PACKAGE 2: Disc, cover.

❏ RCA Victor EPA-821 .... 4/56   170-200
DISC 3: Black label, no dog on label, with
horizontal silver line.
G2PH-2942-3S/G2PH-2943-3S. Label EP#11.

❏ RCA Victor EPA-821 .... 4/56   80-95
COVER 3: Same as cover 1.

RCA Victor EPA-821 ...... 4/56   250-300
TOTAL PACKAGE 3: Disc, cover.

❏ RCA Victor EPA-821 .... '65   20-30
DISC 4: Black label, dog on side.

❏ RCA Victor EPA-821 .... '65   40-50
COVER 4: Verification pending.

RCA Victor EPA-821 .... '65   60-80
TOTAL PACKAGE 4: Disc, cover.

❏ RCA Victor EPA-821 .... '68   50-65
DISC 5: Orange label.
G2PH-2942-9S/G2PH-2943-10S.

❏ RCA Victor EPA-821 .... '68   50-65
COVER 5: Same as cover 1, except no titles
are shown on front.

RCA Victor EPA-821 .... '68   100-130
TOTAL PACKAGE 5: Disc, cover.

Side 1
Heartbreak Hotel
I Was the One
Side 2
Money Honey
I Forgot to Remember to Forget

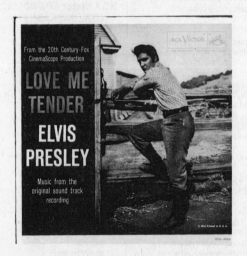

HEARTBREAK HOTEL / I WAS THE ONE

❏ RCA/BMG 07863
64476-7 .... '96   3-5
DISC 1: Colored vinyl. White label with red print.
❏ RCA/BMG 07863
64476-7 .... '96   3-5
COVER 1: Front: Title at top right. 1956 Elvis photo. Back: Titles at left. Different '56 Elvis photo than on front.
RCA/BMG 07863
64476-7.......................... '96   6-10
TOTAL PACKAGE 1: Disc, cover.

Side 1
Heartbreak Hotel
I Was the One
Side 2
Heartbreak Hotel (Alternate take 5 – Previously Unreleased)
I Was the One (Alternate take 2 – Previously Unreleased)

I'M LEAVING IT UP TO YOU

❏ Vegas 45002: Bootleg. Listed for identification only.

HILLBILLY CAT

❏ Rockin' 002: Bootleg. Listed for identification only.

JAILHOUSE ROCK

❏ Pelvis EP-2001: Bootleg. Listed for identification only.

JAILHOUSE ROCK

❏ RCA Victor EPA-4114 ..... 10/57   25-30
DISC 1: Black label, dog on top.
H2WH-6537-4S/H2WH-6538-4S. Label EP#10.
❏ RCA Victor EPA-4114 ..... 10/57   50-70
COVER 1: Front: Titles at right in white print on burgandy stock. RCA Victor logo and "45 EP Economy Package" at upper right, number at upper left. Color Elvis photo. At upper left is "An Original Soundtrack Recording" in a film strip rectangle – the first Elvis EP so marked. This was not used again until 1962, on *Follow That Dream*. Back: Black and white Elvis photo.
RCA Victor EPA-4114 .. 10/57   75-100
TOTAL PACKAGE 1: Disc, cover.

❏ RCA Victor EPA-4114 .... '65   20-30
DISC 2: Black label, dog on side.
❏ RCA Victor EPA-4114 .... '65   40-50
COVER 2: Same as cover 1.
RCA Victor EPA-4114 ...... '65   60-80
TOTAL PACKAGE 2: Disc, cover.

❏ RCA Victor EPA-4114 .... '68   50-65
DISC 3: Orange label.
H2WH-6537-9S/H2WH-6538-9S.
H2WH-6537-9S/H2WH-6538-10S.
❏ RCA Victor EPA-4114 .... '68   50-65
COVER 3: Same as cover 1.
RCA Victor EPA-4114 ...... '68   100-130
TOTAL PACKAGE 3: Disc, cover.

Side 1
Jailhouse Rock
Young and Beautiful

Side 2
I Want to Be Free
Don't Leave Me Now
(You're So Square) Baby I Don't Care

JUST FOR YOU (ELVIS PRESLEY)

❏ RCA Victor EPA-4041 .... 3/57   20-30
DISC 1: Black label, dog on top, without horizontal silver line.
H2WH-4127-5S/H2WH-4128-7S. Label EP#3.
❏ RCA Victor EPA-4041 .... 3/57   80-95
COVER 1: EP Front: Title at top, black print, white stock. RCA Victor logo and number at upper right. No song titles shown. Color Elvis photo. Back: Text only. Lists 25 other RCA EPs, including EPA-4006 (*Love Me Tender*).
RCA Victor EPA-4041 .... 3/57   100-125
TOTAL PACKAGE 1: Disc, cover.

❏ RCA Victor EPA-4041 .... 3/57   30-40
DISC 2: Black label, dog on top, with horizontal silver line.
❏ RCA Victor EPA-4041 .... 3/57   80-95
COVER 2: Same as cover 1.
RCA Victor EPA-4041 .... 3/57   110-135
TOTAL PACKAGE 2: Disc, cover.

❏ RCA Victor EPA-4041 .... 3/57   170-200
DISC 3: Black label, no dog on label, with horizontal silver line.
❏ RCA Victor EPA-4041 .... 3/57   80-95
COVER 3: Same as cover 1.
RCA Victor EPA-4041 .... 3/57   250-300
TOTAL PACKAGE 3: Disc, cover.

❏ RCA Victor EPA-4041 .... '65   20-30
DISC 4: Black label, dog on side.
H2WH-4127-9S/H2WH-4128-10S. Label EP#12, but without side numbers.
❏ RCA Victor EPA-4041 .... '65   40-50
COVER 4: Verification pending.
RCA Victor EPA-4041 ...... '65   60-80
TOTAL PACKAGE 4: Disc, cover.

❏ RCA Victor EPA-4041 .... '68   50-65
DISC 5: Orange label.
H2WH-4127-9S/H2WH-4128-9S.
❏ RCA Victor EPA-4041 .... '68   50-65
COVER 5: Verification pending.
RCA Victor EPA-4041 ...... '68   100-130
TOTAL PACKAGE 5: Disc, cover.

Side 1
I Need You So
Have I Told You Lately

Side 2
Blueberry Hill
Is It So Strange

KID GALAHAD

❑ RCA Victor EPA-4371 .... 9/62   25-30
DISC 1: Black label, dog on top.
N2PH-3137-5S/N2PH-3138-5S. Label EP#3.

❑ RCA Victor EPA-4371 .... 9/62   35-50
COVER 1: Front: Titles at right in black print
on beige stock. RCA Victor logo and number
at upper right. Color Elvis photo. Back: Three
black and white Elvis photos.

RCA Victor EPA-4371 .... 9/62   60-80
TOTAL PACKAGE 1: Disc, cover.

❑ RCA Victor EPA-4371 .... '65   15-20
DISC 2: Black label, dog on side.
N2PH-3137-6S/N2PH-3138-6S. Label EP#12.

❑ RCA Victor EPA-4371 .... '65   35-50
COVER 2: Same as cover 1.

RCA Victor EPA-4371 ...... '65   50-70
TOTAL PACKAGE 2: Disc, cover.

❑ RCA Victor EPA-4371 .... '68   50-65
DISC 3: Orange label.
N2PH-3137-6S/N2PH-3138-8S.

❑ RCA Victor EPA-4371 .... '68   50-65
COVER 3: Verification pending.

RCA Victor EPA-4371 ...... '68   100-130
TOTAL PACKAGE 3: Disc, cover.

Side 1
King of the Whole Wide World
This Is Living
Riding the Rainbow

Side 2
Home Is Where the Heart Is
I Got Lucky
A Whistling Tune

KING CREOLE

❑ RCA Victor EPA-4319 .... 8/58   25-30
DISC 1: Black label, dog on top.
J2PH-4407-1S/J2PH-4408-2S. Label EP#5.

❑ RCA Victor EPA-4319 .... 8/58   55-70
COVER 1: Front: Titles at right in blue print on
white stock. RCA Victor logo, number, and "45
EP Economy Package" at upper right. RCA
copyright notice and "Printed in U.S.A." at
lower right. Color Elvis photo. Back: Text only.
Has plug for *Hard Headed Woman / Don't Ask
Me Why* at bottom.

RCA Victor EPA-4319 .... 8/58   80-100
TOTAL PACKAGE 1: Disc, cover.

❑ RCA Victor EPA-4319 .... 8/58   25-30
DISC 2: Same as disc 1.

❑ RCA Victor EPA-4319 .... 8/58   55-70
COVER 2: Same as cover 1, except there is
no RCA copyright notice and "Printed in
U.S.A." at lower right on front.

RCA Victor EPA-4319 .... 8/58   80-100
TOTAL PACKAGE 2: Disc, cover.

❑ RCA Victor EPA-5122 ..... 11/59   30-40
DISC 3: Black label, dog on top.
J2PH-4407-3S/J2PH-4408-3S. Label EP#8.

❑ RCA Victor EPA-5122 ..... 11/59   30-40
COVER 3: Front: Titles at right in blue print on
white stock. RCA Victor logo and number at
upper right. Gold Standard logo at upper left.
No mention of "Economy Package." No
copyright notice and "Printed in U.S.A." at
lower right. Color Elvis photo. Back: Text only.
Plug for *Hard Headed Woman / Don't Ask Me
Why* is replaced by paragraph about "The Aim
of the Gold Standard Series."

RCA Victor EPA-5122 .. 11/59   60-80
TOTAL PACKAGE 3: Disc, cover.

❑ RCA Victor EPA-5122 ..... 11/59   5000-7500
DISC 4: Maroon label. Listed based on one –
and only one – person's report of it. Many
collectors have doubts about the existence of
a maroon label of this EP. We cannot confirm
it; however, if one should turn up, this price
range is a reality.

❑ RCA Victor EPA-5122 ..... 11/59   30-40
COVER 4: Same as cover 3.

RCA Victor EPA-5122 .. 11/59   5000-7500
TOTAL PACKAGE 4: Disc, cover.

❑ RCA Victor EPA-5122 .... '65   20-30
DISC 5: Black label, dog on side.
J2PH-4407-1S/J2PH-4408-2S. Label EP#12, but without
side numbers.

❑ RCA Victor EPA-5122 .... '65   40-50
COVER 5: Front: Titles at right in blue print on
white stock. RCA Victor logo and number at
upper right. No mention of "Economy
Package." No copyright notice and "Printed in
U.S.A." at lower right. Color Elvis photo. Back:
Text only. Plug for *Hard Headed Woman /
Don't Ask Me Why* is replaced by paragraph
about "The Aim of the Gold Standard Series."

RCA Victor EPA-5122 ...... '65   60-80
TOTAL PACKAGE 5: Disc, cover.

❑ RCA Victor EPA-5122 .... '68   50-65
DISC 6: Orange label.
J2PH-4407-1S/J2PH-4408-2S.

❑ RCA Victor EPA-5122 .... '68   50-65
COVER 6: Same as cover 5.

RCA Victor EPA-5122 ...... '68   100-130
TOTAL PACKAGE 6: Disc, cover.

On all Gold Standard EPs, the term "Gold
Standard" appears only on covers – not on
labels.

Side 1
King Creole
New Orleans

Side 2
As Long As I Have You
Lover Doll

KING CREOLE, VOL. 2

❏ RCA Victor EPA-4321 .... 8/58   25-30
   DISC 1: Black label, dog on top.
   J2PH-4409-1S/J2PH-4410-2S. Label EP#5.
   J2PH-4409-3S/J2PH-4410-3S. Label EP#8.
❏ RCA Victor EPA-4321 .... 8/58   55-70
   COVER 1: Front: Titles at right in light blue
   print on dark blue stock. RCA Victor logo,
   number, and "45 EP Economy Package" at
   upper right. RCA copyright notice and "Printed
   in U.S.A." at lower right. Color Elvis photo.
   Back: Text only. Has plug for *Hard Headed
   Woman / Don't Ask Me Why* at bottom.
RCA Victor EPA-4321 .... 8/58   80-100
TOTAL PACKAGE 1: Disc, cover.

❏ RCA Victor EPA-4321 .... '65   20-30
   DISC 2: Black label, dog on side.
❏ RCA Victor EPA-4321 .... '65   55-70
   COVER 2: Same as cover 1, including the
   then outdated plug for "Elvis' great new single:
   Hard Headed Woman / Don't Ask Me Why" at
   bottom on back.
RCA Victor EPA-4321 ...... '65   75-100
TOTAL PACKAGE 2: Disc, cover.

❏ RCA Victor EPA-4321 .... '68   50-65
   DISC 3: Orange label.
   J2PH-4409-6S/J2PH-4410-6S.
❏ RCA Victor EPA-4321 .... '68   50-65
   COVER 3: Same as cover 1.
RCA Victor EPA-4321 ...... '68   100-130
TOTAL PACKAGE 3: Disc, cover.

Side 1
Trouble
Young Dreams
Side 2
Crawfish
Dixieland Rock

KING OF ROCK AND ROLL

❏ Rockin 001: Bootleg. Listed for identification
   only.

LOVE ME TENDER

❏ RCA Victor EPA-4006 ..... 11/56   20-30
   DISC 1: Black label, dog on top, without
   horizontal silver line.
   G2WH-7523-1S/G2WH-7524-1S. Label EP#4.
❏ RCA Victor EPA-4006 ..... 11/56   55-70
   COVER 1: Front: Titles at top in black print on
   white stock. RCA Victor logo and number at
   upper right. Color Elvis photo. Back: Text
   only.
RCA Victor EPA-4006 .. 11/56   75-100
TOTAL PACKAGE 1: Disc, cover.

❏ RCA Victor EPA-4006 ..... 11/56   30-40
   DISC 2: Black label, dog on top, with
   horizontal silver line.
❏ RCA Victor EPA-4006 ..... 11/56   55-70
   COVER 2: Same as cover 1.

❏ RCA Victor EPA-4006 .. 11/56   85-110
TOTAL PACKAGE 2: Disc, cover.

❏ RCA Victor EPA-4006 ..... 11/56   170-200
   DISC 3: Black label, no dog on label, with
   horizontal silver line.
   G2WH-7523-2S/G2WH-7524-2S. Label EP#11.
❏ RCA Victor EPA-4006 ..... 11/56   55-70
   COVER 3: Same as cover 1.
RCA Victor EPA-4006 .. 11/56   225-275
TOTAL PACKAGE 3: Disc, cover.

❏ RCA Victor EPA-4006 .... '65   20-30
   DISC 4: Black label, dog on side.
   G2WH-7523-1S/G2WH-7524-8S. Label EP#12.
❏ RCA Victor EPA-4006 .... '65   40-50
   COVER 4: Front: Same as cover 1, except no
   titles are shown. Number is changed to tiny
   print and moved to lower right. Back: Same as
   cover 1, except copyright notice is changed
   from "Radio Corporation of America" to RCA,
   New York, N.Y." Tiny "2" lower left above
   catalog number.
RCA Victor EPA-4006 ...... '65   60-80
TOTAL PACKAGE 4: Disc, cover.

❏ RCA Victor EPA-4006 .... '68   50-65
   DISC 5: Orange label.
   G2WH-7523-1S/G2WH-7524-8S.
   G2WH-7523-8S/G2WH-7524-8S.
❏ RCA Victor EPA-4006 .... '68   50-65
   COVER 5: Same as cover 4, except selection
   number does not appear on front.
RCA Victor EPA-4006 ...... '68   100-130
TOTAL PACKAGE 5: Disc, cover.

Side 1
Love Me Tender
Let Me
Side 2
Poor Boy
We're Gonna Move

LOVING YOU, VOL. I

❏ RCA Victor EPA 1-1515 .... 7/57   20-30
   DISC 1: Black label, dog on top, without
   horizontal silver line.
❏ RCA Victor EPA 1-1515 .... 7/57   55-70
   COVER 1: Front: Titles at top in black print on
   white stock. RCA Victor logo and number at
   upper right. Color Elvis photo. Back: Three
   black and white Elvis photos.
RCA Victor EPA 1-1515 . 7/57   75-100
TOTAL PACKAGE 1: Disc, cover.

❏ RCA Victor EPA 1-1515 .... 7/57   30-40
   DISC 2: Black label, dog on top, with
   horizontal silver line.
   H2WH-2764-4S/H2WH-2765-2S. Label EP#1.
❏ RCA Victor EPA 1-1515 .... 7/57   55-70
   COVER 2: Same as cover 1.
RCA Victor EPA 1-1515 . 7/57   85-110
TOTAL PACKAGE 2: Disc, cover.

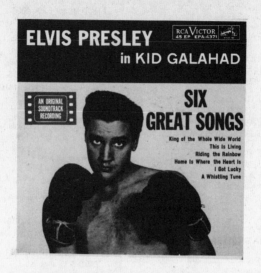

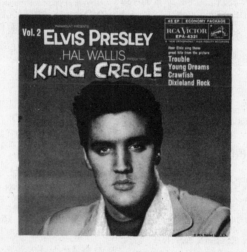

❑ RCA Victor EPA 1-1515 ...... '65   20-30
DISC 3: Black label, dog on side.
H2WH-2764-1S/H2WH-2765-6S. Label EP#14, but without
side numbers.

❑ RCA Victor EPA 1-1515 ...... '65   40-50
COVER 3: Verification pending.

RCA Victor EPA 1-1515 ...'65   60-80
TOTAL PACKAGE 3: Disc, cover.

❑ RCA Victor EPA 1-1515 ...... '68   50-65
DISC 4: Orange label.
H2WH-2764-6S/H2WH-2765-15S.

❑ RCA Victor EPA 1-1515 ...... '68   50-65
COVER 4: Verification pending.

RCA Victor EPA 1-1515 ...'68   100-130
TOTAL PACKAGE 4: Disc, cover.

Side 1
Loving You
Party

Side 2
(Let Me Be Your) Teddy Bear
True Love

LOVING YOU, VOL. II

❑ RCA Victor EPA 2-1515 ....7/57   20-30
DISC 1: Black label, dog on top, without
horizontal silver line.
H2WH-2766-1S/H2WH-2767-1S. Label EP#5.

❑ RCA Victor EPA 2-1515 ....7/57   55-70
COVER 1: Front: Titles at top in black print on
white stock. RCA Victor logo and number at
upper right. Color Elvis photo. Back: Three
black and white Elvis photos (different than
those on Vol. I).

**RCA Victor
EPA 2-1515 ....7/57   75-100**
TOTAL PACKAGE 1: Disc, cover.

❑ RCA Victor EPA 2-1515 ....7/57   30-40
DISC 2: Black label, dog on top, with
horizontal silver line. Some copies of this disc
have the silver line on side 2 but not on side
1.

❑ RCA Victor EPA 2-1515 ....7/57   55-70
COVER 2: Same as cover 1.

**RCA Victor
EPA 2-1515 ....7/57   85-110**
TOTAL PACKAGE 2: Disc, cover.

❑ RCA Victor EPA 2-1515 ...... '65   20-30
DISC 3: Black label, dog on side.
H2WH-2766-7S/H2WH-2767-9S. Label EP#14, but without
side numbers.

❑ RCA Victor EPA 2-1515 ...... '65   40-50
COVER 3: Front: Same as cover 1, except no
titles are shown. Back: Same as cover 1,
except a tiny "2" is added before
Trademark/Copyright notice.

RCA Victor EPA 2-1515 ...'65   60-80
TOTAL PACKAGE 3: Disc, cover.

❑ RCA Victor EPA 2-1515 ...... '68   50-65
DISC 4: Orange label.
H2WH-2766-7S/H2WH-2767-9S.

❑ RCA Victor EPA 2-1515 ...... '68   50-65
COVER 4: Same as cover 3.

RCA Victor EPA 2-1515 ...'68   100-130
TOTAL PACKAGE 4: Disc, cover.

Side 1
Lonesome Cowboy
Hot Dog

Side 2
Mean Woman Blues
Got a Lot o' Livin' to Do

MR. ROCK 'N ROLL

❑ Pelvis: Bootleg. Listed for identification only.

MOST TALKED-ABOUT NEW PERSONALITY IN THE LAST TEN YEARS OF RECORDED MUSIC (12 Great New Sides From His New Albums!!! LPM-1254; EPB-1254; EPA-747) (2 EPs)

❑ RCA Victor EPB-1254 ....3/56   1000-2000
DISCS 1: Black label, dog on top, without
horizontal silver line. Promotional issue only.
Disc 1 (547-0793) (Side 1) G2WH-1850-1S/(Side 4) G2WH-1853-1S. Label EP#4.
Disc 2 (547-0794) (Side 2) G2WH-1851-1S/(Side 3) G2WH-1852-1S. Label EP#4.
Unlike the sleeve, the discs make no
reference to either LPM-1254 or EPA-747.

❑ RCA Victor EPB-1254 ....3/56   2500-3000
COVER 1: Single pocket, white paper sleeve
with green print. Front: Green and white Elvis
photo. Back is blank.

❑ RCA Victor EPB-1254 ....3/56   25-75
INSERT 1: Copy of Dee-Jay Digest, a
newsletter for radio
announcers, used within the sleeve to
separate the two discs.

RCA Victor EPB-1254 ....3/56   3500-5000
TOTAL PACKAGE 1: Disc, cover, insert.

Side 1
Blue Suede Shoes
I'm Counting on You
I Got a Woman

Side 2
One-Sided Love Affair
I Love You Because
Just Because

Side 3
Tutti Frutti
Tryin' to Get to You
I'm Gonna Sit Right Down and Cry (Over You)

Side 4
I'll Never Let You Go (Little "Darlin')
Blue Moon
Money Honey

MOVIE SPOT AND PROMOTIONAL EPs: see *MOVIE SPOTS AND PROMOTIONALS* in LP section

MY BABY'S GONE
❑ No label used: Bootleg. Listed for identification only.

NEVER BEEN TO SPAIN
❑ Vegas 45001: Bootleg. Listed for identification only.

PEACE IN THE VALLEY
❑ RCA Victor EPA-4054 .... 3/57　　20-30
DISC 1: Black label, dog on top, without horizontal silver line.
H2WH-1334-1S/H2WH-1335-1S. Label EP#3.
A quantity of labels for Side 1 of this EP were pressed on an Eddie Fisher release (RCA Victor 47-6913).

❑ RCA Victor EPA-4054 .... 3/57　　40-50
COVER 1: Titles at top in black print on white stock. Front: RCA Victor logo and number at upper right. Includes subtitles with contents. Black and white Elvis photo. RCA copyright notice and "Printed in U.S.A." at lower left. Back: Text only. Has Elvis' name above "*Peace in the Valley.*"

RCA Victor EPA-4054 .... 3/57　60-80
TOTAL PACKAGE 1: Disc, cover.

❑ RCA Victor EPA-4054 .... 3/57　　30-40
DISC 2: Black label, dog on top, with horizontal silver line.
❑ RCA Victor EPA-4054 .... 3/57　　40-50
COVER 2: Same as cover 1.

RCA Victor EPA-4054 .... 3/57　70-90
TOTAL PACKAGE 2: Disc, cover.

❑ RCA Victor EPA-5121 ..... 11/59　　25-35
DISC 3: Black label, dog on top.
❑ RCA Victor EPA-5121 ..... 11/59　　30-40
COVER 3: Titles at top in black print on white stock. Front: RCA Victor logo and number at upper right. Gold Standard logo at upper left. Omits subtitles of contents. Black and white Elvis photo. RCA copyright notice and "Printed in U.S.A." at lower left followed by "RE." Back: Text only. Has Elvis' name below "*Peace in the Valley.*" Paragraph about "The Aim of the Gold Standard Series" is added at bottom.

RCA Victor EPA-5121 .. 11/59　55-75
TOTAL PACKAGE 3: Disc, cover.

❑ RCA Victor EPA-5121 ..... 11/59　　575-650
DISC 4: Maroon label.
H2WH-1334-1S/H2WH-1335-1S. Label EP#5.
❑ RCA Victor EPA-5121 ..... 11/59　　30-40
COVER 4: Same as cover 3.

RCA Victor EPA-5121 .. 11/59　600-700
TOTAL PACKAGE 4: Disc, cover.

❑ RCA Victor EPA-5121 .... '65　　20-30
DISC 5: Black label, dog on side.
H2WH-1334-1S/H2WH-1335-7S. Label EP#13.

❑ RCA Victor EPA-5121 .... '65　　30-40
COVER 5: Same as cover 3, except does not have copyright notice and "Printed in U.S.A." at lower left on front. Also, has a "2" added at lower left.

RCA Victor EPA-5121 ...... '65　50-70
TOTAL PACKAGE 5: Disc, cover.

❑ RCA Victor EPA-5121 .... '68　　50-65
DISC 6: Orange label.
H2WH-1334-1S/H2WH-1335-1S.
H2WH-1334-1S/H2WH-1335-7S.
H2WH-1334-7S/H2WH-1335-15S.
❑ RCA Victor EPA-5121 .... '68　　50-65
COVER 6: Same as cover 5, except back has "Printed in U.S.A." added.

RCA Victor EPA-5121 ...... '68　100-130
TOTAL PACKAGE 6: Disc, cover.

On all Gold Standard EPs, the term "Gold Standard" appears only on covers – not on labels.

Side 1
(There'll Be) Peace in the Valley (For Me)
It Is No Secret (What God Can Do)
Side 2
I Believe
Take My Hand, Precious Lord

PERFECT FOR PARTIES HIGHLIGHT ALBUM
Various artists collection
❑ RCA Victor SPA-7-37 ...... 11/56　　40-50
DISC 1: Black label, dog on top, without horizontal silver line. Has "NOT FOR SALE" on one line. Elvis also acts as narrator on this disc, introducing each selection. Offered through mail order coupon ads.
G2NH-7231-6S/G2NH-7232-6S. Polystyrene pressing. (May be the first EP with Elvis pressed on polystyrene.)
❑ RCA Victor SPA-7-37 ...... 11/56　　80-100
COVER 1: Paper, red, black and white. Front: RCA Victor logo and number at upper right. Black and white photo of Elvis and of LPM-1382. Back: Text, no photo. Has number, "SPA 7-37," at upper right.

RCA Victor SPA-7-37 ... 11/56　120-150
TOTAL PACKAGE 1: Disc, cover.

❑ RCA Victor SPA-7-37 ...... 11/56　　40-50
DISC 2: Black label, dog on top, with horizontal silver line. Has "NOT FOR SALE" on two lines.
G2NH-7231-8S/G2NH-7232-7S. Serial numbers are both stamped and engraved on side one, but only stamped on side two. Polystyrene pressing.
❑ RCA Victor SPA-7-37 ...... 11/56　　80-100
COVER 2: Same as cover 1, except does not have selection number anywhere on back.

RCA Victor SPA-7-37 ... 11/56　120-150
TOTAL PACKAGE 2: Disc, cover.

❏ RCA Victor SPA-7-37 ...... 11/56　40-50
DISC 3: Black label, dog on top, with horizontal silver line. Has "NOT FOR SALE" on one line.

❏ RCA Victor SPA-7-37 ...... 11/56　80-100
COVER 3: Same as cover 2.

RCA Victor SPA-7-37 ... 11/56　120-150
TOTAL PACKAGE 3: Disc, cover.

❏ RCA Victor SPA-7-37 ...... 11/56　40-50
DISC 4: Same as either discs 1, 2 or 3.

❏ RCA Victor SPA-7-37 ...... 11/56　60-100
COVER 4: Not really a cover, this is merely a black and white piece of paper. Printed on one side only, this sheet is pasted on a generic 1956 RCA paper sleeve. Has "Perfect for Parties" in circular print at top. No photo or mention of Elvis or anyone – only drawings of a record, party hat, beverage glass and a couple of party favors. No doubt intended for temporary use only.

RCA Victor SPA-7-37 ... 11/56　100-150
TOTAL PACKAGE 4: Disc, sleeve.

There seems to be no consistent record/cover combination. Copies of any of these discs may be found with any of the covers listed.

This EP was shipped in a brown mailer/envelope, from "Radio Corporation of America, Box 484, Philadelphia, Pa.," which makes no reference to Elvis nor to this EP.
Counterfeit Identification: Fakes have a white label and are therefore easily identified. Originals are on a black label. Fake covers are made of cardboard similar to that found on most EPs and LPs. Original covers are also made of cardboard stock, but much thinner – about the thickness of a post card.

Side 1
Introduction by Elvis Presley
Love Me (Elvis Presley)
Introduction by Elvis Presley
Anchor's Aweigh (Tony Cabot)
Introduction by Elvis Presley
That's a Puente (Tito Puente)

Side 2
Introduction by Elvis Presley
Rock Me But Don't Roll Me (Tony Scott)
Introduction by Elvis Presley
Happy Face Baby (Three Suns)
Introduction by Elvis Presley
Prom to Prom (Dave Pell)
Closing Comments by Elvis Presley

PERFECT FOR PARTIES EP SLICKS

❏ RCA Victor........................ 11/56　400-500
Set of 15 EP front cover slicks, including most of those featured in the *Perfect for Parties* EP (preceding listing), and others on RCA Victor. Offered to juke box operators for display behind the glass on juke boxes. Includes the following titles or artists:
1. *Elvis*
2. *Elvis Presley*
3. George Williams & Orchestra

4. Henri Rene & Orchestra
5. Tito Puente & Orchestra
6. Perez Prado & Orchestra
7. Tony Martin
8. Tony Scott
9. Julius Larosa
10. Tony Cabot
11. Tony Cabot
12. Ames Brothers
13. Bobby Dukoff
14. Three Suns
15. Harry Belafonte

POP TRANSCRIBED SPOT
Various artists collection

❏ RCA Victor 0646 .... 10/57　500-600
DISC 1: Black label, dog on top. Promotional issue for radio stations only. No actual selection number given, 0646 being the identification number on Side 1. Has 30 second sales pitch for and excerpts of RCA's new EP and LPs, including *Jailhouse Rock.*). H08W-0646-1S/H08W-0647-1S.
COVER 1: None made.

RCA Victor 0646 .... 10/57　500-600
TOTAL PACKAGE 1: Disc.

Side 1
Helen Morgan (Gogi Grant)
Jennie (Jennie Smith)
Hi Fi in Focus (Chet Atkins)
Side 2
Jailhouse Rock (Elvis Presley)
Blue Starr (Kay Starr)
Search for Paradise (Robert Merrill – not credited on label)

POP TRANSCRIBED 30 SEC. SPOT
Various artists collection

❏ RCA Victor 3736 .... 4/58　500-600
DISC 1: Black label, dog on top. Promotional issue for radio stations only. No actual selection number given, 3736 being the identification number on Side A. Announcer Vaughn Monroe gives a sales pitch for and introduces excerpts of four RCA LPs, including *Elvis' Golden Records.* Side B is titled "Red Seal Transcribed 30 Sec. Spot." J80W-3736-1S/J80W-3637-1S.
COVER 1: None made.

RCA Victor 3736 .... 4/58　500-600
TOTAL PACKAGE 1: Disc.

Side A
Elvis - Golden Record Album (Elvis Presley)
Gigi - (Gogi Grant & Tony Martin)
Side B
Presenting Tozzi (Excerpts From)
Mighty Fortress (Robert Shaw Chorale)

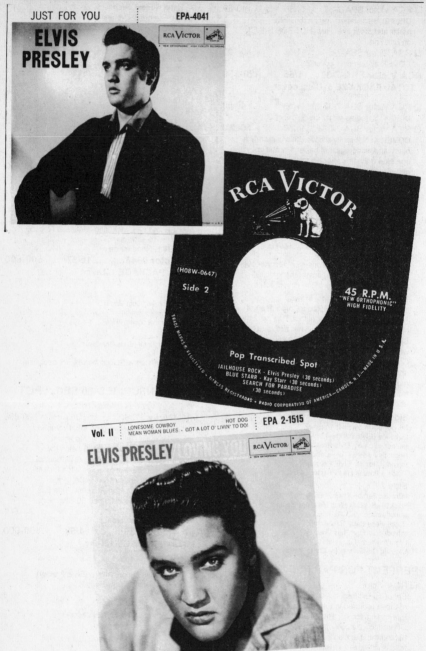

PRO-12 (RCA Victor Promotion Disc)

Various artists collection

❑ RCA Victor PRO-12......... 12/56   750-1000
DISC 1: White label, black print. Promotional issue only.
J7OH-2287-1/J7OH-2288-1.

❑ RCA Victor PRO-12......... 12/56   2250-3000
COVER 1: Paper sleeve. Custom made for WOHO radio, Toledo, Ohio. Promotional issue only. Front: Reads: "WOHO (1470 KC) Featuring RCA Victor." RCA Victor logo and number at upper right. Back is blank. We are uncertain as to how and why this item was offered.

RCA Victor PRO-12...... 12/56   3000-4000
TOTAL PACKAGE 1: Disc, cover.

Side 1
Old Shep (Elvis Presley)
I'm Moving On (Hank Snow)

Side 2
Cattle Call (Eddy Arnold with Hugo Winterhalter & Chorus)
Four Walls (Jim Reeves)

RCA FAMILY RECORD CENTER

Various artists collection

❑ RCA Victor PR-121 .... 2/62   1500-2000
DISC 1: White label, black print. Has an announcer introducing excerpts of eight new tracks from RCA. Produced for in-store play only.
N2NQ-1647-3/N2NQ-1648-3. Has LP-size (¼-inch) hole. Serial numbers are engraved.
COVER 1: None made.

Side 1
Good Luck Charm (Elvis Presley)
The Way You Look Tonight (Peter Nero)
Younger Than Springtime (Paul Anka)
Frenesi (Living Strings)

Side 2
Twistin' the Night Away (Sam Cooke)
Easy Street (Al Hirt)
Make Someone Happy (Perry Como)
Moon River (Henry Mancini)

REAL ELVIS

❑ RCA Victor EPA-940 .... 9/56   20-30
DISC 1: Black label, dog on top, without horizontal silver line.
G2WH-6136-1S/G2WH-6137-1S. Label EP#4.

❑ RCA Victor EPA-940 .... 9/56   80-95
COVER 1: Front: Titles at top in white print on black stock. RCA Victor logo and number at upper right. Black and white Elvis photo. Back: Black and white Elvis photo.

RCA Victor EPA-940 ...... 9/56   100-125
TOTAL PACKAGE 1: Disc, cover.

❑ RCA Victor EPA-940 .... 9/56   30-40
DISC 2: Black label, dog on top, with horizontal silver line.

❑ RCA Victor EPA-940 .... 9/56   80-95
COVER 2: Same as cover 1.

RCA Victor EPA-940 ...... 9/56   110-135
TOTAL PACKAGE 2: Disc, cover.

❑ RCA Victor EPA-940 .... 9/56   170-200
DISC 3: Black label, no dog on label, with horizontal silver line.

❑ RCA Victor EPA-940 .... 9/56   80-95
COVER 3: Same as cover 1.

RCA Victor EPA-940 ...... 9/56   250-300
TOTAL PACKAGE 3: Disc, cover.

❑ RCA Victor EPA-5120 ..... 11/59   30-40
DISC 4: Black label, dog on top.

❑ RCA Victor EPA-5120 ..... 11/59   70-85
COVER 4: Front: Titles at left in white print on red stock. RCA Victor logo and number at upper right. Gold Standard logo at upper left. Has "RE" at lower right, following copyright notice. Black and white Elvis photo. Back: Black and white Elvis photo. Paragraph about "The Aim of the Gold Standard Series" is added at bottom right.

RCA Victor EPA-5120 ..11/59   100-125
TOTAL PACKAGE 4: Disc, cover.

❑ RCA Victor EPA-5120 ..... 11/59   625-725
DISC 5: Maroon label.
G2WH-6136-7S/G2WH-6137-7S. Label EP#5.

❑ RCA Victor EPA-5120 ..... 11/59   70-85
COVER 5: Same as cover 4.

RCA Victor EPA-5120 ..11/59   700-800
TOTAL PACKAGE 5: Disc, cover.

❑ RCA Victor EPA-5120 .... '65   20-30
DISC 6: Black label, dog on side.
G2WH-6136-1S/G2WH-6137-7S.

❑ RCA Victor EPA-5120 .... '65   70-85
COVER 6: Same as cover 4.

RCA Victor EPA-5120 ...... '65   90-115
TOTAL PACKAGE 6: Disc, cover.

❑ RCA Victor EPA-5120 .... '68   50-65
DISC 7: Orange label.
G2WH-6136-7S/G2WH-6137-15S.

❑ RCA Victor EPA-5120 ....:. '68   50-65
COVER 7: Same as cover 4.

RCA Victor EPA-5120 ...... '68   100-130
TOTAL PACKAGE 7: Disc, cover.

On all Gold Standard EPs, the term "Gold Standard" appears only on covers – not on labels.

Side 1
Don't Be Cruel
I Want You, I Need You, I Love You

Side 2
Hound Dog
My Baby Left Me

ROCK AND ROLL ROOTS

Various artists collection

❑ Rock and Roll Roots............'78   20-30
DISC 1: Orange label, black print. Demo disc for the syndicated oldies show, Rock and Roll Roots, plays at 33 rpm. Mentions Elvis twice. Promotional issue only. Only 100 pressed.
COVER 1: None made.

Rock and Roll Roots........'78   20-30
TOTAL PACKAGE 1: Disc.

SPA 7-61 (Untitled 45 EP Sampler)

Various artists collection

❑ RCA SPA 7-61 ....10/57   1000-1500
DISC 1: Black label, dog on top, without horizontal silver line. Has "NOT FOR SALE" on two lines. Previews RCA extended plays, including *Jailhouse Rock*. Promotional issue only.
H2NH-7490-1S/N2NH-7491-1S. Label EP#6.
COVER 1: None made.

RCA SPA 7-61 ....10/57   1000-1500
TOTAL PACKAGE 1: Disc.

Side 1
Howard University Choir
Versatones
Jeannie Smith
Jim Reeves
Paul Lavalle
Robert Merrill

Side 2
Elvis Presley
Billy Mure
Sabres
Gogi Grant
Nick Venet
Lane Bros.

SPD-15 (10 EPs)

Various artists collection

❑ RCA Victor SPD-15 ....12/55   800-1000
DISCS 1: Set of 10 black label (dog on top) extended plays. Has one Elvis EP, numbered 599-9089, representing sides 7 and 14 of 20.

❑ RCA Victor SPD-15 ....12/55   2500-5000
BOX 1: Price is an estimate of what the box *might* be worth. Although we have yet to verify a box for this set, it is likely one was made. It is even possible there are differences between this box and box 3.

❑ RCA Victor SPD-15 ....12/55   15-25
INSERTS 1: Since we know of no box for this set, we also have no knowledge of what inserts were used.

RCA Victor SPD-15 ......12/55   800-1000
TOTAL PACKAGE 1: Discs. (Until one is verified, we have not included a box or inserts in the price.)

❑ RCA Victor SPD-15 /
599-9089 ....11/56   400-500
DISC 2: Price for just the black label Elvis EP from SPD-15 boxed set.
(Side 7) G2WH-1073-1S/(Side 14) G2WH-1074-1S. Label EP#6.

RCA Victor SPD-15/
599-9089....................11/56   400-500
TOTAL PACKAGE 2: Disc.

❑ RCA Victor SPD-15 ....12/55   800-1000
DISCS 3: Juke box edition. Set of 10 gray label (dog on top) extended plays. Has one Elvis EP, numbered 599-9089, representing sides 7 and 14 of 20.

❑ RCA Victor SPD-15 ....12/55   2500-5000
BOX 3: Price is an estimate of what the box *might* be worth. Although we have yet to verify a box for this set, it is likely one was made. It is even possible there are differences between this box and box 2.

❑ RCA Victor SPD-15 ....12/55   15-25
INSERT 3A: A sheet of juke box title strips was probably included with this set.

❑ RCA Victor SPD-15 ....12/55   15-25
INSERTS 3B: Since we know of no box for this set, we also have no knowledge of what inserts were used.

RCA Victor SPD-15 ......12/55   800-1000
TOTAL PACKAGE 3: Discs. (Until one is verified, we have not included a box or inserts in the price.)

❑ RCA Victor SPD-15/
599-9089 ....11/56   400-500
DISC 4: Price for just the gray label Elvis EP from SPD-15 boxed set.
(Side 7) G2WH-1073-1S/(Side 14) G2WH-1074-1S. Label EP#6.

RCA Victor SPD-15/
599-9089....................11/56   400-500
TOTAL PACKAGE 4: Disc.

SAVE-ON-RECORDS Bulletin for June

Various artists collection

❑ RCA Victor SPA-7-27 ....6/56   100-125
DISC 1: Black label, dog on top, with horizontal silver line.
G7NH-4747-1/G7NH-4748-1.
The title, *Save-On-Records*, does not appear anywhere on label.

❑ RCA Victor SPA-7-27 ....6/56   150-175
COVER 1: Red, white, blue and pink paper sleeve. Neither selection number nor track listings appear anywhere on sleeve. Has excerpts of 10 tracks by 10 different artists, including *I'm Gonna Sit Right Down and Cry (Over You)* by Elvis, which is shown on label as *Gonna Sit Right Down and Cry*. Issued as part of an RCA factory direct mail order discount program.

❑ RCA Victor........................6/56   125-150
   INSERT 1: "RCA Victor Save-On-Records
   Coupon Book." Book, priced at $3.98,
   included a $1.00 discount coupon for Elvis
   Presley (LPM-1254). We have yet to find a
   copy of the coupon book intact and still with
   the Presley LP certificate. Coupon book is
   pictured on the front of cover 1.

**RCA Victor......................6/56   375-450
TOTAL PACKAGE 1: Disc, cover, insert.**

Side 1
Rubinstein Plays Liszt (Liebestraum)
Voi Che Sapete (Risë Stevens)
Beethoven: Symphony 9 (A. Toscanini)
Jalousie Excerpt (Arthur Fiedler and the Boston Pops
   Orchestra)
Symphonie Fantastique (Boston Symphony)
Side 2
Intermezzo (Frankie Carle)
Moonlight Cocktail Excerpt (Al Nevins' Orchestra)
[I'm] Gonna Sit Right Down and Cry (Elvis Presley)
Adventure in Time (Sauter-Finegan)
Great Gettin' Up Morning (Harry Belafonte)

SOUND OF LEADERSHIP
(SOUVENIR OF THE MIAMI
MEETING, JUNE, 1956) (8 EPs)
Various artists collection

❑ RCA Victor SPD-19...........6/56   800-1000
   DISCS 1: Boxed set of eight gray label (dog
   on top) extended plays. Includes four-page
   introductory brochure and nine paper
   separator inserts, listed separately below. Has
   one Elvis track, *Heartbreak Hotel*, on disc
   599-9113 (on side 16 of 16). Made as a
   souvenir for employees attending a June 1956
   RCA Victor company convention. All discs are
   labeled "Not for Sale."
❑ RCA Victor SPD-19...........6/56   800-900
   BOX 1: Gold box. Front: White stock with gold
   and black print. Has RCA Victor logo at top
   center, number at upper left. Back is blank.
❑ RCA Victor........................11/56   50-75
   INSERT 1A: Four-page insert, titled "The
   Sound of Leadership." White with black print.
   Back page lists contents.
❑ RCA Victor........................11/56   15-25
   INSERTS 1B: Introductory Contrary to
   Custom (Form 3K693) and All-Time Red Seal
   Best Sellers inserts. Other separator sheets
   may be white with no printing, or may include
   some of the same ones listed for SPD-26,
   Great Country/Western Hits.

**RCA Victor SPD-19........6/56   1800-2200
TOTAL PACKAGE 1: Discs, box, inserts.**

❑ RCA Victor SPD-19/599-91146/56   300-400
   DISC 2: Price for just the EP with the Elvis
   track, from SPD-19 boxed set.
   (Side 8) G2NH-3710-1S/(Side 16) G2NH-3725-1S.

**RCA Victor SPD-19/
599-9114......................6/56   300-400
TOTAL PACKAGE 2: Disc.**

Side 1
Vesti la Giubba (Enrico Caruso)
O Sole Mio (Enrico Caruso)
Side 16
Hot Diggity (Perry Como)
Heartbreak Hotel (Elvis Presley)

STRICTLY ELVIS (ELVIS VOL. 3)

❑ RCA Victor EPA-994.......11/56   20-30
   DISC 1: Black label, dog on top, without
   horizontal silver line.
❑ RCA Victor EPA-994.......11/56   80-95
   COVER 1: Front: Titles at top in black print on
   white stock. RCA Victor logo and number at
   upper right corner. Color Elvis photo. Back:
   Text only – excerpted from the liner notes on
   LPM-1382. Portion beginning "Of special
   interest" refers to the Jordanaires.

**RCA Victor EPA-994 ....11/56   100-125
TOTAL PACKAGE 1: Disc, cover.**

❑ RCA Victor EPA-994.......11/56   30-40
   DISC 2: Black label, dog on top, with
   horizontal silver line.
❑ RCA Victor EPA-994.......11/56   80-95
   COVER 2: Same as cover 1.

**RCA Victor EPA-994 ....11/56   110-135
TOTAL PACKAGE 2: Disc, cover.**

❑ RCA Victor EPA-994.......11/56   170-200
   DISC 3: Black label, no dog on label, with
   horizontal silver line.
   G2WH-7213-4S/G2WH-7214-4S. Label EP#11.
❑ RCA Victor EPA-994.......11/56   80-95
   COVER 3: Same as cover 1.

**RCA Victor EPA-994 ....11/56   250-300
TOTAL PACKAGE 3: Disc, cover.**

❑ RCA Victor EPA-994...........'65   20-30
   DISC 4: Black label, dog on side.
❑ RCA Victor EPA-994...........'65   40-50
   COVER 4: Same as cover 1, except no titles
   shown on front.

**RCA Victor EPA-994 ....'65   60-80
TOTAL PACKAGE 4: Disc, cover.**

❑ RCA Victor EPA-994...........'68   50-65
   DISC 5: Orange label.
   G2WH-7213-6S/G2WH-7214-6S.
❑ RCA Victor EPA-994...........'68   50-65
   COVER 5: Same as cover 4.

**RCA Victor EPA-994 ....'68   100-130
TOTAL PACKAGE 5: Disc, cover.**

Side 1
Long Tall Sally
First in Line
Side 2
How Do You Think I Feel
How's the World Treating You

TV GUIDE PRESENTS ELVIS PRESLEY

❑ RCA Victor GB-MW-
8705 ....9/56　　1000-1200
DISC 1: Blue label. Four track, open-end interview. Single-sided. Promotional issue only.
GB-MW-8705-1/(Side two is a blank pressing.)
Counterfeit Identification: Original discs have locked grooves (needle has to be lifted from disc to pass to next track) and have the identification numbers stamped in the vinyl trail-off. Counterfeits do not have locked grooves and have the identification numbers engraved in the vinyl.

❑ RCA Victor GB-MW-
8705 ....9/56　　150-200
INSERT 1A: "Suggested continuity," a pink, four-page suggested interview script.

❑ RCA Victor GB-MW-
8705 ....9/56　　150-200
INSERT 1B: Gray card, provides background on the interview and pictures the September 8-14, 1956 issue of *TV Guide* with Elvis on the cover.
Counterfeit Identification: Fakes of the inserts reportedly are marked and identified as reproductions.
COVER 1: None made.

RCA Victor GB-MW-
8705............................9/56　　1300-1600
TOTAL PACKAGE 1: Disc, inserts.

❑ RCA Victor GB-MW-
8705 ....9/56　　1000-1200
DISC 2: White label. Four track, open-end interview. Single-sided. Promotional issue only.
GB-MW-8705-1/(Side two is a blank pressing.)
❑ RCA Victor GB-MW-
8705 ....9/56　　150-200
INSERT 2A: "Suggested continuity," a pink, four-page suggested interview script.

❑ RCA Victor GB-MW-
8705 ....9/56　　150-200
INSERT 2B: Gray card, provides background on the interview and pictures the September 8-14, 1956 issue of *TV Guide* with Elvis on the cover.
Counterfeit Identification: Fakes of the inserts reportedly are marked and identified as reproductions.
COVER 2: None made.

RCA Victor GB-MW-
8705............................9/56　　1300-1600
TOTAL PACKAGE 2: Disc, inserts.

Side 1
"Pelvis" Nickname
Adult's Reaction
First Public Appearance
How "Rockin' Motion" Started

THAT'S ALL RIGHT

❑ Sun EP-100: Bootleg. Listed for identification only.

TICKLE ME

❑ RCA Victor EPA-4383 ....6/65　　25-30
DISC 1: Black label, dog on side.
SPKB-5387-1S/SPKB-5388-1S. Label EP#14.
SPKB-5387-6S/SPKB-5388-6S. Label EP#15.
❑ RCA Victor EPA-4383 ....6/65　　55-70
COVER 1: Titles on right in yellow and white print on red stock. RCA Victor logo and number at upper right. At bottom, reads: "Coming Soon! Special Elvis Anniversary LP Album" (which was *Elvis for Everyone*). Back: Pictures five other Elvis EPs, much the same as *Viva Las Vegas* but with *Follow That Dream* replaced by *Viva Las Vegas*.

RCA Victor EPA-4383 ....6/65　　80-100
TOTAL PACKAGE 1: Disc, cover.

❑ RCA Victor EPA-4383 ....7/65　　25-30
DISC 2: Same as disc 1.
❑ RCA Victor EPA-4383 ....7/65　　55-70
COVER 2: Same as cover 1, except reads: "Ask for Special Elvis Anniversary LP Album" at bottom on front.

RCA Victor EPA-4383 ....7/65　　80-100
TOTAL PACKAGE 2: Disc, cover.

❑ RCA Victor EPA-4383 ....'68　　25-30
DISC 3: Same as disc 1.
❑ RCA Victor EPA-4383 ....'68　　75-95
COVER 3: Same as cover 1, except no mention of "Special Elvis Anniversary LP Album." Black strip at bottom of cover.

RCA Victor EPA-4383 ......'68　　100-125
TOTAL PACKAGE 3: Disc, cover.

❑ RCA Victor EPA-4383 ....'68　　150-200
DISC 4: Orange label.
SPKB-5387-3S/SPKB-5388-4S.
❑ RCA Victor EPA-4383 ....'68　　150-200
COVER 4: Same as cover 1, except there is no mention of "Special Elvis Anniversary LP Album."

RCA Victor EPA-4383 ......'68　　300-400
TOTAL PACKAGE 4: Disc, cover.

Side 1
I Feel That I've Known You Forever
Slowly But Surely
Side 2
Night Rider
Put The Blame On Me
Dirty Feeling

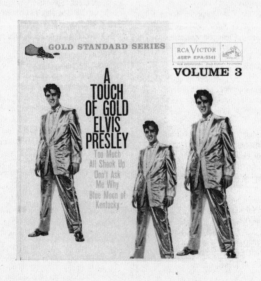

TOUCH OF GOLD, VOLUME I

❑ RCA Victor EPA-5088 .... 4/59   40-50
DISC 1: Black label, dog on top.
K2PH-1245-1S/K2PH-1246-1S. Label EP#6.
K2PH-1245-3S/K2PH-1246-3S. Label EP#3.

❑ RCA Victor EPA-5088 .... 4/59   40-50
COVER 1: Front: Titles at right in blue on
burgandy or brown stock. RCA Victor logo
and number at upper right. Gold Standard
Series logo at upper left. One color photo of
Elvis in his gold suit. Back: Text only.

❑ RCA Victor........................... '59   45-50
INSERT 1: "Loyal Elvis Fan" 3¼" x 2¼"
signature card, with Elvis' picture. Though no
marks on card tie it to *A Touch of Gold*, it was
included with some copies of this EP.
May also have an insert thanking buyers of
RCA records. Also, the plastic bag in which
the EP was packaged has a gold and black
printed area, reading: "Gold Standard Series,
Only $1.29." Neither makes mention of Elvis
or of this EP.

RCA Victor EPA-5088 .... 4/59   125-150
TOTAL PACKAGE 1: Disc, cover, insert.

❑ RCA Victor EPA-5088 .... 4/59   365-400
DISC 2: Maroon label.
K2PH-1245-1S/K2PH-1246-1S. Label EP#6.

❑ RCA Victor EPA-5088 .... '59   40-50
COVER 2: Same as cover 1.

❑ RCA Victor........................... '59   45-50
INSERT 2: "Loyal Elvis Fan" 3¼" x 2¼"
signature card, with Elvis' picture. Though no
marks on card tie it to *A Touch of Gold*, it was
included with some copies of this EP.
May also have an insert thanking buyers of
RCA records. Also, the plastic bag in which
the EP was packaged has a gold and black
printed area, reading: "Gold Standard Series,
Only $1.29." Neither makes mention of Elvis
or of this EP.

RCA Victor EPA-5088 .... 4/59   450-500
TOTAL PACKAGE 2: Disc, cover, insert.

❑ RCA Victor EPA-5088 .... '65   20-30
DISC 3: Black label, dog on side.
K2PH-1245-1S/K2PH-1246-1S. Label EP#12, but without
side numbers.

❑ RCA Victor EPA-5088 .... '65   40-50
COVER 3: Same as cover 1.

RCA Victor EPA-5088 ...... '65   60-80
TOTAL PACKAGE 3: Disc, cover.

❑ RCA Victor EPA-5088 .... '68   75-100
DISC 4: Orange label.
K2PH-1245-1S/K2PH-1246-1S.

❑ RCA Victor EPA-5088 .... '68   75-100
COVER 4: Verification pending.

RCA Victor EPA-5088 ...... '68   150-200
TOTAL PACKAGE 4: Disc, cover.

On all Gold Standard EPs, the term "Gold
Standard" appears only on covers – not on
labels.

Side 1
Hard Headed Woman
Good Rockin' Tonight
Side 2
Don't
I Beg of You

TOUCH OF GOLD, VOLUME II

❑ RCA Victor EPA-5101 .... 9/59   40-50
DISC 1: Black label, dog on top.

❑ RCA Victor EPA-5101 .... 9/59   65-75
COVER 1: Front: Titles at bottom center in
orange on black stock. RCA Victor logo and
number at upper right. Gold Standard Series
logo at upper left. Two color photos of Elvis in
his gold suit. Back: Pictures *Elvis' Gold
Records, Vol. 2.*

❑ RCA Victor........................... '59   45-50
INSERT 1: "Loyal Elvis Fan" 3¼" x 2¼"
signature card, with Elvis' picture. Though no
marks on card tie it to *A Touch of Gold*, it
was included with some copies of this EP. (Card is
pictured above.)
May also have an insert thanking buyers of
RCA records. The plastic bag in which the EP
was packaged has a gold and black printed
area, reading: "Gold Standard Series, Only
$1.29." Neither makes mention of Elvis or of
this EP.

RCA Victor EPA-5101 .... 9/59   150-175
TOTAL PACKAGE 1: Disc, cover, insert.

❑ RCA Victor EPA-5101 .... 9/59   365-400
DISC 2: Maroon label.
K2PH-2605-1S/K2PH-2606-1S. Label EP#7.

❑ RCA Victor EPA-5101 .... 9/59   65-75
COVER 2: Same as cover 1

❑ RCA Victor........................... '59   45-50
INSERT 2: "Loyal Elvis Fan" 3¼" x 2¼"
signature card, with Elvis' picture. Though no
marks on card tie it to *A Touch of Gold*, it was
included with some copies of this EP.
May also have an insert thanking buyers of
RCA records. Also, the plastic bag in which
the EP was packaged has a gold and black
printed area, reading: "Gold Standard Series,
Only $1.29." Neither makes mention of Elvis
or of this EP.

RCA Victor EPA-5101 .... 9/59   475-525
TOTAL PACKAGE 2: Disc, cover, insert.

❏ RCA Victor EPA-5101 .... '65   20-30
DISC 3: Black label, dog on side.
K2PH-2605-1S/K2PH-2606-1S. Label EP#12.
❏ RCA Victor EPA-5101 .... '65   65-75
COVER 3: Same as cover 1.
RCA Victor EPA-5101 ...... '65   85-100
TOTAL PACKAGE 3: Disc, cover.

❏ RCA Victor EPA-5101 .... '68   75-100
DISC 4: Orange Label.
K2PH-2605-1S/K2PH-2606-1S.
❏ RCA Victor EPA-5101 .... '68   75-100
COVER 4: Verification pending.
RCA Victor EPA-5101 ...... '68   150-200
TOTAL PACKAGE 4: Disc, cover.

On all Gold Standard EPs, the term "Gold Standard" appears only on covers – not on labels.

Side 1
Wear My Ring Around Your Neck
Treat Me Nice

Side 2
One Night
That's All Right

TOUCH OF GOLD, VOLUME 3

❏ RCA Victor EPA-5141 .... 1/60   40-50
DISC 1: Black label, dog on top.
❏ RCA Victor EPA-5141 .... 1/60   85-100
COVER 1: Front: Titles at bottom middle in blue on white stock. RCA Victor logo and number at upper right. Gold Standard Series logo at upper left. Three color photos of Elvis in his gold suit. Back: Pictures first two volumes of *A Touch of Gold*.
May also have an insert thanking buyers of RCA records. Also, the plastic bag in which the EP was packaged has a gold and black printed area, reading: "Gold Standard Series, Only $1.29." Neither makes mention of Elvis or of this EP.
Inexplicably, RCA switched from Roman to Arabic numbering for this release, giving us Vols. I and II, then 3.
RCA Victor EPA-5141 .... 1/60   125-150
TOTAL PACKAGE 1: Disc, cover.

❏ RCA Victor EPA-5141 .... 1/60   425-450
DISC 2: Maroon label.
K2PH-6305-1S/K2PH-6306-1S. Label EP#5.
❏ RCA Victor EPA-5141 .... 1/60   85-100
COVER 2: Same as cover 1.
May also have an insert thanking buyers of RCA records. Also, the plastic bag in which the EP was packaged has a gold and black printed area, reading: "Gold Standard Series, Only $1.29." Neither makes mention of Elvis or of this EP.
RCA Victor EPA-5141 .... 1/60   510-550
TOTAL PACKAGE 2: Disc, cover.

❏ RCA Victor EPA-5141 .... '65   20-30
DISC 3: Black label, dog on side.
K2PH-6305-1S/K2PH-6306-1S. Label EP#12.
❏ RCA Victor EPA-5141 .... '65   85-100
COVER 3: Same as cover 1.
RCA Victor EPA-5141 ...... '65   105-130
TOTAL PACKAGE 3: Disc, cover.

❏ RCA Victor EPA-5141 .... '68   75-100
DISC 4: Orange label.
K2PH-6305-1S/K2PH-6306-1S.
❏ RCA Victor EPA-5141 .... '68   75-100
COVER 4: Verification pending.
RCA Victor EPA-5141 ...... '68   150-200
TOTAL PACKAGE 4: Disc, cover.

On all Gold Standard EPs, the term "Gold Standard" appears only on covers – not on labels.

Side 1
All Shook Up
Don't Ask Me Why

Side 2
Too Much
Blue Moon of Kentucky

TUPPERWARE'S HIT PARADE

Various artists collection
❏ Tupperware Home Parties THP-11973
BS-474 .... 1/73   50-75
DISC 1: Approximately half-minute excerpts of 11 songs by 11 artists including *All Shook Up* by Elvis. Single-sided sales tool disc, made for Tupperware representatives.
THP-11973-A/THP-11973-B.
COVER 1: None made.
Tupperware Home Parties THP-11973
BS-474 .... 1/73   50-75
TOTAL PACKAGE 1: Disc.

Side A
Just Walkin' in the Rain (Johnnie Ray)
All Shook Up (Elvis Presley)
Mack the Knife (Bobby Darin)
Mr. Sandman (Chordettes)
Kiss of Fire (Georgia Gibbs)
I'm Walkin the Floor over You (Ernest Tubb)

VIVA LAS VEGAS

❑ RCA Victor EPA-4382 .... 6/64   25-30
DISC 1: Black label, dog on top.
RPKB-0390-3S/RPKB-0391-3S. Label EP#3.

❑ RCA Victor EPA-4382 .... 6/64   55-70
COVER 1: Titles at left in yellow and white print on orange stock. RCA Victor logo and number at upper right. Color Elvis photo. Back: Pictures five other Elvis EPs, much the same as *Tickle Me* but with *Follow That Dream* instead of *Viva Las Vegas.*

RCA Victor EPA-4382 .... 6/64   80-100
TOTAL PACKAGE 1: Disc, cover.

❑ RCA Victor EPA-4382 .... '65   20-30
DISC 2: Black label, dog on side.

❑ RCA Victor EPA-4382 .... '65   40-50
COVER 2: Same as cover 1.

RCA Victor EPA-4382 ...... '65   60-80
TOTAL PACKAGE 2: Disc, cover.

❑ RCA Victor EPA-4382 .... '68   75-100
DISC 3: Orange label.
RPKB-0390-2S/RPKB-0391-2S.

❑ RCA Victor EPA-4382 .... '68   75-100
COVER 3: Verification pending.

RCA Victor EPA-4382 ...... '68   150-200
TOTAL PACKAGE 3: Disc, cover.

Side 1
If You Think I Don't Need You
I Need Somebody to Lean On

Side 2
C'mon Everybody
Today, Tomorrow and Forever

WOHO FEATURING RCA VICTOR: see
PRO-12

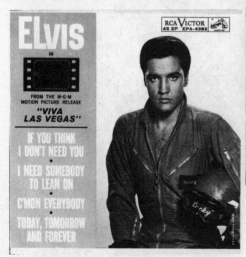

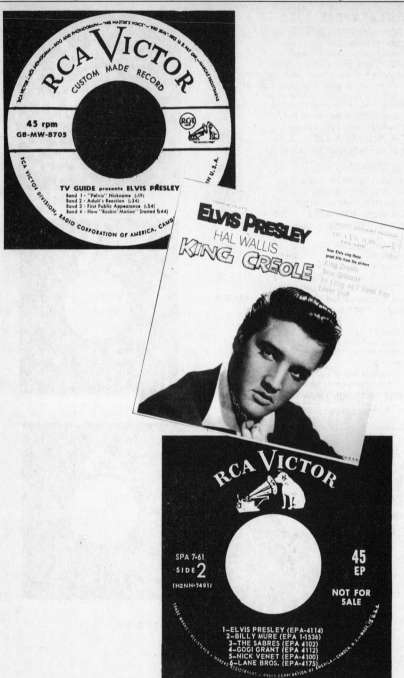

LONG PLAY ALBUMS

ABERBACH PRESENTS ALL TIME GREATS, VOL. 3

Various artists collection

❏ ATG (S) ATG-VOL-3   10-20
DISC 1: White label with brown print.
Promotional issued from the Aberbach
Publishing Group.
ATG-VOL-3-A/ATG-VOL-3-B. Identification numbers are engraved.

❏ ATG ATG-VOL-3   10-20
COVER 1: Gatefold. Front, back, and inside
panels have text only.
INNER SLEEVE 1: White, no printing.

ATG (S) ATG-VOL-3   20-40
TOTAL PACKAGE 1: Disc, cover.

AGE OF ROCK

Various artists mentioned

❏ EMR Enterprises (M) EMR
RH-8 .... '69   100-125
DISC 1: Complete one hour radio show.
Issued to promote the book *The Age of Rock.*
Not a various artists *music* collection, but
does discuss many stars, including Elvis.
Includes *Tutti Frutti, Love Me Tender* and
Blue Suede Shoes.
YB-320-P1/YB-321-P2. Identification numbers are engraved.
COVER 1: White, no printing.
INNER SLEEVE 1: White, no printing.

❏ EMR Enterprises EMR
RH-8 .... '69
INSERT 1: Verification pending. Assumption:
Script or cue sheet of some type.

EMR Enterprises (M) EMR
RH-8 .... '69   100-125
TOTAL PACKAGE 1: Disc, cover.

ALL STAR ROCK – VOLUME 11

Various artists collection

❏ Original Sound Recordings (SP)
OSR-11 .... 2/72   20-25
DISC 1: Orange label, black print.
U-3323 ORS-VOL-11/U-3324 ORS-VOL-11. Identification
numbers are engraved. (Oddly, it is "ORS," not "OSR.")

❏ Original Sound Recordings
OSR-11 .... 2/72   20-25
COVER 1: Similar to that shown for *Rock
Rock Rock (All Star Rock – Volume 11,* but
with shorter title. Has silhouettes of dancing
girls.
INNER SLEEVE 1: White, no printing.
First issued as *ROCK ROCK ROCK (ALL
STAR ROCK, VOLUME 11).* See that listing
for more information.

Original Sound Recordings (SP)
OSR-11 .... 2/72   40-50
TOTAL PACKAGE 1: Disc, cover.

❏ Original Sound Recordings (SP)
OSR-11 .... '70s   15-20
DISC 2: Yellow label, black print.

❏ Original Sound Recordings
OSR-11 .... '70s   15-20
COVER 2: Same as cover 1, except does not
have silhouettes of dancing girls.
INNER SLEEVE 2: White, no printing.

Original Sound Recordings (SP)
OSR-11 .... '70s   30-40
TOTAL PACKAGE 2: Disc, cover.

Side 1
American Pie (Don McLean)
Brand New Key (Melanie)
Let's Stay Together (Al Green)
Day After Day (Badfinger)
Never Been to Spain (Three Dog Night)
Until It's Time for You to Go (Elvis Presley)
Country Wine (Raiders)

Side 2
The Way of Love (Cher)
Hurting Each Other (Carpenters)
Joy (Apollo 100)
My World (Bee Gees)
Everything I Own (Bread)
Feelin' All Right (Joe Cocker)
Down by the Lazy River (Osmonds)

ALL TIME CHRISTMAS FAVORITES (5 LPs)

Various artists collection
Boxed set of five LPs, each one featuring two
artists (one per side). All have white labels
with red print. Identification numbers are
engraved on all discs, which are individually
listed below.

❏ Collector's Edition (SP) CE-505
1A/1B 11/78   10-20
DISC 1:
CE-505-A/CE-505-B.

❏ Collector's Edition (SP) CE-505
2A/2B 11/78   10-20
DISC 2:
CE-505-C/CE-505-D.

❏ Collector's Edition (SP) CE-505
3A/3B 11/78   10-20
DISC 3:
CE-505-E/CE-505-F.

❏ Collector's Edition (SP) CE-505
4A/4B 11/78   10-20
DISC 4:
CE-505-G/CE-505-H.

❏ Collector's Edition (SP) CE-505
5A/5B 11/78   50-75
DISC 5:
CE-505-I/CE-505-J.

❏ Collector's Edition
   CE-505 .... 11/78   100-125
   BOX 1: Slipcover: Front: Collector's Edition
   logo at lower right. Color photos of Santa
   Claus at left. Back is blank. Record case: No
   print except for gold foil on spine. Spelling and
   title errors abound on this set, as noted below.
   For example, the company name on the box
   is Collector's Edition, but on the labels is
   "Collector's Addition."
   INNER SLEEVES 1: White, no printing.

Collector's Edition (SP)
   CE-505 .... 11/78   **200-300**
   TOTAL PACKAGE 1: Discs, box/slipcover.

Disc 1

Side 1 (Lynn Anderson)
Ding-A-Ling the Christmas Bells [sic]
Frosty the Snowman
A Wistle, A Wisker Away [sic]
Rudolph the Red Nosed Reindeer
Soon It Will Be Christmas

Side 2 (Charlie Pride) (sic)
Christmas in My Home Town
Little Drummer Boy
Deck the Halls
O Holy Night
Silent Night

Disc 2

Side 1(Barbara Streisand) (sic)
Jingle Bells
Gounod's Ave Maria
The Best Gift
The Christmas Song
Sleep in Heavenly Peace

Side 2 (Frank Sinatra)
The Christmas Song
Silent Night
Mistletoe and Holly
I'll Be Home for Christmas
The First Noel

Disc 3

Side 1 (Andy Williams)
Sleigh Ride
Christmas Holiday
Winter Wonderland
Mary's Boy Child
Silver Bells

Side 2 (Glen Campbell)
It Must Be Getting Close to Christmas
Have Yourself a Merry [Little] Christmas
Blue Christmas
The Christmas [Song]
Pretty Paper

Disc 4

Side 1 (Dean Martin)
[I'm Dreaming of a] White Christmas
It's a Marshmallow World [In the Winter]
Silver Bells
[Walking in a] Winter Wonderland
Silent Night

Side 2 (Elvis Presley)
Oh Come All Ye Faithful (shown as "Come All Ye
   Faithful")
The First Noel (shown as "Noel")
I'll Be Home for Christmas
Silver Bells
Winter Wonderland (shown as "Walking in a Winter
   Wonderland")

Disc 5

Side 1 (Tammy Wynette)
Away in the Manger
Silent Night
O Little Town of Bethlehem
Joy to the World
It Came Upon a Midnight Clear

Side 2 (Johnny Mathis)
Walking in a Winter Wonderland
Sleigh Ride
I'm Dreaming of a White Xmas
Silver Bells
Blue Christmas

ALL TIME GREATS, VOL. 1
Various artists collection
❏ Promo (S) .... '70s   15-25
   DISC 1: Verification pending. Has one Elvis
   track.
❏ Promo .... '70s   15-25
   COVER 1: Verification pending.
Promo (S) .... **'70s**   **30-50**
   TOTAL PACKAGE 1: Disc, cover.

ALL TIME GREATS, VOL. 3
Various artists collection
❏ Promo (S) .... '70s   15-25
   DISC 1: Verification pending. Has one Elvis
   track.
❏ Promo .... '70s   15-25
   COVER 1: Verification pending.
Promo (S) .... **'70s**   **30-50**
   TOTAL PACKAGE 1: Disc, cover.

ALMOST IN LOVE (With *Stay Away, Joe*)
❏ RCA/Camden (ST)
   CAS-2440 .... 11/70   20-25
   DISC 1: Blue label. Rigid vinyl. Side 2, Track
   5 is *Stay Away, Joe.*
   ZCRS-5966-1S/ZCRS-5967-1S.
   ZCRS-5966-2S/ZCRS-5967-2S.
   ZCRS-5966-3S/ZCRS-5967-3S.
❏ RCA/Camden
   CAS-2440 .... 11/70   10-15
   COVER 1: Front: Tan with color Elvis photo.
   RCA logo at upper left and Camden logo at
   upper right. Back: Shows Side 2, Track 5 as
   "Stay Away, Joe." Pictures three other
   Camden LPs.

INNER SLEEVE 1: White, no printing. (Some Camden LPs had no inner sleeves at all.)

RCA/Camden (ST)

CAS-2440 .... 11/70   30-40

TOTAL PACKAGE 1: Disc, cover.

❑ RCA/Camden (ST)
CAS-2440 .... 11/70   20-25
DISC 2: Same as disc 1.
❑ RCA/Camden
CAS-2440 .... 11/70   15-20
COVER 2: Designate promo. Same as cover 1, but with "Not for Sale" stamped on back.
INNER SLEEVE 2: White, no printing. (Some Camden LPs had no inner sleeves at all.)

RCA/Camden (ST)

CAS-2440 .... 11/70   35-45

TOTAL PACKAGE 2: Disc, cover.

❑ RCA/Camden (ST)
CAS-2440 .... '71   10-15
DISC 3: Blue label. Flexible vinyl. Side 2, Track 5 is *Stay Away, Joe.*
❑ RCA/Camden
CAS-2440 .... '71   10-15
COVER 3: Same as cover 1, except has a "2" on back at lower left.
INNER SLEEVE 3: White, no printing. (Some Camden LPs had no inner sleeves at all.)

RCA/Camden (ST)

CAS-2440 71   20-30

TOTAL PACKAGE 3: Disc, cover.

Side 1
Almost in Love
Long Legged Girl (With the Short Dress On)
Edge of Reality
My Little Friend
A Little Less Conversation
Side 2
Rubberneckin'
Clean Up Your Own Backyard
U.S. Male
Charro
Stay Away, Joe

ALMOST IN LOVE (With *Stay Away*)

❑ RCA/Camden (SP)
CAS-2440 .... 3/73   10-15
DISC 1: Blue label. Rigid vinyl. Side 2, Track 5 is *Stay Away.* Since *Stay Away* is mono, the designation is changed here from "ST" to "SP."
ZCRS-5966-3S/ZCRS-5967-3S.
❑ RCA/Camden CAS-2440 ... 3/73   10-15
COVER 1: Same as cover 1 with *Stay Away, Joe,* (previous listing) except shows Side 2, Track 5 as "Stay Away." and has "RE" on back.

INNER SLEEVE 1: White, no printing. (Some Camden LPs had no inner sleeves at all.)

RCA/Camden (SP)

CAS-2440 .... 3/73   20-30

TOTAL PACKAGE 1: Disc, cover.

❑ RCA/Camden (SP)
CAS-2440 .... '73   5-10
DISC 2: Blue label. Flexible vinyl. Side 2, Track 5 is *Stay Away.*
ZCRS-5966-3S/ZCRS-5967-11S.
ZCRS-5966-2S/ZCRS-5967-14S.
❑ RCA/Camden CAS-2440 ..... '73   5-10
COVER 2: Same as cover 1.
INNER SLEEVE 2: White, no printing. (Some Camden LPs had no inner sleeves at all.)

RCA/Camden (SP)

CAS-2440 .... '73   10-20

TOTAL PACKAGE 2: Disc, cover.

Side 1
Almost in Love
Long Legged Girl (With the Short Dress On)
Edge of Reality
My Little Friend
A Little Less Conversation
Side 2
Rubberneckin'
Clean Up Your Own Backyard
U.S. Male
Charro
Stay Away

ALMOST IN LOVE (Pickwick)

❑ Pickwick/Camden (SP)
CAS-2440 .... 12/75   2-5
DISC 1: Black label. Multi-color Pickwick logo at center. Side 2, Track 5 is *Stay Away.*
ZCRS-5966-3S/ZCRS-5967-12S.
CAS-2440A-8/CAS-2440B. Identification numbers are engraved.
❑ Pickwick/Camden
CAS-2440 .... 12/75   3-5
COVER 1: Front: White with color photo of Elvis. Camden logo at upper left, Pickwick logo at lower left. Back: Shows Side 2, Track 5 as "Stay Away."
INNER SLEEVE 1: White, no printing.

Pickwick/Camden (SP)

CAS-2440 .... 12/75   5-10

TOTAL PACKAGE 1: Disc, cover.

Side 1
Almost in Love
Long Legged Girl (With the Short Dress On)
Edge of Reality
My Little Friend
A Little Less Conversation
Side 2
Rubberneckin'
Clean Up Your Own Backyard
U.S. Male
Charro
Stay Away

ALOHA FROM HAWAII VIA SATELLITE (2 LPs)

❑ RCA (Q) VPSX-6089.........2/73   10-20
DISCS 1: Reddish-orange label.

(Disc 1) CPRT-4748/CPRT-4749. **(Disc 2)** CPRT-4750/CPRT-4751. On side 1, "CPRT-4748" is stamped, but the "8" is crossed out and another "8" stamped next to it.

(Disc 1) CPRT-4748/CPRT-4749. **(Disc 2)** CPRT-4750/CPRT-4751. On side 1, "CPRT-4748" is stamped, but the "8" is crossed out and another "8" stamped next to it. Also, on side 2, "CPRT-4748" is stamped, but the "8" is crossed out and a "9" engraved.

(Disc 1) CPRT-4748/CPRT-4749. **(Disc 2)** CPRT-4750/CPRT-4751. On side 1, "CPRT-4748" is stamped, but the "8" is crossed out and a "9" engraved.

(Disc 1) CPRT-4748-1-A2/CPRT-4749-1-B5. **(Disc 2)** CPRT-4750-1-B-2/CPRT-4751-2-B3.

❑ RCA VPSX-6089...............2/73   60-70
COVER 1: Contents not printed on covers. There is no Saturn-shaped contents sticker, nor is there a QuadraDisc sticker. On this issue, stickers were on shrink wrap. Front has die-cut (5½" diameter) hole which allows inner sleeve to show. Double pocket cover.

❑ RCA VPSX-6089...............2/73   4-8
INNER SLEEVES 1: Two identical sleeves. Side 1 shows Elvis on stage. It is this shot that is displayed through the hole in those covers that are die-cut. Pictures and plugs *Elvis As Recorded at Madison Square Garden*. Side 2 is merely photo trickery. Depicts Elvis, wearing the jumpsuit shown on the *Madison Square Garden* cover, standing and singing on the grass, near the ocean, flanked by 14 Hawaiian girls – a ridiculous concoction. These sleeves were used with all issues of this LP, including CPD2-2642.

❑ RCA VPSX-6089...............2/73   15-25
SHRINK STICKER 1A: Saturn-shaped contents sticker. Black print on gold stock.

❑ RCA VPSX-6089...............2/73   5-10
SHRINK STICKER 1B: QuadraDisc sticker. Black, white, and gold sticker.

RCA (Q) VPSX-6089 ....2/73   75-100
TOTAL PACKAGE 1: Discs, cover, inner sleeves, stickers.

❑ RCA (Q) VPSX-6089.........2/73   10-20
DISCS 2: Same as discs 1.

❑ RCA VPSX-6089...............2/73   2000-4000
COVER 2: Same as cover 1, but with a "Chicken of the Sea Sneak Preview" sticker applied to front, on the shrink wrap. Because these LPs were shrink wrapped first, the QuadraDisc sticker (on front) and Saturn-shaped contents sticker (on back) are also on the shrink instead of the actual cover. These copies were distributed within the Van Camps, or Chicken of the Sea, organization. Promotional issue only. Includes an insert card, listed separately below. Front has die-cut (5½" diameter) hole which allows inner sleeve to show. Double pocket cover.

Price here is for cover with shrink wrap and three stickers still properly attached to cover. Stickers by themselves are priced separately below.

❑ RCA VPSX-6089...............2/73   4-8
INNER SLEEVES 2: Same as inner sleeves 1.

❑ RCA VPSX-6089...............2/73   100-150
INSERT 2: Pictures Elvis at left, a can of Chicken of the Sea tuna at upper right, and programming schedule at lower right. Printed on just one side.

❑ RCA VPSX-6089...............2/73   700-800
SHRINK STICKER 2A: Chicken of the Sea, multi-color (red, yellow, green, black, and white) sticker. Used only on cover 2.

❑ RCA VPSX-6089...............2/73   15-25
SHRINK STICKER 2B: Saturn-shaped contents sticker. Black print on gold stock.

❑ RCA VPSX-6089...............2/73   5-10
SHRINK STICKER 2C: QuadraDisc sticker. Black, white, and gold sticker.

RCA (Q) VPSX-6089 ....2/73   2500-5000
TOTAL PACKAGE 2: Discs, cover, inner sleeves, stickers.

❑ RCA (Q) VPSX-6089.........2/73   10-20
DISCS 3: Same as discs 1.

❑ RCA VPSX-6089...............2/73   60-70
COVER 3: Contents not printed on cover. A gold, Saturn-shaped sticker, listing the contents, applied directly to either front or back cover. Also on front is a gold and black "QuadraDisc" sticker, used because covers indicate "Stereo" instead of quadraphonic. Front has die-cut (5½" diameter) hole which allows inner sleeve to show. Double pocket cover.

❑ RCA VPSX-6089...............2/73   4-8
INNER SLEEVES 3: Same as inner sleeves 1.
SHRINK STICKERS 3: Not priced separately since they are applied directly to cover.

RCA (Q) VPSX-6089 ....2/73   75-100
TOTAL PACKAGE 3: Discs, cover with stickers, inner sleeves.

❑ RCA (Q) VPSX-6089.........2/73   10-20
DISCS 4: Same as discs 1.

❑ RCA VPSX-6089...............2/73   500-975
COVER 4: Front: Has two white stickers, listing contents and playing times. Promotional issue only. Otherwise, same as cover 1.

❑ RCA VPSX-6089...............2/73   4-8
INNER SLEEVES 4: Same as inner sleeves 1.
SHRINK STICKERS 4: Not priced separately since they are applied directly to cover.

RCA (Q) VPSX-6089 ....2/73   500-1000
TOTAL PACKAGE 4: Discs, cover with stickers, inner sleeves.

❑ RCA (Q) VPSX-6089 .... 2/73   10-20
  DISCS 5: Same as discs 1.

❑ RCA VPSX-6089 .... 2/73   70-80
  COVER 5: Designate promo. Same as cover 3, but with "Not for Sale" stamped on back.

❑ RCA VPSX-6089 .... 2/73   4-8
  INNER SLEEVES 5: Same as inner sleeves 1.
  SHRINK STICKERS 5: Not priced separately since they are applied directly to cover.

RCA (Q) VPSX-6089 .... 2/73   80-110
  TOTAL PACKAGE 5: Discs, cover with stickers, inner sleeves.

❑ RCA (Q) VPSX-6089 .... '74   10-12
  DISCS 6: Orange label.
  (Disc 1) CPRT-4748-22Q/CPRT-4749-24. **(Disc 2)** CPRT-4750-20Q/CPRT-4751-20Q.
  (Disc 1) CPRT-4748-25/CPRT-4749-24Q. **(Disc 2)** CPRT-4750-23/CPRT-4751-22.

❑ RCA VPSX-6089 .... '74   15-20
  COVER 6: Front: Has Quadradisc/RCA logo at lower right. Contents printed on back, in Saturn-shaped background. Double pocket cover.

❑ RCA VPSX-6089 .... 2/73   4-8
  INNER SLEEVES 6: Same as inner sleeves 1.

RCA (Q) VPSX-6089 .... '74   30-40
  TOTAL PACKAGE 6: Discs, cover, inner sleeves.

❑ RCA (Q) VPSX-6089 .... '74   10-12
  DISCS 7: Orange label.
  (Disc 1) CPRT-4748-22Q/CPRT-4749-24. **(Disc 2)** CPRT-4750-20Q/CPRT-4751-20Q.
  (Disc 1) CPRT-4748-25/CPRT-4749-24Q. **(Disc 2)** CPRT-4750-23/CPRT-4751-22.

❑ RCA VPSX-6089 .... '74   15-20
  COVER 7: Front: Has Quadradisc/RCA logo at lower right. Contents printed on back, in Saturn-shaped background. Double pocket cover. Back: Has "RE" at lower left corner.

❑ RCA VPSX-6089 .... 2/73   4-8
  INNER SLEEVES 7: Same as inner sleeves 1.

❑ RCA VPSX-6089 .... 2/73   50-60
  SHRINK STICKER 7A: Black, 2¼" x 3½" sticker with yellow letters and border. Reads: "Including Steamroller Blues." VPSX-6089-3 at bottom.

❑ RCA VPSX-6089 .... 2/73   5-10
  SHRINK STICKER 7B: QuadraDisc sticker. Black, white, and gold sticker.

RCA (Q) VPSX-6089 .... '74   85-100
  TOTAL PACKAGE 7: Discs, cover, inner sleeves, stickers.

❑ RCA (Q) CPD2-2642 .... '75   10-12
  DISCS 8: Orange Label.
  (Disc 1) CPRT-4748-24/CPRT-4749-25. **(Disc 2)** CPRT-4750-23/CPRT-4751-23.
  (Disc 1) CPRT-4748-27/CPRT-4749-32. **(Disc 2)** CPRT-4750-25/CPRT-4751-24.
  (Disc 1) CPD2-2642 is crossed out and CPRT-4748-27 is stamped./CPRT- 4750-25. **(Disc 2)** CPRT-4750-25/CPRT-4751-24.

❑ RCA CPD2-2642 .... '75   15-20
  COVER 8: Reflects number change. Has "RE" on back, otherwise, same as cover 6.

❑ RCA VPSX-6089 .... 2/73   4-8
  INNER SLEEVES 8: Same as inner sleeves 1.

RCA (Q) CPD2-2642 .... '75   30-40
  TOTAL PACKAGE 8: Discs, cover, inner sleeves.

❑ RCA (Q) VPSX-6089 .... '76   8-10
  DISCS 9: Tan label.

❑ RCA VPSX-6089 .... '76   12-15
  COVER 9: Reflects number change. Has "RE" on back, otherwise, same as cover 3.

❑ RCA VPSX-6089 .... 2/73   4-8
  INNER SLEEVES 9: Same as inner sleeves 1.

RCA (Q) VPSX-6089 .... '76   25-30
  TOTAL PACKAGE 9: Discs, cover, inner sleeves.

❑ RCA (Q) CPD2-2642 .... 11/77   4-6
  DISCS 10: Black label, dog near top.

❑ RCA CPD2-2642 .... 11/77   5-10
  COVER 10: Reflects selection number change.

❑ RCA CPD2-2642 .... '77   40-60
  SHRINK STICKER 10: Announces the "Memories of Elvis" NBC-TV show.

❑ RCA VPSX-6089 .... 2/73   4-8
  INNER SLEEVES 10: Same as inner sleeves 1.

RCA (Q) CPD2-2642 .... '77   55-85
  TOTAL PACKAGE 10: Discs, cover, inner sleeves, sticker.

❑ RCA (S) CPL2-2642 .... '84   4-6
  DISCS 11: Black label, dog near top.

❑ RCA CPL2-2642 .... '84   4-6
  COVER 11: Reflects prefix change. Standard, single pocket, does not have die-cut hole on front.
  INNER SLEEVES 11: White, no printing.

RCA (S) CPL2-2642 .... '84   8-12
  TOTAL PACKAGE 11: Discs, cover.

Disc 1

Side 1
Introduction: Also Sprach Zarathustra
See See Rider
Burning Love
Something
You Gave Me a Mountain
Steamroller Blues

Side 2
My Way
Love Me
Johnny B. Goode
It's Over
Blue Suede Shoes
I'm So Lonesome I Could Cry
I Can't Stop Loving You
Hound Dog

Disc 2

Side 3
What Now My Love
Fever
Welcome to My World
Suspicious Minds
Introductions By Elvis

Side 4
I'll Remember You
Medley: Long Tall Sally/Whole Lot-ta Shakin' Goin' On
An American Trilogy
A Big Hunk O' Love
Can't Help Falling in Love

ALOHA FROM HAWAII VIA SATELLITE (2 LPs) (Record Club)

❑ RCA (ST) R213736 .... '73   20-30
DISCS 1: RCA Orange label. Dynaflex vinyl.
Record Club issue – though not indicated as
such. This edition is stereo, not quad. To
really confuse the issue, some copies of this
LP were shipped with an orange label disc 1
and a tan label disc 2.
(Disc 1) R213736-A-1S/R213736-B-1S/. **(Disc 2)**
R213736-C-4S/R213736-D-1S.

❑ RCA R213736 .... '73   25-35
COVER 1: Contents printed on back, in
Saturn-shaped background. Since this is
stereo there is no QuadraDisc reference.
Does not have die-cut hole, as photo on inner
sleeve is also printed on cover.

❑ RCA VPSX-6089 .... 2/73   4-8
INNER SLEEVES 1: Two identical sleeves.
Side 1 shows Elvis on stage. It is this shot
that is displayed through the hole in those
covers that are die-cut. Pictures and plugs
*Elvis As Recorded at Madison Square
Garden*. Side 2 is merely photo trickery.
Depicts Elvis, wearing the jumpsuit shown on
the *Madison Square Garden* cover, standing
and singing on the grass, near the ocean,
flanked by 14 Hawaiian girls.

RCA (ST) R213736............ '73   50-75
TOTAL PACKAGE 1: Discs, cover, inner
sleeves.

❑ RCA (ST) R213736 .... '76   20-25
DISCS 2: Tan label. Dynaflex vinyl. Record
Club issue – though not indicated as such.
This edition is stereo, not quad.
(Disc 1) R213736-A-1S/R213736-B-1S/**(Disc 2)** R213736-
C-4S/R213736-D-2S.

❑ RCA R213736 .... '76   20-30
COVER 2: Same as cover 1, but with "RE"
added to back.

❑ RCA VPSX-6089 .... 2/73   4-8
INNER SLEEVES 2: Same as inner sleeves
1.

RCA (ST) R213736............ '76   45-65
TOTAL PACKAGE 2: Discs, cover, inner
sleeves.

❑ RCA (Q) VPSX-6089 .... '77   5-10
DISCS 3: Black label, dog near top.

❑ RCA R213736 .... '77   20-30
COVER 3: Same as cover 1, except has "RE"
on back.
INNER SLEEVES 3: White, no printing.

RCA (Q) VPSX-6089 .... '77   25-40
TOTAL PACKAGE 3: Discs, cover.

Disc 1

Side 1
Introduction: Also Sprach Zarathustra
See See Rider
Burning Love
Something
You Gave Me a Mountain
Steamroller Blues

Side 2
My Way
Love Me
Johnny B. Goode
It's Over
Blue Suede Shoes
I'm So Lonesome I Could Cry
I Can't Stop Loving You
Hound Dog

Disc 2

Side 3
What Now My Love
Fever
Welcome to My World
Suspicious Minds
Introductions By Elvis

Side 4
I'll Remember You
Medley: Long Tall Sally/Whole Lot-ta Shakin' Goin' On
An American Trilogy
A Big Hunk O' Love
Can't Help Falling in Love

ALOHA REHEARSAL SHOW – KUI LEE CANCER BENEFIT

❑ Amiga 5-73-210: Bootleg. Listed for
identification only.

ALTERNATE ALOHA

❑ RCA Victor (ST)
6985-1-R .... '88   5-6
DISC 1: Black label, dog near top.
6985-1-R-A-2/6985-1-R-B-2. Identification numbers are
engraved.

❑ RCA/BMG 6985-1-R............. '88   5-6
COVER 1: Front: White. Has artist's rendering
of Elvis, but with no lettering whatsoever.
Back: UPC bar code at upper right and
BMG/RCA logo at lower right.

❑ RCA/BMG 6985-1-R............. '88   2-3
INNER SLEEVE 1: Lavender print on white
stock. Liner notes on side 1; technical
production notes on side 2.

❑ RCA 6985-1-R .... '88   3-5
SHRINK STICKER 1: Red print on white
stock. Describes *The Alternate Aloha* LP.

**RCA Victor (ST)
6985-1-R........................ '88   15-20**
TOTAL PACKAGE 1: Disc, cover, inner
sleeve, sticker.

❑ RCA Victor (ST) 6985-1-R .. '88   5-6
 DISC 2: Same as disc 1.
RCA/BMG 6985-1-R................ '88   10-12
 COVER 2: Designate promo. Same as cover
 1, but with "Not for Sale" stamped on back.
RCA/BMG 6985-1-R................ '88   2-3
 INNER SLEEVE 2: Same as inner sleeve 1.
RCA 6985-1-R.......................... '88   1-5
 SHRINK STICKER 2: Same as sticker 1.
RCA Victor (ST)
 6985-1-R........................'88   20-25
 TOTAL PACKAGE 2: Disc, cover, inner
 sleeve, sticker.

Card stock jacket, with printing on cover – not
on slicks.
Disc 1
Side 1
Introduction: Also Sprach Zarathustra
See See Rider
Burning Love
Something
You Gave Me a Mountain
Steamroller Blues
My Way
Love Me
It's Over
Blue Suede Shoes
I'm So Lonesome I Could Cry
Side 2
What Now My Love
Fever
Welcome to My World
Suspicious Minds
I'll Remember You
An American Trilogy (shown as "American Trilogy")
A Big Hunk O' Love (shown as "Big Hunk O' Love")
Can't Help Falling in Love
Blue Hawaii

ALWAYS ON MY MIND

❑ RCA (SP) AFL1-5430........6/85   12-15
 DISC 1: Purple vinyl. Gold "Elvis 50th
 Anniversary" label.
 AFL1-5430A-10/AFL1-5430B-10. Identification numbers are
 engraved.
❑ RCA AFL1-5430................6/85   4-5
 COVER 1: Multi-color with artist's rendering of
 Elvis on front and back. UPC bar code at
 upper right and RCA logo at lower right on
 back.
 INNER SLEEVE 1: White, no printing.
❑ RCA AFL1-5430................6/85   4-5
 SHRINK STICKER 1: White print on blue
 stock. Highlights contents and purple vinyl
 pressing.
RCA (SP) AFL1-5430......6/85   20-25
 TOTAL PACKAGE 1: Disc, cover, sticker.

❑ RCA (SP) AFL1-5430........6/85   12-15
 DISC 2: Same as disc 1.
❑ RCA AFL1-5430................6/85   8-10
 COVER 2: Designate promo. Same as cover
 1, but with "Not for Sale" stamped on back.
 INNER SLEEVE 2: White, no printing.

❑ RCA AFL1-5430................6/85   4-5
 SHRINK STICKER 2: Same as sticker 1.
RCA (SP) AFL1-5430......6/85   25-30
 TOTAL PACKAGE 2: Disc, cover, sticker.

❑ RCA (SP) AFL1-5430.......8/85   10-12
 DISC 3: Black vinyl. Gold, black and white
 "Elvis 50th Anniversary" label.
❑ RCA AFL1-5430................8/85   4-5
 COVER 3: Same as cover 1.
 INNER SLEEVE 3: White, no printing.
RCA (SP) AFL1-5430 .....8/85   15-20
 TOTAL PACKAGE 3: Disc, cover.

Card stock jacket, with printing on cover – not
on slicks.
Don't Cry Daddy is monaural on this LP.
Side A
Separate Ways
Don't Cry Daddy
My Boy
Solitaire
Bitter They Are, Harder They Fall
Hurt
Side B
Pieces of My Life
I Miss You
It's Midnight
I've Lost You
You Gave Me a Mountain
Unchained Melody
Always on My Mind

AMERICA'S No. 1s
Various artists collection
❑ America's No. 1s   10-15
 DISC 1: Price range is for any individual disc
 containing at least one Elvis track. Includes a
 one-page cue sheet.

AMERICAN CHRISTMAS (FROM THE ARCHIVES OF SATURDAY EVENING POST) (12 LPs)
Various artists collection
Complete 12-hour radio show. Boxed set of
12 LPs. All discs have white labels with red
print. Identification numbers are engraved on
all discs, which are individually listed below.
Issued only to radio stations.
❑ Otis Conner Prod. (SP)
 1A/1B................12/84   5-10
 DISC 1:
 S-AMC-1-00A/S-AMC-1-00B.
❑ Otis Conner Prod. (SP)
 2A/2B................12/84   5-10
 DISC 2:
 S-AMC-2-00A/S-AMC-2-00B.
❑ Otis Conner Prod. (SP)
 3A/3B................12/84   5-10
 DISC 3:
 S-AMC-3-00A/S-AMC-3-00B.
❑ Otis Conner Prod. (SP)
 4A/4B................12/84   5-10

DISC 4:
S-AMC-4-00A/S-AMC-4-00B.
❏ Otis Conner Prod. (SP)
5A/5B 12/84   5-10
DISC 5:
S-AMC-5-00A/S-AMC-5-00B.
❏ Otis Conner Prod. (SP)
6A/6B 12/84   5-10
DISC 6:
S-AMC-6-00A/S-AMC-6-00B.
❏ Otis Conner Prod. (SP)
7A/7B 12/84   5-10
DISC 7:
S-AMC-7-00A/S-AMC-7-00B.
❏ Otis Conner Prod. (SP)
8A/8B 12/84   5-10
DISC 8:
S-AMC-8-00A/S-AMC-8-00B.
❏ Otis Conner Prod. (SP)
9A/9B 12/84   5-10
DISC 9:
S-AMC-9-00A/S-AMC-9-00B.
❏ Otis Conner Prod. (SP)
10A/10B 12/84   5-10
DISC 10:
S-AMC-10-00A/S-AMC-10-00B.
❏ Otis Conner Prod. (SP)
11A/11B 12/84   5-10
DISC 11:
S-AMC-11-00A/S-AMC-11-00B.
❏ Otis Conner Prod. (SP)
12A/12B 12/84   5-10
DISC 12:
S-AMC-12-00A/S-AMC-12-00B.
❏ Otis Conner Prod............12/84   20-30
BOX 1: White slick with red print, applied to a blank, black box.
INNER SLEEVES 1: White, no printing.
❏ Otis Conner Prod............12/84   15-25
INSERT 1: 14 pages of cue sheets and program notes.

Otis Conner Prod.
(SP) 12/84   **125-200**
TOTAL PACKAGE 1: Discs, box, inserts.

Elvis Contents:

Hour 1
Blue Christmas (Side 2, Segment 5)

Hour 3
Silent Night (Side 2, Segment 4)

Hour 7
Santa Claus Is Back in Town (Side 2, Segment 4)

Hour 10
Silver Bells (Side 2, Segment 4)

Hour 12
Merry Christmas Baby (Side 1, Segment 1)

AMERICAN COUNTRY COUNTDOWN (3 LPs)
Various artists collections.
❏ American Country
Countdown (S)   10-15
DISC 1: Price range is for any individual disc containing at least one Elvis track.
❏ American Country
Countdown (S)   25-35
COMPLETE SET 1: Boxed set of three LPs. Each is a complete three-hour, weekly radio show with three pages of cue sheets and program notes. Boxes are white and have a drawing of a western hat and boots. Issued only to subscribing radio stations. Price range is for any complete set containing at least one Elvis track.

AMERICAN DREAM, VOLUME 1
❏ Claudia 197-79: Bootleg. Listed for identification only.

AMERICAN TOP 40 (3 LPs)
Various artists collections.
❏ American Top 40 (S)   10-15
DISC 1: Price range is for any individual disc containing at least one Elvis track.
❏ American Top 40 (S)   25-35
COMPLETE SET 1: Boxed set of three LPs. Each is a complete three-hour, weekly radio show with three pages of cue sheets and program notes. Issued only to subscribing radio stations. Price range is for any complete set containing at least one Elvis track.

AMERICA'S OWN
❏ Geneva 2001: Bootleg. Listed for identification only.

APRIL '64 POP SAMPLER
Various artists collection
❏ RCA Victor (SP)
SPS 33-272 ....4/64   500-750
DISC 1: Side 1: Black label, no dog. "Stereo" at bottom. Promotional issue only.
RNRS-3736-1S/RNRS-3737-1S.
COVER 1: White, no printing.
INNER SLEEVE 1: White, no printing.
RCA Victor (SP)
SPS 33-272 ....4/64   **500-750**
TOTAL PACKAGE 1: Disc.

All tracks except *Saeta* (Carlos Montoya) are stereo.

Side 1
The Pink Panther Theme (Henry Mancini & Orchestra)
Prism Song (Gale Garnett)
It Took a Miracle (Solomon King)
Give Me This Mountain (Blackwood Brothers)
I Met God in the Morning (George Beverly Shea)
What Now My Love (Frankie Fanelli)
Mayibuye (Miriam Makeba)
Saeta (Carlos Montoya)

Side 2
Exactly Like You (Ames Brothers)
You Don't Knock (Don Gibson)
Hobo Flats (Joe Williams)
Medley: Old Piano Roll Blues (Frankie Carle)
Jitterbug Waltz (Chet Atkins)
Kissin' Cousins (Elvis Presley)
Always in My Heart (Los Indios Tabajaras)

APRIL '65 POP SAMPLER

Various artists collection

❑ RCA Victor (SP)
SPS 33-331 ....4/65   500-750
DISC 1: Black label, no dog. "Stereo
Dynagroove" at bottom. Promotional issue
only.
SNRS-3309-1S/SNRS-3310-1S.
COVER 1: White, no printing.
INNER SLEEVE 1: White, no printing.

RCA Victor (SP)
SPS 33-331 ....4/65   500-750
TOTAL PACKAGE 1: Disc.

All tracks except *Chapines* (Juan Serrano) are
stereo.

Side 1
Love Theme from "In Harm's Way" (Jerry Goldsmith
    Orchestra)
Oh, What a Beautiful Mornin' (Ethel Ennis)
Shine on Harvest Moon (Frankie Carle)
I Could Have Danced All Night (Peter Nero)
Bossa Antigua (Paul Desmond Featuring Jim Hall)
Cameroon (Mariam Makeba)
Hello Dolly (The Melachrino Stings and Orchestra)

Side 2
Chapines (Juan Serrano)
The Meanest Girl in Town (Elvis Presley)
Never on Sunday (Mariachi Los Comperos)
The Other Side of You (Connie Smith)
People (Joe Williams)
Plastered (Don Bowman)
I Stepped over the Line (Don Robertson)

APRIL '66 POP SAMPLER

Various artists collection

❑ RCA Victor (ST)
SPS 33-403 ....4/66   500-750
DISC 1: Black label, no dog. "Stereo
Dynagroove" at bottom. Promotional issue
only.
TNRS-3146-1S/TNRS-3147-1S.
COVER 1: White, no printing.
INNER SLEEVE 1: White, no printing.

RCA Victor (ST)
SPS 33-403 ....4/66   500-750
TOTAL PACKAGE 1: Disc.

Side 1
My Fair Sadie (Various Artists)
It's Just an Old Hawaiian Custom (Ray Kinney)
Solo and Some Trust in Chariots (Rod McKuen)
That Old Feeling (Brook Benton)
Medley: Baia and Solamente Una Vez (Frankie Carle)
Cheers (Group 1, Directed By George Wilkins)
Columbus Stockade Blues (Willie Nelson)

Side 2
Stand At Your Window (The Blue Boys with Bud
    Logan)
Big Boss Man (Charlie Rich)
Of Thee I Sing (Tommy Leonetti)
Bill Bailey (Marilyn Maye)
Frankie and Johnny (Elvis Presley)
Solo Busanova (Hugo Montenegro)
Dominique (The Provocative Strings of Zacharias)

ARMED FORCES RADIO & TELEVISION SERVICE

Listed individually, alphanumerically, are
some AFRTS albums we know of that have
Elvis on one full side. There are surely others,
but this is our first attempt to individually
document them, so we'll begin with the few we
have verified. All were made for either public
service radio broadcasting or for play on
Armed Forces Radio Network stations.
AFRTS issues of a commercial Elvis album
will be found under each specific title.

❑ P-4627/P-4628 ....'56   100-200
DISC 1:
SSL-8591/SSL-8592.
COVER 1: None made.
INNER SLEEVE 1: Brown, no printing.

P-4627/P-4628....................'56   100-200
TOTAL PACKAGE 1: Disc.

Side 1 (Red Nichols)
Bugler's Lament
The Wail of the Winds
Glory, Glory
Corky
Panama

Side 2 (Elvis Presley)
I Forgot to Remember to Forget (shown as "I
    Forgot to Remember")
Mystery Train
Heartbreak Hotel
I Was the One

❑ P-4839/P-4840 ....'56   100-200
DISC 1:
SSL-8895/SSL-8896.
COVER 1: None made.
INNER SLEEVE 1: Brown, no printing.

P-4839/P-4840....................'56   100-200
TOTAL PACKAGE 1: Disc.

Side 1 (Elvis Presley)
My Baby Left Me
I Want You, I Need You, I Love You
You're a Heartbreaker
That's All Right
Milkcow Blues Boogie

Side 2 (Hugo Winterhalter)
The Little Musicians
This Is Real
Flaherty's Beguine
Canadian Sunset (Eddie Heywood, piano solo)

❑ P-4991/P-4992 .... '56　　100-200
DISC 1:
SSL-9137/SSL-9138.
COVER 1: None made.
INNER SLEEVE 1: Brown, no printing.

P-4991/P-4992 .... '56　　100-200
TOTAL PACKAGE 1: Disc.

Side 1 (Richard Maltby)
Raucous Maracas
Pagan Love Song
The Birth of the Blues
Theme from War and Peace

Side 2 (Elvis Presley)
Anyway You Want Me (That's How I Will Be)
Love Me Tender
I'll Never Let You Go (Little Darlin')
Blue Moon
Just Because

❑ P-7867/P-7868 .... '56　　35-50
DISC 1: Has one Elvis track. No other
information available.
COVER 1: None made.
INNER SLEEVE 1: Brown, no printing.

P-7867/P-7868 .... '56　　35-50
TOTAL PACKAGE 1: Disc.

❑ P-7979/P-7980 .... '57　　35-50
DISC 1: Has one Elvis track, the title of which
is not yet known to us. No other information
available.
COVER 1: None made.
INNER SLEEVE 1: Brown, no printing.

P-7979/P-7980 .... '57　　35-50
TOTAL PACKAGE 1: Disc.

❑ P-9918/P-9919 .... '56　　100-200
DISC 1:
SSL-18036/SSL-18037.
COVER 1: None made.
INNER SLEEVE 1: Brown, no printing.

P-9918/P-9919 .... '56　　100-200
TOTAL PACKAGE 1: Disc.

Side 1 (Elvis Presley – Paradise Hawaiian Style)
Paradise Hawaiian Style
Drums of the Islands
Sand Castles

Side 2 (Julius La Rosa)
Once to Every Heart
It's Just a Matter of Time
You're Gonna Hear from Me

ARMY ROTC PRESENTS "COUNTRY LINE":
see *COUNTRY LINE*

AUGUST 1959 SAMPLER
Various artists collection
❑ RCA Victor (SP)
SP-33-27 .... 8/59　　750-1000
DISC 1: Black label, dog on top. "Living
Stereo" at bottom. Promotional issue only.
K2NY-4491-1S/K2NY-4491-2S.
COVER 1: None made.

INNER SLEEVE 1: White, no printing.
RCA Victor (SP)
SP-33-27 .... 8/59　　750-1000
TOTAL PACKAGE 1: Disc.

All songs except *Blue Moon of Kentucky*
(Elvis Presley) are true stereo.
Side 1
Warsaw Concerto (Hugo Winterhalter's Orchestra)
Volare (Melachrino Strings and Orchestra)
Blessed Assurance (George Beverly Shea)
Wunderbar (Howard Keel & Anne Jeffreys)
Guadalajara (Xavier Cugat's Orchestra)
Gypsy Lament (Esquivel's Orchestra)
The Merry Old Land of Oz (Shorty Rogers' Orchestra)
Side 2
Someday (Jim Reeves)
Blue Moon of Kentucky (Elvis Presley)
The 3rd Man Theme (Buddy Morrow's Orchestra)
You're Driving Me Crazy (Perez Prado's Orchestra)
The Song Is You (Pat Suzuki)
Intro; Darling Cora (Harry Belafonte)

AUGUST '65 POP SAMPLER
Various artists collection
❑ RCA Victor (SP)
SPS-33-347 .... 8/65　　500-750
DISC 1: Black label, no dog. "Stereo
Dynagroove" at bottom. Promotional issue
only.
SNRS-5639-2S/SNRS-5640-1S.
COVER 1: White, no printing.
INNER SLEEVE 1: White, no printing.
RCA Victor (SP)
SPS-33-347 .... 8/65　　500-750
TOTAL PACKAGE 1: Disc.

All tracks except *Your Cheatin' Heart* (Elvis
Presley) are stereo.
Side 1
Tatahi Arahoho (Tahitian Native Group)
In the Middle of a Memory (Carl Belew)
Get Me to the Church on Time (Marilyn Maye)
Take a Letter, Miss Gray (Justin Tubb)
Overture from "My Fair Lady" (Paul Lavalle)
You've Lost That Lovin' Feelin' (Floyd Cramer)
Side 2
Catchin' on Fast (Peggy March & Bennie Thomas)
The Devil's Grin (Lorne Greene)
Begin the Beguine (Los Indios Tabajaras)
Little Ole You (Jim Reeves)
Twangsville (Duane Eddy)
Your Cheatin' Heart (Elvis Presley)

AVON VALENTINE FAVORITES
Various artists collection
❑ RCA Special Products (SP)
DPL1-0751 .... 1/86　　3-5
DISC 1: Custom Avon label; maroon, white
and pink with heart on lace. Sold only by Avon
representatives, as part of a Valentine
promotion.
DPL1-0751A-1/DPL1-0751B-2.

❏ RCA Special Products
DPL1-0751 .... 1/86   3-5
COVER 1: Front: RCA Special Products logo
at lower left. Color photo of an unidentified
couple. Back: Color photos of the nine acts
heard, including Elvis.
INNER SLEEVE 1: White, no printing.
❏ RCA Special Products
DPL1-0751 .... 1/86   2-4
MAILER 1: White cardboard mailer, with
selection number printed on it.
RCA Special Products (SP)
DPL1-0751 .... 1/86   8-15
TOTAL PACKAGE 1: Disc, cover, mailer.

Card stock jacket, with printing on cover – not
on slicks.
Can't Help Falling in Love is monaural on this
LP.
Side 1
Lady (Kenny Rogers)
My Funny Valentine (Tony Bennett)
Feels So Right (Alabama)
Theme from "Love Story" (Henry Mancini)
It's Impossible (Perry Como)
Side 2
Tonight, I Celebrate My Love (Peabo Bryson & Roberta
    Flack)
Chances Are (Johnny Mathis)
Can't Help Falling Love (Elvis Presley)
And I Love Her (Jose Feliciano)
Crazy (Kenny Rogers)

BABY, I DON'T CARE

❏ Astra 500: Bootleg. Listed for identification
only.

BACK IN MEMPHIS (RCA)

❏ RCA Victor (ST)
LSP-4429 .... 11/70   15-20
DISC 1: Orange label. Rigid vinyl.
XPRS-2470-5S/XPRS-2471-5S. Identification numbers are
stamped. XPRS-2470-30S/XPRS-2471-31S. Identification
numbers are engraved.
❏ RCA Victor LSP-4429 ...... 11/70   12-15
COVER 1: Black-and-white photos of Elvis on
front and back. Front: Selection number at
upper left, "Victor Stereo" at upper right. Back:
Has note at upper left about playing disc both
mono and stereo phonographs, and titles at
lower right.
❏ RCA Victor 21-112-1
pt 54 .... 8/70   3-5
INNER SLEEVE 1: Black-and-white. Pictures
RCA's Elvis LP catalog front and back, most
recent being *Worldwide Gold Award Hits, Vol.
1* (side 2, row 4, column 4).
RCA Victor (ST)
LSP-4429 .... 11/70   30-40
**TOTAL PACKAGE 1: Disc, cover, inner
sleeve.**

❏ RCA Victor (ST)
LSP-4429 .... 11/70   15-20
DISC 2: Orange label. Rigid vinyl.

❏ RCA Victor LSP-4429 ...... 11/70   15-20
COVER 2: Designate promo. Same as cover
1, but with "Not for Sale" stamped on back.
❏ RCA Victor 21-112-1
pt 54 .... 8/70   3-5
INNER SLEEVE 2: Black-and-white. Pictures
RCA's Elvis LP catalog front and back, most
recent being *Worldwide Gold Award Hits, Vol.
1* (side 2, row 4, column 4).
RCA Victor (ST)
LSP-4429 .... 11/70   35-45
**TOTAL PACKAGE 2: Disc, cover, inner
sleeve.**

❏ RCA Victor (ST)
LSP-4429 .... '71   10-15
DISC 3: Orange label. Flexible vinyl.
❏ RCA Victor LSP-4429 .... '71   12-15
COVER 3: Same as cover 1.
❏ RCA Victor .... '70s   2-4
INNER SLEEVE 3: Black-and-white. Pictures
RCA Elvis catalog front and back. Any of
several sleeves may be found on reissues
from this period.
RCA Victor (ST)
LSP-4429 .... '71   25-35
**TOTAL PACKAGE 3: Disc, cover, inner
sleeve.**

❏ RCA Victor (ST) LSP-4429 .. '76   4-8
DISC 4: Tan label.
XPRS-2470-35/XPRS-2471-32S. XPRS-2470-33S/XPRS-
2471-32S.
❏ RCA Victor LSP-4429 .... '76   12-15
COVER 4: Same as cover 1.
❏ RCA Victor .... '70s   2-4
INNER SLEEVE 4: Black-and-white. Pictures
RCA Elvis catalog front and back. Any of
several sleeves may be found on reissues
from this period.
RCA Victor (ST)
LSP-4429 .... '76   20-25
**TOTAL PACKAGE 4: Disc, cover, inner
sleeve.**

❏ RCA Victor (ST) LSP-4429 .. '76   4-6
DISC 5: Black label, dog near top.
❏ RCA LSP-4429 .... '76   5-10
COVER 5: Reflects logo change.
❏ RCA Victor .... '70s   2-4
INNER SLEEVE 5: Black-and-white. Pictures
RCA Elvis catalog front and back. Any of
several sleeves may be found on reissues
from this period.
RCA Victor (ST)
LSP-4429 .... '76   10-20
**TOTAL PACKAGE 5: Disc, cover, inner
sleeve.**

❏ RCA Victor (ST)
AFL1-4429 .... '77   3-5
DISC 6: Black label, dog near top.

❑ RCA AFL1-4429 .... '77   5-8
COVER 6: Reflects prefix change.
Only copies with a sticker bearing the "AFL1"
prefix, wrapped around cover at top of spine
have been verified. We have yet to find a
printed AFL1-4429 cover.

❑ RCA Victor .... '70s   2-4
INNER SLEEVE 6: Black-and-white. Pictures
RCA Elvis catalog front and back. Any of
several sleeves may be found on reissues
from this period.

RCA Victor (ST)
AFL1-4429 .... '77   10-18
TOTAL PACKAGE 6: Disc, cover, inner
sleeve.

❑ RCA Victor (ST)
AYL1-3892 .... '80   3-5
DISC 7: Black label, dog near top.
KPRS-2468 and AFL1-4428A both stamped and both crossed
out. AYL1-3892A is engraved. KPRS-2469 and AFL1-4428B
are both stamped and both crossed out. AYL1-3892B then
engraved.

❑ RCA AYL1-3892 .... '80   5-6
COVER 7: Reflects number change.
INNER SLEEVE 7: White, no printing.

RCA Victor (ST)
AYL1-3892 .... '80   8-12
TOTAL PACKAGE 7: Disc, cover.

Previously issued as one-half of the two-LP
set *From Memphis to Vegas / From Vegas to
Memphis.*

Side 1
Inherit the Wind
This Is the Story
Stranger in My Own Home Town
A Little Bit of Green
And the Grass Won't Pay No Mind

Side 2
Do You Know Who I Am
From a Jack to a King
The Fair Is Moving On
You'll Think of Me
Without Love

BACK IN MEMPHIS (AFRTS)

❑ Armed Forces Radio & Television Service
(S) P-12299/P12300 .... '69   75-100
DISC 1:
P-12299 RL 22-1/P12300 RL 22-1. Identification numbers
are engraved.
COVER 1: None made.
INNER SLEEVE 1: Brown, no printing.

Armed Forces Radio & Television
Service (M) P-12299/
P12300 .... '69   75-100
TOTAL PACKAGE 1: Disc.

BACK IN PORTLAND (APRIL 27, 1973)

❑ Live Archives EPE-1012: Bootleg. Listed for
identification only.

BEATLEMANIA / ELVISMANIA

❑ Professional Studio Mix JCL-7777: Bootleg.
Listed for identification only.

BEGINNING (1954-1955)

❑ Marvenco (M) 101 .... '88   6-12
DISC 1: Pink vinyl. Custom, full color label.
Pictures Elvis, Scotty and Bill. Number "101"
appears in trail off, but not on label.
L-30024X EP-ARM-101-B/L-30024 EP-ARM-101-A.
(Indication that side 2 is marked as "A" is correct.)
Identification numbers are engraved.

❑ Marvenco 101 .... '88   3-4
COVER 1: Front: Colorized, black-and-white
photo of Elvis, Scotty and Bill; same as on
label. Back: Has 8¼", die-cut hole, to expose
label and pink vinyl disc. Also has gold
"Certified Limited Production" numbered
sticker at upper right, which bears the copy
number. Number "101" appears on disc but
not on cover.
INNER SLEEVE: Since disc is displayed
through die-cut hole in front cover, no sleeve
is used.

❑ Marvenco .... '88   2-3
INSERT 1A: Full color, 12-page booklet.

❑ Marvenco .... '88   1-2
INSERT 1B: "Elvis Personal Management
Contract." Black lettering with blue border, on
white stock. Has gold "Certified Reproduction"
sticker at lower left. Printed on just one side.

❑ Marvenco 101 .... '88   1-2
INSERT 1C: Three-page, press release.
Discusses the recordings and their release by
Marvenco. Page one is on Marvenco
letterhead. This insert may not have been in
all copies.

Marvenco (M) 101 .... '88   15-25
TOTAL PACKAGE 1: Disc, cover, inserts.

❑ Marvenco (M) 101 .... '88   6-12
DISC 2: Black vinyl. Custom, full color label.
Pictures Elvis, Scotty and Bill. Number "101"
appears in trail off, but not on label.

❑ Marvenco 101 .... '88   3-4
COVER 2: Same as cover 1.
INNER SLEEVE: Since disc is displayed
through die-cut hole in front cover, no sleeve
is used.

❑ Marvenco .... '88   2-3
INSERT 2A: Full color, 12-page booklet.

❑ Marvenco .... '88   1-2
INSERT 2B: "Elvis Personal Management
Contract." Black lettering with blue border, on
white stock. Has gold "Certified Reproduction"
sticker at lower left. Printed on just one side.

❑ Marvenco 101......................'88　　1-2
INSERT 2C: Three page, press release. Discusses the recordings and their release by Marvenco. Page one is on Marvenco letterhead. This insert may not have been in all copies.
Marvenco (M) 101.............'88　　15-25
TOTAL PACKAGE 2: Disc, cover, inserts.

Card stock jacket, with printing on cover – not on slicks.

Side 1
Biff Collie Interview
Scotty Moore Tells the Story of the First Year

Side 2
Good Rockin' Tonight (shown as "There's Good Rockin' Tonight")
Baby, Let's Play House
Blue Moon of Kentucky
I Got a Woman (shown as "I've Got a Woman")
That's All Right (shown as "That's Alright Little Mama")
Elvis Interview

BEGINNING YEARS

❑ Louisiana Hayride (M)
LH-3061 ....8/83　　400-500
DISC 1: White label advance pressing from RCA Indianapolis, maker of this LP. Numbers are handwritten on label. Shipped in the standard LP cover, along with a shipping memo. Only three were made.

❑ Louisiana Hayride
LH-3061 ....8/83　　3-4
COVER 1: Double pocket. Mostly blue, with black-and-white photo of Elvis on front, inside front, and back.
INNER SLEEVE 1: White, no printing.

❑ RCA Records ....8/83　　1-2
INSERT 1: RCA shipping memo.

Louisiana Hayride (M)
LH-3061.......................8/83　　400-500
TOTAL PACKAGE 1: Disc, cover, shipping memo.

❑ Louisiana Hayride (M)
LH-3061 ....5/84　　6-8
DISC 2: Blue label with white print. 50,000 copies made.
LH-3061-A1/LH-3061-B1. Both sides have "Masterphonics" in trail off. Identification numbers are engraved.

❑ Louisiana Hayride
LH-3061 ....8/83　　8-10
COVER 2: Same as cover 1.

❑ Louisiana Hayride
LH-3061 ....5/84　　2-3
INSERT 2A: *D.J. Fontana Remembers Elvis*, a 20-page, black-and-white booklet.

❑ Louisiana Hayride
LH-3061 ....5/84　　1-2
INSERT 2B: Four-page copy of Elvis' Louisiana Hayride contract.

❑ Louisiana Hayride
LH-3061...........................5/84　　1-2
INSERT 2C: Full color, 10" x 10" promotional flyer for *Presleyana: Elvis Presley Record Price Guide, 2nd Edition.*
Louisiana Hayride (M)
LH-3061 ....5/84　　20-25
TOTAL PACKAGE 2: Disc, cover, inserts.

Card stock jacket, with printing on cover – not on slicks. (instead of cardboard stock with printed slicks applied).
Contents of this LP were split into two other LPs: *First Live Recordings* and *Hillbilly Cat.*

Side 1
That's All Right (shown as "That's All Right Momma")
Blue Moon of Kentucky
Good Rockin' Tonight
I Got a Woman

Side 2
Tweedle Dee
Baby, Let's Play House (shown as "I Wanna Play House with You")
Maybellene
That's All Right (shown as "That's All Right Momma")
Hound Dog

BEHIND CLOSED DOORS

❑ Audifon AFNS-66072-4: Bootleg. Listed for identification only.

BEST OF CHRISTMAS

Various artists collection
❑ RCA Victor (ST)
CPL1-7013 ....11/85　　3-4
DISC 1: Black label, dog near top.
CPL1-7013A-10/CPL1-7013A-11-S.

❑ RCA CPL1-7013..............11/85　　3-4
COVER 1: Front: RCA logo at bottom center. Color, with hand-carved, wooden figurines all of the acts (except Jessi Colter) heard on this LP, including one of Elvis. Back: Text only.
INNER SLEEVE 1: White, no printing.

RCA Victor (ST)
CPL1-7013 ....11/85　　6-10
TOTAL PACKAGE 1: Disc, cover.

Card stock jacket, with printing on cover – not on slicks.

Side 1
Christmas in Dixie (Alabama)
Light of the Stable (Judds)
Silent Night, Holy Night (Waylon Jennings & Jessi Colter)
Blue Christmas (Earl Conley)

Side 2
It's Christmas (Ronnie Milsap)
Hard Candy Christmas (Dolly Parton)
Silver Bells (Elvis Presley)
Pretty Paper (Willie Nelson)

BEST OF COUNTRY SESSIONS

Various artists collection

❑ Country Sessions
    USA (S) 122 ....'83   50-70
    DISC 1: Complete radio show. Has two tracks
    by Elvis. Issued only to radio stations. More
    information needed, such as number of discs,
    length of show, type of cover or box, and
    description of insert(s).

❑ Country Sessions
    USA 122 ....'83
    COVER 1: Verification pending. Not yet
    priced.

❑ Country Sessions
    USA 122 ....'83
    INSERT 1: Program notes and cue sheets.
    Likely but verification is still pending. Not yet
    priced.

Country Sessions USA (S)
122 ....'83   50-70
    **TOTAL PACKAGE 1: Disc(s), cover/box,
    insert(s).**

BEST OF ELVIS

❑ His Master's Voice DLP-1159: Bootleg.
    Listed for identification only.

BEST OF THE '50s

Various artists collection

❑ RCA Victor (SP)
    AEL1-5800 ....6/86   4-6
    DISC 1: Black label, dog near top.
    AEL1-5800A-1S/AEL1-5800B-1OS.

❑ RCA AEL1-5800 ....6/86   4-6
    COVER 1: Front: No logo or number. Color
    photo of unidentified, dancing couple. Back:
    RCA logo and number at lower right. UPC bar
    code at upper left.
    INNER SLEEVE 1: White, no printing.
    INSERT 1: Return mail card, part of an
    RCA/Nashville customer survey. Makes no
    mention of Elvis or this LP.

RCA Victor (SP)
AEL1-5800 ....6/86   8-12
    TOTAL PACKAGE 1: Disc, cover.

Card stock jacket, with printing on cover – not
on slicks.

Side 1
I'm Movin' On (Hank Snow)
Slow Poke (Pee Wee King)
A Satisfied Mind (Porter Wagoner)
Cattle Call (Eddy Arnold)
Four Walls (Jim Reeves)

Side 2
Geisha Girl (Hank Locklin)
Oh Lonesome Me (Don Gibson)
The Three Bells (Browns)
He'll Have to Go (Jim Reeves)
Love Me Tender (Elvis Presley)

BEST OF THE '60s

Various artists collection

❑ RCA Victor (SP)
    AEL1-5802 ....6/86   4-6
    DISC 1: Black label, dog near top.
    AEL1-5802A-1S/AEL1-5802B-1S.

❑ RCA AEL1-5802 ....6/86   4-6
    COVER 1: Front: No logo or number. Color
    photo of unidentified couple. Back: RCA logo,
    number and UPC bar code at lower right.
    INNER SLEEVE 1: White, no printing.
    INSERT 1: Return mail card, part of an
    RCA/Nashville customer survey. Makes no
    mention of Elvis or this LP.

RCA Victor (SP)
AEL1-5802 ....6/86   8-12
    TOTAL PACKAGE 1: Disc, cover.

Card stock jacket, with printing on cover – not
on slicks.

Side 1
Please Help Me I'm Falling (Hank Locklin)
I've Been Everywhere (Hank Snow)
The End of the World (Skeeter Davis)
Abilene (George Hamilton IV)
Crying in the Chapel (Elvis Presley)

Side 2
Welcome to My World (Jim Reeves)
Make the World Go Away (Eddy Arnold)
The Ballad of the Green Berets (SSgt. Barry Sadler)
Pop a Top (Jim Ed Brown)
The Easy Part's Over (Charley Pride)

BEST OF THE '70s

Various artists collection

❑ RCA Victor (SP)
    AEL1-5837 ....6/86   4-6
    DISC 1: Black label, dog near top.
    AEL1-5837-A-1S/AEL1-5837-B-1S. Identification numbers
    are engraved.

❑ RCA AEL1-5837 ....6/86   4-6
    COVER 1: Front: No logo or number. Color
    photo of unidentified, dancing couple. Back:
    RCA logo and number at bottom center. UPC
    bar code at upper right.
    INNER SLEEVE 1: White, no printing.
    INSERT 1: Return mail card, part of an
    RCA/Nashville customer survey. Makes no
    mention of Elvis or this LP.

RCA Victor (SP)
AEL1-5837 ....6/86   8-12
    TOTAL PACKAGE 1: Disc, cover.

Card stock jacket, with printing on cover – not
on slicks.

Side 1
9 to 5 (Dolly Parton)
Burning Love (Elvis Presley)
Good Hearted Woman (Waylon Jennings & Willie
    Nelson)
The Door Is Always Open (Dave & Sugar)
It Was Almost Like a Song (Ronnie Milsap)

Side 2
When You're Hot You're Hot (Jerry Reed)
She's Actin' Single (Gary Stewart)

Amanda (Waylon Jennings)
Kiss an Angel Good Morning (Charley Pride)
Thank God I'm a Country Boy (John Denver)

BEST OF THE '50s, '60s and '70s

Various artists collection

❑ RCA Victor (SP)

AEL1-5838 ....6/86   4-6

DISC 1: Black label, dog near top.
AEL1-5838-A-1S/AEL1-5838-B-1S.

❑ RCA AEL1-5838................6/86   4-6

COVER 1: Front: No logo or number. Color
photo of three unidentified, dancing couples.
Back: RCA logo and number at lower left.
UPC bar code at lower right.
INNER SLEEVE 1: White, no printing.
INSERT 1: Return mail card, part of an
RCA/Nashville customer survey. Makes no
mention of Elvis or this LP.

RCA Victor (SP)

AEL1-5838 ....6/86   8-12
TOTAL PACKAGE 1: Disc, cover.

Card stock jacket, with printing on cover – not
on slicks.

Side 1
9 to 5 (Dolly Parton)
It Was Almost Like a Song (Ronnie Milsap)
Amanda (Waylon Jennings)
I'm Movin' On (Hank Snow)
Oh Lonesome Me (Don Gibson)

Side 2
When You're Hot You're Hot (Jerry Reed)
Love Me Tender (Elvis Presley)
The End of the World (Skeeter Davis)
Kiss an Angel Good Morning (Charley Pride)
Make the World Go Away (Eddy Arnold)

BEST YEARS

❑ Bootleg. Listed for identification only.

BETWEEN TAKES WITH ELVIS (3 LPs)

❑ Creative Radio (M)

(No Number) 7/89   20-30

DISCS 1: Label has black print on silver
stock. Promotional issue only. Only 500
copies made. Mostly dialogue but with some
music segments (listed below), all of which
are previously unissued Elvis recordings.
(Disc 1) OE-CR-1A L-33140/OE-CR-2 L-33140. **(Disc 2)**
OE-CR-3 L- 33140/OE-CR-4 L-33140. **(Disc 3)** OE-CR-5 L-
33140/OE-CR-6 L-33140. Identification numbers are
engraved.

❑ Creative Radio

(No Number) 7/89   10-20

COVER 1: Single pocket. White stock; gray
print on front and black on back. Though not
packaged inside covers (which were shrink
wrapped at the factory), each LP set came
with the bonus single, *NEARER MY GOD TO
THEE / You Gave Me a Molehill.* See that
listing for more info.
INNER SLEEVES 1: White, no printing.

Creative Radio (M)

(No Number) 7/89   30-50
TOTAL PACKAGE 1: Disc, cover.

Card stock jacket, with printing on cover – not
on slicks.

Disc 1

Side 1
You Gave Me a Mountain
Hawaiian Wedding Song

Side 2
Burning Love
For the Good Times
Always on My Mind
Separate Ways
You Gave Me a Mountain
Love Me
El Paso
How the Web Was Woven

Disc 2

Side 1
(Let Me Be Your) Teddy Bear
A Big Hunk O' Love
See See Rider
For the Good Times
Hawaiian Wedding Song
Never Been to Spain

Side 2
Burning Love
For the Good Times
You Gave Me a Mountain
Until It's Time for You to Go
Polk Salad Annie
I Can't Stop Loving You
An American Trilogy
Funny How Time Slips Away
Cattle Call
Over the Rainbow
I'll Remember You
Nearer My God to Thee
The Lighthouse
I, John
I Need Your Loving
For the Good Times

Disc 3

Side 1
Funny How Time Slips Away
Burning Love
Help Me Make It Through the Night
Run On
I, John
Lead Me, Guide Me
Nearer My God to Thee

Disc 3

Side 2
Discussion and interviews

BIG BOSS MAN

❑ CFR 10793: Bootleg. Listed for identification
only.

BIG COUNTRY HITS

Various artists collection

❑ Pickwick (S) JS-6166 ....'75   10-20
DISC 1: Has one Elvis track, *Promised Land.*

❑ Pickwick JS-6166 .... '75   10-20
  COVER 1: Pictures a country setting.
  INNER SLEEVE 1: White, no printing.
Pickwick (S) JS-6166 .... '75   20-40
  TOTAL PACKAGE 1: Disc, cover.

BILLBOARD TOP ROCK'N ROLL HITS – 1956

Various artists collection

❑ Billboard/Rhino (M) R1-70599
  DPL1-0890 .... '89   3-5
  DISC 1: Multi-color label, large "Billboard" at top, tiny "Rhino" at bottom.
  DPL1-0890A 05250/DLP1-0890B 055250X.
❑ Billboard/Rhino R1-70599
  DPL1-0890 .... '89   3-5
  COVER 1: Front: Text only. Back: Black-and-white photos of several of the artists heard, including one of Elvis. Rhino logo and number at lower right. UPC bar code at upper right.
  INNER SLEEVE 1: White, no printing.
Billboard/Rhino (M) R1-70599
  DPL1-0890 .... '89   6-10
  TOTAL PACKAGE 1: Disc, cover.

❑ Billboard/Rhino (M) R1-70599
  DPL1-0890 .... '89   3-5
  DISC 2: Same as disc 1.
❑ Billboard/Rhino R1-70599
  DPL1-0890 .... '89   3-6
  COVER 2: Designate promo. Same as cover 1, except upper right corner is cut at an angle.
  INNER SLEEVE 2: White, no printing.
Billboard/Rhino (M) R1-70599
  DPL1-0890 .... '89   6-12
  TOTAL PACKAGE 2: Disc, cover.

Card stock jacket, with printing on cover – not on slicks.

Side 1
Don't Be Cruel (Elvis Presley)
Be-Bop-A-Lula (Gene Vincent)
Blue Suede Shoes (Carl Perkins)
I'm in Love Again (Fats Domino)
See You Later Alligator (Bill Haley & His Comets)

Side 2
Hound Dog (Elvis Presley)
The Fool (Sanford Clark)
The Green Door (Jim Lowe)
Why Do Fools Fall in Love (Teenagers)
Flying Saucers (Buchanan & Goodman)

BILLBOARD TOP ROCK'N ROLL HITS – 1957

Various artists collection

❑ Billboard/Rhino (M) R1-70618
  DPL1-0827 .... '88   3-5
  DISC 1: Multi-color label, large "Billboard" at top, tiny "Rhino" at bottom.
  R1-70618A DPL1-0827 20931/R1-70618B DPL1-0827 20931-X. Identification numbers are engraved.

❑ Billboard/Rhino R1-70618
  DPL1-0827 .... '88   3-5
  COVER 1: Front: Text only. Back: Seven black-and-white photos of artists heard, including one of Elvis. Rhino logo and number at lower right. UPC bar code at upper right.
  INNER SLEEVE 1: White, no printing.
Billboard/Rhino (M) R1-70618
  DPL1-0827 .... '88   6-10
  TOTAL PACKAGE 1: Disc, cover.

❑ Billboard/Rhino (M) R1-70618
  DPL1-0827 .... '88   3-5
  DISC 2: Same as disc 1.
❑ Billboard/Rhino R1-70618
  DPL1-0827 .... '88   3-6
  COVER 2: Designate promo. Same as cover 1, except upper right corner is cut at an angle.
  INNER SLEEVE 2: White, no printing.
Billboard/Rhino (M) R1-70618
  DPL1-0827 .... '88   6-12
  TOTAL PACKAGE 2: Disc, cover.

Card stock jacket, with printing on cover – not on slicks.

Side 1
All Shook Up (Elvis Presley)
Wake Up Little Susie (Everly Brothers)
Diana (Paul Anka)
Party Doll (Buddy Knox)
That'll Be the Day (Crickets)

Side 2
Jailhouse Rock (Elvis Presley)
Little Darlin' (Diamonds)
Peggy Sue (Buddy Holly)
School Day (Chuck Berry)
Whole Lot of Shakin' Going On (Jerry Lee Lewis)

BILLBOARD TOP ROCK'N ROLL HITS – 1958

Various artists collection

❑ Billboard/Rhino (M) R1-70619
  DPL1-0828 .... '88   3-5
  DISC 1: Multi-color label, large "Billboard" at top, tiny "Rhino" at bottom.
  R1-70619A DPL1-0828 20963/R1-70619B DPL1-0828 20963-X. Identification numbers are engraved.
❑ Billboard/Rhino R1-70619
  DPL1-0828 .... '88   3-5
  COVER 1: Front: Text only. Back: Seven black-and-white photos of artists heard, including one of Elvis. Rhino logo and number at lower right. UPC bar code at upper right.
  INNER SLEEVE 1: White, no printing.
Billboard/Rhino (M) R1-70619
  DPL1-0828 .... '88   6-10
  TOTAL PACKAGE 1: Disc, cover.

❑ Billboard/Rhino (M) R1-70619
  DPL1-0828 .... '88   3-5
  DISC 2: Same as disc 1.

❏ Billboard/Rhino R1-70619
DPL1-0828 .... '88   3-6
COVER 2: Designate promo. Same as cover
1 except upper right corner is cut at an angle.
INNER SLEEVE 2: White, no printing.
Billboard/Rhino (M) R1-70619
DPL1-0828 .... '88   6-12
TOTAL PACKAGE 2: Disc, cover.

Card stock jacket, with printing on cover – not
on slicks.

Side 1
At the Hop (Danny and the Juniors)
Tequila (Champs)
To Know Him Is to Love Him (Teddy Bears)
It's Only Make Believe (Conway Twitty)
Get a Job (Silhouettes)
Side 2
Hard Headed Woman (Elvis Presley)
Little Star (Elegants)
Bird Dog (Everly Brothers)
Yakety Yak (Coasters)
Great Balls of Fire (Jerry Lee Lewis)

BILLBOARD TOP ROCK'N ROLL HITS – 1959
Various artists collection
❏ Billboard/Rhino (M) R1-70620
DPL1-0829 .... '88   3-5
DISC 1: Multi-color label, large "Billboard" at
top, tiny "Rhino" at bottom.
R1-70620A DPL1-0829 20946/R1-70620B DPL1-0829
20946-X. Identification numbers are engraved.
❏ Billboard/Rhino R1-70620
DPL1-0829 .... '88   3-5
COVER 1: Front: Text only. Back: Seven
black-and-white photos of artists heard,
including one of Elvis. Rhino logo and number
at lower right. UPC bar code at upper right.
Billboard/Rhino (M) R1-70620
DPL1-0829 .... '88   6-10
TOTAL PACKAGE 1: Disc, cover.

❏ Billboard/Rhino (M) R1-70620
DPL1-0829 .... '88   3-5
DISC 2: Same as disc 1.
❏ Billboard/Rhino R1-70620
DPL1-0829 .... '88   3-6
COVER 2: Designate promo. Same as cover
1, except upper right corner is cut at an angle.
INNER SLEEVE 2: White, no printing.
Billboard/Rhino (M) R1-70620
DPL1-0829 .... '88   6-12
TOTAL PACKAGE 2: Disc, cover.

Card stock jacket, with printing on cover – not
on slicks.
Side 1
Mack the Knife (Bobby Darin)
Venus (Frankie Avalon)
Lonely Boy (Paul Anka)
Stagger Lee (Lloyd Price)
Kansas City (Wilbert Harrison)

Side 2
A Big Hunk O' Love (Elvis Presley)
The Happy Organ (Dave "Baby" Cortez)
Charlie Brown (Coasters)
16 Candles (Crests)
Sleep Walk (Santo & Johnny)

BILLBOARD TOP ROCK'N ROLL HITS – 1960
Various artists collection
❏ Billboard/Rhino (M) R1-70621
DPL1-0830 .... '88   3-5
DISC 1: Multi-color label, large "Billboard" at
top, tiny "Rhino" at bottom.
R1-70621A DPL1-0830 20930/R1-70621B DPL1-0830
20930-X. Identification numbers are engraved.
❏ Billboard/Rhino R1-70621
DPL1-0830 .... '88   3-5
COVER 1: Front: Text only. Back: Seven
black-and-white photos of artists heard,
including one of Elvis. Rhino logo and number
at lower right. UPC bar code at upper right.
INNER SLEEVE 1: White, no printing.
Billboard/Rhino (M) R1-70621
DPL1-0830 .... '88   6-10
TOTAL PACKAGE 1: Disc, cover.

❏ Billboard/Rhino (M) R1-70621
DPL1-0830 .... '88   3-5
DISC 2: Same as disc 1.
❏ Billboard/Rhino R1-70621
DPL1-0830 .... '88   3-6
COVER 2: Designate promo. Same as cover
1 except upper right corner is cut at an angle.
INNER SLEEVE 2: White, no printing.
Billboard/Rhino (M) R1-70621
DPL1-0830 .... '88   6-12
TOTAL PACKAGE 2: Disc, cover.

Card stock jacket, with printing on cover – not
on slicks.

Side 1
It's Now Or Never (Elvis Presley)
Cathy's Clown (Everly Brothers)
The Twist (Chubby Checker)
Save the Last Dance for Me (Drifters)
Running Bear (Johnny Bear)
Side 2
Stuck on You (Elvis Presley)
Handy Man (Jimmy Jones)
Walk, Don't Run (Ventures)
Alley-Oop (Hollywood Argyles)
Stay (Maurice Williams and the Zodiacs)

BILLBOARD'S GREATEST CHRISTMAS HITS (1955 - PRESENT)
Various artists collection
❏ Billboard/Rhino (M) R1-70636
DPL1-0885 .... '89   3-5
DISC 1: Multi-color label, large "Billboard" at
top, "Rhino" at bottom.
DPL1-0885A/DPL1-0885B. Identification numbers are
engraved. R1-70636A/R1- 70636B is engraved and crossed
out.

❏ Billboard/Rhino R1-70636
DPL1-0885 .... '89   3-5
COVER 1: Front: Text only. Back: Six black-
and-white photos of artists heard, including
one of Elvis and Col. Parker. Rhino logo and
number at lower right. UPC bar code at upper
right.
INNER SLEEVE 1: White, no printing.
Billboard/Rhino (M) R1-70636
DPL1-0885 .... '89   6-10
TOTAL PACKAGE 1: Disc, cover.

❏ Billboard/Rhino (M) R1-70636
DPL1-0885 .... '88   3-5
DISC 2: Same as disc 1.
❏ Billboard/Rhino R1-70636
DPL1-0885 .... '88   3-6
COVER 2: Designate promo. Same as cover
1, except upper right corner is cut at an angle.
INNER SLEEVE 2: White, no printing.
Billboard/Rhino (M) R1-70636
DPL1-0885 .... '88   6-12
TOTAL PACKAGE 2: Disc, cover.

Card stock jacket, with printing on cover – not
on slicks.

Side 1
Jingle Bell Rock (Bobby Helms)
Rockin' Around the Christmas Tree (Brenda Lee)
The Chipmunk Song (Chipmunks & David Seville)
The Little Drummer Boy (Harry Simeone Chorale)
Mary's Boy Child (Harry Belafonte)
Side 2
Blue Christmas (Elvis Presley)
Nuttin' for Christmas (Barry Gordon)
Please Come Home for Christmas (Charles Brown)
White Christmas (Drifters)
Grandma Got Run Over By a Reindeer (Elmo 'N Patsy)

BILLBOARD'S 1979 YEARBOOK (5 LPs)

Various artists collection
Complete five-hour radio show. Reviews news
events and music of 1979. Issued only to
radio stations. Includes one Elvis song,
Hound Dog (shown on side 4 cue sheet as
"You Ain't Nothin' But a Hound Dog"). All discs
have white labels with black print, engraved
identification numbers, and are listed
individually below.
❏ Billboard (SP) Side 1/
Side 3 .... 12/79   10-20
DISC 1:
ROK-1 CX-274A/ROC-3 CX-274B.
❏ Billboard (SP) Side 2/
Side 4 .... 12/79   10-20
DISC 2:
ROK-2 CX-275A/ROC-4 CX-275B.
❏ Billboard (SP) Side 5/
Side 7 .... 12/79   10-20
DISC 3:
ROC-5 CX-276A/ROK-7 CX-276B.

❏ Billboard (SP) Side 6/
Side 9 .... 12/79   10-20
DISC 4:
ROK-6 CX-277A/ROC-9 CX-278B.
❏ Billboard (SP) Side 8/
Side 10 .... 12/79   10-20
DISC 5:
ROK-8 CX-278A/ROC-10 CX-278B.
❏ Billboard.......................... 12/79   20-40
BOX 1: Front: Mustard slick with brown and
red print. Has "Music in the Air" logo at upper
right. Back is blank.
❏ Billboard.......................... 12/79   5-10
INSERTS 1: 10 pages of cue sheets and
program notes.
Billboard (SP) 12/79   100-175
TOTAL PACKAGE 1: Disc, box, inserts.

BIRTHDAY TRIBUTE TO ELVIS

❏ Creative Radio (SP) (No
Number) 1/88   15-20
DISC 1: Blue label with black print. Issued to
radio stations only.
ELVIS-B-SP-A L-29417/ELVIS-B-SP-B L-29417.
Identification numbers are engraved.
COVER 1: None made.
INNER SLEEVE 1: White, no printing.
❏ Creative Radio 1/88   3-5
INSERT 1: One page of programming
information.
Creative Radio (SP) (No
Number) 1/88   20-25
TOTAL PACKAGE 1: Disc, insert.

Side 1
Elvis Medley
That's All Right
Heartbreak Hotel
All Shook Up
(Let Me Be Your) Teddy Bear
Blue Suede Shoes
Side 2
Love Me Tender
Jailhouse Rock
Suspicious Minds
Hound Dog
My Way
Don't Be Cruel
I'll Remember You

BLACK STAR

❏ Bilko EPE-1588: Bootleg. Listed for
identification only.

BLUE CHRISTMAS

Various artists collection
❏ Welk Music Group (SP)
WM-3002........................ 10/84   30-40
DISC 1: White label, blue print. Issued by the
publisher of *Blue Christmas*, presenting 16
different versions of the song, plus other
Christmas tunes. Promotional issue only.
3002-A/WM-3002-B. Identification numbers are engraved.

❑ Welk Music Group

WM-3002........................10/84   30-40

COVER 1: Front and Back: White with blue print. Text only.

INNER SLEEVE 1: White, no printing.

Welk Music Group (SP)

WM-3002 ....10/84   60-80

TOTAL PACKAGE 1: Disc, cover.

Side 1

Blue Christmas (Elvis Presley)
Blue Christmas (Living Voices)
Blue Christmas (Chet Atkins)
Blue Christmas (Willie Nelson)
Blue Christmas (Mickey Gilley)
Blue Christmas (Lawrence Welk)
Blue Christmas (Jim Reeves)
Blue Christmas (Ernest Tubb)
Blue Christmas (Tammy Wynette)
Blue Christmas (Jackie Gleason)

Side 2

Blue Christmas (Glen Campbell)
Blue Christmas (Beach Boys)
Blue Christmas (Danny Davis and the Nashville Brass)
Blue Christmas (Johnny Mathis)
Blue Christmas (Merle Haggard)
Christmas Is (Percy Faith)
Mele Kalikimaka (Bing Crosby)
Ding-A-Ling the Christmas Bell (Lynn Anderson)
Christmas in Los Angeles (Lawrence Welk)
Brazilian Sleighbells (Percy Faith)

BLUE HAWAII

❑ RCA Victor (M)

LPM-2426........................10/61   20-25

DISC 1: Black label, "Long Play" at bottom.
M2PP-2996-1S/M2PP-2997-4S. Label LP#1.
M2PP-2996-2S/M2PP-2997-2S. Label LP#2.
M2PP-2996-3S/M2PP-2997-8S. Label LP#1.
M2PP-2996-6S/M2PP-2997-11S. Label LP#2.
M2PP-2996-15S/M2PP-2997-15S. Label LP#2.
M2PP-2996-19S/M2PP-2997-19S. Label LP#2.

❑ RCA Victor LPM-2426 .....10/61   50-75

COVER 1: Front: RCA logo at upper right and number at lower left. Has red sticker announcing the inclusion of *Rock-A-Hula Baby* and *Can't Help Falling in Love*. Sticker is permanently affixed to cover and therefore not priced separately. Has blue "An Original Soundtrack Recording" film strip logo at lower right. Back: At lower right has "Important" note about playing mono and stereo records, followed by "Miracle Surface" pitch and some technical notes.

INNER SLEEVE 1: Generic RCA sleeve. Makes no mention of Elvis or this LP.

STICKER 1: Not priced separately since it is applied directly to cover.

RCA Victor (M)

LPM-2426 ....10/61   70-100

TOTAL PACKAGE 1: Disc, cover with sticker.

❑ RCA Victor (M)

LPM-2426........................11/63   20-25

DISC 2: Black label, "Mono" at bottom.

❑ RCA Victor LPM-2426 .....11/63   25-30

COVER 2: Same as cover 1, except does not have red sticker on cover. Price reflects RCA's continued use of this same cover, with no discernible differences.

❑ RCA Victor (No Number) ...9/63   8-10

INNER SLEEVE 2: Turquoise, black and white. Front: RCA's Elvis LP catalog, most recent being *It Happened at the World's Fair* (side 1, row 4, column 5). Back: RCA Elvis EPs and 45s catalog.

RCA Victor (M)

LPM-2426 ....11/63   50-65

TOTAL PACKAGE 2: Disc, cover, inner sleeve.

❑ RCA Victor (M)

LPM-2426........................10/64   10-20

DISC 3: Black label, "Monaural" at bottom.
M2PP-2996-22S/M2PP-2997-22S. Label LP#12.

❑ RCA Victor LPM-2426 .....10/64   25-30

COVER 3: Same as cover 2.

❑ RCA Victor

21-112-1 40A....................10/64   4-8

INNER SLEEVE 3: Red, black and white. Front: RCA's Elvis LP catalog, most recent being *Kissin' Cousins* (side 1, row 1, column 6). Back: RCA Elvis EPs and 45s catalog.

RCA Victor (M)

LPM-2426 ....10/64   40-60

TOTAL PACKAGE 3: Disc, cover, inner sleeve.

❑ RCA Victor (ST)

LSP-2426 ....10/61   30-40

DISC 4: Black label, "Living Stereo" at bottom.
M2PY-2998-3S/M2PY-2999-5S. Label LP#7.

❑ RCA Victor LSP-2426 ......10/61   110-125

COVER 4: Front: RCA logo at upper right and number at upper left. Has red sticker announcing the inclusion of *Rock-A-Hula Baby* and *Can't Help Falling in Love*. Sticker is permanently affixed to cover and therefore not priced separately. "Living Stereo" at upper right. Does not have blue "An Original Soundtrack Recording" film strip logo at lower right. Back: At lower right has "Important" note about playing mono and stereo records, followed by "Miracle Surface" pitch and some technical notes.

INNER SLEEVE 4: Generic RCA sleeve. Makes no mention of Elvis or this LP.

STICKER 4: Not priced separately since it is applied directly to cover.

RCA Victor (ST)

LSP-2426 ....10/61   140-160

TOTAL PACKAGE 4: Disc, cover, sticker.

❑ RCA Victor (ST)

LSP-2426 ....10/61   30-40

DISC 5: Same as disc 4.
M2PY-2998-3S/M2PY-2999-5S. Label LP#7.

❏ RCA Victor LSP-2426...... 10/61   30-45
COVER 5: Front: RCA logo at upper right and
number at upper left. Without red sticker
announcing the inclusion of *Rock-A-Hula
Baby* and *Can't Help Falling in Love*. "Living
Stereo" at upper right. Does not have blue "An
Original Soundtrack Recording" film strip logo
at lower right. Back: At lower right has
"Important" note about playing mono and
stereo records, followed by "Miracle Surface"
pitch and some technical notes.
INNER SLEEVE 5: Generic RCA sleeve.
Makes no mention of Elvis or this LP.

RCA Victor (ST)
LSP-2426................... 10/61   60-85
TOTAL PACKAGE 5: Disc, cover, inner
sleeve.

❏ RCA Victor (ST)
LSP-2426 .... 10/64   10-20
DISC 6: Black label, RCA logo in white at top
and "Stereo" at bottom.
M2PY-2996-17S/M2PY-2997-14S. Label LP#16.

❏ RCA Victor LSP-2426...... 10/64   25-30
COVER 6: Similar to cover 2, except has "RE"
at lower left on front and back. Has "Victor
Stereo" at upper right on front.

❏ RCA Victor 21-112-1
40A.................................... 10/64   4-8
INNER SLEEVE 6: Red, black and white.
Front: RCA's Elvis LP catalog, most recent
being *Kissin' Cousins* (side 1, row 1, column
6). Back: RCA Elvis EPs and 45s catalog.

RCA Victor (ST)
LSP-2426................... 10/64   40-60
TOTAL PACKAGE 6: Disc, cover, inner
sleeve.

❏ RCA Victor (ST)
LSP-2426 .... 11/68   20-25
DISC 7: Orange label. Rigid vinyl.
M2PY-2998-12S/M2PY-2999-12.

❏ RCA Victor LSP-2426...... 11/68   8-10
COVER 7: Similar to cover 2, except has "RE"
on front at bottom left. Back gives both LPM
and LSP numbers, though mono (LPM) was
no longer being made at this time.

❏ RCA Victor 21-112-1
40D.................................... 6/68   4-6
INNER SLEEVE 7: Red, black and white.
Front: RCA's Elvis LP catalog, most recent
being *Elvis' Gold Records, Vol. 4* (side 1, row
4, column 5). Back: RCA's Elvis LP and Twin
Pack Stereo 8 catalog. May also be found
with inner sleeves 40B and 40C. See chapter
on inner sleeves for more information.

RCA Victor (ST)
LSP-2426................... 11/68   35-40
TOTAL PACKAGE 7: Disc, cover, inner
sleeve.

❏ RCA Victor (ST)
LSP-2426 .... '71   10-15
DISC 8: Orange label. Flexible vinyl.

M2PY-2998-20S/M2PY-2999-22S. Identification numbers are
engraved.

❏ RCA Victor LSP-2426.......... '71   4-8
COVER 8: Same as cover 6, except has "RE"
on front and back. Makes no reference to a
mono (LPM-2426) issue.

❏ RCA Victor.......................... '70s   2-4
INNER SLEEVE 8: Black-and-white. Pictures
RCA Elvis catalog front and back. Any of
several sleeves may be found on reissues
from this period.

RCA Victor (ST)
LSP-2426....................... '71   15-25
TOTAL PACKAGE 8: Disc, cover, inner
sleeve.

❏ RCA Victor (ST)
LSP-2426 .... '76   4-8
DISC 9: Tan label.

❏ RCA LSP-2426.................... '76   4-8
COVER 9: Same as cover 7.

❏ RCA Victor.......................... '70s   2-4
INNER SLEEVE 9: Black-and-white. Pictures
RCA Elvis catalog front and back. Any of
several sleeves may be found on reissues
from this period.

RCA Victor (ST)
LSP-2426....................... '76   10-20
TOTAL PACKAGE 9: Disc, cover, inner
sleeve.

❏ RCA Victor (ST)
LSP-2426 .... '76   4-6
DISC 10: Black label, dog near top.

❏ RCA LSP-2426.................... '76   4-6
COVER 10: Reflects logo change.

❏ RCA Victor.......................... '70s   2-4
INNER SLEEVE 10: Black-and-white.
Pictures RCA Elvis catalog front and back.
Any of several sleeves may be found on
reissues from this period.

RCA Victor (ST)
LSP-2426....................... '76   10-18
TOTAL PACKAGE 10: Disc, cover, inner
sleeve.

❏ RCA (ST) LSP-2426.......... 5/77   800-1000
DISC 11: Black label, dog near top. Blue vinyl.
Experimental pressing only, not intended for
sale or distribution.
COVER 11: None made.
M2PY-2998-20S/M2PY-2999-22S. Identification numbers are
engraved.
M2PY-2998-20S/M2PY-2999-22S. Identification numbers
are engraved.
M2PY-2998-20S/M2PY-2999-22S. Identification numbers
are engraved.
M2PY-2998-20S/M2PY-2999-22S. Identification numbers
are engraved.

RCA LSP-2426................ 5/77   800-1000
TOTAL PACKAGE 11: Disc.

❏ RCA (ST) AFL1-2426 .... 9/77   3-5
DISC 12: Black label, dog near top.

❏ RCA AFL1-2426 .... 9/77   3-5
M2PY-2998-24/M2PY-2999-27 is engraved but crossed out,
then AFL1- 2426A/AFL1-2426B is stamped.
COVER 12: Reflects prefix change. Includes
copies with a sticker bearing the "AFL1"
prefix, wrapped around cover at top of spine.

❏ RCA Victor .... '70s   2-4
INNER SLEEVE 12: Black-and-white.
Pictures RCA Elvis catalog front and back.
Any of several sleeves may be found on
reissues from this period.
M2PY-2998-20S/M2PY-2999-22S. Identification numbers are
engraved.
M2PY-2998-20S/M2PY-2999-22S. Identification numbers
are engraved.

RCA (ST) AFL1-2426 ...... 9/77   8-15
**TOTAL PACKAGE 12: Disc, cover inner
sleeve.**

❏ RCA (ST) AFL1-2426 .... 9/77   3-5
DISC 13: Black label, dog near top.
❏ RCA AFL1-2426 .... 9/77   8-10
M2PY-2998-24/M2PY-2999-27 is engraved but crossed out,
then AFL1- 2426A/AFL1-2426B is stamped.
COVER 13: Designate promo. Same as cover
12, but with "Not for Sale" stamped on back.
❏ RCA Victor .... '70s   2-4
INNER SLEEVE 13: Black-and-white.
Pictures RCA Elvis catalog front and back.
Any of several sleeves may be found on
reissues from this period.
M2PY-2998-20S/M2PY-2999-22S. Identification numbers are
engraved.
M2PY-2998-20S/M2PY-2999-22S. Identification numbers
are engraved.

RCA (ST) AFL1-2426 ...... 9/77   15-20
**TOTAL PACKAGE 13: Disc, cover, inner
sleeve.**

❏ RCA Victor (ST)
AYL1-3683 .... 5/80   3-5
DISC 14: Black label, dog near top.
AYL1-3683A/AYL1-3683-B. First, "AFL1-2426A/AFL1-2426B"
is stamped but crossed out. Then "M2PY-2998-24/M2PY-
2999-27" is engraved, but also crossed out. Finally, the
correct number is engraved.
❏ RCA AYL1-3683 .... 5/80   3-5
COVER 14: Front: RCA logo and number at
upper right and "Best Buy Series" at upper
left. Back: Does not have "Important" note
about playing mono and stereo records, or
"Miracle Surface" pitch and technical notes.
Indicates "Previously released as AFL1-
2426."
Includes copies with a sticker bearing the
"AYL1" prefix, wrapped around cover at top of
spine.
INNER SLEEVE 14: White, no printing.
M2PY-2998-20S/M2PY-2999-22S. Identification numbers are
engraved.
M2PY-2998-20S/M2PY-2999-22S. Identification numbers are
engraved.

RCA Victor (ST)
AYL1-3683 .... 5/80   6-10
TOTAL PACKAGE 14: Disc, cover.

Side 1
Blue Hawaii
Almost Always True

Aloha Oe
No More
Can't Help Falling in Love
Rock-a-Hula Baby
Moonlight Swim
Side 2
Ku-u-i-po
Ito Eats
Slicin' Sand
Hawaiian Sunset
Beach Boy Blues
Island of Love
Hawaiian Wedding Song

BLUE HAWAII BOX

❏ Laurel BPM-501-A: Bootleg. Listed for
identification only.

BORN TO ROCK

❏ EAP SRS-147: Bootleg. Listed for
identification only.

BRIGHTEST STARS OF CHRISTMAS
Various artists collection

❏ RCA Special Products (SP)
DLP1-0086 .... 11/74   5-10
DISC 1: Blue label. Dynaflex vinyl. Made
especially for JCPenney, and sold only in their
stores. Full title on label is "JCPenney
Presents the Brightest Stars of Christmas."
DLP1-0086A-1/DLP1-0086B-1.
DLP1-0086A-2/DLP1-0086B-2.
❏ RCA Special Products
DLP1-0086 .... 11/74   5-10
COVER 1: Front: RCA Special Products logo
at lower right. JCPenney logo at lower left.
Back: Text only.
INNER SLEEVE 1: White, no printing.
M2PY-2998-20S/M2PY-2999-22S. Identification numbers are
engraved.
M2PY-2998-20S/M2PY-2999-22S. Identification numbers are
engraved.

RCA Special Products (SP)
DLP1-0086 .... 11/74   10-20
TOTAL PACKAGE 1: Disc, cover.

Card stock jacket, with printing on cover – not
on slicks.

Side 1
We Wish You a Merry Christmas (Eugene Omandy)
Here Comes Santa Claus (Elvis Presley)
Winter Wonderland (Danny Davis/Nashville Brass)
Home for the Holidays (Perry Como)
Christmas Medley (Henry Mancini)
Side 2
Jingle Bells (Julie Andrews)
Joy to the World (Ed Ames)
Sleigh Ride (Arthur Fiedler and the Boston Pops)
Christmas in My Home Town (Charley Pride)
Hark the Herald Angels Sing (Robert Shaw Chorale)
Silent Night (Sergio Franchi)

BURBANK SESSIONS, VOL. 1

❑ Audifon AFNS-62768: Bootleg. Listed for identification only.

BURBANK SESSIONS, VOL. 2

❑ Audifon AFNS-62968: Bootleg. Listed for identification only.

BURNING LOVE (AND HITS FROM HIS MOVIES, VOL. 2) (Camden)

❑ RCA/Camden (ST)
CAS-2595 .... 11/72   5-10
DISC 1: Blue label, black and white print. Dynaflex vinyl.
BCRS-6448-1S/BCRS-6449-1S. Identification numbers are stamped.
BCRS-6448-1S/BCRS-6449-4S. Identification numbers are engraved.
BCRS-6448-3S/BCRS-6449-3S. Identification numbers are stamped.

❑ RCA/Camden
CAS-2595 .... 11/72   15-20
COVER 1: Right: Starburst at lower left announcing "Special Bonus Photo Inside." RCA/Camden logo at lower right. Back: At lower right is "Coming in Early 1973, Elvis' Satellite Album, "Aloha from Hawaii" announcement.
INNER SLEEVE 1: White, no printing. (Some Camden LPs had no inner sleeves at all.)

❑ RCA/Camden
CAS-2595 .... 11/72   40-45
INSERT 1: Front: 8" x 10" color photo. Back: Promotion for *Elvis As Recorded at Madison Square Garden.*
M2PY-2998-20S/M2PY-2999-22S. Identification numbers are engraved.
M2PY-2998-20S/M2PY-2999-22S. Identification numbers are engraved.

RCA/Camden (ST)
CAS-2595 .... 11/72   60-75
TOTAL PACKAGE 1: Disc, cover, insert.

❑ RCA/Camden (ST)
CAS-2595 .... 11/72   5-10
DISC 2: Same as disc 1.

❑ RCA/Camden
CAS-2595 .... 11/72   20-25
COVER 2: Designate promo. Same as cover 1, but with "Not for Sale" stamped on back.
INNER SLEEVE 2: White, no printing. (Some Camden LPs had no inner sleeves at all.)

❑ RCA/Camden
CAS-2595 .... 11/72   40-45
INSERT 2: Same as insert 1.
M2PY-2998-20S/M2PY-2999-22S. Identification numbers are engraved.
M2PY-2998-20S/M2PY-2999-22S. Identification numbers are engraved.

RCA/Camden (ST)
CAS-2595 .... 11/72   65-80
TOTAL PACKAGE 2: Disc, cover, insert.

❑ RCA/Camden (ST)
CAS-2595 .... '73   7-10
DISC 3: Same as disc 1.

❑ RCA/Camden CAS-2595 ..... '73   8-10
COVER 3: Same as cover 1, except has "RE" on front at lower left and makes no mention of the bonus photo. Inexplicably, some copies purchased on the first day of release – November 1972 – came in this cover.
INNER SLEEVE 3: White, no printing. (Some Camden LPs had no inner sleeves at all.)
M2PY-2998-20S/M2PY-2999-22S. Identification numbers are engraved.
M2PY-2998-20S/M2PY-2999-22S. Identification numbers are engraved.

RCA/Camden (ST)
CAS-2595 .... '73   15-20
TOTAL PACKAGE 3: Disc, cover.

Side 1
Burning Love
Tender Feeling
Am I Ready
Tonight Is So Right for Love
Guadalajara
Side 2
It's a Matter of Time
No More
Santa Lucia
We'll Be Together
I Love Only One Girl

BURNING LOVE (AND HITS FROM HIS MOVIES, VOL. 2) (Pickwick)

❑ Pickwick/Camden (ST)
2595 .... 12/75   4-6
DISC 1: Black label. Multi-color Pickwick logo at center.

❑ Pickwick/Camden 2595 ... 12/75   4-8
COVER 1: Back has announcement for *Elvis Aloha from Hawaii via Satellite*, just as on Camden covers.

Pickwick/Camden (ST)
2595 .... 12/75   8-15
TOTAL PACKAGE 1: Disc, cover.

❑ Pickwick/Camden (ST)
2595 .... '76   2-4
DISC 2: Same as disc 1A.

❑ Pickwick/Camden 2595 .... '76   3-4
COVER 2: Back does not have the announcement for *Elvis Aloha from Hawaii via Satellite*.
INNER SLEEVE 2: White, no printing.

Pickwick/Camden (ST)
2595 .... '76   5-8
TOTAL PACKAGE 2: Disc, cover.

Side 1
Burning Love
Tender Feeling
Am I Ready
Tonight Is So Right for Love
Guadalajara

Side 2
It's a Matter of Time
No More
Santa Lucia
We'll Be Together
I Love Only One Girl

CADILLAC ELVIS

❑ TCB 1-8-35: Bootleg. Listed for identification only.

CAFÉ EUROPA

❑ Tulsa TML-01-4: Bootleg. Listed for identification only.

CANADIAN TRIBUTE

❑ RCA Victor (SP)
KKL1-7065 ....9/78   6-8
DISC 1: Gold vinyl. Custom, Elvis photo label.
KKL1-7065A-12/KKL1-7065B-12.
KKL1-7065A-13/KKL1-7065B-10.
KKL1-7065A-13/KKL1-7065B-11.
❑ RCA Victor KKL1-7065......9/78   6-8
COVER 1: Front: At upper right is embossed, gold foil title on black stock. Back: Has "RCA Record Division, New York, N.Y." at bottom.
❑ RCA Victor KKL1-7065......9/78   2-4
INNER SLEEVE 1: Custom sleeve. Has eight black-and-white photos on side 1 and two on side 2.
M2PY-2998-20S/M2PY-2999-22S. Identification numbers are engraved.
M2PY-2998-20S/M2PY-2999-22S. Identification numbers are engraved.

RCA Victor (SP)
KKL1-7065 ....9/78   15-20
TOTAL PACKAGE 1: Disc, cover, inner sleeve.

❑ RCA Victor (SP)
KKL1-7065 ....9/78   6-8
DISC 2: Same as disc 1.
❑ RCA Victor KKL1-7065......9/78   10-12
COVER 2: Designate promo. Same as cover 1, but with "Not for Sale" stamped on back.
❑ RCA Victor KKL1-7065......9/78   2-4
INNER SLEEVE 2: Custom sleeve. Has eight black-and-white photos on side 1 and two on side 2.
M2PY-2998-20S/M2PY-2999-22S. Identification numbers are engraved.
M2PY-2998-20S/M2PY-2999-22S. Identification numbers are engraved.

RCA Victor (SP)
KKL1-7065 ....9/78   20-25
TOTAL PACKAGE 2: Disc, cover, inner sleeve.

Side 1
Intro-Jailhouse Rock
Intro-(Let Me Be Your) Teddy Bear
Loving You
Until It's Time for You to Go
Early Morning Rain
Vancouver Press Conference (1957)

Side 2
I'm Movin' On
Snowbird
For Lovin' Me
Put Your Hand in the Hand
Little Darlin'
My Way

CELEBRATE THE SEASON WITH TUPPERWARE

Various artists collection

❑ RCA Special Products (SP)
DPL1-0803 ....'87   10-20
DISC 1: Custom, white label with black and red print. Made for Tupperware to be used in conjunction with their home parties.
DPL1-0803A-2/DPL1-0803B-1.
DPL1-0803A-2/DPL1-0803B-2.
❑ RCA Special Products
DPL1-0803 ....'87   10-20
COVER 1: Front: RCA Special Products logo and number at lower left. Back: Color photos of the 10 artists heard on this LP, including Elvis.
INNER SLEEVE 1: White, no printing.
M2PY-2998-20S/M2PY-2999-22S. Identification numbers are engraved.
M2PY-2998-20S/M2PY-2999-22S. Identification numbers are engraved.

RCA Special Products (SP)
DPL1-0803 ....'87   20-40
TOTAL PACKAGE 1: Disc, cover.

Card stock jacket, with printing on cover – not on slicks.

Side 1
Sleigh Ride (Arthur Fiedler and the Boston Pops)
White Christmas (Dolly Parton)
Christmas Medley (Perry Como)
Let It Snow! Let It Snow! (Johnny Mathis)
Santa Claus (I Still Believe in You) (Alabama)

Side 2
The Christmas Song (Nat King Cole)
Winter Wonderland (Anne Murray)
Feliz Navidad (Jose Feliciano)
I'll Be Home for Christmas (Elvis Presley)
New Year's Medley (Henry Mancini)

CHAPPELL MUSIC STORY, VOL. 2 (2 LPs)

Various artists collection

❑ Chappell Music (SP)
C-11580............................'80   25-50
DISCS 1: Excerpts of 225 songs, including *I Will Be Home Again*, by Elvis. Made for radio stations by the publisher (Chappell Music) of those songs. Titles and artists are not identified on cover or label. Promotional issue only.
❑ Chappell Music C-11580 .....'80   25-50
COVER : Verification pending.
Chappell Music (SP)
C-11580..........................'80   50-100
TOTAL PACKAGE : Discs, cover.

CHARTER PUBLICATIONS SOUND SERIES:
see SOUND SERIES

CHRISTMAS COLLECTION (10 LPs)

Various artists collection

Ten Christmas LPs, each by a different artist. Includes *Elvis' Christmas Album* (Pickwick CAS-2428). See that listing for details on that specific LP, including pricing. Some of the albums in this set are likely to be imports, but that may vary from set to set. In the box documented here, the Elvis LP is a U.S. pressing; however, we know of another that has *Christmas with Elvis* (Noel 10145), made in Portugal. Regardless, the set itself is a U.S. issue. The LPs are packaged in a special slipcover.

❑ Snowflake........................12/85   20-40
COVER 1: White slipcover with black, red and gray print. Snowflake logo at bottom center on back.
Nat King Cole *THE CHRISTMAS SONG* (Capitol SM-1967)
Bing Crosby *WHITE CHRISTMAS* (Joker SM-4048)
Frank Sinatra *A JOLLY CHRISTMAS* (Capitol SL-9240)
Anne Murray *CHRISTMAS WISHES* (Capitol SN-16232)
Elvis Presley *ELVIS' CHRISTMAS ALBUM* (Pickwick CAS-2428)
Barbra Streisand *A CHRISTMAS ALBUM* (Columbia CS-9557)
Johnny Mathis *CHRISTMAS WITH JOHNNY MATHIS* (CSP P-18766) (Incorrectly shown on slipcover as "Merry Christmas.")
Harry Simeone Chorale *THE LITTLE DRUMMER BOY* (MCA 15006)
Mormon Tabernacle Choir *IT'S CHRISTMAS* CBS Special Products P-14303
Mantovani and His Orchestra *THE MANTOVANI CHRISTMAS ALBUM* (Pickwick/Contour CN-2040)

CHRISTMAS PROGRAMMING FROM RCA VICTOR

Various artists collection

❑ RCA Victor (M)
SP-33-66 ....11/59   500-600
DISC 1: Black label, "Long Play" at bottom. Promotional issue only.
K2NP-6188-1S/K2NP-6189-1S
❑ RCA Victor SP-33-66 ......11/59   500-600
COVER 1: Paper, 12" x 12" sleeve. White with red, green and black print. Front: RCA Victor logo and number at upper right. Drawing of a dee jay at work, wearing a Santa suit. Back: Pictures 12 RCA Christmas albums, including *Elvis' Christmas Album* (LPM-1951). Several of these tracks appeared on the previously issued October Christmas Sampler (SPS 33-54).
Counterfeit Identification: Fake covers are all black-and-white. Originals have color on both front and back.
INNER SLEEVE 1: Cover serves as an inner sleeve.
M2PY-2998-20S/M2PY-2999-22S. Identification numbers are engraved.

M2PY-2998-20S/M2PY-2999-22S. Identification numbers are engraved.
RCA Victor (M)
SP-33-66....................11/59   1000-1200
TOTAL PACKAGE 1: Disc, cover.

Side 1
Home for the Holidays (Perry Como)
White Christmas (John Klein)
Rudolph the Red-Nosed Reindeer (Boston Pops)
Silent Night (Giorgio Tozzi & Rosalind Elias)
Blue Christmas (Esquivel's Orchestra & Chorus)
Santa Claus Is Comin' to Town (Ralph Hunter)

Side 2
Ding Dong Dandy Christmas (Three Suns)
I'll Be Home for Christmas (Elvis Presley)
O Christmas Tree (Mario Lanza)
Hallelujah Chorus (Royal Philharmonic Orchestra)
Winter Wonderland (George Melachrino Orchestra)
Little Town of Bethlehem (George Beverly Shea)

CHRISTMAS TREASURY FROM AVON

Various artists collection

❑ RCA Special Products (SP)
DPL1-0716 ....11/85   3-5
DISC 1: Custom, red label, white and black print. Made for Avon representatives use as a Christmas bonus item.
DPL1-0716A-3/DPL1-0716B-4.
❑ RCA DPL1-0716..............11/85   3-5
COVER 1: RCA at lower left. Back: Number at lower right. Color photos of 10 artists heard on this LP, including Elvis.
INNER SLEEVE 1: White, no printing.
❑ RCA Special Products
DPL1-0716 ....11/85   1-2
MAILER 1: Brown cardboard mailer, with title and number printed on it.
M2PY-2998-20S/M2PY-2999-22S. Identification numbers are engraved.
RCA Special Products (SP)
DPL1-0716 ....11/85   8-12
TOTAL PACKAGE 1: Disc, cover, mailer.

Card stock jacket, with printing on cover – not on slicks.

Side 1
Medley: Winter Wonderland/Sleigh Ride (Dolly Parton)
Come 'Round the Christmas Tree (Bing Crosby)
The First Noel (Nat King Cole)
Deck the Halls (Julie Andrews)
12 Days of Christmas (John Denver/Muppets)

Side 2
Home for the Holidays (Perry Como)
Silver Bells (Elvis Presley)
Joy to the World (Anne Murray)
Feliz Navidad (Jose Feliciano)
The Christmas Song (Kenny Rogers)

CHRISTMAS WITH ELVIS

❑ Creative Radio (SP) (No Number) 12/87   50-90
DISC 1: Red label with black print. Issued to radio stations only.
L-29023/L-29023X. Identification numbers are engraved.

COVER 1: None made.

❏ Creative Radio 12/87   5-10

INSERT 1: One page of programming instructions.

Creative Radio (SP) (No Number) 12/87   50-100

TOTAL PACKAGE 1: Disc, insert.

Side 1
The Wonderful World of Christmas
I'll Be Home for Christmas
O Come All Ye Faithful
Santa Claus Is Back in Town
Rockin' Around the Christmas Tree (Brenda Lee)
Santa Bring My Baby Back (To Me)
Silver Bells
White Christmas
Sleigh Ride (Salsoul Orchestra)
If I Get Home on Christmas Day

Side 2
Here Comes Santa Claus
Holly Leaves and Christmas Trees
On a Snowy Christmas Night
It Won't Seem Like Christmas
Blue Christmas
If I Can Dream
Winter Wonderland
Silent Night

CHRONOLOGY OF AMERICAN MUSIC (ALL THE NUMBER ONE SONGS) (21 LPs)

Complete five-hour radio show. Issued on 21 LPs from MMP (More Music Productions). Chronologically presents 325 No. 1 rock era hits, from *Rock Around the Clock* (July 9, 1955) through *Me and Mrs. Jones* (December 16, 1972). Included are all of the No. 1 hits by Elvis, which are noted. Identification numbers are engraved on all discs, listed separately below. Issued only to subscribing radio stations.

❏ MMP (M) Side 1/
    Side 21 .... 12/72   10-20
DISC 1:
(1) CF-WCW/(21) CF-WCW.

❏ MMP (M) Side 2/
    Side 22 .... 12/72   15-25
DISC 2:
(2) CF-WCW/(22) CF-WCW.

❏ MMP (M) Side 3/
    Side 23 .... 12/72   15-25
DISC 3:
(3) CF-WCW/(24) CF-WCW.

❏ MMP (M) Side 4/
    Side 24 .... 12/72   15-25
DISC 4:
(4) CF-WCW/(24) CF-WCW.

❏ MMP (M) Side 5/
    Side 25 .... 12/72   15-25
DISC 5:
(5) CF-WCW/(25) CF-WCW.

❏ MMP (M) Side 6/
    Side 26 .... 12/72   15-25
DISC 6:
(6) CF-WCW/(26) CF-WCW.

❏ MMP (M) Side 7/
    Side 27 .... 12/72   15-25
DISC 7:
(7) CF-WCW/(27) CF-WCW.

❏ MMP (M) Side 8/
    Side 28 .... 12/72   15-25
DISC 8:
(8) CF-WCW/(28) CF-WCW.

❏ MMP (M) Side 9/
    Side 29 .... 12/72   15-25
DISC 9:
(9) CF-WCW/(29) CF-WCW.

❏ MMP (M) Side 10/
    Side 30 .... 12/72   15-25
DISC 10:
(10) CF-WCW/(30) CF-WCW.

❏ MMP (M) Side 11/
    Side 31 .... 12/72   15-25
DISC 11:
(11) CF-WCW/(31) CF-WCW.

❏ MMP (M) Side 12/
    Side 32 .... 12/72   15-25
DISC 12:
(12) CF-WCW/(32) CF-WCW.

❏ MMP (M) Side 13/
    Side 33 .... 12/72   15-25
DISC 13:
(13) CF-WCW/(33) CF-WCW.

❏ MMP (M) Side 14/
    Side 34 .... 12/72   15-25
DISC 14:
(14) CF-WCW/(34) CF-WCW.

❏ MMP (M) Side 15/
    Side 35 .... 12/72   15-25
DISC 15:
(15) CF-WCW/(35) CF-WCW.

❏ MMP (M) Side 16/
    Side 36 .... 12/72   15-25
DISC 16:
(16) CF-WCW/(36) CF-WCW.

❏ MMP (M) Side 17/
    Side 37 .... 12/72   15-25
DISC 17:
(17) CF-WCW/(37) CF-WCW.

❏ MMP (M) Side 18/
    Side 38 .... 12/72   15-25
DISC 18:
(18) CF-WCW/(38) CF-WCW.

❏ MMP (M) Side 19/
    Side 39 .... 12/72   15-25
DISC 19:
(19) CF-WCW/(39) CF-WCW.

❏ MMP (M) Side 20/
    Side 40 .... 12/72   15-25
DISC 20:
(20) CF-WCW/(40) CF-WCW.

❏ MMP (M) Side 21/
    Side 41 .... 12/72   15-25
DISC 21:
(21) CF-WCW/(41) CF-WCW.

❏ MMP (M) Side 22 .... 12/72   15-25
BOX 1: None made.
INSERT 1: Verification pending. Assumption:
It is likely there is a programmer's packet of
some type that goes with this set.

MMP (M) MM-333-72..... 12/72   425-525
TOTAL PACKAGE 1: Disc, cover, inserts.

Elvis Contents:

Side 2
Heartbreak Hotel (Track 1)
I Was the One (Track 2)
I Want You, I Need You, I Love You (Track 4)
My Baby Left Me (Track 5)
Don't Be Cruel (Track 6)
Hound Dog (Track 7)
Love Me Tender (Track 9)

Side 3
All Shook Up (Track 3)
(Let Me Be Your) Teddy Bear (Track 5) .
Loving You (Track 6)

Side 4
Jailhouse Rock (Track 6)

Side 5
Don't (Track 1)
I Beg of You (Track 2)
Hard Headed Woman (Track 7)

Side 7
A Big Hunk O' Love (Track 7)

Side 8
Stuck on You (Track 9)

Side 9
It's Now Or Never (Track 6)

Side 10
Are You Lonesome Tonight (Track 5)

Side 11
Surrender (Track 1)

Side 13
Good Luck Charm (Track 5)

Side 31
Suspicious Minds (Track 7)

CLAMBAKE

❏ RCA Victor (M)
LPM-3893........................11/67   100-125
DISC 1: Black label, "Monaural" at bottom.
UPRM-8439-1S/UPRM-8440-1S. Label LP#12.
UPRM-8439-2S/UPRM-8440-2S. Label LP#12.
UPRM-8439-3S/UPRM-8440-3S. Label LP#12.

❏ RCA Victor LPM-3893 ..... 11/67   100-125
COVER 1: Front: RCA logo at upper right and
number at lower left. Has orange rectangle
announcing bonus, autographed photo of
Elvis and Priscilla.

❏ RCA Victor 21-112-1
40C....................................3/67   4-6
INNER SLEEVE 1: Blue, black and white.
Front: RCA's Elvis LP catalog, most recent
being *Spinout* (side 1, row 2, column 7). Back:
RCA Elvis Stereo 8 catalog.

❏ RCA Victor LPM-3893 ..... 11/67   40-50
INSERT 1: 11" x 11" color, wedding photo of
Elvis and Priscilla.
M2PY-2998-20S/M2PY-2999-22S. Identification numbers are
engraved.

RCA Victor (M)
LPM-3893 .... 11/67   250-300
TOTAL PACKAGE 1: Disc, cover, inner
sleeve, insert.

❏ RCA Victor (M)
LPM-3893........................11/67   100-125
DISC 2: Same as disc 2.

❏ RCA Victor LPM-3893 ..... 11/67   125-150
COVER 2: Designate promo. Same as cover
1, but with "Not for Sale" stamped on back.

❏ RCA Victor 21-112-1
40C....................................3/67   4-6
INNER SLEEVE 2: Blue, black and white.
Front: RCA's Elvis LP catalog, most recent
being *Spinout* (side 1, row 2, column 7). Back:
RCA Elvis Stereo 8 catalog.

❏ RCA Victor LPM-3893 ..... 11/67   40-50
INSERT 2: 11" x 11" color, wedding photo of
Elvis and Priscilla.
M2PY-2998-20S/M2PY-2999-22S. Identification numbers are
engraved.

RCA Victor (M)
LPM-3893 .... 11/67   275-325
TOTAL PACKAGE 2: Disc, cover, inner
sleeve, insert.

❏ RCA Victor (ST)
LSP-3893 ....11/67   10-15
DISC 3: Black label, RCA logo in white at top
and "Stereo" at bottom.
UPRS-8441-4S/UPRS-8442-4S. Label LP#16.
UPRS-8441-5S/UPRS-8442-6S. Label LP#16.

❏ RCA Victor LSP-3893 ...... 11/67   25-30
COVER 3: Front: RCA logo at upper right and
number at upper left. Has orange rectangle on
front announcing bonus, autographed photo of
Elvis and Priscilla.

❏ RCA Victor 21-112-1
40C....................................3/67   4-6
INNER SLEEVE 3: Blue, black and white.
Front: RCA's Elvis LP catalog, most recent
being *Spinout* (side 1, row 2, column 7). Back:
RCA Elvis Stereo 8 catalog.

❏ RCA Victor LSP-3893 ...... 11/67   40-50
INSERT 3: 11" x 11" color, wedding photo of
Elvis and Priscilla.
M2PY-2998-20S/M2PY-2999-22S. Identification numbers are
engraved.

RCA Victor (M)
LPM-3893 .... 11/67   80-100
TOTAL PACKAGE 3: Disc, cover, inner
sleeve, insert.

❏ RCA Victor LSP-3893 ...... 11/67   10-15
DISC 4: Same as disc 3.

❏ RCA Victor LSP-3893 ...... 11/67   40-55
COVER 4: Designate promo. Same as cover
3, but with "Not for Sale" stamped on back.

❑ RCA Victor 21-112-1
40C....................................3/67   4-6
INNER SLEEVE 4: Blue, black and white.
Front: RCA's Elvis LP catalog, most recent
being *Spinout* (side 1, row 2, column 7). Back:
RCA Elvis Stereo 8 catalog.

❑ RCA Victor LSP-3893......11/67   40-50
INSERT 4: 11" x 11" color, wedding photo of
Elvis and Priscilla.
M2PY-2998-20S/M2PY-2999-22S. Identification numbers are
engraved.

RCA Victor (M)
LPM-3893..................11/67   100-125
**TOTAL PACKAGE 4: Disc, cover, inner
sleeve, insert.**

❑ RCA Victor (ST)
APL1-2565 ....9/77   3-5
DISC 5: Black label, dog near top
❑ RCA APL1-2565...............9/77   3-5
COVER 5: Reflects prefix change.
❑ RCA Victor..........................'70s   2-4
INNER SLEEVE 5: Black-and-white. Pictures
RCA Elvis catalog front and back. Any of
several sleeves may be found on reissues
from this period.
M2PY-2998-20S/M2PY-2999-22S. Identification numbers are
engraved.

RCA Victor (ST)
APL1-2565 ....9/77   8-15
**TOTAL PACKAGE 5: Disc, cover, inner
sleeve.**

Side 1
Guitar Man
Clambake
Who Needs Money
A House That Has Everything
Confidence
Hey, Hey, Hey

Side 2
You Don't Know Me
The Girl I Never Loved
How Can You Lose What You Never Had
Big Boss Man
Singing Tree
Just Call Me Lonesome

CLASSIC COUNTRY MUSIC – A
SMITHSONIAN COLLECTION
(6 LPs)
Various Artists Collection
❑ RCA/BMG DML6-0914........'90   30-50
Boxed, six disc set. Description of individual
discs pending. Includes 85-page, 6" x 9"
booklet on the history of country music and
the artists featured.
M2PY-2998-20S/M2PY-2999-22S. Identification numbers are
engraved.
RCA/BMG R-042
DML6-0914....................'90   30-50
TOTAL PACKAGE 1: Discs, box, booklet.

Disc 1
Side 1
Soldier's Joy (Gid Tanner & Skillet Lickers)
Jordan Is a Hard Road to Travel (Uncle Dave Macon &
   Fruit Jar Drinkers)
Barbara Allen (Bradley Kincaid)
The Prisoner's Song (Vernon Dalhart)
Wildwood Flower (Carter Family)
Waiting for a Train (Jimmie Rodgers)
Blue Yodel No. 8 (Jimmie Rodgers)
Ragged But Right (Riley Puckett)

Disc 1
Side 2
Can the Circle Be Unbroken (Carter Family)
Silver Haired Daddy of Mine (Gene Autry)
Just Because (Shelton Brothers)
St. Louis Blues (Milton Brown & Brownies)
My Mary (W. Lee O'Daniel & Light Crust Doughboys
   with Leon Huff)
Great Speckled Bird (Roy Acuff & Crazy Tennesseans)
Under the Double Eagle (Bill Boyd & Cowboy
   Ramblers)
I Want to Be a Cowboy's Sweetheart (Patsy Montana &
   Prairie Ramblers)

Disc 2
Side 3
South of the Border (Gene Autry)
Tumbling Tumbleweeds (Sons of the Pioneers)
Cool Water (Sons of the Pioneers)
Rye Whiskey (Tex Ritter)
Steel Guitar Rag (Bob Wills & Texas Playboys)
New San Antonio Rose (Bob Wills & Texas Playboys)
Walking the Floor Over You (Ernest Tubb)
Born to Lose (Ted Daffan's Texans)
You Are My Sunshine (Jimmie Davis)

Disc 2
Side 4
Pistol Packin' Mama (Al Dexter & Troopers)
There's a Star Spangled Banner Waving Somewhere
   (Elton Britt)
The Cattle Call (Eddy Arnold)
Wabash Cannonball (Roy Acuff & Smoky Mountain
   Boys)
Kentucky (Blue Sky Boys)
New Pretty Blonde (Moon Mullican & Showboys)
Philadelphia Lawyer (Maddox Brothers & Rose)
I Am a Pilgrim (Merle Travis)

Disc 3
Side 5
It's Mighty Dark to Travel (Bill Monroe & Blue Grass
   Boys)
Randy Lynn Rag (Lester Flatt, Earl Scruggs & Foggy
   Mountain Boys)
Slippin' Around (Floyd Tillman)
Tramp on the Street (Molly O'Day & Cumberland
   Mountain Folks)
I'm Moving On (Hank Snow & Rainbow Ranch Boys)
Take an Old Cold Tater (Jimmy Dickens)
Tennessee Waltz (Pee Wee King & Golden West
   Cowboys)
Peace in the Valley (Red Foley)

Disc 3

Side 6

Lovesick Blues (Hank Williams)
Your Cheating Heart (Hank Williams)
I Love You a Thousand Ways (Lefty Frizzell)
The Wild Side of Life (Hank Thompson & Brazos Valley Boys)
It Wasn't God Who Made Honky Tonk Angels (Kitty Wells)
Slowly (Webb Pierce)
Country Gentleman (Chet Atkins)
I Really Don't Want to Know (Eddy Arnold)
Sixteen Tons (Tennessee Ernie Ford)

Disc 4

Side 7

Blue Moon of Kentucky (Elvis Presley)
Bye Bye Love (Everly Brothers)
You Win Again (Jerry Lee Lewis)
Young Love (Sonny James)
I Walk the Line (Johnny Cash)
Crazy Arms (Ray Price)
He'll Have to Go (Jim Reeves)
Faded Love (Patsy Cline)
The Battle of New Orleans (Johnny Horton)

Disc 4

Side 8

El Paso (Marty Robbins)
Big Bad John (Jimmy Dean)
When I Stop Dreaming (Louvin Brothers)
Detroit City (Bobby Bare)
We Must Have Been Out of Our Minds (George Jones & Melba Montgomery)
Excuse Me (Buck Owens)
Hello Walls (Faron Young)
Ode to Billie Joe (Bobbie Gentry)

Disc 5

Side 9

King of the Road (Roger Miller)
Green Green Grass of Home (Porter Wagoner)
Funny How Time Slips Away (Willie Nelson)
Gentle on My Mind (Glen Campbell)
Rocky Top (Osborne Brothers)
Coal Miner's Daughter (Loretta Lynn)
Coat of Many Colors (Dolly Parton)
Folsom Prison Blues (Johnny Cash)
Stand By Your Man (Tammy Wynette)

Disc 5

Side 10

Homecoming (Tom T. Hall)
Is Anybody Goin' to San Antone (Charley Pride)
For the Good Times (Ray Price)
Sin City (Flying Burrito Brothers)
After the Fire Is Gone (Loretta Lynn & Conway Twitty)
I Never Go Around Mirrors (Lefty Frizzell)
Why Me, Lord (Kris Kristofferson)
The Grand Tour (George Jones)

Disc 6

Side 11

Love Hurts (Gram Parsons & Emmylou Harris)
Bob Wills Is Still the King (Waylon Jennings)
Who'll Turn Out the Lights (Ronnie Milsap)
Mamas, Don't Let Your Babies Grow Up to Be Cowboys (Willie Nelson & Waylon Jennings)
'Til I Gain Control Again (Rodney Crowell)
Beneath Still Waters (Emmylou Harris)
The Devil Went Down to Georgia (Charlie Daniels)
He Stopped Loving Her Today (George Jones)

Disc 6

Side 12

Old Flame (Alabama)

Forty Hour Week (Alabama)
A Country Boy Can Survive (Hank Williams Jr.)
Don't Get Above Your Raising (Ricky Skaggs)
Honky Tonk Man (Dwight Yoakam)
Kids of the Baby Boom (Bellamy Brothers)
9 to 5 (Dolly Parton)
Grandpa (Judds)

C'MON EVERYBODY (Camden)

❑ RCA/Camden (M)
　CAL-2518 ....7/71　　8-12
　DISC 1: Blue Label. Dynaflex vinyl.
　APRM-4694-1S/APRM-4695-2S.
　APRM-4694-3S/APRM-4695-3S.
　APRM-4694-4S/APRM-4695-4S.

❑ RCA/Camden CAL-2518 ...7/71　　8-12
　COVER 1: Front: RCA/Camden logo and number at upper left. Back: Has titles and a photo of a cast of thousands.
　INNER SLEEVE 1: White, no printing. (Some Camden LPs had no inner sleeves at all.)
　M2PY-2998-20S/M2PY-2999-22S. Identification numbers are engraved.

RCA/Camden (M)
　CAL-2518 ....7/71　　**15-25**
　TOTAL PACKAGE 1: Disc, cover.

❑ RCA/Camden (M)
　CAL-2518 ....7/71　　8-12
　DISC 2: Same as disc 1.

❑ RCA/Camden CAL-2518 ...7/71　　12-18
　COVER 2: Designate promo. Same as cover 1, but with "Not for Sale" stamped on back.
　INNER SLEEVE 2: White, no printing. (Some Camden LPs had no inner sleeves at all.)
　M2PY-2998-20S/M2PY-2999-22S. Identification numbers are engraved.

RCA/Camden (M)
　CAL-2518 ....7/71　　**20-30**
　TOTAL PACKAGE 2: Disc, cover.

Side 1

C'Mon Everybody
Angel
Easy Come, Easy Go
A Whistling Tune
Follow That Dream

Side 2

King of the Whole Wide World
I'll Take Love
Today, Tomorrow and Forever
I'm Not the Marrying Kind
This Is Living

C'MON EVERYBODY (Pickwick)

❑ Pickwick/Camden (M)
　CAS-2518 ....12/75　　2-5
　DISC 1: Black label. Multi-color Pickwick logo at center. Despite "CAS" prefix, this LP is monaural.
　CAS-2518-A1/CAS-2518-B1.

❑ Pickwick/Camden
CAS-2518......................12/75   3-5
COVER 1: Front: Camden logo and number at
upper left. Pickwick logo at right, under title.
Back: Has titles and a photo of a cast of
thousands.
INNER SLEEVE 1: White, no printing.
Pickwick/Camden (M)
CAS-2518 ....12/75   **5-10**
TOTAL PACKAGE 1: Disc, cover.

Side 1
C'Mon Everybody
Angel
Easy Come, Easy Go
A Whistling Tune
Follow That Dream
Side 2
King of the Whole Wide World
I'll Take Love
Today, Tomorrow and Forever
I'm Not the Marrying Kind
This Is Living

COLLECTOR'S CASSETTE (Tape)
❑ Tyro (M) No Number
Used..................................6/90   15-20
TAPE 1: White cassette tape.
❑ Tyro (M) No Number
Used..................................6/90   5-10
INSERT CARD/COVER 1: Black-and-white
card/cover.
Tyro (M) No Number
Used...........................6/90   **20-30**
TOTAL PACKAGE 1: Tape, card/cover.

Cassette offered as a promotional bonus to
buyers of the book, *Elvis: A Tribute to His Life.*
Side 1
I Beg of You
True Love
King Creole (Version 1)
King Creole (Version 2)
Crawfish (With Girl Singer)
Side 2
Party (shown as "Let's Have a Party")
Don't Leave Me Now
When It Rains It Really Pours (shown as "When It
  Rains [It Really Pours]")
New Orleans (shown as "Down in New Orleans")

COLLECTORS EDITION (5 LPs)
❑ RCA Victor (SP) TB-1..........'76   40-60
DISCS 1: Boxed, three-LP (five-disc) set with:
Elvis in Hollywood (2 LP), *Elvis Forever* (1 LP)
and *Elvis* (2 LP). This *Elvis* is the set issued in
the United States as DPL2-0056(e). This
package made in Canada, which is why
identification numbers are not given here, but
offered for sale in the United States through
TV mail order ads.
❑ RCA Victor (SP) TB-1..........'76   40-60
BOX 1: Front: Black stock with gold foil print.
Back: Black stock with white print.
INNER SLEEVES 1: White, no printing.

❑ Roadshow Merchandise...........   15-25
INSERT 1: "Special TV Edition Photo Album,"
a 20-page color booklet. On back cover, at
lower right is "See Elvis in Concert for RCA
Record Tours." A Boxcar reprint of this
booklet came with some issues of *Elvis in
Hollywood.*
M2PY-2998-20S/M2PY-2999-22S. Identification numbers are
engraved.
RCA Victor (SP) TB-1......'76   **100-150**
TOTAL PACKAGE 1: Discs, box, insert.

COLLECTORS GOLD (3 LPs)
Boxed vinyl edition of the set more commonly
found on CD.
❑ RCA/BMG (SP)
3114-1-R 8/91   100-200
DISCS 1:
❑ RCA/BMG 3114-1-R..........8/91   100-200
BOX 1: Front: Color photo (circa-1965) of
Elvis. Back: Titles.
❑ RCA/BMG 3114-1-R..........8/91   10-20
INSERT 1: Booklet, with same color cover as
front of box.
❑ RCA/BMG 3114-1-R..........8/91   3-5
SHRINK STICKER 1: On box, reads: "Special
Limited National Numbered Edition - Edition of
10,000."
M2PY-2998-20S/M2PY-2999-22S. Identification numbers are
engraved.
RCA/BMG (SP)
3114-1-R......................8/91   **225-450**
TOTAL PACKAGE 1: Discs, box, insert,
sticker.

COLONEL PARKER'S BOY
❑ TAKRL 1816: Bootleg. Listed for
identification only.

COMING ATTRACTIONS
Various artists collection
❑ The Source (S) CA 82-7 ....7/82   10-15
DISC 1: One hour radio show, featuring
"*Diner* – A Musical Feast from the '50s."
Includes an Elvis excerpt. Promotional issue
only.
❑ The Source CA 82-7..........7/82   10-15
COVER 1: White with drawing of a diner.
INNER SLEEVE 1: White, no printing.
❑ The Source CA 82-7..........7/82   3-5
INSERT 1: One page cue sheet.
The Source (S)
CA 82-7 ....7/82   **20-40**
TOTAL PACKAGE 1: Disc, cover, insert.

COMING HOME (2 LPs)

Various artists collection

❑ RCA Spec. Prod./BMG (ST)
DVL2-0868 .... '88   2-5
DISC 1A: Black label, dog near top. Made for and sold via mail order by the Beautiful Music Company. One of two separate LPs, sold as a pair.
(**Disc 1**) DVL2-0868-A-1/DVL2-0868-B-1. Identification numbers are engraved.

❑ RCA Spec. Prod./BMG
DVL2-0868 .... '88   2-5
COVER 1A: Single pocket. Front: "CYR-1" at upper left, RCA Special Products and BMG logos at lower left. Number at upper right, Beautiful Music Company address at lower right. Color picture of unidentified couple. Back: Advertising for other LPs from Suffolk Marketing.

❑ RCA Spec. Prod./BMG (ST)
DVL2-0868 .... '88   2-5
DISC 1B: Black label, dog near top. Made for and sold via mail order by the Beautiful Music Company. One of two separate LPs, sold as a pair.
(**Disc 2**) DVL2-0868-C-1/DVL2-0868-D-1. Identification numbers are engraved.

❑ RCA Spec. Prod./BMG
DVL 2-0868 .... '88   2-5
COVER 1B: Single pocket. Front: "CYR-2" at upper left, RCA Special Products and BMG logos at lower left. Number at upper right, Beautiful Music Company address at lower right. Color picture of unidentified couple. Back: Advertising for other LPs from Suffolk Marketing.
INNER SLEEVES 1: White, no printing.

RCA Special Products/BMG (ST)

DVL2-0868 A/B .... '88   10-20
TOTAL PACKAGE 1: Discs, covers.

Card stock jacket, with printing on cover – not on slicks.

Disc 1

Side 1
Coat of Many Colors (Dolly Parton)
I Saw the Light (Hank Williams)
Did You Think to Pray (Charley Pride)
Deck of Cards (Wink Martindale)
Precious Memories (Jim Reeves)
That's Enough (Johnny Cash)

Side 2
Why Me Lord (Kris Kristofferson)
Keep on the Firing Line (Original Carter Family)
A Satisfied Mind (Porter Wagoner)
Me and Jesus (Tom T. Hall)
One Day at a Time (Cristy Lane)
Old Shep (Red Foley)

Disc 2

Side 1
Uncloudy Day (Wille Nelson)
Old Rivers (Walter Brennan)
Wings of a Dove (Ferlin Husky)
How Far Is Heaven (Kitty Wells with Carol Sue)
The Great Speckled Bird (Roy Acuff)

(There'll Be) Peace in the Valley (For Me) (Elvis Presley)

Side 2
It Takes Faith (Marty Robbins)
Tramp on the Street (Molly O'Day)
My Mother's Hungry Eyes (Merle Haggard and the Strangers)
Family Bible (George Jones)
No Charge (Melba Montgomery)
Take My Hand, Precious Lord (Tennessee Ernie Ford)

COMMAND PERFORMANCE

❑ ECP 101: Bootleg. Listed for identification only.

COMPLETE KID GALAHAD SESSION, VOL. 1

❑ TCB 3-30-973: Bootleg. Listed for identification only.

COMPLETE KID GALAHAD SESSION, VOL. 2

❑ TCB 3-30-974: Bootleg. Listed for identification only.

COMPLETE KID GALAHAD SESSION, VOL. 3

❑ TCB 3-30-975: Bootleg. Listed for identification only.

COMPLETE MILLION DOLLAR QUARTET SESSION: see *MILLION DOLLAR QUARTET SESSION*

COMPLETE ON TOUR SESSIONS, VOL. 1

❑ Vicky 0211: Bootleg. Listed for identification only.

COMPLETE PARADISE HAWAIIAN STYLE SESSIONS, VOL. 1

❑ TCB 963-1: Bootleg. Listed for identification only.

COMPLETE PARADISE HAWAIIAN STYLE SESSIONS, VOL. 2

❑ TCB 963-2: Bootleg. Listed for identification only.

COMPLETE PARADISE HAWAIIAN STYLE SESSIONS, VOL. 3

❑ TCB 963-3: Bootleg. Listed for identification only.

COMPLETE SUN SESSIONS (2 LPs)

❑ RCA Victor (M)
6414-1-R 7/87   4-5
DISCS 1: Black label, dog near top.
(**Disc 1**) 6414-1-R-A-1/6414-1-R-B-1. (**Disc 2**) 6414-1-R-C-5/6414-1-R-D-1. Identification numbers are engraved on all except Side C, where they are stamped.

(Disc 1) 6414-1-R-A-4/6414-1-R-B-4. **(Disc 2)** 6414-1-R-C-4/6414-1-R-D-4. Identification numbers are engraved.

❑ RCA 6414-1-R 7/87   8-10
COVER 1: Double pocket. Front: Colorized Elvis photo. Back: Colorized Scotty, Elvis and Bill photo. Inside panels: Five colorized photos of or including Elvis.

❑ RCA/BMG 7/87   2-4
INNER SLEEVES 1: Mustard with black print, with "A 1987 Commemorative Release" on each side.

❑ RCA/BMG 7/87   3-5
INSERT 1A: Color 15" x 22" Elvis signature poster. Has "Sincerely Yours, Elvis" at lower left and RCA logo and number "POS-2" at lower right.

❑ RCA/BMG 7/87   1-2
INSERT 1B: Black-and-white 8" x 10" flyer; ad for *Elvis Talks* on one side and four "1987 Commemorative Collection" LPs pictured on reverse.

❑ RCA Victor 6414-1-R 7/87   4-5
SHRINK STICKER 1: Circular, gold foil "Digitally Remastered" sticker, which has selection number.

RCA Victor (M)
6414-1-R **7/87**   **25-30**
TOTAL PACKAGE 1: Discs, cover, inserts, sticker.

❑ RCA Victor (M)
6414-1-R 7/87   4-5
DISCS 2: Same as discs 1.

❑ RCA 6414-1-R 7/87   12-15
COVER 2: Designate promo. Same as cover 1, but with "Not for Sale" stamped on back.

❑ RCA/BMG 7/87   2-4
INNER SLEEVES 2: Mustard with black print, with "A 1987 Commemorative Release" on each side.

❑ RCA/BMG 7/87   3-5
INSERT 2A: Color 15" x 22" Elvis signature poster. Has "Sincerely Yours, Elvis" at lower left and RCA logo and number "POS-2" at lower right.

❑ RCA/BMG 7/87   1-2
INSERT 2B: Black-and-white 8" x 10" flyer; ad for *Elvis Talks* on one side and four "1987 Commemorative Collection" LPs pictured on reverse.

❑ RCA Victor 6414-1-R 7/87   4-5
SHRINK STICKER 2: Circular, gold foil "Digitally Remastered" sticker, which has selection number.

RCA Victor (M)
6414-1-R **7/87**   **30-35**
TOTAL PACKAGE 1: Discs, cover, inserts, sticker.

Card stock jacket, with printing on cover – not on slicks.

Disc 1

Side A
That's All Right

Blue Moon of Kentucky
Good Rockin' Tonight
I Don't Care if the Sun Don't Shine
Milkcow Blues Boogie
You're a Heartbreaker
Baby, Let's Play House
I'm Left, You're Right, She's Gone

Side B
Mystery Train
I Forgot to Remember to Forget
I Love You Because
Blue Moon
Tomorrow Night
I'll Never Let You Go (Little Darlin')
Just Because
Trying To Get to You

Disc 2

Side C
Harbor Lights
I Love You Because – takes 1 & 2
That's All Right
Blue Moon of Kentucky
I Don't Care if the Sun Don't Shine
I'm Left, You're Right, She's Gone (My Baby's Gone) – take 9
I'll Never Let You Go (Little Darlin')
When It Rains, It Really Pours

Side D
I Love You Because – take 3
I Love You Because – take 4
I Love You Because – take 5
I'm Left, You're Right, She's Gone – take 7
I'm Left, You're Right, She's Gone – take 8
I'm Left, You're Right, She's Gone – take 10
I'm Left, You're Right, She's Gone – take 11
I'm Left, You're Right, She's Gone – take13
I'm Left, You're Right, She's Gone – take 12

COMPLETE WILD IN THE COUNTRY SESSIONS

❑ Laurel LPM 502-D: Bootleg. Listed for identification only.

COMPLETE WILD IN THE COUNTRY SESSIONS, VOL. 1

❑ TCB 81160: Bootleg. Listed for identification only.

COMPLETE WILD IN THE COUNTRY SESSIONS, VOL. 2

❑ TCB 81160: Bootleg. Listed for identification only.

COUNTRY & WESTERN CLASSICS (1955)

Various artists collection

❑ Economic Consultants Inc. (M)
1955 .... '73   10-20
DISC 1: Gold label, black print. Has two Elvis tracks. Mail order offer.
C&W 1955-1/C&W 1955-2. Identification numbers are engraved.

❑ Economic Consultants
Inc. 1955 ....'73   10-20
COVER 1: Front: Brown, with a drawing of a
saddle and a cowboy hat. Back: Text only.
Economic Consultants Inc. (M)
1955................................'73   20-40
TOTAL PACKAGE 1: Disc, cover.

COUNTRY & WESTERN CLASSICS (1956)

Various artists collection

❑ Economic Consultants Inc. (M)
1956 ....'73   10-20
DISC 1: Gold label, black print. Has seven
Elvis tracks. Mail order offer.
C&W 1956-1/C&W 1956-2. Identification numbers are
engraved.

❑ Economic Consultants
Inc. 1956 ....'73   10-20
COVER 1: Front: Brown, with a drawing of a
saddle and a cowboy hat. Back: Text only.
Economic Consultants Inc. (M)
1956................................'73   20-40
TOTAL PACKAGE 1: Disc, cover.

COUNTRY & WESTERN CLASSICS (1957)

Various artists collection

❑ Economic Consultants Inc. (M)
1957 ....'73   10-20
DISC 1: Gold label, black print. Has four
Elvis tracks. Mail order offer.
C&W 1957-1/C&W 1957-2. Identification numbers are
engraved.

❑ Economic Consultants
Inc. 1957 ....'73   10-20
COVER 1: Front: Brown, with a drawing of a
saddle and a cowboy hat. Back: Text only.
Economic Consultants Inc. (M)
1957................................'73   20-40
TOTAL PACKAGE 1: Disc, cover.

COUNTRY & WESTERN CLASSICS (1958)

Various artists collection

❑ Economic Consultants Inc. (M)
1958 ....'73   10-20
DISC 1: Gold label, black print. Has one
Elvis track. Mail order offer.
C&W 1958-1/C&W 1958-2. Identification numbers are
engraved.

❑ Economic Consultants
Inc. 1958 ....'73   10-20
COVER 1: Front: Brown, with a drawing of a
saddle and a cowboy hat. Back: Text only.
Economic Consultants Inc. (M)
1958................................'73   20-40
TOTAL PACKAGE 1: Disc, cover.

COUNTRY CHRISTMAS (3 LPs)

Various artists collection

❑ Time-Life (SP) STL-109...10/88   6-10
DISCS 1: Custom, red label with black-and-
white print. Sold only by Time-Life via mail
order.
(Disc 1) STL-109 Side 1-1/STL-109 Side 2-1. (Disc 2)
STL-109 Side 3- 1/STL-109 Side 4-1. (Disc 3) STL-109 Side
5-1/STL-109 Side 6-1.

❑ Time-Life STL-109............:10/88   6-10
BOX 1: Front: Time-Life logo at bottom
center. Color, winter scene. Back: Text only.
INNER SLEEVES 1: Generic Time-Life, poly-
lined.
Time-Life (SP)
STL-109.....................10/88   15-20
TOTAL PACKAGE 1: Discs, box.

Disc 1

Side 1
Country Christmas (Loretta Lynn)
Santa Claus Is Coming to Town (George Strait)
I'll Be Home for Christmas (Elvis Presley)
Rudolph the Red-Nosed Reindeer (Gene Autry)
Jingle Bells (Willie Nelson)
Santa's Gonna Come in a Stagecoach (Buck Owens)
If We Make It Through December (Merle Haggard)
Pretty Paper (Roy Orbison)
Christmas Prayer (Marty Robbins)

Side 2
Mr. and Mrs. S. Claus (George Jones & Tammy
    Wynette)
Christmas Time's a-Comin' (Bill Monroe)
Carols Kids Used to Sing (Statler Brothers)
Away in a Manger (Reba McEntire)
Tennessee Christmas (Alabama)
Old Toy Trains (Roger Miller)
I Can't Have a Merry Christmas, Mary (Without You)
    (Jerry Lee Lewis)
An Old Christmas Card (Jim Reeves)

Disc 2

Side 1
Blue Christmas (Elvis Presley)
Christmas Boogie (Davis Sisters)
Jingle Bell Rock (Chet Atkins)
Christmas in My Home Town (Charley Pride)
Happy Christmas (Tammy Wynette)
Walkin' the Floor This Christmas (Ernest Tubb)
Blue Christmas Lights (Buck Owens)
Christmas Time in the Valley (Freddy Fender)
The Friendly Beasts (Louvin Brothers)

Side 2
Santa Looked a Lot Like Daddy (Buck Owens)
Santa Claus Is Back in Town (Dwight Yoakam)
It Won't Seem like Christmas (Loretta Lynn)
What a Merry Christmas (Willie Nelson)
If Every Day Was like Christmas (Elvis Presley)
The Midnight Clear (Louvin Brothers)
Here Comes Santa Claus (Gene Autry)
Truckin' Trees for Christmas (Red Simpson)

Disc 3

Side 1
When It's Christmas Time in Texas (George Strait)
Santa! Don't Pass Me By (Freddy Fender)
Nuttin' for Christmas (Homer & Jethro)
Reindeer Boogie (Hank Snow)
It's Christmas (Ronnie Milsap)
My Mom and Santa Claus (George Jones)
White Christmas (Tammy Wynette)

The Little Drummer Boy (Johnny Cash)

Side 2

Christmas in Dixie (Alabama)
Let It Snow, Let It Snow (Charley Pride)
C-h-r-i-s-t-m-a-s (Eddy Arnold)
Lonely Christmas Call (Mickey Gilley)
Hard Candy Christmas (Dolly Parton)
Winter Wonderland (Chet Atkins)
Goin' Home for Christmas (Merle Haggard)
Silent Night (Reba McEntire)

COUNTRY CHRISTMAS, VOL. 2

Various artists collection

❑ RCA Victor (ST)
AYL1-4809 .... 11/83   3-4
   DISC 1: Black label, dog near top.
   AYL1-4809A-1S/AYL1-4809B-1S. Identification numbers are
   engraved.
❑ RCA AYL1-4809 .... 11/83   3-4
   COVER 1: Front: RCA logo at bottom center.
   Color drawing of a Christmas tree trimming
   scene. Back: Text only. Number at bottom
   center. UPC code at upper right.
   INNER SLEEVE 1: White, no printing.
❑ RCA AYL1-4809 .... 11/83   1-2
   SHRINK STICKER: White with red print.
   Announces three titles, including *Silver Bells*
   by Elvis Presley.

RCA Victor (ST)
AYL1-4809 .... 11/83   8-10
TOTAL PACKAGE 1: Disc, cover, sticker.

Side 1

White Christmas (Earl Thomas Conley)
Hard Candy Christmas (Dolly Parton)
Christmas Time's A-Coming (Jerry Reed)
Winter Wonderland (Eddy Arnold)

Side 2

Reflections (Sylvia)
Silver Bells (Elvis Presley)
I've Got What You Want (Louise Mandrell)
Christmas in Dixie (Alabama)

COUNTRY CLASSICS (2 LPs)
(Record Club)

❑ RCA Victor (SP)
R-233299e .... '80   15-20
   DISCS 1: Black label, dog near top.
   (Disc 1) R233299A-6/R233299B-5. **(Disc 2)** R233299C-
   5/R233299D-5.
❑ RCA R-233299e .... '80   15-20
   COVER 1: Single pocket. Front: No logo or
   number shown. Color '70s concert Elvis
   photo. Back: RCA logo and number at lower
   right.
   INNER SLEEVES 1: White, no printing.

RCA Victor (SP)
R-233299e .... '80   30-40
TOTAL PACKAGE 1: Discs, cover.

Disc 1

Side 1

Faded Love
Guitar Man
Blue Moon of Kentucky
Crying in the Chapel

Tomorrow Night

Side 2

I'm Coming Home
(Now and Then There's) A Fool Such As I
From a Jack to a King
I Really Don't Want to Know
That's All Right

Disc 2

Side 3

Have I Told You Lately That I Love You
Tomorrow Never Comes
It's a Sin
He Touched Me
I Love You Because

Side 4

I'm Left, You're Right, She's Gone
Just Call Me Lonesome
(There'll Be) Peace in the Valley (For Me)
There Goes My Everything

COUNTRY COUNTDOWN: see *AMERICAN COUNTRY COUNTDOWN*

COUNTRY CROSSROADS

❑ Country Crossroads
32-83 .... '83   25-50
   DISC 1: Southern Baptist Radio-TV issue.
   Has one track by Elvis.
❑ Country Crossroads
32-83 .... '83   25-50
   COVER 1: Verification pending.

Country Crossroads
32-83 .... '83   50-100
TOTAL PACKAGE : Disc, cover.

COUNTRY GOLD

Various artists collection

❑ RCA Special Products (ST)
DPL1-0561 .... '82   10-12
   DISC 1: Black RCA Special Products label,
   dog near top.
   DPL1-0561A-1/DPL1-0561B-1.
❑ RCA Special Products
DPL1-0561 .... '82   10-12
   COVER 1: Front: RCA Special Products logo
   and number at lower left. Color photo of an
   unidentified couple. Back: same photo as on
   front.
   INNER SLEEVE 1: White, no printing.

RCA Special Products (ST)
DPL1-0561 .... '82   20-25
TOTAL PACKAGE 1: Disc, cover.

Side 1

Here You Come Again (Dolly Parton)
She Left Love All Over Me (Razzy Bailey)
Fire and Smoke (Earl Thomas Conley)
Theme from The Dukes of Hazzard (Waylon Jennings)
Smoky Mountain Rain (Ronnie Milsap)

Side 2

Tennessee River (Alabama)
Sweetest Thing (Juice Newton & Silver Spur)
Never Been So Loved (Charley Pride and the Cherry
   Sisters)
Drifter (Sylvia)

Are You Lonesome Tonight (Elvis Presley)

(ARMY ROTC PRESENTS) COUNTRY LINE

❑ U.S. Army ROTC (M) .... '78   5-10
   DISCS 1: Hosted by Lee Arnold, each disc
   has 24 one-minute shows, with country music
   news and celebrity interviews. Provided to
   radio stations as public service broadcasting.
   Price is for any individual disc in the series,
   whether Elvis is mentioned or not. One show,
   No. 307, April 1-15, 1978, has an interview
   with Vernon Presley. Issued only to
   subscribing stations.
❑ U.S. Army ROTC Prog. .... '78   3-5
   COVER 1: Generic Country Line cover.
   Pictures a pair of cowboy boots.
U.S. Army ROTC (M) ......'78   8-15
   TOTAL PACKAGE 1: Disc, cover.

COUNTRY MEMORIES (2 LPs) (Record Club)

❑ RCA Victor (SP)
   R-244069 .... '78   15-20
   DISCS 1: Black label, dog near top.
   (Disc 1) R244069A-1/R244069B-1. **(Disc 2)** R244069C-
   2/R244069D-1.
   (Disc 1) R244069A-2/R244069B-1. **(Disc 2)** R244069C-
   2/R244069D-1.
❑ RCA R-233299e .... '78   15-20
   COVER 1: Single pocket. Color 1969 Elvis
   photo front and back.
   INNER SLEEVES 1: White, no printing.
RCA Victor (SP)
R-244069 .... '78   30-40
   TOTAL PACKAGE 1: Discs, cover.

Card stock jacket, with printing on cover – not
on slicks.
Disc 1
Side 2
I'll Hold You in My Heart
Welcome to My World
It Keeps Right On A-Hurtin'
Release Me
Make the World Go Away
Side 2
Snowbird
Early Morning Rain
I'm So Lonesome I Could Cry
Funny How Time Slips Away
I'm Moving On
Disc 2
Side 3
Help Me Make It Through the Night
You Don't Know Me
How Great Thou Art
I Washed My Hands in Muddy Water
I Forgot to Remember to Forget
Side 4
Your Cheatin' Heart
Baby, Let's Play House
Whole Lot-ta Shakin' Goin' On
Gentle on My Mind
For the Good Times

COUNTRY MEMORIES (7 LPs)

Various artists collection
Mail order offer only. All discs in this set have
a black, white and red label, and are listed
individually below.
❑ Reader's Digest/BMG
   RBA-066A-1 .... '89   3-4
   DISC 1:
   V1RS-5591-D3/V1RS-5592-D3.
❑ Reader's Digest/BMG
   RBA-066A-2 .... '89   3-4
   DISC 2:
   V1RS-5593-D2/V1RS-5594-D2.
❑ Reader's Digest/BMG
   RBA-066A-3 .... '89   3-4
   DISC 3:
   V1RS-5595-D2/V1RS-5596-D2.
❑ Reader's Digest/BMG
   RBA-066A-4 .... '89   3-4
   DISC 4:
   V1RS-5597-D2/V1RS-5598-D3.
❑ Reader's Digest/BMG
   RBA-066A-5 .... '89   3-4
   DISC 5:
   V1RS-5599-D2/V1RS-5600-D2.
❑ Reader's Digest/BMG
   RBA-066A-6 .... '89   3-4
   DISC 6:
   V1RS-5601-D2/V1RS-5602-D.
❑ Reader's Digest/BMG
   RBA-066A-7 .... '89   3-4
   DISC 7:
   V1RS-5603-D2/V1RS-5604-D2.
❑ Reader's Digest/BMG
   RBA-066AA .... '89   15-20
   BOX 1: Slipcover: Red. Front: Reader's
   Digest/BMG logo at lower left. Pictures 16
   artists, including Elvis, inside stars around
   cover. Back is blank. Record case: White with
   black print. Back is blank.
   INNER SLEEVES 1: Generic, individually
   numbered, plastic sleeves. Front and Back:
   Clear, covered with Reader's Digest Pegasus
   logos. No mention of Elvis.
❑ Reader's Digest/BMG .... '89   5-7
   INSERT 1: 11¼" x 11½" 16-page information
   booklet.
Reader's Digest/BMG Music Service
   (SP) RBA-037A .... '89   40-55
   TOTAL PACKAGE 1: Discs, box, insert.

COUNTRY MUSIC

❑ Time-Life (SP) STW-106 ..... '81   5-10
   DISC 1: Brown and white label.
   STW-106A-1/STW-106B-1.
❑ Time-Life STW-106 .... '81   5-10
   COVER 1: Front: An artist's rendering of the
   same Elvis photo found on the *Kissin' Cousins*
   LP cover.
   INNER SLEEVE 1: White, no printing.
Time-Life (SP) STW-106....81   10-20
   TOTAL PACKAGE 1: Disc, cover.

One of a series of 20 country music LPs, which were generally sold in supermarkets. Card stock jacket, with printing on cover – not on slicks.

Side 1
Blue Moon of Kentucky
Old Shep
When My Blue Moon Turns to Gold Again
Are You Lonesome Tonight
Your Cheatin' Heart

Side 2
Wooden Heart
Suspicious Minds
Little Cabin Home on the Hill
U.S. Male

COUNTRY MUSIC IN THE MODERN ERA (1940s-1970s)

Various artists collection

❑ New World Records (SP)
   NW-207 .... '77   30-40
   DISC 1: Red label, black, blue and white print. Made for public libraries, to be used in their record albums section.
   NW-207A/NW-207B. Identification numbers are engraved.

❑ New World Records
   NW-207 .... '77   30-40
   COVER 1: Gatefold, with six, bound-in pages of lyrics, photos and biographical notes. Front: New World logo at lower left, number at lower right. Black-and-white drawing of a jam session. Back: Text only.
   INNER SLEEVE 1: White, no printing.
New World Records (SP)
   NW-207 .... '77   60-80
   TOTAL PACKAGE 1: Disc, cover.

Side 1
Bouquet of Roses (Eddy Arnold)
Never No More Blues (Lefty Frizzell)
Much Too Young to Die (Ray Price)
Squid Jiggin' Ground (Hank Snow)
There's Poison in Your Heart (Kitty Wells)
Try Me One More Time (Ernest Tubb)
Love Letters in the Sand (Patsy Cline)
Jean's Song (Chet Atkins)
Mystery Train (Elvis Presley)

Side 2
Little Old You (Jim Reeves)
Jimmy Martinez (Marty Robbins)
I'm a Honky-Tonk Girl (Loretta Lynn)
Lorena (Johnny Cash)
Don't Let Him Know (Buck Owens)
All I Love Is You (Roger Miller)
Sing a Sad Song (Merle Haggard)
Coat of Many Colors (Dolly Parton)
Help Me Make It Through the Night (Kris Kristofferson)

COUNTRY SESSIONS

❑ NBC (S) 74 .... '82   30-40
   DISC 1: Purple label, white print. Complete one hour Elvis radio show. Issued only to radio stations.
   CS-126A/CS-126B. Identification numbers are engraved.
   COVER 1: None made.

❑ NBC 74 .... '82   4-8
   INSERT 1: Page of program notes and cue sheets.
NBC (S) 74 .... '82   35-50
   TOTAL PACKAGE 1: Disc, insert.

COUNTRY SIDE (2 LPs)

❑ Creative Radio (SP) (No
   Number) 8/82   35-40
   DISCS 1: Complete two-hour radio show. Black print on silver stock. Issued to radio stations only.
   (Disc 1) EC-1-1 L-28205/EC-1-2 L-28205. **(Disc 2)** EC-2-1 L-28205/EC-2-2 L-28205. Identification numbers are engraved.
   COVER 1: None made.
   INNER SLEEVES 1: White, no printing.
❑ Creative Radio   4-8
   INSERT 1: Two pages, containing programming information and out-cues.
**Creative Radio (SP) (No
Number) 8/82   40-50**
   TOTAL PACKAGE : Discs, insert.

COUNTRY SOFT AND MELLOW (7 LPs)

Various artists collection

Mail order offer only. All discs in this set have a black, white and red label, and are listed individually below. All sides have two Elvis tracks and four tracks by various artists from that same year or years. All identification numbers are engraved.

❑ Reader's Digest/BMG
   RB4-200-1 .... '89   3-4
   DISC 1:
   V1RS-5841-D3/V1RS-5842-D4.
❑ Reader's Digest/BMG
   RB4-200-2 .... '89   3-4
   DISC 2:
   V1RS-5843-D/V1RS-5844-D.
❑ Reader's Digest/BMG
   RB4-200-3 .... '89   3-4
   DISC 3:
   V1RS-5845-D3/V1RS-5846-D3.
❑ Reader's Digest/BMG
   RB4-200-4 .... '89   3-4
   DISC 4:
   V1RS-5847-D2/V1RS-5848-D2.
❑ Reader's Digest/BMG
   RB4-200-5 .... '89   3-4
   DISC 5:
   V1RS-5849-D2/V1RS-5850-D2.
❑ Reader's Digest/BMG
   RB4-200-6 .... '89   3-4
   DISC 6:
   V1RS-5851-D2/V1RS-5852-D2.
❑ Reader's Digest/BMG
   RB4-200-7 .... '89   3-4
   DISC 7:
   V1RS-5853-D1/V1RS-5854-D3.

❑ Reader's Digest/BMG
RB4-200 ....'89   15-20
BOX 1: Front: Gold. Reader's Digest/BMG
logo at bottom center. Back is blank. Record
case: Beige with black print. Back is blank.
INNER SLEEVES 1: Generic, individually
numbered, plastic sleeves. Front and Back:
Clear, covered with Reader's Digest Pegasus
logos. No mention of Elvis.

❑ Reader's Digest/BMG.......... '89   5-7
INSERT 1: 3" x 3" information and program
notes booklet.

Reader's Digest/BMG (SP)
RB4-200 ....'89   **40-55**
TOTAL PACKAGE 1: Discs, box, insert.

COUNTRY SUPER SOUNDS (1956)
Various artists collection

❑ Omega Sales Inc. (M)
O-6-1956 ....'73   10-20
DISC 1: Yellow label. One of a 16-LP set. Has
four Elvis tracks.
CSS-1956-1/CSS-1956-2. Identification numbers are
engraved.

❑ Omega Sales Inc.
O-6-1956 ....'73   10-20
COVER 1: Front: Brown with yellow and white
print. Reads: "Collector's Edition" at upper
right. Back: Lists other LPs available from
Omega Sounds.

Omega Sales Inc. (M)
O-6-1956........................'73   **20-40**
TOTAL PACKAGE 1: Disc, cover.

COUNTRY SUPER SOUNDS (1957)
Various artists collection

❑ Omega Sales Inc. (M)
O-6-1957 ....'73   10-20
DISC 1: Yellow label. One of a 16-LP set. Has
four Elvis tracks.
CSS-1957-1/CSS-1957-2. Identification numbers are
engraved.

❑ Omega Sales Inc.
O-6-1957 ....'73   10-20
COVER 1: Front: Brown with yellow and white
print. Reads: "Collector's Edition" at upper
right. Back: Lists other LPs available from
Omega Sounds.

Omega Sales Inc. (M)
O-6-1957........................'73   **20-40**
TOTAL PACKAGE 1: Disc, cover.

COUNTRY SUPER SOUNDS (1958)
Various artists collection

❑ Omega Sales Inc. (M)
O-6-1958 ....'73   10-20
DISC 1: Yellow label. One of a 16-LP set. Has
one Elvis track.
CSS-1958-1/CSS-1958-2. Identification numbers are
engraved.

❑ Omega Sales Inc.
O-6-1958 ....'73   10-20
COVER 1: Front: Brown with yellow and white
print. Reads: "Collector's Edition" at upper
right. Back: Lists other LPs available from
Omega Sounds.

Omega Sales Inc. (M)
O-6-1958........................'73   **20-40**
TOTAL PACKAGE 1: Disc, cover.

CRUISIN' AMERICA WITH COUSIN BRUCIE (3LPs)
Various artists collections.

❑ Cruisin' America (S).................   10-15
DISC 1: Price range is for any individual disc
containing at least one Elvis track.

❑ Cruisin' America (S).................   25-35
COMPLETE SET 1: Boxed set of three LPs.
Each is a complete three-hour, weekly radio
show with three pages of cue sheets and
program notes. Issued only to subscribing
radio stations. Price range is for any complete
set containing at least one Elvis track.

CURRENT AUDIO MAGAZINE (AUGUST-SEPTEMBER 1972) / ELVIS: HIS FIRST AND ONLY PRESS CONFERENCE
Various artists collection

❑ Current Audio Magazine (SP)
CM-Vol. 1 ....8/72   25-30
DISC 1: Red, black and white label. An audio
magazine, "Not Licensed for Public
Broadcasting." Has a portion of Elvis' 1972
New York press conference.
CM-VOL. 1 NO. 1 AA-2/CM-VOL. 1 NO. 1 B-2. Identification
numbers are engraved.

❑ Current Audio Magazine
CM-Vol. 1 ....8/72   25-30
COVER 1: Gatefold cover. Front: Color photo
of Mick Jagger. Back: "Distributed by Buddah
Records" logo at lower left. Color Elvis photo.
Inside Panels: Seven black-and-white and
duotone photos of those heard on this LP,
including one of Elvis, one of Elvis and Col.
Parker, and one of Col. Parker.
INNER SLEEVE 1: White, no printing.

❑ Current Audio Magazine
CM-Vol. 1 ....8/72   5-10
INSERT 1: Eight-page, black-and-white, fold-
out, photo/text insert, covering an assortment
of topics

Current Audio Magazine (SP)
CM-Vol. 1 ....8/72   **55-70**
TOTAL PACKAGE 1: Disc, cover, insert.

Card stock jacket, with printing on cover – not
on slicks.

Side 1

Mick Jagger Speaks About Mick Jagger
Manson Will Escape! Says Ed Sanders
Current Audio Comedy – Robert Klein
Teddy Kennedy on Youth, Dope, Abortion
Angela Davis Not Guilty!
The Monty Python Flying Circus

Side 2

Elvis Presley's News Conference
The Killer Was a Narc
Bella Abzug
Scoop's Column – Audio Mix By Scoop Nisker
Nader Group Hits Vega, Despite Recall
Crime Watch: Audio's Monthly Crime Column
Sensous You – Jaye P. Morgan Gives Answers to Sex
Test

DATE WITH ELVIS

❑ RCA Victor (M)

LPM-2011..........................9/59   50-100
DISC 1: Black label, "Long Play" at bottom.
K2PP-1148-1S/K2PP-1149-1S. Label LP#3. Identification
numbers are stamped.
K2PP-1148-3S/K2PP-1149-7S. Label LP#4. Identification
numbers are engraved.
K2PP-1148-8S/K2PP-1149-7S. Label LP#3. Identification
numbers are stamped.

❑ RCA Victor LPM-2011 ....9/59   250-300
COVER 1A: Gatefold, though record pocket is
the front instead of back panel and the pocket
opening is at top rather than right side (as with
most gatefold covers). Front: RCA logo and
number at upper right. Contents printed on a
red sticker with white lettering, applied to
front. No titles are printed on cover itself. Back
is an "Elvis 1960" calendar, with March 24
circled in red. Some copies came with a "New
Golden Age of Sound Album" foil banner.
Since banner was wrapped around but not
affixed to cover, it is priced separately below.
COVER 1B: Same as cover 1A, but without
the red sticker.
STICKER 1: Contents printed on a red
sticker with white lettering. Since sticker is
affixed directly to cover and not wrap, it is not
priced separately. Used only on cover 1A.

❑ Alcoa Wrap.......................9/59   200-300
BANNER 1: Aluminum foil wraparound
banner, proclaiming this LP as one of 24
Alcoa Wrap "New Golden Age of Sound
Albums," and announcing a Beautiful Hair
Breck New Golden Age of Sound Preview LP.
Makes no reference to this specific LP or to
Elvis. In fact, a banner from any of the 24
Golden Age of Sound Albums could be used
with *A Date with Elvis*.

RCA Victor (M)

LPM-2011 ....9/59   **300-400**
**TOTAL PACKAGE 1: Disc, cover. (Does
not include banner.)**

❑ RCA Victor (M)
LPM-2011........................11/63   30-40
DISC 2: Black label, "Mono" at bottom.

❑ RCA Victor
LPM-2011.....................9/11/63   75-100
COVER 2: Single pocket cover. Front: RCA
logo and number at upper right. Back:
Contents printed, along with plug for "Elvis
Greatest Hits in 3 History-Making Albums"
(three volumes of *Elvis Golden Records*).

❑ RCA Victor (No Number)...9/63   8-10
INNER SLEEVE 2: Turquoise, black and
white. Front: RCA's Elvis LP catalog, most
recent being *It Happened at the World's Fair*
(side 1, row 4, column 5). Back: RCA Elvis
EPs and 45s catalog.

RCA Victor (M)

LPM-2011 ....11/63   **110-150**
**TOTAL PACKAGE 2: Disc, cover, inner
sleeve.**

❑ RCA Victor (M)
LPM-2011 ....1/65   10-15
DISC 3: Black label, "Monaural" at bottom.

❑ RCA Victor LPM-2011 ....1/65   30-40
COVER 3: Same as cover 2, except has
"RE2" on front and "RE" and "2" (separately)
on back.

❑ RCA Victor 21-112-1
40A 10/64   4-8
INNER SLEEVE 3: Red, black and white.
Front: RCA's Elvis LP catalog, most recent
being *Kissin' Cousins* (side 1, row 1, column
6). Back: RCA Elvis EPs and 45s catalog.

RCA Victor (M)

LPM-2011 ....1/65   **45-65**
**TOTAL PACKAGE 3: Disc, cover, inner
sleeve.**

❑ RCA Victor (SE)
LSP-2011(e) 1/65   10-15
DISC 4: Black label, RCA logo in white at top
and "Stereo Electronically Reprocessed" at
bottom.
RPRS-7867-2S/RPRS-7868-2S. Label LP#15. On *Young and
Beautiful* and *Baby I Don't Care*, songwriter credits follow
song titles.
RPRS-7867-4S/RPRS-7868-1S. Label LP#15. On *Young and
Beautiful* and *Baby I Don't Care*, songwriter credits follow
line under titles about "an M-G-M release, Jailhouse Rock."

❑ RCA Victor LSP-2011e......1/65   20-30
COVER 4: Single pocket cover. Front: RCA
logo and "Stereo Electronically Reprocessed"
at upper right. Selection number at upper left.
"RE2" at lower right. Contents printed below
title. Back: Plugs "Elvis Greatest Hits in 3
History-Making Albums" (three volumes of
Elvis Golden Records), though laid out
differently than on cover 2. Has box at lower
right explaining "Electronic Stereo Now
Available." The 1963 copyright date reflects
RCA's use of the same basic artwork as on
cover 2.

❑ RCA Victor 21-112-1
40A.................................. 10/64   4-8
INNER SLEEVE 4: Red, black and white.
Front: RCA's Elvis LP catalog, most recent
being *Kissin' Cousins* (side 1, row 1, column
6). Back: RCA Elvis EPs and 45s catalog.

RCA Victor (SE)
LSP-2011(e) 1/65   **35-55**
TOTAL PACKAGE 4: Disc, cover, inner
   sleeve.

❑ RCA Victor (SE)
LSP-2011(e).................... 11/68   15-20
DISC 5: Orange label. Rigid vinyl.
❑ RCA Victor LSP-2011e.... 11/68   8-10
COVER 5: Same as cover 4, except has
"SER" at lower left on both front and back.
❑ RCA Victor 21-112-1
40D..................................... 6/68   4-6
INNER SLEEVE 5: Red, black and white.
Front: RCA's Elvis LP catalog, most recent
being *Elvis' Gold Records, Vol. 4* (side 1, row
4, column 5). Back: RCA's Elvis LP and Twin
Pack Stereo 8 catalog. May also be found
with inner sleeves 40B and 40C. See chapter
on inner sleeves for more information.

RCA Victor (SE)
LSP-2011(e) 11/68   **25-35**
TOTAL PACKAGE 5: Disc, cover, inner
   sleeve.

❑ RCA Victor (SE)
LSP-2011(e)......................... '71   10-15
DISC 6: Orange label. Flexible vinyl.
❑ RCA Victor LSP-2011(e) ..... '71   8-10
COVER 6: Same as cover 5.
❑ RCA Victor......................... '70s   2-4
INNER SLEEVE 6: Black-and-white. Pictures
RCA Elvis catalog front and back. Any of
several sleeves may be found on reissues
from this period.

RCA Victor (SE)
LSP-2011(e) .... '71   **20-30**
TOTAL PACKAGE 6: Disc, cover, inner
   sleeve.

❑ RCA Victor (SE)
LSP-2011(e)......................... '76   4-8
DISC 7: Tan label.
RPRS-7867-8S/RPRS-7868-7S.
❑ RCA Victor LSP-2011e........ '76   4-8
COVER 7: Same as cover 4, except has new
RCA logo, "Victor" and "Stereo Effect" at
upper right on front. Has "SER" at lower right
on front and back. Back does not list mono
selection number.
❑ RCA Victor......................... '70s   2-4
INNER SLEEVE 7: Black-and-white. Pictures
RCA Elvis catalog front and back. Any of
several sleeves may be found on reissues
from this period.

RCA Victor (SE)
LSP-2011(e) .... '76   **10-20**
TOTAL PACKAGE 7: Disc, cover, inner
   sleeve.

❑ RCA Victor (SE)
LSP-2011(e)......................... '76   4-6
DISC 8: Black label, dog near top.
❑ RCA LSP-2011e.................. '76   4-6
COVER 8: Reflects logo change. Has "SER"
on back.
❑ RCA Victor......................... '70s   2-4
INNER SLEEVE 8: Black-and-white. Pictures
RCA Elvis catalog front and back. Any of
several sleeves may be found on reissues
from this period.

RCA Victor (SE)
LSP-2011(e) .... '76   **10-18**
TOTAL PACKAGE 8: Disc, cover, inner
   sleeve.

❑ RCA Victor (SE)
AFL1-2011(e)....................... '77   4-5
DISC 9: Black label, dog near top.
❑ RCA AFL1-2011e................ '77   4-5
COVER 9: Reflects prefix change.
Includes copies with a sticker bearing the
"AFL1" prefix, wrapped around cover at top of
spine.
❑ RCA Victor......................... '70s   2-4
INNER SLEEVE 9: Black-and-white. Pictures
RCA Elvis catalog front and back. Any of
several sleeves may be found on reissues
from this period.

RCA Victor (SE)
AFL1-2011(e) .... '77   **10-15**
TOTAL PACKAGE 9: Disc, cover, inner
   sleeve.

On both covers and labels, the electronically
reprocessed stereo designation "(e)" may not
appear following every usage of the selection
number.

Side 1
Blue Moon of Kentucky
Young and Beautiful
(You're So Square) Baby I Don't Care
Milkcow Blues Boogie
Baby Let's Play House

Side 2
Good Rockin' Tonight
Is It So Strange
We're Gonna Move
I Want to Be Free
I Forgot to Remember to Forget

DATIN' WITH ELVIS

❑ Screen 3542: Bootleg. Listed for identification only.

DEAD ON STAGE IN LAS VEGAS, AUGUST 20TH 1977

❑ SUX-004: Bootleg. Listed for identification only.

DECEMBER '62 POP SAMPLER

Various artists collection

❑ RCA Victor (S) SPS
33-191 .... 12/62   500-750
DISC 1: Black label without dog. Has "Living Stereo" at bottom. Various artists sampler.
Promotional issue only.
N2NY-5357-1S/N2NY-5358-1S.
COVER 1: White, no printing.
INNER SLEEVE 1: White, no printing.

RCA Victor (S)
SPS 33-191 .... 12/62   500-750
TOTAL PACKAGE 1: Disc.

Side 1
Diane (Gaylord Carter)
Ivory Tower (Hank Jones & Dean Kay)
Along the Santa Fe Trail (Jimmie Haskell Orchestra & Chorus)
Boulevard of Broken Dreams (Sir Julian at the Organ)
This Could Be the Start of Something (Sacha Distel with Ray Ellis & Orchestra)
Do It Again (Sacha Distel with Ray Ellis & Orchestra)
I Don't Wanna Be Tied (Elvis Presley)

Side 2
Where Do You Come From (Elvis Presley)
Next Door to an Angel (Neil Sedaka)
Joshua (Tokens)
March of the Toys (Marty Gold and His Orchestra)
A Kiss to Build a Dream On (Marty Gold and His Orchestra)
Lover (Zaccarias and His Orchestra) (Camden Release)

DECEMBER '63 POP SAMPLER

Various artists collection

❑ RCA Victor (S)
SPS 33-247 .... 12/63   500-750
DISC 1: Black label without dog. Has "Stereo" at bottom. Various artists sampler.
Promotional issue only.
PNRS-5799-1S/PNRS-5800-1S.
COVER 1: White, no printing.
INNER SLEEVE 1: White, no printing.

RCA Victor (S)
SPS 33-247 .... 12/63   500-750
TOTAL PACKAGE 1: Disc.

All tracks except *Anytime* (Eddie Fisher) are stereo.

Side 1
Main Title from "The Cardinal" (Jerome Moross)
Dixieland Tango (Orchestra Conducted by Jerome Moross)
I Can't Stop Loving You (Hank Locklin)

Oh! Carol (Neil Sedaka)
Charade (Main Title) (Henry Mancini and His Orchestra)
Charade (Vocal) (Henry Mancini and His Orchestra)

Side 2
Fun in Acapulco (Elvis Presley)
One Note (Joe Daley Trio)
Anytime (Eddie Fisher)
Womenfolk (Womenfolk)
Run Molly (Villagers)

DEMO (RADIO PROGRAMS)

Various artists collection

❑ Creative Radio
Shows (SP) D-A .... '87   20-25
DISC 1: Red and pink label with black print.
Various artists sampler of 11 programs available to broadcasters from Creative Radio Shows. Promotional issue only.
D-A L-27375/D-B L-27375-X. Identification numbers are engraved.
COVER 1: None made.
INNER SLEEVE 1: White, no printing.

Creative Radio Shows (SP)
D-A .... '87   20-25
TOTAL PACKAGE 1: Disc.

Side 1
Gary Owens Supertracks
The Elvis Hour
The Rock Files
The Joy of Christmas
Elvis 10th Anniversary Special

Side 2
Beach Boys 25th Anniversary
Memories of Elvis
Spirit of American Rock
The Beatle Invasion
The Buddy Holly Tribute
Lionel Richie Special

DICK CLARK MUSIC MACHINE (3 LPs)

Various artists collection

❑ Diamond P. Enterprises............   30-45
DISCS 1: White labels with blue print.
Complete three-hour syndicated radio show.
Issued only to subscribing stations. Although three discs were sent each week, price is for any of the LPs having at least one Elvis track.
Discs that do not have an Elvis song are valued at $5 to $10 each. Included in this series of at least 77 (the highest number we've seen) shows are ones designated as "Evergreen," which are not timely and can be aired at any time.
INNER SLEEVES 1: White, no printing.

❑ Diamond P. Enterprises............   3-5
INSERTS 1: Cue sheets with program notes.
Price is for any corresponding to discs with an Elvis track.

Diamond P. Enterprises   35-50
TOTAL PACKAGE 1: Discs, insert.

DICK CLARK SOLID GOLD

Various artists collection

❑ Diamond P. Enterprises   10-15
DISC 1: White labels with gold print.
Complete, one-hour syndicated radio show.
Issued only to subscribing stations. Price is
for any LPs having at least one Elvis track.
Discs that do not have an Elvis song are
valued at $5 to $10 each.
INNER SLEEVES 1: White, no printing.

❑ Diamond P. Enterprises   2-5
INSERT 1: Cue sheet with program notes and
weekly theme. Price is for any corresponding
to discs with an Elvis track.

Diamond P. Enterprises **12-20**
TOTAL PACKAGE 1: Disc, insert.

DINER (2 LPs)

Various artists collection

❑ Elektra (SP) E1-60107E ...... '82   5-10
Original Soundtrack LP, the first release of a
non-Elvis soundtrack LP to have an Elvis
track.
DISCS 1: Red label, black and white print.
(Disc 1) E1-60107-E-A2-SH-AR/E1-60107-E-D2-SH-AR.
(Disc 2) E1-60107-E-B2-SH-AR/E1-60107-E-C2-SH-AR.

❑ Elektra E1-60107E .... '82   5-10
COVER 1: Single pocket. Front: Color scene
from film. Back: Text only. Elektra logo and
number at bottom center.

Elektra (SP) E1-60107E.... '82   **10-20**
TOTAL PACKAGE 1: Disc, cover.

❑ Elektra (SP) E1-60107E ...... '82   5-10
DISCS 2: Same as discs 1.

❑ Elektra E1-60107E .... '82   10-15
COVER 2: Designate promo. Same as cover
1, but with "Not for Sale" stamped on back.
INNER SLEEVES 1: White, no printing.

Elektra (SP) E1-60107E.... '82   **15-25**
TOTAL PACKAGE 1: Disc, cover.

Card stock jacket, with printing on cover – not
on slicks.

Disc 1
Side 1
Whole Lotta Shakin' Going [sic] On (Jerry Lee Lewis)
A Teenager in Love (Dion and the Belmonts)
A Thousand Miles Away (Heartbeats)
Somethin' Else (Eddie Cochran)
I Wonder Why (Dion and the Belmonts)
Side 2 (Shows side 4 on cover)
Whole Lot of [sic] Loving (Fats Domino)
Take Out Some Insurance (Jimmy Reed)
Dream Lover (Bobby Darin)
Don't Be Cruel (Elvis Presley)
Goodbye Baby (Jack Scott)
Disc 2
Side 1 (Shows side 3 on cover)
Honey Don't (Carl Perkins)
Mr. Blue (Fleetwoods)
Reconsider Baby (Lowell Fulson)
Ain't Got No Home (Clarence Henry)
Come Go with Me (Del Vikings)

Side 2
Beyond the Sea (Bobby Darin)
Theme from the Motion Picture (Uncredited)
Fascination (Jane Morgan)
Where Or When (Dick Haymes)
It's All in the Game (Tommy Edwards)

DINNER DATE WITH ELVIS

❑ Live Archives 1011: Bootleg. Listed for
identification only.

DOG'S LIFE

❑ Audifon 67361: Bootleg. Listed for
identification only.

DORSEY SHOWS

❑ Golden Archives GA-100: Bootleg. Listed for
identification only.

DOUBLE DYNAMITE (2 LPs)
(Pickwick/Camden)

❑ Pickwick/Camden (SP)
DL2-5001 .... 12/75   12-15
DISCS 1: Black label. Multi-color Pickwick
logo at center.
(Disc 1) DL2-5001-A/DL2-5001-B. (Disc 2) DL2-5001-
C/DL2-5001-D. Identification numbers are engraved.

❑ Pickwick/Camden
DL2-5001 .... 12/75   12-15
COVER 1: Single pocket. Front: Same Elvis
photo as *Elvis As Recorded at Madison
Square Garden* LP. Has Camden logo and
number at upper left and Pickwick logo at
lower right.
INNER SLEEVES 1: White, no printing.

Pickwick/Camden (SP)
DL2-5001 .... 12/75   **25-30**
TOTAL PACKAGE 1: Discs, cover.

Disc 1
Side 1
Burning Love
I'll Be There
Fools Fall in Love
Follow That Dream
You'll Never Walk Alone
Side 2
Flaming Star
Yellow Rose of Texas/The Eyes of Texas
Old Shep
Mama
Disc 2
Side 3
Rubberneckin'
U.S. Male
Frankie and Johnny
If You Think I Don't Need You
Easy Come, Easy Go
Side 4
Separate Ways
(There'll Be) Peace in the Valley (For Me)
Big Boss Man
It's a Matter of Time

DOUBLE DYNAMITE (2 LPs) (RCA/Pair)

❑ RCA Special Products/Pair (SP)
PDL2-1010 .... 5/82　　15-20
DISCS 1: Black label, RCA Special Products logo at top. Pair logo at bottom. Repackage of Camden/Pickwick DL2-5001, less two tracks: *You'll Never Walk Alone* and *If You Think I Don't Need You.*
(Disc 1) PDL2-1010-A-1/PDL2-1010-B-1. **(Disc 2)** PDL2-1010-C-1/PDL2-1010-D-2.

❑ RCA Special Products/Pair
PDL2-1010 .... 5/82　　15-20
COVER 1: Single pocket. Front: Color Elvis photo. RCA Special Products logo and number at lower left. Pair logo at lower right. Back: Black-and-white of same photo as on front.
INNER SLEEVES 1: White, no printing.

RCA Special Products/Pair (SP)
PDL2-1010 .... 5/82　　**30-40**
TOTAL PACKAGE 1: Discs, cover.

Side 1
Burning Love
I'll Be There
Fools Fall in Love
Follow That Dream
You'll Never Walk Alone

Side 2
Flaming Star
Yellow Rose of Texas/The Eyes of Texas
Old Shep
Mama

Disc 2

Side 3
Rubberneckin'
U.S. Male
Frankie and Johnny
If You Think I Don't Need You
Easy Come, Easy Go

Side 4
Separate Ways
(There'll Be) Peace in the Valley (For Me)
Big Boss Man
It's a Matter of Time

DOUBLE TROUBLE

❑ RCA Victor (M)
LPM-3787 .... 6/67　　10-15
DISC 1: Black label, "Monaural" at bottom.
UPRM-3943-3S/UPRM-3944-3S. Label LP#12.
UPRM-3943-4S/UPRM-3944-4S. Label LP#12.

❑ RCA Victor LPM-3787 .... 6/67　　25-30
COVER 1: Front: RCA logo at upper right and number at lower left. Bottom film strip announces bonus color photo of Elvis inside. Back cover is same as front.

❑ RCA Victor 21-112-1
40C .... 3/67　　4-6
INNER SLEEVE 1: Blue, black and white. Front: RCA's Elvis LP catalog, most recent being *Spinout* (side 1, row 2, column 7). Back: RCA Elvis Stereo 8 catalog.

❑ RCA Victor LPM-3787 .... 6/67　　40-50
INSERT 1: Front: 7" x 9" color photo. Back: RCA Elvis catalog selections.

RCA Victor (M)
LPM-3787 .... 6/67　　**80-100**
TOTAL PACKAGE 1: Disc, cover, inner sleeve, insert.

❑ RCA Victor (M)
LPM-3787 .... 6/67　　10-15
DISC 2: Same as disc 1.

❑ RCA Victor LPM-3787 .... 6/67　　45-50
COVER 2: Designate promo. Same as cover 1, but with "Not for Sale" stamped on back.

❑ RCA Victor 21-112-1
40C .... 3/67　　4-6
INNER SLEEVE 2: Blue, black and white. Front: RCA's Elvis LP catalog, most recent being *Spinout* (side 1, row 2, column 7). Back: RCA Elvis Stereo 8 catalog.

❑ RCA Victor LPM-3787 .... 6/67　　40-50
INSERT 2: Front: 7" x 9" color photo. Back: RCA Elvis catalog selections.

RCA Victor (M)
LPM-3787 .... 6/67　　**100-120**
TOTAL PACKAGE 2: Disc, cover, inner sleeve, insert.

❑ RCA Victor (M)
LPM-3787 .... 6/67　　10-15
DISC 3: Same as disc 1.

❑ RCA Victor LPM-3787 .... '68　　35-55
COVER 3: Front: Same as cover 1, except bonus photo announcement is replaced with "Trouble Double."

❑ RCA Victor 21-112-1
40C .... 3/67　　4-6
INNER SLEEVE 3: Blue, black and white. Front: RCA's Elvis LP catalog, most recent being *Spinout* (side 1, row 2, column 7). Back: RCA Elvis Stereo 8 catalog.

RCA Victor (M)
LPM-3787 .... '68　　**50-75**
TOTAL PACKAGE 3: Disc, cover, inner sleeve.

❑ RCA Victor (ST)
LSP-3787 .... 6/67　　10-15
DISC 4: Black label, RCA logo in white at top of label and "Stereo" at bottom.
UPRS-3945-3S/UPRS-3946-3S. Label LP#16.

❑ RCA Victor (S)
LSP-3787 .... 6/67　　25-30
COVER 4: Front: RCA logo at upper right and number at upper left. Bottom film strip announces bonus color photo of Elvis inside. Back cover is same as front.

❑ RCA Victor 21-112-1
40C .... 3/67　　4-6
INNER SLEEVE 4: Blue, black and white. Front: RCA's Elvis LP catalog, most recent being *Spinout* (side 1, row 2, column 7). Back: RCA Elvis Stereo 8 catalog.

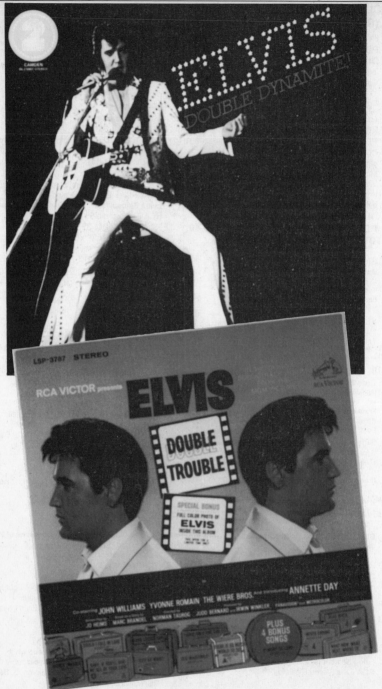

❑ RCA Victor LSP-3787........6/67   40-50
INSERT 4: Front: 7" x 9" color photo. Back:
RCA Elvis catalog selections.
RCA Victor (ST)
LSP-3787.....................6/67   80-100
**TOTAL PACKAGE 4: Disc, cover, inner
   sleeve, insert.**

❑ RCA Victor (ST)
LSP-3787 ....6/67   10-15
DISC 5: Same as disc 4.
❑ RCA Victor LSP-3787........6/67   45-50
COVER 5: Designate promo. Same as cover
4, but with "Not for Sale" stamped on back.
❑ RCA Victor 21-112-1
40C.....................................3/67   4-6
INNER SLEEVE 5: Blue, black and white.
Front: RCA's Elvis LP catalog, most recent
being *Spinout* (side 1, row 2, column 7). Back:
RCA Elvis Stereo 8 catalog.
❑ RCA Victor LSP-3787........6/67   40-50
INSERT 5: Front: 7" x 9" color photo. Back:
RCA Elvis catalog selections.
RCA Victor (S)
LSP-3787.....................6/67   100-120
**TOTAL PACKAGE 5: Disc, cover, inner
   sleeve, insert.**

❑ RCA Victor (ST)
LSP-3787 ....6/67   10-15
DISC 6: Same as disc 4.
❑ RCA Victor LSP-3787..........'68   35-55
COVER 6: Front: Same as cover 4, except
bonus photo announcement is replaced with
"Trouble Double."
❑ RCA Victor 21-112-1
40C.....................................3/67   4-6
INNER SLEEVE 6: Blue, black and white.
Front: RCA's Elvis LP catalog, most recent
being *Spinout* (side 1, row 2, column 7). Back:
RCA Elvis Stereo 8 catalog.
RCA Victor (S)
LSP-3787......................'68   50-75
**TOTAL PACKAGE 6: Disc, cover, inner
   sleeve.**

❑ RCA Victor (ST)
LSP-3787 ....11/68   20-25
DISC 7: Orange label. Rigid vinyl.
❑ RCA Victor (ST)
LSP-3787 ....11/68   8-10
COVER 7: Front: Same as cover 4, except
area previously used for bonus photo
announcement is now blank.
❑ RCA Victor 21-112-1
40D.....................................6/68   4-6
INNER SLEEVE 7: Red, black and white.
Front: RCA's Elvis LP catalog, most recent
being *Elvis' Gold Records, Vol. 4* (side 1, row
4, column 5). Back: RCA's Elvis LP and Twin
Pack Stereo 8 catalog.

May also be found with inner sleeves 40B and
40C. See chapter on inner sleeves for more
information.
RCA Victor (ST)
LSP-3787....................11/68   35-40
**TOTAL PACKAGE 7: Disc, cover, inner
   sleeve.**

❑ RCA Victor (ST)
LSP-3787 ....'76   4-8
DISC 8: Tan label.
❑ RCA LSP-3787 ....'76   4-8
COVER 8: Verification pending.
❑ RCA Victor.........................'70s   2-4
INNER SLEEVE 8: Black-and-white. Pictures
RCA Elvis catalog front and back. Any of
several sleeves may be found on reissues
from this period.
RCA Victor (ST)
LSP-3787......................'76   10-20
**TOTAL PACKAGE 8: Disc, cover, inner
   sleeve.**

❑ RCA Victor (ST)
LSP-3787 ....'76   4-6
DISC 9: Black label, dog near top.
❑ RCA LSP-3787 ....'76   4-6
COVER 9: Reflects logo change.
❑ RCA Victor.........................'70s   2-4
INNER SLEEVE 9: Black-and-white. Pictures
RCA Elvis catalog front and back. Any of
several sleeves may be found on reissues
from this period.
RCA Victor (ST)
LSP-3787......................'76   10-18
**TOTAL PACKAGE 9: Disc, cover, inner
   sleeve.**

❑ RCA Victor (ST)
APL1-2564 ....9/77   3-5
DISC 10: Black label, dog near top.
❑ RCA APL1-2564 ....9/77   3-5
COVER 10: Reflects selection number
change.
Includes copies with a sticker bearing the
"AFL1" prefix, wrapped around cover at top of
spine.
❑ RCA Victor.........................'70s   2-4
INNER SLEEVE 10: Black-and-white.
Pictures RCA Elvis catalog front and back.
Any of several sleeves may be found on
reissues from this period.
RCA Victor (ST)
APL1-2564 ....9/77   8-15
**TOTAL PACKAGE 10: Disc, cover, inner
   sleeve.**

Though once assumed to exist (based on
RCA's 1979 catalog), we have yet to verify
even one copy of this LP with an "AFL1"
prefix. It appears none were made.

Side 1
Double Trouble
Baby If You'll Give Me All Your Love
Could I Fall in Love
Long Legged Girl (With the Short Dress On)
City By Night
Old MacDonald

Side 2
I Love Only One Girl
There Is So Much World to See
It Won't Be Long
Never Ending
Blue River
What Now, What Next, Where To

E-Z COUNTRY PROGRAMMING (NO. 2)
Various artists collection

❑ RCA Victor (M) 11/55   300-350
DISC 1: Light green label, black and red print.
10" various artists sampler of RCA's country
catalog. Promotional issue only.
G7OL-0108-1/G7OL-0109-1.
COVER 1: None made.
INNER SLEEVE 1: Brown, no printing.

RCA Victor (M) 11/55   300-350
TOTAL PACKAGE 1: Disc.

Side 1
When You Said Goodbye (Eddy Arnold)
Hi De Ank Tum (Nita, Rita & Ruby)
Mystery Train (Elvis Presley)
Honey (Chet Atkins)
These Hands (Hank Snow)
The Last Frontier (Sons of the Pioneers)

Side 2
I Forgot to Remember to Forget (Elvis Presley)
I Wore Dark Glasses (Anita Carter)
Rock-A-Bye Baby (Skeeter Bonn)
Love and Marriage (Homer & Jethro)
Love Or Spite (Hank Locklin)
Handful of Sunshine (Stuart Hamblen)

E-Z COUNTRY PROGRAMMING (NO. 3)
Various artists collection

❑ RCA Victor (M) 2/56   300-350
DISC 1: Light green label, black and red print.
10" various artists sampler of RCA's country
catalog. Promotional issue only.
G8OL-0199-1/G8OL-0200-1.
COVER 1: None made.
INNER SLEEVE 1: Brown, no printing.

RCA Victor (M) 2/56   300-350
TOTAL PACKAGE 1: Disc.

Side 1
Heartbreak Hotel (Elvis Presley)
I'm Moving In (Hank Snow)
If It Ain't on the Menu (Hawkshaw Hawkins)
The Poor People of Paris (Chet Atkins)
I Want to Be Loved (Johnnie & Jack, & Ruby Wells)
That's a Sad Affair (Jim Reeves)

Side 2
Do You Know Where God Lives (Eddy Arnold)
If You Were Mine (Jim Reeves)
The Little White Duck (Dorothy Olsen)

Borrowing (Hawkshaw Hawkins)
What Would You Do (Porter Wagoner)
I Was the One (Elvis Presley)

E-Z POP PROGRAMMING (NO. 5)
Various artists collection

❑ RCA Victor (M) 11/55   300-350
DISC 1: Yellow label, black print. 12" various
artists sampler of RCA's pop catalog.
Promotional issue only.
F7OP-9681-1/F7OP-9682-1.
COVER 1: None made.
INNER SLEEVE 1: Brown, no printing.

RCA Victor (M) 11/55   300-350
TOTAL PACKAGE 1: Disc.

Side 1
Dungaree Doll (Eddie Fisher)
Stolen Love (Dinah Shore)
Take My Hand (Rhythmettes)
Not One Goodbye (Jaye P. Morgan)
Don't Go to Strangers (Vaughn Monroe)
The Rock and Roll Waltz (Kay Starr)
I Forgot to Remember to Forget (Elvis Presley)
The Little Laplander (Henri Rene)

Side 2
The Large Large House (Mike Pedicin)
All At Once You Love Her (Perry Como)
When You Said Goodbye (Eddy Arnold)
My Bewildered Heart (Jaye P. Morgan)
Mystery Train (Elvis Presley)
That's All There Is to That (Dinah Shore)
Jean's Song (Chet Atkins)
Everybody's Got a Home But Me (Eddie Fisher)

E-Z POP PROGRAMMING (NO. 6)
Various artists collection

❑ RCA Victor (M) 2/56   300-350
DISC 1: Light yellow label, black print. 10"
various artists sampler of RCA's pop catalog.
Promotional issue only.
G7OL-0197-1/G7OL-0198-1.
COVER 1: None made.
INNER SLEEVE 1: Brown, no printing.

RCA Victor (M) 2/56   300-350
TOTAL PACKAGE 1: Disc.

Side 1
Lipstick and Candy and Rubbersole Shoes (Julius La Rosa)
Mr. Wonderful (Teddi King)
The Bitter with the Sweet (Bill Eckstine)
Forever Darling (Ames Brothers)
Sweet Lips (Jaye P. Morgan)
Do You Know Where God Lives (Eddy Arnold)

Side 2
Grapevine (Billy Eckstine)
Poor People of Paris (Jean's Song) (Chet Atkins)
Juke Box Baby (Perry Como)
Little White Duck (Dorothy Olsen)
I Was the One (Elvis Presley)
Hot Dog Rock and Roll (Singing Dogs)

EARLY DAYS

❏ Rockin' Records 45-001: Bootleg. Listed for identification only.

EARLY ELVIS (1954-1956 LIVE AT THE LOUISIANA HAYRIDE)

❏ Premore (M) PL-589........11/89   10-20
DISC 1: Custom, "Early Elvis" label. White stock with red print. A mail order only, coupon offer from the Solo Cup company.
EP-8906-A/EP-8906-B. Identification numbers are engraved.

❏ Premore PL-589 ....11/89   10-20
COVER 1: Front: Has an artist's rendering of Elvis.
INNER SLEEVE 1: White, no printing.

Premore (M) PL-589 ..... 11/89   20-40
TOTAL PACKAGE 1: Disc, cover.

Card stock jacket, with printing on cover – not on slicks. A cassette tape edition of this package was made, with same selection number (PL-589). Tape and cover/card, with same art as cover 1, are sealed in a cello pack.

Side 1
Introduction
That's All Right (shown as "That's All Right Momma")
Blue Moon of Kentucky
Good Rockin' Tonight
I Got a Woman

Side 2
Tweedle Dee
Baby, Let's Play House (shown as "I Wanna Play House with You")
Maybellene
That's All Right (shown as "That's All Right Momma")
Hound Dog

EARLY '60s (THESE WERE OUR SONGS) (7 LPs)

Various artists collection
Mail order offer only. All discs in this set have a black label with red and white print. Each is listed individually below. All identification numbers are engraved.

❏ Reader's Digest/BMG Direct Marketing
RC4-100-1 .... '89   3-4
DISC 1:
W1RS-5871-2/W1RS-5872-2.

❏ Reader's Digest/BMG Direct Marketing
RC4-100-2 .... '89   3-4
DISC 2:
W1RS-5873-2/W1RS-5874-2.

❏ Reader's Digest/BMG Direct Marketing
RC4-100-3 .... '89   3-4
DISC 3:
W1RS-5875-2/W1RS-5876-2.

❏ Reader's Digest/BMG Direct Marketing
RC4-100-4 .... '89   3-4
DISC 4:
W1RS-5877-2/W1RS-5878-2.

❏ Reader's Digest/BMG Direct Marketing
RC4-100-5 .... '89   3-4
DISC 5:

W1RS-5879-2/W1RS-5880-2.

❏ Reader's Digest/BMG Direct Marketing
RC4-100-6 .... '89   3-4
DISC 6:
W1RS-5881-2/W1RS-5882-2.

❏ Reader's Digest/BMG Direct Marketing
RC4-100-7 ....:......... '89   3-4
DISC 7:
W1RS-5883-2/W1RS-5884-2.
INNER SLEEVES: Generic, individually numbered, plastic sleeves. Front and Back: Clear, covered with Reader's Digest Pegasus logos. Number (RDA/AP1) at lower left on side 2.

❏ Reader's Digest/RCA Music Service
RCA-100-A .... '89   15-20
BOX 1: Slipcover: Blue. Front: Reader's Digest/BMG Direct Marketing logos at lower left. Back is blank. Record case: White with pink print. Back is blank.

Reader's Digest/BMG Direct Marketing (SP) RCA-100A .... '89   40-50
TOTAL PACKAGE 1: Discs, box.

Disc 1

Side 1
Rubber Ball (Bobby Vee)
Good Timin' (Jimmy Jones)
Tell Laura I Love Her (Ray Peterson)
Walk, Don't Run (Ventures)
Walkin' to New Orleans (Fats Domino)
Money (That's What I Want) Barrett Strong

Side 2
Lonely Teenager (Dion)
Baby (You Got What It Takes) (Brook Benton & Dinah Washington)
You're Sixteen (Johnny Burnette)
Devil or Angel (Bobby Vee)
Way Down Yonder in New Orleans (Freddy Cannon)
He Will Break Your Heart (Jerry Butler)

Disc 2

Side 1
Quarter to Three (Gary U.S. Bonds)
Mother-in-Law (Ernie K-Doe)
Dance on Little Girl (Paul Anka)
Little Sister (Elvis Presley)
Pretty Little Angel Eyes (Curtis Lee)
A Little Bit of Soap (Jarmels)

Side 2
Heartaches (Marcels)
Tower of Strength (Gene McDaniels)
(Marie's the Name) His Latest Flame (Elvis Presley)
But I Do (Clarence "Frogman" Henry)
Who Put the Bomp (Barry Mann)
More Money for You and Me Medley (Four Preps)

Disc 3

Side 1
Surfin' Safari (Beach Boys)
Johnny Angel (Shelley Fabares)
Ahab the Arab (Ray Stevens)
Soldier Boy (Shirelles)
Happy Birthday Sweet Sixteen (Neil Sedaka)

\Side 2

She's Not You (Elvis Presley)
Bobby's Girl (Marcie Blane)
You Belong to Me (Duprees)
(Dance with the) Guitar Man (Duane Eddy and the
   Rebelettes)
I Know (Barbara George)
Palisades Park (Freddy Cannon)

Disc 4

Side 1

Baby Workout (Jackie Wilson)
Everybody (Tommy Roe)
Wipe Out (Surfaris)
You've Really Got a Hold on Me (Miracles)
(You're the) Devil in Disguise (Elvis Presley)
Surfer Girl (Beach Boys)

Side 2

Can I Get a Witness (Marvin Gaye)
Hello Stranger (Barbara Lewis)
Judy's Turn to Cry (Lesley Gore)
Louie Louie (Kingsmen)
Denise (Randy and the Rainbows)
Chains (Cookies)

Disc 5

Side 1

Fun, Fun, Fun (Beach Boys)
Dead Man's Curve (Jan and Dean)
California Sun (Rivieras)
Suspicion (Terry Stafford)
Mr. Bass Man (Johnny Cymbal with Ronnie Bright)
Come See About Me (Supremes)

Side 2

Dance, Dance, Dance (Beach Boys)
You Never Can Tell (Chuck Berry)
Surfin' Bird (Trashmen)
The Shoop Shoop Song (It's in His Kiss) (Betty Everett)
Little Honda (Hondells)
I'm on the Outside (Looking in) (Little Anthony and the
   Imperials)

Disc 6

Side 1

Return to Sender (Elvis Presley)
Lovers Who Wander (Dion)
Nadine (Is It You) (Chuck Berry)
Keep Searchin' (We'll Follow the Sun) (Del Shannon)
Pride and Joy (Marvin Gaye)
Hello Josephine (My Girl Josephine) (Fats Domino)

Side 2

Walk on By (Dionne Warwick)
Sweet Nothin's (Brenda Lee)
You Beat Me to the Punch (Mary Wells)
You Don't Own Me (Lesley Gore)
My Heart Has a Mind of Its Own (Connie Francis)
The End of the World (Skeeter Davis)

Disc 7

Side 1

Surfin' U.S.A. (Beach Boys)
The Way You Do the Things You Do (Temptations)
Baby, It's You (Shirelles)
Drag City (Jan and Dean)
Come and Get These Memories (Martha and the
   Vandellas)
When Will I Be Loved (Everly Brothers)

Side 2

Do You Love Me (Contours)
Twist and Shout (Isley Brothers)
New Orleans (Gary U.S. Bonds)
The Peppermint Twist (Joey Dee and the Starliters)
Let's Dance (Chris Montez)

The Loco-Motion (Little Eva)

EARTH NEWS (FOR THE WEEK OF AUGUST 29, 1977)

❑ Earth News (M)
  EN8-22-77 ....8/77   325-350
  DISC 1: Sent only subscribing radio stations.
  Has 14 five-minute programs, 12 devoted to
  Elvis news, music, and interviews. Includes
  excerpts of *Blue Suede Shoes* (1956 live TV
  appearance), *Don't Be Cruel* (1956 live TV
  appearance), *Heartbreak Hotel* (1956 live TV
  appearance), and *Hound Dog*.
  EN-8-22-77-A/EN-8-22-77-B. Identification numbers are
  engraved.
  COVER 1: None made.
  INNER SLEEVE 1: White, no printing.
❑ Earth News EN8-22-77......8/77   6-10
  INSERT 1A: One page script.
❑ Earth News EN8-22-77......8/77   6-10
  INSERT 1B: One page letter expressing the
  need to air this series the week of August 22,
  even though the label indicates August 29.

Earth News (M)
  EN8-22-77 ....8/77   350-375
  TOTAL PACKAGE 1: Disc, inserts.

Side 1
1956 Elvis Interview
Blue Suede Shoes (From Dorsey Brothers TV Show)
1956 Elvis Interview
Don't Be Cruel (From Ed Sullivan Show)
Heartbreak Hotel (From Dorsey Brothers TV Show)
1956 Elvis Interview
Jay Thompson's Elvis Interview
Elvis Sails Interview
Dick Clark/Elvis Phone Call
The Truth About Me

Side 2
1956 Elvis Interview
1961 Elvis Interview
Red West Interview
The Truth About Me
Hound Dog
Willie Mae Thornton Interview
The Truth About Me
In the Ghetto
Steve Bender Interview
Medley: Hey Mr. Presley/I Dreamed I Was Elvis/My
   Baby's Crazy About Elvis/Elvis Presley for
   President

EASY LISTENING HITS OF THE '60s AND '70s

Various artists collection
Mail order offer only. All discs in this set have
a black label with red and white print. Each is
listed individually below. All identification
numbers are engraved.
❑ Reader's Digest/BMG Direct Marketing
  RB4-040-1 ....'89   3-4
  DISC 1:
  V1RS-5561-1/V1RS-5562-1.
  V1RS-5561-1/V1RS-5562-2.

❑ Reader's Digest/BMG Direct Marketing
RB4-040-2 .... '89   3-4
DISC 2:
V1RS-5563-1/V1RS-5564-D-1.
V1RS-5563-1/V1RS-5564-D-2.

❑ Reader's Digest/BMG Direct Marketing
RB4-040-3 .... '89   3-4
DISC 3:
V1RS-5565-D1/V1RS-5566-D2.
V1RS-5565-D3/V1RS-5566-D1.

❑ Reader's Digest/BMG Direct Marketing
RB4-040-4 .... '89   3-4
DISC 4:
V1RS-5567-D1/V1RS-5568-D1.
V1RS-5567-D2/V1RS-5568-D3.

❑ Reader's Digest/BMG Direct Marketing
RB4-040-5 .... '89   3-4
DISC 5:
V1RS-5569-D2/V1RS-5570-1.
V1RS-5569-D2/V1RS-5570-4.

❑ Reader's Digest/BMG Direct Marketing
RB4-040-6 .... '89   3-4
DISC 6:
V1RS-5571-1/V1RS-5572-D1.
V1RS-5571-D2/V1RS-5572-D2.

❑ Reader's Digest/BMG Direct Marketing
RB4-040-7 .... '89   3-4
DISC 7:
V1RS-5573-2/V1RS-5574-2.

❑ Reader's Digest/RCA Music Service
RBA-040-A .... '89   15-20
BOX 1: Slipcover: Yellow. Front: Reader's
Digest/BMG Direct Marketing logos at lower
left. Back is blank. Record case: White with
maroon print. Back is blank.
INNER SLEEVES 1: Generic, individually
numbered, plastic sleeves. Front and Back:
Clear, covered with Reader's Digest Pegasus
logos. Number (RDA/AP1) at lower left on
side 2.

❑ Reader's Digest
RBU-040-E .... '89   4-6
INSERT 1: 4" X 4," 64-page "Music Program
Notes" booklet. Has duotone photos of 20
acts, including Elvis ("Aloha" concert).

**Reader's Digest/BMG Direct Marketing
(SP) RBA-040A .... '89   40-55
TOTAL PACKAGE : Discs, box, insert.**

Disc 1

Side 1: You Light Up My Life
You Light Up My Life (Debby Boone)
Never Gonna Fall Again (Eric Carmen)
Touch Me in the Morning (Diana Ross)
When I Need You (Leo Sayer)
Ain't No Way to Treat a Lady (Helen Reddy)
Shadows in the Moonlight (Anne Murray)

Side 2: You Light Up My Life
Just When I Needed You Most (Randy Van Warmer)
Do You Know Where You're Going To (Diana Ross)
This Will Be (Natalie Cole)
All I Ever Need Is You (Sonny & Cher)
Until It's Time for You to Go (Elvis Presley)
Deja Vu (Dionne Warwick)

Disc 2

Side 1: Make Your Own Kind of Music
Make Your Own Kind of Music (Mama Cass)
The Way of Love (Cher)
It's Not Unusual (Tom Jones)
Medley: I Say a Little Prayer/By the Time I Get to
Phoenix (Glen Campbell & Anne Murray)
Up, Up and Away (5th Dimension)
Wouldn't It Be Nice (Beach Boys)

Side 2: Make Your Own Kind of Music
Everybody's Talkin' (Nilsson)
This Is My Song (Petula Clark)
Jean (Oliver)
You're My World (Helen Reddy)
When Will I Be Loved (Everly Brothers)
The Last Waltz (Engelbert Humperdinck)

Disc 3

Side 1: Feelings
You and Me Against the World (Helen Reddy)
Still (Commodores featuring Lionel Richie)
I Just Fall in Love Again (Anne Murray)
All By Myself (Eric Carmen)
We're All Alone (Rita Coolidge)
You Are So Beautiful (Joe Cocker)

Side 2: Soft 'n' Country
You Needed Me (Anne Murray)
Watching Scotty Grow (Bobby Goldsboro)
Afternoon Delight (Starland Vocal Band)
It Was Almost like a Song (Ronnie Milsap)
I'm Easy (Keith Carradine)
I Will Always Love You (Dolly Parton)

Disc 4

Side 1: No. 1 Easy Listening Hits
Three Times a Lady (Commodores)
I'll Never Love This Way Again (Dionne Warwick)
Love Will Keep Us Together (Captain & Tennille)
Breaking Up Is Hard to Do (Neil Sedaka)
One Less Bell to Answer (5th Dimension)
Laughter in the Rain (Neil Sedaka)

Side 2: Good Times in the '70s
Making Our Dreams Come True (Cyndi Grecco)
Delta Dawn (Helen Reddy)
Escape (Rupert Holmes)
Two Doors Down (Dolly Parton)
My Sweet Gypsy Rose (Tony Orlando & Dawn)

Disc 5

Side 1: No. 1 Easy Listening Hits
I'll Never Fall in Love Again (Tom Jones)
The Fool on the Hill (Sergio Mendes)
Don't Sleep in the Subway (Petula Clark)
Wichita Lineman (Glen Campbell)
It Must Be Him (Vikki Carr)
Can't Help Falling in Love (Elvis Presley)

Side 2: Simply Folk
Good Morning Starshine (Oliver)
Where Have All the Flowers Gone (Kingston Trio)
Willow Weep for Me (Chad & Jeremy)
Tell It All Brother (Kenny Rogers and the First Edition)
Let It Be Me (Glen Campbell & Bobbie Gentry)
The Last Farewell (Roger Whittaker)

Disc 6

Side 1: The Great Instrumental Hits
Theme from Romeo and Juliet (Henry Mancini)
Feels So Good (Chuck Mangione)
Brian's Song (Michel Legrand)
Music Box Dancer (Frank Mills)
Moon River (Henry Mancini)
Song from M*A*S*H (Al DeLory and His Orchestra)

Side 2: Soulfully Yours

Stop in the Name of Love (Supremes)
Show and Tell (Al Wilson)
I Heard It Through the Grapevine (Gladys Knight and the Pips)
How Sweet It Is (To Be Loved By You) (Marvin Gaye)
I'm Gonna Make You Love Me (Supremes &Temptations)

Disc 7

Side 1: Unforgettable Stars, Unforgettable Moments

My Way (Elvis Presley)
Mame (Louis Armstrong)
Happy (Bobby Darin)
New World Coming (Mama Cass)
I'll Have to Say I Love You in a Song (Jim Croce)

Side 2: Reflections

The Times of Your Life (Paul Anka)
Try to Remember/The Way We Were (Gladys Knight and the Pips)
Autumn of My Life (Bobby Goldsboro)
All I Have to Do Is Dream (Richard Chamberlain)
Memories (Elvis Presley)

ELVIS

❏ RCA Victor (M)
   LPM-1382........................11/56   125-150
   DISC 1A: Black label, "Long Play" at bottom.
   G2WP-7207-1S/G2WP-7208-1S. Label LP#1.
   G2WP-7207-14S/G2WP-7208-14S. Label LP#1. Numbers on side 1 are stamped, but those on side 2 are engraved.
   G2WP-7207-17S/G2WP-7208-20S. Label LP#1.

❏ RCA Victor LPM-1382.....11/56   125-150
   COVER 1: This disc may be found in any of the covers shown as 1A through 1L, individually described below.
   INNER SLEEVE 1: Generic RCA sleeve. Makes no mention of Elvis or this LP.

RCA Victor (M)
   LPM-1382..................11/56   250-300
   TOTAL PACKAGE 1A: Disc, cover.

❏ RCA Victor (M)
   LPM-1382........................11/56   175-250
   DISC 1B: Black label, "Long Play" at bottom. Label shows the sequence of titles as "Band" 1 through 6 on each side.
   G2WP-7207-3S/G2WP-7208-3S. Has "New Orthophonic" High Fidelity centered on label, above hole.
   G2WP-7207-5S/G2WP-7208-5S. Has "New Orthophonic" High Fidelity centered on label, above hole.
   G2WP-7207-6S/G2WP-7208-5S. Has "New Orthophonic" High Fidelity on both sides, centered on label above hole.
   G2WP-7207-6S/G2WP-7208-5S. Has "New Orthophonic" High Fidelity only on side 1 (centered on label above hole).
   G2WP-7207-6S/G2WP-7208-7S. Has "New Orthophonic" High Fidelity on both sides, (centered on label above hole).
   G2WP-7207-8S/G2WP-7208-8S. Has "New Orthophonic" High Fidelity centered on label, above hole.

❏ RCA Victor LPM-1382.....11/56   125-150
   COVER 1: This disc may be found in any of the covers shown as 1A through 1L, individually described below.
   INNER SLEEVE 1: Generic RCA sleeve. Makes no mention of Elvis or this LP.

RCA Victor (M)
   LPM-1382..................11/56   300-400
   TOTAL PACKAGE 1B: Disc, cover.

❏ RCA Victor (M)
   LPM-1382........................11/56   500-600
   DISC 1C: Black label, "Long Play" at bottom. Mistakenly pressed with an alternative take of *Old Shep*, not available on any other authorized U.S. vinyl release. Any copy with a "15S" matrix on side 2 (matrix on side 1 is irrelevant) is likely to have the alternative; however, playing the track is the way to be certain. Alternative is different throughout, instrumentally and vocally – especially Elvis' phrasing – but here are two lyric variations. Words in all upper case are exclusive to the alternative take (which can now be heard on the 1992 CD boxed set *Elvis – The King of Rock 'N' Roll, The Complete '50s Masters*): 1) "As the years fast did roll, Old Shep he grew old AND his eyes were fast growing dim." 2) "He came to my side and he looked up at me, and HE laid his old head on my knee." Price would apply to any other pressing with the alternative take, regardless of identification number.
   G2WP-7207-12S/G2WP-7208-15S.

❏ RCA Victor LPM-1382.....11/56   125-150
   COVER 1: This disc may be found in any of the covers shown as 1A through 1L, individually described below.
   INNER SLEEVE 1: Generic RCA sleeve. Makes no mention of Elvis or this LP.

RCA Victor (M)
   LPM-1382..................11/56   625-750
   TOTAL PACKAGE 1C: Disc, cover.

❏ RCA Victor (M)
   LPM-1382........................11/56   500-600
   DISC 1D: Black label, "Long Play" at bottom. Mistakenly pressed with an alternative take of *Old Shep*, not available on any other authorized U.S. vinyl release. Any copy with a "17S" matrix on side 2 (matrix on side 1 is irrelevant) is likely to have the alternative; however, playing the track is recommended way to be certain. May also appear on some "19S" pressings (G2WP-7207-18S/ G2WP-7208-19S); however, price applies to any pressing with the alternative take, regardless of identification number. See disc 1C for alternative take identification.
   G2WP-7207-17S/G2WP-7208-17S. Label LP#1.

❏ RCA Victor LPM-1382.....11/56   125-150
   COVER 1: This disc may be found in any of the covers shown as 1A through 1L, individually described below.
   INNER SLEEVE 1: Generic RCA sleeve. Makes no mention of Elvis or this LP.

RCA Victor (M)
   LPM-1382..................11/56   625-750
   TOTAL PACKAGE 1D: Disc, cover.

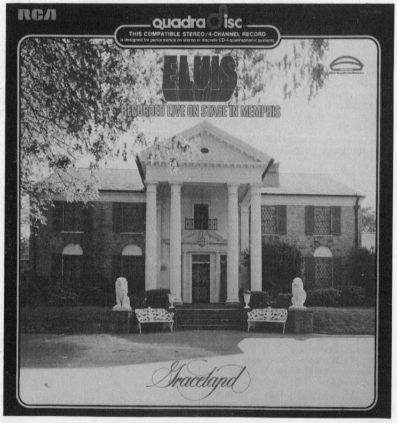

❑ RCA Victor LPM-1382 ..... 11/56   125-150
COVER 1A: Front: RCA logo and number at upper right. No song titles listed. Back: Pictures (clockwise) the following LPs: *Soft and Sweet; Walt Disney Song Carousel; Relax with Victor Herbert; (Matt) Dennis Anyone; Serenade to Love; Frankie Carle Plays Cole Porter; Music for Reading; Lavalle at Work.* At bottom, reads: "Listen to these . . . and give yourself a treat!"
May contain any of the discs shown as 1A through 1D.

❑ RCA Victor LPM-1382 ..... 11/56   125-150
COVER 1B: Same as cover 1A except back pictures (clockwise): *Voodoo Suite; Down to Eartha; Champagne for Dinner; Wanderin' with Eddy Arnold; Have You Met Miss Carroll; Sax in Silk; Always (Hugo Winterhalter); Music for Relaxation.* At bottom, reads: "Listen to these musical favorites in many moods!"
May contain any of the discs shown as 1A through 1D.

❑ RCA Victor LPM-1382 ..... 11/56   125-150
COVER 1C: Same as cover 1A except back pictures (clockwise): *A Sentimental Date with Perry Como; Lonesome Gal (Lurlean Hunter); The Jazz Workshop (Four Brass, One Tenor); Jaye P. Morgan; The Immortal Ladies (George Melachrino); The Sound of Glenn Miller; My Reverie (Three Suns); George Beverly Shea – Inspirational Songs.* At bottom, reads: "More Great pop and jazz albums to fit every mood!"
May contain any of the discs shown as 1A through 1D.

❑ RCA Victor LPM-1382 ..... 11/56   125-150
COVER 1D: Same as cover 1A except back pictures (clockwise*): Lena Horne; Shorty Rogers and His Giants; Dinner in Caracas; Masquerade; Carousel; Flirtation Walk; Belafonte; Teddi King.* At bottom, reads: "Hear these other great pop and jazz albums."
May contain any of the discs shown as 1A through 1D.

❑ RCA Victor LPM-1382 ..... 11/56   125-150
COVER 1E: Same as cover 1A except back pictures (clockwise): *Dinah Shore; America's Favorite Marches; Soft and Sweet; Mambo Mania; Peter Pan; Juke Box Saturday Night; Mario Lanza – A Kiss; Music for Dining.* At bottom, reads: "For added listening pleasure . . . try these!"
May contain any of the discs shown as 1A through 1D.

❑ RCA Victor LPM-1382 ..... 11/56   125-150
COVER 1F: Same as cover 1A except back pictures (clockwise): *Mark Twain and Other Folk Favorites - Harry Belafonte; Kay Starr; Inside Sauter-Finegan; So Smooth; I Love You; Glenn Miller; Student Prince; Music for Two People Alone.* At bottom, reads: "You'll enjoy these best selling favorites!"
May contain any of the discs shown as 1A through 1D.

❑ RCA Victor LPM-1382 ..... 11/56   125-150
COVER 1G: Same as cover 1A except back pictures (clockwise): *Brahms Violin Concerto; Salome; Dance of the Seven Veils; Horowitz; Rubinstein (Chopin); Gâté Parisienne; Pictures at an Exhibition; Student Prince (Mario Lanza); Arturo Toscanini.*
May contain any of the discs shown as 1A through 1D.

❑ RCA Victor LPM-1382 ..... 11/56   125-150
COVER 1H: Same as cover 1A except back pictures (clockwise): *An Adventure in High Fidelity; Toscanini Plays Your Favorites; Stokowski; Magic for a Summer Night; A Kiss and Other Love Songs By Mario Lanza; The Pines...The Fountains of Rome; Toscanini and the NBC Symphony Orchestra; Beethoven's Symphonies Nos. 1 and 9; Oklahoma Suite (Morton Gould and His Orchestra).* At bottom, reads: "Enjoy memorable music . . . memorably performed!"
May contain any of the discs shown as 1A through 1D.

❑ RCA Victor LPM-1382 ..... 11/56   125-150
COVER 1I: Same as cover 1A except back pictures (clockwise): *Rhapsody (Stokowski); David Oistrakh; Tchaikovsky Concerto No. 1 (Gilels- Reiner); Symphonie Fantastique; Madam Butterfly; The Magic Mario Lanza; A Toscanini Omnibus; Beethoven's Fifth Symphony (Boston Symphony Orchestra).*
May contain any of the discs shown as 1A through 1D.

❑ RCA Victor LPM-1382 ..... 11/56   125-150
COVER 1J: Same as cover 1A except back pictures (clockwise): *Eroica; Horowitz; Swan Lake; Rhapsody in Blue; Classical Music for People Who Hate Classical Music; Beethoven's Symphonies Nos. 5 and 8; With Love from a Chorus; Victory at Sea.* At bottom, reads: "You'll want to own these other concert favorites."
May contain any of the discs shown as 1A through 1D.

❑ RCA Victor LPM-1382 ..... 11/56   125-150
COVER 1K: Same as cover 1A except back pictures (clockwise): *Verdi: Aida; Iturbi; Pathetique; Sleeping Beauty; Sylvia Coppelia; Artur Rubinstein; Heifetz; Forever the Waltz.* At bottom, reads: "Hear these magnificent performances!"
May contain any of the discs shown as 1A through 1D.

❑ RCA Victor LPM-1382 ..... 11/56   125-150
COVER 1L: Same as cover 1A except back is text only and pictures no albums.

❑ RCA Victor (M)
LPM-1382 .... 11/63   30-40
DISC 2: Black label, "Mono" at bottom.

❑ RCA Victor LPM-1382 ..... 11/56   35-50
COVER 2: Front: RCA logo at upper right and number at lower left. "RE" at lower right. Lists contents. Back: All text, no photos.

☐ RCA Victor (No Number)...9/63   8-10
INNER SLEEVE 2: Turquoise, black and white. Front: RCA's Elvis LP catalog, most recent being *It Happened at the World's Fair* (side 1, row 4, column 5). Back: RCA Elvis EPs and 45s catalog.

RCA Victor (M)
LPM-1382 .... 11/63   75-100
TOTAL PACKAGE 2: Disc, cover, inner sleeve.

☐ RCA Victor (M)
LPM-1382............................'64   10-15
DISC 3: Black label, "Monaural" at bottom.
☐ RCA Victor (M)
LPM-1382............................'64   35-50
COVER 3: Same as cover 2.
☐ RCA Victor 21-112-1
40A..................................10/64   4-8
INNER SLEEVE 3: Red, black and white. Front: RCA's Elvis LP catalog, most recent being *Kissin' Cousins* (side 1, row 1, column 6). Back: RCA Elvis EPs and 45s catalog.

RCA Victor (M)
LPM-1382 .... '64   50-75
TOTAL PACKAGE 3: Disc, cover, inner sleeve.

☐ RCA Victor (SE)
LSP-1382(e)......................2/62   100-125
DISC 4: Black label, RCA logo in silver at top and "Stereo Electronically Reprocessed" at bottom.
M2PY-4729-3S/M2PY-4730-3S.
☐ RCA Victor LSP-1382(e) ...2/62   50-75
COVER 4: Front: RCA logo and "Stereo Electronically Reprocessed" at upper right and number at upper left. "RE" at lower right. Lists contents. Back: All text, no photos. Has box of text at upper left "From the Originators of Electronically Reprocessed Stereo." Price reflects RCA's use of this same cover, with no discernible differences, until 1968.
INNER SLEEVE 4: White, no printing.

RCA Victor (SE)
LSP-1382(e) 2/62   150-200
TOTAL PACKAGE 4: Disc, cover.

☐ RCA Victor (SE)
LSP-1382(e)....................10/64   10-15
DISC 5: Black label, RCA logo in white at top and "Stereo" at bottom.
M2PY-4729-2S/M2PY-4730-4S. Label LP#17.
☐ RCA Victor
LSP-1382(e)....................10/64   35-40
COVER 5: Same as cover 4.
☐ RCA Victor 21-112-1
40A..................................10/64   4-8
INNER SLEEVE 5: Red, black and white. Front: RCA's Elvis LP catalog, most recent being *Kissin' Cousins* (side 1, row 1, column 6). Back: RCA Elvis EPs and 45s catalog.

RCA Victor (SE)
LSP-1382(e) 10/64   50-65
TOTAL PACKAGE 5: Disc, cover, inner sleeve.

☐ RCA Victor (SE)
LSP-1382(e)....................11/68   15-20
DISC 6: Orange label. Rigid vinyl.
☐ RCA Victor
LSP-1382(e)....................11/68   8-10
COVER 6: Same as cover 4, except has "SER" on back and a "2" (separately), and a red sticker indicating "Stereo effect reprocessed from mono," etc.
☐ RCA Victor 21-112-1
40D..................................6/68   4-6
INNER SLEEVE 6: Red, black and white. Front: RCA's Elvis LP catalog, most recent being *Elvis' Gold Records, Vol. 4* (side 1, row 4, column 5). Back: RCA's Elvis LP and Twin Pack Stereo 8 catalog. May also be found with inner sleeves 40B and 40C. See chapter on inner sleeves for more information.

RCA Victor (SE)
LSP-1382(e) 11/68   25-35
TOTAL PACKAGE 6: Disc, cover, inner sleeve.

☐ RCA Victor (SE)
LSP-1382(e)........................'71   10-15
DISC 7: Orange label. Flexible vinyl.
☐ RCA Victor LSP-1382(e) .....'71   4-8
COVER 7: Same as cover 6, except has "SER" on both front and back, and a "2" on back.
☐ RCA Victor........................'70s   2-4
INNER SLEEVE 7: Black-and-white. Pictures RCA Elvis catalog front and back. Any of several sleeves may be found on reissues from this period.

RCA Victor (SE)
LSP-1382(e) .... '71   15-25
TOTAL PACKAGE 7: Disc, cover, inner sleeve.

☐ RCA Victor (SE)
LSP-1382(e)........................'76   4-8
DISC 8: Tan label.
☐ RCA Victor LSP-1382(e) .....'76   4-8
COVER 8: Same as cover 7, except has "SER" only on front and does not have red sticker on back.
☐ RCA Victor........................'70s   2-4
INNER SLEEVE 8: Black-and-white. Pictures RCA Elvis catalog front and back. Any of several sleeves may be found on reissues from this period.

RCA Victor (SE)
LSP-1382(e) .... '76   10-20
TOTAL PACKAGE 8: Disc, cover, inner sleeve.

❑ RCA Victor (SE)
LSP-1382(e)........................ '76   4-6
DISC 9: Black label, dog near top.

❑ RCA LSP-1382(e) .... '76   4-6
COVER 9: Reflects logo change.

❑ RCA Victor......................... '70s   2-4
INNER SLEEVE 9: Black-and-white. Pictures
RCA Elvis catalog front and back. Any of
several sleeves may be found on reissues
from this period.

RCA Victor (SE)
LSP-1382(e) ....'76   10-18
TOTAL PACKAGE 9: Disc, cover, inner
sleeve.

❑ RCA Victor (SE)
AFL1-1382(e)...................... '77   3-5
DISC 10: Black label, dog near top.

❑ RCA AFL1-1382(e)............. '77   3-5
COVER 10: Reflects prefix change. Includes
copies with a sticker bearing the "AFL1"
prefix, wrapped around cover at top of spine.

❑ RCA Victor......................... '70s   2-4
INNER SLEEVE 10: Black-and-white.
Pictures RCA Elvis catalog front and back.
Any of several sleeves may be found on
reissues from this period.

RCA Victor (SE)
AFL1-1382(e) ....'77   8-15
TOTAL PACKAGE 10: Disc, cover, inner
sleeve.

❑ RCA (M) AFM1-5199.........8/84   6-8
DISC 11: Digitally remastered, quality mono
pressing. Gold "Elvis 50th Anniversary" label.
AFM1-5999A-1/AFM1-5999B-1. Identification numbers are
engraved.

❑ RCA AFM1-5199 ....8/84   6-8
COVER 11: Reflects prefix change. Wrapped
with gold "The Definitive Rock Classic"
banner, listed separately below. Back: UPC
bar code at upper right.

❑ RCA (M) AFM1-5199.........8/84   2-4
BANNER 11: Gold stock with black print. Has
50th Anniversary drawing of Elvis. Reads: "A
Collectible, the Definitive Rock Classic
Restored to Original Mono, Digitally
Remastered, Quality Pressing, on Heavy
Virgin Vinyl." Used only on cover 11.

RCA (M) AFM1-5199.......8/84   15-20
TOTAL PACKAGE 11: Disc, cover, banner.

On both covers and labels, the electronically
reprocessed stereo designation "(e)" may not
appear following every usage of the selection
number.

Side 1
Rip It Up
Love Me
When My Blue Moon Turns to Gold Again
Long Tall Sally
First in Line
Paralyzed

Side 2
So Glad You're Mine
Old Shep
Reddy Teddy
Anyplace Is Paradise
How's the World Treating You
How Do You Think I Feel
Also see *LEGENDARY PERFORMER*
(Volume 1) (Experimental Picture Discs)

ELVIS

❑ King Kong: Bootleg. Listed for identification
only.

ELVIS

❑ Long Playing Record 27443: Bootleg. Listed
for identification only.
❑ Neuphone: Bootleg. Listed for identification
only.

ELVIS (2 LPs)

❑ RCA Victor (SP)
DPL2-0056(e)....................8/73   20-25
DISCS 1: Mustard color label. Dynaflex vinyl
(though quite rigid for Dynaflex). Marketed
mail order through Brookville Records.
(Disc 1) DPL2-0056A-1/DPL2-0056-B-1. (Disc 2) DPL2-
0056C-1/DPL2-0056-D-1.

❑ RCA Special Products
DPL2-0056(e)....................8/73   20-25
COVER 1: Single pocket. RCA Special
Products logo at upper left and Brookville logo
at upper right. Even though both prefix
"0056(e)" and, text at lower left on front,
indicate LP is reprocessed, some tracks are
true stereo.

❑ RCA Victor......................... '70s   2-4
INNER SLEEVE 1: Black-and-white. Pictures
RCA Elvis catalog front and back. Any of
several sleeves may be found on reissues
from this period.

RCA Victor (SP)
DPL2-0056(e) 8/73   40-55
TOTAL PACKAGE 1: Discs, cover, inner
sleeves.

❑ RCA Victor (SP)
DPL2-0056(e)....................9/73   10-15
DISCS 2: Blue label, black and white print.
Dynaflex vinyl.
(Disc 1) DPL2-0056A-2/DPL2-0056-B-1. (Disc 2) DPL2-
0056C-4/DPL2-0056-D-3.
(Disc 1) DPL2-0056A-2/DPL2-0056-B-3. (Disc 2) DPL2-
0056C-3/DPL2-0056-D-1.
(Disc 1) DPL2-0056A-4/DPL2-0056-B-3. (Disc 2) DPL2-
0056C-3/DPL2-0056-D-3.
(Disc 1) DPL2-0056A-4/DPL2-0056-B-3. (Disc 2) DPL2-
0056C-3/DPL2-0056-D-1.
(Disc 1) DPL2-0056A-4/DPL2-0056-B-2. (Disc 2) DPL2-
0056C-10/DPL2-0056-D-7. Identification numbers are
stamped on disc 1 and engraved on disc 2.

❑ RCA Victor
DPL2-0056(e)....................9/73   10-15
COVER 2: Same as cover 1, except has "RE"
at lower right (on front) and there is no
mention of Brookville Records.

THIS ALBUM HAS BEEN BANDED FOR DJ USE

ELVIS   DJL1-0606
As Recorded Live on Stage in Memphis
Elvis Presley
Side A
1 SEE SEE RIDER 2:55
2 I GOT A WOMAN 2:48
3 LOVE ME 1:28
4 TRYING TO GET TO YOU 2:00
5 Medley: LONG TALL SALLY/WHOLE
    LOT-TA SHAKIN' GOIN' ON/MAMA DON'T
    DANCE/FLIP, FLOP AND FLY/
    JAILHOUSE ROCK/HOUND DOG 3:21
6 WHY ME LORD 2:34
7 HOW GREAT THOU ART 3:21

Side B
1 Medley: BLUEBERRY HILL/I CAN'T
    STOP LOVING YOU 2:50
2 HELP ME 2:30
3 AN AMERICAN TRILOGY 3:50
4 LET ME BE THERE 3:26
5 MY BABY LEFT ME 2:18
6 LAWDY, MISS CLAWDY 1:54
7 CAN'T HELP FALLING IN LOVE 1:34
8 CLOSING—VAMP :50

PROMOTIONAL ALBUM—NOT FOR SALE

❑ RCA Victor.........................'70s   2-4
INNER SLEEVE 2: Black-and-white. Pictures
RCA Elvis catalog front and back. Any of
several sleeves may be found on reissues
from this period.
RCA Victor (SP)
DPL2-0056(e) 9/73   25-35
TOTAL PACKAGE 2: Disc, cover.

❑ RCA Victor (ST)
DPL2-0056 ....'77   1000-2000
DISCS 3: Black label. Tan, marble vinyl.
Experimental pressing only, not intended for
sale or distribution.
DPL2-0056A-9/DPL2-0056B-5. Identification numbers are
stamped.
COVER 3: None made.
RCA Victor (ST)
DPL2-0056 ....'77   1000-2000
TOTAL PACKAGE 3: Disc.

Repackaged in 1978 as *Elvis Commemorative
Album.*
Card stock jacket, with printing on cover – not
on slicks.
Disc 1
Side 1
Hound Dog
I Want You, I Need You, I Love You
All Shook Up
Don't
I Beg of You
Side 2
A Big Hunk O' Love
Love Me
Stuck on You
Good Luck Charm
Return to Sender
Disc 2
Side 3
Don't Be Cruel
Loving You
Jailhouse Rock
Can't Help Falling in Love
I Got Stung
Side 4
(Let Me Be Your) Teddy Bear
Love Me Tender
Hard Headed Woman
It's Now or Never
Surrender

ELVIS (By Jerry Hopkins)

❑ American Foundation for the
Blind ....'71   50-100
DISCS 1: Green label. A reading by Larry
Robinson of the Jerry Hopkins book, *Elvis*, on
two 16 2/3 rpm discs. Issued in plain paper
sleeves – no cover used.
85261/85262
85279/85280
American Foundation for the
Blind..............................'71   50-100
TOTAL PACKAGE 1: Discs.

ELVIS (Including: Fool, It's Impossible, Where Do I Go From Here, I'll Take You Home Again Kathleen, and Others)

❑ RCA Victor (ST)
APL1-0283 ....7/73   20-25
DISC 1: Orange label. Dynaflex vinyl.
APL1-0283-A-7/APL1-0283-B-5.
APL1-0283-A-7S/APL1-0283-B-5S.
APL1-0283-A-8S/APL1-0283-B-6S.
APL1-0283-A-9S/APL1-0283-B-7S.
❑ RCA APL1-0283 ....7/73   20-25
COVER 1: Front: RCA logo and number at
lower left. Back: Pictures *Elvis As Recorded at
Madison Square Garden* and *Elvis Aloha from
Hawaii via Satellite.*
❑ RCA Victor 21-112-1
PT 54B 7/73   3-5
INNER SLEEVE 1: Black-and-white. Pictures
RCA's Elvis LP catalog front and back, most
recent being *Elvis As Recorded at Madison
Square Garden* (side 2, row 2, column 6).
RCA Victor (ST)
APL1-0283 ....7/73   45-55
**TOTAL PACKAGE 1: Disc, cover, inner
sleeve.**

❑ RCA Victor (ST)
APL1-0283 ....7/73   20-25
DISC 2: Same as disc 1.
❑ RCA APL1-0283 ....7/73   25-30
COVER 2: Designate promo. Same as cover
1, but with "Not for Sale" stamped on back.
❑ RCA Victor 21-112-1
PT 54B 7/73   3-5
INNER SLEEVE 2: Black-and-white. Pictures
RCA's Elvis LP catalog front and back, most
recent being *Elvis As Recorded at Madison
Square Garden* (side 2, row 2, column 6). May
also be found with inner sleeve 55B.
RCA Victor (ST)
APL1-0283 ....7/73   50-60
**TOTAL PACKAGE 2: Disc, cover, inner
sleeve.**

Side 1
Fool
Where Do I Go from Here
Love Me, Love the Life I Lead
It's Still Here
It's Impossible
Side 2
(That's What You Get) For Lovin' Me
Padre
I'll Take You Home Again, Kathleen
I Will Be True
Don't Think Twice, It's All Right

ELVIS (NBC-TV Special)

❑ RCA Victor (SP)
    LPM-4088.........................12/68   20-25
    DISC 1: Orange label, rigid disc.
    WPRM-8051-6S/WPRM-8052-6S.
    WPRM-8051-7S/WPRM-8052-2S.
    WPRM-8051-9S/WPRM-8052-10S.

❑ RCA Victor LPM-4088 ..... 12/68   20-25
    COVER 1: Front: RCA logo and number at
    upper left, "Victor" at upper right. Back: Has
    six color photos of Elvis from the TV show.
    This was the first RCA orange label Elvis LP
    and first to have the then-new, extra bold RCA
    logo. With monaural phased out – the
    previous LP to this one, *Speedway*, being the
    last – this LP became the first with the box of
    text on the back about "RCA Stereo Records."

❑ RCA Victor 21-112-1
    40D.....................................6/68   4-6
    INNER SLEEVE 1: Red, black and white.
    Front: RCA's Elvis LP catalog, most recent
    being *Elvis' Gold Records, Vol. 4* (side 1, row
    4, column 5). Back: RCA's Elvis LP and Twin
    Pack Stereo 8 catalog. May also be found
    with inner sleeves 40B and 40C. See chapter
    on inner sleeves for more information.

RCA Victor (SP)
    LPM-4088 .... 12/68   40-50
    TOTAL PACKAGE 1: Disc, cover, inner
    sleeve.

❑ RCA Victor (SP)
    LPM-4088.........................12/68   15-20
    DISC 2: Same as disc 1.

❑ RCA Victor LPM-4088 ..... 12/68   25-35
    COVER 2: Designate promo. Same as cover
    1, but with "Not for Sale" stamped on back.

❑ RCA Victor 21-112-1
    40D.....................................6/68   4-6
    INNER SLEEVE 2: Red, black and white.
    Front: RCA's Elvis LP catalog, most recent
    being *Elvis' Gold Records, Vol. 4* (side 1, row
    4, column 5). Back: RCA's Elvis LP and Twin
    Pack Stereo 8 catalog. May also be found
    with inner sleeves 40B and 40C. See chapter
    on inner sleeves for more information.

RCA Victor (SP)
    LPM-4088 .... 12/68   50-60
    TOTAL PACKAGE 2: Disc, cover, inner
    sleeve.

❑ RCA Victor (SP)
    LPM-4088...........................'71   10-15
    DISC 3: Orange label, flexible disc.
    WPRM-8051-6S/WPRM-8052-11S.

❑ RCA Victor LPM-4088 .... '71   15-20
    COVER 3: Same as cover 1.

❑ RCA Victor.........................'70s   2-4
    INNER SLEEVE 3: Black-and-white. Pictures
    RCA Elvis catalog front and back. Any of
    several sleeves may be found on reissues
    from this period.

RCA Victor (SP)
    LPM-4088 .... '71   25-35
    TOTAL PACKAGE 3: Disc, cover, inner
    sleeve.

❑ RCA Victor (SP)
    LPM-4088...........................'76   12-15
    DISC 4: Tan label.

❑ RCA Victor LPM-4088 ....'76   5-10
    COVER 4: Same as cover 1.

❑ RCA.....................................'76   40-50
    SHRINK STICKER 6: Announces "Memories
    of Elvis" NBC-TV show.

❑ RCA Victor.........................'70s   2-4
    INNER SLEEVE 4: Black-and-white. Pictures
    RCA Elvis catalog front and back. Any of
    several sleeves may be found on reissues
    from this period.

RCA Victor (SP)
    LPM-4088 .... '76   60-75
    TOTAL PACKAGE 4: Disc, cover, inner
    sleeve.

❑ RCA Victor (SP)
    LPM-4088...........................'76   4-6
    DISC 5: Black label, dog near top.
    WPRM-8051-13S/WPRM-8052-9S.

❑ RCA LPM-4088 ....'76   4-6
    COVER 5: Reflects logo change.

❑ RCA.....................................'76   40-50
    SHRINK STICKER 5: Announces "Memories
    of Elvis" NBC-TV show.

❑ RCA Victor.........................'70s   2-4
    INNER SLEEVE 5: Black-and-white. Pictures
    RCA Elvis catalog front and back. Any of
    several sleeves may be found on reissues
    from this period.

RCA Victor (SP)
    LPM-4088 .... '76   50-70
    TOTAL PACKAGE 5: Disc, cover, sticker,
    inner sleeve.

❑ RCA Victor (SP)
    AFM1-4088..........................'77   3-5
    DISC 6: Black label, dog near top.

❑ RCA AFM1-4088 ....'77   10-15
    COVER 6: Reflects selection number change.
    Includes copies with a sticker bearing the
    "AFM1" prefix, wrapped around cover at top of
    spine.

❑ RCA.....................................'77   40-50
    SHRINK STICKER 6: Announces "Memories
    of Elvis" NBC-TV show.

❑ RCA Victor.........................'70s   2-4
    INNER SLEEVE 6: Black-and-white. Pictures
    RCA Elvis catalog front and back. Any of
    several sleeves may be found on reissues
    from this period.

RCA Victor (SP)
    AFM1-4088 .... '77   55-75
    TOTAL PACKAGE 6: Disc, cover, inner
    sleeve, sticker.

❑ RCA Victor (SP)
AFM1-4088 .... '77   3-5
DISC 6: Black label, dog near top.

❑ RCA AFM1-4088 .... '77   3-5
COVER 6: Reflects selection number change. Includes copies with a sticker bearing the "AFM1" prefix, wrapped around cover at top of spine.

❑ RCA Victor......................... '70s   2-4
INNER SLEEVE 6: Black-and-white. Pictures RCA Elvis catalog front and back. Any of several sleeves may be found on reissues from this period.

RCA Victor (SP)
AFM1-4088 .... '77   8-15
TOTAL PACKAGE 6: Disc, cover, inner sleeve.

❑ RCA Victor (SP)
AYM1-3894 ....2/81   3-5
DISC 7: Black label, dog near top.
AYM1-3094a-14S. Side 2 has WPRM-8051-10S stamped but crossed out, then has AFL1-4088B stamped but crossed out, then has AYM1-3094B engraved.

❑ RCA AYM1-3894 ....2/81   3-5
COVER 7: Reflects selection number change. Part of RCA's "Best Buy Series."
INNER SLEEVE 7: White, no printing.

RCA Victor (SP)
AYM1-3894 .... 2/81   6-10
TOTAL PACKAGE 7: Disc, cover.

Side 1
Trouble/Guitar Man
Lawdy Miss Clawdy/Baby What Do You Want Me to Do
Medley: Heartbreak Hotel/Hound Dog/One Night/All Shook Up/Can't Help Falling in Love/Jailhouse Rock/Love Me Tender

Side 2
Where Could I Go But to the Lord/Up Above My Head/Saved
Blue Christmas
Memories
Medley: Nothingville/Big Boss Man/Guitar Man/Little Egypt/Trouble/Guitar Man
If I Can Dream

If I Can Dream here is not the actual version from the TV show. That recording has never been issued by RCA; however, it has been bootleged. Despite the monaural ("LPM") prefix, there are several stereo tracks on this LP.

ELVIS (ONE NIGHT WITH YOU)

❑ RCA Special Products (SP)
DVM1-0704 .... 1/84   10-15
DISC 1: Black custom label with gold print. Available only through the HBO® cable television channel.
DVM1-0704A-1/DVM1-0704B-1.

❑ RCA Special Products
DVM1-0704 ....1/84   30-35
COVER 1: Front: Gold stock, with an artist's rendering of Elvis. HBO® logo at lower right. Title, *Elvis* in hot pink lettering on front and back. Back: RCA Special Products logo and number at left. HBO® and Elvis 50th Anniversary logos at lower right.
INNER SLEEVE 1: White, no printing.

❑ RCA Special Products
DVM1-0704 ....1/84   8-10
INSERT 1: Bonus 24" x 36" duotone poster. Has LP number at lower left.

❑ RCA Special Products
DVM1-0704 ....1/84   12-15
SHRINK STICKER 1: White print on gold stock. Reads: "Includes Songs Featured in the HBO® Special, *Elvis*, One Night with You."

RCA Special Products (SP)
DVM1-0704 .... 1/84   60-75
TOTAL PACKAGE 1: Disc, cover, insert, sticker.

First issued as *Elvis (NBC TV Special)*, LPM-4088.
Card stock jacket, with printing on cover – not on slicks.

Side 1
Trouble/Guitar Man
Lawdy Miss Clawdy/Baby What Do You Want Me to Do
Medley: Heartbreak Hotel/Hound Dog/One Night/All Shook Up/Can't Help Falling in Love/Jailhouse Rock/Love Me Tender

Side 2
Where Could I Go But to the Lord/Up Above My Head/Saved
Blue Christmas
Memories
Medley: Nothingville/Big Boss Man/Guitar Man/Little Egypt/Trouble/Guitar Man
If I Can Dream

ELVIS (SPEAKS TO YOU) (2 LPs)

❑ Green Valley (SP) GV-2001/
2003 ....4/78   10-15
DISCS 1: Disc one; black print on green stock. Disc two; black print on red stock. Disc one is exactly the same as the previously issued *Elvis Exclusive Live Press Conference*.
(Disc 1) Green Valley Elvis Interview Side One RE-1/Green Valley Elvis Interview Side Two RE-1. **(Disc 2)** GV-2003-A/GV-2003-B. Identification numbers are engraved.

❑ Green Valley GV-2001/
2003 ....4/78   10-15
COVER 1: Double pocket. Full color Elvis photos front and back.
INNER SLEEVES 1: White, no printing.

Green Valley (SP) GV-2001/
2003...........................4/78   20-30
TOTAL PACKAGE : Discs, cover.

Though labeled as a "1961 Press Conference," the event actually took place March 8, 1960.

Disc 1
Side 1
1961 Press Conference Memphis, Tennessee
Side 2
1961 Press Conference Memphis, Tennessee
Disc 2
Side 1
How Great Thou Art (Jordanaires)
Elvis Interview
Side 2
Jordanaires Conversation
From Graceland to the Promised Land (Jordanaires)

ELVIS - A CANADIAN TRIBUTE: see
CANADIAN TRIBUTE

ELVIS - A COLLECTORS EDITION: see
COLLECTORS EDITION

ELVIS - A LEGENDARY PERFORMER: see
LEGENDARY PERFORMER

ELVIS: A THREE HOUR SPECIAL (3 LPs)
❑ Drake-Chenault (SP).........8/77   150-225
DISCS 1: Boxed, three-LP set.
❑ Drake-Chenault (SP).........8/77   50-100
BOX 1: Verification pending.
INNER SLEEVES 1: White, no printing.
❑ Drake-Chenault.................8/77   5-15
INSERT 1: Three pages of cue sheets and
programming information. Issued only to radio
stations.
Drake-Chenault (SP) 8/77   200-350
TOTAL PACKAGE 1: Disc, box (?), insert.

ELVIS, A WAY OF LIFE
❑ Neuphone: Bootleg. Listed for identification
only.

ELVIS ALOHA FROM HAWAII VIA
SATELLITE: see *ALOHA FROM HAWAII*
VIA SATELLITE

ELVIS ARON PRESLEY (8 LPs)
Limited-edition boxed set. Discs have silver
label stock with blue and white lettering. Each
of the following eight LPs is in a special
cardboard cover/sleeve and is described and
priced below. Each has its own title. All have
identification numbers and Elvis' signature
engraved.
❑ RCA Victor (M)
CPL8-3699-1 ....7/80   4-6
DISC 1: *An Early Live Performance.*
CPL8-3699-1A-2S/CPL8-3699-1B-2S.
CPL8-3699-1A-3S/CPL8-3699-1B-2S.
Side 1
Heartbreak Hotel
Long Tall Sally
Blue Suede Shoes
Money Honey
Side 2
An Elvis Monolog

❑ RCA Victor (M)
CPL8-3699-2 ....7/80   4-6
DISC 2: *An Early Benefit Performance*
CPL8-3699-2A-4S/CPL8-3699-2B-2S.
Side 1
Heartbreak Hotel
All Shook Up
(Now and Then There's) A Fool Such As I
I Got a Woman
Love Me
Introductions
Such a Night
Reconsider Baby
Side 2
I Need Your Love Tonight
That's All Right
Don't Be Cruel
One Night
Are You Lonesome Tonight
It's Now or Never
Swing Down Sweet Chariot
Hound Dog

❑ RCA Victor (SP)
CPL8-3699-3 ....7/80   4-6
DISC 3: *Collectors' Gold from the Movie*
Years
CPL8-3699-3A-2S/CPL8-3699-3B-1S.
Side 1
They Remind Me Too Much of You
Tonight Is So Right for Love
Follow That Dream
Wild in the Country
Datin'
Side 2
Shoppin' Around
Can't Help Falling in Love
A Dog's Life
I'm Falling in Love Tonight
Thanks to the Rolling Sea
Contrary to contents listed, *Tonight Is So
Right for Love* does not appear on this LP.
The song heard is *Tonight Is All Right for
Love*. Except for *Can't Help Falling in Love*, all
tracks are stereo.
❑ RCA Victor (SP)
CPL8-3699-4 ....7/80   4-6
DISC 4: *The TV Specials*
CPL8-3699-4A-3S/CPL8-3699-4B-3S.
CPL8-3699-4A-4S/CPL8-3699-4B-4S.
Side 1
Jailhouse Rock
Suspicious Minds
Lawdy Miss Clawdy
Baby What You Want Me to Do
Blue Christmas
Side 2
You Gave Me a Mountain
Welcome to My World
Tryin' to Get to You
I'll Remember You
My Way

❑ RCA Victor (SP)
CPL8-3699-5 ....7/80   4-6
DISC 5: *The Las Vegas Years*
CPL8-3699-5A-3S/CPL8-3699-5B-3S.

Side 1
Polk Salad Annie
You've Lost That Lovin'Feelin'
Sweet Caroline
Kentucky Rain
Are You Lonesome Tonight

Side 2
My Babe
In the Ghetto
An American Trilogy
Little Sister/Get Back
Yesterday

❏ RCA Victor (SP)
CPL8-3699-6 ....7/80   4-6
DISC 6: *Lost Singles*
CPL8-3699-6A-2S/CPL8-3699-6B-2S.
CPL8-3699-6A-3S/CPL8-3699-6B-3S.

Side 1
I'm Leavin'
The First Time Ever I Saw Your Face
Hi-Heel Sneakers
Softly, As I Leave You

Side 2
Unchained Melody
Fool
Rags to Riches
It's Only Love
America the Beautiful
Unchained Melody, America the Beautiful and
Softly, As I Leave You are monaural here.

❏ RCA Victor (M)
CPL8-3699-7 ....7/80   4-6
DISC 7: *Elvis at the Piano (S) / The Concert
Years, Part 1*
CPL8-3699-7A-3S/CPL8-3699-7B-3S.
Side 1 is stereo. Side 2 is a monaural live
concert.

Side 1
It's Still Here
I'll Take You Home Again Kathleen
Beyond the Reef
I Will Be True

Side 2
Also Sprach Zarathustra
See See Rider
I Got a Woman/Amen
Love Me
If You Love Me (Let Me Know)
Love Me Tender
All Shook Up
(Let Me Be Your) Teddy Bear/Don't Be Cruel

❏ RCA Victor (M)
CPL8-3699-8 ....7/80   4-6
DISC 8: *The Concert Years – Concluded*
CPL8-3699-8A-2S/CPL8-3699-8B-3S.
CPL8-3699-8A-3S/CPL8-3699-8B-3S.

Side 1
Hound Dog
The Wonder of You
Burning Love
Dialog/Introductions/Johnny B. Goode
Introductions/Long Live Rock and Roll
T-r-o-u-b-l-e
Why Me Lord

Side 2
How Great Thou Art
Let Me Be There

An American Trilogy
Funny How Time Slips Away
Little Darlin'
Mystery Train/Tiger Man
Can't Help Falling In Love
Listed as "Long Live Rock and Roll" but
actually it is just a few lines from Chuck
Berry's *School Day.*

❏ RCA Victor CPL8-3699......7/80   20-25
BOX 1: Front: Silver stock with gold,
embossed signature, "Elvis Aron Presley."
Back: Silver stock with blue print. Has
"Limited Edition" sticker at lower left, with one
of the letters of Elvis' name, followed by
edition number. Below that is "EAP-3699."

❏ RCA Victor CPL8-3699......7/80   25-30
INNER SLEEVES 1: Price is for all eight
sleeves. Covers have a full color Elvis photo
on side one; contents and a black-and-white
photo on side two.

❏ RCA Victor CPL8-3699......7/80   10-15
INSERT 1: 20-page photo and information
booklet.

❏ RCA Victor CPL8-3699......7/80   3-5
SHRINK STICKER 1: Silver foil with blue
print. Reads: "25th Anniversary Limited
Edition" and highlights contents.
LIMITED EDITION STICKER 1: Since this
sticker is affixed to cover and not shrink wrap,
it is not priced separately.

RCA Victor (SP)
CPL8-3699 ....7/80   **100-125**
**TOTAL PACKAGE 1: Discs, box, inner
    sleeves, sticker.**

❏ RCA Victor (SP)
CPL8-3699 ....7/80   32-48
DISCS 2: Same as discs 1 through 8.

❏ RCA Victor (SP) NS (Box
Number) 7/80   180-200
BOX 2: Same as box 1, except has "Reviewer
Series" sticker. Used on complimentary and
review copies only. For this edition, only the
"NS" prefix is used, followed by the specific
box number.

❏ RCA Victor CPL8-3699......7/80   25-30
INNER SLEEVES 2: Price is for.all eight
sleeves. Covers have a full color Elvis photo
on side one; contents and a black-and-white
photo on side two.

❏ RCA Victor CPL8-3699......7/80   10-15
INSERT 2: 20-page photo and information
booklet.

❏ RCA Victor CPL8-3699......7/80   3-5
SHRINK STICKER 2: Silver foil with blue
print. Reads: "25th Anniversary Limited
Edition" and highlights contents.
LIMITED EDITION STICKER 2: Since this
sticker is affixed to cover and not shrink wrap,
it is not priced separately.

RCA Victor (SP)
CPL8-3699 ....7/80   250-300
**TOTAL PACKAGE 2: Discs, box, inner
    sleeves, sticker.**

LSP-2075 (e)

STEREO
Electronically Reprocessed

50,000,000 ELVIS FANS CAN'T BE WRONG

ELVIS' GOLD RECORDS — Volume 2

A FOOL SUCH AS I
I NEED YOUR LOVE TONIGHT
WEAR MY RING AROUND YOUR NECK
DONCHA' THINK IT'S TIME
I BEG OF YOU
A BIG HUNK O' LOVE
DON'T
MY WISH CAME TRUE
ONE NIGHT
I GOT STUNG

MAGIC MILLIONS
RCA VICTOR
A "New Orthophonic" High Fidelity Recording

As an additional challenge to the Presley collector, there are 11 different limited edition numbers found on this set – one letter prefix for each letter in the spelling of Elvis Aron Presley. To complete the collection requires 11 different box sets, one each with the letters: E-L-V-I-S-A-R-O-N-P-Y. The remaining letters (R-E-S-L-E) in the name are duplicates. Similar limited edition numbers appeared on cassette and eight-track boxed sets.

Value: It is safe to approximate that a full set of the 11 boxes necessary to spell *Elvis Aron Presley*, would be valued somewhat higher than 11 times the worth of a single set. To locate a specific letter can be far more difficult than simply finding a copy of the set.

ELVIS ARON PRESLEY (Cassettes)

❏ RCA Victor (SP)
CPK8-3699.......................7/80   10-20
CASSETTES 1: Four double cassettes.

❏ RCA Victor CPK8-3699.....7/80   20-25
BOX 1: Front: Silver stock with gold, embossed signature, "Elvis Aron Presley." Back: Silver stock with blue print. Has "Limited Edition" sticker at lower left, with one of the letters of Elvis' name, followed by edition number. Below that is "EAPK-3699."

❏ RCA Victor CPK8-3699.....7/80   25-30
INSERT 1A: Eight color photos. Covers have a full color Elvis photo on side one; contents and a black-and-white photo on side two. The photos are the same as used in the LP edition for inner sleeves. Other details about this set are identical to CPL8-3699, the LP boxed edition.

❏ RCA Victor CPK8-3699.....7/80   10-15
INSERT 1B: 20-page photo and information booklet.

❏ RCA Victor CPK8-3699.....7/80   3-5
SHRINK STICKER 1: Silver foil with blue print. Reads: "25th Anniversary Limited Edition" and highlights contents.
LIMITED EDITION STICKER 1: Since this sticker is affixed to cover and not shrink wrap, it is not priced separately.

RCA Victor (SP)
CPK8-3699 ....7/80   70-100
TOTAL PACKAGE 1: Cassettes, box, inserts, sticker.

ELVIS ARON PRESLEY (8-Tracks)

❏ RCA Victor (SP)
CPS8-3699.......................7/80   8-12
TAPES 1: Four double-length 8-track cartridges.

❏ RCA Victor CPS8-3699.....7/80   10-15
BOX 1: Front: Silver stock with gold, embossed signature, "Elvis Aron Presley." Back: Silver stock with blue print. Has "Limited Edition" sticker at lower left, with one of the letters of Elvis' name, followed by edition number. Below that is "EAPS-3699."

❏ RCA Victor CPS8-3699.....7/80   25-30
INSERT 1A: Eight color photos. Covers have a full color Elvis photo on side one; contents and a black-and-white photo on side two. The photos are the same as used in the LP edition for inner sleeves. Other details about this set are identical to CPL8-3699, the LP boxed edition.

❏ RCA Victor CPS8-3699.....7/80   10-15
INSERT 1B: 20-page photo and information booklet.

❏ RCA Victor CPS8-3699.....7/80   3-5
SHRINK STICKER 1: Silver foil with blue print. Reads: "25th Anniversary Limited Edition" and highlights contents.
LIMITED EDITION STICKER 1: Since this sticker is affixed to cover and not shrink wrap, it is not priced separately.

RCA Victor (SP)
CPS8-3699 ....7/80   40-50
TOTAL PACKAGE 1: Tapes, box, inserts, sticker.

Even though the contents of this box set are the same as the cassette package, the price reflects the less desirable – now extinct – eight-track format.

ELVIS ARON PRESLEY (EXCERPTS FROM THE 8-RECORD 25TH ANNIVERSARY ALBUM)

❏ RCA (SP) DJL1-3729........7/80   50-60
DISC 1: Silver stock with blue and white lettering. Distributed exclusively to retail locations for in-store play. Has only excerpts of the songs listed.
DJL1-3729-A-2S/DJL1-3729-B-2S. Identification numbers are engraved.

❏ RCA DJL1-3729 ....7/80   50-65
COVER 1: Silver and blue duotone, front and back.
INNER SLEEVE 1: White, no printing.

RCA (SP) DJL1-3729......7/80   100-125
TOTAL PACKAGE 1: Disc, cover.

Contrary to contents listed, *Tonight Is So Right for Love* is not on this LP. The song included is *Tonight Is All Right for Love*. Also, *Thanks to the Rolling Sea* is shown on neither cover nor label. We list it in its proper place below.

Side 1
Also Sprach Zarathustra
See See Rider
Heartbreak Hotel
Long Tall Sally
Introduction/Heartbreak Hotel
Hi-Heel Sneakers
In the Ghetto
My Babe
Welcome to My World
Beyond the Reef
Baby What You Want Me to Do
Tonight Is So Right for Love*
Thanks to the Rolling Sea**
Datin'
All Shook Up
(Let Me Be Your) Teddy Bear/Don't Be Cruel
Swing Down Sweet Chariot
How Great Thou Art
America the Beautiful

Side 2
Polk Salad Annie
You've Lost That Lovin' Feelin'
Little Darlin'
Hound Dog
I'll Take You Home Again Kathleen
Shoppin' Around
Yesterday
Blue Suede Shoes
Reconsider Baby
Are You Lonesome Tonight
An American Trilogy
Love Me Tender
Burning Love
T-r-o-u-b-l-e
Unchained Melody
Why Me Lord
Can't Help Falling in Love
My Way

ELVIS ARON PRESLEY (SELECTIONS FROM THE 8-RECORD 25TH ANNIVERSARY ALBUM)

❏ RCA (SP) DJL1-3781 ....7/80   50-60
DISC 1: Silver stock with blue and white lettering. Issued to radio stations. Has 12 *complete* tracks, unlike the similar DJL1-3729 (above), which has 37 excerpts. Promotional issue only.
DJL1-3781-A-1S/DJL1-3781-B-1S. Identification numbers are engraved.
DJL1-3781-A-2S/DJL1-3781-B-2S. Identification numbers are engraved.

❏ RCA DJL1-3781 ....7/80   50-65
COVER 1: Silver and blue duotone, front and back.
INNER SLEEVE 1: White, no printing.
RCA (SP) DJL1-3781 ......7/80   **100-125**
TOTAL PACKAGE 1: Disc, cover.

Side 1
Long Tall Sally
Elvis Monolog
Heartbreak Hotel
All Shook Up
Datin'
Lawdy Miss Clawdy/Baby What You Want Me to Do

Side 2
Are You Lonesome Tonight
Hi-Heel Sneakers
Beyond the Reef
(Let Me Be Your) Teddy Bear/Don't Be Cruel
How Great Thou Art
Little Darlin'

ELVIS ARON PRESLEY FOREVER (2 LPs)

❏ RCA Special Products/Pair (SP)
PDL-2-1185 ....'88   '12-15
DISCS 1: Black label, RCA Special Products logo at top. Pair logo at bottom.
(Disc 1) PDL2-1185-A-2/PDL2-1185-B-1. **(Disc 2)** PDL2-1185-C-1/ PDL2-1185-D-2. Identification numbers are engraved. On side 1, the "1185" was engraved, then crossed out and "1186" put next to it. Then, "1185" is added again.

❏ RCA Special Products/Pair
PDL2-111859 ....'88   12-15
COVER 1: Single pocket. Front: Colorized Elvis photo. RCA Special Products logo and number at lower left. Pair logo at lower right. Back: Black-and-white of same photo as on front.
INNER SLEEVES 1: White, no printing.
RCA Special Products/Pair (SP)
PDL-2-1185 ....'88   25-30
TOTAL PACKAGE 1: Discs, cover.

Card stock jacket, with printing on cover – not on slicks.

Disc 1

Side 1
Blue Hawaii
Hawaiian Wedding Song
No More
Early Morning Rain

Side 2
Pieces of My Life
I Can Help
Bringing It Back
Green, Green Grass of Home

Disc 2

Side 1
Mean Woman Blues
Loving You
Got a Lot o' Livin' to Do
Blueberry Hill

Side 2
T-r-o-u-b-l-e
And I Love You So
Woman Without Love
Shake a Hand

ELVIS AS RECORDED AT MADISON SQUARE GARDEN

❏ RCA Victor (ST)
LSP-4776 ....6/72   8-10
DISC 1: Orange label. Dynaflex vinyl.
BPRS-5144-3S/BPRS-5145-3S. Identification numbers are stamped.
BPRS-5144-4S/BPRS-5145-4S. Identification numbers are stamped.
BPRS-5144-5S/BPRS-5145-5S. Identification numbers are stamped.
BPRS-5144-5S/BPRS-5145-6S. Identification numbers are engraved.

❑ RCA Victor LSP-4776........6/72   10-15
COVER 1: Front: RCA Victor logo and
number at upper left. Back: Pictures *Elvis
Now* and *Elvis Sings Hits from His Movies*,
Vol. 1.

❑ RCA Victor 21-112-1
PT 54A 8/71   3-5
INNER SLEEVE 1: Black-and-white. Pictures
RCA's Elvis LP catalog front and back, most
recent being *Love Letters from Elvis* (side 2,
row 4, column 5). May also be found with
inner sleeves 56A or 57A.

RCA Victor (ST)
LSP-4776.....................6/72   20-30
**TOTAL PACKAGE 1: Disc, cover, inner
sleeve.**

❑ RCA Victor (ST)
LSP-4776 ....6/72   8-10
DISC 2: Orange label. Dynaflex vinyl.
BPRS-5144-3S/BPRS-5145-3S. Identification numbers are
stamped.
BPRS-5144-4S/BPRS-5145-4S. Identification numbers are
stamped.
BPRS-5144-5S/BPRS-5145-5S. Identification numbers are
stamped.
BPRS-5144-5S/BPRS-5145-6S. Identification numbers are
engraved.

❑ RCA Victor LSP-4776........6/72   70-85
COVER 2: Same as cover 1 except has white,
4" x 6" contents and running times sticker at
upper left for radio station airplay.
Counterfeit Identification: Counterfeit
stickers exist but can be identified by the
misspelling of the title *Love Me*, which reads:
"Live Me."

❑ RCA Victor 21-112-1
PT 54A 8/71   3-5
INNER SLEEVE 2: Black-and-white. Pictures
RCA's Elvis LP catalog front and back, most
recent being *Love Letters from Elvis* (side 2,
row 4, column 5). May also be found with
inner sleeves 56A or 57A.

RCA Victor (ST)
LSP-4776.....................6/72   80-100
**TOTAL PACKAGE 2: Disc, cover, inner
sleeve.**

❑ RCA Victor (ST)
LSP-4776 ....6/72   8-10
DISC 3: Same as disc 1.

❑ RCA Victor LSP-4776........6/72   40-45
COVER 3: Same as cover 1 except has a
white 4" x 6" sticker at lower right, which is
rubber stamped "Promotional Album Not For
Sale." Printing on this cover is slightly darker
than on cover 1, especially noticeable on
Elvis' face.

❑ RCA Victor 21-112-1
PT 54A 8/71   3-5
INNER SLEEVE 3: Black-and-white. Pictures
RCA's Elvis LP catalog front and back, most
recent being *Love Letters from Elvis* (side 2,
row 4, column 5). May also be found with
inner sleeves 56A or 57A.

RCA Victor (ST)
LSP-4776.....................6/72   50-60
**TOTAL PACKAGE 3: Disc, cover, inner
sleeve.**

❑ RCA Victor (ST) SPS-33-571-1
(LSP-4776) 6/72   150-250
DISCS 4: White label. Dynaflex vinyl. Double
LP in double pocket cover. Has the same
music as the single disc version but is banded
for dee jay convenience. Promotional issue
only.
(Disc 1) BPRS-6351-2S/BPRS-6352-2S.
(Disc 2) BPRS-6353-2S/BPRS-6354-2S.

❑ RCA Victor SPS-33-571-1
(LSP-4776) 6/72   100-150
COVER 4: White, double pocket. Has
contents and running times printed on two,
white 4" x 6" stickers at left side, on front.
There is no printing whatsoever on the cover
itself.

❑ RCA Victor 21-112-1
PT 54A/56A/57A.................8/71   3-5
INNER SLEEVES 4: Black-and-white.
Pictures RCA's Elvis LP catalog front and
back. Any two of the three listed (54A, 56A, or
57A) may be found in this LP.

RCA Victor (ST) SPS-33-571-1
(LSP-4776) 6/72   300-400
**TOTAL PACKAGE 4: Discs, cover, inner
sleeves.**

❑ RCA Victor (ST)
LSP-4776 ....'77   1000-2000
DISC 5: Picture disc. Side 1 has large picture
of Elvis as shown on front cover of *Aloha from
Hawaii via Satellite*, and small photo of front
cover of *Elvis As Recorded At Madison
Square Garden*. Side 2 pictures the scene
with Elvis and the Hawaiian women, as used
on the inner sleeves of the *Aloha* album.
Experimental item only.
BPRS-5144/BPRS-5145.

❑ RCA LSP-4776 ....'77   3-5
COVER 5: Same as cover 1.

RCA Victor (ST)
LSP-4776......................'77   1000-2000
TOTAL PACKAGE 5: Disc, cover.

❑ RCA Victor (ST)
LSP-4776 ....'76   4-8
DISC 6: Tan label. Dynaflex vinyl.
BPRS-5144-1S/BPRS-5145-1S.

❑ RCA Victor LSP-4776..........'76   4-8
COVER 6: Same as cover 1, except has a "2"
on back at lower right.

❑ RCA Victor........................'70s   2-4
INNER SLEEVE 6: Black-and-white. Pictures
RCA Elvis catalog front and back. Any of
several sleeves may be found on reissues
from this period.

RCA Victor (ST)
   LSP-4776........................'76   **10-20**
   TOTAL PACKAGE 6: Disc, cover, inner
   sleeve.

❏ RCA Victor (ST)
   LSP-4776 ....'76   3-5
   DISC 7: Black label, dog near top.
❏ RCA LSP-4776....................'76   4-6
   BPRS-5144-1S/BPRS-5145-8S.
❏ RCA Victor LSP-4776..........'76   4-8
   COVER 7: Same as cover 1, except has a "2"
   on back at lower right.
❏ RCA Victor.........................'70s   2-4
   INNER SLEEVE 7: Black-and-white. Pictures
   RCA Elvis catalog front and back. Any of
   several may be found on reissues from this
   period.

RCA Victor (ST)
   LSP-4776........................'76   **10-18**
   TOTAL PACKAGE 7: Disc, cover, inner
   sleeve.

❏ RCA Victor (ST)
   AFL1-4776 ....'77   3-4
   DISC 8: Black label, dog near top.
❏ RCA AFL1-4776..................'77   4-8
   COVER 8: Reflects prefix change. Includes
   copies with a sticker bearing the "AFL1"
   prefix, wrapped around cover at top of spine.
❏ RCA Victor.........................'70s   2-4
   INNER SLEEVE 8: Black-and-white. Pictures
   RCA Elvis catalog front and back. Any of
   several sleeves may be found on reissues
   from this period.

RCA Victor (ST)
   AFL1-4776......................'77   **10-15**
   TOTAL PACKAGE 8: Disc, cover, inner
   sleeve.

❏ RCA Victor (ST)
   AFL1-4776 ....'77   3-4
   DISC 9: Black label, dog near top.
❏ RCA AFL1-4776..................'77   8-10
   COVER 9: Designate promo. Same as cover
   7, but with "Not for Sale" stamped on back.
❏ RCA Victor.........................'70s   2-4
   INNER SLEEVE 9: Black-and-white. Pictures
   RCA Elvis catalog front and back. Any of
   several sleeves may be found on reissues
   from this period.

RCA Victor (ST)
   AFL1-4776......................'77   **15-20**
   TOTAL PACKAGE 9: Disc, cover, inner
   sleeve.

❏ RCA Victor (ST)
   AQL1-4776 ....'80   2-5
   DISC 10: Black label, dog near top. Dynaflex
   vinyl.
   AQL1-4776A/AQL1-4776B-11.

❏ RCA AQL1-4776..................'80   2-5
   COVER 10: Reflects prefix change. Front:
   Same as cover 1, except has "RE-1" at lower
   left. Back: "RE-1" at lower left, and "2" at
   lower right. Pictures only *Elvis Now* omitting
   mention of *Elvis Sings Hits from His Movies,*
   Volume 2.
   INNER SLEEVE 10: White, no printing.

RCA Victor (ST)
   AQL1-4776 ....'80   **5-10**
   TOTAL PACKAGE 10: Disc, cover.

Side 1
Introduction: Also Sprach Zarathustra
That's All Right
Proud Mary
Never Been to Spain
You Don't Have to Say You Love Me
You've Lost That Lovin' Feelin'
Polk Salad Annie
Love Me
All Shook Up
Heartbreak Hotel
Medley:Teddy Bear/Don't Be Cruel
Love Me Tender

Side 2
The Impossible Dream
Introductions by Elvis
Hound Dog
Suspicious Minds
For the Good Times
American Trilogy
Funny How Time Slips Away
I Can't Stop Loving You
Can't Help Falling in Love
Closing Riff

ELVIS AS RECORDED LIVE ON STAGE IN
   MEMPHIS: see *ELVIS RECORDED LIVE*
   ON STAGE IN MEMPHIS

ELVIS BACK IN MEMPHIS: see *BACK IN*
   MEMPHIS

ELVIS' CHRISTMAS ALBUM

❏ RCA Victor (M)
   LOC-1035.........................11/57   75-100
   DISC 1: Black label, "Long Play" at bottom.
   H2PP-6526-1S/H2PP-6527-1S. Label LP#1.
❏ RCA Victor LOC-1035 .....11/57   100-125
   COVER 1: Gatefold. Includes 12-page,
   bound-in booklet. Page 11 has RCA's Elvis
   EP and singles catalog, page 12 is glued to
   inside back cover. Photos are "From the new
   Elvis Presley motion picture, "Jailhouse
   Rock," most in color. Lettering on spine is in
   gold ink. Front: Red, with 3" x 3" photo of Elvis
   amidst Christmas presents and ornaments.
   Back: Color Elvis photo, no lettering. May be
   accompanied by gold foil, gift-giving sticker.
   Since sticker was attached to outer plastic
   bag, and not directly to cover, it is priced
   separately below.
   (See sticker 1.)
   INNER SLEEVE 1: Generic RCA sleeve.
   Makes no mention of Elvis or this LP.

❑ RCA Victor LOC-1035 ..... 11/57   325-375
STICKER 1: A (approximately) 3" x 4" gold foil, gift giving sticker, with black print. Has "To" and "From" blanks to be filled in by buyer. Priced separately since it is not attached to cover.

RCA Victor (M)
LOC-1035 .... 11/57   500-600
TOTAL PACKAGE 1: Disc, cover, sticker.

❑ RCA Victor (M)
LOC-1035........................ 11/57   15000-20000
DISC 2: Red vinyl. Black label, "Long Play" at bottom. Souvenir pressing made by a plant employee. Not intended for sale or distribution. Likely a one-of-a-kind item.
H2PP-6526-1S/H2PP-6527-1S. Label LP#1.

❑ RCA Victor LOC-1035 ..... 11/57   100-125
COVER 2: Same as cover 1.
INNER SLEEVE 2: Generic RCA sleeve. Makes no mention of Elvis or this LP.

RCA Victor (M)
LOC-1035 .... 11/57   15000-22000
TOTAL PACKAGE 2: Disc, cover.

❑ RCA Victor (M)
LOC-1035........................ 11/57   75-100
DISC 3: Same as disc 1.

❑ RCA Victor LOC-1035 ..... 11/57   150-175
COVER 3: Same as cover 1, except lettering on spine is in *silver* ink.
INNER SLEEVE 3: Generic RCA sleeve. Makes no mention of Elvis or this LP.

❑ RCA Victor LOC-1035 ..... 11/57   325-375
STICKER 3: A (approximately) 3" x 4" gold foil, gift giving sticker, with black print. Has "To" and "From" blanks to be filled in by buyer. Priced separately since it is not attached to cover.

RCA Victor (M)
LOC-1035 .... 11/57   550-650
TOTAL PACKAGE 3: Disc, cover, sticker.

❑ RCA (M) AFM1-5486......... 7/85   12-15
DISC 4: Green vinyl. Gold "Elvis 50th Anniversary" label. (July release date is correct.)
AFM1-5486A-1/AFM1-5486-B-1. Identification numbers are engraved.

❑ RCA AFM1-5486 .... 7/85   4-5
COVER 4: Gatefold. Includes 12-page (not bound-in) booklet. Page 11 has RCA's 50th Anniversary LP and singles catalog, page 12 is glued to inside back cover. Has same *Jailhouse Rock*, photos as cover 1.
INNER SLEEVE 4: White, no printing.

❑ RCA AFM1-5486 .... 7/85   4-5
STICKER 4: Circular. White print on red stock. Reads: "Restored to Original Mono. Digitally Remastered. Pressed on Green Vinyl. A Collectible."

RCA (M) AFM1-5486 .... 7/85   20-25
TOTAL PACKAGE 4: Disc, cover, sticker.

❑ RCA (M) AFM1-5486......... 7/85   12-15
DISC 5: Same as disc 4.

❑ RCA AFM1-5486 .... 7/85   8-10
COVER 5: Designate promo. Same as cover 3, but with "Not for Sale" stamped on back.
INNER SLEEVE 5: White, no printing.

❑ RCA AFM1-5486 .... 7/85   4-5
STICKER 5: Circular. White print on red stock. Reads: "Restored to Original Mono. Digitally Remastered. Pressed on Green Vinyl. A Collectible."

RCA (M) AFM1-5486 .... 7/85   25-30
TOTAL PACKAGE 5: Disc, cover, sticker.

❑ RCA (M) AFM1-5486 .... 12/85   6-10
DISC 6: Black vinyl. Gold "Elvis 50th Anniversary" label. Despite being black vinyl, many are found in covers with sticker reading: "Pressed on Green Vinyl."
AFM1-5486A-1 A4/AFM1-5486-B-1 A4. Identification numbers are engraved.

❑ RCA AFM1-5486 .... 12/85   4-5
COVER 6: Gatefold. Same as cover 3, except 12-page booklet is loose – neither bound-in nor glued. Price includes booklet.

❑ RCA AFM1-5486 .... 7/85   4-5
STICKER 6: Circular. White print on red stock. Reads: "Restored to Original Mono. Digitally Remastered. Pressed on Green Vinyl. A Collectible." Applied to cover 5 by mistake.
INNER SLEEVE 6: White, no printing.

RCA (M) AFM1-5486 ..... 12/85   15-20
TOTAL PACKAGE 6: Disc, cover, sticker.

Covers 3, 4 and 5 are card stock, with printing on cover – not on slicks.

Side 1
Santa Claus Is Back in Town
White Christmas
Here Comes Santa Claus
I'll Be Home for Christmas
Blue Christmas
Santa Bring My Baby Back (To Me)

Side 2
Oh Little Town of Bethlehem
Silent Night
(There'll Be) Peace in the Valley (For Me)
I Believe
Take My Hand, Precious Lord
It Is No Secret (What God Can Do)

ELVIS' CHRISTMAS ALBUM

❑ RCA Victor (M)
LPM-1951.......................11/58   50-75
DISC 1: Black label, "Long Play" at bottom.
Repackage of the preceding LP (LOC-1035,
Nos. 1 and 2) in new, single pocket cover.
Omits photos that were in the 1957 issue.
H2PP-6526-8S/H2PP-6527-14S. Label LP#1.
H2PP-6526-18S/H2PP-6527-22S. Label LP#1.
H2PP-6526-21S/H2PP-6527-23S. Label LP#1.

❑ RCA Victor LPM-1951.....11/58   100-125
COVER 1: Front: RCA logo and number at
upper right. Pictures Elvis with a snowy
countryside scene in the background. Back:
Four color Elvis pictures, three of which show
him in uniform.
INNER SLEEVE 1: Generic RCA sleeve.
Makes no mention of Elvis or this LP.

RCA Victor (M)
LPM-1951 .... 11/58   150-200
TOTAL PACKAGE 1: Disc, cover.

❑ RCA Victor (M)
LPM-1951.......................11/63   30-40
DISC 2: Black label, "Mono" at bottom.
H2PP-6526-10S/H2PP-6527-13S.

❑ RCA Victor LPM-1951.....11/63   20-30
COVER 2: Front: RCA logo at upper right,
number and "RE" at lower left. Pictures Elvis
with a snowy countryside scene in the
background. Back: Pictures *His Hand in Mine*
and three Elvis RCA EPs.

❑ RCA Victor (No Number)...9/63   8-10
INNER SLEEVE 2: Turquoise, black and
white. Front: RCA's Elvis LP catalog, most
recent being *It Happened at the World's Fair*
(side 1, row 4, column 5). Back: RCA Elvis
EPs and 45s catalog.

RCA Victor (M)
LPM-1951 .... 11/63   60-80
**TOTAL PACKAGE 2: Disc, cover, inner
sleeve.**

❑ RCA Victor (M)
LPM-1951.......................11/64   10-15
DISC 3: Black label, "Monaural" at bottom.

❑ RCA Victor LPM-1951.....11/64   20-25
COVER 3: Same as cover 2, except has "RE"
at lower left on front and has a blue stripe
across the top on front.

❑ RCA Victor 21-112-1
40A.................................10/64   4-8
INNER SLEEVE 3: Red, black and white.
Front: RCA's Elvis LP catalog, most recent
being *Kissin' Cousins* (side 1, row 1, column
6). Back: RCA Elvis EPs and 45s catalog.

RCA Victor (M)
LPM-1951 .... 11/64   35-50
**TOTAL PACKAGE 3: Disc, cover, inner
sleeve.**

❑ RCA Victor (SE)
LSP-1951(e) 11/64   10-15
DISC 4: Black label, RCA logo in white at top
and "Stereo" at bottom.
RPRS-6163-3S/RPRS-6164-3S. Label LP#15.
RPRS-6163-6S/RPRS-6164-10S. Label LP#15.
RPRS-6163-14S/RPRS-6164-22S. Label LP#17.

❑ RCA Victor
LSP-1951(e) 11/64   20-25
COVER 4: Front: RCA logo and "Stereo
Electronically Reprocessed" at upper right
and number at upper left. "RE" at lower left.
Back: Pictures *His Hand in Mine* and three
Elvis RCA EPs.

❑ RCA Victor 21-112-1
40A.................................10/64   4-8
INNER SLEEVE 4: Red, black and white.
Front: RCA's Elvis LP catalog, most recent
being *Kissin' Cousins* (side 1, row 1, column
6). Back: RCA Elvis EPs and 45s catalog.

RCA Victor (SE)
LSP-1951(e) 11/64   35-50
**TOTAL PACKAGE 4: Disc, cover, inner
sleeve.**

❑ RCA Victor (SE)
LSP-1951(e) 11/68   35-45
DISC 5: Orange label. Rigid vinyl.

❑ RCA Victor
LSP-1951(e) 11/68   20-25
COVER 5: Same as cover 4, except has a red
sticker directly on cover indicating "Stereo
effect reprocessed from mono," etc.

❑ RCA Victor 21-112-1
40D.................................6/68   4-6
INNER SLEEVE 5: Red, black and white.
Front: RCA's Elvis LP catalog, most recent
being *Elvis' Gold Records, Vol. 4* (side 1, row
4, column 5). Back: RCA's Elvis LP and Twin
Pack Stereo 8 catalog. May also be found
with inner sleeves 40B and 40C. See chapter
on inner sleeves for more information.

RCA Victor (SE)
LSP-1951(e) 11/68   60-75
**TOTAL PACKAGE 5: Disc, cover, inner
sleeve.**

On both covers and labels, the electronically
reprocessed stereo designation "(e)" may not
appear following every usage of the selection
number.

Side 1
Santa Claus Is Back in Town
White Christmas
Here Comes Santa Claus
I'll Be Home for Christmas
Blue Christmas
Santa Bring My Baby Back (To Me)

Side 2
Oh Little Town of Bethlehem
Silent Night
(There'll Be) Peace in the Valley (For Me)
I Believe
Take My Hand, Precious Lord
It Is No Secret (What God Can Do)

ELVIS' CHRISTMAS ALBUM

❑ RCA/Camden (M)
   CAL-2428 ....11/70   15-25
   DISC 1: Blue label, Rigid Vinyl. Repackage of
   LPM-1951. Added are *If Everyday Was Like
   Christmas* and *Mama Liked the Roses*.
   Omitted are (*There'll Be) Peace in the Valley
   (For Me)*, *I Believe, Take My Hand, Precious
   Lord*, and *It Is No Secret (What God Can Do*).
   ZCRM-5799-1S/ZCRM-5800-1S. Identification numbers are
   engraved.
   ZCRM-5799-2S/ZCRM-5800-3S. Identification numbers are
   engraved.
   ZCRM-5799-8S/ZCRM-5800-8S. Identification numbers are
   stamped.

❑ RCA/Camden
   CAL-2428 ....11/70   12-15
   COVER 1: Front: RCA logo and number at
   upper left and Camden logo at upper right.
   Back: Pictures three other Camden LPs, one
   of which is *Almost in Love* (CAS-2440).
   Covers for this LP (2428) and 2440 were
   made at the same time, which explains how
   an LP with a lower number pictures one that is
   12 numbers higher. This LP lists *Stay Away*
   among the contents of 2440, but first
   pressings had *Stay Away, Joe* instead.
   INNER SLEEVE 1: White, no printing. (Some
   Camden LPs had no inner sleeves at all.)

RCA/Camden (M)
   CAL-2428 ....11/70   30-40
   TOTAL PACKAGE 1: Disc, cover.

❑ RCA/Camden (M)
   CAL-2428 ....11/70   15-25
   DISC 2: Same as disc 1.
❑ RCA/Camden
   CAL-2428 ....11/70   18-20
   COVER 2: Designate promo. Same as cover
   1, but with "Not for Sale" stamped on back.
   INNER SLEEVE 2: White, no printing. (Some
   Camden LPs had no inner sleeves at all.)

RCA/Camden (M)
   CAL-2428 ....11/70   35-45
   TOTAL PACKAGE 2: Disc, cover.

❑ RCA/Camden (M)
   CAL-2428 ....'71   8-12
   DISC 3: Blue label. Flexible vinyl.
❑ RCA/Camden CAL-2428 .....'71   10-15
   COVER 3: Same as cover 1.
   INNER SLEEVE 3: White, no printing.

RCA/Camden (M)
   CAL-2428 ....'71   20-30
   TOTAL PACKAGE 3: Disc, cover.

❑ RCA/Camden (M)
   CAL-2428 ....'71   10-12
   DISC 4: Same as disc 1 or 2.
❑ RCA/Camden CAL-2428 .....'71   5-8
   COVER 4: Same as cover 1, except has a "2"
   or a "3" at lower left on back.
   INNER SLEEVE 4: White, no printing.

RCA/Camden (M)
   CAL-2428 ....'71   **15-20**
   TOTAL PACKAGE 4: Disc, cover.

Side 1
Blue Christmas
Silent Night
White Christmas
Santa Claus Is Back in Town
I'll Be Home for Christmas

Side 2
If Every Day Was Like Christmas
Here Comes Santa Claus (Down Santa Claus Lane)
Oh Little Town of Bethlehem
Santa Bring My Baby Back (To Me)
Mama Liked the Roses

ELVIS' CHRISTMAS ALBUM

❑ Pickwick/Camden (M)
   CAS-2428 ....12/75   4-5
   DISC 1: Black label. Multi-color Pickwick logo
   at center.
❑ Pickwick/Camden
   CAS-2428 ....12/75   4-5
   CAS-2428-A-8/CAS-2428-B-8. Identification numbers are
   engraved. CAS-2428-A-38/CAS-2428-B-38. Identification
   numbers are stamped.
   COVER 1: Front: Pickwick logo at upper left,
   Camden logo at upper right. Color Elvis photo.
   Back: Pictures three other Camden LPs. Does
   not have Christmas trim border. Does not say
   "Previously Released."
   NOTE: Some copies of this LP were found
   with the original Camden CAL-2426 cover but
   a Pickwick record inside.
   INNER SLEEVE 1: Generic Pickwick sleeve.
   Makes no mention of Elvis or this LP.

Pickwick/Camden (M)
   CAS-2428 ....12/75   8-10
   TOTAL PACKAGE 1: Disc, cover.

❑ Pickwick/Camden (M)
   CAS-2428 ....12/76   2-4
   DISC 2: Same as disc 1.
❑ Pickwick/Camden
   CAS-2428 ....12/76   3-4
   COVER 2: Same as cover 1, except has
   Christmas trim border and "Previously
   Released," on back.
   INNER SLEEVE 2: Generic Pickwick sleeve.
   Makes no mention of Elvis or this LP.

Pickwick/Camden (M)
   CAS-2428 ....12/76   5-8
   TOTAL PACKAGE 2: Disc, cover.

❑ Pickwick/Camden (M)
   CAS-2428 ....12/76   4-5
   DISC 3: Same as disc 2.
❑ Pickwick/Camden
   CAS-2428 ....12/76   15-20
   COVER 3: Same as cover 2, except
   Christmas trim border and "Previously
   Released," on back, as well as all text, are in
   green ink.

INNER SLEEVE 3: Generic Pickwick sleeve. Makes no mention of Elvis or this LP.

Pickwick/Camden (M)

CAS-2428 .... 12/76   20-25
TOTAL PACKAGE 3: Disc, cover.

❏ Pickwick/Camden (M)
CAS-2428........................ 12/86   15-25
DISC 4: Black, RCA Special Products label.
<small>ZCRM-5799 CAL-2428-A/ZCRM-5800 CAL-2428-B. All identification numbers are engraved except "ZCRM-5800," which is stamped.</small>

❏ Pickwick/Camden
CAS-2428........................ 12/86   15-25
COVER 4: Same as cover 1, except has RCA Special Products at upper left on front. Back has "The Special Music Company" added at top center and 1986 copyright date at bottom.
INNER SLEEVE 4: Generic Pickwick sleeve. Makes no mention of Elvis or this LP.

Pickwick/Camden (M)

CAS-2428 .... 12/86   30-50
TOTAL PACKAGE 4: Disc, cover.

❏ Pickwick/Camden (M)
CAS-2428........................ 12/86   2-4
DISC 5: Same as disc 2.

❏ Pickwick/Camden
CAS-2428........................ 12/86   3-4
COVER 5: Same as cover 2, except has "Dist. in Canada" on back (this is still a U.S. release).
INNER SLEEVE 5: Generic Pickwick sleeve. Makes no mention of Elvis or this LP.

Pickwick/Camden (M)

CAS-2428 .... 12/86   5-8
TOTAL PACKAGE 5: Disc, cover.

In November 1978, Pickwick issued a specially-wrapped package of seven LPs, including this one. After the holidays, they replaced this LP with *Frankie and Johnny*. See *PICKWICK PACK* for more on this set. This LP is also one of 10 included in *A CHRISTMAS COLLECTION*. See that listing for more information.

Side 1
Blue Christmas
Silent Night
White Christmas
Santa Claus Is Back in Town
I'll Be Home for Christmas

Side 2
If Every Day Was Like Christmas
Here Comes Santa Claus (Down Santa Claus Lane)
Oh Little Town of Bethlehem
Santa Bring My Baby Back (To Me)
Mama Liked the Roses

ELVIS COMEDY RECORD

❏ **SUX 002:** Bootleg. Listed for identification only.

ELVIS COMMEMORATIVE ALBUM (2 LPs)

❏ RCA Special Products (SP)
DPL2-0056(e)...................... '78   30-35
DISCS 1: Gold vinyl. Black label, dog near top. TV mail order offer.
<small>**(Disc 1)** DPL2-0056A-3/DPL2-0056B-3. **(Disc 2)** DPL2-0056C-4/DPL2-0056D-5.</small>
<small>**(Disc 1)** DPL2-0056A-9/DPL2-0056B-2. **(Disc 2)** DPL2-0056C-4/DPL2-0056D-5.</small>

❏ RCA Special Products
DPL2-0056(e)...................... '78   30-35
COVER 1: Double pocket. Has gold and black "Limited Edition Reg. No." sticker applied directly to cover, and therefore included in above price range. Repackage of the 1973 Special Products *Elvis* set, which is pictured at lower left on front and back of this cover. May or may not have a gold sticker listing contents.
INNER SLEEVES 1: White, no printing.

❏ RCA Victor DPL2-0056(e) ...'78   5-10
INSERT 1: "Registered Certificate of Ownership." Number on this 6¼" x 4¼" certificate corresponds to number on sticker (on front cover).

❏ RCA Victor DPL2-0056(e) ...'78   15-20
STICKER 1: Gold sticker that lists contents.

RCA Special Products (SP)

DPL2-0056(e) .... '78   **80-100**
TOTAL PACKAGE 1: Discs, cover, insert, sticker.

Disc 1

Side 1
Hound Dog
I Want You, I Need You, I Love You
All Shook Up
Don't
I Beg of You

Side 2
A Big Hunk O' Love
Love Me
Stuck on You
Good Luck Charm
Return to Sender

Disc 2

Side 3
Don't Be Cruel
Loving You
Jailhouse Rock
Can't Help Falling in Love
I Got Stung

Side 4
(Let Me Be Your) Teddy Bear
Love Me Tender
Hard Headed Woman
It's Now or Never
Surrender

ELVIS COUNTRY

❏ RCA Special Products (SP)
DPL1-0647 ....4/84   10-15
DISC 1: Black label, dog near top. Made for
ERA Records.
DPL1-0647-A-1/DPL1-0647-B-1.

❏ RCA Special Products
DPL1-0647 ....4/84   15-20
COVER 1: Front: Artist's rendering of Elvis,
with desert background. Back: ERA logo and
number (BU-3930) at lower left, RCA Special
Products logo, number, and UPC bar code at
lower right.
INNER SLEEVE 1: White, no printing.

RCA Special Products (SP)

DPL1-0647 ....4/84   25-35
TOTAL PACKAGE 1: Disc, cover.

Card stock jacket, with printing on cover – not
on slicks.

Side 1
Are You Lonesome Tonight
Suspicion
Your Cheatin' Heart
Blue Moon of Kentucky
Don't
I Forgot to Remember to Forget
Help Me Make It Through the Night

Side 2
Kentucky Rain
I Really Don't Want to Know
Hurt
There's a Honky Tonk Angel (Who Will Take Me Back
In)
Always on My Mind
Green, Green Grass of Home

ELVIS COUNTRY ("I'M 10,000 YEARS OLD")

❏ RCA Victor (ST)
LSP-4460 ....1/71   20-25
DISC 1: Orange label. Rigid vinyl.
ZPRS-1825-8S/ZPRS-1826-8S.
ZPRS-1825-9S/ZPRS-1826-7S.

❏ RCA Victor LSP-4460........1/71   5-10
COVER 1: Front: Colorized photo of Elvis at
age two. RCA logo and number at upper left,
"Victor Stereo" at upper right. Back: Black-
and-white Elvis photo from a 1970 Las Vegas
concert.

❏ RCA Victor 21-112-1
pt 54 ....8/70   3-5
INNER SLEEVE 1: Black-and-white. Pictures
RCA's Elvis LP catalog front and back, most
recent being *Worldwide Gold Award Hits, Vol.
1* (side 2, row 4, column 4).

❏ RCA Victor LSP-4460........1/71   10-15
INSERT 1: Colorized 5" x 7" photo of Elvis at
age two, same as on front cover of LP. Back
has a black-and-white Elvis photo.

❏ RCA Victor LSP-4460........1/71   15-20
SHRINK STICKER 1: Announces the
inclusion of the bonus photo.

❏ RCA Victor (ST)
LSP-4460.....................1/71   55-75
TOTAL PACKAGE 1: Disc, cover, inner
sleeve, insert, sticker.

❏ RCA Victor (ST)
LSP-4460 ....1/71   20-25
DISC 2: Same as disc 1.

❏ RCA Victor LSP-4460........1/71   10-15
COVER 2: Designate promo. Same as cover
1, but with "Not for Sale" stamped on back.

❏ RCA Victor 21-112-1
pt 54 ....8/70   3-5
INNER SLEEVE 2: Black-and-white. Pictures
RCA's Elvis LP catalog front and back, most
recent being *Worldwide Gold Award Hits, Vol.
1* (side 2, row 4, column 4).

❏ RCA Victor LSP-4460........1/71   10-15
INSERT 2: Colorized 5" x 7" photo of Elvis at
age two, same as on front cover of LP. Back
has a black-and-white Elvis photo.

❏ RCA Victor LSP-4460........1/71   15-20
SHRINK STICKER 2: Announces the
inclusion of the bonus photo.

RCA Victor (ST)

LSP-4460.....................1/71   60-80
TOTAL PACKAGE 2: Disc, cover, inner
sleeve, insert, sticker.

❏ RCA Victor (ST)
LSP-4460 ....1/71   10-15
DISC 3: Orange label. Flexible vinyl.
ZPRS-1825-1S/ZPRS-1826-2S. Identification numbers are
stamped.
ZPRS-1825-9S/ZPRS-1826-9S. Identification numbers are
engraved.

❏ RCA Victor LSP-4460........1/71   5-10
COVER 3: Same as cover 1.

❏ RCA Victor..........................'70s   2-4
INNER SLEEVE 3: Black-and-white. Pictures
RCA Elvis catalog front and back. Any of
several sleeves may be found on reissues
from this period.

❏ RCA Victor LSP-4460........1/71   10-15
INSERT 3: Colorized 5" x 7" photo of Elvis at
age two, same as on front cover of LP. Back
has a black-and-white Elvis photo.

❏ RCA Victor LSP-4460........1/71   15-20
SHRINK STICKER 3: Announces the
inclusion of the bonus photo.

RCA Victor (ST)

LSP-4460.....................1/71   40-65
TOTAL PACKAGE 3: Disc, cover, inner
sleeve, insert, sticker.

❏ RCA Victor (ST)
LSP-4460 ....1/71   5-10
DISC 4: Same as disc 2.
ZPRS-1825-4S/ZPRS-1826-5S.

❏ RCA Victor LSP-4460........1/71   15-20
COVER 4: Designate promo. Same as cover
1, but with "Not for Sale" stamped on back.

❑ RCA Victor 21-112-1
pt 54 ....8/70   3-5
INNER SLEEVE 4: Black-and-white. Pictures RCA's Elvis LP catalog front and back, most recent being *Worldwide Gold Award Hits, Vol. 1* (side 2, row 4, column 4).

❑ RCA Victor LSP-4460........1/71   10-15
INSERT 4: Colorized 5" x 7" photo of Elvis at age two, same as on front cover of LP. Back has a black-and-white Elvis photo.

❑ RCA Victor LSP-4460........1/71   15-20
SHRINK STICKER 4: Announces the inclusion of the bonus photo.

RCA Victor (ST)
LSP-4460.....................1/71   45-70
TOTAL PACKAGE 4: Disc, cover, inner sleeve, insert, sticker.

❑ RCA Victor (ST)
LSP-4460 ....'76   15-18
DISC 5: Tan label. Two label printings exist, one with "Side 1/Side 2" and another with "Side A/Side B."
ZPRS-1825-7S/ZPRS-1826-7.

❑ RCA Victor LSP-4460..........'76   4-8
COVER 5: Same as cover 1, except has "RE" on back at lower left.

❑ RCA Victor..........................'70s   2-4
INNER SLEEVE 5: Black-and-white. Pictures RCA Elvis catalog front and back. Any of several sleeves may be found on reissues from this period.

RCA Victor (ST)
LSP-4460.......................'76   20-30
TOTAL PACKAGE 5: Disc, cover, inner sleeve.

❑ RCA Victor LSP-4460..........'76   3-6
DISC 6: Black label, dog near top.

❑ RCA LSP-4460....................'76   3-6
COVER 6: Same as cover 1, except has "RE" on back at lower left.

❑ RCA Victor..........................'70s   2-4
INNER SLEEVE 6: Black-and-white. Pictures RCA Elvis catalog front and back. Any of several sleeves may be found on reissues from this period.

RCA Victor LSP-4460.......'76   10-20
TOTAL PACKAGE 6: Disc, cover, inner sleeve.

❑ RCA Victor (ST)
LSP-4460 ....5/77   1000-2000
DISC 7: Tan label. Green vinyl. Experimental pressing only, not intended for sale or distribution.
COVER 7: None made.

RCA Victor (ST)
LSP-4460.....................5/77   1000-2000
TOTAL PACKAGE 7: Disc.

❑ RCA Victor (ST)
LSP-4460 ....5/77   1000-2000
DISC 8: Tan label. Blue vinyl. Experimental pressing only, not intended for sale or distribution.
COVER 8: None made.

RCA Victor (ST)
LSP-4460.....................5/77   1000-2000
TOTAL PACKAGE 8: Disc.

❑ RCA Victor (ST)
AFL1-4460...........................'77   3-4
DISC 9: Black label, dog near top.

❑ RCA AFL1-4460 ....'77   3-4
COVER 9: Reflects prefix change. Includes copies with a sticker bearing the "AFL1" prefix, wrapped around cover at top of spine.

❑ RCA Victor..........................'70s   2-4
INNER SLEEVE 9: Black-and-white. Pictures RCA Elvis catalog front and back. Any of several sleeves may be found on reissues from this period.

RCA Victor (ST)
AFL1-4460.....................'77   8-12
TOTAL PACKAGE 9: Disc, cover, inner sleeve.

❑ RCA Victor (ST)
AYL1-3956 ....5/81   2-5
DISC 10: Black label, dog near top.
AYL1-3956A/AYL1-3956B. Identification numbers are engraved. ZPRS-1825-7S/ZPRS-1826-7S is stamped but crossed out. AFL1-4460A/AFL1-4460B is engraved but also crossed out.

❑ RCA AYL1-3956 ....5/81   2-5
COVER 10: Reflects selection number change. Part of RCA's "Best Buy Series." Includes copies with a sticker bearing the "AYL1" prefix, wrapped around cover at top of spine.
INNER SLEEVE 10: White, no printing.

RCA Victor (ST)
AYL1-3956 ....5/81   5-10
TOTAL PACKAGE 10: Disc, cover.

Side 1
Snowbird
Tomorrow Never Comes
Little Cabin on the Hill
Whole Lot-ta Shakin' Goin' On
Funny How Time Slips Away
I Really Don't Want to Know

Side 2
There Goes My Everything
It's Your Baby, You Rock It
The Fool
Faded Love
I Washed My Hands in Muddy Water
Make the World Go Away

ELVIS COUNTRY CLASSICS: see *COUNTRY CLASSICS*

ELVIS EXCLUSIVE INTERVIEW (ELVIS WITH RAY GREEN BACKSTAGE)

❑ Creative Radio Network (M)
CRN-E1 .... 5/88   165-185
DISC 1: Red label with black print. First pressings have full-length versions of all songs. Just 100 copies were made of this edition, which can be identified by looking at Side B. The grooved area on that side is about 3½" wide as opposed to 2¼" on the second pressing. Does not have "Elvis" engraved in the trail off on Side B.
ERG-A L-31232/ERG-B L-31232-X. Identification numbers are engraved.

❑ Creative Radio Network
CRN-E1 .... 5/88   10-15
COVER 1: Front: Red, white and blue, no photos, text only. Back: Duotone photo of Ray Green and Elvis.
INNER SLEEVE 1: White, no printing.

Creative Radio Network (M)
CRN-E1 .... 5/88   175-200
TOTAL PACKAGE 1: Disc, cover.

❑ Creative Radio Network (M)
CRN-E1 .... 5/88   10-15
DISC 2: Red label with black print. Side 1 ("A") is identical to disc 1. Side 2 ("B") has only excerpts of songs. The grooved area on side 2 is about 2¼" wide.
ERG-A L-31232/ERG-B L-31232-X - Identification numbers are engraved. Also has "Elvis" engraved on side B.

❑ Creative Radio Network
CRN-E1 .... 5/88   10-15
COVER 2: Same as cover 1.
INNER SLEEVE 2: White, no printing.

Creative Radio Network (M)
CRN-E1 .... 5/88   20-30
TOTAL PACKAGE 2: Disc, cover.

ELVIS EXCLUSIVE LIVE PRESS CONFERENCE (MEMPHIS, TENNESSEE – FEBRUARY, 1961)

❑ Green Valley (M)
GV-2001 .... 10/77   5-10
DISC 1: Green label.
Green Valley Elvis Interview Side One RE-1/Green Valley Elvis Interview Side Two RE-1. Identification numbers are engraved.

❑ Green Valley GV-2001 .... 10/77   20-35
COVER 1: Flimsy stock, as is often used on import LPs. Front: Black, white and red. Text only. Back: Drawing of Elvis, liner notes. Black 1½" stripe at top does not wrap around the spine. Does not have the number on label or jacket.
INNER SLEEVE 1: White, no printing.

Green Valley (M)
GV-2001 .... 10/77   25-45
TOTAL PACKAGE 1: Disc, cover.

❑ Green Valley (M)
GV-2001 .... 10/77   5-10
DISC 2: Same as disc 1.

❑ Green Valley GV-2001 .... 12/77   10-15
COVER 2: Artwork and print same as cover 1, except black stripe on back wraps around onto spine. Also, jacket is more rigid than cover 1 but is still made of card stock, with printing on cover – not on slicks..
INNER SLEEVE 2: White, no printing.

❑ Green Valley GV-2001 .... 12/77   5-10
INSERT 2: Script for interview.

Green Valley (M)
GV-2001 .... 12/77   20-35
TOTAL PACKAGE 2: Disc, cover, script.

Reused as one disc in the two-LP *Elvis (Speaks to You)*, then reissued later as *Elvis the King Speaks*. Though labeled as a "1961 Press Conference," the event actually took place March 8, 1960.

Side 1
Elvis Live
Side 2
Elvis Live

ELVIS FEVER

❑ Bootleg. Listed for identification only.

ELVIS 50th ANNIVERSARY (THE 50th BIRTHDAY RADIO SPECIAL) (6 LPs)

Complete six-hour radio show. All discs in this set, listed and priced individually below, have a silver label with black print. All identification numbers are engraved. Issued only to subscribing radio stations.

❑ Creative Radio (SP)
1A/1B 8/85   20-25
DISC 1:
1-A L-19711/1-B L-19711X.

❑ Creative Radio (SP)
2A/2B 8/85   20-25
DISC 2:
2-A L-19711/2-B L-19711X

❑ Creative Radio (SP)
3A/3B 8/85   20-25
DISC 3:
3-A L-19777/3-B L-19777X.

❑ Creative Radio (SP)
4A/4B 8/85   20-25
DISC 4:
4-A L-19776/4-B L-19776X.

❑ Creative Radio (SP)
5A/5B 8/85   20-25
DISC 5:
5-A L-19769/5-B L-19769X.

❑ Creative Radio (SP)
6A/6B 8/85   20-25
DISC 6:
6-A L-19779/6-B L-19779X.
BOX 1: Plain, no printing.
INNER SLEEVES 1: White, no printing.

❑ Creative Radio...................8/85   5-10
INSERT 1: Seven pages of script and
programmer's notes.

Creative Radio (SP)
1A-6B 8/85   125-160
TOTAL PACKAGE 1: Discs, insert.

Disc 1
Side 1
See See Rider
The Elvis Medley
That's All Right
Blue Moon of Kentucky
Pledging My Love
(Let Me Be Your) Teddy Bear
Blue Suede Shoes
Million Dollar Quartet
Side 2
What Now My Love
I Was the One
All Shook Up
Lawdy, Miss Clawdy
I Can't Stop Loving You
Kentucky Rain
Way Down
Disc 2
Side 1
Elvis Montage
Heartbreak Hotel
Treat Me Nice
Steamroller Blues
Burning Love
I Want You, I Need You, I Love You
Hound Dog
Side 2
I'll Remember You
Hard Headed Woman
Love Me Tender
What'd I Say
Rip It Up
An American Trilogy
G.I. Blues
Frankfurt Special
Disc 3
Side 1
Elvis Montage
Don't Be Cruel
She's Not You
Trouble/Guitar Man
Love Me
Jailhouse Rock
(Marie's the Name) His Latest Flame
Side 2
Gospel Medley
Welcome to My World
You Gave Me a Mountain
A Fool such As I
Moody Blue
The Last Farewell
Too Much
Disc 4
Side 1
Elvis Montage
Stuck on You
If You Talk in Your Sleep
Old Shep
A Big Hunk O' Love
I Got Stung
Don't

It's Now Or Never
Side 2
Such a Night
Unchained Melody
Little Darlin'
I Need Your Love Tonight
Are You Sincere
(You're the) Devil in Disguise
Little Sister
Can't Help Falling in Love
Disc 5
Side 1
Elvis Montage
Good Luck Charm
Crying in the Chapel
Something
Release Me
I'm So Lonesome I Could Cry
The Impossible Dream
Side 2
Wooden Heart
How Great Thou Art
Green, Grass of Home
Johnny B. Goode
For the Heart
It's Over
Surrender
Return to Sender
In the Ghetto
Disc 6
Side 1
That's All Right
Baby, What You Want Me to Do
Blue Suede Shoes
If I Can Dream
Promised Land
Tryin' to Get to You
Don't Cry Daddy
Let It Be Me
Side 2
Are You Lonesome Tonight
One Night
Suspicious Minds
The Wonder of You
You'll Never Walk Alone
Memories
My Way

ELVIS FOR EVERYONE

❑ RCA Victor (M)
    LPM-3450...........................7/65   20-30
DISC 1: Black label, "Monaural" at bottom.
SPRM-5390-1S/SPRM-5391-1S. Label LP#12.
SPRM-5390-5S/SPRM-5391-5S. Label LP#12.
❑ RCA Victor LPM-3450 ....7/65   25-35
COVER 1: Front: RCA logo at lower right and
number at lower left. Has color photo of Elvis
standing near a cash register. Has his name
in red print. Back: Pictures 15 earlier Elvis LPs
in color.
❑ RCA Victor 21-112-1
    40B 4/65   4-6
INNER SLEEVE 1: Red, black and white.
Front: RCA's Elvis LP catalog, most recent
being *Roustabout* (side 1, row 1, column 5).
Back: RCA Elvis EPs and 45s catalog.

RCA Victor (M)
LPM-3450 .... 7/65   **50-70**
TOTAL PACKAGE 1: Disc, cover, inner sleeve.

❑ RCA Victor (M)
   LPM-3450 .... 7/65   20-30
   DISC 2: Same as disc 1.
❑ RCA Victor LPM-3450 .... 7/65   40-50
   COVER 2: Designate promo. Same as cover 1, but with "Not for Sale" stamped on back.
❑ RCA Victor 21-112-1
   40B 4/65   4-6
   INNER SLEEVE 2: Red, black and white. Front: RCA's Elvis LP catalog, most recent being *Roustabout* (side 1, row 1, column 5). Back: RCA Elvis EPs and 45s catalog.

RCA Victor (M)
LPM-3450 .... 7/65   **65-85**
TOTAL PACKAGE 2: Disc, cover, inner sleeve.

❑ RCA Victor (SP)
   LSP-3450 .... 7/65   20-30
   DISC 3: Black label, RCA logo in white at top and the word "Stereo" at bottom.
   SPRS-5392-4S/SPRS-5393-2S. Label LP#16.
   SPRS-5392-6S/SPRS-5393-6S. Label LP#16.
❑ RCA Victor LSP-3450 .... 7/65   25-35
   COVER 3: Front: RCA logo at upper right and number at upper left. Has color photo of Elvis standing near a cash register. Back: Pictures 15 earlier Elvis LPs in color. Price reflects RCA's use of this same cover, with no discernible differences, until 1976.
❑ RCA Victor 21-112-1 40B .. 4/65   4-6
   INNER SLEEVE 3: Red, black and white. Front: RCA's Elvis LP catalog, most recent being *Roustabout* (side 1, row 1, column 5). Back: RCA Elvis EPs and 45s catalog.

RCA Victor (SP)
LSP-3450 .... 7/65   **50-70**
TOTAL PACKAGE 3: Disc, cover, inner sleeve.

❑ RCA Victor (SP)
   LSP-3450 .... 7/65   20-30
   DISC 4: Same as disc 3.
❑ RCA Victor LSP-3450 .... 7/65   40-50
   COVER 4: Designate promo. Same as cover 3, but with "Not for Sale" stamped on back.
❑ RCA Victor 21-112-1
   40B 4/65   4-6
   INNER SLEEVE 4: Red, black and white. Front: RCA's Elvis LP catalog, most recent being *Roustabout* (side 1, row 1, column 5). Back: RCA Elvis EPs and 45s catalog.

RCA Victor (SP)
LSP-3450 .... 7/65   **65-85**
TOTAL PACKAGE 4: Disc, cover, inner sleeve.

❑ RCA Victor (SP)
   LSP-3450 .... 11/68   20-25
   DISC 5: Orange label. Rigid vinyl.
❑ RCA Victor LSP-3450 ...... 11/68   8-10
   COVER 5: Similar to cover 3, except Elvis' name is in orange print instead of red. Also, other print on front is not as dark as on cover 3.
❑ RCA Victor 21-112-1
   40D 6/68   4-6
   INNER SLEEVE 5: Red, black and white. Front: RCA's Elvis LP catalog, most recent being *Elvis' Gold Records, Vol. 4* (side 1, row 4, column 5). Back: RCA's Elvis LP and Twin Pack Stereo 8 catalog. May also be found with inner sleeves 40B and 40C. See chapter on inner sleeves for more information.

RCA Victor (SP)
LSP-3450 .... 11/68   **30-40**
TOTAL PACKAGE 5: Disc, cover, inner sleeve.

❑ RCA Victor (SP)
   LSP-3450 .... '71   10-15
   DISC 6: Orange label. Flexible vinyl.
   SPRS-5392-10S/SPRS-5393-9S.
❑ RCA Victor LSP-3450 .... '71   8-10
   COVER 6: Same as cover 5.
❑ RCA Victor .... '70s   2-4
   INNER SLEEVE 6: Black-and-white. Pictures RCA Elvis catalog front and back. Any of several sleeves may be found on reissues from this period.

RCA Victor (SP)
LSP-3450 .... '71   **20-25**
TOTAL PACKAGE 6: Disc, cover, inner sleeve.

❑ RCA Victor (ST)
   LSP-3450 .... '76   4-8
   DISC 7: Tan label.
❑ RCA LSP-3450 .... '76   4-8
   COVER 7: Same as cover 5.
❑ RCA Victor .... '70s   2-4
   INNER SLEEVE 7: Black-and-white. Pictures RCA Elvis catalog front and back. Any of several sleeves may be found on reissues from this period.

RCA Victor (ST)
LSP-3450 .... '76   **10-20**
TOTAL PACKAGE 7: Disc, cover, inner sleeve.

❑ RCA Victor (ST)
   LSP-3450 .... '76   4-6
   DISC 8: Black label, dog near top.
❑ RCA LSP-3450 .... '76   4-6
   COVER 8: Reflects logo change.
❑ RCA Victor .... '70s   2-4
   INNER SLEEVE 8: Black-and-white. Pictures RCA Elvis catalog front and back. Any of several sleeves may be found on reissues from this period.

RCA Victor (ST)
LSP-3450......................'76   10-18
TOTAL PACKAGE 8: Disc, cover, inner sleeve.

❑ RCA Victor (SP)
AFL1-3450 ....'77   3-5
DISC 9: Black label, dog near top.

❑ RCA AFL1-3450 ....'77   3-5
COVER 9: Reflects prefix change. Includes copies with a sticker bearing the "AFL1" prefix, wrapped around cover at top of spine.

❑ RCA Victor.........................'70s   2-4
INNER SLEEVE 9: Black-and-white. Pictures RCA Elvis catalog front and back. Any of several sleeves may be found on reissues from this period.

RCA Victor (SP)
AFL1-3450......................'77   8-15
TOTAL PACKAGE 9: Disc, cover, inner sleeve.

❑ RCA Victor (SP)
AYL1-4232 ....2/82   3-5
DISC 10: Black label, dog near top.
AYL1-4232A-2/AYL1-4232B-1.

❑ RCA AYL1-4232 ....2/82   3-5
COVER 10: Reflects selection number change. Part of RCA's "Best Buy Series." Includes copies with a sticker bearing the "AYL1" prefix, wrapped around cover at top of spine.
INNER SLEEVE 10: White, no printing.

RCA Victor (SP)
AYL1-4232 ....2/82   6-10
TOTAL PACKAGE 10: Disc, cover.

Finders Keepers, Losers Weepers; For the Millionth and the Last Time; I Met Her Today; Memphis, Tennessee and *Santa Lucia* are the only stereo tracks on this LP.

Side 1
Your Cheatin' Heart
Summer Kisses, Winter Tears
Finders Keepers, Losers Weepers
In My Way
Tomorrow Night
Memphis, Tennessee

Side 2
For the Millionth and the Last Time
Forget Me Never
Sound Advice
Santa Lucia
I Met Her Today
When It Rains It Really Pours

ELVIS FOREVER (2 LPs)

❑ RCA Special Products (SP)
KSL2-7031 ....'74   15-25
DISCS 1: Mustard color label. Made in Canada but sold in U.S. via TV mail order.
(Disc 1) KSL2-7031-A-2/KSL2-7031-B. (Disc 2) KSL2-7031-C-3/KSL2-7031-D. Identification numbers are engraved.

❑ RCA Special Products
KSL2-7031 ....'74   15-20
COVER 1: Single pocket. Front: RCA Special Products logo and number at lower left. At upper right is: "Deluxe 2 Record $6.98 As Seen On TV." Has color shot of Elvis from "Aloha" concert. Back: Color Elvis photo. "Made in Canada," etc., at bottom.
INNER SLEEVE 1: White, no printing.

RCA (SP) KSL2-7031........'74   30-45
TOTAL PACKAGE 1: Discs, cover.

❑ RCA (SP) KSL2-7031..........'74   15-20
DISCS 2: Mustard color label, but noticeably lighter than discs 1.
(Disc 1) KSL2-7031-A-2/KSL2-7031-B8. (Disc 2) KSL2-7031-C-3/KSL2-7031-D8. dentification numbers are engraved. This pressing has an "8" added to the numbers on sides B and D.

❑ RCA Special Products
KSL2-7031 ....'74   8-12
COVER 2: Same as cover 1, except does not have "Deluxe 2 Record $6.98 As Seen On TV" at upper right. Instead, reads: "2 Record Set, Ensemble de 2 Disques." Back: Same as cover 1, except has "Distributed by Tee Vee Records," etc. added below RCA copyright notice, at lower right.
INNER SLEEVES 2: White, no printing.

RCA Special Products (SP)
KSL2-7031 ....'74   25-35
TOTAL PACKAGE 2: Discs, cover.

Disc 1
Side 1
Treat Me Nice
I Need Your Love Tonight
That's When Your Heartaches Begin
G.I. Blues
Blue Hawaii
Easy Come, Easy Go

Side 2
Suspicion
Puppet on a String
Heartbreak Hotel
One Night
Memories
Blue Suede Shoes

Disc 2
Side 3
Are You Lonesome Tonight
Hi-Heel Sneakers
Old Shep
Rip It Up
Such a Night
(Now and Then There's) A Fool Such As I

Side 4
Tutti Frutti
In the Ghetto
Wear My Ring Around Your Neck
Wooden Heart
Crying in the Chapel
Don't Cry Daddy

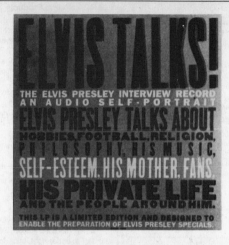

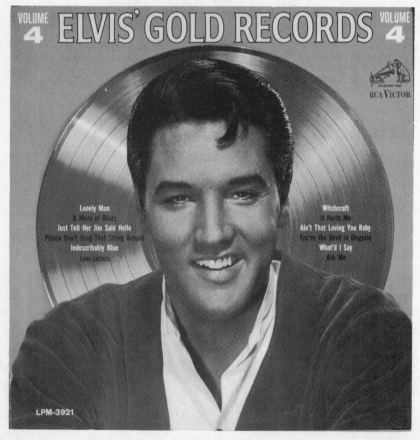

ELVIS FRIENDS REMEMBER

☐ Allied 4704: Bootleg. Listed for identification only.

ELVIS' GOLDEN RECORDS

☐ RCA Victor (M)
LPM-1707...........................4/58   50-60
DISC 1: Black label, "Long Play" at bottom.
H2WP-8398-1S/H2WP-8399-2S. Label LP#2.
H2WP-8398-21S/H2WP-8399-21S. Label LP#2.

☐ RCA Victor LPM-1707.......4/58   60-70
COVER 1: Front: RCA logo and number at upper right. Title is in light blue letters. Contents are *not* opened on front. Stock is flat (not glossy). Back: Contents spread across all three columns of liner notes. Title and artist lines are centered.

☐ RCA Victor No Number.......'58   8-12
INNER SLEEVE 1: Black, white and red. Pictures *Loving You*, as one of five LPs in the "Popular" category.

☐ RCA Victor...........................'58   80-100
INSERT 1: Coupon with a "Fabulous Offer!" of a 12-page 8" x 10" Elvis photo booklet for 25¢. Insert is not marked in any way to identify it with *Elvis Golden Records*; however it did come in some copies of this LP. No verification exists that it came with any other Elvis albums. (Note: price is for coupon, not for photo booklet.)

☐ RCA Victor (M)
LPM-1707.....................4/58   200-250
TOTAL PACKAGE 1: Disc, cover, insert, inner sleeve.

☐ RCA Victor (M)
LPM-1707...........................'58   50-60
DISC 2: Same as disc 1.

☐ RCA Victor LPM-1707.........'58   40-50
COVER 2: Same as cover 1, except has "RE" to the right of selection number and slick is on glossy stock.

☐ RCA Victor No Number.......'58   8-12
INNER SLEEVE 2: Black, white and red. Pictures *Loving You*, as one of five LPs in the "Popular" category.

☐ RCA Victor (M)
LPM-1707.......................'58   100-125
TOTAL PACKAGE 2: Disc, cover, inner sleeve.

☐ RCA Victor (M)
LPM-1707.......................11/63   30-40
DISC 3: Black label, "Mono" at bottom.
H2WP-8398-10S/H2WP-8399-10S. Label LP#10.

☐ RCA Victor LPM-1707.....11/63   20-30
COVER 3: Front: RCA logo at upper right and number (with "RE") at lower left. Title is in white letters. Contents are printed at top. Stock is glossy. Back: Contents are at top right. Title and artist lines are flush left. Box at lower right with "Important Note."

☐ RCA Victor (No Number)...9/63   8-10
INNER SLEEVE 3: Turquoise, black and white. Front: RCA's Elvis LP catalog, most recent being *It Happened at the World's Fair* (side 1, row 4, column 5). Back: RCA Elvis EPs and 45s catalog.

☐ RCA Victor (M)
LPM-1707..................11/63   60-80
TOTAL PACKAGE 3: Disc, cover, inner sleeve.

☐ RCA Victor (M)
LPM-1707.......................10/64   10-15
DISC 4: Black label, "Monaural" at bottom.

☐ RCA Victor (M)
LPM-1707.......................10/64   10-20
H2WP-8398-32S/H2WP-8399-30S. Label LP#12.
COVER 4: Same as cover 3, except has "RE2" after selection number, on back.

☐ RCA Victor 21-112-1
40A.................................10/64   4-8
INNER SLEEVE 4: Red, black and white. Front: RCA's Elvis LP catalog, most recent being *Kissin' Cousins* (side 1, row 1, column 6). Back: RCA Elvis EPs and 45s catalog.

☐ RCA Victor (M)
LPM-1707..................10/64   25-45
TOTAL PACKAGE 4: Disc, cover, inner sleeve.

☐ RCA Victor (SE)
LSP-1707(e).....................2/62   100-150
DISC 5: Black label, RCA logo in silver at top and "Stereo" at bottom.
M2WY-4733-2S/M2WY-4734-2S. Label LP#9.
M2WY-4733-3S/M2WY-4734-3S. Label LP#9.

☐ RCA Victor LSP-1707(e) ...2/62   100-150
COVER 5: Front: A 1¼" black strip runs across top, which has number at left and "Stereo Electronically Reprocessed" at right in white letters. RCA logo at upper right below black stripe. Has "RE" at lower right. Back: Same as cover 3 except has box of text at upper left "From the Originators of Electronically Reprocessed Stereo."
INNER SLEEVE 5: White, no printing.

☐ RCA Victor (SE)
LSP-1707(e) 2/62   200-300
TOTAL PACKAGE 5: Disc, cover.

☐ RCA Victor (SE)
LSP-1707(e)....................10/64   10-20
DISC 6: Black label, RCA logo in white at top and "Stereo" at bottom.
M2WY-4733-6S/M2WY-4734-5S. Label LP#15.

☐ RCA Victor
LSP-1707(e) 10/64   10-20
COVER 6: Front: Catalog Number at upper left and "Stereo Electronically Reprocessed" at right in white letters. Has "RE" at lower right. Back: Same as cover 3 except has box of text at upper left "From the Originators of Electronically Reprocessed Stereo."

❏ RCA Victor 21-112-1
40A...................10/64   4-8
INNER SLEEVE 6: Red, black and white.
Front: RCA's Elvis LP catalog, most recent
being *Kissin' Cousins* (side 1, row 1, column
6). Back: RCA Elvis EPs and 45s catalog.

RCA Victor (SE)
LSP-1707(e) 10/64   25-50
TOTAL PACKAGE 6: Disc, cover, inner
sleeve.

❏ RCA Victor (SE)
LSP-1707(e)....................11/68   20-25
DISC 7: Orange label. Rigid vinyl.
❏ RCA Victor
LSP-1707(e)....................11/68   8-10
COVER 7: Verification pending.
❏ RCA Victor 21-112-1
40D....................6/68   4-6
INNER SLEEVE 7: Red, black and white.
Front: RCA's Elvis LP catalog, most recent
being *Elvis' Gold Records, Vol. 4* (side 1, row
4, column 5). Back: RCA's Elvis LP and Twin
Pack Stereo 8 catalog. May also be found
with inner sleeves 40B and 40C. See chapter
on inner sleeves for more information.

RCA Victor (SE)
LSP-1707(e) 11/68   30-40
TOTAL PACKAGE 7: Disc, cover, inner
sleeve.

❏ RCA Victor (SE)
LSP-1707(e)......................'71   10-15
DISC 8: Orange label. Flexible vinyl.
M2WY-4733-12S/M2WY-4734-13S. Identification numbers
are engraved.
❏ RCA Victor LSP-1707(e) ..... '71   4-8
COVER 8: Front: RCA logo and number at
upper left and "Victor, Stereo Reprocessed
from Monophonic" at upper right, all in yellow
print on a black stripe across top. Black
border around entire cover. "SER" at bottom
left. Back: Same as cover 3, except does not
have box with "Important Note." Has box at
upper left with information about stereo
records. Spine is black with yellow print.
❏ RCA Victor........................'70s   2-4
INNER SLEEVE 8: Black-and-white. Pictures
RCA Elvis catalog front and back. Any of
several may be found on reissues from this
period.

RCA Victor (SE)
LSP-1707(e) ....'71   15-25
TOTAL PACKAGE 8: Disc, cover, inner
sleeve.

❏ RCA Victor (SE)
LSP-1707(e)........................'76   4-8
DISC 9: Tan label.
❏ RCA Victor LSP-1707(e) ..... '76   4-8
COVER 9: Verification pending.

❏ RCA Victor........................'70s   2-4
INNER SLEEVE 9: Black-and-white. Pictures
RCA Elvis catalog front and back. Any of
several sleeves may be found on reissues
from this period.

RCA Victor (SE)
LSP-1707(e) ....'76   10-20
TOTAL PACKAGE 9: Disc, cover, inner
sleeve.

❏ RCA Victor LSP-1707(e) .....'76   4-6
DISC 10: Black label, dog near top.
❏ RCA LSP-1707(e)................'76   4-6
COVER 10: Reflects logo change.
❏ RCA Victor........................'70s   2-4
INNER SLEEVE 10: Black-and-white.
Pictures RCA Elvis catalog front and back.
Any of several sleeves may be found on
reissues from this period.

RCA Victor LSP-1707(e) ..'76   10-18
TOTAL PACKAGE 10: Disc, cover, inner
sleeve.

❏ RCA Victor (SE)
AFL1-1707(e) ....'77   3-5
DISC 11: Black label, dog near top.
❏ RCA AFL1-1707(e)..............'77   3-5
COVER 11: Reflects prefix change. Includes
copies with a sticker bearing the "AFL1"
prefix, wrapped around cover at top of spine.
❏ RCA Victor........................'70s   2-4
INNER SLEEVE 11: Black-and-white.
Pictures RCA Elvis catalog front and back.
Any of several sleeves may be found on
reissues from this period.

RCA Victor (SE)
AFL1-1707(e) ....'77   8-15
TOTAL PACKAGE 11: Disc, cover, inner
sleeve.

❏ RCA Victor (SE)
AQL1-1707(e)......................'79   3-5
DISC 12: Black label, dog near top.
❏ RCA AQL1-1707(e) ....'79   3-5
COVER 12: Reflects prefix change, with
"RE1" on back cover.
❏ RCA Victor........................'70s   2-4
INNER SLEEVE 12: Black-and-white.
Pictures RCA Elvis catalog front and back.
Any of several sleeves may be found on
reissues from this period.

RCA Victor (SE)
AQL1-1707(e)................'79   8-15
TOTAL PACKAGE 12: Disc, cover, inner
sleeve.

❏ RCA (M) AFM1-5196.........8/84   5-8
DISC 13: Digitally remastered, quality mono
pressing. Gold "Elvis 50th Anniversary" label.
AFM-5196A-1/AFM1-5196B-1. Identification numbers are
engraved.

❏ RCA AFM1-5196 .... 8/84   5-8
COVER 13: Reflects prefix change. Front: Has white border around edge of cover. Wrapped with gold "The Definitive Rock Classic" banner, listed separately below. Back: UPC bar code at upper right. Spine is white with black print.
INNER SLEEVE 13: White, no printing.

❏ RCA AFM1-5196 .... 8/84   3-5
BANNER 13: Gold stock with black print. Has 50th Anniversary drawing of Elvis. Reads: "A Collectible, the Definitive Rock Classic Restored to Original Mono, Digitally Remastered, Quality Pressing, on Heavy Virgin Vinyl."

RCA (M) AFM1-5196 .... 8/84   15-20
TOTAL PACKAGE 13: Disc, cover, banner.

❏ RCA (M) AFM1-5196 .... '84   3-5
DISC 14: Same as disc 12.

❏ RCA AFM1-5196 .... '84   2-4
COVER 14: Front: Thin white stripes at top and bottom. Wrapped with gold "The Definitive Rock Classic" banner, listed separately below. Back: UPC bar code at upper right. Spine is red with white print.

❏ RCA AFM1-5196 .... 8/84   3-5
BANNER 14: Gold stock with black print. Has 50th Anniversary drawing of Elvis. Reads: "A Collectible, the Definitive Rock Classic Restored to Original Mono, Digitally Remastered, Quality Pressing, on Heavy Virgin Vinyl."

RCA (M) AFM1-5196 .... '84   10-15
TOTAL PACKAGE 14: Disc, cover, banner.

On covers and labels, the electronically reprocessed stereo designation "(e)" may not appear following every usage of the selection number. Covers 12 and 13 are card stock, with printing on cover – not on slicks.

Side 1
Hound Dog
Loving You
All Shook Up
Heartbreak Hotel
Jailhouse Rock
Love Me
Too Much

Side 2
Don't Be Cruel
That's When Your Heartaches Begin
(Let Me Be Your) Teddy Bear
Love Me Tender
Treat Me Nice
Any Way You Want Me (That's How I Will Be)
I Want You, I Need You, I Love You

ELVIS' GOLDEN RECORDS

❏ RCA/BMG (M) 7863-
67462 .... 7/97   5-10
DISC 1: Verification pending.

❏ RCA/BMG (M) 7863-
67462 .... 7/97   5-10
COVER 1: Front: Same cover as earlier issues of this title. Indicates a "limited edition."

**RCA/BMG (M) 7863-
67462 .... 7/97   10-20**
TOTAL PACKAGE 1: Disc, cover, inner sleeve (sleeve verification pending).

Contains the 14 tracks from the original vinyl issue, plus the following bonus tracks:
My Baby Left Me
I Was the One
That's All Right
Baby, Let's Play House
Mystery Train
Blue Suede Shoes

ELVIS' GOLD RECORDS, VOL. 2 (50,000,000 ELVIS FANS CAN'T BE WRONG)

❏ RCA Victor (M)
LPM-2075 .... 12/59   50-75
DISC 1: Black label, "Long Play" at bottom. Title on label is "Elvis' Gold Records, Vol. 2."
K2PP-2713-1S/K2PP-2714-1S. Label LP#1.
K2PP-2713-5S/K2PP-2714-4S. Label LP#1.
K2PP-2713-14S/K2PP-2714-10S. Label LP#2.

❏ RCA Victor LPM-2075 ..... 12/59   100-125
COVER 1: Front: RCA logo and number at upper right. Back: Color, 12" x 12" Elvis photo. No lettering whatsoever.
INNER SLEEVE 1: Generic RCA sleeve. Makes no mention of Elvis or this LP.

**RCA Victor (M)
LPM-2075 .... 12/59   150-200**
TOTAL PACKAGE 1: Disc, cover.

❏ RCA Victor (M)
LPM-2075 .... 11/63   30-40
DISC 2: Black label, "Mono" at bottom.
Label LP#10.

❏ RCA Victor LPM-2075 ..... 11/63   30-40
COVER 2: Front: RCA logo at upper right and number at lower left. Has "RE" at lower right.

❏ RCA Victor (No Number) ...9/63   8-10
INNER SLEEVE 2: Turquoise, black and white. Front: RCA's Elvis LP catalog, most recent being *It Happened at the World's Fair* (side 1, row 4, column 5). Back: RCA Elvis EPs and 45s catalog.

**RCA Victor (M)
LPM-2075 .... 11/63   70-90**
TOTAL PACKAGE 2: Disc, cover, inner sleeve.

❏ RCA Victor (M)
LPM-2075 .... 10/64   10-15
DISC 3: Black label, "Monaural" at bottom. Title on label is "50,000,000 Elvis Presley Fans Can't Be Wrong, Elvis' Gold Records – Vol. 2."
K2PP-2713/K2PP-2714. No take ("S") number used on this pressing. Label LP#1.
K2PP-2713-13S/K2PP-2714-18S. Label LP#12.

❏ RCA Victor LPM-2075 ..... 10/64   20-30
COVER 3: Front: RCA logo at upper right and number at lower left. Has "RE" at lower right. Back: Color, 12" x 12" Elvis photo. Has box of text at upper left "From the Originators of Electronically Reprocessed Stereo." Since this information should only appear on reprocessed stereo releases, its use here is clearly a mistake. Box of text at upper right has "Important" note about playing mono and stereo records, and "Miracle Surface" pitch.

❏ RCA Victor 21-112-1
40A 10/64   4-8
INNER SLEEVE 3: Red, black and white. Front: RCA's Elvis LP catalog, most recent being *Kissin' Cousins* (side 1, row 1, column 6). Back: RCA Elvis EPs and 45s catalog.

RCA Victor (M)
LPM-2075 .... 10/64   **35-55**
TOTAL PACKAGE 3: Disc, cover, inner sleeve.

❏ RCA Victor (M)
LPM-2075 .... 10/64   10-15
DISC 4: Black label, "Monaural" at bottom. Title on label is just "Elvis' Gold Records – Volume 2."
K2PP-2713-17S/K2PP-2714-14S. Label LP#12.

❏ RCA Victor LPM-2075 ..... 10/64   20-30
COVER 4: Same as cover 3.

❏ RCA Victor 21-112-1
40A 10/64   4-8
INNER SLEEVE 4: Red, black and white. Front: RCA's Elvis LP catalog, most recent being *Kissin' Cousins* (side 1, row 1, column 6). Back: RCA Elvis EPs and 45s catalog.

RCA Victor (M)
LPM-2075 .... 10/64   **35-55**
TOTAL PACKAGE 4: Disc, cover, inner sleeve.

❏ RCA Victor (SE)
LSP-2075(e) 2/62   100-150
DISC 5: Black label, RCA logo in silver at top and "Stereo Electronically Reprocessed" at bottom. Title on label is "50,000,000 Elvis Presley Fans Can't Be Wrong, Elvis' Gold Records – Vol. 2."
M2PY-4737-3S/M2PY-4738-3S. Label LP#9.

❏ RCA Victor LSP-2075(e) ... 2/62   10-20
COVER 5: Front: RCA logo and "Stereo Electronically Reprocessed" at upper right and number at upper left. Has "RE" at lower right. Back: Color, 12" x 12" Elvis photo. Has box of text at upper left "From the Originators of Electronically Reprocessed Stereo," box of text at upper right with "Important" note about playing mono and stereo records, and "Miracle Surface" pitch. Price reflects RCA's use of this same cover, with no discernible differences, until 1968.
INNER SLEEVE 5: White, no printing.

RCA Victor (SE)
LSP-2075(e) 2/62   **100-200**
TOTAL PACKAGE 5: Disc, cover.

❏ RCA Victor (SE)
LSP-2075(e) 10/64   10-20
DISC 6: Black label, RCA logo in white at top and "Stereo" at bottom.
M2PY-4737-1S/M2PY-4738-4S. Label LP#15.

❏ RCA Victor
LSP-2075(e) 10/64   10-20
COVER 6: Same as cover 5.

❏ RCA Victor 21-112-1
40A 10/64   4-8
INNER SLEEVE 6: Red, black and white. Front: RCA's Elvis LP catalog, most recent being *Kissin' Cousins* (side 1, row 1, column 6). Back: RCA Elvis EPs and 45s catalog.

RCA Victor (SE)
LSP-2075(e) 10/64   **25-50**
TOTAL PACKAGE 6: Disc, cover, inner sleeve.

❏ RCA Victor (SE)
LSP-2075(e) 11/68   20-25
DISC 7: Orange label. Rigid vinyl.

❏ RCA Victor
LSP-2075(e) 11/68   8-10
COVER 7: Verification pending.

❏ RCA Victor 21-112-1
40D 6/68   4-6
INNER SLEEVE 7: Red, black and white. Front: RCA's Elvis LP catalog, most recent being *Elvis' Gold Records, Vol. 4* (side 1, row 4, column 5). Back: RCA's Elvis LP and Twin Pack Stereo 8 catalog. May also be found with inner sleeves 40B and 40C. See chapter on inner sleeves for more information.

RCA Victor (SE)
LSP-2075(e) 11/68   **30-40**
TOTAL PACKAGE 7: Disc, cover, inner sleeve.

❏ RCA Victor (SE)
LSP-2075(e) .... '71   10-15
DISC 8: Orange label. Flexible vinyl.

❏ RCA Victor LSP-2075(e) ..... '71   4-8
COVER 8: Front: "Victor" and "Stereo Effect Reprocessed from Monophonic" at upper right; "RCA" and number at upper left. Has "SER" at lower left. Back: Color, 12" x 12" Elvis photo. Has box of text about stereo records at upper right and "SER" at lower left.

❏ RCA Victor   2-4
INNER SLEEVE 8: Black-and-white. Pictures RCA Elvis catalog front and back. Any of several sleeves may be found on reissues from this period.

RCA Victor (SE)
LSP-2075(e) .... '71   **15-25**
TOTAL PACKAGE 8: Disc, cover, inner sleeve.

❏ RCA Victor (SE)
LSP-2075(e).........................'76   4-8
DISC 9: Tan label.
M2PY-4737-15S/M2PY-4738-13S.

❏ RCA Victor LSP-2075(e).....'76   4-8
COVER 9: Front: RCA logo at upper left and "Victor" at upper right. "SER" at bottom left. Back: Number at upper right.

❏ RCA Victor..........................'70s   2-4
INNER SLEEVE 9: Black-and-white. Pictures RCA Elvis catalog front and back. Any of several sleeves may be found on reissues from this period.

**RCA Victor (SE)
LSP-2075(e) ....'76   10-20
TOTAL PACKAGE 9: Disc, cover, inner sleeve.**

❏ RCA Victor LSP-2075(e).....'76   4-6
DISC 10: Black label, dog near top.

❏ RCA LSP-2075(e) ....'76   4-6
COVER 10: Reflects logo change.

❏ RCA Victor..........................'70s   2-4
INNER SLEEVE 10: Black-and-white. Pictures RCA Elvis catalog front and back. Any of several sleeves may be found on reissues from this period.

**RCA Victor LSP-2075(e) ..'76   10-18
TOTAL PACKAGE 10: Disc, cover, inner sleeve.**

❏ RCA Victor (SE)
AFL1-2075(e)......................'77   3-5
DISC 11: Black label, dog near top.

❏ RCA AFL1-2075(e)................'77   3-5
COVER 11: Reflects prefix change. Includes copies with a sticker bearing the "AFL1" prefix, wrapped around cover at top of spine.

❏ RCA Victor..........................'70s   2-4
INNER SLEEVE 11: Black-and-white. Pictures RCA Elvis catalog front and back. Any of several sleeves may be found on reissues from this period.

**RCA Victor (SE)
AFL1-2075(e) ....'77   8-15
TOTAL PACKAGE 11: Disc, cover, inner sleeve.**

❏ RCA (M) AFM1-5197.........8/84   5-8
DISC 12: Digitally remastered, quality mono pressing. Gold "Elvis 50th Anniversary" label.
AFM1-5197A-1/AFM1-5197B-1. Identification numbers are engraved.

❏ RCA AFM1-5197 ....8/84   5-8
COVER 12: Reflects prefix change. Wrapped with gold "The Definitive Rock Classic" banner, listed separately below. Back: UPC bar code at upper right.

❏ RCA AFM1-5197 ....8/84   3-5
BANNER 12: Gold stock with black print. Has 50th Anniversary drawing of Elvis. Reads: "A Collectible, the Definitive Rock Classic Restored to Original Mono, Digitally Remastered, Quality Pressing, on Heavy Virgin Vinyl."

**RCA (M) AFM1-5197.......8/84   15-20
TOTAL PACKAGE 11: Disc, cover, banner.**

On covers and labels, the electronically reprocessed stereo designation "(e)" may not appear following every usage of the selection number. Cover 12 is card stock, with printing on cover – not on slicks.

Side 1
I Need Your Love Tonight
Don't
Wear My Ring Around Your Neck
My Wish Came True
I Got Stung

Side 2
One Night
A Big Hunk O' Love
I Beg of You
(Now and Then There's) A Fool Such As I
Doncha' Think It's Time

ELVIS' GOLD RECORDS, VOL. 2 (50,000,000 ELVIS FANS CAN'T BE WRONG)

❏ RCA/BMG (M) 7863-67463 .'97   5-10
DISC 1: Verification pending.

❏ RCA/BMG (M) 7863-67463 .'97   5-10
COVER 1: Front: Same "gold suit" cover as earlier issues of this title. Back: Color Elvis photo, but a different one than on previous issues. Indicates a "limited edition."

**RCA/BMG (M) 7863-67463..........................'97   10-20
TOTAL PACKAGE 1: Disc, cover, inner sleeve (sleeve verification pending).**

Side 1
A Big Hunk O' Love
My Wish Came True
(Now and Then There's) A Fool Such As I
I Need Your Love Tonight
Don't
I Beg of You
Santa Bring My Baby Back (To Me)
Santa Claus Is Back in Town
Party
Paralyzed

Side 2
One Night
I Got Stung
King Creole
Wear My Ring Around Your Neck
Doncha' Think It's Time
Mean Woman Blues
Playing for Keeps
Hard Headed Woman
Got a Lot O' Livin' to Do
(There'll Be) Peace in the Valley (For Me)

ELVIS' GOLDEN RECORDS, VOLUME 3

❏ RCA Victor (M)
   LPM-2765.........................9/63   30-40
   DISC 1: Black label, "Mono" at bottom.
   PPRM-4168-10S/PPRM-4169-1S. Label LP#11.
   PPRM-4168-11S/PPRM-4169-2S. Label LP#1.
   PPRM-4168-12S/PPRM-4169-3S. Label LP#10.

❏ RCA Victor LPM-2765.......9/63   40-50
   COVER 1: Front: RCA logo at upper right and
   number at lower left. Has color photo of Elvis
   in the middle of a gold record. Back: Pictures
   Gold Records, Volumes 1 and 2, and *His
   Hand in Mine.*

❏ RCA Victor (No Number)...9/63   8-10
   INNER SLEEVE 1: Turquoise, black and
   white. Front: RCA's Elvis LP catalog, most
   recent being *It Happened at the World's Fair*
   (side 1, row 4, column 5). Back: RCA Elvis
   EPs and 45s catalog.
   INSERT 1: Some buyers of this LP received
   an 8" x 10" photo booklet from record
   retailers; however, this booklet was not
   packaged with the LP.

RCA Victor (M)
   LPM-2765.....................9/63   80-100
   TOTAL PACKAGE 1: Disc, cover, inner
      sleeve.

❏ RCA Victor (M)
   LPM-2765.......................10/64   10-15
   DISC 2: Black label, "Monaural" at bottom.
   PPRM-4168-12S/PPRM-4169-3S. Label LP#12.
   PPRM-4168-15S/PPRM-4169-6S. Label LP#12.

❏ RCA Victor LPM-2765.....10/64   40-50
   COVER 2: Same as cover 1.

❏ RCA Victor 21-112-1
   40A................................10/64   4-8
   INNER SLEEVE 2: Red, black and white.
   Front: RCA's Elvis LP catalog, most recent
   being *Kissin' Cousins* (side 1, row 1, column
   6). Back: RCA Elvis EPs and 45s catalog.

RCA Victor (M)
   LPM-2765.................10/64   55-70
   TOTAL PACKAGE 2: Disc, cover, inner
      sleeve.

❏ RCA Victor (ST)
   LSP-2765 ....9/63   75-100
   DISC 3: Black label, RCA logo in silver at top
   and "Stereo" at bottom.
   PPRS-4170-3S/PPRS-4171-3S. Label LP#16.
   PPRS-4170-5S/PPRS-4171-5S. Label LP#16.

❏ RCA Victor LSP-2765.......9/63   40-50
   COVER 3: Front: RCA logo at upper right and
   number at upper left. Has color photo of Elvis
   in the middle of a gold record. Back: Pictures
   Gold Records, Volumes 1 and 2, and *His
   Hand in Mine.*

❏ RCA Victor (No Number)...9/63   8-10
   INNER SLEEVE 3: Turquoise, black and
   white. Front: RCA's Elvis LP catalog, most
   recent being *It Happened at the World's Fair*
   (side 1, row 4, column 5). Back: RCA Elvis
   EPs and 45s catalog.
   INSERT 3: Some buyers of this LP received
   an 8" x 10" photo booklet from record
   retailers; however, this booklet was not
   packaged with the LP.

RCA Victor (ST)
   LSP-2765.....................9/63   125-160
   TOTAL PACKAGE 3: Disc, cover, inner
      sleeve.

❏ RCA Victor (ST)
   LSP-2765 ....10/64   10-20
   DISC 4: Black label, RCA logo in white at top
   and "Stereo" at bottom.
   PPRS-4170-3S/PPRS-4171-3S. Label LP#16.

❏ RCA Victor LSP-2765......10/64   10-20
   COVER 4: Same as cover 3.

❏ RCA Victor 21-112-1
   40A 10/64   4-8
   INNER SLEEVE 4: Red, black and white.
   Front: RCA's Elvis LP catalog, most recent
   being *Kissin' Cousins* (side 1, row 1, column
   6). Back: RCA Elvis EPs and 45s catalog.

RCA Victor (ST)
   LSP-2765...................10/64   25-50
   TOTAL PACKAGE 4: Disc, cover, inner
      sleeve.

❏ RCA Victor (ST)
   LSP-2765 ....11/68   20-25
   DISC 5: Orange label. Rigid vinyl.

❏ RCA Victor LSP-2765......11/68   8-10
   COVER 5: Verification pending.

❏ RCA Victor 21-112-1
   40D....................................6/68   4-6
   INNER SLEEVE 5: Red, black and white.
   Front: RCA's Elvis LP catalog, most recent
   being *Elvis' Gold Records, Vol. 4* (side 1, row
   4, column 5). Back: RCA's Elvis LP and Twin
   Pack Stereo 8 catalog. May also be found
   with inner sleeves 40B and 40C. See chapter
   on inner sleeves for more information.

RCA Victor (ST)
   LSP-2765..................11/68   30-40
   TOTAL PACKAGE 5: Disc, cover, inner
      sleeve.

❏ RCA Victor (ST)
   LSP-2765 ....'76   4-8
   DISC 6: Tan label.

❏ RCA Victor LSP-2765..........'76   4-8
   COVER 6: Verification pending.

❏ RCA Victor........................'70s   2-4
   INNER SLEEVE 6: Black-and-white. Pictures
   RCA Elvis catalog front and back. Any of
   several sleeves may be found on reissues
   from this period.

RCA Victor (ST)
LSP-2765.......................'76   10-20
TOTAL PACKAGE 6: Disc, cover, inner
sleeve.

❑ RCA Victor (ST)
LSP-2765 ....'76   4-6
DISC 7: Black label, dog near top.
❑ RCA LSP-2765....................'76   4-6
COVER 7: Verification pending.
❑ RCA Victor.........................'70s   2-4
INNER SLEEVE 7: Black-and-white. Pictures
RCA Elvis catalog front and back. Any of
several sleeves may be found on reissues
from this period.
RCA Victor (ST)
LSP-2765.......................'76   10-18
TOTAL PACKAGE 7: Disc, cover, inner
sleeve.

❑ RCA Victor (ST)
AFL1-2765 ....'77   3-5
DISC 8: Black label, dog near top.
PPRS-4170-14S/PPRS-4171-19S.
❑ RCA AFL1-2765.................'77   3-5
COVER 8: Reflects prefix change. Includes
copies with a sticker bearing the "AFL1"
prefix, wrapped around cover at top of spine.
❑ RCA Victor.........................'70s   2-4
INNER SLEEVE 8: Black-and-white. Pictures
RCA Elvis catalog front and back. Any of
several sleeves may be found on reissues
from this period.
RCA Victor (ST)
AFL1-2765....................'77   8-15
TOTAL PACKAGE 8: Disc, cover, inner
sleeve.

Side 1
It's Now or Never
Stuck on You
Fame and Fortune
I Gotta Know
Surrender
I Feel So Bad

Side 2
Are You Lonesome Tonight
(Marie's the Name) His Latest Flame
Little Sister
Good Luck Charm
Anything That's Part of You
She's Not You

ELVIS' GOLD RECORDS, VOLUME 4

❑ RCA Victor (M)
LPM-3921...........................2/68   750-1000
DISC 1: Black label, "Monaural" at bottom.
UPRM-8481-1S/UPRM-8482-5S. Label LP#12.
❑ RCA Victor LPM-3921 ....2/68   750-1000
COVER 1: Front: RCA logo at upper right and
number at lower left. Has color photo of Elvis
in front of a gold record. Back: Pictures five
other Elvis LPs.

❑ RCA Victor 21-112-1
40C.....................................3/67   4-6
INNER SLEEVE 1: Blue, black and white.
Front: RCA's Elvis LP catalog, most recent
being *Spinout* (side 1, row 2, column 7). Back:
RCA Elvis Stereo 8 catalog.
INSERT: None! The color 8" x 10" Elvis
(circa-1962) photo that is sometimes referred
to as a "Gold IV bonus photo" was never
packaged with this LP. Still, prices in the $200
to $300 range have been paid for this publicity
photo.
RCA Victor (M)
LPM-3921 ....2/68   1500-2000
TOTAL PACKAGE 1: Disc, cover, inner
sleeve.

❑ RCA Victor (SP)
LSP-3921 ....2/68   10-20
DISC 2: Black label, RCA logo in white at top
and "Stereo" at bottom.
UPRS-8483-4S/UPRS-8484-4S. Label LP#16.
UPRS-8483-8S/UPRS-8484-8S. Label LP#16.
❑ RCA Victor LSP-3921........2/68   15-20
COVER 2: Front: RCA logo at upper right and
number at upper left. Has color photo of Elvis
in front of a gold record. Back: Pictures five
other Elvis LPs.
❑ RCA Victor 21-112-1
40C.....................................3/67   4-6
INNER SLEEVE 2: Blue, black and white.
Front: RCA's Elvis LP catalog, most recent
being *Spinout* (side 1, row 2, column 7). Back:
RCA Elvis Stereo 8 catalog.
RCA Victor (SP)
LSP-3921....................2/68   30-50
TOTAL PACKAGE 2: Disc, cover, inner
sleeve.

❑ RCA Victor (SP)
LSP-3921 ....2/68   10-20
DISC 3: Same as disc 2.
❑ RCA Victor LSP-3921........2/68   25-30
COVER 3: Designate promo. Same as cover
2, but with "Not for Sale" stamped on back.
Though the idea of a designate promo of
LPM-3921 (monaural, cover 1) is not
unthinkable, we have yet to verify a copy.
❑ RCA Victor 21-112-1
40C.....................................3/67   4-6
INNER SLEEVE 3: Blue, black and white.
Front: RCA's Elvis LP catalog, most recent
being *Spinout* (side 1, row 2, column 7). Back:
RCA Elvis Stereo 8 catalog.
RCA Victor (SP)
LSP-3921....................2/68   40-60
TOTAL PACKAGE 3: Disc, cover, inner
sleeve.

❑ RCA Victor (SP)
LSP-3921 ....11/68   20-25
DISC 4: Orange label. Rigid vinyl.

❑ RCA Victor LSP-3921......11/68   8-10
COVER 4: Same as cover 2.

❑ RCA Victor 21-112-1
40D...................................6/68   4-6
INNER SLEEVE 4: Red, black and white.
Front: RCA's Elvis LP catalog, most recent
being *Elvis' Gold Records, Vol. 4* (side 1, row
4, column 5). Back: RCA's Elvis LP and Twin
Pack Stereo 8 catalog. May also be found
with inner sleeves 40B and 40C. See chapter
on inner sleeves for more information.

RCA Victor (SP)
LSP-3921...................11/68   30-40
TOTAL PACKAGE 4: Disc, cover, inner
sleeve.

❑ RCA Victor (SP)
LSP-3921.........................11/68   10-15
DISC 5: Orange label. Flexible vinyl.

❑ RCA Victor LSP-3921......11/68   8-10
COVER 5: Same as cover 2, except reflects
logo change and has "RE" at lower left on
front. Back: "RE2" at lower left corner.

❑ RCA Victor 21-112-1
40D...................................6/68   4-6
INNER SLEEVE 5: Red, black and white.
Front: RCA's Elvis LP catalog, most recent
being *Elvis' Gold Records, Vol. 4* (side 1, row
4, column 5). Back: RCA's Elvis LP and Twin
Pack Stereo 8 catalog. May also be found
with inner sleeves 40B and 40C. See chapter
on inner sleeves for more information.

RCA Victor (SP)
LSP-3921...................11/68   20-30
TOTAL PACKAGE 5: Disc, cover, inner
sleeve.

❑ RCA Victor (SP)
LSP-3921 ....'76   10-12
DISC 6: Tan label.

❑ RCA Victor LSP-3921..........'76   10-12
UPRS-8483-13S/UPRS-8484-3S.
COVER 6: Same as cover 2, except reflects
logo change and has "RE" at lower left on
front. Back does not list mono number.

❑ RCA Victor.........................'70s   2-4
INNER SLEEVE 6: Black-and-white. Pictures
RCA Elvis catalog front and back. Any of
several sleeves may be found on reissues
from this period.

RCA Victor (SP)
LSP-3921.......................'76   20-25
TOTAL PACKAGE 6: Disc, cover, inner
sleeve.

❑ RCA Victor (SP)
AFL1-3921 ....'76   10-12
DISC 7: Tan label.

❑ RCA Victor AFL1-3921........'76   10-15
COVER 7: Reflects prefix change. Unusual
because the "AFL1" prefix is printed on both
the label and cover (as opposed to using an
"AFL1" sticker on the jacket to cover the
"LSP" prefix.)

❑ RCA Victor.........................'70s   2-4
INNER SLEEVE 7: Black-and-white. Pictures
RCA Elvis catalog front and back. Any of
several sleeves may be found on reissues
from this period.

RCA Victor (SP)
AFL1-3921.....................'76   25-30
TOTAL PACKAGE 7: Disc, cover, inner
sleeve.

❑ RCA Victor (SP)
LSP-3921 ....'76   4-6
DISC 8: Black label, dog near top.

❑ RCA LSP-3921 ....'76   4-6
COVER 8: Verification pending.

❑ RCA Victor.........................'70s   2-4
INNER SLEEVE 8: Black-and-white. Pictures
RCA Elvis catalog front and back. Any of
several sleeves may be found on reissues
from this period.

RCA Victor (SP)
LSP-3921.......................'76   10-18
TOTAL PACKAGE 8: Disc, cover, inner
sleeve.

❑ RCA Victor (SP)
AFL1-3921...........................'77   3-5
DISC 9: Black label, dog near top.

❑ RCA AFL1-3921 ....'77   3-5
COVER 9: Reflects prefix change. Includes
copies with a sticker bearing the "AFL1"
prefix, wrapped around cover at top of spine.

❑ RCA Victor.........................'70s   2-4
INNER SLEEVE 9: Black-and-white. Pictures
RCA Elvis catalog front and back. Any of
several sleeves may be found on reissues
from this period.

RCA Victor (SP)
AFL1-3921.....................'77   8-15
TOTAL PACKAGE 9: Disc, cover, inner
sleeve.

All songs are stereo except *Ain't That Loving*
You Baby, which was recorded only in
monaural.

Side 1
Love Letters
Witchcraft
It Hurts Me
What'd I Say
Please Don't Drag That String Around
Indescribably Blue

Side 2
Devil In Disguise
Lonely Man
A Mess of Blues
Ask Me
Ain't That Loving You Baby
Just Tell Her Jim Said Hello

ELVIS' GOLD RECORDS, VOLUME 5

❑ RCA Victor (ST)
AFL1-4941 ....2/84   7-10
DISC 1: Black label, dog near top. Flexible
vinyl.
AFL1-4941-A-7S/AFL1-4941-B-7S.

❑ RCA AFL1-4941 ....2/84   8-10
COVER 1: Front: Number at upper right, but
no RCA logo on front. Full color photo of Elvis
from '68 Special. Back: RCA logo and number
at lower right. Has color photo of Elvis in
concert. UPC bar code at upper right.
INNER SLEEVE 1: White, no printing.

RCA Victor (ST)
AFL1-4941 .... 2/84   15-20
TOTAL PACKAGE 1: Disc, cover.

❑ RCA Victor (ST)
AFL1-4941 ....2/84   7-10
DISC 2: Same as disc 1.

❑ RCA AFL1-4941 ....2/84   12-15
COVER 2: Designate promo. Same as cover
1, but with "Not for Sale" stamped on back.
INNER SLEEVE 2: White, no printing.

RCA Victor (ST)
AFL1-4941 .... 2/84   20-25
TOTAL PACKAGE 2: Disc, cover.

Side 1
Suspicious Minds
Kentucky Rain
In the Ghetto
Clean Up Your Own Backyard
If I Can Dream
Side 2
Burning Love
If You Talk in Your Sleep
For the Heart
Moody Blue
Way Down

ELVIS GOSPEL 1957-1971 (KNOWN ONLY TO HIM)

❑ RCA (SP) 9586-1-R.............'89   15-20
DISC 1: Red label, black and silver print with
lightning bolt RCA logo.
9586-1-R-A/9586-1-R-B. Identification numbers are
engraved.

❑ RCA 9586-1-R.....................'89   15-20
COVER 1: Front: No number or logo. Back:
RCA and BMG logos and number at lower left.
UPC bar code at upper right. Duotone photo
of Elvis with the Imperials Quartet (circa
1971).
INNER SLEEVE 1: White, no printing.

RCA (SP) 9586-1-R...........'89   30-40
TOTAL PACKAGE 1: Disc, cover.

❑ RCA (SP) 9586-1-R.............'89   15-20
DISC 2: Same as disc 1.

❑ RCA 9586-1-R ....'89   20-25
COVER 2: Designate promo. Same as cover
1, but with "Not for Sale" stamped on back.
INNER SLEEVE 2: White, no printing.

RCA (SP) 9586-1-R...........'89   35-45
TOTAL PACKAGE 2: Disc, cover.

Card stock jacket, with printing on cover – not
on slicks.

Side A
(There'll Be) Peace in the Valley (For Me)
Take My Hand, Precious Lord
I'm Gonna Walk Dem Golden Stairs
I Believe in the Man in the Sky
Joshua Fit the Battle
Swing Down Sweet Chariot
Stand By Me
Side B
Where Could I Go But to the Lord
Run On
So High
We Call on Him
Who Am I
Lead Me, Guide Me
Known Only to Him

ELVIS – GREATEST HITS VOLUME ONE:
see GREATEST HITS VOLUME ONE

ELVIS' GREATEST SHIT

❑ Dog Vomit SUX-005: Bootleg. Listed for
identification only.

ELVIS: HIS FIRST AND ONLY PRESS
CONFERENCE: see CURRENT AUDIO
MAGAZINE

ELVIS! HIS GREATEST HITS: see HIS
GREATEST HITS

ELVIS HOUR (Discs 1 - 13)

In its entirety, *The Elvis Hour* (on disc) is
made up of 52 individual discs, each with a
one-hour, complete radio show. They were
issued over approximately a three-year
period, in four sets of 13 LPs. Each set and
LP is listed individually below. On all,
identification numbers are engraved.
Recently, these were available from the
producer for $10 each, or $450 for all 52
discs. There are many incorrect titles shown
on the cue sheets for the 52 discs. We have
chosen to use the proper titles and have
made the appropriate corrections.

❑ Creative Radio Shows (SP)
EH-001 ....'86   8-10
DISC 1:
EH-HR1A/EH-HR1B.

❑ Creative Radio Shows (SP)
EH-002 ....'86   8-10
DISC 2:
EH-HR2A/EH-HR2B.

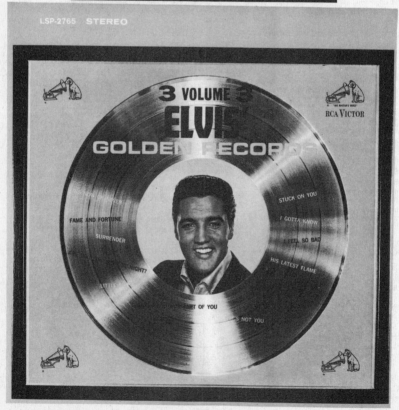

❏ Creative Radio Shows (SP)
   EH-003 .... '86   8-10
   DISC 3:
   EH-HR3A/EH-HR3B.
❏ Creative Radio Shows (SP)
   EH-004 .... '86   8-10
   DISC 4:
   EH-HR4A/EH-HR4B.
❏ Creative Radio Shows (SP)
   EH-005 .... '86   8-10
   DISC 5:
   EH-HR5A/EH-HR5B.
❏ Creative Radio Shows (SP)
   EH-006 .... '86   8-10
   DISC 6:
   EH-HR6A/EH-HR6B.
❏ Creative Radio Shows (SP)
   EH-007 .... '86   8-10
   DISC 7:
   EH-HR7A/EH-HR7B.
❏ Creative Radio Shows (SP)
   EH-008 .... '86   8-10
   DISC 8:
   EH-HR8A/EH-HR8B.
❏ Creative Radio Shows (SP)
   EH-009 .... '86   8-10
   DISC 9:
   EH-HR9A/EH-HR9B.
❏ Creative Radio Shows (SP)
   EH-010 .... '86   8-10
   DISC 10:
   EH-HR10A/EH-HR10B.
❏ Creative Radio Shows (SP)
   EH-011 .... '86   8-10
   DISC 11:
   EH-HR11A/EH-HR11B.
❏ Creative Radio Shows (SP)
   EH-012 .... '86   8-10
   DISC 12:
   EH-HR12A/EH-HR12B.
❏ Creative Radio Shows (SP)
   EH-013 .... '86   8-10
   DISC 13:
   EH-HR13-1/EH-HR13-2.
❏ Creative Radio Shows .... '86   8-10
   INSERT 1A: 13 pages of cue sheets and
   programming information.
❏ Creative Radio Shows .... '86   1-2
   INSERT 1B: Cover letter asking that all
   records be returned after airing.

Creative Radio Shows ..... '86   100-150
TOTAL PACKAGE 1: 13 Discs, inserts.

Disc 1
Side 1
See See Rider
Something
Pledging My Love
My Baby Left Me
The Wonder of You
You Don't Have to Say You Love Me

Side 2
U.S. Male
Suspicious Minds
From a Jack to a King
Return to Sender
Blue Suede Shoes
The Last Farewell
Too Much

Disc 2
Side 1
A Big Hunk O' Love
That's All Right
I Want You, I Need You, I Love You
What'd I Say
Stuck on You
Are You Lonesome Tonight

Side 2
Way Down
Rip It Up
Got a Lot o' Livin' to Do
Don't
Don't Be Cruel
I'll Never Fall in Love Again
Promised Land
Tryin' to Get to You

Disc 3
Side 1
Hound Dog
Heartbreak Hotel
Don't Cry Daddy
Let It Be Me
One Night
In the Ghetto

Side 2
(Now and Then There's) A Fool Such As I
Moody Blue
What Now My Love
Blue Eyes Cryin' in the Rain
Hard Headed Woman
Gospel Medley

Disc 4
Side 1
Jailhouse Rock
(Let Me Be Your) Teddy Bear
All Shook Up
I Can't Stop Loving You
You've Lost That Lovin' Feeling
Good Luck Charm

Side 2
Little Sister
Kentucky Rain
I Got Stung
Don't
It's Now Or Never
Such a Night
Unchained Melody
Little Darlin'

Disc 5
Side 1
Jailhouse Rock
Heartbreak Hotel
I'll Remember You
Hard Headed Woman
Love Me Tender
Are You Lonesome Tonight
(You're the) Devil in Disguise

Side 2

I Really Don't Want to Know
Lawdy, Miss Clawdy
For the Heart
Hound Dog
Got a Lot o' Livin' to Do
She's Not You
Blue Suede Shoes
I'm So Lonesome I Could Cry

Disc 6

Side 1

Treat Me Nice
Love Me Tender
Help Me
Bitter They Are, Harder They Fall
My Baby Left Me
Frankie and Johnny
Love Letters

Side 2

I Got Stung
Steamroller Blues
Burning Love
I Just Can't Help Believing
Miss Misunderstood (David Bellamy)
Tomorrow Never Comes
Rock and Roll Medley

Disc 7

Side 1

Hard Headed Woman
Country Medley
Why Me Lord
Love Me
Blue Suede Shoes
If I Can Dream

Side 2

Mary in the Morning
Make the World Go Away
Patch It Up
I've Lost You
I Beg of You
The Elvis Medley

Disc 8

Side 1

Wear My Ring Around Your Neck
G.I. Blues
Easy Come, Easy Go
Got a Lot o' Livin' to Do
Follow That Dream
Double Trouble
Can't Help Falling in Love

Side 2

Return to Sender
Fever
In the Ghetto
Whole Lot-ta Shakin' Goin' On
The Last Farewell
Any Way You Want Me (That's How I Will Be)
Let Me Be There
Bridge over Troubled Water

Disc 9

Side 1

Stuck on You
Let Yourself Go
She's Not You
Only the Lonely (Roy Orbison)
She Thinks I Still Care
Reconsider, Baby
Make the World Go Away

Side 2

Viva Las Vegas
The Lady Loves Me
One Broken Heart for Sale
Don't
I Just Can't Help Believing
An American Trilogy

Disc 10

Side 1

Too Much
All Shook Up
Don't Be Cruel
Something
If You Talk in Your Sleep
Blue Hawaii
I Need Your Love Tonight

Side 2

From a Jack to a King
Hound Dog
That's All Right
I Got a Woman
Such a Night
You'll Think of Me
My Way

Disc 11

Side 1

Suspicious Minds
Frankfort Special
Wooden Heart
Pocketful of Rainbows
(Marie's the Name) His Latest Flame
Always on My Mind

Side 2

Let Me Be There
Are You Lonesome Tonight
Love Me
The Next Step Is Love
Swing Low, Sweet Chariot
The Impossible Dream
Your Cheating Heart
Tomorrow Never Comes
Johnny B. Goode

Disc 12

Side 1

A Big Hunk O' Love
There Goes My Everything
I Gotta Know
I Keeps Right on A-Hurtin'
I Got Stung
I'll Remember You
I Need Your Love Tonight

Side 2

Young Dreams
King Creole
Gentle on My Mind
When It Rains It Really Pours
Release Me
Have I Told You Lately That I Love You
Trouble/Guitar Man Medley
If I Can Dream

Disc 13
Side 1
I Can't Stop Loving You
Heartbreak Hotel
Hound Dog
All Shook Up
(You're the) Devil in Disguise
That's All Right
Rip It Up
You Don't Have to Say You Love Me
I Really Don't Want to Know
Side 2
Promised Land
Surrender
Wild in the Country
Rock-A-Hula Baby
It's Easy for You
You've Lost That Lovin' Feeling
My Baby Left Me
For the Good Times

ELVIS HOUR (Discs 14 - 26)
☐ Creative Radio Shows (SP)
EH-014 .... '87   8-10
DISC 1:
EH-HR14A/EH-HR14B.
☐ Creative Radio Shows (SP)
EH-015 .... '87   8-10
DISC 2:
EH-HR15A/EH-HR15B.
☐ Creative Radio Shows (SP)
EH-016 .... '87   8-10
DISC 3:
EH-HR16A/EH-HR16B.
☐ Creative Radio Shows (SP)
EH-017 .... '87   8-10
DISC 4:
EH-HR17A/EH-HR17B.
☐ Creative Radio Shows (SP)
EH-018 .... '87   8-10
DISC 5:
EH-HR18A/EH-HR18B.
☐ Creative Radio Shows (SP)
EH-019 .... '87   8-10
DISC 6:
EH-HR19A/EH-HR19B.
☐ Creative Radio Shows (SP)
EH-020 .... '87   8-10
DISC 7:
EH-HR20A/EH-HR20B.
☐ Creative Radio Shows (SP)
EH-021 .... '87   8-10
DISC 8:
EH-HR21A/EH-HR21B.
☐ Creative Radio Shows (SP)
EH-022 .... '87   8-10
DISC 9:
EH-HR22A/EH-HR22B.
☐ Creative Radio Shows (SP)
EH-023 .... '87   8-10
DISC 10:
EH-HR23A/EH-HR23B.
☐ Creative Radio Shows (SP)
EH-024 .... '87   8-10
DISC 11:
EH-HR24A/EH-HR24B.

☐ Creative Radio Shows (SP)
EH-025 .... '87   8-10
DISC 12:
EH-HR25A/EH-HR25B.
☐ Creative Radio Shows (SP)
EH-026 .... '87   8-10
DISC 13:
EH-HR26-A/EH-HR26-B.
☐ Creative Radio Shows .... '87   8-10
INSERT 1A: 13 pages of cue sheets and
programming information.
☐ Creative Radio Shows .... '87   1-2
INSERT 1B: Cover letter asking that all
records be returned to syndicator after airing.
Creative Radio Shows ..... '87   100-150
TOTAL PACKAGE 1: 13 Discs, inserts.

Disc 14
Side 1
Tryin' to Get to You
Blue Suede Shoes (Buddy Holly)
I Forgot to Remember to Forget
When My Blue Moon Turns to Gold Again
Release Me
The Next Step Is Love
Patch It Up
Side 2
Hound Dog
My Baby Left Me
Heartbreak Hotel
Never Gonna Fall in Love Again
Don't Be Cruel
Love Coming Down
You Gave Me a Mountain
Disc 15
Side 1
Hurt
I Got a Woman
Love Me
Just Pretend
What Now My Love
I Feel So Bad
I'll Remember You
Side 2
Follow That Dream
Fun in Acapulco
Jailhouse Rock
Faded Love
Help Me Make It Through the Night
Lawdy, Miss Clawdy
One Night
If I Can Dream
Disc 16
Side 1
Steamroller Blues
Johnny B. Goode
It's Over
I Can't Stop Loving You
You'll Think of Me
Love Me Tender
Side 2
Viva Las Vegas
Tutti Frutti
Stranger in My Own Hometown
Return to Sender
Fever
In the Ghetto
Let It Be Me

Disc 17

Side 1
Good Luck Charm
Plantation Rock
Proud Mary
For Lovin' Me
Tutti Frutti
I Feel So Bad
Rock-A-Hula Baby
(Marie's the Name) His Latest Flame

Side 2
Love Me Tender
King Creole
Didja Ever
I'm Beginning to Forget You
Mary in the Morning
Party
Are You Lonesome Tonight
Never Been to Spain

Disc 18

Side 1
Elvis Hit Medley
Gentle on My Mind
I Was the One
A Big Hunk O' Love
An American Trilogy

Side 2
Shake, Rattle and Roll
I Got a Woman
Memories
Moody Blue
Down By the Riverside (Million Dollar Quartet)
Swing Low, Sweet Chariot
Concert Medley
It's Impossible

Disc 19

Side 1
Trouble
Hurt
(Let Me Be Your) Teddy Bear
Got a Lot o' Livin' to Do
What's She Really Like
(Now and Then There's) A Fool Such As I
Frankfort Special

Side 2
Bossa Nova Baby
Let It Be Me
I Need Your Love Tonight
One Night
Tomorrow Never Comes
(There'll Be) Peace in the Valley (For Me)
I Just Can't Help Believing

Disc 20

Side 1
Blue Suede Shoes
Money Honey
Memories
In the Ghetto
Don't Cry Daddy
Welcome to My World
Wild in the Country
Surrender

Side 2
Help Me Make It Through the Night
G.I. Blues
Frankfort Special
Your Cheating Heart
The Elvis Medley
You've Lost That Lovin' Feeling
Release Me

Disc 21

Side 1
Follow That Dream
Kissin' Cousins
King Creole
Crawfish
Don't Ask Me Why
Return to Sender
Viva Las Vegas
Girls! Girls! Girls!
The Lady Loves Me

Side 2
I Got a Woman/Amen
Love Me
Hawaiian Wedding Song
Let Yourself Go
I've Got a Thing About You Baby
My Way
Can't Help Falling in Love

Disc 22

Side 1
(You're the) Devil in Disguise
You Gave Me a Mountain
I Want You, I Need You, I Love You
Hound Dog
A Big Hunk O' Love
You Don't Have to Say You Love Me
Bridge over Troubled Water

Side 2
The Wonder of You
Tryin' to Get to You
The Last Farewell
That's All Right
You'll Never Walk Alone
It's Now Or Never

Disc 23

Side 1
Johnny B. Goode
And I Love You So
Burning Love
Steamroller Blues
You'll Think of Me
Don't Be Cruel
I'll Remember You

Side 2
She's Not You
Trouble/Guitar Man
Hurt
Muddy Water
Faded Love
How Great Thou Art

Disc 24

Side 1
From a Jack to a King
I Really Don't Want to Know
I Just Can't Help Believing
Rock Hits Medley
When My Blue Moon Turns to Gold Again
Stuck on You

Side 2
What'd I Say
It's Only Make Believe (Conway Twitty)
The Sound of Your Cry
Funny How Time Slips Away
Little Sister
The Impossible Dream
Tryin' to Get to You

Disc 25

Side 1

Heartbreak Hotel
Old Shep
What's She Really Like
When It Rains It Really Pours
That's All Right
Kentucky Rain
Inherit the Wind

Side 2

(Let Me Be Your) Teddy Bear
Blue Suede Shoes
Too Much Monkey Business
Hound Dog
Love Me Tender
Promised Land
What Now My Love
I Love You Because

Disc 26

Side 1

The Wonder of You
Patch It Up
Wear My Ring Around Your Neck
Fairytale
(Now and Then There's) A Fool Such As I
Stuck on You
Follow That Dream
Got a Lot o' Livin' to Do

Side 2

Mean Woman Blues
Let Me Be There
My Baby Left Me
Lawdy, Miss Clawdy
If You Talk in Your Sleep
An American Trilogy

ELVIS HOUR (Discs 27 - 39)

❑ Creative Radio Shows (SP)
EH-027 .... '87　　　 8-10
DISC 1:
EH-HR27A/EH-HR27B.

❑ Creative Radio Shows (SP)
EH-028 .... '87　　　 8-10
DISC 2:
EH-HR28A/EH-HR28B.

❑ Creative Radio Shows (SP)
EH-029 .... '87　　　 8-10
DISC 3:
EH-HR29A/EH-HR29B.

❑ Creative Radio Shows (SP)
EH-030 .... '87　　　 8-10
DISC 4:
EH-HR30A/EH-HR30B.

❑ Creative Radio Shows (SP)
EH-031 .... '87　　　 8-10
DISC 5:
EH-HR31A/EH-HR31B.

❑ Creative Radio Shows (SP)
EH-032 .... '87　　　 8-10
DISC 6:
EH-HR32A/EH-HR32B.

❑ Creative Radio Shows (SP)
EH-033 .... '87　　　 8-10
DISC 7:
EH-HR33A/EH-HR33B.

❑ Creative Radio Shows (SP)
EH-034 .... '87　　　 8-10
DISC 8:
EH-HR34A/EH-HR34B.

❑ Creative Radio Shows (SP)
EH-035 .... '87　　　 8-10
DISC 9:
EH-HR35A/EH-HR35B.

❑ Creative Radio Shows (SP)
EH-036 .... '87　　　 8-10
DISC 10:
EH-HR36A/EH-HR36B.

❑ Creative Radio Shows (SP)
EH-037 .... '87　　　 8-10
DISC 11:
EH-HR37A/EH-HR37B.

❑ Creative Radio Shows (SP)
EH-038 .... '87　　　 8-10
DISC 12:
EH-HR38A/EH-HR38B.

❑ Creative Radio Shows (SP)
EH-039 .... '87　　　 8-10
DISC 13:
EH-HR39-A/EH-HR39-B.

❑ Creative Radio Shows .... '87　　　 8-10
**INSERT 1A: 13 pages of cue sheets and
programming information.**

❑ Creative Radio Shows .... '87　　　 1-2
**INSERT 1B: Cover letter asking that all
records be returned to syndicator after airing.**

Creative Radio Shows ..... '87　　 100-150
TOTAL PACKAGE 1: 13 Discs, inserts.

Disc 27

Side 1

Hound Dog
The Elvis Medley
(Let Me Be Your) Teddy Bear
Loving You
Proud Mary
You've Lost That Lovin' Feeling

Side 2

Ain't That Loving You Baby
Thinking About You
I Can Help
Are You Lonesome Tonight
Hound Dog
Suspicious Minds

Disc 28

Side 1

Mystery Train
I Miss You
Hurt
Shake, Rattle and Roll
Pledging My Love
Steamroller Blues
Witchcraft
Love Letters

Side 2

Crying in the Chapel
Something
Never Been to Spain
Wooden Heart
How Great Thou Art
The Elvis Medley
Can't Help Falling in Love

Disc 29

Side 1

Surrender
Blue Suede Shoes
Don't Cry Daddy
I'm Gonna Sit Right Down and Cry (Over You)
Bitter They Are, Harder They Fall
Don't Think Twice, It's All Right
Playing for Keeps

Side 2

Green, Green Grass of Home
Loving You (Donna Fargo)
What'd I Say
Too Much
Pieces of My Life
Release Me

Disc 30

Side 1

For the Heart
G.I. Blues
Any Way You Want Me (That's How I Will Be)
Viva Las Vegas
It's Impossible
Always on My Mind

Side 2

(You're the) Devil in Disguise
Reddy Teddy
Mean Woman Blues
A Mess of Blues
Bossa Nova Baby
Please Don't Drag That String Around
I Just Can't Help Believing
My Way

Disc 31

Side 1

I Got a Woman/Amen
Love Me
Rock Hits Medley
Tutti Frutti
I'll Take You Home Again Kathleen
Concert Medley

Side 2

Jailhouse Rock
(Marie's the Name) His Latest Flame
Help Me Make It Through the Night
Welcome to My World
You Gave Me a Mountain
From a Jack to a King
Are You Lonesome Tonight

Disc 32

Side 1

I Can't Stop Loving You
Let It Be Me
Let Yourself Go
Little Sister
I Want You, I Need You, I Love You
You Don't Have to Say You Love Me

Side 2

The Next Step Is Love
Burning Love
The Wonder of You
Love Me Tender
Can't Help Falling in Love
The Impossible Dream
What'd I Say

Disc 33

Side 1

Stuck on You
Fame and Fortune

Kentucky Rain
I Was the One
Don't Be Cruel
The Elvis Medley

Side 2

(Now and Then There's) A Fool Such As I
A Big Hunk O' Love
For the Good Times
The Last Farewell
Shake, Rattle and Roll
Johnny B. Goode
Moody Blue
Swing Low, Sweet Chariot
If I Can Dream

Disc 34

Side 1

Release Me
Treat Me Nice
Don't Think Twice, It's All Right
Viva Las Vegas
Promised Land
If I Can Dream

Side 2

See See Rider
I Got a Woman
An American Trilogy
Whole Lot-ta Shakin' Goin' On
Funny How Time Slips Away
Memories
My Way

Disc 35

Side 1

Return to Sender
That's All Right
I'll Remember You
Guitar Man
Movie Songs Medley
Good Luck Charm
She's Not You
You've Lost That Lovin' Feeling

Side 2

Welcome to My World
I'm So Lonesome I Could Cry
Tomorrow Never Comes
Johnny B. Goode
For the Heart
Jailhouse Rock
Blue Suede Shoes
Don't Be Cruel

Disc 36

Side 1

It's Now Or Never
Concert Songs Medley
(You're the) Devil in Disguise
Wild in the Country
I Just Can't Help Believing
Crying in the Chapel
One Broken Heart for Sale
Blue Hawaii

Side 2

Roustabout
You Gave Me a Mountain
I've Got a Thing About You Baby
Are You Lonesome Tonight
Hawaiian Wedding Song
You've Lost That Lovin' Feeling

Disc 37

Side 1
Treat Me Nice
Return to Sender
Hound Dog
Jailhouse Rock
What Now My Love
For the Heart
Baby, I Don't Care

Side 2
I Forgot to Remember to Forget
Mystery Train
Make the World Go Away
Trouble/Guitar Man
I Can't Stop Loving You

Disc 38

Side 1
Wear My Ring Around Your Neck
King Creole
Dixieland Rock
Johnny B. Goode
And I Love You So
It's Only Love
When My Blue Moon Turns to Gold Again
She Thinks I Still Care

Side 2
Young Dreams
Shoppin' Around
I Want You, I Need You, I Love You
Such a Night
Suspicious Minds
The Wonder of You
(There'll Be) Peace in the Valley (For Me)
The Impossible Dream

Disc 39

Side 1
My Baby Left Me
When It Rains It Really Pours
That's All Right
Blue Moon of Kentucky
Pledging My Love
(Let Me Be Your) Teddy Bear
Blue Suede Shoes
Million Dollar Quartet

Side 2
I Was the One
I Love You Because
Love Me
Reddy Teddy
Heartbreak Hotel
Love Letters
Tryin' to Get to You

ELVIS HOUR (Discs 40 - 52)

❏ Creative Radio Shows (SP)
  EH-040 .... '88   8-10
  DISC 1:
  EH-HR40A/EH-HR40B.
❏ Creative Radio Shows (SP)
  EH-041 .... '88   8-10
  DISC 2:
  EH-HR41A/EH-HR41B.
❏ Creative Radio Shows (SP)
  EH-042 .... '88   8-10
  DISC 3:
  EH-HR42A/EH-HR42B.

❏ Creative Radio Shows (SP)
  EH-043 .... '88   8-10
  DISC 4:
  EH-HR43A/EH-HR43B.
❏ Creative Radio Shows (SP)
  EH-044 .... '88   8-10
  DISC 5:
  EH-HR44A/EH-HR44B.
❏ Creative Radio Shows (SP)
  EH-045 .... '88   8-10
  DISC 6:
  EH-HR45A/EH-HR45B.
❏ Creative Radio Shows (SP)
  EH-046 .... '88   8-10
  DISC 7:
  EH-HR46A/EH-HR46B.
❏ Creative Radio Shows (SP)
  EH-047 .... '88   8-10
  DISC 8:
  EH-HR47A/EH-HR47B.
❏ Creative Radio Shows (SP)
  EH-048 .... '88   8-10
  DISC 9:
  EH-HR48A/EH-HR48B.
❏ Creative Radio Shows (SP)
  EH-049 .... '88   8-10
  DISC 10:
  EH-HR49A/EH-HR49B.
❏ Creative Radio Shows (SP)
  EH-050 .... '88   8-10
  DISC 11:
  EH-HR50A/EH-HR50B.
❏ Creative Radio Shows (SP)
  EH-051 .... '88   8-10
  DISC 12:
  EH-HR51A/EH-HR51B.
❏ Creative Radio Shows (SP)
  EH-052 .... '88   8-10
  DISC 13:
  EH-HR352A/EH-HR52-B.
❏ Creative Radio Shows ....'88   8-10
  INSERT 1A: 13 pages of cue sheets and
  programming information.
❏ Creative Radio Shows ....'88   1-2
  INSERT 1B: Cover letter asking that all
  records be returned to syndicator after airing.
Creative Radio Shows ..... '88   100-150
  TOTAL PACKAGE 1: 13 Discs, inserts.

Disc 40

Side 1
All Shook Up
Let Me Be There
Any Day Now
For the Heart
You Don't Have to Say You Love
If You Love Me
I Just Can't Help Believing

Side 2
Stuck on You
Girls! Girls! Girls!
Wooden Heart
Girl of My Best Friend
Any Way You Want Me (That's How I Will Be)
Proud Mary
Blue Suede Shoes
In the Ghetto

Disc 41

Side 1
Good Luck Charm
I Can't Help Believing
Hound Dog
She's Not You
Don't Be Cruel
You've Lost That Lovin' Feeling
Crying in the Chapel
How Great Thou Art

Side 2
See See Rider
That's All Right
Hurt
Fame and Fortune
Got a Lot o' Livin' to Do
Rags to Riches
Too Much Monkey Business
Concert Medley

Disc 43

Side 1
The Wonder of You
It's Only Love
Tutti Frutti
I Was the One
Party
The Lady Loves Me
Pocketful of Rainbows

Side 2
What Now My Love
Polk Salad Annie
I've Lost You
Hard Headed Woman
When My Blue Moon Turns to Gold Again
Reddy Teddy
Witchcraft
He'll Have to Go

Disc 44

Side 1
Little Darlin'
Love Me
Unchained Melody
Tryin' to Get to You
Way Down
Hot Dog
Lover Doll
Burning Love

Side 2
The Last Farewell
Too Much Monkey Business
Didja Ever
Blue Suede Shoes
Mean Woman Blues
Long Tall Sally
Are You Lonesome Tonight
Love Me Tender

Disc 45

Side 1
Whole Lot-ta Shakin' Goin' On
I Don't Care If the Sun Don't Shine
King Creole

Jailhouse Rock
Clean Up Your Own Back Yard
Good Luck Charm
Plantation Rock
I Got a Woman

Side 2
Return to Sender
One Night
The Next Step Is Love
Let It Be Me
That's When Your Heartaches Begin
I'll Remember You

Disc 46

Side 1
Patch It Up
The Elvis Medley
Help Me Make It Through the Night
For the Good Times
Why Me, Lord
Mary in the Morning

Side 2
(Let Me Be Your) Teddy Bear
It's Now Or Never
Treat Me Nice
Thinking About You
Fun in Acapulco
Shoppin' Around
Faded Love
Somebody Bigger Than You and I

Disc 47

Side 1
Suspicious Minds
She Thinks I Still Care
One Broken Heart for Sale
She's Not You
Reconsider, Baby
Lawdy, Miss Clawdy
Steamroller Blues
Are You Sincere

Side 2
Bossa Nova Baby
The Elvis Medley
My Baby Left Me
How Great Thou Art
Tomorrow Never Comes
Let Yourself Go
I Need Your Love Tonight
Are You Sincere

Disc 48

Side 1
Lawdy, Miss Clawdy
One Night
Don't
Mary in the Morning
I Just Can't Help Believing
Girls! Girls! Girls!
Roustabout

Side 2
I've Got a Thing About You Baby
Polk Salad Annie
Hawaiian Wedding Song
High Heel Sneakers
And I Love You So
So Glad You're Mine
You've Lost That Lovin' Feeling

Disc 49

Side 1

Never Been to Spain
Heartbreak Hotel
A Big Hunk O' Love
(Now and Then There's) A Fool Such As I
The Wonder of You
A Mess of Blues
Tomorrow Night
What's She Really Like

Side 2

Wear My Ring Around Your Neck
Don't Be Cruel
Blue Suede Shoes
My Baby Left Me
Love Letters
Playing for Keeps
Burning Love
Can't Help Falling in Love

Disc 50

Side 1

That's All Right
Shake, Rattle and Roll
Let Yourself Go
Doncha' Think It's Time
What'd I Say
I Was the One
All Shook Up
Hound Dog

Side 2

Follow That Dream
Fame and Fortune
That's When Your Heartaches Begin
Suspicious Minds
Promised Land
I'll Remember You
An American Trilogy

Disc 51

Side 1

Whole Lot-ta Shakin' Goin' On
Memories
(Marie's the Name) His Latest Flame
Early Morning Rain
Can't Help Falling in Love
Hurt
Muddy Water

Side 2

Too Much
Bossa Nova Baby
Let It Be Me
(Let Me Be Your) Teddy Bear
Such a Night
You'll Think of Me
Unchained Melody
Concert Medley
It's Impossible

Disc 52

Side 1

(You're the) Devil in Disguise
If You Talk in Your Sleep
Old Shep
Loving You
Jailhouse Rock
Treat Me Nice
I'll Take You Home Again Kathleen
Little Darlin'

Side 2

You Don't Have to Say You Love Me
I Really Don't Want to Know
U.S. Male

Welcome to My World
You Gave Me a Mountain
Let Me Be There
My Baby Left Me
For the Good Times

ELVIS IN CONCERT (2 LPs)

❏ RCA Victor (ST)
   APL2-2587 ....10/77   5-8
   DISCS 1: Blue, custom "Elvis" label.
   (Disc 1) APL2-2587-A-2S/APL2-2587-B-3S. **(Disc 2)** APL2-2587-C-1S/APL2-2587-D-2S. Identification numbers are engraved.
   (Disc 1) APL2-2587A-4S/APL2-2587B-4S. **(Disc 2)** APL2-2587C-5S/APL2-2587D-5S. Identification numbers are stamped on disc 1 and engraved on disc 2.
   (Disc 1) APL2-2587A-7S/APL2-2587B-6S. **(Disc 2)** APL2-2587C-15S/APL2-2587D-15S. Identification numbers are stamped.
   (Disc 1) APL2-2587A-10S/APL2-2587B-10S. **(Disc 2)** APL2-2587C-5S/APL2- 2587D-17S. Identification numbers are stamped.

❏ RCA Victor APL2-2587....10/77   8-12
   COVER 1: Double pocket, full color Elvis photo on each of the four panels. Front: Number at upper right. Back: RCA logo and number at lower left.

❏ RCA Victor 21-112-1
   PT 54F..............................7/77   2-4
   INNER SLEEVE 1: Black-and-white. Pictures RCA's Elvis LPs front and back, most recent being *Moody Blue* (side 2, row 5, column 1).

❏ Boxcar/RCA......................7/77   5-8
   INSERT 1: Four-page, Boxcar/RCA, color brochure. Pictures 18 other Elvis albums, most recent being *Moody Blue.*

RCA Victor (ST)
   APL2-2587 ....10/77   20-30
   TOTAL PACKAGE 1: Discs, cover, inner
      sleeve, insert.

❏ RCA Victor (ST)
   APL2-2587 ....10/77   5-8
   DISCS 2: Same as discs 1.

❏ RCA Victor APL2-2587....10/77   12-15
   COVER 2: Designate promo. Same as cover 1, but with "Not for Sale" stamped on back.

❏ RCA Victor 21-112-1
   PT 54F..............................7/77   2-4
   INNER SLEEVE 2: Black-and-white. Pictures RCA's Elvis LPs front and back, most recent being *Moody Blue* (side 2, row 5, column 1).

❏ Boxcar/RCA......................7/77   5-8
   INSERT 2: Four-page, Boxcar/RCA, color brochure. Pictures 18 other Elvis albums, most recent being *Moody Blue.*

RCA Victor (ST)
   APL2-2587 ....10/77   25-35
   TOTAL PACKAGE 2: Discs, cover, inner
      sleeve, insert.

❏ RCA Victor (ST)
   CPL2-2587 ....'82   10-15
   DISCS 3: Black label, dog near top.

❏ RCA CPL2-2587..................'82   30-35
   COVER 3: Reflects prefix change.
   INNER SLEEVE 3: White, no printing.

RCA Victor (ST)
CPL2-2587 .... '82   **40-50**
TOTAL PACKAGE 3: Discs, cover.

Disc 1
Side 1
Elvis' Fans Comments/Opening Riff
Also Sprach Zarathustra/Opening Riff
See See Rider
That's All Right
Are You Lonesome Tonight
Medley: Teddy Bear/Don't Be Cruel
Elvis' Fans Comments
You Gave Me a Mountain
Jailhouse Rock

Side 2
Elvis' Fans Comments
How Great Thou Art
Elvis' Fans Comments
I Really Don't Want to Know
Elvis Introduces His Father
Closing Riff

Disc 2
Side 3
Medley: I Got a Woman/Amen
Elvis Talks
Love Me
If You Love Me (Let Me Know)
Medley: O Sole Mio (Sherrill Nielsen Solo)/It's Now or
  Never
Trying to Get to You

Side 4
Hawaiian Wedding Song
Fairytale
Little Sister
Early Morning Rain
What'd I Say
Johnny B. Goode
And I Love You So

ELVIS IN HOLLYWOOD (2 LPs)
❑ RCA Special Products (SP)
  DPL2-0168 .... 1/76   **10-15**
  DISCS 1: Blue label, black and white print.
  Flexible vinyl. Sold by Brookville Marketing via
  TV mail order.
  (Disc 1) DPL2-0168-A-1/DPL2-0169-B-2. **(Disc 2)** DPL2-0168-C-1/DPL2- 0169-D-2. Identification numbers are stamped.
  (Disc 1) DPL2-0168-A-3/DPL2-0169-B-3. **(Disc 2)** DPL2-0168-C-3/DPL2-0169-D-4. Identification numbers are engraved.
  (Disc 1) DPL2-0168-A-6/DPL2-0169-B-6. **(Disc 2)** DPL2-0168-C-6/DPL2-0169-D-8. Identification numbers are stamped.
❑ RCA Special Products
  DPL2-0168 .... 1/76   **20-25**
  COVER 1: Single pocket. RCA logo and
  number at upper left, Brookville logo at upper
  right. Color Elvis photos on front and back.
  INNER SLEEVES 1: White, no printing.
❑ Roadshow Merchandise...........   **10-15**
  INSERT 1: "Special TV Edition Photo Album,"
  a 20-page color booklet. On back cover, at
  lower right is "See Elvis in Concert for RCA
  Record Tours." 1977 reissues came with a
  very similar booklet from Boxcar, which has,
  on back at lower right: "Our Sincere Thanks
  for Your Everlasting Loyalty."

❑ RCA Special Products
  DPL2-0168 .... 1/76   **20-25**
  STICKER 1: Yellow 3" x 6" sticker applied
  directly to top left corner. Reads: "2 Record
  Set – 20 Great Songs Plus Photo Album."
  Also lists song titles.

RCA Special Products (SP)
DPL2-0168 .... 1/76   **60-80**
**TOTAL PACKAGE 1: Discs, cover, insert,
  sticker.**

❑ RCA Special Products (SP)
  DPL2-0168 .... 1/76   **10-15**
  DISCS 2: Same as discs 1.
❑ RCA Special Products
  DPL2-0168 .... 1/76   **30-50**
  COVER 2: Same as cover 1, but with a white
  sticker listing times and titles for dee jays.
  Promotional issue only.)
  INNER SLEEVES 2: White, no printing.
❑ Roadshow Merchandise...........   **10-15**
  INSERT 2: "Special TV Edition Photo Album,"
  a 20-page color booklet. On back cover, at
  lower right is "See Elvis in Concert for RCA
  Record Tours." 1977 reissues came with a
  very similar booklet from Boxcar, which has,
  on back at lower right: "Our Sincere Thanks
  for Your Everlasting Loyalty."
❑ RCA Special Products
  DPL2-0168 .... 1/76   **20-25**
  STICKER 2: Yellow 3" x 6" sticker applied
  directly to top left corner. Sticker Reads: "2
  Record Set - 20 Great Songs Plus Photo
  Album." Also lists song titles.

RCA Special Products (SP)
DPL2-0168 .... 1/76   **70-100**
**TOTAL PACKAGE 2: Discs, cover, insert,
  sticker.**

Card stock jacket, with printing on cover – not
on slicks.

Disc 1
Side A
Jailhouse Rock
Rock-A-Hula Baby
G.I. Blues
Kissin' Cousins
Wild in the Country

Side B
King Creole
Blue Hawaii
Fun in Acapulco
Follow That Dream
Girls! Girls! Girls!

Disc 2
Side C
Viva Las Vegas
Bossa Nova Baby
Flaming Star
Girl Happy
Frankie and Johnny

Side D
Roustabout
Spinout
Double Trouble
Charro
They Remind Me Too Much of You

ELVIS IN NASHVILLE (1956 - 1971)

❑ RCA (SP) 8468-1-R............ '88   18-25
DISC 1: Black label, dog on top. Although it
has not been confirmed, this appears to be
the first pressing of this release and the last of
the RCA black labels.
8468-1-R-A/8468-1-R-B. Identification numbers are
handwritten.

❑ RCA 8468-1-R...................... '88   12-15
COVER 1: Front: Blue, with duotone Elvis
photo. No label name or number on front.
Back: Text only. BMG and RCA logos at
bottom. UPC bar code at upper right.
INNER SLEEVE 1: White, no printing.

RCA (SP) 8468-1-R...........'88   30-40
TOTAL PACKAGE 1: Disc, cover.

❑ RCA (SP) 8468-1-R............. '88   18-25
DISC 2: Same as disc 1.
❑ RCA 8468-1-R...................... '88   15-20
COVER 2: Designate promo. Same as cover
1, but with "Not for Sale" stamped on back.
INNER SLEEVE 2: White, no printing.

RCA (SP) 8468-1-R...........'88   35-45
TOTAL PACKAGE 2: Disc, cover.

❑ RCA (SP) 8468-1-R............. '88   8-10
DISC 3: Red label, black and silver print with
lightning bolt RCA logo. This was one of the
first RCA releases to use the Red label.
8468-1-R-A/8468-1-R-B. Identification numbers are
engraved.
❑ RCA 8468-1-R...................... '88   12-15
COVER 3: Same as cover 1.
INNER SLEEVE 3: White, no printing.

RCA (SP) 8468-1-R...........'88   20-25
TOTAL PACKAGE 3: Disc, cover.

❑ RCA (SP) 8468-1-R............. '88   8-10
DISC 4: Same as disc 3.
❑ RCA 8468-1-R...................... '88   15-20
COVER 4: Designate promo. Same as cover
1, but with "Not for Sale" stamped on back.
INNER SLEEVE 4: White, no printing.

RCA (SP) 8468-1-R...........'88   25-30
TOTAL PACKAGE 4: Disc, cover.

❑ RCA (SP) 8468-1-R............. '88   8-10
DISC 3: Black label, dog on top.
8468-1-R-A/8468-1-R-B. Identification numbers are
handwritten.
❑ RCA 8468-1-R...................... '88   8-10
COVER 3: Same as cover 1.
INNER SLEEVE 3: White, no printing.

RCA (SP) 8468-1-R...........'88   15-20
TOTAL PACKAGE 3: Disc, cover.

Card stock jacket, with printing on cover – not
on slicks.

Side 1
I Got a Woman
A Big Hunk O' Love
Working on the Building
Judy
Anything That's Part of You
Night Rider
Where No One Stands Alone

Side 2
Just Call Me Lonesome
Guitar Man
Little Cabin Home on the Hill
It's Your Baby, You Rock It
Early Morning Rain (shown as "Early Mornin' Rain")
It's Still Here
I, John

ELVIS IN PERSON AT THE INTERNATIONAL HOTEL, LAS VEGAS, NEVADA

❑ RCA Victor (ST)
LSP-4428 ....11/70   20-25
DISC 1: Orange label. Rigid vinyl.
XPRS-2468-30S/XPRS-2469-31S.
❑ RCA Victor LSP-4428......11/70   20-25
COVER 1: Front: RCA logo and number at
upper left, "Victor Stereo" at upper right.
Black-and-white Elvis photo. Back: Three
black-and-white Elvis photos.
❑ RCA Victor 21-112-1
pt 54 ....8/70   3-5
INNER SLEEVE 1: Black-and-white. Pictures
RCA's Elvis LP catalog front and back, most
recent being *Worldwide Gold Award Hits, Vol.
1* (side 2, row 4, column 4).

RCA Victor (ST)
LSP-4428................... 11/70   45-55
TOTAL PACKAGE 1: Disc, cover, inner
sleeve.

❑ RCA Victor (ST)
LSP-4428 ....11/70   20-25
DISC 2: Same as disc 1.
❑ RCA Victor LSP-4428......11/70   30-35
COVER 2: Designate promo. Same as cover
1, but with "Not for Sale" stamped on back.
❑ RCA Victor 21-112-1
pt 54 ....8/70   3-5
INNER SLEEVE 2: Black-and-white. Pictures
RCA's Elvis LP catalog front and back, most
recent being *Worldwide Gold Award Hits, Vol.
1* (side 2, row 4, column 4).

RCA Victor (ST)
LSP-4428................... 11/70   55-65
TOTAL PACKAGE 2: Disc, cover, inner
sleeve.

❑ RCA Victor (ST)
LSP-4428 ....'71   10-15
DISC 3: Orange label. Flexible vinyl.
XPRS-2468-5S/XPRS-2469-5S.
❑ RCA Victor LSP-4428...........'71   25-30
COVER 3: Same as cover 1.

❑ RCA Victor 21-112-1
pt 54 ....8/70 3-5
INNER SLEEVE 3: Black-and-white. Pictures
RCA's Elvis LP catalog front and back, most
recent being *Worldwide Gold Award Hits, Vol.
1* (side 2, row 4, column 4).

RCA Victor (ST)
LSP-4428.....................'71 40-50
**TOTAL PACKAGE 3: Disc, cover, inner
 sleeve.**

❑ RCA Victor (ST)
LSP-4428 ....'71 10-15
DISC 4: Same as disc 3.
❑ RCA Victor LSP-4428..........'71 35-40
COVER 4: Designate promo. Same as cover
2.
❑ RCA Victor 21-112-1
pt 54 ....8/70 3-5
INNER SLEEVE 4: Black-and-white. Pictures
RCA's Elvis LP catalog front and back, most
recent being *Worldwide Gold Award Hits, Vol.
1* (side 2, row 4, column 4).

RCA Victor (ST)
LSP-4428.....................'71 50-60
**TOTAL PACKAGE 4: Disc, cover, inner
 sleeve.**

❑ RCA Victor (ST)
LSP-4428 ....'76 10-12
DISC 5: Tan label.
XPRS-2468-6S/XPRS-2469-5S.
❑ RCA Victor LSP-4428..........'76 10-12
COVER 5: Same as cover 1, except has a "3"
on back at lower right.
❑ RCA Victor.....................'70s 2-4
INNER SLEEVE 5: Black-and-white. Pictures
RCA Elvis catalog front and back. Any of
several sleeves may be found on reissues
from this period.

RCA Victor (ST)
LSP-4428.....................'76 20-25
**TOTAL PACKAGE 5: Disc, cover, inner
 sleeve.**

❑ RCA Victor (ST)
LSP-4428 ....'76 4-6
DISC 6: Black label, dog near top.
❑ RCA LSP-4428.................'76 4-6
XPRS-2468-32S/XPRS-2469-35S.
COVER 6: Same as cover 4.
❑ RCA Victor.....................'70s 2-4
INNER SLEEVE 6: Black-and-white. Pictures
RCA Elvis catalog front and back. Any of
several sleeves may be found on reissues
from this period.
RCA Victor (ST)
LSP-4428.....................'76 10-18
**TOTAL PACKAGE 6: Disc, cover, inner
 sleeve.**

❑ RCA Victor (ST)
AFL1-4428............'77 3-5
DISC 7: Black label, dog near top.
❑ RCA AFL1-4428 ....'77 3-5
COVER 7: Reflects prefix change.
Includes copies with a sticker bearing the
"AFL1" prefix, wrapped around cover at top of
spine.
❑ RCA Victor.....................'70s 2-4
INNER SLEEVE 7: Black-and-white. Pictures
RCA Elvis catalog front and back. Any of
several sleeves may be found on reissues
from this period.

RCA Victor (ST)
AFL1-4428.....................'77 8-15
**TOTAL PACKAGE 7: Disc, cover, inner
 sleeve.**

❑ RCA Victor (ST)
AYL1-3892 ....2/81 3-5
DISC 8: Black label, dog near top.
❑ RCA AYL1-3892.................2/81 3-5
COVER 8: Reflects selection number change.
Part of RCA's "Best Buy Series." Includes
copies with a sticker bearing the "AYL1"
prefix, wrapped around cover at top of spine.
INNER SLEEVE 8: White, no printing.
RCA Victor (ST)
AYL1-3892 ....2/81 6-10
TOTAL PACKAGE 8: Disc, cover.

Previously issued as one-half of the two-LP
set *From Memphis to Vegas / From Vegas to
Memphis.*

Side 1
Blue Suede Shoes
Johnny B. Goode
All Shook Up
Are You Lonesome Tonight
Hound Dog
I Can't Stop Loving You
My Babe

Side 2
Medley: Mystery Train/Tiger Man
Words
In the Ghetto
Suspicious Minds
Can't Help Falling in Love

**ELVIS IN THE GREATEST SHOW ON
EARTH: see *GREATEST SHOW ON
EARTH***

ELVIS IS BACK!

❑ RCA Victor (M)
LPM-2231 ....4/60 40-50
DISC 1: Black label, "Long Play" at bottom of
the label.
L2WP-1965-5S/L2WP-1966-5S. Label LP#1. Side 2, song 4
is shown as The Girl Next Door.
L2WP-1965-5S/L2WP-1966-5S. Label LP#12. Side 2, song 4
is *Girl Next Door Went A-Walking.*
L2WP-1965-5S/L2WP-1966-6S. Label LP#1.
L2WP-1965-6S/L2WP-1966-5S. Label LP#1.

❏ RCA Victor LPM-2231 ....4/60   120-125

COVER 1: Gatefold; however, front and back cover slicks are transposed, resulting in the record pocket having the "Elvis Is Back!" (and Elvis in civilian clothes) slick. Contents not printed anywhere on cover. Front: Does *not* have a sticker listing contents. (Does not apply to covers showing any signs of sticker removal.) RCA logo and number in box at upper right. RCA copyright notice at lower left. Inside panels have 15 black-and-white army snapshot Elvis photos. Back: Color Elvis photo.

❏ RCA Victor 21-112-1
Pt. 22C 4/60   8-12

INNER SLEEVE 1: Black, white and red. Pictures *Elvis' Gold Records, Volume 2* (Side 1, row 2, column 4).

❏ RCA Victor...........................'59   30-40

INSERT 1: "Loyal Elvis Fan" 3¾" x 2¼" signature card, with Elvis' picture. Though no marks on card tie it to this LP, it was included with some copies, as well as with some *Touch of Gold* EPs

RCA Victor (M)
LPM-2231 ....4/60   200-225
TOTAL PACKAGE 1: Disc, cover, inner sleeve, insert.

❏ RCA Victor (M)
LPM-2231..........................4/60   40-50
DISC 2: Same as disc 1.

❏ RCA Victor LPM-2231 ....4/60   100-110
COVER 2: Same as cover 1 except does have yellow, 3" x 3¼" contents sticker, applied on front under title. Sticker is permanently affixed to cover and not priced separately.

❏ RCA Victor 21-112-1
Pt. 22C 4/60   8-12
INNER SLEEVE 2: Black, white and red. Pictures *Elvis' Gold Records, Volume 2* (Side 1, row 2, column 4).

RCA Victor (M)
LPM-2231 ....4/60   150-175
TOTAL PACKAGE 2: Disc, cover, inner sleeve.

❏ RCA Victor (M)
LPM-2231.......................11/63   30-40
DISC 3: Black label, "Mono" at bottom.
Label LP#10. On side 2, song 4 is shown as *Girl Next Door Went A-Walking*.
COVER 3: Verification pending.

❏ RCA Victor (No Number)....9/63   8-10
INNER SLEEVE 3: Turquoise, black and white. Front: RCA's Elvis LP catalog, most recent being *It Happened at the World's Fair* (side 1, row 4, column 5). Back: RCA Elvis EPs and 45s catalog.

RCA Victor (M)
LPM-2231 ....11/63   50-75
TOTAL PACKAGE 3: Disc, cover, inner sleeve.

❏ RCA Victor (M)
LPM-2231......................10/64   10-15
DISC 4: Black label, "Monaural" on bottom.
On side 2, song 4 is shown as Girl Next Door Went A-Walking.

❏ RCA Victor LPM-2231 .....10/64   35-50
COVER 4: Gatefold. Front and back cover slicks are correctly applied; record pocket has photo of Elvis in uniform. Front: Contents printed directly on cover, below title. RCA logo and number in box at upper right. RCA copyright notice followed by "RE," at lower left. Inside panels same as cover 1.

❏ RCA Victor 21-112-1
40A...................................10/64   4-8
INNER SLEEVE 4: Red, black and white. Front: RCA's Elvis LP catalog, most recent being *Kissin' Cousins* (side 1, row 1, column 6). Back: RCA Elvis EPs and 45s catalog.

RCA Victor (M)
LPM-2231 ....10/64   50-75
TOTAL PACKAGE 4: Disc, cover, inner sleeve.

❏ RCA Victor (ST)
LSP-2231 ....4/60   100-125
DISC 5: Black label, "Living Stereo" at bottom. Has titles and credits in a type size as tiny as used on any Elvis LP.
L2WP-1967-3S/L2WP-1968-2S. Label LP#7.

❏ RCA Victor LSP-2231........4/60   150-175
COVER 5: Gatefold; however, front and back cover slicks are transposed, resulting in the record pocket having the "Elvis Is Back!" (Elvis in civilian clothes) slick. Contents not printed anywhere on cover. Front: May or may not have sticker listing contents. (Does not apply to covers showing any signs of sticker removal.) RCA logo in box at upper right, number at upper left. Has "Living Stereo" and "Miracle Surface" black stripe across top. RCA copyright notice at lower left. Inside panels have 15 black-and-white army snapshot Elvis photos. Back: Color Elvis photo.
INNER SLEEVE 5: Generic RCA sleeve. Makes no mention of Elvis or this LP.

RCA Victor (ST)
LSP-2231 ....4/60   250-300
TOTAL PACKAGE 5: Disc, cover.

❏ RCA Victor (ST)
LSP-2231 ....10/64   10-20
DISC 6: Black label, RCA logo in white at top and "Stereo" at bottom.
Side 2, song 4 is shown as Girl Next Door Went A-Walking.

❑ RCA Victor LSP-2231...... 10/64   35-50

COVER 6: Gatefold. Front and back cover slicks are correctly applied; record pocket has photo of Elvis in uniform. Front: Contents printed directly on cover, below title. RCA logo in box at upper right, number at upper left. Has "Living Stereo" and "Miracle Surface" black stripe across top. RCA copyright notice followed by "RE," at lower left. Inside panels same as cover 5.

❑ RCA Victor 21-112-1
40A.................................. 10/64   4-8

INNER SLEEVE 6: Red, black and white. Front: RCA's Elvis LP catalog, most recent being *Kissin' Cousins* (side 1, row 1, column 6). Back: RCA Elvis EPs and 45s catalog.

RCA Victor (ST)
LSP-2231.................. 10/64   50-80
TOTAL PACKAGE 6: Disc, cover, inner sleeve.

❑ RCA Victor (ST)
LSP-2231 .... 11/68   20-25
DISC 7: Orange label. Rigid vinyl.
❑ RCA Victor LSP-2231...... 11/68   15-20
COVER 7: Same as cover 6.
❑ RCA Victor 21-112-1
40D..................................... 6/68   4-6
INNER SLEEVE 7: Red, black and white. Front: RCA's Elvis LP catalog, most recent being *Elvis' Gold Records, Vol. 4* (side 1, row 4, column 5). Back: RCA's Elvis LP and Twin Pack Stereo 8 catalog. May also be found with inner sleeves 40B and 40C. See chapter on inner sleeves for more information.

RCA Victor (ST)
LSP-2231.................. 11/68   40-50
TOTAL PACKAGE 7: Disc, cover, inner sleeve.

❑ RCA Victor (ST)
LSP-2231 .... '76   10-12
DISC 8: Tan label.
❑ RCA Victor LSP-2231.......... '76   10-12
COVER 8: Verification pending.
❑ RCA Victor......................... '70s   2-4
INNER SLEEVE 8: Black-and-white. Pictures RCA Elvis catalog front and back. Any of several sleeves may be found on reissues from this period.

RCA Victor (ST)
LSP-2231....................... '76   20-30
TOTAL PACKAGE 8: Disc, cover, inner sleeve.

❑ RCA Victor (ST)
LSP-2231 .... '76   4-8
DISC 9: Black label, dog near top.
L2WP-1967-15S/L2WP-1968-11S. Identification numbers are stamped on side 1 and engraved on side 2.

❑ RCA LSP-2231 .... '76   4-8
COVER 9: Single pocket. Front: RCA logo and number at upper right. Blue border around cover. Has "RE3" at lower left. Back is same as cover 6.
❑ RCA Victor......................... '70s   2-4
INNER SLEEVE 9: Black-and-white. Pictures RCA Elvis catalog front and back. Any of several sleeves may be found on reissues from this period.

RCA Victor (ST)
LSP-2231....................... '76   10-20
TOTAL PACKAGE 9: Disc, cover, inner sleeve.

❑ RCA Victor (ST)
AFL1-2231........................... '77   3-5
DISC 10: Black label, dog near top.
❑ RCA AFL1-2231 .... '77   3-5
COVER 10: Reflects prefix change.
❑ RCA Victor......................... '70s   2-4
INNER SLEEVE 10: Black-and-white. Pictures RCA Elvis catalog front and back. Any of several sleeves may be found on reissues from this period. Includes copies with a sticker bearing the "AFL1" prefix, wrapped around cover at top of spine.

RCA Victor (ST)
AFL1-2231..................... '77   8-15
TOTAL PACKAGE 10: Disc, cover, inner sleeve.

Side 1
Make Me Know It
Fever
The Girl of My Best Friend
I Will Be Home Again
Dirty, Dirty Feeling
Thrill of Your Love

Side 2
Soldier Boy
Such a Night
It Feels So Right
The Girl Next Door
Like a Baby
Reconsider, Baby

ELVIS LAKELAND, FLORIDA SHOW

❑ TCB LSP-1976: Bootleg. Listed for identification only.

ELVIS LEGENDARY CONCERT PERFORMANCES: see *LEGENDARY CONCERT PERFORMANCES*

ELVIS LIVE

❑ Nugget 1071: Bootleg. Listed for identification only.

ELVIS LOVE SONGS: see *LOVE SONGS*

ELVIS MEDLEY

❑ RCA Victor (SP)
AHL1-4530 .... 10/82   5-7
DISC 1: Black label, dog near top. Flexible vinyl.
AHL1-4530-A-1/AHL1-4530-B-1. Both sides have "AHL1-4430-1" engraved, but scratched out with correct number then stamped. Both have "Denny Woodland" engraved.

❑ RCA AHL1-4530 .... 10/82   5-7
COVER 1: Front: RCA logo and number at lower right. Cover's main photo is same as used earlier on *From Elvis Presley Boulevard, Memphis, Tennessee.* Back: Four color Elvis photos. UPC bar code at upper right.
INNER SLEEVE 1: White, no printing.

RCA Victor (SP)
AHL1-4530 .... 10/82   **10-15**
TOTAL PACKAGE 1: Disc, cover.

❑ RCA Victor (SP)
AHL1-4530 .... 10/82   5-7
DISC 2: Same as disc 1.
❑ RCA AHL1-4530 .... 10/82   10-15
COVER 2: Designate promo. Same as cover 1, but with "Not for Sale" stamped on back.
INNER SLEEVE 2: White, no printing.

RCA Victor (SP)
AHL1-4530 .... 10/82   **15-20**
TOTAL PACKAGE 2: Disc, cover.

Card stock jacket, with printing on cover – not on slicks.
Suspicious Minds is monaural on this LP.

Side 1
The Elvis Medley (Jailhouse Rock/Teddy Bear/Don't Be Cruel/ Burning Love/Suspicious Minds)
Jailhouse Rock
(Let Me Be Your) Teddy Bear
Hound Dog
Don't Be Cruel

Side 2
Burning Love
Suspicious Minds
Always on My Mind
Heartbreak Hotel
Hard Headed Woman

ELVIS MEETS THE BEATLES

❑ BSR LTD. ES LP-50: Bootleg. Listed for identification only.

ELVIS MEMORIES . . . (3 LPs)

❑ ABC Radio (SP)
ASP-1003 .... 12/78   300-350
DISCS 1: Boxed, three-LP set supplied by ABC Radio to subscribing stations. Originally broadcast nationwide January 7, 1979.
(Disc 1) ASP-1003-1/ASP-1003-2. **(Disc 2)** ASP-1003-3/ASP-1003-4. **(Disc 3)** ASP-1003-5/ASP-1003-6. Identification numbers are engraved.

❑ ABC Radio ASP-1003 ..... 12/78   125-175
BOX 1: Front: Eight identical duotone "Aloha concert" Elvis photos in a circle, alternating with "Elvis Memories . . . " eight times. Back: Text only.

INNER SLEEVES 1: White, no printing.
❑ ABC Radio ASP-1003 ..... 12/78   20-40
INSERT 1A: 16-page "Program Operation Instructions" booklet.
❑ ABC Radio ASP-1003 ..... 12/78   5-10
INSERT 1B: Four pages of "Commercial/Final Program Instructions."

ABC Radio (SP)
ASP-1003 .... 12/78   **475-575**
TOTAL PACKAGE 1: Discs, box, inserts.

Disc 1

Side 1
Memories
Elvis Memories (Jingle/Logo)
That's All Right
Good Rockin' Tonight
Mystery Train
I Want You, I Need You, I Love You
Heartbreak Hotel

Side 2
Burning Love
Rip It Up
Follow That Dream
Loving You
Love Me Tender
Hound Dog
Don't Be Cruel
Way Down
Moody Blue
(You're the) Devil in Disguise
Suspicion

Disc 2

Side 3
Elvis Memories (Jingle/Logo)
(Marie's the Name) His Latest Flame
All Shook Up
(Let Me Be Your) Teddy Bear
Jailhouse Rock
It's Now Or Never
Elvis Memories (Jingle/Logo)
I Got Stung
One Night
Wear My Ring Around Your Neck
Stuck on You

Side 4
Elvis Memories (Jingle/Logo)
My Wish Came True
Good Luck Charm
And the Grass Won't Pay No Mind
Fame and Fortune
Kentucky Rain
In the Ghetto

Disc 3

Side 5
Viva Las Vegas
Don't Cry Daddy
Separate Ways
You Don't Have to Say You Love Me
Elvis Memories (Jingle/Logo)
Blue Christmas
Are You Lonesome Tonight
Can't Help Falling in Love

Side 6
Elvis Memories (Jingle/Logo)
My Way
How Great Thou Art
Crying in the Chapel
If I Can Dream

The Wonder of You
Memories

ELVIS MEMORIES (MICHELOB PRESENTS HIGHLIGHTS OF *ELVIS MEMORIES*)

❑ ABC/Michelob (SP)
OCC-810 .... 12/78   50-100
DISC 1: Has Michelob logo. Highlights from ABC Radio's three-hour *Elvis Memories*. Distributed exclusively within the Michelob organization.
OCC-810A-1/OCC-810B-2. Identification numbers are stamped on side 1 and engraved on side 2.

❑ ABC/Michelob
OCC-810 .... 12/78   50-100
COVER 1: Front: Michelob logo at upper left. Eight identical duotone "Aloha concert" Elvis photos in a circle, alternating with "Elvis Memories . . . " eight times. Back: Copy of handwritten letter of explanation from Michelob's Bob McDowell. RCA and ABC credits at bottom.
INNER SLEEVES 1: White, no printing.

ABC/Michelob (SP)
OCC-810 .... 12/78   **100-200**
TOTAL PACKAGE 1: Disc, cover.

Card stock jacket, with printing on cover – not on slicks.

Side 1
Memories
Heartbreak Hotel
Love Me Tender
Hound Dog
Don't Be Cruel
Jailhouse Rock
It's Now or Never

Side 2
Viva Las Vegas
Separate Ways
You Don't Have to Say You Love Me
Are You Lonesome Tonight
Can't Help Falling in Love
If I Can Dream

ELVIS MEMORIES (Reel Tape)

❑ ABC Radio 12/78   40-50
TAPE 1: Seven-inch reel tape with "Promotional Ad Spots for Elvis Memories." Sent to subscribing radio stations for advance promotion of their upcoming airing of *Elvis Memories*. Price includes box.

ABC Radio 12/78   **40-50**
TOTAL PACKAGE 1: Tape, box.

❑ ABC Radio 12/78   10-20
TAPE 2: Five-inch reel tape with commercials to be run during the show. Sent to radio stations running *Elvis Memories*. Price includes box.

ABC Radio 12/78   **10-20**
TOTAL PACKAGE 2: Tape, box.

ELVIS MEMORIES – COLLECTOR'S CASSETTE (Tape)

❑ RCA (SP) DPK1-0904 .... '91   5-10
TAPE 1: Not issued on LP, this cassette is packaged in an Elvis Cologne box. Made for and sold only by JCPenney stores.

❑ RCA DPK1-0904 .... '91   3-5
SLIP COVER 1: Has the same artwork as used on "Elvis" Cologne tote bags. Reads: "An exclusive recording, including *Come What May* – released for the first time in an Elvis collection Special Edition."

❑ RCA/Elvis Cologne .... '91   3-5
BOX 1: Cologne box. Front reads: "Cassette Tape, Exclusive Collection of Elvis Recordings." Back lists contents.

❑ RCA (SP) DPK1-0904 .... '91   10-20
TOTAL PACKAGE : Tape, cologne box, slip cover.

Side 1
You Don't Have to Say You Love Me
It's Now Or Never
Come What May
Puppet on a String

Side 2
Can't Help Falling in Love (shown as "*I Can't Help Falling in Love With You*")
(Let Me Be Your) Teddy Bear
Love Letters
Memories

ELVIS MEMORIES ARE FOREVER (ELVIS SPEAKS: HISTORICAL DOCUMENTATION)

❑ Memphis Flash
JL-12645 .... 9/77   10-20
DISC 1: Black label with yellow and red print.
❑ Memphis Flash
JL-12645 .... 9/77   10-20
COVER 1: Front: Color "Aloha" photo of Elvis. Back: Nine color Elvis photos.
INNER SLEEVE 1: White, no printing.

Memphis Flash
JL-12645 .... 9/77   **10-20**
TOTAL PACKAGE 1: Disc, cover.

ELVIS MEMORIES OF CHRISTMAS: see *MEMORIES OF CHRISTMAS*

ELVIS NOW

❑ RCA Victor (ST)
LSP-4671 .... 2/72   10-15
DISC 1: Orange label. Dynaflex vinyl.
APRS-2007-2S/APRS-2008-1S.
APRS-2007-3S/APRS-2008-3S.
APRS-2007-5S/APRS-2008-5S.

❑ RCA Victor LSP-4671 .... 2/72   10-15
COVER 1: Front: RCA logo and number at upper right. Color Elvis photo. Back: Pictures *Worldwide 50 Gold Award Hits, Vol. 1* and *Elvis the Other Sides: Worldwide Gold Award Hits, Vol. 2*.

❏ RCA Victor 21-112-1
PT 54A 8/71   3-5
INNER SLEEVE 1: Black-and-white. Pictures
RCA's Elvis LP catalog front and back, most
recent being *Love Letters from Elvis* (side 2,
row 4, column 5). May also be found with
inner sleeve 55A.
RCA Victor (ST)
LSP-4671.....................2/72   25-35
**TOTAL PACKAGE 1: Disc, cover, inner
sleeve.**

❏ RCA Victor (ST)
LSP-4671 ....2/72   10-15
DISC 2: Same as disc 1.
❏ RCA Victor LSP-4671........2/72   70-80
COVER 2: Same as cover 1 except has white,
4" x 6" contents and running times sticker at
upper left, and cut corner at lower right. Used
for radio station airplay.
❏ RCA Victor 21-112
1PT 54A 8/71   3-5
INNER SLEEVE 2: Black-and-white. Pictures
RCA's Elvis LP catalog front and back, most
recent being *Love Letters from Elvis* (side 2,
row 4, column 5). May also be found with
inner sleeve 55A.
RCA Victor (ST)
LSP-4671.....................2/72   80-100
**TOTAL PACKAGE 2: Disc, cover, inner
sleeve.**

❏ RCA Victor (ST)
LSP-4671 ....'76   12-15
DISC 3: Tan label. Dynaflex vinyl.
APRS-2007-5S/APRS-2008-5S.
❏ RCA Victor LSP-4671..........'76   8-10
COVER 3: Verification pending.
❏ RCA Victor.........................'70s   2-4
INNER SLEEVE 3: Black-and-white. Pictures
RCA Elvis catalog front and back. Any of
several sleeves may be found on reissues
from this period.
RCA Victor (ST)
LSP-4671.......................'76   20-30
**TOTAL PACKAGE 3: Disc, cover, inner
sleeve.**

❏ RCA Victor (ST)
LSP-4671 ....'76   4-6
DISC 4: Black label, dog near top.
❏ RCA LSP-4671....................'76   4-6
COVER 4: Verification pending.
❏ RCA Victor.........................'70s   2-4
INNER SLEEVE 4: Black-and-white. Pictures
RCA Elvis catalog front and back. Any of
several sleeves may be found on reissues
from this period.
RCA Victor (ST)
LSP-4671.......................'76   10-18
**TOTAL PACKAGE 4: Disc, cover, inner
sleeve.**

❏ RCA Victor (ST)
AFL1-4671...........................'77   3-5
DISC 5: Black label, dog near top.
❏ RCA AFL1-4671 ....'77   3-5
COVER 5: Reflects prefix change. Includes
copies with a sticker bearing the "AFL1"
prefix, wrapped around cover at top of spine.
❏ RCA Victor.........................'70s   2-4
INNER SLEEVE 5: Black-and-white. Pictures
RCA Elvis catalog front and back. Any of
several sleeves may be found on reissues
from this period.
RCA Victor (ST)
AFL1-4671.....................'77   8-15
**TOTAL PACKAGE 5: Disc, cover, inner
sleeve.**

Side 1
Help Me Make It Through the Night
Miracle of the Rosary
Hey Jude
Put Your Hand in the Hand
Until It's Time for You to Go
Side 2
We Can Make the Morning
Early Morning Rain
Sylvia
Fools Rush In (Where Angels Fear to Tread)
I Was Born About Ten Thousand Years Ago
Also see *LEGENDARY PERFORMER
(Volume 1) (Experimental Picture Discs)*

ELVIS ON TOUR

❏ Amiga 2-72-020: Bootleg. Listed for
identification only.
❏ Lisa LMP 72-01: Bootleg. Listed for
identification only.

ELVIS PRESLEY

❏ RCA Victor (M)
LPM-1254 ....3/56   125-150
DISC 1: Black label, "Long Play" at bottom.
G2PP-1282-3S/G2PP-1283-5S. Label LP#1.
G2PP-1282-6S/G2PP-1283-5S. Label LP#2.
❏ RCA Victor LPM-1254 ....3/56   175-200
COVER 1: Front: Black-and-white Elvis photo
is centered. RCA logo and number at upper
right. "Elvis" at left in light pink. Back: Four
black-and-white Elvis photos. Number at
upper right. Box of text at lower right explains
"New Orthophonic Recordings," "Blunted
Needles," and "Gruve/Gard."
INNER SLEEVE 1: Generic RCA sleeve. No
mention of Elvis or this LP.
RCA Victor (M)
LPM-1254 ....3/56   300-350
TOTAL PACKAGE 1: Disc, cover.

❏ RCA Victor (M)
LPM-1254 ....11/63   30-40
DISC 2: Black label, "Mono" at bottom.
G2PP-1282-20S/G2PP-1283-12S. Label LP#1.

❑ RCA Victor LPM-1254 ..... 11/63   60-100
COVER 2: Front: Black-and-white Elvis photo
is left of center. RCA logo at upper right and
number and "RE" at lower left. "Elvis" at left in
dark pink. Back: Four black-and-white Elvis
photos. Number at upper right followed by
"RE." Box of text at lower right is replaced by
"Important" notes on mono/stereo and
"Miracle Surface."

❑ RCA Victor (No Number)... 9/63   8-10
INNER SLEEVE 2: Turquoise, black and
white. Front: RCA's Elvis LP catalog, most
recent being *It Happened at the World's Fair*
(side 1, row 4, column 5). Back: RCA Elvis
EPs and 45s catalog.

RCA Victor (M)
LPM-1254 .... 11/63   100-150
TOTAL PACKAGE 2: Disc, cover, inner
sleeve.

❑ RCA Victor (M)
LPM-1254 .... 10/64   20-30
DISC 3: Black label, "Monaural" at bottom.

❑ RCA Victor LPM-1254 ..... 10/64   25-35
COVER 3: Verification pending.

❑ RCA Victor 21-112-1
40A 10/64   4-8
INNER SLEEVE 3: Red, black and white.
Front: RCA's Elvis LP catalog, most recent
being *Kissin' Cousins* (side 1, row 1, column
6). Back: RCA Elvis EPs and 45s catalog.

RCA Victor (M)
LPM-1254 .... 10/64   50-75
TOTAL PACKAGE 3: Disc, cover, inner
sleeve.

❑ RCA Victor (SE)
LSP-1254(e) 2/62   100-150
DISC 4: Black label, RCA logo in silver at top
and "Stereo Electronically Reprocessed" at
bottom.
M2PY-4727-3S/M2PY-4728-3S. Label LP#9.
M2PY-4727-8S/M2PY-4728-2S. Label LP#9. Identification
numbers are engraved on side 1 and stamped on side 2.

❑ RCA Victor LSP-1254(e) ... 2/62   100-150
COVER 4: Front: RCA logo and "Stereo
Electronically Reprocessed" at upper right
and number at upper left. Has "RE" at lower
right. Back: Four black-and-white Elvis
photos. Has box of text at upper left "From the
Originators of Electronically Reprocessed
Stereo," and box of text at lower right with
"Important" note about playing mono and
stereo records, and "Miracle Surface" pitch.
INNER SLEEVE 4: White, no printing.

RCA Victor (SE)
LSP-1254(e) 2/62   200-300
TOTAL PACKAGE 4: Disc, cover.

❑ RCA Victor (SE)
LSP-1254(e) 10/64   10-20
DISC 5: Black label, RCA logo in white at top
and "Stereo" at bottom.

❑ RCA Victor
LSP-1254(e) 10/64   15-20
COVER 5: Same as cover 4, except has a "2"
at lower left on back.

❑ RCA Victor 21-112-1
40A 10/64   4-8
INNER SLEEVE 5: Red, black and white.
Front: RCA's Elvis LP catalog, most recent
being *Kissin' Cousins* (side 1, row 1, column
6). Back: RCA Elvis EPs and 45s catalog.

RCA Victor (SE)
LSP-1254(e) 10/64   30-50
TOTAL PACKAGE 5: Disc, cover, inner
sleeve.

❑ RCA Victor (SE)
LSP-1254(e) 11/68   20-25
DISC 6: Orange label. Rigid vinyl.

❑ RCA Victor 11/68   10-20
COVER 6: Verification pending.

❑ RCA Victor 21-112-1
40D 6/68   4-6
INNER SLEEVE 6: Red, black and white.
Front: RCA's Elvis LP catalog, most recent
being *Elvis' Gold Records, Vol. 4* (side 1, row
4, column 5). Back: RCA's Elvis LP and Twin
Pack Stereo 8 catalog. May also be found
with inner sleeves 40B and 40C. See chapter
on inner sleeves for more information.

RCA Victor (SE)
LSP-1254(e) 11/68   30-50
TOTAL PACKAGE 6: Disc, cover, inner
sleeve.

❑ RCA Victor (SE)
LSP-1254(e) .... '76   5-10
DISC 7: Tan label.

❑ RCA LSP-1254(e) .... '76   8-10
COVER 7: Verification pending.

❑ RCA Victor .... '70s   2-4
INNER SLEEVE 7 Black-and-white. Pictures
RCA Elvis catalog front and back. Any of
several sleeves may be found on reissues
from this period.

RCA Victor (SE)
LSP-1254(e) .... '76   15-25
TOTAL PACKAGE 7: Disc, cover, inner
sleeve.

❑ RCA Victor (SE)
LSP-1254(e) .... '76   4-6
DISC 8: Black label, dog near top.

❑ RCA LSP-1254(e) .... '76   4-6
COVER 8: Verification pending.

❑ RCA Victor .... '70s   2-4
INNER SLEEVE 8: Black-and-white. Pictures
RCA Elvis catalog front and back. Any of
several sleeves may be found on reissues
from this period.

RCA Victor (SE)
LSP-1254(e) ....'76   10-18
**TOTAL PACKAGE 8: Disc, cover, inner
sleeve.**

❏ RCA Victor (SE)
AFL1-1254(e) ....'77   3-5
DISC 9: Black label, dog near top.
❏ RCA AFL1-1254(e).............'77   3-5
COVER 9: Reflects prefix change. Includes
copies with a sticker bearing the "AFL1"
prefix, wrapped around cover at top of spine.
❏ RCA Victor.........................'70s   2-4
INNER SLEEVE 9 Black-and-white. Pictures
RCA Elvis catalog front and back. Any of
several sleeves may be found on reissues
from this period.

RCA Victor (SE)
AFL1-1254(e) ....'77   8-15
**TOTAL PACKAGE 9: Disc, cover, inner
sleeve.**

❏ RCA Victor (SE)
AFL1-1254(e) ....'77   3-5
DISC 10: Black label, dog near top.
❏ RCA AFL1-1254(e).............'77   8-10
COVER 10: Designate promo. Same as cover
9, but with "Not for Sale" stamped on back.
❏ RCA Victor.........................'70s   2-4
INNER SLEEVE 10 Black-and-white. Pictures
RCA Elvis catalog front and back. Any of
several sleeves may be found on reissues
from this period.

RCA Victor (SE)
AFL1-1254(e) ....'77   15-20
**TOTAL PACKAGE 10: Disc, cover, inner
sleeve.**

❏ RCA (M) AFM1-5198.........8/84   5-8
DISC 11: Digitally remastered, quality mono
pressing. Gold "Elvis 50th Anniversary" label.
AFM1-5198A-1/AFM1-5198B-1. Identification numbers are
engraved.
AFM1-5198A-1/AFM1-5198B-2. Identification numbers are
engraved.
❏ RCA AFM1-5198 ....8/84   5-8
COVER 11: Reflects number change.
Wrapped with gold "The Definitive Rock
Classic" banner, listed separately below.
Back: UPC bar code at upper right. This cover
is made of card stock, with printing on cover –
not on slicks.
❏ RCA AFM1-5198 ....8/84   3-5
BANNER 11: Gold stock with black print. Has
50th Anniversary drawing of Elvis. Reads: "A
Collectible, the Definitive Rock Classic
Restored to Original Mono, Digitally
Remastered, Quality Pressing, on Heavy
Virgin Vinyl."

RCA (M) AFM1-5198.......8/84   15-20
TOTAL PACKAGE 11: Disc, cover.

On both covers and labels, the electronically
reprocessed stereo designation "(e)" may not
appear following every usage of the selection
number.

Side 1
Blue Suede Shoes
I'm Counting on You
I Got a Woman
One-Sided Love Affair
I Love You Because
Just Because

Side 2
Tutti Frutti
Tryin' to Get to You
I'm Gonna Sit Right Down and Cry (Over You)
I'll Never Let You Go (Little Darlin')
Blue Moon
Money Honey
Also see *LEGENDARY PERFORMER
(Volume 1) (Experimental Picture Discs)*

ELVIS PRESLEY

❏ Singer's SODD-13: Bootleg. Listed for
identification only.

ELVIS PRESLEY BIRTHDAY
TRIBUTE

Complete four-hour radio show with songs
and interviews.
❏ United Stations (SP) Elvis
BO-5 ....1/89   100-150
DISCS 1: Four LPs, numbered 1, 2, 3, and 4.
❏ United Stations Elvis
BO-5 ....1/89   25-40
COVER 1: Single-pocket cover.
❏ United Stations Elvis
BO-5 ....1/89   5-10
INSERT 1: Four pages of cue sheets and
program notes.

United Stations (SP) Elvis
BO-5 ....1/89   130-200
TOTAL PACKAGE : Disc, cover, inserts.

For individual birthday radio shows from
United Stations, see *SOLID GOLD COUNTRY
(All-Elvis Shows)*

ELVIS PRESLEY COLLECTION
(3 LPs)

❏ RCA Special Products (SP)
DML3-0632.......................7/84   20-30
DISCS 1: Black label, dog near top. Flexible
vinyl. Boxed set produced for mail order sales
by Candlelite Music.
(Side 1) DML3-0632A-1/DML30632B-2. (Side 2) DML3-
0632C-1/DML30632D-1. (Side 3) DML3-0632E-
1/DML30632F-1.
❏ RCA Special Products
DML3-0632.......................7/84   45-55
BOX 1: Front: Pink and black, with black-and-
white Elvis photo. Candlelite logo at upper left
and number at lower right. RCA number at
lower left. Back of box is blank.
INNER SLEEVES 1: White, no printing.

❏ RCA Special Products
DML3-0632 ....7/84   10-15
INSERT 1: Twelve-page, 12" x 12"
photo/story booklet.
RCA Special Products (SP)
DML3-0632..................7/84   **75-100**
TOTAL PACKAGE 1: Discs, box, insert.

Disc 1

Side 1
Don't Be Cruel
Loving You
Trouble
I Was the One
When My Blue Moon Turns to Gold Again

Side 2
Are You Lonesome Tonight
Hard Headed Woman
Don't
Little Sister

Disc 2

Side 3
One Night
A Big Hunk O' Love
(Marie's the Name) His Latest Flame
I Got Stung
I Want You, I Need You, I Love You

Side 4
Jailhouse Rock
The Wonder of You
Too Much
Love Me

Disc 3

Side 5
All Shook Up
Heartbreak Hotel
Crying in the Chapel
(Let Me Be Your) Teddy Bear
Can't Help Falling in Love

Side 6
Hound Dog
Love Me Tender
Return to Sender
It's Now or Never

ELVIS PRESLEY (1954-1961) (2 LPs)

❏ Time-Life (SP) STL-106 ....9/86   8-10
DISCS 1: Custom "Rock 'N' Roll Era" label.
One in a series of mail order "Rock 'N' Roll
Era" sets from Time-Life. Sold only by Time-
Life via mail order.
(Disc 1) STL-106A-1/STL-106B-5. **(Disc 2)** STL-106C-
1/STL-106DB-1.

❏ Time-Life STL-106.............9/86   12-15
BOX 1: Front: Two color Elvis portraits. Time-
Life logo at lower left. Back: Text only.
INNER SLEEVES 1: White, only printing is
Time-Life logo.

❏ Time-Life STL-106.............9/86   2-4
INSERT 1: Black-and-white, 11¾" x 18"
poster/brochure.
Time-Life (SP) STL-106..9/86   25-30
TOTAL PACKAGE 1: Discs, box, insert.

Disc 1

Side 1
That's All Right
Heartbreak Hotel
Hound Dog
Love Me Tender
Don't Be Cruel
All Shook Up

Side 2
I Want You, I Need You, I Love You
Jailhouse Rock
Love Me
(Let Me Be Your) Teddy Bear
Too Much

Disc 2

Side 3
Hard Headed Woman
One Night
Wear My Ring Around Your Neck
(Now and Then There's) A Fool Such As I
Don't
A Big Hunk O' Love

Side 4
It's Now or Never
Stuck on You
Are You Lonesome Tonight
Little Sister
Can't Help Falling in Love

ELVIS PRESLEY INTERVIEW RECORD – AN AUDIO SELF-PORTRAIT

❏ RCA (M) DJM1-0835 ....10/84   40-50
DISC 1: Gold "Elvis 50th Anniversary" label.
Promotional issue only.
DJM1-0835-A-1/DJM1-0835-B-1. Both sides have "DJL1"
engraved, then crossed out and "DJM1" added. Identification
numbers are engraved. Both sides have "January 8th, 1935"
stamped. Commercially issued as *Elvis Talks!*
DJM1-0835-A-1/DJM1-0835-B-2. Both sides have "DJL1"
engraved, then crossed out and "DJM1" added. Identification
numbers are engraved. Both sides have "January 8th, 1935"
stamped.
DJM1-0835-A-1S/DJM1-0835-B-2S. Both sides have "DJL1"
engraved, then crossed out and "DJM1" added. Identification
numbers are engraved. Both sides have "January 8th, 1935"
stamped.

❏ RCA DJM1-0835 ....10/84   40-50
COVER 1: Front: Black stock with gold and
white print. RCA logo and number at lower
left. Back: Pictures six LP releases from the
"Golden Celebration."
INNER SLEEVE 1: White, no printing.
RCA (M) DJM1-0835 .....10/84   80-100
TOTAL PACKAGE 1: Disc, cover.

Side 1
The 1956 Interviews
Elvis Presley: Excerpt from a *TV Guide* Interview 1956
Colonel Tom Parker: Excerpt from a *TV Guide*
     Interview 1956
Vernon and Gladys Presley: Tupelo, Mississippi,
     September 26,1956
Elvis Presley: Tupelo, Mississippi, September 26, 1956

Side 2
The 1960-61 Interview
Image Change Since Discharge from the Army – By
     Accident or Design?
Elvis Talks About His Mother
How Does Elvis View Himself?

Does He Enjoy His Work?
How Does He Relax?
Does He Have Any Time to Read? If So, What Does He Read?
Does He Like Himself?
Does He Like to Work?
If He Were Starting Out Again (in 1961) Would He Do Anything Differently? Does He Have Any Specific Goals for the Future?
Does He Think He Has Changed Much As a Person?
How Does He View the Criticism That Has Been Leveled at Some of the People Surrounding Him?
If He Were a Father and Could Only Give His Child One Piece of Advice, What Would That Be?

ELVIS PRESLEY IS ALIVE AND WELL AND SINGING IN LAS VEGAS, VOL. 1

❏ Kings' Voice: Bootleg. Listed for identification only.

ELVIS PRESLEY – STILL THE KING (4 LPs)

Complete three-hour radio show. All discs in this set, listed individually below, have a red label with white print. All identification numbers are engraved.

❏ Westwood (S) EP-87 .... '87		30-40
DISC 1:		
ETK-87-1/ETK-87-5.		
❏ Westwood (S) EP-87 .... '87		30-40
DISC 2:		
ETK-87-2/ETK-87-6.		
❏ Westwood (S) EP-87 .... '87		30-40
DISC 3:		
ETK-87-3/ETK-87-7.		
❏ Westwood (S) EP-87 .... '87		30-40
DISC 4:		
ETK-87-4/ETK-87-8.		
COVER: White, no printing.		
Westwood (S) EP-87 .... '87		**120-160**
TOTAL PACKAGE 1: Discs.		

ELVIS PRESLEY STORY (1975) (13 LPs)

Complete 13-hour radio show. All discs in this set, listed individually below, have a white label with black print except for "Elvis Presley," which is in pink. They also have a 1975 copyright date at bottom. On all discs, identification numbers and a 1974 copyright date are engraved. A 12-hour version of this program aired in 1971 but was produced only on reel tapes.

❏ Watermark (M) 1A/2B .... '75	50-60
DISC 1:	
EPS-1A/EPS-2B.	
❏ Watermark (M) 1B/3A .... '75	50-60
DISC 2:	
EPS-1B/EPS-1B.	
❏ Watermark (M) 2A/3B .... '75	50-60
DISC 3:	
EPS-2A/EPS-3B.	

❏ Watermark (M) 4A/5B .... '75	50-60
DISC 4:	
EPS-4A/EPS-5B.	
❏ Watermark (SP) 6A/4B .... '75	50-60
DISC 5:	
EPS-6A/EPS-5B.	
❏ Watermark (SP) 5A/6B .... '75	50-60
DISC 6:	
EPS-5A/EPS-6B.	
❏ Watermark (S) 7A/8B .... '75	50-60
DISC 7:	
EPS-7A/EPS-8B.	
❏ Watermark (S) 9A/7B .... '75	50-60
DISC 8:	
EPS-9A/EPS-7B.	
❏ Watermark (S) 8A/9B .... '75	50-60
DISC 9:	
EPS-8A/EPS-9B.	
❏ Watermark (S) 10A/13B ...... '75	50-60
DISC 10:	
EPS-10A/EPS-13B.	
❏ Watermark (S) 12A/10B ...... '75	50-60
DISC 12:	
EPS-12A/EPS-10B.	
❏ Watermark (S) 11A/12B ...... '75	50-60
DISC 12:	
EPS-11A/EPS-12B.	
❏ Watermark (S) 13A/11B ...... '75	50-60
DISC 13:	
EPS-13A/EPS-11B.	
INNER SLEEVES: White, no printing.	
❏ Watermark .... '75	75-100
INSERT 1: 48-page programmer's "Manual of Operations."	
Watermark .... '75	**750-900**
TOTAL PACKAGE 1: Discs, insert.	

Chapter 1
Side A
Introduction: Medley of Elvis' Hits
Old Shep
Jesus Knows What I Need (Comparison of versions by the Statesmen Quartet and by Elvis)

Side B
That's All Right (Arthur Crudup)
Hound Dog (Willie Mae Thornton)
Early '50s Medley: Harbor Lights (Sammy Kaye)/Rag Mop (Ames Brothers)/Tennessee Waltz (Patti Page)/Cry of the Wild Goose (Frankie Lane)/You Belong to Me (Jo Stafford)/My Heart Cries for You (Guy Mitchell)/Come-On-A My House (Rosemary Clooney)/Cry (Johnny Ray)
Working on the Building (Comparison of versions by the Blackwood Brothers and by Elvis)

Chapter 2
Side A
That's All Right
Blue Moon of Kentucky
Good Rockin' Tonight
You're a Heartbreaker
Just Because

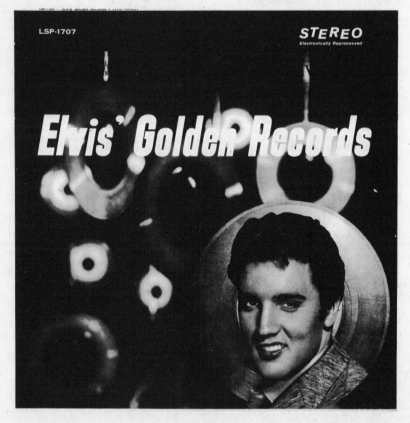

Side B

Milkcow Blues Boogie
The Truth About Me
Baby Let's Play House
I'm Left, You're Right, She's Gone
Blue Moon
I Forgot to Remember to Forget
Mystery Train

Chapter 3

Side A

Heartbreak Hotel
I Was the One
Heartbreak Hotel (Stan Freberg)
Medley: Reddy Teddy/Blueberry Hill/Money Honey/Rip
    It Up/I Got a Woman/Lawdy Miss Clawdy/Long Tall
    Sally/Shake, Rattle and Roll/Tutti Frutti
Blue Suede Shoes
I Want You, I Need You, I Love You

Side B

Hound Dog
Don't Be Cruel
Love Me
Love Me Tender
One-Sided Love Affair
Too Much

Chapter 4

Side A

All Shook Up
Loving You
(Let Me Be Your) Teddy Bear
Gotta Lot O' Livin' to Do
(There'll Be) Peace in the Valley (For Me)

Side B

Medley of Songs about Elvis
Party
Jailhouse Rock
Baby I Don't Care
Oh Little Town of Bethlehem
Blue Christmas
Don't

Chapter 5

Side A

King Creole
Dear 53310761 (The Thirteens)
Wear My Ring Around Your Neck
Hard Headed Woman
If We Never Meet Again
Elvis Sails Interview

Side B

Trouble
I Got Stung
(Now and Then There's) A Fool Such As I
My Wish Came True
A Big Hunk O' Love
I Will Be Home Again

Chapter 6

Side A

I'm Hanging Up My Rifle (Bill Parsons)
Dirty, Dirty Feeling
Stuck On You
It's Now Or Never
Fever
G.I. Blues

Side B

Wooden Heart
Flaming Star
Are You Lonesome Tonight
I Slipped, I Stumbled, I Fell
His Hand in Mine

Surrender
I'm Comin' Home

Chapter 7

Side A

Medley of Elvis' Film Songs
Blue Hawaii
I Feel So Bad
Can't Help Falling in Love
Good Luck Charm
Return to Sender

Side B

One Broken Heart for Sale
Medley of Elvis' Film Songs
Bossa Nova Baby
Happy Ending
Memphis, Tennessee
Fun in Acapulco

Chapter 8

Side A

(You're the) Devil in Disguise
Santa Lucia
What'd I Say
Crying in the Chapel
Ain't That Loving You Baby
Your Cheatin' Heart

Side B

Little Egypt
Medley of Silly Elvis Film Songs
Down by the Riverside/When the Saints Go Marching
    In
Puppet on a String
Do the Clam
When It Rains It Really Pours

Chapter 9

Side A

Old MacDonald
Long Lonely Highway
Down in the Alley
Tomorrow Is a Long Time
Paradise Hawaiian Style

Side B

If Everyday Was Like Christmas
There Ain't Nothing Like a Song
He's Your Uncle, Not Your Dad
Big Boss Man
How Great Thou Art

Chapter 10

Side A

Guitar Man
U.S. Male
A Little Less Conversation
Memories
Yellow Rose of Texas/The Eyes of Texas
If I Can Dream

Side B

Songs from NBC-TV Special
Only the Strong Survive
Gentle on My Mind
In the Ghetto

Chapter 11

Side A

Songs from *Elvis in Person at the International Hotel,*
    Las Vegas, Nevada
Don't Cry Daddy
Kentucky Rain

Side B
Songs from *On Stage*
You've Lost That Lovin' Feeling
The Wonder of You
The Next Step Is Love

Chapter 12
Side A
Patch It Up
Bridge over Troubled Water
Rags to Riches
There Goes My Everything
Whole Lot'ta Shakin' Goin' On
I'm Leavin'

Side B
Help Me Make It Through the Night
An American Trilogy
Don't Think Twice
Also Sprach Zarathustra/See See Rider
Hound Dog
Burning Love
It's a Matter of Time

Chapter 13
Side A
Separate Ways
My Way
I'm So Lonesome I Could Cry
Raised on Rock
Talk About the Good Times
Steamroller Blues

Side B
Medley of Elvis Hits
I've Got a Thing About You Baby
Help Me
Promised Land

ELVIS PRESLEY STORY (1977) (13 LPs)

Revised edition to reflect the death of Elvis.
All discs in this set have a white label with
black print except for "Elvis Presley," which is
in blue. They also have a 1977 copyright date
at bottom. On all discs, identification numbers
and a 1977 copyright date are engraved.
INNER SLEEVES: White, no printing.

❑ Watermark............................ '77　　50-100
INSERT 1: 48-page programmer's "Manual of
Operations."

Watermark........................ '77　　600-750
TOTAL PACKAGE 1: Discs, insert.

Price is based on $45 to $50 per disc, instead
of $50 to $60, as shown for the 1975 edition.
The contents of the 1977 edition are exactly
the same as those for the 1975 edition, with
the following exceptions:

Chapter 1
Side A
August 16, 1977 news bulletin regarding Elvis' death is
added.

Chapter 12
Side A
Revised script regarding Elvis' concert tours.

Chapter 13
Side B
Medley of Elvis' Hits
I've Got a Thing About You Baby
Medley of Elvis' Hits Through 1977

ELVIS PRESLEY STORY (5 LPs)
❑ RCA Special Products (SP)
DML5-0263........................7/77　　30-40
DISCS 1: Black label, dog near top. Flexible
vinyl. Boxed set produced for mail order sales
by Candlelite Music.
(Disc 1) DML5-0263A-1/DML5-0263B-1. (Disc 2) DML5-
0263C-1/DML5-0263D-1. (Disc 3) DML5-0263E-1/DML5-
0263F-1. (Disc 4) DML5- 0263G-1/DML5-0263H-1. (Disc
5) DML5-0263I-1/DML5-0263J-1.
(Disc 1) DML5-0263A-2/DML5-0263B-2. (Disc 2) DML5-
0263C-2/DML5-0263D-2. (Disc 3) DML5-0263E-2/DML5-
0263F-3. (Disc 4) DML5- 0263G-2/DML5-0263H-2. (Disc
5) DML5-0263I-2/DML5-0263J-3.

❑ RCA Special Products
DML5-0263........................7/77　　20-35
BOX 1: Slipcover: Black with white and
yellow/gold lettering. Has color Elvis portrait.
RCA Special Products logo and number at
lower right. Candlelite logo at upper left. Back
is blank. Record case: Contents and liner
notes on front. Back is blank.
INNER SLEEVES 1: White, no printing.

RCA Special Products (SP)
DML5-0263................. 7/77　　50-75
TOTAL PACKAGE 1: Discs, box.

Disc 1
Side 1
It's Now or Never
Treat Me Nice
For the Good Times
I Got Stung
Ask Me
Return to Sender

Side 2
The Wonder of You
Hound Dog
Make the World Go Away
(Marie's the Name) His Latest Flame
Loving You

Disc 2
Side 3
One Night
You Don't Know Me
Blue Christmas
Good Luck Charm
Blue Suede Shoes
Surrender

Side 4
In the Ghetto
Too Much
Help Me Make It Through the Night
I Was the One
Love Me
Little Sister

Disc 3

Side 5

Can't Help Falling in Love
Trouble
Memories
Wear My Ring Around Your Neck
Blue Hawaii
Burning Love

Side 6

Love Me Tender
Stuck on You
Funny How Time Slips Away
All Shook Up
Puppet on a String
Jailhouse Rock

Disc 4

Side 7

Heartbreak Hotel
Can't Help Falling in Love
I Just Can't Help Believing
I Beg of You
Don't Cry Daddy
Hard Headed Woman
Are You Lonesome Tonight

Side 8

(Let Me Be Your) Teddy Bear
Hawaiian Wedding Song
A Big Hunk O' Love
I'm Yours
(Now and Then There's) A Fool Such As I
Don't

Disc 5

Side 9

I Want You, I Need You, I Love You
Kissin' Cousins
I Can't Stop Loving You
(You're the) Devil in Disguise
Suspicion
Don't Be Cruel

Side 10

She's Not You
From a Jack to a King
I Need Your Love Tonight
Wooden Heart
Have I Told You Lately That I Love You
You Don't Have to Say You Love Me
Also see *ELVIS – HIS SONGS OF INSPIRATION*

ELVIS PRESLEY STORY

❏ EAP: Bootleg. Listed for identification only.

ELVIS PRESLEY SUN COLLECTION: see
SUN COLLECTION

ELVIS PRESLEY YEARS (7 LPs)

Various artists collection

Mail order offer only. All discs in this set have a black, white and red label, and are listed individually below. All sides have two Elvis tracks and four tracks by various artists from that same year or years. All identification numbers are engraved.

❏ Reader's Digest/BMG
  RBA-236A-1 .... '91   3-6
  DISC 1: 1954-1955/1956
  X1RS-5901-3/X1RS-5902-3.

❏ Reader's Digest/BMG
  RBA-236A-2 .... '91   3-6
  DISC 2: 1957/1958
  X1RS-5903-3/X1RS-5904-1.

❏ Reader's Digest/BMG
  RBA-236A-3 .... '91   3-6
  DISC 3: 1959/1960-1961
  X1RS-5905-2/X1RS-5906-3.

❏ Reader's Digest/BMG
  RBA-236A-4 .... '91   3-6
  DISC 4: 1962-1963/1964-1965
  X1RS-5907-3/X1RS-5908-1.

❏ Reader's Digest/RCA Music Service
  RBA-236A-5 .... '91   3-6
  DISC 5: 1966-1967/1968-1969
  X1RS-5909-1/X1RS-5910-1.

❏ Reader's Digest/BMG
  RBA-236A-6 .... '91   3-6
  DISC 6: 1970-1971/1972-1973
  X1RS-5911-5/X1RS-5912-2.

❏ Reader's Digest/BMG
  RBA-236A-7 .... '91   3-6
  DISC 7: 1974-1975/1976-1977
  X1RS-5913-1/X1RS-5914-1.

❏ Reader's Digest/BMG
  RBA-236A .... '91   15-20
  BOX 1: Front: Large portrait of Elvis, with smaller ones of Buddy Holly, Chuck Berry, the Beach Boys, Linda Ronstadt, Donna Summer, and the Supremes. Reader's Digest/BMG logo and number at lower right. Back is blank. Record case: Blue with blue and red print. Back is blank.
  INNER SLEEVES 1: Generic, individually numbered, plastic sleeves. Front and Back: Clear, covered with Reader's Digest Pegasus logos. No mention of Elvis.

❏ Reader's Digest/BMG .... '91   5-7
  INSERT 1: 3" x 3" information and program notes booklet.

Reader's Digest/BMG (SP)
  RBA-236A .... '91   40-60
  TOTAL PACKAGE 1: Discs, box, insert.

ELVIS RECORDED LIVE ON STAGE IN MEMPHIS

❏ RCA Victor (ST)
  CPL1-0606 .... 6/74   8-10
  DISC 1: Orange label. Dynaflex vinyl. Title shown on label is "Elvis As Recorded Live on Stage in Memphis." (No "As" on cover.)
  CPL1-0606A-1S/CPL1-0606B-1S.
  CPL1-0606A-2S/CPL1-0606B-2S.

❏ RCA CPL1-0606 .... 6/74   12-15
  COVER 1: Front: Pictures the Graceland mansion. RCA logo and number at upper left, Mid-South Coliseum logo at upper right. Back: Pictures the entrance to Graceland.

❑ RCA Victor 21-112-1
PT56D.............................6/74   3-5
INNER SLEEVE 1: Black-and-white. Pictures
RCA Elvis cassette tape catalog front and
back, most recent being *Elvis, Aloha from
Hawaii via Satellite* (side 2, row 3, column 5).

RCA Victor (ST)
CPL1-0606 ....6/74   25-30
TOTAL PACKAGE 1: Disc, cover, inner
sleeve.

❑ RCA Victor (ST)
DJL1-0606.........................6/74   150-200
DISC 2: Orange label. Dynaflex vinyl.
Banded edition for radio stations, made so
dee jays could easily select a specific track for
airplay. Promotional issue only.....
DJL1-0606C-3S/DJL1-0606D-3S.

❑ RCA CPL1-0606...............6/74   150-200
COVER 2: Same as cover 1 except has white,
4" x 6" contents and running times sticker at
upper left. Promo number (DJL1-0606)
appears only on sticker; not on cover. Title
shown on sticker is "Elvis As Recorded Live
on Stage in Memphis."

❑ RCA Victor 21-112-1
PT56D.............................6/74   3-5
INNER SLEEVE 2: Black-and-white. Pictures
RCA Elvis cassette tape catalog front and
back, most recent being *Elvis, Aloha from
Hawaii via Satellite* (side 2, row 3, column 5).

RCA Victor (ST)
DJL1-0606..................6/74   300-400
TOTAL PACKAGE 2: Disc, cover, inner
sleeve.

❑ RCA (Q) APD1-0606.........6/74   100-150
DISC 3: Quadradisc. Orange label. Flexible
vinyl. Reportedly, this pressing has some
dialogue by Elvis which can only be heard on
a quad system. We can neither confirm this,
nor can we describe the variation. Neither this
disc nor any of the covers show "Victor."
APD1-0606A-1Q/APD1-0606B-3Q.

❑ RCA APD1-0606 ....6/74   100-150
COVER 3: Front: Same photo of Graceland
used on cover 1, but reduced about 15% to fit
within a black border. Back: Same as cover 1
except for prefix change. Has Quadradisc
logo at top center.

❑ RCA Victor 21-112-1
PT56D.............................6/74   3-5
INNER SLEEVE 3: Black-and-white. Pictures
RCA Elvis cassette tape catalog front and
back, most recent being *Elvis, Aloha from
Hawaii via Satellite* (side 2, row 3, column 5).

RCA (Q) APD1-0606 ....6/74   200-300
TOTAL PACKAGE 3: Disc, cover, inner
sleeve.

❑ RCA Victor (ST)
CPL1-0606..........................'76   10-15
DISC 4: Tan label.

❑ RCA Victor CPL1-0606........'76   8-10
COVER 4: Verification pending.

❑ RCA Victor........................'70s   2-4
INNER SLEEVE 4: Black-and-white. Pictures
RCA Elvis catalog front and back. Any of
several sleeves may be found on reissues
from this period.

RCA Victor (ST)
CPL1-0606 ....'76   20-30
TOTAL PACKAGE 4: Disc, cover, inner
sleeve.

❑ RCA Victor (ST)
AFL1-0606...........................'77   3-5
DISC 5: Black label, dog near top.

❑ RCA Victor AFL1-0606........'77   3-5
AFL1-0606A-31/AFL1-0606B-30. On both sides, "CP" is
stamped but crossed out, and "AF" is stamped below.
COVER 5: Reflects prefix change.
Includes copies with a sticker bearing the
"AFL1" prefix, wrapped around cover at top of
spine.

❑ RCA Victor........................'70s   2-4
INNER SLEEVE 5: Black-and-white. Pictures
RCA Elvis catalog front and back. Any of
several sleeves may be found on reissues
from this period.

RCA Victor (ST)
AFL1-0606.....................'77   8-15
TOTAL PACKAGE 5: Disc, cover, inner
sleeve.

❑ RCA Victor (ST)
AQL1-4776 ....'79   3-5
DISC 6: Black label, dog near top.

❑ RCA Victor AQL1-4776 ....'79   3-5
COVER 6: Reflects number change.

❑ RCA Victor........................'70s   2-4
INNER SLEEVE 6: Black-and-white. Pictures
RCA Elvis catalog front and back. Any of
several sleeves may be found on reissues
from this period.

RCA Victor (ST)
AQL1-4776 ....'79   8-15
TOTAL PACKAGE 6: Disc, cover, inner
sleeve.

Side 1
See See Rider
I Got a Woman
Love Me
Tryin' to Get to You
Medley: Long Tall Sally/Whole Lot-ta Shakin' Goin'
    On/Your Mama Don't Dance/Flip, Flop and Fly
Jailhouse Rock/Hound Dog
Why Me
How Great Thou Art

Side 2

Medley: Blueberry Hill/I Can't Stop Loving You
Help Me
An American Trilogy
Let Me Be There
My Baby Left Me
Lawdy, Miss Clawdy
Can't Help Falling in Love
Closing Vamp

ELVIS REMEMBERED (3 LPs)

Complete three-hour radio show with songs and interviews.

❏ Creative Radio Shows (M)
1A-3B .... '77   275-300
DISCS 1: White, unprinted labels with handwritten "Elvis HR 1A/B," "HR- 2A/B," "HR-3A/B" on each disc.
(Disc 1) 816-1A/816-1B. **(Disc 2)** 816-2A/816-2B. **(Disc 3)** 816-3A/816-3B. Identification numbers are engraved.
COVER 1: None issued.

❏ Creative Radio Shows
1A-3B .... '77   5-10
INSERT 1A: Three pages of cue sheets with programming information.

❏ Creative Radio Shows .... '77   2-3
INSERT 1B: One page, "Handling Instructions."

❏ Creative Radio Shows .... '77   2-3
INSERT 1C: Flyer advertising radio shows featuring: Elvis, Beatles, Beach Boys, Buddy Holly; Frank Sinatra, and John Wayne.

Creative Radio Shows (M)
1A-3B .... '77   300-375
TOTAL PACKAGE 1: Discs, inserts.

❏ Creative Radio Shows (M)
1A-3B .... '78   85-95
DISCS 2: Printed labels; silver stock with black print. Otherwise, same as discs 1.

❏ Creative Radio Shows
1A-3B .... '78   5-10
INSERT 2A: Three pages of cue sheets with programming information.

❏ Creative Radio Shows .... '78   2-3
INSERT 2B: One page, "Handling Instructions."

Creative Radio Shows (M)
1A-3B .... '78   90-110
TOTAL PACKAGE 2: Discs, inserts.

Disc 1

Side 1

Heartbreak Hotel
Medley of Elvis Hits
Medley: Hound Dog/King Creole/Don't Be Cruel/(Let Me Be Your) Teddy Bear/Blue Suede Shoes/Reconsider Baby/Hard Headed Woman/Loving You
All Shook Up
That's All Right
I Really Don't Want to Know
Hound Dog
Make the World Go Away

Side 2

Jailhouse Rock

I Forgot to Remember to Forget
Money Honey
Are You Sincere
You Gave Me a Mountain
Such a Night
Fame and Fortune

Disc 2

Side 1

Medley: I Got Stung/A Big Hunk O' Love/One Broken Heart for Sale/Return to Sender/Surrender/Down by the Riverside
How Great Thou Art
Treat Me Nice
I Can't Stop Loving You/I Got a Woman/Amen
I Want You, I Need You, I Love You
Where Did They Go Lord

Side 2

It's Now or Never
In the Ghetto
I Beg of You
She Wears My Ring
Wear My Ring Around Your Neck

Disc 3

Side 1

Love Me Tender
I Can Help
(Now and Then There's) A Fool Such As I
Crying in the Chapel
If I Can Dream
Suspicious Minds
My Way

Side 2

See See Rider
Hurt
There Goes My Everything
Green, Green Grass of Home
There's a Honky-Tonk Angel (Who'll Take Me Back In)
Memories
Also see *Elvis Remembered* in the EP chapter.

ELVIS ROCKS AND THE GIRLS ROLL

❏ Pink & Black LPM-1510: Bootleg. Listed for identification only.

ELVIS ROCKS LITTLE ROCK

❏ Bilko LPM-1589: Bootleg. Listed for identification only.

ELVIS, SCOTTY AND BILL – THE FIRST YEAR: see *FIRST YEAR*

ELVIS SINGS COUNTRY FAVORITES

❏ Reader's Digest/RCA Music Service (SP)
RDA-242/D .... '84   25-30
DISC 1: Black, white and red label. Mail order bonus from Reader's Digest with the purchase of *The Great Country Entertainers*.
PIRS-5746-1/PIRS-5747-1

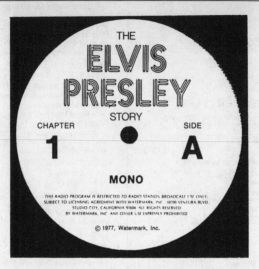

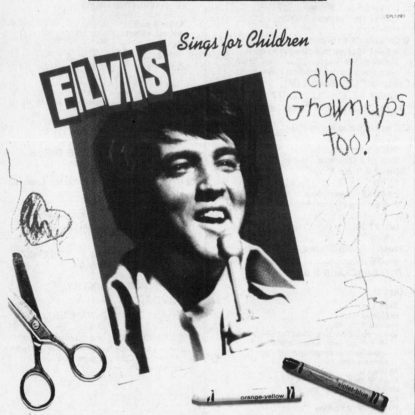

❏ Reader's Digest/RCA Music
RDA-242/D.......................... '84   25-45
COVER 1: Front: Reader's Digest and RCA
Music Service logos at lower right. Color Elvis
photo. Back: Contents and a picture of a
guitar.
INNER SLEEVE 1: White, no printing.

**Reader's Digest/RCA Music Service
(SP) RDA-242/D .... '84   50-75**
TOTAL PACKAGE 1: Disc, cover.

Card stock jacket, with printing on cover – not
on slicks.

Side 1
Make the World Go Away
I'm Movin' On
Are You Lonesome Tonight
Faded Love
Your Cheatin' Heart
Gentle on My Mind

Side 2
Release Me
Welcome to My World
I Can't Stop Loving You
Funny How Time Slips Away
I'm So Lonesome I Could Cry
You Gave Me a Mountain

ELVIS SPECIAL

❏ Bootleg. Listed for identification only.

❏ **ELVIS SINGS BURNING LOVE: see**
BURNING LOVE

ELVIS SINGS FLAMING STAR
(Camden)

❏ RCA/Camden (SP)
CAS-2304.......................... 4/69   15-20
DISC 1: Blue label. Rigid vinyl. Repackage of
*Singer Presents Elvis Singing Flaming Star
and Others.*
WCRS-8154-3S/WCRS-8155-3S.

❏ RCA/Camden CAS-2304...4/69   15-20
COVER 1: Front: RCA logo and number at
upper left, Camden logo and "Stereo" at upper
right. Color Elvis (*Stay Away Joe*) photo.
Back: Pictures six other Elvis LPs (four
volumes of *Gold Hits*, and two sacred
albums.) Has a "1" at lower left.
INNER SLEEVE 1: White, no printing. (Some
Camden LPs had no inner sleeves at all.)

**RCA/Camden (SP)
CAS-2304 .... 4/69   30-40**
TOTAL PACKAGE 1: Disc, cover.

❏ RCA/Camden (SP)
CAS-2304.......................... 4/69   15-20
DISC 2: Same as disc 1.
❏ RCA/Camden CAS-2304...4/69   20-25
COVER 2: Designate promo. Same as cover
1, but with "Not for Sale" stamped on back.
INNER SLEEVE 2: White, no printing. (Some
Camden LPs had no inner sleeves at all.)

❏ RCA/Camden (SP)
CAS-2304 .... 4/69   35-45
TOTAL PACKAGE 2: Disc, cover.

❏ RCA/Camden (SP)
CAS-2304.......................... '69   15-20
DISC 3: Same as disc 1.
❏ RCA/Camden CAS-2304..... '69   8-10
COVER 3: Same as cover 1, except has a "2"
or "3" at lower left on back.
INNER SLEEVE 3: White, no printing. (Some
Camden LPs had no inner sleeves at all.)

**RCA/Camden (SP)
CAS-2304 .... '69   25-30**
TOTAL PACKAGE 3: Disc, cover.

❏ RCA/Camden (SP)
CAS-2304.......................... '69   10-15
DISC 4: Blue label. Flexible vinyl.
❏ RCA/Camden CAS-2304..... '69   8-10
COVER 4: Same as cover 1, except has a "2"
or "3" at lower left on back.
INNER SLEEVE 4: White, no printing. (Some
Camden LPs had no inner sleeves at all.)

**RCA/Camden (SP)
CAS-2304 .... '69   20-25**
TOTAL PACKAGE 4: Disc, cover.

Tiger Man is monaural, all other tracks are
stereo.

Side 1
Flaming Star
Wonderful World
Night Life
All I Needed Was the Rain
Too Much Monkey Business

Side 2
Yellow Rose of Texas/The Eyes of Texas
She's a Machine
Do the Vega
Tiger Man

ELVIS SINGS FLAMING STAR
(Pickwick)

❏ Pickwick/Camden (SP)
CAS-2304........................ 12/75   2-4
DISC 1: Black label. Multi-color Pickwick logo
at center.
CAS-2304-A/CAS-2304-B.
❏ Pickwick/Camden
CAS-2305........................ 12/75   3-4
COVER 1: Front: Pickwick logo at upper left,
Camden logo and number at upper right.
Color Elvis (*Stay Away Joe*) photo. Back:
Pictures two Camden Elvis LPs.
INNER SLEEVE 1: White, no printing.

**Pickwick/Camden (SP)
CAS-2304 .... 12/75   5-10**
TOTAL PACKAGE 1: Disc, cover.

❏ Pickwick/Camden (SP)
CAS-2304........................ 12/76   2-4
DISC 2: Same as disc 1.

❑ Pickwick/Camden
CAS-2304........................12/76   2-3
COVER 2: Same as cover 1, except has a "2" at lower left on back. Copies may exist with a "3," as is the case with the RCA/Camden release.

Pickwick/Camden (SP)
CAS-2304 .... 12/76   4-8
TOTAL PACKAGE 2: Disc, cover.

Side 1
Flaming Star
Wonderful World
Night Life
All I Needed Was the Rain
Too Much Monkey Business

Side 2
Yellow Rose of Texas/The Eyes of Texas
She's a Machine
Do the Vega
Tiger Man

ELVIS SINGS FOR CHILDREN AND GROWNUPS TOO!

❑ RCA Victor (SP)
CPL1-2901 ....7/78   4-6
DISC 1: Black label, dog near top.
CPL1-2901-A/CPL1-2901-B. Identification numbers are engraved.
CPL1-2901A-1S/CPL1-2901-B-1S. Identification numbers are stamped
CPL1-2901A-2S/CPL1-2901-B-1S. Identification numbers are stamped.

❑ RCA CPL1-2901................7/78   5-8
COVER 1: Gatefold. Front: Color Elvis photo. Number at upper right. Back: Has a removable "Special Memories of Elvis Greeting Card" attached to the back cover. Greeting card is described and priced separately below. Under the removable card, printed on the cover, is a photo of the front of the greeting card. Has two slits cut to hold card in place. Inside panels have only contents and lyrics. This marked the first time an Elvis LP came with printed lyrics.

❑ RCA Victor 21-112-1
PT 54F 7/77   2-4
INNER SLEEVE 1: Black-and-white. Pictures RCA's Elvis LPs front and back, most recent being *Moody Blue* (side 2, row 5, column 1). May also be found with unprinted, white inner sleeve.

❑ Boxcar...............................7/78   3-5
INSERT 1: Attached to back cover is a 5½" x 6¾" "Special Memories of Elvis Greeting Card."

RCA Victor (SP)
CPL1-2901 .... 7/78   15-25
TOTAL PACKAGE : Disc, cover, inner sleeve, insert.

❑ RCA Victor (SP)
CPL1-2901 ....7/78   4-6
DISC 2: Same as disc 1.

❑ RCA CPL1-2901................7/78   5-10
COVER 2: Designate promo. Same as cover 1, but with "Not for Sale" stamped on back.

❑ RCA Victor 21-112-1
PT 54F 7/77   2-4
INNER SLEEVE 2: Black-and-white. Pictures RCA's Elvis LPs front and back, most recent being *Moody Blue* (side 2, row 5, column 1). May also be found with unprinted, white inner sleeve.

❑ Boxcar...............................7/78   3-5
INSERT 2: Attached to back cover is a 5½" x 6¾" "Special Memories of Elvis Greeting Card."

RCA Victor (SP)
CPL1-2901 .... 7/78   20-30
TOTAL PACKAGE 2: Disc, cover, inner sleeve, insert.

❑ RCA Victor (SP)
CPL1-2901 ....'81   4-6
DISC 3: Same as disc 1.

❑ RCA CPL1-2901.................'81   3-5
COVER 3: Same as cover 1, except has "Special Memories of Elvis Greeting Card" printed directly on back cover. Since there is no card, cover does not have the two slits.
INNER SLEEVE 3: White, no printing.

RCA Victor (SP)
CPL1-2901 .... '81   8-12
TOTAL PACKAGE 3: Disc, cover.

❑ RCA Victor (SP)
CPL1-2901 ....'81   4-6
DISC 4: Same as disc 1.

❑ RCA CPL1-2901.................'81   20-25
COVER 4: Single Pocket cover. Has "Special Memories of Elvis Greeting Card" printed directly on back cover. Since there is no card, cover does not have two slits.
INNER SLEEVE 4: White, no printing.

RCA Victor (SP)
CPL1-2901 .... '81   25-30
TOTAL PACKAGE 4: Disc, cover.

Though not identified as such on disc or cover, *Big Boots* is a previously unreleased take.

Side 1
(Let Me Be Your) Teddy Bear
Wooden Heart
Five Sleepyheads
Puppet on a String
Angel
Old MacDonald

Side 2
How Would You Like to Be
Cotton Candy Land
Old Shep
Big Boots
Have a Happy

ELVIS SINGS HITS FROM HIS MOVIES, VOLUME 1 (Camden)

❑ RCA/Camden (ST)
CAS-2567...........................6/72   8-12
DISC 1: Blue label. Dynaflex vinyl. Label
makes no reference to "Volume 1."
BCRS-5270-3S/BCRS-5271-3S.

❑ RCA/Camden CAS-2567...6/72   8-12
COVER 1: Front: RCA/Camden logo and
number at upper right. Color Elvis photo.
Back: Elvis photo and four other RCA LPs
pictured in color.
INNER SLEEVE 1: White, no printing. (Some
Camden LPs had no inner sleeves at all.)

RCA/Camden (ST)
CAS-2567 .... 6/72   15-25
TOTAL PACKAGE 1: Disc, cover.

❑ RCA/Camden (ST)
CAS-2567...........................6/72   8-12
DISC 2: Same as disc 1.

❑ RCA/Camden CAS-2567...6/72   12-18
COVER 2: Designate promo. Same as cover
1, but with "Not for Sale" stamped on back.
INNER SLEEVE 2: White, no printing. (Some
Camden LPs had no inner sleeves at all.)

RCA/Camden (ST)
CAS-2567 .... 6/72   20-30
TOTAL PACKAGE 2: Disc, cover.

Side 1
Down by the Riverside/When the Saints Go Marching
In
They Remind Me Too Much of You
Confidence
Frankie and Johnny
Guitar Man
Side 2
Long Legged Girl (With a Short Dress On)
You Don't Know Me
How Would You Like to Be
Big Boss Man
Old MacDonald

ELVIS SINGS HITS FROM HIS MOVIES, VOLUME 1 (Pickwick)

❑ Pickwick/Camden (ST)
CAS-2567.......................12/75   2-5
DISC 1: Black label. Multi-color Pickwick logo
at center.
CAS-2567A/CAS-2567B. Identification numbers are
engraved.

❑ Pickwick/Camden
CAS-2567.......................12/75   3-5
COVER 1: Same as RCA/Camden cover 1
(above), except Pickwick logo is at lower left
on front, and number is at upper right. Back
has "Previously released on Camden
Records."
INNER SLEEVE 1: White, no printing.

Pickwick/Camden (ST)
CAS-2567 .... 12/75   5-10
TOTAL PACKAGE 1: Disc, cover.

Side 1
Down by the Riverside/When the Saints Go Marching
In
They Remind Me Too Much of You
Confidence
Frankie and Johnny
Guitar Man
Side 2
Long Legged Girl (With a Short Dress On)
You Don't Know Me
How Would You Like to Be
Big Boss Man
Old MacDonald

ELVIS SINGS INSPIRATIONAL FAVORITES

❑ Reader's Digest/RCA Music Service (SP)
RD4A-181/D ....'83   7-10
DISC 1: Black, white and red label. Mail order
bonus from Reader's Digest with the purchase
of the 1983 edition of *Elvis! His Greatest Hits.*
J1RS-5695-4/J1RS-5696-1.
J1RS-5695-4/J1RS-5696-2.

❑ Reader's Digest/RCA Music Service
RDA-181/D ....'83   7-10
COVER 1: Prefix differs from one used on
disc. Front: Reader's Digest and RCA Music
Service logos at upper left. Has color Elvis
photo. Back: Contents, and drawing of a
church scene.
INNER SLEEVE 1: White, no printing.
INSERT: 24-page "Reader's Digest Music"
catalog. Has nothing to do with Elvis or this
LP.

Reader's Digest/RCA Music Service
(SP) RD4A-181/D .... '83   15-20
TOTAL PACKAGE 1: Disc, cover.

Card stock jacket, with printing on cover – not
on slicks.
Side 1
How Great Thou Art
Somebody Bigger Than You and I
In the Garden
It Is No Secret (What God Can Do)
His Hand in Mine
Take My Hand, Precious Lord
Side 2
Crying in the Chapel
(There'll Be) Peace in the Valley (For Me)
Put Your Hand in the Hand
Where Did They Go, Lord
I Believe
You'll Never Walk Alone

ELVIS SINGS THE WONDERFUL WORLD OF CHRISTMAS

❑ RCA Victor (ST)
LSP-4579 .... 10/71   8-10
DISC 1: Orange label. Dynaflex vinyl.
APRS-1673-B1L/APRS-1674-A2E.
APRS-1673-1S/APRS-1674-2S.
APRS-1673-1S/APRS-1674-32S.
APRS-1673-2S/APRS-1674-2S.
APRS-1673-3S/APRS-1674-4S.
APRS-1673-5S/APRS-1674-6S.

❑ RCA Victor LSP-4579......10/71   10-15
  COVER 1: Front: RCA Victor logo and
  number at upper left. Pictures 12 items
  associated with Christmas and winter,
  including snowmen at lower corners, each
  with Elvis' face in black-and-white. Back:
  pictures three other inspirational LPs by Elvis.
  Dynaflex logo at lower right.
❑ RCA Victor 21-112-1PT
  55A.....................................8/71   3-5
  INNER SLEEVE 1: Black-and-white. Pictures
  RCA Elvis Stereo 8 tape catalog front and
  back, most recent being a four-tape issue of
  Worldwide 50 Gold Award Hits, Vol. 1 (side 2,
  row 3, column 6).
❑ RCA Victor..........................8/71   20-25
  INSERT 1: Color 5" x 7" Elvis postcard.
  Signed "Season's Greetings, Elvis."
❑ RCA Victor LSP-4579......10/71   15-20
  SHRINK STICKER 1: Red and white,
  announces the bonus, autographed postcard.

RCA Victor (ST)

LSP-4579...................10/71   55-75
  **TOTAL PACKAGE 1: Disc, cover, inner
  sleeve, insert, sticker.**

❑ RCA Victor (ST)
  LSP-4579 ....10/71   8-10
  DISC 2: Same as disc 1.
❑ RCA Victor LSP-4579......10/71   20-25
  COVER 2: Designate promo. Same as cover
  1, but with "Not for Sale" stamped on back.
❑ RCA Victor 21-112-1 PT
  55A.....................................8/71   3-5
  INNER SLEEVE 2: Black-and-white. Pictures
  RCA Elvis Stereo 8 tape catalog front and
  back, most recent being a four-tape issue of
  Worldwide 50 Gold Award Hits, Vol. 1 (side 2,
  row 3, column 6).
❑ RCA Victor..........................8/71   20-25
  INSERT 2: Color 5" x 7" Elvis postcard.
  Signed "Season's Greetings, Elvis."
❑ RCA Victor LSP-4579......10/71   15-20
  SHRINK STICKER 2: Red and white,
  announces the bonus, autographed postcard.

RCA Victor (ST)

LSP-4579...................10/71   65-85
  **TOTAL PACKAGE 2: Disc, cover, inner
  sleeve, insert, sticker.**

❑ RCA (ST) ANL1-1936..........'75   3-4
  DISC 3: Orange label. Flexible vinyl.
  ANL1-1936A-34/ANL1-1936B-38. On side 1, whatever
  number was stamped is crossed out and "1936" engraved.
❑ RCA ANL1-1936.................'75   3-4
  COVER 3: Reflects number change. Front:
  RCA logo moved to upper right. Back: No
  mention of Dynaflex.
❑ RCA Victor........................'70s   2-4
  INNER SLEEVE 3: Black-and-white. Pictures
  RCA Elvis catalog front and back. Any of
  several sleeves may be found on reissues
  from this period.

❑ RCA (ST) ANL1-1936........'75   8-12
  **TOTAL PACKAGE 3: Disc, cover, inner
  sleeve.**

❑ RCA (ST) ANL1-1936..........'76   20-25
  DISC 4: Tan label.
❑ RCA ANL1-1936.................'76   20-25
  COVER 4: Verification pending.
❑ RCA Victor........................'70s   2-4
  INNER SLEEVE 4: Black-and-white. Pictures
  RCA Elvis catalog front and back. Any of
  several may be found on reissues from this
  period.

❑ RCA (ST) ANL1-1936........'76   40-50
  **TOTAL PACKAGE 4: Disc, cover, inner
  sleeve.**

❑ RCA (ST) ANL1-1936..........'76   3-5
  DISC 5: Black label, dog near top.
❑ RCA ANL1-1936.................'76   3-5
  COVER 5: Verification pending.
❑ RCA Victor........................'70s   2-4
  INNER SLEEVE 5: Black-and-white. Pictures
  RCA Elvis catalog front and back. Any of
  several sleeves may be found on reissues
  from this period.

❑ RCA (ST) ANL1-1936........'76   8-15
  **TOTAL PACKAGE 5: Disc, cover, inner
  sleeve.**

Side 1
O Come, All Ye Faithful
The First Noel
On a Snowy Christmas Night
Winter Wonderland
The Wonderful World of Christmas
It Won't Seem Like Christmas (Without You)

Side 2
I'll Be Home on Christmas Day
If I Get Home on Christmas Day
Holly Leaves and Christmas Trees
Merry Christmas Baby
Silver Bells

ELVIS TALKS!

❑ RCA Victor (M)
  6313-1-R 7/87   10-12
  DISC 1: Black label, dog near top. Mail order
  LP offer. Commercial issue of the same
  interviews as found on *Elvis Presley Interview
  Record* (DJM1-0835). Label indicates
  "Stereo," which of course is not the case.
  6313-1-R-A/6313-1-R-B. Identification numbers are
  engraved.
❑ RCA Victor 6313-1-R.........7/87   12-15
  COVER 1: Text only on front and back. Cover
  correctly indicates this LP is "Mono."
❑ RCA/BMG..........................7/87   1-2
  INNER SLEEVE 1: Mustard with black print,
  with "A 1987 Commemorative Release" on
  each side.

RCA Victor (M)
6313-1-R 7/87   25-30
TOTAL PACKAGE 1: Disc, cover, inner sleeve.

___

❏ RCA Victor (M)
6313-1-R 7/87   10-12
DISC 2: Same as disc 1.

❏ RCA Victor 6313-1-R......... 7/87   18-20
COVER 2: Designate promo. Same as cover 1, but with "Not for Sale" stamped on back.

❏ RCA/BMG......................... 7/87   1-2
INNER SLEEVE 2: Mustard with black print, with "A 1987 Commemorative Release" on each side.

RCA Victor (M)
6313-1-R 7/87   30-35
TOTAL PACKAGE 2: Disc, cover, inner sleeve.

___

Card stock jacket, with printing on cover – not on slicks.

Side 1
The 1956 Interviews
Elvis Presley: Excerpt from a *TV Guide* Interview 1956
Colonel Tom Parker: Excerpt from a *TV Guide* Interview 1956
Vernon and Gladys Presley: Tupelo, Mississippi, September 26,1956
Elvis Presley: Tupelo, Mississippi, September 26, 1956

Side 2
The 1960-61 Interview
Image Change Since Discharge from the Army – By Accident or Design?
Elvis Talks About His Mother
How Does Elvis View Himself?
Does He Enjoy His Work?
How Does He Relax?
Does He Have Any Time to Read? If So, What Does He Read?
Does He Like Himself?
Does He Like to Work?
If He Were Starting Out Again (in 1961) Would He Do Anything Differently?
Does He Have Any Specific Goals for the Future?
Does He Think He Has Changed Much As a Person? How Does He View the Criticism That Has Been Leveled at Some of the People Surrounding Him?
As a Father, Who Could Only Give His Child One Piece of Advice, What Would It Be?

ELVIS TAPES

❏ Great Northwest Music Company (M)
GNW-4005 .... '77   4-6
DISC 1: Green label with black print.
GNM-4005A/GNM-4005B. Identification numbers are engraved.

❏ Great Northwest Music Company
GNW-4005 .... '77   4-6
COVER 1: Front: Collage of five black-and-white photos of Elvis in Vancouver. Back: Black-and-white photo of Elvis on stage in Vancouver.
INNER SLEEVE 1: White, no printing.

Great Northwest Music Company (M)
GNW-4005 .... '77   8-15
TOTAL PACKAGE 1: Disc, cover.

ELVIS 10TH ANNIVERSARY (6 LPs)

Complete six-hour radio show. All discs in this set, listed individually below, have a silver label with black print. All identification numbers are engraved. Issued only to subscribing radio stations. As of press time, this set is being offered by the producer for $150.

❏ Creative Radio 1A/1B........ 8/87   18-20
DISC 1:
E-10-1-A L-28121/E-10-1-B L-28121-X.

❏ Creative Radio 2A/2B........ 8/87   18-20
DISC 2:
E-10-2-A L-28120/E-10-2-B L-28120-X.

❏ Creative Radio 3A/3B........ 8/87   18-20
DISC 3:
E-10-3-A L-28149/E-10-3-B L-28149-X.

❏ Creative Radio 4A/4B........ 8/87   18-20
DISC 4:
E-10-4-A L-28149/E-10-4-B L-28149-X.

❏ Creative Radio 5A/5B........ 8/87   18-20
DISC 5:
E-10-5-A L-28157/E-10-5-B L-28157-X.

❏ Creative Radio 6A/6B........ 8/87   18-20
DISC 6:
E-10-6-A L-28156/E-10-6-B L-28156-X.

❏ Creative Radio................... 8/87   40-50
BOX 1: White slick with title in gold print is applied to a plain black box.

❏ Creative Radio................... 8/87   5-10
INSERT 1: Eight pages of programming information and cue sheets.

Creative Radio................ 8/87   125-175
TOTAL PACKAGE 1: Discs, box, insert.

___

Disc 1
Side A
Elvis Medley
Love Me
All Shook Up
A Big Hunk O' Love
That's All Right
(Let Me Be Your) Teddy Bear
Blue Suede Shoes
I Just Can't Help Believing

Side B
I Was the One
Rip It Up
Don't
(Marie's the Name) His Latest Flame
Loving You
My Baby Left Me
Wonder of You

Disc 2
Side A
Elvis Medley
Hound Dog
Welcome to My World
(You're the) Devil in Disguise
Wear My Ring Around Your Neck
Tryin' to Get to You
Mean Woman Blues

Side B

(Now and Then There's) A Fool Such As I
Tomorrow Never Comes
What Now My Love
Whole Lot-ta Shakin' Goin' On
An American Trilogy
G.I. Blues
Frankfort Special

Disc 3

Side A

Elvis Medley
Heartbreak Hotel
Easy Come, Easy Go
Got a Lot O' Livin' to Do
If You Talk in Your Sleep
Old Shep

Side B

Patch It Up
Steamroller Blues
Burning Love
Memories
In the Ghetto
Don't Cry Daddy
Too Much
All Shook Up
Don't Be Cruel

Disc 4

Side A

That's All Right (Live)
Didja Ever
Good Luck Charm
Johnny B. Goode
For the Heart
Hurt
How Great Thou Art
Green, Green Grass of Home

Side B

Polk Salad Annie
I'll Remember You
Hard Headed Woman
Love Me Tender
I Want You, I Need You, I Love You
Lawdy, Miss Clawdy

Disc 5

Side A

You Gave Me a Mountain
Shake, Rattle and Roll
I Can't Stop Loving You
The Impossible Dream
Let It Be Me
Jailhouse Rock
Treat Me Nice

Side B

Moody Blue
Little Darlin'
Are You Lonesome Tonight
Young and Beautiful
Follow That Dream
Fame and Fortune
Return to Sender
Little Sister
Can't Help Falling in Love

Disc 6

Side A

See See Rider
Baby What You Want Me to Do
Blue Suede Shoes
If I Can Dream
Unchained Melody
Tryin' to Get to You

Suspicious Minds

Side B

It's Now Or Never
Way Down
Kentucky Rain
What Now My Love
You'll Never Walk Alone
My Way

ELVIS – THAT'S THE WAY IT IS: see *THAT'S THE WAY IT IS*

ELVIS THE ENTERTAINER

❑ Rooster RLP-501: Bootleg. Listed for identification only.

ELVIS THE KING (1954-1965) (2 LPs)

❑ Time-Life (SP) STL-126.......'89 35-45
 DISCS 1: Custom "Rock 'N' Roll Era" label.
 The second Elvis box in a series of "Rock 'N'
 Roll Era" sets from Time-Life. Sold only by
 Time-Life via mail order.
 (Disc 1) STL-126A-1/STL-126B-1. **(Disc 2)** STL-126C-
 1/STL-126D-1.

❑ Time-Life STL-126...............'89 35-45
 BOX 1: Front: Photo of Elvis from Tupelo Fair
 concert. Back: Text only.
 INNER SLEEVES 1: White, only printing is
 Time-Life logo.

❑ Time-Life STL-126...............'89 5-10
 INSERT 1: Black-and-white, 11¾" x 18"
 poster/brochure.

Time-Life (SP) STL-126....'89 75-100
 TOTAL PACKAGE 1: Discs, box, insert.

Disc 1

Side 1

Good Rockin' Tonight
My Baby Left Me
Anyway You Want Me (That's How I Will Be)
Blue Suede Shoes
Lawdy, Miss Clawdy
That's When Your Heartaches Begin

Side 2

Mystery Train
Treat Me Nice
Money Honey
(You're So Square) Baby I Don't Care
Loving You

Disc 2

Side 3

Party
I Feel So Bad
Return to Sender
(You're the) Devil in Disguise
I Got Stung
I Need Your Love Tonight

Side 4

(Marie's the Name) His Latest Flame
Such a Night
Good Luck Charm
A Mess of Blues
Crying in the Chapel

ELVIS: THE KING SPEAKS: see *KING SPEAKS (FEBRUARY 1961, MEMPHIS, TENNESSEE)*

ELVIS: THE FIRST LIVE RECORDINGS: see
FIRST LIVE RECORDINGS

ELVIS: THE LEGEND LIVES ON: see
LEGEND LIVES ON

ELVIS: THE OTHER SIDES: see
*WORLDWIDE GOLD AWARD HITS VOL. 2
– THE OTHER SIDES*

ELVIS TODAY

❑ RCA Victor (ST)
  APL1-1039 ....5/75   25-30
  DISC 1: Orange label. Flexible vinyl.
  APL1-1039-A-40-S/APL1-1039-B-4S. Identification numbers
  are engraved.

❑ RCA APL1-1039................5/75   20-25
  COVER 1: Front: Color Elvis photo. Number
  at lower right. Back: RCA logo at upper left,
  number at upper right. Pictures four other
  Elvis LPs. Has "0698" at bottom of spine.
  Price reflects RCA's use of this same cover,
  with no discernible differences, until 1977.

❑ RCA Victor 21-112-1
  PT 54C 11/73   3-5
  INNER SLEEVE 1: Black-and-white. Pictures
  RCA's Elvis LP catalog front and back, most
  recent being *Elvis As Recorded at Madison
  Square Garden* (side 2, row 4, column 2). May
  also be found with inner sleeve 54D.

❑ RCA Victor (ST)
  APL1-1039 ....5/75   10-15
  SHRINK STICKER 1: Announces the
  inclusion of the hit single *T-r-o-u-b-l-e*.

RCA Victor (ST)
APL1-1039 ....5/75   60-75
  **TOTAL PACKAGE 1: Disc, cover, inner
  sleeve, sticker.**

❑ RCA Victor (ST)
  APL1-1039 ....5/75   25-30
  DISC 2: Same as disc 1.

❑ RCA APL1-1039................5/75   30-35
  COVER 2: Designate promo. Same as cover
  1, but with "Not for Sale" stamped on back.

❑ RCA Victor 21-112-1
  PT 54C 11/73   3-5
  INNER SLEEVE 2: Black-and-white. Pictures
  RCA's Elvis LP catalog front and back, most
  recent being *Elvis As Recorded at Madison
  Square Garden* (side 2, row 4, column 2). May
  also be found with inner sleeve 54D.

❑ RCA Victor (ST)
  APL1-1039 ....5/75   10-15
  SHRINK STICKER 2: Announces the
  inclusion of the hit single *T-r-o-u-b-l-e*.

RCA Victor (ST)
APL1-1039 ....5/75   70-85
  **TOTAL PACKAGE 2: Disc, cover, inner
  sleeve, sticker.**

❑ RCA (Q) APD1-1039.........5/75   95-115
  DISC 3: Quadradisc. Orange label. Flexible
  vinyl.

APD1-1039A-1/APD1-1039B-1.

❑ RCA APD1-1039 ....5/75   95-115
  COVER 3: Same as cover 1 except has
  Quadradisc logo at top center and "0798" at
  bottom of spine. .

❑ RCA Victor 21-112-1
  PT 54C 11/73   3-5
  INNER SLEEVE 3: Black-and-white. Pictures
  RCA's Elvis LP catalog front and back, most
  recent being *Elvis As Recorded at Madison
  Square Garden* (side 2, row 4, column 2). May
  also be found with inner sleeve 54D.

❑ RCA Victor (ST)
  APL1-1039 ....5/75   10-15
  SHRINK STICKER 3: Announces the
  inclusion of the hit single *T-r-o-u-b-l-e*.

RCA (Q) APD1-1039 ....5/75   200-250
  **TOTAL PACKAGE 3: Disc, cover, inner
  sleeve, sticker.**

❑ RCA Victor (ST)
  APL1-1039 ....5/75   8-10
  DISC 4: Tan label. In some areas only a tan
  label issue was available.
  APL1-1039-A-31-S/APL1-1039-B-21S. Identification
  numbers are engraved.
  APL1-1039-A-31-S/APL1-1039-B-30S. Identification
  numbers are engraved.

❑ RCA APL1-1039................5/75   10-15
  COVER 4: Same as cover 1.

❑ RCA Victor........................5/75   3-5
  INNER SLEEVE 4: Black-and-white. Pictures
  RCA Elvis catalog front and back. Any of
  several sleeves may be found on reissues
  from this period.

RCA Victor (ST)
APL1-1039 ....5/75   20-30
  **TOTAL PACKAGE 4: Disc, cover, inner
  sleeve.**

❑ RCA Victor (ST)
  AFL1-1039...........................'77   3-5
  DISC 5: Black label, dog near top.

❑ RCA AFL1-1039 ....'77   3-5
  COVER 5: Reflects prefix change. Includes
  copies with a sticker bearing the "AFL1"
  prefix, wrapped around cover at top of spine.

❑ RCA Victor.........................'70s   2-4
  INNER SLEEVE 5: Black-and-white. Pictures
  RCA Elvis catalog front and back. Any of
  several sleeves may be found on reissues
  from this period.

RCA Victor (ST)
AFL1-1039....................'77   8-15
  **TOTAL PACKAGE 5: Disc, cover, inner
  sleeve.**

❑ RCA Victor (ST)
  AFL1-1039...........................'77   1000-2000
  DISC 6: Picture disc. Side 1 has eight
  "dancing" pictures of Elvis. Side 2 has one
  Elvis photo, same as used on *Legendary
  Performer, Vol. 3* picture disc, side 1.
  Experimental item only.

❑ RCA AFL1-1039 .... '77   3-5
   COVER 6: Same as cover 1.

RCA Victor (ST)
AFL1-1039 .... '77   1000-2000
TOTAL PACKAGE 5: Disc, cover.

❑ RCA Victor (Q)
   APD1-1039 .... '77   60-75
   DISC 7: Quadradisc. Black label, dog near
   top.
   APD1-1039A-1/APD1-1039B-1.
❑ RCA Victor (Q)
   APD1-1039 .... '77   65-75
   COVER 7: Same as cover 3.
❑ RCA Victor .... '70s   2-4
   INNER SLEEVE 7: Black-and-white. Pictures
   RCA Elvis catalog front and back. Any of
   several may be found on reissues from this
   period.

RCA Victor (Q)
APD1-1039 .... '77   125-150
**TOTAL PACKAGE 7: Disc, cover, inner
   sleeve.**

Side A
T-r-o-u-b-l-e
And I Love You So
Susan When She Tried
Woman Without Love
Shake a Hand

Side B
Pieces of My Life
Fairytale
I Can Help
Bringing It Back
Green Green Grass of Home

**ELVIS VINTAGE 1955: see *VINTAGE 1955
ELVIS***

**ELVIS WITH RAY GREEN BACKSTAGE: see
*ELVIS EXCLUSIVE INTERVIEW***

ELVIS' WITCHCRAFT ALBUM (50,000,000 WITCHES & WIZARDS CAN'T BE WRONG)

❑ TCB LSP-2908: Bootleg. Listed for
   identification only.

EPIC OF THE '70s (6 LPs)
Various artists collection
Complete six-hour radio show. Has music of
the '70s and interviews with most of the artists
featured. Includes *Burning Love* as well as
comments by Elvis (Disc 4, side 2). Issued to
subscribing radio stations only. All discs have
blue labels with silver print. Each is listed
individually below. All identification numbers
are engraved.

❑ Century 21 Productions (SP)
   1A/2A .... '76   15-20
   DISC 1:
   7PV-43585-1A/7PV-43585-2A.

❑ Century 21 Productions (SP)
   1B/2B .... '76   15-25
   DISC 2:
   7PV-43585-1B/7PV-43585-2B.
❑ Century 21 Productions (SP)
   3A/4A .... '76   15-25
   DISC 3:
   7PV-43585-3A/7PV-43585-4A.
❑ Century 21 Productions (SP)
   3B/4B .... '76   15-25
   DISC 4:
   7PV-43585-3B/7PV-43585-4B.
❑ Century 21 Productions (SP)
   5A/6A .... '76   15-25
   DISC 5:
   7PV-43585-5A/7PV-43585-6A.
❑ Century 21 Productions (SP)
   5B/6B .... '76   15-25
   DISC 6:
   7PV-43585-5B/7PV-43585-6B.
   INNER SLEEVES 1: White, no printing.
   COVER/BOX 1: Verification pending.
❑ Century 21 Productions .... '76   10-15
   INSERT 1: Six pages of cue sheets and
   program notes.

Century 21 Productions (SP) .... '76   100-200
TOTAL PACKAGE 1: Discs, insert.

ESSENTIAL ELVIS – THE FIRST MOVIES

❑ RCA Victor (M)
   6738-1-R 1/88   10-12
   DISC 1: Black label, dog near top. Flexible
   vinyl.
   6738-1-R-A/6738-1-R-B. Identification numbers are
   engraved.
❑ RCA Victor 6738-1-R 1/88   10-15
   COVER 1: Gatefold. RCA lightning bolt logo
   and number at upper right. Color and duotone
   Elvis photos pictured on all four panels.
   INNER SLEEVE 1: White, no printing.

RCA Victor (M)
6738-1-R 1/88   20-25
TOTAL PACKAGE 1: Disc, cover.

❑ RCA Victor (M)
   6738-1-R 1/88   10-12
   DISC 2: Same as disc 1.
❑ RCA Victor 6738-1-R 1/88   15-20
   COVER 2: Designate Promo. Same as cover
   1 but with "Not For Sale" stamped on back.
   INNER SLEEVE 2: White, no printing.
   Card stock jacket, with printing on cover – not
   on slicks.

RCA Victor (M)
6738-1-R 1/88   25-30
TOTAL PACKAGE 2: Disc, cover.

Card stock jacket, with printing on cover – not
on slicks.

Side 1
Love Me Tender
Let Me
Poor Boy
We're Gonna Move
Loving You
Party
Hot Dog
(Let Me Be Your) Teddy Bear
Loving You
Mean Woman Blues
Got a Lot o' Livin' to Do

Side 2
Loving You
Party
Lonesome Cowboy
Jailhouse Rock
Treat Me Nice
Young and Beautiful
Don't Leave Me Now
I Want to Be Free
Baby I Don't Care
Jailhouse Rock
Got a Lot o' Livin' to Do
Love Me Tender

ESSENTIAL ELVIS, VOLUME 2: see
STEREO '57

ETERNAL ELVIS

❏ Bootleg. Listed for identification only.

EXCLUSIVE INTERVIEW: see *ELVIS*
EXCLUSIVE INTERVIEW

EXCLUSIVE LIVE PRESS CONFERENCE:
see *ELVIS EXCLUSIVE LIVE PRESS*
CONFERENCE

FAMILY CHRISTMAS COLLECTION (5 LPs)

Various artists collection

❏ Time-Life (SP) STL-131 .. 10/90   20-25
DISCS 1: White label with red and black print.
Sold only by
Time-Life via mail order. Identification
numbers are engraved. Has three Elvis
tracks.
(Disc 1) STL-131-R1-S1-1/STL-131-R1-S2-1.
(Disc 2) STL-131-R2-S3- 1/STL-131-R2-S4-1.
(Disc 3) STL-131-R3-S5-1/STL-131-R3-S6-1.
(Disc 4) STL-131- R4-S7-1/STL-131-R4-S8-1.
(Disc 5) STL-131-R5-S9-1/STL-131-R5-S10-1.

❏ Time-Life STL-131 .... 10/88   5-10
BOX 1: Front: Time-Life logo at lower right.
White with red and gold print. Back: Tan with
black print. Text only.
INNER SLEEVES 1: Generic, Time-Life poly-
lined.

Time-Life (SP)
STL-131 .... 10/90   25-35
TOTAL PACKAGE 1: Discs, box.

FEBRUARY SAMPLER 59-7

Various artists collection

❏ RCA Victor/Camden (M)
SP-33-59-7 .... 2/59   600-800
DISC 1: Side 1: RCA Victor black label, with
"Long Play" at bottom. Side 2: RCA Camden
label with "Long Play" at bottom. Various
artists sampler with tunes from both RCA
Victor and RCA Camden LPs. Promotional
issue only. Despite its higher number, RCA
issued this disc eight months before SP-33-
54.
J2NP-8230/K3N8-0023.
COVER 1: None made.
INNER SLEEVE 1: White, no printing.

RCA Victor/Camden (M)
SP-33-59-7 .... 2/59   600-800
TOTAL PACKAGE 1: Disc.

Side 1
Hearts of Paris (Ray Hartley with Don Walker
  Orchestra)
The Stranger of Galilee (Blackwood Brothers)
Countdown (Buddy Morrow and His Orchestra)
That's All Right (Elvis Presley)

Side 2
Wabash Cannonball (Eddy Arnold)
The Old Rugged Cross (Three Suns)
The Sheik of Araby (Fats Waller)
Colonel Bogey (Norwegian Military Band)

FELTON JARVIS TALKS ABOUT ELVIS (OPEN-ENDED)

❏ RCA (M) FJ-1981 .... 1/81   200-250
DISC 1: Red label with black print. An open-
end interview with Felton Jarvis, mostly
discussing the *Guitar Man* LP. Promotional
issue only.
J-1981-1-A/J-1981-1-B. Identification numbers are
engraved. Also has "Randy's Roost" engraved on both sides.
COVER 1: White, no printing.
INNER SLEEVE 1: White, no printing.

❏ RCA FJ-1981 .... 1/81   20-25
INSERT 1A: Six pages of script on three
sheets.

❏ RCA AAL1-3917 .... 1/81   50-75
INSERT 1B: Belt buckle. Front: Silver and
black, with "Elvis." Back: Engraved the
contents of the *Guitar Man* LP. Though other
color buckles exist, only silver and black
buckles were sent with the *Felton Jarvis Talks
About Elvis* LP. We have yet to learn why
other color buckles were made – or exactly
who made them – but we do know they are
not an official part of this promotional
package.
RCA (M) FJ-1981 .... 1/81   270-350
TOTAL PACKAGE 1: Disc, inserts.

IMPORTANT HANDLING
INSTRUCTIONS

IT IS YOUR OBLIGATION TO RETURN THE ENCLOSED

PROGRAM *ELVIS* TO CREATIVE RADIO SHOWS

AFTER YOUR BROADCAST.

PLEASE RETURN THE SHOW VIA U.S. MAIL, SPECIAL

4TH CLASS RATE. ATTACHED IS A LABEL FOR YOUR

CONVENIENCE. THANK YOU.

Creative Radio Shows   1414 W. Olive Avenue · Burbank

ELVIS

HR 1·A

50 BELOVED SONGS OF FAITH (3 LPs)

Various artists collection
Unusual because records 1 and 2 have RCA/BMG artists, but record 3 has CBS/Columbia artists and is on the CBS label.

❑ Reader's Digest/BMG Direct Marketing (ST) BMR3-100 (Record 1) .... '90   2-4
DISC 1A: Black label, red and white print. A via mail order from the Beautiful Music Company. One of three separate LPs, sold as a set.
WIRS-6031-1/WIRS-6032-1. Identification numbers are engraved.

❑ Reader's Digest/BMG Direct Marketing (ST) BMR3-100 (Record 2) .... '90   2-4
DISC 1B: Black label, red and white print. A via mail order from the Beautiful Music Company. One of three separate LPs, sold as a set.
WIRS-6033-1/WIRS-6034-1. Identification numbers are engraved.

❑ CBS Special Products (ST) P-21633 (Record 3) .... '90   2-4
DISC 1C: Red label, yellow and black print. A via mail order from the Beautiful Music Company. One of three separate LPs, sold as a set.
AS-21633-1A/BS-21633-1A. Identification numbers are engraved.

❑ Reader's Digest/Beautiful Music Co. (ST) BMR3-100 (DIR-1) .... '90   2-4
COVER 1A: Front: "DIR-1" at upper left. Reader's Digest logo at lower right, number at upper right. Back: Text only.

❑ Reader's Digest/Beautiful Music Co. (ST) BMR3-100 (DIR-2) .... '90   2-4
COVER 1B: Front: "DIR-2" at upper left. Reader's Digest logo at lower right, number at upper right. Back: Text only.

❑ Reader's Digest/Beautiful Music Co. (ST) BMR3-100 (DIR-3) .... '90   2-4
COVER 1C: Cover is same as 1A and 1B, with no mention of the CBS connection. Front: "DIR-3" at upper left. Reader's Digest logo at lower right, number at upper right. Back: Text only.
INNER SLEEVES 1: White, no printing.

Reader's Digest/BMG Direct Marketing (ST) BMR3-100.............. '90   15-25
TOTAL PACKAGE 1: Discs, covers.

Card stock jacket, with printing on cover – not on slicks.

Disc 1

Side 1
In the Garden (Loretta Lynn)
The Family That Prays (Porter Wagoner)
I Need Thee Every Hour (Scott Singers)
Softly and Tenderly (Guy & Ralna)
Beyond the Sunset (Red Foley)
May the Good Lord Bless and Keep You (Kate Smith)
Crying in the Chapel (Elvis Presley)

Side 2
I Love to Tell the Story (Pat Boone)
It Is No Secret (Jim Reeves)
A Beautiful Life (Statler Brothers)
One Day At a Time (Cristy Lane)
Nearer My God to Thee (Jack Halloran Chorus)
I'll Fly Away (Charley Pride)
What a Friend (Norma Zimmer/Jim Roberts)
Bless This House (Perry Como)

Disc 2

Side 1
Wings of a Dove (Dolly Parton)
Precious Memories (Jimmy Dean)
Swing Low, Sweet Chariot (Doris Ackers)
I Saw the Light (Hank Williams Jr.)
Whispering Hope (Browns)
Someone to Care (Jimmy Davis)
Standing on the Promises (Johnson Family)
Blessed Assurance (George Beverly Shea)

Side 2
Take My Hand, Precious Lord (Eddy Arnold)
Beautiful Isle of Somewhere (Three Suns)
Peace in the Valley (Floyd Cramer)
Abide with Me (Don Hustad Chorale)
He Touched Me (Bill Gaither Trio)
Jesus Is Coming Soon (Oak Ridge Boys)
Jesus Loves Me (Tennessee Ernie Ford)

Disc 3

Side 1
In the Sweet By and By (Johnny Cash)
Me and Jesus (Tammy Wynette & George Jones)
Amazing Grace (Willie Nelson)
The Bible Tells Me So (Roy Rogers & Dale Evans)
Will the Circle Be Unbroken (Carter Family)
Great Speckled Bird (Roy Acuff)
When the Roll Is Called Up Yonder (Marty Robbins)
How Great Thou Art (Jim Roberts)
Bringing in the Sheaves (Burl Ives)
Church in the Wildwood (Mike Curb Congregation)

Side 2
When They Ring Those Bells (David Houston)
Brighten the Corner (Anita Kerr)
Old Rugged Cross (Ray Price)
Help Me (Larry Gatlin)
Lily of the Valley (Wayne Newton)
Rock of Ages (B.J. Thomas)
Family Bible (George Jones)
Just a Closer Walk with Thee (Anita Bryant)
Sweet Hour of Prayer (Jim Nabors)
The Lord's Prayer (Mormon Tabernacle Choir)

50 YEARS – 50 HITS (3 LPs)

❑ RCA Special Products (SP) SVL3-0710 .... 1/85   15-20
DISCS 1: Black label, dog near top. Sold via TV mail order and through the RCA Record Club.
(**Disc 1**) SVL3-0710A-2/SVL3-0710B-2. (**Disc 2**) SVL3-0710C-1/SVL3-0710D-1. (**Disc 3**) SVL3-0710E-1/SVL3-0710F-2.

❑ RCA Special Products SVL3-0710 .... 1/85   15-20
COVER 1: Single pocket. RCA Special Products logo and number at lower right. Same color Elvis photo used on both front and back.
INNER SLEEVES 1: White, no printing.

RCA Special Products (SP)
SVL3-0710 .... 1/85   **30-40**
TOTAL PACKAGE 1: Discs, cover.

Card stock jacket, with printing on cover – not on slicks.

Disc 1
Side 1
Heartbreak Hotel
Don't Be Cruel
I Want You, I Need You, I Love You
Too Much
Viva Las Vegas
Hound Dog
Old Shep

Side 2
The Wonder of You
Loving You
Kissin' Cousins
Suspicion
All Shook Up
Love Me Tender
What'd I Say
Don't

Disc 2
Side 3
One Broken Heart for Sale
Danny Boy
(Let Me Be Your) Teddy Bear
Good Luck Charm
Suspicious Minds
Treat Me Nice
Return to Sender
If I Can Dream

Side 4
A Big Hunk O' Love
One Night
Such a Night
Love Me
Don't Cry Daddy
Wear My Ring Around Your Neck
It's Now Or Never
My Wish Came True

Disc 3
Side E
I Got Stung
(Now and Then There's) A Fool Such As I
Blue Hawaii
Kentucky Rain
Can't Help Falling in Love
Stuck on You
(Such an) Easy Question
Hard Headed Woman
I Beg of You

Side F
You Don't Have to Say You Love Me
Crying in the Chapel
She's Not You
Puppet on a String
Moody Blue
Surrender
In the Ghetto
Memories

50th ANNIVERSARY: see *ELVIS 50TH ANNIVERSARY*

50,000,000 ELVIS FANS CAN'T BE WRONG: see *ELVIS' GOLD RECORDS, VOLUME 2*

FINAL DAYS
❑ Bootleg. Listed for identification only.

FIRST LIVE RECORDINGS
❑ Music Works (M)
PB-3601 .... 2/84   7-10
DISC 1: Black label with white print.
PB-3601A-1/PB-3601B-1. Identification numbers are engraved.
❑ Music Works PB-3601 .... 2/84   8-10
COVER 1: Front: Music Works logo at lower left. Duotone Elvis photo. Back: Liner notes and duotone Elvis photo.
INNER SLEEVE 1: White, no printing.

Music Works (M)
PB-3601 .... 2/84   15-20
TOTAL PACKAGE 1: Disc, cover.

Contents of this LP makes up about half of *The Beginning Years*. Card stock jacket, with printing on cover – not on slicks.

Side 1
Introduction with Elvis Presley and Horace Logan
Baby Let's Play House (shown as "I Wanna Play House with You")
Maybelline
Tweedle Dee

Side 2
That's All Right (shown as "That's All Right Momma")
Recollections by Frank Page
Hound Dog

FIRST OF ELVIS (EARLY 50'S MELODIES)
❑ Show-Land LP-2001 .... '79   50-75
DISC 1: Verification pending.
❑ Show-Land LP-2001 .... '79   50-75
COVER 1: White, paper sleeve. Front: Black-and-white photocopy of the "First Picture Known of Elvis Presley Performing with a Band."

Show-Land LP-2001 .... '79   100-150
TOTAL PACKAGE 1: Disc, cover.

Side 1
Introduction
That's All Right (shown as "That's All Right Little Mama")
Melodies . . . and Interviews
Blue Moon of Kentucky
Special Interview of Elvis Presley, Age 12 at Tupelo, Mississippi

Side 2
Good Rockin' Tonight (shown as "There's Good Rockin' Tonight")
Melodies . . . Talks and Interviews
I Got a Woman (shown as "I've Got a Woman Away Over Town")
Elvis Introducing Melodies, Him and Guitar

FIRST YEAR (ELVIS, SCOTTY AND BILL)

❑ Golden Editions Limited (M)
GEL-101 ....'79   4-8
DISC 1: White label with mustard color print. Reportedly made in 1979, before the Virgin-distributed edition (package 2), but warehoused until after Virgin distributed theirs. Definitely a more deluxe package than package 2.
GEL-101-A-3/GEL-101-B-4. Identification numbers are engraved. (Between the two sides, four numbers are crossed out.)

❑ Golden Editions Limited
GEL-101 ....'79   4-8
COVER 1: Gatefold. Front: All print is gold foil. Has duotone photo of Scotty Moore, Elvis Presley and Bill Black. Back: All print is white. Has black-and-white photo of Scotty and Elvis. Inside panels: Contents on left and 15-photo collage on right.
INNER SLEEVE 1: White, no printing.

❑ Golden Editions Limited
GEL-101 ....'79   4-6
INSERT 1A: 12-page photo/story booklet.

❑ Golden Editions Limited
GEL-101 ....'79   2-3
INSERT 1B: One-page copy of a July 1954 personal management contract between W.S. "Scotty" Moore and Elvis, Vernon and Gladys Presley.

Golden Editions Limited (M)
GEL-101 ....'79   15-25
TOTAL PACKAGE 1: Disc, cover, inserts.

❑ Golden Editions Limited (M)
KING-1 ....6/79   3-5
DISC 2: Black label with mustard color print.
KING-1-A2/KING-1-B2. Identification numbers are engraved. Also engraved on side 1 is "Gone But Not Forgotten" and "A Poeky Prime Cut." On side 2 is "If Not For You King!"

❑ Golden Editions Limited
KING-1 ....6/79   3-5
COVER 2: Double pocket, unlike gatefold cover 1. Front pocket has the booklet and contract. Uses thinner cover stock than cover 1. Front: Has gold ink instead of gold foil, except on "Special Collector's Edition, at upper left, and Golden Editions logo, at upper right, both of which are white. Has duotone photo of (L-R) Scotty Moore, Elvis Presley and Bill Black. Back: All print is white. Has black-and-white photo of Scotty and Elvis. At lower right is "Distributed By Virgin Records Ltd." Inside panels: Contents on left and 15-photo collage on right.
INNER SLEEVE 2: White, no printing.

❑ Golden Editions Limited
GEL-101 ....'79   4-6
INSERT 2A: 12-page photo/story booklet.

❑ Golden Editions Limited
GEL-101 ....'79   2-3
INSERT 2B: One-page copy of a July 1954 personal management contract between W.S. "Scotty" Moore and Elvis, Vernon and Gladys Presley.

Golden Editions Limited (M)
KING-1 ....'79   12-20
TOTAL PACKAGE 2: Disc, cover, inserts.

Most of this material appeared previously on *The First Years*. Card stock jacket, with printing on cover – not on slicks.

Side 1
Biff Collie Interview
Good Rockin' Tonight (shown as "There's Good Rockin' Tonight")
Baby, Let's Play House
Blue Moon of Kentucky
I've Got a Woman
That's All Right (shown as "That's All Right Little Mama")
Elvis Interview (With Bob Hoffer)

Side 2
Scotty Moore Tells the Story of the First Year

FIRST YEARS

❑ HALW (M) HALW-0001 ...12/78   12-25
DISC 1: Pink label with black print. Side 1 is titled The
First Year (not "Years," as shown on cover), Side 2 is *Elvis Presley Live*.
HALW-0000-1/HALW-0000-2. Identification numbers are engraved. Side 1 also has "Mastercraft Memphis" engraved.

❑ HALW HALW-0001 ....12/78   12-25
COVER 1: All print is black-and-white, including photo of Scotty, Elvis and Bill on front. Print quality is sharp (unauthorized reissues have poorly reproduced cover art). Has limited edition number stamped at upper right on front. Cover indicates "10,000 Albums" made. Covers incorrectly state that the live recordings are from a concert at "Cook's Hoedown Club in Houston, Texas." The show was actually at the Eagle's Hall in Houston.
INNER SLEEVE 1: White, no printing.

HALW (M)
HALW-0001 ....12/78   25-50
TOTAL PACKAGE 1: Disc, cover.

❑ HALW (M) HALW-0001 ...12/78   12-25
DISC 2: Same as disc 1.

❑ HALW HALW-0001 ....12/78   8-10
COVER 2: Same as cover 1, except has no edition number.
INNER SLEEVE 2: White, no printing.

HALW (M)
HALW-0001 ....12/78   20-35
TOTAL PACKAGE 2: Disc, cover.

Side 1

Scotty Moore Tells the Story: First Meeting; Discovery of Elvis By Sam Phillips; The First Recording Session; The Second Recording Session; Shows with the Starlite Wranglers; On Their Own (Elvis, Scotty and Bill); Stranded in Shreveport, Louisiana; Grand Ole Opry Appearance; Louisiana Hayride Appearance.

Side 2

Elvis Presley Live: Good Rockin' Tonight (shown as "There's Good Rockin' Tonight"); Baby, Let's Play House; Blue Moon of Kentucky; I Got a Woman (shown as "I've Got a Woman"); That's All Right (shown as "That's Alright Little Mama").

FIRST YEARS – RECORDED LIVE DECEMBER 1954 / FEBRUARY 1955

❑ Black Belt: Bootleg. Listed for identification only.

FOR ELVIS FANS ONLY

❑ Lisa 6772: Bootleg. Listed for identification only.

FOR LP FANS ONLY

❑ RCA Victor (M)
LPM-1990..........................3/59   100-125
DISC 1: Black label, "Long Play" at bottom.
J2PP-8070-1S/J2PP-8071-1S. Label LP#1.
J2PP-8070-7S/J2PP-8071-4S. Label LP#1.

❑ RCA Victor LPM-1990.......3/59   150-175
COVER 1: Front: RCA logo and number at upper right. Color Elvis photo. Titles in yellow at upper right. Back: Color photo of Elvis in uniform. No other printing whatsoever. Elvis' name is on the spine but does not appear on either the front or back. Lettering on spine is larger than on just about any other single Elvis album.
INNER SLEEVE 1: Generic RCA "Popular Sound Spectacular for '59" sleeve (or other generic RCA sleeves). None mention Elvis or this LP.

RCA Victor (M)
LPM-1990 .... 3/59   250-300
TOTAL PACKAGE 1: Disc, cover.

❑ RCA Victor (M)
LPM-1990........................11/63   35-45
DISC 2: Black label, "Mono" at bottom.

❑ RCA Victor LPM-1990.....11/63   35-45
COVER 2: Front: RCA logo at upper left and number at lower left. "RE" at lower left. Black box at upper right with title and contents. Color Elvis photo. Back: Color photo of Elvis in uniform.

❑ RCA Victor (No Number)...9/63   8-10
INNER SLEEVE 2: Turquoise, black and white. Front: RCA's Elvis LP catalog, most recent being *It Happened at the World's Fair* (side 1, row 4, column 5). Back: RCA Elvis EPs and 45s catalog.

RCA Victor (M)
LPM-1990 .... 11/63   75-100
TOTAL PACKAGE 2: Disc, cover, inner sleeve.

❑ RCA Victor (M)
LPM-1990..........................1/65   25-35
DISC 3: Black label, "Monaural" at bottom.
J2PP-8070-4S/J2PP-8071-4S. Label LP#12.

❑ RCA Victor LPM-1990 ....1/65   25-35
COVER 3: Front: RCA logo at upper left and number at lower left. "RE" at lower left. Black box at upper right with title and contents. Color Elvis photo. Back: Color photo of Elvis in uniform. Has "Electronic Stereo Now Available" box of text at lower left and numbers at upper right.

❑ RCA Victor 21-112-1
40A....................................10/64   4-8
INNER SLEEVE 3: Red, black and white. Front: RCA's Elvis LP catalog, most recent being *Kissin' Cousins* (side 1, row 1, column 6). Back: RCA Elvis EPs and 45s catalog.

RCA Victor (M)
LPM-1990 .... 1/65   50-75
TOTAL PACKAGE 3: Disc, cover, inner sleeve.

❑ RCA Victor (SE)
LSP-1990(e) 1/65   10-20
DISC 4: Black label, RCA logo in white at the top and "Stereo" at bottom.
RPRS-7865-2S/RPRS-7866-2S. Label LP#15.

❑ RCA Victor LSP-1990(e) ...1/65   225-325
COVER 4: Front: RCA logo and number at upper left. "RE" at lower left, "Stereo Electronically Reprocessed" and black box with title and contents at upper right. Color Elvis photo. Back: Same Elvis photo as on front. Black box at upper right is the only other printing.

❑ RCA Victor 21-112-1
40A....................................10/64   4-8
INNER SLEEVE 4: Red, black and white. Front: RCA's Elvis LP catalog, most recent being *Kissin' Cousins* (side 1, row 1, column 6). Back: RCA Elvis EPs and 45s catalog.

RCA Victor (SE)
LSP-1990(e) 1/65   250-350
TOTAL PACKAGE 4: Disc, cover, inner sleeve.

❑ RCA Victor (SE)
LSP-1990(e) 1/65   10-20
DISC 5: Same as disc 4.

❑ RCA Victor LSP-1990(e) ...1/65   20-30
COVER 5: Front: RCA logo and number at upper left. "RE" at lower left. "Stereo Electronically Reprocessed" and black box with title and contents at upper right. Color Elvis photo. Back: Color photo of Elvis in uniform. Has "Electronic Stereo Now Available" box of text at lower left and numbers at upper right.

❑ RCA Victor 21-112-1
40A.................................10/64   4-8
INNER SLEEVE 5: Red, black and white.
Front: RCA's Elvis LP catalog, most recent
being *Kissin' Cousins* (side 1, row 1, column
6). Back: RCA Elvis EPs and 45s catalog.

RCA Victor (SE)
LSP-1990(e) **1/65**   **35-60**
TOTAL PACKAGE 5: Disc, cover, inner
   sleeve.

❑ RCA Victor (SE)
LSP-1990(e)..........................'68   20-25
DISC 6: Orange label. Rigid vinyl.
❑ RCA Victor LSP-1990(e) ..... '68   8-10
COVER 6: Same as cover 5, except has
"SER" at lower left on front.
❑ RCA Victor 21-112-1
40D.....................................6/68   4-6
INNER SLEEVE 6: Red, black and white.
Front: RCA's Elvis LP catalog, most recent
being *Elvis' Gold Records, Vol. 4* (side 1, row
4, column 5). Back: RCA's Elvis LP and Twin
Pack Stereo 8 catalog. May also be found
with inner sleeves 40B and 40C. See chapter
on inner sleeves for more information.

RCA Victor (SE)
LSP-1990(e) .... **'68**   **30-40**
TOTAL PACKAGE 6: Disc, cover, inner
   sleeve.

❑ RCA Victor (SE)
LSP-1990(e)..........................'76   10-15
DISC 7: Tan label.
❑ RCA LSP-1990(e) .... '76   10-15
COVER 7: Verification pending.
❑ RCA Victor...........................'70s   2-4
INNER SLEEVE 7: Black-and-white. Pictures
RCA Elvis catalog front and back. Any of
several sleeves may be found on reissues
from this period.

RCA Victor (SE)
LSP-1990(e) .... **'76**   **25-35**
TOTAL PACKAGE 7: Disc, cover, inner
   sleeve.

❑ RCA Victor (SE)
LSP-1990(e)..........................'76   4-8
DISC 8: Black label, dog near top.
❑ RCA LSP-1990(e) .... '76   4-8
COVER 8: Verification pending.
❑ RCA Victor...........................'70s   2-4
INNER SLEEVE 8: Black-and-white. Pictures
RCA Elvis catalog front and back. Any of
several sleeves may be found on reissues
from this period.

RCA Victor (SE)
LSP-1990(e) .... **'76**   **10-18**
TOTAL PACKAGE 8: Disc, cover, inner
   sleeve.

❑ RCA Victor (SE)
AFL1-1990(e) ....'77   3-5
DISC 9: Black label, dog near top.
❑ RCA Victor AFL1-1990(e)....'77   3-5
COVER 9: Reflects selection number change.
Includes copies with a sticker bearing the
"AFL1" prefix, wrapped around cover at top of
spine.
❑ RCA Victor..........................'70s   2-4
INNER SLEEVE 9: Black-and-white. Pictures
RCA Elvis catalog front and back. Any of
several sleeves may be found on reissues
from this period.

RCA Victor (SE)
AFL1-1990(e) .... **'77**   **8-15**
TOTAL PACKAGE 9: Disc, cover, inner
   sleeve.

On both covers and labels, the electronically
reprocessed stereo designation "(e)" may not
appear following every usage of the selection
number.

Side 1
That's All Right
Lawdy Miss Clawdy
Mystery Train
Playing for Keeps
Poor Boy

Side 2
My Baby Left Me
I Was the One
Shake, Rattle and Roll
I'm Left, You're Right, She's Gone
You're a Heartbreaker

FOREVER YOUNG, FOREVER BEAUTIFUL (RECORDED LIVE AT HOME – 1958)

❑ Memphis Flash (M)
JL-92447 ....5/78   20-40
DISC 1: Color portrait of Elvis on both sides.
❑ Memphis Flash
JL-92447 ....5/78   25-50
COVER 1: Front: Color portrait (same as on
labels) of Elvis. Back: Color photo of Elvis.
❑ Memphis Flash
JL-92447 ....5/78   5-10
INNER SLEEVE 1: 14 black-and-white photos
of Elvis.

Memphis Flash (M)
JL-92447 .... **5/78**   **50-100**
TOTAL PACKAGE 1: Disc, cover, inner
   sleeve.

Counterfeits exist; however, none meet the
descriptions given above.

Side 1
I Understand
Happy, Happy Birthday Baby
I Can't Help It (If I'm Still in Love with You) (By Anita
   Wood)
Who's Sorry Now (By Anita Wood)
Who's Sorry Now (By Anita Wood)
Happy, Happy Birthday Baby

Side 2

Happy, Happy Birthday Baby
Happy, Happy Birthday Baby
Happy, Happy Birthday Baby
Happy, Happy Birthday Baby
Happy, Happy Birthday Baby
Tumbling Tumbleweeds/Baby, Don't You Know
Tomorrow Night
Little Darlin'
Just a Closer Walk with Thee

14 #1 COUNTRY HITS

Various artists collection

❑ RCA Victor (ST)

AHL1-7004 .... '85   3-5
DISC 1: Black label, dog near top.
AHL1-7004A-1S/AHL1-7004B-1S.

❑ RCA AHL1-7004 .... '85   3-5
COVER 1: Front: No logo or number. Back:
Text only. RCA logo at lower left, number and
UPC bar code at upper right.
INNER SLEEVE 1: White, no printing.

RCA Victor (ST)

AHL1-7004 .... '85   6-10
TOTAL PACKAGE 1: Disc, cover.

Card stock jacket, with printing on cover – not
on slicks.

Side 1

9 to 5 (Dolly Parton)
Nobody (Sylvia)
Somewhere Between (Earl Thomas Conley)
Lady Down on Love (Alabama)
Guitar Man (Elvis Presley)
Just to Satisfy You (Waylon and Special Guest)
All Roads Lead to You (Steve Wariner)

Side 2

(There's) No Gettin' Over Me (Ronnie Milsap)
Friends (Razzy Bailey)
Lucille (You Won't Do Your Daddy's Will) (Waylon
Jennings)
She Got the Goldmine (I Got the Shaft) (Jerry Reed)
I Got Mexico (Eddy Raven)
Never Been So Loved (Charley Pride)
I Will Always Love You (Dolly Parton)

FRANK SINATRA SHOW (WELCOME HOME ELVIS)

❑ No label name: Bootleg. Listed for
identification only.

FRANKIE AND JOHNNY (RCA)

❑ RCA Victor (M)

LPM-3553 .... 4/66   10-15
DISC 1: Black label, "Monaural" at bottom.
SPRM-7386-1S/SPRM-7387-7S. Label LP#12.
SPRM-7386-5S/SPRM-7387-5S. Label LP#12.

❑ RCA Victor LPM-3553 .... 4/66   25-30
COVER 1: Front: RCA Victor logo at upper
right and number at lower left. Color Elvis
photo. Back: Ten color Elvis photos.

❑ RCA Victor 21-112-1

40B 4/65   4-6
INNER SLEEVE 1: Red, black and white.
Front: RCA's Elvis LP catalog, most recent
being *Roustabout* (side 1, row 1, column 5).
Back: RCA Elvis EPs and 45s catalog.

❑ RCA Victor LPM-3553 ......4/66   60-75
INSERT 1: 11¾" x 11¾" color print of an Elvis
portrait. Back is blank.

❑ RCA Victor LPM-3553 ......4/66   20-25
SHRINK STICKER 1: Announces the bonus,
color Elvis photo.

RCA Victor (M)

LPM-3553 .... 4/66   120-150
TOTAL PACKAGE 1: Disc, cover, inner
sleeve, insert, sticker.

❑ RCA Victor (M)

LPM-3553 .... 4/66   10-15
DISC 2: Black label, "Monaural" at bottom.
SPRM-7386-5S/SPRM-7387-5S. Label LP#12.

❑ RCA Victor LPM-3553 .... 4/66   45-50
COVER 2: Designate promo. Same as cover
1, but with "Not for Sale" stamped on back.

❑ RCA Victor 21-112-1

40B 4/65   4-6
INNER SLEEVE 2: Red, black and white.
Front: RCA's Elvis LP catalog, most recent
being *Roustabout* (side 1, row 1, column 5).
Back: RCA Elvis EPs and 45s catalog.

❑ RCA Victor LPM-3553 .... 4/66   60-75
INSERT 2: 11¾" x 11¾" color print of an Elvis
portrait. Back is blank.

❑ RCA Victor LPM-3553 .... 4/66   20-25
SHRINK STICKER 2: Announces the bonus,
color Elvis photo.

RCA Victor (M)

LPM-3553 .... 4/66   140-170
TOTAL PACKAGE 2: Disc, cover, inner
sleeve, insert, sticker.

❑ RCA Victor (ST)

LSP-3553 .... 4/66   10-15
DISC 3: Black label, RCA logo in white at top
and "Stereo" at bottom.
SPRS-7388-4S/SPRS-7389-5S. Label LP#16.
SPRS-7388-5S/SPRS-7389-2S. Label LP#16.

❑ RCA Victor LSP-3553 ....4/66   25-30
COVER 3: Front: RCA Victor logo at upper
right and number at upper left. Color Elvis
photo. Back. Ten color Elvis photos.

❑ RCA Victor 21-112-1

40B 4/65   4-6
INNER SLEEVE 3: Red, black and white.
Front: RCA's Elvis LP catalog, most recent
being *Roustabout* (side 1, row 1, column 5).
Back: RCA Elvis EPs and 45s catalog.

❑ RCA Victor LSP-3553 ....4/66   60-75
INSERT 3: 11¾" x 11¾" color print of an Elvis
portrait. Back is blank.

❑ RCA Victor LSP-3553 ....4/66   20-25
SHRINK STICKER 3: Announces the bonus,
color Elvis photo.

RCA Victor (ST)

LSP-3553.....................4/66   120-150
TOTAL PACKAGE 3: Disc, cover, inner
sleeve, insert, sticker.

❑ RCA Victor (ST)
LSP-3553 ....4/66   10-15
DISC 4: Black label, RCA logo in white at top
and "Stereo" at bottom.
SPRS-7388-5S/SPRS-7389-2S. Label LP#16.

❑ RCA Victor LSP-3553........4/66   45-50
COVER 4: Designate promo. Same as cover
3, but with "Not for Sale" stamped on back.

❑ RCA Victor 21-112-1
40B....................................4/65   4-6
INNER SLEEVE 4: Red, black and white.
Front: RCA's Elvis LP catalog, most recent
being *Roustabout* (side 1, row 1, column 5).
Back: RCA Elvis EPs and 45s catalog.

❑ RCA Victor LSP-3553........4/66   60-75
INSERT 4: 11¾" x 11¾" color print of an Elvis
portrait. Back is blank.

❑ RCA Victor LSP-3553........4/66   20-25
SHRINK STICKER 4: Announces the bonus,
color Elvis photo.

RCA Victor (ST)

LSP-3553.....................4/66   140-170
TOTAL PACKAGE 4: Disc, cover, inner
sleeve, insert, sticker.

One month after Elvis' death, RCA announced
reissues of six Elvis soundtrack albums from
the '60s, one of which is *Frankie and Johnny*
(APL1-2559). This information appears in the
Phonolog New Release Reporter for the week
September 26, 1977. Though the other five
albums do exist, we have not verified any
copies of this one. It may have been
withdrawn at the last moment to avoid conflict
with the Pickwick issue of *Frankie and
Johnny*, or a few may have actually been
made before it was pulled from the catalog.
Until a copy is verified, we hesitate to price it.
If it does exist, it is a very rare item.

Side 1
Frankie and Johnny
Come Along
Petunia, the Gardener's Daughter
Chesay
What Every Woman Lives For
Look Out, Broadway

Side 2
Beginner's Luck
[Medley] Down by the Riverside/When the Saints Go
  Marching In
Shout It Out
Hard Luck
Please Don't Stop Loving Me
Everybody Come Aboard

FRANKIE AND JOHNNY (Pickwick)

❑ Pickwick/Camden (ST)
ACL-7007 ....'76   5-7
DISC 1: Black label. Multi-color Pickwick logo
at center. Omits two tracks from the RCA
Victor issue: *Chesay* and *Everybody Come
Aboard*.
ACL-7007A/ACL-7007B. Identification numbers are
engraved.

❑ Pickwick/Camden
ACL-7007 ....'76   5-8
COVER 1: Front: Camden logo at upper right
and Pickwick logo at upper right. Color Elvis
photo is same as found on *Elvis Now*. Back:
Four black-and-white Elvis photos. (All photos
on cover are '70s concert shots and have
nothing whatsoever to do with *Frankie and
Johnny*.)
INNER SLEEVE 1: White, no printing.

Pickwick/Camden (ST)
ACL-7007 ....'76   10-15
TOTAL PACKAGE 1: Disc, cover.

In early 1979, Pickwick reissued a package of
seven Elvis LPs. Since it was issued after the
'78 Christmas season, *Elvis' Christmas Album*
was replaced with *Frankie and Johnny*. See
Pickwick Pack.

Side 1
Frankie and Johnny
Come Along
Petunia, the Gardener's Daughter
What Every Woman Lives For
Look Out, Broadway

Side 2
Beginner's Luck
[Medley] Down by the Riverside/When the Saints Go
  Marching In
Shout It Out
Hard Luck
Please Don't Stop Loving Me

FRANTIC FIFTIES (AS BROADCAST IN "THE WORLD TODAY" DECEMBER 28th and 29th, 1959)

❑ Mutual Broadcast System (M)
RW-4082 ....1/60   150-250
DISC 1: Green label, silver print. Recaps "The
Voices and Events Which Made the Frantic
Fifties." Promotional issue for Mutual Network
affiliate radio stations only. Segment on Rock
and Roll has an excerpt of *Hound Dog* by
Elvis.
L8OP-1032-1/L8OP-1033-1. Identification numbers
(stamped) indicate this disc was pressed by RCA Victor.

❑ Mutual Broadcast System
RW-4082 ....1/60   150-250
COVER 1: Front: Text only. Back: Text only.
Has "Operation Newsbeat – Mutual's News
Concept for Modern Radio" at top.
INNER SLEEVE 1: White, no printing.

Mutual Broadcast System (M)
RW-4082.....................1/60   300-500
TOTAL PACKAGE 1: Disc, cover.

FROM ELVIS IN MEMPHIS (RCA)

❑ RCA Victor (ST)
LSP-4155 ....6/69   20-25
DISC 1: Orange label. Rigid vinyl.
XPRS-1366-4S-A1/XPRS-1367-A2.
XPRS-1366-4S/XPRS-1367-1S.
XPRS-1366-4S/XPRS-1367-7S.
XPRS-1366-6S/XPRS-1367-6S.
XPRS-1366-7S/XPRS-1367-7S.

❑ RCA Victor LSP-4155........6/69   20-25
COVER 1: Front: RCA logo and number at upper left, "Victor Stereo" at upper right. Color Elvis photo. Back: Color Elvis photo. Pictures "Elvis," the TV Special album.

❑ RCA Victor 21-112-1
40D.....................................6/68   4-6
INNER SLEEVE 1: Red, black and white. Front: RCA's Elvis LP catalog, most recent being *Elvis' Gold Records, Vol. 4* (side 1, row 4, column 5). Back: RCA's Elvis LP and Twin Pack Stereo 8 catalog. May also be found with inner sleeves 40B and 40C. See chapter on inner sleeves for more information.

❑ RCA Victor LSP-4155........6/69   30-40
INSERT 1: Color 8" x 10" Elvis photo, signed "Sincerely, Elvis Presley." Back lists other Elvis RCA releases.

❑ RCA Victor LSP-4155........6/69   5-10
SHRINK STICKER 1: Announces bonus photo.

RCA Victor (ST)
LSP-4155......................6/69   **80-100**
TOTAL PACKAGE 1: Disc, cover, inner sleeve, insert, sticker.

❑ RCA Victor (ST)
LSP-4155 ....6/69   20-25
DISC 2: Same as disc 1.

❑ RCA Victor LSP-4155........6/69   30-35
COVER 2: Designate promo. Same as cover 1, but with "Not for Sale" stamped on back.

❑ RCA Victor 21-112-1
40D.....................................6/68   4-6
INNER SLEEVE 2: Red, black and white. Front: RCA's Elvis LP catalog, most recent being *Elvis' Gold Records, Vol. 4* (side 1, row 4, column 5). Back: RCA's Elvis LP and Twin Pack Stereo 8 catalog. May also be found with inner sleeves 40B and 40C. See chapter on inner sleeves for more information.

❑ RCA Victor LSP-4155........6/69   30-40
INSERT 2: Color 8" x 10" Elvis photo, signed "Sincerely, Elvis Presley." Back lists other Elvis RCA releases.

❑ RCA Victor LSP-4155........6/69   5-10
SHRINK STICKER 2: Announces bonus photo.

RCA Victor (ST)
LSP-4155......................6/69   **90-110**
TOTAL PACKAGE 2: Disc, cover, inner sleeve, insert, sticker.

❑ RCA Victor (ST)
LSP-4155 ....'71   10-15
DISC 3: Orange label. Flexible vinyl.

❑ RCA Victor LSP-4155..........'71   20-25
COVER 3: Same as cover 1.

❑ RCA Victor..........................'70s   2-4
INNER SLEEVE 3: Black-and-white. Pictures RCA Elvis catalog front and back. Any of several sleeves may be found on reissues from this period.

RCA Victor (ST)
LSP-4155......................'71   **30-45**
TOTAL PACKAGE 3: Disc, cover, inner sleeve.

❑ RCA Victor (ST)
LSP-4155 ....'76   12-15
DISC 4: Tan label.

❑ RCA Victor LSP-4155..........'76   12-15
COVER 4: Verification pending.

❑ RCA Victor..........................'70s   2-4
INNER SLEEVE 4: Black-and-white. Pictures RCA Elvis catalog front and back. Any of several sleeves may be found on reissues from this period.

RCA Victor (ST)
LSP-4155......................'76   **25-30**
TOTAL PACKAGE 4: Disc, cover, inner sleeve.

❑ RCA Victor (ST)
LSP-4155 ....'76   10-15
DISC 5: Black label, dog near top.

❑ RCA LSP-4155....................'76   10-15
COVER 5: Verification pending.

❑ RCA Victor..........................'70s   2-4
INNER SLEEVE 5: Black-and-white. Pictures RCA Elvis catalog front and back. Any of several sleeves may be found on reissues from this period.

RCA Victor (ST)
LSP-4155......................'76   **10-18**
TOTAL PACKAGE 5: Disc, cover, inner sleeve.

❑ RCA Victor (ST)
AFL1-4155...........................'77   3-5
DISC 6: Black label, dog near top.
AFL1-4155A-12/AFL1-4155B-15.

❑ RCA AFL1-4155 ....'77   3-5
COVER 6: Reflects prefix change. Includes copies with a sticker bearing the "AFL1" prefix, wrapped around cover at top of spine.

❑ RCA Victor..........................'70s   2-4
INNER SLEEVE 6: Black-and-white. Pictures RCA Elvis catalog front and back. Any of several sleeves may be found on reissues from this period.

RCA Victor (ST)
AFL1-4155......................'77   **8-15**
TOTAL PACKAGE 6: Disc, cover, inner sleeve.

"Good Times" ($20–$30).

"Elvis Recorded Live on Stage in Memphis" ($300–$400).

"Reconsider Baby" ($20–$25).

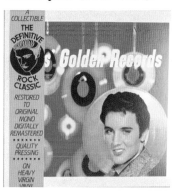

"Elvis' Golden Records." Digitally remastered monaural ($10–$15).

"Elvis' Golden Records, Vol. 2." Digitally remastered monaural ($10–$15).

"Elvis." Digitally remastered monaural ($10–$15).

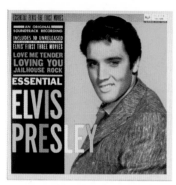

"Essential Elvis: The First Movies" ($20–$25).

"Elvis Aron Presley Forever" ($25–$30).

"Elvis Recorded Live on Stage in Memphis." Quadraphonic ($200–$300).

"Good Rockin' Tonight" ($60–$80).

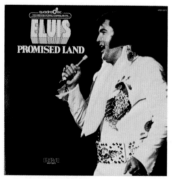

"Promised Land." Quadraphonic ($200–$250).

"Elvis Today." Quadraphonic ($200–$250).

Elvis Presley lipstick. Tube attached to display card
($1,000–$1,500). Tube without card ($400–$600).

Elvis Presley record case ($500–$750). Elvis Presley guitar,
with carrying case ($2,500–$3,000). Guitar without case
($1,000–$2,000).

Side 1
Wearin' That Loved On Look
Only the Strong Survive
I'll Hold You in My Arms (Till I Can Hold You in My Heart)
Long Black Limousine
It Keeps Right On A-hurtin'
I'm Moving On

Side 2
Power of My Love
Gentle On My Mind
After Loving You
True Love Travels on a Gravel Road
Any Day Now
In the Ghetto

FROM ELVIS IN MEMPHIS (MFSL)

❑ Mobile Fidelity Sound Lab (ST)
   MFSL 1-059 .... '82   25-40
   DISC 1: White label, black and mustard print. Manufactured from original stereo master tapes, produced in Japan at half-speed using special plating and High-Definition Super Vinyl, for maximum reproduction.
   MFSL 1-059-A1/MFSL 1-059-B2. These numbers, and "M.T. Orthofon" are engraved, but "H-111/H-121" is stamped.

❑ Mobile Fidelity Sound Lab
   MFSL 1-059 .... '82   25-40
   COVER 1: Front: Yellow stripe across top with "Original Master Recording." Back: Has "Original Master Recording" across top. Does not picture the "Elvis" TV Special album. Front and back Elvis photos are identical to those on the RCA Victor issue.
   INNER SLEEVE 1: Plastic, no printing.
   INSERT 1: Generic MFSL "Limited Editions from the Original Masters" catalog. No mention of Elvis or this LP.

Mobile Fidelity Sound Lab (ST)
   MFSL 1-059 .... '82   50-80
   TOTAL PACKAGE 1: Disc, cover.

Side 1
Wearin' That Loved On Look
Only the Strong Survive
I'll Hold You in My Arms (Till I Can Hold You in My Heart)
Long Black Limousine
It Keeps Right On A-hurtin'
I'm Moving On

Side 2
Power of My Love
Gentle On My Mind
After Loving You
True Love Travels on a Gravel Road
Any Day Now
In the Ghetto

FROM ELVIS PRESLEY BOULEVARD, MEMPHIS, TENNESSEE (RECORDED LIVE)

❑ RCA Victor (ST)
   APL1-1506 ....5/76   10-12
   DISC 1: Tan label. Flexible vinyl. One of only two Elvis LPs to have been issued originally on the tan label, the other being *The Sun Sessions.*
   APL1-1506A-1S/APL1-1506B-2S.
   APL1-1506A-2S/APL1-1506B-2S.

❑ RCA APL1-1506 ....5/76   10-12
   COVER 1: Front: RCA logo at lower left, number at upper left. Color Elvis photo. Back: Text only. RCA logo and number at lower right.

❑ RCA Victor 21-112-1PT
   54B 7/73   3-5
   INNER SLEEVE 1: Black-and-white. Pictures RCA's Elvis LP catalog front and back, most recent being *Elvis As Recorded at Madison Square Garden* (side 2, row 2, column 6). May also be found with inner sleeve 54D

❑ RCA APL1-1506 ....5/76   5-10
   SHRINK STICKER 1: Announces the inclusion of the hits *Hurt* and *For the Heart.*

RCA Victor (ST)
   APL1-1506 ....5/76   30-40
   TOTAL PACKAGE 1: Disc, cover, inner sleeve, sticker.

❑ RCA Victor (ST)
   APL1-1506 ....5/76   10-12
   DISC 2: Same as disc 1.

❑ RCA APL1-1506 ....5/76   15-20
   COVER 2: Designate promo. Same as cover 1, but with "Not for Sale" stamped on back.

❑ RCA Victor 21-112-1PT
   54B 7/73   3-5
   INNER SLEEVE 2: Black-and-white. Pictures RCA's Elvis LP catalog front and back, most recent being *Elvis As Recorded at Madison Square Garden* (side 2, row 2, column 6). May also be found with inner sleeve 54D

❑ RCA APL1-1506 ....5/76   5-10
   SHRINK STICKER 2: Announces the inclusion of the hits *Hurt* and *For the Heart.*

RCA Victor (ST)
   APL1-1506 ....5/76   35-45
   TOTAL PACKAGE 2: Disc, cover, inner sleeve, sticker.

❑ RCA Victor (ST)
   APL1-1506 ....'77   4-6
   DISC 3: Black label, dog near top.
   APL1-1506A-5/APL1-1506B-4. Both sides have a "1" before the last number, which is crossed out. After, the correct number is added.

❑ RCA APL1-1506/
   AFL1-1506.........................'77   4-6
   COVER 3: Same as cover 1, but with a wrap-around sticker added to top of spine with "AFL1-1506," so it shows on front and back.

❑ RCA Victor......................... '70s   2-4
   INNER SLEEVE 3: Black-and-white. Pictures
   RCA Elvis catalog front and back. Any of
   several may be found on reissues from this
   period.

RCA Victor (ST)
APL1-1506 .... '77   10-18
   TOTAL PACKAGE 3: Disc, cover, inner
   sleeve.

❑ RCA (ST) AFL1-1506.......... '77   3-5
   DISC 4: Black label, dog near top.
❑ RCA AFL1-1506.................. '77   3-5
   COVER 4: Reflects prefix change.
❑ RCA Victor......................... '70s   2-4
   INNER SLEEVE 4: Black-and-white. Pictures
   RCA Elvis catalog front and back. Any of
   several may be found on reissues from this
   period.

RCA (ST) AFL1-1506 .... '77   8-15
   TOTAL PACKAGE 4: Disc, cover, inner
   sleeve.

Side 1
Hurt
Never Again
Blue Eyes Crying in the Rain
Danny Boy
The Last Farewell
Side 2
For the Heart
Bitter They Are, Harder They Fall
Solitaire
Love Coming Down
I'll Never Fall in Love Again

FROM ELVIS WITH LOVE (2 LPs)

❑ RCA Victor (SP)
   R-234340 .... '78   12-15
   DISCS 1: RCA Record Club issue. Black
   label, dog near top.
   (Disc 1) R-234340 A-1/R-234340D-2. Identification
   numbers are engraved on side 1 and stamped on side 2.
   (Disc 2) R-234340 B-1/R-234340C-1. Identification
   numbers are engraved on both sides.
❑ RCA R-234340 .... '78   12-15
   COVER 1: Single pocket. Front: RCA logo
   and number at upper right. Color "Aloha" Elvis
   photo. Back: Silhouette of front cover photo.
❑ RCA Victor 21-112-1PT
   54F 7/77   4-8
   INNER SLEEVES 1: Black-and-white.
   Pictures RCA's Elvis LPs front and back, most
   recent being *Moody Blue* (side 2, row 5,
   column 1). On side 1, at bottom left, is the
   number 21-112-1 PT 54F.

RCA Victor (SP)
R-234340 .... '78   30-40
   TOTAL PACKAGE 1: Discs, cover, inner
   sleeves.

Disc 1
Side 1
Love Me Tender
Can't Help Falling in Love

The Next Step Is Love
I Need Your Love Tonight
I Can't Stop Loving You
Side 2
I Want You, I Need You, I Love You
I Love You Because
Love Letters
A Thing Called Love
A Big Hunk O' Love
Disc 2
Side 3
Love Me
Without Love
Faded Love
Loving You
You've Lost That Lovin' Feelin'
Side 4
Have I Told You Lately That I Love You
You Don't Have to Say You Love Me
True Love
Ain't That Loving You Baby
Please Don't Stop Loving Me

FROM HOLLYWOOD TO VEGAS

❑ Brookville BRLP-301: Bootleg. Listed for
   identification only.

FROM LAS VEGAS TO NIAGARA FALLS

❑ Live Productions LVLP-1897/1898: Bootleg.
   Listed for identification only.

FROM MEMPHIS TO VEGAS / FROM VEGAS TO MEMPHIS (2 LPs)

❑ RCA Victor (ST)
   LSP-6020 ....11/69   35-50
   DISCS 1: Orange label. Rigid vinyl. On side 2,
   label incorrectly shows writers of *Words* as
   Tommy Boyce and Bobby Hart, and shows
   writer of *Suspicious Minds* as Frances
   Zambon. This was the first multi-disc Elvis
   album.
   (Disc 1) XPRS-2468-4S/XPRS-2469-3S. **(Disc 2)** XPRS-
   2470-4S/XPRS-2471-4S. Identification numbers are
   engraved.
   (Disc 1) XPRS-2468-4S/XPRS-2469-4S. **(Disc 2)** XPRS-
   2470-3S/XPRS-2471-4S.
   (Disc 1) XPRS-2468-5S/XPRS-2469-5S. **(Disc 2)** XPRS-
   2470-5S/XPRS-2471-5S. Identification numbers are
   stamped.
❑ RCA Victor LSP-6020......11/69   20-25
   COVER 1: Double pocket. Front: Titled *Elvis
   in Person at the International Hotel, Las
   Vegas, Nevada*, has RCA logo and number at
   upper left, "Victor Stereo" at upper right.
   Black-and-white Elvis photo. Back: Titled *Elvis
   Back in Memphis*, also has RCA logo and
   number at upper left, "Victor Stereo" at upper
   right. Black-and-white Elvis photo. Inside
   panels have four black-and-white Elvis
   photos. Price reflects RCA's use of this same
   cover, with no discernible differences, until
   1976.

❑ RCA Victor 21-112-1
   40D....................................6/68   8-12
   INNER SLEEVES 1: Red, black and white.
   Front: RCA's Elvis LP catalog, most recent
   being *Elvis' Gold Records, Vol. 4* (side 1, row
   4, column 5). Back: RCA's Elvis LP and Twin
   Pack Stereo 8 catalog. May also be found
   with inner sleeves 40B and 40C. See chapter
   on inner sleeves for more information.
❑ RCA Victor............................ '69   40-50
   INSERTS 1: Includes two of the following four
   8" x 10" black-and-white Elvis photos, all of
   which have RCA catalog selections on the
   back. Price is for any two of the following
   photos:

   a) Elvis sitting, holding his guitar. (Guitar neck
   does not show.) Right profile of Elvis,
   microphone at lower right. Signed "Sincerely,
   Elvis Presley."
   b) Elvis in leather suit, sitting, holding his
   guitar. (Guitar neck shows.) Right profile of
   Elvis, microphone at lower right. Signed
   "Sincerely Yours, Elvis Presley."
   c) Elvis in leather suit, standing, holding
   microphone. No guitar in photo. Signed "My
   Sincere Thanks, Elvis Presley."
   d) Elvis not in leather suit. Standing, left
   profile shot, from shoulders up. Signed
   "Thanks, Elvis."
❑ RCA Victor............................ '69   50-75
   SHRINK STICKER 1: Announces bonus Elvis
   photos.
RCA Victor (ST)
   LSP-6020.................11/69   150-200
   **TOTAL PACKAGE 1: Discs, cover, inner
   sleeves, inserts, sticker.**

❑ RCA Victor (ST)
   LSP-6020........................11/69   35-50
   DISCS 2: Same as discs 1.
❑ RCA Victor LSP-6020......11/69   30-35
   COVER 2: Designate promo. Same as cover
   1, but with "Not for Sale" stamped on back.
❑ RCA Victor 21-112-1
   40D....................................6/68   8-12
   INNER SLEEVES 2: Red, black and white.
   Front: RCA's Elvis LP catalog, most recent
   being *Elvis' Gold Records, Vol. 4* (side 1, row
   4, column 5). Back: RCA's Elvis LP and Twin
   Pack Stereo 8 catalog. May also be found
   with inner sleeves 40B and 40C. See chapter
   on inner sleeves for more information.
❑ RCA Victor............................ '69   40-50
   INSERTS 2: Includes two of the four 8" x 10"
   black-and-white Elvis photos listed above.
❑ RCA Victor............................ '69   50-75
   SHRINK STICKER 2: Announces bonus Elvis
   photos.
RCA Victor (ST)
   LSP-6020.................12/69   175-225
   **TOTAL PACKAGE 2: Discs, cover, inner
   sleeves, inserts, sticker.**

❑ RCA Victor (ST)
   LSP-6020........................12/69   20-25
   DISCS 3: Orange label. Rigid vinyl. On side 2,
   correctly shows writers of *Words* as Barry,
   Robin and Maurice Gibb, and writer of
   Suspicious Minds as Mark James.
   (Disc 1) XPRS-2468-6S/XPRS-2469-5S. **(Disc 2)** XPRS-
   2470-5S/XPRS-2471-5S.
❑ RCA Victor LSP-6020......11/69   20-25
   COVER 3: Same as cover 1.
❑ RCA Victor 21-112-1
   40D....................................6/68   8-12
   INNER SLEEVES 3: Red, black and white.
   Front: RCA's Elvis LP catalog, most recent
   being *Elvis' Gold Records, Vol. 4* (side 1, row
   4, column 5). Back: RCA's Elvis LP and Twin
   Pack Stereo 8 catalog. May also be found
   with inner sleeves 40B and 40C. See chapter
   on inner sleeves for more information.
❑ RCA Victor............................ '69   40-50
   INSERTS 3: Includes two of the four 8" x 10"
   black-and-white Elvis photos listed above.
❑ RCA Victor............................ '69   50-75
   SHRINK STICKER 3: Announces bonus Elvis
   photos.
RCA Victor (ST)
   LSP-6020...................12/69   140-185
   **TOTAL PACKAGE 3: Discs, cover, inner
   sleeves, inserts, sticker.**

❑ RCA Victor (ST)
   LSP-6020............................'71   10-20
   DISCS 4: Orange label. Flexible disc.
❑ RCA Victor LSP-6020...........'71   10-20
   COVER 4: Verification pending.
❑ RCA Victor 21-112-1
   40D.................................... '70s   4-8
   INNER SLEEVES 4: Black-and-white.
   Pictures RCA Elvis catalog front and back.
   Any of several sleeves may be found on
   reissues from this period.
RCA Victor (ST)
   LSP-6020........................'71   25-50
   **TOTAL PACKAGE 4: Discs, cover, inner
   sleeves.**

❑ RCA Victor (ST)
   LSP-6020 .... '76   12-15
   DISCS 5: Tan label.
   (Disc 1) XPRS-2468-36S/XPRS-2469-32S. **(Disc 2)** XPRS-
   2470-35S/XPRS-2471-32S.
❑ RCA LSP-6020.....................'76   12-15
   COVER 5: Same as cover 1.
❑ RCA Victor........................'70s   4-8
   INNER SLEEVES 5: Black-and-white.
   Pictures RCA Elvis catalog front and back.
   Any of several sleeves may be found on
   reissues from this period.
RCA Victor (ST)
   LSP-6020........................'76   30-40
   **TOTAL PACKAGE 5: Discs, cover, inner
   sleeves.**

❏ RCA Victor (ST)
LSP-6020 .... '76   5-8
DISCS 6: Black label, dog near top.
❏ RCA LSP-6020 .... '76   5-8
COVER 6: Covers are slightly smaller, and
paper stock is of a lighter weight than is found
on cover 1.
❏ RCA Victor......................... '70s   4-8
INNER SLEEVES 6: Black-and-white.
Pictures RCA Elvis catalog front and back.
Any of several sleeves may be found on
reissues from this period.

RCA Victor (ST)
LSP-6020...................... '76   **15-25**
TOTAL PACKAGE 6: Discs, cover, inner
sleeves.

Disc 1
Side 1
Blue Suede Shoes
Johnny B. Goode
All Shook Up
Are You Lonesome Tonight
Hound Dog
I Can't Stop Loving You
My Babe
Side 2
Medley: Mystery Train/Tiger Man
Words
In the Ghetto
Suspicious Minds
Can't Help Falling in Love
Disc 2
Side 3
Inherit the Wind
This Is My Story
Stranger in My Own Home Town
A Little Bit of Green
And the Grass Won't Pay No Mind
Side 4
Do You Know Who I Am
From a Jack to a King
The Fair Is Moving On
You'll Think of Me
Without Love (There Is Nothing)

FROM THE BEACH TO THE BAYOU
❏ Graceland GL-1001: Bootleg. Listed for
identification only.
❏ Moon 8135: Bootleg. Listed for identification
only.

FROM THE DARK TO THE LIGHT
❏ Tiger TR-101: Bootleg. Listed for
identification only.

FROM THE WAIST UP
❏ Golden Archives GA-150: Bootleg. Listed for
identification only.

FUN IN ACAPULCO
❏ RCA Victor (M)
LPM-2756........................12/63   30-40
DISC 1: Black label, "Mono" at bottom.

PPRM-4434-1S/PPRM-4435-1S. Label LP#10.
PPRM-4434-2S/PPRM-4435-2S. Label LP#11.
❏ RCA Victor LPM-2756 .....12/63   30-40
COVER 1: Front: RCA Victor logos at upper
right and left (the first time this was done on a
front cover), and number at lower left. Color
Elvis photo. Back: 13 color Elvis photos (one
for each song title). Price reflects RCA's
continued use of this same cover, with no
discernible differences.
❏ RCA Victor (No Number)...9/63   8-10
INNER SLEEVE 1: Turquoise, black and
white. Front: RCA's Elvis LP catalog, most
recent being *It Happened at the World's Fair*
(side 1, row 4, column 5). Back: RCA Elvis
EPs and 45s catalog.

RCA Victor (M)
LPM-2756 .... 12/63   **70-90**
TOTAL PACKAGE 1: Disc, cover, inner
sleeve.

❏ RCA Victor (M)
LPM-2756 ....10/64   10-15
DISC 2: Black label, "Monaural" at bottom.
PPRM-4434-2S/PPRM-4435-2S. Label LP#12.
❏ RCA Victor LPM-2756 .....10/64   30-40
COVER 2: Same as cover 1.
❏ RCA Victor 21-112-1
40A 10/64   4-8
INNER SLEEVE 2: Red, black and white.
Front: RCA's Elvis LP catalog, most recent
being *Kissin' Cousins* (side 1, row 1, column
6). Back: RCA Elvis EPs and 45s catalog.

RCA Victor (M)
LPM-2756 .... 10/64   **45-65**
TOTAL PACKAGE 2: Disc, cover, inner
sleeve.

❏ RCA Victor (ST)
LSP-2756 ....12/63   40-50
DISC 3: Black label, RCA logo in silver at top
and "Stereo" at bottom.
PPRS-4436-1S/PPRS-4437-1S. Label LP#14.
PPRS-4436-2S/PPRS-4437-2S. Label LP#14.
❏ RCA Victor LSP-2756......12/63   40-50
COVER 3: Front: RCA Victor logos at upper
right and left. Number at upper left. Color Elvis
photo. Back: 13 color Elvis photos (one for
each song title).
❏ RCA Victor (No Number)...9/63   8-10
INNER SLEEVE 3: Turquoise, black and
white. Front: RCA's Elvis LP catalog, most
recent being *It Happened at the World's Fair*
(side 1, row 4, column 5). Back: RCA Elvis
EPs and 45s catalog.

RCA Victor (ST)
LSP-2756.................. 12/63   **90-110**
TOTAL PACKAGE 3: Disc, cover, inner
sleeve.

❏ RCA Victor (ST)
LSP-2756 ....10/64   10-15
DISC 4: Black label, RCA logo in white at top
and "Stereo" at bottom.

PPRS-4436-3S/PPRS-4437-3S. Label LP#16.

❑ RCA Victor LSP-2756...... 10/64   30-40
COVER 4: Same as cover 3.

❑ RCA Victor 21-112-1
40A.................................10/64   4-8
INNER SLEEVE 4: Red, black and white.
Front: RCA's Elvis LP catalog, most recent
being *Kissin' Cousins* (side 1, row 1, column
6). Back: RCA Elvis EPs and 45s catalog.

RCA Victor (ST)
LSP-2756.................. 10/64   45-65
TOTAL PACKAGE 4: Disc, cover, inner
sleeve.

❑ RCA Victor (ST)
LSP-2756 ....11/68   20-25
DISC 5: Orange label. Rigid vinyl.

❑ RCA Victor LSP-2756...... 11/68   8-10
COVER 5: Verification pending.

❑ RCA Victor 21-112-1
40D....................................6/68   4-6
INNER SLEEVE 5: Red, black and white.
Front: RCA's Elvis LP catalog, most recent
being *Elvis' Gold Records, Vol. 4* (side 1, row
4, column 5). Back: RCA's Elvis LP and Twin
Pack Stereo 8 catalog. May also be found
with inner sleeves 40B and 40C. See chapter
on inner sleeves for more information.

RCA Victor (ST)
LSP-2756.................. 11/68   35-40
TOTAL PACKAGE 5: Disc, cover, inner
sleeve.

❑ RCA Victor (ST)
LSP-2756 ....'76   10-15
DISC 6: Tan label.

❑ RCA Victor LSP-2756..........'76   10-15
COVER 6: Verification pending.

❑ RCA Victor.........................'70s   2-4
INNER SLEEVE 6: Black-and-white. Pictures
RCA Elvis catalog front and back. Any of
several sleeves may be found on reissues
from this period.

RCA Victor (ST)
LSP-2756.......................'76   20-30
TOTAL PACKAGE 6: Disc, cover, inner
sleeve.

❑ RCA Victor (ST)
LSP-2756 ....'76   4-6
DISC 7: Black label, dog near top.

❑ RCA LSP-2756....................'76   4-6
COVER 7: Front: "RE" in small letters at lower
left corner.

❑ RCA Victor.........................'70s   2-4
INNER SLEEVE 7: Black-and-white. Pictures
RCA Elvis catalog front and back. Any of
several sleeves may be found on reissues
from this period.

RCA Victor (ST)
LSP-2756.......................'76   10-18
TOTAL PACKAGE 7: Disc, cover, inner
sleeve.

❑ RCA Victor (ST)
AFL1-2756...........................'77   3-5
DISC 8: Black label, dog near top.

❑ RCA AFL1-2756 ....'77   3-5
COVER 8: Reflects prefix change. Includes
copies with a sticker bearing the "AFL1"
prefix, wrapped around cover at top of spine.

❑ RCA Victor.........................'70s   2-4
INNER SLEEVE 8: Black-and-white. Pictures
RCA Elvis catalog front and back. Any of
several sleeves may be found on reissues
from this period.

RCA Victor (ST)
AFL1-2756.....................'77   8-15
TOTAL PACKAGE 8: Disc, cover, inner
sleeve.

Side 1
Fun in Acapulco
Vino, Dinero Y Amor
Mexico
El Toro
Marguerita
The Lady Was a Bullfighter
No Room to Rhumba In a Sports Car

Side 2
I Think I'm Gonna Like It Here
Bossa Nova Baby
You Can't Say No In Acapulco
Guadalajara
Love Me Tonight
Slowly But Surely

G.I. BLUES

❑ RCA Victor (M)
LPM-2256 ....10/60   20-25
DISC 1: Black label, "Long Play" at bottom.
L2PP-3657-1S/L2PP-3658-1S. Label LP#1.

❑ RCA Victor LPM-2256 .....10/60   400-450
COVER 1: Front: RCA Victor logo at upper
right, number at lower left. Has red, heart-
shaped sticker applied to cover, announcing
the inclusion of *Wooden Heart*. (Sticker is a
permanent part of cover – not merely a shrink
wrap sticker.) Color Elvis photo. Back: Four
color Elvis photos.

❑ RCA Victor
(No Number)....................10/60   10-20
INNER SLEEVE 1: Brown, black and white.
Front: RCA's Elvis LP catalog, most recent
being *Elvis Is Back!* (side 1, row 1). Back:
RCA Elvis EPs and an explanation of
stereophonic sound. This sleeve not only
appeared with 1960 issues of *G.I. Blues*, but
has also been found with other RCA albums
issued that year.
STICKER 1: Not priced separately since it is
applied directly to cover.

RCA Victor (M)
LPM-2256 .... 10/60   425-500
TOTAL PACKAGE 1: Disc, cover with sticker, inner sleeve.

❑ RCA Victor (M)
LPM-2256........................12/60   20-25
DISC 2: Same as disc 1.
❑ RCA Victor LPM-2256 ..... 12/60   50-55
COVER 2: Same as cover 1, except without heart-shaped sticker. Price reflects RCA's continued use of this same cover, with no discernible differences.
❑ RCA Victor
(No Number) 10/60   10-20
INNER SLEEVE 2: Brown, black and white. Front: RCA's Elvis LP catalog, most recent being *Elvis Is Back!* (side 1, row 1). Back: RCA Elvis EPs and an explanation of stereophonic sound. This sleeve not only appeared with 1960 issues of *G.I. Blues*, but has also been found with other RCA albums issued that year.

RCA Victor (M)
LPM-2256 .... 12/60   80-100
TOTAL PACKAGE 2: Disc, cover, inner sleeve.

❑ RCA Victor (M)
LPM-2256........................11/63   30-40
DISC 3: Black label, "Mono" at bottom.
❑ RCA Victor LPM-2256 ..... 11/63   50-55
COVER 3: Same as cover 2.
❑ RCA Victor (No Number)...9/63   8-10
INNER SLEEVE 3: Turquoise, black and white. Front: RCA's Elvis LP catalog, most recent being *It Happened at the World's Fair* (side 1, row 4, column 5). Back: RCA Elvis EPs and 45s catalog.

RCA Victor (M)
LPM-2256 .... 11/63   90-105
TOTAL PACKAGE 3: Disc, cover, inner sleeve.

❑ RCA Victor (M)
LPM-2256........................10/64   10-15
DISC 4: Black label, "Monaural" at bottom.
L2PP-3657-19S/L2PP-3658-20S. Label LP#12.
L2PP-3657-20S/L2PP-3658-18S. Label LP#12.
❑ RCA Victor LPM-2256 ..... 10/64   30-35
COVER 4: Same as cover 2.
❑ RCA Victor 21-112-1
40A................................. 10/64   4-8
INNER SLEEVE 4: Red, black and white. Front: RCA's Elvis LP catalog, most recent being *Kissin' Cousins* (side 1, row 1, column 6). Back: RCA Elvis EPs and 45s catalog.

RCA Victor (M)
LPM-2256 .... 10/64   45-60
TOTAL PACKAGE 4: Disc, cover, inner sleeve.

❑ RCA Victor (ST)
LSP-2256 ....10/60   50-75
DISC 5: Black label, "Living Stereo" at bottom.
L2PY-3659-2S/L2PY-3660-7S. Label LP#7.
❑ RCA Victor LSP-2256......10/60   400-450
COVER 5: Front: RCA Victor logo at upper right, number at lower left. Has red, heart-shaped sticker applied to cover, announcing the inclusion of *Wooden Heart*. (Sticker is a permanent part of cover – not merely a shrink wrap sticker.) Color Elvis photo. Back: Four color Elvis photos.
❑ RCA Victor
(No Number)....................10/60   10-20
INNER SLEEVE 5: Brown, black and white. Front: RCA's Elvis LP catalog, most recent being Elvis Is Back! (side 1, row 1). Back: RCA Elvis EPs and an explanation of stereophonic sound. This sleeve not only appeared with 1960 issues of *G.I. Blues,* but has also been found with other RCA albums issued that year.
STICKER 5: Not priced separately since it is applied directly to cover.

RCA Victor (ST)
LSP-2256 .... 10/60   450-550
TOTAL PACKAGE 5: Disc, cover with sticker, inner sleeve.

❑ RCA Victor (ST)
LSP-2256 ....12/60   40-50
DISC 6: Same as disc 5.
❑ RCA Victor LSP-2256......12/60   60-65
COVER 6: Same as cover 5, except without heart-shaped sticker.
❑ RCA Victor
(No Number)....................10/60   10-20
INNER SLEEVE 6: Brown, black and white. Front: RCA's Elvis LP catalog, most recent being *Elvis Is Back!* (side 1, row 1). Back: RCA Elvis EPs and an explanation of stereophonic sound. This sleeve not only appeared with 1960 issues of *G.I. Blues*, but has also been found with other RCA albums issued that year.

RCA Victor (ST)
LSP-2256 .... 12/60   110-135
TOTAL PACKAGE 6: Disc, cover, inner sleeve.

❑ RCA Victor (ST)
LSP-2256 ....10/64   10-20
DISC 7: Black label, RCA logo in white at the top and "Stereo" at bottom.
L2PY-3659-3S/L2PY-3660-3S. Label LP#16.
❑ RCA Victor LSP-2256......10/64   25-30
COVER 7: Verification pending.
❑ RCA Victor 21-112-1
40A................................. 10/64   4-8
INNER SLEEVE 7: Red, black and white. Front: RCA's Elvis LP catalog, most recent being *Kissin' Cousins* (side 1, row 1, column 6). Back: RCA Elvis EPs and 45s catalog.

RCA Victor (ST)
LSP-2256...................10/64　　40-60
TOTAL PACKAGE 7: Disc, cover, inner sleeve.

❑ RCA Victor (ST)
LSP-2256 ....11/68　　20-25
DISC 8: Orange label. Rigid vinyl.
❑ RCA Victor LSP-2256......11/68　　8-10
COVER 8: Verification pending.
❑ RCA Victor 21-112-1
40D.....................................6/68　　4-6
INNER SLEEVE 8: Red, black and white. Front: RCA's Elvis LP catalog, most recent being *Elvis' Gold Records, Vol. 4* (side 1, row 4, column 5). Back: RCA's Elvis LP and Twin Pack Stereo 8 catalog. May also be found with inner sleeves 40B and 40C. See chapter on inner sleeves for more information.

RCA Victor (ST)
LSP-2256...................11/68　　35-40
TOTAL PACKAGE 8: Disc, cover, inner sleeve.

❑ RCA Victor (ST)
LSP-2256 ....'71　　10-15
DISC 9: Orange label. Flexible vinyl.
❑ RCA Victor LSP-2256..........'71　　4-8
COVER 9: Verification pending.
❑ RCA Victor.........................'70s　　2-4
INNER SLEEVE 9: Black-and-white. Pictures RCA Elvis catalog front and back. Any of several sleeves may be found on reissues from this period.

RCA Victor (ST)
LSP-2256........................'71　　15-25
TOTAL PACKAGE 9: Disc, cover, inner sleeve.

❑ RCA Victor (ST)
LSP-2256 ....'76　　12-15
DISC 10: Tan label.
❑ RCA LSP-2256....................'76　　12-15
COVER 10: Verification pending.
❑ RCA Victor.........................'70s　　2-4
INNER SLEEVE 10: Black-and-white. Pictures RCA Elvis catalog front and back. Any of several sleeves may be found on reissues from this period.

RCA Victor (ST)
LSP-2256........................'76　　25-30
TOTAL PACKAGE 10: Disc, cover, inner sleeve.

❑ RCA Victor (ST)
LSP-2256 ....'76　　4-6
DISC 11: Black label, dog near top.
❑ RCA LSP-2256....................'76　　4-6
COVER 11: Verification pending. Front: "RE" in small letters at lower left corner.

❑ RCA Victor.........................'70s　　2-4
INNER SLEEVE 11: Black-and-white. Pictures RCA Elvis catalog front and back. Any of several sleeves may be found on reissues from this period.

RCA Victor (ST)
LSP-2256........................'76　　10-18
TOTAL PACKAGE 11: Disc, cover, inner sleeve.

❑ RCA Victor (ST)
AFL1-2256...........................'77　　3-5
AFL1-2256A-1/AFL1-2256B-1.
DISC 12: Black label, dog near top.
❑ RCA AFL1-2256 ....'77　　3-5
COVER 12: Verification pending. Includes copies with a sticker bearing the "AFL1" prefix, wrapped around cover at top of spine.
❑ RCA Victor.........................'70s　　2-4
INNER SLEEVE 12: Black-and-white. Pictures RCA Elvis catalog front and back. Any of several sleeves may be found on reissues from this period.

RCA Victor (ST)
AFL1-2256.....................'77　　8-15
TOTAL PACKAGE 12: Disc, cover, inner sleeve.

❑ RCA Victor (ST)
AYL1-3735 ....9/80　　3-5
DISC 13: Black label, dog near top.
AYL1-3735A/AYL1-3736B. Identification numbers are engraved. L2PY-3659- 9S/L2PY-3660-15S is stamped but crossed out. Then AFL1-2256A/AFL1-2256B is stamped but crossed out.
❑ RCA Victor AYL1-3735......9/80　　3-5
COVER 13: Reflects prefix change.

RCA Victor (ST)
AYL1-3735 ....9/80　　6-10
TOTAL PACKAGE 13: Disc, cover.

Side 1
Tonight Is So Right for Love
What's She Really Like
Frankfort Special
Wooden Heart
G.I. Blues

Side 2
Pocket Full of Rainbows
Shoppin' Around
Big Boots
Didja' Ever
Blue Suede Shoes
Doin' the Best I Can

G.I. BLUES/LOVING YOU (Picture Disc): see *LOVING YOU/G.I. BLUES*

GENE PRICE COUNTRY EXPRESS
Various artists collections.

❑ Dept. of the U.S. Army (S)........　　10-15
DISC 1: Price range is for any individual disc containing at least one Elvis track. Monthly public service radio show, issued only to radio stations.

❏ Dept. of the U.S. Army (S)........   15-25
COMPLETE SET 1: Set of two LPs. includes cue sheets and program notes. Covers (yellow with title in red, white and blue) are gatefold. Price range is for any complete set containing at least one Elvis track.

GIBSON GOLD

Various artists collection
❏ RCA Special Products (S)
DPL2-0778 .... '87   20-25
DISCS 1: Black label, dog near top. Promotional issue made for the Gibson Appliance company.
(Disc 1) DPL2-0778A-1/DPL2-0778B-1. **(Disc 2)** DPL2-0778C-1/DPL2-0778D-1.
❏ RCA Special Products
DPL2-0778 .... '87   20-25
COVER 1: Gatefold. Front: RCA Special Products logo at upper left. Black with gold record. Back: Text inside gold record. Inside panels: Photos of 13 artists heard on this LP, including Elvis.
INNER SLEEVE 1: White, no printing.
RCA Special Products (S)
DPL2-0778 .... '87   **40-50**
TOTAL PACKAGE : Disc, cover.

GIFT OF MUSIC: see *QSP PRESENTS A GIFT OF MUSIC*

GIRL HAPPY

❏ RCA Victor (M)
LPM-3338......................... 4/65   10-15
DISC 1: Black label, "Monaural" at bottom.
SPRM-2012-1S/SPRM-2013-1S. Label LP#12.
SPRM-2012-1S/SPRM-2013-2S. Label LP#12.
SPRM-2012-5S/SPRM-2013-5S. Label LP#12.
❏ RCA Victor LPM-3338.......4/65   35-40
COVER 1: Front: RCA logo at upper right and number at lower left. Color Elvis photo. Back: Color Elvis photo superimposed on a boat.
❏ RCA Victor 21-112-1
40B.....................................4/65   4-6
INNER SLEEVE 1: Red, black and white. Front: RCA's Elvis LP catalog, most recent being *Roustabout* (side 1, row 1, column 5). Back: RCA Elvis EPs and 45s catalog.
BONUS PRINT: This 16" x 20" color print of a painting by June Kelly (Elvis in a red jacket with blue background) was given away by records stores around the time of the release of *Girl Happy*. Although not included with the record, many regard it a bonus item for this album. Its price range is $50 to $75.
RCA Victor (M)
LPM-3338 .... 4/65   **50-60**
TOTAL PACKAGE 1: Disc, cover, inner sleeve.

❏ RCA Victor (ST)
LSP-3338 ....4/65   10-15
DISC 2: Black label, RCA logo in white at top and "Stereo" at bottom.

SPRS-2014-3S/SPRS-2015-3S. Label LP#16.
❏ RCA Victor LSP-3338........4/65   35-40
COVER 2: Front: RCA logo at upper right and number at upper left. Color Elvis photo. Back: Color Elvis photo superimposed on a boat.
❏ RCA Victor 21-112-1
40B 4/65   4-6
INNER SLEEVE 2: Red, black and white. Front: RCA's Elvis LP catalog, most recent being *Roustabout* (side 1, row 1, column 5). Back: RCA Elvis EPs and 45s catalog.
BONUS PRINT: This 16" x 20" color print of a painting by June Kelly (Elvis in a red jacket with blue background) was given away by records stores around the time of the release of *Girl Happy*. Although it was not included with the record, most collectors consider it a bonus item for this album. It sells for approximately $50 - $75.
RCA Victor (ST)
LSP-3338 .... 4/65   **50-60**
TOTAL PACKAGE 2: Disc, cover.

❏ RCA Victor (ST)
LSP-3338 ....11/68   20-25
DISC 3: Orange label. Rigid vinyl.
❏ RCA Victor LSP-3338......11/68   8-10
COVER 3: Verification pending.
❏ RCA Victor 21-112-1
40D.....................................6/68   4-6
INNER SLEEVE 3: Red, black and white. Front: RCA's Elvis LP catalog, most recent being *Elvis' Gold Records, Vol. 4* (side 1, row 4, column 5). Back: RCA's Elvis LP and Twin Pack Stereo 8 catalog. May also be found with inner sleeves 40B and 40C. See chapter on inner sleeves for more information.
RCA Victor (ST)
LSP-3338 .... 11/68   **35-40**
TOTAL PACKAGE 3: Disc, cover, inner sleeve.

❏ RCA Victor (ST)
LSP-3338 ....'71   10-15
DISC 4: Orange label. Flexible vinyl.
SPRS-2014-3S/SPRS-2015-3S.
❏ RCA Victor LSP-3338..........'71   4-8
COVER 4: Verification pending.
❏ RCA Victor..........................'70s   2-4
INNER SLEEVE 4: Black-and-white. Pictures RCA Elvis catalog front and back. Any of several sleeves may be found on reissues from this period.
RCA Victor (ST)
LSP-3338 ....'71   **15-25**
TOTAL PACKAGE 4: Disc, cover, inner sleeve.

❏ RCA Victor (ST)
LSP-3338 ....'76   12-15
DISC 5: Tan label.
❏ RCA Victor LSP-3338..........'76   12-15
COVER 5: Verification pending.

❑ RCA Victor.......................... '70s   2-4
INNER SLEEVE 5: Black-and-white. Pictures RCA Elvis catalog front and back. Any of several sleeves may be found on reissues from this period.

RCA Victor (ST)
LSP-3338....................... '76   25-30
TOTAL PACKAGE 5: Disc, cover, inner sleeve.

❑ RCA Victor (ST)
LSP-3338 .... '76   4-6
DISC 6: Black label, dog near top.
❑ RCA LSP-3338.................... '76   4-6
COVER 6: Similar to cover 2, except paper stock is of a lighter weight and has "RE" in lower left corner.
❑ RCA Victor.......................... '70s   2-4
INNER SLEEVE 6: Black-and-white. Pictures RCA Elvis catalog front and back. Any of several sleeves may be found on reissues from this period.

RCA Victor (ST)
LSP-3338....................... '76   10-18
TOTAL PACKAGE 6: Disc, cover, inner sleeve.

❑ RCA Victor (ST)
AFL1-3338 .... '77   3-5
DISC 7: Black label, dog near top.
❑ RCA AFL1-3338................... '77   3-5
COVER 7: Reflects prefix change. Includes copies with a sticker bearing the "AFL1" prefix, wrapped around cover at top of spine.
❑ RCA Victor.......................... '70s   2-4
INNER SLEEVE 7: Black-and-white. Pictures RCA Elvis catalog front and back. Any of several sleeves may be found on reissues from this period.

RCA Victor (ST)
AFL1-3338..................... '77   8-15
TOTAL PACKAGE 7: Disc, cover, inner sleeve.

Side 1
Girl Happy
Spring Fever
Fort Lauderdale Chamber of Commerce
Startin' Tonight
Wolf Call
Do Not Disturb
Side 2
Cross My Heart and Hope to Die
The Meanest Girl in Town
Do The Clam
Puppet on a String
I've Got to Find My Baby
You'll Be Gone

GIRLS, GIRLS, AND MORE GIRLS

❑ Eternal: Bootleg. Listed for identification only.

GIRLS! GIRLS! GIRLS!

❑ RCA Victor (M)
LPM-2621 .... 11/62   20-25
DISC 1: Black label, "Long Play" at bottom.
N2PP-3293-1S/N2PP-3293-2S. Label LP#5. Has songwriter credits for *We're Comin' in Loaded* under title.
N2PP-3293-4S/N2PP-3293-3S. Label LP#5. Has songwriter credits for *We're Comin' in Loaded* under title.
N2PP-3293-5S/N2PP-3293-5S. Label LP#2. Has songwriter credits for *We're Comin' in Loaded* on same line as title.
❑ RCA Victor LPM-2621 ..... 11/62   55-75
COVER 1: Front: RCA logo at upper right and number at lower left. Color Elvis photo. Back: Two color Elvis photos from the film and four earlier soundtrack albums pictured.
INNER SLEEVE 1: Generic RCA sleeve. No mention of this LP.
❑ RCA Victor...................... 11/62   125-150
INSERT 1: Color 11" x 11" 1963 calendar. Front: Calendar and seven color Elvis photos. Back: Lists other RCA Elvis albums and EPs. Two later printings of the 1963 calendar exist, each with a different back side, but neither was actually included with the *Girls! Girls! Girls!* LP.

RCA Victor (M)
LPM-2621 .... 11/62   200-250
TOTAL PACKAGE 1: Disc, cover, insert.

❑ RCA Victor (M)
LPM-2621....................... 11/63   30-40
DISC 2: Black label, "Mono" at bottom.
❑ RCA Victor LPM-2621 ..... 11/63   20-30
COVER 2: Verification pending.
❑ RCA Victor (No Number)...9/63   8-10
INNER SLEEVE 2: Turquoise, black and white. Front: RCA's Elvis LP catalog, most recent being *It Happened at the World's Fair* (side 1, row 4, column 5). Back: RCA Elvis EPs and 45s catalog.

RCA Victor (M)
LPM-2621 .... 11/63   60-80
TOTAL PACKAGE 2: Disc, cover, inner sleeve.

❑ RCA Victor (M)
LPM-2621......................... 10/64   10-15
DISC 3: Black label, "Monaural" at bottom.
❑ RCA Victor LPM-2621 ..... 10/64   10-20
COVER 3: Verification pending.
❑ RCA Victor 21-112-1
40A 10/64   4-8
INNER SLEEVE 3: Red, black and white. Front: RCA's Elvis LP catalog, most recent being *Kissin' Cousins* (side 1, row 1, column 6). Back: RCA Elvis EPs and 45s catalog.

RCA Victor (M)
LPM-2621 .... **10/64**   **25-45**
TOTAL PACKAGE 3: Disc, cover, inner
sleeve.

❑ RCA Victor (ST)
LSP-2621 .... 11/62   60-75
DISC 4: Black label, "Living Stereo" at bottom.
N2PY-3295-1S/N2PY-3296-1S. Label LP#8.
N2PY-3295-5S/N2PY-3296-5S. Label LP#7.
❑ RCA Victor LSP-2621...... 11/62   60-75
COVER 4: Front: RCA logo at upper right and
number at upper left. Color Elvis photo. Back:
Two color Elvis photos from the film and four
earlier soundtrack albums pictured.
INNER SLEEVE 4: Generic RCA sleeve. No
mention of this LP.
❑ RCA Victor........................ 11/62   125-150
INSERT 4: Color 11" x 11" 1963 calendar.
Front: Calendar and seven color Elvis photos.
Back: Lists other RCA Elvis albums and EPs.
Two later printings of the 1963 calendar exist,
each with a different back side, but neither
was actually included with the *Girls! Girls!
Girls!* LP.

RCA Victor (ST)
LSP-2621 .... **11/62**   **250-300**
TOTAL PACKAGE 4: Disc, cover, insert.

❑ RCA Victor (ST)
LSP-2621 .... 10/64   10-20
DISC 5: Black label, RCA logo in white at top
and "Stereo" at bottom.
N2PY-3295-6S/N2PY-3296-6S. Label LP#16.
❑ RCA Victor LSP-2621...... 10/64   35-45
COVER 5: Same as cover 4. NOTE: Because
RCA used the same cover for many reissues,
the price for this cover reflects part of this total
package.
❑ RCA Victor 21-112-1
40A.................................... 10/64   4-8
INNER SLEEVE 5: Red, black and white.
Front: RCA's Elvis LP catalog, most recent
being *Kissin' Cousins* (side 1, row 1, column
6). Back: RCA Elvis EPs and 45s catalog.

RCA Victor (ST)
LSP-2621 .... **10/64**   **50-75**
TOTAL PACKAGE 5: Disc, cover, inner
sleeve.

❑ RCA Victor (ST)
LSP-2621 .... 11/68   20-25
DISC 6: Orange label. Rigid vinyl.
❑ RCA Victor LSP-2621...... 11/68   8-10
COVER 6: Verification pending.
❑ RCA Victor 21-112-1
40D.................................... 6/68   8-10
INNER SLEEVE 6: Red, black and white.
Front: RCA's Elvis LP catalog, most recent
being *Elvis' Gold Records, Vol. 4* (side 1, row
4, column 5). Back: RCA's Elvis LP and Twin
Pack Stereo 8 catalog. May also be found
with inner sleeves 40B and 40C.

RCA Victor (ST)
LSP-2621 .... **11/68**   **35-45**
TOTAL PACKAGE 6: Disc, cover, inner
sleeve.

❑ RCA Victor (ST)
LSP-2621 .... '71   10-15
DISC 7: Orange label. Flexible vinyl.
❑ RCA Victor LSP-2621.......... '71   4-8
COVER 7: Verification pending.
❑ RCA Victor........................ '70s   2-4
INNER SLEEVE 7: Black-and-white. Pictures
RCA Elvis catalog front and back. Any of
several sleeves may be found on reissues
from this period.

RCA Victor (ST)
LSP-2621 .... **'71**   **15-25**
TOTAL PACKAGE 7: Disc, cover, inner
sleeve.

❑ RCA Victor (ST)
LSP-2621 .... '76   12-15
DISC 8: Tan label.
❑ RCA Victor LSP-2621.......... '76   12-15
COVER 8: Verification pending.
❑ RCA Victor........................ '70s   2-4
INNER SLEEVE 8: Black-and-white. Pictures
RCA Elvis catalog front and back. Any of
several sleeves may be found on reissues
from this period.

RCA Victor (ST)
LSP-2621 .... **'76**   **25-30**
TOTAL PACKAGE 8: Disc, cover, inner
sleeve.

❑ RCA Victor (ST)
LSP-2621 .... '76   4-6
DISC 9: Black label, dog near top.
❑ RCA LSP-2621 .... '76   4-6
COVER 9: Front: "RE" in small letters at lower
left corner.
❑ RCA Victor........................ '70s   2-4
INNER SLEEVE 9: Black-and-white. Pictures
RCA Elvis catalog front and back. Any of
several sleeves may be found on reissues
from this period.

RCA Victor (ST)
LSP-2621 .... **'76**   **10-18**
TOTAL PACKAGE 9: Disc, cover, inner
sleeve.

❑ RCA Victor (ST)
AFL1-2621............................ '77   3-5
DISC 10: Black label, dog near top.
❑ RCA Victor AFL1-2621 .... '77   3-5
COVER 10: Reflects prefix change. Includes
copies with a sticker bearing the "AFL1"
prefix, wrapped around cover at top of spine.

RCA Victor (ST)
AFL1-2621 .... **'77**   **8-15**
TOTAL PACKAGE 10: Disc, cover, inner
sleeve.

Side 1

Girls! Girls! Girls!
I Don't Want to Be Tied
Where Do You Come From
I Don't Want To
We'll Be Together
A Boy Like Me, A Girl Like You
Earth Boy

Side 2

Return to Sender
Because of Love
Thanks to the Rolling Sea
Song of the Shrimp
The Walls Have Ears
We're Coming In Loaded

GOLDEN CELEBRATION (3 LPs)

Complete three-hour radio show. All discs in this set, listed individually below, have a gold label with black print. All identification numbers are engraved. Issued only to subscribing radio stations.

- ❏ Westwood One 11/84   40-60
  DISC 1: Westwood One logo on label.
  Elvis-A/Elvis-D.
- ❏ Westwood One 11/84   40-60
  DISC 2: Westwood One logo on label.
  Elvis-B/Elvis-E.
- ❏ Westwood One 11/84   40-60
  DISC 3: Westwood One logo on label.
  Elvis-C/Elvis-F.
  COVER 1: White, no printing.
  INNER SLEEVES 1: Clear plastic, no printing.
- ❏ Westwood One 11/84   5-10
  INSERT 1: Three pages of titles, times and programming instructions.

Westwood One 11/84   125-200
  TOTAL PACKAGE 1: Discs, insert.

Hour 1 (Discs 1 & 2)

All Shook Up
That's All Right
Good Rockin' Tonight
I Got a Woman
Maybelline
Heartbreak Hotel
Money Honey
Hound Dog
Too Much
Long Tall Sally
I Was the One
Baby, Let's Play House

Hour 2 (Discs 1 & 3)

Blue Moon of Kentucky
Tutti Frutti
Swing Down, Sweet Chariot
Love Me Tender
Jailhouse Rock
Can't Help Falling in Love
Don't
Big Hunk O' Love
Earth Angel
Stuck on You
It's Now or Never
Such a Night
Get Back

Hour 3 (Discs 2 & 3)

Heartbreak Hotel
Shake, Rattle and Roll

Hard Headed Woman
Blue Suede Shoes
Tiger Man
Lawdy, Miss Clawdy
Baby What You Want Me to Do
Love Me
Tryin' To Get To You
Mystery Train Medley
In the Ghetto
Are You Lonesome Tonight
Burning Love
Don't Be Cruel
Little Sister
If I Can Dream

GOLDEN CELEBRATION (Cassette)

- ❏ RCA Victor (M) (No
  Number) 9/84   25-35
  TAPE 1: Promotional only, "Advance Cassette" sampler of the boxed set.

**RCA Victor (M) (No
Number) 9/84   25-35**
  TOTAL PACKAGE 1: Tape.

Side 1

The Sun Sessions – Outtakes: Blue Moon of Kentucky
The Dorsey Brothers Stage Show: Shake, Rattle and Roll/Flip, Flop and Fly/I Gotta Woman (sic)
The Milton Berle Show: Hound Dog/Dialogue
The Steve Allen Show: I Want You, I Need You, I Love You
The Mississippi-Alabama Fair and Dairy Show: Blue Suede Shoes

Side 2

The Ed Sullivan Show: (There'll Be) Peace in the Valley (For Me)
Elvis at Home: The Fool
Collector's Treaures: Dark Moon
Elvis in Burbank: Tiger Man
Tryin' to Get to You

GOLDEN CELEBRATION (6 LPs)

Flexible vinyl. Each of the following six discs is in a special cardboard cover/sleeve and is described and priced separately. Each has its own title and is on the gold "Elvis 50th Anniversary" label. All have identification numbers engraved, and "January 8th, 1935" stamped.

- ❏ RCA (M) CPM6-5172-1
  (A/B) 10/84   5-8
  DISC 1:
  CPM6-5172-A-1/CPM6-B-1. Identification numbers are stamped.
  CPM6-5172-A-3/CPM6-B-1. Identification numbers are engraved.

Side 1 The Sun Sessions – Outtakes
Memphis Tennessee, 1954 and 1955

Harbor Lights
That's All Right
Blue Moon of Kentucky
I Don't Care If the Sun Don't Shine
I'm Left, You're Right, She's Gone (My Baby's Gone)
I'll Never Let You Go (Little Darlin')
When It Rains, It Really Pours

Side 2 The Dorsey Brothers Stage Show, New York, N.Y. 1956
Shake, Rattle and Roll/Flip, Flop and Fly
I Got a Woman
Baby, Let's Play House
Tutti Frutti
Blue Suede Shoes
Heartbreak Hotel

❑ RCA Victor (M) CPM6-5172-2
(C/D)..............................10/84   5-8
DISC 2:
CPM6-5172-C-1/CPM6-D-1.

Side 3 The Dorsey Brothers Stage Show, New York, N.Y. 1956
Tutti Frutti
I Was the One
Blue Suede Shoes
Heartbreak Hotel
Money Honey
Heartbreak Hotel

Side 4 The Milton Berle Show, California, 1956
Heartbreak Hotel
Blue Suede Shoes/Dialogue/Blue Suede Shoes
  (Reprise)
Hound Dog/Dialogue
I Want You, I Need You, I Love You
The Steve Allen Show, New York, 1956
Dialogue/I Want You, I Need You, I Love You
Introduction/Hound Dog

❑ RCA Victor (M) CPM6-5172-3
(E/F) 10/84   5-8
DISC 3:
CPM6-5172-E-1/CPM6-F-1.

Side 5 The Mississippi-Alabama Fair and Dairy Show, Tupelo, Mississippi, September 26, 1956
Heartbreak Hotel
Long Tall Sally
Introductions and Presentations/I Was the One
I Want You, I Need You, I Love You
I Got a Woman

Side 6 The Mississippi-Alabama Fair and Dairy Show, Tupelo, Mississippi, September 26, 1956
Don't Be Cruel
Reddy Teddy
Love Me Tender
Hound Dog
Vernon and Gladys Presley
Nick Adams
A Fan
Elvis

❑ RCA Victor (M) CPM6-5172-4
(G/H) 10/84   5-8
DISC 4:
CPM6-5172-G-1/CPM6-H-1.

Side 7 The Mississippi-Alabama Fair and Dairy Show, Tupelo, Mississippi, September 26, 1956
Love Me Tender
I Was the One
I Got a Woman
Don't Be Cruel
Blue Suede Shoes
Baby, Let's Play House
Hound Dog/Announcements

Side 8 The Ed Sullivan Show, California and New York, 1956
Don't Be Cruel
Love Me Tender
Reddy Teddy
Hound Dog
Dont' Be Cruel
Love Me Tender
Love Me
Hound Dog

❑ RCA Victor (M) CPM6-5172-5
(I/J) 10/84   5-8
DISC 5:
CPM6-5172-I-1/CPM6-J-1.

Side 9 The Ed Sullivan Show, New York, January 6, 1957
Hound Dog
Love Me Tender
Heartbreak Hotel
Don't Be Cruel
Too Much
When My Blue Moon Turns to Gold Again
(There'll Be) Peace in the Valley (For Me)

Side 10 Elvis at Home, Germany, 1958-60
Danny Boy
Soldier Boy
The Fool
Earth Angel
He's Only a Prayer Away

❑ RCA Victor (M) CPM6-5172-6
(K/L)..............................10/84   5-8
DISC 6:
CPM6-5172-K-1/CPM6-L-1.

Side 11 Collector's Treasures, Discovered at Graceland
Excerpt from an Interview for *TV Guide*
My Heart Cries for You
Dark Moon
Write to Me from Naples
Suppose

Side 12 Elvis, Burbank, California, June 27, 1968
Blue Suede Shoes
Tiger Man
That's All Right
Lawdy, Miss Clawdy
Baby, What You Want Me to Do/Monologue
Love Me
Are You Lonesome Tonight
Baby, What You Want Me to Do (Reprise)
Monologue/Blue Christmas/Monologue
One Night/Tryin' to Get to You

❑ RCA Victor
CPM6-5172 ....10/84   20-25
BOX/SLIPCOVER 1: Front: Gold stock with embossed drawing of Elvis (50th Anniversary logo). Back: RCA logo at upper left. UPC bar code at upper right. Gold "A Numbered Collectible" sticker at lower left. Text only.

❑ RCA Victor
CPM6-5172 ....10/84   15-20
INNER SLEEVES 1: Price for all six sleeves. Covers have black-and-white Elvis photos on both sides. On spine, LPs are numbered 1 through 6, (CPM6-5172-1, CPM6-5172-2, etc.) but discs have only letters (CPM6-5172-A, CPM6-5172-B, etc.) and side numbers (side 1, side 2, etc.).

❑ RCA CPM6-5172............. 10/84   5-10
  INSERT 1A: Color 8" x 10" Elvis photo. Has
  number at lower right. Back is blank.
❑ RCA CPM/CPK6-5172 .... 10/84   2-3
  INSERT 1B: Black-and-white 8" x 10" flyer.
  Pictures this set and other releases in the
  "Elvis 50th Anniversary" series. Has LP and
  cassette number at bottom.
  INSERT 1C: White 9" x 12" envelope, used to
  hold inserts 1A and 1B. Plain, no printing.
❑ RCA CPM/CPK6-5172 .... 10/84
  SHRINK STICKER 1: Gold foil, 2½" x 3½"
  with black print. Lists highlights of set and
  announces bonus photo.

RCA (M) CPM6-5172..... 10/84   75-100
  **TOTAL PACKAGE 1: Discs, box, inserts,
    sticker, inner sleeves.**

GOLDEN YEARS OF COUNTRY (25 LPs)

Various artists collection
Complete 25-hour radio show, with one LP for
each year from 1955 through 1979. Has eight
songs by Elvis, listed below. Issued only to
subscribing radio stations. First issued in
1978 on 24 discs, then in 1979 a 25th disc
was added. Each disc is listed individually
below. All identification numbers are
engraved.

❑ Drake-Chenault 1955 Part 1/
  Part 2.................................'78   5-8
  DISC 1:
  1955-A/1955-B REL 6-78.
❑ Drake-Chenault 1956 Part 1/
  Part 2.................................'78   5-8
  DISC 2:
  1956-A/1956-B.
❑ Drake-Chenault 1957 Part 1/
  Part 2.................................'78   5-8
  DISC 3:
  1957-A/1957-B.
❑ Drake-Chenault 1958 Part 1/
  Part 2.................................'78   5-8
  DISC 4:
  1958-A/1958-B.
❑ Drake-Chenault 1959 Part 1/
  Part 2.................................'78   5-8
  DISC 5:
  1959-A/1959-B.
❑ Drake-Chenault 1960 Part 1/
  Part 2.................................'78   5-8
  DISC 6:
  1960-A/1960-B.
❑ Drake-Chenault 1961 Part 1/
  Part 2.................................'78   5-8
  DISC 7:
  1961-A/1961-B.
❑ Drake-Chenault 1962 Part 1/
  Part 2.................................'78   5-8
  DISC 8:
  1962-A/1962-B.

❑ Drake-Chenault 1963 Part 1/
  Part 2.................................'78   5-8
  DISC 9:
  1963-A/1963-B.
❑ Drake-Chenault 1964 Part 1/
  Part 2.................................'78   5-8
  DISC 10:
  1964-A/1964-B.
❑ Drake-Chenault 1965 Part 1/
  Part 2.................................'78   5-8
  DISC 11:
  1965-A/1965-B.
❑ Drake-Chenault 1966 Part 1/
  Part 2.................................'78   5-8
  DISC 12:
  1966-A/1966-B.
❑ Drake-Chenault 1967 Part 1/
  Part 2.................................'78   5-8
  DISC 13:
  1967-A/1967-B.
❑ Drake-Chenault 1968 Part 1/
  Part 2.................................'78   5-8
  DISC 14:
  1968-A/1968-B.
❑ Drake-Chenault 1969 Part 1/
  Part 2.................................'78   5-8
  DISC 15:
  1969-A/1969-B.
❑ Drake-Chenault 1970 Part 1/
  Part 2.................................'78   5-8
  DISC 16:
  1970-A/1970-B.
❑ Drake-Chenault 1971 Part 1/
  Part 2.................................'78   5-8
  DISC 17:
  1971-A/1971-B.
❑ Drake-Chenault 1972 Part 1/
  Part 2.................................'78   5-8
  DISC 18:
  1972-A/1972-B.
❑ Drake-Chenault 1973 Part 1/
  Part 2.................................'78   5-8
  DISC 19:
  1973-A/1973-B.
❑ Drake-Chenault 1974 Part 1/
  Part 2.................................'78   5-8
  DISC 20:
  1974-A/1974-B.
❑ Drake-Chenault 1975 Part 1/
  Part 2.................................'78   5-8
  DISC 21:
  1975-A/1975-B.
❑ Drake-Chenault 1976 Part 1/
  Part 2.................................'78   5-8
  DISC 22:
  1976-A/1976-B.
❑ Drake-Chenault 1977 Part 1/
  Part 2.................................'78   5-8
  DISC 23:
  1977-A/1977-B.
❑ Drake-Chenault 1978 Part 1/
  Part 2.................................'78   5-8
  DISC 24:
  1978-A/1978-B.

❑ Drake-Chenault 1979 Part 1/

Part 2 .... '80   5-8

DISC 25:

1979-A/1979-B.

BOX 1: Verification pending.

❑ Drake-Chenault .... '80   25-50

INSERT 1: 55-page operations manual, with
cue sheets and program notes.

Drake-Chenault (SP) .... '80   150-250

TOTAL PACKAGE : Discs, insert.

Elvis Contents:

1955 (Side 2)
I Forgot to Remember to Forget (Segment D)

1956 (Side 1)
Heartbreak Hotel (Segment B)
I Want You, I Need You, I Love You (Segment B)

1956 (Side 2)
Don't Be Cruel (Segment F)

1957 (Side 1)
Jailhouse Rock (Segment C)

1958 (Side 2)
I Beg of You (Segment D)

1974 (Side 2)
Take Good Care of Her (Segment E)

1977 (Side 1)
Way Down (Segment C)

GOOD ROCKIN' TONIGHT

❑ Bopcat LP-100: Bootleg. Listed for
identification only.

GOOD ROCKIN' TONIGHT (2 LPs)

❑ RCA Special Products (SP)
SVL2-0824 .... 1/88   30-40
DISCS 1: Black label, dog near top. Sold via
TV mail order ads.
(Disc 1) SVL2-0824-A-1/SVL2-0824-B-1. **(Disc 2)** SVL2-
0824-C-1/SVL2-0824-D-1. Identification numbers are
engraved.

❑ RCA Special Products
SVL2-0824 .... 1/88   30-40
COVER 1: Single pocket. Front: RCA Special
Products logo and number at left and BMG
logo at lower right. Has artist's rendering of
Elvis. Back: Pictures *Elvis: 50 Years, 50 Hits*.
INNER SLEEVES 1: White, no printing.

RCA Special Products (SP)
SVL2-0824 .... 1/88   60-80
TOTAL PACKAGE 1: Discs, cover.

Card stock jacket, with printing on cover – not
on slicks.

Disc 1

Side 1
Good Rockin' Tonight
Jailhouse Rock
Blue Suede Shoes
Little Sister
Tryin' to Get to You
Lawdy, Miss Clawdy
Heartbreak Hotel
That's All Right

Side 2
Hound Dog
Tutti Frutti
Hard Headed Woman
I Got a Woman
Baby, Let's Play House
I Feel So Bad
Mean Woman Blues
I Got Stung

Disc 2

Side 3
One Night
It Feels So Right
I Want You with Me
Too Much
Money Honey
Rip It Up
Down in the Alley

Side 4
Mystery Train
(Let Me Be Your) Teddy Bear
A Big Hunk O' Love
So Glad You're Mine
Like a Baby
I Was the One
Soldier Boy

GOOD TIMES

❑ RCA Victor (ST)
CPL1-0475 .... 3/74   10-15
DISC 1: Orange label. Dynaflex vinyl.
CPL1-0475-A-1S/CPL1-0475-B-1S.
CPL1-0475-A-2S/CPL1-0475-B-2S.

❑ RCA CPL1-0475 .... 3/74   10-15
COVER 1: Front: RCA logo and number at
upper left. Color Elvis photo. Back. Text only.

❑ RCA Victor 21-112-1
PT 54C 11/73   3-5
INNER SLEEVE 1: Pictures
RCA's Elvis LP catalog front and back, most
recent being *Elvis As Recorded at Madison
Square Garden* (side 2, row 4, column 2).

❑ RCA CPL1-0475 .... 3/74   20-30
SHRINK STICKER 1: Black, red and white.
Announces *I've Got a Thing About You Baby*
and *Take Good Care of Her*.

RCA Victor (ST)
CPL1-0475 .... 3/74   **45-65**
**TOTAL PACKAGE 1: Disc, cover, sticker,
inner sleeve.**

❑ RCA Victor (ST)
CPL1-0475 .... 3/74   10-15
DISC 2: Same as disc 1.

❑ RCA CPL1-0475 .... 3/74   10-15
COVER 2: Same as cover 1.

❑ RCA Victor 21-112-1
PT 54C 11/73   3-5
INNER SLEEVE 1: Black-and-white. Pictures
RCA's Elvis LP catalog front and back, most
recent being *Elvis As Recorded at Madison
Square Garden* (side 2, row 4, column 2).

❑ RCA CPL1-0475 .... 3/74   55-60
SHRINK STICKER 2: Pink. Announces *My
Boy*.

RCA Victor (ST)

CPL1-0475 ....**3/74**   **80-100**
TOTAL PACKAGE 2: Disc, cover, sticker, inner sleeve.

Some copies have both stickers 1 and 2. For those, a price range of $100 to $125 is suggested.

❑ RCA Victor (ST)
CPL1-0475 ....3/74   10-15
DISC 3: Same as disc 1.

❑ RCA Victor CPL1-0475 .....3/74   15-20
COVER 3: Designate promo. Same as cover 1, but with "Not for Sale" stamped on back.

❑ RCA Victor 21-112-1
PT 54C 11/73   3-5
INNER SLEEVE 1: Black-and-white. Pictures RCA's Elvis LP catalog front and back, most recent being *Elvis As Recorded at Madison Square Garden* (side 2, row 4, column 2).

❑ RCA CPL1-0475.................3/74   20-30
SHRINK STICKER 3: Black, red and white. Announces *I've Got a Thing About You Baby* and *Take Good Care of Her*.

RCA Victor (ST)

CPL1-0475 ....**3/74**   **50-70**
TOTAL PACKAGE 3: Disc, cover, sticker, inner sleeve.

❑ RCA Victor (ST)
CPL1-0475 ....3/74   10-15
DISC 4: Same as disc 1.

❑ RCA Victor CPL1-0475 .....3/74   15-20
COVER 4: Designate promo. Same as cover 1, but with "Not for Sale" stamped on back.

❑ RCA Victor 21-112-1
PT 54C 11/73   3-5
INNER SLEEVE 1: Black-and-white. Pictures RCA's Elvis LP catalog front and back, most recent being *Elvis As Recorded at Madison Square Garden* (side 2, row 4, column 2).

❑ RCA CPL1-0475.................3/74   55-60
SHRINK STICKER 4: Pink. Announces *My Boy*.

RCA Victor (ST)

CPL1-0475 ....**3/74**   **85-105**
TOTAL PACKAGE 4: Disc, cover, sticker, inner sleeve.

For any designate promos with both stickers 1 and 2, a price range of $105 to $130 is suggested.

❑ RCA Victor (ST)
CFL1-0475 ....'76   4-6
DISC 5: Black label, dog near top.
CPL1-0475-A-30/CPL1-0475-B-30.

❑ RCA Victor CFL1-0475........'76   4-6
COVER 5: Verification pending.

❑ RCA Victor.........................'70s   2-4
INNER SLEEVE 5: Black-and-white. Pictures RCA Elvis catalog front and back. Any of several sleeves may be found on reissues from this period.

RCA Victor (ST)

CFL1-0475.....................**'76**   **10-18**
TOTAL PACKAGE 5: Disc, cover, inner sleeve.

❑ RCA Victor (ST)
AFL1-0475...........................'77   3-5
DISC 6: Black label, dog near top.

❑ RCA AFL1-0475 ....'77   3-5
COVER 6: Reflects prefix change. Includes copies with a sticker bearing the "AFL1" prefix, wrapped around cover at top of spine.

❑ RCA Victor.........................'70s   2-4
INNER SLEEVE 6: Black-and-white. Pictures RCA Elvis catalog front and back. Any of several sleeves may be found on reissues from this period.

RCA Victor (ST)

AFL1-0475.....................**'77**   **8-15**
TOTAL PACKAGE 6: Disc, cover, inner sleeve.

Side 1
Take Good Care of Her
Loving Arms
I Got a Feelin' in My Body
If That Isn't Love
She Wears My Ring

Side 2
I've Got a Thing About You Baby
My Boy
Spanish Eyes
Talk About the Good Times
Good Time Charlie's Got the Blues

GOOD TIMES

❑ Musique 1240: Bootleg. Listed for identification only.

GOT A LOT O' LIVIN' TO DO

❑ Pirate PR-101: Bootleg. Listed for identification only.

GREAT HITS OF 1956-'57

❑ Reader's Digest/RCA Music Service (SE)
RB4-072/D........................8/87   10-15
DISC 1: Black, white and red label. Mail order bonus from *Reader's Digest* to buyers of an unrelated boxed set – one that has no Elvis tracks.
T1RS-5831-5/T1RS-5831-5.

❏ Reader's Digest/RCA Music Service
RBA-072/D ....8/87　　10-15
COVER 1: Front: Prefix differs from one used
on disc. Reader's Digest and RCA Music
Service logos at bottom center. Black-and-
white *Jailhouse Rock* Elvis photo. Back:
Black-and-white Louisiana Hayride Elvis
photo. (Cover and disc have different
prefixes.)
INNER SLEEVE 1: White, no printing.

**Reader's Digest/RCA Music Service
(SE) RB4-072/D...........8/87　　20-30
TOTAL PACKAGE 1: Disc, cover.**

Card stock jacket, with printing on cover – not
on slicks.

Side 1
Hound Dog
Don't Be Cruel
Love Me Tender
I Want You, I Need You, I Love You
Heartbreak Hotel
Playing for Keeps

Side 2
Blue Suede Shoes
I Was the One
Love Me
(Let Me Be Your) Teddy Bear
Anyway You Want Me (That's How I Will Be)
Too Much

GREAT PERFORMANCES

❏ RCA (SP) 2227-1-R.............'90　　12-15
DISC 1: Red label, black print with lightning
bolt RCA logo.
2227-1-R-A-1/2227-1-R-B-1. Identification numbers are
engraved.

❏ RCA 2227-1-R......................'90　　12-15
COVER 1: Front: No logo or number. Duotone
Elvis (1956) photo. Back: RCA and BMG
logos and number at lower right. Duotone
Elvis (circa 1956) photo.

❏ RCA 2227-1-R......................'90　　3-5
INNER SLEEVE 1: Front: Three duotone Elvis
(1956) photos. Back: Text only.

❏ RCA 2227-1-R......................'90　　4-5
SHRINK STICKER 1: Silver with black print.
Announces "The Legendary 7-18-53 Acetate
of *My Happiness.*"

**RCA (SP) 2227-1-R...........'90　　30-40
TOTAL PACKAGE 1: Disc, cover, inner
　　sleeve, sticker.**

❏ RCA (SP) 2227-1-R.............'90　　12-15
DISC 2: Same as disc 1.

❏ RCA 2227-1-R......................'90　　18-20
COVER 2: Designate promo. Same as cover
1, but with small hole drilled at upper right (if
facing front).

❏ RCA 2227-1-R......................'90　　3-5
INNER SLEEVE 2: Front: Three duotone Elvis
(1956) photos. Back: Text only.

❏ RCA 2227-1-R....................'90　　4-5
SHRINK STICKER 2: Silver with black print.
Announces "The Legendary 7-18-53 Acetate
of *My Happiness.*"

**RCA (SP) 2227-1-R...........'90　　35-45
TOTAL PACKAGE 2: Disc, cover, inner
　　sleeve, sticker.**

Card stock jacket, with printing on cover – not
on slicks.

Side 1
My Happiness
That's All Right
Shake, Rattle & Roll/Flip, Flop & Fly
Heartbreak Hotel
Blue Suede Shoes
Reddy Teddy
Don't Be Cruel
(Let Me Be Your) Teddy Bear
Got o' Lot of Livin' to Do
Jailhouse Rock
Treat Me Nice

Side 2
King Creole
Trouble
Fame and Fortune
Return to Sender
Always on My Mind
An American Trilogy (shown as "American Trilogy")
If I Can Dream
Unchained Melody
Memories

GREATEST HITS, VOLUME ONE

❏ RCA Victor (ST)
AHL1-2347 ....11/81　　8-10
DISC 1: Black label, dog near top.
AHL1-2347-A-1S/AHL1-2347-B-1S. Identification numbers
are engraved.
AHL1-2347-A-1S/AHL1-2347-B-2S. Identification numbers
are engraved.

❏ RCA AHL1-2347..............11/81　　10-15
COVER 1: Front: Textured, white stock with
embossed, red lettering on "Elvis." Has
embossed, blue border on triangle. Back:
RCA logo, number and UPC bar code at lower
left. Has embossed, blue border around color
Elvis photo.
INNER SLEEVE 1: White, no printing.

**RCA Victor (ST)
AHL1-2347 ....11/81　　20-25
TOTAL PACKAGE 1: Disc, cover.**

❏ RCA Victor (ST)
AHL1-2347 ....11/81　　8-10
DISC 2: Same as disc 1.

❏ RCA Victor (ST)
AHL1-2347 ....11/81　　15-20
COVER 2: Designate promo. Same as cover
1, but with "Not for Sale" stamped on back.
INNER SLEEVE 2: White, no printing.

**RCA Victor (ST)
AHL1-2347 ....11/81　　25-30
TOTAL PACKAGE 2: Disc, cover.**

❏ RCA Victor (ST)
AHL1-2347 ....'83   8-10
DISC 3: Same as disc 1.

❏ RCA AHL1-2347 ....'83   8-10
COVER 3: Front: Flat stock, no embossed print. Back: RCA logo, number and UPC bar code at lower left. Border around color Elvis photo is not embossed.
INNER SLEEVE 3: White, no printing.

RCA Victor (ST)
AHL1-2347 ....'83   **15-20**
TOTAL PACKAGE 3: Disc, cover.

Side A
The Wonder of You
A Big Hunk O' Love (Unreleased live)
There Goes My Everything
Suspicious Minds
What'd I Say (Unreleased live)
Side B
Don't Cry Daddy (Unreleased live)
Steamroller Blues (Unreleased live)
The Sound of Your Cry
Burning Love
You'll Never Walk Alone

GREATEST MOMENTS IN MUSIC

❏ RCA Special Products (SP)
DML1-0413 ....'80   7-10
DISC 1: Black label, dog near top. Included as a bonus with Candlelite's *The Legendary Recordings of Elvis Presley*.
DML1-0413-A-1/DML1-0413-B-1. Identification numbers are engraved.

❏ RCA DML1-0413 ....'80   7-10
COVER 1: Front: RCA logo at lower right, number at upper right. Candlelite logo at upper left. Color Elvis photo is same as on *Paradise Hawaiian Style*. Back: Text only.
INNER SLEEVE 1: White, no printing.

RCA Special Products (SP)
DML1-0413 ....'80   **15-20**
TOTAL PACKAGE 1: Disc, cover.

Card stock jacket, with printing on cover – not on slicks.
Concert recordings are stereo, studio tracks are monaural.
Side 1
True Love
Sweet Caroline
Harbor Lights
Rags to Riches
Let It Be Me
Side 2
Your Cheating Heart
Yesterday
Blueberry Hill
Words
Bridge over Troubled Water

GREATEST SHOW ON EARTH

❏ RCA Special Products (ST)
DML1-0348 ....'78   7-10
DISC 1: Black label, dog near top. Included as a bonus with Candlelite's *Memories of Elvis*. Title shown on the label as *Elvis in the Greatest Show on Earth*. May have "Special Products" at top of label or on left side.
DML1-0348-A-1/DML1-0348-B-1. Identification numbers are engraved.

❏ RCA Special Products
DML1-0348 ....'78   7-10
COVER 1: Front: RCA dog logo at lower right, number at upper right. Candlelite logo at upper left. Black-and-white '68 TV Special Elvis photo. Back: Text only.
INNER SLEEVE 1: White, no printing.

RCA Special Products (ST)
DML1-0348 ....'78   **15-20**
TOTAL PACKAGE 1: Disc, cover.

Card stock jacket, with printing on cover – not on slicks.
Side 1
I'll Remember You
Without Love
Gentle on My Mind
It's Impossible
What Now My Love
Side 2
Until It's Time for You to Go
Early Morning Rain
Something
The First Time Ever I Saw Your Face
The Impossible Dream

GREATEST SHOW ON EARTH

❏ Eagle LP-1932: Bootleg. Listed for identification only.

GUITAR MAN

❏ RCA Victor (ST)
AAL1-3917 ....1/81   8-10
DISC 1: Black label, dog near top.
AAL1-3917A-2S/AAL1-3917B-2S. Identification numbers are stamped but "Randy's Roost" is engraved in both sides.

❏ RCA AAL1-3917 ....1/81   8-10
COVER 1: Front: RCA logo and number at lower right. Color *Charro* Elvis photo – shows just head and shoulders. Back: UPC bar code at upper right. Same photo as on front, but pictures Elvis from the waist up.
INNER SLEEVE 1: White, no printing.

❏ RCA 1/81   3-5
INSERT 1: Color, 8" x 10" flyer promoting the film *This Is Elvis*, which has an Elvis ('68 TV Special) photo from the film.

❏ RCA AAL1-3917 ....1/81   5-10
SHRINK STICKER 1: Announces the inclusion of the hits *Guitar Man* and *Lovin' Arms*.

RCA Victor (ST)
AAL1-3917 .... 1/81   25-35
TOTAL PACKAGE 1: Disc, cover, insert, sticker.

❑ RCA Victor (ST)
AAL1-3917 .... 1/81   8-10
DISC 2: Same as disc 1.

❑ RCA AAL1-3917 .... 1/81   12-15
COVER 2: Designate promo. Same as cover 1, but with "Not for Sale" stamped on back.
INNER SLEEVE 2: White, no printing.

❑ RCA....................................1/81   3-5
INSERT 2: Color, 8" x 10" flyer promoting the film *This Is Elvis*, which has an Elvis ('68 TV Special) photo from the film.

❑ RCA AAL1-3917 .... 1/81   5-10
SHRINK STICKER 2: Announces the inclusion of the hits *Guitar Man* and *Lovin' Arms*.

RCA Victor (ST)
AAL1-3917 .... 1/81   30-40
TOTAL PACKAGE 1: Disc, cover, insert, sticker.

All tracks have Elvis' original vocals with updated instrumentation. Card stock jacket, with printing on cover – not on slicks. Also see *FELTON JARVIS TALKS ABOUT ELVIS*

Side 1
Guitar Man
After Loving You
Too Much Monkey Business
Just Call Me Lonesome
Lovin' Arms

Side 2
You Asked Me To
Clean Up Your Own Backyard
She Thinks I Still Care
Faded Love
I'm Movin' On

HAPPY HOLIDAYS, VOLUME 18
Various artists collection
❑ RCA Special Products (SP)
DPL1-0608 .... '83   4-6
DISC 1: Black RCA Special Products label, dog near top. Made for and sold exclusively by True Value Hardware Stores.
DPL1-0608A-1/DPL1-0608B-1.

❑ RCA Special Products
DPL1-0608 .... '83   4-6
COVER 1: Front: RCA Special Products logo and number at lower right. True Value logo at upper left. Back: Nine black-and-white photos of artists heard on this LP, including Elvis.
INNER SLEEVE 1: White, no printing.

RCA Special Products (SP)
DPL1-0608 .... '83   8-12
TOTAL PACKAGE 1: Disc, cover.

Side 1
Christmas Is . . . (Jack Jones)
Winter Wonderland (Anne Murray)

Sleigh Ride (Boston Pops Arthur Fiedler)
The Twelve Days of Christmas
If Every Day Was like Christmas (Elvis Presley)

Side 2
Christmas (Roger Whittaker)
The Little Drummer Boy (Harry Simeone Chorale)
O Holy Night (Nat King Cole)
Christmas Is the Warmest Time of the Year (Ed Ames)
I Wish It Could Be Christmas Forever (Perry Como)

HAPPY HOLIDAYS, VOLUME 20
Various artists collection
❑ RCA Special Products (SP)
DPL1-0713 .... '85   4-6
DISC 1: Black RCA Special Products label, dog near top. Made for and sold exclusively by True Value Stores.
DPL1-0713A-2/DPL1-0713B-2.

❑ RCA Special Products
DPL1-0713 .... '83   4-6
COVER 1: Front: RCA Special Products logo and number at lower right. True Value logo at upper left. Back: 15 black-and-white photos of artists heard on this LP, including Elvis.
INNER SLEEVE 1: White, no printing.

RCA Special Products (SP)
DPL1-0713 .... '85   8-12
TOTAL PACKAGE 1: Disc, cover.

Card stock jacket, with printing on cover – not on slicks.

Side 1
The Little Drummer Boy (Bing Crosby)
Medley: (Kate Smith)
Silent Night (Roger Whittaker and Chorus)
The Christmas Song (Mel Torme)
Blue Christmas (Elvis Presley)
Medley: (Mantovani Orchestra & Chorus)
Ave Maria (Sergio Franchi)

Side 2
Sleigh Ride (Carpenters)
Toyland (Perry Como /Ray Charles Singers)
It's Christmas (Ronnie Milsap)
O Little Town of Bethlehem (George Beverly Shea)
Medley: (Robert Shaw Chorale)
I Wonder As I Wander (Leontyne Price & Arthur Fiedler)
O Holy Night (Mario Lanza)

HAPPY HOLIDAYS, VOLUME 21
Various artists collection
❑ RCA Special Products (SP)
DPL1-0739 .... '86   4-6
DISC 1: Black RCA Special Products label, dog near top. Made for and sold exclusively by True Value Hardware Stores.
DPL1-0739A-1/DPL1-0739B-1.

❑ RCA Special Products
DPL1-0739 .... '83   4-6
COVER 1: Front: RCA Special Products logo and number at lower right. True Value logo at upper left. Back: 12 color photos of artists heard on this LP, including Elvis.
INNER SLEEVE 1: White, no printing.

RCA Special Products (SP)
DPL1-0739 .... '85   **8-12**
TOTAL PACKAGE 1: Disc, cover.

Card stock jacket, with printing on cover – not on slicks.

Side 1
Have Yourself a Merry Little Christmas (Royal Philharmonic)
A Christmas Toast (Bing Crosby)
Angels from the Realm of Glory (Julie Andrews)
Good King Wenceslas (Ames Brothers)
Silver Bells (Elvis Presley)
Santa Claus Is Comin' to Town (Tommy Dorsey Orchestra)

Side 2
Happy Holidays (Alabama)
God Rest Ye Merry Gentlemen (Nat King Cole)
I Wonder as I Wander (Canadian Brass)
Christmas Eve in My Home Town (Bobby Vinton)
Jingle Bells (Glenn Miller Orchestra)

HARUM SCARUM

❑ RCA Victor (M)
LPM-3468 .... 10/65   **10-15**
DISC 1: Black label, "Monaural" at bottom.
SPRM-6762-1S/SPRM-6763-2S. Label LP#12.
SPRM-6762-2S/SPRM-6763-2S.
SPRM-6762-4S/SPRM-6763-4S. Label LP#12.

❑ RCA Victor LPM-3468 ..... 10/65   **30-40**
COVER 1: Front: RCA Victor logo at upper right, number at lower left. Color Elvis photo.
Back: Five color Elvis photos from the film.

❑ RCA Victor 21-1121
40B 4/65   **4-6**
INNER SLEEVE 1: Red, black and white.
Front: RCA's Elvis LP catalog, most recent being *Roustabout* (side 1, row 1, column 5).
Back: RCA Elvis EPs and 45s catalog.

❑ RCA Victor LPM-3468 ..... 10/65   **45-65**
INSERT 1: Color 11¾" x 11¾" photo of Elvis wearing a kaffiyeh. Back is blank.

❑ RCA Victor LPM-3468 ..... 10/65   **20-25**
SHRINK STICKER 1: Announces the bonus, color Elvis photo.

RCA Victor (M)
LPM-3468 .... 10/65   **110-150**
TOTAL PACKAGE 1: Disc, cover, inner sleeve, insert, sticker.

❑ RCA Victor (M)
LPM-3468 .... 10/65   **10-15**
DISC 2: Same as disc 1.

❑ RCA Victor LPM-3468 ..... 10/65   **50-60**
COVER 2: Designate promo. Same as cover 1, but with "Not for Sale" stamped on back.

❑ RCA Victor 21-112-1
40B 4/65   **4-6**
INNER SLEEVE 2: Red, black and white.
Front: RCA's Elvis LP catalog, most recent being *Roustabout* (side 1, row 1, column 5).
Back: RCA Elvis EPs and 45s catalog.

❑ RCA Victor LPM-3468 ..... 10/65   **45-65**
INSERT 2: Color 11¾" x 11¾" photo of Elvis wearing a kaffiyeh. Back is blank.

❑ RCA Victor LPM-3468 ..... 10/65   **20-25**
SHRINK STICKER 2: Announces the bonus, color Elvis photo.

RCA Victor (M)
LPM-3468 .... 10/65   **130-170**
TOTAL PACKAGE 2: Disc, cover, inner sleeve, insert, sticker.

❑ RCA Victor (ST)
LSP-3468 .... 10/65   **10-20**
DISC 3: Black label, RCA logo in white at top and "Stereo" at bottom.
SPRS-6764-1S/SPRS-6765-1S. Label LP#16.
SPRS-6764-1S/SPRS-6765-2S. Label LP#16.

❑ RCA Victor LSP-3468 ...... 10/65   **20-40**
COVER 3: Front: RCA Victor logo at upper right, number at upper left. Color Elvis photo.
Back: Five color Elvis photos from the film.

❑ RCA Victor 21-112-1
40B 4/65   **4-6**
INNER SLEEVE 3: Red, black and white.
Front: RCA's Elvis LP catalog, most recent being *Roustabout* (side 1, row 1, column 5).
Back: RCA Elvis EPs and 45s catalog.

❑ RCA Victor LSP-3468 ...... 10/65   **45-65**
INSERT 3: Color 11¾" x 11¾" photo of Elvis wearing a kaffiyeh. Back is blank.

❑ RCA Victor LSP-3468 ...... 10/65   **20-25**
SHRINK STICKER 3: Announces the bonus, color Elvis photo.

RCA Victor (ST)
LSP-3468 .... 10/65   **100-155**
TOTAL PACKAGE 3: Disc, cover, inner sleeve, insert, sticker.

❑ RCA Victor (ST)
APL1-2558 .... 9/77   **3-5**
DISC 4: Black label, dog near top.

❑ RCA Victor APL1-2558 ...... 9/77   **3-5**
APL1-2558A-2/APL1-2558B-2.
COVER 4: Reflects number change.

❑ RCA Victor .... '70s   **2-4**
INNER SLEEVE 4: Black-and-white. Pictures RCA Elvis catalog front and back. Any of several sleeves may be found on reissues from this period. Includes copies with a sticker bearing the "AFL1" prefix, wrapped around cover at top of spine.

RCA Victor (ST)
APL1-2558 .... 9/77   **8-15**
TOTAL PACKAGE 4: Disc, cover, inner sleeve.

❑ RCA Victor (ST)
AYL1-3734 .... 9/80   **3-5**
DISC 5: Black label, dog near top.
AYL1-3734A/AYL1-3734B. Identification numbers are engraved. APL1-2558A-2/APL1-2558B-2 is stamped but crossed out.

❑ RCA Victor AYL1-3734 ...... 9/80   **3-5**
COVER 5: Reflects number change.
INNER SLEEVE 5: White, no printing.

RCA Victor (ST)
AYL1-3734 .... 9/80   **6-10**
TOTAL PACKAGE 5: Disc, cover.

Side 1
Harem Holiday
My Desert Serenade
Go East, Young Man
Mirage
Kismet
Shake That Tambourine

Side 2
Hey Little Girl
Golden Coins
So Close, Yet So Far
Animal Instinct
Wisdom of the Ages

HAVING FUN WITH ELVIS ON STAGE (Boxcar)

❑ Boxcar (M) (No Number)...8/74   75-100
DISC 1: White label with black and orange print. Sold only at 1974 Elvis personal appearances. No music – has only Elvis talking on stage.
Elvis Side 1/Elvis Side 2.

❑ Boxcar 8/74   75-100
COVER 1: Front: Boxcar logo at upper left. Six black-and-white photos of Elvis in concert. Back: U.S. map with Elvis appearances noted.

❑ RCA Victor 21-112-1
PT 54B 7/73   3-5
INNER SLEEVE 1: Black-and-white. Pictures RCA's Elvis LP catalog front and back, most recent being *Elvis As Recorded at Madison Square Garden* (side 2, row 2, column 6). May also be found with inner sleeves 54C. See chapter on inner sleeves for more information.

Boxcar (M)
(No Number) 8/74   **150-200**
TOTAL PACKAGE 1: Disc, cover, inner sleeve.

HAVING FUN WITH ELVIS ON STAGE (RCA Victor)

❑ RCA Victor (M)
CPM1-0818 .... 10/74   10-15
DISC 1: Orange label. Dynaflex vinyl. Reissue of (preceding) Boxcar LP. No music – has only Elvis talking on stage.
CPM1-0818A-1/CPM1-0818B-1.
CPM1-0818A-2S/CPM1-0818B-10S.
CPM1-0818A-2S/CPM1-0818B-11S.

❑ RCA Victor
CPM1-0818 .... 10/74   15-20
COVER 1: Front: RCA logo and number at upper left. Six black-and-white photos of Elvis in concert. Back: U.S. map with Elvis appearances noted.

❑ RCA Victor 21-112-1
PT 54C 11/73   3-5
INNER SLEEVE 1: Black-and-white. Pictures RCA's Elvis LP catalog front and back, most recent being *Elvis.As Recorded at Madison Square Garden* (side 2, row 4, column 2).

RCA Victor (M)
CPM1-0818 .... 10/74   **30-40**
TOTAL PACKAGE 1: Disc, cover, inner sleeve.

❑ RCA Victor (M)
CPM1-0818 .... 10/74   10-15
DISC 2: Same as disc 1.

❑ RCA Victor
CPM1-0818 .... 10/74   20-25
COVER 2: Designate promo. Same as cover 1, but with "Not for Sale" stamped on back.

❑ RCA Victor 21-112-1
PT 54C 11/73   3-5
INNER SLEEVE 2: Black-and-white. Pictures RCA's Elvis LP catalog front and back, most recent being *Elvis As Recorded at Madison Square Garden* (side 2, row 4, column 2).

RCA Victor (M)
CPM1-0818 .... 10/74   **35-45**
TOTAL PACKAGE 2: Disc, cover, inner sleeve.

❑ RCA Victor (M)
CPM1-0818 .... '76   10-12
DISC 3: Tan label.

❑ RCA Victor CPM1-0818....... '76   10-12
COVER 3: Verification pending.

❑ RCA Victor .... '70s   2-4
INNER SLEEVE 3: Black-and-white. Pictures RCA Elvis catalog front and back. Any of several sleeves may be found on reissues from this period.

RCA Victor (M)
CPM1-0818 .... '76   **20-25**
TOTAL PACKAGE 3: Disc, cover, inner sleeve.

❑ RCA Victor (M)
AFM1-0818 .... '77   12-15
DISC 4: Black label, dog near top.

❑ RCA AFM1-0818 .... '77   12-15
COVER 4: Reflects prefix change.

❑ RCA Victor .... '70s   2-4
INNER SLEEVE 4: Black-and-white. Pictures RCA Elvis catalog front and back. Any of several sleeves may be found on reissues from this period.

RCA Victor (M)
AFM1-0818 .... '77   **25-35**
TOTAL PACKAGE 4: Disc, cover, inner sleeve.

HE TOUCHED ME

❑ RCA Victor (ST)
LSP-4690 ....4/72   10-15
DISC 1: Orange label. Dynaflex vinyl.
BPRS-1083-1S/BPRS-1084-1S.
BPRS-1083-3S/BPRS-1084-3S. Identification numbers are
stamped.
BPRS-1083-6S/BPRS-1084-6S. Identification numbers are
engraved.

❑ RCA Victor LSP-4690........4/72   15-20
COVER 1: Front: RCA Victor logo and
number at upper right. Back: Pictures *How
Great Thou Art* and *His Hand in Mine.*

❑ RCA Victor 21-112-1
PT 56A 8/71   3-5
INNER SLEEVE 1: Black-and-white. Pictures
RCA Elvis cassette tape catalog front and
back, most recent being four-tape issue of
Worldwide 50 Gold Award Hits (side 2, row 3,
column 5). May also be found with inner
sleeve 57A. See chapter on inner sleeves for
more information.

RCA Victor (ST)
LSP-4690 ....4/72   30-40
   **TOTAL PACKAGE 1: Disc, cover, inner
   sleeve.**

❑ RCA Victor (ST)
LSP-4690 ....4/72   10-15
DISC 2: Same as disc 1.

❑ RCA Victor LSP-4690........4/72   70-80
COVER 2: Same as cover 1 except has
contents and running times on a white 4" x 6"
sticker, applied at upper left on front.
Promotional issue only.
Counterfeit Identification: Counterfeit
stickers exist and are difficult to identify.

❑ RCA Victor 21-112-1
PT 56A 8/71   3-5
INNER SLEEVE 2: Same as Inner Sleeve 1.

RCA Victor (ST)
LSP-4690.....................4/72   80-100
   **TOTAL PACKAGE 2: Disc, cover with
   sticker, inner sleeve.**

❑ RCA Victor (ST)
LSP-4690 ....'76   4-8
DISC 3: Tan label. Dynaflex vinyl.

❑ RCA LSP-4690...................'76   4-8
COVER 3: Same as cover 1, except paper
stock is of a lighter weight.

❑ RCA Victor........................'70s   2-4
INNER SLEEVE 3: Black-and-white. Pictures
RCA Elvis catalog front and back. Any of
several sleeves may be found on reissues
from this period.

RCA Victor (ST)
LSP-4690.....................'76   10-20
   **TOTAL PACKAGE 3: Disc, cover, inner
   sleeve.**

❑ RCA Victor (ST)
LSP-4690 ....'76   4-6
DISC 4: Black label, dog near top. Dynaflex
vinyl.

❑ RCA LSP-4690....................'76   4-6
COVER 4: Verification pending.

❑ RCA Victor.........................'70s   2-4
INNER SLEEVE 4: Black-and-white. Pictures
RCA Elvis catalog front and back. Any of
several sleeves may be found on reissues
from this period.

RCA Victor (ST)
LSP-4690......................'76   10-18
   **TOTAL PACKAGE 4: Disc, cover, inner
   sleeve.**

❑ RCA Victor (ST)
AFL1-4690...........................'77   3-5
DISC 5: Black label, dog near top. Dynaflex
vinyl.
AFL1-4690A/AFL1-4690B. Identification numbers are
engraved. Stamped but crossed out are BPRS-1083/BPRS-
1084.

❑ RCA Victor AFL1-4690........'77   3-5
COVER 5: Reflects prefix change. Front: "RE"
at lower left. Back: "RE" at lower right.
Includes copies with a sticker bearing the
"AFL1" prefix, wrapped around cover at top of
spine.

❑ RCA Victor.........................'70s   2-4
INNER SLEEVE 5: Black-and-white. Pictures
RCA Elvis catalog front and back. Any of
several sleeves may be found on reissues
from this period.

RCA Victor (ST)
AFL1-4690....................'77   8-15
   **TOTAL PACKAGE 5: Disc, cover, inner
   sleeve.**

Side 1
He Touched Me
I've Got Confidence
Amazing Grace
Seeing Is Believing
He Is My Everything
Bosom of Abraham

Side 2
An Evening Prayer
Lead Me, Guide Me
There Is No God But God
A Thing Called Love
I, John
Reach Out to Jesus

HE WALKS BESIDE ME (FAVORITE SONGS OF FAITH AND INSPIRATION)

❑ RCA Victor (ST)
AFL1-2772........................3/78   3-5
DISC 1: Black label, dog near top.
AFL1-2772A-1S/AFL1-2772B-2S.
AFL1-2772A-4S/AFL1-2772B-2S.
AFL1-2772A-5S/AFL1-2772B-1S.
AFL1-2772A-5S/AFL1-2772B-2S.

❑ RCA AFL1-2772 .... 3/78   3-5
  COVER 1: Front: Number at upper left. Color
  Elvis photo. Back: Color picture of a church
  steeple.

❑ RCA Victor 21-112-1
  PT 54F 7/77   2-4
  INNER SLEEVE 1: Black-and-white. Pictures
  RCA's Elvis LPs front and back, most recent
  being *Moody Blue* (side 2, row 5, column 1).

❑ RCA/Boxcar.............................   5-8
  INSERT 1: Color, 5¾" x 5¾" 20-page photo
  booklet and RCA catalog.

❑ RCA AFL1-2772 .... 3/78   2-4
  SHRINK STICKER 1: Blue with white print.
  Reads: "Includes Limited Edition Mini-Photo
  Album." Has selection number at bottom.

RCA Victor (ST)
AFL1-2772 .... 3/78   15-25
  TOTAL PACKAGE 1: Disc, cover, inner
    sleeve, insert, sticker.

❑ RCA Victor (ST)
  AFL1-2772 .... 3/78   3-5
  DISC 2: Same as disc 1.

❑ RCA AFL1-2772 .... 3/78   5-10
  COVER 2: Designate promo. Same as cover
  1, but with "Not for Sale" stamped on back.

❑ RCA Victor 21-112-1
  PT 54F 7/77   2-4
  INNER SLEEVE 2: Black-and-white. Pictures
  RCA's Elvis LPs front and back, most recent
  being *Moody Blue* (side 2, row 5, column 1).

❑ RCA/Boxcar.............................   5-8
  INSERT 2: Color, 5¾" x 5¾" 20-page photo
  booklet and RCA catalog.

❑ RCA AFL1-2772 .... 3/78   2-4
  SHRINK STICKER 2: Blue with white print.
  Reads: "Includes Limited Edition Mini-Photo
  Album." Has selection number at bottom.

RCA Victor (ST
AFL1-2772 .... 3/78   20-30
  TOTAL PACKAGE 2: Disc, cover, inner
    sleeve, insert, sticker.

Though not identified as such, *Miracle of the
Rosary* is a previously unreleased alternative
mix.

Side A
He Is My Everything
Miracle of the Rosary
Where Did They Go Lord
Somebody Bigger Than You and I
An Evening Prayer
The Impossible Dream (Unreleased Version)

Side B
If I Can Dream (Unreleased Version)
Padre
Known Only to Him
Who Am I
How Great Thou Art

HEART OF DIXIE
Various artists collection

❑ A&M (SP) SP-3930 .... '89   5-8
  DISC 1: Original soundtrack release.
  SP-03930-A ES-1/SP-03930-B ES-1. Identification numbers
  are engraved.

❑ A&M SP-3930 .... '89   10-12
  COVER 1: Front: No logo or number. Color
  photos of film stars. Back: A&M logo at lower
  right. Four color photos of film scenes. UPC
  bar code at upper right.
  INNER SLEEVE 1: White, no printing.

A&M (SP) SP-3930 .... '89   15-20
  TOTAL PACKAGE 1: Disc, cover.

Card stock jacket, with printing on cover – not
on slicks.

Side 1
Moanin' Blues (Prelude)
Delbert McClinton & the Snakes
Light's Out (John Cowan & the Snakes
I Want You, I Need You, I Love You (Elvis Presley)
The Wayward Wind (Rebecca Russell and the Snakes)

Side 2
Blue Suede Shoes (Elvis Presley)
Since I Met You Baby (Ivory Joe Hunter)
Willie and the Hand Jive (Kenny Vance)
Taylor's Cafe (Gladhand Band)
Faith, Hope and Glory (Delbert McClinton, Rebecca
    Russell and the Snakes)

HEARTBREAK HOTEL
Various artists collection

❑ RCA (SP) 8533-1-R .... '88   8-10
  DISC 1: Original soundtrack release. Red,
  black and silver label.
  8533-1-RA-1S/8533-1-RB-10+. Identification numbers are
  engraved.
  8533-1-RA-2S/8533-1-RB-10+. Identification numbers are
  engraved.

❑ RCA 8533-1-R .... '88   10-15
  COVER 1: Front: No logo or number. Color
  photo of "Elvis" and four characters from the
  film, in a pink Cadillac. Back: RCA logo at
  lower right, BMG at lower left. UPC bar code
  at upper right. Three color scenes from film.
  INNER SLEEVE 1: Generic RCA sleeve.
  Makes no mention of Elvis or this LP.

RCA (SP) 8533-1-R .... '88   20-25
  TOTAL PACKAGE 1: Disc, cover.

Card stock jacket, with printing on cover – not
on slicks.

Side 1
Heartbreak Hotel (Elvis Presley)
One Night (Elvis Presley)
Drift Away (Dobie Gray)
Can't Help Falling in Love (David Keith)
Burning Love (Elvis Presley)
Love Me (David Keith)

Side 2
Reddy Teddy (Elvis Presley)
I'm Eighteen (Alice Cooper)
Soul on Fire (Charlie Schlatter with Zulu Time)
If I Can Dream (Elvis Presley)
Heartbreak Hotel (David Keith and Charlie Schlatter
    with Zulu Time)

HELLO CAROL! (SOCIAL SECURITY PRESENTS MUSIC YOU CAN'T FORGET)

❏ Social Security (M)
157-169 .... '74   25-35
DISC 1: A series of 15-minute shows, hosted by Carol Channing. Sent to radio stations as public service programming. The Elvis segment contains: *Spanish Eyes, That's All Right, Love Me Tender* and *Don't Be Cruel.*
COVER 1: Verification pending.
Social Security (M)
157-169.......................... **'74**   **25-35**
TOTAL PACKAGE 1: Disc

HILLBILLY CAT

❏ Music Works (M)
PB-3602 ....7/84   7-10
DISC 1: Contents of this LP makes up about half of *The Beginning Years.*
PB-3602-1/PB-3602-1. Identification numbers are engraved.
❏ Music Works PB-36029.....7/84   8-10
COVER 1: Front: Music Works logo at lower left, number at upper right. Duotone Elvis photo. Back: Liner notes and duotone Elvis photo.
INNER SLEEVE 1: White, no printing.
Music Works (M)
PB-3602.......................7/84   **15-20**
TOTAL PACKAGE 1: Disc, cover.

Card stock jacket, with printing on cover – not on slicks.

Side 1
Introduction of Louisiana Hayride with Frank Page
Elvis Presley with Horace Logan
That's All Right Momma
Elvis talks about his musical style with Horace Logan
Blue Moon of Kentucky

Side 2
Recollections by Frank Page of Elvis Presley and Colonel Tom Parker
Good Rockin' Tonight
I Got a Woman

HILLBILLY CAT LIVE

❏ Spring Fever SFLP-301: Bootleg. Listed for identification only.

HILLBILLY CAT 1954-1974

❏ Brookville BRLP-311: Bootleg. Listed for identification only.

HIS GREATEST HITS (8 LPs)

Mail order offer only. All discs in this set have a black, white and red label, and are listed individually below.
❏ Reader's Digest/RCA Music Service (SP)
RD4A-010-1 .... '79   25-30
DISC 1:
J1RS-5681-1/J1RS-5682-1.

❏ Reader's Digest/RCA Music Service (SP)
RD4A-010-2 .... '79   25-30
DISC 2:
J1RS-5683-1/J1RS-5684-1.
❏ Reader's Digest/RCA Music Service (SP)
RD4A-010-3 .... '79   25-30
DISC 3:
J1RS-5685-3/J1RS-5686-1.
❏ Reader's Digest/RCA Music Service (SP)
RD4A-010-4 .... '79   25-30
DISC 4:
J1RS-5687-1/J1RS-5688-1.
❏ Reader's Digest/RCA Music Service (SP)
RD4A-010-5 .... '79   25-30
DISC 5:
J1RS-5689-1/J1RS-5690-1.
❏ Reader's Digest/RCA Music Service (SP)
RD4A-010-6 .... '79   25-30
DISC 6:
J1RS-5691-2/J1RS-5692-2.
❏ Reader's Digest/RCA Music Service (SP)
RD4A-010-7 .... '79   25-30
DISC 7:
J1RS-5693-4/J1RS-5694-1.
❏ Reader's Digest/RCA Music Service (SP)
RD4A-010-8 .... '79   25-30
DISC 8:
J1RS-5695-4/J1RS-5696-1.
❏ Reader's Digest/RCA Music Service
RD10/A................................ '79   175-200
BOX 1: Slipcover: White. Front has "*Reader's Digest Commemorative Album. Elvis! His Greatest Hits.*" Back is blank. Record case: White with blue print. Back is blank. Number is different than is shown on discs.
INNER SLEEVES 1: Generic, individually numbered, Reader's Digest, plastic lined sleeves. Front: Beige, with drawings of horns and a keyboard. Back: Blank.
Reader's Digest/RCA Music Service (SP) RD4A-010.............. **'79   400-500**
TOTAL PACKAGE 1: Discs, box.

Disc 1
Side 1
Heartbreak Hotel
Don't Be Cruel
I Want You, I Need You, I Love You
Blue Suede Shoes
Anyway You Want Me (That's How I Will Be)
Hound Dog
Side 2
Love Me Tender
Too Much
Love Me
I Was the One
Playing for Keeps
(Let Me Be Your) Teddy Bear
Disc 2
Side 1
All Shook Up
Loving You
Treat Me Nice
Blue Christmas
That's When Your Heartaches Begin
Jailhouse Rock

Side 2

Don't
I Beg of You
Wear My Ring Around Your Neck
One Night
King Creole
Hard Headed Woman

Disc 3

Side 1

I Got Stung
(Now and Then There's) A Fool Such As I
I Need Your Love Tonight
My Wish Came True
Doncha' Think It's Time
A Big Hunk O' Love

Side 2

Are You Lonesome Tonight
Stuck on You
I Gotta Know
Fame and Fortune
A Mess of Blues
It's Now Or Never

Disc 4

Side 1

Can't Help Falling in Love
Surrender
Little Sister
Flaming Star
I Feel So Bad
(Marie's the Name) His Latest Flame

Side 2

Return to Sender
Good Luck Charm
Follow That Dream
Wooden Heart
She's Not You
Rock-a-Hula Baby

Disc 5

Side 1

Blue Hawaii
(You're the) Devil in Disguise
One Broken Heart for Sale
Bossa Nova Baby
Such a Night
King of the Whole Wide World

Side 2

Kissin' Cousins
Ask Me
Ain't That Loving You Baby
Viva Las Vegas
Kiss Me Quick
What'd I Say

Disc 6

Side 1

Suspicious Minds
In the Ghetto
(Such an) Easy Question
Don't Cry Daddy
If I Can Dream
Puppet on a String

Side 2

You Don't Have to Say You Love Me
Burning Love
The Wonder of You
Steamroller Blues
Kentucky Rain
My Way

Disc 7

Side 1

Mystery Train
I'm Left, You're Right, She's Gone
I Forgot to Remember to Forget
Baby, Let's Play House
That's All Right
You're a Heartbreaker

Side 2

Your Cheatin' Heart
I Really Don't Want to Know
When My Blue Moon Turns to Gold Again
There Goes My Everything
Have I Told You Lately That I Love You
I Can't Stop Loving You

Disc 8

Side 1

How Great Thou Art
Somebody Bigger Than You and I
In the Garden
It Is No Secret (What God Can Do)
His Hand in Mine
Take My Hand, Precious Lord

Side 2

Crying in the Chapel
(There'll Be) Peace in the Valley (For Me)
Put Your Hand in the Hand
Where Did They Go Lord
I Believe
You'll Never Walk Alone

HIS GREATEST HITS (7 LPs)

Mail order offer only. All discs in this set have
a black, white and red label, and are listed
individually below. (Omits disc 8 from previous
set.)

❑ Reader's Digest/RCA Music Service (SP)
   RD4A-010-2/1 .... '83   3-5
   DISC 1:
   J1RS-5681-2/J1RS-5682-1.

❑ Reader's Digest/RCA Music Service (SP)
   RD4A-010-2/2 .... '83   3-5
   DISC 2:
   J1RS-5683-5/J1RS-5684-2.

❑ Reader's Digest/RCA Music Service (SP)
   RD4A-010-2/3 .... '83   3-5
   DISC 3:
   J1RS-5685-4/J1RS-5686-2.

❑ Reader's Digest/RCA Music Service (SP)
   RD4A-010-2/4 .... '83   3-5
   DISC 4:
   J1RS-5687-1/J1RS-5688-2.

❑ Reader's Digest/RCA Music Service (SP)
   RD4A-010-2/5 .... '83   3-5
   DISC 5:
   J1RS-5689-1/J1RS-5690-2.

❑ Reader's Digest/RCA Music Service (SP)
   RD4A-010-2/6 .... '83   3-5
   DISC 6:
   J1RS-5691/J1RS-5692-2.

❑ Reader's Digest/RCA Music Service (SP)
   RD4A-010-2/7 .... '83   3-5
   DISC 7:
   J1RS-5693-4/J1RS-5694-1.

❏ Reader's Digest/RCA Music Service
010/A..................................... '83   25-35
  BOX 1: Slipcover: Front: "Collector's Edition"
  at upper right. Reader's Digest/RCA Music
  Service logo at upper left. Has color drawings
  of Elvis. Back: Yellow, no printing. Record
  case: White with blue print, including duotone
  reproduction of drawings on slipcover. Back is
  blank. Number is different than is shown on
  discs.
  INNER SLEEVES 1: Generic, individually
  numbered, Reader's Digest, plastic lined
  sleeves. Front and Back: Red, black and blue
  with number (RDA/GP2-D) at bottom.

❏ Reader's Digest/RCA Music
  Service 010/A...................... '83   5-10
  INSERT 1: Duotone, 11¼" x 11½" 12-page
  information booklet, *Elvis! His Greatest Hits.*

Reader's Digest/RCA Music (SP)
RD4A-010-2................... '83   60-100
TOTAL PACKAGE 1: Discs, box, insert.

❏ Reader's Digest/RCA Music Service
010/A..................................... '90   10-20
  BOX 2: Same as box 1, except back and trim
  of box is white instead of yellow. The LPs in
  this set are the same as discs 1 through 7.

❏ Reader's Digest/RCA Music Service
010/A..................................... '83   5-10
  INSERT 2: Duotone, 11¼" x 11½" 12-page
  information booklet, *Elvis! His Greatest Hits.*

Reader's Digest/RCA Music (SP)
010/A .... '90   40-50
TOTAL PACKAGE 2: Discs, box, insert.

Disc 1
Side 1
Heartbreak Hotel
Don't Be Cruel
I Want You, I Need You, I Love You
Blue Suede Shoes
Anyway You Want Me (That's How I Will Be)
Hound Dog
Side 2
Love Me Tender
Too Much
Love Me
I Was the One
Playing for Keeps
(Let Me Be Your) Teddy Bear

Disc 2
Side 1
All Shook Up
Loving You
Treat Me Nice
Blue Christmas
That's When Your Heartaches Begin
Jailhouse Rock
Side 2
Don't
I Beg of You
Wear My Ring Around Your Neck
One Night
King Creole
Hard Headed Woman

Disc 3
Side 1
I Got Stung
(Now and Then There's) A Fool Such As I
I Need Your Love Tonight
My Wish Came True
Doncha' Think It's Time
A Big Hunk O' Love
Side 2
Are You Lonesome Tonight
Stuck on You
I Gotta Know
Fame and Fortune
A Mess of Blues
It's Now Or Never

Disc 4
Side 1
Can't Help Falling in Love
Surrender
Little Sister
Flaming Star
I Feel So Bad
(Marie's the Name) His Latest Flame
Side 2
Return to Sender
Good Luck Charm
Follow That Dream
Wooden Heart
She's Not You
Rock-a-Hula Baby

Disc 5
Side 1
Blue Hawaii
(You're the) Devil in Disguise
One Broken Heart for Sale
Bossa Nova Baby
Such a Night
King of the Whole Wide World
Side 2
Kissin' Cousins
Ask Me
Ain't That Loving You Baby
Viva Las Vegas
Kiss Me Quick
What'd I Say

Disc 6
Side 1
Suspicious Minds
In the Ghetto
(Such an) Easy Question
Don't Cry Daddy
If I Can Dream
Puppet on a String
Side 2
You Don't Have to Say You Love Me
Burning Love
The Wonder of You
Steamroller Blues
Kentucky Rain
My Way

Disc 7
Side 1
Mystery Train
I'm Left, You're Right, She's Gone
I Forgot to Remember to Forget
Baby, Let's Play House
That's All Right
You're a Heartbreaker

Side 2
Your Cheatin' Heart
I Really Don't Want to Know
When My Blue Moon Turns to Gold Again
There Goes My Everything
Have I Told You Lately That I Love You
I Can't Stop Loving You

HIS HAND IN MINE (RCA)

❏ RCA Victor (M)
LPM-2328.........................12/60   40-50
DISC 1: Black label, "Long Play" at bottom.
L2PP-4729-3S/L2PP-4730-3S. Label LP#1.
L2PP-4729-13S/L2PP-4730-2S. Label LP#2.

❏ RCA Victor LPM-2328.....12/60   60-75
COVER 1: RCA Victor logo at upper right,
number at lower left. Color Elvis photo. Back:
Pictures *Peace in the Valley* EP. Has
"Important Notice" about "New Orthophonic"
recordings at lower right.
INNER SLEEVE 1: Generic RCA sleeve.
Makes no mention of Elvis or this LP.

RCA Victor (M)
LPM-2328 ....12/60   **100-125**
TOTAL PACKAGE 1: Disc, cover.

❏ RCA Victor (M)
LPM-2328.........................11/63   30-40
DISC 2: Black label, "Mono" at bottom.

❏ RCA Victor LPM-2328.....11/63   20-30
COVER 2: Verification pending.

❏ RCA Victor (No Number)...9/63   8-10
INNER SLEEVE 2: Turquoise, black and
white. Front: RCA's Elvis LP catalog, most
recent being *It Happened at the World's Fair*
(side 1, row 4, column 5). Back: RCA Elvis
EPs and 45s catalog.

RCA Victor (M)
LPM-2328 ....11/63   **60-80**
TOTAL PACKAGE 2: Disc, cover, inner
     sleeve.

❏ RCA Victor (M)
LPM-2328.........................10/64   10-20
DISC 3: Black label, "Monaural" at bottom.

❏ RCA Victor LPM-2328.....10/64   10-20
COVER 3: Verification pending.

❏ RCA Victor 21-112-1
40A...................................10/64   4-8
INNER SLEEVE 3: Red, black and white.
Front: RCA's Elvis LP catalog, most recent
being *Kissin' Cousins* (side 1, row 1, column
6). Back: RCA Elvis EPs and 45s catalog.

RCA Victor (M)
LPM-2328 ....10/64   **25-50**
TOTAL PACKAGE 3: Disc, cover, inner
     sleeve.

❏ RCA Victor (ST)
LSP-2328 ....12/60   75-100
DISC 4: Black label, "Living Stereo" at bottom.
L2PY-4731-4S/L2PY-4732-4S. Label LP#7.

❏ RCA Victor (ST)
LSP-2328 ....12/60   75-100
COVER 4: RCA Victor logo at upper right,
number at upper left. Color Elvis photo. Back:
Pictures *Peace in the Valley* EP. Has Miracle
Surface logo and "Important Notice" about a
"True Stereophonic Record" at lower right.
Price reflects RCA's continued use of this
same cover, with no discernible differences.
INNER SLEEVE 4: Generic RCA sleeve.
Makes no mention of Elvis or this LP.

RCA Victor (ST)
LSP-2328...................12/60   **150-200**
TOTAL PACKAGE 4: Disc, cover.

❏ RCA Victor (ST)
LSP-2328 ....10/64   525-600
DISC 5: Black label, RCA logo in *silver* at top
and "Stereo" at bottom.
L2PY-4731-4S/L2PY-4732-4S. Label LP#13
L2PY-4731-12S/L2PY-4732-12S. Label LP#13

❏ RCA Victor LSP-2328......10/64   75-100
COVER 5: Same as cover 4.

❏ RCA Victor 21-112-1
40A...................................10/64   4-8
INNER SLEEVE 5: Red, black and white.
Front: RCA's Elvis LP catalog, most recent
being *Kissin' Cousins* (side 1, row 1, column
6). Back: RCA Elvis EPs and 45s catalog.

RCA Victor (ST)
LSP-2328...................10/64   **600-700**
TOTAL PACKAGE 5: Disc, cover, inner
     sleeve.

❏ RCA Victor (ST)
LSP-2328 ....11/64   10-20
DISC 6: Black label, RCA logo in white at top
and "Stereo" at bottom.
L2PY-4731-4S/L2PY-4732-3S. Label LP#16.
L2PY-4731-13S/L2PY-4732-1S. Label LP#16.

❏ RCA Victor LSP-2328......11/64   75-100
COVER 6: Same as cover 4.

❏ RCA Victor 21-112-1
40A...................................11/64   4-8
INNER SLEEVE 6: Red, black and white.
Front: RCA's Elvis LP catalog, most recent
being *Kissin' Cousins* (side 1, row 1, column
6). Back: RCA Elvis EPs and 45s catalog.

RCA Victor (ST)
LSP-2328...................11/64   **90-130**
TOTAL PACKAGE 6: Disc, cover, inner
     sleeve.

❏ RCA Victor (ST)
LSP-2328 ....11/68   20-25
DISC 7: Orange label. Rigid vinyl.

❏ RCA Victor LSP-2328......11/68   20-25
COVER 7: Same as cover 4, except has "RE"
at lower left corner of back cover.

❑ RCA Victor 21-112-1
40D....................................6/68   4-6
INNER SLEEVE 7: Red, black and white.
Front: RCA's Elvis LP catalog, most recent
being *Elvis' Gold Records, Vol. 4* (side 1, row
4, column 5). Back: RCA's Elvis LP and Twin
Pack Stereo 8 catalog. May also be found
with inner sleeves 40B and 40C. See chapter
on inner sleeves for more information.

RCA Victor (ST)
LSP-2328.................... 11/68   45-55
**TOTAL PACKAGE 7: Disc, cover, inner
sleeve.**

❑ RCA (ST) ANL1-1319........3/76   4-8
DISC 8: Orange label. Flexible vinyl. This was
the last Elvis LP to be issued on the orange
RCA label. Does not have "Victor" on label –
very unusual for an RCA commercial orange
label.
ANL1-1319-A/ANL1-1319-B. Correct numbers are engraved.
Previous numbers for this LP, L2PY-4731/L2PY-4732, are
stamped and may or may not be crossed out.

❑ RCA ANL1-1319................3/76   4-8
COVER 8: Front: RCA logo and number at
lower right, number by itself at upper right.
Color photo is a cropped version of the one on
covers 1A-6A. Back: Listing of other RCA mid-
line ($5.98) product. "RE" at bottom left.
INNER SLEEVE 8: White, no printing.

RCA (ST) ANL1-1319......3/76   10-20
TOTAL PACKAGE 8: Disc, cover.

❑ RCA Victor (ST)
LSP-2328 ....'76   10-15
DISC 9: Tan label.

❑ RCA LSP-2328....................'76   4-8
L2PY-4731-16S/L2PY-4732-16S.
COVER 9: Front: RCA logo and number at
upper right. "Victor" and "Stereo" at upper
right. Back: Same as cover 4, but with a "4" at
lower left.

❑ RCA Victor.........................'70s   2-4
INNER SLEEVE 9: Black-and-white. Pictures
RCA Elvis catalog front and back. Any of
several sleeves may be found on reissues
from this period.

RCA Victor (ST)
LSP-2328.......................'76   15-25
**TOTAL PACKAGE 9: Disc, cover, inner
sleeve.**

❑ RCA Victor (ST)
AYL1-3935 ....5/81   3-5
DISC 10: Yellow label.
AYL1-3935-A/AYL1-3935-B. Identification numbers are
engraved. Has ANL1- 1319A-2S stamped but crossed out.
Also has AYL1-3935 engraved twice, but with one crossed
out.

❑ RCA AYL1-3935................5/81   3-5
COVER 10: Reflects prefix change. Part of
RCA's "Best Buy Series. " Includes copies
with a sticker bearing the "AYL1" prefix,
wrapped around cover at top of spine.

RCA Victor (ST)
AYL1-3935 ....5/81   6-10
TOTAL PACKAGE 10: Disc, cover.

Side 1
His Hand in Mine
I'm Gonna Walk Dem Golden Stairs
In My Father's House
Milky White Way
Known Only to Him
I Believe in the Man in the Sky

Side 2
Joshua Fit the Battle
Jesus Knows What I Need
Swing Down Sweet Chariot
Mansion over the Hilltop
If We Never Meet Again
Working on the Building

HIS HAND IN MINE (AFRTS)

❑ Armed Forces Radio & Television Service
(M) R-313/R-314 ....'60   200-300
DISC 1:
SSL-14027/SSL-14028.
COVER 1: None made.
INNER SLEEVE 1: Brown, no printing.

**Armed Forces Radio & Television
Service (M) R-313/
R-314 ....'60   200-300**
TOTAL PACKAGE 1: Disc.

Side 1
His Hand in Mine
I'm Gonna Walk Dem Golden Stairs
In My Father's House
Milky White Way
Known Only to Him
I Believe in the Man in the Sky

Side 2
Joshua Fit the Battle
Jesus Knows What I Need
Swing Down Sweet Chariot
Mansion over the Hilltop
If We Never Meet Again
Working on the Building

HIS SONGS OF FAITH AND INSPIRATION
(2 LPs)

❑ RCA Special Products (SP)
DVL2-0728 ....2/86   25-40
DISCS 1: Black label, dog near top. Mail order
LP, sold via TV ads.
(Disc 1) DVL2-0728A-1/DVL2-0728B-7. **(Disc 2)** DVL2-
0728C-1/DVL2-0728D-1.

❑ RCA Special Products
DVL2-0728 ....2/86   25-40
COVER 1: Single pocket. Front: RCA Special
Products logo and number at lower right. An
artist reproduced, more or less, the color
photo used on ANL1-1319 (*His Hand in Mine*,
orange label issue). Back: Pictures *Elvis: 50
Years, 50 Hits.*
INNER SLEEVES 1: White, no printing.

RCA Special Products (SP)

DVL2-0728 .... 2/86   50-80
TOTAL PACKAGE 1: Disc, cover.

Card stock jacket, with printing on cover – not
on slicks.

Disc 1

Side 1

How Great Thou Art
Stand by Me
Joshua Fit the Battle
So High
In My Father's House (Are Many Mansions)
He Touched Me
I've Got Confidence
It Is No Secret (What God Can Do)
He Is My Everything

Side 2

Working on the Building
In the Garden
We Call on Him
His Hand in Mine
By and By
Farther Along
Known Only to Him
I Believe in the Man in the Sky
You'll Never Walk Alone

Disc 2

Side 3

An Evening Prayer
Mansion over the Hilltop
Milky White Way
Reach Out to Jesus
Who Am I
Take My Hand, Precious Lord
I'm Gonna Walk Dem Golden Stairs (shown as "Gonna
 Walk Dem Golden Stairs")
If the Lord Wasn't Walking by My Side
(There'll Be) Peace in the Valley (For Me)

Side 4

Crying in the Chapel
Where No One Stands Alone
He Knows Just What I Need
Bosom of Abraham
Where Could I Go But to the Lord
Without Him
Swing Down, Sweet Chariot
Amazing Grace
If We Never Meet Again

HIS SONGS OF INSPIRATION

❑ RCA Special Products (SP)
DML1-0264 .... '77   7-10
DISC 1: Black label, dog near top. Offered by
Candlelight Music as a bonus to customers of
The Elvis Presley Story.

DPL1-0264A-2/DPL1-0264B-2. Both label and cover show
"DML1" as the prefix, however "DPL1" is stamped in the
vinyl.

DPL1-0264A-2/DPL1-0264B-3.

DPL1-0264A-3/DPL1-0264B-2. This black label pressing has
no dog on it.

❑ RCA Special Products
DML1-0264 .... '77   7-10
COVER 1: Front: RCA Special Products logo
and number at lower right, Candlelite logo at
top center. Color Elvis photo is same as on
Elvis (LPM-1382), but is flopped (negative
reversed). Back: Text only.

INNER SLEEVE 1: White, no printing.

RCA Special Products (SP)

DML1-0264 .... '77   15-20
TOTAL PACKAGE 1: Disc, cover.

Card stock jacket, with printing on cover – not
on slicks.

Side 1

Crying in the Chapel
Put Your Hand in the Hand
I Believe
How Great Thou Art
If I Can Dream

Side 2

(There'll Be) Peace in the Valley (For Me)
Amazing Grace
An American Trilogy
Follow That Dream
You'll Never Walk Alone

HISTORY OF COUNTRY MUSIC HANK WILLIAMS / ELVIS PRESLEY

❑ Sunrise Media (M)
SM-3011 .... '81   8-12
DISC 1: Red label with black print. Four songs
by each artist. Side 1 is by Hank Williams,
side 2 by Elvis.

SM-3011-A S-10290/SM-3011-B S-10291. Identification
numbers are engraved. Both sides also have two sets of
numbers crossed out.

❑ Sunrise Media SM-3011 ...... '81   8-12
COVER 1: Front: Color picture of a guitar,
rope, hat and boots. Back: Text only.
INNER SLEEVE 1: White, no printing.

Sunrise Media (M)

SM-3011 .... '81   15-25
TOTAL PACKAGE 1: Disc, cover.

Side 1 Hank Williams

I Can't Help It (If I'm Still in Love with You)
Half As Much
Honky Tonk Blues
Why Don't You Love Me

Side 2 Elvis Presley

Heartbreak Hotel
(Let Me Be Your) Teddy Bear
Love Me Tender
Jailhouse Rock

HOME-RECORDED ELVIS

❑ TO 300: Bootleg. Listed for identification
only.

HOT SUMMER NIGHT

❑ Chips CLPI-1501: Bootleg. Listed for
identification only.

HOW GREAT THOU ART (AS SUNG BY ELVIS)

❑ RCA Victor (M)

LPM-3758..........................3/67   15-25

DISC 1: Black label, "Mono Dynagroove" at bottom. Full title on label is *How Great Thou Art As Sung By Elvis Presley*. This was the only commercial Elvis release to be labeled "Dynagroove."

TPRM-1893-2S/TPRM-1894-1S.

TPRM-1893-2S/TPRM-1894-2S.

TPRM-1893-3S/TPRM-1894-3S.

❑ RCA Victor LPM-3758.......3/67   20-30

COVER 1: Front: RCA Victor Dynagroove logo at upper right, number at lower left. Color Elvis photo. Back: Color Elvis photo.

❑ RCA Victor 21-112-1

40C....................................3/67   4-6

INNER SLEEVE 1: Blue, black and white. Front: RCA's Elvis LP catalog, most recent being *Spinout* (side 1, row 2, column 7). Back: RCA Elvis Stereo 8 catalog.

RCA Victor (M)

LPM-3758 ....3/67   40-60

TOTAL PACKAGE 1: Disc, cover, inner sleeve.

❑ RCA Victor (ST)

LSP-3758 ....3/67   15-25

DISC 2: Black label, RCA logo in white at top and "Stereo Dynagroove" at bottom. Full title on label is *How Great Thou Art As Sung By Elvis Presley*. This was the only commercial Elvis release to be labeled "Dynagroove."

TPRS-1895-2S/TPRS-1896-2S.

TPRS-1895-4S/TPRS-1896-3S.

❑ RCA Victor LSP-3758........3/67   20-30

COVER 2: Front: RCA Victor Dynagroove logo at upper right, number at upper left. Color Elvis photo. Back: Color Elvis photo.

❑ RCA Victor 21-112-1

40C....................................3/67   4-6

INNER SLEEVE 2: Blue, black and white. Front: RCA's Elvis LP catalog, most recent being *Spinout* (side 1, row 2, column 7). Back: RCA Elvis Stereo 8 catalog.

RCA Victor (ST)

LSP-3758.....................3/67   40-60

TOTAL PACKAGE 2: Disc, cover, inner sleeve.

❑ RCA Victor (ST)

LSP-3758 ....11/68   20-25

DISC 3: Orange label. Rigid vinyl.

❑ RCA Victor LSP-3758......11/68   35-50

COVER 3: Front: RCA Victor Dynagroove logo at upper right, number at lower left. Color Elvis photo. Back: "Grammy Award Winner" Logo in upper left corner. "RE" at lower left. Color Elvis photo.

❑ RCA Victor 21-112-1

40D...................................6/68   4-6

INNER SLEEVE 3: Red, black and white. Front: RCA's Elvis LP catalog, most recent being *Elvis' Gold Records, Vol. 4* (side 1, row 4, column 5). Back: RCA's Elvis LP and Twin Pack Stereo 8 catalog. May also be found with inner sleeves 40B and 40C. See chapter on inner sleeves for more information.

RCA Victor (ST)

LSP-3758...................11/68   60-80

TOTAL PACKAGE 3: Disc, cover, inner sleeve.

❑ RCA Victor (ST)

LSP-3758 ....11/68   20-25

DISC 4: Orange label. Rigid vinyl.

❑ RCA Victor LSP-3758......11/68   8-10

COVER 4: Front: RCA logo and number at upper left. "Victor" and "Stereo" at upper right. "RE" at lower left. Back: "RE" at lower left. Does not show mono number.

❑ RCA Victor 21-112-1

40D...................................6/68   4-6

INNER SLEEVE 4: Red, black and white. Front: RCA's Elvis LP catalog, most recent being *Elvis' Gold Records, Vol. 4* (side 1, row 4, column 5). Back: RCA's Elvis LP and Twin Pack Stereo 8 catalog. May also be found with inner sleeves 40B and 40C. See chapter on inner sleeves for more information.

RCA Victor (ST)

LSP-3758...................11/68   30-40

TOTAL PACKAGE 4: Disc, cover, inner sleeve.

❑ RCA Victor (ST)

LSP-3758 ....'71   10-15

DISC 5: Orange label. Flexible vinyl.

TPRS-1895-17S/TPRS-1896-18S.

❑ RCA Victor LSP-3758..........'71   8-10

COVER 5: Same as cover 4.

❑ RCA Victor........................'70s   2-4

INNER SLEEVE 5: Black-and-white. Pictures RCA Elvis catalog front and back. Any of several may be found on reissues from this period.

RCA Victor (ST)

LSP-3758......................'71   20-30

TOTAL PACKAGE 5: Disc, cover, inner sleeve.

❑ RCA Victor (ST)

LSP-3758 ....'76   10-15

DISC 6: Tan label.

TPRS-1895-17S/TPRS-1896-16S.

❑ RCA LSP-3758...................'76   8-10

COVER 6: Same as cover 4.

❑ RCA Victor........................'70s   2-4

INNER SLEEVE 6: Black-and-white. Pictures RCA Elvis catalog front and back. Any of several may be found on reissues from this period.

RCA Victor (ST)

LSP-3758......................'76   **20-25**
TOTAL PACKAGE 6: Disc, cover, inner
  sleeve.

❑ RCA Victor (ST)
  LSP-3758 ....'76   4-6
  DISC 7: Black label, dog near top.
  TPRS-1895-18S/TPRS-1896. Identification numbers are
  stamped on side 1 and engraved on side 2.

❑ RCA LSP-3758....................'76   4-6
  COVER 7: Front: RCA logo and number at
  upper left, "Victor Stereo" at upper right. "RE"
  at lower left. Back: "RE" at lower left.
  Otherwise, same as cover 2.

❑ RCA Victor........................'70s   2-4
  INNER SLEEVE 7: Black-and-white. Pictures
  RCA Elvis catalog front and back. Any of
  several may be found on reissues from this
  period.

RCA Victor (ST)

LSP-3758......................'76   **10-18**
TOTAL PACKAGE 7: Disc, cover, inner
  sleeve.

❑ RCA Victor (ST)
  AFL1-3758 ....'77   3-5
  DISC 8: Black label, dog near top.

❑ RCA AFL1-3758.................'77   3-5
  COVER 8: Reflects prefix change. Includes
  copies with a sticker bearing the "AFL1"
  prefix, near or covering the printed "LSP"
  prefix.

❑ RCA Victor........................'70s   2-4
  INNER SLEEVE 8: Black-and-white. Pictures
  RCA Elvis catalog front and back. Any of
  several sleeves may be found on reissues
  from this period.

RCA Victor (ST)

AFL1-3758....................'77   **8-15**
TOTAL PACKAGE 8: Disc, cover, inner
  sleeve.

❑ RCA Victor (ST)
  AQL1-3758..........................'79   5-10
  DISC 9: Black label, dog near top.

❑ RCA AQL1-3758 ....'79   5-10
  COVER 9: Reflects prefix change.

❑ RCA Victor........................'70s   2-4
  INNER SLEEVE 9: Black-and-white. Pictures
  RCA Elvis catalog front and back. Any of
  several sleeves may be found on reissues
  from this period.

RCA Victor (ST)

AQL1-3758....................'79   **8-15**
TOTAL PACKAGE 9: Disc, cover, inner
  sleeve.

Side 1
How Great Thou Art
In the Garden
Somebody Bigger Than You and I
Farther Along
Stand By Me

Without Him

Side 2
So High
Where Could I Go But to the Lord
By and By
If The Lord Wasn't Walking by My Side
Run On
Where No One Stands Alone
Crying in the Chapel

I GOT LUCKY (Camden)

❑ RCA/Camden (M)
  CAL-2533 ....10/71   8-10
  DISC 1: Blue label. Dynaflex vinyl.
  ACRM-5837-1S/ACRM-5838-1S.
  ACRM-5837-2S/ACRM-5838-2S.
  ACRM-5837-3S/ACRM-5838-3S.

❑ RCA/Camden
  CAL-2533 ....10/71   15-20
  COVER 1: Front: RCA/Camden logo and
  number at upper left. Color Elvis photo. Back:
  Pictures four other Camden LPs.
  INNER SLEEVE 1: White, no printing. (Some
  Camden LPs had no inner sleeves at all.)

RCA/Camden (M)

CAL-2533 ....10/71   **25-30**
TOTAL PACKAGE 1: Disc, cover.

❑ RCA/Camden (M)
  CAL-2533 ....10/71   8-10
  DISC 2: Same as disc 1.

❑ RCA/Camden
  CAL-2533 ....10/71   20-25
  COVER 2: Designate promo. Same as cover
  1, but with "Not for Sale" stamped on back.
  INNER SLEEVE 2: White, no printing. (Some
  Camden LPs had no inner sleeves at all.)

RCA/Camden (M)

CAL-2533 ....10/71   **30-35**
TOTAL PACKAGE 2: Disc, cover.

Side 1
I Got Lucky
What a Wonderful Life
I Need Somebody to Lean On
Yoga Is As Yoga Does
Ridin' the Rainbow

Side 2
Fools Fall in Love
The Love Machine
Home Is Where the Heart Is
You Gotta Stop
If You Think I Don't Need You

I GOT LUCKY (Pickwick)

❑ Pickwick/Camden (M)
  CAS-2533.......................12/75   2-5
  DISC 1: Black label. Multi-color Pickwick logo
  at center. Despite the "CAS" (stereo) Pickwick
  prefix, all tracks are monaural.
  CAS-2533-A-4/CAS-2533-B-5.

❏ Pickwick/Camden
CAS-2533......................12/75   3-5
COVER 1: Similar to RCA/Camden cover 1,
except: Titles and contents are in red script
print; Pickwick logo at upper left; number and
"Camden" at upper right. Back: Pictures four
Elvis Camden LPs.
INNER SLEEVE 1: White, no printing.
Pickwick/Camden (M)
CAS-2533..................12/75   5-10
TOTAL PACKAGE 1: Disc, cover.

Side 1
I Got Lucky
What a Wonderful Life
I Need Somebody to Lean On
Yoga Is As Yoga Does
Ridin' the Rainbow
Side 2
Fools Fall in Love
The Love Machine
Home Is Where the Heart Is
You Gotta Stop
If You Think I Don't Need You

I WANNA BE A ROCK'N'ROLL STAR

❏ Viktorie NS-13026: Bootleg. Listed for
identification only.

I WAS THE ONE

❏ RCA (ST) AHL1-4678........4/83   7-10
DISC 1: Pink and black "Elvis" label. This was
the first Elvis LP on a custom label and the
first to not have RCA (with our without
"Victor") prominently shown on label.
AHL1-4678-A-1/AHL1-4678-B-1. Identification numbers are
engraved. Both sides also have "Denny Woodland" engraved
in trail off.
❏ RCA AHL1-4678................4/83   8-10
COVER 1: Front: Number at lower right. Has
artist Bill Rieser's rendering of '50s Elvis.
Back: RCA logo and number at lower right,
UPC bar code at upper right. Has another of
Rieser's Elvis drawings.
❏ RCA AHL1-4678................4/83   1-2
INNER SLEEVE 1: Front: Black, with RCA
copyright notice at lower right. Back: Black,
with selection number at lower left. (Though
this may appear to be a generic sleeve, the
selection number indicates it belongs only
with this LP.)
RCA (ST) AHL1-4678......5/83   15-20
**TOTAL PACKAGE 1: Disc, cover, inner
sleeve.**

Collection of 1955-1961 recordings with slight
vocal backing differences and/or stereo
instrumentation enhancements.
Side 1
My Baby Left Me
(You're So Square) Baby I Don't Care
Little Sister
Don't
Wear My Ring Around Your Neck
Paralyzed

Side 2
Baby, Let's Play House
I Was the One
Rip It Up
Young and Beautiful
Reddy Teddy

I'M LEAVIN'

❏ Bootleg. Listed for identification only.

IF WE CAN DREAM

❏ TCB LPM-4088: Bootleg. Listed for
identification only.

IN MY WAY (SONGS FROM WILD IN THE COUNTRY AND BLUE HAWAII)

❏ Laurel LPM-8660: Bootleg. Listed for
identification only.

IN PERSON – ELVIS AND HIS SHOW

❏ Golden Archives GA-200: Bootleg. Listed for
identification only.

IN THE BEGINNING

Various artists collection
❏ ATV (M) VM1......................'80   25-35
DISC 1: Beige label with brown print. Has one
Elvis track, *Lawdy, Miss Clawdy.*
❏ ATV VM1 ....'80   25-35
COVER 1: Front: Brown with white print. Title
at top, artists listed in center. ATV logo at
lower left. Back: Text only.
ATV (M) VM1....................'80   50-70
TOTAL PACKAGE 1: Disc, cover.

INTERNATIONAL HOTEL, LAS VEGAS NEVADA PRESENTS ELVIS, AUGUST-1969-AUGUST

Specially prepared, complimentary gift box
given to invited guests at the Showroom
Internationale on July 31, 1969 (media
performance) and August 1 (official opening
night). Box and contents listed separately
below.
❏ RCA................................7/69   1500-2000
BOX 1: Oversize, 12¾" x 12¾". Front: Orange
RCA logo at lower right. Title is in white, 6" x
6" box with orange and pink print at upper
right. International Hotel logo at upper right.
Black-and-white Elvis photo, same as first
used on *From Memphis to Vegas / From
Vegas to Memphis.* Back: Black, no printing.
❏ RCA Victor (ST)
LSP-4088 ....6/69   40-50
INSERT 1A: Copy of Elvis *(NBC-TV Special)*;
orange label, rigid disc. See that listing for
complete information on this LP.

Heart of Dixie
Original Motion Picture Soundtrack

1. **MOANIN' BLUES**-Prelude .34
(K. Vance, P. Namanworth)
OPC Muse Publishing, Inc. (ASCAP)
2. **LITTLE BITTY PRETTY ONE**-
Delbert McClinton & The Snakes 2:21
(R. Byrd) Recordo Music Publishers (BMI)
3. **LIGHTS OUT**-John Cowan & The Snakes 2:05
(S. David, M. Rebennack) SBK Blackwood Music Inc
under license from ATV (Venice) (BMI)

SIDE 1   4. **NIGHT TIME IS THE RIGHT TIME**-
Charlie Jacobs & The Snakes 3:09
(L. Herman) Screen Gems EMI Music Inc. (BMI)
5. **I WANT YOU, I NEED YOU, I LOVE YOU**-
Elvis Presley 2:38
(I. Kosloff, G. Mysels) Elvis Presley Music,
administered by Unichappell Music, Inc. (BMI)
6. **THE WAYWARD WIND**-Rebecca Russell &
The Snakes 3:33
(S. Lebowsky, H. Newman) Programs International Publishing, Inc. (ASCAP)

SP 3930 Stereo (SP 03930 A)
Produced by Kenny Vance for Red Cart Productions
Executive Producers: Steve Tisch & Maureen Crowe
Compilation ℗ 1989 A&M Records, Inc.
All Rights Reserved.

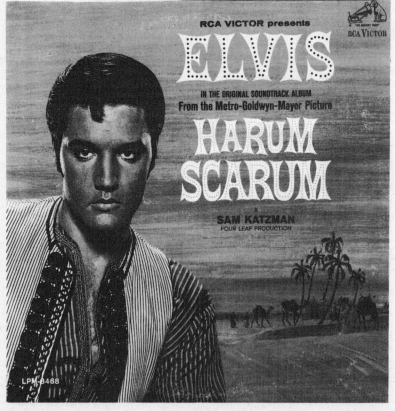

RCA VICTOR presents
ELVIS
IN THE ORIGINAL SOUNDTRACK ALBUM
From the Metro-Goldwyn-Mayer Picture
HARUM SCARUM
A
SAM KATZMAN
FOUR LEAF PRODUCTION

LPM-3468

❑ RCA Victor (ST)
LSP-4155 ....6/69　　　40-50
INSERT 1B: Copy of *From Elvis in Memphis*; orange label, rigid disc. See that listing for complete information on this LP.

❑ RCA Victor..........................7/69　　　50-100
INSERT 1C: Nine-page press release – a summary of Elvis' life and career – page one of which is on RCA Records Public Affairs letterhead.

❑ RCA PJ-3170 ....'69　　　20-30
INSERT 1D: RCA, 36-page, full-color, 1969 *Elvis' Records & Tapes* catalog (with pink, red and white cover). Has number on back cover at lower right.

❑ RCA....................................'69　　　10-15
INSERT 1E: RCA 1969 Elvis pocket calender. Has color photo of Elvis in his gold suit on one side.

❑ RCA..................................6/69　　　50-75
INSERT 1F: Color 8" x 10" Elvis photo, signed "Sincerely, Elvis Presley." Back announces Elvis' International Hotel engagement. This photo first appeared as a bonus with *From Elvis in Memphis*.

❑ RCA....................................'69　　　50-80
INSERT 1G: Two black-and-white, glossy 8" x 10" Elvis photos with blank backs. The two photos are pictures taken from the NBC-TV Special. Price is for both photos.

❑ RCA....................................'69　　　50-100
INSERT 1H: Single page, reading: "Dear Friend, Enclosed is a special promotion package with our compliments. Sincerely, Elvis & the Colonel." Has two black-and-white Elvis photos, one at upper left and one at upper right. Included with box but not actually packaged inside it.

RCA Victor......................7/69　2000-2500
TOTAL PACKAGE 1: Box, inserts.

INTERNATIONAL HOTEL, LAS VEGAS NEVADA PRESENTS ELVIS 1970

Specially prepared, complimentary gift box given to invited guests at the Showroom Internationale on January 26, 1970 (Elvis' opening night). Box and contents listed separately below.

❑ RCA..............................11/69　　1100-1300
BOX 1: Oversize, 12¾" x 12¾". Front: Orange RCA logo at lower right. Title is in white, 6" x 6" box with orange and pink print at upper right. International Hotel logo at upper right. Black-and-white Elvis photo, same as first used on *From Memphis to Vegas / From Vegas to Memphis*. Back: Black, no printing.

❑ RCA Victor (ST)
LSP-6020 ....11/69　　　60-85
INSERT 1A: Copy of *From Memphis to Vegas / From Vegas to Memphis*; orange label, rigid disc. See that listing for complete information on this LP.

❑ RCA Victor 47-9791...........1/70　　　20-25
INSERT 1B: Orange label 45 rpm of *Kentucky Rain / My Little Friend*, with picture sleeve. See that listing for complete information on this single.

❑ RCA..................................7/69　　　50-100
INSERT 1C: Nine-page press release – a summary of Elvis' life and career – page one of which is on RCA Records Public Affairs letterhead.

❑ RCA....................................'70　　　20-30
INSERT 1D: RCA, full-color, spiral-bound 1970 *Elvis' Records & Tapes* catalog (with red, white and black cover).

❑ RCA..............................12/69　　　8-12
INSERT 1E: RCA 1970 Elvis pocket calender. Has black-and-white photo of Elvis in leather suit, from '68 TV Special, on one side.

❑ RCA..................................1/70　　　50-100
INSERT 1F: Black-and-white, 8" x 10" Elvis photo, signed "Thanks, Elvis." Back announces Elvis' International Hotel engagement ("January 26th thru February 23rd.")

❑ RCA..................................1/70　　　40-50
INSERT 1G: 16-page photo booklet. Color front and back covers, black-and-white photos inside. Elvis photo on front is identical to the one on the picture sleeve for *Suspicious Minds / You'll Think of Me*.

❑ RCA....................................'69　　　150-300
INSERT 1H: Four-page, complimentary dinner menu. Color front and back covers, black, red and white print inside. Elvis photo on front is identical to the one on the picture sleeve for *Suspicious Minds / You'll Think of Me*.

RCA..............................1/70　1500-2000
TOTAL PACKAGE 1: Box, inserts.

INTERNATIONAL HOTEL, LAS VEGAS NEVADA PRESENTS ELVIS (V.I.P. BOX)

❑ RCA Victor........................7/69　　2000-2500
BOX 1: Same as previous International Hotel boxes, except does *not* have printed, white 6" x 6" box with International Hotel logo and engagement dates. This box, sometimes referred to as the "V.I.P. Box," was reportedly printed without a date so it could be used for any performance or promotion. Price is for box only.

INTERVIEWS WITH ELVIS (CANADA 1957)

❑ Gusto (M) SD-995 ....'78　　　20-30
DISC 1: Blue label with black, yellow and brown print. Label makes no reference to Starday.
SD-995A/AD-995B. Identification numbers are engraved.

❑ Gusto/Starday (M) SD-995.. '78   20-30
COVER 1: Front: Shows both Gusto and
Starday logos, and number, at upper left. Has
a collage of five Elvis photos, two color and
three black-and-white. Back: Four Elvis
photos, one color and three black-and-white.
INNER SLEEVE 1: White, no printing.
Gusto (M) SD-995 .... '78   **40-60**
  TOTAL PACKAGE 1: Disc, cover.

Repackage of interviews previously issued as
The Elvis Tapes.

IT HAPPENED AT THE WORLD'S FAIR

❑ RCA Victor (M)
  LPM-2697 .... 4/63   20-25
DISC 1: Black label, "Long Play" at bottom.
PPRM-2727-3S/PPRM-2728-4S. Label LP#5.
PPRM-2727-5S/PPRM-2728-6S. Label LP#1.

❑ RCA Victor LPM-2697 .... 4/63   70-75
COVER 1: Front: RCA logo at upper right,
number at lower left. Color Elvis photo. Back:
Two color Elvis photos from film.

❑ RCA Victor LPM-2697 .... 4/63   200-250
INSERT 1: Color, 8" x 10," signed Elvis photo.
Has three different poses and is signed
"Sincerely, Elvis Presley." Back lists other
RCA Elvis releases.
Counterfeit Identification: Reproductions of
this photo have been circulating over the past
few years, and are easily identified by the
distorted images and colors in the picture.
INNER SLEEVE 1: Generic RCA sleeve.
Makes no mention of Elvis or this LP.
RCA Victor (M)
  LPM-2697 .... 4/63   **300-350**
  TOTAL PACKAGE 1: Disc, cover, insert.

❑ RCA Victor (ST)
  LSP-2697 .... 4/63   50-75
DISC 2: Black label, "Living Stereo" at bottom.
PPRS-2729-2S/PPRS-2730-3S. Label LP#8.
PPRS-2729-5S/PPRS-2730-2S.

❑ RCA Victor LSP-2697 .... 4/63   50-75
COVER 2: Front: RCA logo at upper right,
number at upper left. Color Elvis photo. Back:
Two color Elvis photos from film.

❑ RCA Victor LPM-2697 .... 4/63   200-250
INSERT 2: Color, 8" x 10," signed Elvis photo.
Has three different poses and is signed
"Sincerely, Elvis Presley." Back lists other
RCA Elvis releases.
Counterfeit Identification: Reproductions of
this photo have been circulating over the past
few years, and are easily identified by the
distorted images and colors in the picture.
INNER SLEEVE 2: Generic RCA sleeve.
Makes no mention of Elvis or this LP.
RCA Victor (ST)
  LSP-2697 .... 4/63   **300-400**
  TOTAL PACKAGE 2: Disc, cover, insert.

❑ RCA Victor (ST)
  LSP-2697 .... 10/64   10-20
DISC 3: Black label, RCA logo in white at top
and "Stereo" at bottom.

❑ RCA Victor LSP-2697 ...... 10/64   45-50
COVER 3: Same as cover 2. NOTE: Because
RCA used the same cover for many reissues,
the price for this cover reflects part of this total
package.

❑ RCA Victor 21-112-1
  40A 10/64   4-8
INNER SLEEVE 3: Red, black and white.
Front: RCA's Elvis LP catalog, most recent
being Kissin' Cousins (side 1, row 1, column
6). Back: RCA Elvis EPs and 45s catalog.
RCA Victor (ST)
  LSP-2697 .... 10/64   **60-80**
  TOTAL PACKAGE 3: Disc, cover, inner sleeve.

❑ RCA Victor (ST)
  APL1-2568 .... 9/77   3-5
DISC 4: Black label, dog near top.
APL1-2568A-2/APL1-2568B-3.

❑ RCA Victor APL1-2568 ...... 9/77   3-5
COVER 4: Reflects prefix change.

❑ RCA Victor .... '70s   2-4
INNER SLEEVE 4: Black-and-white. Pictures
RCA Elvis catalog front and back. Any of
several may be found on reissues from this
period.
RCA Victor (ST)
  APL1-2568 .... 9/77   **8-15**
  TOTAL PACKAGE 4: Disc, cover, inner sleeve.

Side 1
Beyond the Bend
Relax
Take Me to the Fair
They Remind Me Too Much of You
One Broken Heart for Sale
Side 2
I'm Falling in Love Tonight
Cotton Candy Land
A World of Our Own
How Would You Like to Be
Happy Ending

JAILHOUSE ROCK SESSIONS

❑ Laurel 2502: Bootleg. Listed for identification
only.

JOURNEY INTO YESTERDAY (1956)
Various artists collection

❑ Economic Consultants Inc. (M)
  1956 .... '73   10-20
DISC 1: Yellow label. One of 16 LP series,
each presenting music of a specific year. Mail
order offer.
EC-1956-1/EC-1956-2. Identification numbers are engraved.

❑ Economic Consultants Inc.
1956 .... '73   10-20
COVER 1: Front: Black with title on a scroll.
Back: Text only.

Economic Consultants Inc. (M)
1956 .... '73   20-40
TOTAL PACKAGE 1: Disc, cover.

Elvis Contents:
Side 1
Blue Suede Shoes (Track 2)
Side 2
Tutti Frutti (Track 3)

JOURNEY INTO YESTERDAY (1969)

Various artists collection

❑ Economic Consultants Inc. (M)
1969 .... '73   10-20
DISC 1: Yellow label. One of 16 LP series,
each presenting music of a specific year. Mail
order offer.
EC-1969-1/EC-1969-2. Identification numbers are engraved.
❑ Economic Consultants Inc.
1969 .... '73   10-20
COVER 1: Front: Black with title on a scroll.
Back: Text only.

Economic Consultants Inc. (M)
1969 .... '73   20-40
TOTAL PACKAGE 1: Disc, cover.

Elvis Contents:
Side 2
Suspicious Minds (Track 1)
In the Ghetto (Track 2)

JOY OF CHRISTMAS (18 LPs)

Various artists collection

Black, red and green labels. Complete 18-
hour radio show. This edition programmed for
adult contemporary formats. The first 12 hours
are hosted by Gene Norman, the last six are
music only. Issued only to subscribing radio
stations. Identification numbers are engraved
on all discs, listed individually below.

❑ Creative Radio Shows
1A/1B 11/87   5-10
DISC 1:
JA-1-A L-26188/JA-1-B L-26188-X
❑ Creative Radio Shows
2A/2B 11/87   5-10
DISC 2:
JA-2-A L-26187/JA-2-B L-26187-X
❑ Creative Radio Shows
3A/3B 11/87   5-10
DISC 3:
JA-3-A L-26186/JA-3-B L-26186-X
❑ Creative Radio Shows
4A/4B 11/87   5-10
DISC 4:
JA-4-A L-26194/JA-4-B L-26194-X
❑ Creative Radio Shows
5A/5B 11/87   5-10
DISC 5:

JA-5-A L-26189/JA-5-B L-26189-X
❑ Creative Radio Shows
6A/6B 11/87   5-10
DISC 6:
JA-6-A L-26211/JA-6-B L-26211-X
❑ Creative Radio Shows
7A/7B 11/87   5-10
DISC 7:
JA-7-A L-26210/JA-7-B L-26210-X
❑ Creative Radio
Shows 8A/8B 11/87   5-10
DISC 8:
JA-8-A L-26209/JA-8-B L-26209-X
❑ Creative Radio Shows
9A/9B 11/87   5-10
DISC 9:
JA-9-A L-26212/JA-9-B L-26212-X
❑ Creative Radio Shows
10A/10B 11/87   5-10
DISC 10:
JA-10-A L-26213/JA-10-B L-26213-X
❑ Creative Radio Shows
11A/11B 11/87   5-10
DISC 11:
JA-11-A L-26215/JA-11-B L-26215-X
❑ Creative Radio Shows
12A/12B 11/87   5-10
DISC 12:
JA-12-A L-26214/JA-12-B L-26214-X
❑ Creative Radio Shows
13A/13B 11/87   5-10
DISC 13:
JA-13-A/JA-13-B.
❑ Creative Radio Shows
14A/14B 11/87   5-10
DISC 14:
JA-14-A/JA-14-B.
❑ Creative Radio Shows
15A/15B 11/87   5-10
DISC 15:
JA-15-A/JA-15-B.
❑ Creative Radio Shows
16A/16B 11/87   5-10
DISC 16:
JA-16-A/JA-16-B.
❑ Creative Radio Shows
17A/17B 11/87   5-10
DISC 17:
JA-17-A/JA-17-B.
❑ Creative Radio Shows
18A/18B 11/87   5-10
DISC 18:
JA-18-A/JA-18-B.
COVER/BOX 1: None made.
❑ Creative Radio Shows 11/87   15-20
INSERT 1: Programmer's packet, including:
a) Introductory letter; b) Scheduling info page;
c) Co-op ad mat; d) 18 pages of programming
notes and cue sheets; e) Notice to return
program when through; f) Return mailing
label.

Creative Radio Shows
(SP) 11/87   100-200
TOTAL PACKAGE 1: Discs, insert.

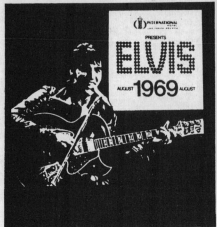
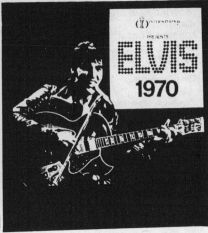

Elvis Contents:

Hour 2
Silver Bells

Hour 3
Blue Christmas

Hour 6
Blue Christmas

Hour 8
If Everyday Was like Christmas

Hour 11
O Come, All Ye Faithful

Hour 14
Blue Christmas

Hour 16
Oh Little Town of Bethlehem

Hour 17
Silver Bells

JOY OF CHRISTMAS (18 LPs)

Various artists collection

Black, red and green labels. Complete 18-hour radio show. This edition programmed for country music formats. The first 12 hours are hosted by Gene Norman, the last six are music only. Issued only to subscribing radio stations.
COVER 1: None made.

❏ Creative Radio Shows 11/87   15-20
INSERT 1: Programmer's packet of: a) Introductory letter; b) Scheduling info page; c) Co-op ad mat; d) 18 pages of programming notes and cue sheets; e) Notice to return program when through; f) Return mailing label.

Creative Radio (SP) 11/87   **100-200**
TOTAL PACKAGE 1: Discs, insert.

Elvis Contents:

Hour 7
Here Comes Santa Claus (Segment A)

Hour 9
Blue Christmas (Segment D)
I'll Be Home on Christmas Eve (Segment D)

Hour 10
Oh Come, All Ye Faithful (Segment D)

Hour 11
Holly Leaves and Christmas Trees (Segment E)

Hour 13
Oh Come, All Ye Faithful (Segment F)

Hour 15
Blue Christmas (Segment A)

Hour 16
Silver Bells (Segment B)

Hour 18
Blue Christmas (Segment F)

JUNE '62 POPULAR SAMPLER

Various artists collection

❏ RCA Victor (ST)
SPS 133-51 .... 6/62   500-750
DISC 1: Black label, "Living Stereo" at bottom. Canadian issue only.

10N2NY-1101-1S/10N2NY-1101-1S.
COVER 1: None made.
INNER SLEEVE 1: White, no printing.
RCA Victor (ST)
SPS 133-51 .... 6/62   **500-750**
TOTAL PACKAGE 1: Disc.

Side 1
Baby, We're Really in Love (Don Gibson)
Kiss Me Quick (Elvis Presley)
Something Blue (Elvis Presley)
Rock-A-Bye Boogie (Porter Wagoner & Skeeter Davis)
Sally Goodin (Gordon Terry)
Ev'rything I've Got (Peter Nero)
Side 2
Tracks not yet known.

JUST LET ME HEAR SOME OF THAT ROCK 'N' ROLL MUSIC (2 LPs)

Various artists collection

❏ Goodman Group (M)
GG-PRO-1 .... '79   25-50
DISCS 1: Excerpts of 100 songs, including three by Elvis. Made for radio stations by the music publisher (The Goodman Group). Promotional issue only.
(Disc 1.) GGPRO-1 Record 1 Side A/GGPRO-1 Record 1 Side B. **(Disc 2)** GGPRO-1 Record 2 Side A/GGPRO-1 Record 2 Side B. Identification numbers are engraved.

❏ Goodman Group
GG-PRO-1 .... '79   25-50
COVER 1: Double pocket. Text only.
INNER SLEEVES 1: White, no printing.
Goodman Group (M)
GG-PRO-1 .... '79   **50-100**
TOTAL PACKAGE 1: Discs, cover.

Elvis Contents:

Disc 1 (Side A)
Big Boss Man (Track 3)

Disc 2 (Side A)
Promised Land (Track 2)
Reconsider Baby (Track 3)
Besides Elvis, on this LP are: Dion; Clarence "Frogman" Henry; Chuck Berry; Jackie Wilson; Jorgen Ingmann; El Dorados; Pat Boone; Jimmy Reed; Linda Ronstadt; Bo Diddley; Monotones; John Lee Hooker; Animals; Gene Chandler; Jerry Butler; Spaniels; McGuire Sisters; Tune Weavers; Tony Orlando & Dawn; Charms; Fontane Sisters; Jerry Keller; Rod Stewart; Flamingos; Yardbirds; Rita Coolidge; Little Walter; Gentrys; Peter & Gordon; Sensations; Lee Andrews and the Hearts; Johnny Rivers; Lonnie Mack; Mike Douglas; Johnny Cymbal; Spiral Starecase; Moonglows; Dee Clark; Dells; Clovers; Ray Charles; Johnnie & Joe; Otis Redding; Chantays; Bobby Vinton; Fleetwoods; Bill Haley and His Comets; Faye Adams; Rays; Beach Boys; Dale Hawkins; Creedence Clearwater Revival; Pearl Bailey; Aaron Neville; Harvey and the Moonglows; Beatles; Capris; Pozo-Seco Singers; Ronnie

Hawkins; Jimmy McCracklin; Vibrations; Julie Rodgers; Gene Allison; and the Dovells.

KICKIN' BACK (THE 1974 HILTON DRESS REHEARSAL)

❑ Live Archives EPE-1013: Bootleg. Listed for identification only.

KING CREOLE

❑ RCA Victor (M)
LPM-1884........................8/58   75-100
DISC 1: Black label, "Long Play" at bottom.
J2PP-4183-6S/J2PP-4184-4S. Label LP#1. Shows first ititials and last names of all songwriters. Refers to *King Creole* as "A Paramount Film."
J2PP-4183-8S/J2PP-4184-10S. Label LP#2. Shows full names of all songwriters. Refers to *King Creole* as "A Paramount Picture."

❑ RCA Victor LPM-1884.......8/58   75-100
COVER 1: Front: RCA logo and number in blue ink at upper right. No contents listed on front. Color Elvis photo. Back: Three black-and-white film scenes pictured. "Important Notice" at right makes no reference to "Miracle Surface."
INNER SLEEVE 1: Generic RCA sleeve. Makes no mention of Elvis or this LP.
INSERT 1: None! The black-and-white, signed 8" x 10" photo of Elvis in army dress uniform (reads: "Best Wishes, Elvis Presley") was not packaged with this LP, but was almost certainly given away by local record stores at the time of this release. It has been recently discovered inside copies of the LP, and still sealed inside a copy in its original record store plastic bag. It is often referred to as the "King Creole Bonus Photo," and is valued at $200 to $250.

RCA Victor (M)
LPM-1884 ....8/58   150-200
TOTAL PACKAGE 1: Disc, cover.

❑ RCA Victor (M)
LPM-1884........................11/63   30-40
DISC 2: Black label, "Mono" at bottom.
❑ RCA Victor LPM-1884.....11/63   30-40
COVER 2: Front: RCA logo at upper right, number at lower left, both in black ink. Contents are listed at top. RCA copyright notice at lower right is followed by "RE." Color Elvis photo. Back: Three black-and-white film scenes pictured. Has number followed by "RE" at upper right. "Important Notice" at right refers to RCA's "Miracle Surface."
❑ RCA Victor (No Number)...9/63   8-10
INNER SLEEVE 2: Turquoise, black and white. Front: RCA's Elvis LP catalog, most recent being *It Happened at the World's Fair* (side 1, row 4, column 5). Back: RCA Elvis EPs and 45s catalog.

RCA Victor (M)
LPM-1884 ....11/63   75-90
TOTAL PACKAGE 2: Disc, cover, inner sleeve.

❑ RCA Victor (M)
LPM-1884........................10/64   25-35
DISC 3: Black label, "Monaural" at bottom.
J2PP-4183-6S/J2PP-4184-4S. Label LP#12.
❑ RCA Victor LPM-1884 .....10/64   30-35
COVER 3: Verification pending.
❑ RCA Victor 21-112-1
40A.................................10/64   4-8
INNER SLEEVE 3: Red, black and white. Front: RCA's Elvis LP catalog, most recent being *Kissin' Cousins* (side 1, row 1, column 6). Back: RCA Elvis EPs and 45s catalog.

RCA Victor (M)
LPM-1884 ....10/64   60-75
TOTAL PACKAGE 3: Disc, cover, inner sleeve.

❑ RCA Victor (SE)
LSP-1884(e) 2/62   100-150
DISC 4: Black label, RCA logo in silver at top and "Stereo Electronically Reprocessed" at bottom.
M2WS-4735-1S/M2PY-4736-1S. Label LP#9.
❑ RCA Victor LSP-1884(e) ...2/62   25-50
COVER 4: Front: RCA logo and "Stereo Electronically Reprocessed" at upper right, number at upper left, all in black ink. Contents are listed at top. RCA copyright notice at lower right is followed by "RE." Color Elvis photo. Back: Three black-and-white film scenes pictured. Has box of text at upper left "From the Originators of Electronically Reprocessed Stereo."
INNER SLEEVE 4: White, no printing.

RCA Victor (SE)
LSP-1884(e) 2/62   125-200
TOTAL PACKAGE 4: Disc, cover.

❑ RCA Victor (SE)
LSP-1884(e) 10/64   10-20
DISC 5: Black label, RCA logo in white at top and "Stereo" at bottom.
M2PY-4735-1S/M2PY-4736-1S. Label LP#17.
❑ RCA Victor
LSP-1884(e) 10/64   35-45
COVER 5: Same as cover 4. NOTE: Because RCA used the same cover for many reissues, the price for this cover reflects part of this total package.
❑ RCA Victor 21-112-1
40A.................................10/64   4-8
INNER SLEEVE 5: Red, black and white. Front: RCA's Elvis LP catalog, most recent being *Kissin' Cousins* (side 1, row 1, column 6). Back: RCA Elvis EPs and 45s catalog.

RCA Victor (SE)
LSP-1884(e) 10/64   50-75
TOTAL PACKAGE 5: Disc, cover, inner sleeve.

❑ RCA Victor (SE)
LSP-1884(e) 11/68   20-25
DISC 6: Orange label. Rigid vinyl.

❑ RCA Victor
LSP-1884(e)................... 11/68   8-10
COVER 6: Verification pending.

❑ RCA Victor 21-112-1
40D................................... 6/68   4-6
INNER SLEEVE 6: Red, black and white.
Front: RCA's Elvis LP catalog, most recent
being *Elvis' Gold Records, Vol. 4* (side 1, row
4, column 5). Back: RCA's Elvis LP and Twin
Pack Stereo 8 catalog. May also be found
with inner sleeves 40B and 40C. See chapter
on inner sleeves for more information.

RCA Victor (SE)
LSP-1884(e) 11/68   35-40
TOTAL PACKAGE 6: Disc, cover, inner
sleeve.

❑ RCA Victor (SE)
LSP-1884(e)........................ '71   10-15
DISC 7: Orange label. Flexible vinyl.

❑ RCA Victor
LSP-1884(e)................... 11/68   4-8
COVER 7: Front: Has number at upper left
and a red sticker at upper right, reading
"Stereo Effect Reprocessed from
Monophonic." No print on spine. Back: Note
about stereo records at upper left; number at
upper right. Has "SER" and "3" at lower left.

❑ RCA Victor......................... '70s   2-4
INNER SLEEVE 7: Black-and-white. Pictures
RCA Elvis catalog front and back. Any of
several sleeves may be found on reissues
from this period.

RCA Victor (SE)
LSP-1884(e) .... '71   15-25
TOTAL PACKAGE 7: Disc, cover, inner
sleeve.

❑ RCA Victor (SE)
LSP-1884(e)........................ '76   10-12
DISC 8: Tan label.

❑ RCA LSP-1884(e) .... '76   10-12
COVER 8: Verification pending.

❑ RCA Victor......................... '70s   2-4
INNER SLEEVE 8: Black-and-white. Pictures
RCA Elvis catalog front and back. Any of
several sleeves may be found on reissues
from this period.

RCA Victor (SE)
LSP-1884(e) .... '76   20-30
TOTAL PACKAGE 8: Disc, cover, inner
sleeve.

❑ RCA Victor (SE)
LSP-1884(e)........................ '76   4-6
DISC 9: Black label, dog near top.

❑ RCA LSP-1884(e) .... '76   4-6
COVER 9: Verification pending.

❑ RCA Victor......................... '70s   2-4
INNER SLEEVE 9: Black-and-white. Pictures
RCA Elvis catalog front and back. Any of
several sleeves may be found on reissues
from this period.

RCA Victor (SE)
LSP-1884(e) .... '76   10-18
TOTAL PACKAGE 9: Disc, cover, inner
sleeve.

❑ RCA Victor (SE)
AFL1-1884(e) .... '77   3-5
DISC 10: Black label, dog near top.
AFL1-1884A-1/AFL1-1884B-1.

❑ RCA AFL1-1884(e).............. '77   3-5
COVER 10: Reflects prefix change.
Includes copies with a sticker bearing the
"AFL1" prefix, wrapped around cover at top of
spine.

❑ RCA Victor......................... '70s   2-4
INNER SLEEVE 10: Black-and-white.
Pictures RCA Elvis catalog front and back.
Any of several sleeves may be found on
reissues from this period.

RCA Victor (SE)
AFL1-1884(e) .... '77   8-15
TOTAL PACKAGE 10: Disc, cover, inner
sleeve.

❑ RCA Victor (SE)
AYL1-3733 .... 9/80   3-5
DISC 11: Black label, dog near top.
AYL1-3733A/AYL1-3734B. Identification numbers are
engraved. Has both M2PY-4735- 10S/M2PY-4736-8S and
AFL1-1884A/AFL1-1884B stamped but crossed out.

❑ RCA AYL1-3733 .... 9/80   3-5
COVER 11: Reflects prefix change. Part of
RCA's "Best Buy Series." Includes copies with
a sticker bearing the "AYL1" prefix, wrapped
around cover at top of spine.

RCA Victor (SE)
AYL1-3733 .... 9/80   6-10
TOTAL PACKAGE 11: Disc, cover.

On both covers and labels, the electronically
reprocessed stereo designation "(e)" may not
appear following every usage of the selection
number.

Side 1
King Creole
As Long As I Have You
Hard Headed Woman
Trouble
Dixieland Rock

Side 2
Don't Ask Me Why
Lover Doll
Crawfish
Young Dreams
New Orleans

KING CREOLE
❑ Original Sound: Bootleg. Listed for
identification only.

KING CREOLE ACETATES
❑ Creole REC-456: Bootleg. Listed for
identification only.

KING GOES WILD

❑ Wilde PRP-207: Bootleg. Listed for identification only.

KING OF LAS VEGAS LIVE

❑ Hazbin 351: Bootleg. Listed for identification only.

KING SPEAKS (FEBRUARY 1961, MEMPHIS, TENNESSEE)

❑ Green Valley (M)
GV-2004 .... 12/77   5-7
DISC 1: Green label, black print.
❑ Great Northwest Music Company
GNW-4006 .... 12/77   5-8
COVER 1: White cover. (Note Green Valley disc in a Great Northwest cover.)
INNER SLEEVE 1: White, no printing.
Great Northwest Music Company/Green Valley (M)
GNW-4006 .... 12/77   10-15
TOTAL PACKAGE 1: Disc, cover.

❑ Great Northwest Music Company (M)
GNW-4006 .... 12/77   4-6
DISC 2: Red label. Offers a slightly different presentation of the press conference first issued as *Elvis Exclusive Live Press Conference* (Memphis, Tennessee, February 1961).
❑ Great Northwest Music Company (M)
GNW-4006 .... 12/77   4-6
COVER 2: Brown cover.
Great Northwest Music Company (M)
GNW-4006 .... 12/77   8-12
TOTAL PACKAGE 2: Disc, cover.

Though labeled as a "1961 Press Conference," the event actually took place March 8, 1960. Card stock jacket, with printing on cover – not on slicks.

KING, YESTERDAY AND TODAY

❑ Bootleg. Listed for identification only.

KING'S GOLD (Tapes)

❑ Media Entertainment (SP) ... '85   50-60
TAPES 1: Three reel-to-reel tapes, issued only to radio stations.
❑ Media Entertainment .... '85   5-10
INSERT 1: Three cue sheets with times and programming information.
Media Entertainment
(SP) .... '85   55-70
TOTAL PACKAGE 1: Tapes, insert.

KISSIN' COUSINS

❑ RCA Victor (M)
LPM-2894 ....3/64   20-30
DISC 1: Black label, "Mono" at bottom.
RPRM-0228-2S/RPRM-0229-2S. Label LP#11.
RPRM-0228-4S/RPRM-0229-4S. Label LP#11.
❑ RCA Victor LPM-2894 ....3/64   30-40
COVER 1: Front: RCA Victor logo at upper right, number at lower left. Color Elvis photo. At lower right is black-and-white, 2½" x 2¼" photo of six characters in the film (two of which are Elvis). Back: Six film-related, color Elvis photos.
❑ RCA Victor (No Number) ...9/63   8-10
INNER SLEEVE 1: Turquoise, black and white. Front: RCA's Elvis LP catalog, most recent being *It Happened at the World's Fair* (side 1, row 4, column 5). Back: RCA Elvis EPs and 45s catalog.
INSERT I: None! Reportedly, an 8" x 10" signed black-and-white Elvis photo (apparently from a shoot for *Viva Las Vegas*) reading: "Best Wishes, Elvis Presley" was given out at record stores. This photo was also given away free with a box of popcorn purchase at movie theaters that year. Now often referred to as the "Kissin Cousins Bonus Photo," its price range is $50 to $75.
RCA Victor (M)
LPM-2894 .... 3/64   60-80
TOTAL PACKAGE 1: Disc, cover, inner sleeve.

❑ RCA Victor (M)
LPM-2894 ....3/64   20-30
DISC 2: Same as disc 1.
❑ RCA Victor LPM-2894 ....3/64   110-150
COVER 2: Same as cover 1, except does not have black-and-white, 2½" x 2¼" photo of film stars.
❑ RCA Victor (No Number) ...9/63   8-10
INNER SLEEVE 2: Turquoise, black and white. Front: RCA's Elvis LP catalog, most recent being *It Happened at the World's Fair* (side 1, row 4, column 5). Back: RCA Elvis EPs and 45s catalog.
RCA Victor (M)
LPM-2894 .... 3/64   150-200
TOTAL PACKAGE 2: Disc, cover, inner sleeve.

❑ RCA Victor (M)
LPM-2894 ....10/64   50-80
DISC 3: Black label, "Monaural" at bottom.
RPRM-0228-2S/RPRM-0229-6S. Label LP#12.
❑ RCA Victor LPM-2894 .....10/64   30-40
COVER 3: Same as Cover 1
❑ RCA Victor 21-112-1
40A 10/64   4-8
INNER SLEEVE 3: Red, black and white. Front: RCA's Elvis LP catalog, most recent being *Kissin' Cousins* (side 1, row 1, column 6). Back: RCA Elvis EPs and 45s catalog.

RCA Victor (M)
LPM-2894 .... 10/64   **85-125**
TOTAL PACKAGE 3: Disc, cover, inner
  sleeve.

❑ RCA Victor (M)
  LPM-2894 .... 10/64   45-50
  DISC 4: Same as disc 3.
  RPRM-0228-2S/RPRM-0229-6S. Label LP#12.
❑ RCA Victor LPM-2894 ..... 10/64   110-150
  COVER 4: Same as Cover 2
❑ RCA Victor 21-112-1
  40A 10/64   4-8
  INNER SLEEVE 4: Red, black and white.
  Front: RCA's Elvis LP catalog, most recent
  being *Kissin' Cousins* (side 1, row 1, column
  6). Back: RCA Elvis EPs and 45s catalog.

RCA Victor (M)
LPM-2894 .... 10/64   **150-200**
TOTAL PACKAGE 4: Disc, cover, inner
  sleeve.

❑ RCA Victor (ST)
  LSP-2894 .... 3/64   40-50
  DISC 5: Black label, RCA logo in silver at top
  and "Stereo" at bottom.
  RPRS-0230-1S/RPRS-0231-1S. Label LP#13.
  RPRS-0230-4S/RPRS-0231-2S. Label LP#14.
❑ RCA Victor LSP-2894 .... 3/64   50-65
  COVER 5: Front: RCA Victor logo at upper
  right, number at upper left. Color Elvis photo.
  At lower right is black-and-white, 2½" x 2¼"
  photo of six characters in the film (two of
  which are Elvis). Back: Six film- related, color
  Elvis photos.
❑ RCA Victor (No Number) ... 9/63   8-10
  INNER SLEEVE 5: Turquoise, black and
  white. Front: RCA's Elvis LP catalog, most
  recent being *It Happened at the World's Fair*
  (side 1, row 4, column 5). Back: RCA Elvis
  EPs and 45s catalog.
  INSERT I: None! Reportedly, an 8" x 10"
  signed black-and-white Elvis photo
  (apparently from a shoot for *Viva Las Vegas*)
  reading: "Best Wishes, Elvis Presley" was
  given out at record stores. This photo was
  also given away free with a box of popcorn
  purchase at movie theaters that year. Now
  often referred to as the "Kissin Cousins Bonus
  Photo," its price range is $50 to $75.

RCA Victor (ST)
LSP-2894 .... 3/64   **100-125**
TOTAL PACKAGE 5: Disc, cover, inner
  sleeve.

❑ RCA Victor (ST)
  LSP-2894 .... 3/64   40-50
  DISC 6: Same as disc 5.
❑ RCA Victor LSP-2894 .... 3/64   125-140
  COVER 6: Same as cover 5, except does not
  have black-and-white, 2½" x 2¼" photo of film
  stars.

❑ RCA Victor (No Number) ... 9/63   8-10
  INNER SLEEVE 6: Turquoise, black and
  white. Front: RCA's Elvis LP catalog, most
  recent being *It Happened at the World's Fair*
  (side 1, row 4, column 5). Back: RCA Elvis
  EPs and 45s catalog.

RCA Victor (ST)
LSP-2894 .... 3/64   **175-200**
TOTAL PACKAGE 6: Disc, cover, inner
  sleeve.

❑ RCA Victor (ST)
  LSP-2894 .... 10/64   10-20
  DISC 7: Black label, RCA logo in white at top
  and "Stereo" at bottom.
❑ RCA Victor LSP-2894 ...... 10/64   25-30
  COVER 7: Same as cover 5, except has "RE"
  at lower left.
❑ RCA Victor 21-112-1
  40A 10/64   4-8
  INNER SLEEVE 7: Red, black and white.
  Front: RCA's Elvis LP catalog, most recent
  being *Kissin' Cousins* (side 1, row 1, column
  6). Back: RCA Elvis EPs and 45s catalog.

RCA Victor (ST)
LSP-2894 .... 10/64   **40-60**
TOTAL PACKAGE 7: Disc, cover, inner
  sleeve.

❑ RCA Victor (ST)
  LSP-2894 .... 11/68   20-25
  DISC 8: Orange label. Rigid vinyl.
❑ RCA Victor LSP-2894 ...... 11/68   8-10
  COVER 8: Same as cover 5, except has "RE"
  at lower left and has RCA (not RCA Victor)
  logo.
❑ RCA Victor 21-112-1
  40D 6/68   4-6
  INNER SLEEVE 8: Red, black and white.
  Front: RCA's Elvis LP catalog, most recent
  being *Elvis' Gold Records, Vol. 4* (side 1, row
  4, column 5). Back: RCA's Elvis LP and Twin
  Pack Stereo 8 catalog. May also be found
  with inner sleeves 40B and 40C. See chapter
  on inner sleeves for more information.

RCA Victor (ST)
LSP-2894 .... 11/68   **35-40**
TOTAL PACKAGE 8: Disc, cover, inner
  sleeve.

❑ RCA Victor (ST)
  LSP-2894 .... '71   10-15
  DISC 9: Orange label. Flexible vinyl.
❑ RCA LSP-2894 .... '71   4-8
  COVER 9: Same as cover 7.
❑ RCA Victor .... '70s   2-4
  INNER SLEEVE 9: Black-and-white. Pictures
  RCA Elvis catalog front and back. Any of
  several sleeves may be found on reissues
  from this period.

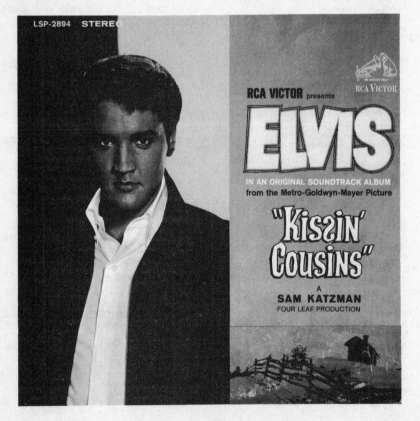

RCA Victor (ST)
LSP-2894.......................'71   15-25
TOTAL PACKAGE 9: Disc, cover, inner
  sleeve.

❑ RCA Victor (ST)
  LSP-2894 ....'76   10-12
  DISC 10: Tan label.
❑ RCA Victor LSP-2894..........'76   10-12
  COVER 10: Same as cover 8.
❑ RCA Victor.........................'70s   2-4
  INNER SLEEVE 10: Black-and-white.
  Pictures RCA Elvis catalog front and back.
  Any of several sleeves may be found on
  reissues from this period.

RCA Victor (ST)
LSP-2894.......................'76   20-30
TOTAL PACKAGE 10: Disc, cover, inner
  sleeve.

❑ RCA (ST) LSP-2894............'77   1000-1500
  DISC 11: Black label, dog near top. Blue vinyl.
  Experimental pressing only, not intended for
  sale or distribution.
  COVER 11: None made.
  INNER SLEEVE 11: White, no printing.
RCA (ST) LSP-2894..........'77   1000-1500
  TOTAL PACKAGE 11: Disc.

❑ RCA Victor (ST)
  LSP-2894 ....'77   4-6
  DISC 12: Black label, dog near top. Black
  vinyl.
  RPRS-0230-5S/RPRS-0231-8S.
❑ RCA LSP-2894....................'77   4-6
  COVER 12: Same as cover 8.
❑ RCA Victor.........................'70s   2-4
  INNER SLEEVE 12: Black-and-white.
  Pictures RCA Elvis catalog front and back.
  Any of several sleeves may be found on
  reissues from this period.

RCA Victor (ST)
LSP-2894.......................'77   10-18
TOTAL PACKAGE 12: Disc, cover, inner
  sleeve.

❑ RCA (ST) AFL1-2894 ....'77   3-5
  DISC 13: Black label, dog near top.
❑ RCA AFL1-2894 ....'77   3-5
  COVER 13: Reflects prefix change. Includes
  copies with a sticker bearing the "AFL1"
  prefix, wrapped around cover at top of spine.
❑ RCA Victor.........................'70s   2-4
  INNER SLEEVE 13: Black-and-white.
  Pictures RCA Elvis catalog front and back.
  Any of several sleeves may be found on
  reissues from this period.
RCA (ST) AFL1-2894 ....'77   8-15
  TOTAL PACKAGE 13: Disc, cover, inner
  sleeve.

❑ RCA (ST) AYL1-4115........9/81   3-5
  DISC 14: Black label, dog near top.

AYL1-4115A-12/AYL1-4115B-9S. Side B also has RPRS-
0231-9S and AYL1- 2894B stamped but crossed out.
❑ RCA AYL1-4115 ....9/81   3-5
  COVER 14: Reflects prefix change. Part of
  "Best Buy Series." Includes copies with a
  sticker bearing the "AYL1" prefix.
  INNER SLEEVE 14: White, no printing.
RCA (ST) AYL1-4115......9/81   6-10
  TOTAL PACKAGE 14: Disc, cover.

Side 1
Kissin' Cousins (No. 2)
Smokey Mountain Boy
There's Gold in the Mountains
One Boy, Two Little Girls
Catchin' On Fast
Tender Feeling

Side 2
Anyone (Could Fall In Love With You)
Barefoot Ballad
Once Is Enough
Kissin' Cousins
Echoes of Love
(It's a) Long Lonely Highway

**KNOWN ONLY TO HIM: see *ELVIS GOSPEL
1957-1971***

LAST CONCERT
❑ Audifon 1054: Bootleg. Listed for
  identification only.

LAST FAREWELL
❑ E.P. PRP-78-1: Bootleg. Listed for
  identification only.

LE DISQUE D'OR
❑ RCA (SP) 6886 807.............'77   7-10
  DISC 1: Red label with silver print. Imported
  from France but widely distributed throughout
  the United States by Impact.
  IMP-6886 807-1/IMP-6886 807-2.
❑ RCA 6886 807 ....'77   8-10
  COVER 1: Front: RCA logo and "Distribution
  Impact" at lower right, number at upper right.
  Color Elvis photo. Back: Pictures 10 other
  albums in the Impact series.
  INNER SLEEVE 1: White, no printing.
RCA (SP) 6886 807 ....'77   15-20
  TOTAL PACKAGE 1: Disc, cover.

Card stock jacket, with printing on cover – not
on slicks.

Side 1
C'mon Everybody
A Whistling Tune
I'll Be There (If You Want Me)
I Love Only One Girl
Easy Come, Easy Go
Santa Lucia

Side 2
Tonight Is So Right for Love
Guadalajara
Angel
A Little Less Conversation
Follow That Dream
Long Legged Girl (With a Short Dress On)

LEAVIN' IT UP TO YOU

❑ Audifon AFNS-66173: Bootleg. Listed for identification only.

LEGEND LIVES ON (7 LPs)

Mail order offer only. All LPs in this set have a black, white and red label, and are listed individually below.

❑ Reader's Digest/RCA Music Service (SP)
RB4-191-1 .... '86   3-5
DISC 1:
S1RS-5871-11/S1RS-5872-1.

❑ Reader's Digest/RCA Music Service (SP)
RB4-191-2 .... '86   3-5
DISC 2:
S1RS-5873-1/S1RS-5874-1.

❑ Reader's Digest/RCA Music Service (SP)
RB4-191-3 .... '86   3-5
DISC 3:
S1RS-5875-1/S1RS-5876-1.

❑ Reader's Digest/RCA Music Service (SP)
RB4-191-4 .... '86   3-5
DISC 4:
S1RS-5877-1/S1RS-5878-1.

❑ Reader's Digest/RCA Music Service (SP)
RB4-191-5 .... '86   3-5
DISC 5:
S1RS-5879-1/S1RS-5880-1.

❑ Reader's Digest/RCA Music Service (SP)
RB4-191-6 .... '86   3-5
DISC 6:
S1RS-5881-1/S1RS-5882-1.

❑ Reader's Digest/RCA Music Service (SP)
RB4-191-7 .... '86   3-5
DISC 7:
S1RS-5883-1/S1RS-5884-1.

❑ Reader's Digest/RCA Music Service
010/A .... '86   25-35
BOX 1: Slipcover: Front: "Collector's Edition" at upper right. Reader's Digest/RCA Music Service logo at bottom center, number at lower left. Color Elvis photo. Back: Record case: White with black and gold print. Back is blank. Number is different than is shown on discs.
INNER SLEEVES 1: Generic, individually numbered, plastic sleeves. Front and Back: Clear, covered with Reader's Digest Pegasus logos. Number (RDA/AP1) at lower left on side 2.

❑ Reader's Digest/RCA Music Service
010/A .... '86   5-10
INSERT 1: Duotone, 11¼" x 11½" 12-page information booklet, *Elvis, The Legend Lives On.*

**Reader's Digest/RCA Music Service
(SP) RBA-191/A 8/86**   50-75
TOTAL PACKAGE 1: Discs, box, insert.

Disc 1 (Elvis Live – Remembering the '50s)
Side 1
Medley: Also Sprach Zarathustra/That's All Right
Medley: Mystery Train/Tiger Man

Elvis Hits Medley
Medley: Long Tall Sally/Whole Lot-ta Shakin' Goin' On
Little Darlin'
Johnny B. Goode

Side 2
See See Rider
Fever
A Big Hunk O' Love
Jailhouse Rock
Love Me
All Shook Up

Disc 2 (Elvis Live – Remembering the '60s)
Side 1
I Just Can't Help Believin'
You Don't Have to Say You Love Me
Little Sister
You've Lost That Lovin' Feelin'
In the Ghetto
Suspicious Minds

Side 2
What Now My Love
Are You Lonesome Tonight
Medley: I Got a Woman/Amen
Medley: O Sole Mio/It's Now or Never
Unchained Melody
Let It Be Me

Disc 3 (Elvis Live – Remembering the '70s)
Side 1
Burning Love
Steamroller Blues
It's Impossible
An American Trilogy
Let Me Be There
Bridge over Troubled Water

Side 2
Kentucky Rain
Don't Cry Daddy
Fairytale
You Gave Me a Mountain
My Way
Bridge over Troubled Water

Disc 4 (Early Elvis)
Side 1
Good Rockin' Tonight
Tryin' to Get to You
Medley: Shake, Rattle and Roll/Flip, Flop and Fly
Heartbreak Hotel
Hound Dog
Don't Be Cruel

Side 2
Rip It Up
Money Honey
Blue Moon
One-Sided Love Affair
Got a Lot o' Livin' to Do
Reddy Teddy

Disc 5 (The 1968 TV Special/Country Favorites)
Side 1
Blue Suede Shoes
Lawdy Miss Clawdy/Baby, What You Want Me to Do
Medley: Heartbreak Hotel/Hound Dog/All Shook Up
Love Me Tender
Blue Christmas
One Night

Side 2

Release Me (And Let Me Love Again)
Help Me Make It Through the Night
Always on My Mind
I'm So Lonesome I Could Cry
I Can't Stop Loving You
Green, Green Grass of Home

Disc 6 (Can't Help Falling in Love/Indescribably Blue)

Side 1

Welcome to My World
And I Love You So
Mary in the Morning
Can't Help Falling in Love
Love Letters
Until It's Time for You to Go

Side 2

Hurt
Separate Ways
Indescribably Blue
Fool
I've Lost You
For the Good Times

Disc 7 (Elvis' Later Hits/In a Reflective Mood)

Side 1

Promised Land
U.S. Male
I'm Leavin'
Early Mornin' Rain
Moody Blue
Way Down

Side 2

The Elvis Medley
Loving Arms
Funny How Time Slips Away
Yesterday
Memories
Life

LEGEND LIVES ON

❑ Presley Collection PCS-1001: Bootleg. Listed for identification only.

LEGEND OF A KING (Picture Discs)

❑ Associated Broadcasters (M)
AB1-1001 .... 8/80   150-250
DISC 1: Test pressing of recording planned for picture disc. White label on both sides, with handwritten title and numbers. Production credits on side 1 only. Promotional issue only.
AB1-1001-A L-2781-P.B./AB1-1001-B L-2781-X. Identification numbers are engraved.
COVER 1: White, no printing.
❑ Associated Broadcasters .... '80   1-2
INSERT 1: One-page flyer on how to order *The Legend of a King* picture disc from Associated Broadcasters.

Associated Broadcasters (M)
AB1-1001 .... 8/80   150-250
TOTAL PACKAGE 1: Disc, insert.

❑ Associated Broadcasters (M)
1001 .... '80   25-35
DISC 2: Picture disc. First pressings are numbered from 3000 through 6000. Edition number, though it may be difficult to spot unless the lighting is just right, is between "Side One" and "Elvis." Has same color Elvis photo on both sides. Sold mail order via radio and TV ads.
ABI-1001-A L-2781-P.B./ABI-1001-B L-2781-X. Identification numbers are engraved.
❑ Associated Broadcasters
1001 .... '80   25-35
COVER 2: Standard, die-cut picture disc cover. Front: Black with white and gold printing. Back: Text only. Several spelling errors are made, including: "shrowd" for *shroud*; "idle" for *idol*; "Jordinaires" for *Jordanaires*; and "Downing" for *Dowling*. List of credits at lower left includes Neal Fisher and Allen Mallad.
INNER SLEEVE 2: None used.
❑ Associated Broadcasters..... '80   1-2
INSERT 2: One-page flyer on how to order *The Legend of a King* picture disc from Associated Broadcasters.

Associated Broadcasters (M)
1001 .... '80   50-75
TOTAL PACKAGE 2: Disc, cover, insert.

❑ Associated Broadcasters (M)
1001 .... '80   15-25
DISC 3: Picture disc. Second pressings are numbered from 6001 through 9000.
❑ Associated Broadcasters
1001 .... '80   15-25
COVER 3: Same as cover 2, except most spelling errors are fixed. Has white stickers with corrections pasted over columns one and three of "Elvis People." "Allen Mallad" is listed in credits at lower left on back.
INNER SLEEVE 3: None used.

Associated Broadcasters (M)
1001 .... '80   30-50
TOTAL PACKAGE 3: Disc, cover.

❑ Associated Broadcasters (M)
1001 .... '80   12-17
DISC 3: Same as disc 3.
❑ Associated Broadcasters
1001 .... '80   12-17
COVER 3: Same as cover 3, except "Allen Mallad" does not appear in credits at lower left on back.

Associated Broadcasters (M)
1001 .... '80   25-35
TOTAL PACKAGE 3: Disc, cover.

❑ Associated Broadcasters (M)
1001 .... '80   12-15
DISC 4: Picture disc. Third pressings are numbered from 00001 through 02999, and 09001 through 15000. Edition number (side 1) is clearly printed in white.

ABI-1001-A (RE) L-2781-P.B./ABI-1001-B (RE) L-2781-X.
Identification numbers are engraved.

❑ Associated Broadcasters
1001 .... '80   12-15
COVER 4: Same as cover 3 except all
spelling errors are corrected. In credits on
back, "Neal Fisher" is omitted and "Sonny
West" is added.

Associated Broadcasters (M)
1001 ....'80   25-30
TOTAL PACKAGE 4: Disc, cover.

❑ Associated Broadcasters (M)
1001 .... '84   12-15
DISC 5: Same as disc 4A.
❑ Associated Broadcasters
1001 .... '84   3-5
COVER/CARD 5: Disc is in clear plastic
sleeve/envelope, with an 11¾" x 11¾"
cardboard card. Card, white with black print,
is printed on only one side, and has the same
information as found on the back of cover 4.

Associated Broadcasters (M)
1001 ....'84   15-20
TOTAL PACKAGE 5: Disc, cover/card.

❑ Associated Broadcasters (M)
1001 .... '85   5-10
DISC 6: Not numbered. Otherwise, same as
disc 4.
❑ Associated Broadcasters
1001 .... '85   3-5
COVER/CARD 6: Same as cover/card 5.
INNER SLEEVE 6: White, no printing.

Associated Broadcasters (M)
1001 ....'85   8-15
TOTAL PACKAGE 6: Disc, cover/card.

Card stock jacket, with printing on cover – not
on slicks.

LEGEND OF A KING
(COMMEMORATIVE EDITION)
(2 LPs)

❑ Associated Broadcasters (M)
(No Number) 12/87   150-180
DISCS 1: Red vinyl. Complete two-hour radio
show, as originally broadcast on KSTN,
Stockton, California. Both have a white label
with red print. Promotional issue only.
(Disc 1) S-1/S-2. **(Disc 2)** S-1/S-2.
COVER 1: None made. Packaged in a clear
plastic sleeve/envelope.
INNER SLEEVES 1: White, no printing.
❑ Associated Broadcasters
(No Number) 12/87   10-20
INSERT 1: Five pages, three of cue sheets
and program information, and two giving
some background on the show.

Associated Broadcasters (M)
(No Number) 12/87   160-200
TOTAL PACKAGE 1: Discs, insert.

LEGEND OF A KING (3 LPs)

Complete three-hour radio show. All discs in
this set, listed individually below, have a silver
label with black print. All identification
numbers are engraved. Issued only to radio
stations.

❑ Associated Broadcasters 1-A, 1-B/1-C,
1-D...................................... '85   65-75
DISC 1A: Time of segment 1-B is 14:25.
S-1 HR-1/S2 HR-1.
❑ Associated Broadcasters 2-A, 2-B/2-C,
2-D...................................... '85   65-75
DISC 1B:
HR-2 S-1/HR-2 S2.
❑ Associated Broadcasters 3-A, 3-B, 3-C/3-D,
3-E...................................... '85   65-75
DISC 1C: Label on side 6 has "Hour 3-D,
"Hour 3-E," and "Program Promos."
HR-3 S-1 RE/S-6 RE.
❑ Associated Broadcasters..........
BOX 1: None made. Discs were issued in
plain, white cardboard jackets.
❑ Associated Broadcasters.....'85   10-20
INSERT 1: Six pages of cue sheets and
programming information.

Associated Broadcasters 1-A, 1-B/1-C,
1-D...............................'85   200-250
TOTAL PACKAGE 1: Discs, insert.

❑ Associated Broadcasters 1-A, 1-B/1-C,
1-D...................................... '85   65-75
DISC 2A: Time of segment 1-B is 15:15,
increased from 14:25 to include an interview
with drummer Johnny Bernero.
1A-RE/S2 HR-1.
❑ Associated Broadcasters 2-A, 2-B/2-C,
2-D...................................... '85   65-75
DISC 2B: Same as disc 1B.
HR-2 S-1/HR-2 S2.
❑ Associated Broadcasters 3-A, 3-B, 3-C/3-D,
3-E...................................... '85   65-75
DISC 2C: Label on side 6 has "Hour 3-D,
"Hour 3-E," "2-60 ABI Records," and "Program
Promos."
HR-3 S-1 RE/3-B RE.
❑ Associated Broadcasters.....'85   50-100
BOX 2: White box with black print. Reads: "A
Broadcast Documentary, Elvis the Legend of
a King," followed by credits and address. Only
100 boxes were made.
INNER SLEEVES 1: White, no printing.
❑ Associated Broadcasters.....'85   10-20
INSERT 2: Seven pages; six of cue sheets
and programming information, and one with
instructions for running ABI Records spots.

Associated Broadcasters
.......................................'85   250-350
TOTAL PACKAGE 2: Discs, box, insert.

Disc 1

Side 1

Rhythm and Blues Collage
Old Shep
Sweet Sweet Spirit
That's All Right
Blue Moon of Kentucky/That's All Right (Reprise)
Good Rockin' Tonight (Reprise)
My Baby's Gone
I'm Left, You're Right, She's Gone
Baby, Let's Play House
Mystery Train

Side 2

Heartbreak Hotel
Hound Dog
Don't Be Cruel
Love Me Tender
Loving You
(Let Me Be Your) Teddy Bear
Got a Lot o' Livin' to Do
Jailhouse Rock
King Creole
G.I. Blues
Flaming Star
Blue Hawaii
Girls! Girls! Girls!
Trouble
Lawdy, Miss Clawdy
You Gave Me a Mountain

Disc 2

Side 3

All Shook Up
(There'll Be) Peace in the Valley (For Me)
Wear My Ring Around Your Neck
(Now and Then There's) A Fool Such As I
My Wish Came True
It's Now Or Never

Side 4

Are You Lonesome Tonight
Surrender
Can't Help Falling in Love
Blue Hawaii
Soundtrack Song Collage
Return to Sender
Little Sister
If I Can Dream
Suspicious Minds

Disc 3

Side 5

Johnny B. Goode
Separate Ways
Welcome to My World
Moody Blue
Way Down
How Great Thou Art
My Way

Side 6

Memories
Beyond the Reef
Hound Dog
Guitar Man (Original Version)
Guitar Man (1980 Version)
Danny Boy
Write to Me from Naples
An American Trilogy

LEGENDARY CONCERT PERFORMANCES (2 LPs)

❑ RCA Victor (ST) R-244047 .. '78   15-20
DISCS 1: Black label, dog near top. RCA
Record Club issue.
(Disc 1) R-244047-A-2/R-244047-B-2. (Disc 2) R-244047-
C-2/R-244047-D-2. Identification numbers are engraved.

❑ RCA (ST) R-244047 .... '78   15-20
COVER 1: Single pocket. RCA logo and
number at lower left. Color Elvis photo on
front, same as on *From Elvis Presley
Boulevard, Memphis, Tennessee.*
INNER SLEEVES 1: White, no printing.

RCA Victor (ST)

R-244047 .... '78   30-40
TOTAL PACKAGE 1: Discs, cover.

Card stock jacket, with printing on cover – not
on slicks.

Disc 1

Side 1

Blue Suede Shoes
Sweet Caroline
Burning Love
Runaway
My Babe

Side 2

Johnny B. Goode
Yesterday
Medley: Mystery Train/Tiger Man
You Gave Me a Mountain
Never Been to Spain

Disc 2

Side 1

See See Rider
Words
Proud Mary
Walk a Mile in My Shoes
Steamroller Blues

Side 2

Polk Salad Annie
Something
Let It Be Me
The Impossible Dream
My Way

LEGENDARY MAGIC OF ELVIS PRESLEY

❑ RCA Special Products (SP)
DVL1-0461 .... '80   7-10
DISC 1: Black label, dog near top. Made for
Candlelite Music and sold by mail order.
DVL1-0461A-1/DVL1-0461B-1.

❑ RCA Special Products
DVL1-0461 .... '80   8-10
COVER 1: Front: RCA Special Products logo
and number at lower left, Candlelite logo at
top center. Color Elvis photo from '68 TV
Special. Back: Scroll of text, same Elvis photo
as on front.
INNER SLEEVE 1: White, no printing.

RCA Special Products (SP)

DVL1-0461 .... '80   15-20
TOTAL PACKAGE 1: Disc, cover.

Card stock jacket, with printing on cover – not on slicks.

Side 1
The Wonder of You
Baby, I Don't Care
My Wish Came True
Suspicious Minds
I Want You, I Need You, I Love You
Little Sister
It's Now Or Never
Too Much
Are You Lonesome Tonight

Side 2
Burning Love
(Now and Then There's) A Fool Such As I
Hard Headed Woman
In the Ghetto
When My Blue Moon Turns to Gold Again
Don't Cry Daddy
Jailhouse Rock
(Marie's the Name) His Latest Flame
One Night

LEGENDARY PERFORMER (Volume 1) (Experimental Picture Discs)

❑ RCA (M) CPL1-0341 .... 1/78   1000-2000
DISC 1: Picture disc, with artwork from *Elvis Presley* (LPM-1254). Experimental pressing, using the contents of CPL1-0341 (though not numbered as such other than in the vinyl) and the cover art of several other Elvis albums as the photo on the disc. Side 2 is white with no printing. This was the very first Elvis picture disc made, with less than a dozen copies pressed. Not intended for sale or distribution.
CPL1-0341A-6/CPL1-0341B-4.
COVER 1: None made.
INNER SLEEVE 1: White, no printing.
RCA (M) CPL1-0341 .... 1/78   1000-2000
TOTAL PACKAGE 1: Disc.

❑ RCA (M) CPL1-0341 .... 1/78   1000-2000
DISC 2: Picture disc, with artwork from *Elvis* (LPM-1382). Otherwise, same as disc 1.
COVER 2: None made.
INNER SLEEVE 2: White, no printing.
RCA (M) CPL1-0341 .... 1/78   1000-2000
TOTAL PACKAGE 2: Disc.

DISC 3: Picture disc, with artwork from *Elvis Now* (LSP-4671). Otherwise, same as disc 1.
COVER 3: None made.
INNER SLEEVE 3: White, no printing.
RCA (M) CPL1-0341 .... 1/78   1000-2000
TOTAL PACKAGE 3: Disc.

There are two or three other pressings in this 1978 experimental series; however, these are only ones we have verified.

Side 1
That's All Right
I Love You Because (Unreleased Version)
Heartbreak Hotel
Don't Be Cruel
Love Me (Unreleased Live Version)
Trying to Get to You (Unreleased Live Version)

Side 2
Love Me Tender
(There'll Be) Peace in the Valley (For Me)
(Now and Then There's) A Fool Such As I
Tonight's All Right for Love
Are You Lonesome Tonight (Unreleased Live Version)
Can't Help Falling in Love

LEGENDARY PERFORMER (Volume 1)

❑ RCA (M) CPL1-0341 .... 1/74   8-10
DISC 1: Custom; black, silver and gold.
CPL1-0341A-1/CPL1-0341B-1.
CPL1-0341A-2/CPL1-0341B-2.
CPL1-0341A-9/CPL1-0341B-6.
❑ RCA CPL1-0341 .... 1/74   12-15
COVER 1: Textured stock. Front: Die cut, 8" hole. White with red and embossed gold print. Back: Text only. RCA logo and number at bottom center.
❑ RCA CPL1-0341 .... 1/74   4-5
INNER SLEEVE 1: Cardboard stock. Front: Color "Aloha" Elvis photo. Back: Text only, black and red print. RCA logo and number at bottom center.
❑ RCA CPL1-0341 .... 1/74   5-10
INSERT 1: 12-page, *The Early Years*, booklet. 4-page color cover around eight black-and-white pages.
RCA (M) CPL1-0341 .... 1/74   30-40
TOTAL PACKAGE 1: Disc, cover, inner sleeve, insert.

❑ RCA (M) CPL1-0341 .... 1/74   8-10
DISC 2: Same as disc 1.
❑ RCA CPL1-0341 .... 1/74   18-20
COVER 2: Designate promo. Same as cover 1, but with "Not for Sale" stamped on back.
❑ RCA CPL1-0341 .... 1/74   4-5
INNER SLEEVE 2: Cardboard. Front: Color "Aloha" Elvis photo. Back: Text only, black and red print. RCA logo and number at bottom center.
❑ RCA (M) CPL1-0341 .... 1/74   5-10
INSERT 2: 12-page, *The Early Years*, booklet. 4-page color cover around eight black-and-white pages.
RCA (M) CPL1-0341 .... 1/74   35-45
TOTAL PACKAGE 2: Disc, cover, inner sleeve, insert.

❑ RCA (M) CPL1-0341 .... 1/86   10-12
DISC 3: Verification pending.
❑ RCA (M) CPL1-0341 .... 1/86   10-12
COVER 3: Flat stock (not textured). Front: Does not have die cut hole. In its place is the color Elvis photo from inner sleeve 1. No embossed print. Otherwise, same as cover 1.
INNER SLEEVE 3: White, no printing. Some copies have been found with inner sleeve 1. For these, make the appropriate price adjustment as shown for inner sleeve 1.
RCA (M) CPL1-0341 .... 1/86   20-25
TOTAL PACKAGE 3: Disc, cover.

Card stock jacket, with printing on cover – not on slicks.

Side 1

That's All Right
I Love You Because (Unreleased Version)
Heartbreak Hotel
Don't Be Cruel
Love Me (Unreleased Live Version)
Trying to Get to You (Unreleased Live Version)

Side 2

Love Me Tender
(There'll Be) Peace in the Valley (For Me)
(Now and Then There's) A Fool Such As I
Tonight's All Right for Love
Are You Lonesome Tonight (Unreleased Live Version)
Can't Help Falling in Love

LEGENDARY PERFORMER (Volume 2)

❑ RCA (SP) CPL1-1349 .... 1/76   8-10
DISC 1: Custom; black, gold and white print.
CPL1-1349-A-1S/CPL1-1349-B-1S. Identification numbers are engraved.
CPL1-1349-A-2S/CPL1-1349-B-2S. Identification numbers are stamped.

❑ RCA CPL1-1349 .... 1/76   12-15
COVER 1: Textured stock. Front: Die cut, 8" hole. White with blue and embossed gold print. Back: Text only. RCA logo and number at bottom center.

❑ RCA CPL1-1349 .... 1/76   4-5
INNER SLEEVE 1: Cardboard stock. Front: Color "Aloha" Elvis photo. Back: Text only, black and blue print. RCA logo and number at bottom center.

❑ RCA CPL1-1349 .... 1/76   5-10
INSERT 1: 16-page, *The Early Years Continued* . . . booklet. Four-page color cover around 12 black-and-white pages.

RCA (SP) CPL1-1349 ...... 1/76   30-40
TOTAL PACKAGE 1: Disc, cover, inner sleeve, insert.

❑ RCA (SP) CPL1-1349 .... 1/76   8-10
DISC 2: Same as disc 1.

❑ RCA CPL1-1349 .... 1/76   18-20
COVER 2: Designate promo. Same as cover 1, but with "Not for Sale" stamped on back.

❑ RCA CPL1-1349 .... 1/76   4-5
INNER SLEEVE 2: Cardboard stock. Front: Color "Aloha" Elvis photo. Back: Text only, black and blue print. RCA logo and number at bottom center.

❑ RCA CPL1-1349 .... 1/76   5-10
INSERT 2: 16-page, *The Early Years Continued* . . . booklet. Four-page color cover around 12 black-and-white pages.

RCA (SP) CPL1-1349 ...... 1/76   35-45
TOTAL PACKAGE 2: Disc, cover, inner sleeve, insert.

❑ RCA Victor (SP)
CPL1-1349 .... '77   45-50
DISC 3: Same as disc 1, but without the false starts and outtakes on *Such a Night* and *Cane and a High Starched Collar*. Mistakenly has only the complete take of both songs. Also, label print is noticeably darker than on disc 1.
CPL1-1349A-31/CPL1-1349B-31. Identification numbers are engraved.

❑ RCA CPL1-1349 .... '77   5-10
COVER 3: Same as cover 1.

❑ RCA CPL1-1349 .... 1/76   4-5
INNER SLEEVE 3: Cardboard stock. Front: Color "Aloha" Elvis photo. Back: Text only, black and blue print. RCA logo and number at bottom center.

❑ RCA CPL1-1349 .... 1/76   5-10
INSERT 3: 16-page, *The Early Years Continued* . . . booklet. Four-page color cover around 12 black-and-white pages.

RCA (SP) CPL1-1349 .... '77   60-75
TOTAL PACKAGE 3: Disc, cover, inner sleeve, insert.

❑ RCA (SP) CPL1-1349 .... 1/86   10-12
DISC 4: Verification pending.

❑ RCA CPL1-1349 .... 1/86   10-12
COVER 4: Flat stock (not textured). Front: Does not have die cut hole. In its place is the color Elvis photo from inner sleeve 1. No embossed print. Otherwise, same as cover 1. Bonus booklet was not included with this edition.
INNER SLEEVE 4: White, no printing. Some copies have been found with inner sleeve 1. For these, make the appropriate price adjustment as shown for inner sleeve 1.

RCA (SP) CPL1-1349 ...... 1/86   20-25
TOTAL PACKAGE 4: Disc, cover.

Card stock jacket, with printing on cover – not on slicks.

Side 1

Harbor Lights
Jay Thompson Interviews Elvis (1956)
I Want You, I Need You, I Love You (Unreleased Take)
Blue Suede Shoes (Unreleased Live Version)
Blue Christmas
Jailhouse Rock
It's Now Or Never

Side 2

Cane and a High Starched Collar
Presentation of Awards to Elvis
Blue Hawaii (Unreleased Version)
Such a Night
Baby What Do You Want Me to Do (Unreleased Live Version)
How Great Thou Art
If I Can Dream

THE LEGEND LIVES ON

LEGENDARY PERFORMER
(Volume 3) (Picture Disc)

❏ RCA (SP) CPL1-3078 ..... 11/78   10-15
DISC 1: Pictures applied to a blue vinyl disc.
Circa 1958 Elvis photo on side A and '68 TV
Special shot on side B, both in color.
CPL1-3078A-3S/CPL1-3078B-4S.
CPL1-3078A-4S/CPL1-3078B-3S.
CPL1-3078A-4S/CPL1-3078B-4S.

❏ RCA CPL1-3078.............. 11/78   5-10
COVER 1: Textured stock. Front: Die cut,
10¼" hole. White with blue and gold print.
Back: Text only. RCA logo and number at
bottom right.
INNER SLEEVE 1: Clear plastic, no printing.

❏ RCA CPL1-3078.............. 11/78   3-5
INSERT 1: 16-page, *Yesterdays* . . . booklet.
Four-page color cover around 12 black-and-
white pages.

RCA (SP) CPL1-3078.... 11/78   20-30
TOTAL PACKAGE 2: Disc, cover, insert.

❏ RCA (SP) CPL1-3078 ..... 11/78   10-15
DISC 2: Same as disc 1.
❏ RCA CPL1-3078.............. 11/78   10-15
COVER 2: Designate promo. Same as cover
1, but with "Not for Sale" stamped on back.
INNER SLEEVE 2: Clear plastic, no printing.
❏ RCA CPL1-3078.............. 11/78   3-5
INSERT 2: 16-page, *Yesterdays* . . . booklet.
Four-page color cover around 12 black-and-
white pages.

RCA (SP) CPL1-3078.... 11/78   25-35
TOTAL PACKAGE 2: Disc, cover, insert.

❏ RCA (SP) CPL1-30 .... '78   200-300
DISC 3: Same as disc 1, except '68 TV
Special photo is on both sides of LP.
Experimental pressing only, not intended for
sale or distribution.
COVER 3: None made.

RCA (SP) CPL1-30............. '78   200-300
TOTAL PACKAGE 3: Disc.

Card stock jacket, with printing on cover – not
on slicks.

Side 1
Hound Dog
Excerpts from [1956 *TV Guide*] Interview
Danny
Fame and Fortune (Unreleased Alternate Version)
Frankfort Special (Unreleased Alternate Version)
Britches
Crying in the Chapel
Side 2
Surrender
Guadalajara (Unreleased Alternate Version)
It Hurts Me (Unreleased Version)
Let Yourself Go (Unreleased Version)
In the Ghetto
Let It Be Me (Unreleased Live Version)

LEGENDARY PERFORMER
(Volume 3)

❏ RCA (SP) CPL1-3082...... 11/78   5-8
DISC 1: Custom; black, gold and white print.
CPL1-3082-A-1S/CPL1-3082-B-11S. Identification numbers
are stamped.
CPL1-3082-A-3S/CPL1-3082-B-10S. Identification numbers
are engraved.

❏ RCA CPL1-3082.............. 11/78   5-10
COVER 1: Textured stock. Front: Die cut, 8"
hole. White with blue and gold print. Back:
Text only. RCA logo and number at bottom
right.

❏ RCA CPL1-3082.............. 11/78   4-5
INNER SLEEVE 1: Cardboard stock. Front:
Color, circa 1958 Elvis photo. Back: Text only,
black and purple print. RCA logo and number
at bottom right.

❏ RCA CPL1-3082.............. 11/78   3-5
INSERT 1: 16-page, *Yesterdays* . . . booklet.
Four-page color cover around 12 black-and-
white pages.

RCA (SP) CPL1-3082.... 11/78   20-30
**TOTAL PACKAGE 1: Disc, cover, inner
sleeve, insert.**

❏ RCA (SP) CPL1-3082...... 11/78   5-8
DISC 2: Same as disc 1.
❏ RCA CPL1-3082.............. 11/78   10-15
COVER 2: Designate promo. Same as cover
1, but with "Not for Sale" stamped on back.
❏ RCA CPL1-3082.............. 11/78   4-5
INNER SLEEVE 2: Cardboard. Front: Color,
circa 1958 Elvis photo. Back: Text only, black
and purple print. RCA logo and number at
bottom right.
❏ RCA CPL1-3082.............. 11/78   3-5
INSERT 2: 16-page, *Yesterdays* . . . booklet.
Four-page color cover around 12 black-and-
white pages.

RCA (SP) CPL1-3082.... 11/78   25-35
**TOTAL PACKAGE 2: Disc, cover, inner
sleeve, insert.**

❏ RCA (SP) CPL1-3082........ 1/86   10-12
DISC 3: Verification pending.
❏ RCA CPL1-3082.............. 1/86   10-12
COVER 3: Flat stock (not textured). Front:
Does not have die cut hole. In its place is the
color Elvis photo from inner sleeve 1.
Otherwise, same as cover 1. Bonus booklet
was not included with this edition.
INNER SLEEVE 3: White, no printing. Some
copies have been found with inner sleeve 1.
For these, make the appropriate price
adjustment as shown for inner sleeve 1.

RCA (SP) CPL1-3082...... 1/86   20-25
TOTAL PACKAGE 3: Disc, cover.

Card stock jacket, with printing on cover – not
on slicks.

Side 1
Hound Dog
Excerpts from [1956 *TV Guide*] Interview
Danny
Fame and Fortune (Unreleased Alternate Version)
Frankfort Special (Unreleased Alternate Version)
Britches
Crying in the Chapel

Side 2
Surrender
Guadalajara (Unreleased Alternate Version)
It Hurts Me (Unreleased Version)
Let Yourself Go (Unreleased Version)
In the Ghetto
Let It Be Me (Unreleased Live Version)

LEGENDARY PERFORMER (Volume 4)

❑ RCA (SP) CPL1-4848 ..... 11/83   8-10
DISC 1: Custom; black, gold and white print.
CPL1-4848-A-1S/CPL1-4848-B-1S. Identification numbers are engraved. Both sides have "AF" engraved, crossed out and "CP" added.

❑ RCA (SP) CPL1-4848 ..... 11/83   10-15
COVER 1: Textured stock. Front: Die cut, 8" hole. White with blue and gold print. Back: Text only. RCA logo and number at bottom right, UPC bar code at upper right.

❑ RCA CPL1-4848 .... 11/83   4-5
INNER SLEEVE 1: Cardboard. Front: Color, circa '66 Elvis photo. Back: Text only, black and purple print. RCA logo and number at bottom right.

❑ RCA CPL1-4848 .... 11/83   3-5
INSERT 1: 12-page, *Memories of the King* booklet. Four-page color cover around eight black-and-white pages.

RCA (SP) CPL1-4848.... 11/83   30-35
TOTAL PACKAGE 1: Disc, cover, inner sleeve, insert.

❑ RCA (SP) CPL1-4848 ..... 11/83   8-10
DISC 2: Same as disc 1.

❑ RCA CPL1-4848 .... 11/83   18-20
COVER 2: Designate promo. Same as cover 1, but with "Not for Sale" stamped on back.

❑ RCA CPL1-4848 .... 11/83   4-5
INNER SLEEVE 2: Cardboard stock. Front: Color, circa 1966 Elvis photo. Back: Text only, black and purple print. RCA logo and number at bottom right.

❑ RCA CPL1-4848 .... 11/83   3-5
INSERT 2: 12-page, "Memories of the King" booklet. Four-page color cover around eight black-and-white pages.

RCA (SP) CPL1-4848.... 11/83   35-40
TOTAL PACKAGE 2: Disc, cover, inner sleeve, insert.

❑ RCA (SP) CPL1-4848 .... 1/86   10-12
DISC 3: Verification pending.

❑ RCA (SP) CPL1-4848........ 1/86   10-12
COVER 3: Flat stock (not textured). Front: Does not have die cut hole. In its place is the color Elvis photo from inner sleeve 1. Otherwise, same as cover 1. Bonus booklet was not included with this edition.
INNER SLEEVE 3: White, no printing. Some copies have been found with inner sleeve 1. For these, make the appropriate price adjustment as shown for inner sleeve 1.

RCA (SP) CPL1-4848...... 1/86   20-25
TOTAL PACKAGE 3: Disc, cover.

Card stock jacket, with printing on cover – not on slicks.

Side 1
When It Rains, It Really Pours
Interview
One Night
I'm Beginning to Forget You
Mona Lisa
Wooden Heart
Plantation Rock

Side 2
The Lady Loves Me
Swing Down, Sweet Chariot
That's All Right
Are You Lonesome Tonight
Reconsider Baby
I'll Remember You

LEGENDARY RECORDINGS OF ELVIS PRESLEY (6 LPs)

Black label, dog near top. Boxed set made for Candlelite Music and sold by mail order. Discs and covers, which have individual titles, are listed separately below. Identification numbers are engraved on discs 1, 2 & 3; stamped on 4, 5 & 6.

❑ RCA Special Products (SP)
DML6-0412-1 .... 8/79   4-5
DISC 1:
DML1-0412-A-2/DML1-0412-B-2.

❑ RCA Special Products
DML6-0412 .... 8/79   4-5
COVER 1: Blue cover, black print. Front: RCA logo at lower right, number at upper right. Candlelite logo at top center. Has embossed image of Elvis. Back: Text only.

❑ RCA Special Products (SP)
DML6-0412-2 .... 8/79   4-5
DISC 2:
DML1-0412-C-1/DML1-0412-D-1.

❑ RCA Special Products
DML6-0412 .... 8/79   4-5
COVER 2: Orange cover, black print. Front: RCA logo at lower right, number at upper right. Candlelite logo at top center. Has embossed image of Elvis. Back: Text only.

❑ RCA Special Products (SP)
DML6-0412-3 .... 8/79   4-5
DISC 3:
DML1-0412-E-1/DML1-0412-F-1.

❑ RCA Special Products
DML6-0412 ....8/79   4-5
COVER 3: Yellow cover, black print. Front:
RCA logo at lower right, number at upper
right. Candlelite logo at top center. Has
embossed image of Elvis. Back: Text only.

❑ RCA Special Products (SP)
DML6-0412-4 ....8/79   4-5
DISC 4:
DML1-0412-G-1/DML1-0412-H-1.

❑ RCA Special Products
DML6-0412 ....8/79   4-5
COVER 4: Green cover, black print. Front:
RCA logo at lower right, number at upper
right. Candlelite logo at top center. Has
embossed image of Elvis. Back: Text only.

❑ RCA Special Products (SP)
DML6-0412-5 ....8/79   4-5
DISC 5:
DML1-0412-I-1/DML1-0412-J-2.

❑ RCA Special Products
DML6-0412 ....8/79   4-5
COVER 5: Purple cover, black print. Front:
RCA logo at lower right, number at upper
right. Candlelite logo at top center. Has
embossed image of Elvis. Back: Text only.

❑ RCA Special Products (SP)
DML6-0412-6 ....8/79   4-5
DISC 6:
DML1-0412-K-1/DML1-0412-L-1.

❑ RCA Special Products
DML6-0412 ....8/79   4-5
COVER 6: Pink cover, black print. Front: RCA
logo at lower right, number at upper right.
Candlelite logo at top center. Has embossed
image of Elvis. Back: Text only.

❑ RCA Special Products
DML6-0412-A....................8/79   50-65
BOX 1: Oversize, 12¾" x 12¾". Front:
Maroon with gold foil stamping. RCA logo at
lower left, number at upper left. Candlelite
logo at top center. Has gold foil stamped
image of Elvis. Back: Blank. Inside Front: Text
only. Inside Back: Blank, with stapled yellow
ribbon, for lifting the LPs out of the box.

RCA Special Products (SP)
DML6-0412-1..............8/79   100-125
TOTAL PACKAGE 1: Discs, box.

❑ RCA Special Products (SP)
DML6-0412 ....'79   25-30
DISCS 2: Black label, dog near top.
(Disc 1) DML6-0412A-1/DML6-0412B-1. **(Disc 2)** DML6-
0412C-1/DML6-0412D-1. **(Disc 3)** DML6-0412-E-1/DML6-
0412-F-1. **(Disc 4)** DML6-0412G-1/DML6-0412H-1. **(Disc
5)** DML6-0412I-1/DML6-0412J-1. **(Disc 6)** DML6-0412K-
1/DML6-0412L-1

❑ RCA Special Products
DML6-0412.........................'79   55-70
BOX 2: Black slip cover; Front: RCA logo at
lower middle, number at upper left. Candlelite
logo at top center. Has gold foil stamped
image of Elvis. Back: Blank. Record case:
Contents and liner notes on front. Back is
blank. Sealed copies of this box had a white
piece of paper listing contents which was
sealed under the shrink wrap, on the backside
of the box but was not applied to cover.
Records came in white inner sleeves.

RCA Special Products (SP)
DML6-0412....................'79   80-100
TOTAL PACKAGE 2: Discs, box.

Disc 1 (Precious Memories)
Side 1
Take My Hand, Precious Lord
Where Could I Go (But to the Lord)
In the Garden
It Is No Secret (What God Can Do)
Stand By Me
Side 2
Mama Liked the Roses
Padre
All That I Am
I'm Leavin'
Forget Me Never (shown as "Forgive Me Never")

Disc 2 (Encore of Golden Performances)
Side 1
Frankie and Johnny
[Medley] Down by the Riverside/When the Saints Go
    Marching In
Girl Happy
Do the Clam
G.I. Blues
Side 2
See See Rider/Also Sprach Zarathustra
Johnny B. Goode
Lawdy, Miss Clawdy/Baby What You Want Me to Do
Whole Lot-ta Shakin' Goin' On/Long Tall Sally
It's Over

Disc 3 (Memories Are Made of This)
Side 1
Snowbird
I Love You Because
Just Because
Release Me
Mystery Train
Side 2
Blue Moon of Kentucky
It Keeps Right on A-Hurtin'
I Don't Care If the Sun Don't Shine
I'm Movin' On
Baby, Let's Play House

Disc 4 (The King of Rock N' Roll)
Side 1
Shake, Rattle and Roll
I Slipped I Stumbled, I Fell
Tutti Frutti
Ain't That Lovin' You Baby
Rip It Up

Side 2
Party
Tiger Man
Paralyzed
Hi-Heel Sneakers
I Got a Woman

Disc 5 (The Home of the Blues)

Side 1
Any Day Now
How's the World Treating You
Only the Strong Survive
Just for Old Times Sake
You've Lost That Lovin' Feelin'

Side 2
They Remind Me Too Much of You
Lonely Blue Boy (Danny)
Indescribably Blue
It Feels So Right
Tell Me Why

Disc 6 (Elvis Forever)

Side 1
Fools Rush In
Please Don't Stop Loving Me
Proud Mary
Never Been to Spain
Don't Think Twice, It's All Right

Side 2
Fools Fall in Love
Walk a Mile in My Shoes
Blue Moon
Witchcraft
Runaway

LET'S BE FRIENDS (Camden)

❏ RCA/Camden (SP)
CAS-2408 .... 4/70 　　15-20
DISC 1: Blue label. Rigid vinyl.
ZCRS-1059-30S/ZCRS-1060-7S. Identification numbers are engraved.
ZCRS-1059-30S/ZCRS-1060-9S. Identification numbers are engraved.
ZCRS-1059-33S/ZCRS-1060-33S. Identification numbers are engraved. This identification number can be found on both rigid and flexible vinyl pressings.

❏ RCA/Camden CAS-2408...4/70 　　10-15
COVER 1: Front: RCA logo and number at upper left, "Camden" and "Stereo." at upper right. Color Elvis photo. Back: Black-and-white Elvis photo. Pictures *Elvis Sings Flaming Star*. At lower left or right, may have a "1," "2" or "3."
INNER SLEEVE 1: White, no printing. (Some Camden LPs had no inner sleeves at all.)

RCA/Camden (SP)
CAS-2408 .... 4/70 　　25-35
TOTAL PACKAGE 1: Disc, cover.

❏ RCA/Camden (SP)
CAS-2408 .... 4/70 　　15-20
DISC 2: Same as disc 1.
❏ RCA/Camden CAS-2408...4/70 　　15-20
COVER 2: Designate promo. Same as cover 1, but with "Not for Sale" stamped on back.
INNER SLEEVE 2: White, no printing. (Some Camden LPs had no inner sleeves at all.)

❏ RCA/Camden (SP)
CAS-2408 .... 4/70 　　30-40
TOTAL PACKAGE 2: Disc, cover.

❏ RCA/Camden (SP)
CAS-2408 ....4/70 　　15-20
DISC 3: Blue label. Flexible vinyl.
❏ RCA/Camden CAS-2408...4/70 　　5-10
COVER 3: Same as cover 1.
INNER SLEEVE 3: White, no printing. (Some Camden LPs had no inner sleeves at all.)

RCA/Camden (SP)
CAS-2408 .... 4/70 　　20-30
TOTAL PACKAGE 3: Disc, cover.

Side 1
Stay Away, Joe
If I'm a Fool (For Loving You)
Let's Be Friends
Let's Forget About the Stars
Mama

Side 2
I'll Be There (If You Ever Want Me)
Almost
Change of Habit
Have a Happy

LET'S BE FRIENDS (Pickwick)

❏ Pickwick/Camden (SP)
CAS-2408 .... 12/75 　　2-5
DISC 1: Black label. Multi-color Pickwick logo at center.
ZCRS-1059-33S/ZCRS-1060-33S. Identification numbers are stamped. Also has CAS-2408-A/CAS2408-B engraved on both sides. ZCRS-1059-35/ZCRS-1060-35.

❏ Pickwick/Camden
CAS-2408 .... 12/75 　　3-5
COVER 1: Front: Same Elvis photo as Camden cover 1 (above), but has a 1" black border around front edge. Pickwick logo at lower left, Camden logo and number at upper right. "Let's Be Friends" and "Elvis" are transposed from their position on Camden cover 1. Back: Same as Camden cover 1, except Pickwick logo and address added at lower right. Also added are a few other miscellaneous notes and a "2" at bottom.
INNER SLEEVE 1: Generic Pickwick sleeve. Makes no mention of Elvis or this LP.

Pickwick/Camden (SP)
CAS-2408 .... 12/75 　　5-10
TOTAL PACKAGE 1: Disc, cover.

❏ Pickwick/Camden (SP)
CAS-2408 ....'77 　　750-1000
DISC 2: Gold vinyl. Experimental pressing, not intended for sale of distribution.
COVER 2: None made.

Pickwick/Camden (SP)
CAS-2408 .... '77 　　750-1000
TOTAL PACKAGE 2: Disc.

❑ Pickwick/Camden (SP)
CAS-2408............................ '77   750-1000
DISC 3: Multi-color, or *splash* vinyl.
Experimental pressing, not intended for sale
of distribution.
COVER 3: None made.
INNER SLEEVE 3: Generic Pickwick sleeve.
Makes no mention of Elvis or this LP.

Pickwick/Camden (SP)
CAS-2408 .... '77   750-1000
TOTAL PACKAGE 3: Disc.

Side 1
Stay Away, Joe
If I'm a Fool (For Loving You)
Let's Be Friends
Let's Forget About the Stars
Mama
Side 2
I'll Be There (If You Ever Want Me)
Almost
Change of Habit
Have a Happy

LIGHTNING STRIKES TWICE – ELVIS PRESLEY / THE SILVER BEATLES

❑ United Distributors (M)
UDL-2382............................ '81   20-30
DISC 1: One side for each artist. Side 1 is by
the Silver Beatles, from their Decca auditions.
Side 2 is by Elvis.
UDL-2382-A/UDL-2382-B. Identification numbers are
engraved.

❑ United Distributors
UDL-2382............................ '81   20-30
COVER 1: White with black print. Front: Title,
artists and number at upper left. Back: blank.
Label name does not appear on cover
anywhere.
INNER SLEEVE 1: White, no printing.

United Distributors (M)
UDL-2382 .... '81   40-60
TOTAL PACKAGE 1: Disc, cover.

Card stock jacket, with printing on cover – not
on slicks.
Side 1 (Silver Beatles)
September in the Rain
Besame Mucho
Sheik of Araby
To Know You
Hello Little Girl
Side 2 (Elvis Presley)
Baby Let's Play House
I Got a Woman (shown as "I've Got a Woman")
That's All Right
Blue Moon of Kentucky
Tweedlee Dee (shown as "Tweedelee Dee")

LIVE EXPERIENCE
❑ E.P. PRP-143: Bootleg. Listed for
identification only.

LIVE EXPERIENCE IN VEGAS, FEBRUARY 1971
❑ Bonthold LP-2999: Bootleg. Listed for
identification only.

LIVE MEMORIES
❑ Silver: Bootleg. Listed for identification only.

LIVE SESSIONS
❑ Memphis Star: Bootleg. Listed for
identification only.

LIVE ON STAGE - HILTON HOTEL
❑ Bootleg. Listed for identification only.

LONG LOST LOVE SONGS
❑ Vault E-1020: Bootleg. Listed for
identification only.

LOST ON TOUR
❑ Bilko LPM-1590: Bootleg. Listed for
identification only.

LOUISIANA HAYRIDE
❑ Louisiana Hayride (M)
NR-8454 .... '76   500-700
DISC 1: Complete radio show. Light yellow
label with black print. Number ("NR8454") is
not in parenthesis. Label printed on side 1
only. Has blanks on label filled in, indicating
this is Program 836 and that the featured
artist is Bobby G. Rice. Issued only to radio
stations.
NR-8454-A/NR-8454-B. Identification numbers are
engraved.
COVER 1: White, no printing.

Louisiana Hayride (M)
NR-8454 .... '76   500-700
TOTAL PACKAGE 1: Disc.

❑ Louisiana Hayride (M)
NR-8454 .... '76   300-350
DISC 2: Gold label with black print. Number
("NR8454") is in parenthesis. Label printed on
side 1 only. Blanks are not filled in.
NR-8454-A/NR-8454-B. Identification numbers are
engraved.
COVER 2: White, no printing.

Louisiana Hayride (M)
NR-8454 .... '76   300-350
TOTAL PACKAGE 2: Disc.

Counterfeit Identification: Fake discs have numbers (NR-8973- A/NR-8973-XB) stamped in vinyl. Originals have those identification numbers engraved. Label does not have "Program" and "Time" lines, and "For One Time Only Use," all of which are on originals. A black-and-white fake cover exists; however, there are no printed covers for originals.

LOVE LETTERS FROM ELVIS

❑ RCA Victor (ST)
LSP-4530 ....5/71   8-10
DISC 1: Orange label. Dynaflex vinyl.
APRS-1392-1S/APRS-1393-1S. Identification numbers are stamped.
APRS-1392-2S/APRS-1393-1S. Identification numbers are stamped.
APRS-1392-3S/APRS-1393-3S. Identification numbers are stamped.
APRS-1392-4S/APRS-1393-3S. Identification numbers are stamped. Though still a Dynaflex disc, this pressing is noticeably more rigid than APRS-1392-2S/APRS-1393-1S.
APRS-1392-30S/APRS-1393-5S. Identification numbers are engraved.

❑ RCA Victor LSP-4530........5/71   20-25
COVER 1: Front: RCA Victor logo and number at top center. Below logo, on one line, is "Love Letters from." Back: Postage stamp size black-and-white Elvis photo.

❑ RCA Victor 21-112-1
pt 57 ....8/70   3-5
INNER SLEEVE 1: Black-and-white. Front: Pictures Camden Elvis catalog, most recent being *Elvis' Christmas Album* (side 1, row 2, column 1). Back: RCA Elvis 3¾-ips reel tapes.

RCA Victor (ST)
LSP-4530.....................5/71   35-45
TOTAL PACKAGE 1: Disc, cover, inner sleeve.

❑ RCA Victor (ST)
LSP-4530 ....5/71   8-10
DISC 2: Same as disc 1.

❑ RCA Victor LSP-4530........5/71   4-8
COVER 2: Front: RCA Victor logo and number at lower right. At top center, on one line, is "Love Letters." On the next line is "from." Has "RE" at lower left. Back: Postage stamp size black-and-white Elvis photo. Price reflects RCA's use of this same cover, with no discernible differences, until 1976.

❑ RCA Victor 21-112-1
pt 57 ....8/70   3-5
INNER SLEEVE 2: Black-and-white. Front: Pictures Camden Elvis catalog, most recent being *Elvis' Christmas Album* (side 1, row 2, column 1). Back: RCA Elvis 3¾-ips reel tapes.

RCA Victor (ST)
LSP-4530.....................5/71   15-25
TOTAL PACKAGE 2: Disc, cover, inner sleeve.

❑ RCA Victor (ST)
LSP-4530 ....5/71   8-10
DISC 3: Same as disc 1.
APRS-1392-4S/APRS-1393-3S.

❑ RCA Victor LSP-4530........5/71   25-35
COVER 3: Designate promo. Same as cover 1, but with "Not for Sale" stamped on back.

❑ RCA Victor 21-112-1
pt 57 ....8/70   3-5
INNER SLEEVE 3: Black-and-white. Front: Pictures Camden Elvis catalog, most recent being *Elvis' Christmas Album* (side 1, row 2, column 1). Back: RCA Elvis 3¾-ips reel tapes.

RCA Victor (ST)
LSP-4530.....................5/71   45-50
TOTAL PACKAGE 3: Disc, cover, inner sleeve.

❑ RCA Victor (ST)
LSP-4530 ....5/71   8-10
DISC 4: Same as disc 1.
APRS-1392-4S/APRS-1393-3S.

❑ RCA Victor LSP-4530........5/71   10-15
COVER 4: Designate promo. Same as cover 2, but with "Not for Sale" stamped on back.

❑ RCA Victor 21-112-1
pt 57 ....8/70   3-5
INNER SLEEVE 4: Black-and-white. Front: Pictures Camden Elvis catalog, most recent being *Elvis' Christmas Album* (side 1, row 2, column 1). Back: RCA Elvis 3¾-ips reel tapes.

RCA Victor (ST)
LSP-4530.....................5/71   25-35
TOTAL PACKAGE 4: Disc, cover, inner sleeve.

❑ RCA Victor (ST)
LSP-4530 ....'76   4-8
DISC 5: Tan label. Dynaflex vinyl.

❑ RCA Victor LSP-4530........5/71   20-25
COVER 5: Same as cover 1.

❑ RCA Victor.........................'70s   2-4
INNER SLEEVE 5: Black-and-white. Pictures RCA Elvis catalog front and back. Any of several sleeves may be found on reissues from this period.

RCA Victor (ST)
LSP-4530.....................'76   25-35
TOTAL PACKAGE 5: Disc, cover, inner sleeve.

❑ RCA Victor (ST)
LSP-4530 ....'76   4-8
DISC 6: Same as disc 5.
APRS-1392-31S/APRS-1393-32S.

❑ RCA Victor LSP-4530..........'76   4-8
COVER 6: Same as cover 2.

❑ RCA Victor.........................'70s   2-4
INNER SLEEVE 6: Black-and-white. Pictures RCA Elvis catalog front and back. Any of several sleeves may be found on reissues from this period.

RCA Victor (ST)
LSP-4530.....................'76   10-20
TOTAL PACKAGE 6: Disc, cover, inner sleeve.

RCA Victor (ST)
LSP-4530 .... '76   12-15
DISC 7: Black label, dog near top.
RCA Victor LSP-4530 .... '76   10-12
COVER 7: Verification pending.
RCA Victor .... '70s   2-4
INNER SLEEVE 7: Black-and-white. Pictures RCA Elvis catalog front and back. Any of several sleeves may be found on reissues from this period.

RCA Victor (ST)
LSP-4530 .... '76   **25-30**
TOTAL PACKAGE 7: Disc, cover, inner sleeve.

RCA Victor (ST)
AFL1-4530 .... '77   12-15
DISC 8: Black label, dog near top. Includes copies with both the "LSP" and "AFL1" prefixes printed on the label.
RCA AFL1-4530 .... '77   10-12
COVER 8: Reflects prefix change. Includes copies with a sticker bearing the "AFL1" prefix, wrapped around cover at top of spine. Used for discs with both the "LSP" and "AFL1" prefixes on label, though only "AFL1" appears on the cover.
RCA Victor .... '70s   2-4
INNER SLEEVE 8: Black-and-white. Pictures RCA Elvis catalog front and back. Any of several sleeves may be found on reissues from this period.

RCA Victor (ST)
AFL1-4530 .... '77   **25-30**
TOTAL PACKAGE 8: Disc, cover, inner sleeve.

Side 1
Love Letters
When I'm Over You
If I Were You
Got My Mojo Working
Heart of Rome

Side 2
Only Believe
This Is Our Dance
Cindy Cindy
I'll Never Know
It Ain't No Big Thing
Life

LOVE ME TENDER (2 LPs)
Various artists collection
Time-Life (SP) STL-133 ...... '91   10-12
DISCS 1: Custom pink label with black-and-white print. Sold only by Time-Life via mail order.
(Disc 1) STL-133A-1/STL-133B-1. **(Disc 2)** STL-133C-1/STL-133D-1. **(Disc 3)** STL-133E-1/STL-133F-1. Identification numbers are engraved.

Time-Life STL-133 .... '91   10-12
COVER 1: Single pocket. Front: Time-Life logo at upper right. Color photo of unidentified couple. Back: Time-Life logo and number at lower right. Another photo of same couple seen on front.
INNER SLEEVES 1: Clear plastic, no printing.
Time-Life (SP) STL-133.... '91   **20-25**
TOTAL PACKAGE 1: Disc, cover.

Card stock jacket, with printing on cover – not on slicks.

Disc 1
Side 1
Love Me Tender (Elvis Presley)
It's All in the Game (Tommy Edwards)
16 Candles (Crests)
Twilight Time (Platters)
Chances Are (Johnny Mathis)
Young Love (Sonny James)
Side 2
He'll Have to Go (Jim Reeves)
Happy, Happy Birthday Baby (Tune Weavers)
For Your Precious Love (Jerry Butler)
In the Still of the Nite (Five Satins)
There's a Moon Out Tonight (Capris)
Maybe (Chantels)
Earth Angel (Penguins)
Disc 2
Side 1
One Summer Night (Danleers)
Where Or When (Dion and the Belmonts)
Love Letters in the Sand (Pat Boone)
Daddy's Home (Shep and the Limelites)
I Only Have Eyes for You (Flamingos)
Goodnight My Love (Jesse Belvin)
Sleep Walk (Santo and Johnny)
Side 2
Are You Lonesome Tonight (Elvis Presley)
I'm Sorry (Brenda Lee)
Smoke Gets in Your Eyes (Platters)
Let It Be Me (Everly Brothers)
Since I Fell for You (Lenny Welch)
Tears on My Pillow (Little Anthony & the Imperials)
Disc 3
Side 1
Over the Mountain, Across the Sea (Johnnie & Joe)
Sea of Love (Phil Phillips)
Lavender Blue (Sammy Turner)
You Belong to Me (Duprees)
Can't Help Falling in Love (Elvis Presley)
Who's Sorry Now (Connie Francis)
Deep Purple (Nino Tempo & April Stevens)

Side 2
It's Only Make Believe (Conway Twitty)
Mr. Lonely (Bobby Vinton)
What in the World's Come over You (Jack Scott)
Since I Don't Have You (Skyliners)
Only Love Can Break a Heart (Gene Pitney)
The End of the World (Skeeter Davis)
Last Date (Floyd Cramer)

LOVE SONGS (16 ORIGINAL HITS)

❑ K-TEL (SP) NU9900 .... 10/81   10-12
DISC 1: Brown, orange, black and white label.
NU-9900-A-11 MR-25305/NU-9900-B-11 MR-25305X.
NU-9900-A-44/NU-9900-B-44.

❑ K-TEL NU9900 .... 10/81   10-12
COVER 1: Front: K-Tel logo and number at
upper right. Color '68 Elvis TV Special photo.
Back: Text only.
INNER SLEEVE 1: White, no printing.

K-TEL (SP) NU9900 ...... 10/81   **20-25**
   TOTAL PACKAGE 1: Disc, cover.

Card stock jacket, with printing on cover – not
on slicks.

Side 1
Suspicious Minds
She's Not You
The Wonder of You
Love Letters
Wooden Heart
I Want You, I Need You, I Love You
Memories
Kentucky Rain

Side 2
Love Me Tender
It's Now or Never
Are You Lonesome Tonight
You Don't Have to Say You Love Me
I Just Can't Help Believin'
Can't Help Falling in Love
Surrender
Loving You (shown as "Lovin' You")

LOVING YOU

❑ RCA Victor (M)
LPM-1515 .... 7/57   100-110
DISC 1: Black label, "Long Play" at bottom.
H2WP-2762-3S/H2WP-2763-3S. Label LP#1.
H2WP-2762-10S/H2WP-2763-13S. Label LP#1.

❑ RCA Victor LPM-1515 .... 7/57   140-175
COVER 1: Front: RCA Victor logo and
number at upper right. No contents shown.
Color Elvis photo. Back: Box of text at lower
right explains "New Orthophonic High Fidelity"
and needle maintenance. Four black-and-
white film scenes pictured.

❑ RCA Victor No Number .... '57   10-15
INNER SLEEVE 1: Full color. Pictures *Elvis
Presley* and *Elvis* as two of the LPs in the
"Best-Selling Long Play Pop Albums"
category.

RCA Victor (M)
LPM-1515 .... 7/57   250-300
   TOTAL PACKAGE 1: Disc, cover, inner
   sleeve.

❑ RCA Victor (M)
LPM-1515 .... 11/63   30-40
DISC 2: Black label, "Mono" at bottom.
H2WP-2762-1S/H2WP-2763-14S. Label LP#10.

❑ RCA Victor LPM-1515 ..... 11/63   60-75
COVER 2: Front: RCA Victor logo at upper
right. Below that is "Loving You, (Let Me Be
Your) Teddy Bear, Mean Woman Blues and
Others." Has number at lower left, and "RE" at
lower right. Color Elvis photo. Back: First
paragraph of liner notes is completely
rewritten, reflecting the passing of six years
since cover 1. Box of text on cover 1 is
replaced by a paragraph on mono/stereo
phonographs, and RCA's "Miracle Surface."
Four black-and-white film scenes pictured.

❑ RCA Victor (No Number) ... 9/63   8-10
INNER SLEEVE 2: Turquoise, black and
white. Front: RCA's Elvis LP catalog, most
recent being *It Happened at the World's Fair*
(side 1, row 4, column 5). Back: RCA Elvis
EPs and 45s catalog.

RCA Victor (M)
LPM-1515 .... 11/63   100-125
   TOTAL PACKAGE 2: Disc, cover, inner
   sleeve.

❑ RCA Victor (M)
LPM-1515 .... 10/64   10-15
DISC 3: Black label, "Monaural" at bottom.

❑ RCA Victor LPM-1515 ..... 10/64   25-35
COVER 3: Verification pending.

❑ RCA Victor 21-112-1
40A 10/64   4-8
INNER SLEEVE 3: Red, black and white.
Front: RCA's Elvis LP catalog, most recent
being *Kissin' Cousins* (side 1, row 1, column
6). Back: RCA Elvis EPs and 45s catalog.

RCA Victor (M)
LPM-1515 .... 10/64   40-60
   TOTAL PACKAGE 3: Disc, cover, inner
   sleeve.

❑ RCA Victor (SE)
LSP-1515(e) 2/62   100-150
DISC 4: Black label, RCA logo in silver at top
and "Stereo Electronically Reprocessed" at
bottom.
M2WY-4731-3S/M2WY-4732-3S. Label LP#9.

❑ RCA Victor LSP-1515(e) ... 2/62   10-20
COVER 4: Front: RCA logo and "Stereo
Electronically Reprocessed" at upper right,
number at upper left – in white print on 1"
black stripe across top. "RE" at lower right.
Back: Has box of text at upper left "From the
Originators of Electronically Reprocessed
Stereo." Four black-and-white film scenes
pictured. Price reflects RCA's continued use
of this same cover, with no discernible
differences.
INNER SLEEVE 4: White, no printing.

RCA Victor (SE)
LSP-1515(e) .... **2/62**　　**100-200**
TOTAL PACKAGE 4: Disc, cover.

❑ RCA Victor (SE)
LSP-1515(e).................... 10/64　　10-20
DISC 5: Black label, RCA logo in white at top
and "Stereo" at bottom.
M2WY-4731-5S/M2WY-4732-6S. Label LP#17.
❑ RCA Victor
LSP-1515(e).................... 10/64　　25-30
COVER 5: Same as cover 4.
❑ RCA Victor 21-112-1
40A................................. 10/64　　4-8
INNER SLEEVE 5: Red, black and white.
Front: RCA's Elvis LP catalog, most recent
being *Kissin' Cousins* (side 1, row 1, column
6). Back: RCA Elvis EPs and 45s catalog.

RCA Victor (SE)
LSP-1515(e) .... **10/64**　　**40-60**
TOTAL PACKAGE 5: Disc, cover, inner
sleeve.

❑ RCA Victor (SE)
LSP-1515(e).................... 11/68　　20-25
DISC 6: Orange label. Rigid vinyl.
❑ RCA Victor
LSP-1515(e).................... 11/68　　8-10
COVER 6: Verification pending.
❑ RCA Victor 21-112-1
40D................................. 6/68　　4-6
INNER SLEEVE 6: Red, black and white.
Front: RCA's Elvis LP catalog, most recent
being *Elvis' Gold Records, Vol. 4* (side 1, row
4, column 5). Back: RCA's Elvis LP and Twin
Pack Stereo 8 catalog.
May also be found with inner sleeves 40B and
40C. See chapter on inner sleeves for more
information.

RCA Victor (SE)
LSP-1515(e) .... **11/68**　　**35-40**
TOTAL PACKAGE 6: Disc, cover, inner
sleeve.

❑ RCA Victor (SE)
LSP-1515(e)......................... '71　　10-15
DISC 7: Orange label. Flexible vinyl.
❑ RCA Victor
LSP-1515(e).................... 11/68　　4-8
COVER 7: Verification pending.
❑ RCA Victor......................... '70s　　2-4
INNER SLEEVE 7: Black-and-white. Pictures
RCA Elvis catalog front and back. Any of
several sleeves may be found on reissues
from this period.

RCA Victor (SE)
LSP-1515(e) .... '71　　**15-25**
TOTAL PACKAGE 7: Disc, cover, inner
sleeve.

❑ RCA Victor (SE)
LSP-1515(e)........................ '76　　10-15
DISC 8: Tan label.
❑ RCA Victor LSP-1515(e) ..... '76　　4-8
COVER 8: Verification pending.
❑ RCA Victor......................... '70s　　2-4
INNER SLEEVE 8: Black-and-white. Pictures
RCA Elvis catalog front and back. Any of
several sleeves may be found on reissues
from this period.

RCA Victor (SE)
LSP-1515(e) .... '76　　**15-25**
TOTAL PACKAGE 8: Disc, cover, inner
sleeve.

❑ RCA (SE) LSP-1515(e) .... '76　　4-6
DISC 9: Black label, dog near top.
❑ RCA LSP-1515(e)................. '76　　4-6
M2WY-4731-9/M2WY-9. Identification numbers are
engraved.
COVER 9: Front: RCA logo and number at
upper left. "Victor" and "Stereo Effect
Reprocessed from Monophonic" at upper
right. "SER" at bottom left. Blue border around
cover. Back: Has note about RCA stereo
records at top center.
❑ RCA Victor......................... '70s　　2-4
INNER SLEEVE 9: Black-and-white. Pictures
RCA Elvis catalog front and back. Any of
several sleeves may be found on reissues
from this period.

RCA (SE) LSP-1515(e) ..... '76　　**10-18**
TOTAL PACKAGE 9: Disc, cover, inner
sleeve.

❑ RCA Victor (SE)
AFL1-1515(e)...................... '77　　3-5
DISC 10: Black label, dog near top.
❑ RCA AFL1-1515(e)............... '77　　3-5
COVER 10: Reflects prefix change.
❑ RCA Victor......................... '70s　　2-4
INNER SLEEVE 10: Black-and-white.
Pictures RCA Elvis catalog front and back.
Any of several sleeves may be found on
reissues from this period. Includes copies with
a sticker bearing the "AFL1" prefix, wrapped
around cover at top of spine.

RCA Victor (SE)
AFL1-1515(e) .... '77　　**8-15**
TOTAL PACKAGE 10: Disc, cover, inner
sleeve.

On both covers and labels, the electronically
reprocessed stereo designation "(e)" may not
appear following every usage of the selection
number.

Side 1
Mean Woman Blues
(Let Me Be Your) Teddy Bear
Loving You
Got a Lot o' Livin' to Do
Lonesome Cowboy
Hot Dog
Party

Side 2
Blueberry Hill
True Love
Don't Leave Me Now
Have I Told You Lately That I Love You
I Need You So

LOVING YOU

❑ Gold Suit GSR-10001: Bootleg. Listed for identification only.

LOVING YOU / G.I. BLUES (Picture Disc)

❑ RCA Victor (M) LPM-1515........   4000-6000
DISC 1: Experimental picture disc. Photo imbedded in vinyl on both sides is the front cover art of a *G.I. Blues* LP. This one-of-a-kind test pressing was discovered by Ed Bonja (Elvis' Tour Manager and photographer in the '70s), while cleaning out Col. Parker's office. When asked about it, Parker indicated it was a demo being considered for a promotion, but was rejected because he did not like the way the disc cut off Elvis' name and the movie title. Plays five songs from the standard *Loving You* album (*Loving You; Got a Lot o' Livin' to Do; Lonesome Cowboy; Blueberry Hill;* and *True Love*). The remaining five tracks are assorted instrumentals, by unidentified artists that have nothing whatsoever to do with Elvis. Believed to have been produced in the early to mid-'60s, this may be the very first RCA picture disc. The cover containing this disc is described under *Loving You*, as "Cover 2."
AL - BL. Identification numbers are stamped on respective sides.

RCA Victor (M) LPM-1515.....   4000-6000
   TOTAL PACKAGE 1: Disc, cover.

Side 1
Loving You
Got a Lot o' Livin' to Do
Lonesome Cowboy
Instrumental (Title not yet known)
Theme from "The Three Penny Opera" (Moritat)

Side 2
Blueberry Hill
True Love
Bei Mir Bist Du Schoen
Tonight (From "West Side Story")
Am I Blue

LOVING YOU RECORDING SESSIONS

❑ Vik EPP-254: Bootleg. Listed for identification only.

MCA MUSIC (4 LPs)

❑ MCA (SP) (No Number)   40-60
DISCS 1: Excerpts of 200 songs by various artists, including five of Elvis songs. Promotional issue only.
COVER/BOX 1: Verification pending.

MCA (SP) (No Number).........   40-60
   TOTAL PACKAGE 1: Discs, cover or box.

MAHALO FROM ELVIS

❑ Pickwick/Camden (ST)
   ACL-7064 ....5/78   8-12
   DISC 1: Black label. Multi-color Pickwick logo at center.
   ONE-A-KEEL ACL-7064-A/A-1-KEEL ACL-7064-B.
   Identification numbers are engraved.
   B-One KEEL ACL-7064-A-1/A-KEEL ACL-7064-B.
   Identification numbers are stamped.
   Three B-KEEL ACL-7064-A-1/A-Two-KEEL ACL-7064-B.
   Identification numbers are engraved.
   B-KEEL ACL-7064-A-1/Two-B-KEEL ACL-7064-B1.
   Identification numbers are engraved.

❑ Pickwick/Camden
   ACL-7064 ....5/78   8-12
   COVER 1: Front: Pickwick logo at upper left, Camden logo and number at upper right. Color, '70s concert Elvis photo. Back: Text and a drawing of some trees.
   INNER SLEEVE 1: Generic Pickwick sleeve. Makes no mention of Elvis or this LP.

Pickwick/Camden (ST)
   ACL-7064 ....5/78   15-25
   TOTAL PACKAGE 1: Disc, cover.

Blue Hawaii, Early Morning Rain, Hawaiian Wedding Song, and *Ku-u-i-po* were recorded in 1973 for the *Aloha from Hawaii Via Satellite* TV special. They are included in the show but are not on the *Aloha from Hawaii via Satellite* soundtrack. *No More,* recorded at the same time as the other songs on side 1, is not used in the TV special.

Side 1
Blue Hawaii
Early Morning Rain
Hawaiian Wedding Song
Ku-u-i-po
No More

Side 2
Relax
Baby, If You'll Give Me All Your Love
One Broken Heart for Sale
So Close, Yet So Far (shown as "So Close, Yet So Far (From Paradise)")
Happy Ending

MAIN EVENT – ELVIS VS. THE BEATLES

❑ Superstar 10: Bootleg. Listed for identification only.

(1957) MARCH OF DIMES GALAXY OF STARS (DISCS FOR DIMES)
Various artists collection

❑ N.F.I.P. (M) GM-8M-0653/
   0654 ....12/56   1700-1800
   DISC 1: White and blue-green label. 16" transcription with 20 entertainers, including Elvis, speaking on behalf of the 1957 March of Dimes campaign. Issued only to radio stations.

COVER 1: None made.

❑ N.F.I.P. GM-8M-0653/
　0654 .... 12/56　　100-200
　INSERT 1: 16 pages of dee jay
　announcements.
　INNER SLEEVE 1: Brown, no printing.

N.F.I.P. (M) GM-8M-0653/
　0654 .... 12/56　　1800-2000
　TOTAL PACKAGE 1: Disc, insert.

Side 1
Howard Miller (Instructions – Not for Broadcast)
Eddie Fisher
Julie London
Denise Lor
Jim Lowe
Mills Brothers
Guy Mitchell
Vaughn Monroe
Elvis Presley
Gale Robbins

Side 2
Pat Boone
Sammy Davis Jr.
Gogi Grant
Bill Hayes
Eartha Kitt
Ray Price
Johnnie Ray
Henri Rene
Dinah Shore
Margaret Whiting
Andy Williams

(1957) MARCH OF DIMES GALAXY OF STARS (DISC JOCKEY INTERVIEWS)

Various artists collection

❑ N.F.I.P. (M) GM-8M-0657/
　0658 .... 12/56　　1700-1800
　DISC 1: White and blue-green label. 16"
　transcription with six vocal acts, including
　Elvis, providing an open-end interview on
　behalf of the 1957 March of Dimes campaign,
　and introducing one of their songs. The Elvis
　track is *Love Me Tender*. Issued only to radio
　stations.
　COVER 1: None made.

❑ N.F.I.P. GM-8M-0657/
　0658 .... 12/56　　50-75
　INSERT 1A: a) Cover letter to Station
　Managers, on National Foundation for
　Infantile Paralysis (N.F.I.P.) letterhead; b)
　Listing of National Committee and State
　Chairmen; c) Five-page script for the open-
　end interview with Elvis Presley.

❑ N.F.I.P. GM-8M-0657/
　0658 .... 12/56　　50-75
　INSERT 1B: Five, five-page scripts for the
　open-end interviews with the other stars on
　this disc: Jill Corey, Andy Williams, Alan Dale,
　Mills Brothers, and Guy Mitchell.
　INNER SLEEVE 1: Brown, no printing.

N.F.I.P. (M) GM-8M-0657/
　0658 .... 12/56　　1800-2100
　TOTAL PACKAGE 1: Disc, inserts.

Side 1
I Love My Baby (Jill Corey)
Love Me Tender (Elvis Presley)
Baby Doll (Andy Williams)

Side 2
Your Love Is My Love (Alan Dale)
Paper Doll (Mills Brothers)
Singing the Blues (Guy Mitchell)

MEMORIES

❑ TAKRL 24911: Bootleg. Listed for
　identification only.

MEMORIES OF CHRISTMAS

❑ RCA Victor (SP)
　CPL1-4395 .... 8/82　　3-5
　DISC 1: Black label, dog near top.
　CPL1-4395-A-1S/CPL1-4395-B-1S. Identification numbers
　are engraved.

❑ RCA CPL1-4395 .... 8/82　　6-8
　COVER 1: Front: Color Elvis photo, circa
　1964 pose. No RCA logo or number shown.
　Back: RCA logo and number at lower right.
　UPC bar code at upper right. Color photo of
　Graceland with Christmas lights.
　INNER SLEEVE 1: White, no printing.

❑ RCA Victor CPL1-4395 ...... 8/82　　6-8
　INSERT 1: Red and white 7" x 9" 1982-83
　calendar, which has a color Elvis photo,
　signed "Season's Greetings, Elvis."

❑ RCA Victor CPL1-4395 ...... 8/82　　3-4
　SHRINK STICKER 1: Announces the
　inclusion of the bonus 1982-83, autographed
　calendar.

RCA Victor (SP)
　CPL1-4395 .... 8/82　　20-25
　TOTAL PACKAGE 1: Disc, cover, insert,
　sticker.

❑ RCA Victor (SP)
　CPL1-4395 .... 8/82　　3-5
　DISC 2: Same as disc 1.

❑ RCA CPL1-4395 .... 8/82　　10-12
　COVER 2: Designate promo. Same as cover
　1, but with "Not for Sale" stamped on back.
　INNER SLEEVE 2: White, no printing.

❑ RCA Victor CPL1-4395 ...... 8/82　　6-8
　INSERT 2: Red and white 7" x 9" 1982-83
　calendar, which has a color Elvis photo,
　signed "Season's Greetings, Elvis."

❑ RCA Victor CPL1-4395 ...... 8/82　　3-4
　SHRINK STICKER 2: Announces the
　inclusion of the bonus 1982-83, autographed
　calendar.

RCA Victor (SP)
　CPL1-4395 .... 8/82　　25-30
　TOTAL PACKAGE 2: Disc, cover, insert,
　sticker.

Card stock jacket, with printing on cover – not
on slicks.

Side 1
O Come, All Ye Faithful (Unreleased take)
Silver Bells
I'll Be Home on Christmas Day (Unreleased take)
Blue Christmas
Santa Claus Is Back in Town

Side 2
Merry Christmas Baby (Unreleased, complete version)
If Everyday Was Like Christmas
Christmas Message by Elvis/Silent Night

MEMORIES OF ELVIS (3 LPs)

Complete three-hour radio show. All discs in
this set, listed individually below, have a silver
label with black print. All identification
numbers are engraved. Issued only to
subscribing radio stations.

❏ Creative Radio 1A/1B 10/87   15-20
DISC 1:
MEM-1-A L-27586/MEM-1-B L-27586X.

❏ Creative Radio 2A/2B 10/87   15-20
DISC 2:
MEM-2-A L-27586/MEM-2-B L-27586X.

❏ Creative Radio 3A/3B 10/87   15-20
DISC 3:
MEM-3-A L-27586/MEM-3-B L-27586X.

COVER 1: Single pocket. White, no printing.

❏ Creative Radio 10/87   5-10
INSERT 1: Three pages of programming
information and cue sheets.

Creative Radio (SP) 10/87   50-65
TOTAL PACKAGE 1: Discs, inserts.

Disc 1
Side 1
Elvis Medley
I Want You, I Need You, I Love You
Love Me Tender
Blue Suede Shoes
Harbor Lights
That's All Right
Wear My Ring Around Your Neck

Side 2
I Can't Stop Loving You
An American Trilogy
It's Now Or Never
Are You Lonesome Tonight
What'd I Say
Heartbreak Hotel

Disc 2
Side 1
The Wonder of You
All Shook Up
Lawdy, Miss Clawdy
Kentucky Rain
Too Much
I'll Remember You
Rock Medley
If I Can Dream

Side 2
Treat Me Nice
Can't Help Falling in Love
Hound Dog
Steamroller Blues
Don't Cry Daddy
Return to Sender

In the Ghetto
Disc 3
Side 1
Love Me
Elvis Medley
(Now and Then There's) A Fool Such As I
Good Luck Charm
There Goes My Everything
(You're the) Devil in Disguise
A Big Hunk O' Love
Suspicious Minds

Side 2
Follow That Dream
I Got a Woman
Impossible Dream
(Marie's the Name) His Latest Flame
You Gave Me a Mountain
Don't Be Cruel
Memories

MEMORIES OF ELVIS (4 LPs)

Complete four-hour radio show. Issued only to
subscribing radio stations.

❏ United Stations 8/89   40-60
DISCS: Four, labeled "Hour 1, Side 1" through
"Hour 4, Side 2."

❏ United Stations 8/89
COVER 1: Verification pending. May have
been a generic cover, picturing logos of other
United shows.

❏ United Stations 8/89   5-10
INSERT 1: Four pages of programming
information and cue sheets.

United Stations (SP) 8/89   45-70
TOTAL PACKAGE 1: Discs, cover, inserts.

Disc 1
Side 1
Interview (Charlie Daniels)
The Elvis Presley Medley
Interview (Mac Davis)
That's All Right (shown as "That's All Right Mama")
Baby Let's Play House
Interview (Johnny Cash)
Heartbreak Hotel
I was the One
Interview (John Lennon)
I Want You, I Need You, I Love You
Blue Suede Shoes
Interview (Freddy Fender)
Don't Be Cruel
Hound Dog
Interview (Paul McCartney)

Disc 1
Side 2
Love Me Tender
Any Way You Want Me
Interview (Little Richard)
Too Much
Playing for Keeps (shown as "Playin' For Keeps")
Interview (Sonny James)
All Shook Up
That's When Your Heartaches Begin
Interview (Tammy Wynette)
Teddy Bear
Loving You

Disc 2

Side 1

Interview (Jim Ed Brown)
Jailhouse Rock
Treat Me Nice
Interview (June Carter Cash)
Don't
I Beg of You
Interview (Carl Perkins)
Wear My Ring Around Your Neck
Hard Headed Woman
Interview (Conway Twitty)
I Got Stung
One Night

Disc 2

Side 2

Interview (Tom Jones)
(Now and Then There's) A Fool Such As I (shown as
    "Now and Then")
A Big Hunk O' Love (shown as "Big Hunk O' Love")
Interview (Bo Diddley)
Stuck on You
Fame and Fortune
Interview - John Schneider
It's Now or Never
A Mess of Blues
Interview (Johnny Tillotson)
Are You Lonesome Tonight
I Gotta Know

Disc 3

Side 1

Interview (Oak Ridge Boys)
Surrender
Interview (Terry Stafford)
Wooden Heart
I Feel So Bad
Interview (Fabian)
Little Sister
(Marie's the Name) His Latest Flame
Interview (Pat Boone)
Can't Help Falling in Love
Rock-A-Hula Baby

Disc 3

Side 2

Interview (Charlie Daniels)
Good Luck Charm
Anything That's Part of You
Interview (Paul McCartney)
Follow That Dream
She's Not You
Interview (Don Everly)
Return to Sender
Where Do You Come From
Interview (Bill Medley)
One Broken Heart For Sale
(You're the) Devil in Disguise
Interview (Johnny Rivers)
Kissin' Cousins
Viva Las Vegas
Interview (Roger Miller)
Ain't That Loving You Baby
Ask Me

Disc 4

Side 1

Interview (Roy Orbison)
Crying in the Chapel
If I Can Dream
Interview (Mac Davis)
In the Ghetto
Suspicious Minds
Interview (Don McLean)

Don't Cry Daddy
Kentucky Rain
Interview (Ray Peterson)
The Wonder of You
You Don't Have to Say You Love Me

Disc 4

Side 2

Interview (Merle Haggard)
Burning Love
Separate Ways
Interview (Chris Lowe)
Always on My Mind
Promised Land (shown as "Promise Land")
Interview (Brenda Lee)
Way Down
My Way

MEMORIES OF ELVIS (A LASTING TRIBUTE TO THE KING OF ROCK 'N' ROLL (5 LPs)

Black label, dog near top. Boxed set made for
Candlelite Music and sold by mail order.
Discs, all of which have a slightly shortened
subtitle, *Memories of Elvis* (Tribute to the
King), are listed separately below.

❑ RCA Special Products
   DPL5-0347-1 .... '78   3-5
   DISC 1:
   DPL5-0347A-1/DPL5-0347B-1.

❑ RCA Special Products
   DPL5-0347-2 .... '78   3-5
   DISC 2:
   DPL5-0347C-1/DPL5-0347D-1.

❑ RCA Special Products
   DPL5-0347-3 .... '78   3-5
   DISC 3:
   DPL5-0347E-1/DPL5-0347F-1.

❑ RCA Special Products
   DPL5-0347-4 .... '78   3-5
   DISC 4:
   DPL5-0347G-1/DPL5-0347H-1.

❑ RCA Special Products
   DPL5-0347-5 .... '78   3-5
   DISC 5:
   DPL5-0347I-1/DPL5-0347J-3.

❑ RCA Special Products
   DPL5-0347 .... '78   15-20
   BOX 1: Slipcover: Front: RCA logo at lower
   right, number at upper right. Candlelite logo at
   upper left. Has artist Robert Charles Howe's
   color rendering of Elvis, from the '50s, '60s
   and '70s. Back: Blank. Record case: Text
   only. White with black print.
   INNER SLEEVES 1: White, no printing.

❑ RCA Special Products
   DPL5-0347-5 .... '78   5-10
   INSERT 1A: Duotone, 16-page *Musical
   History's Finest Hour* booklet.

❑ RCA Special Products
   DPL5-0347-5 .... '78   5-10
   INSERT 1B: LP-size print of the Howe portrait
   used on front cover of box. Included only with
   the first 5,000 sets.

RCA Special Products (SP)

DPL5-0347 .... '78   60-100

TOTAL PACKAGE 1: Discs, box, inserts.

Disc 1

Side 1

One Broken Heart for Sale
Young and Beautiful
A Mess of Blues
The Next Step Is Love
I Gotta Know
Love Letters

Side 2

When My Blue Moon Turns to Gold Again
If Everyday Was Like Christmas
Steamroller Blues
Anyway You Want Me (That's How I Will Be)
(Such An) Easy Question
That's When Your Heartaches Begin

Disc 2

Side 3

Kentucky Rain
Money Honey
My Way
Girls! Girls! Girls!
Lonely Man
U.S. Male

Side 4

My Wish Came True
Kiss Me Quick
As Long As I Have You
Bossa Nova Baby
I Forgot to Remember to Forget
Such a Night

Disc 3

Side 5

I Really Don't Want to Know
Doncha' Think It's Time
His Hand in Mine
That's All Right
Nothingville (Medley)
Baby, I Don't Care

Side 6

Playing for Keeps
King of the Whole Wide World
Don't Ask Me Why
Flaming Star
I'm Left, You're Right, She's Gone
What'd I Say

Disc 4

Side 7

There Goes My Everything
Patch It Up
Reconsider Baby
Good Rockin' Tonight
You Gave Me a Mountain
Rock-A-Hula Baby

Side 8

Mean Woman Blues
It Hurts Me
Fever
I Want to Be Free
Viva Las Vegas
Old Shep

Disc 5

Side 9

Anything That's Part of You
My Baby Left Me

Wild in the Country
Memphis, Tennessee
Don't Leave Me Now
I Feel So Bad

Side 10

Separate Ways
Polk Salad Annie
Fame and Fortune
Trying to Get to You
I've Lost You
King Creole

Also see *THE GREATEST SHOW ON EARTH*

MEMPHIS MEMORIES

❑ Memories 69 ST-1697: Bootleg. Listed for
identification only.

MEMPHIS RECORD (2 LPs)

❑ RCA Victor (ST)

6221-1-R 7/87   4-5

DISCS 1: Black label, dog near top.

(Disc 1) 6621-1-R-A-1/6621-1-R-B-1. (Disc 2) 6621-1-R-C-10/6621-1-R-D-10. Identification numbers are engraved. Sides are shown as "A," "B," "C" and "D."

(Disc 1) 6621-1-R-A-4/6621-1-R-B-1. (Disc 2) 6621-1-R-C-12/6621-1-R-D-12. Identification numbers are engraved. Sides are shown as "1," "2," "3" and "4." Print is smaller than on labels using "A," "B," "C" and "D."

❑ RCA 6621-1-R 7/87   4-5

COVER 1: Double pocket. Configured, when
opened, to simulate two 25" x 12½"
newspaper pages. Other than red letters on
"Elvis" and "Extra," cover is black-and-white,
including five late '60s Elvis photos.

❑ RCA/BMG.........................7/87   2-4

INNER SLEEVES 1: Mustard with black print,
with "A 1987 Commemorative Release" on
each side.

❑ RCA/BMG.........................'87   8-10

INSERT 1A: Color, 15" x 22" Elvis signature
poster. Has "Sincerely Yours, Elvis" at lower
left and RCA logo and number "POS-2" at
lower right.

❑ RCA/BMG.........................7/87   2-4

INSERT 1B: Black-and-white, 8" x 10" flyer;
ad for *Elvis Talks* on one side and four "1987
Commemorative Collection" LPs pictured on
reverse.

❑ RCA 6621-1-R 7/87   3-5

SHRINK STICKER 1: Circular, gold foil
"Digitally Remastered" sticker, which has
selection number.

RCA Victor (ST)

6221-1-R......................7/87   25-35

**TOTAL PACKAGE 1: Discs, cover, inner
sleeves, inserts, sticker.**

❑ RCA Victor (ST)

6221-1-R 7/87   4-5

DISCS 2: Same as discs 1.

❑ RCA 6621-1-R 7/87   8-10

COVER 2: Designate promo. Same as cover
1, but with "Not for Sale" stamped on back.

❏ RCA/BMG..........................7/87   2-4
  INNER SLEEVES 2: Mustard with black print,
  with "A 1987 Commemorative Release" on
  each side.

❏ RCA/BMG..........................'87   8-10
  INSERT 2A: Color, 15" x 22" Elvis signature
  poster. Has "Sincerely Yours, Elvis" at lower
  left and RCA logo and number "POS-2" at
  lower right.

❏ RCA/BMG..........................7/87   2-4
  INSERT 2B: Black-and-white, 8" x 10" flyer;
  ad for *Elvis Talks* on one side and four "1987
  Commemorative Collection" LPs pictured on
  reverse.

❏ RCA 6621-1-R...................7/87   3-5
  SHRINK STICKER 2: Circular, gold foil
  "Digitally Remastered" sticker, which has
  selection number.

RCA Victor (ST)
  6621-1-R......................7/87   30-40
  TOTAL PACKAGE 2: Discs, cover, inner
  sleeves, inserts, sticker.

After Loving You, while listed correctly on
covers, is shown as "After Lovin' You" on the
labels. Card stock jacket, with printing on
cover – not on slicks.

Disc 1

Side A (1)
Stranger in My Own Home Town
Power of My Love
Only the Strong Survive
Any Day Now
Suspicious Minds

Side B (2)
Long Black Limousine
Wearin' That Loved On Look
I'll Hold You in My Heart
After Loving You
Rubberneckin'
I'm Movin' On

Disc 2

Side C (3)
Gentle on My Mind
True Love Travels on a Gravel Road
It Keeps Right on A-Hurtin'
You'll Think of Me
Mama Liked the Roses
Don't Cry Daddy

Side D (4)
In the Ghetto
The Fair Is Moving On
Inherit the Wind
Kentucky Rain
Without Love
Who Am I

MEMPHIS, TENNESSEE

❏ Original Audifon 67670: Bootleg. Listed for
  identification only.
❏ Rock Sound Fifty Seven M.T. 57-01:
  Bootleg. Listed for identification only.

**MICHELOB PRESENTS HIGHLIGHTS OF
ELVIS MEMORIES: see** *ELVIS MEMORIES
(MICHELOB PRESENTS HIGHLIGHTS OF
ELVIS MEMORIES)*

MILLION DOLLAR QUARTET (COMPLETE MILLION DOLLAR QUARTET SESSION)

*(Elvis Presley/Carl Perkins/Jerry Lee
Lewis/JohnnyCash)*

❏ RCA (M) 2023-1-R.............3/90   8-10
  DISC 1: Red label, black print with lightning
  bolt RCA logo. Also shows a nameless Sun
  Records (78 rpm) label.
  2023-1-R-A-1/2023-1-R-B-1. Identification numbers are
  engraved.

❏ RCA 2023-1-R....................3/90   8-10
  COVER 1: Front: No logo or number. Four
  colorized (blue, pink, yellow, and green tint)
  Quartet session photos – all of the same shot.
  Back: RCA, BMG and Sun logos and number
  at lower right. UPC bar code at lower right.
  Four colorized (blue, pink, yellow, and green
  tint) Elvis (circa 1956) photos.

❏ RCA 2023-1-R....................3/90   1-2
  INNER SLEEVE 1: Front: Five black-and-
  white (with pink tint) Quartet, and Elvis (circa
  1956). RCA, BMG and Sun logos and number
  at lower right. Back: Text only.

❏ RCA 2023-1-R....................3/90   5-10
  INSERT 1: Black-and-white, 8" x 10" glossy of
  the same Quartet photo as on front cover.
  Promotional issue only.

❏ RCA 2023-1-R....................3/90   3-5
  SHRINK STICKER 1: Red with white print.
  Announces "First U.S. Commercial Release"
  of these recordings.

RCA (M) 2023-1-R...........3/90   25-35
  TOTAL PACKAGE 1: Disc, cover, inner
  sleeve, insert, sticker.

❏ RCA (M) 2023-1-R.............3/90   8-10
  DISC 2: Same as disc 1.

❏ RCA 2023-1-R....................3/90   12-15
  COVER 2: Designate promo. Same as cover
  1, but with a ¾-inch notch cut into lower right
  corner.

❏ RCA 2023-1-R....................3/90   1-2
  INNER SLEEVE 2: Front: Five black-and-
  white (with pink tint) Quartet, and Elvis (circa
  1956). RCA, BMG and Sun logos and number
  at lower right. Back: Text only.

❏ RCA 2023-1-R....................3/90   5-10
  INSERT 2: Black-and-white, 8" x 10" glossy of
  the same Quartet photo as on front cover.
  Promotional issue only.

❏ RCA 2023-1-R....................3/90   3-5
  SHRINK STICKER 2: Red with white print.
  Announces "First U.S. Commercial Release"
  of these recordings.

RCA (M) 2023-1-R...........3/90   30-40
  TOTAL PACKAGE 2: Disc, cover, inner
  sleeve, insert, sticker.

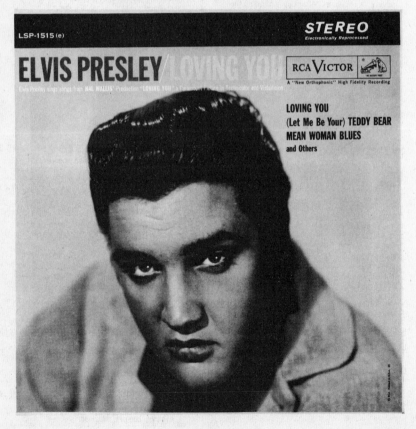

Though Elvis is not the lead vocalist on all of the following tracks, some participation on his part is presumed. Card stock jacket, with printing on cover – not on slicks.

Side A
You Belong to My Heart
When God Dips His Love in My Heart
Just a Little Talk with Jesus
Jesus Walked That Lonesome Valley
I Shall Not Be Moved
(There'll Be) Peace in the Valley (For Me)
Down By the Riverside
I'm in a Crowd But So Alone
Farther Along
Blessed Jesus (Take My Hand)
As We Travel Along the Jericho Road
I Just Can't Make It By Myself
Little Cabin Home on the Hill
Summertime Is Past and Gone
I Hear a Sweet Voice Calling
Sweetheart You Done Me Wrong
Keeper of the Key
Crazy Arms
Don't Forbid Me
Too Much Monkey Business
Brown Eyed Handsome Man
Out of Sight, Out of Mind
Brown Eyed Handsome Man

Side B
Don't Be Cruel
Don't Be Cruel
Paralyzed
Don't Be Cruel
There's No Place like Home
When the Saints Go Marchin' In
Softly and Tenderly
Is It So Strange
That's When Your Heartaches Begin
Brown Eyed Handsome Man
Rip It Up
I'm Gonna Bid My Blues Goodbye
Crazy Arms
That's My Desire
End of the Road
Black Bottom Stomp
You're the Only Star in My Blue Heaven
Elvis [Farewell]

MILLION DOLLAR QUARTET

❏ One Million Dollar OMD-001: Bootleg. Listed for identification only.

❏ S 5001: Bootleg. Listed for identification only.

MILLION DOLLAR QUARTET, VOLUME ONE

(Elvis Presley/Carl Perkins/Jerry Lee Lewis/Johnny Cash)

❏ Sun 1008 .... 11/77   200-300
COVER 1: Only slicks exist – no discs made. Actual covers were never fabricated. Front: Sun logo and number at upper right. Has black-and-white photo of the Quartet in front of a large Sun logo. Back is blank.

Sun 1008 .... 11/77   200-300
TOTAL PACKAGE 1: Cover slick.

MISTLETOE AND MEMORIES
Various artists collection
❏ RCA (ST) 8372-1-R .... '88   5-10
DISC 1: Red label, black and silver print with lightning bolt RCA logo.
8372-1-R-A-1S/8372-1-R-B-1S. Identification numbers are engraved.

❏ RCA 8372-1-R .... '88   5-10
COVER 1: Front: No logo or number. Back: RCA and BMG logos and number at lower right. UPC bar code at upper right.
INNER SLEEVE 1: White, no printing.

RCA (ST) 8372-1-R .... '88   10-20
TOTAL PACKAGE 1: Disc, cover.

Card stock jacket, with printing on cover – not on slicks.

Side A
Santa Claus (I Still Believe in You) (Alabama)
Blue Christmas (K.T. Oslin)
O Come, All Ye Faithful (Elvis Presley)
Silent Night (Kenny Rogers)
White Christmas (Dolly Parton)

Side B
Silver Bells (The Judds)
It's Not Christmas (Ronnie Milsap)
This Time of Year (Michael Johnson)
In a Manger (Baillie and the Boys)

MONOLOGUE LP
❏ Bullet: Bootleg. Listed for identification only.

MOODY BLUE
DISC 1: None made.
❏ RCA AFK1-2428 ....5/77   3500-5000
COVER 1: Only slicks exist of this item. Finished cardboard covers were not made because the wrong prefix was printed on the slicks. "AFK" indicates a cassette, not a record album. All but three slicks – saved as souvenirs – were shredded. The three were first sold in Feb;uary 1978. The reworked cover is inexplicably different and visually inferior. The most noticeable change is that Elvis' photo has been reduced from 7½" tall to just 3". Also, his right hand does not show on this cover. On the released edition (see cover 4) Elvis' right hand shows but is awkwardly positioned. Strangely, every appearance we've seen of *Moody Blue* on an RCA inner sleeve pictures this slick and not the one actually manufactured into a cover. Slick is printed on one side only.

RCA AFK1-2428 .... 5/77   3500-5000
TOTAL PACKAGE 1: Cover slick.

❏ RCA (ST) AFL1-2428 ....5/77   1000-2000
DISC 2: Colored vinyl – any color other than blue or black. Includes, but not limited to: white, red, green, yellow, gold, as well as combinations of colors. All were experimental or sample pressings of some sort. None of these were intended for sale or distribution. Black label, dog near top.
COVER 2: None made.

RCA (ST) AFL1-2428 ...... 5/77   1000-2000
TOTAL PACKAGE 2: Disc.

❑ RCA (ST) AFL1-2428 ....5/77   1000-2000
DISC 3: Picture disc. Price is for any *Moody Blue* picture disc, all of which were made under the same conditions as outlined for disc 2.
COVER 3: None made.

RCA (ST) AFL1-2428 ...... 5/77   1000-2000
TOTAL PACKAGE 3: Disc.

❑ RCA (ST) AFL1-2428 ....6/77   '3-5
DISC 4: Blue vinyl. Black label, dog near top.
AFL1-2428-A-1S/AFL1-2428-B-2S. Identification numbers are engraved. Also has "Masterfonics GAM" engraved on both sides.
AFL1-2428-A-2S/AFL1-2428-B-2S. Identification numbers are engraved. Also has "Masterfonics GAM" engraved on both sides.

❑ RCA AFL1-2428 ....6/77   3-5
COVER 4: Corrected printing. Front: Number at upper right. Color Elvis photo is three inches tall, and his right hand is shown (see cover 1). Unlike cover 1, most of this cover is wasted. Back: RCA logo and number at lower right. Color Elvis photo.

❑ RCA Victor 21-112-1
PT 54E 4/77   2-4
INNER SLEEVE 4: Black-and-white. Pictures RCA's Elvis LP catalog front and back, most recent being *The Sun Sessions* (side 2, row 1, column 1). May also be found with inner sleeve 54F.

❑ RCA AFL1-2428-1 ....6/77   1-2
SHRINK STICKER 4A: Blue, white print. Reads: "The Blue Album." Has selection number at bottom.

❑ RCA AFL1-2428-2 ....6/77   1-2
SHRINK STICKER 4B: Blue, white print. Reads: "Contains the Hits *Moody Blue* and *Way Down*." Has number at bottom.

RCA (ST) AFL1-2428 ...... 6/77   10-18
TOTAL PACKAGE 4: Disc, cover, inner sleeve, stickers.

❑ RCA (ST) AFL1-2428 ....6/77   3-5
DISC 5: Same as disc 4.

❑ RCA AFL1-2428 ....6/77   5-10
COVER 5: Designate promo. Same as cover 4, but with "Not for Sale" stamped on back.

❑ RCA Victor 21-112-1
PT 54E 4/77   2-4
INNER SLEEVE 5: Black-and-white. Pictures RCA's Elvis LP catalog front and back, most recent being *The Sun Sessions* (side 2, row 1, column 1). May also be found with inner sleeve 54F.

❑ RCA AFL1-2428-1 ....6/77   1-2
SHRINK STICKER 5A: Blue, white print. Reads: "The Blue Album." Has selection number at bottom.

❑ RCA AFL1-2428-2 ....6/77   1-2
SHRINK STICKER 5B: Blue, white print. Reads: "Contains the Hits *Moody Blue*" and "*Way Down*." Has number at bottom.

RCA (ST) AFL1-2428 ...... 6/77   18-25
TOTAL PACKAGE 5: Disc, cover, inner sleeve, stickers.

❑ RCA (ST) AFL1-2428 ....7/77   150-200
DISC 6: Black vinyl. Black label, dog near top.
AFL1-2428-A-1S/AFL1-2428-B-2S. Identification numbers are engraved. Also has "Masterfonics GAM" engraved on both sides. Black vinyl copies with a tan label are Canadian pressings.

❑ RCA AFL1-2428 ....7/77   3-5
COVER 6: Same as cover 4.

❑ RCA Victor 21-112-1
PT 54E 4/77   2-4
INNER SLEEVE 6: Black-and-white. Pictures RCA's Elvis LP catalog front and back, most recent being *The Sun Sessions* (side 2, row 5, column 1). May also be found with inner sleeve 54F.

RCA (ST) AFL1-2428 ...... 7/77   150-200
TOTAL PACKAGE 6: Disc, cover, inner sleeve.

❑ RCA Victor (ST)
AQL1-2428 ....'80s   8-10
DISC 7: Black vinyl. Black label, dog near top.

❑ RCA AQL1-2428................'80s   8-10
AQL1-2428-A-32/AQL1-2428-B-32.
COVER 7: Reflects prefix change.

❑ RCA Victor..........................'70s   2-4
INNER SLEEVE 7: Black-and-white. Pictures RCA Elvis catalog front and back. Any of several sleeves may be found on reissues from this period.

RCA Victor (ST)
AQL1-2428 .... '80s   20-25
TOTAL PACKAGE 7: Disc, cover, inner sleeve.

Side A
Unchained Melody
If You Love Me (Let Me Know)
Little Darlin'
He'll Have to Go
Let Me Be There

Side B
Way Down
Pledging My Love
Moody Blue
She Thinks I Still Care
It's Easy for You

MOVIE SPOTS (Film Commercials Made for Radio Stations)

Most of Elvis films had specially produced radio spots that were supplied by the movie studio to radio stations on 7", 10", and 12" discs. These often contained an assortment of announcements for the film, usually made in 10, 20, 30, and 60 second lengths. Most movie spots have excerpts of Elvis songs from the film being advertised. Although prices will vary – with higher values attached to the older releases, especially pre-1960 ones – these discs will usually fall into the $200 to $400 range for near-mint copies.

Ones containing more of Elvis and less of some pitchman are more valuable than those where the reverse is the case.

MOVING AHEAD WITH MUSIC (2 LPs)
Various artists collection

❑ Pickwick (S) CL-001 .... '70s   15-20
  DISCS 1: Black label. Multi-color Pickwick logo at center. Promotional issue only. Sampler of Pickwick LPs, including *Almost in Love* and *Burning Love and Hits from His Movies*. Has two Elvis tracks: *U.S. Male* and *Burning Love*.

❑ Pickwick CL-001 .... '70s   15-20
  COVER 1: Double pocket. Front: Still life scene, no artists pictured. Inside Panels: Pictures Pickwick LPs, including *Burning Love and Hits from His Movies*.
  INNER SLEEVE 1: Generic Pickwick. No mention of Elvis or this LP.

Pickwick (S) CL-001 .... '70s   30-40
  TOTAL PACKAGE 1: Discs, cover.

MUSIC YOU CAN'T FORGET
Various artists collection

❑ GSS (M) CC-167 .... '70s   15-20
  DISC 1: Show No. 167 in a public service series sponsored by the Social Security Administration and hosted by Carol Channing. Included in this show are *Love Me Tender*, *Spanish Eyes*, *That's All Right*, and *Don't Be Cruel* by Elvis.

❑ GSS CC-167 .... '70s   15-20
  COVER 1: Verification pending.

GSS (M) CC-167 .... '70s   30-40
  TOTAL PACKAGE 1: Disc.

MY WAY, VOLUME 1 (CHARLOTTE, NORTH CAROLINA FEBRUARY 21, 1977)

❑ Presleyana PRP-1987-88-1: Bootleg. Listed for identification only.

NASHVILLE OUTTAKES & EARLY INTERVIEWS

❑ Wizardo 312: Bootleg. Listed for identification only.

NATIONAL MUSIC SURVEY
Various artists collections.

❑ National Music Survey (S)   10-15
  DISC 1: Price range is for any individual disc containing at least one Elvis track.

❑ National Music Survey (S)   25-35
  COMPLETE SET 1: Single pocket set of three LPs. Each is a complete three-hour, weekly radio show with three pages of cue sheets and program notes. Issued only to subscribing radio stations. Price range is for any complete set containing at least one Elvis track.

1954-1955 THE BEGINNING see *BEGINNING (1954-1955)*

1955 SUN DAYS

❑ Sun 1009 ....11/77   200-300
  COVER 1: Only slicks exist – no discs made. Actual covers were never fabricated. Front: Sun logo and number at upper right. Lists the artists planned for this LP: *Elvis Presley*, Charlie Rich, Jerry Lee Lewis, Carl Perkins, Roy Orbison, and Johnny Cash. Also has a large Sun logo. Back is blank.

Sun 1009 ....11/77   200-300
  TOTAL PACKAGE 1: Cover slick.

1961 HAWAII BENEFIT CONCERT

❑ Golden Archives GA-200: Bootleg. Listed for identification only.

NOVEMBER / DECEMBER SAMPLER 59-44 thru 59-47
Various artists collection

❑ RCA Victor (SP)
  SPS-33-57 ....11/59   600-750
  DISC 1: Black label, "Living Stereo" at bottom. Various artists sampler. Promotional issue only.
  K2NY-5894-1S/K2NY-5895-1S.
  COVER 1: None made.
  INNER SLEEVE 1: White, no printing.

RCA Victor (SP)
  SPS-33-57 ....11/59   600-750
  TOTAL PACKAGE 1: Disc.

Side 1
My Tane (sic) (Jerry Byrd)
It Could Happen to You (Lena Horne)
Kalamazoo (New Glenn Miller Qrchestra)
Oklahoma Medley (Frankie Carle)
San Antonio Rose (Ames Brothers)
I Shall Not Be Moved (Kay Starr)
Comes Love (Marty Gold's Orchestra)

Side 2
I Beg of You (Elvis Presley)
I'm Sitting on Top of the World (Dave Gardner)
Camp Meetin' Time (Del Wood)
At the Jazz Band Ball (Dukes of Dixieland)
I Know That You Know (Chet Atkins)
Cha-Con-Cha (Tito Puente's Orchestra)
Riff Blues (Ray Martin and His Orchestra)

NUMBER ONE HITS

❏ RCA Victor (SP)

6382-1-R ....7/87　　　3-5

DISC 1: Black label, dog near top.

6382-1-R-A-1/6382-1-R-B-1. Identification numbers are engraved. Some songwriter credits are on a second line, under titles.

6382-1-RA-5/6382-1-RB-5. Identification numbers are engraved.

All songwriter credits are on same line as titles.

6382-1-RA-9/6382-1-RB-9. Identification numbers are engraved.

Some songwriter credits are on a second line, under titles.

❏ RCA 6382-1-R ....7/87　　　3-5

COVER 1: Front: No label or number shown. Color 1956 Elvis photo. Back: RCA logo and UPC bar code at lower right. Number appears only on spine. Color Elvis photo is a reduction (2" x 3") of the one on front.

❏ RCA/BMG..........................7/87　　　1-2

INNER SLEEVE 1: Mustard with black print, with "A 1987 Commemorative Release" on each side.

❏ RCA/BMG..........................7/87　　　8-10

INSERT 1A: Color 15" x 22" Elvis signature poster. Has "Sincerely Yours, Elvis" at lower left and RCA logo and number "POS-2" at lower right.

❏ RCA/BMG..........................7/87　　　2-4

INSERT 1B: Black-and-white 8" x 10" flyer; ad for *Elvis Talks* on one side and four "1987 Commemorative Collection" LPs pictured on reverse.

❏ RCA 6382-1-R ....7/87　　　3-5

SHRINK STICKER 1: Circular, gold foil "Digitally Remastered" sticker, which has selection number.

RCA Victor (SP)

6382-1-R ....7/87　　　20-30

TOTAL PACKAGE 1: Disc, cover, inner sleeve, sticker, inserts.

❏ RCA Victor (SP)

6382-1-R ....7/87　　　3-5

DISCS 2: Same as disc 1.

❏ RCA 6621-1-R...................7/87　　　8-10

COVER 2: Designate promo. Same as cover 1, but with "Not for Sale" stamped on back.

❏ RCA/BMG..........................7/87　　　1-2

INNER SLEEVE 2: Mustard with black print, with "A 1987 Commemorative Release" on each side.

❏ RCA/BMG..........................7/87　　　8-10

INSERT 2A: Color 15" x 22" Elvis signature poster. Has "Sincerely Yours, Elvis" at lower left and RCA logo and number "POS-2" at lower right.

❏ RCA/BMG..........................7/87　　　2-4

INSERT 2B: Black-and-white 8" x 10" flyer; ad for *Elvis Talks* on one side and four "1987 Commemorative Collection" LPs pictured on reverse.

❏ RCA 6382-1-R ....7/87　　　3-5

SHRINK STICKER 2: Circular, gold foil "Digitally Remastered" sticker, which has selection number.

RCA Victor (SP)

6382-1-R......................7/87　　　25-35

TOTAL PACKAGE 2: Disc, cover, inner sleeve, sticker, inserts.

Card stock jacket, with printing on cover – not on slicks.

Side A

Heartbreak Hotel
I Want You, I Need You, I Love You
Hound Dog
Don't Be Cruel
Love Me Tender
Too Much
All Shook Up
(Let Me Be Your) Teddy Bear
Jailhouse Rock

Side B

Don't
Hard Headed Woman
A Big Hunk O' Love
Stuck on You
It's Now or Never
Are You Lonesome Tonight
Surrender
Good Luck Charm
Suspicious Minds

OCTOBER CHRISTMAS SAMPLER
59-40-41

Various artists collection

❏ RCA Victor (SP)

SPS-33-54 ....10/59　　　600-750

DISC 1: Black label, "Living Stereo" at bottom. Various artists sampler. Promotional issue only.

K2NY-5481-1S/K2NY-2230-1S.

COVER 1: None made.

INNER SLEEVE 1: White, no printing.

RCA Victor (SP)

SPS-33-54 ....10/59　　　600-750

TOTAL PACKAGE 1: Disc.

All songs except Elvis' *Blue Christmas* and *Have Yourself a Merry Little Christmas* (Gisele MacKenzie) are true stereo.

Side 1

Blue Christmas (Elvis Presley)
Have Yourself a Merry Little Christmas (Gisele MacKenzie)
White Christmas (John Klein)
Blue Christmas (Esquivel)
Winter Wonderland (Melachrino Strings)
Santa Claus Is Comin' to Town (Ralph Hunter)

Side 2

O Little Town of Bethlehem (George Beverly Shea)
Home for the Holidays (Perry Como)
What a Friend We Have in Jesus (Johnson Family)
A Christmas Festival (Boston Pops)
O Christmas Tree (Mario Lanza)
Silent Night (Giorgio Tozzi & Rosalind Elias)

OCTOBER 1960 POPULAR STEREO SAMPLER

Various artists collection

❑ RCA Victor (ST)

　SPS 33-96 .... 10/60 　　500-750
　DISC 1: Black label, "Living Stereo" at bottom.
　L2NY-3813-1S/L2NY-3813-1S.
　COVER 1: None made.
　INNER SLEEVE 1: White, no printing.

RCA Victor (ST)

　SPS 33-96 .... 10/60 　　500-750
　TOTAL PACKAGE 1: Disc.

Side 1
Flowers for the Cats (Shorty Rogers)
Am I That Easy to Forget (Skeeter Davis)
The Battle of San Juan Hill (Jimmy Driftwood)
Sunrise Serenade; Beg Your Pardon (Frankie Carle)
Little Drummer Boy (Hugo & Luigi)
Tonight Is So Right for Love (Elvis Presley)
Side 2
One More Dance (Mariam Makeba)
And the Angels Sing (Ames Brothers)
Lullaby of Broadway (Schory's Ensemble)
Zion Stands (George Beverly Shea)
On That Happy Golden Shore (Blackwood Brothers)
There's a Promise (Lyman)
I Need Thee Every Hour (Laymen Singers)
Wonderful (Nashville All-Stars)

OCTOBER 1960 POPULAR STEREO SAMPLER

Various artists collection

❑ RCA Victor (ST)

　SPS 33-9 .... 10/60 　　500-750
　DISC 1: Black label, "Living Stereo" at bottom.
　Canadian issue only. Contents same as U.S.
　version, though not in exact same sequence.
　1OL2NY-1156-1S/1OL2NY-1156-1S.
　COVER 1: None made.
　INNER SLEEVE 1: White, no printing.

RCA Victor (ST)

　SPS 33-9 .... 10/60 　　500-750
　TOTAL PACKAGE 1: Disc.

OCTOBER '61 POP SAMPLER

Various artists collection

❑ RCA Victor (ST)

　SPS 33-141 .... 10/61 　　500-750
　DISC 1: Black label without dog. Has "Living
　Stereo" at bottom. Various artists sampler.
　Promotional issue only.
　M2NY-3177-1S/M2NY-3178-1S.
　COVER 1: None made.
　INNER SLEEVE 1: White, no printing.

RCA Victor (ST)

　SPS 33-141 .... 10/61 　　500-750
　TOTAL PACKAGE 1: Disc.

Side 1
My Blue Heaven (Henri Rene's Orchestra)
Jerico (Ray Martin's Orchestra)
I'm Waiting for Ships That Never Come In (Jim Reeves)

Don't Get Around Much Anymore (Sam Cooke)
Jingle Bells (Chet Atkins)
Side 2
Blue Hawaii (Elvis Presley)
You Go to My Head (New Glenn Miller Orchestra)
Unchained Melody (Floyd Cramer)
Say a Prayer (Don McNeill)
Rock of Ages (George Beverly Shea)
The Way of the Cross (Blackwood Brothers)

OFFICIAL GRAMMY AWARDS ARCHIVE COLLECTION (VOL. 4, THE GREAT SINGERS)

Various artists collection

❑ Franklin Mint (SP)

　GRAM-4 .... '85 　　100-150
　DISCS 1: Black and silver label. Four-LP
　boxed set, this being No. 4 in a limited edition
　set of 14, sold mail order by the Franklin Mint
　Record Society. This boxed set, titled *The
　Great Singers*, features eight different artists,
　one on each side of each LP. All discs are red
　vinyl. Elvis is heard on just one of the 56
　discs, although the complete 14-box series is
　valued at $700 to $900.
　FMRS-GMY-016A-1/FMRS-GMY-016B-1. Identification
　numbers are engraved. (Elvis side is B-side.)
　INNER SLEEVE 1: Generic Franklin Mint,
　poly-lined sleeve. No mention of Elvis or this
　LP.

❑ Franklin Mint GRAM-4 .... '85 　　20-25
　BOX 1: Silver, linen stock with red print. Has
　color sticker of a gramophone applied to
　center. Back is blank.

❑ Franklin Mint GRAM-4 .... '85 　　15-20
　INSERT 1A: Black-and-white, 20-page
　booklet. Has biographical sketches of each
　performer.

❑ Franklin Mint GRAM-4 .... '85 　　1-2
　INSERT 1B: One-page letter on Franklin Mint
　Record Society letterhead, introducing this
　set.

Franklin Mint (SP)

　GRAM-4 .... '85 　　150-200
　TOTAL PACKAGE 1: Disc, box, inserts.

Box 1 (All-Time Winners)
Disc 1
Side A: Barbra Streisand; Paul Simon; Simon &
　　Garfunkel
Side B: Count Basie; Quincy Jones
Disc 2
Side A: Henry Mancini; John Williams
Side B: Glen Campbell; Peter, Paul & Mary
Disc 3
Side A: Herb Alpert; George Benson
Side B: Roger Miller; Johnny Cash
Disc 4
Side A: Aretha Franklin; Ray Charles
Side B: Duke Ellington; Stevie Wonder

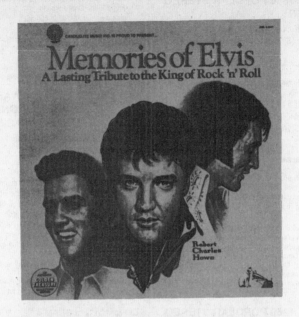

Box 2 (Record of the Year)

Disc 1
Side A: Bobby Darin; Petula Clark; Herb Alpert; Joni Mitchell; Glen Campbell; Fifth Dimension
Side B: Blood, Sweat & Tears; James Taylor; Ramsey Lewis Trio; Anne Murray; Sammy Davis Jr.; Percy Faith

Disc 2
Side A: Beatles; Linda Ronstadt; Carpenters; Harry Nilsson; Janis Ian; Barry Manilow
Side B: Chicago; Debby Boone; Perry Como; Jeannie C. Riley; Jack Jones; Carole King

Disc 3
Side A: Carly Simon; Ray Stevens; Gloria Gaynor; Jim Croce; Chuck Mangione; Willie Nelson
Side B: Johnny Cash; Peggy Lee; Nat "King" Cole; Getz & Gilberto; Tony Bennett; Bobbie Gentry

Disc 4
Side A: Mamas and the Papas; Louis Armstrong; Dave Brubeck; Stevie Wonder; Christopher Cross; Three Dog Night
Side B: Diana Ross & Lionel Richie; Maria Muldaur; Roberta Flack; Toto; Washington & Withers; Joe Jackson

Box 3 (Great Performances of the Rock Era, Vol. 1)

Disc 1
Side A: Beach Boys; Monkees; Jefferson Airplane
Side B: Byrds; Association

Disc 2
Side A: Blood, Sweat & Tears; Chicago
Side B: Crosby, Stills & Nash; Doobie Brothers

Disc 3
Side A: REO Speedwagon; Toto
Side B: Rolling Stones; Pretenders

Disc 4
Side A: Fleetwood Mac; Supertramp
Side B: Styx; Police

Box 4 (The Great Singers)

Disc 1
Side A: Frank Sinatra
Side B: Judy Garland

Disc 2
Side A: Billie Holiday
Side B: Tony Bennett

Disc 3
Side A: Lena Horne
Side B: Nat "King" Cole

Disc 4
Side A: Peggy Lee
Side B: Elvis Presley
    Blue Suede Shoes
    Are You Lonesome Tonight
    Rock-A-Hula Baby
    Wooden Heart
    Blue Hawaii
    Can't Help Falling in Love (shown as "Can't Help Falling in Love with You")

Box 5 (Pop Performances, Vol. 1)

Disc 1
Side A: Janis Joplin; Brook Benton; Linda Ronstadt; Joe Cocker; Helen Reddy; Carole King
Side B: Joan Baez; Gordon Lightfoot; America; Bread; Seals & Crofts; New Seekers

Disc 2
Side A: Carpenters; Dave Loggins; Deodato; Englebert Humperdinck; Captain & Tennille; B.J. Thomas

Side B: Boz Scaggs; George Harrison; Van McCoy; Lou Rawls; Glen Campbell; Vicki Sue Robinson

Disc 3
Side A: Linda Ronstadt; James Taylor; Barry DeVorzon; Billy Preston; England Dan & John Ford Coley; Gino Vannelli
Side B: Barry Manilow; Earth, Wind & Fire; Melissa Manchester; Jose Feliciano; Commodores; Dionne Warwick

Disc 4
Side A: Emmylou Harris; Quincy Jones & James Ingram; Manhattan Transfer; Leo Sayer; Robert John; Judy Collins
Side B: Go Go's; Barry Manilow; Ambrosia; Andy Gibb; Laura Branigan; Lionel Richie

Box 6 (Best New Artist)

Disc 1
Side A: Bobby Darin
Side B: Cream; Derek and the Dominoes; Eric Clapton

Disc 2
Side A: Harry Chapin
Side B: Carly Simon

Disc 3
Side A: Sonny & Cher; Cher
Side B: Bill Withers

Disc 4
Side A: Loggins & Messina
Side B: Carpenters

Box 7 (The Big Band Sound)

Disc 1
Side A: Count Basie; Duke Ellington
Side B: Stan Kenton; Woody Herman

Disc 2
Side A: Glenn Miller; Larry Elgart; Ray Anthony
Side B: Les Brown; Glen Gray; Si Zentner

Disc 3
Side A: Thad Jone & Mel Lewis; Rob McConnell
Side B: Billy May; Neal Hefti; Gerry Mulligan; Quincy Jones

Disc 4
Side A: Dizzy Gillespie; Toshino Akiyoshi & Lew Tabackin; Maynard Ferguson
Side B: Gil Evans; Don Ellis; Buddy Rich

Box 8 (Rhythm & Blues, Vol. 1)

Disc 1
Side A: Muddy Waters; Dinah Washington; Jesse Belvin; Coasters; Hank Ballard and the Midnighters; Etta James
Side B: Jackie Wilson; Sam Cooke; Jimmy Reed; Ernie K-Doe; Little Johnny Taylor; Little Eva

Disc 2
Side A: Martha and the Vandellas; Lenny Welch; Major Lance; Barbara Lewis; Joe Tex; Supremes
Side B: Temptations; Impressions; Wilson Pickett; Junior Walker and the All Stars; James Brown; Capitols

Disc 3
Side A: Aretha Franklin; Percy Sledge; Otis & Carla; Miracles; Jackie Wilson
Side B: Etta James; Sam & Dave; Marvin Gaye & Tammi Terrell; Booker T and the MGs; Mel & Tim; Otis Redding

Disc 4
Side A: Marvin Gaye; Aretha Franklin; Johnnie Taylor; Archie Bell and the Drells; Sam & Dave; Temptations
Side B: B.B. King; Ike & Tina Turner; Clarence Carter; Edwin Starr; Isaac Hayes; Staple Singers

Box 9 (Songs of the Year)
Disc 1
Side A: Bruce Johnston; Neil Sedaka; Paul Williams; Leo Sayer; Armanda McBroom; Peter Allen
Side B: Dolly Parton; Don Schlitz; David Allan Coe; Tom T. Hall; Dallas Frazier; Larry Gatlin
Disc 2
Side A: Paul Williams; Morris Albert; Joe Brooks; Bobby Russell; Jim Weatherly; Charlie Rich
Side B: Andre Previn; Johnny Mercer; Steve Allen; John Barry; Anthony Newley; Henry Mancini
Disc 3
Side A: McFadden & Whitehead; Delfonics; K.C. and the Sunshine Band; Sly and the Family Stone; Chic
Side B: Gilbert O'Sullivan; Joe South; Bobby Russell; John Hartford; Roger Miller; Gordon Lightfoot
Disc 4
Side A: Dottie West; Hank Cochran; Jessi Colter; Shel Silverstein; Ed Bruce; Willie Nelson
Side B: James Taylor; Jackie DeShannon; Otis Redding; Marvin Gaye; Allen Tjoussaint; Earth, Wind & Fire

Box 10 (Folk Performances)
Disc 1
Side A: Ewan MacCall; Mountain Ramblers; Fred McDowell; Fleix Dukes & Fred McDowell; Leadbelly
Side B: Woody Guthrie; Pete Seeger
Disc 2
Side A: Harry Belafonte; Harry Belafonte & Mariam Makeba; Mariam Makeba; Kingston Trio
Side B: Joan Baez; Bob Dylan; Judy Collins; Bob Dylan; Odetta
Disc 3
Side A: Brothers Four; Limeliters; Rooftop Singers; New Christy Minstrels; Clancy Brothers & Tommy Makem; Irish Rovers
Side B: Richard & Mimi Farina; John Hartford; Judy Collins; Incredible String Band; Chieftains
Disc 4
Side A: Bob Dylan; Joan Baez; Arlo Guthrie
Side B: T-Bone Walker; Koko Taylor; Albert Collins; Queen Ida and the Bon Temps Zydeco Band; B.B. King

Box 11 (Stage & Original Cast Recordings)
Disc 1
Side A: Gypsy; Camelot; Flower Drum Song; Sound of Music; Redhead
Side B: Bye Bye Birdie; What Makes Sammy Run; Do I Hear a Waltz; Fiddler on the Roof
Disc 2
Side A: Half a Sixpence; Apple Tree; Mame; Man of La Mancha
Side B: Cabaret; Hallelujah Baby; Sweet Charity
Disc 3
Side A: Hair; Godspell; Two Gentlemen of Verona; Raisin; Your Arms Are Too Short to Box with God
Side B: 1776; Company; The Rothschilds; I Love My Wife; Annie
Disc 4
Side A: A Chorus Line; A Little Night Music; On the 20th Century; Sweeney Todd; Ballroom

Side B: A Day in Hollywood, a Night in the Ukraine; Ain't Misbehavin'; One Mo' Time

Box 12 (The Producer's Choice)
Disc 1
Side A: Quincy Jones
Side B: Arif Mardin
Disc 2
Side A: Bill Szymczyk
Side B: Richard Perry
Disc 3
Side A: Ted Templeman
Side B: Gamble & Huff
Disc 4
Side A: Thom Bell
Side B: Billy Sherrill

Box 13 (Jazz Vocalists)
Disc 1
Side A: Billie Holiday; Sarah Vaughan; Peggy Lee; Lena Horne; Carmen McRae; Helen Merrill
Side B: Jimmy Rushing; Joe Williams; Mel Torme; Mark Murphy; Johnny Hartman; Joao Gilberto
Disc 2
Side A: Helen Humes; Mel Torme; Billie Holiday; Ernestine Anderson; Etta Jones
Side B: Joe Williams; Carmen McRae; Jackie & Roy; Maxine Sullivan; Sarah Vaughan; Chaka Khan; Helen Merrill
Disc 3
Side A: Eddie Jefferson; Mark Murphy; Jackie & Roy; Lambert, Hendricks & Ross; Janet Lawson; Quire
Side B: Hi-Lo's; Lambert, Hendricks & Ross; Manhattan Transfer; Quire; Jon Hendricks & Company; Manhattan Transfer
Disc 4
Side A: Slam Stewart; Jimmy Rowles; Dave Frishberg; Mel Torme; Jackie & Roy; Bobby Troup
Side B: Irene Kral; Mel Torme; Helen Humes; Dave Frishberg; Etta Jones; Sarah Vaughan

Box 14 (Album of the Year)
Disc 1
Side A: Andy Williams; Tonny Bennett; Barry Manilow
Side B: Henry Mancini; Nat "King" Cole; Stan Getz
Disc 2
Side A: Fifth Dimension; Glen Campbell; Harry Nilsson; Janis Ian
Side B: Harry Belafonte; James Taylor
Disc 3
Side A: Blood, Sweat & Tears; Peter Frampton
Side B: Jackson Browne; Linda Ronstadt
Disc 4
Side A: Quincy Jones; Donald Fagen
Side B: Supertramp; Fleetwood Mac

OLD & HEAVY GOLD (1956)
Various artists collection
❑ Economic Consultants Inc. (M)
1956 .... '73   10-20
DISC 1: Gold label with black print. One of a multi-LP set. Mail order offer. Has five Elvis tracks.
OHG-1956 Side 1/OHG-1956 Side 2. Identification numbers are engraved.

❑ Economic Consultants Inc.
1956 .... '73   10-20
COVER 1: Front: Black with oval drawing of a
pirate with a treasure chest. Back: Two large
gold coins with song titles.
Economic Consultants Inc. (M)
1956................................'73   20-40
TOTAL PACKAGE 1: Disc, cover.

OLD & HEAVY GOLD (1957)
Various artists collection
❑ Economic Consultants Inc. (M)
1957 .... '73   10-20
DISC 1: Gold label with black print. One of a
multi-LP set. Mail order offer. Has five Elvis
tracks.
OHG-1957 Side 1/OHG-1957 Side 2. Identification numbers
are engraved.
❑ Economic Consultants Inc.
1957 .... '73   10-20
COVER 1: Front: Black with oval drawing of a
pirate with a treasure chest. Back: Two large
gold coins with song titles.
Economic Consultants Inc. (M)
1957................................'73   20-40
TOTAL PACKAGE 1: Disc, cover.

OLD & HEAVY GOLD (1958)
Various artists collection
❑ Economic Consultants Inc. (M)
1958 .... '73   10-20
DISC 1: Gold label with black print. One of a
multi-LP set. Mail order offer. Has one Elvis
track.
OHG-1958 Side 1/OHG-1958 Side 2. Identification numbers
are engraved.
❑ Economic Consultants Inc.
1958 .... '73   10-20
COVER 1: Front: Black with oval drawing of a
pirate with a treasure chest. Back: Two large
gold coins with song titles.
Economic Consultants Inc. (M)
1958................................'73   20-40
TOTAL PACKAGE 1: Disc, cover.

OLD & HEAVY GOLD (1960)
Various artists collection
❑ Economic Consultants Inc. (M)
1960 .... '73   10-20
DISC 1: Gold label with black print. One of a
multi-LP set. Mail order offer. Has two Elvis
tracks.
OHG-1960 Side 1/OHG-1960 Side 2. Identification numbers
are engraved.
❑ Economic Consultants Inc.
1960 .... '73   10-20
COVER 1: Front: Black with oval drawing of a
pirate with a treasure chest. Back: Two large
gold coins with song titles.

Economic Consultants Inc. (M)
1960................................'73   20-40
TOTAL PACKAGE 1: Disc, cover.

OLD & HEAVY GOLD (1961)
Various artists collection
❑ Economic Consultants Inc. (M)
1961 .... '73   10-20
DISC 1: Gold label with black print. One of a
multi-LP set. Mail order offer. Has one Elvis
track.
OHG-1961 Side 1/OHG-1961 Side 2. Identification numbers
are engraved.
❑ Economic Consultants Inc.
1961 .... '73   10-20
COVER 1: Front: Black with oval drawing of a
pirate with a treasure chest. Back: Two large
gold coins with song titles.
Economic Consultants Inc. (M)
1961................................'73   20-40
TOTAL PACKAGE 1: Disc, cover.

OLD & HEAVY GOLD (1962)
Various artists collection
❑ Economic Consultants Inc. (M)
1962 .... '73   10-20
DISC 1: Gold label with black print. One of a
multi-LP set. Mail order offer. Has two Elvis
tracks.
OHG-1962 Side 1/OHG-1962 Side 2. Identification numbers
are engraved.
❑ Economic Consultants Inc.
1962 .... '73   10-20
COVER 1: Front: Black with oval drawing of a
pirate with a treasure chest. Back: Two large
gold coins with song titles.
Economic Consultants Inc. (M)
1962................................'73   20-40
TOTAL PACKAGE 1: Disc, cover.

ON STAGE FEBRUARY, 1970
❑ RCA Victor (ST)
LSP-4362 ....6/70   20-25
DISC 1: Orange label. Rigid vinyl. .
ZPRS-1422-B1B/ZPRS-1423-B2D.
ZPRS-1422-2S/ZPRS-1423-3S.
ZPRS-1422-5S/ZPRS-1423-4S.
ZPRS-1422-30S/ZPRS-1423-8S.
❑ RCA Victor LSP-4362........6/70   10-12
COVER 1: Front: RCA logo and number at
upper left, "Victor Stereo" at upper right.
Black-and-white Elvis Las Vegas concert
photo. Back: Black-and-white Elvis Las Vegas
concert photo. Has red print in four places on
right side.
❑ RCA Victor 21-112-1
40C 3/67   4-6
INNER SLEEVE 1: Blue, black and white.
Front: RCA's Elvis LP catalog, most recent
being *Spinout* (side 1, row 2, column 7). Back:
RCA Elvis Stereo 8 catalog.

RCA Victor (ST)
LSP-4362......................6/70   35-45
TOTAL PACKAGE 1: Disc, cover, inner sleeve.

❏ RCA Victor (ST)
LSP-4362 ....6/70   20-25
DISC 2: Same as disc 1.

❏ RCA Victor LSP-4362........6/70   15-20
COVER 2: Designate promo. Same as cover 1, but with "Not for Sale" stamped on back.

❏ RCA Victor 21-112-1
40C......................................3/67   4-6
INNER SLEEVE 2: Blue, black and white. Front: RCA's Elvis LP catalog, most recent being *Spinout* (side 1, row 2, column 7). Back: RCA Elvis Stereo 8 catalog.

RCA Victor (ST)
LSP-4362.....................6/70   40-50
TOTAL PACKAGE 2: Disc, cover, inner sleeve.

❏ RCA Victor (ST)
LSP-4362 ....'71   10-15
DISC 3: Orange label. Flexible vinyl.
ZPRS-1422-2S/ZPRS-1423-2S.
ZPRS-1422-8S/ZPRS-1423-7S. Identification numbers are engraved.

❏ RCA Victor (ST)
LSP-4362 ....'71   10-12
COVER 3: Same as cover 1.

❏ RCA Victor...........................'70s   2-4
INNER SLEEVE 3: Black-and-white. Pictures RCA Elvis catalog front and back. Any of several sleeves may be found on reissues from this period.

RCA Victor (ST)
LSP-4362.......................'71   20-30
TOTAL PACKAGE 3: Disc, cover, inner sleeve.

❏ RCA Victor (ST)
LSP-4362 ....'76   10-15
DISC 4: Tan label.

❏ RCA LSP-4362.....................'76   10-15
COVER 4: Verification pending.

❏ RCA Victor...........................'70s   2-4
INNER SLEEVE 4: Black-and-white. Pictures RCA Elvis catalog front and back. Any of several sleeves may be found on reissues from this period.

RCA Victor (ST)
LSP-4362.......................'76   25-35
TOTAL PACKAGE 4: Disc, cover, inner sleeve.

❏ RCA Victor (ST)
LSP-4362 ....'76   4-6
DISC 5: Black label, dog near top.

❏ RCA LSP-4362.....................'76   4-6
ZPRS-1422-33S/ZPRS-1423-33S.

COVER 5: Same as cover 1, except on back all print is white and there is a "2" at lower right.

❏ RCA Victor..........................'70s   2-4
INNER SLEEVE 5: Black-and-white. Pictures RCA Elvis catalog front and back. Any of several sleeves may be found on reissues from this period.

RCA Victor (ST)
LSP-4362.......................'76   10-18
TOTAL PACKAGE 5: Disc, cover, inner sleeve.

❏ RCA Victor (ST)
LSP-4362 ....'76   4-6
DISC 6: Same as disc 5.

❏ RCA LSP-4362 ....'76   5-10
COVER 6: Designate promo. Same as cover 5, but with "Not for Sale" stamped on back.

❏ RCA Victor..........................'70s   2-4
INNER SLEEVE 6: Black-and-white. Pictures RCA Elvis catalog front and back. Any of several sleeves may be found on reissues from this period.

RCA Victor (ST)
LSP-4362.......................'76   15-20
TOTAL PACKAGE 6: Disc, cover, inner sleeve.

❏ RCA (ST) AFL1-4362 ....'77   3-5
DISC 7: Black label, dog near top.

❏ RCA AFL1-4362 ....'77   3-5
COVER 7: Front: Reflects prefix change. Back: Same black-and-white photo of Elvis wearing a jumpsuit as on cover 1. Includes copies with a sticker bearing the "AFL1" prefix, wrapped around cover at top of spine.

❏ RCA Victor..........................'70s   2-4
INNER SLEEVE 7: Black-and-white. Pictures RCA Elvis catalog front and back. Any of several sleeves may be found on reissues from this period.

RCA (ST) AFL1-4362 ....'77   10-12
TOTAL PACKAGE 7: Disc, cover, inner sleeve.

❏ RCA Victor (ST)
AQL1-4362 ....2/83   8-10
DISC 8: Black label, dog near top.
AQL1-4362A 33S/AQL1-4362B 34S. Matrix is a mess. On side 1 "ZPRS- 1422-33S" is stamped but crossed out. Then "AFL1-4362A" is stamped with the "AF" crossed out and the "AQ" added. On side 2 "ZPRS-1423-34S" is stamped but crossed out. Then "AFL1-4362B" is engraved with the "AF" crossed out and the "AQ" added.

❏ RCA AQL1-4362................2/83   20-30
COVER 8: Front: Reflects prefix change. Omits "Victor Stereo." Back: Black-and-white photo of Elvis shirt and pants instead of a jumpsuit. Areas in red print on cover 1 are now in white.
INNER SLEEVE 8: White, no printing.

RCA Victor (ST)
AQL1-4362 ....2/83   30-40
TOTAL PACKAGE 8: Disc, cover.

Side 1
See See Rider
Release Me
Sweet Caroline
Runaway
The Wonder of You

Side 2
Polk Salad Annie
Yesterday
Proud Mary
Walk a Mile in My Shoes
Let It Be Me (Je T'appartiens)

ON A COUNTRY ROAD

Various artists collections.

❑ On a Country Road (S)   10-15
   DISC 1: Price range is for any individual disc
   containing at least one Elvis track.

On a Country Road (S)   25-35
   COMPLETE SET 1: Set of three LPs. Each is
   a complete three-hour, weekly radio show
   with three pages of cue sheets and program
   notes. Issued only to subscribing radio
   stations. Price range is for any complete set
   containing at least one Elvis track.

ON STAGE IN THE U.S.A.

❑ Wizardo 304: Bootleg. Listed for
   identification only.

ON THE RECORD – EVENTS OF 1977 (Compiled by the United Press International Audio News)

❑ Caedmon (M) TC-1572 ..... 1/78   30-40
   DISC 1: White, blue and black label. United
   Press International news service recap of
   1977's top news stories. Has excerpts of *All
   Shook Up,* from *Elvis As Recorded at
   Madison Square Garden* and *Hound Dog.*
   Issued only to radio stations.
   TC1572A/TC1572B. Identification numbers are engraved.

❑ Caedmon TC-1572 .... 1/78   30-40
   COVER 1: Caedmon logo and number at
   upper right. Black-and-white photos, front and
   back, of some of the people and events
   making news in 1977, including a '68 TV
   Special shot of Elvis.

**Caedmon (M)
   TC-1572 .... 1/78   60-80**
   TOTAL PACKAGE 1: Disc, cover.

ONE NIGHT WITH YOU: see *ELVIS (ONE
   NIGHT WITH YOU)*

ORIGINAL ELVIS PRESLEY MEDLEY (Jellybean/Elvis)

❑ Disconet Program Service
   (SP) .... '79   30-40
   DISC 1: Volume 3, Program 9 of a
   promotional only series. The A-side of this LP
   is by a group called Jellybean. Issued only to
   Disconet subscribers.

❑ Disconet Program Service
   (SP) .... '79   5-10
   COVER 1: Black, no printing.

**Disconet Program
   Service (SP) .... '79   35-50**
   TOTAL PACKAGE 1: Disc, cover.

Side 1 (Jellybean)
Side 2 (Elvis Presley)
Easy Going Remixed – Far Medley Medley: Good Luck
Charm/It's Now Or Never/Return to Sender/All
Shook Up/Jailhouse Rock/Don't Be Cruel/(Let Me
Be Your) Teddy Bear/Hound Dog/Blue Suede
Shoes

ORIGINAL ELVIS PRESLEY MEDLEY (Fear/Elvis)

❑ Disconet Program Service
   (SP) .... '80   30-40
   DISC 1: Volume 3, Program 9 of a
   promotional only series. The A-side of this LP
   is by a group called Fear. Issued only to
   Disconet subscribers.
   MP307A/MWDN309B. Identification numbers are engraved.

❑ Disconet Program Service
   (SP) .... '80   5-10
   COVER 1: Has die-cut, 3¾" center hole, with
   drawings of a tonearm above and below.
   Reads: "For Promotional Use of Subscriber –
   Not for Sale."
   INNER SLEEVE 1: White, no printing.

**Disconet Program
   Service (SP) .... '80   35-50**
   TOTAL PACKAGE 1: Disc, cover.

Side 1 (Fear)
Side 2 (Elvis Presley)
Easy Going Remixed – Far Medley Medley: Good Luck
Charm/It's Now Or Never/Return to Sender/All
Shook Up/Jailhouse Rock/Don't Be Cruel/(Let Me
Be Your) Teddy Bear/Hound Dog/Blue Suede
Shoes

The volume and program number given us for
this disc is identical to the previous one listed.
We don't yet know which – if either – is
incorrect.

ORIGINAL ELVIS PRESLEY MEDLEY (Pseudo Echo - Bonnie Tyler/Elvis)

❑ Disconet Program Service
   (SP) .... '86   30-40
   DISC 1: Volume 8, Program 9 of a
   promotional only series. The A-side of this LP
   has one song by Pseudo Echo and one by
   Bonnie Tyler. Issued only to Disconet
   subscribers.

❑ Disconet Program Service
   (SP) .... '86   5-10
   COVER 1: Black die-cut, no printing.

Disconet Program
Service (SP) .... '86   **35-50**
TOTAL PACKAGE 1: Disc, cover.

Side 1 (Pseudo Echo/Bonnie Tyler)
Side 2 (Elvis Presley)
Easy Going Remixed – Far Medley Medley: Good Luck Charm/It's Now Or Never/Return to Sender/All Shook Up/Jailhouse Rock/Don't Be Cruel/(Let Me Be Your) Teddy Bear/Hound Dog/Blue Suede Shoes

ORIGINAL BEATLES MEDLEY
(Beatles/Elvis)

□ Disconet Program Service
(SP) .... '80   30-40
DISC 1: Volume 8, Program 9 of a promotional only series. Issued only to Disconet subscribers.
□ Disconet Program Service
(SP) .... '80   5-10
COVER 1: Black die-cut, no printing.
Disconet Program
Service (SP) .... '80   **35-50**
TOTAL PACKAGE 1: Disc, cover.

The volume and program number given us for this disc is identical to the previous one listed. We don't yet know which – if either – is incorrect.

Side 1 (Beatles)
Side 2 (Elvis Presley)
Easy Going Remixed – Far Medley Medley: Good Luck Charm/It's Now Or Never/Return to Sender/All Shook Up/Jailhouse Rock/Don't Be Cruel/(Let Me Be Your) Teddy Bear/Hound Dog/Blue Suede Shoes

OTHER SIDES: see *WORLDWIDE 50 GOLD AWARD HITS, VOL. 2*

OUR MEMORIES OF ELVIS

□ RCA Victor (ST)
AQL1-3279 .... 2/79   8-10
DISC 1: Black label, dog on top. The first of two volumes of the "Pure Elvis" sound – Elvis and his band sans *sweetening* (backing vocals and orchestration).
AQL1-3279-A-1S/AQL1-3279-B-1S. Identification numbers are stamped.
AQL1-3279-A-3S/AQL1-3279-B-3S. Identification numbers are engraved.
□ RCA AQL1-3279 .... 2/79   8-10
COVER 1: Front: No logo or number shown. Color photo of Elvis' father, Vernon, and Colonel Tom Parker standing in front of the Graceland Mansion. At upper right is a tiny, color Elvis photo in the "Memories of Elvis Series" logo. Back: RCA logo at lower left. Color Elvis photo.
□ RCA Victor 21-112-1
PT 54F 7/77   2-4
INNER SLEEVE 1: Black-and-white. Pictures RCA's Elvis LPs front and back, most recent being *Moody Blue* (side 2, row 5, column 1).

□ RCA AQL1-3279 .... 2/79   30-40
SHRINK STICKER 1A: Rectangular, 2½" x 4" with black-and-white picture of Elvis in circle. Reads: "Featuring The Hit Single: Are You Sincere," and shows the selection number AQL1-3279-2.
□ RCA AQL1-3279 .... 2/79   30-40
SHRINK STICKER 1B: Round, 2" brown. Reads: "Contains the Hit Single: Are You Sincere," and shows the selection number AQL1-3279. Since copies are not known to exist with both stickers, total package price includes either one.

RCA Victor (ST)
AQL1-3279 .... 2/79   **80-100**
TOTAL PACKAGE 1: Disc, cover, sticker, inner sleeve.

□ RCA Victor (ST)
AQL1-3279 .... 2/79   8-10
DISC 2: Same as disc 1.
□ RCA AQL1-3279 .... 2/79   18-20
COVER 2: Designate promo. Same as cover 1, but with "Not for Sale" stamped on back.
□ RCA Victor 21-112-1
PT 54F 7/77   2-4
INNER SLEEVE 2: Black-and-white. Pictures RCA's Elvis LPs front and back, most recent being *Moody Blue* (side 2, row 5, column 1).
□ RCA AQL1-3279 .... 2/79   30-40
SHRINK STICKER 2A: Rectangular, 2½" x 4" with black-and-white picture of Elvis in circle. Reads: "Featuring The Hit Single: Are You Sincere," and shows the selection number AQL1-3279-2.
□ RCA AQL1-3279 .... 2/79   30-40
SHRINK STICKER 2B: Round, 2" brown. Reads: "Contains the Hit Single: Are You Sincere," and shows the selection number AQL1-3279. Since copies are not known to exist with both stickers, total package price includes either one.

RCA Victor (ST)
AQL1-3279 .... 2/79   **90-110**
TOTAL PACKAGE 2: Disc, cover, sticker, inner sleeve.

Side 1
Are You Sincere (Unreleased Version)
It's Midnight
My Boy
Girl of Mine
Take Good Care of Her
I'll Never Fall in Love Again

Side 2
Your Love's Been a Long Time Coming
Spanish Eyes
Never Again
She Thinks I Still Care
Solitaire

ॉ

OUR MEMORIES OF ELVIS, VOLUME 2 (MORE OF THE PURE ELVIS SOUND)

❑ RCA Victor (ST)

AQL1-3448 ....7/79   8-10

DISC 1: Black label, dog near top.

AQL1-3448-A-1S/AQL1-3448-B-1S. Identification numbers are stamped on side 1 and engraved on side 2.

AQL1-3448-A-3S/AQL1-3448-B-1S. Identification numbers are engraved on both sides.

AQL1-3448-A-3S/AQL1-3448-B-2S. Identification numbers are engraved on both sides.

AQL1-3448-A-17/AQL1-3448-B-2S. Identification numbers are stamped on side 1 and engraved on side 2.

❑ RCA AQL1-3448 ....7/79   8-10

COVER 1: Front: Number at lower left. Color Elvis photo. Back: RCA logo and number at lower left. Color Elvis photo. At upper right is a tiny, color Elvis photo in the "Memories of Elvis Series" logo. Pictures *Our Memories of Elvis (Volume 1)* at lower right.

❑ RCA Victor 21-112-1

PT 54F 7/77   2-4

INNER SLEEVE 1: Black-and-white. Pictures RCA's Elvis LPs front and back, most recent being *Moody Blue* (side 2, row 5, column 1).

❑ RCA Victor AQL1-3448 .....7/79   40-50

SHRINK STICKER 1: Circular, blue and white. Announces the inclusion of *There's a Honky Tonk Angel (Who'll Take Me Back In)* and *I Got a Feelin' in My Body*.

RCA Victor (ST)

AQL1-3448 ....7/79   60-75

TOTAL PACKAGE 1: Disc, cover, sticker, inner sleeve.

❑ RCA Victor (ST)

AQL1-3448 ....7/79   8-10

DISC 2: Same as disc 1.

❑ RCA AQL1-3448 ....7/79   12-15

COVER 2: Designate promo. Same as cover 1, but with "Not for Sale" stamped on back.

❑ RCA Victor 21-112-1

PT 54F 7/77   2-4

INNER SLEEVE 2: Black-and-white. Pictures RCA's Elvis LPs front and back, most recent being *Moody Blue* (side 2, row 5, column 1).

❑ RCA Victor AQL1-3448 .....7/79   40-50

SHRINK STICKER 2: Circular, blue and white. Announces the inclusion of *There's a Honky Tonk Angel (Who'll Take Me Back In)* and *I Got a Feelin' in My Body*.

RCA Victor (ST)

AQL1-3448 ....7/79   65-80

TOTAL PACKAGE 2: Disc, cover, sticker, inner sleeve.

Side A
I Got A Feelin' in My Body
Green Green Grass of Home
For the Heart
She Wears My Ring
I Can Help

Side B
Way Down

There's a Honky Tonk Angel (Who'll Take Me Back In)
Find Out What's Happening
Thinking About You
Don't Think Twice, It's All Right (Unreleased Complete Studio Jam)
Also see *PURE ELVIS*

PAIR OF KINGS (ELVIS PRESLEY / FRANK SINATRA)

❑ Loota 4902: Bootleg. Listed for identification only.

PARADISE, HAWAIIAN STYLE

❑ RCA Victor (M)

LPM-3643 ....6/66   15-20

DISC 1: Black label, "Monaural" at bottom.

TPRM-3844-1S/TPRM-3845-1S. At top of label is "Paradise, Hawaiian Style, Elvis Presley."

TPRM-3844-3S/TPRM-3845-3S. Label LP#12. At top of label is "RCA Victor Presents Elvis in the Original Soundtrack Album from the Paramount Picture Paradise, Hawaiian Style – a Hal Wallis Production."

❑ RCA Victor LPM-3643 ....6/66   25-30

COVER 1: Front: RCA logo at upper right, number at lower left. Color Elvis photo. Back: Nine postage stamp size, studio posed Elvis photos.

❑ RCA Victor 21-112-1

40B 4/65   4-6

INNER SLEEVE 1: Red, black and white. Front: RCA's Elvis LP catalog, most recent being *Roustabout* (side 1, row 1, column 5). Back: RCA Elvis EPs and 45s catalog.

RCA Victor (M)

LPM-3643 ....6/66   45-60

TOTAL PACKAGE 1: Disc, cover, inner sleeve.

❑ RCA Victor (M)

LPM-3643 ....6/66   15-20

DISC 2: Same as disc 1.

❑ RCA Victor LPM-3643 ....6/66   35-45

COVER 2: Designate promo. Same as cover 1, but with "Not for Sale" stamped on back.

❑ RCA Victor 21-112-1

40B 4/65   4-6

INNER SLEEVE 2: Red, black and white. Front: RCA's Elvis LP catalog, most recent being *Roustabout* (side 1, row 1, column 5). Back: RCA Elvis EPs and 45s catalog.

RCA Victor (M)

LPM-3643 ....6/66   55-70

TOTAL PACKAGE 2: Disc, cover, inner sleeve.

❑ RCA Victor (ST)

LSP-3643 ....6/66   15-20

DISC 3: Black label, RCA logo in white at top and "Stereo" at bottom.

TPRS-3846-1S/TPRS-3847-1S. Label LP#16. At top of label is "Paradise, Hawaiian Style, Elvis Presley."

TPRS-3846-2S/TPRS-3847-2S. Label LP#16. At top of label is "Paradise, Hawaiian Style, Elvis Presley."

❑ RCA Victor LSP-3643........6/66   25-30
COVER 3: Front: RCA logo at upper right, number at upper left. Color Elvis photo. Back: Nine postage stamp-size, studio posed Elvis photos.

❑ RCA Victor 21-112-1
40B....................................4/65   4-6
INNER SLEEVE 3: Red, black and white. Front: RCA's Elvis LP catalog, most recent being *Roustabout* (side 1, row 1, column 5). Back: RCA Elvis EPs and 45s catalog.

RCA Victor (ST)
LSP-3643.....................6/66   **45-60**
TOTAL PACKAGE 3: Disc, cover, inner sleeve.

❑ RCA Victor (ST)
LSP-3643 ....6/66   15-20
DISC 4: Same as disc 3.

❑ RCA Victor LSP-3643........6/66   35-45
COVER 4: Designate promo. Same as cover 1, but with "Not for Sale" stamped on back.

❑ RCA Victor 21-112-1
40B....................................4/65   4-6
INNER SLEEVE 4: Red, black and white. Front: RCA's Elvis LP catalog, most recent being *Roustabout* (side 1, row 1, column 5). Back: RCA Elvis EPs and 45s catalog.

RCA Victor (ST)
LSP-3643.....................6/66   **55-70**
TOTAL PACKAGE 4: Disc, cover, inner sleeve.

❑ RCA Victor (ST)
LSP-3643 ....6/66   40-50
DISC 5: Same as disc 3 EXCEPT vinyl is flexible, like the ones from the '70s identified as "Dynaflex."

❑ RCA Victor LSP-3643........6/66   25-30
COVER 5: Same as cover 3

❑ RCA Victor 21-112-1
40B....................................4/65   4-6
INNER SLEEVE 5: Red, black and white. Front: RCA's Elvis LP catalog, most recent being *Roustabout* (side 1, row 1, column 5). Back: RCA Elvis EPs and 45s catalog.

RCA Victor (ST)
LSP-3643.....................6/66   **70-85**
TOTAL PACKAGE 5: Disc, cover, inner sleeve.

❑ RCA Victor (ST)
LSP-3643 ....11/68   20-25
DISC 6: Orange label. Rigid vinyl.

❑ RCA Victor LSP-3643......11/68   8-10
COVER 6: Verification pending.

❑ RCA Victor 21-112-1
40D...................................6/68   4-6
INNER SLEEVE 6: Red, black and white. Front: RCA's Elvis LP catalog, most recent being *Elvis' Gold Records, Vol. 4* (side 1, row 4, column 5). Back: RCA's Elvis LP and Twin Pack Stereo 8 catalog. May also be found with inner sleeves 40B and 40C. See chapter on inner sleeves for more information.

RCA Victor (ST)
LSP-3643....................11/68   **35-40**
TOTAL PACKAGE 6: Disc, cover, inner sleeve.

❑ RCA Victor (ST)
LSP-3643 ....'71   10-15
DISC 7: Orange label. Flexible vinyl.
TPRS-3846-2S/TPRS-3847-4S. At top of label is "Paradise, Hawaiian Style, Elvis Presley."

❑ RCA Victor LSP-3643..........'71   4-8
COVER 7: Same as cover 2, except has mono/stereo "Library of Congress Card Numbers" note on back at lower right.

❑ RCA Victor.........................'70s   2-4
INNER SLEEVE 7: Black-and-white. Pictures RCA Elvis catalog front and back. Any of several sleeves may be found on reissues from this period.

RCA Victor (ST)
LSP-3643.......................'71   **15-25**
TOTAL PACKAGE 7: Disc, cover, inner sleeve.

❑ RCA Victor (ST)
LSP-3643 ....'76   10-15
DISC 8: Tan label.

❑ RCA Victor LSP-3643..........'76   10-15
COVER 8: Verification pending.

❑ RCA Victor.........................'70s   2-4
INNER SLEEVE 8: Black-and-white. Pictures RCA Elvis catalog front and back. Any of several sleeves may be found on reissues from this period.

RCA Victor (ST)
LSP-3643.......................'76   **25-35**
TOTAL PACKAGE 8: Disc, cover, inner sleeve.

❑ RCA Victor (ST)
LSP-3643 ....'76   4-6
DISC 9: Black label, dog near top.
TPRS-3846-7/TPRS-3847-7. Identification numbers are engraved.

❑ RCA LSP-3643....................'76   4-6
COVER 9: Front: RCA logo and number at upper left. "Victor" and "Stereo" at upper right. "RE" at lower left. Back: Same as cover 6, except mono number is not listed.

❑ RCA Victor.........................'70s   2-4
INNER SLEEVE 9: Black-and-white. Pictures RCA Elvis catalog front and back. Any of several sleeves may be found on reissues from this period.

RCA Victor (ST)

LSP-3643......................'76   10-15
TOTAL PACKAGE 9: Disc, cover, inner
sleeve.

❏ RCA Victor (ST)
AFL1-3643 ....'77   3-5
DISC 10: Black label, dog near top.
❏ RCA AFL1-3643 ....'77   3-5
COVER 10: Reflects prefix change.
❏ RCA Victor........................'70s   2-4
INNER SLEEVE 10: Black-and-white.
Pictures RCA Elvis catalog front and back.
Any of several sleeves may be found on
reissues from this period.

RCA Victor (ST)

AFL1-3643......................'77   8-15
TOTAL PACKAGE 10: Disc, cover, inner
sleeve.

Side 1
Paradise, Hawaiian Style
Queenie Wahine's Papaya
Scratch My Back (I'll Scratch Yours)
Drums of the Islands
Datin'

Side 2
A Dog's Life
A House of Sand
Stop Where You Are
This Is My Heaven
Sand Castles

PARADISE, HAWAIIAN STYLE (AFRTS)

❏ Armed Forces Radio & Television Service
(M) P-9918/9919 ....'66   50-100
DISC 1:
SSL-18036/SSL-18037
COVER 1: None made.
INNER SLEEVE 1: Brown, no printing.

Armed Forces Radio & Television Service (M)

P-9918/9919 ....'66   50-100
TOTAL PACKAGE 1: Disc.

Side 1
Elvis Presley – Paradise, Hawaiian Style
Paradise, Hawaiian Style (With the Jordanaires)
Drums of the Islands (With the Jordanaires)
Sand Castles
Julius LaRosa – You're Gonna Hear from Me
Once to Every Heart
It's Just a Matter of Time
You're Gonna Hear from Me

PERSONALLY ELVIS (2 LPs)

❏ Silhouette Music (M)
10001/10002 ....'79   10-15
DISCS 1: Blue label with silver print. Has no
Elvis music, only interviews with him.
(Disc 1) SM-10001-A/SM-10001-B. **(Disc 2)** SM-10002-
A/SM-10002-B. Identification numbers are engraved.

❏ Silhouette Music
10001/10002 ....'79   10-15
COVER 1: Double pocket. Color Elvis photos,
circa '57 and '58, on all four panels.
INNER SLEEVES 1: White, no printing.
❏ Silhouette Music ....'79   2-4
INSERT 1: 8" x 10" transfer, a silhouette of
Elvis' bust. Unfortunately, some transfers
were packed facing one of the records and did
indeed transfer an image onto the vinyl
causing a permanent blemish.
❏ Silhouette Music ....'79   8-10
STICKER 1: Black, 1¼" x 1½" with gold
letters. Reads "Special Free Elvis Presley Gift
Inside Each Album Set."

Silhouette Music (M) 10001/10002............................'79   30-45

TOTAL PACKAGE 1: Discs, cover, sticker,
insert.

Disc 1
Side 1
1955 Texarkana
1956 Municipal Auditorium, San Antonio
Side 2
1956 Warwick Hotel, New York
Disc 2
Side 1
1956 County Coliseum, San Antonio
Honolulu
Side 2
1956 Warwick Hotel, New York (continued)

PICKWICK PACK (7 LPs)

❏ Pickwick/Camden (SP)....11/78   40-60
SET 1: Specially wrapped package of the
following seven Pickwick LPs:
I Got Lucky
Separate Ways
Mahalo from Elvis
Elvis' Christmas Album
You'll Never Walk Alone
Elvis Sings Hits from His Movies, Vol. 1
Burning Love (And Hits from His Movies)
See individual listings for complete
information on these LPs.
❏ Pickwick/Camden 11/78   110-140
BAND 1: Cardboard wrapper with information
about the package.

Pickwick/Camden (SP) 11/78   150-200

TOTAL PACKAGE 1: Albums, band.

❏ Pickwick/Camden (SP)......2/79   40-60
SET 2: Specially wrapped package of the
following seven Pickwick LPs (with *Elvis'
Christmas Album* replaced by *Frankie and
Johnny*):
I Got Lucky
Separate Ways
Mahalo from Elvis
Frankie and Johnny
You'll Never Walk Alone
Elvis Sings Hits from His Movies, Vol. 1
Burning Love (And Hits from His Movies)

See individual listings for complete
information on these LPs.

❑ Pickwick/Camden 2/79 110-140
BAND 2: Cardboard wrapper with information
about the package.

Pickwick/Camden
(SP) 2/79 **150-200**
TOTAL PACKAGE 2: Albums, band.

All seven albums are shrink-wrapped. The
outer band identifies the package, which
actually has no title. We simply named it
"Pickwick Pack" in an earlier Elvis book, and
the name stuck.

PLANTATION ROCK
❑ Audifon AFNS-63760: Bootleg. Listed for
identification only.

PLAY IT HOT
❑ Laurel LPM-3002: Bootleg. Listed for
identification only.

PLAYBOY MUSIC HALL OF FAME WINNERS (3 LPs)
Various artists collection

❑ Playboy (S) PB-7473............'78 75-100
DISCS 1: Gray label, white and black print.
Mail order offer available exclusively from
Playboy magazine. The one Elvis track is an
otherwise unreleased version of *(It's a) Long
Lonely Highway.* This track, lifted from the
Tickle Me film's audio track, is not the only
screwy item on this LP – the Beatles' *Kansas
City* is from a live concert performance.
(Disc 1) PB-7473-1-1/PB-7473-2-1. (Disc 2) PB-7473-
3/PB-7473-4. (Disc 3) PB-7473-5/PB-7473-6. Identification
numbers are engraved.

❑ Playboy PB-7473.................'78 75-100
COVER 1: Triple pocket. Front and Inside
Front: Playboy Rabbit logo. Inside panels:
Star-shaped cutouts to display names on
inner sleeves of artists heard on this LP.
Back: Text and Rabbit logo.

❑ Playboy PB-7473.................'78 15-25
INNER SLEEVES 1: Silver with black print.
Has artists' names in position to show through
star-cuts on inside panels. For that reason,
the inner sleeves are essential to this cover.

Playboy (S) PB-7473 ....'78 **175-225**
TOTAL PACKAGE 1: Discs, cover, inner
 sleeves.

Card stock jacket, with printing on cover – not
on slicks.

Disc 1
Side 1
Playboy's Theme (Cy Coleman)
Oh! Look at Me Now (Frank Sinatra)
Windy (Wes Montgomery)
Date with Oscar (Lionel Hampton)
A-Tisket A-Tasket (Ella Fitzgerald)
Side 2
A Taste of Honey (Herb Alpert)

Joogie Boogie (Dizzy Gillespie)
One O'Clock Jump (Count Basie)
Do Nothin' Til You Hear from Me (Duke Ellington)
Exotica (John Coltrane)
Disc 2
Side 1
Mack the Knife (Louis Armstrong)
The Sophisticated Rabbit (Shelly Manne)
Theme: Harlem Folk Dance (Stan Kenton)
The Mooche (Duke Ellington)
Side 2
Pilgrim's Progress (Paul Desmond)
Crazy Time (Dave Brubeck)
Don't Blame Me (Miles Davis)
Disc 3
Side 1
All of Me (Frank Sinatra)
Ain't Misbehavin' (Count Basie)
I Wonder Who's Kissing Her Now (Ray Charles)
**(It's a) Long Lonely Highway (shown as "Movin'
Down the Line") (Elvis Presley)**
Kansas City (Beatles)
Side 2
Peoples Peoples (Jimi Hendrix)
Goin' Down Slow (Duane Allman)
Five Long Years (Eric Clapton)
Playboy's Theme (Cy Coleman)

PLEASE RELEASE ME
❑ 1ST Records 161: Bootleg. Listed for
identification only.

POT LUCK WITH ELVIS
❑ RCA Victor (M)
LPM-2523.........................6/62 35-45
DISC 1: Black label, "Long Play" at bottom.
N2PP-1885-3S/N2PP-1886-3S. Label LP#3.
N2PP-1885-4S/N2PP-1886-4S. Label LP#1.
❑ RCA Victor LPM-2523 ....6/62 45-55
COVER 1: Front: RCA Victor logo and
number at lower left. This was the first Elvis
LP that didn't have the RCA Victor logo at
upper right. Color Elvis photo. Back: Black-
and-white photos of four Elvis LPs and one
EP. Price reflects RCA's continued use of this
same cover, with no discernible differences.
INNER SLEEVE 1: Generic RCA sleeves.
Makes no mention of Elvis or this LP.
RCA Victor (M)
LPM-2523 ....6/62 80-100
TOTAL PACKAGE 1: Disc, cover.

❑ RCA Victor (M)
LPM-2523........................10/64 50-65
DISC 2: Black label, "Monaural" at bottom.
N2PP-1885-5S/N2PP-1886-6S. Label LP#12.
❑ RCA Victor LPM-2523 .....10/64 45-55
COVER 2: Same as cover 1.
❑ RCA Victor 21-112-1
40A 10/64 4-8
INNER SLEEVE 2: Red, black and white.
Front: RCA's Elvis LP catalog, most recent
being *Kissin' Cousins* (side 1, row 1, column
6). Back: RCA Elvis EPs and 45s catalog.

RCA Victor (M)
LPM-2523 .... 10/64   100-125
TOTAL PACKAGE 2: Disc, cover, inner sleeve.

❑ RCA Victor (ST)
LSP-2523 .... 6/62   50-75
DISC 3: Black label, "Living Stereo" at bottom.
N2PY-1887-1S/N2PY-1888-1S. Label LP#8.
N2PY-1887-4S/N2PY-1888-4S. Label LP#7.

❑ RCA Victor LSP-2523........6/62   50-75
COVER 3: Front: RCA Victor logo at lower left, number at upper left. Color Elvis photo. Back: Black-and-white photos of four Elvis LPs and one EP.
INNER SLEEVE 3: White, no printing.

RCA Victor (ST)
LSP-2523 .... 6/62   100-150
TOTAL PACKAGE 3: Disc, cover.

❑ RCA Victor (ST)
LSP-2523 .... 10/64   10-20
DISC 4: Black label, RCA logo in white at top and "Stereo" at bottom.

❑ RCA Victor LSP-2523......10/64   40-45
COVER 4: Verification pending.

❑ RCA Victor 21-112-1
40A..................................... 10/64   4-8
INNER SLEEVE 4: Red, black and white. Front: RCA's Elvis LP catalog, most recent being *Kissin' Cousins* (side 1, row 1, column 6). Back: RCA Elvis EPs and 45s catalog.

RCA Victor (ST)
LSP-2523 .... 10/64   50-75
TOTAL PACKAGE 4: Disc, cover, inner sleeve.

❑ RCA Victor (ST)
LSP-2523 .... 11/68   20-25
DISC 5: Orange label. Rigid vinyl.

❑ RCA Victor LSP-2523......11/68   8-10
COVER 5: Verification pending.

❑ RCA Victor 21-112-1
40D..................................... 6/68   4-6
INNER SLEEVE 5: Red, black and white. Front: RCA's Elvis LP catalog, most recent being *Elvis' Gold Records, Vol. 4* (side 1, row 4, column 5). Back: RCA's Elvis LP and Twin Pack Stereo 8 catalog. May also be found with inner sleeves 40B and 40C.

RCA Victor (ST)
LSP-2523 .... 11/68   35-40
TOTAL PACKAGE 5: Disc, cover, inner sleeve.

❑ RCA Victor (ST)
LSP-2523 .... '76   10-15
DISC 6: Tan label.

❑ RCA LSP-2523.................... '76   6-8
COVER 6: Verification pending.

❑ RCA Victor........................ '70s   2-4
INNER SLEEVE 6: Black-and-white. Pictures RCA Elvis catalog front and back. Any of several may be found on reissues from this period.

RCA Victor (ST)
LSP-2523...................... '76   20-25
TOTAL PACKAGE 6: Disc, cover, inner sleeve.

❑ RCA Victor (ST)
LSP-2523 .... '76   4-6
DISC 7: Black label, dog near top.

❑ RCA LSP-2523 .... '76   4-6
COVER 7: Same as cover 4, except has "RE" at lower left on front and "RE2" at corner on back.

❑ RCA Victor........................ '70s   2-4
INNER SLEEVE 7: Black-and-white. Pictures RCA Elvis catalog front and back. Any of several may be found on reissues from this period.

RCA Victor (ST)
LSP-2523...................... '76   10-18
TOTAL PACKAGE 7: Disc, cover, inner sleeve.

❑ RCA Victor (ST)
AFL1-2523........................... '77   3-5
DISC 8: Black label, dog near top.

❑ RCA AFL1-2523 .... '77   3-5
COVER 8: Reflects prefix change.

❑ RCA Victor........................ '70s   2-4
INNER SLEEVE 8: Black-and-white. Pictures RCA Elvis catalog front and back. Any of several may be found on reissues from this period.

RCA Victor (ST)
AFL1-2523...................... '77   8-15
TOTAL PACKAGE 8: Disc, cover, inner sleeve.

Side 1
Kiss Me Quick
Just for Old Times Sake
Gonna Get Back Home Somehow
(Such an) Easy Question
Steppin' Out of Line
I'm Yours

Side 2
Something Blue
Suspicion
I Feel That I've Known You Forever
Night Rider
Fountain of Love
That's Someone You Never Forget

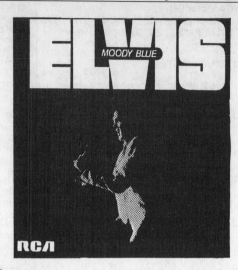

PRESLEYMANIA, VOL. 1

❏ Memphis King LP-2903: Bootleg. Listed for identification only.

PROMISED LAND

❏ RCA Victor (ST)
APL1-0873 .... 1/75   25-30
DISC 1: Orange label. Dynaflex vinyl.
APL1-0873-A-3S/APL1-0873-B-2S.

❏ RCA (ST) APL1-0873........1/75   20-25
COVER 1: Front: RCA logo and number at lower left, number also at upper right. Color '70s Elvis concert photo. Back: Color photos of four other Elvis LPs. Has "0698" at base of spine.

❏ RCA Victor 21-112-1
PT 55B 4/74   3-5
INNER SLEEVE 1: Black-and-white. Pictures RCA Elvis Stereo 8 tape catalog front and back, most recent being *Elvis As Recorded at Madison Square Garden.* (side 2, row 4, column 6).

RCA Victor (ST)

APL1-0873 .... 1/75   **50-60**
TOTAL PACKAGE 1: Disc, cover, inner sleeve.

❏ RCA Victor (ST)
APL1-0873 .... 1/75   25-30
DISC 2: Same as disc 1.

❏ RCA Victor APL1-0873......1/75   25-30
COVER 2: Designate promo. Same as cover 1, but with "Not for Sale" stamped on back.

❏ RCA Victor 21-112-1
PT 55B 4/74   3-5
INNER SLEEVE 2: Black-and-white. Pictures RCA Elvis Stereo 8 tape catalog front and back, most recent being *Elvis As Recorded at Madison Square Garden.* (side 2, row 4, column 6).

RCA Victor (ST)

APL1-0873 .... 1/75   **55-65**
TOTAL PACKAGE 2: Disc, cover, inner sleeve.

❏ RCA (Q) APD1-0873.........1/75   100-125
DISC 3: Quadradisc. Orange label.
APD1-0873-A-2Q/APD1-0873-B-1Q.

❏ RCA APD1-0873 .... 1/75   100-125
COVER 3: Front: Quadradisc logo at upper left. RCA logo and number at lower left, number also at upper right. Color '70s Elvis concert photo. Back: Color photos of four other Elvis LPs. Has "0798" at base of spine.

❏ RCA Victor 21-112-1
PT 54C 11/73   3-5
INNER SLEEVE 3: Black-and-white. Pictures RCA's Elvis LP catalog front and back, most recent being *Elvis As Recorded at Madison Square Garden* (side 2, row 4, column 2).

RCA (Q) APD1-0873 .... 1/75   200-250
TOTAL PACKAGE 3: Disc, cover, inner sleeve.

❏ RCA Victor (ST)
APL1-0873 .... 1/75   6-10
DISC 4: Tan label. Dynaflex vinyl.
APL1-0873A-1S/APL1-0873B-1S.
APL1-0873A-10/APL1-0873B-10.
APL1-0873A-30/APL1-0873B-30.

❏ RCA Victor APL1-0873......1/75   6-10
COVER 4: Same as cover 1.

❏ RCA Victor 21-112-1
PT 55B 4/74   3-5
INNER SLEEVE 4: Black-and-white. Pictures RCA Elvis Stereo 8 tape catalog front and back, most recent being *Elvis As Recorded at Madison Square Garden.* (side 2, row 4, column 6).

RCA Victor (ST)

APL1-0873 .... 1/75   **15-20**
TOTAL PACKAGE 4: Disc, cover, inner sleeve.

❏ RCA Victor (ST)
APL1-0873 .... 1/75   6-10
DISC 5: Same as disc 4.

❏ RCA Victor APL1-0873......1/75   12-15
COVER 5: Designate promo. Same as cover 1, but with "Not for Sale" stamped on back.

❏ RCA Victor 21-112-1
PT 55B 4/74   3-5
INNER SLEEVE 5: Black-and-white. Pictures RCA Elvis Stereo 8 tape catalog front and back, most recent being *Elvis As Recorded at Madison Square Garden.* (side 2, row 4, column 6).

RCA Victor (ST)

APL1-0873 .... 1/75   **20-25**
TOTAL PACKAGE 5: Disc, cover, inner sleeve.

❏ RCA Victor (ST)
LSP-0873 .... '76   4-6
DISC 6: Black label, dog near top.

❏ RCA LSP-0873 .... '76   4-6
COVER 6: Reflects prefix change. Includes copies with a sticker bearing the "AFL1" prefix, wrapped around cover at top of spine.

❏ RCA Victor.......................... '70s   2-4
INNER SLEEVE 6: Black-and-white. Pictures RCA Elvis catalog front and back. Any of several sleeves may be found on reissues from this period.

RCA Victor (ST)

LSP-0873........................ '76   **10-18**
TOTAL PACKAGE 6: Disc, cover, inner sleeve.

❏ RCA Victor (ST)
AFL1-0873............................ '77   3-5
DISC 7: Black label, dog near top.

❑ RCA AFL1-0873 .... '77　　3-5
　　COVER 7: Reflects prefix change.
❑ RCA Victor.......................... '70s　　2-4
　　INNER SLEEVE 7: Black-and-white. Pictures
　　RCA Elvis catalog front and back. Any of
　　several sleeves may be found on reissues
　　from this period.

RCA Victor (ST)
　　AFL1-0873 .... '77　　**10-18**
　　**TOTAL PACKAGE 7: Disc, cover, inner
　　sleeve.**

❑ RCA Victor (ST)
　　AFL1-0873 .... '77　　3-5
　　DISC 8: Black label, dog near top.
❑ RCA AFL1-0873 .... '77　　8-10
　　COVER 8: Designate promo. Same as cover
　　7, but with "Not for Sale" stamped on back.
❑ RCA Victor.......................... '70s　　2-4
　　INNER SLEEVE 8: Black-and-white. Pictures
　　RCA Elvis catalog front and back. Any of
　　several sleeves may be found on reissues
　　from this period.

RCA Victor (ST)
　　AFL1-0873 .... '77　　**15-20**
　　**TOTAL PACKAGE 8: Disc, cover, inner
　　sleeve.**

❑ RCA Victor (Q)
　　APD1-0873.......................... '77　　50-75
　　DISC 9: Quadradisc. Black label, dog near
　　top.
　　APD1-0873-A₁2Q/APD1-0873-B-1Q.
❑ RCA APD1-0873 .... 7/77　　50-75
　　COVER 9: Same as cover 3.
❑ RCA Victor 21-112-1
　　PT 54F .... 7/77　　2-4
　　INNER SLEEVE 9: Black-and-white. Pictures
　　RCA's Elvis LPs front and back, most recent
　　being *Moody Blue* (side 2, row 5, column 1).

RCA Victor (Q)
　　APD1-0873 .... '77　　**100-150**
　　**TOTAL PACKAGE 9: Disc, cover, inner
　　sleeve.**

May have a generic "Factory Sealed" sticker,
but it makes no mention of Elvis or this LP.

Side A
Promised Land
There's a Honky Tonk Angel
Help Me
Mr. Songman
Love Song of the Year

Side B
It's Midnight
Your Love's Been a Long Time Coming
If You Talk in Your Sleep
Thinking About You
You Asked Me To

PURE ELVIS

❑ RCA (ST) DJL1-3455 ....8/79　　250-300
　　DISC 1: White label with black print.
　　Promotional issue only. "Pure Elvis" is the title
　　on the cover but not on labels, which give only
　　"Our Memories Of Elvis, Vol. 2" as the title.
　　DJL1-3455-A-1S/DJL1-3455-B-2S. Identification numbers
　　are engraved.
❑ RCA DJL1-3455 ....8/79　　250-300
　　COVER 1: Front: RCA logo and number at
　　lower left. "Not for Sale" at upper right. Black-
　　and-white Elvis '70s concert photo. Back: Text
　　only.
❑ RCA Victor 21-112-1
　　PT 54F..............................7/77　　2-4
　　INNER SLEEVE 1: Black-and-white. Pictures
　　RCA's Elvis LPs front and back, most recent
　　being *Moody Blue* (side 2, row 5, column 1).
　　INSERT: A one-page, in-house memo
　　regarding this LP has been thought by some
　　to be an insert sent with the album. This is not
　　the case. Titled "The Real Sound of Elvis," the
　　memo was nothing more than "RCA Internal
　　Correspondence," which defined for
　　distributors the "Pure Elvis" sound.

RCA (ST) DJL1-3455 ......8/79　　**500-600**
　　**TOTAL PACKAGE : Disc, cover, inner
　　sleeve.**

The four songs on side 1 are *unsweetened*,
which constitutes the "pure Elvis" sound. The
same songs on side 2 are presented exactly
as originally issued. This LP was a
promotional item for *Our Memories of Elvis,
Volume 2.*

Side 1
I Got a Feelin' in My Body
For the Heart
She Wears My Ring
Find Out What's Happening

Side 2
I Got a Feelin' in My Body
For the Heart
She Wears My Ring
Find Out What's Happening

PURE GOLD

❑ RCA (SP) ANL1-0971(e) ...6/75　　5-7
　　DISC 1: Orange label. Flexible vinyl.
　　ANL1-0971A-1/ANL1-0971B-1.
　　ANL1-0971A-2/ANL1-0971B-2. Pressings using these same
　　identification numbers can be found with varying degrees of
　　flexibility – from nearly rigid to very thin.
❑ RCA ANL1-0971(e) ....6/75　　5-7
　　COVER 1: Front: RCA logo at lower left,
　　number at upper right. Color Elvis '70s concert
　　photo. Back: Pictures 18 RCA LPs in the
　　"Pure Gold" series, including this one.
　　INNER SLEEVE 1: White, no printing.

RCA (SP)
　　ANL1-0971(e) ....6/75　　**10-15**
　　TOTAL PACKAGE 1: Disc, cover.

❑ RCA (SP) ANL1-0971(e) ...6/75　　5-7
　　DISC 2: Same as disc 1.

❑ RCA ANL1-0971(e) 6/75   8-12
COVER 2: Designate promo. Same as cover
1, but with "Not for Sale" stamped on back.
INNER SLEEVE 2: White, no printing.
RCA (SP)
ANL1-0971(e) 6/75   15-20
TOTAL PACKAGE 2: Disc, cover.

❑ RCA (SP) ANL1-0971(e).....'76   4-6
DISC 3: Yellow label.
❑ RCA ANL1-0971(e) ....'76   4-6
COVER 3: Verification pending.
INNER SLEEVE 3: White, no printing.
RCA (SP) ANL1-0971(e) ...'76   8-12
TOTAL PACKAGE 3: Disc, cover.

❑ RCA (SP) AYL1-3732......11/80   3-5
DISC 4: Yellow label.
AYL1-3732A/AYL1-3732B. Identification numbers are
engraved. Also ANL1-0971A- 6/ANL1-0971B-6 is stamped
but crossed out. On side B only, AML7-0971-B is stamped
but crossed out.

❑ RCA AYL1-3732.............11/80   3-5
COVER 4: Reflects selection number change.
Part of RCA's "Best Buy Series." Includes
copies with a sticker bearing the "AYL1"
prefix, wrapped around cover at top of spine.
INNER SLEEVE 4: White, no printing.
RCA (SP) AYL1-3732....11/80   6-10
TOTAL PACKAGE 4: Disc, cover.

Side A
Kentucky Rain
Fever
It's Impossible
Jailhouse Rock
Don't Be Cruel
Side B
I Got a Woman
All Shook Up
Loving You
In the Ghetto
Love Me Tender

QSP PRESENTS A GIFT OF MUSIC
Various artists collection
❑ RCA Special Products (SP)
QSP1-0034 ....'84   20-30
DISC 1: Red label, black and white print. A
promotional sampler made for QSP, a direct
sales subsidiary of *Reader's Digest.*
QSP1-0034A-1/QSP1-0034B-1.
❑ RCA QSP1-0034 ....'84   20-30
COVER 1: Front: RCA logo on label of a gold
record album. Back: Number at upper right.
Text and illustrations.
INNER SLEEVE 1: White, no printing.
RCA Special Products (SP)
QSP1-0034 ....'84   40-60
TOTAL PACKAGE 1: Disc, cover.

Card stock jacket, with printing on cover – not
on slicks.
Side A
Islands in the Stream (Kenny Rogers & Dolly Parton)
Sweet Dreams (Are Made of This) (Eurythmics)

The Best of Times (Perry Como)
The Wayward Wind (James Galway & Sylvia)
Say It Isn't So (Hall & Oates)
Return of the Jedi (Charles Gerhardt and the National
Philharmonic Orchestra)
Side B
Dixieland Delight (Alabama)
Hooked on Big Bands (Larry Elgart and His Manhattan
Swing Orchestra)
Love Me Tender (Elvis Presley)
Burning Bridges (Charley Pride)
Theme from "Dallas" (Joe Reisman Orchestra)
God Bless America (Leontyne Price)

QSP PRESENTS A GIFT OF MUSIC
Various artists collection
❑ RCA Special Products (S)
QSP1-0037.......................'80s   20-30
DISC 1: Red label, black and white print. A
promotional sampler made for QSP, a direct
sales subsidiary of *Reader's Digest.* Has one
Elvis track, *Can't Help Falling in Love.*
QSP1-0037A-1/QSP1-0037B-1.
❑ RCA QSP1-0037 ....'80s   20-30
COVER 1: Verification pending.
INNER SLEEVE 1: White, no printing.
RCA Special Products (S)
QSP1-0037 ....'80s   40-60
TOTAL PACKAGE 1: Disc, cover.

❑ RCA Special Products (S)
QSP1-0037.......................'80s   55-70
DISC 2: Same as disc 1, except has a very
large RCA logo pressed into the vinyl, similar
to what might be found on a picture disc.
❑ RCA QSP1-0037 ....'80s   20-30
COVER 2: Same as cover 1.
INNER SLEEVE 2: White, no printing.
RCA Special Products (S)
QSP1-0037 ....'80s   75-100
TOTAL PACKAGE 2: Disc, cover.

Card stock jacket, with printing on cover – not
on slicks.

RCA RADIO VICTROLA DIVISION SPOTS
❑ RCA Victor (M) 0401 ....10/56   800-1200
DISC 1: Maroon label, silver print. Single-
sided disc with four 50-second radio
commercials for RCA's Victrolas, as well as
for the bonus SPD-22 and SPD-23 EPs. Elvis
is the announcer on all of the spots, which
also include excerpts of songs from the two
SPD extended plays. Issued only to radio
stations running the spots.
COVER 1: None made.
INNER SLEEVE 1: Plain, no printing.
RCA Victor (M) 0401.....10/56   1000-1500
TOTAL PACKAGE 1: Disc.

RCA VICTOR

NOVEMBER/DECEMBER SAMPLER
59-44 thru 59-47

SPS
33-67
K2NY-5895

SIDE 2

NOT FOR
SALE

1-I BEG OF YOU (LPM-2075) 2-I'M SITTING ON
TOP OF THE WORLD (Excerpt LPM-2083, Side1)
3-CAMP MEETIN' TIME (LSP-2091)
4-AT THE JAZZ BAND BALL (LPM-2097)
5-I KNOW THAT YOU KNOW (LSP-2103)
6-CHA-CON-CHA (LSP-2113)
7-RIFF BLUES (Theme) (LSP-2140)
1. Presley 2. Gardner 3. Wood
4. Dukes of Dixieland
5. Atkins 6. Puente's Orch.
7. Arr and cond. by
Martin

LIVING STEREO

The Playboy
Music Hall of Fame
Winners

Celebrating Playboy's Silver Anniversary

RCA UNTITLED SAMPLERS

Each of the following RCA samplers is a collection of tunes by various artists. All were promotional issues only and each includes at least one Elvis track, shown in boldface type. As prices suggest, the RCA samplers rank among the rarest of all Elvis collectibles. Though some collectors do not consider them as essential as all-Elvis releases, there are still not enough of these discs to satisfy the demand. Some are so scarce that only one or two copies are known to exist. Untitled samplers are listed in alphanumeric order, with cross references provided for titled ones. Worth noting are the other selections RCA chose to feature on these samplers, and how often Elvis was surrounded by music totally unlike his.

SP-33-4

❑ SP-33-4 (M) 7/56   1000-1500
DISC 1: Black label, "Long Play" at bottom.
J2NP-1779-1/J2NP-1780-1A.
COVER 1: None made.
INNER SLEEVE 1: White, no printing.
SP-33-4 (M) 7/56   1000-1500
TOTAL PACKAGE 1: Disc.

Side 1
Magyar Melodies (Gypsy Sandor)
Pretending (Andy Russell)
My Bucket's Got a Hole in It (Bob Scobey)
Dodging a Divorcee (Skitch Henderson)
Frenesi (Herb Jeffries)
Usted (Luis Arcaraz)
Francisco Guayabal (Deny Mor)
Hot Timbales (Tito Puente)
El Chicero (Billo)
Oye Este Ritmo (M. Lopez)
The Lord's Prayer (Jerome)

Side 2
I'm Movin' on to Glory (Hank Snow)
Babalu (La Playa)
Twilight in Turkey (Tommy Dorsey)
Just Say I Love Her (Lou Monte)
Don't Be Cruel (Elvis Presley)
I'm Glad I'm Not You (Grant-Martin)
Holiday for Strings (Glenn Miller)
Pavan for a Dead Princess (Fritz Reiner)
Trio in G (Beethoven) (Heifetz-Primrose)
Marriage of Figaro (G. Tozzi)
Capriccio (W. Landowska)
A Mighty Fortress (Robert Shaw)

SP-33-10P

❑ SP-33-10P (M) 8/58   900-1200
DISC 1: Black label, "Long Play" at bottom.
J2NP-6273-1A/J2NP-6274-1 B1. Identification numbers are engraved on side 1 and stamped on side 2.
COVER 1: None made.
INNER SLEEVE 1: White, no printing.
SP-33-10P (M).................8/58   900-1200
TOTAL PACKAGE 1: Disc.

Side 1
Under the Bridges of Paris (Dissell & O'Reilly)
Maria Elena (Los Indios Tabajaras)
In Spain They Say Si Si (Tony Martin)
Freilach Merengue (Johnny Conquet)
The World Is Your Balloon (Tony Perkins)
Cheerful Little Earfull (Dave Pell)
Speak Easy (Clegg)

Side 2
Love, Love, Love (George Feyer)
Oye Negra (Xavier Cugat)
The Queen's Fancy (J. Lewis)
Diamonds Are a Girl's Best Friend (Lena Horne)
Pampa (Adios Pampa Mia) (Perez Prado)
King Creole (Elvis Presley)
Medley (M. Davis)

SPS-33-27: see *AUGUST 1959 SAMPLER*
SPS-33-54: see *OCTOBER CHRISTMAS SAMPLER*
SP-33-59-7: see *FEBRUARY SAMPLER*
SP-33-66: see *CHRISTMAS PROGRAMMING FROM RCA VICTOR*
SPS 33-96: see *OCTOBER 1960 POPULAR STEREO SAMPLER*
SPS 33-141: see *OCTOBER '61 POP SAMPLER*
SPS 33-57: see *NOVEMBER/DECEMBER SAMPLER*
SPS 33-191: see *DECEMBER '62 POP SAMPLER*
SPS 33-219: see *SEPTEMBER '63 POP SAMPLER*
SPS 33-247: see *DECEMBER '63 POP SAMPLER*
SPS 33-272: see *APRIL '64 POP SAMPLER*
SPS 33-331: see *APRIL '65 POP SAMPLER*
SPS 33-347: see *AUGUST '65 POP SAMPLER*
SPS 33-403: see *APRIL '66 POP SAMPLER*

RADIO RECORDERS REVISITED

❑ Laurel 06184: Bootleg. Listed for identification only.

RADIO THRILLS

❑ Moon 101: Bootleg. Listed for identification only.

RADIO'S MILLION PERFORMANCE SONGS

Various artists collection
❑ CBS Songs (SP)
SNGS-101 ....'84   25-30
DISC 1: Yellow label, black print. Promotional issue only.
SNGS A-101-RE2A/SNGS B-101-RE-1A. Identification numbers are engraved.

❑ CBS Songs SNGS-101 .... '84   25-30

COVER 1: Front: CBS Songs logo at upper right. 13 black-and-white photos of artists heard on this LP, including Elvis. Back: 14 black-and-white photos, the same poses as the ones on front – but larger.
INNER SLEEVE 1: White, no printing.

CBS Songs (SP)

SNGS-101 .... '84   **50-60**
TOTAL PACKAGE 1: Disc, cover.

Card stock jacket, with printing on cover – not on slicks.

Side 1

Ain't That a Shame (Fats Domino)
Don't Be Cruel (Elvis Presley)
Handy Man (Jimmy Jones)
Come Softly to Me (Fleetwoods)
I Hear You Knocking (Gale Storm)
I'm Walkin' (Fats Domino)
Mockingbird (Inez & Charlie Foxx)

Side 2

Elusive Butterfly (Bob Lind)
Hard Day's Night (Beatles)
Four Walls (Jim Reeves)
Put a Little Love in Your Heart (Jackie De Shannon)
Weekend in New England (Barry Manilow)
Nobody Does It Better (Carly Simon)
Wasted Days and Wasted Nights (Freddie Fender)
With Pen in Hand (Bobby Goldsboro)

RAISED ON ROCK / FOR OL' TIMES SAKE

❑ RCA Victor (ST)
APL1-0388 .... 11/73   10-15
DISC 1: Orange label. Dynaflex vinyl.
APL1-0388A-1/APL1-0388B-1.
APL1-0388A-2/APL1-0388B-2.
APL1-0388A-2/APL1-0388B-4S.

❑ RCA APL1-0388 .... 11/73   15-20
COVER 1: Front: RCA logo and number at middle right. Color Elvis '70s concert photo. Title at top is *Raised on Rock*. Back: Same photo as on front. Title at top is *For Ol' Times Sake*. Has "0598" at base of spine.

❑ RCA Victor 21-112-1
PT 54C 11/73   3-5
INNER SLEEVE 1: Black-and-white. Pictures RCA's Elvis LP catalog front and back, most recent being *Elvis As Recorded at Madison Square Garden* (side 2, row 4, column 2). May also be found with inner sleeve 57B.

RCA Victor (ST)

APL1-0388 .... 11/73   **30-40**
TOTAL PACKAGE 1: Disc, cover, inner sleeve.

❑ RCA Victor (ST)
APL1-0388 .... 11/73   10-15
DISC 2: Same as disc 1.
❑ RCA Victor APL1-0388.... 11/73   20-25
COVER 2: Designate promo. Same as cover 1, but with "Not for Sale" stamped on back.

❑ RCA Victor 21-112-1
PT 54C 11/73   3-5
INNER SLEEVE 2: Black-and-white. Pictures RCA's Elvis LP catalog front and back, most recent being *Elvis As Recorded at Madison Square Garden* (side 2, row 4, column 2). May also be found with inner sleeve 57B.

RCA Victor (ST)

APL1-0388 .... 11/73   **35-45**
TOTAL PACKAGE 2: Disc, cover, inner sleeve.

❑ RCA (ST) AFL1-0388 .... '76   15-20
DISC 3: Tan label.
❑ RCA AFL1-0388 .... '76   15-20
COVER 3: Verification pending.
❑ RCA Victor .... '70s   2-4
INNER SLEEVE 3: Black-and-white. Pictures RCA Elvis catalog front and back. Any of several may be found on reissues from this period.

RCA (ST) AFL1-0388 .... '76   30-40

TOTAL PACKAGE 3: Disc, cover, inner sleeve.

❑ RCA (ST) APL1-0388 .... '77   3-5
DISC 4: Black label, dog near top.
AFL1-0388A-1/AFL1-0388B-1.
❑ RCA APL1-0388 .... '77   3-5
COVER 4: Same as cover 1, except does not have "0598" at base of spine.
❑ RCA Victor .... '70s   2-4
INNER SLEEVE 4: Black-and-white. Pictures RCA Elvis catalog front and back. Any of several sleeves may be found on reissues from this period.

RCA (ST) APL1-0388 .... '77   8-15

TOTAL PACKAGE 4: Disc, cover, inner sleeve.

Side A

Raised on Rock
Are You Sincere
Find Out What's Happening
I Miss You
Girl of Mine

Side B

For Ol' Times Sake
If You Don't Come Back
Just a Little Bit
Sweet Angeline
Three Corn Patches

RALPH EMERY SHOW

Various artists collections.

❑ Ralph Emery Show (S)   10-15
DISC 1: Price range is for any individual disc containing at least one Elvis track.

❑ Ralph Emery Show (S)............. 35-50
COMPLETE SET 1: Set of five LPs. Each is a complete one-hour, weekly radio show with five pages of cue sheets and program notes. Issued only to subscribing radio stations. Price range is for any complete set containing at least one Elvis track.

REACH OUT AND TOUCH (7 LPs)
Various artists collection
Mail order offer only. All discs in this set have a black, white and red label, and are listed individually below. All identification numbers are engraved. Reportedly has one or more Elvis tracks.

❑ Reader's Digest/BMG
RBA-037-1 .... '91   3-4
DISC 1:
X1RS-5631-1/X1RS-5632-1.

❑ Reader's Digest/BMG
RBA-037-2 .... '91   3-4
DISC 2:
X1RS-5633-1/X1RS-5634-1.

❑ Reader's Digest/BMG
RBA-037-3 .... '91   3-4
DISC 3:
X1RS-5635-1/X1RS-5636-1.

❑ Reader's Digest/BMG
RBA-037-4 .... '91   3-4
DISC 4:
X1RS-5637-1/X1RS-5638-1.

❑ Reader's Digest/BMG
RBA-037-5 .... '91   3-4
DISC 5:
X1RS-5639-1/X1RS-5640-1.

❑ Reader's Digest/BMG
RBA-037-6 .... '91   3-4
DISC 6:
X1RS-5641-1/X1RS-5642-3.

❑ Reader's Digest/BMG
RBA-037-7 .... '91   3-4
DISC 7:
X1RS-5643-1/X1RS-5644-1.

❑ Reader's Digest/BMG
RBA-037A .... '91   15-20
BOX 1: Slipcover: White with rust print. Front: Reader's Digest/BMG logo at lower right. Back is blank. Record case: White with pink and gold print. Back is blank.
INNER SLEEVES 1: Generic, individually numbered, plastic sleeves. Front and Back: Clear, covered with Reader's Digest Pegasus logos. No mention of Elvis.

❑ Reader's Digest/BMG.......... '91   5-7
INSERT 1: 3" x 3" information and program notes booklet.

Reader's Digest/BMG Music (SP)
RBA-037A .... '91   40-55
TOTAL PACKAGE 1: Discs, box, insert.

REBIRTH OF BEALE STREET
Various artists collection

❑ Beale Street (SP) BS-1........'83   90-100
DISC 1: Brown label, yellow print. Collection of songs from 1923 to 1983 by Memphis recording artists. Limited-edition, numbered promotional only LP made by the City of Memphis.
BS-1-A L-14232/BS-1-B L-14232-X. Identification numbers are engraved.

❑ Beale Street BS-1................'83   90-100
COVER 1: Front: Beale Street logo at lower right. "A Limited Edition of 1000" and copy number at upper right. Back: Color photo of Lou Rawls, duotone of W.C. Handy at upper left.
INNER SLEEVE 1: White, no printing.

❑ Beale Street BS-1................'83   10-20
INSERT 1: Eight-page, 11¾" x 11¾" color booklet, *Beale St. Reborn.* Tells the Beale Street story – past and present.

Beale Street (SP) BS-1.....'83   200-225
TOTAL PACKAGE 1: Disc, cover, insert.

Side 1
Birth of the Blues (Lou Rawls)
Rebirth of Beale Street (Lou Rawls)
Memphis Blues (Handy's Blues)
St. Louis Blues (Handy's Orchestra)
Midnight Frolic Drag (Charlie Williamson Orchestra)
Judge Harsh Blues (Furry Lewis)
So Glad Troubles Don't Last Always (Illinois Central)
Fourth Street Mess Around (Memphis Jug Band)
Three O'Clock Blues (B.B. King)

Side 2
Yes, Yes, I've Done My Duty (Sunset Travelers)
Mystery Train (Little Junior's Blue Flames)
Mystery Train (Elvis Presley)
That's All Right (Elvis Presley)
Walking the Dog (Rufus Thomas)
Birth of the Blues (Lou Rawls)
Rebirth of Beale Street (Lou Rawls)

RECONSIDER BABY

❑ RCA (SP) AFL1-5418........4/85   12-15
DISC 1: Blue vinyl. Gold, black and white "Elvis 50th Anniversary" label.
AFL1-5418A-1/AFL1-5418B-1. Identification numbers are engraved.

❑ RCA AFL1-5418 ....4/85   4-5
COVER 1: Front: No lettering. Colorized Elvis (circa 1955) photo. Back: Two duotone Elvis (circa 1957) photos. UPC bar code at upper right.
INNER SLEEVE 1: White, no printing.

❑ RCA AFL1-5418 ....4/85   4-5
SHRINK STICKER 1: Circular, blue and white. Announces "Newly Discovered Versions of *Tomorrow Night* and *Ain't That Lovin' You Baby*, and that LP is blue vinyl.
RCA (SP)
AFL1-5418..................4/85   20-25
TOTAL PACKAGE 1: Disc, cover, sticker.

❑ RCA (SP) AFL1-5418 .... 8/85   10-12
DISC 2: Black vinyl. Gold, black and white "Elvis 50th Anniversary" label.
❑ RCA AFL1-5418 .... 2/85   4-5
COVER 2: Same as cover 1.
INNER SLEEVE 2: White, no printing.
RCA (SP) AFL1-5418 ..... 8/85   **15-20**
   TOTAL PACKAGE 2: Disc, cover.

Card stock jacket, with printing on cover – not on slicks.

Side A
Reconsider Baby
Tomorrow Night
So Glad You're Mine
One Night
When It Rains, It Really Pours
My Baby Left Me
Ain't That Loving You Baby (Fast version)

Side B
I Feel So Bad
Down in the Alley
Hi-Heel Sneakers
Stranger in My Own Home Town
Merry Christmas Baby

RECORD REPORT WITH CHARLIE TUNA

Various artists covered.

❑ Filmways Radio .... '77-78   5-10
DISCS 1: Silver labels with black print. Syndicated radio show providing music news and interviews. Hosted by Charlie Tuna, a Los Angeles dee jay. Each disc has 10, five-minute shows, enough for one week of programs. Price is for any individual disc in the series that mentions Elvis. Issued only to subscribing stations.
INNER SLEEVES 1: White, no printing.
Filmways Radio .... '77-78   **5-10**
   TOTAL PACKAGE 1: Disc.

RECORDED LIVE ON STAGE IN MEMPHIS: see *ELVIS RECORDED LIVE ON STAGE IN MEMPHIS*

REFLECTIONS OF ELVIS (3 LP)

❑ Diamond P. Productions
  (S) 8/77   345-390
DISCS 1: Complete three-hour radio show. Issued only to subscribing radio stations.
COVER 1: None made.
INNER SLEEVES 1: White, no printing.
❑ Diamond P. Productions.... 8/77   5-10
INSERT 1: Three pages of cue sheets and program notes.
Diamond P. Productions
  (S) 8/77   **350-400**
   TOTAL PACKAGE 1: Discs, insert.

REMEMBERING (2 LPs)

❑ RCA Special Products/Pair (SP)
  PDL2-1037 .... 12/83   12-15
DISCS 1: Black label, dog near top. RCA Special Products logo at top. Pair logo at bottom. Title on labels read: "Elvis Presley, Remembering."
(**Disc 1**) PDL2-1037-A-3/PDL2-1037-B-1. (**Disc 2**) PDL2-1037-C-1/PDL2-1037-D-3.
❑ RCA Special Products/Pair
  PDL2-1037 .... 12/83   12-15
COVER 1: Single pocket. Front: RCA Special Products logo and number at lower left. Pair logo at lower right. Color Elvis (circa 1956) photo. Title on front and back cover is "Remembering Elvis." Back: Black-and-white copy of same photo as on front.
INNER SLEEVES 1: White, no printing.
RCA Special Products/Pair (SP)
  PDL2-1037 .... 12/83   **25-30**
   TOTAL PACKAGE 1: Discs, cover.

Card stock jacket, with printing on cover – not on slicks.

Disc 1
Side 1
Blue Moon of Kentucky
Young and Beautiful
Milkcow Blues Boogie
Baby, Let's Play House

Side 2
Good Rockin' Tonight
We're Gonna Move
I Want to Be Free
I Forgot to Remember to Forget

Disc 2
Side 1
Kiss Me Quick
Just for Old Times Sake
Gonna Get Back Home Somehow
(Such an) Easy Question

Side 2
Suspicion
I Feel That I've Known You Forever
Night Rider
Fountain of Love

RETURN OF THE ROCKER

❑ RCA Victor (SP)
  5600-1-R 6/86   7-10
DISC 1: Black label, dog near top.
5600-1-R-A-1/5600-1-R-B-1. Identification numbers are engraved.
❑ RCA 5600-1-R 6/86   8-10
COVER 1: Front: No logo or number. Color Elvis painting by Mark Chickinelli is reproduced. Back: RCA logo at lower left, number and UPC bar code at upper right.
INNER SLEEVE 1: White, no printing.
RCA Victor (SP)
  5600-1-R 6/86   **15-20**
   TOTAL PACKAGE 1: Disc, cover.

❑ RCA Victor (SP)
5600-1-R 6/86   7-10
DISC 2: Same as disc 1.

❑ RCA 5600-1-R....................6/86   12-15
COVER 2: Designate promo. Same as cover
1, but with "Not for Sale" stamped on back.
INNER SLEEVE 2: White, no printing.

RCA Victor (SP)
5600-1-R........................6/86   20-25
TOTAL PACKAGE 2: Disc, cover.

Card stock jacket, with printing on cover – not
on slicks.

Side A
King of the Whole Wide World
(Marie's the Name) His Latest Flame
Little Sister
A Mess of Blues
Like a Baby
I Want You With Me

Side B
Stuck on You
Return to Sender
Make Me Know It
Witchcraft
I'm Comin' Home
Follow That Dream

ROBERT W. MORGAN FOR TODAY'S ARMY

Various artists collections.

❑ U.S. Army (S)   10-15
DISC 1: Price range is for any individual disc
containing at least one Elvis track. A public
service radio show.

❑ U.S. Army (S)   5-10
COVER 1: Gatefold, with red, white and blue
title.

U.S. Army (S)........................   15-25
TOTAL PACKAGE 1: Disc, cover.

For a complete set of five LPs – each a
complete one-hour, weekly radio show with
five pages of cue sheets and program notes –
multiply the price range shown above times
the number of discs containing at least one
Elvis track.

ROBERT W. SARNOFF – 25 YEARS OF RCA LEADERSHIP

Various artists collection

❑ RCA Victor (S)
RWS-0001...........................'73   750-1000
DISC 1: Orange label. Dynaflex vinyl. In-
house promotional issue only. Made as
souvenirs for Sarnoff's retirement party.
CPRS-5501/CPRS-5502.

❑ RCA RWS-0001 ....'73   750-1000
COVER 1: Front: Black-and-white photo of
Robert W. Sarnoff. Back: Text only.
INNER SLEEVE 1: White, no printing.

RCA Victor (S)
RWS-0001 ....'73   1500-2000
TOTAL PACKAGE 1: Disc, cover.

Side 1 - Band 1 (The Post-War Years: Crooners/ Comedy/Mambo)
Because (Perry Como)
My Two Front Teeth (Spike Jones)
Be My Love (Mario Lanza)
The Thing (Phil Harris)
Anytime (Eddie Fisher)
Ghost Riders in the Sky (Vaughn Monroe)
Cherry Pink and Apple Blossom White (Perez Prado)
Oh My Pa-Pa (Eddie Fisher)

Side 1 - Band 2 (From the Golden Classics to the Presley Era)
Tchaikovsky Violin Concerto (Jascha Heifetz)
Chopin "Polonaise in A♭" (Artur Rubinstein)
Puccini "Un-beldi" from *Madam Butterfly* (Leontyne Price)
Liszt "Hungarian Rhapsody No. 2" (Vladimir Horowitz)
The Symphony of the Air/Beethoven Symphony No. 9 (Arturo Toscanini)
Hound Dog (Elvis Presley)
Don't Be Cruel (Elvis Presley)
Heartbreak Hotel (Elvis Presley)
In the Ghetto (Live) (Elvis Presley)

Side 1 - Band 3 (Broadway's Brightest Lights)
Hello Dolly/Fiddler on the Roof
Hair/South Pacific
The Sound of Music

Side 1 - Band 4 (The Closing Fifties)
Day-O (The Banana Boat Song) (Harry Belafonte)
Mathilda (Harry Belafonte)
Tchaikovsky "Piano Concerto No. 1" (Van Cliburn)
The Kennedy Wit (John F. Kennedy)

Side 2 - Band 1 (The Middle Years: Soundtracks/Instrumentals/Country)
Victory at Sea (Richard Rodgers-Robert Russell Bennett)
Peter Gunn (Henry Mancini)
Moon River (Henry Mancini)
I Will Follow Him (Little Peggy March)
Sugar Lips (Al Hirt)
Ballad of the Green Berets (SSgt. Barry Sadler)
Bouquet of Roses (shown as "Big Bouquet of Roses") (Eddy Arnold)
The Three Bells (Browns)
Kiss an Angel Good Morning (Charley Pride)
I'm So Afraid of Losing You Again (Charley Pride)
He'll Have to Go (Jim Reeves)
Tennessee Waltz (Chet Atkins and the Boston Pops)

Side 2 - Band 2 (Rock Begins)
Last Train to Clarksville (Monkees)
I'm a Believer (Monkees)
These Eyes (Guess Who)
Light My Fire (Jose Feliciano)
Somebody to Love (Jefferson Airplane)

Side 2 - Band 3 (The New RCA)
A Few Words from Neil Armstrong (Neil Armstrong)
Grazing in the Grass (Friends of Distinction)
Take Me Home Country Roads (John Denver)
Everybody Plays the Fool (Main Ingredient)
Troglodye (Caveman) (Jimmy Castor Bunch)
Space Oddity (David Bowie)
It's Impossible (Perry Como)
Without You (Harry Nilsson)

Side 2 - Band 4 (Epilog)
Keep the Dream Alive/The January 15 Benefit Concert
for the Martin Luther King Jr. Center for Social
Change/Precious Lord (Linda Hopkins)

ROCK ME GENTLY

❑ Astra AST-400: Bootleg. Listed for
identification only.

ROCK'N ROLL FOREVER

❑ RCA Special Products (M)
DML1-0437 .... '81   7-10
DISC 1: Black label, dog near top. Offered by
Candlelite Music as a mail order bonus. Title
shown on label as "Rock and Roll Forever."
DML1-0437A-1/DML1-0437B-1.

❑ RCA DML1-0437 .... '81   8-10
COVER 1: Front: Nipper (but not RCA) logo at
lower right, number at upper right. Candlelite
logo at top center. Duotone Elvis *Loving You*
photo. Back: Same photo as on front.
INNER SLEEVE 1: White, no printing.

RCA Special Products (M)
DML1-0437 .... '81   15-20
TOTAL PACKAGE 1: Disc, cover.

Label indicates "Stereo" but songs are all true
monaural.
Card stock jacket, with printing on cover – not
on slicks.

Side A
One Night
(Let Me Be Your) Teddy Bear
Love Me Tender
Don't Be Cruel
I Want You, I Need You, I Love You

Side B
Jailhouse Rock
Heartbreak Hotel
Blue Suede Shoes
Hound Dog
All Shook Up

ROCK AND ROLL ROOTS

Various artists collection

❑ Rock and Roll Roots............ '78   10-20
DISCS 1: Light blue labels with dark blue
print. Complete three-hour syndicated radio
show. Ran for about six months during 1978.
Issued only to subscribing stations. Although
three discs were sent each week, price is for
any of the LPs having an Elvis track. *Roots*
discs that do *not* have an Elvis song are
valued at $5 to $10 each.
INNER SLEEVES 1: White, no printing.

❑ Rock and Roll Roots............ '78   5-10
INSERTS 1: Cue sheets with program notes.
Price is for any corresponding to discs with an
Elvis track.

Rock and Roll Roots........ '78   15-30
TOTAL PACKAGE 1: Disc, insert.

Elvis Contents:
Program 3
Hound Dog (Side 1B)
Program 7
(Let Me Be Your) Teddy Bear (Side 1A)
Program 8
Hard Headed Woman (Side 2A)
Program 18
Return to Sender (Side 3A)

ROCK AND ROLL: THE EARLY DAYS

Various artists collection

❑ RCA Victor (M)
AFM1-5463......................7/85   4-5
DISC 1:
AFM1-5463-A-2/AFM1-5463-B-1. Identification numbers are
engraved.

❑ RCA AFM1-5463 ....7/85   4-5
COVER 1: Front: No logo or number.
Colorized photos of five artists heard on the
LP, including Elvis. Back: RCA logo at lower
right, number and UPC bar code at upper
right. Eight colorized photos (different poses
than on front) of artists heard on the LP,
including Elvis.
INNER SLEEVE 1: White, no printing.

❑ RCA AFM1-5463 ....7/85   3-5
INSERT 1: Four-page brochure, offering the
Rock and Roll: The Early Days videocassette.
16 black-and-white photos of artists on the
tape, including two of Elvis.

❑ RCA AFM1-5463 ....7/85   3-5
SHRINK STICKER 1: Black-and-white,
announces the availability of *Rock and Roll:
The Early Days* videocassette.

RCA Victor (M)
AFM1-5463.................7/85   15-20
TOTAL PACKAGE 1: Disc, cover, insert,
sticker.

❑ RCA Victor (M)
AFM1-5463......................7/85   4-5
DISC 2:

❑ RCA AFM1-5463 ....7/85   8-10
COVER 2: Designate promo. Same as cover
1, but with "Not for Sale" stamped on back.
INNER SLEEVE 2: White, no printing.

❑ RCA AFM1-5463 ....7/85   3-5
INSERT 2: Four-page brochure, offering the
Rock and Roll: The Early Days videocassette.
16 black-and-white photos of artists on the
tape, including two of Elvis.

❑ RCA AFM1-5463 ....7/85   3-5
SHRINK STICKER 2: Black-and-white,
announces the availability of *Rock and Roll:
The Early Days* videocassette.

RCA Victor (M)
AFM1-5463.................7/85   20-25
TOTAL PACKAGE 2: Disc, cover, insert,
sticker.

Card stock jacket, with printing on cover – not on slicks.

Side 1
Sh Boom (Chords)
Good Rockin' Tonight (Wynonie "Mr. Blues" Harris)
Hound Dog (Willie Mae "Big Mama" Thornton)
I'm Your Hoochie Coochie Man (Muddy Waters)
Shake, Rattle and Roll ("Big" Joe Turner)
Rock Around the Clock (Bill Haley & His Comets)

Side 2
That's All Right (Elvis Presley)
Blue Suede Shoes (Carl Perkins)
Maybelline (Chuck Berry)
Bo Diddley (Bo Diddley)
Tutti Frutti (Little Richard)
Great Balls of Fire (Jerry Lee Lewis)

ROCK MY SOUL
❑ Teddy Bear IMP-1108: Bootleg. Listed for identification only.

ROCK ROCK ROCK (ALL STAR ROCK – VOLUME 11)
Various artists collection
❑ Original Sound Recordings (SP)
OSR-11 ....2/72   20-25
DISC 1: Orange label, black print.
U-3323 ORS-VOL-11/U-3324 ORS-VOL-11. Identification numbers are engraved.
❑ Original Sound Recordings
OSR-11 ....2/72   20-25
COVER 1: Front: OSR logo and number at upper right. Black, yellow and white drawing. Back: Text and black-and-white reduction of front cover drawing.
INNER SLEEVE 1: White, no printing.
Original Sound Recordings (SP)
OSR-11 ....2/72   **40-50**
TOTAL PACKAGE 1: Disc, cover.

Side 1
American Pie (Don McLean)
Brand New Key (Melanie)
Let's Stay Together (Al Green)
Day After Day (Badfinger)
Never Been to Spain (Three Dog Night)
Until It's Time for You to Go (Elvis Presley)
Country Wine (Raiders)

Side 2
The Way of Love (Cher)
Hurting Each Other (Carpenters)
Joy (Apollo 100)
My World (Bee Gees)
Everything I Own (Bread)
Feelin' All Right (Joe Cocker)
Down by the Lazy River (Osmonds)
Reissued as *ALL STAR ROCK – VOLUME 11*. See that listing for more information.

ROCK, ROLL & REMEMBER (6 LPs)
Various artists collection
Complete six-hour radio show, based on Dick Clark's book of the same title. Has two Elvis songs as well as an Elvis telephone interview with Clark. All discs are listed individually below. Identification numbers are engraved on all.
❑ Dick Clark Productions DPE-402
Side 1A/1B...........................'77   12-20
DISC 1:
DPE-402-1-A/DPE-402-1-B.
❑ Dick Clark Productions DPE-402
Side 2A/2B...........................'77   12-20
DISC 2:
DPE-402-2-A/DPE-402-2-B.
❑ Dick Clark Productions DPE-402
Side 3A/3B...........................'77   12-20
DISC 3:
DPE-402-3-A/DPE-402-3-B.
❑ Dick Clark Productions DPE-402 Side
4A/4B................................'77   12-20
DISC 4:
DPE-402-4-A/DPE-402-4-B.
❑ Dick Clark Productions DPE-402
Side 5A/5B...........................'77   12-20
DISC 5:
DPE-402-5-A/DPE-402-5-B.
❑ Dick Clark Productions DPE-402
Side 6A/6B...........................'77   12-20
DISC 6:
DPE-402-6-A/DPE-402-6-B.
❑ Dick Clark Productions
DPE-402............................'77   10-15
BOX 1: Red and white, generic Dick Clark "Rock, Roll & Remember" box. No mention of Elvis or this program.
INNER SLEEVES 1: White, no printing.
❑ Dick Clark Productions
DPE-402............................'77   5-10
INSERT 1: Six pages of cue sheets and program notes.
Dick Clark Productions (SP)
DPE-402 ....'77   **100-150**
TOTAL PACKAGE 1: Discs, box, insert.

Elvis Contents:
Side 1A
I Want You, I Need You, I Love You (Track 6)
Side 5A
Wear My Ring Around Your Neck (Track 2)

ROCK, ROLL & REMEMBER, 1982 (4 LPs)
❑ United Stations Pgm. 30
(SP) ....'82   160-170
DISCS 1: Complete four-hour radio show. Issued only to subscribing radio stations. Has 48 songs by Elvis.
❑ United Stations Pgm. 30......'82   10-15
BOX 1: Black-and-white.
INNER SLEEVES 1: White, no printing.

Our Memories Of Elvis - Vol. 2
Elvis Presley

Side A Stereo
DJL1-3455-A

NOT FOR SALE

1 I Got A Feelin' In My Body 3:33
2 For The Heart 3:27
3 She Wears My Ring 3:20
4 Find Out What's Happening 2:37

TMKS ® RCA CORP —MADE IN U S A

❑ United Stations Pgm. 30......'82 | 5-15
INSERT 1: Four pages of cue sheets and
program notes.
United Stations
Pgm. 30 (SP).................'82 | **175-200**
TOTAL PACKAGE 1: Discs, box, inserts.

ROCK, ROLL & REMEMBER, 1985 (4 LPs)

❑ United Stations Pgm. 152
(SP)....................................'85 | 135-150
DISCS 1: Complete four-hour radio show.
Issued only to subscribing radio stations. Has
48 songs by Elvis. Repackage of the 1982
show.

❑ United Stations Pgm. 152....'85 | 3-5
COVER 1: Single pocket. Red and white,
generic "Rock Roll & Remember" cover.
INNER SLEEVES 1: White, no printing.

❑ United Stations Pgm. 152....'85 | 5-10
INSERT 1: Four pages of cue sheets and
program notes.
United Stations
Pgm. 152 (SP)...............'85 | **145-170**
TOTAL PACKAGE : Disc, cover, insert.

ROCKER

❑ RCA (M) AFM1-5182.......10/84 | 10-12
DISC 1: Gold, black and white "Elvis 50th
Anniversary" label.
AFM1-5182A-1/AFM1-5182B-1. Identification numbers are
engraved.

❑ RCA AFM1-5182.............10/84 | 10-12
COVER 1: No logo or number shown. Black-
and-white Elvis (circa 1957) photo. Back: RCA
logo at lower right, number at upper left. UPC
bar code at upper right. Black-and-white Elvis
(circa 1957) photo.
INNER SLEEVE 1: White, no printing.
RCA (M) AFM1-5182.....10/84 | **20-25**
TOTAL PACKAGE 1: Disc, cover.

❑ RCA (M) AFM1-5182.......11/84 | 10-12
DISC 2: Same as disc 1.

❑ RCA AFM1-5182.............11/84 | 15-18
COVER 2: Designate promo. Same as cover
1, but with "Not for Sale" stamped on back.
INNER SLEEVE 2: White, no printing.
RCA (M) AFM1-5182.....11/84 | **25-30**
TOTAL PACKAGE 2: Disc, cover.

Card stock jacket, with printing on cover – not
on slicks.

Side A
Jailhouse Rock
Blue Suede Shoes
Tutti Frutti
Lawdy Miss Clawdy
I Got a Woman
Money Honey

Side B
Ready Teddy

Rip It Up
Shake, Rattle and Roll
Long Tall Sally
(You're So Square) Baby I Don't Care
Hound Dog

ROCKIN' IN NEW YORK CITY

❑ Mystery Train: Bootleg. Listed for
identification only.

ROCKIN' REBEL

❑ Golden Archives GA-250: Bootleg. Listed for
identification only.

ROCKIN' REBEL, VOL. II

❑ Golden Archives GA-300: Bootleg. Listed for
identification only.

ROCKIN' REBEL, VOL. III

❑ Golden Archives GA-350: Bootleg. Listed for
identification only.

ROCKIN' TV 1956

❑ Bootleg. Listed for identification only.

ROCKIN' THE NATION

❑ Gladys 85858: Bootleg. Listed for
identification only.

ROCKIN' WITH ELVIS – APRIL FOOL'S DAY

❑ Live Stage 72722: Bootleg. Listed for
identification only.

ROCKIN' WITH ELVIS – NEW YEAR'S EVE (DEC. 31, 1976) PITTSBURGH, PA.

❑ Spirit of America 7677: Bootleg. Listed for
identification only.

ROUGH CUT DIAMONDS

❑ Diamond LPS-2000: Bootleg. Listed for
identification only.

ROUGH CUT DIAMONDS, VOLUME 2

❑ Diamond LPS-3000: Bootleg. Listed for
identification only.

ROUSTABOUT

❑ RCA Victor (M)
LPM-2999.......................10/64 | 30-40
DISC 1: Black label, "Mono" at bottom.
RPRM-5276-3S/RPRM-5277-12S. Label LP#10.

❑ RCA Victor LPM-2999 ..... 10/64   45-50
  COVER 1: Front: RCA Victor logo at top
  center, number at lower left. Color Elvis photo,
  behind which is a 2" Elvis photo. Back: Five
  color Elvis photos, one of which is a reduction
  of the main pose on the front. Price reflects
  RCA's use of this same cover, with no
  discernible differences, until 1968.
❑ RCA Victor 21-112-1
  40A 10/64   4-8
  INNER SLEEVE 1: Red, black and white.
  Front: RCA's Elvis LP catalog, most recent
  being *Kissin' Cousins* (side 1, row 1, column
  6). Back: RCA Elvis EPs and 45s catalog.

RCA Victor (M)
LPM-2999 .... 10/64   **80-100**
**TOTAL PACKAGE 1: Disc, cover, inner
  sleeve.**

❑ RCA Victor (M)
  LPM-2999 .... 10/64   30-40
  DISC 2: Same as disc 1.
❑ RCA Victor LPM-2999 ..... 10/64   65-75
  COVER 2: Same as cover 1 except at lower
  right on back, "Not for Sale, Promotion issue
  only" is rubber stamped. May also have a
  white and red sticker on front cover, reading
  "Promo Only." Issued only to radio stations.
  White cardboard mailers, with the same
  "Promo Only" sticker on it, exist.
❑ RCA Victor 21-112-1
  40A 10/64   4-8
  INNER SLEEVE 2: Red, black and white.
  Front: RCA's Elvis LP catalog, most recent
  being *Kissin' Cousins* (side 1, row 1, column
  6). Back: RCA Elvis EPs and 45s catalog.

RCA Victor (M)
LPM-2999 .... 10/64   **100-125**
**TOTAL PACKAGE 2: Disc, cover, inner
  sleeve.**

❑ RCA Victor (M)
  LPM-2999 .... 1/65   10-15
  DISC 3: Black label, "Monaural" at bottom.
  RPRM-5276-1S/RPRM-5277-11S. Label LP#12.
  RPRM-5276-4S/RPRM-5277-4S. Label LP#12.
❑ RCA Victor LPM-2999 .... 1/65   45-50
  COVER 3: Same as cover 1.
❑ RCA Victor 21-112-1
  40A 10/64   4-8
  INNER SLEEVE 3: Red, black and white.
  Front: RCA's Elvis LP catalog, most recent
  being *Kissin' Cousins* (side 1, row 1, column
  6). Back: RCA Elvis EPs and 45s catalog.

RCA Victor (M)
LPM-2999 .... 1/65   **60-75**
**TOTAL PACKAGE 3: Disc, cover, inner
  sleeve.**

❑ RCA Victor (ST)
  LSP-2999 .... 10/64   550-650
  DISC 4: Black label, RCA logo in silver at top
  and "Stereo" at bottom. "Elvis Presley" at
  bottom of label.
  RPRS-5278-1S/RPRS-5279-1S. Label LP#13.
❑ RCA Victor LSP-2999 ..... 10/64   45-50
  COVER 4: Front: RCA Victor logo at top
  center, number at upper left. Color Elvis
  photo, behind which is a 2" Elvis photo. Back:
  Five color Elvis photos, one of which is a
  reduction of the main pose on the front. Price
  reflects RCA's use of this same cover, with no
  discernible differences, until 1976 or '77.
❑ RCA Victor 21-112-1
  40A 10/64   4-8
  INNER SLEEVE 4: Red, black and white.
  Front: RCA's Elvis LP catalog, most recent
  being *Kissin' Cousins* (side 1, row 1, column
  6). Back: RCA Elvis EPs and 45s catalog.

RCA Victor (ST)
LSP-2999 .... 10/64   **600-700**
**TOTAL PACKAGE 4: Disc, cover, inner
  sleeve.**

❑ RCA Victor (ST)
  LSP-2999 .... 11/64   10-20
  DISC 5: Black label, RCA logo in white at top
  and "Stereo" at bottom. "Elvis Presley" under
  title, at top.
  RPRS-5278-2S/RPRS-5279-4S. Label LP#16.
  RPRS-5278-3S/RPRS-5279-3S. Label LP#16.
  RPRS-5278-4S/RPRS-5279-4S. Label LP#16.
❑ RCA Victor LSP-2999 ...... 11/64   25-30
  COVER 5: Same as cover 4.
❑ RCA Victor 21-112-1
  40A 10/64   4-8
  INNER SLEEVE 5: Red, black and white.
  Front: RCA's Elvis LP catalog, most recent
  being *Kissin' Cousins* (side 1, row 1, column
  6). Back: RCA Elvis EPs and 45s catalog.

RCA Victor (ST)
LSP-2999 .... 11/64   **40-60**
**TOTAL PACKAGE 5: Disc, cover, inner
  sleeve.**

❑ RCA Victor (ST)
  LSP-2999 .... 11/68   20-25
  DISC 6: Orange label. Rigid vinyl.
  RPRS-5278-5S/RPRS-5279-4S.
  RPRS-5278-7S/RPRS-5279-7S.
❑ RCA Victor LSP-2999 ...... 11/68   8-10
  COVER 6: Same as cover 4.
❑ RCA Victor 21-112-1
  40D 6/68   4-6
  INNER SLEEVE 6: Red, black and white.
  Front: RCA's Elvis LP catalog, most recent
  being *Elvis' Gold Records, Vol. 4* (side 1, row
  4, column 5). Back: RCA's Elvis LP and Twin
  Pack Stereo 8 catalog. May also be found
  with inner sleeves 40B and 40C. See chapter
  on inner sleeves for more information.

RCA Victor (ST)
LSP-2999...................**11/68**   **35-40**
TOTAL PACKAGE 6: Disc, cover, inner sleeve.

❏ RCA Victor (ST)
LSP-2999 ....'71   10-15
DISC 7: Orange label. Flexible vinyl.
RPRS-5278-5S/RPRS-5279-4S.

❏ RCA Victor LSP-2999.........'71   4-8
COVER 7: Same as cover 4, except inking is noticeably darker. This change is especially obvious with its darker blue color sky (top of cover).

❏ RCA Victor.........................'70s   2-4
INNER SLEEVE 7: Black-and-white. Pictures RCA Elvis catalog front and back. Any of several sleeves may be found on reissues from this period.

RCA Victor (ST)
LSP-2999.......................**'71**   **15-25**
TOTAL PACKAGE 7: Disc, cover, inner sleeve.

❏ RCA Victor (ST)
LSP-2999 ....'76   10-15
DISC 8: Tan label.

❏ RCA LSP-2999...................'76   4-8
COVER 8: Verification pending.

❏ RCA Victor.........................'70s   2-4
INNER SLEEVE 8: Black-and-white. Pictures RCA Elvis catalog front and back. Any of several sleeves may be found on reissues from this period.

RCA Victor (ST)
LSP-2999.......................**'76**   **15-25**
TOTAL PACKAGE 8: Disc, cover, inner sleeve.

❏ RCA Victor (ST)
LSP-2999 ....'76   4-6
DISC 9: Black label, dog near top.

❏ RCA LSP-2999...................'76   4-6
COVER 9: Has "RE" in corner.

❏ RCA Victor.........................'70s   2-4
INNER SLEEVE 9: Black-and-white. Pictures RCA Elvis catalog front and back. Any of several sleeves may be found on reissues from this period.

RCA Victor (ST)
LSP-2999.......................**'76**   **10-18**
TOTAL PACKAGE 9: Disc, cover, inner sleeve.

❏ RCA Victor (ST)
AFL1-2999 ....'77   3-5
DISC 10: Black label, dog near top.

❏ RCA Victor AFL1-2999........'77   3-5
COVER 10: Reflects prefix change.

❏ RCA Victor.........................'70s   2-4
INNER SLEEVE 10: Black-and-white. Pictures RCA Elvis catalog front and back. Any of several sleeves may be found on reissues from this period.

RCA Victor (ST)
AFL1-2999.....................**'77**   **8-15**
TOTAL PACKAGE 10: Disc, cover, inner sleeve.

Side 1
Roustabout
Little Egypt
Poison Ivy League
Hard Knocks
It's a Wonderful World
Big Love, Big Heartache
Side 2
One Track Heart
It's Carnival Time
Carny Town
There's a Brand New Day on the Horizon
Wheels on My Heels

SAVAGE YOUNG ELVIS (Cassette)

❏ RCA Special Products/Realistic (M)
DPK1-0679........................7/84   10-15
TAPE 1: Cassette tape of an Elvis package that was never available on LP. Marketed through Radio Shack stores. Realistic selection number: 51-3024.

❏ RCA Special Products/Realistic
DPK1-0679........................7/84   10-15
COVER/CARD 1: Cassette and cover/card are sealed in a cello pack. Front: Pink, turquoise, black and white, 12" x 12" photo card. RCA and Realistic logos and numbers at lower right. Black-and-white Elvis (1956) photo. Back: Two black-and-white Elvis (1956) photos.

RCA Special Products/Realistic (M)
DPK1-0679.................**7/84**   **20-30**
TOTAL PACKAGE 1: Tape, cover/card.

Side 1
Blue Suede Shoes
All Shook Up
Little Sister
Mystery Train
Milkcow Blues Boogie
Side 2
Hard Headed Woman
Rip It Up
Blue Moon
Ain't That Lovin' You Baby
My Baby Left Me

SEASON'S GREETINGS FROM ELVIS

❏ RCA EPC-2: Bootleg. Listed for identification only.

SEPARATE WAYS (Camden)

❑ RCA/Camden (SP)
CAS-2611......................... 12/72   8-10
DISC 1: Blue label. Dynaflex vinyl.
BCRS-6495-11S/BCRS-6496-4S.
BCRS-6495-14S/BCRS-6496-11S.
BCRS-6495-15S/BCRS-6496-7S.
BCRS-6495-16S/BCRS-6496-7S.

❑ RCA/Camden
CAS-2611......................... 12/72   8-10
COVER 1: Front: RCA/Camden logo and
number at bottom center. Color Elvis ('70s
concert) photo superimposed on an artist's
rendition of a highway scene. Back: Pictures
nine other RCA/Camden LPs in color.
INNER SLEEVE 1: White, no printing. (Some
Camden LPs had no inner sleeves at all.)

❑ RCA/Camden
CAS-2611......................... 12/72   10-15
INSERT 1: Color 3" x 5" Elvis greeting card,
signed "Happy Birthday to You in 1973,
Sincerely, Elvis Presley."

RCA/Camden (SP)
CAS-2611 .... 12/72   30-35
TOTAL PACKAGE 1: Disc, cover, insert.

❑ RCA/Camden (SP)
CAS-2611......................... 12/72   8-10
DISC 2: Same as disc 1.

❑ RCA/Camden
CAS-2611......................... 12/72   12-15
COVER 2: Designate promo. Same as cover
1, but with "Not for Sale" stamped on back.
INNER SLEEVE 2: White, no printing. (Some
Camden LPs had no inner sleeves at all.)

❑ RCA/Camden
CAS-2611......................... 12/72   10-15
INSERT 2: Same as insert 1.

RCA/Camden (SP)
CAS-2611 .... 12/72   35-40
TOTAL PACKAGE 2: Disc, cover, insert.

Card stock jacket, with printing on cover – not
on slicks.

Side 1
Separate Ways
Sentimental Me
In My Way
I Met Her Today
What Now, What Next, Where To
Side 2
Always on My Mind
I Slipped, I Stumbled, I Fell
Is It So Strange
Forget Me Never
Old Shep

SEPARATE WAYS (Pickwick)

❑ Pickwick/Camden (SP)
CAS-2611 .... 12/75   2-5
DISC 1: Black label. Multi-color Pickwick logo
at center.

❑ Pickwick/Camden
CAS-2611......................... 12/75   3-5
CAS-2611A/CAS-2611B.
COVER 1: Front: Pickwick logo at bottom
center. Camden logo and number at upper
left. Back: Plug for the *Aloha from Hawaii* TV
special (on RCA/Camden issue) is replaced
by a '70s concert Elvis photo.
INNER SLEEVE 1: White, no printing.

Pickwick/Camden (SP)
CAS-2611 .... 12/75   5-10
TOTAL PACKAGE 1: Disc, cover.

❑ Pickwick/Camden (SP)
CAS-2611........................... '77   750-1000
DISC 2: Gold vinyl. Experimental pressing,
not intended for sale or distribution.
COVER 2: None made.

Pickwick/Camden (SP)
CAS-2611 .... '77   500-750
TOTAL PACKAGE 2: Disc.

Side 1
Separate Ways
Sentimental Me
In My Way
I Met Her Today
What Now, What Next, Where To
Side 2
Always on My Mind
I Slipped, I Stumbled, I Fell
Is It So Strange
Forget Me Never
Old Shep

SEPTEMBER '63 POP SAMPLER
Various artists collection

❑ RCA Victor (S)
SPS 33-219 .... 10/63   500-750
DISC 1: Black label with "Stereo Dynagroove"
at bottom. Promotional issue only.
PNRS-4198/PNRS-4199.
COVER 1: White, no printing.
INNER SLEEVE 1: White, no printing.

RCA Victor (S)
SPS 33-219 .... 10/63   500-750
TOTAL PACKAGE 1: Disc.

Side 1
900 Miles (Odetta)
The Midnight Special (Limeliters)
Guitar Child (Duane Eddy)
All Keyed Up (Floyd Cramer)
Don't Tell Me Your Troubles (Don Gibson)
The Wreck of Number Nine (Hank Snow)
Nobody Knows the Trouble I've Seen (Sam Cooke)
Side 2
Excerpts (Three Suns)
Nola (Sid Ramin and His Orchestra)
Let's Fall in Love (Voices of Hugo & Luigi Chorus)
Piano Excerpts: (Frankie Carle/Floyd Cramer/Peter
   Nero)
Excerpts (Ann-Margret/Kitty Kallen/Della Reese)
Are You Lonesome Tonight (Elvis Presley)

SCOTT MUNI'S WORLD OF ROCK (3 LPs)

Various artists collections.

❑ Scott Muni's World of Rock (S)   10-15
DISC 1: Price range is for any individual disc containing at least one Elvis track.

❑ Scott Muni's World of Rock (S)   25-35
COMPLETE SET 1: Set of three LPs. Each is a complete three-hour, weekly radio show with three pages of cue sheets and program notes. Issued only to subscribing radio stations. Price range is for any complete set containing at least one Elvis track.

SHELBY SINGLETON MUSIC, INC. (AND AFFILIATES) PRESENTS SONGS FOR THE SEVENTIES (2 LPs)

Various artists collection

❑ Shelby Singleton Music (M)
#1 ....12/69   125-175
DISCS 1: White label, black print. Promotional issued for radio stations only.
(Disc 1) XSBV-130484-1A 1-A/XSBV-130485-1A 1-B. **(Disc 2)** XSBV-130486-1A 2-A/XSBV-130487-1A 2-B.

❑ Shelby Singleton Music
1 ....12/69   125-150
COVER 1: Double pocket. Front and Back: White with blue print. Inside panels: Blank.
INNER SLEEVES 1: White, no printing.

❑ Shelby Singleton Music
#1 ....12/69   50-75
INSERT 1: Spiralbound, 66-page song and lyrics book. Cover is same as LP cover 1.

Shelby Singleton Music (M)
#1 ....12/69   300-400
TOTAL PACKAGE 1: Discs, cover, insert.

Disc 1 (Pop/R&B)

Side 1
Turn the World Around (Eddy Arnold)
The Wedding Cake (Connie Francis)
Reconsider Me (Johnny Adams)
Little Tin God (Michael Henry Martin)
Jim Dandy (Lavern Baker)
I Almost Called Your Name (Margaret Whiting)
Got You on My Mind (Cookie and the Cupcakes)
Then I'll Be Over You (Al Martino)
Walk Through This Life with You (Ella Washington)
Such a Night (Elvis Presley)
Good Lovin' (David Clayton Thomas)
Kiddio (Brook Benton)

Side 2
Soulshake (Peggy Scott & Jo Jo Benson)
Wings of My Love (Connie Francis)
From This Moment On (Eddy Arnold)
Since You Don't Care (Sylvie Vartan)
San Francisco Is a Lonely Town (O.C. Smith)
Billy & Sue (B.J. Thomas)
Proud Woman (Johnny Adams)
Gone Like the Wind (Connie Francis)
Next Stop Paradise (Jesse Pearson)
Revenge (Brook Benton)
Chains of Love (B.J. Thomas)
Taste of Tears (Johnny Mathis)

Disc 2 (Country)

Side 1
Before the Next Teardrop Falls (Duane Dee)
Little Tin God (Stu Phillips)
If the Whole World Stopped Loving (Roy Drusky)
I'm Only a Woman (Lucille Starr)
Reconsider Me (Ray Pillow)
San Francisco Is a Lonely Town (Ben Peters)
There Never Was a Time (Jeannie C. Riley)
Turn the World Around (Eddy Arnold)
The Artist (Jeannie C. Riley)
Truck Driving Son of a Gun (Dave Dudley)
I Almost Called Your Name (Margaret Whiting)
Shiny Red Automobile (George Morgan)

Side 2
That's a No No (Lynn Anderson)
From This Moment On (Eddy Arnold)
The Wedding Cake (Jeannie C. Riley)
From Heaven to Heartache (Bobby Lewis)
The Day After Forever (Mike Douglas)
Then I'll Be over You (Eddy Arnold)
Cry, Cry, Cry (Connie Smith)
A Lifetime of Regret (Red Sovine)
Taste of Tears (Jeannie C. Riley)
Someone Like You (Waylon Jennings)
Country Girl (Jeannie C. Riley)
War Baby (Dee Mullins)

SHOCK, RATTLE 'N' ROLL

❑ Pink & Black LPM-1500: Bootleg. Listed for identification only.

SINGER PRESENTS ELVIS SINGING FLAMING STAR AND OTHERS

❑ RCA Victor (SP)
PRS-279 ....11/68   50-60
DISC 1: Mustard color label. Rigid vinyl. Made exclusively for and sold only at Singer Sewing Centers.
WNRS-2363-5S/WNRS-2364-4S. Serial sumbers are stamped, but engraved is "A-1" (side 1) and "A-4 (side 2).
WNRS-2363-5S/WNRS-2364-5S. Serial sumbers are stamped, but engraved is "A-3" in engraved on both sides.
WNRS-2363-6S/WNRS-2364-4S. Identification numbers are stamped, but engraved is "A-5-B" (side 1) and "A-3-G" (side 2).

❑ RCA PRS-279 ....11/68   50-65
COVER 1: Front: RCA logo at upper left. This was the first Elvis RCA LP to not have "Victor" on front cover. Number not shown. Color Elvis (*Charro*) photo. Back: Number at upper right. Pictures six other Elvis LPs. Has plug for the Singer Company at bottom.
INNER SLEEVE 1: White, no printing.
INSERT 1: An 8" x 10" Elvis photo was distributed by Singer to buyers of this album; however, the photo was not packaged with the LP.

RCA Victor (SP)
PRS-279 ....11/68   100-125
TOTAL PACKAGE 1: Disc, cover.

Tiger Man is monaural – other tracks are stereo.

Side 1
Flaming Star
Wonderful World
Night Life
All I Needed Was the Rain
Too Much Monkey Business

Side 2
Yellow Rose of Texas/The Eyes of Texas
She's a Machine
Do the Vega
Tiger Man

60 YEARS OF COUNTRY MUSIC (2 LPs)

Various artists collection

❑ RCA Victor (SP)
CPL1-4351 .... 6/82   5-10
DISCS 1: Black label, dog near top.
(Disc 1) CPL2-4351A-2S/CPL2-4351B-1S. (Disc 2) CPL2-4351C-1S/CPL2- 4351D-1S.

❑ RCA CPL1-4351 .... 6/82   5-10
COVER 1: Double pocket. Front: RCA (letters) logo at lower right, number at upper right. Color photo of dog, Nipper, and gramophone. Back: Color photos of 10 different RCA and Bluebird labels. UPC bar code at upper right. Inside panels: Liner notes and session information.
INNER SLEEVES 1: White, no printing.

RCA Victor (SP)
CPL1-4351 .... 6/82   10-20
TOTAL PACKAGE 1: Disc, cover.

Card stock jacket, with printing on cover – not on slicks.

Disc 1

Side A
Arkansaw Traveler (Henry C. Gilliland & A.C. Robertson)
The Prisoner's Song (Vernon Dalhart)
Blue Yodel (Jimmie Rodgers)
Wildwood Flower (Carter Family)
My Swiss Moonlight Lullaby (Wilf Carter)
Loveless Love (Milton Brown & His Musical Brownies)

Side B
Under the Double Eagle (Bill Boyd)
Sunny Side of Life (Blue Sky Boys)
Jolie Blonde (Hackberry Ramblers)
Orange Blossom Special (Bill Monroe & His Blue Grass Boys)
Star-Spangled Banner Somewhere (Elton Britt)
Cool Water (Sons of the Pioneers)

Disc 2

Side C
I'm Movin' On (Hank Snow)
Heartbreak Hotel (Elvis Presley)
I Can't Stop Loving You (Don Gibson)
He'll Have to Go (Jim Reeves)
Yakety Axe (Chet Atkins)
Make the World Go Away (Eddy Arnold)

Side D
When You're Hot, You're Hot (Jerry Reed)
Kiss an Angel Good Morning (Charley Pride)
Good Hearted Woman (Waylon Jennings)
Jolene (Dolly Parton)
It Was Almost Like a Song (Ronnie Milsap)
Old Flame (Alabama)

SOCIAL SECURITY PRESENTS DONNA FARGO (2 LPs)

❑ Dept. of Health Education and Welfare (M)
DHEW .... '77   12-15
Each double pocket LP has a dozen, five-minute, public service radio show. Issued by the U.S. Department of Health, Education, and Welfare, only to radio stations. Price is for any with an Elvis track.
DISCS 1: Labels may either be gold and pink, with no photo, or black-and-white with a photo of Donna Fargo.

❑ Dept. of Health Education and Welfare
DHEW .... '77   12-15
COVER 1: Double pocket. Front: May be pink or white, with a black-and-white photo of Donna Fargo. U.S. Department of Health, Education, and Welfare number at lower right. Back: Text only. Inside panels are blank.
INNER SLEEVES 1: White, no printing.

Dept. of Health Education and Welfare (M) DHEW .... '77   25-30
TOTAL PACKAGE 1: Discs, cover.

'68 COMEBACK

❑ Memphis MKS-101: Bootleg. Listed for identification only.

'68 COMEBACK, VOL. 2

❑ Amiga MKS-102: Bootleg. Listed for identification only.

SOLD OUT

❑ EP PRP-251: Bootleg. Listed for identification only.

SOLID GOLD: see *DICK CLARK SOLID GOLD*

SOLID GOLD COUNTRY

Various artists collections.

❑ United Stations   10-15
Complete syndicated radio show. Issued only to subscribing stations. Although three to five discs were sent each week, price is for any of the LPs having at least one Elvis track. Discs that do not have an Elvis song are valued at $5 to $10 each. Discs containing all-Elvis shows are listed in the preceding section. A four-hour version of the 1989 birthday show is listed under *ELVIS PRESLEY BIRTHDAY TRIBUTE.*
INNER SLEEVES 1: White, no printing.

❑ United Stations   4-8
INSERTS 1: Cue sheets with program notes. Price is for any corresponding to discs with an Elvis track.

United Stations 15-25
TOTAL PACKAGE 1: Disc, insert.

SOLID GOLD COUNTRY
(All-Elvis Shows)

Complete syndicated all-Elvis radio shows. Thus far there are 41 Elvis shows in this series, each individually titled. All are listed chronologically by air date. Price includes a page of cues and programming information. Issued only to subscribing stations. Shows featuring various artists are listed in a section that follows.

❏ United Stations .... '84   35-50
   DISC 1: *Birthday Tribute (1-6-84)*
❏ United Stations .... '85   30-40
   DISC 2: *A Golden Celebration (1-7-85)*
❏ United Stations .... '85   30-40
   DISC 3: *G.I. Blues (4-8-85)*
❏ United Stations .... '85   30-40
   DISC 4: *Live on Vinyl (6-24-85)*
❏ United Stations .... '85   30-40
   DISC 5: *Elvis Presley's Greatest Country Hits (7-8-85)*
❏ United Stations .... '85   30-40
   DISC 6: *Memorial Salute to Elvis Presley (8-12-85)*
❏ United Stations .... '85   30-40
   DISC 7: *The RCA Signing (11-18-85)*
❏ United Stations .... '85   30-40
   DISC 8: *An Elvis Christmas Celebration (12-16-85)*
❏ United Stations .... '86   20-30
   DISC 9: *Elvis Presley Birthday Tribute (1-6-86)*
❏ United Stations .... '86   20-30
   DISC 10: *Elvis Presley's Love Songs (2-10-86)*
❏ United Stations .... '86   20-30
   DISC 11: *Elvis Presley's Posthumous Releases (3-10-86)*
❏ United Stations .... '86   20-30
   DISC 12: *Elvis Presley's No. 1 Hits (4-18-86)*
❏ United Stations .... '86   20-30
   DISC 13: *Elvis Presley's Double-Sided Hits (5-5-86)*
❏ United Stations .... '86   20-30
   DISC 14: *Live on Vinyl (6-23-86)*
❏ United Stations .... '86   20-30
   DISC 15: *Salute to the Jordanaires (8-1-86)*
❏ United Stations .... '86   20-30
   DISC 16: *Elvis Presley Memorial Tribute (8-14-86)*
❏ United Stations .... '86   20-30
   DISC 17: *Elvis Presley's Remakes (8-31-86)*
❏ United Stations .... '86   20-30
   DISC 18: *Elvis Presley's Gold Albums (10-13-86)*
❏ United Stations .... '86   20-30
   DISC 19: *Elvis Presley's Movie (11-10-86)*
❏ United Stations .... '86   20-30
   DISC 20: *An Elvis Christmas Celebration (12-22-86)*

❏ United Stations .... '87   20-30
   DISC 21: *Elvis Presley Birthday Tribute (1-5-87)*
❏ United Stations .... '87   20-30
   DISC 22: *Elvis Presley's Love Songs (2-9-87)*
❏ United Stations .... '87   20-30
   DISC 23: *Elvis Presley's Gold Singles (3-2-87)*
❏ United Stations .... '87   20-30
   DISC 24: *Elvis Presley's Title Tracks (4-20-87)*
❏ United Stations .... '87   20-30
   DISC 25: *Elvis Presley Memorial Tribute (5-18-87)*
❏ United Stations .... '87   20-30
   DISC 26: *Live on Vinyl (6-22-87)*
❏ United Stations .... '87   20-30
   DISC 27: *Elvis Presley's Two-Sided Hits (7-20-87)*
❏ United Stations .... '87   20-30
   DISC 28: *Elvis Presley – Year by Year (8-10-87)*
❏ United Stations .... '87   20-30
   DISC 29: *Elvis Presley's Posthumous Records (9-14-87)*
❏ United Stations .... '87   20-30
   DISC 30: *Salute to Elvis Presley (9-28-87)*
❏ United Stations .... '87   20-30
   DISC 31: *Songs of Broken Romance (11-2-87)*
❏ United Stations .... '87   20-30
   DISC 32: *An Elvis Christmas Celebration (12-19-87)*
❏ United Stations .... '88   20-30
   DISC 33: *Elvis Presley Birthday Tribute (1-2-88)*
❏ United Stations .... '88   20-30
   DISC 34: *G.I. Blues (3-21-88)*
❏ United Stations .... '88   20-30
   DISC 35: *The Sun Sessions (4-18-88)*
❏ United Stations .... '88   20-30
   DISC 36: *The Movies (7-18-88)*
❏ United Stations .... '89   20-30
   DISC 37: *Christmas with Elvis (12-25-89)*
❏ United Stations 90   20-30
   DISC 38: *Elvis Presley Birthday Tribute, Part 1 (1-4-90)*
❏ United Stations 90   20-30
   DISC 39: *Elvis Presley Birthday Tribute, Part 2 (1-5-90)*
❏ United Stations 90   20-30
   DISC 40: *On Stage in Las Vegas (6-15-90)*
❏ United Stations 90   20-30
   DISC 41: *Christmas with Elvis (12-21-90)*

SOLID GOLD SCRAPBOOK
(All-Elvis Shows)

Complete syndicated all-Elvis radio shows. Thus far there are 21 Elvis shows in this series, each individually titled. All are listed chronologically by air date. Price includes a page of cues and programming information. Issued only to subscribing stations. Shows featuring various artists are listed in a section that follows.

❑ United Stations .... '87   20-30
  DISC 1: *Elvis Presley Profile (1-7-87)*
❑ United Stations .... '88   20-30
  DISC 2: *Elvis Presley Profile (1-7-88)*
❑ United Stations .... '88   20-30
  DISC 3: *Elvis' Golden Records, Vol. 3 (9-5-88)*
❑ United Stations .... '88   20-30
  DISC 4: *Elvis' Flip Sides (10-11-88)*
❑ United Stations .... '88   20-30
  DISC 5: *Elvis' Movie Music (11-15-88)*
❑ United Stations .... '89   20-30
  DISC 6: *Elvis Rockers – A Birthday Tribute (1-6-89)*
❑ United Stations .... '89   20-30
  DISC 7: *Elvis' Greatest Love Songs (2-14-89)*
❑ United Stations .... '89   20-30
  DISC 8: *Songs Covered by Elvis (3-6-89)*
❑ United Stations .... '89   20-30
  DISC 9: *Elvis' Nashville Recording Sessions (5-23-89)*
❑ United Stations .... '89   20-30
  DISC 10: *Elvis During the British Invasion (6-27-89)*
❑ United Stations .... '89   20-30
  DISC 11: *Elvis Presley Tribute (8-16-89)*
❑ United Stations .... '89   20-30
  DISC 12: *The Army Years (10-5-89)*
❑ United Stations .... '89   20-30
  DISC 13: *20th Anniversary of [Elvis'] Last Song to Hit the charts (11-1-89)*
❑ United Stations 90   20-30
  DISC 14: *Elvis' 55th Birthday Tribute (1-8-90)*
❑ United Stations 90   20-30
  DISC 15: *30th Anniversary of First Gold LP (2-20-90)*
❑ United Stations 90   20-30
  DISC 16: *Elvis Sails (3-23-90)*
❑ United Stations 90   20-30
  DISC 17: *Elvis in Hollywood (4-20-90)*
❑ United Stations 90   20-30
  DISC 18: *Elvis – The Floyd Cramer Sessions (6-13-90)*
❑ United Stations 90   20-30
  DISC 19: *Elvis in Hollywood (9-29-90)*
❑ United Stations 90   20-30
  DISC 20: *Elvis Gold (10-17-90)*
❑ United Stations 91   20-30
  DISC 21: *Elvis' Golden Decade: 1956-'65 (5-21-91)*

SOLID GOLD SCRAPBOOK
(STARRING DICK BARTLEY)
Various artists collection

❑ United Stations (SP)   10-15
  DISCS: White labels, mustard and blue print. Syndicated oldies radio show, usually boxed in sets of five one-hour shows. Price is for any individual discs in the series with an Elvis track. Issued only to subscribing radio stations. LPs that do not have an Elvis song are valued at $5 to $10 each.
  INNER SLEEVES 1: White, no printing.
❑ United Stations   4-8
  INSERTS 1: Cue sheets with program notes. Price is for any corresponding to discs with an Elvis track.
United Stations (SP)   15-25
  TOTAL PACKAGE 1: Disc, insert.

SOMETHING FOR EVERYBODY

❑ RCA Victor (M)
  LPM-2370 ....6/61   60-75
  DISC 1: Black label, "Long Play" at bottom.
  M2WP-2149-1S/M2WP-2150-1S. Label LP#2.
  M2WP-2149-6S/M2WP-2150-6S. Label LP#1.
❑ RCA Victor LPM-2370 ....6/61   65-75
  COVER 1: Front: RCA Victor logo at upper right, number at lower left. Color Elvis photo. Back: Black-and-white photos: *Wild in the Country* film scene, *Elvis By Request* Compact 33 Double, and *Wild in the Country / I Feel So Bad*, Compact 33 Single.
  INNER SLEEVE 1: Generic RCA sleeves. Makes no mention of Elvis or this LP.
RCA Victor (M)
  LPM-2370 .... 6/61   125-150
  TOTAL PACKAGE 1: Disc, cover

❑ RCA Victor (M)
  LPM-2370 ....11/63   30-40
  DISC 2: Black label, "Mono" at bottom.
❑ RCA Victor LPM-2370 .....11/63   30-40
  COVER 2: Verification pending.
❑ RCA Victor No Number 9/63   8-10
  INNER SLEEVE 2: Turquoise, black and white. Front: RCA's Elvis LP catalog, most recent being *It Happened at the World's Fair* (side 1, row 4, column 5). Back: RCA Elvis EPs and 45s catalog.
RCA Victor (M)
  LPM-2370 .... 11/63   70-90
  TOTAL PACKAGE 2: Disc, cover, inner sleeve.

❑ RCA Victor (M)
  LPM-2370 ....10/64   10-15
  DISC 3: Black label, "Monaural" at bottom.
❑ RCA Victor LPM-2370 ....'64   25-35
  COVER 3: Front: Same as cover 1. Back: Photos of Compact 33s are replaced by one of the *Viva Las Vegas* EP. Has "RE" at lower left.

❑ RCA Victor 21-112-1
40A 10/64   4-8
INNER SLEEVE 3: Red, black and white.
Front: RCA's Elvis LP catalog, most recent
being *Kissin' Cousins* (side 1, row 1, column
6). Back: RCA Elvis EPs and 45s catalog.

RCA Victor (M)
LPM-2370 .... 10/64   40-60
TOTAL PACKAGE 3: Disc, cover, inner
sleeve.

❑ RCA Victor (ST)
LSP-2370 .... 7/61   75-100
DISC 4: Black label, "Living Stereo" at bottom.
M2WY-2151-6S/M2WY-2152-2S. Label LP#7.

❑ RCA Victor LSP-2370 .... 7/61   75-100
COVER 4: Front: RCA Victor logo at upper
right, number at upper left. Color Elvis photo.
Back: Black-and-white photos: *Wild in the
Country* film scene, *Elvis By Request*
Compact 33 Double, and *Wild in the Country /
I Feel So Bad*, Compact 33 Single.
INNER SLEEVE 4: Generic RCA sleeves.
Makes no mention of Elvis or this LP.

RCA Victor (ST)
LSP-2370 .... 7/61   150-200
TOTAL PACKAGE 4: Disc, cover.

❑ RCA Victor (ST)
LSP-2370 .... '64   35-45
DISC 5: Black label, RCA logo in silver at top
and "Stereo" at bottom.

❑ RCA Victor LSP-2370 .... '64   35-45
COVER 5: Front: Same as cover 4. Back:
Photos of Compact 33s are replaced by *Elvis'
Christmas Album* and *His Hand in Mine*. The
Wild in the Country photo is replaced by one
of the *Viva Las Vegas* EP. Has "RE" at top
right.

❑ RCA Victor No Number 9/63   8-10
INNER SLEEVE 5: Turquoise, black and
white. Front: RCA's Elvis LP catalog, most
recent being *It Happened at the World's Fair*
(side 1, row 4, column 5). Back: RCA Elvis
EPs and 45s catalog.

RCA Victor (ST)
LSP-2370 .... '64   80-100
TOTAL PACKAGE 5: Disc, cover, inner
sleeve.

❑ RCA Victor (ST)
LSP-2370 .... 10/64   15-20
DISC 6: Black label, RCA logo in white at top
and "Stereo" at bottom.

❑ RCA Victor LSP-2370 ...... 10/64   20-30
COVER 6: Front: Same as cover 4. Back:
Photos of Compact 33s are replaced by one
of the *Viva Las Vegas* EP. Has "RE" at lower
left.

❑ RCA Victor 21-112-1
40A 10/64   4-8
INNER SLEEVE 6: Red, black and white.
Front: RCA's Elvis LP catalog, most recent
being *Kissin' Cousins* (side 1, row 1, column
6). Back: RCA Elvis EPs and 45s catalog.

RCA Victor (ST)
LSP-2370 .... 10/64   40-60
TOTAL PACKAGE 6: Disc, cover, inner
sleeve.

❑ RCA Victor (ST)
LSP-2370 .... 11/68   20-25
DISC 7: Orange label. Rigid vinyl.
M2WY-2151-5S/M2WY-2152-6S. Label LP#7.

❑ RCA Victor LSP-2370 ...... 11/68   8-10
COVER 7: Front: Same as cover 4. Back:
Photos of *Elvis (NBC-TV Special), How Great
Thou Art* and *His Hand in Mine*. Has "RE2" at
lower left.

❑ RCA Victor 21-112-1
40D 6/68   4-6
INNER SLEEVE 7: Red, black and white.
Front: RCA's Elvis LP catalog, most recent
being *Elvis' Gold Records, Vol. 4* (side 1, row
4, column 5). Back: RCA's Elvis LP and Twin
Pack Stereo 8 catalog. May also be found
with inner sleeves 40B and 40C. See chapter
on inner sleeves for more information.

RCA Victor (ST)
LSP-2370 .... 11/68   35-40
TOTAL PACKAGE 7: Disc, cover, inner
sleeve.

❑ RCA Victor (ST)
LSP-2370 .... '71   10-15
DISC 8: Orange label. Flexible vinyl.

❑ RCA LSP-2370 .... '71   4-6
COVER 8: Same as cover 7.

❑ RCA Victor .... '70s   2-4
INNER SLEEVE 8: Black-and-white. Pictures
RCA Elvis catalog front and back. Any of
several sleeves may be found on reissues
from this period.

RCA Victor (ST)
LSP-2370 .... '71   15-25
TOTAL PACKAGE 8: Disc, cover, inner
sleeve.

❑ RCA Victor (ST)
LSP-2370 .... '76   5-8
DISC 9: Tan label.

❑ RCA LSP-2370 .... '76   4-6
COVER 9: Same as cover 7.

❑ RCA Victor .... '70s   2-4
INNER SLEEVE 9: Black-and-white. Pictures
RCA Elvis catalog front and back. Any of
several sleeves may be found on reissues
from this period.

RCA Victor (ST)
LSP-2370.......................'76   **10-20**
TOTAL PACKAGE 9: Disc, cover, inner
  sleeve.

❑ RCA Victor (ST)
LSP-2370 ....'76   4-6
  DISC 10: Black label, dog near top.
❑ RCA LSP-2370...................'76   4-6
  COVER 10: Same as cover 7.
❑ RCA Victor.........................'70s   2-4
  INNER SLEEVE 10: Black-and-white.
  Pictures RCA Elvis catalog front and back.
  Any of several sleeves may be found on
  reissues from this period.

RCA Victor (ST)
LSP-2370.......................'76   **10-18**
TOTAL PACKAGE 10: Disc, cover, inner
  sleeve.

❑ RCA Victor (ST)
AFL1-2370 ....'77   3-5
  DISC 11: Black label, dog near top.
❑ RCA AFL1-2370..................'77   3-5
  COVER 11: Reflects prefix change.
❑ RCA Victor.........................'70s   2-4
  INNER SLEEVE 11: Black-and-white.
  Pictures RCA Elvis catalog front and back.
  Any of several sleeves may be found on
  reissues from this period.

RCA Victor (ST)
AFL1-2370.....................'77   **8-15**
TOTAL PACKAGE 11: Disc, cover, inner
  sleeve.

❑ RCA (ST) AYL1-4116.......5/81   3-5
  DISC 12: Black label, dog near top.
  AYL1-4116A-1S/AYL1-4116B-1S. Identification numbers are
  stamped. Also side 1 has AFL1-2370A-16 stamped but
  crossed out and side 2 has AFL1-2370B engraved.
❑ RCA AYL1-4116................5/81   3-5
  COVER 12: Reflects prefix change. Part of
  RCA's "Best Buy Series." Includes copies with
  a sticker bearing the "AYL1" prefix, wrapped
  around cover at top of spine.
  INNER SLEEVE 12: White, no printing.

RCA (ST) AYL1-4116......5/81   6-10
TOTAL PACKAGE 12: Disc, cover.

❑ RCA (ST) AYL1-4116........'80s   8-10
  DISC 13: Black label, dog near top.
  AYL1-4116A 16/AFL1-2370A 16
  AYL1-4116B 15/AFL1-2370 B-15
  Identification numbers are stamped. Also, side 1 has AFL1-
  2370A stamped but crossed out and side 2 has AFL1-2370
  B-15 engraved.

❑ RCA AYL1-4116 ....'80s   8-10
  COVER 13: Front: Catalog number and
  "STEREO" at upper left below white RCA
  logo. "Victor" does not appear on cover. Has
  "Previously released as AFL-2370" in small
  print at lower left. Back: White with black print.
  Side A designated as "The Ballad Side" and
  Side B designated as "The Rhythm Side".
  UPC code at upper right corner with small "2"
  at lower right.
  INNER SLEEVE 13: White, no printing.

RCA (ST) AYL1-4116...... '80s   15-20
TOTAL PACKAGE 13: Disc, cover.

Side 1
There's Always Me
Give Me the Right
It's a Sin
Sentimental Me
Starting Today
Gently

Side 2
I'm Comin' Home
In Your Arms
Put the Blame on Me
Judy
I Want You with Me
I Slipped, I Stumbled, I Fell

SONGS FOR THE SEVENTIES: *see SHELBY
SINGLETON MUSIC, INC. (AND
AFFILIATES) PRESENTS SONGS FOR
THE SEVENTIES*

SONGS HOLLYWOOD FORGOT
❑ Bootleg. Listed for identification only.

SONGS OF FAITH AND INSPIRATION (3 LPs)
Various artists collection

❑ Time-Life (SP) STL-127.......'89   10-12
  DISCS 1: White label with blue and red print.
  Sold only by Time-Life via mail order. Artists
  names are not shown on labels.
  (Disc 1) STL-127A/STL-128. **(Disc 2)** STL-127C/STL-127D.
  (Disc 3) STL-127E/STL-127F.
❑ Time-Life STL-127...............'89   10-12
  COVER 1: Single pocket. Front: Time-Life
  logo at bottom center. Back: Text only.
  INNER SLEEVES 1: White, no printing.

Time-Life (SP) STL-127....'89   20-25
TOTAL PACKAGE 1: Discs, cover.

Card stock jacket, with printing on cover – not
on slicks.

Disc 1

Side 1
Pray Every Day (Buck Owens)
Where No One Stands Alone (Don Gibson)
Old Brush Arbors (George Jones)
Were You There (Johnny Cash)
I Am a Pilgrim (Bill Monroe)
I'll Fly Away (Red Foley)
God Be with You (Jim Reeves)

Side 2
What Would You Give (Webb Pierce)
Crying in the Chapel (Rex Allen)
Wings of a Dove (Ferlin Husky)
I Saw the Light (Hank Williams)
Just a Closer Walk with Thee (Pasty Cline)
Thank God (Roy Acuff)
His Hand in Mine (Elvis Presley)

Disc 2
Side 1
Dust on the Bible (Kitty Wells)
The Old Rugged Cross (Eddy Arnold)
Turn Your Radio On (Grandpa Jones)
What a Friend We Have in Jesus (Merle Haggard)
What Would You Do (Porter Wagoner)
May the Good Lord Bless and Keep You (Tammy Wynette)

Side 2
Rank Stranger (Stanley Brothers)
Golden Streets of Glory (Dolly Parton)
Rock of Ages (Ray Price)
The Great Speckled Bird (Roy Acuff)
Peace in the Valley (Red Foley)
How Great Thou Art (Elvis Presley)
Talk About Suffering (Ricky Skaggs & Tony Rice)

Disc 3
Side 1
Dust on Mother's Bible (Buck Owens)
It Is No Secret (Eddy Arnold)
One Day at a Time (Merle Haggard)
The Christian Life (Louvin Brothers)
Lord I've Been Ready for Years (Oak Ridge Boys)
Everybody (Loretta Lynn)
He Turned the Water into Wine (Johnny Cash)

Side 2
Throw Out the Life Line (Wilburn Brothers)
Precious Memories (Tennessee Ernie Ford)
Family Bible (Claude Gray)
If We Never Meet Again (Ernest Tubb)
Amazing Grace (George Jones)
Will the Circle Be Unbroken (Nitty Gritty Dirt Band)

SOUND IDEAS (6 LPs)
Various artists collection

❑ Welk Music Group (S)
Number Not Known............. '86   25-35
DISCS 1: Has excerpts of songs published by Welk Music, including two Elvis tracks. Promotional issue only.
❑ Welk Music Group............... '86   25-35
BOX 1: Verification pending.

Welk Music Group (S)
Number Not Known...... '86   **50-70**
TOTAL PACKAGE 1: Discs, box.

SOUND OF '77 – MOR (5 LPs)
Various artists collection
Complete five-hour radio show recapping select music and events of 1977. Along with *Moody Blue*, this contains a medley of Elvis tunes. Identification numbers are engraved on all discs, listed separately below. Sides 1, 3, 5, 7 and 9 are identical to the Rock edition (next listing) with some rock songs on the remaining sides being replaced by MOR (Middle of the Road) tunes. The format is indicated in the matrix with an "R" (rock), "M" (MOR), or "RM" (both). The Elvis tribute is identical on both shows. Issued only to radio stations.

❑ Billboard Side 1/Side 6 ....12/77   10-20
DISC 1:
BB-77 1RM/BB-77 6M.
❑ Billboard Side 2/Side 7 ....12/77   10-20
DISC 2:
BB-77 2M/BB-77 7RM.
❑ Billboard Side 3/Side 8 ....12/77   10-20
DISC 3:
BB-77 3RM/BB-77 8M.
❑ Billboard Side 4/Side 9 ....12/77   10-20
DISC 4:
BB-77 4M/BB-77 9RM.
❑ Billboard Side 5/
Side 10 ....12/77   10-20
DISC 5:
BB-77 5RM/BB-77 10M.
❑ Billboard BB-77................12/77   25-50
BOX 1: Front: Black slick with white print. Billboard logo at upper left. Back is blank.
INNER SLEEVES 1: White, no printing.
❑ Billboard BB-77................12/77   10-15
INSERT 1: Five pages of cue sheets and program notes, appropriate for both the rock and MOR versions of this show.

Billboard (SP) BB-77....12/77   **100-175**
TOTAL PACKAGE 1: Discs, box, insert.

Elvis Contents:
Side 7
Moody Blue (Track 1)
Side 10
Elvis Medley: That's All Right/Baby, Let's Play House/Mystery Train/I Forgot to Remember to Forget/Just Because/Heartbreak Hotel/My Way. (Track 1)

SOUND OF '77 – ROCK (5 LPs)
Various artists collection
Complete radio show recaping select music and events of 1977. Along with *Moody Blue*, this contains a medley of Elvis tunes. Identification numbers are engraved on all discs, listed separately below. Issued only to radio stations.
❑ Billboard Side 1/Side 6 ....12/77   10-20
DISC 1:
BB-77 1RM/BB-77 6R.
❑ Billboard Side 2/Side 7 ....12/77   10-20
DISC 2:
BB-77 2R/BB-77 7RM.

❏ Billboard Side 3/Side 8 .... 12/77   10-20
  DISC 3:
  BB-77 3RM/BB-77 8R.

❏ Billboard Side 4/Side 9 .... 12/77   10-20
  DISC 4:
  BB-77 4R/BB-77 9RM.

❏ Billboard Side 5/
  Side 10 .... 12/77   10-20
  DISC 5:
  BB-77 5RM/BB-77 10R.

❏ Billboard BB-77 .... 12/77   25-50
  BOX 1: Front: Black slick with white print.
  Billboard logo at upper left. Back is blank.
  INNER SLEEVES 1: White, no printing.

❏ Billboard BB-77 .... 12/77   10-15
  INSERT 1: Five pages of cue sheets and
  program notes, approprate for both the rock
  and MOR versions of this show.

Billboard (SP) BB-77 .... 12/77   100-175
  TOTAL PACKAGE 1: Discs, box, insert.

Elvis Contents:

Side 7
Moody Blue (Track 1)

Side 10
Elvis Medley: That's All Right/Baby, Let's Play
  House/Mystery Train/I Forgot to Remember to
  Forget/Just Because/Heartbreak Hotel/My Way.
  (Track 1)

SOUND SERIES VOLUME VI
Various artists collection

❏ Charter Publications CH-12473   15-25
  DISC 1: White label. Issued with a song book
  and demonstration soundsheet. Promotional
  issue only.

❏ Charter Publications CH-12473   15-25
  COVER 1:

❏ Charter Publications CH-12473   10-15
  SONG BOOK 1: Has the sheet music for the
  songs, but not the lyrics.

❏ Eva-Tone   3-5
  SOUNDSHEET 1: Verification pending.

Charter Publications
  CH-12473 40-70
  **TOTAL PACKAGE : Disc, cover, song
  book, soundsheet.**

From the information we have received, it is
not clear which artists are heard on the album.
On the cover, songwriters Jimmy Webb and
Lennon & McCartney are listed, as are Elvis
Presley, Chicago, Bill Holcombe, Eugene
Magill, Caesar Ciovannini, and Leonard Mass.
We suspect that Elvis is not heard on the
soundsheet, but thus far we're unable to say
for certain. It is also not yet known which Elvis
track(s) are included.

Side 1
God Bless America
Just You N' Me
Elvis Presley in Concert
House of the Rising Sun
Bessa Brillante
Festive Overture

Gentle Journey
Skylab March

Side 2
Didn't We
California Dreamin'
Eight Days a Week
Road Rock and Hammer
Four of a Kind
All That Jazz (Rock)
If I Fell
The Sound of Silence
Sound of the Sea

SOUNDS OF SOLID GOLD (10 LPs)
Various artists collection

Boxed set, provided to radio stations as public
service broadcasting. Programs 1 through 3
are a tribute to Elvis and are valued at $15 to
$25 each. The remaining discs are $5 to $10.
Issued in 1978. Each side (program) runs
slightly under 15 minutes. Labels indicate
"Volume L1."

SOUNDS OF SOLID GOLD, VOL. 2 (7 LPs)
Various artists collection

Yellow label, red print. Boxed set, provided to
radio stations as public service broadcasting.
Discs, valued at $15 to $25 with an Elvis
track, or $5 to $10 without, are listed
individually below, one side of each being
devoted to a particular year. All identification
numbers are engraved. By the time Vol. 12
came out, labels were changed to black with
gold and white printing; however no Elvis
tracks are on that disc. There are other
volumes in this series with Elvis tracks, and
prices for them should be no different than the
ones listed here.

❏ United States Marine Corp (M) Program
  1/Promos
  DISC 1: 1960/Promos
  14V-70755-2/14V-70755-1.

❏ United States Marine Corp (M) Programs 2/3
  DISC 2: 1969/1959
  14V-70756-1/14V-70756-2.

❏ United States Marine Corp (M) Programs 4/5
  DISC 3: 1963/1968
  14V-70757-1/14V-70757-2.

❏ United States Marine Corp (M) Programs 6/7
  DISC 4: 1961/1955
  14V-70758-1/14V-70758-2.

❏ United States Marine Corp (M) Programs 8/9
  DISC 5: 1962/1965
  14V-70759-1/14V-70759-2.

❏ United States Marine Corp (M) Programs
  10/11
  DISC 6: 1956/1964
  14V-70760-1/14V-70760-2.

❏ United States Marine Corp (M) Programs
  12/13
  DISC 7: 1957/1966
  14V-70761-1/14V-70761-2.

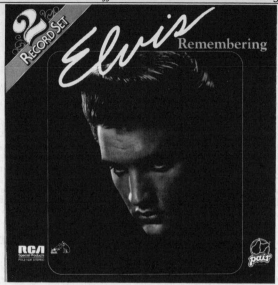

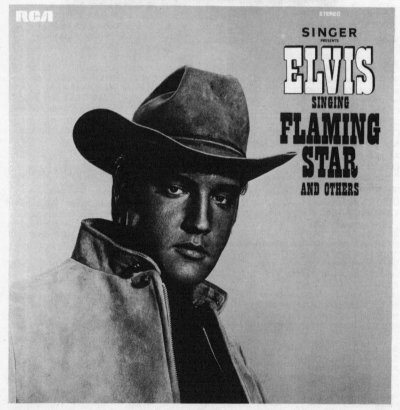

❏ United States Marine Corp Vol. 2
BOX 1: White. Front: Color drawing. Back:
Black-and-white photo of the show's host,
Marv Brooks. Listing of contents.
INNER SLEEVES 1: White, no printing.

SOUNDS OF SOLID GOLD, VOL. 4 (7 LPs)

Various artists collection

❏ United States Marine Corp (M) Programs 1/2
DISC 1: 1971/1963
62V-71403-1/62V-71403-2.

❏ United States Marine Corp (M) Programs 3/4
DISC 2: 1956/1969
62V-71403-3/62V-71403-4

❏ United States Marine Corp (M) Programs 5/6
DISC 3: 1970/1960
62V-71403-5/62V-71403-6

❏ United States Marine Corp (M) Programs 7/8
DISC 4: 1958/1971
62V-71403-7/62V-71403-8.

❏ United States Marine Corp (M) Programs 9/10
DISC 5: 1965/1961
62V-71403-9/62V-71403-10.

❏ United States Marine Corp (M) Programs 11/12
DISC 6: 1970/1959
62V-71403-11/62V-71403-12.

❏ United States Marine Corp (M) Program 13/Promos
DISC 7: 1966/Promos
62V-71403-13/62V-71403-14.

❏ United States Marine Corp Vol. 4
BOX 1: White. Front: Color drawing. Back:
Black-and-white photo of the show's host,
Marv Brooks. Listing of contents.
INNER SLEEVES 1: White, no printing.

Elvis Contents:

Program 6 (1960)
Are You Lonesome Tonight (Track 2)

SOUNDTRACK OF THE '60s (3 LPs)

Various artists collections.

❏ Soundtrack of the '60s (S)   10-15
DISC 1: Price range is for any individual disc
containing at least one Elvis track.

❏ Soundtrack of the '60s (S)   25-35
For a complete set of three LPs – each a
complete one-hour, weekly radio show with
three pages of cue sheets and program notes
– multiply the price range shown above times
the number of discs containing at least one
Elvis track. Boxes are white and have a
drawing of a western hat and boots. Issued
only to subscribing radio stations.

SOUPY SALES MOLDY OLDIES

Various artists collection

❏ NBC Radio (SP)
Show #49 .... 3/87   10-20
DISC 1: Shows air dates as March 7-8, 1987.
Though we have only verified show #49, it
appears there are other discs in the series. If
so, any with an Elvis track would have the
same price range. Includes single-page cue
sheet. May or may not have a special cover or
box.

NBC Radio (SP)
Show #49 .... 3/87   10-20
TOTAL PACKAGE 1: Disc(s), cover/box, insert(s).

Side 1
Blue Moon (Marcels)
Bristol Stomp (Dovells)
Stand By Me (Ben E. King)
Little Sister (Elvis Presley)
I'm Walkin (Fats Domino)
Dizzy (Tommy Roe)
Shotgun (Jr. Walker & All Stars)
Just My Imagination (Temptations)
She Loves You (Beatles)

Side 2
Wake Up Little Susie (Everly Brothers)
Walk Right Back (Everly Brothers)
Cathy's Clown (Everly Brothers)
Bye Bye Love (Everly Brothers)
Soul Finger (Bar-Kays)
Red Rubber Ball (Cyrkle)

SOUTHERN GENTLEMAN

❏ Schonbrunn HCV-542: Bootleg. Listed for
identification only.

SPECIAL CHRISTMAS PROGRAMMING (Tape)

❏ RCA Victor (M) EPC-1 ..... 11/67   150-175
TAPE 1: Boxed, full-track 7½-ips reel tape.
Amber, plastic reel has red, white and green
label on top side. Promotional issue only for
radio stations to air December 3, 1967. This
same program was made available on disc
(see next listing).

❏ RCA Victor EPC-1 .... 11/67   150-175
BOX 1: Front: Full-track 7½-ips at upper right.
Color Elvis photo, same as on cover of *Elvis
Christmas Album* (LPM/LSP-1951). Back:
"Sequence" of program is printed.

❏ RCA Victor 11/67   40-50
INSERT 1: Four-page "Elvis Special
Christmas Program Script." Color Elvis photo
on page one, same as on front cover of
Kissin' Cousins.

RCA Victor (M) EPC-1 .. 11/67   350-400
TOTAL PACKAGE 1: Tape, box, insert.

Although not included in the package sent to radio stations, there also exists four posters, of three different sizes, postcards, and publicity flyers – all of which promotes this show. Since this is a full-track recording, playing side 2 will result in hearing side 1 backwards.

Side 1
Here Comes Santa Claus
Blue Christmas
O, Little Town of Bethlehem
Silent Night
I'll Be Home for Christmas
I Believe
If Everyday Was Like Christmas
How Great Thou Art
His Hand in Mine
Special Elvis Christmas Message
I'll Be Home for Christmas

SPECIAL CHRISTMAS PROGRAMMING (LP)

❑ RCA Victor (M)
No Number......................11/67　　950-1400
DISC 1: White label, black print. Promotional issue only for radio stations to air December 3, 1967. This same program was made available on a reel tape (see previous listing).
UNRM-5697/UNRM-5698.
COVER 1: White, no printing.
❑ RCA Victor......................11/67　　50-100
INSERT 1: Script sheet with running times and program information. A 10" red vinyl bootleg exists of this material. There are no legitimate 10" LPs, nor are there any authorized colored vinyl discs of this show.

RCA Victor (M)
No Number ....11/67　1000-1500
TOTAL PACKAGE 1: Disc, insert.

Side 1
Here Comes Santa Claus
Blue Christmas
O, Little Town of Bethlehem
Silent Night
I'll Be Home for Christmas

Side 2
I Believe
If Everyday Was Like Christmas
How Great Thou Art
His Hand in Mine
Special Elvis Christmas Message
I'll Be Home for Christmas

SPECIAL DELIVERY FROM ELVIS

❑ Flaming Star FSR-3: Bootleg. Listed for identification only.

SPECIAL PALM SUNDAY PROGRAMMING

❑ RCA Victor (M)
SP 33-461 ....4/67　　600-650
DISC 1: White label, black print. Reads: "Complete half-hour radio program with spot announcements and selections from the RCA Victor album *How Great Thou Art* (LPM/LSP-3758." Promotional issue only.
UNRM-3932-1S/UNRM-3933-2S. Identification numbers are stamped.
Counterfeit Identification: Fakes have identification numbers engraved. Originals have those numbers stamped in the vinyl.
COVER 1: White, no printing.
❑ RCA Victor (M)
SP 33-461 ....4/67　　50-100
INSERT 1: Cue sheet with running times and program information.

RCA Victor (M)
SP 33-461 ....4/67　　650-750
TOTAL PACKAGE 1: Disc, insert.

Side 1
How Great Thou Art
In the Garden
Somebody Bigger Than You and I
Stand by Me

Side 2
Without Him
Where Could I Go But to the Lord
Where No One Stands Alone
Crying in the Chapel
How Great Thou Art (Excerpt)

SPEEDWAY

❑ RCA Victor (M)
LPM-3989........................6/68　　800-1000
DISC 1: Black label, "Monaural" at bottom.
WPRM-1034-1S/WPRM-1035-1S. Label LP#12.
❑ RCA Victor LPM-3989 ....6/68　　800-1000
COVER 1: Front: Nipper logo at top center, number at lower left. Seven color Elvis photos. Back: 12 color Elvis photos.
❑ RCA Victor 21-112-1
40D.....................................6/68　　4-6
INNER SLEEVE 1: Red, black and white. Front: RCA's Elvis LP catalog, most recent being *Elvis' Gold Records, Vol. 4* (side 1, row 4, column 5). Back: RCA's Elvis LP and Twin Pack Stereo 8 catalog.
❑ RCA Victor........................6/68　　25-40
INSERT 1: Color 8" x 10" Elvis (circa 1962) photo, signed "Sincerely, Elvis Presley." Back lists other RCA Elvis records.
❑ RCA Victor LPM-3989 ....6/68　　20-25
SHRINK STICKER 1: Red and white, reads: "Special Bonus, for a limited time only, full color photo of Elvis."

RCA Victor (M)
LPM-3989 ....6/68　1650-2050
TOTAL PACKAGE 1: Disc, cover, inner sleeve, insert, sticker.

□ RCA Victor (ST)
LSP-3989 ....6/68   10-20
DISC 2: Black label, RCA logo in white at top
and "Stereo" at bottom.
WPRM-1034-6S/WPRM-1035-4S. Label LP#16.
WPRS-1036-8S/WPRS-1037-7S. Label LP#16.

□ RCA Victor LSP-3989........6/68   20-25
COVER 2: Front: Nipper logo at top center,
number at upper left. Seven color Elvis
photos. Back: 12 color Elvis photos. Price
reflects RCA's continued use of this same
cover, with no discernible differences.

□ RCA Victor 21-112-1
40D.....................................6/68   4-6
INNER SLEEVE 2: Red, black and white.
Front: RCA's Elvis LP catalog, most recent
being *Elvis' Gold Records, Vol. 4* (side 1, row
4, column 5). Back: RCA's Elvis LP and Twin
Pack Stereo 8 catalog.

□ RCA Victor........................6/68   25-40
INSERT 2: Color 8" x 10" Elvis (circa 1962)
photo, signed "Sincerely, Elvis Presley." Back
lists other RCA Elvis records.

□ RCA Victor LSP-3839........6/68   20-25
SHRINK STICKER 2: Red and white, reads:
"Special Bonus, for a limited time only, full
color photo of Elvis."

RCA Victor (ST)
LSP-3839.....................6/68   80-115
TOTAL PACKAGE 2: Disc, cover, inner
  sleeve, insert, sticker.

□ RCA Victor (ST)
LSP-3989 ....11/68   20-25
DISC 3: Orange label. Rigid vinyl.

□ RCA Victor LSP-3989......11/68   8-10
COVER 3: Same as cover 2.

□ RCA Victor 21-112-1
40D................................ ....6/68   4-6
INNER SLEEVE 3: Red, black and white.
Front: RCA's Elvis LP catalog, most recent
being *Elvis' Gold Records, Vol. 4* (side 1, row
4, column 5). Back: RCA's Elvis LP and Twin
Pack Stereo 8 catalog. May also be found
with inner sleeves 40B and 40C. See chapter
on inner sleeves for more information.

RCA Victor (ST)
LSP-3989...................11/68   35-40
TOTAL PACKAGE 3: Disc, cover, inner
  sleeve.

□ RCA Victor (ST)
LSP-3989 ....'71   10-15
DISC 4: Orange label. Flexible vinyl.

□ RCA Victor LSP-3989..........'71   4-8
COVER 4: Same as cover 2.

□ RCA Victor........................'70s   2-4
INNER SLEEVE 4: Black-and-white. Pictures
RCA Elvis catalog front and back. Any of
several sleeves may be found on reissues
from this period.

RCA Victor (ST)
LSP-3989.....................'71   15-25
TOTAL PACKAGE 4: Disc, cover, inner
  sleeve.

□ RCA Victor (ST)
LSP-3989 ....'76   4-8
DISC 5: Tan label.

□ RCA LSP-3989 ....'76   4-8
COVER 5: Front: RCA logo and catalog
number at upper left, and "Victor" and
"Stereo" at upper right. Both front and back
have "RE" at lower left.

□ RCA Victor........................'70s   2-4
INNER SLEEVE 5: Black-and-white. Pictures
RCA Elvis catalog front and back. Any of
several sleeves may be found on reissues
from this period.

RCA Victor (ST)
LSP-3989.....................'76   10-20
TOTAL PACKAGE 5: Disc, cover, inner
  sleeve.

□ RCA Victor (ST)
LSP-3989 ....'76   4-6
DISC 6: Black label, dog near top.

□ RCA LSP-3989 ....'76   4-6
COVER 6: Front: "RE" in small letters at lower
left corner.

□ RCA Victor........................'70s   2-4
INNER SLEEVE 6: Black-and-white. Pictures
RCA Elvis catalog front and back. Any of
several sleeves may be found on reissues
from this period.

RCA Victor (ST)
LSP-3989.....................'76   10-18
TOTAL PACKAGE 6: Disc, cover, inner
  sleeve.

□ RCA Victor (ST)
AFL1-3989..........................'77   3-5
DISC 7: Black label, dog near top.

□ RCA AFL1-3989 ....'77   3-5
COVER 7: Reflects prefix change.

□ RCA Victor........................'70s   2-4
INNER SLEEVE 7: Black-and-white. Pictures
RCA Elvis catalog front and back. Any of
several sleeves may be found on reissues
from this period.

RCA Victor (ST)
AFL1-3989....................'77   8-15
TOTAL PACKAGE 7: Disc, cover, inner
  sleeve.

This is the only standard catalog RCA Presley
release with a solo track by another artist
(*Your Groovy Self* by Nancy Sinatra).

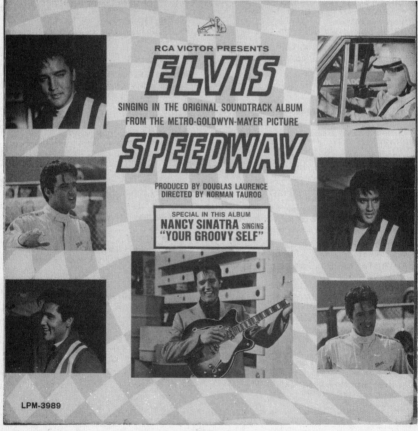

Side 1
Speedway
There Ain't Nothing Like a Song (Duet with Nancy Sinatra)
Your Time Hasn't Come Yet, Baby
Who Are You (Who Am I)
He's Your Uncle, Not Your Dad
Let Yourself Go

Side 2
Your Groovy Self (By Nancy Sinatra)
Five Sleepy Heads
Western Union
Mine
Goin' Home
Suppose

SPINOUT

❑ RCA Victor (M)
    LPM-3702........................10/66   10-15
    DISC 1: Black label, "Monaural" at bottom.
    TPRM-5314-1S/TPRM-5315-2S. Label LP#12.
    TPRM-5314-5S/TPRM-5315-5S. Label LP#12.
❑ RCA Victor LPM-3702.....10/66   25-55
    COVER 1: Front: RCA Victor logo at upper
    right, number at lower left. Color Elvis photo.
    Back: Nine color Elvis photos.
❑ RCA Victor 21-112-1
    40B....................................4/65   4-6
    INNER SLEEVE 1: Red, black and white.
    Front: RCA's Elvis LP catalog, most recent
    being *Roustabout* (side 1, row 1, column 5).
    Back: RCA Elvis EPs and 45s catalog.
❑ RCA Victor..........................4/65   40-50
    INSERT 1: Color 11¾" x 11¾" photo of Elvis,
    similar (same sitting, different pose) to photo
    on front cover of LP. Back is blank.
❑ RCA Victor LPM-3702.....10/66   20-25
    SHRINK STICKER 1: Announces the bonus,
    color Elvis photo.

RCA Victor (M)
    LPM-3702.................10/66   100-150
    TOTAL PACKAGE 1: Disc, cover, inner
       sleeve, insert, sticker.

❑ RCA Victor (M)
    LPM-3702........................10/66   10-15
    DISC 2: Same as disc 1.
❑ RCA Victor LPM-3702.....10/66   45-75
    COVER 2: Designate promo. Same as cover
    1, but with "Not for Sale" stamped on back.
❑ RCA Victor 21-112-1
    40B....................................4/65   4-6
    INNER SLEEVE 2: Red, black and white.
    Front: RCA's Elvis LP catalog, most recent
    being *Roustabout* (side 1, row 1, column 5).
    Back: RCA Elvis EPs and 45s catalog.
❑ RCA Victor..........................4/65   40-50
    INSERT 2: Color 11¾" x 11¾" photo of Elvis,
    similar (same sitting, different pose) to photo
    on front cover of LP. Back is blank.
❑ RCA Victor LPM-3702.....10/66   20-25
    SHRINK STICKER 2: Announces the bonus,
    color Elvis photo.

RCA Victor (M)
    LPM-3702.................10/66   120-170
    TOTAL PACKAGE 2: Disc, cover, inner
       sleeve, insert, sticker.

❑ RCA Victor (ST)
    LSP-3702........................10/66   10-20
    DISC 3: Black label, RCA logo in white at top
    and "Stereo" at bottom.
    TPRS-5316-1S/TPRS-5317-1S. Label LP#16.
    TPRS-5316-8S/TPRS-5317-8S. Label LP#16.
❑ RCA Victor LSP-3702......10/66   25-50
    COVER 3: Front: RCA Victor logo at upper
    right, number at upper left. Color Elvis photo.
    Back: Nine color Elvis photos.
❑ RCA Victor 21-112-1
    40B....................................4/65   4-6
    INNER SLEEVE 3: Red, black and white.
    Front: RCA's Elvis LP catalog, most recent
    being *Roustabout* (side 1, row 1, column 5).
    Back: RCA Elvis EPs and 45s catalog.
❑ RCA Victor..........................4/65   40-50
    INSERT 3: Color 11¾" x 11¾" photo of Elvis,
    similar (same sitting, different pose) to photo
    on front cover of LP. Back is blank.
❑ RCA Victor LSP-3702......10/66   20-25
    SHRINK STICKER 3: Announces the bonus,
    color Elvis photo.

RCA Victor (ST)
    LSP-3702.................10/66   100-150
    TOTAL PACKAGE 3: Disc, cover, inner
       sleeve, insert, sticker.

❑ RCA Victor (ST)
    APL1-2560 ....9/77   3-5
    DISC 4: Black label, dog near top.
    APL1-2560-1/APL1-2560B-4.
❑ RCA APL1-2560 ....9/77   3-5
    COVER 4: Reflects number change.
❑ RCA Victor..........................'70s   2-4
    INNER SLEEVE 4: Black-and-white. Pictures
    RCA Elvis catalog front and back. Any of
    several may be found on reissues from this
    period.

RCA Victor (ST)
    APL1-2560 ....9/77   8-15
    TOTAL PACKAGE 4: Disc, cover, inner
       sleeve.

❑ RCA Victor (ST)
    AYL1-3684 ....5/80   3-5
    DISC 5: Black label, dog near top.
    AYL1-3684A/AYL1-3684B. Also, APL1-2560A-3/ APL1-
    2560B-5 is stamped but crossed out.
❑ RCA AYL1-3684 ....5/80   3-5
    COVER 5: Reflects number change.
    INNER SLEEVE 5: White, no printing.

RCA Victor (ST)
    AYL1-3684 ....5/80   6-10
    TOTAL PACKAGE 5: Disc, cover.

Side 1
Stop, Look and Listen
Adam and Evil
All That I Am
Never Say Yes
Am I Ready
Beach Shack

Side 2
Spinout
Smorgasbord
I'll Be Back
Tomorrow Is a Long Time
Down in the Alley
I'll Remember You

SPOTLIGHT ON ELVIS

❏ Bootleg. Listed for identification only.

STANDING ROOM ONLY, VOLUME 2

❏ Eagle NOTN-3003: Bootleg. Listed for identification only.

STANDING ROOM ONLY, VOLUME 3

❏ Eagle NOTN-3004: Bootleg. Listed for identification only.

STARS OF CHRISTMAS (SELECTED ESPECIALLY FOR AVON)

Various artists collection

❏ RCA Special Products/BMG (ST)
DPL1-0842 .... '88   4-5
DISC 1: Blue label, white and rust print.
Available only from Avon distributors.
DPL1-0842-A-2/DPL1-0842-B-1.

❏ RCA Special Products/BMG
DPL1-0842 ....,... '88   4-5
COVER 1: Front: No logo or number. Back:
RCA Special Products and BMG logos at
bottom left. 12 color photos of artists heard,
including Elvis (same pose as on *A Legendary
Performer, Vol. 3*).
INNER SLEEVE 1: Clear plastic, no printing.

❏ Avon Products   2-5
INSERT 1: Color, 20-page, 8" x 11" booklet,
with color photos of each artist, song lyrics,
and comments. Has "FSC #5233-1" on back
page.

RCA Special Products/BMG (ST)
DPL1-0842 .... '88   **10-15**
TOTAL PACKAGE 1: Disc, cover, insert.

Card stock jacket, with printing on cover – not
on slicks.

Side 1
Beneath the Christmas Star (Judy Collins)
Let It Snow! Let It Snow! (Johnny Mathis))
Santa Claus Is Comin' to Town (Pointer Sisters)
Jingle Bells (Jose Feliciano)
Rockin' Around the Christmas Tree (Forester Sisters)
White Christmas (Bing Crosby)

Side 2
It's the Most Wonderful Time (Andy Williams)
Twelve Days of Christmas (Roger Whittaker)
Merry Christmas, Darling (Carpenters)
If Every Day Was like Christmas (Elvis Presley)
I Saw Three Ships (James Galway)
Silent Night (Kenny Rogers)

STEPPIN' OUT OF LINE

❏ Laurel 2427: Bootleg. Listed for identification
only.

STEREO '57 (ESSENTIAL ELVIS, VOLUME 2)

❏ RCA (S) 9589-1-R 2/89   8-10
DISC 1: Red, black and silver label. RCA
lightning bolt logo on disc and cover.
9589-1-R-A-1/9589-1-R-B. Identification numbers are
engraved.

❏ RCA 9589-1-R 2/89   8-10
COVER 1: Gatefold. RCA lightning bolt logo
and number at upper right. Color Elvis photo
on front, black-and-white and duotone Elvis
photos on three remaining panels.
INNER SLEEVE 1: Generic RCA sleeve. No
mention of this LP.

❏ RCA 9589-1-R 2/89   3-5
SHRINK STICKER 1: Circular, yellow and
red, reads: "Rare Unreleased Elvis
Collectibles Complete with Studio Dialog &
Extra Takes. Historic Presley Recordings."

RCA (S) 9589-1-R 2/89   **20-25**
TOTAL PACKAGE 1: Disc, cover, sticker.

Card stock jacket, with printing on cover – not
on slicks.

Side 1
I Beg of You
Is It So Strange
Have I Told You Lately That I Love You
It Is No Secret (What God Can Do)
Blueberry Hill
Mean Woman Blues
(There'll Be) Peace in the Valley (For Me)
Have I Told You Lately That I Love You

Side 2
Blueberry Hill
That's When Your Heartaches Begin
It Is So Strange
I Beg of You
(There'll Be) Peace in the Valley (For Me)
I Beg of You

STILL THE KING: see *ELVIS PRESLEY – STILL THE KING*

SUN COLLECTION

❏ RCA (M) HY-1001 ....8/75   10-15
DISC 1: British import that was widely
distributed in the United States. Green, black
and white label. Does not have "Starcall" on
label.
HY-1001-A-1E A2AA/HY-1001-B-2E A3B. Identification
numbers are engraved.

❑ RCA HY-1001 .... 8/75   10-15
  COVER 1: Front: Starcall logo at upper right,
  RCA Records and Tapes logo at lower right.
  Color, artist's rendering of a circa 1956 Elvis.
  Back: Lower half pictures six other LPs in the
  Starcall series.
  INNER SLEEVE 1: White, no printing.
RCA (M) HY-1001 .... 8/75   20-30
  TOTAL PACKAGE 1: Disc, cover.

❑ RCA (M) HY-1001 .... 10/75   5-10
  DISC 2: Same as disc 1, except has "Starcall"
  on right side of label.
  HY-1001-A-1E A2D/HY-1001-B-2E A1N. Identification
  numbers are engraved.
❑ RCA HY-1001 .... 10/75   5-10
  COVER 2: Front: Starcall logo at upper right,
  RCA Records and Tapes logo at lower right.
  "Imported & Distributed by Peters
  International" sticker at lower left. Color,
  artist's rendering of a circa 1956 Elvis. Back:
  Nearly identical to U.S. issue, with three
  columns of discographical and session notes
  by Roy Carr. Black-and-white Elvis (circa
  1956) photo.
  INNER SLEEVE 2: White, no printing.
RCA (M) HY-1001 .... 10/75   10-20
  TOTAL PACKAGE 2: Disc, cover.

  Card stock jacket, with printing on cover – not
  on slicks.

  Side A
  That's All Right
  Blue Moon of Kentucky
  I Don't Care If the Sun Don't Shine
  Good Rockin' Tonight
  Milkcow Blues Boogie
  You're a Heartbreaker
  I'm Left, You're Right, She's Gone
  Baby Let's Play House

  Side B
  Mystery Train
  I Forgot to Remember to Forget
  I'll Never Let You Go (Little Darlin')
  Tryin' to Get to You
  I Love You Because (1st Version)
  Blue Moon
  Just Because
  I Love You Because (2nd Version)

SUN SESSIONS
❑ RCA Victor (M)
  APM1-1675 .... 3/76   8-10
  DISC 1: Tan label. U.S. version of *The Sun
  Collection*
  APM1-1675-A-2S/APM1-1675-B-2S. Identification numbers
  are engraved.
  APM1-1675-A-4S/APM1-1675-B-4S. Identification numbers
  are stamped.
❑ RCA APM1-1675 .... 3/76   8-10
  COVER 1: Front: RCA logo and number at
  bottom, number also at upper right. Color,
  artist's rendering of Elvis, circa 1956. Back:
  Three columns of discographical and session
  notes by Roy Carr. Black-and-white Elvis
  (circa 1956) photo.

❑ RCA Victor 21-112-1
  PT 54D 6/75   3-5
  INNER SLEEVE 1: Black-and-white. Pictures
  RCA's Elvis LP catalog front and back, most
  recent being *Elvis As Recorded at Madison
  Square Garden* (side 2, row 2, column 6). May
  also be found with inner sleeve 54C.
RCA Victor (M)
  APM1-1675 .... 3/76   20-25
  TOTAL PACKAGE 1: Disc, cover, inner
    sleeve.

❑ RCA Victor (M)
  APM1-1675 .... 3/76   8-10
  DISC 2: Same as disc 1.
❑ RCA APM1-1675 .... 3/76   12-15
  COVER 2: Designate promo. Same as cover
  1, but with "Not for Sale" stamped on back.
❑ RCA Victor 21-112-1
  PT 54D 6/75   3-5
  INNER SLEEVE 2: Black-and-white. Pictures
  RCA's Elvis LP catalog front and back, most
  recent being *Elvis As Recorded at Madison
  Square Garden* (side 2, row 2, column 6). May
  also be found with inner sleeve 54C.
RCA Victor (M)
  APM1-1675 .... 3/76   25-30
  TOTAL PACKAGE 2: Disc, cover, inner
    sleeve.

❑ RCA Victor (M)
  APM1-1675 .... '76   4-6
  DISC 3: Black label, dog near top.
  APM1-1675-A-3S/APM1-1675-B-3S.
❑ RCA Victor (M)
  APM1-1675 .... '76   4-6
  COVER 3: Same as cover 1.
❑ RCA Victor 21-112-1
  PT 54D 6/75   3-5
  INNER SLEEVE 3: Black-and-white. Pictures
  RCA's Elvis LP catalog front and back, most
  recent being *Elvis As Recorded at Madison
  Square Garden* (side 2, row 2, column 6). May
  also be found with inner sleeve 54C.
RCA Victor (M)
  APM1-1675 .... 3/76   10-20
  TOTAL PACKAGE 3: Disc, cover, inner
    sleeve.

❑ RCA Victor (M)
  AFM1-1675 .... '77   3-5
  DISC 4: Black label, dog near top.
❑ RCA AFM1-1675 .... '77   3-5
  COVER 4: Reflects prefix change.
❑ RCA Victor .... '70s   2-4
  INNER SLEEVE 4: Black-and-white. Pictures
  RCA Elvis catalog front and back. Any of
  several sleeves may be found on reissues
  from this period.

RCA Victor (M)
AFM1-1675 .... '77 8-15
TOTAL PACKAGE 4: Disc, cover, inner sleeve.

❑ RCA Victor (ST)
AYM1-3893 .... 2/81 3-5
DISC 5: Black label, dog near top.
AYM1-3893A/AYM1-3893-B. Identification numbers are engraved. Also APM1-1675-A-4S/APM1-1675-B-4S is stamped but crossed out.

❑ RCA AYM1-3893 .... 2/81 3-5
COVER 5: Reflects number change.
INNER SLEEVE 5: White, no printing.

RCA Victor (ST)
AYM1-3893 .... 2/81 6-10
TOTAL PACKAGE 5: Disc, cover.

This was the first of two standard catalog, RCA's Elvis LPs, first issued on the tan label the other being *From Elvis Presley Boulevard, Memphis, Tennessee.*

Side A
That's All Right
Blue Moon of Kentucky
I Don't Care If the Sun Don't Shine
Good Rockin' Tonight
Milkcow Blues Boogie
You're a Heartbreaker
I'm Left, You're Right, She's Gone
Baby Let's Play House

Side B
Mystery Train
I Forgot to Remember to Forget
I'll Never Let You Go (Little Darlin')
Tryin' to Get to You
I Love You Because (1st Version)
Blue Moon
Just Because
I Love You Because (2nd Version)

SUN STORY (2 LPs)
Various artists collection
❑ Rhino (M) RNDA-71103 .... 1/86 5-8
DISCS 1: Yellow label, black print.
(Disc 1) RNLP-71103A-1 13662/RNLP-71103B-1 13662-X.
(Disc 2) RNLP- 71103C-1 13663/RNLP-71103D-1 13663-X.
Identification numbers are engraved.

❑ Rhino RNDA-71103 .... 1/86 5-8
COVER 1: Single pocket. Front: Five colorized photos of artists heard on this LP, including Elvis. Back: Sun logo at bottom center, Rhino logo, number and UPC bar code at lower right.
INNER SLEEVES 1: White, no printing.

❑ Rhino RNDA-71103 .... 1/86 4-5
INSERT 1: Four-page, 11" x 11" *The Sun Story* booklet. Has 12 black-and-white photos of Sun artists, including Elvis.

❑ Rhino RNDA-71103 .... 1/86 3-4
SHRINK STICKER 1: Yellow and brown, 3" x 6½" announcing 11 selections and the "Souvenir Booklet Enclosed."

Rhino (M)
RNDA-71103 .... 1/86 20-25
TOTAL PACKAGE 1: Disc, cover, insert, sticker.

Card stock jacket, with printing on cover – not on slicks.

Disc 1
Side 1
Good Rockin' Tonight (Elvis Presley)
Rocket 88 (Jackie Brenston)
Blue Suede Shoes (Carl Perkins)
Mystery Train (Junior Parker)
Folsom Prison Blues (Johnny Cash)
Sitting by My Window (Five Tinos)
Ooby Dooby (Roy Orbison)

Side 2
Whole Lotta Shakin' Goin' On (Jerry Lee Lewis)
Matchbox (Carl Perkins)
Lonely Weekends (Charlie Rich)
Mona Lisa (Carl Mann)
My Bucket's Got a Hole in It (Sonny Burgess)
Flyin' Saucers Rock 'N' Roll (Billy Riley)
Great Balls of Fire (Jerry Lee Lewis)

Disc 2
Side 1
Get Rhythm (Johnny Cash)
Devil Doll (Roy Orbison)
Just Walkin' in the Rain (Prisonaires)
Straight A's in Love (Johnny Cash)
Ubangi Stomp (Warren Smith)
Bear Cat (Rufus Thomas)
That's All Right (Elvis Presley)

Side 2
Honey Don't (Carl Perkins)
High School Confidential (Jerry Lee Lewis)
Red Hot (Billy Riley)
I Walk the Line (Johnny Cash)
Who Will the Next Fool Be (Charlie Rich)
Raunchy (Bill Justis)
Breathless (Jerry Lee Lewis)

SUN YEARS – INTERVIEWS AND MEMORIES
DISC 1: None made.

❑ Sun (M) 1001 .... 8/77 50-100
COVER 1: White stock with black print. Sun logo and number at upper right. Nine black-and-white photos and one drawing of Elvis. Only slicks were made of this item, and it was never manufactured as a finished cover. Printed on one side only. Title shown on front as *Interviews and Memories of: The Sun Years.*

Sun (M) 1001 .... 8/77 50-100
TOTAL PACKAGE 1: Cover slick.

❑ Sun (M) 1001 .... 9/77 5-8
DISC 2: Yellow, '50s style Sun label with *Memphis, Tennessee* at bottom.
S-1001-A/S-1001-B. Identification numbers are engraved.

❑ Sun 1001 ....9/77   5-8
   COVER 2: Light yellow stock with brown print.
   Sun logo and number at upper right. Front:
   Nine brown and white photos and one
   drawing of Elvis. Title shown as *Interviews
   and Memories of: The Sun Years.* Back: Two
   Elvis brown and white photos.
   INNER SLEEVE 2: White, no printing.

Sun (M) 1001 ....9/77   10-15
   TOTAL PACKAGE 2: Disc, cover.

❑ Sun (M) 1001 ....9/77   5-8
   DISC 3: Yellow, Sun International label with
   "Nashville, U.S.A." at bottom.
   S-1001-A XSY-151483-1A/S-1001-B XSY-151484-1A.
   Identification numbers are engraved.
   S-1001-A XSY-151483-1B/S-1001-B XSY-151484-1B.
   Identification numbers are engraved.
   S-1001-A XSY-151483-1C/S-1001-B XSY-151484-1C.
   Identification numbers are engraved.
   S-1001-A XSY-151483-1C/S-1001-B XSY-151484-1D.
   Identification numbers are engraved.

❑ Sun 1001 ....9/77   5-8
   COVER 3: White stock with brown print.
   Otherwise, same as cover 2.
   INNER SLEEVE 3: White, no printing.

Sun (M) 1001 ....9/77   10-15
   TOTAL PACKAGE 3: Disc, cover.

❑ Sun (M) 1001 ....9/77   5-8
   DISC 4: Same as disc 3.

❑ Sun 1001 ....9/77   5-8
   COVER 4: Dark yellow stock with brown print.
   Otherwise, same as cover 2.
   INNER SLEEVE 4: White, no printing.

Sun (M) 1001 ....9/77   10-15
   TOTAL PACKAGE 4: Disc, cover.

Side 1 (The Sun Years)
Parts from Actual Recording Sessions with the Voice of
Sam Phillips, the Voice of Elvis Presley, Plus
Excerpts of Elvis Presley's Sun Recordings, Issued
and Unissued.

Side 2 (Interviews and Music)
Interviews By Jay Thompson At Wichita Falls, Texas,
Charlie Walker At San Antonio, Texas Plus Various
Other Rare Elvis Presley Talking Intros on Stage
and Television.

SUPER '60s (7 LPs)
Various artists collection
Mail order offer only. All discs in this set have
a black, white and red label, and are listed
individually below. All identification numbers
are stamped.

❑ Reader's Digest/RCA Music Service
   RBA-037-1 ....'89   3-4
   DISC 1:
   W1RS-5551-3/W1RS-5552-3.
❑ Reader's Digest/RCA Music Service
   RBA-037-2 ....'89   3-4
   DISC 2:
   W1RS-5553-3/W1RS-5554-1.
❑ Reader's Digest/RCA Music Service
   RBA-037-3 ....'89   3-4
   DISC 3:
   W1RS-5555-2/W1RS-5556-3.

❑ Reader's Digest/RCA Music Service
   RBA-037-4 ....'89   3-4
   DISC 4:
   W1RS-5557-3/W1RS-5558-1.
❑ Reader's Digest/RCA Music Service
   RBA-037-5 ....'89   3-4
   DISC 5:
   W1RS-5559-1/W1RS-5560-1.
❑ Reader's Digest/RCA Music Service
   RBA-037-6 ....'89   3-4
   DISC 6:
   W1RS-5561-5/W1RS-5562-2.
❑ Reader's Digest/RCA Music Service
   RBA-037-7 ....'89   3-4
   DISC 7:
   W1RS-5563-1/W1RS-5564-1.
❑ Reader's Digest/RCA Music Service
   RBA-037A ....'89   15-20
   BOX 1: Slipcover: White. Front: Reader's
   Digest/BMG logo at lower right. Back is blank.
   Record case: White with blue print. Back is
   blank.
   INNER SLEEVES 1: Generic, individually
   numbered, plastic sleeves. Front and Back:
   Clear, covered with Reader's Digest Pegasus
   logos. No mention of Elvis.
❑ Reader's Digest/RCA Music
   Service ....'89   5-7
   INSERT 1: 4" x 4" information and program
   notes booklet.

**Reader's Digest/RCA Music Service
(SP) RBA-037A ....'89   40-55**
   TOTAL PACKAGE 1: Discs, box, insert.

SUPER SONGS (3 LPs)
Various artists collection
❑ Mutual (S)   15-25
   DISC 1: Issued only to radio stations. Has one
   Elvis track.
❑ Mutual..   15-25
   COVER 1: Verification pending.
Mutual (S)   30-50
   TOTAL PACKAGE 1: Disc, cover.

SUPERSTAR OUTTAKES
❑ E.P. PRP-254: Bootleg. Listed for
   identification only.

SUPERSTAR OUTTAKES. VOL. 2
❑ E.P. PRP-258: Bootleg. Listed for
   identification only.

SWEET DREAMS OF COUNTRY
(7 LPs)
Various artists collection
Mail order offer only. All discs in this set have
a black, white and red label, and are listed
individually below. All identification numbers
are engraved.

❑ Reader's Digest/BMG
  RCA-049A .... '90   3-5
  DISC 1:
  W1RS-5731-3/W1RS-5732-3.
❑ Reader's Digest/BMG
  RCA-049A .... '90   3-5
  DISC 2:
  W1RS-5733-2/W1RS-5734-2.
❑ Reader's Digest/BMG
  RCA-049A .... '90   3-5
  DISC 3:
  W1RS-5735-2/W1RS-5736-2.
❑ Reader's Digest/BMG
  RCA-049A .... '90   3-5
  DISC 4:
  W1RS-5737-1/W1RS-5738-1.
❑ Reader's Digest/BMG
  RCA-049A .... '90   3-5
  DISC 5:
  W1RS-5739-1/W1RS-5740-1.
❑ Reader's Digest/BMG
  RCA-049A .... '90   3-5
  DISC 6:
  W1RS-5741-1/W1RS-5742-1.
❑ Reader's Digest/BMG
  RCA-049A .... '90   3-5
  DISC 7:
  W1RS-5743-2/W1RS-5744-2.
❑ Reader's Digest/RCA Music Service
  049 .... '90   10-15
  BOX 1: Slipcover: Front: Blue. "Digitally
  Remastered" at bottom right. Back is blank.
  Record case is white with blue print.
  INNER SLEEVES 1: Generic, individually
  numbered, plastic sleeves. Front and Back:
  Clear, covered with Reader's Digest Pegasus
  logos.
❑ Reader's Digest/RCA Music Service
  RCA-049A .... '90   2-4
  INSERT 1: 3" x 3" "Music Program Notes"
  booklet. booklet, Elvis, The Legend Lives On.
Reader's Digest/RCA Music Service (S)
  RCA-049A .... **'90**   **40-55**
  TOTAL PACKAGE 1: Discs, box, insert.

TV GUIDE PRESENTS ELVIS
❑ Hound Dawg HD-1000: Bootleg. Listed for
  identification only.

THAT'S THE WAY IT IS
❑ RCA Victor (ST)
  LSP-4445 .... 12/70   45-75
  DISC 1: Orange label. Rigid vinyl.
  ZPRS-1867-3S/ZPRS-1868-3S.
❑ RCA Victor LSP-4445 ...... 12/70   8-10
  COVER 1: Front: RCA logo and number at
  upper left, "Victor Stereo" at upper right.
  Black-and-white Elvis photo. Back: 12 black-
  and-white Elvis photos.

❑ RCA Victor 21-112-1
  pt 54 .... 8/70   4-6
  INNER SLEEVE 1: Black-and-white. Pictures
  RCA's Elvis LP catalog front and back, most
  recent being *Worldwide Gold Award Hits, Vol.
  1* (side 2, row 4, column 4).
RCA Victor (ST)
  LSP-4445 .... **12/70**   **60-90**
  **TOTAL PACKAGE 1: Disc, cover, inner
  sleeve.**

❑ RCA Victor (ST)
  LSP-4445 .... 12/70   20-25
  DISC 2: Same as disc 1.
❑ RCA Victor LSP-4445 ...... 12/70   12-15
  COVER 2: Designate promo. Same as cover
  1, but with "Not for Sale" stamped on back.
❑ RCA Victor 21-112-1
  pt 54 .... 8/70   3-5
  INNER SLEEVE 2: Black-and-white. Pictures
  RCA's Elvis LP catalog front and back, most
  recent being Worldwide Gold Award Hits, Vol.
  1 (side 2, row 4, column 4).
RCA Victor (ST)
  LSP-4445 .... **12/70**   **35-45**
  **TOTAL PACKAGE 2: Disc, cover, inner
  sleeve.**

❑ RCA Victor (ST)
  LSP-4445 .... '71   10-15
  DISC 3: Orange label. Flexible vinyl.
  ZPRS-1867-A3D/ZPRS-1868-A2E.
  ZPRS-1867-9S/ZPRS-1868-7S.
❑ RCA Victor LSP-4445 .... '71   4-8
  COVER 3: Same as cover 1.
❑ RCA Victor .... '70s   2-4
  INNER SLEEVE 3: Black-and-white. Pictures
  RCA Elvis catalog front and back. Any of
  several sleeves may be found on reissues
  from this period.
RCA Victor (ST)
  LSP-4445 .... **'71**   **15-25**
  **TOTAL PACKAGE 3: Disc, cover, inner
  sleeve.**

❑ RCA Victor (ST)
  LSP-4445 .... '76   10-15
  DISC 4: Tan label.
  ZPRS-1867-5S/ZPRS-1868-6S.
  ZPRS-1867-9S/ZPRS-1868-9S.
❑ RCA Victor LSP-4445 .... '76   4-8
  COVER 4: Same as cover 1.
❑ RCA Victor .... '70s   2-4
  INNER SLEEVE 4: Black-and-white. Pictures
  RCA Elvis catalog front and back. Any of
  several sleeves may be found on reissues
  from this period.
RCA Victor (ST)
  LSP-4445 .... **'76**   **15-25**
  **TOTAL PACKAGE 4: Disc, cover, inner
  sleeve.**

❑ RCA Victor (ST)
  LSP-4445 .... '76   4-6
  DISC 5: Black label, dog near top.
❑ RCA LSP-4445 .... '76   4-6
  COVER 5: Same as cover 1.
❑ RCA Victor .... '70s   2-4
  INNER SLEEVE 5: Black-and-white. Pictures
  RCA Elvis catalog front and back. Any of
  several sleeves may be found on reissues
  from this period.

RCA Victor (ST)
  LSP-4445 .... '76   10-18
  TOTAL PACKAGE 5: Disc, cover, inner
  sleeve.

❑ RCA Victor (ST)
  AFL1-4445 .... '77   3-5
  DISC 6: Black label, dog near top.
❑ RCA AFL1-4445 .... '77   3-5
  AFL1-4445A/AFL1-4445B. Also has ZPRS-1867-30S stamped
  on side 1.
  COVER 6: Reflects prefix change.
❑ RCA Victor .... '70s   2-4
  INNER SLEEVE 6: Black-and-white. Pictures
  RCA Elvis catalog front and back. Any of
  several sleeves may be found on reissues
  from this period.

RCA Victor (ST)
  AFL1-4445 .... '77   8-15
  TOTAL PACKAGE 6: Disc, cover, inner
  sleeve.

❑ RCA Victor (ST)
  AYL1-4114 .... 9/81   3-5
  DISC 7: Black label, dog near top.
  AYL1-4114A/AYL1-4114B. Also has ZPRS-1867-30S stamped
  but crossed out on side 1. Has AFL1-4445A/AFL1-4445B
  stamped (on sides 1 and 2).
❑ RCA AYL1-4114 .... 9/81   3-5
  COVER 7: Reflects prefix change. Part of
  RCA's "Best Buy Series." Includes copies with
  a sticker bearing the "AYL1" prefix, wrapped
  around cover at top of spine.
  INNER SLEEVE 7: White, no printing.

RCA Victor (ST)
  AYL1-4114 .... 9/81   6-10
  TOTAL PACKAGE 7: Disc, cover.

Side 1
I Just Can't Help Believin'
Twenty Days and Twenty Nights
How the Web Was Woven
Patch It Up
Mary in the Morning
You Don't Have to Say You Love Me
Side 2
You've Lost That Lovin' Feelin'
I've Lost You
Just Pretend
Stranger in the Crowd
The Next Step Is Love
Bridge over Troubled Water
  Only *I Just Can't Help Believing, Patch It
  Up, You've Lost That Lovin' Feelin', I've
  Lost You,* and *Bridge over Troubled Water*
  are from the film.

THAT'S THE WAY IT IS
❑ Amiga 2 71-190: Bootleg. Listed for
  identification only.
❑ Lisa LMP 70-01: Bootleg. Listed for
  identification only.

**THESE WERE OUR SONGS: see *EARLY
'60s (THESE WERE OUR SONGS)***

30 YEARS OF NO. 1 COUNTRY HITS (7 LPs)
Various artists collection
Mail order offer only. All discs in this set have
a black, white and red label, and are listed
individually below.
❑ Reader's Digest/RCA Music Service
  RB4-215-1 .... '86   3-4
  DISC 1:
  T1RS-5621-1/T1RS-5622-1.
❑ Reader's Digest/RCA Music Service
  RB4-215-2 .... '86   3-4
  DISC 2:
  T1RS-5623-1/T1RS-5624-1.
❑ Reader's Digest/RCA Music Service
  RB4-215-3 .... '86   3-4
  DISC 3:
  T1RS-5625-1/T1RS-5626-1.
❑ Reader's Digest/RCA Music Service
  RB4-215-4 .... '86   3-4
  DISC 4:
  T1RS-5627-1/T1RS-5628-1.
❑ Reader's Digest/RCA Music Service
  RB4-215-5 .... '86   3-4
  DISC 5:
  T1RS-5629-1/T1RS-5630-1.
❑ Reader's Digest/RCA Music Service
  RB4-215-6 .... '86   3-4
  DISC 6:
  T1RS-5631-1/T1RS-5632-1.
❑ Reader's Digest/RCA Music Service
  RB4-215-7 .... '86   3-4
  DISC 7:
  T1RS-5633-1/T1RS-5634-1.
❑ Reader's Digest/RCA Music Service
  RBA-215A .... '86   15-20
  BOX 1: Slipcover: Brown. Front: Reader's
  Digest/RCA Music Service at upper right.
  Back is blank. Record case: White with rust
  print. Back is blank.
  INNER SLEEVES 1: Generic, individually
  numbered, plastic sleeves. Front and Back:
  Clear, covered with Reader's Digest Pegasus
  logos. Number (RDA/AP2) at lower left on
  side 2. No mention of Elvis.
❑ Reader's Digest/RCA Music
  Service .... '86   5-7
  INSERT 1: Duotone, 11¼" x 11½", 12-page
  information booklet.
**Reader's Digest/RCA Music Service
  (SP) RBA-215A .... '86   40-55**
  TOTAL PACKAGE 1: Discs, box, insert.

Disc 1

Side 1 (1950-1951)
Chattanoogie Shoe Shine Boy (Red Foley)
Kentucky Waltz (Eddy Arnold)
I'm Movin' On (Hank Snow)
Slow Poke (Pee Wee King)
Why Don't You Love Me (Hank Williams)
Shotgun Boogie (Tennessee Ernie Ford)

Side 2 (1952-1953)
Dear John Letter (Jean Shepard & Ferlin Husky)
Kaw-Liga (Hank Williams)
Mexican Joe (Jim Reeves)
The Wild Side of Life (Hank Thompson)
It Wasn't God (Who Made Honky-Tonk Angels) (Kitty Wells)
Jambalaya (Hank Williams)

Disc 2

Side 1 (1954-1956)
Cattle Call (Eddy Arnold)
Slowly (Webb Pierce)
In the Jailhouse Now (Webb Pierce)
I Don't Hurt Anymore (Hank Snow)
Why Baby Why (Red Sovine & Webb Pierce)
I Forgot to Remember to Forget (Elvis Presley)

Side 2 (1957-1958)
Oh Lonesome Me (Don Gibson)
Gone (Ferlin Husky)
(Let Me Be Your) Teddy Bear (Elvis Presley)
Guess Things Happen That Way (Johnny Cash)
Bye Bye Love (Everly Brothers)
Great Balls of Fire (Jerry Lee Lewis)

Disc 3

Side 1 (1959-1960)
White Lightning (George Jones)
Country Girl (Faron Young)
Please Help Me I'm Falling (Hank Locklin)
He'll Have to Go (Jim Reeves)
Wings of a Dove (Ferlin Husky)
The Three Bells (The Browns)

Side 2 (1961-1962)
Hello Walls (Faron Young)
I Fall to Pieces (Patsy Cline)
Walk On By (Leroy Van Dyke)
She's Got You (Patsy Cline)
She Thinks I Still Care (George Jones)
I've Been Everywhere (Hank Snow)

Disc 4

Side 1 (1963-1964)
Once a Day (Connie Smith)
Dang Me (Roger Miller)
I Guess I'm Crazy (Jim Reeves)
Lonesome 7-7203 (Hawkshaw Hawkins)
Still (Bill Anderson)
Abilene (George Hamilton IV)

Side 2 (1965-1966)
Make the World Go Away (Eddy Arnold)
Giddy Up Go (Red Sovine)
Take Good Care of Her (Sonny James)
Girl on the Billboard (Del Reeves)
There Goes My Everything (Jack Greene)
This Is It (Jim Reeves)

Disc 5

Side 1 (1967-1969)
Okie from Muskogee (Merle Haggard)
For Loving You (Bill Anderson & Jan Howard)
Galveston (Glen Campbell)
All the Time (Jack Greene)
Fist City (Loretta Lynn)
Honey (Bobby Goldsboro)

Side 2 (1970-1971)
Hello Darlin' (Conway Twitty)
Coal Miner's Daughter (Loretta Lynn)
Fightin' Side of Me (Merle Haggard)
When You're Hot, You're Hot (Jerry Reed)
Kiss an Angel Good Morning (Charley Pride)
Help Me Make It Through the Night (Sammi Smith)

Disc 6

Side 1 (1972-1973)
Eleven Roses (Hank Williams Jr.)
One's on the Way (Loretta Lynn)
Funny Face (Donna Fargo)
Old Dogs, Children, and Watermelon Wine (Tom T. Hall)
Come Live with Me (Roy Clark)
You've Never Been This Far Before (Conway Twitty)

Side 2 (1974-1975)
Somebody Done Somebody Wrong Song (B.J. Thomas)
Pure Love (Ronnie Milsap)
I'm a Ramblin' Man (Waylon Jennings)
When Will I Be Loved (Linda Ronstadt)
If We Make It Through December (Merle Haggard)
Rhinestone Cowboy (Glen Campbell)

Disc 7

Side 1 (1976-1977)
Here You Come Again (Dolly Parton)
Good Hearted Woman (Waylon Jennings & Willie Nelson)
Heaven's Just a Sin Away (Kendalls)
Cherokee Maiden (Merle Haggard)
Don't It Make My Brown Eyes Blue (Crystal Gayle)
Moody Blue (Elvis Presley)

Side 2 (1978-1979)
Backside of Thirty (John Conlee)
Two Doors Down (Dolly Parton)
Nobody Likes Sad Songs (Ronnie Milsap)
Do You Know You Are My Sunshine (Statler Brothers)
It Must Be Love (Don Williams)
Someone Loves You Honey (Charley Pride)

THIS IS ELVIS (2 LPs)

❑ RCA Victor (SP)
CPL2- 4031 ....4/80   5-7
DISCS 1: Black label, dog near top.
(Disc 1) CPL2-4031-A-1S/CPL2-4031-B-1S. **(Disc 2)** CPL2-4031-C-1S/CPL2-4031-D-1S. Identification numbers are engraved.

❑ RCA CPL2-4031.................4/80   5-7
COVER 1: Double pocket. Front: Number at lower right. Black-and-white Elvis photo. Back: RCA logo and number at lower right, UPC bar code at upper right. Color Elvis photo. Inside panels: Large, color Elvis ('68 TV Special) photo, bordered by 28 Elvis photos, both color and black-and-white.

❑ RCA CPL2-4031.................4/80   4-6
INNER SLEEVES 1: (Disc 1 sleeve) Front: Black-and-white Elvis (in uniform) photo. Back: Lists contents. (Disc 2 sleeve) Front: Black-and-white Elvis (recording, circa 1972). Back: Lists contents.

❑ RCA CPL2-4031.................4/80   10-15
SHRINK STICKER 1: Round (2" diameter) red sticker reads: "Contains Previously Unreleased Material."

RCA Victor (SP)
CPL2- 4031 .... 4/80   25-35
TOTAL PACKAGE 1: Discs, cover, inner sleeves, sticker.

❏ RCA Victor (SP)
CPL2- 4031 .... 4/80   5-7
DISCS 2: Same as discs 1.
❏ RCA CPL2-4031 .... 4/80   10-15
COVER 2: Designate promo. Same as cover 1, but with a ½-inch notch cut into upper left corner.
❏ RCA CPL2-4031 .... 4/80   4-6
INNER SLEEVES 2: (Disc 1 sleeve) Front: Black-and-white Elvis (in uniform) photo. Back: Lists contents. (Disc 2 sleeve) Front: Black-and-white Elvis (recording, circa 1972). Back: Lists contents.
❏ RCA CPL2-4031 .... 4/80   10-15
SHRINK STICKER 2: Round (2" diameter) red sticker reads: "Contains Previously Unreleased Material."

RCA Victor (SP)
CPL2- 4031 .... 4/80   30-45
TOTAL PACKAGE 2: Discs, cover, sticker, inner sleeves.

Card stock jacket, with printing on cover – not on slicks.
Disc 1
Side 1
(Marie's The Name) His Latest Flame
Moody Blue
That's All Right
Shake, Rattle and Roll/Flip, Flop and Fly (Dorsey TV Show)
Heartbreak Hotel (Unreleased, from the Dorsey TV Show)
Hound Dog (Unreleased, from the Milton Berle Show)
Excerpt from Hy Gardner Interview (Unreleased)
My Baby Left Me
Side 2
Merry Christmas Baby
Mean Woman Blues (Unreleased)
Don't Be Cruel (Unreleased, from the Ed Sullivan Show)
(Let Me Be Your) Teddy Bear
Jailhouse Rock
Army Swearing In (Unreleased)
G.I. Blues
Excerpt from Departure for Germany Press Conference (Elvis Sails)
Excerpt from Home from Germany Press Conference (Unreleased)
Disc 2
Side 1
Too Much Monkey Business (Unreleased)
Love Me Tender
I Got a Thing About You Baby
I Need Your Love Tonight
Blue Suede Shoes (Unreleased)
Viva Las Vegas
Suspicious Minds/Excerpt from Jay Cees Award to Elvis (Unreleased)
Promised Land
Side 2
Madison Square Garden Press Conference

Always on My Mind (Unreleased)
Are You Lonesome Tonight
My Way
An American Trilogy (Unreleased)
Memories

THOSE FABULOUS '50s (3 LPs)
Various artists collection
❏ Sessions (S) DVL2-0877 ..... '89   3-5
DISC 1:
DVL2-0877-A1/DVL2-0877-B1.
❏ Sessions (S) DVL2-0877 ..... '89   3-5
DISC 2:
DVL2-0877-C1/DVL2-0877-D1.
❏ Sessions (S) MSM-35152.... '89   3-5
DISC 3: Disc three numbers are quite different than those on discs 1 and 2.
MSM35152A/MSM35152B.
❏ Sessions (S) DVL2-0877 ..... '89   8-10
COVER 1: Single pocket. Front: Black-and-white photo of a '50s pajama party, with copies of the *Loving You* LP and *Elvis Presley* EP shown. Also, there is an Elvis photo on the wall. Sessions logo at bottom right. Back: RCA Special Products/BMG logo at bottom left. Sessions logo at bottom right.
INNER SLEEVES 1: White, no printing.
Sessions (S) DVL2-0877 .. '89   20-25
TOTAL PACKAGE 1: Discs, cover.

Mail order only offer. All discs have a purple label with black and red print. All identification numbers are engraved. Specific Elvis tracks not yet known.

THROUGH THE YEARS
❏ Bootleg. Listed for identification only.

(ELVIS SINGS SONGS FROM) TICKLE ME
❏ Audition Supertone US-533310761: Bootleg. Listed for identification only.

TIGER MAN ON TOUR
❏ Bootleg. Listed for identification only.

TIME-LIFE TREASURY OF CHRISTMAS (3 LPs)
Various artists collection
❏ Time-Life (SP)
STL-107 .... 10/86   10-15
DISCS 1: Custom, red label with black-and-white print. Sold only by Time-Life via mail order.
(Disc 1) STL-107A-1/STL-107B-1. **(Disc 2)** STL-107C-1/STL-107D-1. **(Disc 3)** STL-107E-1/STL-107F-1.
❏ Time-Life STL-107 .... 10/86   5-10
BOX 1: Front: Time-Life logo at lower right. Color, winter scene. Back: Text only.
INNER SLEEVES 1: Generic, Time-Life poly-lined.

Time-Life (SP)
STL-107 .... 10/86   **15-20**
TOTAL PACKAGE 1: Discs, box.

Disc 1
Side 1
White Christmas (Bing Crosby)
Winter Wonderland/Sleigh Ride (Dolly Parton)
The Little Drummer Boy (Harry Simeone Chorale)
O Little Town of Bethlehem (Andre Previn)
The Twelve Days of Christmas (Roger Whittaker)
Hark, the Herald Angels Sing (Nat King Cole)
O Holy Night (Perry Como)

Side 2
The Christmas Song (Carpenters)
Christmas Medley (Robert Shaw Chorale)
Night Before Christmas (Fred Waring)
Here Comes Santa Claus (Elvis Presley)
Santa's Beard (Beach Boys)
Christmas in My Home Town (Charley Pride)
Away in a Manger (Ed Ames)
Silent Night (Jim Reeves)

Disc 2
Side 1
Home for the Holidays (Perry Como)
Rudolph the Red-Nosed Reindeer (Gene Autry)
Feliz Navidad (Jose Feliciano)
Good King Wesceslas (Morton Gould)
Jingle Bell Rock (Bobby Helms)
Christmas Medley (Arthur Fiedler and the Boston Pops)
Ave Maria (Leontyne Price)

Side 2
Ding Dong Merrily on High (Roger Whittaker)
If Every Day Was like Christmas (Elvis Presley)
Rockin' Around the Christmas Tree (Brenda Lee)
Santa Claus Is Coming to Town (Perry Como)
Jingle Bells (Jim Reeves)
What Child Is This (Andre Previn)
Adeste Fideles (Luciano Pavarotti)

Disc 3
Side 1
I'll Be Home for Christmas (Perry Como)
God Rest Ye Merry Gentlemen (Julie Andrews)
Christmas in Dixie (Alabama)
Do You Hear What I Hear (Bing Crosby)
Christmas Medley (Robert Shaw Chorale)
Blue Christmas (Glen Campbell)
It Came upon a Midnight Clear (Robert Page)
Have Yourself a Merry Little Christmas (Judy Garland)

Side 2
Mary's Boy Child (Harry Belafonte)
Rocking (Roger Whittaker)
Let It Snow, Let It Snow, Let It Snow
The First Noel (Sergio Franchi)
Silver Bells (Sergio Franchi)
Holly Jolly Christmas (Burl Ives)
Christmas (Perry Como and the Fontane Sisters)
We Wish You a Merry Christmas (Eugene Ormandy & Orchestra)

TIME-LIFE TREASURY OF CHRISTMAS, VOL. 2 (3 LPs)
Various artists collection
❏ Time-Life (SP)
STL-108 .... 10/87   10-15
DISCS 1: Custom, red label with black-and-white print. Sold only by Time-Life via mail order.

(**Disc 1**) STL-108S1-2/STL-108-S2-2. (**Disc 2**) STL-108-S1-2/STL-108-S2-2. (**Disc 3**) STL-108-S1-2/STL-108S2-2. Identification numbers are engraved.

❏ Time-Life STL-107 .... 10/87   5-10
BOX 1: Front: Time-Life logo at lower right. Color, winter scene. Back: Text only.
INNER SLEEVES 1: Generic, Time-Life poly-lined.

Time-Life (SP)
STL-108 .... 10/87   **15-20**
TOTAL PACKAGE 1: Discs, box.

Disc 1
Side 1
The Christmas Song (Nat King Cole)
Jingle Bells (Bing Crosby and the Andrews Sisters)
The Little Drummer Boy (Roger Whittaker)
Sleigh Ride (Arthur Fiedler and the Boston Pops)
I Heard the Bells on Christmas Day (Harry Belafonte)
Up on the House Top (Eddy Arnold)
Irish Carol (Julie Andrews)
Jolly Old St. Nicholas (Chet Atkins)

Side 2
Bless This House (Perry Como)
Christmas Medley (Canadian Brass)
Christmas Is for Children (Glen Campbell)
Blue Christmas (Elvis Presley)
Frosty the Snowman (Red Foley)
An Old Christmas Card (Jim Reeves)
In Dulci Jubilo (Vienna Choir Boys)
O Come All Ye Faithful (Ed Ames)

Disc 2
Side 1
Silent Night (Sergio Franchi)
There's No Christmas like a Home Christmas (Perry Como)
Christmas Day (The Beach Boys)
Tennessee Christmas (Alabama)
Home for Christmas (Morton Gould)
Coventry Carol (Choir of King's College)
The Holly and the Ivy (Roger Whittaker)
O Holy Night (Luciano Pavarotti)

Side 2
White Christmas (Perry Como)
Winter Wonderland (Andrews Sisters)
I'll Be Home for Christmas (Bing Crosby)
The Twelve Days of Christmas (Robert Shaw Chorale)
The Gifts They Gave (Harry Belafonte)
Toy Trumpet (Arthur Fiedler & Boston Pops & Al Hirt)
God Rest Ye Merry Gentlemen (Roger Whittaker)
Good King Wenceslas (Ames Brothers)

Disc 3
Side 1
Rudolph the Red-Nosed Reindeer (Bing Crosby)
C-h-r-i-s-t-m-a-s (Jim Reeves)
Twinkle Twinkle Little Me (Supremes)
Jingle Bell Rock (Chet Atkins)
That Special Time of Year (Gladys Knight and the Pips)
Pretty Paper (Willie Nelson)
Old Toy Trains (Roger Miller)
Christmas Medley (Robert Shaw Chorale)

Side 2
Medley (Perry Como)
Do You Hear What I Hear (Ed Ames)
Shepherds in the Field (Choir of King's College)
Joy to the World (Julie Andrews)
O Come, O Come, Emmanuel (Virgil Fox)
Gesu Bambino (Luciano Pavarotti)
Ave Maria (Renate Tebaldi)
Hallelujah/Messiah (Robert Shaw Chorale)

TO ELVIS: LOVE STILL BURNING

❑ Fotoplay (SP) FSP-1001 ...5/78   15-20
  DISC 1: Picture disc. On both sides is a
  reproduction of an Elvis painting by the late
  Marge Nichols. Neither "Side One," "Side
  Two," the "PIC" logo, nor disclaimer are
  printed on disc.
  RD-7801-A/RD-7801-B. Identification numbers are
  engraved.
  COVER 1: None made.

❑ Fotoplay FSP-1001 ....5/78   5-10
  INSERT 1: Since cardboard covers were not
  yet made, 600 albums, each with a black-and-
  white 11" x 11" insert sheet, were distributed
  in plastic bags. Identified on insert sheet, at
  lower left, as a "Special Collector's Prevue
  Copy." Bag has no printing.

Fotoplay (SP)
**FSP-1001......................5/78   20-30
TOTAL PACKAGE 1: Disc, insert.**

❑ Fotoplay (SP)
  FSP-1001/TK-605 ....5/78   200-300
  DISC 2: Picture disc. Same in appearance as
  disc 1; however, the music heard is *Part 3*, an
  album by KC and the Sunshine Band (TK-
  605). A one-of-a-kind, experimental item to
  test the picture disc process. Not issued with
  cover.
  TK-605-A/TK-605-B. Identification numbers are engraved.
  COVER 2: None made.

Fotoplay (SP)
**FSP-1001......................5/78   200-300
TOTAL PACKAGE 2: Disc.**

❑ Fotoplay (SP) FSP-1001 ...5/78   10-15
  DISC 3: Same as disc 1.
❑ Fotoplay FSP-1001 ....6/78   15-25
  COVER 3: White stock with black print.
  Standard, die-cut picture disc cover. Some
  copies of disc 4 may also be found in this
  cover.

Fotoplay (SP)
**FSP-1001......................5/78   25-40
TOTAL PACKAGE 3: Disc, cover.**

❑ Fotoplay (SP) FSP-1001 ...6/78   5-10
  DISC 4: Same as disc 1, except does have
  "Side One," "Side Two," the "PIC" logo, and a
  disclaimer printed on disc.
❑ Fotoplay FSP-1001 ....6/78   5-10
  COVER 4: Black stock with white print.
  Standard, die-cut picture disc cover.

Fotoplay (SP)
**FSP-1001.................. ...6/78   10-20
TOTAL PACKAGE 4: Disc, cover.**

Side 1
I Remember Elvis Presley (Danny Mirror)
What Will We Do Without You (Bobby Fisher)
Goodbye King of Rock & Roll (Leon Everette)
Dark Cloud over Memphis (Johnny Tollison)
Candy Bars for Elvis (Barry Tiffin)
Goodbye Elvis (Jim Whittington)

Side 2
The Day the Beat Stopped (Ral Donner)
Just a Country Boy (Frankie Allen)
Elvis, the Man from Tupelo (George Pickard)
For Every Star That Rises (Michael Morgan)
The Passing of a King (Tony Copeland)
An authorized and lawful compilation, this LP
was both the first Elvis picture disc, and the
world's first *commercially issued* picture disc
album – by anyone. Has 11 Elvis tribute
songs, but no music by Presley himself. Card
stock jacket, with printing on cover – not on
slicks.

TO KNOW HIM IS TO LOVE HIM

❑ Black Belt LP-1: Bootleg. Listed for
  identification only.

TODAY: see *ELVIS TODAY*

TOP TEN HITS (2 LPs)

❑ RCA/BMG (SP)
  6383-1-R 7/87   4-6
  DISCS 1: Black label, dog near top.
  (Disc 1) 6383-1-R-A-1/6383-1-R-B-1. **(Disc 2)** 6383-1-R-
  C-1/6383-1-R-D-1. Identification numbers are engraved.
  Shows sides as "A," "B," "C" and "D."
  (Disc 1) 6383-1-R-A-2/6383-1-R-B-5. **(Disc 2)** 6383-1-R-
  C-1/6383-1-R-D-5. Identification numbers are engraved.
  Shows sides as "1," "2," "3" and "4."
  (Disc 1) 6383-1-R-A-5/6383-1-R-B-5. **(Disc 2)** 6383-1-R-
  C-5/6383-1-R-D-5. Identification numbers are engraved.
  Shows sides as "1," "2," "3" and "4."

❑ RCA/BMG 6383-1-R..........7/87   4-6
  COVER 1: Single pocket. Front: No logo or
  number. Color Elvis (1956) photo. Back: RCA
  logo and UPC bar code at lower right. Number
  is on spine (and part of bar code) but does not
  appear on front or back.

❑ RCA/BMG........................7/87   2-4
  INNER SLEEVES 1: Mustard with black print,
  with "A 1987 Commemorative Release" on
  each side.

❑ RCA/BMG........................7/87   8-10
  INSERT 1A: Color 15" x 22" Elvis signature
  poster. Has "Sincerely Yours, Elvis" at lower
  left and RCA logo and number "POS-2" at
  lower right.

❑ RCA/BMG........................7/87   2-4
  INSERT 1B: Black-and-white 8" x 10" flyer; ad
  for *Elvis Talks* on one side and four "1987
  Commemorative Collection" LPs pictured on
  reverse.

❑ RCA 6383-1-R...................7/87   3-5
  SHRINK STICKER 1: Circular, gold foil
  "Digitally Remastered" sticker, which has
  selection number.

RCA/BMG (SP)
**6383-1-R.......................7/87   25-35
TOTAL PACKAGE 1: Discs, cover, inner
    sleeves, inserts, sticker.**

❑ RCA/BMG (SP)
  6383-1-R 7/87   4-6
  DISCS 2: Same as discs 1.

❏ RCA 6383-1-R.................7/87   8-10
   COVER 2: Designate promo. Same as cover 1, but with "Not for Sale" stamped on back.

❏ RCA/BMG.........................7/87   2-4
   INNER SLEEVES 2: Mustard with black print, with "A 1987 Commemorative Release" on each side.

❏ RCA/BMG.........................7/87   8-10
   INSERT 2A: Color 15" x 22" Elvis signature poster. Has "Sincerely Yours, Elvis" at lower left and RCA logo and number "POS-2" at lower right.

❏ RCA/BMG.........................7/87   2-4
   INSERT 2B: Black-and-white 8" x 10" flyer; ad for *Elvis Talks* on one side and four "1987 Commemorative Collection" LPs pictured on reverse.

❏ RCA 6383-1-R.................7/87   3-5
   SHRINK STICKER 2: Circular, gold foil "Digitally Remastered" sticker, which has selection number.

RCA/BMG (SP)

6383-1-R.....................7/87   30-40
   TOTAL PACKAGE 2: Discs, cover, inner sleeves, inserts, sticker.

Card stock jacket, with printing on cover – not on slicks.

Disc 1

Side A
Heartbreak Hotel
I Want You, I Need You, I Love You
Hound Dog
Don't Be Cruel
Love Me Tender
Love Me
Too Much
All Shook Up
(Let Me Be Your) Teddy Bear
Jailhouse Rock

Side B
Don't
I Beg of You
Wear My Ring Around Your Neck
Hard Headed Woman
One Night
I Got Stung
(Now and Then There's) A Fool Such As I
I Need Your Love Tonight
Big Hunk O' Love

Disc 2

Side C
Stuck on You
It's Now Or Never
Are You Lonesome Tonight
Surrender
I Feel So Bad
Little Sister
(Marie's the Name) His Latest Flame
Can't Help Falling in Love
Good Luck Charm
She's Not You

Side D
Return to Sender
(You're the) Devil in Disguise
Bossa Nova Baby
Crying in the Chapel

In the Ghetto
Suspicious Minds
Don't Cry Daddy
The Wonder of You
Burning Love

TRANSCRIBED RADIO INTERVIEW WITH JERRY LEIBER AND MIKE STOLLER FOR "JAILHOUSE ROCK"

❏ MGM Air-View (M)
   MGM-12-232 ....10/57   500-1000
   DISC 1: Red plastic transcription. Has an interview with *Jailhouse Rock* songwriters Jerry Leiber and Mike Stoller, plus commentary by Dick Simmons. Elvis is talked about but is not heard on this disc. Side 2 has the same interview, but without the announcer – for stations preferring an open-end broadcast.
   COVER 1: None made.
   INNER SLEEVE 1: Brown, no printing.

❏ MGM Air-View 10/57   25-50
   INSERT 1: Interview trancript and introductory note. Not included with this disc, but offered from NSS via the introductory note, is a black-and-white photo still of Elvis with Leiber and Stoller (still No. 1719X43).

MGM Air-View (M)
   MGM-12-232.............10/57   500-1000
   TOTAL PACKAGE 1: Disc, insert.

TRIBUTE TO ELVIS

❏ Country Sessions USA (S)
   126 ....'83   50-100
   DISC 1: Complete radio show. Promotional issue only.
   COVER 1: Verification pending.
   INNER SLEEVE 1: White, no printing.

❏ Country Sessions USA
   126 ....'83
   INSERT 1: Verification pending. Assumption: Cue sheet and program notes.

Country Sessions USA (S)
   126.................................'83   50-100
   TOTAL PACKAGE 1: Disc, insert.

TRIBUTE TO DORSEY, VOLUME 1

❏ RCA Victor (M)
   LPM-1432......................4/57   10-15
   DISC 1: Black label, dog on top.
   G2JP-9434-1S/G2JP-9435-1S. Label LP#3.

❏ RCA Victor LPM-1432 .... 4/57 35-40
 COVER 1: Front: RCA logo and number at
 upper right. Duotone photo of a trombone.
 Back: Five black-and-white photos of Tommy
 Dorsey, alone and with others. One pictures
 Tommy and Jimmy Dorsey with Elvis. This
 photo is reproduced on the Side 3 inner
 sleeve in *Elvis – A Golden Celebration.* This
 was the first time Elvis was pictured on an LP
 by another artist.
 INNER SLEEVE 1: Generic RCA sleeve.
 Makes no mention of Elvis or this LP.
RCA Victor (M)
 LPM-1432 .... 4/57 **45-55**
 TOTAL PACKAGE 1: Disc, cover.

TROUBLE BOUND

❏ TAKRL 24912: Bootleg. Listed for
 identification only.

TUPELO MISS. FLASH LIVE

❏ Bootleg. Listed for identification only.

20 YEARS OF NO. 1 HITS
(1956 - 1975) (7 LPs)
   Various artists collection
 Mail order offer only. All discs in this set have
 a black, white and red label, and are listed
 individually below. Except where noted
 otherwise, all identification numbers are
 stamped.
❏ Reader's Digest/RCA Music Service
 RBA-243-1 .... '86 3-4
 DISC 1:
 T1RS-5961-1/T1RS-5962-1.
❏ Reader's Digest/RCA Music Service
 RBA-243-2 .... '86 3-4
 DISC 2:
 T1RS-5963-1/T1RS-5964-1.
❏ Reader's Digest/RCA Music Service
 RBA-243-3 .... '86 3-4
 DISC 3:
 T1RS-5965-3/T1RS-5966-1.
❏ Reader's Digest/RCA Music Service
 RBA-243-4 .... '86 3-4
 DISC 4:
 T1RS-5967-1/T1RS-5968-1. Identification numbers are
 engraved on side B.
❏ Reader's Digest/RCA Music Service
 RBA-243-5 .... '86 3-4
 DISC 5:
 T1RS-5969-1/T1RS-5970-1. Identification numbers are
 engraved.
❏ Reader's Digest/RCA Music Service
 RBA-243-6 .... '86 3-4
 DISC 6:
 T1RS-5971-1/T1RS-5972-1.
❏ Reader's Digest/RCA Music Service
 RBA-243-7 .... '86 3-4
 DISC 7:
 T1RS-5973-1/T1RS-5974-1.

❏ Reader's Digest/RCA Music Service
 RBA-215A .... '86 15-20
 BOX 1: Slipcover: Brown. Front: Reader's
 Digest/RCA Music Service at lower right. Back
 is blank. Record case: White with black print.
 Back is blank.
 INNER SLEEVES 1: Generic, individually
 numbered, plastic sleeves. Front and Back:
 Clear, covered with Reader's Digest Pegasus
 logos. No mention of Elvis.
❏ Reader's Digest/RCA Music
 Service .... '86 5-7
 INSERT 1: Duotone, 11¼" x 11½", 12-page
 information booklet.
Reader's Digest/RCA Music Service
(SP) RBA-243A .... '86 **40-55**
 TOTAL PACKAGE 1: Discs, box, insert.

 Contains eight Elvis tracks:
 Hound Dog
 Don't Be Cruel
 Stuck on You
 Are You Lonesome Tonight
 Surrender
 Good Luck Charm
 Suspicious Minds

25 GOLDEN YEARS IN LOWERY
COUNTRY (2 LPs)
   Various artists collection
❏ Lowery Group (SP) LG-1 ..... '80 25-30
 DISCS 1: White labels, black print.
 Promotional issue only.
 (Disc 1) LM-1A/LM-1B. **(Disc 2)** LM-1C/LM-1D.
❏ Lowery Group LG-1 .... '80 25-30
 COVER 1: Double pocket. White with black
 print. Text only on all four panels.
 INNER SLEEVES 1: White, no printing.
Lowery Group (SP) LG-1 . '80 **50-60**
 TOTAL PACKAGE 1: Disc, cover.

 All tracks are stereo except *Ahab the Arab,*
 Be-Bop-A-Lula, Go Away with Me, No One
 But You, and *That's All You Gotta Do.*
Disc 1
Side 1
 Young Love (Sonny James)
 Spanish Fireball (Hank Snow)
 No One But You (Red Foley & Kitty Wells)
 Be-Bop-A-Lula (Gene Vincent)
 Go Away with Me (Wilburn Brothers)
 I Have But One Goal (Bill Lowery and the Smith
  Brothers)
Side 2
 Walk On By (Leroy Van Dyke)
 Ahab the Arab (Ray Stevens)
 That's All You Gotta Do (Brenda Lee)
 If the Good Lord's Willing (Johnny Cash)
 Misery Loves Company (Porter Wagoner)

Disc 2

Side 1
Games People Play (Freddy Weller)
Down in the Boondocks (Billy Joe Royal)
(How Can I) Unlove You (Lynn Anderson)
Children (Johnny Cash)
Walk a Mile in My Shoes (Elvis Presley)
These Are Not My People (Freddy Weller)

Side 2
Rose Garden (Lynn Anderson)
Traces (Sonny James)
I Take It Back (Sandy Posey)
All My Hard Times (Roy Drusky)
Fool Me (Lynn Anderson)
9,999,999 Tears (Dickie Lee)

U.S.A.F. PRESENTS ROGER CARROLL

Various artists collections.

❑ U.S.A.F. (S) 10-15
DISC 1: Price range is for any individual disc
containing at least one Elvis track.

❑ U.S.A.F. (S) 20-30
COMPLETE SET 1: Boxed set of two LPs.
Each is a complete public service radio show
with two pages of cue sheets and program
notes. Boxes are white and have a drawing of
Roger Carroll. Issued only to radio stations.
Price range is for any complete set containing
at least one Elvis track.

U.S.A.F. PRESENTS WOLFMAN JACK

Various artists collections.

❑ U.S.A.F. (S) 10-15
DISC 1: Price range is for any individual disc
containing at least one Elvis track.

❑ U.S.A.F. (S) 20-30
COMPLETE SET 1: Set of two LPs. Each is a
complete public service radio show with two
pages of cue sheets and program notes.
Issued only to radio stations. Price range is
for any complete set containing at least one
Elvis track.

UNFINISHED BUSINESS

❑ Reel to Reel 380: Bootleg. Listed for
identification only.

UNFORGETTABLE FIFTIES (4 LPs)

Various artists collection
Mail order offer only.
❑ Heartland/RCA Special Products (M)
1072 .... '88   2-4
DISC 1: Black label, dog near top.
DVL3-0867-A1/DVL3-0867-B1.
❑ Heartland/RCA Special Products (M)
1072 .... '88   2-4
DISC 2: Black label, dog near top.
DVL3-0867-C1/DVL3-0867-D1.
❑ Heartland/RCA Special Products (M)
1072 .... '88   2-4
DISC 3: Black label, dog near top.
DVL3-0867-E1/DVL3-0867-F1.

❑ Heartland (M) 1072 .... '88   2-4
DISC 4: Orange label. (No mention of RCA.)
MSM-35148A/MSM-35148B.
❑ Heartland/RCA Special Products
1072 .... '88   5-10
COVER 1: Single pocket. Heartland logo at
lower left. Pictures assorted '50s items. Back:
Text only.
INNER SLEEVES 1: White, no printing.
Heartland/RCA Special Products
(M) 1072 .... '88   15-25
TOTAL PACKAGE 1: Discs, cover.

Disc 1
Sh-Boom (Crew-Cuts)
Music, Music Music (Teresa Brewer)
Catch a Falling Star (Perry Como)
I'm Walking Behind You (Eddie Fisher)
Whatever Will Be Will Be (Que Sera Sera) (shown as "Que Sera Sera") (Doris Day)
April Love (Pat Boone)
Oh Lonesome Me (Don Gibson)
Hearts of Stone (Fontane Sisters)
The Naughty Lady of Shady Lane (Ames Brothers)
Volare (Domenico Modugno)
This Ole House (Rosemary Clooney)
Slowpoke (Pee Wee King)
Patricia (Perez Prado and His Orchestra)

Disc 2
Sincerely (McGuire Sisters)
Love Me Tender (Elvis Presley)
Be My Love (Mario Lanza)
Little Things Mean a Lot (Kitty Kallen)
Mona Lisa (Nat King Cole)
You Belong to Me (Jo Stafford)
Love Is a Many Splendored Thing (Four Aces)
Cherry Pink and Apple Blossom White (Perez Prado)
He'll Have to Go (Jim Reeves)
Tennessee Waltz (Patti Page)
Round and Round (Perry Como)
Tammy (Debbie Reynolds)

Disc 3
That's Amore (Dean Martin)
Chattanoogie Shoe Shine Boy (Red Foley)
My Prayer (Platters)
Don't Be Cruel (Elvis Presley)
The Rock and Roll Waltz (Kay Starr)
Blue Tango (Leroy Anderson)
You, You, You (Ames Brothers)
Cattle Call (Eddy Arnold)
Oh My Pa-Pa (Eddie Fisher)
The Wayward Wind (Gogi Grant)
Sixteen Tons (Tennessee Ernie Ford)
Autumn Leaves (Roger Williams)
Chances Are (Johnny Mathis)

Disc 4
The Three Bells (Browns)
Because of You (Tony Bennett)
Mack the Knife (Bobby Darin)
The Thing (Phil Harris)
Mister Sandman (Chordettes)
Moonglow and Theme from Picnic (Morris Stoloff)
Hot Diggity (Perry Como)
Heartaches by the Number (Guy Mitchell)
Purple People Eater (Sheb Wooley)
Sugartime (McGuire Sisters)
Rag Mop (Ames Brothers)
Goodnight Irene (Gordon Jenkins and the Weavers)

UNRELEASED TRACKS

☐ Tonto TS-200: Bootleg. Listed for identification only.

VALENTINE GIFT FOR YOU

☐ RCA (SP) AFL1-5353........2/85   12-15
DISC 1: Red vinyl. Gold, black and white "Elvis 50th Anniversary" label.
AFL1-5353A-1/AFL1-5353B-3. Identification numbers are engraved.

☐ RCA AFL1-5353................2/85   4-5
COVER 1: Front: No logo or number. Color Elvis (1956) photo. Back: RCA logo and number at upper left. UPC bar code at lower right.
INNER SLEEVE 1: White, no printing.

☐ RCA AFL1-5353................2/85   4-5
SHRINK STICKER 1: Red and white, reads: "The Gift of Love! This LP is Pressed on Special Red Vinyl."

RCA (SP) AFL1-5353......2/85   20-25
TOTAL PACKAGE 1: Disc, cover, sticker.

☐ RCA (SP) AFL1-5353........2/85   12-15
DISC 2: Same as disc 1.

☐ RCA AFL1-5353................2/85   8-10
COVER 2: Designate promo. Same as cover 1, but with "Not for Sale" stamped on back.
INNER SLEEVE 2: White, no printing.

☐ RCA AFL1-5353................2/85   4-5
SHRINK STICKER 2: Red and white, reads: "The Gift of Love! This LP is Pressed on Special Red Vinyl."

RCA (SP) AFL1-5353......2/85   25-30
TOTAL PACKAGE 2: Disc, cover, sticker.

☐ RCA (SP) AFL1-5353........8/85   10-12
DISC 3: Black vinyl. Gold, black and white "Elvis 50th Anniversary" label.

☐ RCA AFL1-5353................2/85   4-5
COVER 3: Same as cover 1.
INNER SLEEVE 3: White, no printing.

RCA (SP) AFL1-5353......8/85   15-20
TOTAL PACKAGE 3: Disc, cover.

Card stock jacket, with printing on cover – not on slicks.

Side A
Are You Lonesome Tonight
I Need Somebody to Lean On
Young and Beautiful
Playing for Keeps
Tell Me Why
Give Me the Right
It Feels So Right

Side B
I Was the One
Fever
Tomorrow Is a Long Time
Love Letters
Fame and Fortune
Can't Help Falling in Love

VEGAS FEVER

☐ Graceland PL-3137-8: Bootleg. Listed for identification only.

VEGAS YEARS 1972-1975

☐ TAKRL 24913: Bootleg. Listed for identification only.

VINTAGE 1955 ELVIS

☐ Oak (M) 1003......................'90   30-40
DISC 1: Beige label with black print. Title on label and back of cover is "Vintage 55 Elvis."
NR-18245-A/NR-18245-B. Identification numbers are engraved.

☐ Oak 1003............................'90   30-40
COVER 1: Front: No logo or number. Black-and-white Elvis (circa 1956) photo. Back: Text only. Oak logo and number at lower right.

Oak (M) 1003 ....'90   60-80
TOTAL PACKAGE 1: Disc, cover.

Card stock jacket, with printing on cover – not on slicks.

Side 1
Interview (Biff Collie)
Baby Let's Play House
I Got a Woman (shown as "I've Got a Woman")
Good Rockin' Tonight (shown as "There's Good Rockin' Tonight")
That's All Right (shown as "That's All Right Little Mama")

Side 2
Scotty Moore Tells the Beginning of Elvis

VIVA LAS VEGAS

☐ Lucky LR-711: Bootleg. Listed for identification only.

WRCA PLAYS THE HITS FOR YOUR CUSTOMERS

Various artists collection

☐ RCA (ST) DJL1-1785 ....4/76   300-350
DISC 1: White label, black print. Simulated radio show from make believe station WRCA, complete with dee jay host and WRCA jingles. Made for in-store play to promote new RCA albums, one of which was *The Sun Sessions*. Promotional issue only.
DJL1-1785A-1/DJL1-1785B-1.
COVER 1: White, no printing.
INNER SLEEVE 1: White, no printing.

RCA (ST) DJL1-1785 ......4/76   300-350
TOTAL PACKAGE 1: Disc.

Side 1
Sarah Smile (Hall & Oates)
Roll Me Through the Rushes (Rosie)
Get Up & Boogie (Silver Convention)
Don't Stop Now (The Brothers)
Turn the Beat Around (Vicki Sue Robinson)
That's All Right (Elvis Presley)
Suspicious Minds (Waylon Jennings & Jessi Colter)
That'll Be the Day (Pure Prairie League)

Side 2
Say You Love Me (D.J. Rogers)
It's Cool (The Tymes)
Hey, What's That Dance You're Doin' (Choice Four)
Disaster Movie Suite (Henry Mancini & Orchestra)
Caravan (Chet Atkins & Les Paul)
From the People to the People (Roger Whittaker)
In Trance (The Scorpions)
Heaven and Hell (Vangelis)
Label indicates stereo, but entire LP is monaural. Some tracks are edited.

WE'RE PLAYING YOUR SONG (2 LPs)

Various artists collection

❏ Pickwick (S) RPS-1 .... '80   10-20
DISC 1: A sampler of assorted Pickwick LPs, including tracks from *Almost in Love* and *Elvis' Christmas Album*. Promotional issue only.

❏ Pickwick RPS-1 .... '80   10-20
COVER 1: Double pocket. Inside panels picture other Pickwick LPs, including *Almost in Love* by Elvis.

Pickwick (S) RPS-1 .... '80   20-40
TOTAL PACKAGE 1: Disc, cover.

Elvis Contents:

Side 2
Burning Love (Track 1)
U.S. Male (Track 2)

Side 3
Blue Christmas (Track 7)

WELCOME HOME ELVIS

❏ Memphis Flag 8500: Bootleg. Listed for identification only.

WELCOME TO MY WORLD

❏ RCA Victor (SP)
APL1-2274 .... 4/77   6-8
DISC 1: Black label, dog near top.
APL1-2274-A-1S/APL1-2274-B-1S. Identification numbers are engraved.
APL1-2274-A-2S/APL1-2274-B-1S. Identification numbers are engraved.

❏ RCA APL1-2274 .... 4/77   6-8
COVER 1: Front: Number at upper right. Color reproduction of an Elvis ('70s concert) portrait. Back: RCA logo and number at lower right. Reduced version of portrait on front.

❏ RCA Victor 21-112-1
PT 54E 4/77   2-4
INNER SLEEVE 1: Black-and-white. Pictures RCA's Elvis LP catalog front and back, most recent being *The Sun Sessions* (side 2, row 5, column 1).

RCA Victor (SP)
APL1-2274 .... 4/77   15-20
TOTAL PACKAGE 1: Disc, cover, inner sleeve.

❏ RCA Victor (SP)
APL1-2274 .... 4/77   6-8
DISC 2: Same as disc 1.

❏ RCA APL1-2274 .... 4/77   10-12
COVER 2: Designate promo. Same as cover 1, but with "Not for Sale" stamped on back.

❏ RCA Victor 21-112-1
PT 54E 4/77   2-4
INNER SLEEVE 2: Black-and-white. Pictures RCA's Elvis LP catalog front and back, most recent being *The Sun Sessions* (side 2, row 5, column 1).

RCA Victor (SP)
APL1-2274 .... 4/77   20-25
TOTAL PACKAGE 2: Disc, cover, inner sleeve.

❏ RCA Victor (SP)
AFL1-2274 .... '77   3-5
DISC 3: Black label, dog near top.

❏ RCA AFL1-2274 .... '77   3-5
COVER 3: Reflects prefix change.

❏ RCA Victor .... '70s   2-4
INNER SLEEVE 3: Black-and-white. Pictures RCA Elvis catalog front and back. Any of several sleeves may be found on reissues from this period.

RCA Victor (SP)
AFL1-2274 .... '77   8-15
TOTAL PACKAGE 3: Disc, cover, inner sleeve.

❏ RCA Victor (SP)
AQL1-2274 .... '77   2-4
DISC 4: Black label, dog near top.

❏ RCA AQL1-2274 .... '77   2-4
COVER 4: Reflects prefix change.

❏ RCA Victor .... '70s   2-4
INNER SLEEVE 4: Black-and-white. Pictures RCA Elvis catalog front and back. Any of several sleeves may be found on reissues from this period.

RCA Victor (SP)
AQL1-2274 .... '77   6-12
TOTAL PACKAGE 4: Disc, cover, inner sleeve.

Side A
Welcome to My World (Live)
Help Me Make It Through the Night
Release Me (And Let Me Love Again) (Live)
I Really Don't Want to Know
For the Good Times (Live)

Side B
Make the World Go Away (Live)
Gentle on My Mind
I'm So Lonesome I Could Cry (Live)
Your Cheatin' Heart
I Can't Stop Loving You (Live – Unreleased)
This was the first Elvis LP issued with the '70s black label, with the dog near the top.

WHITE CHRISTMAS (UNFORGETTABLE CHRISTMAS SONGS), VOL. 1

Various artists collection

☐ Scana (SP) 27022 .... 11/86   5-7
DISC 1: White label, red print. German-made LP that was widely distributed in the United States.
27022-A/27022-B. Identification numbers are engraved.

☐ Scana 27022 .... 11/86   5-7
COVER 1: Front: Red cover with color photos of Elvis Presley, Dean Martin, Nat King Cole, and Mahalia Jackson; black-and-whites of Bing Crosby and Frank Sinatra. Back: Text only.
INNER SLEEVE 1: White, no printing except "N23/1/1" at lower right on side 1.

Scana (SP) 27022 .... 11/86   10-15
TOTAL PACKAGE 1: Disc, cover.

Card stock jacket, with printing on cover – not on slicks.

Side 1
White Christmas (Bing Crosby)
Jingle Bells (Frank Sinatra)
Winter Wonderland (Dean Martin)
Happiest Christmas Tree (Nat King Cole)
Silent Night (Mahalia Jackson)

Side 2
You're All I Want for Christmas (Bing Crosby)
The Christmas Waltz (Frank Sinatra)
Frosty the Snowman (Nat King Cole)
O Little Town of Bethlehem (Mahalia Jackson)
Santa Bring My Baby Back to Me (Elvis Presley)

WHITE CHRISTMAS (UNFORGETTABLE CHRISTMAS SONGS), VOL. 2

Various artists collection

☐ Scana (SP) 27023 .... 11/86   5-7
DISC 1: White label, red print. German-made LP that was widely distributed in the United States.
27023-A/27023-B. Identification numbers are engraved.

☐ Scana 27022 .... 11/86   5-7
COVER 1: Front: Green cover with color photos of Elvis Presley, Dean Martin, Nat King Cole, and Mahalia Jackson; black-and-whites of Bing Crosby and Frank Sinatra. Back: Text only.
INNER SLEEVE 1: White, no printing except "N15/5/7" at lower right on side 1.

Scana (SP) 27023 .... 11/86   10-15
TOTAL PACKAGE 1: Disc, cover.

Card stock jacket, with printing on cover – not on slicks.

Side 1
I'll Be Home for Christmas (Frank Sinatra)
Here Comes Santa Claus (Bing Crosby and the
    Andrews Sisters)
Mrs. Santa Claus (Nat King Cole)
Rudolph the Red Nosed Reindeer (Dean Martin)

Santa Claus Is Back in Town (Elvis Presley)
Side 2
Have Yourself a Merry Little Christmas (Frank Sinatra)
Buon Natale (Nat King Cole)
The Christmas Blues (Dean Martin)
Joy to the World (Mahalia Jackson)
White Christmas (Bing Crosby)

WORLD IN SOUND – 1977

☐ Associated Press (M)
AP-1977 .... 1/78   40-50
DISC 1: Red with black print. Associated Press' news service recap of 1977's top news stories. Has an excerpt of *Hound Dog*, from *Elvis in Concert*. Issued only to radio stations.
AP-1977-1/AP-1977-2. Identification numbers are engraved.

☐ Associated Press
AP-1977 .... 1/78   40-50
COVER 1: Associated Press logo at upper right. Black-and-white photos, front and back, of some of the people and events making news in 1977, including one of Elvis (from Madison Square Garden press conference).
INNER SLEEVE 1: White, no printing.

Associated Press (M)
AP-1977 .... 1/78   80-100
TOTAL PACKAGE 1: Disc, cover.

WORLD OF ELVIS PRESLEY

Each disc is a complete one-hour weekly radio show, part of a series that ran from April 25, through November 20, 1983 – a total of 30 programs. Each is listed and priced individually below. White label with black print. All identification numbers are engraved.

☐ World of Elvis Presley
    (SP) .... '83   35-60
DISC 1:
CS-112-A/CS-112-B.

☐ World of Elvis Presley
    (SP) .... '83   35-60
DISC 2:
EP-2-A/EP-2-B.

☐ World of Elvis Presley
    (SP) .... '83   75-100
DISC 3:
EP-3-A/EP-3-B.

☐ World of Elvis Presley
    (SP) .... '83   35-60
DISC 4:
EP-4-A/EP-4-B.

☐ World of Elvis Presley
    (SP) .... '83   35-60
DISC 5:
EP-5-A/EP-5-B.

☐ World of Elvis Presley
    (SP) .... '83   35-60
DISC 6:
EP-6-A/EP-6-B.

☐ World of Elvis Presley
    (SP) .... '83   35-60
DISC 7:
EP-7-A/EP-7-B.

❑ World of Elvis Presley
   (SP) .... '83   35-60
   DISC 8:
   EP-8-A/EP-8-B.

❑ World of Elvis Presley
   (SP) .... '83   35-60
   DISC 9:
   EP-9-A/EP-9-B.

❑ World of Elvis Presley
   (SP) .... '83   35-60
   DISC 10:
   EP-10-A/EP-10-B.

❑ World of Elvis Presley
   (SP) .... '83   35-60
   DISC 12:
   EP-11-A/EP-11-B.

❑ World of Elvis Presley
   (SP) .... '83   35-60
   DISC 12:
   EP-12-A/EP-12-B.

❑ World of Elvis Presley
   (SP) .... '83   35-60
   DISC 13:
   EP-13-A/EP-13-B.

❑ World of Elvis Presley
   (SP) .... '83   35-60
   DISC 14:
   EP-14-A/EP-14-B.

❑ World of Elvis Presley
   (SP) .... '83   35-60
   DISC 15:
   EP-15-A/EP-15-B.

❑ World of Elvis Presley
   (SP) .... '83   35-60
   DISC 16:
   EP-16-A/EP-16-B.

❑ World of Elvis Presley
   (SP) .... '83   35-60
   DISC 17:
   EP-17-A/EP-17-B.

❑ World of Elvis Presley
   (SP) .... '83   35-60
   DISC 18:
   EP-18-A/EP-18-B.

❑ World of Elvis Presley
   (SP) .... '83   35-60
   DISC 19:
   EP-19-A/EP-19-B.

❑ World of Elvis Presley
   (SP) .... '83   35-60
   DISC 20:
   EP-20-A/EP-20-B.

❑ World of Elvis Presley
   (SP) .... '83   35-60
   DISC 21:
   EP-21-A/EP-21-B.

❑ World of Elvis Presley
   (SP) .... '83   35-60
   DISC 22:
   EP-22-A/EP-22-B.

❑ World of Elvis Presley
   (SP) .... '83   35-60
   DISC 23:
   EP-23-A/EP-23-B.

❑ World of Elvis Presley
   (SP) .... '83   35-60
   DISC 24:
   EP-24-A/EP-24-B.

❑ World of Elvis Presley
   (SP) .... '83   35-60
   DISC 25:
   EP-25-A/EP-25-B.

❑ World of Elvis Presley
   (SP) .... '83   35-60
   DISC 26:
   EP-26-A/EP-26-B.

❑ World of Elvis Presley
   (SP) .... '83   35-60
   DISC 27:
   EP-27-A/EP-27-B.

❑ World of Elvis Presley
   (SP) .... '83   35-60
   DISC 28:
   EP-28-A/EP-28-B.

❑ World of Elvis Presley
   (SP) .... '83   35-60
   DISC 29:
   EP-29-A/EP-29-B.

❑ World of Elvis Presley
   (SP) .... '83   35-60
   DISC 30:
   EP-30-A/EP-30-B.
   COVER: None made.
   INNER SLEEVES: White, no printing.

❑ World of Elvis Presley .... '83   3-5
   INSERTS: Each disc is accompanied by a
   one page cue/script. Price is for any. Fewer
   copies of Program No. 3 were made. All
   others are of equal value.

Program 1

Side 1
That's All Right
Good Rockin' Tonight
All Shook Up
Blue Moon of Kentucky
Shake, Rattle and Roll
Jailhouse Rock
Blue Suede Shoes
Heartbreak Hotel

Side 2
Hound Dog
Don't Be Cruel
Stuck on You
Are You Lonesome Tonight
Surrender
Amazing Grace
In the Ghetto
Memories
My Way

Program 2

Side 1
Viva Las Vegas
A Mess of Blues
Little Sister
(Marie's the Name) His Latest Flame
I'm Left, You're Right, She's Gone
It's Now Or Never
Double Trouble
If I Can Dream
Just Because

Side 2
A Mess of Blues
Love Me Tender
Suspicion
Elvis Interview
She's Not You
Fame and Fortune
Suspicious Minds
You Don't Have to Say You Love Me

Program 3
Verification pending
Program 4
Side 1
Memphis, Tennessee
King of the Whole Wide World
Home Is Where the Heart Is
Hound Dog
It's Now Or Never
I Want You, I Need You, I Love You
Anyway You Want Me (That's How I Will Be)
I Was the One

Side 2
Playing for Keeps
(Let Me Be Your) Teddy Bear
Since I Met You Baby
Memphis Music Medley
That's All Right
I Love You Because
I Don't Care If the Sun Don't Shine
Blue Moon

Program 5
Side 1
Heartbreak Hotel
Hard Headed Woman
I Got Stung
I Gotta Know
Good Luck Charm
Blue Moon of Kentucky
Blue Moon of Kentucky (Alternate Take)
Too Much

Side 2
Loving You
Don't
Jailhouse Rock
I Beg of You
Let It Be Me
Anything That's Part of You
Don't Cry Daddy
(Now and Then There's) A Fool Such As I
Easy Come, Easy Go

Program 6
Side 1
Blue Suede Shoes
Blue Suede Shoes (Carl Perkins)
A Big Hunk O' Love
Wear My Ring Around Your Neck
All Shook Up
I Feel So Bad
Ain't That Loving You Baby
Suspicious Minds

Side 2
Baby, Let's Play House
Milkcow Blues Boogie
I Forgot to Remember to Forget
Can't Help Falling in Love
(You're the) Devil in Disguise
Viva Las Vegas
An American Trilogy

Program 7
Side 1
I Want You, I Need You, I Love You
I Love You Because
Love Me Tender
Help Me Make It Through the Night
Always on My Mind
Loving You
I'll Take Love
Love Me
If You Love Me (Let Me Know)

Side 2
Ain't That Loving You Baby
Love Letters
The Wonder of You
The Next Step Is Love
You Don't Have to Say You Love Me
I'm Yours
Can't Help Falling in Love

Program 8
Side 1
Hound Dog
You've Lost That Lovin' Feeling (Righteous Brothers)
Kissin' Cousins
Crying in the Chapel
Treat Me Nice
Let Yourself Go
Stuck on You
You've Lost That Lovin' Feeling

Side 2
(Let Me Be Your) Teddy Bear
Are You Lonesome Tonight
Rags to Riches
Fame and Fortune
It's Impossible
Polk Salad Annie

Program 9
Side 1
Shake, Rattle and Roll
Return to Sender
She's Not You
I Hear a Symphony
Your Cheating Heart
Don't Be Cruel
In the Ghetto

Side 2
Lawdy, Miss Clawdy
Baby, What You Want Me to Do
Kentucky Rain
Too Much
Little Sister
Surrender
If I Can Dream
My Way

Program 10
Side 1
Welcome to My World
Heartbreak Hotel
I Gotta Know
Wear My Ring Around Your Neck
Burning Love
Anyway You Want Me (That's How I Will Be)
I'm So Lonesome I Could Cry

Side 2
Good Rockin' Tonight
Hurt
Fever
Such a Night
Anything That's Part of You
It's Now Or Never

Don't
Also Sprach Zarathustra/See See Rider

Program 11

Side 1

Suspicious Minds
California Dreamin' (Mamas and the Papas)
Early Morning Rain
What'd I Say
Hard Headed Woman
I Can't Stop Loving You
I Got Stung
It Hurts Me
All Shook Up

Side 2

Just Because
Johnny B. Goode
And I Love You So
What a Wonderful Life
I Want You, I Need You, I Love You
A Mess Of Blues
Loving You
Let Me Be There

Program 12

Side 1

That's All Right
Make Love to Me (Jo Stafford)
Lawdy, Miss Clawdy
(Let Me Be Your) Teddy Bear
Medley: Little Sister/Get Back
I Really Don't Want to Know
Frankie and Johnny
A Big Hunk O' Love

Side 2

Follow That Dream
Treat Me Nice
Steamroller Blues
Blue Suede Shoes
Milkcow Blues Boogie
Tryin' to Get to You
Surrender
You Don't Have to Say You Love Me

Program 13

Side 1

I'm Movin' On
I Was the One
How Do You Keep the Music Playing (Patti Austin &
James Ingram)
(Now and Then There's) A Fool Such As I
It's Now Or Never
Tryin' to Get to You

Side 2

Suspicion
Shake, Rattle and Roll
Little Darlin'
Help Me Make It Through the Night
Memories
An American Trilogy

Program 14

Side 1

Heartbreak Hotel
Only the Strong Survive
Gentle on My Mind
Don't Be Cruel
Kentucky Rain
Any Day Now
T-r-o-u-b-l-e
One Broken Heart for Sale

Side 2

The Next Step Is Love
Easy Come, Easy Go

Rags to Riches
I Forgot to Remember to Forget
Good Rockin' Tonight
The Wonder of You
Can't Help Falling in Love

Program 15

Side 1

Too Much
I Love You Because
Blue Suede Shoes
I Feel So Bad
That's All Right
Blue Moon of Kentucky
Power of My Love
Old Shep

Side 2

It Keeps Right on A-Hurtin'
Love Me
I'll Never Fall in Love Again
Where Do You Come From
Funny How Time Slips Away
It's Still Here
Fairytale

Program 16

Side 1

I Got Stung
(Now and Then There's) A Fool Such As I
Wearin' That Love On Look
Lawdy, Miss Clawdy
Tiger Man
Let Me Be There
That's When Your Heartaches Begin
Blue Suede Shoes

Side 2

Mystery Train
Baby, What You Want Me to Do
Harbor Lights
Suspicious Minds
I'm So Lonesome I Could Cry
Follow That Dream
Unchained Melody

Program 17

Side 1

Stuck on You
I'm Left, You're Right, She's Gone
A Hundred Pounds of Clay (Gene McDaniels)
Steamroller Blues
Shoppin' Around
(You're the) Devil in Disguise
Ain't That Lovin' You Baby
Save the Last Dance for Me (Drifters)
I Got a Woman

Side 2

Polk Salad Annie
Let's Be Friends
Rags to Riches
Burning Love
Johnny B. Goode
You've Lost That Lovin' Feeling

Program 18

Side 1

I Want You, I Need You, I Love You
I Was the One
Like to Get to Know You (Spanky and Our Gang)
Heartbreak Hotel
Only the Strong Survive
For the Good Times
The Next Step Is Love
If You Love Me (Let Me Know)
Love Me Tender

Side 2

It's Now Or Never
Hard Headed Woman
I'm Movin' On
It Hurts Me
Money Honey
In the Ghetto
Loving You

Program 19

Side 1

Bo Diddley (Bo Diddley)
A Big Hunk O' Love
Too Much Monkey Business
Don't
Hurt
Guitar Man
Return to Sender
Good Luck Charm
Always on My Mind

Side 2

You Asked Me To
Let It Be Me
Kissin' Cousins
Night Life
(Let Me Be Your) Teddy Bear
Don't Be Cruel
I'm Leavin'

Program 20

Side 1

Love Me
I'll Remember You
If You Love Me (Let Me Know)
If I Can Dream
The Wonder of You
Loving You
An Evening Prayer
Can't Help Falling in Love

Side 2

Medley: Little Sister/Get Back
Yesterday
Power of My Love
Medley: I Got a Woman/Amen
This Is Living
Unchained Melody
Blue Eyes Cryin' in the Rain

Program 21

Side 1

Let Me Be There
Mystery Train
Hawaiian Wedding Song
Hound Dog
For the Heart
From a Jack to a King
Your Cheating Heart

Side 2

Anyway You Want Me (That's How I Will Be)
Love Me Tender (James Brown)
Love Letters
Steamroller Blues
Memories
In the Ghetto
The Last Farewell

Program 22

Side 1

Good Rockin' Tonight
Jailhouse Rock
Only the Strong Survive
(Now and Then There's) A Fool Such As I
Little Darlin'
Way Down

Any Day Now
Release Me

Side 2

Pledging My Love
One Broken Heart for Sale
High Heel Sneakers
Too Much
It's Now Or Never
Solitaire

Program 23

Side 1

Kentucky Rain
Wearin' That Loved On Look
Stranger in My Own Home Town
Don't Be Cruel
In the Ghetto
I Was the One
Don't Cry Daddy
Yesterday

Side 2

(Let Me Be Your) Teddy Bear
Suspicious Minds
Clean Up Your Own Back Yard
The Wonder of You
A Little Bit of Green
The Fair Is Moving On

Program 24

Side 1

Viva Las Vegas
Little Sister
(Marie's the Name) His Latest Flame
I'm Left, You're Right, She's Gone
It's Now Or Never
Double Trouble
If I Can Dream

Side 2

A Mess of Blues
Love Me Tender
Suspicion
Interview
She's Not You
Fame and Fortune
Suspicious Minds
You Don't Have to Say You Love Me

Program 25

Side 1

Don't Be Cruel
Don't Be Cruel (Otis Blackwell)
Return to Sender
Fever
I Don't Care If the Sun Don't Shine
King Creole
When My Blue Moon Turns to Gold Again
You Gave Me a Mountain
One Broken Heart for Sale

Side 2

Treat Me Nice
I Got a Woman
Love Me
All Shook Up
Paralyzed
I Need Somebody to Lean On
Don't Ask Me Why
Lonely Man

Program 26

Side 1

Guitar Man
Bossa Nova Baby
Fame and Fortune
Anything That's Part of You

Anyway You Want Me (That's How I Will Be)
Long Tall Sally
Blue Suede Shoes
Love Me

Side 2
Burning Love
I Need Somebody to Lean On
Don't Cry Daddy
Moody Blue
Way Down
Crying in the Chapel
Let It Be Me

Program 27
Side 1
Poor People of Paris (Lex Baxter)
Heartbreak Hotel
The Wayward Wind (Gogi Grant)
I Want You, I Need You, I Love You
My Prayer (Platters)
Hound Dog
Don't Be Cruel
Love Me Tender
Singing the Blues (Guy Mitchell)
Too Much
All Shook Up

Side 2
Love Letters in the Sand (Pat Boone)
(Let Me Be Your) Teddy Bear
Wake Up Little Susie (Everly Brothers)
Jailhouse Rock
Tequila (Champs)
Don't
Theme from "A Summer Place" (Percy Faith Orchestra)
Stuck on You
Itsy Bitsy Teenie Weenie Yellow Polka Dot Bikini (Brian Hyland)
It's Now Or Never
Good Luck Charm
Suspicious Minds

Program 28
Side 1
Blue Suede Shoes
Blue Moon of Kentucky
Save the Last Dance for Me (Drifters)
A Mess Of Blues
G.I. Blues
Blue Eyes Cryin' in the Rain
Blue Moon
Moody Blue

Side 2
Blueberry Hill
Blue Hawaii
Beach Boy Blues
Mean Woman Blues
Milkcow Blues Boogie
Indescribably Blue

Program 29
Program 29 is a repeat of Program 4.
Side 1
Memphis, Tennessee
King of the Whole Wide World
Home Is Where the Heart Is
Hound Dog
It's Now Or Never
I Want You, I Need You, I Love You
Anyway You Want Me (That's How I Will Be)
I Was the One

Side 2
Playing for Keeps
(Let Me Be Your) Teddy Bear

Since I Met You Baby
Memphis Music Medley
That's All Right
I Love You Because
I Don't Care If the Sun Don't Shine
Blue Moon

Program 30
Program 30 is a repeat of Program 5.

Side 1
Heartbreak Hotel
Hard Headed Woman
I Got Stung
I Gotta Know
Good Luck Charm
Blue Moon of Kentucky
Blue Moon of Kentucky (Alternate Take)
Too Much

Side 2
Loving You
Don't
Jailhouse Rock
I Beg of You
Let It Be Me
Anything That's Part of You
Don't Cry Daddy
(Now and Then There's) A Fool Such As I
Easy Come, Easy Go

WORLDWIDE 50 GOLD AWARD HITS, VOL. 1 (4 LPs)

❑ RCA Victor (M)
  LPM-6401 ....8/70   40-45
  DISCS 1: Orange label. Rigid vinyl.
  (Disc 1) ZPRM-1508-1S/ZPRM-1509-3S. **(Disc 2)** ZPRM-1510-1S/ZPRM-1511-1S. **(Disc 3)** ZPRM-1512-1S/ZPRM-1513-1S. **(Disc 4)** ZPRM-1514-31S/ZPRM-1515-35S.

❑ RCA Victor LPM-6401 ....8/70   20-25
  BOX 1: Front: RCA logo and number at upper left, "Victor Mono" at upper right. Gold record titles 1 through 25. Back: Same as front except has gold record titles 26 through 50. On both sides, above fourth column, is: "Special Bonus New Photo Book." This was the first commercial Elvis album to not have his picture anywhere on the cover.

❑ RCA Victor 21-112-1
  pt 54 ....8/70   3-5
  INNER SLEEVE 1A: Black-and-white. Pictures RCA's Elvis LP catalog front and back, most recent being *Worldwide Gold Award Hits, Vol. 1* (side 2, row 4, column 4).

❑ RCA Victor 21-112-1
  pt 55 ....8/70   3-5
  INNER SLEEVE 1B: Black-and-white. Pictures RCA Elvis Stereo 8 tape catalog front and back, most recent being *Worldwide 50 Gold Award Hits, Vol. 1* (side 2, row 3, column 5).

❑ RCA Victor 21-112-1
  pt 56 ....8/70   3-5
  INNER SLEEVE 1C: Black-and-white. Pictures RCA Elvis cassette tape catalog front and back, most recent being *Worldwide 50 Gold Award Hits, Vol. 1* (side 2, row 3, column 4).

❑ RCA Victor 21-112-1

  pt 57 ....8/70   3-5
  INNER SLEEVE 1D: Black-and-white. Front:
  Pictures Camden Elvis catalog, most recent
  being *Elvis' Christmas Album* (Side 1, row 2,
  column 1). Back: RCA Elvis 3 ¾ ips reel
  tapes.
❑ RCA Victor...........................1/70   30-40
  INSERT 1A: 16-page photo booklet. Color
  front and back covers, black-and-white photos
  inside. Elvis photo on front is identical to the
  one on the picture sleeve for *Suspicious
  Minds / You'll Think of Me*. This is the booklet
  intended as the bonus album for this release;
  however, some sets have been found to
  contain a substitute photo booklet (1B).
❑ RCA Victor...........................1/70   30-40
  INSERT 1B: 16-page photo booklet. Elvis
  photo on front is from a Las Vegas concert,
  with him wearing a jumpsuit. Reads:
  "Souvenir Photo Album" at lower left.

RCA Victor (M)
  LPM-6401 ....8/70   100-125
  **TOTAL PACKAGE 1: Discs, box, inner
    sleeves, insert.**

❑ RCA Victor (M)
  LPM-6401..........................8/70   10-20
  DISCS 2: Orange label. Flexible vinyl.
  (Disc 1) ZPRM-1508-5S/ZPRM-1509-4S. **(Disc 2)** ZPRM-
  1510-4S/ZPRM-1511-5S. **(Disc 3)** ZPRM-1512-31S/ZPRM-
  1513-4S. **(Disc 4)** ZPRM-1514-4S/ZPRM-1515-4S. All
  identification numbers are stamped except on sides 2, 4 and
  6, which are engraved.
  (Disc 1) ZPRM-1508-7S/ZPRM-1509-7S. **(Disc 2)** ZPRM-
  1510-7S/ZPRM-1511-7S. **(Disc 3)** ZPRM-1512-7S/ZPRM-
  1513-9S. **(Disc 4)** ZPRM-1514-7S/ZPRM-1515-8S.
❑ RCA Victor LPM-6401.......8/70   20-25
  BOX 2: Front: RCA logo and number at upper
  left, "Victor Mono" at upper right. Gold record
  titles 1 through 25. Back: Same as front
  except has gold record titles 26 through 50.
  On both sides, above fourth column, is:
  "Special Bonus New Photo Book." This was
  the first commercial Elvis album to not have
  his picture anywhere on the cover.
❑ RCA Victor 21-112-1
  pt 54 ....8/70   3-5
  INNER SLEEVE 2A: Black-and-white.
  Pictures RCA's Elvis LP catalog front and
  back, most recent being *Worldwide Gold
  Award Hits, Vol. 1* (side 2, row 4, column 4).
❑ RCA Victor 21-112-1
  pt 55 ....8/70   3-5
  INNER SLEEVE 2B: Black-and-white.
  Pictures RCA Elvis Stereo 8 tape catalog front
  and back, most recent being *Worldwide 50
  Gold Award Hits, Vol. 1* (side 2, row 3, column
  5).
❑ RCA Victor 21-112-1
  pt 56 ....8/70   3-5
  INNER SLEEVE 2C: Black-and-white.
  Pictures RCA Elvis cassette tape catalog front
  and back, most recent being *Worldwide 50
  Gold Award Hits, Vol. 1* (side 2, row 3, column
  4).

❑ RCA Victor 21-112-1
  pt 57 ....8/70   3-5
  INNER SLEEVE 2D: Black-and-white. Front:
  Pictures Camden Elvis catalog, most recent
  being *Elvis' Christmas Album* (Side 1, row 2,
  column 1). Back: RCA Elvis 3¾-ips reel tapes.
❑ RCA Victor...........................1/70   30-40
  INSERT 2A: 16-page photo booklet. Color
  front and back covers, black-and-white photos
  inside. Elvis photo on front is identical to the
  one on the picture sleeve for *Suspicious
  Minds / You'll Think of Me*. This is the booklet
  intended as the bonus album for this release;
  however, some sets have been found to
  contain a substitute photo booklet (1B).
❑ RCA Victor...........................1/70   30-40
  INSERT 2B: 16-page photo booklet. Elvis
  photo on front is from a Las Vegas concert,
  with him wearing a jumpsuit. Reads:
  "Souvenir Photo Album" at lower left.

RCA Victor (M)
  LPM-6401 ....8/70   75-100
  **TOTAL PACKAGE 2: Discs, box, inner
    sleeves,
    insert (either).**

❑ RCA Victor (M)
  LPM-6401..........................'76   10-20
  DISCS 3: Tan label.
  (Disc 1) ZPRM-1508-31S/ZPRM-1509-31S. **(Disc 2)** ZPRM-
  1510-32S/ZPRM-1511-31S. **(Disc 3)** ZPRM-1512-
  32S/ZPRM-1513-31S. **(Disc 4)** ZPRM-1514-35S/ZPRM-
  1515-39S. All identification numbers are stamped except on
  side 5, which is engraved.
❑ RCA Victor LPM-6401 ....'76   10-20
  BOX 3: Same as box 1, except no mention of
  bonus photo booklet. That area is left blank.
  Has "RE" at lower left on front and back.
❑ RCA Victor...........................'70s   8-16
  INNER SLEEVES 3: Four black-and-white
  sleeves. Pictures RCA Elvis catalog front and
  back. Any of several sleeves may be found
  here.

RCA Victor (M)
  LPM-6401 ....'76   30-40
  **TOTAL PACKAGE 3: Discs, box, inner
    sleeves.**

❑ RCA Victor (M)
  LPM-6401..........................5/77   1000-1500
  DISC 4: Tan label. Blue vinyl. Disc 1 (sides
  1/2) only. Experimental pressing, not intended
  for sale or distribution.
  BOX/COVER 4: None made.
RCA Victor (M)
  LPM-6401 ....5/77   1000-1500
  TOTAL PACKAGE 4: Disc.

❑ RCA Victor (M)
  LPM-6401..........................'77   8-12
  DISCS 5: Black label, dog near top.
❑ RCA LPM-6401 ....'77   8-12
  BOX 5: Same as box 3.

❑ RCA Victor........................ '70s   8-16
INNER SLEEVES 5: Four black-and-white sleeves. Pictures RCA Elvis catalog front and back. Any of several sleeves may be found here.

RCA Victor (M)
LPM-6401 .... '77   20-35
TOTAL PACKAGE 5: Discs, box, inner sleeves.

Disc 1
Side 1
Heartbreak Hotel
I Was the One
I Want You, I Need You, I Love You
Don't Be Cruel
Hound Dog
Love Me Tender
Side 2
Anyway You Want Me (That's How I Will Be)
Too Much
Playing for Keeps
All Shook Up
That's When Your Heartaches Begin
Loving You
Disc 2
Side 3
(Let Me Be Your) Teddy Bear
Jailhouse Rock
Treat Me Nice
I Beg of You
Don't
Wear My Ring Around Your Neck
Hard Headed Woman
Side 4
I Got Stung
(Now and Then There's) A Fool Such As I
A Big Hunk O' Love
Stuck on You
A Mess of Blues
It's Now Or Never
Disc 3
Side 5
I Gotta Know
Are You Lonesome Tonight
Surrender
I Feel So Bad
Little Sister
Can't Help Falling in Love
Side 6
Rock-A-Hula Baby
Anything That's Part of You
Good Luck Charm
She's Not You
Return to Sender
Where Do You Come From
One Broken Heart for Sale
Disc 4
Side 7
(You're the) Devil in Disguise
Bossa Nova Baby
Kissin' Cousins
Viva Las Vegas
Ain't That Loving You Baby
Wooden Heart
Side 8
Crying in the Chapel
If I Can Dream

In the Ghetto
Suspicious Minds
Don't Cry Daddy
Kentucky Rain
Excerpts from *Elvis Sails*

WORLDWIDE 50 GOLD AWARD HITS, VOL. 1 (2 Cassettes)
❑ RCA Victor (M) PK-6401 ...8/70   10-20
TAPES 1: Boxed set of two cassettes.
(Tape 1) PK-6402. (Tape 2) PK-6403.
❑ RCA Victor PK-6402..........8/70   3-5
TAPE COVER 1A: Blue and white cassette slipcover listing contents. Has number at bottom.
❑ RCA Victor PK-6403..........8/70   3-5
TAPE COVER 1B: Blue and white cassette slipcover listing contents. Has number at bottom.
❑ RCA Victor PK-6401..........8/70   20-30
BOX 1: Front: RCA logo and number at upper left, "Victor Cassette" at upper right. Gold record titles 1 through 25. Back: Same as front except has gold record titles 26 through 50. On both sides, above fourth column, is: "Special Bonus New Photo Book."
❑ RCA Victor........................ 1/70   30-40
INSERT 1A: 16-page photo booklet. Color front and back covers, black-and-white photos inside. Elvis photo on front is identical to the one on the picture sleeve for Suspicious Minds / You'll Think of Me. This is the booklet intended as the bonus album for this release; however, some sets have been found to contain a substitute photo booklet, listed below.
❑ RCA Victor........................ 1/70   30-40
INSERT 1B: 16-page photo booklet. Elvis photo on front is from a Las Vegas concert, with him wearing a jumpsuit. Reads: "Souvenir Photo Album" at lower left.
RCA Victor (M)
PK-6401...................... 8/70   60-100
TOTAL PACKAGE 1: Tapes, covers, box, insert (either).

❑ RCA Victor (M) PK-6401 ..... '73   10-20
TAPES 2: Verification pending. Assumption: Same as tapes 1.
❑ RCA Victor PK-6402............ '73   3-5
TAPE COVER 2A: Verification pending. Assumption: Same as tape cover 1A.
❑ RCA Victor PK-6403............ '73   3-5
TAPE COVER 2B: Verification pending. Assumption: Same as tape cover 1B.
❑ RCA Victor PK-6401............ '73   15-20
BOX 2: Same as box 1, except no mention of bonus photo booklet. That text is replaced by the RCA logo and number.
RCA Victor (M) PK-6401 .. '73   30-50
TOTAL PACKAGE 2: Tapes, covers, box.

Tape 1

Side 1

Heartbreak Hotel
I Was the One
I Want You, I Need You, I Love You
Don't Be Cruel
Hound Dog
Love Me Tender
Anyway You Want Me (That's How I Will Be)
Too Much
Playing for Keeps
All Shook Up
That's When Your Heartaches Begin
Loving You

Side 2

(Let Me Be Your) Teddy Bear
Jailhouse Rock
Treat Me Nice
I Beg of You
Don't
Wear My Ring Around Your Neck
Hard Headed Woman
I Got Stung
(Now and Then There's) A Fool Such As I
A Big Hunk O' Love
Stuck on You
A Mess of Blues
It's Now Or Never

Tape 2

Side 1

I Gotta Know
Are You Lonesome Tonight
Surrender
I Feel So Bad
Little Sister
Can't Help Falling in Love
Rock-A-Hula Baby
Anything That's Part of You
Good Luck Charm
She's Not You
Return to Sender
Where Do You Come From
One Broken Heart for Sale

Side 2

(You're the) Devil in Disguise
Bossa Nova Baby
Kissin' Cousins
Viva Las Vegas
Ain't That Loving You Baby
Wooden Heart
Crying in the Chapel
If I Can Dream
In the Ghetto
Suspicious Minds
Don't Cry Daddy
Kentucky Rain
Excerpts from *Elvis Sails*

WORLDWIDE 50 GOLD AWARD HITS, VOL. 1 (Two 8-Tracks)

❑ RCA Victor (M)
P8S-6401 .... 8/70   15-25
TAPES 1: Boxed set of two 8-track cartridges. Each has a yellow, black and white label listing contents. Number is on front of cartridge. Even though this set is supposed to be mono, cartridge reads: "Stereo Effect Reprocessed from Monophonic."
(Tape 1) P8S-6402. (Tape 2) P8S-6403.

TAPE COVERS 1: Red and white generic cartridge slipcovers. Make no mention of Elvis or this set.

❑ RCA Victor PK-6401 .... 8/70   25-35
BOX 1: Front: RCA logo and number at upper left, "Victor 8-Track Cartridge" at upper right. Gold record titles 1 through 25. Back: Same as front except has gold record titles 26 through 50. On both sides, above fourth column, is: "Special Bonus New Photo Book."

❑ RCA Victor 1/70   30-40
INSERT 1: 16-page photo booklet. Color front and back covers, black-and-white photos inside. Elvis photo on front is identical to the one on the picture sleeve for *Suspicious Minds / You'll Think of Me*. This is the booklet intended as the bonus album for this release; however, some sets have been found to contain a substitute photo booklet, listed below: (Price is for either.) 16-page photo booklet. Elvis photo on front is from a Las Vegas concert, with him wearing a jumpsuit. Reads: "Souvenir Photo Album" at lower left.

RCA Victor (M)

P8S-6401 .... 8/70   60-100
TOTAL PACKAGE 1: Tapes, box, insert.

❑ RCA Victor P8S-6401 .... '73   15-25
TAPES 2: Verification pending. Assumption: Same as tapes 1.

❑ RCA Victor P8S-6401 .... '73
TAPE COVERS 2: Red and white generic cartridge slipcovers. Make no mention of Elvis or this set.

❑ RCA Victor P8S-6401 .... '73   20-25
BOX 2: Same as box 1, except no mention of bonus photo booklet. That text is replaced by the RCA logo and number.

RCA Victor (M)

P8S-6401 .... '73   35-50
TOTAL PACKAGE 2: Tapes, box.

Tape 1

Side 1

Heartbreak Hotel
I Was the One
I Want You, I Need You, I Love You
Don't Be Cruel
Hound Dog
Love Me Tender
Anyway You Want Me (That's How I Will Be)
Too Much
Playing for Keeps
All Shook Up
That's When Your Heartaches Begin
Loving You

Side 2

(Let Me Be Your) Teddy Bear
Jailhouse Rock
Treat Me Nice
I Beg of You
Don't
Wear My Ring Around Your Neck
Hard Headed Woman
I Got Stung
(Now and Then There's) A Fool Such As I
A Big Hunk O' Love

Stuck on You
A Mess of Blues
It's Now Or Never

Tape 2

Side 1

I Gotta Know
Are You Lonesome Tonight
Surrender
I Feel So Bad
Little Sister
Can't Help Falling in Love
Rock-A-Hula Baby
Anything That's Part of You
Good Luck Charm
She's Not You
Return to Sender
Where Do You Come From
One Broken Heart for Sale

Side 2

(You're the) Devil in Disguise
Bossa Nova Baby
Kissin' Cousins
Viva Las Vegas
Ain't That Loving You Baby
Wooden Heart
Crying in the Chapel
If I Can Dream
In the Ghetto
Suspicious Minds
Don't Cry Daddy
Kentucky Rain
Excerpts from *Elvis Sails*

WORLDWIDE GOLD AWARD HITS, PARTS 1 & 2 (2 LPs)

❑ RCA Victor (M)
R-213690 .... '74   75-125
DISCS 1: RCA Record Club issue.
Orange/tan labels. Dynaflex vinyl.
(Disc 1 - Tan) ZPRM-1508-6S/ZPRM-1509-5S. (Disc 2 - Orange) ZPRM-1510-5S/ZPRM-1511- 31S. Inexplicably, the only copy of this set we've seen – one bought in 1974 – has one orange and one tan label disc. Verification is pending on an orange label of disc 1.)

❑ RCA Victor R-213690 .... '74   15-20
COVER 1: Single pocket. Front: RCA logo and number above fourth column of gold record titles. Back: Text only.

❑ RCA Victor 21-112-1
pt 54 .... 8/70   3-5
INNER SLEEVE 1A: Black-and-white.
Pictures RCA's Elvis LP catalog front and back, most recent being *Worldwide Gold Award Hits, Vol. 1* (side 2, row 4, column 4).

❑ RCA Victor 21-112-1
pt 55 .... 8/70   3-5
INNER SLEEVE 1B: Black-and-white.
Pictures RCA Elvis Stereo 8 tape catalog front and back, most recent being *Worldwide 50 Gold Award Hits, Vol. 1* (side 2, row 3, column 5).

RCA Victor (M)
R-213690 .... '74   100-150
TOTAL PACKAGE 1: Discs, cover, inner sleeves.

❑ RCA Victor (M) R-213690.... '74   10-12
DISCS 2: RCA Record Club. Tan label.
Dynaflex vinyl.
(Disc 1) ZPRM-1508-6S/ZPRM-1509-5S. (Disc 2) ZPRM-1510-5S/ZPRM-1511-31S.

❑ RCA Victor R-213690 .... '74   15-20
COVER 2: Same as cover 1.

❑ RCA Victor .... '70s   4-8
INNER SLEEVES 2: Two black-and-white sleeves. Pictures RCA Elvis catalog front and back. Any of several sleeves may be found here.

RCA Victor (M)
R-213690 .... '74   30-40
TOTAL PACKAGE 2: Discs, cover, inner sleeves.

❑ RCA Victor (M)
R-213690 .... '77   5-8
DISCS 3: RCA Record Club. Black label, dog near top.

❑ RCA R-213690 .... '77   5-8
COVER 3: Reflects logo change.

❑ RCA Victor .... '70s   4-8
INNER SLEEVES 3: Two black-and-white sleeves. Pictures RCA Elvis catalog front and back. Any of several sleeves may be found here.

RCA Victor (M)
R-213690 .... '77   15-25
TOTAL PACKAGE 3: Discs, cover, inner sleeves.

Card stock jacket, with printing on cover – not on slicks.

Disc 1

Side 1

Heartbreak Hotel
I Was the One
I Want You, I Need You, I Love You
Don't Be Cruel
Hound Dog
Love Me Tender

Side 2

Anyway You Want Me (That's How I Will Be)
Too Much
Playing for Keeps
All Shook Up
That's When Your Heartaches Begin
Loving You

Disc 2

Side 3

(Let Me Be Your) Teddy Bear
Jailhouse Rock
Treat Me Nice
I Beg of You
Don't
Wear My Ring Around Your Neck
Hard Headed Woman

Side 4

I Got Stung
(Now and Then There's) A Fool Such As I
A Big Hunk O' Love
Stuck on You
A Mess of Blues
It's Now Or Never

WORLDWIDE GOLD AWARD HITS, PARTS 3 & 4 (2 LP)

❏ RCA Victor (M) R-214657 ... '78   5-8
DISCS 1: RCA Record Club. Black label, dog near top.
(Disc 1) R-214657A-1/R-214657B-1. **(Disc 2)** R-214657C-1/R-214657D-1.
(Disc 1) R-214657A-1/R-214657B-1. **(Disc 2)** R-214657C-1/R-214657D-2.

❏ RCA R-214657 .... '78   5-8
COVER 1: Single pocket. Front: RCA logo and number above gold record title 5, *Little Sister.* Back: Text only.
INNER SLEEVES 1: White, no printing.

RCA Victor (M)
R-214657 .... '78   10-20
TOTAL PACKAGE 1: Discs, cover.

Card stock jacket, with printing on cover – not on slicks.

Disc 1

Side 1
I Gotta Know
Are You Lonesome Tonight
Surrender
I Feel So Bad
Little Sister
Can't Help Falling in Love

Side 2
Rock-A-Hula Baby
Anything That's Part of You
Good Luck Charm
She's Not You
Return to Sender
Where Do You Come From
One Broken Heart for Sale

Disc 2

Side 1
(You're the) Devil in Disguise
Bossa Nova Baby
Kissin' Cousins
Viva Las Vegas
Ain't That Loving You Baby
Wooden Heart

Side 2
Crying in the Chapel
If I Can Dream
In the Ghetto
Suspicious Minds
Don't Cry Daddy
Kentucky Rain
Excerpts from *Elvis Sails*

WORLDWIDE 50 GOLD AWARD HITS, VOL. 2 – ELVIS, THE OTHER SIDES

❏ RCA Victor (M)
LPM-6402 .... 8/71   20-30
DISCS 1: Orange label. Flexible vinyl. Boxed set of four LPs.
(Disc 1) APRM-5522-2S/APRM-5523-2S. **(Disc 2)** APRM-5524-11S/APRM-5525-2S. **(Disc 3)** APRM-5526-4S/APRM-5527-2S. **(Disc 4)** APRM-5528-2S/APRM-5529-2S.
(Disc 1) APRM-5522-3S/APRM-5523-3S. **(Disc 2)** APRM-5524-12S/APRM-5525-3S. **(Disc 3)** APRM-5526-3S/APRM-5527-3S. **(Disc 4)** APRM-5528-3S/APRM-5529-3S.

❏ RCA Victor LPM-6402 .... 8/71   15-25
BOX 1: Front: RCA logo and number, and picture of envelope with "Special Bonus Number One" at upper left. "Victor Mono" and "Large Full Color Pullout Portrait Reproduction of Elvis – Special Bonus Number Two" at upper right. No Elvis photos on cover except for two tiny ones on envelope at upper left. Back: Same as front except has different songs listed.

❏ RCA Victor 21-112-1
PT 54A 8/71   3-5
INNER SLEEVE 1A: Black-and-white. Pictures RCA's Elvis LP catalog front and back, most recent being *Love Letters from Elvis* (side 2, row 4, column 5).

❏ RCA Victor 21-112-1
PT 55A 8/71   3-5
INNER SLEEVE 1B: Black-and-white. Pictures RCA Elvis Stereo 8 tape catalog front and back, most recent being a four-tape issue of *Worldwide 50 Gold Award Hits, Vol. 1* (side 2, row 3, column 6).

❏ RCA Victor 8/71   3-5
INNER SLEEVE 1C: Black-and-white. Pictures RCA Elvis cassette tape catalog front and back, most recent being four-tape issue of *Worldwide 50 Gold Award Hits* (side 2, row 3, column 5). On side 2, at bottom right, is the number 21-112-1 PT 56A.

❏ RCA Victor 8/71   3-5
INNER SLEEVE 1D: Black-and-white. Front: Pictures Camden Elvis catalog, most recent being *C'mon Everybody* (side 1, row 2, column 3). Back: RCA Elvis 3¾-ips reel tapes. On side 1, at bottom right, is the number 21-112-1 PT 57A.

❏ RCA 8/71   15-25
INSERT 1A: White 5¼" x 3½" envelope, with black and red print. Reads: "Something from Elvis' Wardrobe for You," and contains a swatch at cloth.

❏ All Star Shows 8/71   15-25
INSERT 1B: Tri-folded 11" x 33" Elvis (circa 1970 concert) poster print. Back is blank.

RCA Victor (M)
LPM-6402 .... 8/71   75-125
TOTAL PACKAGE 1: Discs, box, inner sleeves, inserts.

❏ RCA Victor (M)
LPM-6402 .... '76   10-20
DISCS 2: Tan label. Dynaflex vinyl.
(Disc 1) APRM-5522-4S/APRM-5523-5S. **(Disc 2)** APRM-5524-11S/APRM-5525-5S. **(Disc 3)** APRM-5526-5/APRM-5527-4S. **(Disc 4)** APRM-5528-2S/APRM-5529-5S.
(Disc 1) APRM-5522-5/APRM-5523-8. **(Disc 2)** APRM-5524-13/APRM-5525-6S. **(Disc 3)** APRM-5526-6/APRM-5527-5. **(Disc 4)** APRM-5528-4/APRM-5529-8.

❏ RCA Victor LPM-6402 .... '76   10-20
BOX 2: Same as box 1, except no mention of bonuses. That area is left blank. Has "RE" at lower left.

❏ RCA Victor.........................'70s　　8-16
INNER SLEEVES 2: Four black-and-white sleeves. Pictures RCA Elvis catalog front and back. Any of several sleeves may be found here.

RCA Victor (M)
LPM-6402 ....'76　　30-40
TOTAL PACKAGE 2: Discs, box, inner sleeves.

❏ RCA Victor LPM-6402.........'77　　8-12
DISCS 3: Black label, dog near top.
❏ RCA Victor LPM-6402.........'77　　8-12
BOX 3: Verification pending. Assumption: Nearly the same as box 1 except no references are made to bonus items.
❏ RCA Victor.........................'70s　　8-16
INNER SLEEVES 3: Four black-and-white sleeves. Pictures RCA Elvis catalog front and back. Any of several sleeves may be found here.

RCA Victor (M)
LPM-6402 ....'76　　20-35
TOTAL PACKAGE 3: Discs, box, inner sleeves.

Disc 1
Side 1
Puppet on a String
Witchcraft
Trouble
Poor Boy
I Want To Be Free
Doncha' Think It's Time
Young Dreams
Side 2
The Next Step Is Love
You Don't Have to Say You Love Me
Paralyzed
My Wish Came True
When My Blue Moon Turns to Gold Again
Lonesome Cowboy
Disc 2
Side 3
My Baby Left Me
It Hurts Me
I Need Your Love Tonight
Tell Me Why
Please Don't Drag That String Around
Young and Beautiful
Side 4
Hot Dog
New Orleans
We're Gonna Move
Crawfish
King Creole
I Believe in the Man in the Sky
Dixieland Rock
Disc 3
Side 5
The Wonder of You
They Remind Me Too Much of You
Mean Woman Blues
Lonely Man
Any Day No
Don't Ask Me Why

Side 6
(Marie's the Name) His Latest Flame
I Really Don't Want to Know
Baby, I Don't Care
I've Lost You
Let Me
Love Me
Disc 4
Side 7
Got a Lot o' Livin to Do
Fame and Fortune
Rip It Up
There Goes My Everything
Lover Doll
One Night
Side 8
Just Tell Her Jim Said Hello
Ask Me
Patch It Up
As Long As I Have You
You'll Think of Me
Wild in the Country

YOU AIN'T NOTHING BUT THE KING
❏ King LPS-2722: Bootleg. Listed for identification only.

YOU ARE THERE
❏ E 168: Bootleg. Listed for identification only.

YOU'LL NEVER WALK ALONE (Camden)
❏ RCA/Camden (SP)
CALX-2472 ....3/71　　15-20
DISC 1: Blue label, black and white print. Flexible vinyl.
ACRS-4523-1S/ACRS-4524-1S. Identification numbers are engraved.
ACRS-4523-3S/ACRS-4524-3S. Identification numbers are stamped.
❏ RCA/Camden CAL-2472 ...3/71　　15-20
COVER 1: Front: The only lettering is "Elvis." Color Elvis (circa '70) photo. Back: RCA logo and number at upper left, Camden logo at upper right. Pictures four other Camden Elvis LPs. Cover indicates Dynaflex but disc does not. Has a "3" at lower right.
INNER SLEEVE 1: White, no printing. (Some Camden LPs had no inner sleeves at all.)
RCA/Camden (SP)
CALX-2472 ....3/71　　30-40
TOTAL PACKAGE 1: Disc, cover.

❏ RCA/Camden (SP)
CALX-2472 ....3/71　　15-20
DISC 2: Same as cover 1.
❏ RCA/Camden CAL-2472 ...3/71　　20-25
COVER 2: Designate promo. Same as cover 1, but with "Not for Sale" stamped on back.
INNER SLEEVE 2: White, no printing. (Some Camden LPs had no inner sleeves at all.)
RCA/Camden (SP)
CALX-2472 ....3/71　　35-45
TOTAL PACKAGE 2: Disc, cover.

❑ RCA/Camden (SP)
CALX-2472........................3/71   15-20
DISC 3: Same as disc 1.
❑ RCA/Camden CALX-2472...'73   15-20
COVER 3: Same as cover 1, except has a "7"
on back at lower right.
INNER SLEEVE 3: White, no printing.

RCA/Camden (SP)
CALX-2472...................3/71   30-40
TOTAL PACKAGE 3: Disc, cover.

❑ RCA/Camden (SP)
CAL-2472............................'74   10-12
DISC 4: Blue label, black and white print.
Flexible vinyl. "X" is dropped from prefix.
ACRS-4523-3S/ACRS-4524-8S.
❑ RCA/Camden CAL-2472.....'74   10-12
COVER 4: Same as cover 1, except has "RE"
on back at lower left and "3" at lower right.
Also, "X" is dropped from prefix.
INNER SLEEVE 4: White, no printing.

RCA/Camden (SP)
CAL-2472.....................'74   20-25
TOTAL PACKAGE 4: Disc, cover.

Side 1
You'll Never Walk Alone
Who Am I
Let Us Pray
(There'll Be) Peace in the Valley (For Me)
We Call on Him

Side 2
I Believe
It Is No Secret (What God Can Do)
Sing You Children
Take My Hand Precious Lord
Even though label and cover indicate this is a
mono LP, *You'll Never Walk Alone, Who Am I,
Let Us Pray* and *We Call On Him* are true
stereo.

YOU'LL NEVER WALK ALONE
(Pickwick)

❑ Pickwick/Camden (SP)
CAS-2472......................12/75   2-5
DISC 1: Black label. Multi-color Pickwick logo
at center.
CAS-2472A/CAS-2472B. Identification numbers are
engraved.
❑ Pickwick/Camden
CAS-2472........................12/75   3-5
COVER 1: Same photos and LPs pictured as
RCA/Camden cover 1. Front: Pickwick logo at
upper right, Camden logo and number at
upper left. Back: Same as RCA/Camden
cover. Has a "2" at lower right.
INNER SLEEVE 1: Generic Pickwick sleeve.
Makes no mention of Elvis or this LP.

Pickwick/Camden (SP)
CAS-2472...................12/75   5-10
TOTAL PACKAGE 1: Disc, cover.

Side 1
You'll Never Walk Alone
Who Am I
Let Us Pray
(There'll Be) Peace in the Valley (For Me)
We Call on Him

Side 2
I Believe
It Is No Secret (What God Can Do)
Sing You Children
Take My Hand Precious Lord

YOUR MUSICAL SOUVENIR FROM QSP

Various artists collection

❑ RCA Special Products (SP)
QSP1-0042...............................   25-35
DISC 1: Red label, black and white print. A
promotional sampler made for QSP, a direct
sales subsidiary of *Reader's Digest*. Has one
Elvis track, *Blue Suede Shoes*.
QSP1-0042A-1/QSP1-0042B-1.
❑ RCA QSP1-0042......................   25-35
COVER 1: Verification pending.
INNER SLEEVE 1: White, no printing.

RCA Special Products (SP)
QSP1-0042..........................   50-70
TOTAL PACKAGE 1: Disc, cover.

Card stock jacket, with printing on cover – not
on slicks.

Side A
Verification pending.

Side B
We Built This City (Starship)
Blue Suede Shoes (Elvis Presley)
Missing You (Diana Ross)
Lost in the Fifties Tonight (Ronnie Milsap)
Forty Hour Week (Alabama)
American Patrol (Glenn Miller Orchestra)

YOUR SPECIAL MUSICAL SOUVENIR FROM QSP

Various artists collection

❑ RCA Special Products (S)
QSP1-0047...............................   25-35
DISC 1: Red label, black and white print. A
promotional sampler made for QSP, a direct
sales subsidiary of *Reader's Digest*. Has one
Elvis track, *Are You Lonesome Tonight*.
QSP1-0047A-1/QSP1-0047B-1.
❑ RCA QSP1-0047......................   25-35
COVER 1: Verification pending.
INNER SLEEVE 1: White, no printing.

RCA Special Products (S)
QSP1-0047..........................   50-70
TOTAL PACKAGE 1: Disc, cover.

Card stock jacket, with printing on cover – not
on slicks.

COMPACT DISCS

Here you will find all known domestic compact discs by Elvis, as well as many of the various artists compilations that contain at least one track by Presley.

Unlike a vinyl record, where the country of origin is usually quite clear, CDs present more of a challenge in this regard. While our objective is to include all *United States* releases," there are many discs in this category with such diverse derivations as: 1) Made in Japan for distribution in the U.S. 2) Made in Canada for distribution in the U.S. 3) Made in _____ (fill in blank with any number of countries) for distribution in the U.S. 4) Made in the U.S.A. for export to _____ (fill in blank). 5) Inserts made in the U.S. and discs made in _____ (fill in blank). 6) Inserts made in the U.S. and discs made in _____ (fill in blank) — just to name a few.

Through all of this, we have decided that as long as there is some stateside involvement in the production of a CD, it qualifies for inclusion in this guide.

Just as it is assumed in appraising a vinyl album that the cover or jacket is included – unless noted otherwise – each CD is presumed to have both a front cover insert and rear, tray insert. All compact discs should also be in their appropriate containers, which may range from conventional jewel boxes (single or multi-disc plastic cases) to something more extravagant.

Disc sets made exclusively for promotional use are of course identified as such and priced accordingly; however, standard catalog releases with notched or drilled cases and inserts are not. Unlike *designate promos* of vinyl albums, these quickie promotional copies of CDs have yet to justify a separate pricing structure. They likely never will.

The release dates shown are believed to be accurate within a few weeks in either direction. Some CDs are announced a month or two before they are actually in the stores; others are sent a month or more in advance to the media. We have tried to give the date of general release, or *street date* – when the disc became available to the public.

Our objective is to provide the month and year of issue. When only the year is known, it is shown without a month noted. For those few items for which we show no release date, we welcome such information from readers – as well as corrections to existing data that may be in error.

Since the number of bootleg Elvis compact discs outnumber the legitimate ones, it is inevitable that folks who do not know the difference will be surprised to not find ones in that category listed here. Their usual reaction is to think they have something so rare (and valuable) that even we didn't know of its existence.

Hopefully a future edition of this guide will have bootleg CDs listed and, identified as such, just as we have done in the vinyl record chapters of this book. Meanwhile, here are just *some* of the labels known to have unauthorized and/or illegally-issued Elvis CDs: AJ Records; American Rejects; Bilko; Captain Marvel Jr.; Chips; Circle; Claudia; Cupido; Diamond; Dizzy Document; Miss Prissie; Famous Groove; Fort Baxter; Flashback; Great Dane; King; Live Archives; Mac; Majo; Moon; Mystery Train; PEAF; Ranwood; Rock Legends; Roma Victoria; SD; Savanah; Sunset; Tiger; Tod; 2001; Vault; Vicky; Whitehaven; and Yellow Dog. Remember, this is only a partial listing. Some CDs in this category have no label name, which would never be the case with an authorized release.

Vinyl collectors occasionally use the word *stock* to indicate a commercial, or store stock copy, as to differentiate it from a promotional release. In this chapter, and in the world of CD collecting, *stock* takes on an added meaning.

When describing the colors used on the non-playing surface (top side) of a compact disc, one with the elemental metallic disc used as the primary background is called stock. The reference being that there is no color added to the underlying, aluminum-coated disc. Most CDs are stock with black (or another color) print. Discs with pictures of Elvis silk-screened on the top side are so indicated as are those displaying other works of art.

One area of confusion is regarding RCA/BMG's "Elvis in the '90s" black label. Some discs from this period have the text in what is often described as silver ink, but it is merely the portion of stock metal *not* inked – giving the appearance of silver print. Some others actually have silver printed on the disc. Since values are as of yet unaffected by these variations, we refer to both as having silver print. A third variation from this batch have the text printed in an off-white ink. One version of the black label has the RCA Nipper/gramophone logo at the top, while another has the RCA lightning bolt logo at the top.

The most common type of cover found on Elvis CDs is the *4-page insert.* This cover insert is a 9½" x 4¾" sheet of paper, or card stock, folded in half.

Also very common are *insert booklets,* which are at least eight pages, and are saddle stitched in the middle. An insert booklet doubles as the front cover and is slid into the front of the jewel box, whereas a booklet (no mention of "insert") is larger and usually used in oversize boxed sets.

We have tried to indicate which Elvis CDs came packaged in custom printed, 12¼" x 5½," cardboard long boxes, although there are surely some we have missed. Having a custom long box, one that likely pictures art identical to the front cover insert, can add $4 to $8 to the total value, especially if the box is sealed and has a shrink wrap sticker. Presley CDs in generic long boxes – ones making no mention of Elvis or of a specific disc – add very little to the overall value, if anything at all. The same can be said for plastic blister packs.

The number of tracks indicated for a disc is not necessarily the number of songs heard during the program – the most common exception to the count being medleys. Most medleys include several songs, but constitute only one track.

If the title of a CD you have is listed in this guide, but the description differs to some degree from your copy, you probably have a reissue – or even a reissue of a reissue.

We have made no attempt to document and describe *every* reissue of every Elvis Presley CD. Fortunately this information has already been chronicled in an easily available book, *Elvis: For CD Fans Only: Second Edition*, by Dale Hampton. For anyone wanting to plunge deeper into the Elvis CD world, we recommend this publication. For more information, contact: RuJak Publications, 4500 Sunset Road, Knoxville, TN 37914..

AFTERNOON IN THE GARDEN

RCA/BMG 67457-2.........3/97   **15-18**
Disc has a blue photo of a concert crowd,
  with yellow text. Includes 12-page insert
  booklet. Has 24 tracks.

ALL-TIME BEST LOVE SONGS: see
DO YOU LOVE ME?

ALMOST IN LOVE

RCA/BMG
CAD1-2440 ....12/96   **12-15**
Disc is stock with black print. Includes
  insert. Special Products mail order offer
  from Avon. Has 10 tracks.

ALOHA FROM HAWAII VIA
SATELLITE

RCA/BMG 52642-2.........4/92   **15-18**
Disc is black with silver print. Includes 8-
  page insert booklet. Has 25 tracks.

ALTERNATE ALOHA

RCA/BMG 6985-2-R 5/88   **15-18**
Disc has a color drawing of Elvis (same art
  as used on the LP cover), with text in
  black print. Includes 8-page insert
  booklet. Has 24 tracks.

ALWAYS ON MY MIND

RCA Victor
PCD1-5430 ....7/85   **20-25**
Disc is stock with blue and white print.
  Pressed in Japan for U.S. release.
  Includes 4-page insert. Has 13 tracks.

RCA/BMG
PCD1-5430 ....1/88   **10-15**
Disc is stock with blue and white print.
  Pressed in U.S. Includes 4-page insert.
  Has 13 tracks.

AMAZING GRACE (HIS GREATEST
SACRED PERFORMANCES) (2 CDs)

RCA/BMG 66421-2.......10/94   **25-30**
Discs are lavender with black print.
  Includes 32-page booklet. Slipcase on
  jewel box has same artwork as insert.
  Has 56 tracks.

ARE YOU LONESOME TONIGHT/
I GOTTA KNOW

RCA/BMG 8994-2-RH ......'89   **10-20**
Disc is stock with black print. Includes
  single sheet insert. "Gold Standard
  Single, Commemorative Juke Box
  Series." Has two tracks. Also sold as
  part of a 5-disc set with juke box title
  strips. Value of set is $100 to $125.

AS TIME GOES BY: see MANY MOODS
OF ROMANCE

BACK IN MEMPHIS

RCA/BMG 61081-2 ....10/92   **12-15**
Disc is black with silver print. Includes 6-
  page insert booklet. Has 10 tracks.

BACK TO THE '50s (2 CDs)

Various Artists Compilation

Heartland
DVC 2-1068-1/2 ....'93   **25-30**
Includes insert. Mail order offer. Has two
  Elvis tracks.

BEST OF CHRISTMAS

Various Artists Compilation

RCA/BMG 7013-2-R ....'90   **12-15**
Includes insert. Has one Elvis track.

BILLBOARD GREATEST
CHRISTMAS HITS
(1955–PRESENT)

Various Artists Compilation

Rhino R2-70636 ....'89   **10-12**
Disc is stock with green and mustard color
  print. Includes 4-page insert. Has 10
  tracks, one by Elvis.

BILLBOARD TOP ROCK'N ROLL
HITS (1956)

Various Artists Compilation

Rhino R2-70599 ....'89   **10-12**
Disc is stock with black and green print.
  Includes 4-page insert. Has 10 tracks,
  two by Elvis.

BILLBOARD TOP ROCK'N ROLL
HITS (1957)

Various Artists Compilation

Rhino R2-70618 ....'88   **10-12**
Disc is stock with black and blue print.
  Includes 4-page insert. Has 10 tracks,
  two by Elvis.

BILLBOARD TOP ROCK'N ROLL
HITS (1958)

Various Artists Compilation

Rhino R2-70619 ....'88   **10-12**
Disc is stock with black and red print.
  Includes 4-page insert. Has 10 tracks,
  one by Elvis.

BILLBOARD TOP ROCK'N ROLL
HITS (1959)

Various Artists Compilation

Rhino R2-70620 ....'88   **10-12**
Disc is stock with black and red print.
  Includes 4-page insert. Has 10 tracks,
  one by Elvis.

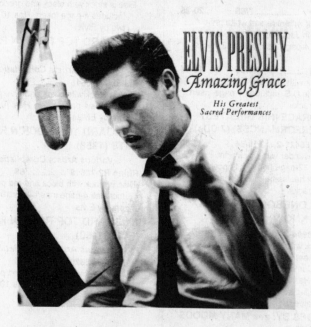

BILLBOARD TOP ROCK'N ROLL HITS (1960)

Various Artists Compilation

Rhino R2-70621 ....'88   **15-20**
Disc is stock with black and orange print. Includes 4-page insert. Has 10 tracks, two by Elvis.

BILLBOARD TOP ROCK'N ROLL HITS (1957–1961) (5 CDs)

Various Artists Compilation

Rhino R2-72004 ....'89   **50-55**
Discs are identical to those described under individual listings (previous), but packaged together in this set. Has 50 tracks, six by Elvis.

BLUE CHRISTMAS

RCA/BMG 59800-2 ....7/92   **10-15**
Disc is black with silver print. Includes insert. Has eight tracks.

BLUE HAWAII

RCA/BMG 3683-2-R 4/88   **12-15**
Disc is stock with black print. Includes 4-page insert. Has 14 tracks.

RCA/BMG 66959-2 ....4/97   **15-18**
Blue picture disc. Includes 8-page insert booklet. Has 22 tracks, including eight bonus cuts.

RCA/BMG 67459-2 ....4/97   **20-25**
Rust picture disc with blue print. Collectors Edition. The 28-page booklet and disc are part of a deluxe hard cover book. Included in the 22 tracks are eight alternates and outtakes.

BLUE SUEDE SHOES (2 CDs)

(Original Ballet Soundtrack)

RCA/BMG 67458-2.........4/97   **25-35**
Discs are stock with blue print and artwork. Includes 16-page booklet. The 36 tracks contain overdubs.

BLUE SUEDE SHOES/ TUTTI FRUTTI

RCA/BMG 8993-2-RH ......'89   **10-20**
Disc is stock with black print. Includes single sheet insert. "Gold Standard Single, Commemorative Juke Box Series." Has two tracks. Also sold as part of a 5-disc set with juke box title strips. Value of set is $100 to $125.

BURNING LOVE AND HITS FROM HIS MOVIES, VOL. 2 (RCA CAMDEN CLASSICS)

RCA/Camden/BMG
CAD1-2595 ....8/87   **7-10**
Disc is stock with black and blue print. Includes 4-page insert. Has 10 tracks.

CAN'T HELP FALLING IN LOVE/ ROCK-A-HULA BABY

RCA/BMG 8991-2-RH ......'89   **10-20**
Disc is stock with black print. Includes single sheet insert. "Gold Standard Single, Commemorative Juke Box Series." Has two tracks. Also sold as part of a 5-disc set with juke box title strips. Value of set is $100 to $125.

CELEBRATION OF COUNTRY 'N' POP MUSIC (4 CDs)

Various Artists Compilation

RCA/BMG/Reader's Digest
RB7-218C-1/2/3/4 ....'95   **55-60**
Includes 48-page booklet. Mail order offer. Has two Elvis tracks.

CELEBRATION OF FAITH & JOY (4 CDs)

Various Artists Compilation

RCA/BMG/Reader's Digest
RBD-196/CD1 ....'93   **55-60**
Includes insert. Mail order offer. Has four Elvis tracks.

CHRISTMAS CLASSICS

RCA/BMG 9801-2-R 7/89   **10-15**
Disc is stock with black print. Includes 4-page insert. Has nine tracks.

CHRISTMAS CLASSICS, VOL. 1

Various Artists Compilation

RCA/BMG 66301-2 ....'93   **12-15**
Includes insert. Has one Elvis track.

CHRISTMAS CLASSICS, VOL. 2

Various Artists Compilation

RCA/BMG 66302-2 ....'93   **12-15**
Includes insert. Has one Elvis track.

CHRISTMAS IN AMERICA (3 CDs)

Various Artists Compilation

RCA/BMG/Reader's Digest
RBD-177/CD1 ....'88   **45-50**
Includes inserts. Mail order offer. Has one Elvis track.

CHRISTMAS MEMORIES FROM ELVIS & ALABAMA

Audio Treasures
ATCD 2106-2 ....5/91   15-20
Disc is stock with red print. RCA Special Products release. Includes insert. Has 10 tracks, five by each artist.

Audio Treasures
ATCD 2106-2 ....10/96   15-20
Disc is stock with red print. RCA Special Products release. Includes insert. Same disc as used for *Country Christmas* Pop-Out CD ornament. Has 12 tracks, six by each artist.

CHRISTMAS WITH ELVIS

RCA/BMG
DIR 9003-2 ....8/97   20-25
Red and white picture disc. Includes 4-page insert. Special Products mail order offer from Razor & Tie Direct LLC. Has 20 tracks.

CLASSIC COUNTRY MUSIC II (A SMITHSONIAN COLLECTION) (4 CDs)

Various Artists Compilation
RCA/BMG RD 042-2 ....'90   65-75
Discs are packaged in an LP-sized box with a 92-page booklet. Mail order offer. Contains one Elvis track. Individual discs sell for $15 to $20.

COLLECTORS GOLD (3 CDs)

RCA/BMG 3114-2-R 8/91   30-40
Disc 1: turquoise with black print. Disc 2: orange with black print. Disc 3: pink with black print. Includes: 1) Long box, with shrink sticker reading "Contains 48 Unreleased Performances." 2) Color, 20-page insert booklet. Has 50 tracks.

RCA/BMG 3114-2-R 9/91   250-350
Same discs as above. Special Collectors Edition includes: 1) Wooden, 12" x 12" box. 2) Certificate of Limited Edition Authenticity. 3) Color, 20-page insert booklet. All CDs are in one jewel box. Reportedly 300 sets made. Mail order offer. Has 50 tracks.

COMMAND PERFORMANCES (ESSENTIAL 60's MASTERS II) (2 CDs)

RCA/BMG 66601-2 ....7/95   30-35
Disc 1: Copper matte picture disc. Disc 2: Green matte picture disc. Slipcase on jewel box has same artwork as insert. Contains 24-page booklet with liner notes and movie poster memorabilia. Has 62 tracks.

COMPLETE 50's MASTERS: see KING OF ROCK 'N' ROLL

CONTEMPORARY COUNTRY, VOL. 1 (THE LATE '70s)

Various Artists Compilation
Time-Life TCD-140 ....'91   15-20
Includes 8-page insert booklet. Mail order offer. Has one Elvis track.

CONTEMPORARY COUNTRY, VOL. 3 (THE LATE '70s)

Various Artists Compilation
Time-Life TCD-142 ....'93   15-20
Includes 8-page insert booklet. Mail order offer. Has one Elvis track.

CONTEMPORARY COUNTRY, VOL. 4 (THE EARLY '80s)

Various Artists Compilation
Time-Life TCD-143 ....'93   15-20
Includes 8-page insert booklet. Mail order offer. Has one Elvis track.

COUNTRY CHRISTMAS (2 CDs)

Various Artists Compilation
Time-Life
TCD-109 A/B ....'88   20-25
Includes inserts. Has three Elvis tracks.

COUNTRY CHRISTMAS (3 CDs)

Various Artists Compilation
RCA/BMG/ Reader's Digest
RBD-166/CD1 ....'92   45-50
Includes 40-page booklet. Mail order offer. Has two Elvis tracks.

COUNTRY CHRISTMAS (Elvis and Jim Reeves)

RCA/BMG
DDX2508-3 ....10/93   25-30
This is a Deco Disc Pop-Out CD and Ornament. Tracks are from *Elvis Presley's Country Christmas* and *Jim Reeves' Holiday Hits*. Each artist has six tracks.

COUNTRY CHRISTMAS (Elvis and Alabama)

RCA/BMG
DDX2517-3 ....10/93   25-30
This is a Deco Disc Pop-Out CD and Ornament. Tracks are from *Elvis Presley's Country Style Christmas* and *Alabama's Down Home Christmas*. Each artist has six tracks.

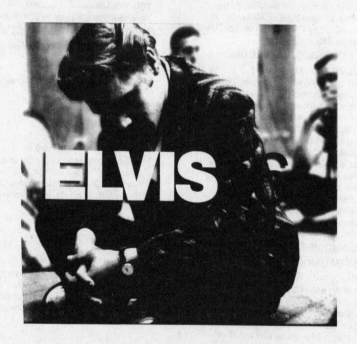

COUNTRY CHRISTMAS, VOL. 2

Various Artists Compilation

RCA/BMG 4809-2-R ....'87   12-15
Includes insert. Has one Elvis track.

COUNTRY MEMORIES (4 CDs)

Various Artists Compilation

RCA/BMG/Reader's Digest
RBD-066/CD1 ....'89   55-60
Includes 64-page booklet. Mail order offer.
Has six Elvis tracks.

COUNTRY SOFT 'N' MELLOW (4 CDs)

Various Artists Compilation

RCA/BMG/Reader's Digest
RBD-200/CD1 ....'89   55-60
Includes 64-page booklet. Mail order offer.
Has three Elvis tracks.

COUNTRY SONGS THAT WILL LAST FOREVER (4 CDs)

Various Artists Compilation

RCA/BMG/Reader's Digest
RBD-202/CD1 ....'93   55-60
Includes insert. Mail order offer. Has two
Elvis tracks.

COUNTRY SWEET 'N' SENTIMENTAL (4 CDs)

Various Artists Compilation

RCA/BMG/Reader's Digest
RBD-241/CD1 ....'93   55-60
Includes 48-page insert booklet. Mail order
offer. Has two Elvis tracks.

COUNTRY USA – 1954

Various Artists Compilation

Time-Life TCD-117........... '90   15-20
Includes inserts. Mail order offer. Has one
Elvis track.

COUNTRY USA – 1955

Various Artists Compilation

Time-Life TCD-118........... '90   15-20
Includes inserts. Mail order offer. Has two
Elvis tracks.

COUNTRY USA – 1956

Various Artists Compilation

Time-Life TCD-119........... '90   15-20
Includes inserts. Mail order offer. Has two
Elvis tracks.

COUNTRY USA – 1958

Various Artists Compilation

Time-Life TCD-112........... '89   15-20
Includes inserts. Mail order offer. Has one
Elvis track.

COUNTRY USA – 1959

Various Artists Compilation

Time-Life TCD-113 ....'90   15-20
Includes inserts. Mail order offer. Has one
Elvis track.

DATE WITH ELVIS

RCA/BMG 2011-2-R 1/89   10-15
Disc is stock with black print. Includes 4-
page insert. Has 10 tracks.

DICK CLARK'S ROCK 'N' ROLL CHRISTMAS (2 CDs)

Various Artists Compilation

Time-Life/BMG TCD-805
R129-02 A/B 12/97   15-25
Includes inserts. Mail order offer. Has three
Elvis tracks.

DINER

(Original Motion Picture Soundtrack)

Various Artists Compilation

Elektra 60107-2 ....'87   14-18
Includes insert. Has 20 tracks, one by
Elvis.

DO YOU LOVE ME? (ALL-TIME BEST LOVE SONGS)

Various Artists Compilation

RCA/BMG 66812-2 ....'96   15-18
Includes 8-page insert cover. Has one Elvis
track.

DOUBLE DYNAMITE

RCA Victor/Pair
PDC2-1010 ....'87   15-20
Disc is stock with black and blue print.
Pressed in Japan. Includes 4-page
insert. Has 16 tracks.

RCA/BMG/Pair/Ariola
PDC2-1010 ....'92   10-12
Disc is stock with black and blue print.
Pressed in U.S.A. Ariola misspelled
"Arila." Includes 4-page insert. Has 16
tracks.

DON'T BE CRUEL: see KING OF ROCK 'N' ROLL

EARLY '60s (THESE WERE OUR SONGS) (3 CDs)

Various Artists Compilation

RCA/BMG/Reader's Digest
RCD-100/CD1 ....'90   45-50
Includes 48-page insert booklet. Mail order
offer. Has 84 tracks, including five by
Elvis.

EASY LISTENING HITS OF THE '60s & '70s (4 CDs)

Various Artists Compilation

RCA/BMG/Reader's Digest
RBD-040/CD1 ....'89   55-60
Includes 64-page booklet. Mail order offer. Has 80 tracks, including four by Elvis.

ELVIS

RCA Victor
PCD1-1382 ....9/84   250-300
Disc is stock with blue and white print. Pressed in Japan for U.S. release. Includes 4-page insert. Has 12 tracks.

RCA Victor
PCD1-5199 ....11/84   30-40
Disc is stock with blue and white print. Pressed in U.S. Includes 4-page insert. Has 12 tracks.

ELVIS ("THE FOOL ALBUM")

RCA/BMG 50283-2 ....3/94   12-15
Disc is black with silver print. Includes 8-page insert booklet. Has 10 tracks.

ELVIS

(NBC-TV SPECIAL)

RCA/BMG 61021-2 ....8/91   12-15
Disc is stock with black print. Includes 8-page insert booklet. Has 31 music tracks and dialog.

ELVIS: A LEGENDARY PERFORMER, VOL. 1

RCA/BMG
CAD1-2705 ....8/89   7-10
Disc is stock with black and blue print. Includes 4-page insert. Has 10 tracks.

ELVIS: A LEGENDARY PERFORMER, VOL. 2

RCA/BMG
CAD1-2706 ....1/90   7-10
Disc is stock with black and blue print. Includes 4-page insert. Has 10 tracks.

ELVIS: A LEGENDARY PERFORMER (VOLUMES 1 & 2)

RCA/BMG CAD1-2705/
CAD1-2706 ....10/92   25-35
Special Products limited edition package of the previous two CDs, in a 12" x 15" gift box. Includes: 1) Outer box. 2) Tee shirt picturing the Elvis Commemorative U.S. Postage Stamp. Mail order offer. Has 20 tracks.

ELVIS ARON PRESLEY "FOREVER"

RCA/BMG/Pair
PDC2-1185 ....12/87   15-25
Disc is stock with black and blue print. Includes 4-page insert. Has 16 tracks.

ELVIS AS RECORDED AT MADISON SQUARE GARDEN

RCA/BMG 54776-2 ....4/92   12-15
Disc is black with silver print. Includes 8-page booklet. Has 22 tracks.

ELVIS AT HIS ROMANTIC BEST

RCA/BMG
DPC1-0984 ....7/91   20-30
Disc is stock with black and red print. Includes 4-page insert. Special Products mail order offer from Avon. Has 14 tracks.

ELVIS BIRTHDAY TRIBUTE

Creative Radio 12/92   30-40
Disc is pink. Intended for radio broadcast. Includes 4-page insert with cue information. Has 13 tracks.

ELVIS' CHRISTMAS ALBUM

RCA Victor
PCD1-5486 ....8/85   15-25
Disc is stock with blue and white print. Pressed in Japan for U.S. release. Includes 16-page insert booklet. Has 12 tracks.

RCA/BMG
PCD1-5486 ....2/90   10-15
Disc is stock with blue and white print. Pressed in U.S. Includes 16-page insert booklet. Has 12 tracks.

ELVIS' CHRISTMAS ALBUM (RCA CAMDEN CLASSICS)

RCA/Camden/BMG
CAD1-2428 ....8/87   7-10
Disc is stock with black and blue print. Includes 4-page insert. Has 10 tracks.

RCA/Camden/BMG
CAD1-2428 ....9/95   7-10
Disc is green with black and silver print. Cover is different from above pressing. Includes 4-page insert. Has 10 tracks.

ELVIS – COMMAND PERFORMANCES: see COMMAND PERFORMANCES

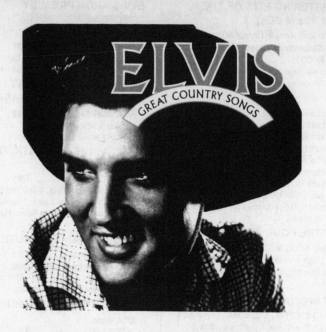

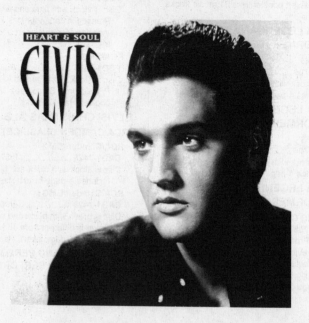

ELVIS COUNTRY
(I'M 10,000 YEARS OLD)

RCA/BMG 66279-2 ....7/93   12-15
Disc is black with silver print. Includes 4-page insert. Has 12 tracks, plus random, annoying snippets of *I Was Born About Ten Thousand Years Ago*.

ELVIS COUNTRY

RCA/BMG 6330-2-R 10/88   20-30
Disc is stock with black print. Includes 4-page insert, the front cover of which mistakenly has art identical to that used on the previous release, *Elvis Country (I'm 10,000 Years Old)*. Has eight tracks.

RCA/BMG 6330-2-R 11/88   10-15
Disc is stock with black print. Includes 4-page insert, the front cover of which now has the same art as on the *I Was the One* LP. Has eight tracks.

RCA/BMG 66405-2 ....6/94   10-15
Disc is red and black with silver print. Includes 4-page insert. Has eight tracks.

ELVIS DOUBLE FEATURE
(Speedway & Clambake)

RCA/BMG/Pair PDC2-1250 (CXD-3017) 9/89   20-25
Disc is stock with black and blue print. Includes 4-page insert. Has 17 tracks, one by Nancy Sinatra.

ELVIS DOUBLE FEATURES
(4 CDs)

RCA/BMG 61835-2 ....1/93   100-150
Packaged in a felt-lined metal film canister. All discs have two color pictures of Elvis. A QVC Home Shopping Channel, exclusive mail order offer. Includes: 1) Disc 1: *Kid Galahad & Girls! Girls! Girls!* Disc 2: *It Happened at the World's Fair & Fun in Acapulco*. Disc 3: *Viva Las Vegas & Roustabout*. Disc 4: *Harum Scarum & Girl Happy*. 2) Color, 20-page booklet. 3) "Elvis, the King of Rock & Roll" pin. 4) Certificate of limited edition authenticity—15,000 sets made. 5) Four black and white 8" x 10" Elvis photos from films featured on CD. 6) Single, card stock page of "Recording Data." Has 91 tracks.

ELVIS DOUBLE FEATURES
(HARUM SCARUM & GIRL HAPPY)

RCA/BMG 66128-2 ....2/93   13-18
Disc is black with silver print. Includes 16-page booklet. Has 22 tracks.

ELVIS DOUBLE FEATURES
(VIVA LAS VEGAS & ROUSTABOUT)

RCA/BMG 66129-2 ....2/93   13-18
Disc is black with silver print. Includes 16-page booklet. Has 24 tracks.

ELVIS DOUBLE FEATURES
(KID GALAHAD & GIRLS! GIRLS! GIRLS!)

RCA/BMG 66130-2 ....2/93   13-18
Disc is black with silver print. Includes 16-page booklet. Has 23 tracks.

ELVIS DOUBLE FEATURES
(IT HAPPENED AT THE WORLD'S FAIR & FUN IN ACAPULCO)

RCA/BMG 66131-2 ....2/93   13-18
Disc is black with silver print. Includes 16-page booklet. Has 22 tracks.

ELVIS DOUBLE FEATURES
(FRANKIE AND JOHNNY & PARADISE, HAWAIIAN STYLE)

RCA/BMG 66360-2 ....6/94   13-18
Disc is black with silver print. Includes 12-page booklet. Has 23 tracks.

ELVIS DOUBLE FEATURES
(SPINOUT & DOUBLE TROUBLE)

RCA/BMG 66361-2 ....6/94   13-18
Disc is black with silver print. Includes 12-page booklet. Has 18 tracks.

ELVIS DOUBLE FEATURES
(KISSIN' COUSINS, CLAMBAKE & STAY AWAY JOE)

RCA/BMG 66362-2 ....6/94   13-18
Disc is black with silver print. Includes 12-page booklet. Has 24 tracks.

ELVIS DOUBLE FEATURES
(FLAMING STAR, FOLLOW THAT DREAM & WILD IN THE COUNTRY)

RCA/BMG 66557-2 ....3/95   13-18
Disc is black with silver print. Includes 12-page booklet. Has 20 tracks.

ELVIS DOUBLE FEATURES
(EASY COME, EASY GO & SPEEDWAY)

RCA/BMG 66558-2 ....3/95   13-18
Disc is black with silver print. Includes 12-page booklet. Has 20 tracks.

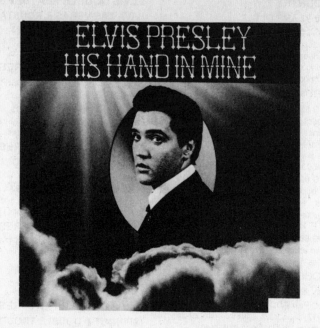

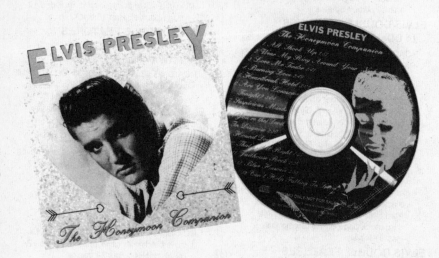

ELVIS DOUBLE FEATURES
(LIVE A LITTLE, LOVE A LITTLE, CHARRO!, TROUBLE WITH GIRLS & CHANGE OF HABIT)

RCA/BMG 66559-2 ....3/95   13-18
Disc is black with silver print. Includes 12-page booklet. Has 20 tracks.

ELVIS! ELVIS! ELVIS!
(THE KING AND HIS MOVIES)

RCA/BMG
DPC 11624......................8/97   25-30
Disc is stock with black print. Included with the 128-page book *Elvis! Elvis! Elvis!* by Peter Guttmacher. Has 15 tracks.

ELVIS 15th ANNIVERSARY (6 CDs)

Creative Radio 8/92   125-135
Discs are black with gold print. Intended for radio broadcast. Includes folder of loose cue sheets. No inserts in jewel boxes. Only 500 pressed. Has 87 music tracks plus talk.

ELVIS '56

RCA/BMG 66817-2.........4/96   20-25
Dark black and white picture disc with white print. Collectors edition CD and 28-page booklet are packaged in a hardcover book. Has 22 tracks.

RCA/BMG 66856-2.........4/96   13-18
Light black and white picture disc with white print. Includes 8-page booklet. Has 22 tracks.

ELVIS '56 ADVANCE MUSIC

RCA/BMG
RADV-66856-2.................2/96   75-100
Disc is stock with black print. Promotional issue. Includes insert. Has 22 tracks.

ELVIS FOR EVERYONE!

RCA/BMG 3450-2-R 10/90   25-30
Disc is stock with black print. Includes 4-page insert. Has 12 tracks.

RCA/BMG 53450-2 ....4/95   15-20
Disc is stock with silver print. Includes 8-page insert booklet. Has 12 tracks.

ELVIS FROM NASHVILLE TO MEMPHIS: see FROM NASHVILLE TO MEMPHIS

ELVIS' GOLDEN RECORDS

RCA Victor
PCD1-1707 ....5/84   250-300
Disc is stock with blue and white print. Pressed in Japan for U.S. release. Includes 8-page booklet. Has 14 tracks.

RCA Victor
PCD1-5196 ....11/84   30-40
Disc is stock with blue and white print. Pressed in U.S. Includes 8-page booklet. Has 14 tracks.

RCA/BMG 67462-2 ....7/97   13-18
Disc is made to simulate a gold record with dark blue label and silver print. Includes 8-page booklet. Back cover has new artwork. Has 20 tracks, including six bonus cuts.

ELVIS' GOLD RECORDS, VOL. 2
(50,000,000 ELVIS FANS CAN'T BE WRONG)

RCA Victor
PCD1-2075 ....9/84   250-300
Disc is stock with blue and white print. Pressed in Japan for U.S. release. Includes 4-page insert. Has 10 tracks.

RCA Victor
PCD1-5197 ....11/84   30-40
Disc is stock with blue and white print. Pressed in U.S. Includes 4-page booklet. Has 10 tracks.

RCA Victor
PCD1-5197 ....'85   700-1000
Disc has same art as is used on insert (and LP) cover, picturing Elvis in his gold suit. Only text shown is the word "Sample" at bottom, in black print. Experimental disc, reportedly only 50 made. Includes 4-page insert. Has 10 tracks.

RCA/BMG 67463-2 ....7/97   13-18
Disc is made to simulate a gold record with red label and silver print. Includes 8-page booklet. Back cover has new artwork. Has 20 tracks, including 10 bonus cuts.

ELVIS' GOLDEN RECORDS VOL. 3

RCA/BMG 2765-2-R 4/90   12-15
Disc is stock with black print. Includes single sheet insert printed on both sides. Has 12 tracks.

RCA/BMG 67464-2 ....7/97   13-18
Disc is made to simulate a gold record with light blue label and silver print. Includes 8-page booklet. Back cover has new artwork. Has 18 tracks, including six bonus cuts.

A HUNDRED YEARS FROM NOW

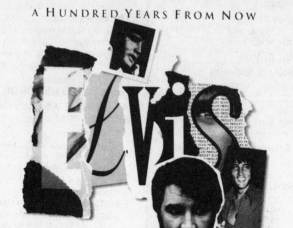

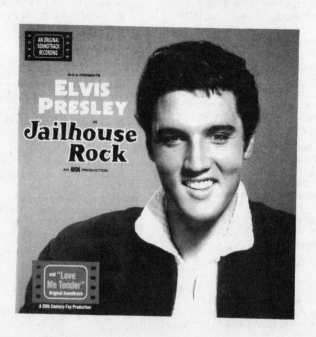

ELVIS' GOLD RECORDS, VOL. 4

RCA/BMG 1297-2-R ....7/90　　**12-15**
Disc is stock with black print. Includes 4-
page insert. Has 12 tracks.

RCA/BMG 67465-2 ....7/97　　**13-18**
Disc is made to simulate a gold record with
green label and silver print. Includes 8-
page booklet. Back cover has new
artwork. Has 18 tracks, including six
bonus cuts.

ELVIS' GOLD RECORDS, VOL. 5

RCA Victor
PCD1-4941 ....5/84　　**15-25**
Disc is stock with blue and white print.
Pressed in Japan for U.S. release.
Includes 4-page insert. Has 10 tracks.

RCA/BMG
PCD1-4941 ....3/88　　**12-15**
Disc is stock with blue and white print.
Pressed in U.S. Includes 4-page insert.
Has 10 tracks.

RCA/BMG 67466-2 ....7/97　　**13-18**
Disc is made to simulate a gold record with
medium blue label and silver print.
Includes 8-page booklet. Back cover has
new artwork. Has 16 tracks, including six
bonus cuts.

ELVIS GOSPEL (1957 – 1971)
(KNOWN ONLY TO HIM)

RCA/BMG 9586-2-R ....4/89　　**14-18**
Disc is stock with black print. Includes 4-
page insert. Has 14 tracks.

ELVIS: GREAT COUNTRY SONGS

RCA/BMG 66880-2.......10/96　　**14-18**
Disc is red with silver and gold print.
Includes 12-page insert booklet. Has 24
tracks.

ELVIS' GREATEST JUKEBOX HITS

RCA/BMG 67565-2.........9/97　　**14-18**
Disc is black, made to simulate a 45 rpm
record with yellow label and black print.
Includes insert. Has 23 tracks.

ELVIS! HIS GREATEST HITS
(4 CDs)

RCA/BMG/Reader's Digest
RDU 010 ....10/96　　**55-60**
Turquoise and gray picture discs with
turquoise and white print. Includes 48-
page insert booklet. Special Collectors
Edition mail order offer. Has 84 tracks.

ELVIS – HIS LIFE AND MUSIC
(4 CDs)

RCA/BMG ....8/94　　**90-100**

Discs are stock with black print. Tracks are
from *Elvis' Gold Records*, Vol. 1-4. This
numbered, limited edition box set
includes: 1) 16-page sessions journal; 2)
176-page book, *Elvis: His Life and Music*
by Timothy Frew. Set comes in hard
black slipcase. First sold through QVC
Home Shopping Channel. Has 48
tracks.

ELVIS IN CONCERT

RCA/BMG 52587-2 ....5/92　　**15-20**
Disc is black with silver print. Includes 8-
page insert booklet. Has 32 tracks.

ELVIS IN HOLLYWOOD

RCA/BMG 15811-2 ....12/93　　**45-55**
Elvis is not heard on this disc, although it
does have interviews with people who
knew him. Offered as a bonus item, by
mail order from QVC Home Shopping
Channel, to buyers of an Elvis set.
Included in the package, but not in the
CD price range, are a VHS cassette of
Elvis in Hollywood, 16-page booklet, and
four Elvis prints. Disc has a picture of
Elvis, as does the cardboard disc holder.
With 5000 pressed and only 250 sold,
the balance were returned to RCA and
destroyed.

ELVIS IN NASHVILLE (1956-1971)

RCA/BMG 8468-2-R .....10/88　　**20-25**
Disc is stock with black print. Includes 8-
page insert booklet. Has 14 tracks.

ELVIS IN PERSON AT THE
INTERNATIONAL HOTEL

RCA/BMG 53892-2 ....10/92　　**12-15**
Disc is black with silver print. Includes 8-
page insert booklet. Has 12 tracks.

ELVIS IS BACK!

RCA/BMG 2231-2-R .....11/88　　**12-15**
Disc is stock with black print. Includes 4-
page insert. Has 12 tracks.

RCA/BMG/DCC
GZS-1111-2 ....6/97　　**30-40**
Disc is 24 kt. gold with black print. Includes
8-page insert. Numbered, limited edition.
Has 12 tracks.

ELVIS MANIA (2 CDs)

Various Artists Compilation
Live Gold
LG 40004/50005 ....'91　　**20-25**
Includes insert booklet. Contains 52 novelty
and tribute songs. Has Elvis interview.
Pressed in Czechoslovakia for U.S.
release.

ELVIS MANIA 2

Various Artists Compilation

Live Gold LG 120012 ....'92   **15-18**
Includes insert booklet. Contains 27 novelty
and tribute songs. Has portions of
several Elvis songs. Pressed in
Czechoslovakia for U.S. release.

ELVIS/NBC-TV SPECIAL: see ELVIS
(NBC-TV SPECIAL)

ELVIS NOW

RCA/BMG 54671-2 ....7/93   **12-15**
Disc is black with silver print. Includes 4-
page insert. Has 10 tracks.

ELVIS PRESLEY

RCA Victor

PCD1-1254 ....5/84   **250-300**
Disc is stock with blue and white print.
Pressed in Japan for U.S. release.
Includes 4-page insert. Has 12 tracks.

RCA Victor

PCD1-5198 ....11/84   **30-40**
Disc is stock with blue and white print.
Pressed in U.S. Includes 4-page insert.
Has 12 tracks.

RCA/BMG 66659-2.........7/95   **25-30**
Disc is 24 kt. gold with black print. Includes
4-page insert. Limited Collectors Edition.
Has 12 tracks.

ELVIS PRESLEY & JIM REEVES
CHRISTMAS FAVORITES

Audio Treasures

ATCD-2107-2..................5/91   **15-20**
Disc is stock with black and red print. RCA
Special Products offer. Includes insert.
Has 10 tracks, five by each artist.

Audio Treasures

ATCD-2107-2................10/96   **10-15**
Although this disc has the same number as
above, it is actually a reissue of *Country
Christmas*. RCA Special Products offer.
Includes insert. Has 12 tracks, six by
each artist.

ELVIS PRESLEY: 1954 – 1961

Time-Life TCD-106......... 3/88   **15-20**
Disc is stock with black print. Includes 8-
page booklet insert. Mail order offer. Has
22 tracks.

ELVIS PRESLEY BIRTHDAY
TRIBUTE (4 CDs)

Unistar 01/03-01/08........1/92   **100-125**
Discs are stock with blue print. Intended for
radio broadcast. Limited edition.

Includes cue sheets for 4-hour show.
Has 58 tracks.

ELVIS PRESLEY COLLECTION
(LOVE SONGS) (2 CDs)

RCA/BMG/Time-Life

69400-2 ....9/97   **20-25**
Red and black picture discs with silver and
black print. Includes 16-page insert
booklet. First in a series of Elvis Time-
Life CDs. Mail order offer. Has 31 tracks.

ELVIS PRESLEY COLLECTION
(ROCK 'N' ROLL) (2 CDs)

RCA/BMG/Time-Life

69401-2 ....11/97   **20-25**
Blue and black picture discs with silver and
black print. Includes 16-page insert
booklet. Second in a series of Elvis
Time-Life CDs. Mail order offer. Has 31
tracks.

ELVIS PRESLEY COLLECTION
(MOVIE MAGIC) (2 CDs)

RCA/BMG/Time-Life

69404-2 ....12/97   **20-25**
Mustard and black picture discs with silver
and black print. Includes 16-page insert
booklet. Third in a series of Elvis Time-
Life CDs. Mail order offer. Has 31 tracks.

ELVIS PRESLEY GOSPEL
TREASURY (2 CDs)

RCA/BMG/Heartland

DMC2-1427 ....12/96   **20-25**
Discs are stock with black print. Includes 4-
page insert. Has 26 tracks.

ELVIS PRESLEY: GREAT
PERFORMANCES

RCA/BMG/Pair PDC2-1251

(CXD-3018) 1/90   **10-12**
Disc is stock with black and blue print.
Includes 4-page insert. Has 16 tracks.

ELVIS PRESLEY INTERVIEWS
(TALKING WITH THE KING)
(3 CDs)

Laserlight Digital

55 581 ....9/96   **15-20**
Discs are stock and yellow with black print.
This is an Audio Book Set on CD. Discs
are: 1) *In the Beginning*. 2) *Eye of the
Hurricane*. 3) *On the Road Interviews*.
Includes inserts. Interviews only. Discs
are also listed separately.

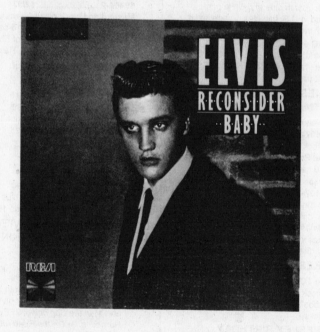

ELVIS PRESLEY LOVE SONGS

RCA/BMG 67595-2.........1/98   **14-18**
Disc is stock with yellow, silver and black artwork and print. Includes insert. Mail order offer. Has 18 tracks.

ELVIS PRESLEY PLATINUM
(A LIFE IN MUSIC) (4 CDs)

RCA/BMG 67469-2.........7/97   **60-70**
These are picture discs. Includes 48-page booklet. Limited time offer. Has 100 tracks; 77 are previously unreleased performances.

ELVIS PRESLEY PLATINUM IN-STORE SAMPLER

RCA/BMG
RJC-67568-2....................8/97   **75-100**
Disc is stock with black print. Includes insert. Used to promote *Elvis Presley Platinum* box set. Has 12 tracks.

ELVIS PRESLEY PLATINUM SAMPLER

RCA/BMG
RDJ-67529-2....................5/97   **75-125**
Disc is white with black print. Includes insert. Used to promote *Elvis Presley Platinum* box set at a BMG Marketing convention. Has four tracks.

ELVIS PRESLEY RADIO SPECIAL

RCA/BMG
RDJ-66121-2.................11/92   **50-75**
Disc is stock with black print. Promotional issue only, made for radio stations to plug the box set, *King of Rock 'N' Roll (Complete 50's Masters)*. Includes single sheet insert. Also includes a prepaid postcard with a few survey questions and mailing list update. Has 17 tracks plus excerpts of Elvis being interviewed.

ELVIS PRESLEY SINGS LEIBER & STOLLER

RCA/BMG 3026-2-R 4/91   **15-20**
Disc is stock with black print. Includes 6-page insert. Has 21 tracks.

ELVIS PRESLEY YEARS (4 CDs)
Various Artists Compilation

RCA/BMG/Reader's Digest
RBD-236/CD1 ....'91   **60-70**
Discs are stock with black and blue print. In multi-disc jewel box. Includes 48-page booklet. Mail order offer. Has 84 tracks, 28 by Elvis.

ELVIS RECORDED LIVE ON STAGE IN MEMPHIS

RCA/BMG 50606-2 ....3/94   **12-15**
Disc is black with silver print. Includes 8-page booklet. Has 16 tracks.

ELVIS SINGS FOR CHILDREN AND GROWNUPS TOO!

RCA/BMG
CAD1-2704 ....8/89   **7-10**
Disc is stock with black and blue print. Includes 4-page insert. Has 10 tracks. RCA Special Products issue.

ELVIS SINGS HITS FROM HIS MOVIES, VOL. 1

RCA/BMG
CAD1-2567 ....6/96   **10-12**
Disc is stock and black with blue print. Special Products mail order offer from Avon. Has 10 tracks.

ELVIS SINGS THE WONDERFUL WORLD OF CHRISTMAS

RCA/BMG 4579-2-R 8/88   **12-15**
Disc is stock with black print. Includes 4-page insert. Has 12 tracks. RCA Special Products issue.

ELVIS TAPES

Jerden JRCD-7005 ....'92   **10-15**
Disc is stock with black and green print. Contains two Elvis interviews.

ELVIS TAPES, VOL. 2

Jerden JRCD-7017 ....9/97   **15-18**
Disc is stock with black and green print. Contains three Elvis interviews.

ELVIS – THAT'S THE WAY IT IS:
see THAT'S THE WAY IT IS

ELVIS, THE KING: 1954 – 1965

Time-Life TCD-126 ....'90   **15-20**
Disc is stock with black and red print. Includes 8-page booklet. Has 22 tracks.

ELVIS – THE OTHER SIDES
(WORLDWIDE GOLD AWARD HITS, VOL. 2) (2 CDs)

RCA/BMG 66921-2.........8/96   **25-30**
Each gold and black picture disc has its own jewel box and unique inserts. Includes: 1) Numbered long box with shrink sticker promoting contents and 25th anniversary of LP release. 2) Special 12-page souvenir booklet. 3) Original First Day of Issue Elvis stamp on limited edition RCA envelope. Has 50 tracks.

ELVIS – THE TRIBUTE
A BIOGRAPHY (3 CDs)

**Entertainment Radio
Network** 9/94   **100-125**
Disc 1: Red and black picture disc. Disc 2:
Blue and black picture disc. Disc 3:
Purple and black picture disc. Limited
edition. Includes cue sheets for 3-hour
radio broadcast promoting "Elvis - The
Tribute" show on Pay-Per-View. Has 47
tracks.

ELVIS THE KING OF ROCK 'N' ROLL:
see KING OF ROCK 'N' ROLL

ELVIS TODAY

RCA/BMG 51039-2 ....4/92   **12-15**
Disc is black with silver print. Includes 8-
page booklet. Has 10 tracks.

ELVIS 20TH ANNIVERSARY RADIO
SHOW (3 CDs)

**Creative Radio
818 991 3892** 8/97   **60-75**
Discs are gold with silver print. Intended for
radio broadcast. Includes cue sheets for
3-hour radio show. Has 44 tracks.

ELVIS 20TH ANNIVERSARY
SAMPLER

RCA/BMG 67537-2.........6/97   **10-20**
Black and white picture disc with blue and
gold print. Includes 4-page insert. Has
six tracks. Special Products issue for
Blockbuster Music stores.

ELVIS 24 KARAT HITS!

**RCA/BMG/DCC
GZS-1117-2** 9/97   **30-40**
Disc is 24 kt. gold with black print. Includes
12-page insert. Numbered, limited
edition. Has 24 tracks.

ELVIS WALK A MILE IN MY SHOES:
see WALK A MILE IN MY SHOES

ELVIS: 15th ANNIVERSARY RADIO
SHOW: see ELVIS 15th
ANNIVERSARY

ESSENTIAL ELVIS
(THE FIRST MOVIES)

RCA/BMG 6738-2-R 1/88   **14-18**
Disc is stock with black print. Includes 8-
page booklet. Has 27 tracks.

ESSENTIAL ELVIS, VOL. 2:

see STEREO '57

ESSENTIAL ELVIS, VOL. 3:

see HITS LIKE NEVER BEFORE

ESSENTIAL ELVIS, VOL. 4:

see HUNDRED YEARS FROM NOW

ESSENTIAL 60's MASTERS:

see FROM NASHVILLE TO MEMPHIS

ESSENTIAL 60's MASTERS II:

see ELVIS COMMAND
PERFORMANCES

ESSENTIAL 70's MASTERS:

see WALK A MILE IN MY SHOES

EYE OF THE HURRICANE

**Laserlight Digital
12 788** 9/96   **6-8**
Disc is stock and yellow with black print.
This is an Audio Book on CD. Includes
4-page insert. Contains only interviews.

FAMILY CHRISTMAS COLLECTION
(4 CDs)

Various Artists Compilation
**Time-Life
TCD-131A/B/C/D** ....'90   **50-60**
Includes inserts. Has three Elvis tracks.

FEEL 21 AGAIN/RARITIES, VOL. 4

Various Artists Compilation
Westwood One ....'91   **40-60**
Includes insert. Has one Elvis track. Radio
promotional CD.

50 BELOVED SONGS OF FAITH
(2 CDs)

Various Artists Compilation
**RCA/BMG/Reader's Digest
BMD2-100** ....'90   **25-30**
Includes insert. Mail order offer. Has one
Elvis track.

50 CHRISTMAS FAVORITES
(2 CDs)

Various Artists Compilation
**Time-Life
TCD-130 A/B** ....'90   **25-30**
Includes inserts. Mail order offer. Has two
Elvis tracks.

50 GREATEST HITS (2 CDs)

RCA/BMG 15018-2 ....'91   **150-200**
Discs are stock with black and red print.
Two CDs in a long box. RCA Special
Products, mail order offer.

50,000,000 ELVIS FANS CAN'T BE
WRONG: see ELVIS' GOLD
RECORDS,VOL. 2

50 WORLDWIDE GOLD HITS, VOL. 1 (2 CDs)

RCA/BMG 6401-2-R 8/88   35-45
Discs are light gold with black print on the
top side and the same gold tint on the
playing side. CDs are in two jewel
boxes, each with a 4-page insert.

RCA/BMG 6401-2-R 8/89   20-30
Discs are light gold with black print on the
top side, but the playing side is
stock—no gold tint. CDs are in two jewel
boxes, each with a 4-page insert.

RCA/BMG 56401-2-R 4/96   20-30
Discs are dark gold with silver outer band.
Slipcase on multi-disc jewel box has
same artwork as on 4-page insert.

50 YEARS – 50 HITS (2 CDs)

RCA/BMG
SVC2-0710-1/2 ....9/90   25-30
Discs are stock with black and red print.
Includes 4-page insert. Two discs in one
jewel box. RCA Special Products, mail
order offer.

FIRESIDE CHRISTMAS (2 CDs)

Various Artists Compilation
RCA/BMG/Pair
PCD2-1219 ....'88   15-20
Includes insert. Has one Elvis track.

FOR LP FANS ONLY

RCA/BMG 1990-2-R 4/89   10-15
Disc is stock with black print. Includes 4-
page insert. Has 10 tracks.

FORREST GUMP

**(Original Motion Picture Soundtrack)
(2 CDs)**
Various Artists Compilation
Epic E2K 66329-2 ....'94   20-25
Includes 14-page insert. Has one Elvis
track.

14 #1 COUNTRY HITS

Various Artists Compilation
RCA/BMG 7004-2-R ....'89   12-15
Includes insert. Has 14 tracks, one by
Elvis.

FROM ELVIS IN MEMPHIS

RCA/BMG 51456-2 ....8/91   12-15
Disc is stock with black print. Includes 8-
page insert booklet. Has 12 tracks.

FROM ELVIS PRESLEY BOULEVARD, MEMPHIS, TENNESSEE

RCA/BMG 1506-2-R 4/88   12-15

Disc is stock with black print. Includes 4-
page insert. Has 10 tracks.

FROM NASHVILLE TO MEMPHIS (ESSENTIAL 60's MASTERS I) (5 CDs)

RCA/BMG 66160-2 ....9/93   70-80
Disc 1: Lavender with black and white print.
Disc 2: Pink with black and white print.
Disc 3: Red with black and white print.
Disc 4: Orange with black and white
print. Disc 5: Blue with black and white
print. Each disc has its own jewel box,
individual photo of Elvis, and unique
inserts. Includes: 1) Numbered long box
with shrink sticker promoting contents.
2) Color, 94-page booklet. 3) Sheet of
36 "Collectible Stamps of Elvis Presley's
1960's RCA Records Label Covers."
Worth noting is that the preparers of this
set apparently did not know that the first
lines of the *This Time/I Can't Stop
Loving You* medley are from *It's My Way
(Of Loving You)* (written and originally
recorded by Wayne Walker in 1956,
then by Dick Flood in 1960). The track
should read: *It's My Way (Of Loving
You)/This Time/I Can't Stop Loving You.*
Has 130 tracks.

RCA/BMG 66160-2 ....9/93   90-100
Same as above, but designated as a
promotional issue. Two different stickers
with either NFS-1 or PRES-4/2 were on
shrink wrap.

FROM NASHVILLE TO MEMPHIS (OUT OF THE BOX – 6 FROM THE 60's)

RCA/BMG
RDJ 62624-2 ....8/93   25-40
Picture disc is yellow with blue print.
Promotional issue only, used to plug the
box set of the same title. Includes 4-
page insert. Has six tracks.

FROM THE BEGINNING WE MADE MUSIC: see SHAKE, RATTLE & ROLL (FROM THE BEGINNING WE MADE MUSIC)

G.I. BLUES

RCA/BMG 3735-2-R 4/88   **12-15**
Disc is stock with black print. Includes 4-page insert. Showing remarkable lack of concern for accuracy, the cover insert and rear, tray insert both show *What's She Really Like* as "She's All Mine." The disc has the correct title. Also, on both of the inserts and the disc, *Tonight is All Right for Love* is mistakenly shown as "Tonight Is So Right for Love (Alternate Version)." It is of course not an alternate take, but a completely different piece of music which just happens to have very similar lyrics. Has 12 tracks.

RCA/BMG 66960-2 ....4/97   **15-18**
Black and white picture disc. Includes 8-page insert booklet. Has 20 tracks, including eight bonus cuts.

RCA/BMG 67460-2 ....4/97   **20-25**
Dark red picture disc with blue print. Collectors Edition. The 28-page booklet and disc are part of a deluxe hard cover book. Included in the 20 tracks are eight alternates and outtakes.

GOD BLESS THE U.S.A (4 CDs)

Various Artists Compilation

RCA/Reader's Digest
RBD-018/CD1 ....'92   **55-60**
Includes 48-page booklet. Mail order offer. Has three Elvis tracks.

GOLDEN COUNTRY (RCA) OLDIES

Various Artists Compilation

RCA Victor
5962-2-RDJ ....'87   **150-200**
Includes insert. Has two Elvis tracks. Promotional issue only.

GOLDEN DAYS OF ROCK 'N' ROLL (3 CDs)

Various Artists Compilation

RCA/BMG/Reader's Digest
RC7-085-1/2/3 ....'97   **45-50**
Includes 48-page booklet. Mail order offer. Has two Elvis tracks.

GOOD ROCKIN' TONIGHT (2 CDs)

RCA/BMG
SVC2-0824 ....1/88   **75-100**
Discs are stock with black and red print. Includes 4-page insert. Two discs in one jewel box. RCA Special Products, mail order offer. Has 32 tracks.

GOOD TIMES

RCA/BMG 50475-2 ....3/94   **12-15**

Disc is black with silver print. Includes 8-page insert booklet. Has 10 tracks.

GREAT AMERICAN VOCALISTS

Various Artists Compilation

RCA/BMG-9965-2-R ....'90   **20-25**
Disc is stock with black print. Includes 8-page insert. Has 20 tracks, including one by Elvis.

GREAT HITS OF 1956-'57

RCA/BMG/Reader's Digest
RBD-072/CD1 ....7/90   **50-75**
Disc is stock with black print. Includes 4-page insert. Has 12 tracks. Offered as a bonus to buyers of another CD set which had no Elvis tracks.

GREAT PERFORMANCES

RCA/BMG 2227-2-R 8/90   **15-18**
Disc is stock with black print. Includes 6-page insert. Has 20 tracks.

GREAT VICTOR DUETS

Various Artists Compilation

RCA/BMG-9967-2-R ....'90   **20-25**
Disc is stock with black print. Includes 8-page insert. Has 20 tracks, including one by Elvis and Ann-Margret.

GREATEST HITS OF THE '50S

Various Artists Compilation

RCA/BMG DPC1-1056 .....'92   **8-12**
Includes insert. Has one Elvis track.

HAPPY HOLIDAYS, VOL. 25 (2 CDs)

Various Artists Compilation

RCA/BMG DPL2-0936 ......'90   **20-25**
Has one Elvis track. Special Products offer from True Value Hardware.

HAPPY HOLIDAYS, VOL. 28

Various Artists Compilation

RCA/BMG DPC1-1107 .....'93   **10-15**
Has one Elvis track. Special Products offer from True Value Hardware.

HAPPY HOLIDAYS, VOL. 32

Various Artists Compilation

RCA/BMG DPC1-1662 .....'97   **10-15**
Has one Elvis track. Special Products offer from True Value Hardware.

HE TOUCHED ME

RCA/BMG 51923-2 ....3/92   **12-15**
Disc is black with silver print. Includes 8-page lyrics/insert booklet. Has 12 tracks.

HEART AND SOUL

RCA/BMG 66532-2 ....1/95   **14-18**
Disc is black with silver print. Includes 4-page insert. Has 22 tracks.

HEART 'N' SOUL OF ROCK 'N' ROLL (4 CDs)

Various Artists Compilation
RCA/BMG/Reader's Digest
RD7-008-1/2/3/4................'97   55-60
Includes 48-page booklet. Mail order offer. Has one Elvis track.

HEART OF DIXIE

(Original Motion Picture Soundtrack)
Various Artists Compilation
A&M CD 3930 ....'89   14-18
Includes insert. Has 10 tracks, two by Elvis.
A&M CD 3930 ....'89   20-25
Includes insert. Has 10 tracks, two by Elvis. Promotional issue only.

HEARTBREAK HOTEL

(Original Motion Picture Soundtrack)
Various Artists Compilation
RCA/BMG 8533-2-R 11/88   20-25
Disc is stock with black print. Includes 4-page insert. Has 11 tracks, five by Elvis.

HEARTBREAK HOTEL

(HOUND DOG & OTHER TOP TEN HITS)
RCA/BMG 2079-2-R 9/90   8-12
Disc is stock with black print. Includes 4-page insert. Has 8 tracks.

HEARTBREAK HOTEL

(I WAS THE ONE)
RCA/BMG 64475-2.........4/96   8-12
Picture disc. Includes insert. Used to promote *Elvis 56*. Has four tracks.

HIS HAND IN MINE

RCA/BMG 1319-2-R 8/88   12-15
Disc is stock with black print. Includes 4-page insert. Has 15 tracks.

HITS LIKE NEVER BEFORE

(ESSENTIAL ELVIS, VOL. 3)
RCA/BMG 2229-2-R 1/91   14-18
Disc is stock with black print. Includes 8-page insert booklet. Has 24 tracks.

HOLIDAY HAPPENING/ CHRISTMAS RARITIES ON CD, VOL. 8

Various Artists Compilation
Westwood One ....'91   50-75
Includes insert. Has one Elvis track. Promotional issue only.

HOLIDAY MUSIC COLLECTION

Various Artists Compilation
RCA/BMG DPC1-1004 .....'97   15-20

Includes insert. Has one Elvis track.

HOLLYWOOD MEN

Various Artists Compilation
RCA/BMG 9966-2-R ....'90   20-25
Includes insert. Has one Elvis track.

HONEYMOON COMPANION

RCA/BMG RDJ
66124-2 ....11/92   75-100
Disc is stock with pink print and has a hologramed photo of Elvis. Includes single sheet insert. Promotional issue only, made to promote Elvis' original versions of songs used in the film, *Honeymoon in Vegas*. Has 13 tracks.

HOORAY FOR HOLLYWOOD (2 CDs)

Various Artists Compilation
RCA/BMG 66099-2 ....'92   20-25
Includes 16-page booklet. Has one track by Elvis.

HOUND DOG/DON'T BE CRUEL

RCA/BMG 8990-2-RH ......'89   10-20
Disc is stock with black print. Includes single sheet insert. "Gold Standard Single, Commemorative Juke Box Series." Has two tracks. Also sold as part of a 5-disc set with juke box title strips. Value of set is $100 to $125.

HOW GREAT THOU ART (AS SUNG BY ELVIS)

RCA/BMG 3758-2-R 8/88   12-15
Disc is stock with black print. Includes 4-page insert. Has 14 tracks.

HUNDRED YEARS FROM NOW (ESSENTIAL ELVIS, VOL. 4)

RCA/BMG 66866-2 ....7/96   14-18
Disc is gray with black and red print. Includes 8-page insert booklet. Has 22 tracks.

IF EVERY DAY WAS LIKE CHRISTMAS

RCA/BMG 66482-2........10/94   15-18
Disc is red with gold print. Includes 16-page insert booklet. Has 25 tracks.
RCA/BMG 66506-2.......11/94   20-25
Disc is red with gold print. Includes 16-page insert booklet. Special Collectors Edition package opens up to a 12" by 12" three-dimensional "Winter at Graceland" pop-up. Has 25 tracks.

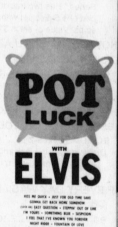

IN THE BEGINNING
Laserlight Digital
12 787 ....9/96   6-8
Disc is stock and yellow with black print.
This is an Audio Book on CD. Includes
4-page insert. Contains only interviews.

JAILHOUSE ROCK AND LOVE ME
TENDER
RCA/BMG 67453-2 ....4/97   15-18
Red and black picture disc. Includes 12-
page insert booklet. Has 20 tracks.

JAILHOUSE ROCK/TREAT ME
NICE
RCA/BMG 8992-2-RH ......'89   10-20
Disc is stock with black print. Includes
single sheet insert. "Gold Standard
Single, Commemorative Juke Box
Series." Has two tracks. Also sold as
part of a 5-disc set with juke box title
strips. Value of set is $100 to $125.

JERRY MAGUIRE
(Original Motion Picture Soundtrack)
Various Artists Compilation
Epic EK 67910 ....'96   15-18
Includes 4-fold insert. Has one Elvis track.

KING CREOLE
RCA/BMG 3733-2-R 4/88   12-15
Disc is stock with black print. Includes 4-
page insert. Has 11 tracks.
RCA/BMG 67454-2 ....4/97   15-18
Brown and white picture disc. Includes 8-
page insert. Has 18 tracks, including
seven bonus cuts.

KING OF ROCK 'N' ROLL
RCA/BMG 62404-2 ....10/92   15-20
Mustard colored picture disc. Includes two
juke box title strips. Made to promote the
box set, *King of Rock 'N' Roll (Complete
50's Masters)*. Has five tracks. (Also
referred to as *Don't Be Cruel*, the first
track listed.) Value of disc without title
strips is $8 to $12.

KING OF ROCK 'N' ROLL
(COMPLETE 50's MASTERS) (5 CDs)
RCA/BMG 66050-2 ....6/92   70-80
All are picture discs of different colors. Disc
1: Black and pale yellow. Disc 2: Black
and pink. Disc 3: Black and turquoise.
Disc 4: Black and pale blue. Disc 5:
Black and lavender titled *Rare and
Rockin'*. Only disc 5 has a sub-title.
Each disc has its own jewel box,
individual photo of Elvis, and unique

inserts. Includes: 1) Numbered long box
with shrink sticker promoting contents.
2) Color 92-page, long box size booklet.
3) Sheet of 36 "Collectible Stamps of
Elvis Presley's 1950's RCA Records
Label Covers." 4) Color, 11" x 5" flyer
advertising the Elvis Home Video
catalog. Has 140 tracks.
RCA/BMG 66050-2 ....5/92   100-150
Promotional issue only. Same as
previously listed, boxed edition, but with
the following items added: 1) Folder
using the same artwork and Elvis photo
as is on the front of the long box. 2)
Black and white 8" x 10" photo of Elvis.
3) Sheet of 36 "Collectible Stamps of
Elvis Presley's 1950's RCA Records
Label Covers" (same as included with
commercial sets). 4) Sticker reading:
"For Promotion Only–Not for Sale." 5)
Two-pages of press release information
on McMullen and Company letterhead
(dated April 29, 1992).
RCA/BMG 102022 ....6/92   100-150
Disc is stock with black and red print.
Promotional issue only, made to plug the
box set of the same title. Has six tracks.

KING OF ROCK 'N' ROLL
(OUT OF THE BOX)
RCA/BMG
RDJ 62328-2....................5/92   35-50
Disc has black and blue print, with an
image of Elvis. Has no cover insert, all
the information is on the rear, tray insert.
Promotional issue only, used to plug the
box set of the same title. Reportedly 800
made. Has four tracks.

KING OF ROCK & ROLL AT HIS
BEST (4 CDs)
RCA/BMG
S4D-4965 SC ....'91   100-150
Discs – all previously issued – are stock
with black and blue print. Packaged in a
long box. Includes: 1) *You'll Never Walk
Alone*. 2) *Burning Love and Hits from
His Movies, Vol. 2*. 3) *Elvis: A Legendary
Performer, Vol. 1*. 4) *Elvis: A Legendary
Performer, Vol. 2*. Mail order offer. Has
39 tracks.

KNOWN ONLY TO HIM: see ELVIS
GOSPEL (1957 – 1971)

LEGEND LIVES ON (4 CDs)

RCA/BMG/Reader's Digest
RBD-191/CD1 ....10/93   55-60
Discs are stock with black and blue print.
  Special Collectors Edition. Includes 48-
  page booklet. Mail order offer. Has 85
  tracks.

LEGEND OF A KING (2 CDs)

Associated Broadcasters
AB1-2CD..........................8/89   100-125
Discs have a color photo of Elvis. Includes
  10-page insert booklet/script. Two CDs
  in one box. Limited edition, 1,000 made
  for radio broadcast. Promotional issue
  only. Has 25 tracks plus interviews.

LEGENDS OF ROCK 'N' ROLL
(THE ESSENTIAL ROCK 'N' ROLL
COLLECTION)

Various Artists Compilation
RCA/BMG/Warner Custom
DMC1-1100 ....'93   30-40
RCA Special Products, mail order offer
  made in conjunction with the U.S. Postal
  Service's "Legends of Rock 'n' Roll and
  Rhythm & Blues" commemorative stamp
  series. Packaged in a "Legends" box.
  Includes 24-page booklet and 20 of the
  commemorative stamps. Has three
  tracks by Elvis. Value of disc alone is
  $12 to $15.

RCA/BMG/Warner Custom
DMC1-1100 ....'93   40-50
Promo version of above set. Box stamped
  "Demonstration – Not For Sale."

LET ME ENTERTAIN YOU

Various Artists Compilation
RCA/BMG 6682-2 ....'96   15-18
This Ann-Margret CD contains a duet with
  Elvis.

"LOST" ALBUM

RCA/BMG 61024-2 ....11/91   14-18
Disc is stock with black print. Includes 4-
  page insert. Elvis is not pictured
  anywhere on this CD. Has 15 tracks.

LOUISIANA HAYRIDE ARCHIVES,
VOL. 1

Branson Gold
BGR-02462 ....7/96   15-20
Disc is stock with black print. Includes
  single-page insert. Has 16 tracks.

LOVE LETTERS FROM ELVIS

RCA/BMG 54350-2 ....10/92   12-15

Disc is black with silver print. Includes 8-
  page insert booklet. Has 11 tracks.

LOVE ME TENDER

RCA/BMG 64885-2.........7/97   10-15
This black and white CD is the first U.S.
  Elvis shaped picture disc. Special
  Products issue for Target Stores. Has
  only one track.

LOVE ME TENDER (2 CDs)

Various Artists Compilation
Time-Life
TCD-133 R103-27 A/B......'91   15-25
Includes insert. Has 40 tracks, including
  three by Elvis.

LOVING YOU

RCA/BMG 1515-2-R 4/88   12-15
Disc is stock with black print. Includes 4-
  page insert. Has 12 tracks.
RCA/BMG 67452-2 ....4/97   15-18
Brown and red picture disc. Includes 8-
  page insert booklet. Has 20 tracks,
  including eight bonus cuts.

MANY MOODS OF ROMANCE
(MY HEART REMINDS ME)

Various Artists Compilation
Time-Life
TCD-301 R974-02 ....'94   15-20
Includes 8-page booklet. Mail order offer.
  Has one Elvis track.

MANY MOODS OF ROMANCE
(AS TIME GOES BY)

Various Artists Compilation
Time-Life
TCD-303 R974-04 ....'94   15-20
Includes 8-page booklet. Mail order offer.
  Has one Elvis track.

MEMORIES OF CHRISTMAS

RCA/BMG 4395-2-R 9/87   12-15
Disc is stock with black print. Includes 4-
  page insert. Has eight tracks.

MEMORIES OF ELVIS (4 CDs)

Unistar 08/09-08/16 ......6/91   100-125
Picture discs with blue print. Limited
  edition. Intended for radio broadcast.
  Includes cue sheets for 4-hour show.
  Has 62 tracks.

MEMORIES OF ELVIS (3 CDs)

Unistar 08/13-08/15........8/93   75-100
Discs are stock with black print. Limited
  edition. Intended for radio broadcast.
  Includes cue sheets for 3-hour show.
  Has 46 tracks.

MEMPHIS RECORD

RCA/BMG 6221-2-R ....7/87　　**15-20**
Disc is stock with blue and white print.
Pressed in Japan for U.S. release.
Includes 12-page insert booklet. Has 23
tracks. This is the first disc distributed by
BMG.

RCA/BMG
6221-2-R ....10/89　　**12-15**
Disc is stock with black print. Pressed in
U.S. Includes 12-page insert booklet.
Has 23 tracks.

MERRY CHRISTMAS

RCA Victor
PCD1-5301 ....11/84　　**300-400**
Disc is stock with blue and white print.
Pressed in Japan for U.S. release. One
of the rarest U.S. CDs. Includes 4-page
insert. Has 10 tracks.

MILLION DOLLAR QUARTET

(ELVIS PRESLEY WITH JERRY LEE LEWIS & CARL PERKINS)

RCA/BMG 2023-2-R ....3/90　　**12-15**
Disc has four pictures of Elvis, and black
print. Has RCA's "Nipper" and Sun's
"rooster/sunray" logos. Includes 6-page
insert booklet. Has 41 tracks.

MIRACLE ON 34th STREET

(Original Motion Picture Soundtrack)
Various Artists Compilation
Fox 11022-2 ....'94　　**15-20**
Includes insert. Has one Elvis track.

MISTLETOE AND MEMORIES

Various Artists Compilation
RCA/BMG 8372-R ....'88　　**12-15**
Includes insert. Has nine tracks, including
one by Elvis.

MONSTER ROCK 'N' ROLL SHOW

Various Artists Compilation
DCC DZS-050 ....'90　　**15-20**
Includes insert. Has two tracks by Elvis.

MOODY BLUE

RCA/BMG 2428-2-R ....5/88　　**15-18**
Disc is light blue with black print. Includes
4-page insert. Has 10 tracks.

RCA/BMG 2428-2-R ....'91　　**12-15**
Disc is dark blue with black print. Includes
4-page insert. Has 10 tracks.

MY FELLOW AMERICANS

(Original Motion Picture Soundtrack)
Various Artists Compilation
TVT TVT 8090-2 ....'96　　**15-20**
Includes insert. Has one Elvis track.

MY HAPPINESS

RCA/BMG
2654-2-RDJ.....................8/90　　**40-60**
Disc is stock with black print. Includes 4-
page insert. Issued to promote the *Great
Performances* CD. Has one track.

MY HEART REMINDS ME: see MANY MOODS OF ROMANCE

MYSTERY TRAIN

(Original Motion Picture Soundtrack)
Various Artists Compilation
RCA/BMG 60367-2-RC ....'89　　**14-18**
Includes insert. Has two Elvis tracks.

NIPPER'S GREATEST CHRISTMAS HITS

Various Artists Compilation
RCA/BMG 9859-2-R ....'89　　**12-15**
Disc is stock with black print. Includes 8-
page insert booklet. Has 20 tracks, one
by Elvis.

NIPPER'S GREATEST HITS THE 50's, VOL. 1

Various Artists Compilation
RCA/BMG 8466-2-R ....'88　　**12-15**
Disc is stock with black print. Includes 8-
page insert booklet. Has 20 tracks, one
by Elvis.

NIPPER'S GREATEST HITS THE 50's, VOL. 2

Various Artists Compilation
RCA/BMG 8467-2-R ....'88　　**12-15**
Disc is stock with black print. Includes 8-
page insert booklet. Has 20 tracks, one
by Elvis.

NIPPER'S GREATEST HITS THE 60's, VOL. 1

Various Artists Compilation
RCA/BMG 8474-2-R ....'88　　**12-15**
Disc is stock with black print. Includes 8-
page insert booklet. Has 20 tracks, one
by Elvis.

NIPPER'S GREATEST HITS THE 60's, VOL. 2

Various Artists Compilation
RCA/BMG 8475-2-R ....'88　　**12-15**
Disc is stock with black print. Includes 8-
page insert booklet. Has 20 tracks, one
by Elvis.

NIPPER'S GREATEST HITS THE 70's, VOL. 1

Various Artists Compilation

RCA/BMG 8476-2-R ....'88   12-15
Disc is stock with black print. Includes 8-page insert booklet. Has 20 tracks, one by Elvis.

RCA/BMG 9684-2-R ....'89   12-15
Disc is stock with black print. Includes 8-page insert booklet. Has 20 tracks, one by Elvis.

NIPPER'S GREATEST HITS THE 80's

Various Artists Compilation

RCA/BMG 9970-2-R ....'90   12-15
Disc is stock with black print. Includes 8-page insert booklet. Has 20 tracks, one by Elvis.

NIPPER'S HOLIDAY FAVORITES

Various Artists Compilation

RCA/BMG
RDJ 62699-2.....................'93   30-40
Includes. Has one Elvis track. RCA Nashville promotional only issue.

NIPPER'S #1 HITS (1956–1986)
(THE BEST OF RCA VICTOR)

Various Artists Compilation

RCA/BMG 9902-2-R ....'89   12-15
Disc is stock with black print. Includes 8-page insert booklet. Has 20 tracks, two by Elvis.

NUMBER ONE HITS

RCA/BMG 6382-2-R 7/87   15-18
Disc is stock with blue and white print. Pressed in Japan for U.S. release. Includes 4-page insert. Has 18 tracks.

RCA/BMG 6382-2-R ....'89   12-15
Disc is stock with black print. Pressed in U.S. Includes 4-page insert. Page 4 does *not* have "RE" beneath selection number, at upper left. Has 18 tracks.

ON STAGE
(FEBRUARY, 1970)

RCA/BMG 54362-2 ....10/91   10-15
Disc is stock with black print. Includes 4-page insert. Has 10 tracks.

ON THE ROAD INTERVIEWS

Laserlight Digital

12 789 ....9/96   6-8
Disc is stock and yellow with black print. This is an Audio Book on CD. Includes 4-page insert. Contains only interviews.

OUT OF THE BOX: see KING OF ROCK 'N' ROLL

OUT OF THE BOX (6 FROM THE 60's): see FROM NASHVILLE TO MEMPHIS (OUT OF THE BOX – 6 FROM THE 60's)

OUT OF THE BOX SAMPLER: see WALK A MILE IN MY SHOES

POT LUCK WITH ELVIS

RCA/BMG 2523-2-R 6/88   20-25
Disc is stock with black print. Includes 4-page insert. Has 12 tracks.

PRECIOUS MEMORIES (2 CDs)

Various Artists Compilation

Time-Life
TCD-127 A/B ....'93   30-40
Includes insert. Also released as *Songs Of Faith And Inspiration*. Mail order offer. Has two Elvis tracks.

PRIVATE PRESLEY CD

Merlin Group

04609-6 ....8/93   25-30
Disc is stock with black print. Promotional issue, offered as a bonus to buyers of the book, *Private Presley*. No insert used. Has 12 tracks which include music and interviews.

PROMISED LAND

RCA/BMG 0873-2-R 4/89   12-15
Disc is stock with black print. Includes 4-page insert. Has 10 tracks.

PURE GOLD

RCA/BMG 53732-2 ....5/92   12-15
Disc is black with silver print. Includes 6-page booklet. Has 10 tracks.

RCA CHRISTMAS 1996

Various Artists Compilation

RCA/BMG
RDJ 64688-2.....................'96   25-30
Includes insert. Has one Elvis track. RCA Nashville promotional only issue.

RCA NASHVILLE 60 YEARS 1928-1988 (3 CDs)

Various Artists Compilation

RCA/BMG 6864-2-RDJ ....'88   150-200
Includes 48-page booklet. Has one Elvis track. RCA Country Music Foundation promotional issue.

RCA RECORDS LABEL (THE 1ST NOTE IN BLACK MUSIC) (3 CDs)

Various Artists Compilation

RCA/BMG 61144-2 ....'92   25-30
Includes 32-page insert booklet. Has one
Elvis track.

RCA/BMG 61144-2 ....'92   40-50
Includes 32-page insert booklet. Has one
Elvis track. Promotional copy of above.

RAISED ON ROCK

RCA/BMG 50388-2 ....3/94   12-15
Disc is black with silver print. Includes 8-
page insert booklet. Has 10 tracks.

RAW ELVIS (COLLECTORS SERIES) (EARLY LIVE RECORDING MARCH 19, 1955)

RCA/BMG/Outwest

9210-2 DRC 11739 ....6/97   14-18
Black and white picture disc. Includes 12-
page insert booklet. Contains five music
tracks and two interviews.

REACH OUT AND TOUCH (4 CDs)

Various Artists Compilation

RCA/BMG/Reader's Digest

RCD-077/CD1 ....'91   55-60
Includes 48-page booklet. Mail order offer.
Has four Elvis tracks.

RECONSIDER BABY

RCA Victor

PCD1-5418 ....4/85   15-18
Disc is stock with blue and white print.
Pressed in Japan for U.S. release.
Includes 4-page insert. Has 12 tracks.

RCA/BMG PCD1-5418 .....'90   10-12
Disc is stock with black print. Pressed in
U.S. Includes 4-page insert. Has 12
tracks.

REMEMBERING ELVIS

RCA/BMG/Pair

PDC2-1037 ....2/88   20-25
Disc is stock with black and blue print.
Includes 4-page insert. RCA Special
Products release. Has 16 tracks.

RETURN OF THE ROCKER

RCA Victor 5600-2-R 6/86   20-25
Disc is stock with blue and white print.
Pressed in Japan for U.S. release.
Includes 4-page insert. Has 12 tracks.

RCA Victor 5600-2-R ....'87   15-20
Disc is stock with blue and white print.
Pressed in U.S. Includes 4-page insert.
Has 12 tracks.

ROCK 'N' ROLL LEGENDS (3 CDs)

Various Artists Compilation

RCA/BMG/Reader's Digest

211C RC7-211-1/2/3 ....'96   45-50
Includes 48-page booklet. Mail order offer.
Has five Elvis tracks.

ROCK 'N' ROLL: THE EARLY DAYS

Various Artists Compilation

RCA Victor

PCD1-5463 ....'85   15-20
Includes insert. Has 13 tracks, including
one by Elvis.

ROCKER

RCA Victor

PCD1-5182 ....11/84   15-20
Disc is stock with blue and white print.
Pressed in Japan for U.S. release.
Includes 4-page insert. Has 12 tracks.

RCA/BMG

PCD1-5182 ....8/88   12-15
Disc is stock with blue and white print.
Pressed in U.S. Includes 4-page insert.
Has 12 tracks.

SANTA CLAUS IS BACK IN TOWN

RCA 11/97   75-100
No label or number, though RCA Records
is thanked. Disc is black with silver print.
Single pocket cover. Includes note from
Priscilla and Lisa Marie. Made for fan
club presidents. Has only the title track.

SELECTIONS FROM *AMAZING GRACE (HIS GREATEST SACRED PERFORMANCES)*

RCA/BMG

RJC 66512-2 ....10/94   35-50
Disc is stock with dark blue print. Used to
promote 2-CD set. Contains 4-page
insert. Has nine tracks.

SHAKE, RATTLE & ROLL (FROM THE BEGINNING WE MADE MUSIC)

RCA/BMG

6382-2-RDJ.....................1/92   75-125
Disc is black with silver print. Includes 4-
page insert. Contains same tracks as
Number One Hits. Promotional issue.
Has 18 tracks.

SHE DEVIL

(Original Motion Picture Soundtrack)

Various Artists Compilation

PolyGram 841583-2 ....'89   15-20
Includes insert. Has one Elvis track.

SIXTIES LEGENDS – ELVIS PRESLEY (2 CDs)

Unistar 05/22-05/24........5/92   50-60
Discs are stock with red print. Intended for radio broadcast. Includes cue sheets for 2-hour show. Has 23 tracks.

SIXTY YEARS – RCA NASHVILLE: see RCA NASHVILLE – SIXTY YEARS

SOLID GOLD HITS OF THE 50's
Various Artists Compilation
RCA/BMG DPC1-0814 .....'88   15-18
Includes insert. Special Products mail order offer from Avon. Has one Elvis track.

SOLID GOLD HITS OF THE 60's
Various Artists Compilation
RCA/BMG DPC1-0815 .....'88   15-18
Includes insert. Special Products mail order offer from Avon. Has one Elvis track.

SOLID GOLD HITS OF THE 70's
Various Artists Compilation
RCA/BMG DPC1-0816 .....'89   15-18
Includes insert. Special Products mail order offer from Avon. Has one Elvis track.

SOMETHING FOR EVERYBODY
RCA/BMG 2370-2-R 10/89   20-25
Disc is stock with black print. Includes 4-page insert. Has 12 tracks.

SONGS OF FAITH & INSPIRATION (2 CDs)
Various Artists Compilation
Time-Life
TCD-127 A/B ....'93   20-25
Includes insert. Also issued as *Precious Memories*. Mail order offer. Has two Elvis tracks.

STEREO '57 (ESSENTIAL ELVIS, VOL. 2)
RCA/BMG 9589-2-R 2/89   14-18
Disc is stock with black print. Includes 10-page booklet. Has 20 tracks.

SUMMER SONGS (2 CDs)
Various Artists Compilation
RCA/BMG DPC2-0981 .....'91   20-25
Includes insert. Special Products mail order offer from Avon. Has one Elvis track.

SUN RECORDS COLLECTION (3 CDs)
Various Artists Compilation
RCA/BMG/Rhino R2 71780/
DRC3-1211 ....'94   50-75

Includes 32-page booklet. Packaged in a special long box, each disc has its own jewel box. Has five Elvis tracks (one with the Million Dollar Quartet).

SUN SESSIONS CD
RCA/BMG 6414-2-R 7/87   15-18
Disc is stock with blue print. Includes 12-page insert booklet. Has 28 tracks. Same as the vinyl set titled *The Complete Sun Sessions*.

SUN STORY
Various Artists Compilation
Rhino RNCD-75884 ....'87   10-15
Disc is yellow with black print. Includes 12-page insert booklet. Has 20 tracks, two by Elvis.

SUN'S GREATEST HITS
Various Artists Compilation
RCA/BMG 66059-2 ....'92   14-18
Disc is yellow with brown print. Includes 16-page insert booklet. Has 17 tracks, four by Elvis. Has RCA's "Nipper" and Sun's "rooster/sunray" logos.

SUPER '60s (4 CDs)
Various Artists Compilation
RCA/BMG/Reader's Digest
RBD-037/CD1 ....'90   55-60
Includes 50-page booklet. Mail order offer. Has five Elvis tracks.

SWEET DREAMS OF COUNTRY (4 CDs)
Various Artists Compilation
RCA/BMG/Reader's Digest
RCD-049/CD1 ....7/90   55-60
Includes inserts. Has seven Elvis tracks.

TEENAGE YEARS (1957–1964)
Various Artists Compilation
Time-Life TCD-161 ....'93   15-20
Includes insert. Mail order offer. Has one Elvis track.

THAT'S THE WAY IT IS
Mobile Fidelity Sound
Lab UDCD-560 ....5/92   30-45
Disc is black "Ultradisc" with "24kt Gold Plated" print. Uses Shape® 2001 pop-up tray. Reissues were packaged in a long box. Includes 12-page booklet. Has 12 tracks.
RCA/BMG 54114-2 ....7/93   12-15
Disc is black with silver print. Includes 4-page insert. Has 12 tracks

THERE'S A RIOT GOIN' ON!
(THE ROCK 'N' ROLL CLASSICS OF LEIBER & STOLLER)
Various Artists Compilation
Rhino R2-70593 ....'91   10-15
Includes insert. Has two tracks by Elvis.

THESE WERE OUR SONGS: see EARLY '60s (THESE WERE OUR SONGS)

THOSE FABULOUS '50s (2 CDs)
Various Artists Compilation
RCA/BMG
DVC2-0877-1/2 ....'89   20-25
Includes insert. RCA Special Products, mail order offer from Sessions Music. Has one Elvis track.

TIME-LIFE HISTORY OF ROCK 'N' ROLL (1954-1956)
Various Artists Compilation
Time-Life TCD-160........... '92   15-20
Includes 24-page insert booklet. Mail order offer. Has two Elvis tracks.

TIME-LIFE TREASURY OF CHRISTMAS, VOL. 1 (2 CDs)
Various Artists Compilation
Time-Life
TCD-107 A/B ....'87   25-30
Includes insert. Mail order offer. Has 53 tracks, two by Elvis.

TIME-LIFE TREASURY OF CHRISTMAS, VOL. 2 (2 CDs)
Various Artists Compilation
Time-Life
TCD-108 A/B ....'87   25-30
Includes insert. Mail order offer. Has 48 tracks, one by Elvis.

TOP TEN HITS (2 CDs)
RCA/BMG
6383-2-R-P 1/2................7/87   25-30
Discs are stock with blue and white print. Pressed in Japan for U.S. release. CDs are in two jewel boxes, each with a 4-page insert. Has 38 tracks.
RCA/BMG
6383-2-R-P 1/2................1/88   20-25
Discs are stock with black print. Pressed in U.S. CDs are in two jewel boxes, each with a 4-page insert. Has 38 tracks.
RCA/BMG 56383-2 ....5/96   20-25
Discs are stock with black print. CDs are in multi-disc jewel box. Slipcase on multi-disc jewel box has same artwork as 4-page insert. Has 38 tracks.

TREASURY OF COUNTRY INSPIRATIONAL FAVORITES (4 CDs)
Various Artists Compilation
RCA/BMG/Reader's Digest
RB7-063C-1/2/3/4 ....'94   55-60
Includes 48-page booklet. Mail order offer. Has three Elvis tracks.

TRUTH ABOUT ME
Rainbo Records.............3/97   30-40
Collectors Set includes: 1) Picture CD. 2) Reprint of the (green) 1956 *Elvis Answers Back!* magazine. 3) 10" gold vinyl disc. 4) Single-sided, gold foil vinyl soundsheet of *The Truth About Me* disc. Both CD and LP contain about 20 minutes of Elvis speaking, whereas 1956 version has only about two minutes. Both also have Elvis' picture on them. Everything is packaged in a 12", plastic gatefold case.

20 YEARS OF NO. 1 HITS (1956 – 1975) (4 CDs)
Various Artists Compilation
RCA/BMG/Reader's Digest
RBD-043/CD1 ....'88   55-60
Includes 64-page booklet. Has seven Elvis tracks.

UNFORGETTABLE FIFTIES (2 CDs)
Various Artists Compilation
RCA/BMG
DVC-0867-1/2 ....'88   15-25
Discs are stock with black print. CDs are in two jewel boxes, each with a single sheet insert. Mail order offer. Has 50 tracks, including two by Elvis.

VALENTINE GIFT FOR YOU
RCA Victor
PCD1-5353 ....8/85   20-25
Disc is stock with blue and white print. Pressed in Japan for U.S. release. Includes 4-page insert. Has 13 tracks.
RCA/BMG
PCD1-5353 ....1/88   12-15
Disc is stock with blue and white print. Pressed in U.S. Includes 4-page insert. Has 13 tracks.

VINTAGE 1955
(Vintage '55 Elvis)
Oak 1003 ....'90   **75-100**
Disc is stock with black print. Includes single sheet insert printed on both sides. Cover insert shows "Vintage 1955" as title, but disc has "Vintage 55 Elvis" (sic). Mail order offer. Has eight tracks.

WALK A MILE IN MY SHOES
(ESSENTIAL 70's MASTERS) (5 CDs)
RCA/BMG 66670-2.......10/95   **70-80**
All are picture discs in different colors. Disc 1: Lavender and black. Disc 2: Aqua and black. Disc 3: Purple and black. Disc 4: Orange and black. Disc 5: Gold and black. Numbered, collectible set includes: 1) Long box with shrink sticker. 2) Color, 94-page booklet. Has 120 tracks.

**RCA/BMG 66670-2
PRES-4/2** 10/95   **90-100**
Promotional version of above release.

WALK A MILE IN MY SHOES
(OUT OF THE BOX SAMPLER)
**RCA/BMG
RJC-66765-2**...................8/95   **40-50**
Dark blue and white picture disc. Used to promote *Essential 70's Masters* box set. Contains 4-page insert. Has 12 tracks.

WE WISH YOU A MERRY CHRISTMAS
Various Artists Compilation
RCA/BMG 2294-2-R ....'90   **12-15**
Includes insert. Has one Elvis track.

WE WISH YOU A MERRY CHRISTMAS
Various Artists Compilation
RCA/BMG DMC1-0992 .....'91   **20-25**
Includes insert. Special Products mail order offer from Avon. Has one Elvis track.

WELCOME TO MY WORLD
RCA/BMG 52274-2 ....5/92   **12-15**
Disc is black with silver print. Includes 8-page insert booklet. Has 10 tracks.

WINDOWS OF THE SOUL
**Erika GLCD
02041313** 9/96   **25-30**
Disc is black with silver print with Elvis in blue. Includes 12-page insert booklet and a phone card. Contains interviews.

YOU'LL NEVER WALK ALONE
(RCA CAMDEN CLASSICS)
**RCA/Camden/BMG
CAD1-2472** 8/87   **7-10**
Disc is stock with black and blue print. Includes 4-page insert. Has nine tracks.

YOUR HIT PARADE: 1956
Various Artists Compilation
Time-Life TCD-125 ....'90   **15-20**
Includes insert. Mail order offer. Has one Elvis track.

YOUR HIT PARADE: THE '50s POP REVIVAL
Various Artists Compilation
Time-Life TCD-137 ....'93   **15-20**
Includes insert. Mail order offer. Has one Elvis track.

YULE FUEL
(1992 Rhino Christmas Sampler)
Various Artists Compilation
Rhino PRO2-90123 ......11/92   **25-35**
Disc is white with green print. Includes 4-page insert. Has 28 tracks, one by Elvis. Promotional issue.

YULE TRAIN
(A Rhino Christmas Sampler)
Various Artists Compilation
Rhino PRO2-90048 ....'90   **25-35**
Includes insert. Has one track by Elvis. Promotional issue.

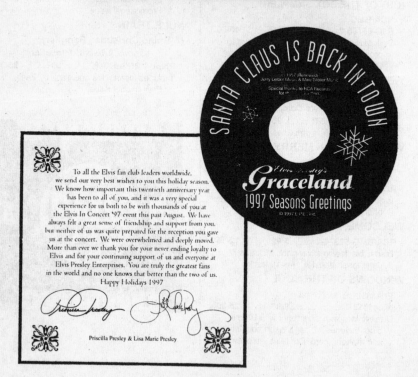

To all the Elvis fan club leaders worldwide,
we send our very best wishes to you this holiday season.
We know how important this twentieth anniversary year
has been to all of you, and it was a very special
experience for us both to be with thousands of you at
the Elvis In Concert '97 event this past August. We have
always felt a great sense of friendship and support from you,
but neither of us was quite prepared for the reception you gave
us at the concert. We were overwhelmed and deeply moved.
More than ever we thank you for your never ending loyalty to
Elvis and for your continuing support of us and everyone at
Elvis Presley Enterprises. You are truly the greatest fans
in the world and no one knows that better than the two of us.
Happy Holidays 1997

Priscilla Presley & Lisa Marie Presley

ELVIS MEMORABILIA

This chapter documents and prices thousands of manufactured articles that bear the name and/or a likeness of Elvis Aron Presley – paraphernalia other than phonograph records. As the time frame indicates, this compilation is strictly limited to items produced during the last 22 years of his lifetime. To attempt a similar post-August 16, 1977 guide book would require even more pages than are found in this entire volume. Furthermore, many recent so-called *collectibles* are widely thought of as riffraff, or contrived. This is not to say that there are no genuinely respectful, and truly collectible Elvis souvenirs from this period, but they are in the minority.

Elvis Presley Enterprises

Any itemization of non-recorded Presley memorabilia begins with Elvis Presley Enterprises merchandise. Within months of Elvis' meteoric rise to fame in early 1956, licenses to manufacture virtually everything under the sun were issued to dozens of avaricious applicants. A glance at this chapter will astound many readers, seeing, perhaps for the first time, the vast assortment of trinkets, doo-dads, and novelties licensed by Elvis Presley Enterprises.

However, E. P. Enterprises was not the only source of legitimate collectibles. Some of the most desirable items listed here were produced by or for companies promoting his records and films.

RCA Victor

RCA Victor developed hundreds of promotional items aimed at furthering interest and sales in Elvis' recordings. While all materials pertaining to actual phonograph record releases, such as bonus photos, are listed in the Records chapters, there are plenty of RCA-created items in this section.

Movie Memorabilia

The 33 films starring Elvis Presley generated a plethora of advertising and promotional merchandise. The release of each film meant an avalanche of assorted audio and visual goodies, all of which are fancied by Elvis fans.

Publications

Elvis has been the subject of several hundred publications. Books and magazines have analyzed every conceivable shred of fact and fiction about the man, his professional as well as his personal life.

Not surprisingly, most of the Elvis publications spewed forth after his death, thus eliminating them from this tome.

Included in the category of publications is sheet music. As a rule, the sheet music and lyrics for Elvis' hit singles would be available from the song's publisher. However, there were some unanticipated booklets of sheet music for Elvis songs that could hardly be considered Presley standards. The following is a mere sampling of curious songs for which sheet music was marketed: *A Dog's Life; Animal Instinct; Catchin' On Fast; El Toro;*

Golden Coins; Have a Happy; I'll Take Love; Ito Eats; Petunia, the Gardener's Daughter; Smorgasbord; Who Needs Money; and *Yoga Is As Yoga Does.*

About the only ilk of Elvis memorabilia not dealt with in this edition is printed items that defy accurate description in a text-only format. Included in this aberrant cluster are Las Vegas and Lake Tahoe signs and trappings, photographs, concert paraphernalia, and postcards. Documenting and sorting collectibles from these categories requires many, many individual comparative illustrations.

Some other noteworthy environs of Elvis memorabilia collecting that we do not attempt to appraise in detail are autographs, awards, and personal items once owned by or given as gifts by Presley. We also avoid the equally troublesome issue of gold and platinum record awards.

Another aspect of Elvis memorabilia collecting that resists inclusion in a price guide is virtually anything once owned by, or given by Elvis.

Included in the latter category are handwritten letters and postcards.

If an Elvis autograph on a piece of paper or a napkin can sell for $100 to $500, which they have, then what about an entire letter in Presley's hand?

One-page letters, usually sent to fans thanking them for their support, etc., have sold in the $5,000 range. Most of the ones we've seen offered were written between 1960 and 1962.

The most exotic – and erotic – letter found thus far is a four-page handwritten letter to his girlfirend, Anita Wood, sent from Germany (November 1958) just after Elvis arrived there.

Elvis confirms in this letter what we always knew about his army years – he was just like any other soldier. In it, he pours his heart out to the girl he left behind, just as so many other boys in that situation have done. Of course he had not yet become involved with Priscilla.

Appraising something so incredibly personal as this is difficult; however, an estimated range of $25,000 or more is likely.

Presley's unrestrained spending and generosity is legendary. A piece of jewelry, for example, given by Elvis is no longer an everyday accessory. The gold and craftsmanship making up one of Elvis' "TCB" ("Taking Care of Business") pendants or "TLC" ("Tender Loving Care") necklaces might be estimated at $150 to $200. Regardless, offers as high as $15,000 have been turned down for an original TCB given by Elvis – its sentimental value to the lucky owner far exceeding the loot.

Exceptions established, ahead is an alphabetical listing of non-recorded Presleyana produced before August 16, 1977. Unless the object is a movie collectible or a publication, look first for the most obvious heading. If it's not there, a cross-reference should point you in the right direction. Movie memorabilia and publications are alphabetically listed in their respective sections.

One important point: The price ranges in this guide are for *near mint* condition items. You must adjust values accordingly when the condition is something less.

Album Covers (Self-standing, cardboard counter displays)
For albums issued from 1960 through 1964 .... $75 - $125
For albums issued from 1965 through 1971 .... $50 - $75
    Though the possibility exists that these units exist for albums issued before 1960
and after 1971, the only ones we have confirmed range from *G.I. Blues* through
Elvis Country. Allowing for such earlier and later discoveries:
For albums issued before 1960 .... $150 - $250
For albums issued after 1971 .... $25 - $50
Anklets (Elvis Presley Enterprises) 1956
Two pairs attached to card .... $1,000 - $2,000
Card/package by itself.. $400 - $800
    (The anklets by themselves are not identified as an Elvis item, thus the
significance of the card.)
    Also see *Dog Tag Anklet.*
Army Yearbook: see 2nd Armored Division
Ashtray: see Coaster
Autograph Book (Elvis Presley Enterprises) 1956 .... $1,000 - $1,200
Bags: see Handbags / Plastic bags / Souvenir opening night package
Ball Point Pen: see Pen
Balloon: see *Follow That Dream* and *Kid Galahad* in Movie Memorabilia Section
Bear: see Teddy bear
Belt (Elvis Presley Enterprises) 1956
Leather belt .... $800 - $1,200
Plastic belt.. $600 - $700
Belt Buckle (Elvis Presley Enterprises) 1956 .... $300 - $500
Billfold (Elvis Presley Enterprises) 1956 .... $650 - $750
Binder (Elvis Presley Enterprises) 1956 .... $1,000 - $1,500
    (Two zipper models are known. One reads: "Love Me Tender," the other "Rock N'
Roll.")
Board Game: see Game
Bobby Sox: see Sox
Bolo Tie (Elvis Presley Enterprises) 1956... $300 - $500
Bookends (Elvis Presley Enterprises) 1956
Pair of bookends .... $800 - $1,200
One bookend.. $400 - $600
    (Approximately 8" tall, each is an ivory or cream colored bust-like figurine of Elvis
holding a guitar.)
Books
    From 1955 through August 1977, thousands of magazines devoted space to Elvis.
However, very few Elvis books – ones exclusively about him – were published
during his lifetime. Most published before 1977 originated in Europe. In the years
since his death, an avalanche of Elvis books have been printed, flowing freely
from virtually every country on earth. For books containing sheet music/lyrics,
see Song Folios / Magazines / Sheet music.
Elvis by Jerry Hopkins (hardbound) 1971
With dust jacket .... $20 - $30
Without dust jacket .... $12 - $25

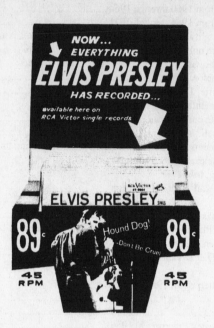

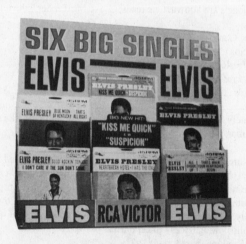

Elvis Presley: Man or Mouse? by Chaw Mank 1959 .... $30 - $50
     (24-page 3½" x 5¾" booklet. Includes three postcard-size insert cards, each with a
     song/poem about Elvis, written by Mank.)

Films and Career of Elvis Presley by Steven and Boris Zmijewsky 1976............ $15 - $20

Meet Elvis Presley by Favius Friedman (paperback) 1971.................................... $15 - $25

Operation Elvis by Alan Levy (hardbound) 1960
     With dust jacket .... $75 - $100
     Without dust jacket .... $35 - $50

Wild in the Country by J.R. Salamanca (Paperback) 1960 .... $30 - $40
     (Pictures Elvis in a scene from the film on the cover.)

The '50s – The Impressions of a Fabulous Decade 1970s.................................... $10 - $20
     (Pictures Elvis on the cover.)

Bracelet (Flasher) (Elvis Presley Enterprises) 1956 .... $100 - $150
     (Square flasher, or double-image photo of Elvis holding a guitar.)

Bracelet (Elvis Presley Enterprises) 1962.. $50 - $100
     (Reads: "Follow That Dream.")

Bracelet (Identification Bracelet) (Elvis Presley Enterprises) 1962 .... $50 - $100
     (Reads: "Love Me Tender.")

Browser Box (RCA Victor) 1956 .... $250 - $500
     (Reads: "Now...Everything Elvis Presley Has Recorded...available here on RCA
     Victor Single Recordings." Pictures the same photo of Elvis on the Steve Allen
     Show – singing to the hound dog – as seen on the picture sleeve for *Hound
     Dog/Don't Be Cruel.*

Browser Box (RCA Victor) 1964 .... $100 - $200
     (Reads: "Six Big Singles." In-store cardboard, counter display. Made to hold six Gold
     Standard Singles: five reissues of 1959 discs and one, *Kiss Me Quick/Suspicion,* billed as
     the "Big New Hit.")

Bubble Gum Card (Elvis Presley Enterprises/Bubbles Inc.) 1956
     Unopened package of 5-cent gum and card .... $200 - $300
     Unopened package of 1-cent gum and card .... $100 - $125
     Any individual card.. $15 - $25
         (Cards numbered 1 through 46 have an "Ask Elvis" question on the back, followed by
         his supposed reply. Cards numbered 47 through 66 picture scenes from the film, *Love
         Me Tender,* and an explanation of that scene on the back.)

Bubble Gum Card Counter Display (Elvis Presley Enterprises/Bubbles Inc.) 1956
     Display box (full) with 24 packages of gum and cards............................... $2,000 - $3,000
         (One 24-count box of 5-cent packages)
     Display box (empty) .... $1,000 - $1,500

Bubble Gum Card (Topps) 1957
     Individual "Hit Stars" card.. $50 - $75

Bubble Gum Card Wrapper (Elvis Presley Enterprises) 1956
     With "5-cent" retail price.. $150 - $250
     With "1-cent" retail price.. $75 - $100

Bubble Gum Wrapper (Topps) 1957
     "Hit Stars" series card .... $50 - $75

Buckle: see Belt Buckle

Bust: see Statuette

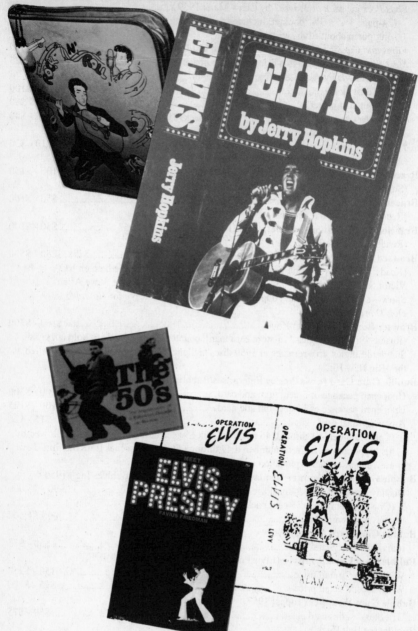

Buttons (Elvis Presley Enterprises) 1956.. $75 - $100
    (Approximate 1" circular buttons, may picture Elvis – with or without text – or may have
    only text.)

Buttons 1950s.. $75 - $100
    (Approximate 3" circular buttons with text only. No manufacturer identification and no
    affiliation with Elvis Presley Enterprises.) Also see *Pin*

Cake Decoration (1956) .... $1,000 - $2,000
    (Multi-color decoration depicts Elvis holding a guitar in front of a microphone. On one
    side there is a cowboy hat and on the other, a dog – a hound dog no doubt.)

Calendars (Pocket): see Pocket Calendars

Carrying Case (Elvis Presley Enterprises) 1956
    With plastic insert tray .... $1,200 - $1,800
    Without plastic insert tray .... $800 - $1,200

Ceramic Tile (Elvis Presley Enterprises) 1956............................... $2,000 - $2,500
    (Square 6" tile. Reads: "Best Wishes, Elvis Presley.")

Charm Bracelet (Elvis Presley Enterprises) 1956
    Bracelet attached to card .... $300 - $400
    Bracelet by itself (no card)... $100 - $200
    Also see *Hit Tunes Charms*

Chewing Gum Card: see Bubble gum card

Chicago American (Faux newspaper) 1971 .... $10 - $20
    (Headline reads: "Elvis Inducted." One of a series of four nostalgic reproductions of
    newspapers featuring news headlines of the 1950s. The other three in the series, which
    are not Elvis related, read: "3 Rock and Roll Stars Die in Air Crash," "Marilyn Weds
    Di Maggio" and "Russians Launch Sputnik." Made by Original Sound Recordings as a
    promotional item for their *Oldies But Goodies* record albums.)

Christmas Card Poster (RCA Victor) 1959 .... $200 - $300
    (Made for display in record stores, this red, white, black and gold poster reads: "Free
    Christmas Card from Elvis to All His Many Fans. Come in Now for your Copy While
    They Last.")

Christmas Cards "From Elvis and the Colonel"
    1956-1959 .... $75 - $100
    1960-1976 .... $50 - $75
    (Cards in this category are mass-distributed, often picturing both Elvis and his manager
    Col. Tom Parker. The Colonel is always pictured wearing a Santa suit. For postcard-
    size, giveaway cards figure about one-half the above price range.)

Christmas Cards (From the Presley home)
    1956-1966 .... $200 - $500
    (Cards in this category are personal ones, mailed directly from Elvis' home in
    Memphis. May be imprinted and/or signed in a variety of ways, including: "Elvis and
    Family," "Priscilla and Elvis," The Presleys," or "Elvis Presley." Return address, 3764
    Highway 51 So., Memphis, Tenn., is usually rubber stamped on back of envelope.)

Coaster (Ashtray) (Elvis Presley Enterprises) 1956 .... $500 - $600
    (Has an autographed photo of Elvis in the glass. Approximately 3 ½" diameter.)

Coin Purse/Key Chain .... $300 - $500
    (Pictures Elvis in a striped shirt)

Coloring Contest: see Girls! Girls! Girls! (Movie Related Memorabilia)

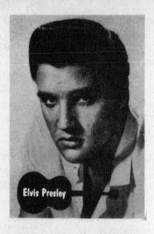

Concert Placards

The most collectible Elvis concert placards are those from the pre-Army years. Before Presleymania struck – in early 1956 – Elvis was often booked on tours with other performers, usually country and western acts. Especially appealing are those where he did *not* receive top billing.

1954-1956: Elvis listed, but *not* headlined .... $500 - $1,000
1956-1958: The Elvis Presley Show... $300 - $600
1960-1961: The Elvis Presley Show... $150 - $250
1969-1977: Elvis in Concert.. $100 - $200

(One exception in the '70s grouping is a placard reading:"Elvis – Extra Special Show by Popular Demand. Sunday Morning, Sept. 2nd at 3:00 A.M. Make your reservations NOW." Only 50 of these placards were made, for placement throughout the Las Vegas Hilton, to announce previously unscheduled show. This 1972 show may have been the only 3:00 a.m. show in Elvis' career. Value: $400-$500.)

Contracts

During his professional career, Elvis signed a number of different contracts for one thing or another. Prices vary widely on originals of these contracts, with value affected most by *when* Elvis signed the contract, since usually only his signature appears. Combine the following price information with an analysis of the historical significance and overall appeal of the contract.

1954-1956: .... $1,500 - $2,000
1956-1958: .... $500 - $1,000
1960-1961: .... $400 - $600
1969-1977: .... $300 - $400

Counter Merchandiser: see Browser Box
Crew Hat: see Hat
Cuff Links (Elvis Presley Enterprises) 1958
  Cuff links in original box.. $600 - $800
  Cuff links by themselves (no box).. $300 - $500
  (Cuff links have "Elvis" printed on them.)
  Also see *Hit Tunes Charms*
Diary (One year) (Elvis Presley Enterprises) 1956 .... $1,000 - $2,000
Diary (Five year) (Elvis Presley Enterprises) 1956.. $2,500 - $3,500
Dog: see Hound Dog
Dog Tag (Elvis Presley Enterprises) 1962 .... $50 - $100
  (Reads: "I'm an Elvis Fan.")
Dog Tag (Elvis Presley Enterprises) 1962 .... $50 - $100
  (Reads: "Presley, Elvis–53310761.")
Dog Tag Anklet (Elvis Presley Enterprises) 1958
  Anklet attached to card .... $50 - $100
  Anklet by itself (no card)... $25 - $50
Dog Tag Bracelet (Boy's) (Elvis Presley Enterprises) 1958
  Bracelet attached to card.. $50 - $100
  Bracelet by itself (no card)... $25 - $50
Dog Tag Bracelet (Girl's) (Elvis Presley Enterprises) 1958
  Bracelet attached to card.. $50 - $100
  Bracelet by itself (no card)... $25 - $50

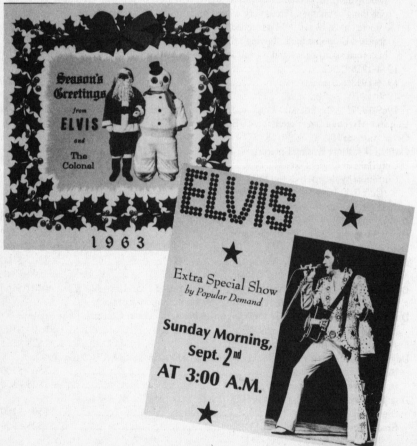

Dog Tag Key Chain (Elvis Presley Enterprises) 1958

Key chain attached to card .... $100 - $150

Key chain by itself (no card) .... $50 - $75

Dog Tag Necklace (Elvis Presley Enterprises) 1958

Necklace attached to card .... $100 - $150

   (Card reads: "Authentic" and has a $1 price.)

Necklace attached to card .... $50 - $75

   (Card has neither "Authentic," nor the $1 price.)

Necklace by itself (no card) .... $25 - $40

Dog Tag Sweater Holder (Elvis Presley Enterprises) 1958

Holder attached to card .... $300 - $400

Holder by itself (no card) .... $150 - $250

Doll (Elvis Presley Enterprises – 18" tall) 1957

Doll with all clothes and in original box .... $3,000 - $4,000

Doll with all clothes, but without original box .... $2,000 - $2,500

Doll with neither clothes nor original box .... $500 - $750

   (Doll is 18" tall. Clothes include brown/beige/red/blue plaid shirt, navy blue denim
pants, black belt, and two blue "suede" shoes.)

Double Trouble Electric Light Display (1967) .... $250 - $300

   (Promotional, in-store display piece. Has same cover as RCA LPM-3787, but made
into a self-standing unit with an electric light bulb behind the cover.)

Drinking Glass: see Glass

Earrings (Elvis Presley Enterprises; picture Elvis) 1956

Earrings attached to card .... $350 - $450

Earrings by themselves (no card) .... $100 - $200

   (Card has two framed pictures of Elvis. Among other tings, card reads: "Elvis
Presley Earrings," "Hound Dog," "Don't Be Cruel" and "Love Me Tender.")

Also see *Hit Tunes Charms*

Easter Postcards (1966-1969)

Mass-distributed, giveaway cards .... $15 - $25

With typewritten messsage from Elvis. Mailed from his home in Memphis .... $100 - $200

Eau de Parfum: see Perfume

Elvis Is Back Electric Light Display (1960) .... $400 - $500

   (Promotional, in-store display piece. Has same photo of Elvis as is found on RCA
LPM/LSP-2231, but made into a self-standing unit with an electric light bulb behind
the cover.)

Elvis NBC-TV Electric Light Display (1968) .... $250 - $300

   (Promotional, in-store display piece. Has same cover as RCA LPM-4088, but made
into a self-standing unit with an electric light bulb behind the cover.)

Elvis Sings on RCA Victor Electric Light Display: see Kissin' Cousins (Elvis Sings on
RCA Victor) Electric Light Display

Fan Club Membership Package (1956)

One "Personal Note to you From EP" with "Elvis Presley, National Headquarters,
Madison, Tenn" at bottom of page .... $250 - $350

One "Elvis Presley Complimentary Fan Club Membership Card" .... $100 - $200

One "Elvis Presley National Fan Club – I Like Elvis and His RCA Records" pin-on
button .... $100 - $200

Complete package (letter, card, button) .... $600 - $900

Flasher Bracelet: see Bracelet

ELVIS REMEMBERS PEARL HARBOR

Hawaii Next Charity Stop

By DON WALKER

BLOCH ARENA, PEARL HARBOR

Saturday
MARCH 25TH
8:30 P.M.
DOORS OPEN 7:15 P.M.

When a 26-year-old ex-GI named Elvis Presley pays $100 to climb up on a stage in Honolulu next March, 20 long and silent years will have passed for 1,102 American seamen entombed in the hull of the valiant battleship "Arizona."

The average age of those shipmates who died during the Pearl Harbor disaster was about the same as that of the guitar-strumming singer who seeks to raise at least $50,000 towards a giant memorial to the "Arizona" crew and all who died for freedom.

Symbol of Freedom

The benefit performance by Presley — only a lad of five at the time war broke out—is symbolic of a new generation of Americans who have not forgotten the price of freedom or how dearly it has been maintained.

Except for the colossal charity benefit in his home-town of

he chose to direct to the fund. Presley plans to buy the first ticket. His will cost $100. Everyone—top Navy brass, commission members and even Col. Tom Parker, Presley's manager who arranged the benefit, will pay. Though ticket costs will be scaled to meet the pocketbooks of all, a number of

TODAY: only a sign on the beach near the rusting hulk of the once mighty battleship marks the spot where the Memorial will stand. The Presley benefit would provide $50,000 of the remaining funds needed.

Memphis Dec. 25, the Honolulu public appearance will be Presley's first since he played the Hawaiian city in 1957 just prior to entry in the Army.

Filling the 4,000 seats in Pearl Harbor's Bloch Arena for the show, sponsored by the Pacific War Memorial Commission, will be a host of other Americans who will have contributed to the "Arizona" Memorial with the purchase of their tickets.

All For Arizona

All proceeds from the show will

said the $50,000 anticipated from the benefit performance will provide "bare essentials" to prepare for the official dedication ceremonies on Memorial Day May 30. Since March 15, 1958 when Congress authorized the construction of the memorial nucleus through contributions, $300,000 has been raised. It was hoped that the final construction of the building would be completed by May 30, 1961—29 years after the murderous Japanese attack in which more than 2,000 Americans lost their lives.

A Proper Tribute

Presley and the Colonel responded to the commissions' cry that fund collections had stirred to a snail's pace and "today the Arizona is but a rusting tomb . . . [while] the proposed memorial will be a

proper tribute."

The commission hopes the Presley show will not only raise money itself but will also serve as a stimulus for obtaining the rest of the $250,000 necessary before the memorial can become a reality.

Film To Follow

Col. Parker said Presley will arrive in Honolulu March 25 for the filming of "Blue Hawaii." It will begin on March 27, the day after the benefit.

The giant museum building will stand on pilings — equal to the height of an 18-story building—over the Pacific near the hulk of the "Arizona." One entire wall of the building has been designed for the Honor Roll of the "Arizona's" crew, who hailed from all 48 states which then comprised the Union.

tugs also will also pay $50 — and their seats. A second performance will be added if the demand is great enough, Col. Parker said.

Parker Answers Plea

A Los Angeles newspaper's plea for help in raising the $250,000 still needed to complete the Memorial prompted Col. Parker to fly to Honolulu several weeks ago to offer Presley's service on the condition—"Every penny of that taken in must go to the fund."

H. Tucker Gratz, chairman of the Pacific War Memorial Commission,

YESTERDAY: Col. Tom Parker (center), Elvis Presley's manager, answered a Pearl Harbor Day plea in a Los Angeles paper by flying to Honolulu to confer with Admiral E. A. Solomons, commander of the 14th Naval District, Pearl Harbor, and H. Tucker Gratz, chairman of the Pacific War Memorial Commission.

"See Elvis in Blue Hawaii" A Hal Wallis Production - Paramount Release. Soon to be filmed in Hawaii.
Reproduced by permission of Music Reporter February 20th Issue

Only $100.00 Tickets are Reserved Seats all others are Reserved Sections.

Flasher Pin: see Pin

Framed Portrait (Elvis Presley Enterprises) 1956.. $750 - $1,000
   (Reads: "Love Me Tender, Sincerely Elvis Presley.")

Frontier Hotel Table Card 1956 .... $50 - $100
   (Purple and orange card commemorating Elvis' first appearance in Las Vegas.)

G.I. Blues LP Electric Light Display (1960) .... $400 - $500
   (Promotional, in-store display piece. Has same cover as RCA LPM/LSP-2256, but
   made into a self-standing unit with an electric light bulb behind the cover.)

Game (Board) (Elvis Presley Enterprises) 1956 .... $1,500 - $2,000
   (Reads: "The Elvis Presley Game – A Party Game for the Young at Heart.")

Glass (Drinking) (Elvis Presley Enterprises) 1956 .... $350 - $450

Gloves: see Mittens

Guitar (Elvis Presley Enterprises/Emenee) 1956-1957
   Guitar with alligator pattern carrying case... $2,500 - $3,000
   Guitar by itself (no case).. $1,000 - $2,000
   Song book .... $50 - $100
      (Book reads: "For Emenee Guitar Including Elvis Presley Song Hits.")

Gum Cards: see Bubble gum cards

Handbag (Clutch) (Elvis Presley Enterprises) 1956...................................... $1,000 - $1,500

Handkerchief (Elvis Presley Enterprises) 1956 .... $500 - $750

Hat (Elvis Presley Enterprises – Magnet) 1956
   Hat with manufacturer's tag attached... $200 - $300
   Hat without special tag.. $150 - $250
      (Tag reads: "Elvis Presley Original Hat.")
   Hat tag by itself (no hat) .... $25 - $50

Hat (Paper U.S. Army hat/ticket. Made to serve as a *G.I. Blues* theater ticket. Also
   promotes both the *G.I. Blues* film and soundtrack album) 1960
   Hat/ticket with box office stub... $100 - $200
   Hat/ticket without box office stub... $75 - $100

Hat (Styrofoam straw hat) (1970s) (Reads: "Elvis Summer Festival" [Nevada hotels] on
   hatband.)... $25 - $50

Hawaiian Lei: see Lei

Herald 1953 (Senior Herald, Humes High School, Memphis, Tennessee) .... $2,000 - $3,000
   (Humes High School yearbook for Elvis' graduating – 12th grade – class. There is little
   price difference between signed and unsigned copies since very few copies exist that are
   not signed by Presley. Besides his senior picture, young Elvis is included in several
   classroom and candid campus shots. He is also mentioned in both the "Class Prophecy,"
   and "Last Will and Testament." Issued in padded hardbound, for seniors, and cardboard
   bound, for underclassmen. 112 pages.
   A limited edition – 1,000 books made – reproduction, nearly identical to the original, was
   published in 1988. These copies, which now sell for $100 to $200, are easily
   distinguished from originals by the 1988 copyright date on page two.

Herald 1952 (Humes High School, Memphis, Tennessee)................................. $250 - $500
   (Humes High School yearbook of Elvis' junior – 11th grade – class. Value is based on
   reports that Elvis is not pictured.)

Herald 1951 (Humes High School, Memphis, Tennessee).................................. $250 - $500
   (Humes High School yearbook of Elvis' sophomore – 10th grade – class. Value is based
   on reports that Elvis is not pictured.)

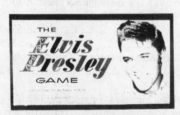

Herald 1950 (Humes High School, Memphis, Tennessee).............................. $2,000 - $3,000
(Humes High School yearbook of Elvis' freshman – 9th grade – class. A larger book than
the 1953 one. A well-groomed Elvis is pictured on page 66 in the Library Club. He is also
seen in a 9th grade group shot on page 84. Elvis is also listed among 9th grade class
members.

Hit Tunes Charms (Hit Tunes Jewelry) 1958
    Bracelet, by itself or with non-Elvis charms... $50 - $75
    "Don't" or "Jail House Rock" charm for bracelet.. $50 - $75
    "Don't" or "Jail House Rock" sweater guard .... $50 - $75
    "Don't" or "Jail House Rock" tie bar.. $50 - $75
    "Don't" or "Jail House Rock" earring (one).. $50 - $75
    Mail order, 24k gold plated 45 rpm shaped jewelry, each with a miniature record label.
    Buyers could select from 26 hit titles, two of which were by Elvis. The record label
    charms were fabricated into bracelets, sweater guards, cuff links, tie bar, and earrings.

Hot Plate Holder: see Ceramic tile

Hound Dog (Elvis Presley Enterprises; 10" dog, and "Hound Dog" hat) 1956 ... $300 - $500
    Hound Dog (Small – approximately 8" to 9" – "Elvis Summer Festival"
    dog with ribbon) 1972... $100 - $150
    Hound Dog (Large – approximately 12" to 15" – "Elvis Summer Festival"
    dog with ribbon) 1972... $300 - $500

Humes Herald: see Herald 1953

Identification Bracelet: see Bracelet

Invitations: see Opening night invitations

Iron-on Emblem: see Patch

Jaycee's Booklet: see United States Jaycees Tribute Booklet

Jeans (Elvis Presley Enterprises/Blue Ridge) 1956
    Pants with "Elvis Presley Jeans" tag.. $250 - $350
    Pants without tag... $200 - $300
    Tag by itself (no pants) .... $25 - $50

Juke Box Title Strips: see Title strips

Key Chain (Flasher, or Double-Image) (Elvis Presley Enterprises/
    Pictorial Prod.) 1956 .... $25 - $50

Key Chain/Coin Purse: see Coin Purse/Key Chain

**Kissin' Cousins (Elvis Sings on RCA Victor) Electric Light
Display** (1964).. $250 - $300
    (Promotional, in-store display piece. Has a photo of Elvis taken from the same
    session as the "Elvis as Josh" shot in the lower left on the back of RCA LPM-2894,
    but made into a self-standing unit with an electric light bulb behind the cover.
    Unlike on the LP cover, the display photo shows Elvis holding a guitar.)

Knoxville Tribune: see Kissin' Cousins (Movie-Related Memorabilia)

Lei (1961) .... $200 - $300
    (Pictures Elvis on one side; promotes the *Blue Hawaii* LP on the reverse)

Lipstick (Elvis Presley Enterprises/Teen-Ager Lipstick Corp.) 1956
    Lipstick in tube (with engraved autographed) still attached to card .... $1,000 - $1,500
    (Heart on card reads: "Keep Me Always on Your Lips, Elvis Presley.")
    Lipstick in tube by itself (no card).. $400 - $600

Locket (Elvis Presley Enterprises) 1957 .... $100 - $200
    (Heart-shaped. Reads: "Elvis Presley.")

Magazines (Published between June 1955 and August 16, 1977)

The focus here is mainly on issues of magazines which at least picture Elvis on the front cover. For any issues containing a feature Elvis story but not picturing him—on either the front or back cover – or for ones that pictures him on the back cover but not on the front, estimate the value at about one-half to two thirds the price of those listed here.

Amazing Elvis Presley 1956.. $100 - $150

Assorted Magazine Supplements (Inserted into local newspapers)

(Price is for any issue with Elvis' picture on the front cover.) These are not weekly TV magazine inserts, which are listed separately—see: *TV Magazine Supplements.*)

Published between 1956 and 1959.. $75 - $100

Published between 1960 and 1969... $40- $80

Published between 1970 and 1977... $30 - $50

Best Songs June 1956.. $75 - $125

Circus Pinups No. 3: The Elvis Years August 1975 .... $25 - $50

Complete TV February 1957 .... $25 - $50

Confidential 1957 .... $25 - $50

(Price is any issue with Elvis' picture on the cover.)

Cool: "Special Issue on Elvis Presley" 1957 .... $100 - $125

Country Music November 1975.. $10 - $20

Country Song Roundup July, 1955 .... $100 - $150

(Pictures Hank Snow on front cover, but headline reads: "Elvis Presley Folk Music Fireball." Elvis' picture appears with story, on page 14.

Country Song Roundup 1956-1960... $50 - $100

(Price is for any issue with Elvis' picture on the front cover.)

Cowboy Songs June, 1955.. $100 - $150

(Has front cover mention of Presley – "Elvis Presley: A Dream Come True" – the first ever on a nationally distributed magazine.)

Dig 1956-1958 .... $75 - $125

(Price is for any issue with Elvis' picture on the front cover.)

Electronic Age Winter '64/'65 .... $100 - $200

(Has "Compliments, Elvis and the Colonel" stamped in gold on front. Has a chapter about Elvis. Made for distribution to RCA stockholders.)

Elvis & Jimmy (Elvis Presley & James Dean) 1956 .... $150 - $250

Elvis & Tom (Elvis Presley & Tom Jones) 1969 .... $25- $35

Elvis Answers Back: see the Singles section of the records chapter, see both *Elvis Presley "Speaks – In Person!"* and *Elvis Presley "The Truth About Me"*

Elvis: His Loves & Marriage 1957 .... $75 - $125

Elvis in the Army 1959... $75 - $125

Elvis: 1971 Presley Album 1971 .... $25 - $35

Elvis 1974 Calendar .... $15 - $25

Elvis Photo Album ("125 Photos Never Before Published") 1956 .... $100 - $200

Elvis Presley ("More Than 100 Pictures – Complete Life Story") 1956 .... $100 - $200

Elvis Presley – Hero Or Heel? 1956 .... $150 - $250

Elvis Presley in Hollywood 1956.. $100 - $200

Elvis Presley Song Hits 1965 .... $50 - $75

Elvis Presley Speaks! 1956 .... $100 - $200

Elvis Song Hits, No. 1 .... $60 - $100
(32-pages. Has *Love Me Tender* Elvis photo on the front cover, and a *Jailhouse Rock,* color photo on back.)
Elvis: The Hollywood Years 1976.. $15 - $25
Elvis: The Intimate Story 1957 .... $100 - $200
Elvis the King Returns 1960 .... $50 - $75
Elvis: The Trials and Triumphs of the Legendary King of Rock & Roll 1976 ..... $15 - $25
Elvis vs. the Beatles 1965.. $100 - $200
Elvis Yearbook 1960 .... $100 - $150
Elvis Years: see Circus
Elvis Yesterday...Today 1975... $15 - $25
Filmland 1957... $50 - $100
Folk and Country Songs 1956-1959 .... $25 - $50
(Price is for any issue with Elvis' picture on the front cover.)
Forum... $15 - $25
(Price is for any issue with Elvis' picture on the front cover.)
Hank Snow Souvenir Photo Album 1955 .... $250 - $450
(Concert tour souvenir photo album. Pictures Hank and Jimmie Rodgers Snow on the cover, but has photos and some background on Elvis inside.)
Hep Cats 1956-1958 .... $100 - $200
(Price is for any issue with Elvis' picture on the front cover.)
Hit Parader 1956-1972.. $15 - $35
(Price is for any issue with Elvis' picture on the front cover.)
Hollywood Rebels 1957 .... $50 - $100
I Love You No. 60 – Here Comes Elvis 1966...................................... $40 - $60
John's Pocket Movie Book 1957 .... $50 - $75
(An action flip book. When pages are flipped briskly, Elvis appears to dance.)
Life April 30, 1956.. $25 - $50
(Has illustrated feature story, but Elvis is not pictured on the front cover.)
Life August 27, 1956... $25 - $50
(Has illustrated feature story, but Elvis is not pictured on the front cover.)
Life March 25, 1957.. $25 - $50
(Has illustrated feature story, but Elvis is not pictured on the front cover.)
Look August 7, 1956.. $25 - $50
(Has illustrated feature story, but Elvis is not pictured on the front cover.)
Look November 13, 1956.. $25 - $50
(Has illustrated feature story, but Elvis is not pictured on the front cover.)
Look May 4, 1971. (Front cover pictures Elvis) .... $15 - $25
Look May 11, 1971 (Part two of story begun May 4)............................ $10 - $20
(Has illustrated feature story, but Elvis is not pictured on the front cover.)
Lowdown 1956... $75 - $100
Modern Screen 1956-1957... $25 - $50
(Price is for any issue with Elvis' picture on the front cover.)
Modern Teen 1960 .... $20 - $40
Motion Picture 1957-1958... $25 - $50
Movie Album, 1965 .... $20 - $30
Movie & TV Show 1960 .... $20 - $40
Movie Digest 1972 .... $10 - $15
(Price is for any issue with Elvis' picture on the front cover.)

Movie Dream Guys 1960 .... $20 - $40
Movie Guide 1962 .... $20 - $40
   (Price is for any issue with Elvis' picture on the front cover.)
Movie Life 1957-1960 .... $20 - $40
   (Price is for any issue with Elvis' picture on the front cover.)
Movie Life Year Book 1958 .... $20 - $40
Movie Mirror 1959 .... $20 - $40
Movie Stars Parade 1957 .... $20 - $40
Movie Stars TV Close-Ups 1960 .... $20 - $40
   (Price is for any issue with Elvis' picture on the front cover.)
Movie Stars TV Close-Ups Parade 1958 .... $20 - $40
Movie TV Album 1957 .... $20 - $40
Movie TV Record Stardom 1960 .... $20 - $40
Movie TV Secrets 1959-1960 .... $20 - $40
   (Price is for any issue with Elvis' picture on the front cover.)
Movie Teen: Special Elvis Issue 1961 .... $35 - $55
Movie Teen Illustrated 1959 .... $20 - $40
Movie World 1959-1960 .... $20 - $40
   (Price is for any issue with Elvis' picture on the front cover.)
Movieland 1957 .... $20 - $40
Movieland and TV Time 1959-1961 .... $20 - $40
   (Price is for any issue with Elvis' picture on the front cover.)
Offical Elvis Presley Album 1956 .... $150 - $250
On the Q.T. 1960 .... $40 - $60
   (Price is for any issue with Elvis' picture on the front cover.)
People January 13, 1975 .... $10 - $20
Personalities 1957 .... $75 - $125
Photoplay
   (Price is for any issue with Elvis' picture on the front cover.)
1957-1959 .... $20 - $30
1960-1976 .... $5 - $15
Popular Screen 1960 .... $15 - $25
Popular TV Movie and Record Stars 1960 .... $15 - $25
Rave 1956-1957 .... $20 - $40
   (Price is for any issue with Elvis' picture on the front cover.)
Record Time – TV Movies 1960 .... $20 - $30
Record Whirl 1956 .... $50 - $75
Rock and Roll Songs 1956-1958 .... $20 30
   (Price is for any issue with Elvis' picture on the front cover.)
Rock & Roll Stars No. 1: The Real Elvis Presley Story 1956 .... $100 - $200
Rock & Roll Stars No. 2: Elvis Answers 10 Important Teenage
   Questions 1957 .... $75 - $125
Rock & Roll Stars No. 3: Elvis in the Army? 1958 .... $50 - $100
Rock 'n' Roll Battlers 1956 .... $75 - $125
Rock 'n' Roll Jamboree 1956 .... $75 - $125
Rock 'n' Roll Rivals 1957 .... $75 - $125
Rock and Roll Roundup 1957 .... $75 - $125
Rolling Stone 1969-1972 .... $10 - $15
   (Price is for any issue with Elvis' picture on the front cover.)

ELVIS IS BACK-
AND TV GUIDE'S GOT HIM!

YES, THE KING HAS RETURNED! HIS FIRST
BIG CIVILIAN ASSIGNMENT -- TO BRING
THE PRESLEY MAGIC BACK TO TELEVISION
IN A TV SPECIAL WITH ANOTHER GENTLEMAN
OF NO LITTLE POPULARITY, FRANK SINATRA!

THE MAY 7 ISSUE OF TV GUIDE FEATURES
ELVIS AND FRANK ON THE COVER...AND
CONTAINS A TERRIFIC ARTICLE ON ELVIS'
RETURN AND HIS POPULARITY -- PAST AND
PRESENT! THERE'S ALSO A SPECIAL STORY
BY A TV GUIDE REPORTER WHO WAS ON
THE SCENE WHEN THE MAY 12 TELEVISION
SHOW WAS TAPED IN MIAMI.

THIS IS ONE MAGAZINE YOU WON'T WANT
TO MISS -- FROM THE FABULOUS AUSTIN
BRIGGS DRAWING OF ELVIS ON THE COVER
TO THE LAST WORD OF THE SONG WRITTEN
TO WELCOME HIM HOME.

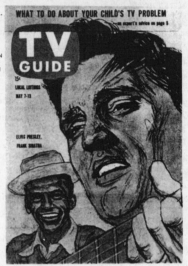

GET THE MAY 7TH ISSUE OF TV GUIDE!
TELL ALL YOUR FRIENDS ABOUT IT, TOO!

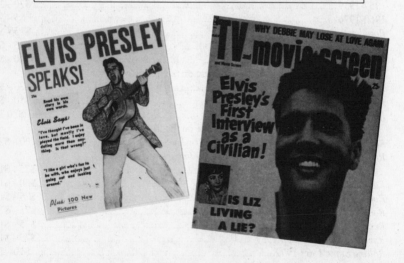

Screen Parade 1958 .... $25 - $50
Screen Stars 1959 .... $25 - $50
Screenland (Plus TV Land) 1965 .... $15 - $25
  (Price is for any issue with Elvis' picture on the front cover.)
Silver Screen 1960 .... $20 - $40
Sixteen .... $20 - $40
  (Price is for any issue with Elvis' picture on the front cover.)
Song Hits Magazine 1956-1963 .... $20 - $40
  (Price is for any issue with Elvis' picture on the front cover.)
Songs and Stars 1965 .... $15 - $25
Songs That Will Live Forever 1956 .... $25 - $35
Souvenir Photo Album: see Photo Albums
Stardom 1960 .... $20 - $40
Starlife TV & Movies Direct from Hollywood 1959 .... $20 - $40
Story of Life .... $8 - $12
Suppressed Annual 1956 .... $40 - $60
TV and Movie Screen 1956-1962 .... $20 - $30
  (Price is for any issue with Elvis' picture on the front cover.)
TV and Screen Life (1960) .... $20 - $30
TV Film Stars 1960 .... $20 - $30
  (Price is for any issue with Elvis' picture on the front cover.)
TV Guide (Week of) September 8-14, 1956 .... $200 - $250
  (Elvis pictured on cover)
TV Guide (Week of) September 22-28, 1956 .... $100 - $150
  (Has illustrated feature story, but Elvis' is not pictured on the front cover.)
TV Guide (Week of) September 29-October 5, 1956 .... $100 - $150
  (Has illustrated feature story, but Elvis' is not pictured on the front cover.)
TV Guide (Week of) May 7-13, 1960 .... $75 - $125
  (Cover has a rendering of Elvis and Frank Sinatra, by *TV Guide* artist, Arthur
  Briggs. Some media copies were accompanied by a one-page flier, headlined:
  "Elvis Is Back – And TV Guide's Got Him")
(Original Art for) *TV Guide* (Week of) May 7-13, 1960 .... $2,500 - $3,500
  (11" x 14½", color art of Elvis and Frank Sinatra, as originally drawn and colored
  by the artist, Arthur Briggs. Originally wrapped in TV Guide art department
  matting.)
TV Guide (Week of) November 30, 1968 .... $15 - $25
  (Has illustrated feature story on the making of the NBC-TV special, but Elvis is
  not pictured on the front cover.)
TV Guide (Week of) March 31, 1973 .... $10 - $20
  (Has illustrated feature story on "Elvis, Aloha from Hawaii via Satellite," but
  Elvis' is not pictured on the front cover.)
TV Guide (Week of) November 10-16, 1973 .... $10 - $20
  (Elvis and others are pictured on cover)
TV Headliner 1957 .... $35 - $50
  (Price is for any issue with Elvis' picture on the front cover.)
TV Picture Life 1959-1960 .... $20 - $40
  (Price is for any issue with Elvis' picture on the front cover.)
TV Movie Fan 1956 .... $35 - $50
TV–Movie Men 1959 .... $20 - $40

TV Radio Mirror 1960 .... $15 - $25

TV Picture Life 1960 .... $15 - $25

TV Record Superstars 1970 .... $15 - $25

TV Screen Diary 1961 .... $40 - $60

    (This was issue No. 1 of a TV Guide clone. No cover date shown.)

TV Star Parade 1958-1960 .... $20 - $40

    (Price is for any issue with Elvis' picture on the front cover.)

TV Magazine Supplements (Inserted into local newspapers, with schedule of upcoming week's shows. Price is for any issue with Elvis' picture on the front cover.These are not feature magazine inserts – such as *Parade* – which are listed separately as *Assorted Magazine Supplements.*)

    Published between 1956 and 1959 .... $25 - $50

    Published between 1960 and 1969 .... $20 - $35

    Published between 1970 and 1977 .... $8 - $15

TV World December 1956 .... $25 - $35

Teen Life 1957 .... $75 - $125

Teen Screen 1961 .... $20 - $30

Teenage Rock and Roll Review October 1956 .... $75 - $125

Teenage Rock and Roll Review December 1956 .... $75 - $125

Teenville 1960 .... $25 - $50

Tommy Sands vs. Belafonte and Elvis 1957 .... $75 - $125

Top Secret 1960 .... $25 - $35

Young Lovers No. 18: The Real Elvis Presley Complete Life Story 1957 .... $200 - $300

Zoo World (Tabloid) September 13, 1973 .... $10 - $15

Medallion (Elvis Presley Enterprises) 1956 .... $200 - $400

    ("I Want You, I Need You, I Love You-Don't Be Cruel-Hound Dog-Heartbreak Hotel.")

Menus (Nevada Hotels)

    August 1969 (International: Las Vegas) .... $600 - $800

    1970 (International: Las Vegas) .... $150 - $250

    1971 (International: Las Vegas) .... $100 - $200

    1971 (Sahara Tahoe: Lake Tahoe) .... $200 - $250

    1972 (Hilton: Las Vegas) .... $60 - $75

    1973 (Hilton: Las Vegas) .... $30 - $50

    (Menu about the size – 7" – and shape of a 45 rpm record.)

    1973 (Hilton: Las Vegas) .... $30 - $50

    (Larger version of above. Reads: "This menu for maitre'd and captain's use only.")

    1973 (Sahara Tahoe: Lake Tahoe) .... $60 - $100

    1974 (Hilton: Las Vegas) .... $60 - $75

    1974 (Sahara Tahoe: Lake Tahoe) .... $75 - $100

    1975 (Hilton: Las Vegas) .... $60 - $75

    (Front pictures Elvis in "Peacock" suit, from the waist up.)

    1975 (Hilton – Cancelled Engagement: Las Vegas) .... $125 - $150

    (Front pictures Elvis in *Aloha from Hawaii* "Eagle" suit – head and shoulders only.)

    1975 (Hilton: Las Vegas) .... $60 - $75

    (Pictures Elvis through die-cut hole. Has a large rainbow and "Hilton Showroom.")

Menu/Photo Album: see Photo album/opening night menu

Mittens (Elvis Presley Enterprises/Nolan) 1956

    Pair of mittens .... $400 - $600

    Single mitten .... $100 - $150

Movie-Related Memorabilia

In this section you will find the most commonly traded collectibles from the film studios, all of which was used in the promotion and exploitation of Elvis' movies. Films appear in chronological order and the items associated with each film are listed alphabetically. This list does not include Elvis Presley Enterprises products that just happen to mention a film title. Such items are listed in their own sections. Among the unusual terms found in this section are:

One-Sheet: A One-sheet is a colorful 27" x 41" paper poster, intended for display by theaters in a case, usually behind glass, outside the building or in the lobby. This is the most commonly circulated movie poster, as every theater uses one-sheets, even if they can not display larger sheets. Usually, theaters in bigger cities order more merchandising paraphernalia than rural and small-town theaters. Though the one-sheet is the only movie poster size listed in this edition, use the following formula to estimate the value of larger sheets:

Three-Sheet: (41" x 81") = 25% to 50% increase over one-sheet price.

Six-Sheet: (81" x 81") = 100% to 125% increase over one-sheet price.

Twenty-Four Sheet: (108" x 162") = 400% to 500% increase over one-sheet price.
Sometimes similar to one-sheets in appearance – but different in size – are the following:

Stills are studio 8' x 10" photo prints showing scenes from the film. Stills for Elvis films can be found in both black-and-white and full color.

Lobby Cards are 11" x 14" and usually issued in sets of eight – each picturing a different scene from the film. Lobby cards are printed (in full color), whereas stills are photographically, or chemically developed prints.

Window Cards are 14" x 22"

Insert Cards are 14" x 36"

Lobby Photos are 22" x 28"

(All sizes are approximate. There may be slight variations in size from one film to another. Occasionally, a card does *not* picture Elvis because he does not appear in the scene from the film, reproduced on the card. Those not picturing Elvis are valued at the low end of the price range. Since stills and cards often turn up individually, prices here are for just one. To appraise a set of six, for example, simply multiply the price by six.)

Love Me Tender (1956)

Insert Card	$200 - $400
Lobby Card	$75 - $100
Lobby Photo	$200 - $400
One-Sheet	$350 - $500
Press Book (20th Century-Fox *Exhibitor's Campaign Book*)	$200 - $300
Standee	$800 - $1200

(Pictures Elvis in costume, holding a guitar. Reads: "Elvis Presley as he appears in his first motion picture Love Me Tender.")

Still	$20 - $25
Theater Pictorial (Magazine)	$200 - $300
Window Card	$125 - $200

Loving You (1957)

Insert Card .... $175 - $300
Lobby Card .... $65 - $85
Lobby Photo .... $175 - $300
One-Sheet .... $200 - $400
Press Book (Paramount *Showmanship Manual*) .... $100 - $200
Standee .... $800 - $1000
  (Pictures Elvis in costume, with his guitar. Reads: "You'll love Elvis in Loving
  You.")
Still .... $20 -$25
Window Card .... $100 -$200

Jailhouse Rock (1957)

Insert Card .... $350 - $500
Lobby Card .... $75 - $125
Lobby Photo .... $350 - $500
One-Sheet .... $900 - $1300
Program .... $100 - $200
  (Four-page theater program. Credits film songs, cast, and others.)
Press Book (MGM Press Book *Advertising-Publicity-Exploitation*) .... $125 - $200
Still .... $20 - $25
Window Card .... $185 - $275

King Creole (1958)

Insert Card .... $150 - $300
Lobby Card .... $60 - $80
Lobby Photo .... $150 - $300
One-Sheet .... $250 - $400
Press Book (Paramount *Showmanship Manual*) .... $75 - $150
Still .... $20 - $25
Window Card .... $100 - $200

King Creole (Reissue–1959)

Insert Card .... $175 - $250
Lobby Card .... $60 - $85
Lobby Photo .... $175 - $250
One-Sheet .... $150 - $300
Press Book (Paramount *Campaign King Creole*) .... $50 - $75
Still .... $15 - $20
Window Card .... $75 - $150

G.I. Blues (1960)

Insert Card .... $100 - $200
Lobby Card .... $30 - $50
Lobby Photo .... $100 - $200
Mug .... $100 - $200
  (Glass mug. Reads: "Hal Wallis' G.I. Blues." Has signatures of Elvis Presley and
  Juliet Prowse.)
One-Sheet .... $150 - $300
Press Book (Paramount *Press Book*) .... $50 - $75
Standee .... $200 - $300
  (Life-size, Elvis in uniform holding a guitar.)

Standee.. $200 - $300
   (Pictures head and shoulder shot of Elvis in uniform with a reduced, full-body photo of
   Juliet Prowse on Elvis' left shoulder. Bottom has three scenes from the film.)
Still.. $10 - $20
Window Card... $50 - $100

Flaming Star (1960)

Insert Card.. $75 - $130
Lobby Card .... $25 - $40
Lobby Photo... $75 - $130
One-Sheet.. $90 - $175
Press Book (20th Century-Fox *Exhibitor's Campaign Manual*)............. $50 - $75
Standee.. $100 - $200
   (Life size and shape, black and white. Pictures Elvis in costume, holding a pistol.)
Standee.. $100 - $200
   (Rectangular. Most prominent picture shows a shirtless Elvis holding a rifle.)
Still.. $10 - $20
Window Card... $45 - $75

Wild in the Country (1961)

Insert Card.. $75 - $125
Lobby Card .... $25 - $40
Lobby Photo... $75 - $125
One-Sheet.. $85 - $150
Press Book (20th Century-Fox *Exhibitor's Campaign Manual*)............. $50 - $75
Still.. $10 - $20
Window Card... $40 - $70

Blue Hawaii (1961)

Coloring Contest Entry Sheet .... $25 - $50
   (Has a drawing of Elvis with guitar, five dancing girls and a beach scene in the
   background, all to be colored.)
Insert Card.. $85 - $150
Lobby Card .... $30 - $50
Lobby Photo... $85 - $150
Mug.. $350 - $450
   (Tiki mug. Reads: "Hal Wallis Production, Elvis Presley, Blue Hawaii a
   Paramount Picture, T.O.A. Convention 1961, New Orleans, La.")
One-Sheet.. $100 - $225
Press Book (Paramount *Merchandising Manual*)................................ $40 - $60
Still.. $10 - $20
Window Card... $50 - $100

Follow That Dream (1962)

Balloon with cardboard base... $50 - $75
   (Balloon reads: "Elvis in Follow That Dream," and plugs the soundtrack EP.)
Insert Card.. $45 - $90
Lobby Card .... $20 - $30
Lobby Photo... $45 - $90
One-Sheet.. $60 - $125
Press Book (United Artists *Pressbook*)... $40 - $60
Still.. $10 - $20
Window Card... $40 - $70

Kid Galahad (1962)

Balloon with cardboard base.. $50 - $75
(Balloon reads: "Elvis in Kid Galahad," and plugs the soundtrack EP.)
Coloring Contest Entry Sheet .... $25 - $50
(Has drawings of Elvis with guitar, Elvis wearing boxing gloves and trunks, and
other scenes to be colored.)
Insert Card.. $45 - $90
Lobby Card .... $20 - $30
Lobby Photo... $45 - $90
One-Sheet... $80 - $150
Press Book (United Artists *Pressbook*)... $25 - $50
Still... $10 - $20
Window Card .... $40 - $70

Girl! Girls! Girls! (1962)

Coloring Contest Entry Sheet .... $25 - $50
(Has a drawing of Elvis and six girls on a boat, to be colored. A "Record
Lane"/Paramount Pictures promotion, with tickets to see Girls! Girls! Girls! being
the significant prizes. Sheet includes color paint palette.)
Insert Card.. $50 - $90
Lobby Card .... $20 - $25
Lobby photo... $50 - $90
One-Sheet... $75 - $125
Press Book (Paramount *Merchandising Manual*).................................. $25 - $50
Still... $10 - $15
Window Card .... $35 - $60

It Happened at the World's Fair (1963)

Insert Card.. $40 - $80
Lobby Card .... $25 - $35
Lobby Photo... $40 - $80
One-Sheet... $50 - $100
Press Book (MGM *Press Book*).. $25 - $50
Still... $10 - $15
Window Card .... $35 - $60

Fun in Acapulco (1963)

Insert Card.. $40 - $85
Lobby Card .... $20 - $25
Lobby Photo... $40 - $85
One-Sheet... $60 - $110
Press Book (Paramount *Merchandising Manual*).................................. $25 - $50
Still... $10 - $15
Window Card .... $35 - $60

Kissin' Cousins (1964)

Button... $50 - $75
(Reads: "I'm a Kissin' Cousin.")
Insert Card.. $40 - $70
Knoxville Tribune (Faux newspaper) .... $100 - $200
(Headline reads: "Anyone for Missiles?" Pictures Elvis, as Jody, and three girls from
the film cast. Newspaper front page, made as a prop for the movie.)
Lobby Card .... $15 - $25

Program

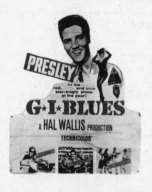

Lobby Photo... $40 - $70
One-Sheet... $50 - $85
Press Book (MGM *Press Book*)................................. $25 - $50
Still... $8 - $12
Window Card.. $25 - $50

Viva Las Vegas (1964)

Insert Card... $150 - $200
Lobby Card... $40 - $60
Lobby Photo.. $150 - $200
One-Sheet (Style A).. $250 - $500
  (Pictures Elvis dancing on left side of poster, Ann-Margret dancing on the right side.)
One-Sheet (Style B).. $300 - $600
  (Pictures Elvis and Ann-Margret close together.)
Press Book (MGM *Press Book*)................................. $25 - $50
Still... $10 - $15
Window Card.. $75 - $130

Roustabout (1964)

Insert Card.. $40 - $80
Lobby Card.. $15 - $25
Lobby Photo.. $40 - $80
One-Sheet... $60 - $100
Press Book (Paramount *Merchandising Manual*)........ $25 - $40
Still... $8 - $12
Window Card.. $25 - $50

Girl Happy (1965)

Insert Card.. $40 - $80
Lobby Card.. $20 - $25
Lobby Photo.. $40 - $80
One-Sheet... $50 - $100
Press Book (MGM *Exhibitor's Campaign Book*)......... $25 - $40
Still... $8 - $12
Window Card.. $30 - $50

Tickle Me (1965)

Insert Card.. $40 - $60
Lobby Card.. $20 - $25
Lobby Photo.. $40 - $75
One-Sheet... $50 - $85
Pen... $20 - $30
  (Has feather on one end that reads: "Elvis Presley in Tickle Me.")
Press Book (Allied Artists *On the Go!*)..................... $25 - $50
Press Pack.. $40 - $60
  (Has feathers inside. Reads: "Elvis At His Best in Tickle Me." Also lists
  song titles in the film.)
Still... $8 - $12
Window Card.. $25 - $40

Harum Scarum (1965)

Insert Card	$50 - $80
Lobby Card	$20 - $30
Lobby Photo	$50 - $80
One-Sheet	$75 - $100
Press Book (MGM *Exhibitor's Campaign Book*)	$25 - $40
Still	$8 - $12
Window Card	$35 - $60

Frankie and Johnny (1966)

Insert Card	$40 - $65
Lobby Card	$20 - $30
Lobby Photo	$50 - $85
One-Sheet	$65 - $90
Press Book (United Artists *Pressbook*)	$25 - $40
Still	$8 - $12
Window Card	$35 - $50

Paradise Hawaiian Style (1966)

Insert Card	$50 - $80
Lobby Card	$20 - $50
Lobby Photo	$50 - $80
One-Sheet	$75 - $125
Press Book (Paramount *Press Book and Merchandising Manual*)	$25 - $40
Still	$8 - $12
Window Card	$35 - $60

Spinout (1966)

Insert Card	$40 - $75
Lobby Card	$20 - $30
Lobby Photo	$40 - $75
One-Sheet	$65 - $90
Press Book (MGM *Exhibitor's Campaign Book*)	$25 - $40
Still	$8 - $12
Window Card	$30 - $50

Fun in Acapulco/Girls! Girls! Girls (Reissue–1966)

Insert Card	$75 - $100
Lobby Card	$30 - $40
Lobby Photo	$100 - $200
One-Sheet	$75 - $150
Press Book (Paramount *Press Book and Merchandising Manual*)	$25 - $40
Still	$8 - $12
Window Card	$40 - $70

Easy Come, Easy Go (1967)

Insert Card	$40 - $75
Lobby Card	$25 - $40
Lobby Photo	$40 - $75
One-Sheet	$65 - $90
Press Book (Paramount *Press Book and Merchandising Manual*)	$25 - $40
Still	$8 - $12
Window Card	$25 - $40

Double Trouble (1967)

Insert Card	$35 - $65
Lobby Card	$15 - $25
Lobby Photo	$35 - $65
One-Sheet	$50 - $80
Press Book (MGM *Press Book*)	$25 - $40
Standee	$100 - $200

(Pictures two Elvises, each holding a guitar, plus other scenes from the film.)

Still	$8 - $12
Window Card	$30 - $50

Also see *Double Trouble Electric Light Display*

Clambake (1967)

Insert Card	$40 - $75
Lobby Card	$15 - $25
Lobby Photo	$40 - $75
One-Sheet	$60 - $95
Press Book (United Artists *Pressbook*)	$25 - $40
Still	$8 - $12
Window Card	$35 - $60

Stay Away Joe (1968)

Insert Card	$40 - $70
Lobby Card	$15 - $25
Lobby Photo	$40 - $70
One-Sheet	$50 - $75
Press Book (MGM *Exhibitor's Campaign Book*)	$25 - $40
Standee	$75 - $125

(Pictures Elvis on a bull, plus other scenes from the film.)

Still	$8 - $12
Window Card	$30 - $50

Speedway (1968)

Insert Card	$40 - $70
Lobby Card	$20 - $25
Lobby Photo	$40 - $70
One-Sheet	$50 - $100
Press Book (MGM *Pressbook*)	$25 - $40
Standee	$75 - $125

(Pictures Elvis dancing with Nancy Sintara.)

Still	$8 - $12
Window Card	$30 - $50

Live a Little, Love a Little (1968)

Insert Card	$40 - $75
Lobby Card	$20 - $25
Lobby Photo	$40 - $75
One-Sheet	$75 - $100
Press Book (MGM *Pressbook*)	$25 - $40
Still	$8 - $12
Window Card	$25 - $40

Charro (1969)

Insert Card	$60 - $90
Lobby Card	$20 - $30
Lobby Photo	$60 - $90
One-Sheet	$80 - $125
Press Book (National General Pictures *Pressbook*)	$25 - $40
Still	$8 - $12
Window Card	$30 - $50

Trouble with Girls (1969)

Insert Card	$50 - $75
Lobby Card	$20 - $25
Lobby Photo	$50 - $75
One-Sheet	$75 - $100
Press Book (MGM *Exhibitor's Campaign Book*)	$25 - $40
Still	$8 - $12
Window Card	$30 - $50

Change of Habit (1969)

Insert Card	$25 - $45
Lobby Card	$20 - $25
Lobby Photo	$25 - $45
One-Sheet	$40 - $70
Press Book (Universal City Studios *Advertising-Publicity-Promotion*)	$25 - $40
Still	$8 - $12
Window Card	$30 - $50

Elvis—That's the Way It Is (1970)

Insert Card	$45 - $75
Lobby Card	$25 - $40
Lobby Photo	$45 - $75
One-Sheet	$65 - $90
Press Book (MGM *Exhibitor's Merchandising Manual*)	$25 - $40
Standee	$100 - $150
(Pictures Elvis holding a microphone.)	
Still	$10 - $15
Window Card	$35 - $50

Elvis on Tour (1972)

Insert Card	$45 - $75
Lobby Card	$25 - $35
Lobby Photo	$45 - $75
One-Sheet	$70 - $100
Press Book (MGM *Pressbook*)	$25 - $40
Still	$10 - $15
Window Card	$35 - $60

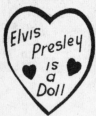

Necklace (Elvis Presley Enterprises) 1956
  Necklace attached to card .... $300 - $500
  Necklace by itself (no card) .... $150 - $250
    (Heart-shaped, with engraving of Elvis)
Necklace (Elvis Presley Enterprises) 1962 .... $50 - $75
    (Reads "Follow That Dream.")
Notebook: see Binder
Opening night invitations (Las Vegas and Lake Tahoe) 1970s
    (Opening night invitations to these engagements were sent to the press and
    assorted VIPs. Most were printed on paper though some were more elaborate.
    Most invited guests also received a personal letter from the publicity office of the
    hotel.)
  Printed (paper) invitation 15-25
  Felt, three-foot, banner/invitation, for January 26, 1972 .... $100 - $200
Overnight Case: see Carrying case
Paint Set (Prenumbered, with oil colors) (Elvis Presley Enterprises) 1956 ...... $800 - $1,200
Pajamas (Elvis Presley Enterprises) 1956 .... $600 - $900
    (Pictures Elvis singing. Lists the songs: "Heartbreak Hotel," "Don't Be Cruel,"
    "Hound Dog," and "I Want You, I Need You.")
Pants: see Jeans
Paper Doll 1957 .... $75 - $100
    (This 7" doll depicts Elvis holding a guitar. Back reads: "This is given free with
    Roxy and comes with Elvis' best wishes.")
Paperweight 1960s .... $15 - $20
    (Has the June Kelly Elvis portrait imbedded in plastic. Reads: "Sincerely Yours,
    Elvis.")
Patches (Iron-on) (Elvis Presley Enterprises) 1956
  Display card with patches attached .... $100 - $200
  Individual patch (no card) .... $40 - $60
    (Heart-shaped. Three variations known, reading: "My Heart Belongs to Elvis
    Presley," "I Love Elvis Presley" or "Elvis Presley Is a Doll.")
    Also see: *Tour Patches/Ribbons*
Pen (Ball point) 1959 .... $40 - $60
    (Yellow and white pen. Bottom has "Elvis Presley, c/o Graceland, 3764 Hi-Way 51
    South, Memphis, Tenn." In black print on yellow. Top has "U.S.A." stamped in
    white.)
Pen (Ball point, Las Vegas concert souvenir) 1970s .... $15 - $25
    (Solid color, with chrome-like top, pocket clip, and tip. Reads: "From Elvis and the
    Colonel.")
Pen (Ball point, RCA) 1972 .... $15 - $25
    (Solid color. Reads: "Elvis Now 1972 Now RCA.")
Pencil (Elvis Presley Enterprises/Union Pencil Co.) 1956
  Complete box of "one dozen packs" of "Elvis Presley Pencils" .... $1,500 - $2,500
  Box by itself (no pencils) .... $100 - $200
    (Box reads: "Sincerely Yours, Elvis Presley.")
  Wrapped 12-pack of pencils .... $300 - $400
  Individual pencil .... $25 - $35
    (Pencil reads: "Sincerely Yours, Elvis Presley.")

Pencil Holder/Sharpener 1957... $100 - $200
   (Square, wooden desktop holder. Has a circular, color Elvis photo on the front. Holds 12
   pencils, or pens. Has a sharpener on the lower right side.)
Pencil Sharpener (Elvis Presley Enterprises) 1956 .... $150 - $250
   (Circular sharpener, with photo of Elvis on the top.)
Pennant .... $50 - $75
   (From the '50s or early '60s. Has six hearts and four stars, and reads: "I Love Elvis.")
Pennant (Elvis Presley Enterprises) 1962... $50 - $75
   (Felt, Tupelo souvenir. Reads: "Birthplace, Elvis Presley, Tupelo, Miss.")
Pennant (RCA/Las Vegas/Tahoe) 1970s... $25 - $35
   (Felt Elvis pennants exist in several colors – red, blue, yellow, white, etc. – and display
   Elvis picture or image from either the '50s, '60s, or '70s. Text may vary, including
   references to a Las Vegas or Tahoe engagement, or such slogans as "The King of Rock
   and Roll – The One and Only Elvis" or "I Love Elvis.")
Perfume ("Eau de Parfum") (Elvis Presley Enterprises) 1957............................. $300 - $500
   (Reads "Elvis Presley's Teddy Bear." Has a 1957 picture of Elvis on label. "Elvis
   Presley Enterprises, Inc." is on two lines.)
Perfume ("Eau de Parfum") (Elvis Presley Enterprises) 1965............................. $50 - $100
   (Reads "Elvis Presley's Teddy Bear." Has a 1965 picture of Elvis on label. "Elvis
   Presley Enterprises, Inc." is on one line.)
Phonograph (Portable "Autograph Model") (Elvis Presley Enterprises) 1956
   Manual record change player.. $1,000 - $1,500
   Automatic record change model .... $1,500 - $2,000
   Printed instructions on "How to Use and Enjoy Your RCA Victor Portable
   Phonograph".. $100 - $150
Photo Album (Elvis Presley Enterprises) 1956 .... $600 - $900
Photo Album (Souvenir Tour Albums and Concert Souvenir Albums)
   In Person – Elvis Presley, Country Music's Mr. Rhythm 1956......................... $400 - $500
   Souvenir Photo Album 1956 .... $300 - $400
      (The first all-Elvis concert souvenir photo album. 12 pages. Reads: "Elvis Presley,
      `Mr. Dynamite' Nation's Only Atomic Powered Singer." Back cover lists seven
      45s, three EPs, and one LP by Elvis.)
   Souvenir Photo Album 1956 .... $300 - $400
      (The second all-Elvis concert souvenir photo album. Reads: "Souvenir Photo
      Album, Elvis Presley." 16 pages. Inside front cover has "Vital Statistics," brief
      Elvis history, and news of the film *Love Me Tender* (from which several of the
      photos are taken.)
   Elvis Presley Photo Folio 1957 .... $200 - $300
      (Features "Jailhouse Rock" photos. Back cover announces "New Elvis' Golden
      Record Album.")
   Photo Album/Opening Night Menu (from the Las Vegas Hilton) 1975 .... $50 - $75
   Miscellaneous Photo Albums from 1970-1977 .... $30 - $60

Photos (Publicity)

1955-1959 (Wallet size, approximately 2½" x 3" / black and white)................... $10 - $20

1955-1959 (4" x 5" / black and white).. $10 - $20

1955-1959 (4" x 5" / color).. $20 - $30

1955-1959 (8" x 10" / black and white).. $30 - $50

1955-1959 (8" x 10" / color).. $40 - $60

1955-1959 (11" x 14" / color).. $50 - $75

1960-1969 (8" x 10" / black and white).. $15 - $25

1960-1969 (8" x 10" / color).. $20 - $30

1970-1977 (8" x 10" / black and white).. $15 - $25

1970-1977 (8" x 10" / color).. $15 - $25

(This section provides only a guide to prices, which vary depending on such variables as print and paper quality. Not included in the above are bonus photos, such as those included with record albums, which are found in the records chapters.)

Pillow (Elvis Presley Enterprises) 1956 .... $700 - $1,000

Pin (Elvis Presley Enterprises) 1956

Pin attached to card... $400 - $500

Pin by itself (no card).. $300 - $400

(Card has a framed picture of Elvis, attached to a guitar. Among other tings, card reads: "Elvis Presley Pin," "Hound Dog," "Don't Be Cruel" and "Love Me Tender.")

Pin (Elvis Presley Enterprises) 1956 .... $100 - $200

(Pictures head and shoulders, color shot of Elvis. 3" pin, reading: "Best Wishes, Elvis Presley.")

Pin (Flasher, or Double-Image Pin) (Elvis Presley Enterprises/Vari-Vue) 1956.... $50 - $100

Pin (Flasher, or Double-Image Pin) (Elvis Presley Enterprises/

Pictorial Products.) 1956.. $50 - $100

Pin (A. Epstein Novelty Co./Bamboo Canes) 1957

(Reads "Wo'nt You Be My Teddy Bear." Note that "won't" is mispelled.)

Pin (Elvis Presley Enterprises) 1950s

Pin attached to red, white and blue ribbon and with a tiny wooden guitar........ $400 - $500

Red and white pin. Reads: "I Like Elvis." (No ribbon or guitar)........................... $50 - $75

Pin (Nevada concerts/RCA) 1970s

Reads "Elvis Summer Festival—International Hotel, RCA Records." .... $50 - $75

Reads "Elvis Summer Festival—Sahara Tahoe, RCA Records." .... $50 - $75

Pin (Nevada concerts/RCA) 1970s... $20 - $30

Tin pin with folding tip. Text only, reading "Elvis in Person," "I Love Elvis" or "Elvis We Love You."

Pinball Machine ("Alive") (Brunswick) 1976 .... $1,500 - $2,000

Plastic Bags 1970-1972.. $15 - $25

(From the Nevada hotels, complimentary, LP-size, printed bags.)

Plate (12" Platter) (Elvis Presley Enterprises) 1956.. $1,000 - $1,500

Pocket Calendars (From RCA Victor, with color Elvis photo on one side)

1963... $75 - $125

1964... $40 - $60

(Uncut sheets of 48 calendars for 1964 have been found. The possibility exists that uncut sheets of other pocket calendars may have survived the paper cutter. Prices for uncut sheets may be approximated by multiplying the number of calendars on one sheet times the price range of an individual calendar.)

1965 through 1969 .... $20 - $30
1970 through 1977 .... $10 - $20
Pocket Watch 1964 .... $200 - $300
(Has a 1964 photo of Elvis wearing a jacket and playing the guitar. Each number on
the face is represented by a letter of Elvis' name. Back of watch has a polished
finish.)
Pocket watch .... $50 - $100
(Same as above except back of watch has a rough, or knurled finish.)
Also see *Wrist Watch*
Polo Shirt: see Shirt
Poodle Skirt: see Skirt
Portrait: see Framed Portrait
Pumps: see Shoes
Purse (Clutch Purse) (Elvis Presley Enterprises) 1956 .... $500 - $750
(Has three pictures of Elvis and his guitar. Lists three song titles: "Heartbreak
Hotel," "Hound Dog" and "I Want You, I Need You.")
Purse: see Handbag
Record Case (Elvis Presley Enterprises) 1956 .... $500 - $750
Record Player: see Phonograph
Ribbons (Tour): see Tour Patches/Ribbons
Ring (Adjustable Ring) (Elvis Presley Enterprises) 1956
Twelve count ring counter display .... $2,500 - $3,000
(Includes all 12 rings.)
Individual Ring (one ring, no display) .... $250 - $350
(Ring has color picture of Elvis.)
Display card by itself (no rings) .... $500 - $600
Ring (Flasher, or Double-Image Ring) 1957 .... $100 - $200
Scarves (Elvis Presley Enterprises) 1956 .... $400 - $500
(Has two drawings of Elvis and guitar and one of him posing. Lists songs: "I Want
You, I Love You," "Love Me Tender," "Don't Be Cruel" and "You're Nothing But A
Hound Dog." Pictures records and a dog. Reads "Best wishes, Elvis Presley.")
International Hotel/RCA "Summer Festival" 28-inch Scarf 1970s .... $200 - $300
Concert Souvenir Autographed Scarves 1970s .... $25 - $40
(Scarf may or may not have the Las Vegas Hilton logo. Most scarves personally
given away by Elvis during his performances were unmarked and are difficult to
authenticate in print. Though they do have value – mostly to the fortunate
recipients – they are not priced here.)
Scrap Book (Elvis Presley Enterprises) 1956 .... $400 - $600
2nd Armored Division (Fort Hood, Texas) .... $1,500 - $2,500
Published by the U.S. Army as a battalion yearbook of sorts, this hardbound souvenir of
boot camp has numerous pictures of Elvis involved in his day-to-day duties.
(A numbered, limited edition – 1,000 books made – reproduction of most of the pages
in the original was published in 1988. This hardbound edition, titled *Elvis Like Any
Other Soldier,* may itself now sell for $100 to $200. However, these are easily
distinguished from originals by the color portrait of private Elvis on their cover.
Originals have no photographs on their cover.)
Senior Herald: see Herald 1953

Sheet Music (Printed Sheet Music for Songs Recorded by Elvis)

1955 .... $50 - $100

1956-1959 .... $40 - $60

1960-1977 .... $20 - $30

   (For sheet music folios that picture Elvis.)

1956-1959 .... $25 - $35

1960-1977 .... $15 - $25

   (For sheet music folios that do not picture Elvis. May be for one of his songs, or – as exists in a few instances – for a song from an Elvis film, but not sung by him. In such cases, his name usually appears on the front cover to attract attention.)

Sheet Music (Other)

Elvis Presley for President .... $50 - $75

   (Sheet music for this Elvis novelty, recorded by Lou Monte (RCA Victor 6704), pictures Elvis.)

Shirt (Elvis Presley Enterprises/Blue Ridge) 1956 .... $250 - $350

   (Green and white, striped shirt.)

Shirt (Elvis Presley Enterprises) 1956 .... $250 - $350

   (Pictures Elvis singing. Lists the titles: "Heartbreak Hotel," "Don't Be Cruel," Hound Dog" and "I Want You, I Need You.")

Shirt (RCA Records) 1976 .... $40 - $60

   (Reads: "For the Heart/Elvis.")

Shirt (Tee Shirt) 1974 .... $150 - $200

   (Shirt is multi-colored, with just about every inch being filled with something Elvis related. Perhaps this shirt can best be identified by the red and black drawings of Elvis and the phrase, "Rock N' Roll Is Here to Stay," which appears several times.)

Shirt (Tee Shirt) 1976 .... $150 - $200

   (Shirt has a multi-colored drawing of Elvis seated at a dining table, surrounded by a dozen well-known, male singing stars. In this "Last Supper"-like scene, most diners are having a hamburger with ketchup.)

Shoes (pumps) (Elvis Presley Enterprises--Faith Shoe Co.), 1956

Pair of pumps with box .... $600 - $900

Single pump (no box) .... $200 - $300

Pumps by themselves (no box) .... $400 - $600

Box by itself (no shoes) .... $200 - $300

Shoes (Sneakers) (Elvis Presley Enterprises) 1956

Pair of sneakers with box .... $600 - $900

Single sneaker (no box) .... $200 - $300

Sneakers by themselves (no box) .... $400 - $600

Box by itself (no shoes) .... $200 - $300

Side Burns Machine Label 1956 .... $100 - $150

   (The only piece of the Elvis Side Burns Machine known to exist today is the label from the front of the machine. A complete vending machine would be valued at several thousand dollars – but we know of none.)

Skirt (Poodle Skirt) (Elvis Presley Enterprises/Little Jean Togs) 1956 .... $1,000 - $1,500

Sneakers: see Shoes

Song Book for Emenee Guitar: see Guitar

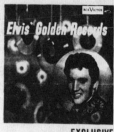

New!
ELVIS'
GOLDEN
RECORD
ALBUM

14 of his
GREATEST HITS
NOW in ONE GREAT
NEW ALBUM!

EXCLUSIVE
ON RCA VICTOR

Song Folios, Magazines and Books

Elvis Presley Album of Juke Box Favorites (Hill & Range) 1956 .... $50 - $75

Full Color Picture Folio Plus Special Giant Size Pin-Up Picture 1963 .... $50 - $75
(Includes bonus, fold-out Elvis pin-up poster.)

Full Color Picture Folio Plus Special Giant Size Pin-Up Picture $25- $50
(Later printing, without the Elvis pin-up poster.)

Love Me Tender Song Folio with Pictures (Hill & Range) 1956 .... $50 - $75

Songs Recorded by Elvis Presley 1968 .... $20 - $30

Songs Recorded by Elvis Presley, Vol. 2 1968 .... $20 - $30

We Call on Him: A Collection of Gospel Songs Recorded by Elvis Presley
Gladys Music, Hill & Range) 1968 .... $30 - $40

Souvenir Menu: see Menus

Souvenir Opening Night Package (Las Vegas Hilton) 1975

Specially printed paper bag with the following items: 1975 photo album/menu,
color tour photo, Summer Festival 1975 Hilton postcard, Elvis and Santa
Claus Christmas postcard, and a 1976 pocket calendar .... $300 - $350

Paper bag by itself (no contents) .... $50 - $100
(This item, though very similar to the Special Souvenir Package, was only given
out on opening night, August 18, 1975.)

Souvenir Photo Album/Folio: see Photo Albums

Sox (Bobby Sox) (Elvis Presley Enterprises), 1956

Two pair attached to card .... $400 - $600

Card/package by itself (no sox) .... $100 - $200
(The sox by themselves are not identified as an Elvis item.)
Also see *Anklets*

Special Souvenir Package (Las Vegas Hilton) 1975

Specially printed paper bag with the following items: 1975 photo album menu, color tour
photo, Summer Festival 1975 Hilton postcard, Elvis and Santa Claus Christmas postcard,
and a 1976 pocket calendar .... $100 - $200

Paper bag by itself (no contents) .... $35 - $55

Standee 1973 .... $150 - $250

(Life-size, color. Pictures Elvis in a scene from the *Aloha from Hawaii via Satellite*
concert, wearing a red lei.)

Statuette (Bronze) (Elvis Presley Enterprises) 1956 .... $750 - $1,000

(8" tall figurine, or bust.)

Statuette (Gold plated) (RCA Victor) 1961 .... $300 - $400

(Elvis figurine, sent by RCA to the news media.)

Stretch Anklets: see Anklets

Sun Labels (1955) 25-30

A small quantity of 45 rpm labels (no rooster) were found at the Sun Records
Memphis warehouse (Select-O-Hits) in 1967. All labels are circular cut but have
never been applied to discs, thus the holes are still LP-size. Most of the labels are for
Milkcow Blues Boogie and *I Forgot to Remember to Forget.*

Sweater Guard: see Hit Tunes Charms

Tag (For shirt or jeans) (Elvis Presley Enterprises) 1956 .... $50 - $75

(Pictures Elvis and his guitar.)

Teddy Bears (Elvis Presley Enterprises) 1957 .... $400 - $600
    (24" bear with ribbons reading: "Elvis Presley" and "Teddy Bear.")
    International Hotel Bear 1971 .... $50 - $100
    (Pink and white bear with a pin-on metal badge.)

Tee-Shirt: see Shirt

Throw Pillow: see Pillow

Tickets (Standard paper tickets for admission to Elvis concerts, filmings, press conferences,
    and other personal appearances. Prices are for complete ticket – not just a stub or
    portion.)
    1955-1960 .... $100 - $200
    1961-1968 .... $50 - $100
    1969-1977 .... $30 - $50

Ticket Stubs (Standard ticket stubs for admission to Elvis concerts, filmings, press
    conferences, and other such personal appearances. Prices are for stubs or portions that
    clearly identify the event.)
    1955-1960 .... $20 - $30
    1961-1968 .... $15 - $25
    1969-1977 .... $10 - $15

Tie: see Bolo Tie

Tie Bar: see Hit Tunes Charms

Tiki Mug: see Blue Hawaii (Movie Related Memorabilia)

Tile: see Ceramic Tile

Title Strips (Available to jukebox operators, these are factory-printed with titles
    of both sides of disc on each strip. Strips were usually made on sheets of 10.
    Prices are for full sheets only.)
    Releases from 1955-1959 .... $20 - $30
    Releases from 1960-1969 .... $15 - $25
    Releases from 1970-1979 .... $10 - $15
    Releases from 1980-1994 .... $8 -$12

Tour Patches/Ribbons 1970-1977 .... $30 - $40

United States Jaycees Tribute Booklet .... $300 - $400
    (Program booklet from the Jaycee's awards ceremony, January 16, 1971, in Memphis.
    Front cover reads: "Ten Outstanding Young Men, Memphis, Tennessee 1970." Includes a
    brief bio and photo of Elvis as well as the other nine winners.)

Victrola: see Phonograph

Wallet (coin purse and key chain) (Elvis Presley Enterprises) 1956 .... $500 - $750
    (Has two Elvis drawings and one photo. Reads: "Elvis Presley–Rock 'n' Roll.")

Wallet (French purse) (Elvis Presley Enterprises) 1956 .... $400 - $600
    (Folding clutch purse with two coin compartments)

Wallet (for cash) (Elvis Presley Enterprises) 1956 .... $400 - $600

Wallet (for photos) (Elvis Presley Enterprises) 1956 .... $400 - $600

Watch, Pocket: see Pocket Watch

Wrist Watch (Mathey-Tissot, self-winding) 1969 5,000-7,500
    (Face has day and date bar at right, "Mathey Tissot" at top and "Automatic" and "Swiss
    Made" at bottom. Has "Elvis Presley" and four stars in raised gold letters, circling the
    bezel. Made at Elvis' request and given by him to friends, family and employees.)

ELVIS MUSIC CHRONOLOGY

(Release date — Title — Format — Label — Selection number)

1954

7/54	*That's All Right/Moon of Kentucky* (78)	Sun 209
7/54	*That's All Right/Moon of Kentucky* (45)	Sun 209
9/54	*Good Rockin' Tonight/I Don't Care If the Sun Don't Shine* (78)	Sun 210
9/54	*Good Rockin' Tonight/I Don't Care If the Sun Don't Shine* (45)	Sun 210

1955

1/55	*You're a Heartbreaker/Milkcow Blues Boogie* (78)	Sun 215
1/55	*You're a Heartbreaker/Milkcow Blues Boogie* (45)	Sun 215
4/55	*Baby Let's Play House/I'm Left, You're Right, She's Gone* (78)	Sun 217
4/55	*Baby Let's Play House/I'm Left, You're Right, She's Gone* (45)	Sun 217
9/55	*Mystery Train/I Forgot to Remember to Forget* (78)	Sun 223
9/55	*Mystery Train/I Forgot to Remember to Forget* (45)	Sun 223
12/55	*Mystery Train/I Forgot to Remember to Forget* (78)	RCA Victor 20-6357
12/55	*Mystery Train/I Forgot to Remember to Forget* (45)	RCA Victor 47-6357
12/55	*That's All Right/Blue Moon of Kentucky* (78)	RCA Victor 20-6380
12/55	*That's All Right/Blue Moon of Kentucky* (45)	RCA Victor 47-6380
12/55	*Good Rockin' Tonight/I Don't Care If the Sun Don't Shine* (78)	RCA Victor 20-6381
12/55	*Good Rockin' Tonight/I Don't Care If the Sun Don't Shine* (45)	RCA Victor 47-6381
12/55	*You're a Heartbreaker/Milkcow Blues Boogie* (78)	RCA Victor 20-6382
12/55	*You're a Heartbreaker/Milkcow Blues Boogie* (45)	RCA Victor 47-6382
12/55	*Baby Let's Play House/I'm Left, You're Right, She's Gone* (78)	RCA Victor 20-6383
12/55	*Baby Let's Play House/I'm Left, You're Right, She's Gone* (45)	RCA Victor 47-6383

1956

1/56	*Heartbreak Hotel/I Was the One* (78)	RCA Victor 20-6420
1/56	*Heartbreak Hotel/I Was the One* (45)	RCA Victor 47-6420
3/56	*Elvis Presley* (EP)	RCA Victor EPA-747
3/56	*Elvis Presley* (EP)	RCA Victor EPB-1254
3/56	*Elvis Presley* (LP)	RCA Victor LPM-1254
4/56	*Heartbreak Hotel* (EP)	RCA Victor EPA-821
5/56	*I Want You, I Need You, I Love You/My Baby Left Me* (78)	RCA Victor 20-6540
5/56	*I Want You, I Need You, I Love You/My Baby Left Me* (45)	RCA Victor 47-6540
7/56	*Don't Be Cruel/Hound Dog* (78)	RCA Victor 20-6604
7/56	*Don't Be Cruel/Hound Dog* (45)	RCA Victor 47-6604
9/56	*Blue Suede Shoes/Tutti Frutti* (78)	RCA Victor 20-6636
9/56	*Blue Suede Shoes/Tutti Frutti* (45)	RCA Victor 47-6636
9/56	*I Got a Woman/I'm Counting on You* (78)	RCA Victor 20-6637
9/56	*I Got a Woman/I'm Counting on You* (45)	RCA Victor 47-6637

9/56	*I'll Never Let You Go (Little Darlin')/I'm Gonna Sit Right Down and Cry (Over You)* (78)	RCA Victor 20-6638
9/56	*I'll Never Let You Go (Little Darlin')/I'm Gonna Sit Right Down and Cry (Over You)* (45)	RCA Victor 47-6638
9/56	*Tryin' to Get to You/I Love You Because* (78)	RCA Victor 20-6639
9/56	*Tryin' to Get to You/I Love You Because* (45)	RCA Victor 47-6639
9/56	*Blue Moon/Just Because* (78)	RCA Victor 20-6640
9/56	*Blue Moon/Just Because* (45)	RCA Victor 47-6640
9/56	*Money Honey/One-Sided Love Affair* (78)	RCA Victor 20-6641
9/56	*Money Honey/One-Sided Love Affair* (45)	RCA Victor 47-6641
9/56	*Lawdy Miss Clawdy/Shake, Rattle and Roll* (78)	RCA Victor 20-6642
9/56	*Lawdy Miss Clawdy/Shake, Rattle and Roll* (45)	RCA Victor 47-6642
9/56	*Elvis Presley* (EP)	RCA Victor EPA-830
9/56	*The Real Elvis* (EP)	RCA Victor EPA-940
10/56	*Love Me Tender/Anyway You Want Me (That's How I Will Be)* (78)	RCA Victor 20-6643
10/56	*Love Me Tender/Anyway You Want Me (That's How I Will Be)* (45)	RCA Victor 47-6643
10/56	*Anyway You Want Me* (EP)	RCA Victor EPA-965
11/56	*Elvis* (LP)	RCA Victor LPM-1382
11/56	*Love Me Tender* (EP)	RCA Victor EPA-4006
11/56	*Elvis (Vol. 1)* (EP)	RCA Victor EPA-992
11/56	*Elvis (Vol. 2)* (EP)	RCA Victor EPA-993
11/56	*Strictly Elvis (Vol. 3)* (EP)	RCA Victor EPA-994

1957

1/57	*Too Much/Playing for Keeps* (78)	RCA Victor 20-6800
1/57	*Too Much/Playing for Keeps* (45)	RCA Victor 47-6800
3/57	*All Shook Up/That's When Your Heartaches Begin* (78)	RCA Victor 20-6870
3/57	*All Shook Up/That's When Your Heartaches Begin* (45)	RCA Victor 47-6870
3/57	*Just for You* (EP)	RCA Victor EPA-4041
3/57	*Peace in the Valley* (EP)	RCA Victor EPA-4054
6/57	*(Let Me Be Your) Teddy Bear/Loving You* (78)	RCA Victor 20-7000
6/57	*(Let Me Be Your) Teddy Bear/Loving You* (45)	RCA Victor 47-7000
7/57	*Loving You* (LP)	RCA Victor LPM-1515
7/57	*Loving You (Vol. 1)* (EP)	RCA Victor EPA 1-1515
7/57	*Loving You (Vol. 2)* (EP)	RCA Victor EPA 2-1515
9/57	*Jailhouse Rock/Treat Me Nice* (78)	RCA Victor 20-7035
9/57	*Jailhouse Rock/Treat Me Nice* (45)	RCA Victor 47-7035
10/57	*Jailhouse Rock* (EP)	RCA Victor EPA-4114
11/57	*Elvis' Christmas Album* (LP)	RCA Victor LOC-1035
11/57	*Elvis Sings Christmas Songs* (EP)	RCA Victor EPA-4108

1958

1/58	*Don't/I Beg of You* (78)	RCA Victor 20-7150
1/58	*Don't/I Beg of You* (45)	RCA Victor 47-7150
4/58	*Elvis' Golden Records* (LP)	RCA Victor LPM-1707
4/58	*Wear My Ring Around Your Neck/Doncha Think It's Time* (78)	RCA Victor 20-7240

4/58	*Wear My Ring Around Your Neck/Doncha Think It's Time* (45)	RCA Victor 47-7240
6/58	*Hard Headed Woman/Don't Ask Me Why* (78)	RCA Victor 20-7280
6/58	*Hard Headed Woman/Don't Ask Me Why* (45)	RCA Victor 47-7280
8/58	*King Creole* (LP)	RCA Victor LPM-1884
8/58	*King Creole* (Vol. 1) (EP)	RCA Victor EPA-4319
8/58	*King Creole* (Vol. 2) (EP)	RCA Victor EPA-4321
10/58	*Elvis Sails* (EP)	RCA Victor EPA-4325
10/58	*One Night/I Got Stung* (78)	RCA Victor 20-7410
10/58	*One Night/I Got Stung* (45)	RCA Victor 47-7410
11/58	*Elvis' Christmas Album* (LP)	RCA Victor LPM-1951
11/58	*Christmas with Elvis* (EP)	RCA Victor EPA-4340

1959

3/59	*For LP Fans Only* (LP)	RCA Victor LPM-1990
3/59	*Mystery Train/I Forgot to Remember to Forget* (Gold Standard) (45)	RCA Victor 447-0600
3/59	*That's All Right/Blue Moon of Kentucky* (Gold Standard) (45)	RCA Victor 447-4601
3/59	*Good Rockin' Tonight/I Don't Care If the Sun Don't Shine* Gold Standard) (45)	RCA Victor 447-0602
3/59	*You're a Heartbreaker/Milkcow Blues Boogie* (Gold Standard) (45)	RCA Victor 447-0603
3/59	*Baby Let's Play House/I'm Left, You're Right, She's Gone* (Gold Standard) (45)	RCA Victor 447-0604
3/59	*Heartbreak Hotel/I Was the One* (Gold Standard) (45)	RCA Victor 447-0605
3/59	*I Want You, I Need You, I Love You/My Baby Left Me* (Gold Standard) (45)	RCA Victor 447-0607
3/59	*Don't Be Cruel/Hound Dog* (Gold Standard) (45)	RCA Victor 447-0608
3/59	*Blue Suede Shoes/Tutti Frutti* (Gold Standard) (45)	RCA Victor 447-0609
3/59	*I Got a Woman/I'm Counting on You* (Gold Standard) (45)	RCA Victor 447-0610
3/59	*I'll Never Let You Go (Little Darlin')/I'm Gonna Sit Right Down and Cry (Over You)* (Gold Standard) (45)	RCA Victor 447-0611
3/59	*Tryin' to Get to You/I Love You Because* (Gold Standard) (45)	RCA Victor 447-0612
3/59	*Blue Moon/Just Because* (Gold Standard) (45)	RCA Victor 447-0613
3/59	*Money Honey/One-Sided Love Affair* (Gold Standard) (45)	RCA Victor 447-0614
3/59	*Lawdy Miss Clawdy/Shake, Rattle and Roll* (Gold Standard) (45)	RCA Victor 447-0615
3/59	*Love Me Tender/Anyway You Want Me (That's How I'll Be)* (Gold Standard) (45)	RCA Victor 447-0616
3/59	*Too Much/Playing for Keeps* (Gold Standard) (45)	RCA Victor 447-0617
3/59	*All Shook Up/That's When Your Heartaches Begin* (Gold Standard) (45)	RCA Victor 447-0618
3/59	*(Now and Then There's) A Fool Such As I/I Need Your Love Tonight* (45)	RCA Victor 47-7506
4/59	*A Touch of Gold (Vol. 1)* (Gold Standard) (EP)	RCA Victor EPA-5088
7/59	*A Big Hunk O' Love/My Wish Came True* (45)	RCA Victor 47-7600
9/59	*A Date with Elvis* (LP)	RCA Victor LPM-2011

9/59	*A Touch of Gold (Vol. 2) (Gold Standard) (EP)*	RCA Victor EPA-5088
11/59	*The Real Elvis (Gold Standard) (EP)*	RCA Victor EPA-5120
11/59	*Peace in the Valley (Gold Standard) (EP)*	RCA Victor EPA-5121
11/59	*King Creole (Gold Standard) (EP)*	RCA Victor EPA-5122
12/59	*Elvis' Gold Records, Vol. 2 (50,000,000 Elvis Fans Can't Be Wrong) (LP)*	RCA Victor LPM-2075

1960

1/60	*A Touch of Gold, Vol. 3 (EP)*	RCA Victor EPA-5141
4/60	*Stuck on You/Fame and Fortune (45)*	RCA Victor 47-7740
4/60	*Stuck on You/Fame and Fortune (Living Stereo) (45)*	RCA Victor 61-7740
4/60	*Elvis Is Back! (LP)*	RCA Victor LPM/LSP-2231
7/60	*It's Now Or Never/A Mess of Blues (45)*	RCA Victor 47-7777
7/60	*It's Now Or Never/A Mess of Blues (Living Stereo) (45)*	RCA Victor 61-7777
10/60	*G.I. Blues (LP)*	RCA Victor LPM/LSP-2256
11/60	*Are You Lonesome Tonight/I Gotta Know (45)*	RCA Victor 47-7810
11/60	*Are You Lonesome Tonight/I Gotta Know (Living Stereo) (45)*	RCA Victor 61-7810
12/60	*His Hand in Mine (LP)*	RCA Victor LPM/LSP 2328

1961

1/61	*Elvis By Request (Flaming Star) (EP)*	RCA Victor LPC-128
2/61	*Surrender/Lonely Man (45)*	RCA Victor 47-7850
2/61	*Surrender/Lonely Man (Living Stereo) (45)*	RCA Victor 47-7850
2/61	*Surrender/Lonely Man (Compact 33 Single)*	RCA Victor 37-7850
2/61	*Surrender/Lonely Man (Stereo Compact 33 Single)*	RCA Victor 68-7850
5/61	*I Feel So Bad/Wild in the Country (45)*	RCA Victor 47-7880
5/61	*I Feel So Bad/Wild in the Country (Compact 33 Single)*	RCA Victor 37-7880
6/61	*Something for Everybody (LP)*	RCA Victor LPM/LSP 2370
8/61	*(Marie's the Name) His Latest Flame/Little Sister (45)*	RCA Victor 47-7908
8/61	*(Marie's the Name) His Latest Flame/Little Sister (Compact 33 Single)*	RCA Victor 37-7908
10/61	*Blue Hawaii (LP)*	RCA Victor LPM/LSP-2426
12/61	*Can't Help Falling in Love/Rock-a-Hula Baby (45)*	RCA Victor 47-7968
12/61	*Can't Help Falling in Love/Rock-a-Hula Baby (Compact 33 Single)*	RCA Victor 37-7968
?/61	*Jailhouse Rock/Treat Me Nice (Gold Standard) (45)*	RCA Victor 447-0619
?/61	*(Let Me Be Your) Teddy Bear/Loving You (Gold Standard) (45)*	RCA Victor 447-0620
?/61	*Don't/I Beg of You (Gold Standard) (45)*	RCA Victor 447-0621
?/61	*Wear My Ring Around Your Neck/Doncha Think It's Time (Gold Standard) (45)*	RCA Victor 447-0622
?/61	*Hard Headed Woman/Don't Ask Me Why (Gold Standard) (45)*	RCA Victor 447-0623
?/61	*One Night/I Got Stung (Gold Standard) (45)*	RCA Victor 447-0624
?/61	*(Now and Then There's) A Fool Such As I/I Need Your*	
?/61	*Love Tonight (Gold Standard) (45)*	RCA Victor 447-0625

1962

2/62	*A Big Hunk O' Love/My Wish Came True* (Gold Standard) (45)	RCA Victor 447-0626
2/62	*Stuck on You/Fame and Fortune* (Gold Standard) (45)	RCA Victor 447-0627
2/62	*It's Now or Never/A Mess of Blues* (Gold Standard) (45)	RCA Victor 447-0628
2/62	*Are You Lonesome Tonight/I Gotta Know* (Gold Standard) (45)	RCA Victor 447-0629
2/62	*Surrender/Lonely Man* (Gold Standard) (45)	RCA Victor 447-0630
2/62	*I Feel So Bad/Wild in the Country* (Gold Standard) (45)	RCA Victor 447-0631
2/62	*Elvis Presley* (Electronically Reprocessed Stereo) (LP)	RCA Victor LSP-1254(e)
2/62	*Elvis* (Electronically Reprocessed Stereo) (LP)	RCA Victor LSP-1382(e)
2/62	*Loving You* (Electronically Reprocessed Stereo) (LP)	RCA Victor LSP-1515(e)
2/62	*Elvis' Golden Records* (Electronically Reprocessed Stereo) (LP)	RCA Victor LSP-1707(e)
2/62	*King Creole* (Electronically Reprocessed Stereo) (LP)	RCA Victor LSP-1884(e)
2/62	*Elvis' Gold Records, Vol. 2 (50,000,000 Elvis Fans Can't Be Wrong)* Electronically Reprocessed Stereo) (LP)	RCA Victor LSP-2075(e)
3/62	*Good Luck Charm/Anything That's Part of You* (45)	RCA Victor 47-7992
3/62	*Good Luck Charm/Anything That's Part of You* (Compact 33 Single)	RCA Victor 37-7992
5/62	*Follow That Dream* (EP)	RCA Victor EPA-4368
6/62	*Pot Luck* (LP)	RCA Victor LPM/LSP-2523
7/62	*She's Not You/Just Tell Her Jim Said Hello* (45)	RCA Victor 47-8041
9/62	*Kid Galahad* (EP)	RCA Victor EPA-4371
10/62	*Return to Sender/Where Do You Come From* (45)	RCA Victor 47-8100
11/62	*Girls! Girls! Girls!* (LP)	RCA Victor LPM/LSP-2621
11/62	*(Marie's the Name) His Latest Flame/Little Sister* (Gold Standard) (45)	RCA Victor 447-0634
11/62	*Can't Help Falling in Love/Rock-a-Hula Baby* (Gold Standard) (45)	RCA Victor 447-0635
11/62	*Good Luck Charm/Anything That's Part of You* (Gold Standard) (45)	RCA Victor 447-0636

1963

2/63	*One Broken Heart for Sale/They Remind Me Too Much of You* (45)	RCA Victor 47-8134
4/63	*It Happened at the World's Fair* (LP)	RCA Victor LPM/LSP-2697
6/63	*(You're the) Devil in Disguise/Please Don't Drag That String Along* (45)	RCA Victor 47-8188
6/63	*She's Not You/Just Tell Her Jim Said Hello* (Gold Standard) (45)	RCA Victor 447-0637
6/63	*Return to Sender/Where Do You Come From* (Gold Standard) (45)	RCA Victor 447-0638
9/63	*Elvis' Gold Records, Vol. 3* (LP)	RCA Victor LPM/LSP-2765
10/63	*Bossa Nova Baby/Witchcraft* (45)	RCA Victor 47-8243
12/63	*Fun in Acapulco* (LP)	RCA Victor LPM/LSP-2756

1964

1/64	*Kissin' Cousins/It Hurts Me* (45)	RCA Victor 47-8307
3/64	*Kissin' Cousins* (LP)	RCA Victor LPM/LSP-2894
4/64	*Kiss Me Quick/Suspicion* (Gold Standard) (45)	RCA Victor 447-0639
4/64	*Viva Las Vegas/What'd I Say* (45)	RCA Victor 47-8360
6/64	*Viva Las Vegas* (EP)	RCA Victor EPA-4382
7/64	*Such a Night/Never Ending* (45)	RCA Victor 47-8400
6/64	*One Broken Heart for Sale/They Remind Me Too Much of You* (Gold Standard) (45)	RCA Victor 447-0640
6/64	*(You're the) Devil in Disguise/Please Don't Drag That String Along* (Gold Standard) (45)	RCA Victor 447-0641
6/64	*Bossa Nova Baby/Witchcraft* (Gold Standard) (45)	RCA Victor 447-0642
9/64	*Ain't That Lovin' You Baby/Ask Me* (45)	RCA Victor 47-8440
10/64	*Roustabout* (LP)	RCA Victor LPM/LSP-2999
11/64	*Blue Christmas/Wooden Heart* (Gold Standard) (45)	RCA Victor 447-0720
11/64	*Elvis' Christmas Album* (Electronically Reprocessed Stereo) (LP)	RCA Victor LSP-1951(e)

1965

1/65	*For LP Fans Only* (Electronically Reprocessed Stereo) (LP)	RCA Victor LSP-1990(e)
1/65	*A Date with Elvis* (Electronically Reprocessed Stereo) (LP)	RCA Victor LSP-2011(e)
2/65	*Do the Clam/You'll Be Gone* (45)	RCA Victor 47-8500
4/65	*Crying in the Chapel/I Believe in the Man in the Sky* (Gold Standard) (45)	RCA Victor 447-0643
4/65	*Girl Happy* (LP)	RCA Victor LPM/LSP-3338
5/65	*Kissin' Cousins/It Hurts Me* (Gold Standard) (45)	RCA Victor 447-0644
5/65	*Such a Night/Never Ending* (Gold Standard) (45)	RCA Victor 447-0645
5/65	*Viva Las Vegas/What'd I Say* (Gold Standard) (45)	RCA Victor 447-0646
5/65	*Elvis Sails* (Gold Standard) (EP)	RCA Victor EPA-5157
6/65	*(Such an) Easy Question/It Feels So Right* (45)	RCA Victor 47-8585
6/65	*Tickle Me* (EP)	RCA Victor EPA -4383
7/65	*Elvis for Everyone* (LP)	RCA Victor LPM/LSP-3450
8/65	*I'm Yours/(It's a) Long Lonely Highway* (45)	RCA Victor 47-8657
10/65	*Puppet on a String/Wooden Heart* (Gold Standard) (45)	RCA Victor 447-0650
10/65	*Harum Scarum* (LP)	RCA Victor LPM/LSP-3468
11/65	*Blue Christmas/Santa Claus Is Back in Town* (Gold Standard) (45)	RCA Victor 447-0647
11/65	*Do the Clam/You'll Be Gone* (Gold Standard) (45)	RCA Victor 447-0648
11/65	*Ain't That Loving You Baby/Ask Me* (Gold Standard) (45)	RCA Victor 447-0649

1966

1/66	*Tell Me Why/Blue River* (45)	RCA Victor 47-8740
2/66	*Joshua Fit the Battle/Known Only to Him* (Gold Standard) (45)	RCA Victor 447-0651

2/66	*Milky White Way/Swing Down Sweet Chariot* (Gold Standard) (45)	RCA Victor 447-0652
3/66	*Frankie and Johnny/Please Don't Stop Loving Me* (45)	RCA Victor 47-8780
4/66	*Frankie and Johnny* (LP)	RCA Victor LPM/LSP-3553
6/66	*Paradise Hawaiian Style* (LP)	RCA Victor LPM/LSP-3643
6/66	*Love Letters/Come What May* (45)	RCA Victor 47-8870
9/66	*Spinout/All That I Am* (45)	RCA Victor 47-8941
10/66	*Spinout* (LP)	RCA Victor LPM/LSP-3702
11/66	*(Such an) Easy Question/It Feels So Right* (Gold Standard) (45)	RCA Victor 447-0653
11/66	*I'm Yours/(It's a) Long Lonely Highway* (Gold Standard) (45)	RCA Victor 447-0654
11/66	*If Everyday Was Like Christmas/How Would You Like to Be* (45)	RCA Victor 47-8950

1967

1/67	*Indescribably Blue/Fools Fall in Love* (45)	RCA Victor 47-9056
2/67	*Easy Come, Easy Go* (EP)	RCA Victor EPA-4387
3/67	*How Great Thou Art (As Sung by Elvis)* (LP)	RCA Victor LPM/LSP-3758
5/67	*Long Legged Girl (With the Short Dress On)/That's Someone You Never Forget* (45)	RCA Victor 47-9115
6/67	*Double Trouble* (LP)	RCA Victor LPM/LSP-3787
8/67	*Judy/There's Always Me* (45)	RCA Victor 47-9287
9/67	*Big Boss Man/You Don't Know Me* (45)	RCA Victor 47-9341
11/67	*Clambake* (LP)	RCA Victor LPM/LSP-3893

1968

1/68	*Guitar Man/High Heel Sneakers* (45)	RCA Victor 47-9425
2/68	*Tell Me Why/Blue River* (Gold Standard) (45)	RCA Victor 447-0655
2/68	*Frankie and Johnny/Please Don't Stop Loving Me* (Gold Standard) (45)	RCA Victor 447-0656
2/68	*Love Letters/Come What May* (Gold Standard) (45)	RCA Victor 447-0657
2/68	*Spinout/All That I Am* (Gold Standard) (45)	RCA Victor 447-0658
2/68	*Elvis' Gold Records, Vol. 4* (LP)	RCA Victor LPM/LSP-3921
3/68	*U.S. Male/Stay Away* (45)	RCA Victor 47-9465
4/68	*You'll Never Walk Alone/We Call on Him* (45)	RCA Victor 47-9600
6/68	*Your Time Hasn't Come Yet Baby/Let Yourself Go* (45)	RCA Victor 47-9547
6/68	*Speedway* (LP)	RCA Victor LPM/LSP-3989
9/68	*A Little Less Conversation/Almost in Love* (45)	RCA Victor 47-9610
11/68	*If I Can Dream/Edge of Reality* (45)	RCA Victor 47-9670
12/68	*Elvis (NBC TV Special)* (LP)	RCA Victor LPM-4088

1969

3/69	*Memories/Charro* (45)	RCA Victor 47-9731
4/69	*How Great Thou Art/His Hand in Mine* (45)	RCA Victor 47-0130
4/69	*Elvis Sings Flaming Star* (LP)	RCA/Camden CAS-2304
4/69	*In the Ghetto/Any Day Now* (45)	RCA Victor 47-9731
5/69	*From Elvis in Memphis* (LP)	RCA Victor LSP-4155

6/69 *Clean Up Your Own Back Yard/The Fair Is Moving On* (45).....RCA Victor 47-9747
9/69 *Suspicious Minds/You'll Think of Me* (45)....................................RCA Victor 47-9764
11/69 *From Memphis to Vegas/From Vegas to Memphis* (LP) ....RCA Victor LSP-6020
11/69 *Don't Cry Daddy/Rubberneckin'* (45) ....RCA Victor 47-9768

1970

2/70 *Kentucky Rain/My Little Friend* (45)...RCA Victor 47-791
4/70 *Let's Be Friends* (LP) ....RCA/Camden CAS-2408
5/70 *The Wonder of You/Mama Liked the Roses* (45) ....RCA Victor 47-9835
6/70 *On Stage—February, 1970* (LP) ....RCA Victor LSP-4362
7/70 *I've Lost You/The Next Step Is Love* (45) ....RCA Victor 47-9873
8/70 *Worldwide 50 Gold Award Hits, Vol. 1* (LP)..........................RCA Victor LPM-6401
10/70 *You Don't Have to Say You Love Me/Patch It Up* (45)..................RCA Victor 47-991
11/70 *Elvis in Person at the International Hotel, Las Vegas, Nevada* (LP)..RCA Victor LSP-4428
11/70 *Back in Memphis* (LP) ....RCA Victor LSP-4429
11/70 *Elvis' Christmas Album* (LP) ....RCA/Camden CAL-2428
11/70 *Almost in Love* (LP) ....RCA/Camden CAS-2440
12/70 *I Really Don't Want to Know/There Goes My Everything* (45) ....RCA Victor 47-9960
12/70 *Elvis—That's the Way It Is* (LP) ....RCA Victor LSP-4445
12/70 *You'll Never Walk Alone/We Call on Him* (Gold Standard) (45) ....RCA Victor 447-0665
12/70 *Your Time Hasn't Come Yet Baby/Let Yourself Go* (Gold Standard) (45) ....RCA Victor 447-0666
12/70 *A Little Less Conversation/Almost in Love* (Gold Standard) (45) ....RCA Victor 447-0667
12/70 *If I Can Dream/Edge of Reality* (Gold Standard) (45)..............RCA Victor 447-0668
12/70 *Memories/Charro* (Gold Standard) (45) ....RCA Victor 447-0669
12/70 *How Great Thou Art/His Hand in Mine* (Gold Standard) (45)..RCA Victor 447-0670
12/70 *In the Ghetto/Any Day Now* (Gold Standard) (45).....................RCA Victor 447-0671
12/70 *Clean Up Your Own Back Yard/The Fair Is Moving On* (Gold Standard) (45) ....RCA Victor 447-0672
12/70 *Suspicious Minds/You'll Think of Me* (Gold Standard) (45) ......RCA Victor 447-0673
?/70 *Indescribably Blue/Fools Fall in Love* (Gold Standard) (45).....RCA Victor447-0659
?/70 *Long Legged Girl (With the Short Dress On)/That's Someone You Never Forget* (Gold Standard) (45) ....RCA Victor 447-0660
?/70 *Judy/There's Always Me* (Gold Standard) (45) ....RCA Victor 447-0661
?/70 *Big Boss Man/You Don't Know Me* (Gold Standard) (45)..........RCA Victor 4470662
?/70 *Guitar Man/High Heel Sneakers* (Gold Standard) (45) ....RCA Victor 4470663
?/70 *U.S. Male/Stay Away* (Gold Standard) (45) ....RCA Victor 447-0664

1971

1/71 *Elvis Country* (LP) ....RCA Victor LSP-4460
2/71 *Rags to Riches/Where Did They Go Lord* (45) ....RCA Victor 47-9980
3/71 *You'll Never Walk Alone* (LP)............................RCA/Camden CALX-2472
5/71 *Life/Only Believe* (45) ....RCA Victor 47-4530

5/71 *Love Letters from Elvis* (LP)..RCA Victor LSP-4530
7/71 *I'm Leavin'/Heart of Rome* (45) ....RCA Victor 47-9998
8/71 *Worldwide Gold Award Hits, Volume 2* (LP) ....RCA Victor LPM-6402
8/71 *Kentucky Rain/My Little Friend* (Gold Standard) (45) ....RCA Victor 447-0675
8/71 *The Wonder of You/Mama Liked the Roses* (Gold
        Standard) (45) ....RCA Victor 447-0676
8/71 *I've Lost You/The Next Step Is Love* (Gold Standard) (45) ....RCA Victor 447-0677
9/71 *C'mon Everybody* (LP)..RCA/Camden CAL-2518
9/71 *It's Only Love/The Sound of Your Cry* (45) ....RCA Victor 48-1017
10/71 *I Got Lucky* (LP) ....RCA/Camden CAL-2533
10/71 *Elvis Sings the Wonderful World of Christmas* (LP) ....RCA Victor LSP-4579
12/71 *Merry Christmas Baby/O Come All Ye Faithful* (45) ....RCA Victor 74-0572

1972

1/72 *Until It's Time for You to Go/We Can Make the Morning* (45) ...RCA Victor 74-0619
2/72 *Elvis Now* (LP)..RCA Victor LSP-4671
2/72 *You Don't Have to Say You Love Me/Patch It Up* (Gold
        Standard) (45) ....RCA Victor 447-0678
2/72 *I Really Don't Want to Know/There Goes My
        Everything* (Gold Standard) (45)..RCA Victor 447-0679
2/72 *Rags to Riches/Where Did They Go Lord* (Gold
        Standard) (45) ....RCAVictor 447-0680
3/72 *He Touched Me/Bosom of Abraham* (45) ....RCA Victor 74-0651
4/72 *He Touched Me* (LP)..RCA Victor LSP-4690
4/72 *An American Trilogy/The First Time Ever I Saw Your
        Face* (45)..RCA Victor 74-0672
5/72 *If Everyday Was Like Christmas/How Would You Like to Be* (Gold
        Standard) (45) ....RCA Victor 447-0681
5/72 *Life/Only Believe* (Gold Standard) (45) ....RCA Victor 447-0682
5/72 *I'm Leavin'/Heart of Rome* (Gold Standard) (45).......................RCA Victor 447-0683
5/72 *It's Only Love/The Sound of Your Cry* (Gold Standard) (45).....RCA Victor 447-0683
6/72 *Elvis Sings Hits from His Movies, Vol. 1* (LP).......................RCA/Camden CAS-2567
6/72 *Elvis as Recorded at Madison Square Garden* (LP)................RCA Victor LSP-4776
8/72 *Burning Love/It's a Matter of Time* (45) ....RCA Victor 74-0679
11/72 *Burning Love and Hits from His Movies, Vol. 2* (LP) ....RCA/Camden CAS-2595
11/72 *Separate Ways/Always on My Mind* (45)....................................RCA Victor 74-0815
12/72 *Separate Ways* (LP) ....RCA/Camden CAS-2611

1973

2/73 *Aloha from Hawaii via Satellite* (EP) ....RCA Victor DTFO-2006
2/73 *Aloha from Hawaii via Satellite* (LP) ....RCA Victor VPSX-6089
3/73 *Almost in Love* (LP) ....RCA/Camden CAS-2440
4/73 *Steamroller Blues/Fool* (45) ....RCA Victor 74-0910
5/73 *An American Trilogy/Until It's Time for You to Go* (Gold
        Standard) (45) ....RCA Victor 447-0685
7/73 *Elvis (Including "Fool")* (LP) ....RCA Victor APL1-0283
8/73 *Elvis* (LP) ....RCA Victor DPL2-0056(e)
9/73 *Raised on Rock/For Ol' Times Sake* (45)...............................RCA Victor APBO-0088

11/73 *Raised on Rock/For Ol' Times Sake* (LP) ....RCA Victor APL1-0388

1974

1/74 *I've Got a Thing About You Baby/Take Good Care*
      of Her (45)..RCA Victor APBO-0196
1/74 *Elvis: A Legendary Performer (Vol. 1)* (LP)..........................RCA Victor CPL1-0341
3/74 *Good Times* (LP)..RCA Victor CPL1-0475
5/74 *If You Talk in Your Sleep/Help Me* (45).................................RCA Victor APBO-0280
6/74 *Elvis Recorded Live on Stage in Memphis* (LP) ....RCA Victor CPL1-0606
6/74 *Elvis Recorded Live on Stage in Memphis*
      (Quadraphonic) (LP)...RCA Victor APD1-0606
6/74 *Let Me Be There* (Mono)/*Let Me Be There* (Stereo) (45) ....RCA Victor JH-10951
10/74 *Promised Land/It's Midnight* (45)....................................RCA Victor PB-10074

1975

1/75 *My Boy/Thinking About You* (45) ....RCA Victor PB-10191
1/75 *Promised Land* (LP)...RCA Victor APL1-0873
1/75 *Promised Land* (Quadraphonic) (LP) ....RCA Victor APD1-0873
3/75 *Steamroller Blues/Burning Love* (Gold Standard) (45) ....RCA Victor GB10156
3/75 *If You Talk in Your Sleep/Raised on Rock* (Gold
      Standard) (45) ....RCA Victor GB-10157
4/75 *T-R-O-U-B-L-E/Mr. Songman* (45).....................................RCA Victor PB-10278
5/75 *Elvis Today* (LP) ....RCA Victor APL1-1039
5/75 *Elvis Today* (Quadraphonic) (LP) ....RCA Victor APD1-1039
6/75 *Pure Gold* (LP) ....RCA Victor ANL1-0971(e)
8/75 *The Sun Collection* (LP)..RCA Victor HY-1001
10/75 *Bringing It Back/Pieces of My Life* (45) ....RCA Victor PB-10401
12/75 *Elvis Sings Flaming Star* (LP) ....Pickwick/Camden CAS-2304
12/75 *Let's Be Friends* (LP)..Pickwick/Camden CAS-2408
12/75 *Almost in Love* (LP) ....Pickwick/Camden CAS-2440
12/75 *Elvis' Christmas Album* (LP)...Pickwick/Camden CAS-2448
12/75 *You'll Never Walk Alone* (LP)...Pickwick/Camden CAS-2472
12/75 *C'mon Everybody* (LP)..Pickwick/Camden CAS-2518
12/75 *I Got Lucky* (LP) ....Pickwick/Camden CAS-2553
12/75 *Elvis Sings Hits from His Movies, Vol. 1* (LP) ....Pickwick/Camden CAS-2567
12/75 *Burning Love and Hits from His Movies, Vol. 2* (LP) ..Pickwick/Camden CAS-2595
12/75 *Separate Ways* (LP) ....Pickwick/Camden CAS-2611
12/75 *Double Dynamite* (LP)...Pickwick/Camden DL2-5001
12/75 *Frankie and Johnny* (LP)..Pickwick/Camden ACL-7007

1976

1/76 *Elvis in Hollywood* (LP)..RCA Victor DPL2-0168
1/76 *Elvis: A Legendary Performer, Vol. 2* (LP) ....RCA Victor CPL1-1349
2/76 *I've Got a Thing About You Baby/Take Good Care of Her* (Gold
      Standard) (45) ....RCA Victor GB-10485
2/76 *Separate Ways/Always on My Mind* (Gold Standard) (45)......RCA Victor GB-10486
2/76 *T-R-O-U-B-L-E/Mr. Songman* (Gold Standard) (45)...............RCA Victor GB-10487

2/76	*Promised Land/It's Midnight* (Gold Standard) (45)................	RCA Victor GB-10488
2/76	*My Boy/Thinking About You* (Gold Standard) (45).................	RCA Victor GB-10489
3/76	*The Sun Sessions* (LP)...	RCA Victor APM1-1675
3/76	*His Hand in Mine* (LP)	RCA Victor ANL1-1319
3/76	*Hurt/For the Heart* (45)	RCA Victor PB-10601
5/76	*From Elvis Presley Boulevard, Memphis, Tennessee* (LP)....	RCA Victor APL1-1506
8/76	*Elvis—A Collectors Edition* (LP)	RCA Victor TB-1
12/76	*Moody Blue/She Thinks I Still Care* (45)	RCA Victor PB-10857

1977

4/77	*Welcome to My World* (LP)	RCA Victor APL1-2274
7/77	*Way Down/Pledging My Love* (45)..	RCA Victor PB-10998
7/77	*The Elvis Presley Story* (LP)...	RCA Victor DML5-026
7/77	*Elvis: His Songs of Inspiration* (LP)......................................	RCA Victor DML1-026
9/77	*Harum Scarum* (LP)...	RCA Victor APL1-2558
9/77	*Spinout* (LP)..	RCA Victor APL1-2560
9/77	*Double Trouble* (LP)	RCA Victor APL1-2561
9/77	*Clambake* (LP)..	RCA Victor APL1-2562
9/77	*It Happened at the World's Fair* (LP)......................................	RCA Victor APL1-2563
10/77	*Elvis in Concert* (LP)	RCA Victor APL2-2587
10/77	*15 Golden Records/30 Golden Hits* (45)	RCA Victor PP-11301
11/77	*My Way/America the Beautiful* (45)..	RCA Victor PB-11165
11/77	*Good Times* (LP)...	RCA Victor CPL1-0475
11/77	*Elvis Recorded Live on Stage in Memphis* (LP)	RCA Victor CPL1-0606
12/77	*20 Golden Hits in Full Color Sleeves* (45)..............................	RCA Victor PP-11340

1978

3/78	*Softly, As I Leave You/Unchained Melody* (45)	RCA Victor PB-11212
4/78	*He Walks Beside Me* (LP)	RCA Victor AFL1-2772
5/78	*Mahalo from Elvis* (LP)	Pickwick/Camden ACL-7064
7/78	*Elvis Sings for Children and Grownups Too!* (LP)	RCA Victor CPL1-2901
8/78	*(Let Me Be Your) Teddy Bear/Puppet on a String* (45)	RCA Victor PB-11320
8/78	*Moody Blue/For the Heart* (Gold Standard) (45)	RCA Victor GB-11326
9/78	*Worldwide Gold Award Hits, Parts 3 and 4* (LP).....................	RCA Victor R-214657
9/78	*From Elvis with Love* (LP)...	RCA Victor R-234340
9/78	*Elvis—Legendary Concert Performances* (LP).........................	RCA Victor R-244047
9/78	*Country Memories* (LP)	RCA Victor R-244069
9/78	*Memories of Elvis* (LP)	RCA Victor DML5-0347
9/78	*The Greatest Show on Earth* (LP)...	RCA Victor DML1-0348
9/78	*Elvis Commemorative Album* (LP)	RCA Victor DPL2-0056(e)
12/78	*Elvis: A Legendary Performer, Vol. 3* (LP)	RCA Victor CPL1-3082

1979

2/79	*Our Memories of Elvis* (LP)...	RCA Victor AQL1-3279
5/79	*Are You Sincere/Solitaire* (45)...	RCA Victor PB-11533
5/79	*Way Down/My Way* (Gold Standard) (45)	RCA Victor GB-11504

8/79	*There's a Honky Tonk Angel (Who Will Take Me Back In)/*	
	I Got a Feelin' in My Body (45) ....RCA Victor PB-11679	
8/79	*Our Memories of Elvis (More of the Pure Elvis Sound)* (LP).RCA VictorAQL1-3449	
8/79	*The Legendary Recordings of Elvis Presley* (LP)................RCA Victor DML6-0412	

1980

4/80	*This Is Elvis* (LP) .... RCA Victor CPL2-4031
5/80	*Are You Sincere/Unchained Melody* (Gold Standard) (45) ..... RCA Victor GB-11988
5/80	*Blue Hawaii* (Best Buy series) (LP)......................................RCA Victor AYL1-3683
5/80	*Spinout* (Best Buy series) (LP) ....RCA Victor AYL1-3684
7/80	*Elvis Aron Presley* (LP) .... RCA Victor CPL8-3699
7/80	*Elvis Country Classics* (LP)..RCA Victor R-233299(e)
8/80	*The Legendary Magic of Elvis Presley* (LP)..........................RCA Victor DVL1-0461
11/80	*Pure Gold* (Best Buy series) (LP)..RCA Victor AYL1-3732
11/80	*King Creole* (Best Buy series) (LP)......................................RCA Victor AYL1-3733
11/80	*Harum Scarum* (Best Buy series) (LP) ....RCA Victor AYL1-3734
11/80	*G.I. Blues* (Best Buy series) (LP)...RCA Victor AYL1-3735

1981

1/81	*Guitar Man/Faded Love* (45)...RCA Victor PB-12158
2/81	*Elvis in Person at the International Hotel, Las Vegas,*	
	Nevada (Best Buy series) (LP) ....RCA Victor AYL1-3892	
2/81	*The Sun Sessions* (Best Buy series) (LP) .... RCA Victor AYM1-3893
2/81	*Elvis (NBC TV Special)* (Best Buy series) (LP)................... RCA Victor AYM1-3894
4/81	*Lovin' Arms/You Asked Me To* (45) ....RCA Victor PB-12205
5/81	*His Hand in Mine* (Best Buy series) (LP).............................RCA Victor AYL1-3935
5/81	*Elvis Country* (Best Buy series) (LP)....................................RCA Victor AYL1-3936
9/81	*Elvis—That's the Way It Is* (Best	
	Buy series) (LP) ....RCA Victor AYL1-4114	
9/81	*Kissin' Cousins* (Best Buy series) (LP)..................................RCA Victor AYL1-4115
9/81	*Something for Everybody* (Best Buy series) (LP) ....RCA Victor AYL1-4116
11/81	*Elvis—Greatest Hits, Vol. 1* (LP) ....RCA Victor AHL1-2347

1982

2/82	*Elvis for Everyone* (Best Buy series) (LP)........................... RCA Victor AYM1-4332
2/82	*You'll Never Walk Alone/There Goes My Everything* (45) .... RCA Victor PB13058
8/82	*Memories of Christmas* (LP)... RCA Victor CPL1-4395
11/82	*The Elvis Medley/Always on My Mind* (45) ....RCA Victor PB-13351
11/82	*The Elvis Medley* (LP) ....RCA Victor AHL1-4530
5/82	*Double Dynamite* (LP)...RCA/Pair PDL2-1010

1983

1/83	*Suspicious Minds/You'll Think of Me* (Gold Standard) (45) ..... RCA VictorGB-13275
4/83	*I Was the One/Wear My Ring Around Your Neck* (45)..............RCA Victor PB13500
5/83	*I Was the One* (LP) ....RCA Victor AHL1-4678
6/83	*Little Sister/Paralyzed* (45)...RCA Victor PB-13547
11/83	*A Country Christmas, Vol. 2* (LP)..RCA Victor AYL1-4809

11/83   *Elvis: A Legendary Performer (Vol. 4) (LP)*.......................... RCA Victor CPL1-4848
12/83   *Remembering Elvis (LP)* ....RCA/Pair PDL2-1037

1984

1/84   *Elvis—HBO Special (LP)* .... RCA Victor DVM1-070
4/84   *Elvis Country (LP)* .... RCA Victor DPL1-0647
5/84   *Elvis Presley (CD)* ....RCA Victor PCD1-1254
5/84   *Elvis (CD)* ....RCA Victor PCD1-1382
5/84   *Elvis' Golden Records (CD)*....................................RCA Victor PCD1-1707
5/84   *Elvis' Gold Records, Vol. 5 (LP)*............................ RCA Victor AFL1-4941
5/84   *Elvis' Gold Records, Vol. 5 (CD)*............................RCA Victor PCD1-4941
5/84   *The Beginning Years (LP)*................................ Louisiana Hayride LH-3061
7/84   *The Elvis Presley Collection (LP)*............................RCA Victor DML3-0632
7/84   *The Savage Young Elvis (Cassette)*........................RCA Victor DPK1-0679
8/84   *Baby, Let's Play House/Hound Dog (45)*....................................RCA Victor PB-1387
8/84   *Elvis' Golden Records (LP)*.. RCA Victor AFM1-5196
8/84   *Elvis' Gold Records, Vol. 2 (50,000,000 Elvis Fans Can't*
         Be Wrong) (LP).. RCA Victor AFM1-5197
8/84   *Elvis Presley (LP)*.. RCA Victor AFM1-5198
8/84   *A Golden Celebration (LP)*................................ RCA Victor CPM6-5172
9/84   *Elvis' Gold Records, Vol. 2 (50,000,000 Elvis Fans Can't*
         Be Wrong) (CD)..RCA Victor PCD1-2075
9/84   *Elvis (LP)* .... RCA Victor AFM1-5199
11/84 *Elvis' Golden Records (CD)*....................................RCA Victor PCD1-5196
11/84 *Elvis' Gold Records, Vol. 2 (50,000,000 Elvis Fans Can't*
         Be Wrong) (CD)..RCA Victor PCD1-5197
11/84 *Elvis Presley (CD)* ....RCA Victor PCD1-5198
11/84 *Elvis (CD)* ....RCA Victor PCD1-5199
11/84 *Rocker (LP)*..RCA Victor AFM1-5182
11/84 *Rocker (CD)*..RCA Victor PCD1-5182
11/84 *Merry Christmas (CD)*...RCA Victor PCD1-5301
12/84 *Elvis' Greatest Hits—Golden Singles, Vol. 1 (45)*....................RCA Victor PB-13897
12/84 *Elvis' Greatest Hits—Golden Singles, Vol. 2 (45)*....................RCA Victor PB-13898
12/84 *Blue Suede Shoes/Promised Land (45)*..RCA Victor PB-13929

1985

1/85   *Elvis: 50 Years—50 Hits (LP)*................................. RCA Victor SVL3-0710
4/85   *Reconsider Baby (LP)*.. RCA Victor AFL1-5418
4/85   *Reconsider Baby (CD)*..RCA Victor PCD1-5418
6/85   *Always on My Mind/My Boy (45)* ....RCA Victor PB-14090
6/85   *Always on My Mind (LP)* .... RCA Victor AFL1-5430
7/85   *Always on My Mind (CD)* ....RCA Victor PCD1-5430
7/85   *Elvis' Christmas Album (LP)* .... RCA Victor AFM1-5486
8/85   *Elvis' Christmas Album (CD)*..............................RCA Victor PCD1-5486
8/85   *A Valentine Gift for You (CD)* ....RCA Victor PCD1-5353
12/85 *Merry Christmas Baby/Santa Claus Is Back in Town (45)*........ RCA Victor PB14237

1986

2/86	*Elvis: His Songs of Faith and Inspiration* (LP) ....RCA Victor DVL2-0728
6/86	*Return of the Rocker* (LP) ....RCA Victor 5600-1-R
6/86	*Return of the Rocker* (CD) ....RCA Victor 5600-2-R
8/86	*Elvis: The Legend Lives On* (LP)...RCA Victor RBA-191/A
?/86	*Good Rockin' Tonight/I Don't Care if the Sun Don't Shine* (45) ......Collectables 4500
?/86	*You're a Heartbreaker/Milkcow Blues Boogie* (45).........................Collectables 4501
?/86	*Baby, Let's Play House/I'm Left, You're Right, She's Gone* (45) ......Collectables 4502
?/86	*I Got a Woman/I'm Counting on You* (45) ....Collectables 4503
?/86	*I'll Never Let You Go (Little Darlin')/I'm Gonna Sit Right Down and Cry (Over You)* (45) ....Collectables 4504
?/86	*Tryin' to Get to You/I Love You Because* (45) ....Collectables 4505
?/86	*Money Honey/One-Sided Love Affair* (45)....................................Collectables 4506
?/86	*Too Much/Playing for Keeps* (45)..Collectables 4507
?/86	*A Big Hunk O' Love/My Wish Came True* (45)..............................Collectables 4508
?/86	*Stuck on You/Fame and Fortune* (45)..Collectables 4509
?/86	*I Feel So Bad/Wild in the Country* (45) ....Collectables 4510
?/86	*She's Not You/Jailhouse Rock* (45) ....Collectables 4511
?/86	*One Broken Heart for Sale/Devil in Disguise* (45) ....Collectables 4512
?/86	*Bossa Nova Baby/Such a Night* (45)..Collectables 4513
?/86	*Love Me/Flaming Star* (45)...Collectables 4514
?/86	*Follow That Dream/When My Blue Moon Turns to Gold Again* (45) ....Collectables 4515
?/86	*Frankie and Johnny/Love Letters* (45)..Collectables 4516
?/86	*U.S. Male/Until It's Time for You to Go* (45)...............................Collectables 4517
?/86	*Old Shep/You'll Never Walk Alone* (45).......................................Collectables 4518
?/86	*Poor Boy/An American Trilogy* (45)..Collectables 4519
?/86	*How Great Thou Art/His Hand in Mine* (45).................................Collectables 4520
?/86	*Big Boss Man/Paralyzed* (45) ....Collectables 4521
?/86	*Fools Fall in Love/Blue Suede Shoes* (45)....................................Collectables 4522
?/86	*The Elvis Medley/Always on My Mind* (45)...................................Collectables 4564

1987 (The BMG Era Begins)

7/87	*The Memphis Record* (LP) ....RCA/BMG 6221-1-R
7/87	*The Memphis Record* (CD) ....RCA/BMG 6221-2-R
7/87	*Elvis Talks!* (LP) ....RCA/BMG 6313-1-R
7/87	*The Number One Hits* (LP) ....RCA/BMG 6382-1-R
7/87	*The Number One Hits* (CD) ....RCA/BMG 6382-2-R
7/87	*The Top Ten Hits* (LP) ....RCA/BMG 6383-1-R
7/87	*The Top Ten Hits* (CD) ....RCA/BMG 6383-2-R-P-1 & 2
7/87	*The Complete Sun Sessions* (LP) ....RCA/BMG 6414-1-R
7/87	*The Sun Sessions* CD (CD) ....RCA/BMG 6414-2-R
8/87	*Great Hits of 1956-57* (LP)..................................... RCA/BMG RBA-072/D
8/87	*You'll Never Walk Alone* (CD) ....RCA/Camden/BMG CAD1-2472
8/87	*Burning Love and Hits from His Movies, Vol. 2* (CD)..RCA/Camden/BMG CAD1-2595
8/87	*Elvis' Christmas Album* (CD)...........................RCA/Camden/BMG CAD1-2428

9/87 *Memories of Christmas* (CD)...RCA/BMG 4395-2-R
12/87 *Elvis Aron Presley "Forever"* (CD) ....RCA/BMG/Pair PDC2-1185
?/87 *Double Dynamite* (CD) ....RCA Victor/Pair PDC2-1010

1988

1/88 *Essential Elvis (The First Movies)* (LP).......................................RCA/BMG 6738-1-R
1/88 *Essential Elvis (The First Movies)* (CD)......................................RCA/BMG 6738-2-R
1/88 *Good Rockin' Tonight* (LP)... RCA/BMG SVL2-0824
1/88 *Good Rockin' Tonight* (CD) ....RCA/BMG SVC2-0824
2/88 *Remembering Elvis* (CD) .... RCA/BMG/Pair PDC2-1037
3/88 *Elvis Presley: 1954-1961* (LP)..Time-Life STL-106
3/88 *Elvis Presley: 1954-1961* (CD)....................................Time-Life TCD-106
4/88 *From Elvis Presley Blvd., Memphis, Tennessee* (CD) ....RCA/BMG 1506-2-R
4/88 *Loving You* (CD) ....RCA/BMG 1515-2-R
4/88 *King Creole* (CD)...RCA/BMG 3733-2-R
4/88 *G.I. Blues* (CD) ....RCA/BMG 3735-2-R
4/88 *Blue Hawaii* (CD) ....RCA/BMG 3683-2-R
5/88 *Moody Blue* (CD) ....RCA/BMG 2428-2-R
5/88 *The Alternate Aloha* (CD) ....RCA/BMG 6985-2-R
6/88 *Pot Luck with Elvis* (CD) ....RCA/BMG 2523-2-R
8/88 *His Hand in Mine* (CD)...RCA/BMG 1319-2-R
8/88 *How Great Thou Art (As Sung by Elvis)* (CD) ....RCA/BMG 3758-2-R
8/88 *50 Worldwide Gold Award Hits, Vol. 1* (CD)............................RCA/BMG 6401-2-R
8/88 *Elvis Sings the Wonderful World of Christmas* (CD) ....RCA/BMG 4579-2-R
10/88 *Elvis Country* (CD) ....RCA/BMG 6330-2-R
10/88 *Elvis in Nashville (1956-1971)* (CD) ....RCA/BMG 8468-2-R
11/88 *Elvis Is Back!* (CD) ....RCA/BMG 2231-2-R

1989

1/89 *A Date with Elvis* (CD) ....RCA/BMG 2011-2-R
2/89 *Essential Elvis, Vol. 2 (Stereo '57)* (LP) ....RCA/BMG 9589-1-R
2/89 *Essential Elvis, Vol. 2 (Stereo '57)* (CD) ....RCA/BMG 9589-2-R
4/89 *Elvis Gospel 1957-1971 (Known Only to Him)* (CD) ....RCA/BMG 9586-2-R
4/89 *For LP Fans Only* (CD)...RCA/BMG 1990-2-R
4/89 *Promised Land* (CD)..RCA/BMG 0873-2-R
7/89 *Christmas Classics* (CD) ....RCA/BMG 9801-2-R
8/89 *Elvis Sings for Children and Grownups Too!* (CD) .... RCA/BMG CAD1-2704
8/89 *Elvis: A Legendary Performer, Vol. 1* (CD) ....RCA/BMG CAD1-2705
9/89 *An Elvis Double Feature: Speedway & Clambake* (CD)..................... RCA/BMG/Pair PDC2-1250 (CXD-3017)
10/89 *Something for Everybody* (CD).....................................RCA/BMG 2370-2-R
?/89 *Hound Dog/Don't Be Cruel* (Gold Standard) (CD) ....RCA/BMG 8990-2-RH
?/89 *Can't Help Falling in Love/Rock-A-Hula Baby* (Gold Standard) (CD) ....RCA/BMG 8991-2-RH
?/89 *Jailhouse Rock/Treat Me Nice* (Gold Standard) (CD).............RCA/BMG 8992-2-RH
?/89 *Blue Suede Shoes/Tutti Frutti* (Gold Standard) (CD) ....RCA/BMG 8993-2-RH
?/89 *Are You Lonesome Tonight/I Gotta Know* (Gold Standard) (CD) ....RCA/BMG 8994-2-RH

?/89   *Elvis, the King (1954-1965)* (LP)...Time-Life STL-126

1990

1/90   *Elvis: A Legendary Performer, Vol. 2* (CD) ....RCA/BMG CAD1-2706
1/90   *Elvis Presley: Great Performances* (CD) .... RCA/BMG/Pair
        PDC2-1251 (CXD-3018)
3/90   *The Million Dollar Quartet* (LP) ....RCA/BMG 2023-1-R
3/90   *The Million Dollar Quartet* (CD) ....RCA/BMG 2023-2-R
4/90   *Elvis' Golden Records, Vol. 3* (CD) ....RCA/BMG 2765-2-R
7/90   *Elvis' Golden Records, Vol. 4* (CD) ....RCA/BMG 1297-2-R
7/90   *Great Hits of 1956-57* (CD).....................RCA/BMG/Reader's Digest RBD-072/CD1
8/90   *The Great Performances* (LP) ....RCA/BMG 2227-1-R
8/90   *The Great Performances* (CD)..RCA/BMG 2227-2-R
9/90   *Heartbreak Hotel (Hound Dog & Other Top Ten Hits)* (CD) ....RCA/BMG 2079-2-R
9/90   *50 Years—50 Hits* (CD)................................. RCA/BMG SVC2-0710-1/2
10/90   *Elvis for Everyone!* (CD) ....RCA/BMG 3450-2-R
?/90   *Vintage '55 Elvis* (LP)..Oak 1003
?/90   *Vintage '55 Elvis* (CD) ....Oak 1003
?/90   *Elvis, the King: 1954-1965* (CD) ....Time-Life TCD-126

1991

1/91   *Essential Elvis, Vol. 3 (Hits Like Never Before)* (CD)................RCA/BMG 2229-2-R
4/91   *Elvis Presley Sings Leiber & Stoller* (CD) ....RCA/BMG 3026-2-R
5/91   *Christmas Memories from Elvis & Alabama* (CD).....Audio Treasures ATCD 2106-2
5/91   *Elvis Presley & Jim Reeves Christmas*
        Favorites (CD) ....Audio Treasures ATCD 2107-2
7/91   *Elvis at His Romantic Best* (CD) ....RCA/BMG DPC1-0984
8/91   *From Elvis in Memphis* (CD)...RCA/BMG 51456-2
8/91   *Collectors Gold* (LP)..RCA/BMG 3114-1-R
8/91   *Collectors Gold* (CD)...RCA/BMG 3114-2-R
8/91   *Elvis (NBC-TV Special)* (CD) ....RCA/BMG 61021-2
10/91   *On Stage (February, 1970)* (CD)..RCA/BMG 54362-2
11/91   *The "Lost" Album* (CD)..RCA/BMG 61024-2
?/91   *The King of Rock & Roll at His Best* (CD) ....RCA/BMG S4D-4965 SC
?/91   *50 Greatest Hits* (CD)..RCA/BMG 15018-2

1992

3/92   *He Touched Me* (CD)...RCA/BMG 51923-2
4/92   *Elvis Today* (LP) ....RCA/BMG 51039-2
4/92   *Aloha from Hawaii via Satellite* (CD) ....RCA/BMG 52642-2
4/92   *Elvis as Recorded at Madison Square Garden* (CD)....................RCA/BMG 54776-2
5/92   *That's the Way It Is* (CD) .... Mobile Fidelity Sound Lab UDCD-560
5/92   *Welcome to My World* (CD)..RCA/BMG 52274-2
5/92   *Elvis in Concert* (CD) ....RCA/BMG 52587-2
5/92   *Pure Gold* (CD)...RCA/BMG 53732-2
6/92   *The King of Rock 'N' Roll (The Complete 50's Masters)* (CD) .....RCA/BMG 66050-2

6/92	*Don't Be Cruel/Ain't That Loving You Baby (Fast Version)* (45)	RCA/BMG 62402-7
6/92	*Blue Christmas/Love Me* (45)	RCA/BMG 62403-7
6/92	*Heartbreak Hotel/Hound Dog* (45)	RCA/BMG 62449-7
7/92	*Blue Christmas* (CD)	RCA/BMG 59800-2
8/92	*Good Rockin' Tonight/I Don't Care if the Sun Don't Shine* (45)	Collectables 4500
8/92	*You're a Heartbreaker/Milkcow Blues Boogie* (45)	Collectables 4501
8/92	*Baby, Let's Play House/I'm Left, You're Right, She's Gone* (45)	Collectables 4502
8/92	*I Got a Woman/I'm Counting on You* (45)	Collectables 4503
8/92	*I'll Never Let You Go (Little Darlin')/I'm Gonna Sit Right Down and Cry (Over You)* (45)	Collectables 4504
8/92	*Tryin' to Get to You/I Love You Because* (45)	Collectables 4505
8/92	*Money Honey/One-Sided Love Affair* (45)	Collectables 4506
8/92	*Too Much/Playing for Keeps* (45)	Collectables 4507
8/92	*A Big Hunk O' Love/My Wish Came True* (45)	Collectables 4508
8/92	*Stuck on You/Fame and Fortune* (45)	Collectables 4509
8/92	*I Feel So Bad/Wild in the Country* (45)	Collectables 4510
8/92	*She's Not You/Jailhouse Rock* (45)	Collectables 4511
8/92	*One Broken Heart for Sale/Devil in Disguise* (45)	Collectables 4512
8/92	*Bossa Nova Baby/Such a Night* (45)	Collectables 4513
8/92	*Love Me/Flaming Star* (45)	Collectables 4514
8/92	*Follow That Dream/When My Blue Moon Turns to Gold Again* (45)	Collectables 4515
8/92	*Frankie and Johnny/Love Letters* (45)	Collectables 4516
8/92	*U.S. Male/Until It's Time for You to Go* (45)	Collectables 4517
8/92	*Old Shep/You'll Never Walk Alone* (45)	Collectables 4518
8/92	*Poor Boy/An American Trilogy* (45)	Collectables 4519
8/92	*How Great Thou Art/His Hand in Mine* (45)	Collectables 4520
8/92	*Big Boss Man/Paralyzed* (45)	Collectables 4521
8/92	*Fools Fall in Love/Blue Suede Shoes* (45)	Collectables 4522

The above (1992) Collectables singles are gold vinyl reissues of previous (1986) black vinyl releases.

10/92	*Elvis in Person at the International Hotel, Las Vegas, Nevada* (CD)	RCA/BMG 53892-2
10/92	*Love Letters from Elvis* (CD)	RCA/BMG 54350-2
10/92	*Back in Memphis* (CD)	RCA/BMG 61081-2
10/92	*King of Rock 'N' Roll (Don't Be Cruel)* (CD)	RCA/BMG 62404-2

1993

1/93	*Kid Galahad/Girls! Girls! Girls!* (CD)	RCA/BMG 61835-2
1/93	*It Happened at the World's Fair/Fun in Acapulco* (CD)	RCA/BMG 61835-2
1/93	*Viva Las Vegas/Roustabout* (CD)	RCA/BMG 61835-2
1/93	*Harum Scarum/Girl Happy* (CD)	RCA/BMG 61835-2

(The above four are part of a TV mail order edition, *Elvis Double Features*, from cable TV's QVC Home Shopping Channel.)

2/93	*Harum Scarum/Girl Happy* (CD)	RCA/BMG 66128-2

2/93	*Viva Las Vegas/Roustabout* (CD)	RCA/BMG 66129-2
2/93	*Kid Galahad/Girls! Girls! Girls!* (CD)	RCA/BMG 66130-2
2/93	*It Happened at the World's Fair/Fun in Acapulco* (CD)	RCA/BMG 66131-2
7/93	*Elvis Country (I'm 10,000 Years Old)* (CD)	RCA/BMG 66279-2
7/93	*Elvis Now* (CD)	RCA/BMG 54671-2
7/93	*That's the Way It Is* (CD)	RCA/BMG 54114-2
8/93	*The Private Presley CD* (CD)	Merlin Group 04609-6
9/93	*From Nashville to Memphis* (CD)	RCA/BMG 66160-2
10/93	*Country Christmas [Elvis & Jim Reeves]* (CD)	RCA/BMG DDX2508-3
10/93	*Country Christmas [Elvis & Alabama]* (CD)	RCA/BMG DDX2517-3
10/93	*The Legend Lives On* (CD)	RCA/BMG/Reader's Digest RBD-191/CD1

1994

3/94	*Elvis ("The Fool Album")* (CD)	RCA/BMG 50283-2
3/94	*Raised on Rock* (CD)	RCA/BMG 50388-2
3/94	*Good Times* (CD)	RCA/BMG 50475-2
3/94	*Elvis Recorded Live on Stage in Memphis* (CD)	RCA/BMG 50606-2
6/94	*Frankie and Johnny/Paradise, Hawaiian Style* (CD)	RCA/BMG 66360-2
6/94	*Spinout/Double Trouble* (CD)	RCA/BMG 66361-2
6/94	*Kissin' Cousins/Clambake/Stay Away Joe* (CD)	RCA/BMG 66362-2
6/94	*Elvis Country* (CD)	RCA/BMG 66405-2
8/94	*Elvis—His Life and Music* (CD)	RCA/BMG
10/94	*Amazing Grace (His Greatest Sacred Performances)* (CD)	RCA/BMG 66421-2
10/96	*If Every Day Was Like Christmas* (CD)	RCA/BMG 66482-2
11/96	*If Every Day Was Like Christmas* (CD)	RCA/BMG 66506-2

1995

1/95	*Heart and Soul* (CD)	RCA/BMG 66532-2
3/95	*Flaming Star/Wild in the Country/ Follow That Dream* (CD)	RCA/BMG 66557-2
3/95	*Easy Come, Easy Go/Speedway* (CD)	RCA/BMG 66558-2
3/95	*Live a Little, Love a Little/Charro!/The Trouble with Girls/ Change of Habit* (CD)	RCA/BMG 66559-2
4/95	*Elvis for Everyone!* (CD)	RCA/BMG 53450-2
7/95	*Elvis Command Performances (The Essential 60's Masters II)* (CD)	RCA/BMG 66601-2
7/95	*Elvis Presley* (CD)	RCA/BMG 66659-2
9/95	*Elvis' Christmas Album* (CD)	RCA/Camden/BMG CAD1-2428
10/95	*Walk a Mile in My Shoes (Essential 70's Masters)* (CD)	RCA/BMG 66670-2

1996

4/96	*Heartbreak Hotel (I Was the One)* (CD)	RCA/BMG 64475-2
4/96	*Elvis 56* (CD)	RCA/BMG 66817-2
4/96	*Elvis 56* (CD)	RCA/BMG 66856-2
4/96	*50 Worldwide Gold Award Hits, Vol. 1* (CD)	RCA/BMG 56401-2-R
5/96	*The Top Ten Hits* (CD)	RCA/BMG 56383-2
6/96	*Elvis Sings Hits from His Movies, Vol. 1* (CD)	RCA/BMG CAD1-2567

7/96	*Essential Elvis, Vol. 4 (A Hundred Years from Now)* (CD) ....RCA/BMG 66866-2
7/96	*The Louisiana Hayride Archives, Vol. 1* (CD)....................Branson Gold BGR-02462
8/96	*Elvis—The Other Sides (Worldwide Gold Award Hits, Vol. 2)* (CD) ....RCA/BMG 66921-2
10/96	*Christmas Memories from Elvis & Alabama* (CD).....Audio Treasures ATCD 2106-2
10/96	*Elvis Presley & Jim Reeves Christmas Favorites* (CD)...Audio Treasures ATCD 2107-2
10/96	*Elvis: Great Country Songs* (CD)..RCA/BMG 66880-2
10/96	*Elvis! His Greatest Hits* (CD)..........................RCA/BMG/Reader's Digest RDU 010
12/96	*Elvis Presley Gospel Treasury* (CD)....................RCA/BMG/Heartland DMC2-1427
12/96	*Almost in Love* (CD) ....RCA/BMG CAD1-2440

1997

3/97	*The Truth About Me* (LP)..Rainbo Records
3/97	*The Truth About Me* (CD)..Rainbo Records
3/97	*An Afternoon in the Garden* (CD)..RCA/BMG 67457-2
4/97	*Loving You* (CD)..RCA/BMG 67452-2
4/97	*Jailhouse Rock and Love Me Tender* (CD)..............................RCA/BMG 67453-2
4/97	*King Creole* (CD)..RCA/BMG 67454-2
4/97	*Blue Hawaii* (CD) ....RCA/BMG 66959-2
4/97	*Blue Hawaii* (CD) ....RCA/BMG 67459-2
4/97	*G.I. Blues* (CD) ....RCA/BMG 66960-2
4/97	*G.I. Blues* (CD) ....RCA/BMG 66960-2
4/97	*Blue Suede Shoes* (CD) ....RCA/BMG 67458-2
6/97	*Elvis Is Back!* (CD) ....RCA/BMG/DCC GZS-1111-2
7/97	*Elvis' Golden Records* (CD)...RCA/BMG 67462-2
7/97	*Elvis' Gold Records, Vol. 2 (50,000,000 Elvis Fans Can't Be Wrong)* (CD)..RCA/BMG 67463-2
7/97	*Elvis' Golden Records, Vol. 3* (CD) ....RCA/BMG 67464-2
7/97	*Elvis' Golden Records, Vol. 4* (CD) ....RCA/BMG 67465-2
7/97	*Elvis' Gold Records, Vol. 5* (CD)..RCA/BMG 67466-2
7/97	*Elvis Presley Platinum (A Life in Music)* (CD) ....RCA/BMG 67469-2
8/97	*Christmas with Elvis* (CD)...RCA/BMG DIR 9003-2
8/97	*Elvis! Elvis! Elvis! (The King and His Movies)* (CD).............RCA/BMG DPC 11624
9/97	*Elvis' Greatest Jukebox Hits* (CD)...RCA/BMG 67565-2
9/97	*Elvis 24 Karat Hits!* (CD)...RCA/BMG/DCC GZS-1117-2
9/97	*Elvis Presley Collection (Love Songs)* (CD)...............RCA/BMG/Time-Life 69400-2
11/97	*Elvis Presley Collection (Rock 'N' Roll)* (CD)............RCA/BMG/Time-Life 69401-2
12/97	*Elvis Presley Collection (Movie Magic)* (CD)............RCA/BMG/Time-Life 69404-2

1998

| 1/98 | *Elvis Presley Love Songs* (CD) ....RCA/BMG 67595-2 |

This chronology focuses on Elvis' commercial music catalog, making no attempt to include promotional-only releases and various artists compilations.

TEST PRESSINGS
&
ACETATES

Test Pressings

During the years of phonograph record manufacturing, several test pressings may have been made for each recording in the course of its production. Separate test pressings may exist, sampling such variations as: A-side only, B-side only, both sides, alternate mixes, and unsweetened takes – before background vocals and/or orchestration are added.

Occasionally, when a record company felt they had a particularly hot new release, they would rush test pressings to select radio stations to allow them to begin programming the tune.

Vinyl test pressings were usually made to sample or *test* the quality of a particular recording after being stamped on a disc. If a pressing were unacceptable, for any of a number of reasons, other test pressings might have followed after the alterations were made. As such, test pressings may exist with drastic differences compared to the final, commercial product. On a test pressing, one may discover, for example: alternate takes, varied mixes, altered lengths, differing lyrics, and altered tempos.

Test pressings may just as likely – perhaps more than likely – offer the listener nothing that is not easily available on the everyday commercial release.

Understandably, the values of test pressings having alternate or unusual takes are higher than those containing commercially available tracks.

Among the most valuable of test pressings are those containing complete songs that are previously unreleased in any form.

Due to the nature and function of test pressings, flaws such as writing, typing, stickers or stampings on the labels do not affect their value nearly as much as they would on conventional records. With most test pressings, song titles and information is written on the label for easy identification.

Unfortunately, counterfeit test pressings also exist. The best way to determine if a pressing is a legitimate copy is to compare the characteristics between a known legitimate copy and the item in question Test pressings generally have the same vinyl characteristics as their promo or stock counterparts. Look for identifying symbols and stampings in the trail-off area of the disc. Remember, many records are produced by the different manufacturers, and symbols and distinctive characteristics call vary.

As with any big ticket collectibles, a buyer is always at an advantage if dealing with someone whose reputation is well-established, and who provides an acceptable guarantee.

Acetates

Due to the limited nature of their use, Elvis acetates are pretty scarce. As a rule, they are more difficult to find than test pressings, and much more so than promotional records. Acetates can be found in seven-, ten- and twelve-inch formats, and they may play at either

33, 45 or 78 rpm speeds. Acetates likely were made for Elvis recordings made during every year of his performing career.

The process used to produce acetates made them fairly expensive in terms of unit costs, a factor which kept their quantities limited. The acetic acid and cellulose composition used in the manufacturing of acetates is very soft and they are not designed for repeated play. The metal core that is sandwiched between the lacquer surfaces makes the disc heavy when compared to a conventional record. These factors make the playing surface of the acetate quite fragile and subject to rapid wear and scratching.

Unlike test pressings, acetates are far less likely to be distributed to radio stations and media people for advance airplay and review. Labeling is usually limited to company name or logo, with blanks for title and reference information.

For the most part, acetates find their way into the hands of collectors the same way as most manufacturing byproducts do, passing from friends and relatives in the industry to fandom. Since the acetate is lathe-cut during the early stages of production, changes are often made before the final version of the track is completed. Because of this, it is not uncommon to find acetates that differ from released versions in the same ways as previously explained for test pressings: alternate takes, varied mixes, altered lengths, differing lyrics, and altered tempos.

Occasionally, "working titles" can be found printed on acetate labels, made when the ultimate title had not been fully decided. is still undecided. One example that come to mind is *Black Star,* a variation of the 1960 film song that later became *Flaming Star.* At other times, the person responsible for preparing a label seems to have had no idea as to the true title. One example of this is a 20th Century-Fox acetate for the tune *We're Gonna Move,* which gives the title as *There's a Leak in This Old Building.* Those of course are merely lyrics from the song. Furthermore, several 20th Century-Fox acetates made for Elvis' first film show the title of the picture as *The Reno Brothers.*

Acetates with such discrepancies are among the most desirable among collectors.

Although a limited specialization – mostly because of their price tags – collecting Elvis acetates is becoming more popular. When contemplating the purchase of an acetate, learn as much about the source as possible.

Since prices on such unique items vary drastically, and are based on countless variables, we can not even begin to list them individually in the guide. For whatever appraisal assistance it may be worth, we can report recent test pressing and acetate sales ranging from as little as $100 to well over $1,000.

This does not take into consideration the most valuable Elvis acetates to surface thus far, the August 1953 personal recording young Elvis made of *My Happiness* backed with *That's When Your Heartaches Begin,* and early '54's *I'll Never Stand in Your Way* (pictured on page 530).

Before being commercially issued by RCA/BMG, offers of over a $100,000.00 were made for these discs. Since their release on CDs, we have heard of no similar offers, but one might assume their values have dropped considerably. Still, a collector with very deep pockets might pay plenty to own the only known copy of either of the first two recordings ever made to contain the singing voice of Elvis Presley.

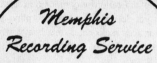

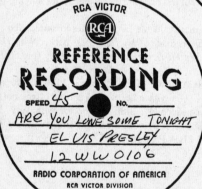

ELVIS 8-TRACK TAPES

Compared to vinyl records, the market for 8-tracks – by Elvis or anyone – is comparatively tiny. Like vinyl releases, however, some 8-track tapes are much harder to find than others.

Usual packaging includes stick-on labels for the plastic cartridges which pictures album cover art; however, some also have stickers affixed to the outer box which picture the art. Most tape cartridges came in generic RCA cardboard boxes, which make no mention of Elvis or any particular selection.

In 1966 when RCA announced the first 20 tapes in the series, each included a bonus 3½" x 5" color photo insert. On the card, in Elvis' own handwriting, is: "I hope you will like the new Stereo 8. Sincerely, Elvis Presley." Since 8-tracks didn't sell particularly well, the bonus photo cards are now quite rare – and are easily worth more than any of the tapes themselves.

All of the necessary ingredients are there to make these tapes a popular collectible, yet very few collectors are involved – comparatively speaking. Though it is probably not a factor – since actually playing Elvis 8-tracks is now unnecessary – it is likely that few collectors still have an 8-track tape player.

Apart from the 8-track boxed sets, such as *Worldwide 50 Gold Award Hits* and *Elvis Aron Presley,* these tapes are not individually priced.

However, except for the quad titles, most Elvis 8-tracks can be found in the $5 to $10 range. Any of the quad issues can bring $20 to $40.

TITLE	LABEL / NUMBER / FORMAT	YEAR
Almost in Love	Camden CAS1-0381 (S)	70
Almost in Love	Pickwick C86-0381 (S)	75
Aloha from Hawaii via Satellite	RCA P8S-5144 (S)	73
Aloha from Hawaii via Satellite, Vol. 1	RCA PQ8-2140 (Q)	73
Aloha from Hawaii via Satellite, Vol. 2	RCA PQ8-2141 (Q)	73
Aloha from Hawaii via Satellite	RCA CPS2-2642 (S)	77
Always on My Mind	RCA APS1-5430 (S)	85
Always on My Mind	RCA S-170138 (BMG Music Club) (S)	85
Back in Memphis	RCA P86-1632 (S)	70
Best of the '50s	RCA S-160523 (BMG Music Club) (M/S)	85
Best of the '60s	RCA S-160685 (BMG Music Club) (S)	85
Best of the '70s	RCA S-160780 (BMG Music Club) (S)	86
Blue Hawaii	RCA P8S-1019 (S)	66
Blue Hawaii	RCA AYS1-3683 (S)	80
Blue Hawaii	RCA P8S-5044 (S)	66
Blue Hawaii / Pot Luck	RCA DPL1-0086 (S)	74
Brightest Stars of Christmas	Camden KKS1-7065 (S)	78
Canadian Tribute	RCA P8S-1280 (S)	67
Clambake	RCA APS1-2565 (S)	77
Clambake	Camden C8S-5052 (S)	71
C'mon Everybody / I Got Lucky	Pickwick C8S-7013 (M)	75
C'mon Everybody / I Got Lucky	RCA S-233299 (BMG Music Club) (S)	80
Country Classics	RCA S-244069 (BMG Music Club) (S)	80
Country Memories		

Date with Elvis	RCA APS1-0387 (SE)	77
Double Dynamite	RCA PDL2-5001 (S)	76
Double Trouble	RCA P8S-1246 (S)	67
Double Trouble	APS1-2564 (S)	77
Elvis	DPS2-0056 (S)	73
Elvis	RCA APS1-0383 (SE)	77
Elvis (Including "Fool")	RCA APS1-0283 (S)	73
Elvis (NBC-TV Special)	RCA P8S-1391 (M/S)	68
Elvis (NBC-TV Special)	RCA AYS1-3894 (M/S)	81
Elvis Aron Presley	RCA CP8S (M/S)	80
Elvis As Recorded at Madison Square Garden	RCA P8S-2054 (S)	73
Elvis As Recorded at Madison Square Garden	RCA PQ8-2054 (Q)	73
Elvis As Recorded at Madison Square Garden	AQS1-4776 (S)	77
Elvis' Christmas Album	Pickwick C8S-9001 (M)	75
Elvis Country	RCA P8S-1655 (S)	71
Elvis Exclusive Live Press Conference	Green Valley (M)	77
Elvis for Everyone	RCA P8S-1078 (S)	66
Elvis' Golden Records	RCA P8S-1244 (SE)	68
Elvis' Golden Records	AQS1-1707 (SE)	71
Elvis' Golden Records, Vol. 2	P8S-2093 (SE)	72
Elvis' Golden Records, Vol. 3	P8S-1057 (S)	66
Elvis' Golden Records, Vol. 4	P8S-1297 (S)	68
Elvis' Greatest Hits, Vol. 1	RCA AHS1-2347 (S)	81
Elvis – His Songs of Inspiration	RCA DMS1-0264 (S)	77
Elvis in Concert	RCA APS2-2587 (S)	77
Elvis in Hollywood	RCA DPS2-0168 (S)	76
Elvis in Person at the International Hotel	RCA P8S-1634 (S)	70
Elvis in Person at the International Hotel	RCA AYS1-3892 (S)	77
Elvis Is Back	RCA P8S-1135 (S)	66
Elvis Medley	RCA AHS1-4530 (S)	82
Elvis Now	RCA P8S-1898 (S)	72
Elvis Presley	RCA APS1-0382 (SE)	77
Elvis Presley, Vols 1 - 3	Candlelite DMS3-0263 (M/S)	77
Elvis Recorded Live on Stage in Memphis	RCA CPS1-0606 (S)	74
Elvis Recorded Live on Stage in Memphis	RCA APT1-0606 (S)	77
Elvis Sings Burning Love & Hits from Movies	Camden C8S-1216 (S)	72
Elvis Sings Burning Love & Hits from Movies	Pickwick C8S-1216 (S)	84
Elvis Sings Country Favorites	Reader's Digest RD-5910 (S)	84
Elvis Sings Flaming Star	Pickwick C8S-7010 (S)	75
Elvis Sings Flaming Star / Let's Be Friends	Camden C8S-5050 (S)	71
Elvis Sings for Children & Grownups Too	RCA CPS1-2901 (S)	78
Elvis Sings His Greatest Hits	Reader's Digest RD8-5773-5 (S)	78
Elvis Sings Hits from His Movies, Vol. 1	Pickwick C8S-0380 (S)	75
Elvis Sings Inspirational Favorites	RCA RD8-577 (S)	82
Elvis Sings Songs of Christmas	RCA P8S-1249 (S)	68
Elvis Sings the Wonderful World of Christmas	RCA P8S-1809 (S)	71
Elvis Sings the Wonderful World of Christmas	RCA ANS1-1936 (S)	73
Elvis Tapes	GNW 8361-1001L (M)	77
Elvis Today	RCA APS1-1039 (S)	75

Elvis Today	RCA APT1-1039 (Q)	75
50 Years – 50 Hits, Vol. 1	RCA SVS2-0710P1 (M/S)	85
50 Years – 50 Hits, Vol. 2	RCA SVS2-0710P2 (M/S)	85
For LP Fans Only	RCA APS1-0386 (SE)	77
Frankie and Johnny	RCA P8S-1100 (S)	66
Frankie and Johnny	RCA APS1-2559 (S)	77
Frankie and Johnny	Pickwick C8S-7007 (S)	76
Frankie and Johnny / Something for Everybody	RCA P8S-5042 (S)	66
From Elvis in Memphis	RCA P8S-1456 (S)	69
From Elvis in Memphis	RCA PQ8-1456 (Q)	74
From Elvis Presley Blvd., Memphis, Tennessee	RCA APS1-1056 (S)	76
From Elvis with Love	RCA S-234340 (BMG Music Club) (M/S)	78
From Memphis to Vegas / Vegas to Memphis	RCA P8S-5076 (S)	69
Fun in Acapulco	RCA P8S-1141 (S)	66
G.I. Blues	RCA P8S-1169 (S)	66
G.I. Blues / Elvis Is Back	RCA P8S-5043 (S)	66
Girl Happy	RCA P8S-1018 (S)	66
Girls! Girls! Girls!	RCA P8S-1139 (S)	66
Golden Celebration	RCA CPSG-5172 (S)	84
Good Times	RCA CPS1-0475 (S)	74
Greatest Moments in Music	Candlelite DMS1-0413 (S)	80
Greatest Show on Earth	Candlelite PSM1-0348 (S)	78
Guitar Man	RCA AAS1-3917 (S)	81
Harum Scarum	RCA P8S-1087 (S)	66
Harum Scarum	RCA APS1-2558 (S)	77
Having Fun with Elvis on Stage	Boxcar (M)	74
Having Fun with Elvis on Stage	RCA CPS1-0818 (M)	74
He Touched Me	RCA P8S-1923 (S)	72
He Walks Beside Me	RCA AFS1-2772 (S)	78
His Hand in Mine	RCA P8S-1136 (S)	66
His Hand in Mine	RCA ANS1-1319 (S)	76
How Great Thou Art	RCA P8S-1218 (S)	67
How Great Thou Art	RCA AQS-3758 (S)	77
How Great Thou Art / His Hand in Mine	RCA P8S-5052 (S)	67
I Got Lucky	Pickwick C8S-7014 (M)	75
I Was the One	RCA APS1-4678 (S)	83
It Happened at the World's Fair	RCA P8S-1140 (S)	66
It Happened at the World's Fair	RCA APS1-2568 (S)	77
King Creole	RCA APS1-0385 (SE)	77
King Creole	RCA AYS1-3733 (SE)	80
Kissin' Cousins	RCA P8S-1142 (S)	66
Legendary Concert Performances	RCA S-244047 (BMG Music Club) (S)	78
Legendary Magic of Elvis Presley	RCA DVS1-0461 (S)	80
Legendary Performer, Vol. 1	RCA CPS1-0341 (M/S)	74
Legendary Performer, Vol. 2	RCA CPS1-1349 (M/S)	76
Legendary Performer, Vol. 3	RCA CPS1-3082 (S)	79
Legendary Performer, Vol. 4	RCA S-134429 (BMG Music Club) (M/S)	84
Legendary Recordings of Elvis Presley	RCA DMS3-0412P1-3 (M/S)	79
Let's Be Friends	Pickwick C8S-7011 (S)	75

Love Letters from Elvis	RCA P8S-1748 (S)	71
Loving You	RCA APS1-0384 (S)	77
Love Songs	K-Tel NU-9908 (M/S)	81
Mahalo from Elvis	Pickwick C8S-7064 (S)	78
Memories of Christmas	RCA CPS1-4395 (S)	82
Memories of Christmas	Candlelite DMS3-0347 (M/S)	78
Memphis Record	RCA S-254097 (BMG Music Club) (S)	85
Moody Blue	RCA AFS1-2428 (S)	77
On Stage – February, 1970	RCA P8S-1594 (S)	70
On Stage – February, 1970	RCA PQ8-1594 (Q)	74
On Stage – February, 1970	RCA AQS1-4362 (S)	77
Other Sides (Worldwide Gold Hits, Vol. 2 - Pt. 1)	RCA P8S-1793 (M)	75
Other Sides (Worldwide Gold Hits, Vol. 2 - Pt. 2)	RCA P8S-1794 (M)	75
Other Sides (Worldwide Gold Hits, Vol. 2 - Pt. 3)	RCA P8S-1795 (M)	75
Other Sides (Worldwide Gold Hits, Vol. 2 - Pt. 4)	RCA P8S-1796 (M)	75
Our Memories of Elvis	RCA AQS1-3279 (S)	79
Our Memories of Elvis, Vol. 2	RCA AQS1-3448 (S)	79
Paradise Hawaiian Style	RCA P8S-1165 (S)	66
Pot Luck with Elvis	RCA P8S-1138 (S)	66
Promised Land	RCA APS1-0873 (S)	75
Promised Land	RCA APT1-0873 (Q)	75
Pure Gold	RCA ANS1-0971 (S)	75
Pure Gold	RCA ANS1-3782 (S)	77
Raised on Rock	RCA APS1-0388 (S)	73
Reconsider Baby	RCA AFS1-5418 (M/S)	85
Reconsider Baby	RCA S-143700 (BMG Music Club) (M/S)	85
Return of the Rocker	RCA APS1-5600 (M/S)	86
Rocker	RCA AFS1-5182 (M)	84
Rock & Roll Forever	RCA CMS1-0437 (M)	81
Roustabout	RCA P8S-1143 (S)	66
Separate Ways	Camden C8S-1227 (S)	73
Separate Ways	Pickwick C8S-1227 (S)	75
Something for Everybody	RCA P8S-1137 (S)	66
Speedway	RCA P8S-1335 (S)	68
Spinout	RCA P8S-1201 (S)	66
Spinout	RCA APS1-2560 (S)	77
Sun Sessions	RCA APS1-1675 (M)	76
Sun Sessions	RCA AYS1-1675 (M)	78
Sun Years	Sun ST-1001 (M)	78
That's the Way It Is	RCA P8S-1652 (S)	70
That's the Way It Is	RCA PQ8-1652 (Q)	74
That's the Way It Is	RCA AYS1-4114 (S)	77
This Is Elvis	RCA CPS2-4031 (S)	80
Top Ten Hits	RCA S-243910 (BMG Music Club) (S)	85
Valentine Gift for You	RCA S-154385 (BMG Music Club) (M/S)	85
Welcome to My World	RCA APS1-2274 (M/S)	77
Worldwide 50 Gold Award Hits, Vol. 1	RCA P8S-6401 (M)	70
Worldwide 50 Gold Award Hits, Parts 1 & 2	RCA S-2136906 (BMG Music Club) (M)	75

Worldwide 50 Gold Award Hits,
   Parts 3 & 4 ....RCA S-2114657 (BMG Music Club) (M)   75
Worldwide 50 Gold Award Hits, Vol. 1- No. 1 .... RCA P8S-1773 (M)   75
Worldwide 50 Gold Award Hits, Vol. 1- No. 2 .... RCA P8S-1774 (M)   75
Worldwide 50 Gold Award Hits, Vol. 1- No. 3 .... RCA P8S-1775 (M)   75
Worldwide 50 Gold Award Hits, Vol. 1- No. 4 .... RCA P8S-1776 (M)   75
You'll Never Walk Alone / Elvis' Christmas Album .... RCA C8S-5051 (M/S)   72
You'll Never Walk Alone / Elvis' Christmas
   Album ....Pickwick C8S-7012 (M/S)   75

BUYERS & SELLERS DIRECTORY

The pages in every Official Price Guide Buyers-Sellers Directory are packed with personal and business ads, certain to appeal to anyone with an interest in music collecting – whether you're buying or selling.

When using the Directory to search for someone who may possibly be a buyer for your records, first please read "What to Expect When Selling Your Records to a Dealer," found in the Introduction.

The Buyers-Sellers Directory is an excellent and inexpensive way to locate those elusive discs you've been seeking for your collection.

To any of the other books in our series. Simply contact our office and ask for complete details.

Osborne Enterprises
Box 255
Port Townsend WA 98368
Phone: (360) 385-1200 — Fax: (360) 385-6572
www.jerryosborne.com — e-mail: jo@jerryosborne.com

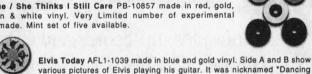

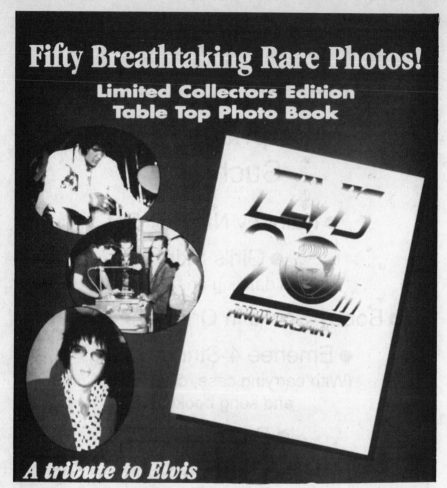

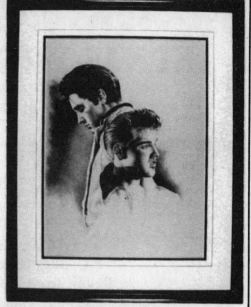